2015/16

THE GUIDE

EDUCATIONAL GRANTS

THIRTEENTH EDITION

Gabriele Zagnojute and Denise Lillya

Additional research by:
Anike Akinola, Ian Pembridge, Jennifer Reynolds
and Emma Weston

DIRECTORY OF So

Published by the Directory of Social Change (Registered Charity no. 800517 in England and Wales)

Head office: 24 Stephenson Way, London NW1 2DP

Northern office: Suite 103, 1 Old Hall Street, Liverpool L3 9HG
Tel: 08450 77 77 07

Visit www.dsc.org.uk to find out more about our books, subscription funding websites and training events. You can also sign up for e-newsletters so that you're always the first to hear about what's new.

The publisher welcomes suggestions and comments that will help to inform and improve future versions of this and all of our titles. Please give us your feedback by emailing publications@dsc.org.uk.

It should be understood that this publication is intended for guidance only and is not a substitute for professional or legal advice. No responsibility for loss occasioned as a result of any person acting or refraining from acting can be accepted by the authors or publisher.

First published 1988
Second edition 1992
Third edition 1994
Fourth edition 1996
Fifth edition 1998
Sixth edition 2000
Seventh edition 2002
Eighth edition 2004
Ninth edition 2006
Tenth edition 2009
Eleventh edition 2011
Twelfth edition 2013
Thirteenth edition 2014

ISBN 978 1 906294 96 0

British Library Cataloguing in Publication Data
A catalogue record for this book is available from the British Library

Cover and text design by Kate Bass
Typeset by Marlinzo Services, Frome
Printed and bound by Page Bros, Norwich

Contents

Foreword

Over the last few years there has been enormous change to the landscape of funding in further and higher education. On the whole, education has become more expensive in England: fees for higher education at £9,000 and the whole cost of courses now passed on to adult learners in further education. At the same time, maintenance support is under ever greater pressure, with some schemes like the Education Maintenance Allowance abolished altogether, and other rates of grants and loans failing to keep pace with inflation. More change is on the way: cuts to hardship funds and Disabled Students' Allowances have been announced, and loans in further education may be extended. And if the picture doesn't appear quite so difficult in the three devolved administrations, there remain strains on the systems there and many groups who can't access adequate support.

Successive NUS research reports have revealed that some groups are particularly vulnerable: disabled students, student parents and carers, students on healthcare courses, and adult learners in further education. Meanwhile, the student support system remains complex, its interaction with benefits even more so, and a greater emphasis on vocational learning and apprenticeships means a growing number of those in education study outside of traditional institutions. Yet access to guidance and support is becoming more fragmented: many advice agencies in the community have suffered closures and budget cuts, and though many universities, colleges and students' unions provide excellent advice centres, here too budgets are under pressure and demand continues to rise.

All this makes *The Guide to Educational Grants* as important a resource as ever. NUS has happily recommended the directory to students, their families and advisers for many years and this edition is no exception. It's an incredibly accessible way to identify potential funds from a huge range of charities that might otherwise remain obscure – and that help may make all the difference to a struggling student.

Of course, NUS will continue to campaign for a fair and comprehensive system of student support. Until that fight is won, we'd urge all students to both make best use of this directory and join us in that fight.

Toni Pearce
NUS National President 2013–2015

Introduction

Welcome to *The Guide to Educational Grants 2015/16*. The core purpose of this guide is to provide up-to-date information on grantmaking charities which offer financial support for people who are in education or training. This is the thirteenth edition of the guide, which is designed to be a practical and valuable tool with which to find funding for educational needs.

This guide contains 1,447 grantmaking charities which gave around £54 million in grants to individuals for educational purposes in the last financial year. Many of the organisations included in this guide also give grants to individuals in need for welfare purposes. These are detailed in the guide's sister publication *The Guide to Grants for Individuals in Need 2015/16*, also published by the Directory of Social Change.

Throughout the research for this edition, we have been collecting detailed financial figures from annual reports and accounts, and gathering comments and feedback about grantmaking from the charities directly. For the second time we carried out the Grants for Individuals in Need and Education (2014) survey, examining a sample of the grantmaking charities contained in the guide. This bore additional statistics, along with many interesting comments on the current grantmaking patterns and the impact of recent government reforms and public spending cuts.

The current climate

In recent years the charitable sector as well as society at large have experienced some significant challenges. With the government welfare reforms and drastic cuts to public expenditure, charitable resources have been stretched more than ever. Many grantmakers have been monitoring the 'perfect storm of local government funding cuts, welfare reform and wider policy changes in the education and voluntary sector for so long that change and uncertainty seem to have become the new normal' (Harpur Trust 2014).

While many grantmaking charities are anticipating a slow recovery from the recession, reduced government funding is having a severe impact on people's lives, especially those who are the poorest and most vulnerable (Aldridge and Maccines 2014). Access to education and training is restricted due to high fees but there is also a range of additional costs for those in schools, colleges, universities and professional training. In light of the big debate on the increase of course fees, expenses such as clothing, accommodation, equipment and books, as well as general living costs, are often underestimated. Furthermore, 'alongside financial poverty many might also suffer a "poverty of experiences": a shortage of encouragement or opportunity to engage in the rich variety of educational and cultural experiences.' (Aldgate and Allhallows Foundation 2013).

In the 21st century the state has rolled back its traditional boundaries of support for citizens and spends less each year on welfare. Work, originally taken off charities, is now being handed back by the Health and Social services in the wholly unrealistic expectation that it can all be done by volunteers, without any need for paid staff to recruit, CRB check, train, organise and support them. ... The country seems to be on a retrograde journey back to the old Victorian welfare values of 'help yourself or go without'. The pace of this process has been accelerated by the recession, and the Government imposed reductions in grant aid to charities. On paper this principle of self-help may be a laudable objective, but there remains a rump of poor, often socially excluded, sometimes mentally impaired, perhaps addicted drug users, or alcohol abusers, people whose problem actually is an inability to help themselves no matter how hard they try, or who cannot try, because it is that inability that is their weakness.

Worcester Municipal Exhibitions Foundation 2012/13

In the last few years government funding to local authorities has been reduced by almost 20% in real terms (Audit Commission 2013). The Audit Commission's findings suggest that many local authorities were fairly resilient to the financial pressures; nevertheless, the impact of spending cuts has not been felt equally across the country and many have been struggling due to the increasing demand for social services support combined with tightened funding. Earlier this year the government announced plans to scrap the funding for Local Welfare Provision Fund, introduced as a replacement for the Social Fund and provided through the Department for Work and Pensions. This has been challenged in a successful judicial review and a fresh decision is expected in December 2014, following a public consultation. If the government continues with its initial plan, local authorities may be forced to reduce or remove current schemes of welfare support. With government support rolling back, families in need are often forced to prioritise basic needs over those related to education.

The voluntary sector has been fulfilling some of the needs previously addressed by the state. Recent changes in the welfare system have not only pressed on financial resources, but also human resources. The lack of clarity caused by complex changes in statutory assistance was noted by some grantmakers: 'in the face of public expenditure cuts and the entitlement criteria for benefits being changed causing confusion, uncertainty and in some cases incorrect decisions, we have tackled the authorities on behalf of our clients' (Perennial 2013). It is frequently the case that individuals are not only discouraged by the complicated system of entitlements but also unaware of such entitlements and of the support that charities provide. More resources of grantmaking charities are now being directed towards money management guidance, debt advice and to improve the general financial literacy of beneficiaries.

Some groups seem to be particularly affected. Recent years have witnessed a rise in demand for support from younger people and despite the overall economic situation improving, those under the age of 25 remain among the most disadvantaged (Citizens Advice 2014a). This point has been extensively commented on both in the trustees' annual reports we reviewed and in our own survey (see page viii). Difficulties are also threatening students with disabilities with the proposed cuts to the Disabled Students' Allowance in 2015. The government's latest budget plan has announced particular allocations for early years education, postgraduate studies or apprenticeship grants for employers (HM Treasury 2014), and some increased support has also been announced for music education (Department for Education 2014a). Nevertheless, statutory funding for education is likely to be further stretched with a £200 million reduction in Education Services Grant paid to local authorities and academies for the year 2015/16 (Department of Education 2014) and changes in support to students and trainees. The Association of Colleges also estimates a significant shortfall in the Department for Education budget in the coming years (AOC 2014), attributable to both government policies and wider societal changes, such as the rising number of children in education (Department of Education 2013).

Grantmaking charities

Many of the above issues were recurring themes in the annual reports and accounts (mainly from 2012/13) of grantmaking charities as well as in our survey. While some organisations believed the period to be 'a year of stabilisation and encouraging growth' (Family Action 2013), the majority of grantmakers referred to current times as a 'challenging environment'. An often-cited topic was a difficult fundraising situation which generated competition among organisations and made charity administrators consider steps to protect the assets, ring-fence funds or reconsider reserves policies. Organisations felt the need to diversify their approach to fundraising by exploring innovative techniques and shifting towards more long-term, secure income rather than relying on donations. It is notable that trustees are becoming 'increasingly business-like' in their approach to charity management (Community Foundation for Merseyside 2013).

As in previous years, a high number of grantmakers saw an increase in applications and some noted record numbers of applications received and/or awards made. Where an increase has been noted it was often because of a greater level of publicity as much as it was owing to a rising demand for support. While our focus here is funding for individuals, it is worth noting the further knock-on effect of cuts in public spending. A number of charities which support both individuals and organisations mentioned increasing demand from other institutions which themselves are experiencing financial difficulties. This, in turn, significantly reduces funds available to individuals.

Corresponding to the results of our survey, discussed in detail on page viii, our research found that there were organisations which witnessed a decrease in applications.

INTRODUCTION

For some this was due to having very specific eligibility requirements and therefore not always being able to find eligible beneficiaries. In other cases this was owing to changes in the local community environment or wider social issues, for example the diminished population of schools in rural areas of the country. As a general observation, however, most grantmaking charities maintain that the demand for support exceeds existing funds.

In response to higher demand, grantmakers followed different routes. Some chose to establish new grant categories to fill in the gaps which had arisen in the current climate; others reduced the amounts given or focused on fewer beneficiaries. A number were forced to cut previously provided support altogether because they were unable to meet the demand or had experienced significant cuts in their own funding. Although a major change of focus and priorities has not been required for all of the charities featured here, the vast majority have made at least some efforts to improve how they reach their beneficiaries, including setting up or developing their websites, establishing new or maintaining ongoing formal or informal partnerships (with local and national bodies, similar organisations, academic institutions and so on), or trying to increase awareness by advertising in the local area or in professional sector publications. In adapting to the still difficult economic circumstances, grantmakers often stressed their attempts and achievements in reducing administrations costs, relying on the help of volunteers, maintaining contacts to signpost beneficiaries to other bodies, and sharing the cost of grants with other charities by requiring applicants to provide evidence of matched funding. The latter is a significant point, as some grantmaking charities will only be able to provide supplementary support and bigger projects will inevitably require seeking help from more than one organisation.

Many trustees' annual reports referred to the increase in support required by young people and by people out of employment and those seeking to gain new qualifications. Furthermore, increasingly more attention was paid to employment-focused vocational training and professional qualifications alongside more conventional academic routes – a high number of charities featured here stated that they were eager to support further education and professional training or to help people into apprenticeships.

Throughout our research we collected extensive financial information on the charitable assets, income, expenditure, grants given and governance costs. The annual accounts and reports we looked at were mainly from 2012/13, (but also from 2012 and, where available, 2013/14). The most common grant total was £2,000 (in the previous edition £1,000). The majority of grantmaking charities contained within the book remain relatively small organisations and almost one-third awarded under £10,000 a year. The total amount of grants awarded by all of the charities featured here remained almost the same as in the previous edition, at about £54 million. It should be noted that full financial details of some, usually smaller, charities could not be obtained and in such instances we estimated the proportion of charitable expenditure awarded in grants,

based on our experience and previous grant-giving patterns. In all cases some deductions, depending on the size of the organisation, had to be made to account for administrative expenses. Where the charity supported both individuals and organisations, the charitable expenditure was halved, and where welfare causes were also assisted, the remaining expenditure was quartered.

Note: the total assets of the charities in the book increased by about 25% on the previous edition. We would like to stress, however, that the assets held will not necessarily represent the charity's grantmaking potential. In some cases assets are protected as permanent endowments or restricted funds and in most instances assets are used to generate income for charitable activities rather than to be distributed as grants.

Higher education

Since the previous edition of this book, the impact of an increase in university fees, in most cases up to £9,000, has been fully experienced. There have been recent claims that in the long run the decision may end up costing more than the system it replaced (Institute for Fiscal Studies 2014), yet speculations on further increases are still ongoing. Despite the much feared deterrent effect on students from disadvantaged backgrounds, there are suggestions that poorer students are entering higher education more than before. UCAS notes an 8% increase in the number of students from disadvantaged backgrounds accepted on university and college courses compared to the year before (UCAS 2014a). After the sudden drop in 2012, the rates are now back to the 2006 to 2010 levels (UCAS 2013). Universities are also reported to be changing their investment patterns and increasing support to attract poorer students (Office for Fair Access 2014). The Independent Commission on Fees (2014), however, maintains that the gap between advantaged and disadvantaged students has narrowed only marginally (from 30.5% in 2010 to 29.8% in 2013). Moreover, as evidenced by a number of remarks from the grantmakers we researched, the prospect of almost £30,000 worth of debt remains a deterrent for some families on low income:

'The reduction in the number of awards for higher education could reflect the unwillingness of students to embark on increasingly costly programmes of study.'
Ruth Hayman Trust 2012

The decision to increase fees has also had an impact on grantmaking patterns, with hardly any charities able to cover the full costs of the course:

'The fees for a student's training are of such a magnitude now that the amount of our support, usually over three years, can only be a contribution to the total amount required. Of necessity the total funds required for fees have to come from a number of different sources.'
The Wall Trust 2012/13

There has been some concern over a decrease in mature students and part-time course attendants (Office for Fair Access 2013). The latest data from UCAS (2014) suggests that at least the numbers of mature students seem to be recovering. While the expenses of mature and part-time students may often be exacerbated by family maintenance and childcare costs, grantmaking charities will often take into account such specific needs.

The National Scholarship Programme, introduced following the reforms to support those entering higher education, ceases to exist as an undergraduate programme from 2015 and the support will be directed to postgraduate students. Some higher education colleges are also losing funding for tuition fees and maintenance loans for the courses commencing in 2014 (UCAS 2014b), and the pressure on finances will be increased, with the funding for higher education institutions reduced for the 2014/15 and 2015/16 cycles (BIS 2014a).

Luckily charities are sympathetic to higher education students and, despite the increase in the cost of entering courses, will try to help by making a contribution towards fees or living expenses and will assist with necessities such as travel, books, equipment, instruments, training materials and educational trips. See the 'How to make an application' section on page 247 for more details on obtaining support.

Schools

Since the previous edition of this book was published, the academies expansion programme has accelerated with 4,167 academies in existence as of September 2014 (Department for Education 2014b) and more schools scheduled to convert or new academies to be sponsored. The conversions, as well as the provision of pupil premiums (given additionally to state-funded schools to help disadvantaged pupils), have in some cases caused demand for school uniforms to reduce and in those instances, charities were able to divert their resources to other educational necessities. In other cases, however, the rebranding of the school and introduction of new uniforms caused additional expenses which charities were approached to help with. Many grantmaking charities maintain that school uniforms and clothing remain one of the most required types of support together with educational outings costs. Notably, the cost of uniforms, schools meals and transport and school trip expenses are reported to have increased (Citizens Advice 2014b).

The Local Government Association (2014) has noted an increased demand for school spaces and a shortfall in funding of those, putting an extra strain on councils as well as the schools concerned. The budget for schools has been ring-fenced by the coalition government between 2010 and 2015; however, there has been a 17% spending cut in real terms to government departments between 2015 and 2019, with no arrangements planned to protect schools or the education budget at this stage (AOC 2014).

As this publication was being prepared, some significant changes had just come into force to the special education needs support arrangements. The new system, effective from September 2014, combines health and care needs with educational ones and will offer educational support up to the age of 25, extending assistance into further education or training. While broadly welcomed, this development is likely to increase in demand due to the closures of some specialist educational establishments:

The closure of special schools and inclusion of children with special needs in mainstream schools has also put a strain on teaching provision, with an increased demand for special needs teaching.   Kelsick's Educational Foundation 2013

Further and vocational education

The previous edition of this guide noted the abolition of the Education Maintenance Allowance in England (still available in Wales, Northern Ireland and Scotland). Support to learners is still provided through the 16–19 Bursary Fund to schools and colleges for those most in need. Support is also provided via schemes such as the Discretionary Learners Allowance, which is available to people on Skills Funding Agency courses, and the Residential Support Scheme (for more information on support for further education see page 375). Further education has been heavily affected by the reduction in funding and the adult skills budget has suffered the most – by 2015/16 it will have been cut by 19% (BIS 2014b). The Education Funding Agency is making cuts in the funding rate of almost 18% for 18-year-old learners in 2014/15, even though a one-year cap has been applied at a 2% rate (Education Funding Agency 2014). Grantmaking charities have already noted a demand for support for further education and many have mentioned having to restructure their giving patterns and allocate more support to further education students to address the gap in this area in particular. Some charities have also already experienced the effect of the withdrawal of grants and free bus travel to post-16 year olds.

Despite the general levels of unemployment falling fairly steadily for the last year (ONS 2014) and as well as the number of people classified as NEETs (Not in Education, Employment or Training) getting lower (NAO 2014; Department for Education 2014c), there is still a concern around young people securing employment. The Institute of Public Policy Research has noted a number of problems in provisions to help young people enter the job market (Dolphin 2014). The requalification option is becoming more and more significant for those unable to find work.

Apprenticeships, including higher apprenticeships which combine vocational and academic qualifications, are on the government's industrial strategy too, with new arrangements for employers that provide places for apprentices and an increasing percentage of businesses are anticipated to engage in the provision of vocational training (Department for Business Innovation and Skills 2014). While high on the agenda, the support is offered to the training providers rather than individuals, therefore it is helpful to know that a number of charitable organisations are willing to offer support. The majority of charities in this guide are also pleased to fund vocational education, including apprenticeships and courses that are likely to lead to employment. Support for fees, training materials, equipment, travel expenses and uniforms for people starting work can all be considered. For more details on apprenticeship training see the section on page 383.

INTRODUCTION

Grants for Individuals in Need and Education survey 2014

In 2014 the research team at DSC for the second time carried out the Grants for Individuals in Need and Education survey, which was sent to grantmaking charities that support individuals in education, provide funding for welfare causes or assist in both areas. We invited charities from around the country to share their views and experiences on the impact of the recent government welfare reforms and the cuts in public spending. The information we gathered complements the data we have collected from the annual reports and accounts by giving a deeper and more personal insight into the current sector environment.

In this year's survey we were, in particular, aiming to see if the recent reforms in the welfare system and public spending policy had had an impact on:

▸ the overall number of applications from individuals;
▸ the types of support required;
▸ the referral agencies in the grantmaking charities' local areas (such as closures), and what impact any such changes had on their charitable work.

These questions are explored in a little more detail below in relation to educational charities.

Number of applications

We asked grantmaking charities whether they had an increase in overall number of applications, a decrease, or if no change in applications has been noticed. Just under half of the respondents (46%) said that they had received around the same number of applications as the previous year. Of the remaining respondents, equal numbers received fewer or more applications than the previous year (27% each). Comments included:

'Requests have come both from other charities and organizations and individuals as a result of cutbacks in funding.'

'Schools seem to be reducing the number of trips/visits/ residential weeks due to the economic downturn and the lack of spending power.'

'Although numbers applying appear to have dropped, we still have sufficient applications to expend all of our funds.'

Number of applications

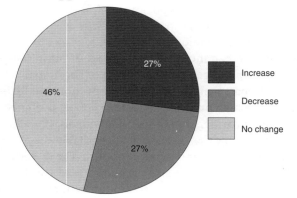

A couple of commenters noted that while enquiries increased, this did not reflect on the number of applications. In addition, some of the respondents

specified that particular types of support increased or decreased, as will be discussed in the following section.

Types of support given

Perhaps unsurprisingly, the greatest number of charities gave support for fees, bursaries and scholarships (88%). A high amount of respondents (69%) also stated that their support was required for additional learning opportunities, such as projects, research, study overseas and so on. This was followed by travel and transport expenses (46%) and school trips or educational visits (35%). Support to people entering a trade or starting work and for living expenses (including accommodation, bills and household essentials) was also frequently given (31% and 27% respectively). School children's necessities were provided for by 23% of the charities and extra-curricular activities by 19%. Those with needs that are traditionally addressed by welfare charities were also supported: to relieve poverty in general (at 12% – the same level of support as given for special educational needs), for utility and household bills (8% each), and for the relief of poverty and sickness, as well as for equipment for those with disabilities (4% each).

Some respondents more specifically noted an increase in applications for support from A-level and university students. Other respondents remarked:

'We have noticed that there is an increased number of applications for help with school fees at the high end schools that until 2008 would have found help from their own resources, i.e., a special bursary.'

'We have noticed a decline in the number of applicants on WEA and similar evening classes, and an increase in the number on part-time postgraduate courses, which are much more costly. We suspect that there has been a decline in evening classes, as fees increase and courses fail to recruit.'

'The level of provision of ESOL in AE and FE, and the huge increase in fees has had an impact on our beneficiaries, as has the massive increase in HE costs for those without family in the UK, or with family with low incomes who cannot get help with fees.'

Among those giving grants for both educational and welfare purposes, educational support was mostly given for: fees, scholarships and bursaries (supported at the same level as general living expenses: 64%); school trips and educational visits (56%); people entering a trade and school children's necessities (supported at the same level as general utility bills (48%).

Groups supported

The greatest amount of support from grantmaking charities (69%) is given to higher education students followed by those in further education (50%). In line with our findings from research on other grantmaking charities, young people in general were supported by a significant proportion – about half of the grantmakers.

Schoolchildren remained a relatively high-priority group, helped by 35% of the respondents, closely followed by people starting work, entering a trade or undertaking apprenticeships (27%) and mature students, at 23%.

Similar to the data on types of support, groups that would normally be helped by welfare charities were mentioned as being supported by the respondents. Among these groups were children, older people and people with disabilities (12% each). About 4% of those surveyed also supported families or one-parent families.

Those grantmakers which support both educational and social welfare causes distributed their assistance more or less equally. The highest supported education-related group was school children/children in general, assisted by 64% of the respondents. Interestingly people entering a trade, starting work or undertaking apprenticeships and further education students were supported slightly more frequently (44%) than those in higher education (40%).

Referral agencies

It appears that the closures/scaling back on the activities of referral agencies have not been noticed by many of the educational charities which responded to our questions. Around 56% of those surveyed stated that they have not noticed a reduction in activities undertaken by Citizens Advice, head teachers, GPs and so on. About 18% of the respondents did notice some closures, often giving specific explanations or examples, and 26% of the respondents noted that the work done by the referral agencies was not relevant to their activities, mainly due to the fact that applications were only accepted from individuals directly. A good number of the referrals to grantmaking educational charities come from universities; however, only a couple of respondents said that they noticed there being fewer resources to support students in some educational establishments or that referrals from universities decreased. The closures were more actively commented on by grantmakers which provide social welfare support or both types of assistance.

'For example due to cut backs in the public sector the level of CAB provision has decreased which in turn has impacted on the level of services they can provide locally. Beneficiaries access us via a range of agencies and channels including community organisations, other funding bodies and in particular word of mouth.'

'The agencies are struggling themselves because of the cutbacks.'

Have you noticed reduction of services provided by referral agencies?

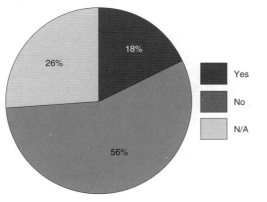

Have you implemented any changes to reach potential beneficiaries?

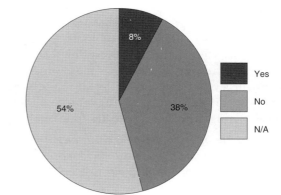

We were interested in finding out whether the charities thought there were any barriers to potential applicants in approaching the grantmaker directly. The majority of those surveyed (81%) had not noticed any, but a small proportion (15%) specified a lack of knowledge of how the application process works, embarrassment, a lack of literacy skills to complete the application forms fully and accurately, limited knowledge of support available in particular areas or professional fields or misunderstanding the charity's eligibility criteria, timelines and types/amount of available support, rendering the applications ineligible in the first place. In addition, some respondents noted delays caused by heavy workloads at advice agencies which, in turn, hinder the successful flow of the application.

'Embarrassment is a big problem. Also, the form puts people off as it is a means tested form. Some find it difficult to complete. We encourage people to call if they need any help.'

Have you noticed any barriers for people applying to you directly?

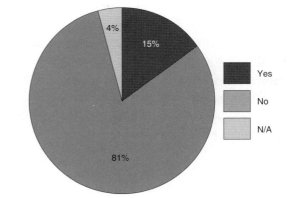

Corresponding to the responses outlined above, 81% of the respondents stated that they are still able to reach their potential beneficiaries and had no problem spending the money available, with 38% considering no steps were needed in order to reach their beneficiaries better. Only 8% specified that they have implemented some changes to their policies and operation or are planning to do so. A number of smaller, more locally based charities felt that they are known well enough in their area of operation or maintained that word of mouth remains the best publicity and ensures that sufficient numbers of beneficiaries approach the trustees for funding.

Those who did undertake some changes noted the following activities: reviewing their guidelines, offering match funding opportunities, registering the information of the organisation on grant-giving databases, running publicity campaigns in local places of public gathering (such as schools, churches, post offices, shops, surgeries and so on), and creating websites. For those which increased their level of publicity, different results were produced – in some instances inviting more applicants and in others deterring ineligible candidates from applying:

> 'The criteria are more widely publicised, including on our website, and we are able to assist individuals in deciding whether or not to apply through our new informal enquiries service.'

> 'Our guidelines have been reviewed to enable us to reach a wider group of beneficiaries as well as provide access to potential match funding.'

Some charities appear to develop partnerships with other organisations in order to help publicise their charitable work. We were interested in taking this point further.

Partnership

It was our aim to find out whether the charities have been working with local agencies, educational establishments and other charitable organisations in their local area in order to reach out to potential beneficiaries and provide support where it is most needed. The majority of the respondents to our survey stated that no partnerships were taking place (67%) and considerably fewer confirmed that they maintain relationships with other bodies (29%) or are considering the possibility of co-operation/already have plans in place to establish such relationships (4%). One respondent admitted that partnership would need to be considered 'if applications started to fall below the funds available'.

Some examples of partnerships included charitable organisations supporting similar causes, local councils and other community groups.

> 'We do get applications from students in institutions where we are already known, but there is no formal partnership.'

Regrettably, as one respondent noted, smaller charities may not always be viewed as worthy partners:

> 'We have been proactive with [other] agencies to get our charity promoted and better known with the administrators. CAB are not in a position to work with us. Perhaps we are simply "too small".'

Are you working in partnership with other bodies?

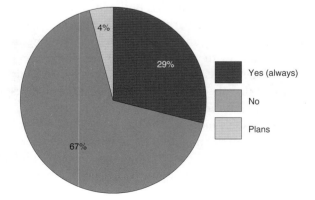

4%
29%
67%

Yes (always)
No
Plans

It should be stressed that overall the experiences of the charities varied. Some grantmaking charities straightforwardly claimed that the changes do not affect their beneficiaries at all and 'are entirely irrelevant to [them] and have no effect whatsoever on [their] charity'. Notably, a high number of charities that responded to the questions were quite specific in their charitable giving. Others, apparently more affected, were asking 'how charities are "expected" to fill the gap in reduced benefits'. It appears that while both changes in the welfare system and the new arrangements in public spending have been in effect for some time, the full impact of these on charities will be unfolding for some time to come.

Eligible and ineligible applications

The DSC Great Giving campaign advocates positive measures to decrease the amount of ineligible applications being submitted to grantmakers. In line with this policy, our survey asked about the number of applications received during the most recent and the previous financial years, and the number of ineligible applications in both years. Overall there was a small increase in the total number of applications (around 10%), while the percentage of ineligible applications remained almost the same as in the previous survey, at about 17%. Interestingly, while some grantmaking charities managed to maintain a low (in many cases inevitable) level of ineligible applications, almost half of the charities making grants for educational purposes had to reject 20% or more of all applications as ineligible.

Finally ...

Both educational and charitable sectors are experiencing difficult and uncertain times. However, the attitudes of grantmaking charities are as inspiring as ever, with most ready to go the extra mile to help those in need. We put together the following sections to help both the grantmaking charities and those requiring assistance. Information includes:

▶ 'Grantmaking charities – their processes and effectiveness': our recommendations for grantmakers
▶ 'About this guide': a description of the types of charities that are included, how they are ordered in the guide and the type of help that they give
▶ 'How to use this guide': an explanation of a typical entry and a flowchart to show you how to identify sources of help
▶ 'How to make an application': some advice on making applications, including an application form template

Most importantly, ensure that you read all eligibility criteria accurately. Do not apply if you are not eligible because the charities will not be able to fund you and it simply wastes everyone's time, including your own. Follow application procedures precisely and make sure that you meet any deadlines. More and more, we are seeing organisations expanding their support beyond just financial grants, and many are offering advice services as well, so take full advantage of these.

We wish you the best of luck in your search for funding.

Acknowledgements

We are extremely grateful to the many charity trustees, staff and volunteers who have provided up-to-date details for inclusion in this guide, and others who have helped. To name them all individually would be impossible. Special thanks go to the grantmaking charities that responded to our Grants for Individuals in Need and Education survey (2014).

Requests for further information

The research for this guide was done as carefully and thoroughly as we were able, but there will still be relevant charities that we have missed and some of the information may be incomplete or will become out of date. If you come across omissions or mistakes in this guide please let us know by calling or emailing the Directory of Social Change's research team (0151 708 0136; email: research@dsc.org.uk) so that we can rectify them for the future.

We are always looking to improve our guides and would appreciate any comments, positive or negative, about this guide, or suggestions on what other information would be useful for inclusion when we research the next edition.

References

Aldgate and Allhallows Foundation (2014), annual report and accounts for the year ended 31 December 2013, London, The Aldgate and Allhallows Foundation

Aldridge, H. and T. Maccines (2014), *Multiple Cuts for the Poorest Families*, Oxford, Oxfam GB

AOC (2014), *The Department for Education budget after 2015*, London, Association of Colleges

Audit Commission (2013), *Tough Times 2013: Councils' responses to financial challenges from 2010/11 to 2013/14*, London, Audit Commission

BIS (2014a), 'Funding for higher education in England for 2014–15: HEFCE grant letter from BIS' [web page], www.hefce.ac.uk, Department for Business, Innovation and Skills, dated 10 February 2014, accessed 23 September 2014

BIS (2014b), *Skills Funding Statement 2013–2016*, London, Department for Business, Innovation and Skills

Citizens Advice (2014a), 'Young people are among hardest hit by sanctions' [online press release], www.citizensadvice.org.uk, dated 2 March 2014, accessed 19 September 2014

Citizens Advice (2014b), 'Citizens Advice: Parents find school uniforms more costly this year than last' [online press release], www.citizensadvice.org.uk, dated 1 September 2014, accessed 17 September 2014

Community Foundation for Merseyside (2013), annual report and accounts 2012/13 for the year ended 31 March 2013, Liverpool, Community Foundation for Merseyside

Department for Business Innovation and Skills (2014), 'Apprenticeships – reasons to be cheerful' [online press release] www.gov.uk, dated 20 August, 2014, accessed 15 September 2014

Department for Education (2014a), 'More funding to help thousands of extra children enjoy music' [online press release], www.gov.uk, dated 22 July 2014, accessed 22 September 2014

Department for Education (2014b), 'Open academies and academy projects awaiting approval: September 2014' [downloadable Excel sheet], www.gov.uk, accessed 15 September 2014

Department for Education (2014c), *The Education Services Grant: Statement of final arrangements for 2015 to 2016*, www.gov.uk

Dolphin, T. (2014), *Remember the Young Ones*, London, The Institute of Public Policy Research

Education Funding Agency (2014), 'Funding for academic year 2014 to 2015 for students aged 16 to 19 and high needs students aged 16 to 25' [letter from Peter Mucklow], www.gov.uk, dated 18 March 2014, accessed 20 September 2014

Family Action (2013), annual report and accounts for the year ended 31 March 2014, London, Family Action

Harpur Trust (2014), annual report and accounts 2012/13, Bedford, The Harpur Trust

HM Treasury (2014), *Budget Report*, www.gov.uk, dated 19 March 2014, accessed 23 September 2014

Independent Commission on Fees (2014), *Analysis of trends in higher education applications, admissions, and enrolments*, www.independentcommissionfees.org.uk, accessed 15 September 2014

Kelsick's Educational Foundation (2013), annual report and accounts for the year ended 31 March 2013, Ambleside, Kelsick's Educational Foundation

Local Government Association (2014), 'Councils warn of £1bn shortfall in funding for new school places' [online press release], www.local.gov.uk, dated 27 August 214, accessed 23 September 2014

NAO (2014), *16- to 18-year-old participation in education and training: report by the Comptroller and Auditor General*, London, National Audit Office

Office for Fair Access (2013), 'OFFA annual report warns over drop in part-time and mature student recruitment' [online press release], www.offa.org.uk, dated 3 July 2013, accessed 19 September 2014

Office for Fair Access (2014), 'Access agreement decisions for 2015–16: a striking change in spending patterns' [online press release], www.offa.org.uk, dated 24 July 2014, accessed 17 September 2014

ONS (2014), 'Labour Market Statistics' [online press release], Office for National Statistics, accessed 18 September 2014

Perennial (2013), annual report and accounts for the year ended 31 December 2013, perennial.org.uk, Gardeners' Royal Benevolent Society

Ruth Hayman Trust (2012), annual report and accounts for the year ended 31 March 2012, www.ruthhaymantrust.org.uk, accessed 23 September 2014

UCAS (2013), *2013 Application Cycle: End of Cycle Report*, Cheltenham, UCAS

UCAS (2014a), 'Record 8% more students from disadvantaged backgrounds get into university' [online press release], www.ucas.com, dated 14 August 2014, accessed 15 September 2014

UCAS (2014b), 'Record numbers of mature students accepted into higher education' [online press release], www.ucas.com, dated 21 August 2014, accessed 15 September 2014

Worcester Municipal Exhibitions Foundation (2012/13), annual report and accounts 2012/13, Worcester, Worcester Municipal Charities

Note: all annual reports and accounts (for which websites are not listed) are available on the Charity Commission for England and Wales website.

Grantmaking charities – their processes and effectiveness

The Directory of Social change has a vision of an independent voluntary sector at the heart of social change. Based upon this vision and our experience of researching this publication for over 25 years, we would like to suggest some ways in which charities that give grants to individuals could seek to encourage greater fairness and more effective practices in grantmaking. They should:

- seek to collaborate with others that have similar objectives. By sharing knowledge and best practice, organisations can contribute towards improving the wider grantmaking landscape. Of the respondents to our survey, only a small proportion (29%) stated that they work in partnership with other organisations often jointly funding individuals and sharing information.
- do as much as possible to decrease the amount of ineligible applications they receive. This is a joint responsibility with applicants, who should make sure that they read criteria carefully and not apply to charities for funding for which they are not eligible. However, grantmakers should facilitate this by ensuring that eligibility criteria and applications guidelines are transparent and easily available. Our research suggests that a growing number of charities choose to move towards electronic application forms and also sometimes consider a two-stage application process. Many willingly offer help and guidance with filling in the application form. Nevertheless, as our survey data indicates, the level of ineligible requests for support remains more or less static.
- ensure, where they are local, that they are very well known within their area of benefit by writing to local Citizens Advice branches, local authorities, schools and other educational establishments and community centres. As evidenced by the comments of the charity trustees during our research, an effective measure of raising the organisation's profile remains word of mouth, particularly with smaller charities. Ideally charities should aim to ensure that needs can be met as rapidly as possible, for example by empowering the clerk or a small number of trustees to make small emergency grants. If trustees can only meet twice a year to consider applications these should cover the peak times, namely May to June when people are running out of money at the end of the academic year or looking forward to funding courses beginning in September, and November to December when people who have started their courses have a much clearer picture of how much money they need.
- form clear policies on who they can support and what they can fund (where the objects of the charities permit it) targeting those most in need. One or two charities in this guide are restricted to making grants to inhabitants of relatively wealthy parishes and appear to have great difficulty finding individuals in need of financial support. The majority, however, receive constant applications and they cannot support all of them.

About this guide

What charities are included?

We have included in this guide grantmaking charities that give or have the potential to give:

- at least £500 a year in educational grants (most give considerably more);
- grants based upon need rather than academic performance;
- funding for levels of education from primary school to first degree level: there may be some that will support pre-school education or postgraduate degrees as well ('education' is defined in its loosest sense, and therefore includes all types of vocational education and training, extracurricular activities and personal or professional development);
- grants to students of more than one educational establishment.

We have not included those that give:

- grants that are solely for postgraduate study;
- awards or scholarships for academic excellence, except where these appear to be particularly relevant to people in need.

About 30% of the charities in this guide also give grants to individuals in need for the relief of poverty and hardship. These, along with many others, are included in the guide's sister publication *The Guide to Grants for Individuals in Need 2015/16*. The charities in this guide often support educational charities, youth organisations, community groups and educational establishments as well; however, the information given relates only to that which is relevant for individuals. *The Directory of Grantmaking Trusts*, also published by the Directory of Social Change, contains funding for organisations.

How charities are ordered

The grantmaking charities are listed in two sections:

1) National charities classified according to:

- Need: for example, disability, independent schools, overseas students (see page 3)
- Occupation of parent or applicant (see page 53)
- Subject being studied (see page 77)

Within each of these sections there is a General section which lists those charities that do not fall into a specific category.

2) Local charities classified by region, county, borough or parish; see page 121 for details about how to use this section.

What are grants given for?

Generally the charities in this guide offer one-off grants for a specific purpose or recurrent support for the duration of the individual's course or project. In some instances support may be given for a specific number of years or, in some rare instances, throughout the individual's education. The majority of the support given is intended to be supplementary and applicants will often need to secure money from different sources; however, small costs of necessities or sometimes even bigger projects may be covered in full. A handful of the grantmakers listed may offer low-interest loans as well.

Grantmakers in this guide can give supplementary help with small grants for:

- uniforms and other school clothing, sport kits, specialist outfits for professionals and clothes for a job interview;
- books, training materials, equipment, tools and specialist instruments;
- small-scale fees associated with the course or training, such as exam, registration or workshop fees;
- living expenses and maintenance costs or accommodation;
- travel costs both in the UK and overseas, including for overseas study, educational trips, voluntary and gap-year experience, field studies or research purposes;
- course, school or training fees, particularly those for professional, technical or vocational courses and qualifications;

- extra-curricular activities aimed at the physical and social development of the individual, including sports, outdoor activities, music (including musical instruments, or the loan musical instruments), arts and so on;
- extra equipment related to disability that cannot be funded from statutory sources;
- childcare costs, particularly for mature students;
- expenses associated with apprenticeships or entering a trade or profession, this can sometimes include business start-up costs;
- some awards may also be given in the form of vouchers, such as for the local school uniform shop.

Supporting information and advice

This guide also contains supporting information and advice on:

- Statutory grants and student support (see page 375)
- Types of schools in the UK and their funding (see page 379)
- Further education and skills training: apprenticeships (see page 383)
- Company sponsorship and career development loans (see page 385)
- Funding for gap years and overseas voluntary work (see page 387)
- Contacts and sources of further information (see page 391)
- Education authority contacts (see page 395)

How to use this guide

Below is a typical charity entry, showing the format we have used to present the information obtained from each of the charities.

On the following page is a flowchart. We recommend that you follow the order indicated in the flowchart to look at each section of the guide and find charities that are relevant to you. You can also use the information in the sections 'About this guide' and 'How to make an application' to help inform your applications.

The Fictitious Trust

£24,000 (120 grants)

Correspondent: Ms I M Helpful, Charities Administrator, 7 Pleasant Road, London SN0 0ZZ (020 7123 4567; email: admin@fictitious.org.uk; website: www.fictitious.org.uk).

CC Number: 112234

Eligibility

Children or young people up to 25 years of age who are in need. Preference is given to children of single parent families and/or those who come from a disadvantaged family background.

Types of grants

Small one-off grants of up to £250 for a wide range of needs, including school uniforms, books, equipment and educational trips in the UK and abroad. Grants are also available for childcare costs.

Annual grant total

In 2013 the trust had an income of £25,000 and an expenditure of £27,000. Grants to 120 individuals totaled £24,000.

Other information

The trust also gives relief-in-need grants to individuals.

Exclusions

No grants for private school or university fees.

Applications

On a form available from the correspondent, submitted either directly by the individual or by the parent or guardian for those under 18. Applications are considered in January, April, July and October.

Award and no. of grants

Total amount given during the financial year in question in grants to individuals for education and how many individual grants were made, if this information was available.

Correspondent

The main person to contact, nominated by the trustees.

Charity Commission number

Note: occasionally some of the organisations are not registered charities.

Eligibility

This states who is eligible to apply for a grant. This can include restrictions on age, family circumstances, occupation of parent, subject to be studied, stage of education, ethnic origin, or place of residence.

Types of grants

Specifies whether the charity gives one-off or recurrent grants, the size of grants given and for which items or costs grants are actually given. This section will also indicate if the charity runs various schemes.

Annual grant total

This shows the total amount of money given in grants to individuals in the last financial year for which there were figures available. Other financial information may be given where relevant.

Other information

This contains miscellaneous further information about the charity, including if they give grants to individuals for relief-in-need, or to organisations.

Exclusions

This field gives information, where available, on what the charity will not fund.

Applications

Including how to apply, who should make the application (i.e. the individual or a third party) and when to submit an application.

How to identify sources of help - a quick reference flowchart

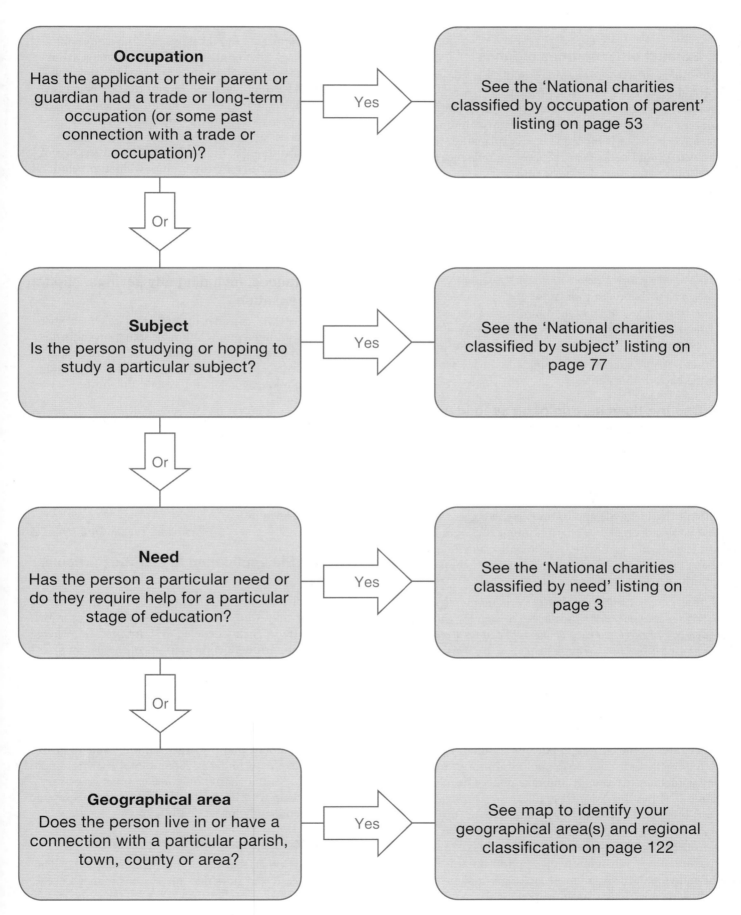

Occupation
Has the applicant or their parent or guardian had a trade or long-term occupation (or some past connection with a trade or occupation)?

Yes → See the 'National charities classified by occupation of parent' listing on page 53

Or

Subject
Is the person studying or hoping to study a particular subject?

Yes → See the 'National charities classified by subject' listing on page 77

Or

Need
Has the person a particular need or do they require help for a particular stage of education?

Yes → See the 'National charities classified by need' listing on page 3

Or

Geographical area
Does the person live in or have a connection with a particular parish, town, county or area?

Yes → See map to identify your geographical area(s) and regional classification on page 122

How to make an application

This section gives you some information on how to make an application, with additional tips from funders' perspectives.

1. Exhaust other sources of funds

All sources of statutory funding should have been applied for and/or received before applying to a charity. Applications, therefore, should include details of these sources and any refusals. Where statutory funding has been received but is inadequate, an explanation that this is the case should be made. A supporting reference from a relevant agency may also be helpful.

If the applicant attends an educational establishment this should also have been approached to see if it has any funds or can give a reduction in fees.

> 'The best way to get help for individual funding is to start by helping yourself – try every avenue to raise as much of the money yourself before and while you approach others for a contribution to your cause. If they can see how determined you are and how hard you've worked already, they'll naturally feel motivated to help you find the remainder.'
> *BBC Performing Arts Fund*

Other possible sources of funding and advice are included at the back of this guide.

2. Use the flowchart on page xv to identify potential sources of funding

Once you have found a grantmaker that may be relevant to you . . .

3. Check eligibility criteria

Submitting ineligible applications is the biggest mistake that applicants make. A charity cannot fund you if you are not eligible and you merely waste both your time and theirs by applying. If you are in any doubt, contact the grantmaker for clarification.

> 'Always read carefully a charity's criteria for eligibility. We, for example, are only allowed to help the children of actors, but three quarters of the applications I receive do not match this basic requirement. You are wasting your time and hopes by applying to a trust which clearly is not allowed to help you.'
> *TACT*

4. Follow the application procedures precisely

Wherever they are available, we have included application procedures in the entries; applicants should take great care to follow these. If there is an application form, use it! Read any guidelines thoroughly and take note of deadlines. Some charities can consider applications throughout the year; others may meet monthly, quarterly or just once a year. Very urgent applications can sometimes be considered between the main meetings. Make sure that the appropriate person submits the application; this could be the individual, their parent or guardian or some professional such as a social worker.

Evidence from our research shows that a large majority of organisations welcome initial contact before a full application is made, so if you are unsure about anything, get in touch with them.

5. Give details of any extenuating or unforeseen circumstances

Potential applicants should think carefully about any circumstances which put them at a disadvantage from other families or students, such as coming from a low-income background, being in receipt of state benefits, being a single parent, having a health problem or disability and so on. Where relevant, try and show how the circumstances you are now in could not have been foreseen (for example, illness, family difficulties, loss of job and so on). Charities are often more willing to help if financial difficulties are a result of unforeseen circumstances rather than a lack of forward planning. The funding in this guide is aimed at those facing the most barriers to education or training.

6. Give clear, honest details about your circumstances, including any savings, capital or compensation

Most trustees will consider the applicant's savings when they are awarding a grant, although sometimes this does not need to affect trustees' calculations. In circumstances where you are certain that your savings are not relevant to grant calculations, you should explain this in the application.

> 'Be open and honest about your circumstances. We have to ensure that we have all the information we need to put your case forwards. If essential details emerge at a later date, this can affect your application. Be honest about how much you want to apply for and don't ask for the most expensive item. If you show that you've done your research, then that helps us too.'
> *Fashion and Textile Children's Trust*

7. Tailor the application to suit the particular charity

For example, if someone is applying to a trade charity on behalf of a child whose parent had lengthy service in that particular trade, then a detailed description (and, where possible, supporting documentation) of the parent's service would be highly relevant. If an application for the same child was being made to a local charity on another occasion, it would not be relevant.

8. Ask for a suitable amount

Ask for an amount that the organisation is able to give. Most grants are for under £300, and local charities often give much less. If a charity only makes small grants, try asking for help with books, travel, childcare expenses and such like, and apply for fees elsewhere.

9. Mention applications to other charities

Explain that other charities are being approached, when this is the case, and state that any surplus money raised will be returned.

10. Offer to supply references

For example, from a teacher, college tutor, support worker and/or another independent person. If the individual has disabilities or medical needs then a report from a doctor would be necessary.

11. Be honest and realistic, not moralising and emotional

Some applications try to morally bribe trustees into supporting the application, or launch into tirades against the current political regime. It is best to confine your application to clear and simple statements of fact.

12. Be clear, concise and provide sufficient detail

Give as much relevant information as possible, in the most precise way. For example, 'place of birth' is sometimes answered with 'Great Britain', but if the charity only gives grants in Liverpool, to answer 'Great Britain' is not detailed enough and the application will be delayed pending further information. Make sure that you write clearly and do not use jargon so your application is easily understood.

13. Say thank you!

Charitable organisations generally like to be kept informed of how their grants have made a difference. It is also important to keep in touch if you are in need of recurrent funding. Feedback also helps charities for future grant giving.

> 'Don't consider the moment the grant appears in your bank account as the end of your relationship with the grantmaker – try to provide updates on the work the grant has helped you to undertake, including photos, videos and other resources.'
> *Royal Geographical Society*

So remember to thank grantmakers for their support and let them know how their funding has helped you.

See below for notes on the application form template.

Using the application form template for financial assistance

Over the page is a general-purpose application form. It has been compiled with the help of Gaddum Centre. It can be photocopied and used whenever convenient and should enable applicants (and agencies or persons applying on behalf of individuals) to state clearly the basic information required by most grantmakers.

Alternatively, applicants can use it as a checklist of points to include in the letter. Applicants using this form should note the following things in particular:

1. It is worth sending a short letter setting out the request in brief, even when using this application form.

2. Because this form is designed to be useful to a wide range of people in need, not all the information asked for in the form will be relevant to every application. For example, not all applicants are in receipt of state benefits, nor do all applicants have HP commitments.

   In such cases, applicants should write N/A (not applicable) in the box or on the line in question.

3. If, similarly, you do not have answers for all the questions at the time of applying – for example, if you have applied to other charities and are still waiting for a reply – you should write 'Pending' under the question: 'Have you written to any other charities? What was the outcome of the application?'

4. The first page is relevant to all applications; the second page is only relevant to people applying for school or college fees. If you are applying for clothing or books for a schoolchild then it may be worth filling out only the first page of the form and submitting a covering letter outlining the reasons for the application.

5. Filling out the weekly income and expenditure parts of the form can be worrying or even distressing. Expenditure when itemised in this way is usually far higher than people expect. It is probably worth filling out this form with the help of a professional.

6. You should always keep a copy of the completed form in case the trust has a specific query.

7. This form should not be used where the trust has its own form, which must be completed.

Application form template

Purpose for which grant is sought	Amount sought from £ this application
Applicant (name) Address Telephone no.	Occupation/School
Date of birth Age	Place of birth
Nationality	Religion (if any)

☐ Single   ☐ Married   ☐ Divorced   ☐ Partnered   ☐ Separated   ☐ Widow/er

Family details: Name	Age	Occupation/School
Parents/ Partner	. . . . . .	. . . .
Brothers/Sisters/ Children	. . . . . .	. . . .
. . . .	. . . . . .	. . . .
. . . .	. . . . . .	. . . .
Others (specify)	. . . . . .	

Income (weekly)	£	p	Expenditure (weekly – *excluding course fees*)	£	p
Father's/husband's wage	. . . . . .		Rent/mortgage	. . . . . .	
Mother's/wife's wage	. . . . . .		Council tax	. . . . . .	
Partner's wage	. . . . . .		Water rate	. . . . . .	
Income Support	. . . . . .		Electricity	. . . . . .	
Jobseeker's Allowance	. . . . . .		Gas	. . . . . .	
Employment and Support Allowance	. . . . . .		Other fuel	. . . . . .	
Pension Credit	. . . . . .		Insurance	. . . . . .	
Working Tax Credit	. . . . . .		Fares/travel	. . . . . .	
Child Tax Credit	. . . . . .		Household expenses (food, laundry etc.).	. . . . . .	
Child Benefit	. . . . . .		Clothing	. . . . . .	
Housing Benefit	. . . . . .		School dinners	. . . . . .	
Attendance Allowance	. . . . . .		Childcare fees	. . . . . .	
Disability Living Allowance	. . . . . .		HP commitments	. . . . . .	
Universal Credit	. . . . . .		Telephone	. . . . . .	
Personal Independence Payments	. . . . . .		TV rental	. . . . . .	
Maintenance payments	. . . . . .		TV licence	. . . . . .	
Pensions	. . . . . .		Other expenditure (specify)		
Other income (specify)	. . . . . .		. . . .	. . . . . .	
. . . .	. . . . . .		. . . .	. . . . . .	
. . . .	. . . . . .		. . . .	. . . . . .	
. . . .	. . . . . .		. . . .	. . . . . .	

Total weekly income £   **Total weekly expenditure** £

Name of school/college/university:

Address

Course:

Is the course ☐ full-time? ☐ part-time?

Date of starting course:

Date of finishing course:

Name of local education authority:

Have you applied for a grant? ☐ YES ☐ NO

What was the outcome of the application?

Give details of any other grants or scholarships awarded:

Have you applied to your school/college/university for help? ☐ YES ☐ NO

What was the outcome of the application?

Have you applied to any other charities? ☐ YES ☐ NO

What was the outcome of the application?

Have you applied for any loans? ☐ YES ☐ NO

What was the outcome of the application?

How much are your school/college fees?

£

Have they been paid in full? ☐ YES ☐ NO

If NO, please give details:

Other costs (e.g. books, clothing, equipment, travel etc.):

How much money do you need to complete the course? £

Examinations passed and other qualifications

Previous employment (with dates)

Any other relevant information (please continue on separate sheet if necessary)

Signature:

Date:

About the Directory of Social Change

DSC has a vision of an independent voluntary sector at the heart of social change. The activities of independent charities, voluntary organisations and community groups are fundamental to achieve social change. We exist to help these organisations and the people who support them to achieve their goals.

We do this by:

- providing practical tools that organisations and activists need, including online and printed publications, training courses, and conferences on a huge range of topics
- acting as a 'concerned citizen' in public policy debates, often on behalf of smaller charities, voluntary organisations and community groups
- leading campaigns and stimulating debate on key policy issues that affect those groups
- carrying out research and providing information to influence policymakers.

DSC is the leading provider of information and training for the voluntary sector and publishes an extensive range of guides and handbooks covering subjects such as fundraising, management, communication, finance and law. We have a range of subscription-based websites containing a wealth of information on funding from charities, companies and government sources. We run more than 300 training courses each year, including bespoke in-house training provided at the client's location. DSC conferences, many of which run on an annual basis, include the Charity Management Conference, the Charity Accountants' Conference and the Charity Law Conference. DSC's major annual event is Charityfair, which provides low-cost training on a wide variety of subjects.

For details of all our activities, and to order publications and book courses, go to www.dsc.org.uk, call 08450 777707 or email publications@dsc.org.uk

National and general sources of help

The entries in this first section are arranged in three groups: 1) classified by need, 2) classified by occupation of parent or applicant, and 3) classified by subject. Charities appear in full in the section that is most relevant (usually the section which occurs first) and are then cross referenced should they also apply in another section.

This breakdown is designed to be the easiest way to identify charities which might be of relevance and as such we have attempted to make the terms as specific as possible. In doing so, this means that there is some crossover between sections. For instance, mature university students could identify charities in the 'Adult and continuing education' and 'Further and higher education' sections, with various other categories possibly being relevant dependent on personal circumstances.

There are a number of grantmakers which do not fall into any specific category; these appear first in the 'General' section.

Charities are arranged alphabetically within each category. We always caution against using these lists alone as a guide to sources of money. Read each main entry carefully as there will usually be other criteria that must be met; for example, someone who is blind should not simply apply to all the charities in the 'blindness' section. See the advice in the 'How to make an application' section on page xvi for more information on how to apply.

1

Classification by subject

National charities classified by need

General

The British and Foreign School Society - Alfred Bourne Trust

£0

Correspondent: Belinda Lawrance, Administrator, Maybrook House, Godstone Road, Caterham, Surrey CR3 6RE (01883 331177; email: enquiries@bfss.org.uk; website: www.bfss.org.uk)

CC Number: 314286

Eligibility
Students aged under 30, who are in the final stage of an initial teacher training course leading to qualified teacher status, and have run into unexpected financial difficulties for reasons outside their control.

Types of grants
Grants are one-off and there is no maximum amount.

Annual grant total
The trust usually has an annual income of around £1,000. In 2013 no grants were made from the trust.

Applications
Note: At the time of writing (July 2014) the British and Foreign School Society (BFSS) is reviewing the arrangements for the administration of this trust and is not accepting applications at present.

Other information
The BFSS is a grant giving organisation and offers funding for educational projects in the UK and around the world. The society also offers a small number of grants for organisations and individuals through its subsidiary trusts of which the Alfred Bourne Trust is one. Eligibility criteria for these subsidiary trusts depend on area of residence and/or particular field of educational activity.

Al-Mizan Charitable Trust

£12,300 (37 grants)

Correspondent: Zahra Shirzad, Grants Officer, 2 Burlington Gardens, London W3 6BA (email: admin@almizantrust.org.uk; website: www.almizantrust.org.uk)

CC Number: 1135752

Eligibility
British citizens, those granted indefinite leave to remain in the UK and asylum seekers who are living in a condition of social or economic deprivation. Preference is given to the following groups:
- Orphans (a child who has lost either both parents or one parent who was the main bread-winner in the family)
- Children and young people under the age of 19 years (particularly those in care or who are carers)
- Individuals who are disabled, incapacitated or terminally ill (particularly those who are severely mentally disabled)
- Single parents (particularly divorcees and widows/widowers with children)
- Estranged or isolated senior citizens
- Individuals with severe medical conditions or their families
- Ex-offenders or reformed drug addicts or alcoholics
- Victims of domestic violence and/or physical or sexual abuse
- Victims of crime, anti-social behaviour and/or terrorism

Types of grants
Mainly one-off grants ranging from £24 – £500, with an average grant being £271.Grants are available both for subsistence costs and those which help break the cycle of poverty by encouraging educational attainment and employability.

Annual grant total
In 2012/13 the trust had assets of £141,000 and an income of £209,000. Grants were made totalling £36,000 with £12,300 of that being awarded to 37 individuals for educational and employability purposes.

Exclusions
No grants for: general appeals; applicants who are not claiming all available benefits; retrospective funding; expenses relating to the practice or promotion of religion; debt, including council tax arrears; fines or criminal penalties; university tuition fees; gap year trips; building work or construction projects; funeral expenses; gifts (including birthdays and festivals); vehicles; and, holidays or recreational outings, unless they serve a medical, social or educational need. No support is given to those who have received a grant in the last twelve months.

Applications
All applications for grant funding must be submitted using the trust's online application system.

Other information
The trust has an informative website.

Lawrence Atwell's Charity (Skinners' Company)

£99,000 (127 grants)

Correspondent: S. Morris, Atwell Administrator, The Skinners' Company, Skinners' Hall, 8 Dowgate Hill, London EC4R 2SP (020 7213 0561; email: atwell@skinners.org.uk; website: www.skinnershall.co.uk/charities/lawrence-atwell-charity.htm)

CC Number: 210773

Eligibility

Young people aged between 16 and 26 who come from low-waged families (total gross income of the household must have been less than £26,000 a year for some time) and who are in need of support for vocational and pre-vocational training or to begin work.

Applicants must be UK citizens, refugees with leave to remain in the UK or asylum seekers in the process of obtaining leave to remain.

Preference is given to applicants who face additional barriers in life, work and training. For example those who: have no or few qualifications after leaving secondary education; have very limited or no support from their families; have a physical or mental disability; are lone parents; have fled persecution in their home countries; are ex-offenders or at risk of offending.

Types of grants

Support is offered towards:
- Vocational training below the level of a first undergraduate degree – for example, NVQ Level 3, BTEC National Diplomas, City and Guilds courses
- 'First step' qualifications to help people become qualified for work – such as, NVQ Level 1/2, BTEC First Diplomas/Certificates and access and foundation courses
- Costs of finding a job – including the costs of attending an interview or buying tools to get someone started

Grants are given according to need, usually in the range of £100–£1,500, and can be one-off or recurrent (reapplication each year is required). The majority of grants are given towards tuition, enrolment, registration and examination fees, however help is also given towards general living expenses, travel costs, household bills, accommodation and specific items, tools, childcare costs, clothing.

Annual grant total

In 2012/13 the charity had assets of £14.5 million and an income of £409,000. Grants to individuals totalled £99,000.

Exclusions

Grants are not provided:
- To people under the age of 16 and over the age of 27
- To international or foreign students who have not lived in the UK for three years prior to the start of their course (including people from EU countries)
- For non-vocational courses such as GCSEs, 'A' levels, or GNVQs
- For higher education courses or courses for which government

funding (such as a student loan) is available
- For courses at Level 4 or above
- For undergraduate/first degrees
- For postgraduate/second degrees
- Towards dance and drama courses which take place at private schools and colleges
- To individuals who are already qualified to work or who have had significant work experience
- To people whose current qualifications are Level 3 or above
- To cover any already existing fees or debts (including loans)
- In cases where it is unclear that the applicant will realistically be able to raise the balance of funds to complete the entire course
- Towards expeditions, travel or study abroad
- For business enterprises or start-up costs

If you are unsure about the level of your qualification see the Qualifications and Curriculum Authority website or visit the Quality Assurance Agency website.

Applications

Applicants are asked to first complete a short pre-application questionnaire available on the charity's website. Eligible applicants can then proceed with an online application. Guidelines for applicants and a useful FAQ section are also available to view on the charity's website. The grants committee meets bi-monthly, in July, September, November, January, March and May, to consider new grant applications from individuals, however emergency grants can also be made.

The charity welcomes informal contact via phone (except on Wednesdays) or email to discuss applications. When making enquires make sure to leave your name, address, day-time phone number and/or your email address.

Other information

The charity also provides assistance to organisations and support to the Skinner's Company's voluntary-aided schools. In 2012/13 grants to schools and organisations totalled £134,000.

There are eight subsidiary charities with the same address and registration number, all for purposes related to education.

Black Family Charitable Trust

£6,000

Correspondent: Dr Thomas Black, Trustee, PO Box 232, Petersfield, Hampshire GU32 9DQ (email: enquires@bfct.org.uk; website: www.bfct.org.uk)

CC Number: 1134661

Eligibility

Schoolchildren, further and higher education students who are in need. The trust's website states that the charity 'primarily aims to help young people to access high quality education, focusing its support particularly on those who would otherwise be denied appropriate education due to a lack of financial resources.'

Types of grants

Means tested bursaries/scholarships and merit based prizes/awards. Projects or research can also be supported.

Annual grant total

In 2012/13 the trust had an income of £7,800 and a total expenditure of £56,000. In previous years most of the support was given to universities and organisations. We estimate that around £6,000 was awarded to individuals for educational purposes.

Applications

In writing to the correspondent.

Other information

Grants are also given to schools (also in developing countries) and other organisations.

The Chizel Educational Trust

£4,300

Correspondent: Geoffrey Bond, Trustee, Burgage Manor, Southwell, Nottingham NG25 0EP

CC Number: 1091574

Eligibility

People under the age of 25 throughout the UK who are in need of financial assistance.

Types of grants

Bursaries, maintenance allowances and grants towards equipment, clothing, instruments, books and travel in the UK or abroad.

Annual grant total

In 2012/13 the trust had an income of £10,500 and an expenditure of £8,900. Financial support is also given to organisations, therefore we estimate that the total of individual grants was around £4,300.

Applications

In writing to the correspondent. Applications are considered twice a year, in June and December.

Other information

Financial assistance is also provided towards the maintenance of Ackworth

School Yorkshire and the Inverness Royal Academy Mollie Stephens Trust.

The Coffey Charitable Trust

£1,000

Correspondent: Christopher Coffey, Trustee, Oaktree House, Over the Misbourne Road, Denham, Uxbridge, Middlesex UB9 5DR (01895 831381; email: coffeytrust@gmail.com)

CC Number: 1043549

Eligibility
People in need in the UK.

Types of grants
Occasional one-off and recurrent grants according to need.

Annual grant total
In 2013/14 the trust had an income of £12,000 and a total expenditure of £6,500. We estimate grants to individuals for educational and social welfare purposes to be around £1,000 each.

Applications
In writing to the correspondent.

Other information
This trust mainly provides grants to Christian organisations and events.

Conservative and Unionist Agents' Benevolent Association

£10,000

Correspondent: Sally Smith, Administrator, Conservative Campaign Headquarters, Millbank Tower, 30 Millbank, London SW1P 4DP (020 7984 8172; email: sally.smith@ conservatives.com)

CC Number: 216438

Eligibility
Children of deceased Conservative or Unionist agents or women organisers.

Types of grants
One-off and recurrent grants towards books, equipment, instruments and fees for schoolchildren.

Annual grant total
In 2012/13 the association had assets of over £2.7 million and an income of £94,000. Grants were made totalling £58,000. We estimate that around £10,000 was spent on educational grants. These are sometimes paid when a parent dies.

Applications
Initial telephone calls are welcomed and application forms are available on request. Applications can be made either directly by the individual or their parent/guardian, or through a member of the management committee or local serving agent. All beneficiaries are allocated a 'visiting agent'.

Other information
The majority of the association's grants are made for relief-in-need purposes.

Peter Alan Dickson Foundation
See entry on page 31

Family Action

Correspondent: David Holmes, Administrator, Family Action, 501–505 Kingsland Road, London E8 4AU (020 7241 7601; email: info@ family-action.org.uk; website: www. family-action.org.uk)

CC Number: 264713

Eligibility
Individuals over the age of 14 who wish to enter further education, undertake training/retraining and otherwise pursue their career.

Types of grants
Educational grants to enable individuals to pursue and advance their career.

Annual grant total
Through the previous programme about £200,000 was being given each year. The amount awarded in new educational grants will only be known after the charitable giving commences.

Applications
An educational grants programme will be opened on 1 September 2014. Further guidelines on eligibility and the application process will be available on the charity's website.

Other information
Previously educational grants were distributed through Barclaycard Horizons Your Education Fund to lone parents. The project was wound up in 2012. Family Action has changed its focus and will now be providing educational support to help individuals pursue education.

The Fenton Trust

£4,000

Correspondent: Fiona MacGillivray, Family Action, 501–505 Kingsland Road, London E8 4AU (020 7241 7609; email: grants.enquiry@family-action.org.uk; website: www.family-action.org.uk)

CC Number: 247552

Eligibility
Any dependent of a member of professional class undergoing a course of education or training or 'poor and deserving members of the professional or middle classes and their dependants.'

Types of grants
Grants are normally of about £200 – £300 and can be given to assist with general educational costs.

Annual grant total
In 2012/13 the trust had an income of £15,500 and an expenditure of £67,100 which is much higher than in previous years. We have estimated that normally the annual total of grants is around £4,000.

Exclusions
Grants are not available for private school fees, loan repayments, childcare costs, living expenses or to postgraduate students.

Applications
Applications should be made via the trust's website and can be submitted at any time. Applicants are also reminded to make sure the application form they have completed is up to date and review the educational grant search on the trust's website prior to applying.

Other information
The grant is paid to the governing body not the individual.

The General Federation of Trade Unions Educational Trust

£1,500

Correspondent: Doug Nicholls, Administrator, Headland House, 308–312 Gray's Inn Road, London WC1X 8DP (020 7520 8340; email: gftuhq@gftu.org.uk; website: www.gftu. org.uk)

CC Number: 313439

Eligibility
Members of a trade union are eligble. Grants will only be considered for the subjects of economic history and theory; industrial law; and the history and principles of industrial relations.

Types of grants
Full-time and part-time students undertaking a course nominated by the recipient's trade union receive a grant of up to £150 (full-time), £50 (part-time) or £100 (Open University). Open University students will be supported after completing the first year. Grants may be paid annually.

Annual grant total

In 2012 the trust had assets of £2.2 million and an income of £811,000. Grants are given to around 15 individuals totalling about £1,500 annually. The 2012 accounts were the latest available at the time of writing (August 2014).

Applications

A nomination form is available from the correspondent and must be signed by the general secretary of the applicant's trade union. Applications are considered quarterly. Proof of trade union membership may be required. Forms signed by lay representatives and local officials are not valid.

Global Educational Trust

£0

Correspondent: Mohammad Yusuf Adrian Bashforth, Administrator, 78 York Street, London W1H 1DP (020 7692 4076; fax: 020 7692 4077; email: info@globaleducationaltrust.org; website: www.globaleducationaltrust.org)

CC Number: 1144969

Eligibility

People in the UK and overseas.

Types of grants

Scholarships and bursaries to allow people to attend school, college or university.

Annual grant total

Although from its website this trust appears to be operational, its accounts had not been submitted to the Charity Commission at the time of writing (August 2014) and were 288 days overdue. Accounts were requested from the correspondent but no response was received.

Applications

In writing to the correspondent.

Other information

The trust also gives grants to organisations in the UK and overseas, it aims to increases literacy rates.

Leverhulme Trade Charities Trust

£1.4 million (258 grants)

Correspondent: Paul Read, Administrator, 1 Pemberton Row, London EC4A 3BG (020 7042 9881; fax: 020 7042 9889; email: pread@ leverhulme.ac.uk; website: www. leverhulme-trade.org.uk)

CC Number: 288404

Eligibility

Students at a recognised UK university who are in need and whose parent or spouse has worked as a commercial traveller, grocer or chemist for at least five years.

Individuals are still eligible if their parent/spouse is unemployed (or deceased) but who fell within one of the three categories when the employment ceased (or at the time of death).

Types of grants

One-off or recurrent grants of up to £3,000 a year to full-time undergraduate students and of up to £5,000 a year to postgraduate students. Support is given towards general educational needs, including tuition and examination fees, living expenses, books, equipment, travel costs and accommodation. Awards are paid to the applicant's university.

Annual grant total

In 2013 the trust had assets of £58.3 million and an income of £2.2 million. Bursaries to 258 individuals totalled around £1.4 million, consisting of £1 million in 200 undergraduate bursaries and £348,000 in 58 postgraduate bursaries.

Applications

Application forms for undergraduate funding together with full guidelines can be accessed from the trust's website. They should be submitted by 1 March or 1 November for consideration in the following six weeks.

Applications for postgraduate funding should be made by the institution on behalf of a qualifying individual. Universities should contact the correspondent in writing.

Other information

In 2013 grants to institutions totalled £1.6 million.

P. and M. Lovell Charitable Trust

£5,600 (19 grants)

Correspondent: The Trustees, Administrator, KPMG, 100 Temple Street, Bristol BS1 6AG (01179 054000; fax: 01179 054065)

CC Number: 274846

Eligibility

People in education who are in need.

Types of grants

One-off grants up to £500 (generally of £300).

Annual grant total

In 2012/13 the trust had assets of £1.9 million, an income of £68,000 and made grants totalling £46,000. Awards to

19 individuals totalled £5,600. The trustees' annual report from 2012/13 specifies that 'the income of the trust is to be distributed solely for charitable purposes to charitable institutions or individuals' while 'the capital may be applied for charitable purposes or retained by the trustees at their discretion.'

Applications

In writing to the correspondent.

Other information

Grants are mostly made to organisations (around £41,000 to 84 institutions in 2012/13).

The Osborne Charitable Trust

£2,000

Correspondent: John Eaton, Administrator, 57 Osborne Villas, Hove, East Sussex BN3 2RA (01273 732500; email: john@eaton207.fsnet.co.uk)

CC Number: 326363

Eligibility

People in education in the UK and overseas.

Types of grants

One-off and recurrent grants according to need and one-off grants in kind. Grants are given to schoolchildren for equipment/instruments and special needs education for fees and equipment/ instruments.

Annual grant total

In 2012/13 the trust had an income of £8,000 and a total expenditure of £8,500. We estimate around £2,000 was made in grants to individuals for education.

Exclusions

No grants for religious or political purposes.

Applications

This trust does not respond to unsolicited applications.

Other information

The trust also makes grants to individuals for social welfare purposes.

Scarr-Hall Memorial Trust

£11,200

Correspondent: Donna Thorley, Administrator, Baker Tilly, Festival Way, Festival Park, Stoke-on-Trent, Staffordshire ST1 5BB

CC Number: 328105

Eligibility

People in education and training throughout the UK.

Types of grants

One-off grants are usually in the range of £100 and £500.

Annual grant total

In 2012/13 the trust had an income of £22,000 and an expenditure of £11,600. We estimate the annual total of grants to individuals to be around £11,200.

Applications

In writing to the correspondent providing an sae and stating all the relevant individual circumstances, reasons why the grant is needed and how much is required.

Victoria Shardlow's Children's Trust

£4,500 (3 grants)

Correspondent: Liz Clifford, Charities Administrator, 9 Menin Way, Farnham GU9 8DY (email: Victoriashardlowtrust@googlemail.com)

Eligibility

Children or young people up to the age of 18 who are coping with 'difficult circumstances and are disadvantaged to participate and benefit from formal or non-formal education.'

Types of grants

Small, one-off grants are awarded towards equipment, fees, transportation costs and educational trips in the UK or abroad. The maximum available grant is £3,000.

Annual grant total

In 2012/13 the trust awarded three individuals with grants ranging between £1,000 and £2,000.

Exclusions

Grants are not given for university fees, gap-year activities and for private school fees or equipment.

Applications

Application forms can be obtained from the correspondent and should be submitted either directly by the individual or by the parent/guardian. Applications are considered in January, April, July and October.

Other information

Support can be given to small registered groups providing educational opportunities for disadvantaged children. The trust has also informed us that larger amounts are given to organisations (for example, Camfed was awarded £20,000 in 2012/13).

This trust is very small and therefore is not registered with the Charity Commission. The correspondent has confirmed that the trust's beneficial area is not restricted and, in practice, applications can be made from anywhere in the world.

Southdown Trust

£17,000 (85 grants)

Correspondent: Hugh Wyatt, Administrator, 9 Nepcote, Findon, Worthing, West Sussex BN14 0SD

CC Number: 235583

Eligibility

Young people in education between the ages of 17 and 26.

Types of grants

One-off and recurrent grants are available for ambitious, entrepreneurial people for educational courses and to 'support individual ventures of general educational benefit'. Examples have included: funding a teaching assistant at a primary school or providing a scholarship for a university student. The trust warns that the awards are modest and normally would not exceed £100–£200.

Annual grant total

In 2012/13 the trust had assets of £1.1 million, an income of £89,000 and a total charitable expenditure of around £45,000. Individual grants totalled £17,000 and were awarded to 85 individuals.

Exclusions

Grants are not made for art, dance, sociology, theatre, law, journalism, counselling, media studies, PhDs or the cost of materials.

Applications

In writing to the correspondent enclosing a CV and a covering letter, specifying what the assistance is required for and providing an sae. Applications should be made directly by the individual.

Other information

Grants are also made to organisations (13 grants totalling £28,000 in 2012/13).

The Stanley Stein Deceased Charitable Trust

£21,000

Correspondent: Michael Lawson, Trustee, Burwood House, 14–16 Caxton Street, London SW1H 0GY (020 7873 1000; email: michael.lawson@williamsturges.co.uk)

CC Number: 1048873

Eligibility

People under the age of 21 who are in need or suffer from illness. People with disabilities, visual or hearing impairment are eligible for help.

Types of grants

One-off and recurrent grants are given according to need towards general educational costs.

Annual grant total

In 2012/13 the trust had an income of £11,700 and an expenditure of £45,000. We estimate that grants to individuals for educational purposes totalled around £21,000.

Applications

On a form available from the correspondent.

Other information

Grants are given for both welfare and education causes.

The Talisman Charitable Trust

£19,500 (12 grants)

Correspondent: Philip Denman, Trustee, Lower Ground Floor Office, 354 Kennington Road, London SE11 4LD (020 7820 0254; website: www.talismancharity.org)

CC Number: 207173

Eligibility

People in the UK who are living on a very low income.

Types of grants

One-off and recurrent grants according to need.

Annual grant total

In 2012/13 the trust had assets of £9.4 million and an income of £199,000. 12 grants for education were made totalling £19,500.

Grants were also made to organisations totalling £59,500 and to individuals for welfare purposes totalling £83,000.

Applications

In writing to the correspondent through a social worker, Citizens Advice or similar third party.

Applications should be on headed paper and include the individual's full name and address, a summary of their financial circumstances, what is needed and how much it will cost. A brief history of the case and a list of any other charities approached should be included as well. Supporting evidence such as medical documentation, a letter from the applicant's school and written quotations would also be helpful.

Applications are considered throughout the year. Only successful applicants will receive a reply.

Note: applications should not be sent by recorded delivery or any signed for services.

Other information

This trust was previously called The Late Baron F. A. d'Erlanger's Charitable Trust.

TIKO Foundation

£12,400 (1 grant)

Correspondent: The Grants Manager, Vicarage House, 58–60 Kensington Church Street, London W8 4DB (020 7368 1642; email: info@tikofoundation.org; website: www.tikofoundation.org)

CC Number: 1145979

Eligibility

Applicants must be entering first (undergraduate) degree and have already received an offer from a high ranking university/universities. Candidates must be academically gifted, reside in the UK and come from a low income background.

Eligibility will initially be checked through an application form and supporting documents.

Types of grants

The foundation grant will finance an applicant's tuition and accommodation expenses for the duration of his or her academic course. Advice and support from trustees is offered throughout the grant award period.

Annual grant total

In 2012/13 the foundation had assets of £32,000 and an income of £8,900. One grant of £12,400 was awarded during the year.

Exclusions

The grant will not provide:
- Funding for a postgraduate degree (for example, MA or BSC), employment training programmes, internships or a first degree already started
- Any other expenses other than course fees and accommodation
- Funding for fees already incurred throughout a degree
- Funding towards anyone who does not meet **all** foundation's eligibility criteria.

Applications

Application forms can be found on the foundation's website. Completed electronic copies should be emailed to the correspondent together with any supporting documentation and a completed Financial Eligibility Checker,

which is also available from the foundation's website. The application round usually opens in October and runs until the end of May the following year.

Other information

The award is not part of an employee training programme and the foundation will not offer any post-graduation work placements or internships.

The award is subject to the applicant achieving excellent grades, taking part in regular monitoring and evaluation of progress, and participating in marketing events.

Madeleine Mary Walker Foundation

£30,000

Correspondent: Paul Benfield, Trustee, 1 Levington Wynd, Nunthorpe, Middlesbrough TS7 0QD (email: m100pfb@yahoo.co.uk)

CC Number: 1062657

Eligibility

People in need of support towards their education up to first degree or equivalent. Priority is given to those living within a 30 mile radius of Stokesley, North Yorkshire.

Types of grants

Assistance can be given towards various educational needs, including the cost of books, equipment/tools, musical instruments, fees, study/travel abroad, field trips and so forth. Grants usually range from £250 to £750.

Annual grant total

In 2012/13 the foundation had assets of £917,000 and an income of £34,000. A total of £30,000 was awarded in grants.

Applications

In writing to the correspondent, providing an sae and a contact telephone number. The trustees usually meet three/four times per year. Applicants may be interviewed.

S. C. Witting Trust

£500 (5 grants)

Correspondent: Witting Trust Administrator, Friends House, 173 Euston Road, London NW1 2BJ

CC Number: 237698

Eligibility

Students following or intending and preparing to follow a course of study at university, ordinarily resident in England.

Types of grants

One-off grants are made for uniforms/clothing, books and equipment/instruments.

Annual grant total

In 2013 the trust gave 5 grants of £100 to individuals in England.

Exclusions

No grants towards debts or loans.

Applications

Applications:
- Must be made in writing with a letter of support from a tutor
- The application must give a short case history, reasons for need and amount needed
- Applications are considered monthly and unsuccessful applications will not be acknowledged unless a stamped envelope is provided
- **No telephone calls**
- **No emails**

Other information

Grants are also made to benefit individuals under the age of 16 or over the age of 60 for welfare purposes.

Toby and Regina Wyles Charitable Trust

£7,000

Correspondent: Ross Badger, Trustee, 3rd Floor, North Dukes Court, 32 Duke Street, St James' London, London SW1Y 6DF (020 7930 7797; email: ross.badger@hhllp.co.uk)

CC Number: 1118376

Eligibility

People in need of assistance to enter or continue their education.

Types of grants

Grants are given towards general educational costs.

Annual grant total

In 2012/13 the trust had assets of £665,000, an income of £171,000 and an expenditure of £55,000. Most of the trust's funding is given to other charitable organisations. The amount of grants awarded to individuals was not specified in the trustees' report of 2012/13, however previously grants to individuals have totalled £7,000.

Applications

In writing to the correspondent.

Other information

Grants are mainly made to organisations.

The Zobel Charitable Trust

£1,500

Correspondent: Stephen Scott, Trustee, Tenison House, Tweedy Road, Bromley, Kent BR1 3NF (020 8464 4242)

CC Number: 1094186

Eligibility
People in education in the UK, particularly in the Christian field.

Types of grants
One-off and recurrent grants according to need.

Annual grant total
This trust generally awards about £1,500 a year to individuals for educational purposes.

Exclusions
No grants for fees.

Applications
This trust does its own research and does not always respond to unsolicited applications.

Other information
Grants are also made to organisations.

Adult and continuing education

Diamond Education Grant
See entry on page 46

Monica Eyre Memorial Foundation

£1,500

Correspondent: Michael Bidwell, Trustee, 5 Clifton Road, Winchester, Hampshire SO22 5BN

CC Number: 1046645

Eligibility
Mature students in need, particularly those with disabilities/special needs in the UK.

Types of grants
Grants towards fees to enable mature students to start or continue courses.

Annual grant total
In 2012/13 the foundation had an income of £5,500 and a total expenditure of £5,000. We estimate the grant total

for individuals for educational purposes was around £1,500.

Applications
In writing to the correspondent. The foundation vets course content and validates enrolment before awarding any funding.

Other information
The foundation also makes grants to organisations and to individuals for welfare purposes.

Gilchrist Educational Trust

£21,000 (44 grants)

Correspondent: Val Considine, Secretary, 20 Fern Road, Storrington, Pulborough, West Sussex RH20 4LW (01903 746723; email: gilchrist.et@ blueyonder.co.uk; website: www. gilchristgrants.org.uk)

CC Number: 313877

Eligibility
Full-time students at a UK university who either 'have made proper provision to fund a degree or higher education course but find themselves facing unexpected financial difficulties which may prevent the completion of it' (normally in the last year of the course); or 'are required, as part of their degree course, to spend a short period studying abroad.'

Types of grants
Both study and travel grants are usually of around £500. Four book prizes are also available to students achieving high grades at Birkbeck College, London University's Department of Extra-Mural Studies.

Annual grant total
In 2012/13 the trust had assets of £1.7 million, an income of £84,000 and a total charitable expenditure of £73,000. Grants to individuals totalled £21,000, out of these 26 were travel grants (£13,300) and 14 study grants (£7,800). Four book prizes were awarded totalling £200.

Exclusions
Support is not given to the following:
- Part-time students
- People seeking funds to enable them to take up a place on a course
- Students seeking help in meeting the cost of maintaining dependents
- Students who have, as part of a course, to spend all or most of an academic year studying in another country
- Those wishing to go abroad under the auspices of independent travel, exploratory or educational projects

Applications
Individuals should contact the grants officer via the above email or by post to the following address: 13 Brookfield Avenue, Larkfield, Aylesford ME20 6RU. Following an initial enquiry, eligible applicants will be sent further list of details required for application. Individuals can submit their applications at any time by post only.

Other information
The trust also gives grants to organisations (£19,500 in 2012/13), British university expeditions for scientific research (£6,500 in 2012/13), and offers a biennial Fieldwork Award of £15,000 'available in even-numbered years and open to small teams of qualified academics and researchers in established posts in university departments or research establishments, most of British nationality, wishing to undertake a field season of over six weeks.'

Business start-up and apprentice-ships/ vocational training

The Oli Bennett Charitable Trust

£4,000

Correspondent: Joy Bennett, Administrator, 'Camelot, Penn Street, Amersham, Buckinghamshire HP7 0PY (01494 717702; email: info@olibennett. org.uk; website: www.olibennett.org.uk)

CC Number: 1090861

Eligibility
Young people between 18 and 30, who are self-employed and are UK residents.

Types of grants
Grants in the range of £1,000 and £1,500 for people starting up their own businesses.

Annual grant total
In 2012 the trust had an income of £4,000 and an expenditure of £9,000. We estimate grants made to individuals for educational purposes totalled around £4,000.

The 2012 accounts are the latest available at the time of writing.

Applications

Application forms are available on the trust's website. Applications are considered every three months. A business plan is required to assess the viability of the idea.

Other information

The trust was set up in memory of Oli Bennett, who died in the September 11 2001 attacks in New York.

City and Guilds Bursaries

£139,000

Correspondent: David Miller, Administrator, City and Guilds of London Institute, 1 Giltspur Street, London EC1A 9DD (020 7294 2468; fax: 020 7294 2400; email: david.miller@ cityandguilds.com; website: www. cityandguilds.com/qualifications-and-apprenticeships/support/bursaries)

CC Number: 312832

Eligibility

UK residents who wish to study or are studying a City and Guilds qualification to improve their financial security.

Most recently preference was given to the following areas: health and social care, engineering, electro-technical, plumbing and heating, and chemical industries.

Types of grants

Educational grants are available for course and exam fees, living costs, books/equipment, travel costs, childcare and other needs. Around 40–60 awards are made each year. Awards are agreed on a case by case basis and determined by the individual course costs.

Annual grant total

In 2012/13 the charity awarded 57 bursaries totalling £139,000.

Exclusions

Retrospective payments, grants for career development or deferred loans taken out with a college or bank are not covered.

Applications

Applications can be made online on the City and Guilds website. They are considered twice a year, in May and October, and can be submitted up to three months before the closing date. For specific deadlines and bursary timetable see the website. Candidates are invited to an interview in London.

Other information

City and Guilds primarily exist to provide qualifications, awards, assessments and support across a range of occupations in industry, commerce and the public services.

The charity warns that the awards are very competitive.

Go Make it Happen: A Project in Memory of Sam Harding

£2,200

Correspondent: Keith Harding, Administrator, 72 New Caledonian Wharf, 6 Odessa Street, London SE16 7TW (020 3592 7921, 07790 622381 (mob); email: keithhard@ hotmail.co.uk; website: www. gomakeithappen.co.uk)

CC Number: 1145369

Eligibility

People between the ages of 18 and 30 to who want to build a career in the tourism and travel industry. The trust has a particular, but not exclusive, focus on young people who have not necessarily followed a 'conventional' academic route and wants to help them 'achieve things in their lives that they would not otherwise be able to achieve.'

Types of grants

Funding is available for training courses, travel expenses and other educational opportunities in the UK and overseas. Some examples include: support for volunteering and internships, language learning, skills-based qualifications and so on.

Annual grant total

In 2012/13 the charity had an income of £7,400 and an expenditure of £2,400. We estimate that grants totalled around £2,200.

Applications

Applications can be made online on the charity's website. The charity will normally make contact within two weeks and may arrange for an interview.

Other information

The charity also provides information and advice on opportunities for working overseas and in travel or tourism generally (both in the UK and abroad).

They also campaign for cycling safety and driver awareness in memory of Sam's tragic death.

The N. and P. Hartley Memorial Trust

£2,000

Correspondent: Virginia Watson, Trustee, 24 Holywell Lane, Leeds LS17 8HA

CC Number: 327570

Eligibility

Priority is firstly given to those living in West Yorkshire, secondly to individuals living in the north of England and thirdly to those elsewhere in the UK and overseas.

Types of grants

One-off grants for vocational training for vocational employment.

Annual grant total

Grants to individuals total between £3,000 and £4,000 each year.

Applications

In writing to the correspondent, preferably through a social worker, Citizens Advice or other welfare agency, for consideration twice yearly. Re-applications from previous beneficiaries are welcomed.

Other information

The trust also makes a number of grants to organisations and to individuals for welfare purposes.

The Prince's Trust

£1.9 million (6,169 grants)

Correspondent: Sarah Haidry, Secretary, Prince's Trust House, 9 Eldon Street, London EC2M 7SL (020 7543 1234; fax: 020 7543 1200; email: sarah.haidry@ princes-trust.org.uk; website: www. princes-trust.org.uk)

CC Number: 1079675, SC041198

Eligibility

Young people between the ages 13 and 30 who are not expecting to achieve five GCSEs (or equivalent) grades A-C, who struggle at school, are not in education or training, are in or leaving care, are long-term unemployed or have been in trouble with the law.

Types of grants

The Prince's Trust aims to change the lives of young people, helping them to develop confidence, learn new skills and get practical and financial support. The following support is offered:
- Development awards – grants of £50–£500 to people aged 14–25 to get into education, training or employment. Previously grants have been given towards IT training, tools and equipment, travel expenses, fees (including licence fees), interview clothes or childcare costs
- Enterprise programme – grants to people aged 18–30 towards test marketing (up to £250) and low interest business start-up loans (in the range of £2,000–£5,000) or, in special circumstances, start-up grants (up to £1,500)

Annual grant total

In 2012/13 the trust had assets of £40.9 million and an income of £57.6 million. A total of £1.9 million was distributed in grants to individuals, consisting of:

Enterprise	434	£936,000
Development awards	5,388	£889,000
Community cash awards	347	£136,000

Note that Community Cash Awards have been discontinued. In 2012 the awards were still made, therefore figures are included in the financial information.

Exclusions

The trust will not fund:

- Retrospective grants
- Gap-year or overseas projects
- Medical treatment
- Course fees that are far above the £500 funding limit
- NVQ Level 4, HNC, HND, university degree or postgraduate courses (or courses of an equivalent level)

Applications

Initial enquiry forms should be completed online on the trust's website. Eligible applicants will then be advised on further procedure.

Potential applicants are also invited to make queries by phone at 0800 842 842, or text 'Call Me' to 07983 385418 to discuss an application.

Other information

The Prince's Trust also runs many programmes which provide young people with personal development, training and opportunities to help them move into work. Details of these can be found on the trust's website.

In April 2012 the trust merged with its sister charity The Prince's Scottish Youth Business Trust.

The Thomas Wall Trust

£47,000 (62 grants)

Correspondent: Deborah French, Chief Accountant, Skinners' Hall, 8 Dowgate Hill, London EC4R 2SP (020 7213 0567; email: information@thomaswalltrust.org. uk; website: www.thomaswalltrust.org. uk)

CC Number: 206121

Eligibility

People who are over the age of 16 and have been resident in the UK for at least three years prior to the beginning of the course to be attended and who are facing financial difficulties stopping them from entering education or employment. Applicants should not have any qualifications for work and be unable to fund their courses through any other means (for example, statutory grants or loans). The courses should be below degree level and leading to employment.

Types of grants

Small, one-off grants (generally of up to £1,000) to overcome financial barriers to work or education. Awards are given towards fees, equipment and other expenses related to vocational, skill-based or technical study and professional training. Interest free loans can also be made. Both full-time and part-time courses are considered for support.

Annual grant total

In 2012/13 the trust had assets of £3.1 million and an income of £139,000. Grants to 62 individuals totalled £47,000.

Exclusions

Grants are not given:

- For undergraduate and postgraduate degree courses or PhD students
- Towards higher education courses that qualify for Student Loan Company funding
- To people earning above £26,000 per year
- To individuals with family income above the average salary (£26,000 per year)
- To persons who are considered 'employable' or 'qualified to work'
- For travel, study or work overseas
- For elective periods or intercalated courses
- Towards business start-up costs
- For GCSEs or A-levels
- To schoolchildren

Applications

Applications should be made online at the trust's website. For the courses starting in September applications should be submitted between January and August and for courses starting at the end of July (or short courses before September) – between January and April. If the funds run out the application round may be closed earlier. Further details on parental income will be required from all applicants under the age of 25.

Other information

Grants are also given to charitable organisations in the field of education and social welfare, especially those that are small or of a pioneering nature. In 2012/13 a total of £27,000 was awarded to 28 organisations.

The trust's website reminds: 'due to limited administration resources, we are unable to deal with telephone enquiries. All information about our application processes can be found by browsing our website. If you do need to contact us the easiest way is by email.'

Due to high demand, on average only about one in ten people get a grant.

Carers

Carers Trust

£51,000

Correspondent: The Administrator, 32–36 Loman Street, London SE1 0EH (0844 800 4361; fax: 0844 800 4362; email: info@carers.org; website: www. carers.org)

CC Number: 1145181

Eligibility

Unpaid carers in the UK, especially those who live near a Princess Royal Trust for Carers Centre.

Types of grants

One-off grants, usually of up to £300. Funding is given to provide support to carers towards equipment, essential items, personal and skills development or other educational activities.

Annual grant total

In 2012/13 the trust had assets of £5.6 million and an income of £8.3 million. During the year a total of £103,000 was awarded in grants to 397 individuals. The trust also makes awards for welfare purposes, therefore we estimate the annual total of educational grants to be around £51,000.

Applications

Applications should be made via your local Carers Service centre. Direct applications are not considered.

Other information

The charity has been formed by merging The Princess Royal Trust for Carers and Crossroads Care in April 2012. Support is mainly channelled through the trust's Network Partners. Information, guidance and advice are also provided through the trust's website and social media.

Grants paid to organisations reached £725,000 and payments to 'Network Partners' totalled £1.3 million in 2012/13.

Children and young people

The French Huguenot Church of London Charitable Trust

£102,000 (50 grants)

Correspondent: Duncan McGowan, Clerk to the Trustees, Haysmacintyre, Fairfax House, 15 Fulwood Place, London WC1V 6AY (email: dmcgowan@haysmacintyre.com)

CC Number: 249017

Eligibility
People under the age of 25. Support is given in the following priority: people who/whose parents are members of the Church; people of French Protestant descent; other people as trustees think fit (preferences are outlined in the following section).

Types of grants
Annual allowances, bursaries and emergency or project grants to school pupils, further/higher education students, people in training or those entering a trade/starting work. Preference is given to French Protestant children attending French schools in London, choristers at schools of the Choir Schools Association, girls at schools of the Girls' Day School Trust and United Learning, and boys in selected independent day schools (list can be received upon request from the trust).

Support can be given for various educational needs, including outfits, necessities, equipment and instruments, books, study of music or other arts, also home/overseas projects. Special allowances for people of French protestant descent are given in modest one-off payments towards books.

Annual grant total
At the time of writing (July 2014) the latest financial information available was from 2012. In 2012 the trust had assets of £10.7 million, an income of £368,000 and a charitable expenditure of £294,000. Educational grants and bursaries to 50 pupils totalled £102,000, including grants to ten young people totalling £900 for overseas projects.

Applications
Applications for grants and bursaries from members of the Church and French Protestant children attending schools in London should be made to the Secretary of the Consistory, 8–9 Soho Square, London W1V 5DD.

Requests for special allowances to people of French Protestant descent and for project grants should be addressed to the correspondent.

Applications from choristers and pupils at the selected schools should be addressed to the educational institution concerned, mentioning the applicant's connection (if any) with the French Protestant Church.

Other information
In addition to the educational fund there also are church and hardship funds mostly supporting organisations. In 2012 awards totalling around £33,000 were made to nine organisations providing assistance mainly to disabled and underprivileged young people.

The trust also awards an annual postgraduate scholarship of £2,500 for Huguenot Research at the Institution of Historical Research at the University of London.

The William Gibbs Trust

£7,500

Correspondent: Antonia Johnson, Trustee, 40 Bathwick Hill, Bath BA2 6LD

CC Number: 282957

Eligibility
Children and young people in education who are of British nationality.

Types of grants
One-off and recurrent grants according to need are given towards general educational needs.

Annual grant total
In 2013 the trust had an income of £9,400 and an expenditure of £15,300. We estimate the annual total of grants to individuals to be around £7,500.

Applications
The trust has previously stated it does not respond to unsolicited applications as the funds are already allocated. Any enquiries should be made in writing.

Other information
Grants are also given to organisations for educational purposes.

The Marillier Trust

£8,500

Correspondent: William Stisted, Trustee, 38 Southgate, Chichester, West Sussex PO19 1DP (01243 787899; email: ws@alhlaw.co.uk)

CC Number: 1100693

Eligibility
Boys between the ages of 5 and 13.

Types of grants
Grants are given for education other than formal teaching in class. The trust will support educational and recreational opportunities, residential trips, after school activities and so on. Loans are also made to individuals.

Annual grant total
In 2012/13 the trust had assets of £990,000 and an income of £39,000. The charitable expenditure totalled £170,000. A total of £8,500 was awarded in grants to individuals (£1,900 for residential trips and £6,600 for after school activities).

Applications
In writing to the correspondent.

Other information
The trust also makes grants to institutions for educational trips, extra-curricular activities, counselling or equipment (in 2012/13 a total of £162,000) and provides human resources (staff, volunteers).

Professionals Aid Council

£24,000 (68 grants)

Correspondent: Finola McNicholl, Administrator, 10 St Christopher's Place, London W1U 1HZ (020 7935 0641; email: admin@pcac.org.uk; website: www.professionalsaid.org.uk)

CC Number: 207292

Eligibility
The dependents of people who are graduates or have worked in a professional occupation requiring that level of education, or those who have a first degree themselves, studying in the UK.

Types of grants
One-off and recurring. Children's education grants for uniforms, travel, equipment/books and educational outings. College or university student grants of £300 to £500 for tuition fees in the final months of a course, medical dental and veterinary courses in the final two years, degree shows, travel expenses and equipment/books.

Annual grant total
In 2012 the charity had assets of £2.15 million and an income of £122,000. During the year there were 18 grants for children's education and 50 grants for further/higher education, totalling £24,000.

These were the latest accounts available at the time of writing (July 2014).

Exclusions

No grants for private tutors, study abroad, ordination or conversion courses, medical electives, IELTS or PLAB tests.

Applications

Initially by filling in the enquiry form on the charity's website or writing to the correspondent.

Other information

The organisation also offers advice and assistance. Grants are also made for welfare purposes.

Red House Youth Projects Trust

£1,200 (4 grants)

Correspondent: The Grants Administrator, Red House Youth Projects, PO Box 1287, North Walsham NR28 8AA (01692 538810; email: grants@redhouseyouthprojects.co.uk; website: www.redhouseyouthprojects.co.uk)

CC Number: 1092828

Eligibility

People under 21 who are resident in Norfolk.

Types of grants

Grants for young people to follow personal ambitions and to undertake community arts/citizenship projects. The trustees' annual report for 2012/13 informs us that: 'Grants would normally not exceed £500.'

Annual grant total

In 2012/13 the trust had assets of £913,000 and an income of £85,000. A total of £11,100 was awarded in grants, the majority of which was received by organisations. 4 grants to individuals totalled £1,200.

Exclusions

No grants for trips abroad. Grants are not made for money already spent.

Applications

On forms available from the trust's website. Applications must be made by the young person, though trustees or staff are willing to help individuals to complete forms. The trust reminds applicants to ensure the correct postage is used when posting an application (a large stamp should be used if the application is in an A4 envelope). Applications must be completed/sent by the following months for submission at the next meeting: February, May, August and November.

Other information

Grants are also available to support the training of adults in charity and voluntary organisations. A grant of up to 50% of costs up to £2,500 would normally be the maximum.

Dr M. Clare Roberts Memorial Fund

£100

Correspondent: Sarah Roberts-Penn, Trustee, 52 Stubbington Way, Fair Oak, Eastleigh, Hampshire SO50 7LR

CC Number: 1107006

Eligibility

Children and young people in the UK looking to expand their 'educational horizons'.

Types of grants

Provision of facilities, equipment or financial assistance.

Annual grant total

In 2012/13 the fund had an income of £540 and an expenditure of £250. Both the income and the expenditure have decreased over the previous few years. We estimate that individual grants totalled around £100.

Applications

In writing to the correspondent.

Other information

Support is also given to institutions towards equipment and facilities not normally provided by the local authorities for the benefit of pupils.

The T. A. K. Turton Charitable Trust

£14,400 (6 grants)

Correspondent: R. Fullerton, Trustee, 47 Lynwood Road, London W5 1JQ (020 8998 1006)

CC Number: 268472

Eligibility

The trust usually supports three pupils in the UK and three in South Africa who are in need. Applicants should demonstrate good academic records (for example good GCSE results or equivalent). Support is given to cover a proportion of the school fees for a two year period, normally leading to A-levels or equivalent university entrance qualifications. Applications are only accepted from schools which have awarded the candidate a bursary of at least 25% of the fees.

Types of grants

Grants are awarded to cover part of the school fees, normally to pupils in their final years of school education. Up to about £3,000 can be awarded per year.

Annual grant total

In 2012/13 the trust had an income of £15,000 and an expenditure of £14,700. We estimate the annual total of grants to be around £14,400.

Applications

According to our research, applications should be made in writing to the correspondent through the school where the candidate proposes to study.

Other information

Our research suggests that since grants are normally given for a two year period, new applications from UK students can now only be considered every two years.

Further and higher education

2 Study Foundation

Correspondent: Office Administrator, 152 City Road, London EC1V 2NX (0844 318 7883; email: info@2studyfoundation.org; website: www.2studyfoundation.org.uk)

CC Number: 1144500

Eligibility

Higher education students in England and Wales.

Types of grants

One-off grants of £500 to £3,000 to alleviate students in financial hardship. Grants are means tested.

Annual grant total

No financial information was available at the time of writing (January 2014). The charity was registered with the Charity Commission in November 2011 and its accounts were not required. Previously the charity has stated that 'they have been inundated with 1,251 applications in 12 days.'

Applications

The trust's website states: 'due to tremendous demand, we have stopped taking applications for the near future. Please do come back and keep checking our site for updates.'

Generally, applicants are invited to request an application form on the foundation's website, using a valid UK University email id (.ac.uk). Applications can be submitted at any time and will be checked with the university for verification. Grants are awarded at the beginning of every term.

The Follett Trust

£9,900

Correspondent: Jamie Westcott, Administrator, The Follett Office, Broadlands House, Primett Road, Stevenage, Hertfordshire SG1 3EE (01438 810400; email: folletttrust@ thefollettoffice.com)

CC Number: 328638

Eligibility

Students in higher education. Some priority may be given to the arts and medical/health concerns.

Types of grants

One-off and recurrent scholarships and grants according to need.

Annual grant total

In 2012/13 the trust had assets of £102,000 and an income of £231,000. A total of £171,000 was spent in charitable expenditure, of which £9,900 was awarded in individual grants.

Applications

It has been previously stated that '**the trust is unable to accept unsolicited applications**.'

Other information

This is a family trust and the trustees' annual report from 2012/13 states that 'the majority of successful applications come from persons and organisations known to the trustees or in which the trustees have a particular interest.'

George Heim Memorial Trust

£2,800

Correspondent: Paul Heim, Trustee, Wearne Wyche, Picts Hill, Langport TA10 9AA (01458252097)

CC Number: 1069659

Eligibility

People aged under the age of 30 who are in further education.

Types of grants

Grants range up to £1,000.

Annual grant total

In 2012/13 the trust had an income of £2,700 and an expenditure of £3,000. We have estimated that the annual total of grants was around £2,800.

Applications

In writing to the correspondent.

The Hockerill Educational Foundation

£49,000

Correspondent: Derek Humphrey, Secretary, 3 The Swallows, Harlow, Essex CM17 0AR (01279 420855; fax: 05603 140931; email: info@hockerillfoundation. org.uk; website: www. hockerillfoundation.org.uk)

CC Number: 311018

Eligibility

The foundation awards grants widely for causes related to religious education, which are usually given under the following categories:

- Students and teaching assistants taking teaching qualifications, or first degrees leading to teaching
- Teachers, teaching assistants and others in an educational capacity seeking professional development through full-time or part-time courses
- Those undertaking research related to the practice of Religious Education in schools or further education
- Students taking other first degree courses, or courses in further education
- Others involved in teaching and leading in voluntary, non-statutory education, including those concerned with adult and Christian education

Grants are also made for gap year projects with an educational focus to those whose home or place of study is in the Dioceses of Chelmsford and St Albans.

Types of grants

Grants of £500 to £1,000 are available for students for help with fees, books, living expenses and travel. Priority is given to those training to be teachers, with a priority to teaching religious education but if funds are available other students with financial difficulties will be funded.

Annual grant total

In 2012/13 grants totalling £49,000 were made to 88 individuals consisting of:

- 54 training for primary education
- 31 for secondary education
- 18 for higher or degrees or diplomas in education
- 3 gap year students

Of the 85 education students, 21 were following courses either partly or directly relating to the teaching of religious education and 64 were taking other education courses or professional development in education.

Exclusions

No grants to schoolchildren, those studying for Christian ministry or mission unless continuing in teaching, and for visits, study or conferences abroad, gap year activities, courses in counselling, therapy or social work, or for courses leading specifically to non-teaching careers such as medicine, law or accountancy. Grants are no longer made to overseas students.

Applications

On a form available from the foundation's website, to be returned by 1 March.

Other information

The charity states that the majority of annual funding is committed to long-term projects or activities in education, but funding is also given to other projects, namely:

- Training and support for the Church of England's educational work, particularly in the dioceses of Chelmsford and St Albans
- Research, development and support grants to organisations in the field of Religious Education

The charity also supports conferences for new religious education teachers and a 'Prize for Innovation in the Teaching of RE'.

The Humanitarian Trust

£0

Correspondent: The Trustees, c/o Prism the Gift Fund, 20 Gloucester Place, London W1U 8HA (020 7486 7760)

CC Number: 208575

Eligibility

British citizens and overseas students under 30 years old on a recognised course of study in the UK and who hold a basic grant for the course.

Types of grants

Grants of £200 are available to graduates and postgraduates and are awarded for 'academic subjects only', and top up fees.

Annual grant total

In 2012/13 the trust had assets of £4.7 million and an income of £127,000. During the year, the trust awarded £36,000 in donations to organisations, £19,600 of which was to academic and educational institutions. No grants were given to individuals.

Exclusions

No grants for domestic expenses such as childcare, overseas courses, fieldwork or travel, theatre, music, journalism or art, drama, sociology, youth work or sports.

Applications

In writing to the correspondent including a CV, income and expenses and total shortfall and two references (from course tutor and head of department). Applications are considered twice a year in March and October.

Helena Kennedy Foundation

£141,000 (102 grants)

Correspondent: The Administrator, Room 243A, University House, University of East London, Water Lane, Stratford E15 4LZ (020 8223 2027; email: enquires@hkf.org.uk; website: www.hkf.org.uk)

CC Number: 1074025

Eligibility

Socially, economically or otherwise disadvantaged students attending a publicly funded further education institution in the UK who are progressing to university education. The main aim of the foundation is to 'tackle social injustice by supporting those who face multiple barriers to participation in education and work to fulfil their potential.' Applicants must be intending to undertake a higher diploma or undergraduate degree for the first time. Students taking a gap year will also be considered.

Types of grants

One-off bursaries of up to £1,500 can be given to 'individuals who have successfully completed a programme of study at a further education sector college and are progressing on to a course in higher education.'

Annual grant total

In 2012/13 the foundation had assets of £520,000 and an income of £347,000. A total of £141,000 was awarded in bursaries to 102 students. The foundation received a record number of applications during the year (435).

Exclusions

Funding is not available to:
- People who have already undertaken a higher education course
- Postgraduate students
- Students at private institutions
- Previous bursary recipients
- Students at international institutions

Applications

Applicants are encouraged to visit the foundation's website or contact the foundation to enquire about eligibility criteria. The applications for courses starting in September are welcomed from January to March each year and application forms can be obtained from the foundation's website. Candidates will need to demonstrate severe financial hardship and barriers to accessing higher education. All applications must be supported by the applicant's educational institution.

Other information

The foundation also provides mentoring, information, one to one advice, specialist and practical support, skills training and work experience opportunities.

A few different support schemes are available (such as the Badged Bursary Scheme, Discover, Article 24 Project), often in partnership with specific institutions, and are open to people on particular courses, universities or with particular experiences. Details of the schemes can be found on the foundation's website.

The Leathersellers' Company Charitable Fund
See entry on page 104

The Sidney Perry Foundation

£271,000 (281 grants)

Correspondent: Lauriann Owens, Secretary, PO Box 2924, Faringdon SN7 7YJ (website: www.the-sidney-perry-foundation.co.uk)

CC Number: 313758

Eligibility

The foundation's primary aim is to assist the first degree students. Applicants must be under the age of 35 when the course starts. Eligible foreign students studying in Britain can also apply. Students undertaking medicine as their second degree and therefore not qualifying for any support are welcomed to apply (see particular exclusions relating to the medicine degree).

Types of grants

One-off and recurrent grants from £300 onwards with an average award of around £900. The maximum general award is of £1,000 and the maximum 'super grant' – of £1,500. In no cases will support exceed £3,000 per individual. Grants are usually towards books and equipment/instruments.

The foundation's website notes that 'grants are considered to be supplemental and to go part of the way to bridge a gap with the applicant finding the bulk of funding elsewhere.'

Annual grant total

At the time of writing (July 2014) the latest financial information available was from 2012. In 2012 the foundation had assets of £3.7 million, an income of £185,000 and made grants to individuals totalling £271,000. This consisted of 255 basic grants (including, 22 'super grants' of £1,200–£1,500), 18 awards totalling £18,000 to young musicians through

Martin Musical Scholarship Fund, 4 grants totalling £12,000 to vocal students through the Guildhall School of Music and four awards totalling £5,300 to Open University Students in engineering.

Exclusions

The foundation is unable to assist:
- The first year of a (three or four year) first degree, save for veterinary, medicine and in exceptional circumstances
- Medical students during their first year if medicine is their second degree
- Medical students during elective periods and intercalated courses
- Second degree courses where the grade in the first is lower than a 2:1, save in exceptional circumstances
- Second degree courses or other postgraduate study unrelated to the first unless they are a necessary part of professional training (e.g. medicine or dentistry)
- Expeditions or courses overseas, emergency funding or clearance of existing debts
- Students over the age of 35 when their course of study commences, save in the most exceptional circumstances
- A Level and GCSE examinations
- Students on access, ESOL, HNC, HND, BTEC, GNVQ and NVQ levels 1–4 and foundation courses
- Those with LEA/SAAS funding, except in exceptional circumstances
- Open University courses (except engineering, which is supported)

Distance learning, correspondence, part-time and short-term courses may only be considered according to circumstances.

Applications

Application forms are available from the foundation's website or the correspondent. Together with a covering letter and other supporting documentation they can be submitted directly by the individual via post by November (the year before the academic year when assistance is necessary). In exceptional circumstances late applications may be considered, with a final cut-off date of 31 January. Incomplete forms will be disregarded. Enclosure of an sae would be appreciated. Applications have to be in writing and supported by signed original references (one of which must be academic). Students are expected to have a confirmed place at an educational establishment and most of the necessary funding already secured before approaching the foundation. Previous beneficiaries should include details of the previous award (amount granted, year received and grant number).

Other information

The foundation is generally unable to deal with student debt or financial problems needing a speedy resolution.

The trustees' annual report from 2012 notes that the governors 'continued to relax some of their current restrictions in order to help students in particular need whose cases they viewed as exceptional.'

Thornton-Smith and Plevins Trust
See entry on page 29

Williamson Memorial Trust

£2,500

Correspondent: Colin Williamson, 6 Windmill Close, Ashington, Pulborough, West Sussex RH20 3LG (01903 893649)

CC Number: 268782

Eligibility
Students on first degree courses.

Types of grants
Grants of not more than £200 a year are made for help with books, fees, living expenses and study or travel abroad. Grants limited to £200 a year to overseas students; the trust is not able to make a more significant contribution towards the higher fees and living expenses that overseas students incur.

Annual grant total
In 2012/13 the trust had an income of £9,300 and a total expenditure of £10,000. Grants are made for education and welfare purposes to individuals and organisations. We estimate the total of grants awarded to individuals for educational purposes was around £2,500.

Exclusions
Grants are not made for postgraduate study.

Applications
Due to a reduction of its funds and the instability of its income, the trust regrets that, to ensure it can meet its existing commitments, very few new applications will be considered. Support will generally only be given to cases known personally to the trustees and to those individuals the trust has existing commitments with.

Gap year/ voluntary work overseas

The Alchemy Foundation

£5,500

Correspondent: R. Stilgoe, Trustee, Trevereux Manor, Limpsfield Chart, Oxted, Surrey RH8 0TL (01883 730600; fax: 01883 730800)

CC Number: 292500

Eligibility
Enterprising individuals in need in the UK.

Types of grants
Grants are made to support voluntary work overseas.

Annual grant total
In 2012/13 the foundation had assets of £2.6 million and an income of £282,000. Approximately £11,000 was given in grants to individuals for relief-in-need and educational purposes.

Applications
In writing to the correspondent. Applications from individuals will only be considered if they are for worthwhile and enterprising voluntary work by young people in the developing world under the auspices of Raleigh International or The Project Trust.

Other information
The foundation gives grants mostly to organisations, namely overseas development, social welfare and disability projects.

John Allatt's Educational Foundation
See entry on page 247

Lady Allen of Hurtwood Memorial Trust
See entry on page 48

The Alvechurch Grammar School Endowment
See entry on page 266

Angus Educational Trust
See entry on page 140

The Arrol Trust

£20,000

Correspondent: C. S. Kennedy, Administrator, Lindsays, Caledonian Exchange, 19A Canning Street, Edinburgh EH3 8HE (01312 291212)

SC Number: SC020983

Eligibility
Young people between the ages of 16 and 25 who are disadvantaged because of their social/economic circumstances or physical/mental disabilities.

Types of grants
Grants are given for activities which will 'broaden individuals' horizons.' Support can be given towards travel in the UK and overseas, educational trips and gap-year or volunteering opportunities.

Annual grant total
In 2013/14 the trust had an income of £17,300 and an expenditure of £23,000. We estimate the annual total of grants to individuals to be around £20,000.

Exclusions
Grants are not made for direct educational expenses, such as course fees.

Applications
Application forms can be requested from the correspondent and must be supported by a reference from the applicant's teacher or employer. Potential candidates may be invited for an interview with the trustees and asked to report back on the completion of their activity.

The Barnabas Trust
See entry on page 112

Jim Bishop Memorial Fund

£2,000

Correspondent: Roger Miller, Trustee, c/o Young Explorers Trust, 6 Manor Road, Burnham on Sea, Somerset TA8 2AS (01278 784658; email: ted@ theyet.org.uk; website: www.theyet.org)

Eligibility
People under 19 who wish to participate in any adventure activity.

Types of grants
Grants of between £50 and £150. Recent grants have been given to enable

participation in expeditions abroad, at sea and in the UK.

Annual grant total
Grants from the Jim Bishop Memorial Fund generally total around £2,000 and are awarded to individuals for educational purposes.

Exclusions
University expeditions will not be supported.

Applications
On a form available from the correspondent or to download from the Young Explorers' Trust website. Applications should include an sae and be submitted by the end of March.

Other information
Jim Bishop was an outstanding young engineer, scientist and explorer who was tragically killed whilst on an international expedition to the Karakorum. He was originally inspired by mountains and adventure as a teenager and he always regarded this initial experience as an important factor in his subsequent life. He endeavoured to encourage this taste for adventure in the young and the Jim Bishop Awards were established by his family and friends to help further these ideals.

The fund is administered by the Young Explorers' Trust.

The Challenger Trust

£0

Correspondent: Sebastian Hare, Challenger Trust, The Lido Centre, 63 Mattock Lane, London W13 9LA (020 8133 6457; email: info@challengertrust. org; website: www.challengertrust.org)

CC Number: 1068226

Eligibility
Young people taking part in overseas expeditions for personal development who can demonstrate a clear financial need which could be significantly relieved by the bursary.

Types of grants
Some support could still be provided for overseas expeditions, however the main emphasis now is on UK-based outdoors programmes.

Annual grant total
In 2012/13 the trust had assets of £62,000, an income of £96,000 and a total charitable expenditure of £115,000. The trust focused solely on the UK school programmes, therefore no individual bursaries were made.

Exclusions
The trust does not provide grants to cover student fees.

Applications
In writing to the correspondent, provided the eligibility criteria are satisfied. The trustees meet at least three times a year.

Other information
The main focus of the trust is funding a number of UK-based outdoors programmes aimed at advancing applicants' educational and employability skills through 'experiential learning'. Grants are also made to schools, local authorities and other educational bodies.

The trustees' annual report from 2012/13 also notes that their 'future plans include incorporating volunteering and community learning elements to complement existing programmes.'

Church Burgesses Educational Foundation
See entry on page 183

Churchill University Scholarships Trust for Scotland

£13,500

Correspondent: The Trustees, c/o MacRae and Kaur LLP, 6th Floor, Atlantic House, 45 Hope Street, Glasgow G2 6AE (01416 116000)

SC Number: SC013492

Eligibility
Students in Scotland.

Types of grants
Grants are given for one-off educational projects of benefit to the community, for example, medical electives or voluntary work overseas in a student's gap year or holiday.

Annual grant total
In 2012/13 the trust had an income of £19,000 and an expenditure of £13,700. Grants totalled approximately £13,500.

Exclusions
Grants are not made for any other educational needs, such as course fees, books or living expenses.

Applications
In writing to the correspondent.

The Cross Trust
See entry on page 131

The Frank Denning Memorial Charity
See entry on page 363

Reg Gilbert International Youth Friendship Trust (GIFT)

£6,200

Correspondent: Alan Aked, 19 Church Street, Beckington, Frome, Somerset BA11 6TG (01373 830232; website: giftfriendshiptrust.org.uk/)

CC Number: 327307

Eligibility
UK citizens aged between 14 and 25 who are visiting a developing country on a project lasting at least six weeks. Applicants must live and volunteer within an indigenous community in the host country, preferably in a 'homestay' environment. Candidates need to demonstrate their own fundraising initiatives, research and preparation for the visit. Normally they would have to be vetted and accepted by an approved overseas project agency but independent travellers may be considered provided a comprehensive and verifiable breakdown of their travel arrangements is submitted.

Types of grants
Grants of up to £500 are given to travellers who can demonstrate need and have already started preparation for the project.

Annual grant total
In 2012/13 the trust had an income of £5,600 and an expenditure of £6,400. We estimate the annual total of grants to be around £6,200.

Exclusions
Grants are not available for proposals leading to academic or vocational qualifications.

Applications
Application forms can be downloaded from the trust's website after the eligibility criteria has been read and understood. An independent academic or professional reference is required together with the application.

Other information
The charity is an autonomous trust under the supervision of the Rotary Club of Frome.

The Mary Grave Trust
See entry on page 198

Hazel's Footprints Trust

£10,100 (15 grants)

Correspondent: The Administrator, Legerwood, Earlston, Berwickshire TD4 6AS (01896 849677; fax: 01896 849677; email: info@hazelsfootprints.org; website: www.hazelsfootprints.org)

SC Number: SC036069

Eligibility

People of any age from the UK and Europe who want to take part in voluntary projects abroad. Proposed projects must be of an educational nature (teaching, community development work and so on) and should last no less than six months (the preferred project duration is one year).

Types of grants

'Footprinter' grants to people who want to take part in voluntary work abroad but are struggling to cover the whole costs themselves.

Annual grant total

In 2012/13 the trust had an income of £229,000 and an expenditure of £92,000. During the year a total of £10,100 was awarded to 15 'footprinters'. Grants can vary from year to year but the trust aims to help on average 15 to 20 individuals per year.

Applications

Application forms can be downloaded from the trust's website. They should be typed, printed off and posted to the correspondent. A photo of the candidate must be attached but no other documents are required nor should be sent. The deadlines for applications are normally by the end March and August. Grants are considered in May and November, respectively. All applicants are notified of the outcome of their application. Candidates may be invited for an interview.

Other information

The trust also awards grants to UK charities working with educational projects in developing countries and makes annual donations to the Otjikondo village school in Namibia. In 2012/13 the Otjikondo grant totalled £11,500 and a further £31,000 was distributed in community grants.

The Hertfordshire Educational Foundation
See entry on page 322

The Holywood Trust
See entry on page 148

The Leadership Trust Foundation

£69,000

Correspondent: Robert Noble, The Leadership Trust, Weston Under Penyard, Ross-on-Wye, Herefordshire HR9 7YH (01989 767667; email: enquiries@leadership.org.uk; website: www.leadership.org.uk)

CC Number: 1063916

Eligibility

Young people, primarily those aged 16 to 25, living within 25 miles of the foundation's office who are undertaking activities designed to enhance their personal development and leadership training with an established and recognised charity.

Types of grants

Bursaries to enable individuals from the charitable sector to undertake training in leadership development. Grants are given to individuals embarking on activities with Raleigh International, Duke of Edinburgh's Award, GAP, British Schools Expedition Society, Jubilee Sailing Trust, Global Young Leaders Conference and so on.

Annual grant total

In 2012 the foundation had an income of £2.1 million and a total expenditure of £2.9 million. It had assets of £2.3 million. Bursaries made to 28 individuals to allow them to attend courses run by the foundation totalled £69,000. The foundation also provides discounts to individuals who were not awarded full bursaries. No small grants were awarded in the year.

The 2012 accounts were the latest available at the time of writing.

Applications

Initially in writing to the correspondent, who will then send an application form to relevant applicants. Completed forms are considered quarterly.

Roger and Miriam Pilkington Charitable Trust

£5,500 (11 grants)

Correspondent: Jane Fagan, Administrator, c/o Brabners Chaffe Street, Horton House, Exchange Flags, Liverpool L2 3YL (01516 003000)

CC Number: 261804

Eligibility

The trustees' report from 2012/13 states that grants are given to:

Enterprising people aged 16 to 25, particularly those who are undertaking imaginative projects abroad which could be said to broaden horizons, giving them experiences which they may not otherwise have; increase awareness of other cultures and ways of living; or help them understand something of social problems outside their immediate environment.

Types of grants

One – off grants only, usually around £500. Due to a great demand grants are spread across a wide selection of projects.

Annual grant total

In 2012/13 the trust had assets of £902,000 and an income of £33,000. A total of £30,000 was spent on charitable activities. Annual grants to individuals totalled in £5,500.

Exclusions

The trustees do not offer support where it should be provided by the education authorities. Long-term funding is not available.

Applications

Our research shows that applications should be submitted in writing to the correspondent. Applications can be made directly by individuals at any time for consideration in March and August. All grants are contingent on the applicant raising a significant proportion of the funds through their own efforts.

Other information

The trust is currently running a grant scheme in seven schools or colleges in the UK and Jersey with applicants being selected by the staff and approved by the trustees. In 2012/13 the grant scheme was allocated £24,500.

The Prince Philip Trust Fund
See entry on page 303

Provincial/Walsh Trust for Bolton

£5,600 (12 grants)

Correspondent: Joan Bohan, Administrator, 237 Ainsworth Lane, Bolton BL2 2QQ (email: Joan.bohan@ntlworld.com; website: www.pwtb.org.uk)

CC Number: 222819

Eligibility

Young people, usually under the age of 25, who live or work within the Bolton Metropolitan Borough.

Types of grants

Grants are mainly one-off and generally range between £500 and £1,500, although higher grants may be awarded. Applicants will be expected to have raised some money through other sources.

Grants are designed to assist people to achieve their personal goals or small projects (particularly helping others) rather than to provide relief-in-need. Character development activities, for example, Operation Raleigh or Health Projects Abroad can be supported. Previously grants have been awarded for specialist equipment, tuition costs, sports activities, volunteering expenses, educational travel.

Annual grant total

In 2012/13 the trust had assets of £988,000 and an income of £37,000. A total of £40,000 was spent in grants, of which £5,600 was given to 12 individuals.

Exclusions

Grants are not awarded for building projects, commercial ventures or for personal loans. Our research also suggests that students or recent ex-students of Bolton School are not normally assisted.

Applications

Application forms are available on the trust's website or can be requested from the correspondent. Supporting information may be provided but the candidates are requested to limit this to three A4 sheets. The trustees usually meet in April and October, but urgent requests can also be considered.

Other information

This charity is a merger of The Provincial Insurance Trust for Bolton and David Walsh Trust.

Grants are also made to organisations and the trustees are eager to support more charitable causes in the area. In 2012/13 grants to 52 organisations totalled £35,000.

The trust is anxious to match fund where possible.

The Sir Philip Reckitt Educational Trust Fund

£34,000

Correspondent: The Trustees, Rollits, Rowntree Wharf, Navigation Road, York YO1 9WE (01904 625790; website: www. spret.org)

CC Number: 529777

Eligibility

People in full-time education who live in Kingston upon Hull, East Riding of Yorkshire, or the county of Norfolk.

Types of grants

Grants are given towards educational travel such as Raleigh International, working in the developing world, Outward Bound-type courses and so on. Travel must be connected with the extracurricular projects of the course. Grants can also be used to help with residence and attendance at conferences, lectures and short educational courses.

Annual grant total

In 2012 the trust had assets of £917,000 and an income of £36,000. Educational grants to individuals totalled £34,000.

At the time of writing (July 2014) this was the most recent financial information available for the trust.

Exclusions

Awards will not normally be made to persons under the age of 14 on the date of travel. Repeat applications for identical activities are not normally considered.

Applications

An application form can be completed and submitted online or can be downloaded and posted to the appropriate address after completion. A reference from the head of the institution of study, an employer or other suitable referee is required.

Note: Applications should be received by the trust more than six weeks before the intended departure date. Those submitted later are not normally considered. Successful applicants must complete a report to be returned to the trustees within three months of the end of the project or period of study.

Other information

Contacts: **Kingston upon Hull and East Riding of Yorkshire** – The Trustees, Sir Philip Reckitt Educational Trust, Rollits, Wilberforce Court, High Street, Hull HU1 1JY (email: hull@spret.org).

Norfolk – The Trustees, Sir Philip Reckitt Educational Trust, c/o Mrs J. Pickering, 99 Yarmouth Road, Ellingham, Bungay NR35 2PH (email: spretrust@googlemail.com).

Saint George's Trust

See entry on page 42
See entry on page 42

The Bassil Shippam and Alsford Trust

£2,300

Correspondent: Iain Macleod, The Bassil Shippam and Alsford Trust, The Corn Exchange, Baffins Lane, Chichester, West Sussex PO19 1GE (01243 786111)

CC Number: 256996

Eligibility

Students in need living in West Sussex.

Types of grants

One-off grants ranging from £100 to £1,000 for gap-year activities and other educational or personal development projects.

Annual grant total

In 2012/13 the trust had assets of £4.1 million, an income of £148,000 and a total charitable expenditure of £84,000. Grants to individuals for educational purposes totalled £2,300.

Exclusions

According to our research, funding cannot be provided towards academic courses.

Applications

In writing to the correspondent. Applications can be submitted at any time directly by individuals and should include a summary of their proposal. The trustees meet three times a year.

Other information

The trust also supports organisations.

W. W. Spooner Charitable Trust

£16,000

Correspondent: Michael Broughton, Trustees, 2 Elliot Road, Watford, Hertfordshire WD17 4DF

CC Number: 313653

Eligibility

Our research suggests that young people who are taking part in voluntary overseas projects and expeditions can be supported. Preference is given for those living in Yorkshire (especially West Yorkshire) and former employees of the Spooner Industries Ltd or their dependents. Scholarships can also be awarded 'for the encouragement of young employees.'

Types of grants

One-off and recurrent grants are available.

Annual grant total

In 2012/13 the trust had assets of £1.7 million and an income of £71,000. A total of £103,000 was spent on charitable activities, of which donations and grants totalled £31,000. According to our research, previously around £16,000 has been awarded in grants to individuals.

Applications

In writing to the correspondent, normally by the end of March, July or October.

Other information

The trust mainly supports charitable and community organisations, clubs/groups.

The Erik Sutherland Gap Year Trust

£100

Correspondent: Viki Sutherland, Administrator, Erik's Gap Year Trust, Torren, Glencoe, Argyll, Scotland PH49 4HX (01855 81107; fax: 01855 811338; email: info@eriks-gap-year-trust. com; website: www.eriks-gap-year-trust. com)

SC Number: SC028293

Eligibility

Young people living in the UK.

Types of grants

Grants for young people who wish to take a gap year or take part in voluntary work overseas before entering higher education. The trust primarily gives partial funding in instances where the young person has a shortfall in funds, though in exceptional cases the trust may 'possibly bear the whole cost of a year out.' The trust aims to help 'one or more' school leavers each year.

Annual grant total

In 2012/13 the trust had an income of £800 and a total expenditure of £100. We estimate that grants to individuals totalled less than £100.

Applications

On a form available to download from the trust's website or from the correspondent.

The Vandervell Foundation

£750 (1 grant)

Correspondent: Valerie Kaye, Administrator, Hampstead Town Hall, 213 Haverstock Hill, London NW3 4QP (020 7435 7546)

CC Number: 255651

Eligibility

Medical students and other students wishing to undertake gap-year opportunities.

Types of grants

One-off grants in the range of £300–£1,000 are given towards medical electives and gap-year projects.

Annual grant total

The latest financial information available at the time of writing (July 2014) was from 2012. In 2012 the foundation had assets of £6.7 million, an income of £301,000 and made grants totalling £351,000. One grant was made to an individual totalling £750.

Exclusions

Grants are not made for projects where the foundation already makes a major grant directly to the organisation, for example Raleigh International.

Applications

In writing to the correspondent. Applications should include a CV and provide a budget. Applications are considered every other month.

Other information

The foundation primarily makes grants to organisations in the fields of education, social welfare and medical research (98 grants totalling £351,000 in 2012).

Warwick Apprenticing Charities
See entry on page 256

See entry on page 256

Wellington Crowthorne Charitable Trust

£4,500

Correspondent: Paul Thompson, Trustee, Wellington College, Crowthorne, Berkshire RG45 7PU (email: pft@wellingtoncollege.org.uk)

CC Number: 277491

Eligibility

People who live in the parishes of Crowthorne, Finchampstead, Sandhurst and Wokingham Without. Preference is given to applicants under the age of 25.

Types of grants

Grants are given to 'promote spiritual, moral, mental and physical capacities of individuals.' Previously grants have been awarded for a wide range of overseas gap-year projects, Outward Bound-type expeditions, school trips and international sports events.

Annual grant total

At the time of writing (July 2014) the latest financial information available was from 2012. In 2012 the trust had an income of £12,000 and an expenditure of £9,600. We estimate that grants to individuals totalled around £4,500.

Applications

In writing to the correspondent. The trustees' meetings are normally held three times a year, although in urgent cases applications can be considered between the meetings.

Other information

Our research suggests that the trust also supports local youth organisations awarding about £5,000 a year.

The trust is maintained and mainly supported by Wellington College.

Illness and disability

Able Kidz

£14,000

Correspondent: Andrew Turner, Trustee, 43 Bedford Street, London WC2E 2HA (0845 123 3997; email: info@ablekidz.com; website: www. ablekidz.com)

CC Number: 1114955

Eligibility

Children with disabilities and young adults under the age of 18 in the UK.

Types of grants

One-off and recurrent grants according to need. Grants are typically made for specialist educational equipment and extra tuition.

Annual grant total

In 2012/13 the charity had an income of £15,200 and a total expenditure of £15,000.

Applications

In writing to the correspondent. Applications are not means tested. They should include the following:

- A summary of the child's circumstances
- What the child requires and how Able Kidz might be able to help
- An outline of the costs involved

The National Association for Colitis and Crohn's Disease (Crohn's and Colitis UK)

£2,000

Correspondent: Caroline Hardy, Administrator, 4 Beaumont House, Beaumont Works, Sutton Road, St Albans AL1 5HH (01727 830038; email: enquiries@crohnsandcolitis.org.

uk; website: www.crohnsandcolitis.org.uk)

CC Number: 1117148, SC038632

Eligibility

People in need between the ages of 15 and 25 who are affected by ulcerative colitis, Crohn's disease or related inflammatory bowel diseases (IBD). Individuals must be on low income, in full/part-time education and have been resident in the UK for at least six months.

Types of grants

Grants of up to £500 are available towards any educational or training needs, including fees, books, equipment, additional costs of university/college en-suite, travel passes, also special educational needs, retraining purposes or other items and services arising as a consequence of having IBD.

Usually up to three grants can be given in any six year period.

Annual grant total

At the time of writing (August 2014) the latest financial information available was from 2012. In 2012 the charity had assets of £3 million and an income of £3.6 million. Personal grants totalled £75,000 awarded to 237 individuals. Educational awards only form a part of the charity's grantmaking activities, therefore we estimate that grants totalled around £2,000.

Applications

Application forms are available to download from the charity's website. The form has two extra sections, one of which should be completed by a doctor to confirm the individual's illness and one to be filled in by a social worker (or health visitor, district nurse, Citizens Advice advisor and so on). Completed applications should be sent to the personal grants fund secretary at: PO Box 334, St Albans, Herts AL1 2WA. Applications are ordinarily considered every six to eight weeks.

Grants are normally made to the shop, school or other agencies, not the applicant.

Other information

Grants are also made for welfare purposes and to institutions for research. Occasionally local grants are made to hospitals. The main role of the association is to provide information and advice to people living with IBD.

Further information on grants can be obtained from Julia Devereux (telephone: 0800 011 4701 or 01727 759654; email: julia.devereux@crohnsandcolitis.org.uk).

The MFPA Trust Fund for the Training Of Handicapped Children in the Arts

£10,400

Correspondent: Tom Yendell, Trustee, 88 London Road, Holybourne, Alton, Hampshire GU34 4EL (01420 88755)

CC Number: 328151

Eligibility

Children with physical or mental disabilities between the ages of 5 and 18 living in the UK.

Types of grants

One-off and recurrent grants towards participation in arts, crafts, painting, music, drama and so on. Awards can be given, for example, towards books, educational outings, equipment and materials or school fees. The maximum grant available is £6,000.

Annual grant total

In 2012/13 the fund had an income of £38,000. Awards to children and grants for art materials totalled £10,400. Grants to individuals are erratic and previously have fluctuated between a few hundred pounds to about £20,000.

Applications

In writing to the correspondent. Applications can be made directly by the individual or through a third party such as their school, college or educational welfare agency. They are considered throughout the year. Candidates should also enclose a letter explaining their needs and a doctor's letter confirming the disability.

Other information

The trust also gives grants to organisations (£45,000 in 2012/13).

The Adam Millichip Foundation

£20,000

Correspondent: Stuart Millichip, Trustee, 17 Boraston Drive, Burford, Tenbury Wells WR15 8AG (07866 424286; email: apply@adammillichipfoundation.org; website: adammillichipfoundation.org/)

CC Number: 1138721

Eligibility

Disabled people in the UK who wish to participate in sports, with the aim of improving the quality of their lives.

Types of grants

Grants have previously been awarded for riding lessons; a specialist bike; ski lessons and a ski slope pass and swimming lessons.

Annual grant total

In 2012/13 the foundation had an income of £12,900 and an expenditure of £8,300. Grants totalled around £8,000.

Exclusions

Grants cannot be awarded for competitive purposes.

Applications

There is a six stage application process which is begun on the foundation's website. Applications are processed on a first come first served basis and can take up to two months once all the information has been gathered.

Other information

This foundation was established in memory of Adam Millichip.

Richard Overall Trust

£7,000

Correspondent: Nicholas Overall, Trustee, New Barn Cottage, Honey Lane, Selborne, Alton GU34 3BY (01420 511175)

CC Number: 1088640

Eligibility

Young people with disabilities participating in physical education.

Types of grants

Grants given according to need.

Annual grant total

In 2012/13 the trust had an income of £2,600 and an expenditure of £7,600. Grants made totalled approximately £7,000.

Applications

In writing to the correspondent.

Snowdon Trust (Formerly known as The Snowdon Award Scheme)

£148,000 (106 grants)

Correspondent: Paul Alexander, Chief Executive Officer, Unit 18, Oakhurst Business Park, Wilberforce Way, Southwater, Horsham, West Sussex RH13 9RT (01403 732899; email: info@snowdonawardscheme.org.uk; website: www.snowdontrust.org)

CC Number: 282754

Eligibility

Students with physical or sensory disabilities who are in or about to enter further/higher education or training in the UK and, because of their disability, have financial needs which are not met elsewhere. Preference is given to people between the ages of 17 and 25.

Types of grants

Bursaries for up to two years are available to people in further/higher education and those training towards employment. Support is aimed to cover additional costs incurred due to the disability which cannot be met in full from statutory sources, including human support (for example sign language interpreters or people to take notes), translators for deaf students, computer equipment, specialist software, adapted or additional accommodation, travel costs, wheelchairs and other mobility equipment or similar expenses.

Grants are normally between £250 and £2,000, in exceptional circumstances up to £2,500 can be awarded.

Annual grant total

In 2012/13 the trust had assets of £1.2 million and an income of £223,000. Grants were made to 106 students totalling £148,000.

Usually a total of around £175,000 is available in grants each year.

Exclusions

The trust does not normally cover expenses for the tuition fees or standard living accommodation and childcare costs, but can occasionally help with the tuition fees if the need is justifiably and directly related to the applicant's disability. Retrospective awards are not made.

Applications

Application forms can be completed online or be downloaded from the trust's website along with full guidance notes. Applications are invited from 1 February to 31 May for consideration in July and from 1 July to 31 August for consideration in October. Applicants are required to provide academic and personal references and supporting documentation, such as medical information of disability, confirmation letter from the place of study, evidence of costs of the support required and a copy of DSA assessment, if applicable.

Other information

This trust also provides mentoring support and advice to beneficiaries and occasionally undertakes research.

Student Disability Assistance Fund (SDAF)

£7,500

Correspondent: Sandra Furmston, Administrative Secretary, BAHSHE Office, 35 Hazelwood Road, Bush Hill Park, Enfield EN1 1JG (020 8482 2412; email: sfurmston@mdx.ac.uk; website: www.studenthealthassociation.co.uk)

CC Number: 253984

Eligibility

Students over the age of 18 on a higher education course in the UK who are affected by disability or illness. Candidates are expected to apply for Disabled Students Allowance (DSA) before applying to the fund. Priority is given to individuals who are not eligible for funding from the local authorities and those who do not qualify for DSA.

Types of grants

One-off grants of up to £500 towards educational aids made necessary by the student's illness or disability. For example, support could be given for special computer equipment and software, additional books, photocopying, extra travel costs for those with mobility problems, cost of note-takers or signers and other special equipment.

Annual grant total

In 2012/13 the fund had an income of £11,600 and an expenditure of £7,700, which is slightly lower than usual. We estimate the annual total of grants to be around £7,500.

Exclusions

Funding is not given for general educational expenses incurred by all students (for example, fees, living costs or compulsory textbooks) and for medical treatment or equipment, unless it is specific to study problems.

Applications

Eligible applicants are asked to apply on an online form on the fund's website. Supporting evidence will have to be posted to the correspondent (full list of required documentation can be found on the fund's website). The deadlines for applications are 1 March, 1 June and 1 November each year. Incomplete applications are not accepted.

Note that the fund 'cannot respond to any telephone enquiries or give information about prospective or pending applications.'

Other information

The fund was formerly known as BASHE (The British Association of Health Services in Higher Education). It can also offer guidance, advice and information.

Blindness

The Amber Trust (Access to Music for Blind People Education and Residential)

£91,000 (134 grants)

Correspondent: Roderic Hill, Trustee, 19 Scarsdale Villas, London W8 6PT (020 7937 9567; email: info@ambertrust. org; website: www.ambertrust.org)

CC Number: 1050503

Eligibility

Children and young people up to and including the age of 18 who are blind or partially sighted.

Types of grants

One-off and recurrent grants for up to one year are awarded to fund three terms of music lessons, music therapy sessions, one-off events, the purchase of musical instruments, specialist software (such as Sibelius), concert tickets or travel to musical activities. After one year applications can be made again but using a reapplication form which allows the trust to monitor the impact of their funding.

Annual grant total

In 2012/13 the trust had assets of £233,000 and an income of £92,000, primarily from general donations. During the year 134 awards were made to 132 individuals. A total of £57,000 was approved and distributed in grants and a further £34,000 had been approved but had not been paid out by the end of the year.

Exclusions

The trust will not make retrospective grants. In some instances the charity will not be able to fund the full costs and the balance will have to be raised from other sources, but the applicants are welcomed to use the AMBER grant to encourage other funding.

Applications

Application forms can be found on the trust's website. Applications should be completed by the child's parents or carers, but can be assisted or prepared by a support worker or teacher. Applications for the purchase of instruments or software should include prices and supplier details. Applications for lessons or music therapy sessions must include full details of the teacher's or therapist's qualifications, experience and CRB clearance. The trustees meet three times a year, in March, July and November. Applications should be received by the end of February, June and October, respectively. All eligible applications will be acknowledged in writing.

When applying for the second and subsequent times, remember to use the reapplication form which can also be found on the trust's website.

Other information

If parents have not found a suitable music teacher or therapist for their child, they are encouraged to get in touch with RNIB's Music Advisory Service providing information and advice on music education at all levels. The service can be contacted on 020 7391 2273 or at mas@rnib.org.uk.

Elizabeth Eagle-Bott Memorial Fund

£30,000

Correspondent: Kathrin John, Administrator, Music Advisory Service, RNIB, 105 Judd Street, London WC1H 9NE (020 7391 2273; email: mas@rnib.org.uk; website: www.rnib.org.uk)

Eligibility

Musicians, normally under the age of 30, who are blind or partially sighted. Candidates must be registered as sight impaired or seriously sight impaired (partially sighted or blind) and be UK citizens. Preference is given to classical musicians, especially organists.

Types of grants

Awards are made towards musical study, projects and various events for the benefit of local, national and international communities. Grants are of up to £10,000 and can be given up to three times each in different years to be used in or outside of the UK within 24 months. Previously grants have been awarded for the purchase of instruments, vocal tuition, music course fees, transcriber and reader costs, purchase or development of accessible and assistive music technology, costs associated with staging concerts and so on.

Annual grant total

In 2012/13 the fund held assets of £60,000 and had an income of £40,000. A total of £41,000 was spent on charitable activities. We estimate that grants to individuals totalled around £30,000.

Applications

Application forms are available by contacting the Royal National Institute of Blind People music advisory service and should be submitted via email by 31 March each year. Applications are assessed in May although the grants panel may meet more than once a year to consider exceptional applications.

Interview and audition expenses will be met by the fund.

Other information

The fund is administered by the Royal National Institute of Blind People.

Grants may also be given to support organisations and individuals assisting blind or partially sighted musicians in their music making.

Gardner's Trust for the Blind

£14,000

Correspondent: Angela Stewart, 117 Charterhouse Street, London EC1M 6AA (020 7253 3757)

CC Number: 207233

Eligibility

Registered blind or partially-sighted people who live in the UK.

Types of grants

Grants are mainly for computer equipment, music equipment and course fees.

Annual grant total

In 2012/13 the trust had assets of almost £3.3 million and an income of £94,000. Education and trade grants totalled £13,000 and music grants £1,000. General aid grants and annual grantees totalled £38,000.

Exclusions

No grants for loan repayments.

Applications

In writing to the correspondent. Applications can be submitted either directly by the individual or by an appropriate third party, but they must also be supported by a third party who can confirm the disability and that the grant is needed. They are considered in March, June, September and December and should be submitted at least three weeks before the meeting.

Other information

The trust also gives grants for welfare purposes and pensions.

Webster and Davidson Mortification for the Blind

£14,000

Correspondent: G. Fulton, Administrator and Secretary, Thorntons Law LLP, Whitehall House, 33 Yeaman Shore, Dundee DD1 4BJ (01382 229111; fax: 01382 202288; email: gfulton@thorntons-law.co.uk; website: www.

thorntons-law.co.uk/practice-areas/wills,-trusts,-executries/charitable-trusts)

SC Number: SC004920

Eligibility

Blind or partially sighted people who are undertaking musical education and are resident, or normally resident, in Britain. Preference will be given to people from Scotland.

Types of grants

Grants, normally of around £1,000, to support the learning and appreciation of music and for specific musical purpose. Generally, but not exclusively, grants are given at secondary school level or to further/higher education students.

Annual grant total

In 2013 the charity had an income of £25,000 and an expenditure of £29,000. We estimate that music awards to individuals totalled around £14,000.

Exclusions

The bursary is not intended to take the place of or supplement Scottish Students' Allowances or other awards derived from public funds.

Applications

Application forms, guidance notes and referee report forms (also available in Braille) can be obtained from the correspondent or can be downloaded from the Thorntons Law LLP website. Applications should be submitted by 31 March.

Other information

Grants are also given to organisations working with visually impaired people to provide funding for educational visits to places of historical or other interest. Organisations from Dundee, Tayside or Scotland are preferred.

Cancer

CLIC Sargent (formerly Sargent Cancer Care for Children)

£6,000

Correspondent: Grants Department, Horatio House, 77–85 Fulham Place, London W6 8JA (020 8752 2878; email: info@clicsargent.org.uk; website: www.clicsargent.org.uk)

CC Number: 1107328

Eligibility

Children and young people aged 24 or under who are living in the UK and are receiving treatment for cancer.

Types of grants

Grants of up to £250, though grants up to £500 may be approved for families who have an exceptional need.

Annual grant total

In 2012/13 the charity distributed more than £1 million in grants to young people and their families. Our research in previous years suggests that educational grants usually account for only a small portion of this expenditure, with the majority of grants given to young people and their families for welfare needs. In previous years, educational grants have totalled £6,000.

Exclusions

No grants are given for school fees.

Applications

Through a healthcare or social care professional, such as a CLIC Sargent Social Worker.

Other information

Details of other grants and services offered by CLIC Sargent are available from a CLIC Sargent Social Worker or the charity's informative website. Alternatively, call 0300 330 0803 for more information, advice and support.

CLIC Sargent was formed in 2005 following a merger between CLIC and Sargent Cancer Care for Children.

Cystic Fibrosis

The Joseph Levy Memorial Fund

£65,000

Correspondent: Roland Gyallay-Pap, Administrator, 1 Bell Street, London NW1 5BY (020 7616 1207; email: roland@jlef.org.uk; website: www. cysticfibrosis.org.uk/who-we-are/support-for-all/welfare-grants)

CC Number: 1079049

Eligibility

Children and young adults up to the age of 25 who have cystic fibrosis.

Types of grants

Grants are available to help individuals develop their career through further/higher education or professional qualifications. Support is given for tuition fees, examination fees, living costs and similar expenses to progress the applicant's career.

Annual grant total

In 2012/13 the fund had assets of £30,000 and an income of £56,000. Grants totalled £65,000.

Applications

In writing to the correspondent by post or email. The deadline for applications is 31 March and awards are decided in mid-June.

Other information

The fund is administered by the Cystic Fibrosis Trust.

Deafness

The Peter Greenwood Memorial Trust for Deaf People

£800

Correspondent: Nicola Storey, Bursary Secretary, Westbrook Building, Great Horton Road, Bradford BD7 1AY (01274 436414 (voice) 01274 433223 (text); email: davemarshall@blueyonder.co.uk; website: www.pgmtrust.org.uk)

CC Number: 327262

Eligibility

Post-school (over 16) students living in England and Wales who are deaf or whose hearing is impaired and who live in England and Wales. Grants are tenable for any higher or further education course or training and mature students and postgraduates can also be supported.

Types of grants

Grants of under £200 towards books, videos, software and equipment that cannot be provided from other sources. The amount of money awarded depends on the trust's funds and the number of eligible applicants.

Annual grant total

In 2012 the trust had an income of £1,100 and a total expenditure of £1,600. We estimate that educational grants to individuals totalled £800, with funding also awarded to organisations working with deaf people.

At the time of writing (July 2014) this was the most recent financial information available for the trust.

Applications

On a form available to download from the trust's website. Each applicant requires a sponsor who can verify their deafness and need. The sponsor must be someone who knows the applicant well and works with them professionally such as a lecturer, teacher, social worker or doctor. See the trust's website for the latest deadline dates for when application forms should be posted.

Other information

Applicants are requested to ask their LEA for assistance before contacting the trust as they often offer special help to deaf students.

Dyslexia

Dyslexia Institute Ltd (Dyslexia Action)

£103,000

Correspondent: Elizabeth Ambekar, Company Secretary, Dyslexia Action House, 10 High Street, Egham, Surrey TW20 9EA (01784 222300; email: GetInvolved@dyslexiaaction.org.uk; website: www.dyslexiaaction.org.uk)

CC Number: 268502, SC039177

Eligibility

People in the UK who have dyslexia or literacy difficulties and are from low income families.

Types of grants

A small number of grants are made from the Learning Fund for subsidised assessment and specific periods of tuition based on educational needs related to dyslexia and literacy difficulties. Grants for one term's tuition are for approximately £400, totalling £2,400 for six terms. A contribution from the individual or their family is required at a minimum of £5 per week. The fund is solely reliant on fundraising activities, therefore the amount of grants given is restricted and varies each year.

The majority of bursary-funded pupils attend the nationwide centres of Dyslexia Action for 1.5 or 2 hours multi-sensory tuition each week during the academic year.

Annual grant total

In 2012/13 the charity had assets of £1.2 million, an income of £7.7 million and a total charitable expenditure of £7 million. Individuals are awarded grants from a restricted Learning Fund only, which provided support totalling £103,000.

Exclusions

Applicants from families where joint annual income is in excess of £22,000 will not be considered without evidence of exceptional circumstances.

Applications

Contact the Dyslexia Action Centre at which the applicant wishes to have tuition. Applications are considered three times a year (one meeting each academic term). Applicants for tuition grants should indicate family income and severity of dyslexia – a full educational psychologist's assessment is normally required.

Note that whilst a grant is awarded to an individual, the payment of fees for tuition is made directly to the Dyslexia Action centre where the tuition will take place.

Other information

The charity also organises training events, conferences, fundraising events, provides guidance, advice and supports schools across England working with children with dyslexia and literacy difficulties who are on free school meals and live in deprived communities.

Meningitis

Meningitis Trust

£126,000

Correspondent: Grants Financial Officer, Fern House, Bath Road, Stroud GL5 3TJ (01453 768000; email: info@ meningitisnow.org; website: www. meningitis-trust.org)

CC Number: 803016

Eligibility

People in need who have meningitis or who have disabilities as a result of meningitis.

Types of grants

One-off and recurrent grants are given towards equipment, re-education and special training, such as sign language lessons.

Annual grant total

In 2012/13 the trust had assets totalling £1.3 million and an income of over £2.6 million. Grants for educational and welfare purposes totalled £251,000 and we have estimated the educational grants figure to be £126,000.

Applications

On a form available from the correspondent or downloaded from the trust's website, where criteria are also posted. An initial telephone call to the grants financial officer on 01453 769043 or the 24-hour helpline on 0800 028 1828 to discuss the application process is welcomed. Applications should be submitted through an appropriate third party and are reviewed on a monthly basis.

Other information

The trust runs a 'family day' for children who have meningitis and their families. The day includes arts, crafts and music for children and gives parents an opportunity to meet the trust's staff and other families. The trust also supports a range of professional counselling, home

visits, therapy and information services. The trust has an informative website.

Renal

The British Kidney Patient Association

£326,000 (574 grants)

Correspondent: Fiona Armitage, Administrator, 3 The Windmills, St Mary's Close, Turk Street, Alton GU34 1EF (01420 541424; email: info@ britishkidney-pa.co.uk; website: www. britishkidney-pa.co.uk)

CC Number: 270288

Eligibility

Dialysis patients and their families on low incomes; transplant patients and those receiving conservative care, if health and quality of life is being seriously affected by their renal condition.

Types of grants

Grants to help with the cost of university or college fees; the cost of books, equipment, lodgings or other expenses involved with educational and job opportunities.

Annual grant total

In 2012 the charity had assets of £3 million, an income of £1.7 million and made grants totalling £652,000 in patient grants for both welfare and educational purposes. In 2012 a record 1148 individuals and families were awarded grants.

These were the latest set of accounts available at the time of writing (August 2014).

Exclusions

The association will not pay loans, court fines or bills already paid.

Applications

Applications are available to download from the BKPA website. Forms must be submitted by a renal social worker or member of the patient's renal team.

Other information

The charity also makes grants to hospitals and supports the Ronald McDonald Houses at the Alder Hey Children's Hospital, Liverpool, Bristol Royal Hospital for Children, Evelina Children's Hospital, London and the Royal Hospital for Sick Children, Yorkhill which provide support for the families of young renal patients attending the units at these hospitals.

They also fund non-laboratory research and provide support services, information and advice to kidney patients, amongst other projects.

Independent and boarding schools

The Athlone Trust

£30,000

Correspondent: John Auber, Trustee, 12 Nasau Road, London SW13 9QE (020 7972 9720; fax: 020 7972 9722; email: john@jrga.co.uk; website: www. athlonetrust.com)

CC Number: 277065

Eligibility

Adopted children under the age of 18 who are in need.

Types of grants

According to our research, the trust can give grants for school fees (including private education). The trust marks that support is increasingly given to families with children who have serious disabilities such as Asperger's Syndrome or Attention Deficit Hyperactivity Disorder (ADHD). In exceptional circumstances one-off grants could be provided to help with the cost of educational essentials for schoolchildren.

Annual grant total

In 2013 the trust had an income of £17,000 and an expenditure of £32,000, which is the highest in the past five years. We estimate that the annual total of grants was around £30,000.

Exclusions

People at college or university are not supported.

Applications

In writing to the correspondent. Applications should be submitted by the applicant's parent/guardian and are usually considered in May and November.

Other information

The trust may consider assisting people who are 19 years old providing they are still at school.

The BMTA Trust Ltd

£144,000 (133 grants)

Correspondent: L. Dolphin, Secretary, Wild Wood, Fairfield Road, Shawford, Winchester SO21 2DA (01962 715025; email: bmtatrust@yahoo.co.uk)

CC Number: 273978

Eligibility

Children between the ages of 13 and 16 who are already attending an independent school with a preference for those whose families are connected with the motor industry. Children in exceptional circumstances of social need are occasionally supported to begin attending an independent or boarding school. The trustees 'aim to consider, primarily, cases brought about by unforeseen disaster rather than giving assistance to fund over-ambitious plans.'

Types of grants

Short-term grants for a maximum of two years at £500 a term 'to enable children to complete their current stage of schooling when families have suffered unforeseen financial difficulties.' Help is given for children attending fee-paying schools.

Assistance may be given up to GCSE level and further education is only funded in exceptional circumstances.

Annual grant total

In 2012/13 the trust has assets of £4.5 million and an income of £144,000. Educational grants to 133 individuals totalled £144,000.

During the year the trust received a grant of £50,000 from The Eleanor Hamilton Educational Trust (EHET) which was all distributed in educational grants to individuals.

The charity further specifies that 14% of the overall grant total was given to beneficiaries with a motor industry connection. Grants for educational purposes constituted 93% of the overall giving with the balance of 7% being awarded for welfare needs.

Applications

By contacting the correspondent via email, letter or phone.

Other information

In 2012/13 a total of £11,300 was awarded to 26 individuals for welfare purposes. Small charities may also be supported.

Buttle UK – School Fees Programme

£766,000 (282 grants)

Correspondent: Alan Cox, Buttle UK, Audley House, 13 Palace Street, London SW1E 5HX (020 7798 6227; email: info@ buttleuk.org; website: www.buttleuk.org)

CC Number: 313007

Eligibility

Children and young people over the age of 11 with medical, emotional, social difficulties or those within precarious households. The following groups are eligible to apply: adopted children and young people; children and young people cared for by grandparents, other

relatives or friends; children and young people from single parent families; children and young people with two carers, where one is severely incapacitated through illness or disability, or is terminally ill. Support is only available where the state education system has been unable to meet the applicant's needs.

Types of grants

The trust funds places within a UK boarding or independent day school.

Annual grant total

In 2012/13 the trust had assets of £46.1 million and both an income and a total charitable expenditure of around £4.6 million. 282 grants were awarded to children totalling £766,000. New awards accounted for 28% of the total and the remainder were renewals. Half of the awards were allocated to the day schools and half to the boarding schools.

Exclusions

The trust cannot assist: children or young people who are looked after by the local authority or other statutory body; where a school has been chosen because of special facilities for a learning or developmental difficulty; where needs could be met within the state day system; children or young people who do not have settled status in the UK or who are normally resident abroad; where the school has been chosen for a particular type of education, such as music, drama or sports.

Applications

Initial communication should be made in writing to the correspondent outlining how the individual meets the eligibility criteria and providing all the relevant details of their health, emotional, social or family difficulties. Eligible applicants will be sent an application form.

Contact details for applicants resident in:

England: Audley House, 13 Palace Street, London SW1E 5HX, info@buttleuk.org, 020 7828 7311

Scotland: PO Box 5075, Glasgow G78 4WA, scotland@buttleuk.org, 01505 850437

Wales: PO Box 2528, Cardiff CF23 0GX, wales@buttleuk.org, 02920 541996

Northern Ireland: PO Box 484, Belfast BT6 0YA, nireland@buttleuk.org, 02890 641164

Further information and guidelines can be found on the trust's website.

Other information

The trust also runs a small grants programme helping individuals in need.

The Emmott Foundation Ltd

£354,000 (106 grants)

Correspondent: Julie and Paul Spillane, Education Officers, 26 Red Lion Square, London WC1R 4AG (01159 376526; email: emmottfoundation@btinternet. com; website: emmottfoundation.org/)

CC Number: 209033

Eligibility

Students aged 16–18 in fee-paying schools (including state boarding schools) who have high academic achievements (a majority of actual or predicted As or A*s at GCSE) and whose parents or guardians 'are no longer able to meet their planned financial commitments for education as a result of a sudden or unexpected family crisis such as death, accident, severe illness, divorce, desertion or loss of employment.' Awards may be granted to students with lower grades in circumstances of exceptional need or where there is a major educational, social or pastoral problem, including domestic violence, bullying, parental drug/alcohol abuse.

Note: grants are made only where the school is willing to make a significant contribution to the fees.

Types of grants

Grants are for sixth form only. Their purpose is to enable pupils to enter or remain in the sixth form in their present school. The grants help only with basic fees, not with incidental expenses (music lessons, travel, books, expeditions and so on). Grants are usually of between £500 and £1,500 per term, paid directly to the school at the start of each sixth form term.

Annual grant total

In 2012/13 the foundation had assets of £9.1 million and an income of £482,000. Direct individual fee assistance to pupils at the sixth form totalled £354,000 distributed between 106 individuals.

Exclusions

Students in other age groups than specified above are not considered.

Applications

Initially in writing to the correspondent. Application forms are sent to eligible applicants. Usually the applicants are visited by the education officers or their equivalent from similar charities. The trustees meet in March, June and November to consider applications.

The foundation invites applicants to contact the education officers with queries regarding their eligibility.

Other information

The foundation also gives annual grants to students in Royal Agriculture College, Cirencester (£9,000 to three students in 2012/13).

Fishmongers' Company's Charitable Trust

£26,000

Correspondent: Peter Woodward, Trustee, Fishmongers' Hall, London Bridge, London EC4R 9EL (020 7626 3531; fax: 020 7929 1389; email: ct@fishhall.org.uk; website: www.fishhall.org.uk/Education–Grants)

CC Number: 263690

Eligibility

Children and young people under the age of 19 who are in need of a sum of money to complete schooling. Preference is given to children of single parent families and/or those with a learning difficulty or disability, or those who come from a disadvantaged or unstable family background. People studying fishery related subjects are also favoured.

Types of grants

Small, one-off grants to assist in cases of short-term need. The trust has previously been giving assistance with school fees, maximum grant being around £1,800.

Annual grant total

In 2013 the trust had assets of £23.7 million, an income of £2 million and a total charitable expenditure of £519,000. Around £428,000 was awarded in educational grants, of which £26,000 was given in grants to individuals.

Applications

Application forms can be requested from the correspondent. They can be submitted directly by the individual or by a parent/guardian for those under the age of 18. The trustees usually meet in March, June/July and October/November.

Note: the correspondent has confirmed that currently individual applications are not accepted.

Other information

The trust also gives to organisations for welfare, medical, environment and heritage causes. The largest recipient of the trust's funding is Gresham's School in Norfolk, but a number of other schools are also supported.

Following the merger of about forty small charities in September 2013, the trust now has a number of restricted funds making awards for specific purposes.

Currently, individual applications are not accepted but a number of scholarships are distributed through educational establishments, mainly where they are 'either of national importance or if their principal purpose is to cater for disabled students.'

IAPS Charitable Trust

£5,600

Correspondent: Richard Flower, Secretary, 11 Waterloo Place, Warwick Street, Leamington Spa CV32 5LA (01926 887833, 01926461508; email: rwf@iaps.org.uk; website: www.iaps.org.uk/about/our-charities)

CC Number: 1143241

Eligibility

Children up to the age of 18 in early, primary or middle school years, both in the UK and overseas. Teachers may receive training or research grants. Preference is given to current and former members of the Independent Association of Prep Schools (IAPS) and their dependents.

Support to 'children of members or deceased members of the teaching profession to continue their education in independent senior schools, where their families' financial circumstances would otherwise prevent them from doing so.'

Children between the ages of 8 and 14 are supported to attend residential music courses in the UK (principally supported courses are the National Schools Symphony Orchestras (NSSO and Young NSSO), the National Preparatory School Orchestras (NPSO) and the Junior Eton Choral Courses (JECC)).

Types of grants

Grants are available to support children's education, including training in music, and also to teachers for training and research.

The trust also provides bursaries of up to £2,500 per year per pupil. Priority is given where 'pupils have already started their education in independent schools and whose families' financial circumstances have changed. The support of the school, or intended school, is essential and all awards are subject to an annual needs assessment review.'

Annual grant total

In 2013/14 the trust had assets of £710,000 and an income of £67,000. Grants to individuals totalled £11,200. The amount awarded solely for educational purposes was not specified in the accounts; we estimate that educational grants totalled around £5,600. Individual grants are made from restricted funds.

The trustees' annual report from 2013/14 notes that 'the charity has an ambition to increase the funds available for bursaries and in particular to be able to support bursaries for younger pupils.'

Exclusions

Support is not given where public funding is available. Gap-year students are not assisted.

Applications

In writing to the correspondent. Applications for general grants are considered at termly meetings, although urgent cases can be decided in between.

Enquiries about application for a bursary should be made to Charles Abram (charlesabram@hotmail.com) and for music grants to John Brett (hmstudy@obh.co.uk, Old Buckenham Hall School, Brettenham Park, Ipswich IP7 7PH) or the intended courses directly.

Other information

In 2012 the IAPS Benevolent Fund and the IAPS Bursary Trust, and in 2013 the IAPS Orchestra Trust, merged with the trust allowing it to extend its work.

The trust also supports organisations and gives welfare grants to members and former members of the IAPS and their dependents. In 2013/14 grants to institutions totalled £38,000.

The trust is also known as 'itrust'.

The Lloyd Foundation

£95,000 (68 grants)

Correspondent: Margaret Keyte, Secretary, 1 Churchill Close, Breaston, Derbyshire DE72 3UD (01332 873772; email: keytelloyd@btintenet.com)

CC Number: 314203

Eligibility

Children (aged between 5 and 25 years old) of British citizens ordinarily living/working overseas.

Assistance is also available to 'teaching members of staff of schools outside the UK conducted in accordance with British educational principles and practice' and to people in need who 'have been employed by the former English School Cairo for at least five years or at the time of its closure.'

Types of grants

The trust may offer scholarships, bursaries, maintenance allowances to school pupils and further/higher education students 'to obtain British type education either overseas or in the UK whilst the family is living/working overseas.' Our research suggests that the grants normally range between £300 and £3,000 and can be given towards general educational purposes, including fees, books, equipment/instruments, living expenses, travel costs, study of music or the arts and so on. According to our research, grants are primarily given to attend the nearest English-medium schools and where no such school exists help can be given towards fees for a school in the UK.

Annual grant total

In 2012/13 the foundation had assets of £3.2 million, an income of £149,000 and made grants totalling around £95,000 to 68 beneficiaries. The trustees' annual report 2012/13 notes that a further 94 applications and enquiries for awards had to be refused due to not meeting the terms of reference of the foundation.

Exclusions

Children under the age of five or those taking postgraduate courses are not normally supported.

Applications

Application forms can be requested from the correspondent. Submissions can be made directly by the individual or through an appropriate third party. The trustees normally meet quarterly.

The McAlpine Educational Endowments Ltd

£116,000 (21 grants)

Correspondent: Brian Arter, Trustee, Eaton Court, Maylands Avenue, Hemel Hempstead, Hertfordshire HP2 7TR (01442 233444)

CC Number: 313156

Eligibility

Children and young people in need in 'preparatory, public or other independent school and any technical college or university.'

Types of grants

Support is given for 'an academic year by year basis, but can be renewed for subsequent years subject to a satisfactory school report for the academic year and the availability of funds.' According to our research, grants normally reach up to £1,800 and are mainly towards the cost of independent school fees for children attending ten schools selected by the trustees. Applicants normally are of academic ability, sound character and leadership potential but, for reasons of financial hardship, would otherwise have to leave the school.

Annual grant total

In 2012/13 the charity had assets of £130,000, an income of £104,000 and

made grants to individuals totalling £116,000. During the year 21 bursaries were made.

Exclusions

Grants for people at specialist schools (such as ballet or music schools, or schools for children with learning difficulties) are not normally considered.

Applications

In writing to the correspondent. The trustees' annual report form 2012/13 states that the trust 'carries out its objectives by receiving applications from individuals or parents in connection with mainstream education.' Applications should normally be made through the selected schools, the list of which is available from the correspondent. Applications are considered during the summer before the new academic year. Note, that because of the long-term nature of the charity's commitments, very few new grants can be considered each year.

The Ogden Trust

£604,000 (80 grants)

Correspondent: Tim Simmons, Chief Executive, Hughes Hall, Wollaston Road, Cambridge CB1 2EW (01223 518164; fax: 01223 761837; email: office@ ogdentrust.com; website: ogdentrust.com/)

CC Number: 1037570

Eligibility

Academically gifted young people in the areas of science, physics and maths who have previously been educated in the state sector and who wish to attend a selection of independent secondary schools at sixth form level to study science subjects at A-level with the intention of studying physics at university. Undergraduate students who are already associated with the trust are also supported (for a list of groups members of which are considered to be associated with the trust, see the trust's website). Applicants must be of British nationality and have a combined parental income of less than £50,000.

Types of grants

The trust offers:

- Sixth Form Science Scholarships – towards school fees and travel costs to 'gifted young scientists wishing to study A-level physics at an independent school in areas of the country where access to good A-Level physics provision in the maintained sector is difficult'
- Undergraduate Science Scholarship – up to £1,500 a year for a maximum of four years payable in two instalments (October and February) available to

students 'already associated with the trust and wishing to study for a physics or related degree at a British university'

Annual grant total

In 2012/13 the trust had assets of £42.8 million and an income of £330,000. Bursaries and scholarships totalled £604,000, consisting of £352,000 in 37 bursaries and £252,000 in 43 undergraduate scholarships.

Exclusions

Postgraduate degrees are not supported (except PGCE physics students).

Applications

The Sixth Form Science Scholarships operate through schools associated with the trust, a list of which can be found on its website. The list is not closed and new schools may submit candidates. Applicants should apply to the school directly using the enquiry form which can be downloaded from the trust's website.

Application forms for the Undergraduate Science Scholarships can be found on the trust's website. Applications should be accompanied by an academic reference and supporting documentation.

Other information

The trust also supports institutions. In 2012/13 a total of £508,000 was awarded in grants.

Reedham Children's Trust

£331,000 (132 grants)

Correspondent: Sarah Smart, Administrator, 23 Inwood Avenue, Coulsdon, Surrey CR5 1LP (020 8660 1461; fax: 020 8763 1293; email: info@ reedham-trust.org.uk; website: www. reedham-trust.org.uk)

CC Number: 312433

Eligibility

Children (normally between the ages of 11 and 16) who are in need of boarding care, due to the death, disability or absence of one or both of their parents (whether natural or through adoption), or their own disability, or other domestic or personal circumstances, such as domestic violence, parental drug/ alcohol abuse.

The trust focuses on social need for boarding, not an educational need or academic ability; however, it closely monitors the progress (both academic and social) of the children assisted.

Types of grants

Grants, on average of around £2,500, towards boarding fees.

Annual grant total

In 2012/13 the trust had assets of £7.1 million and an income of £284,000. Grants were awarded totalling £331,000 in support of 132 children.

Exclusions

The trust will not give support in cases where the local authority should bear the responsibility (for example where a care order is in place).

Children below the age of 11 are supported only in exceptional circumstances and funding after GCSEs can only be continued following a review of the home situation.

Applications

Eligible applicants should contact the trust via email or phone for further guidance on application process. Applications are considered throughout the year and may be made by a parent/guardian, legal or medical professional, through the applicant's school or educational welfare agency, if applicable. The trust will need a confirmation from a professional that boarding school education is in the best interests of the applicant. Applications are normally considered five times a year.

Other information

The trust has a restricted North East Fund to support children in that specific area. In 2012/13 a total of £21,000 was awarded from the fund.

Royal National Children's Foundation

£910,000 (341 grants)

Correspondent: Chris Hughes, Director of Operations, Sandy Lane, Cobham, Surrey KT3 4AW (01932 868622; fax: 01932 866420; email: admin@rncf.org.uk; website: www.rncf.org.uk)

CC Number: 310916

Eligibility

Children between the ages of 7 and 18 who have suffered a trauma, tragedy, neglect or are at risk in some other way, and whose family cannot meet the costs of boarding education unaided.

Types of grants

The foundation provides support towards state and independent boarding school fees. Some pupils in independent day schools are also assisted (normally younger children aged 7–13). Emphasis is on boarding need rather than on educational need.

Annual grant total

In 2012/13 the foundation had assets of £23.4 million and an income of £908,000. A total of £910,000 was spent in support to 341 children.

Exclusions

Support cannot be given on the sole basis of financial difficulties, educational preferences or special needs.

Applications

Eligible applicants should make initial contact with the foundation via phone or email. Application forms will then be provided and should be completed by a parent/guardian or other appropriate third party (such as a legal or medical professional, school or welfare agency, if applicable). Consideration can take around 8–12 weeks. Informal enquiries prior to the application are also welcomed.

Other information

The Royal Wanstead Children's Foundation and Joint Educational Trust have merged to form Royal National Children's Foundation, retaining the registered charity number of the former.

Thornton-Smith and Plevins Trust

£210,000 (79 grants)

Correspondent: Heather Cox, Grants Secretary, 298 Icknield Way, Luton, Bedfordshire LU3 2JS (01582 611675; fax: 01582 890995; email: thornton.smithypt@ntlworld.com)

CC Number: 1137196

Eligibility

Currently the trust mostly supports young people aged 16 to 19 who are in distressed circumstances.

Support may also be given to people under the age of 25 who are in need, including people undertaking work practice or apprenticeships in any trade or profession and young people in preparatory, secondary, higher or further education. Assistance is also given to individuals of the professional or business classes who have fallen into poverty and are unable to make adequate provision for their retirement or old age.

Types of grants

Support is given in grants and loans towards school fees and associated costs or in scholarships to travel overseas for educational purposes. Grants are means tested and are paid per term, subject to reasonable progress. The average award is around £2,700. Preference is given to short-term applications primarily in relation to A-levels.

Annual grant total

In 2012/13 the trust had assets of £11.3 million and an income of £360,000. Grants were made to 79 individuals totalling £210,000 and consisted of £208,000 awarded in grants and loans to assist with school fees and

expenses, and £2,000 given in scholarships for educational travel abroad.

Exclusions

Our research suggests that grants are not normally given for the first degree courses. Support will not be given in circumstances where parents were not in a position to fund the fees when entering the child for the school.

Applications

In writing to the correspondent. Applications should include details of the candidate's education and their parents' financial situation. If the applicant is considered eligible further inquiries are made. Applications are normally considered by 31 March to commence in September.

Other information

This trust was formerly the Thornton-Smith Young People's Trust which has been combined with the Wilfred Maurice Plevins Charity, Thornton-Smith Plevins Common Investment Fund and The Thornton-Smith Trust for efficiency.

To be assisted by The Wilfred Maurice Plevins fund, beneficiaries must also be aged ten or over and be the children of a professional. Beneficiaries older than 25 may only receive assistance from The Thornton-Smith fund.

The trust is directing most grants towards education although support was continued for existing elderly beneficiaries (in 2012/13 £5,700).

Orders

The Journal Children's Fund (in conjunction with the Royal Antediluvian Order of Buffaloes)

£27,000

Correspondent: C. McMahon, Administrator, RAOB GLE Trust Corporation, Grove House, Skipton Road, Harrogate, North Yorkshire HG1 4LA (01423 502438; email: hq@raobgle.org.uk; website: www.raobgle.org.uk)

CC Number: 529575

Eligibility

'The education and preferment of orphan or necessitous children of deceased members of the Royal Antediluvian Order of Buffaloes Grand Lodge of England.' The fund's activities extend worldwide.

Types of grants

Help with the cost of books, clothing and other essentials for schoolchildren. Grants may also be available for those at college or university who are eligible.

Annual grant total

In 2012/13 the fund had assets of £399,000 most of which represented investments and debtors and is therefore not available for grant giving. It had an income of £57,000. Grants were made to individuals for education totalling £27,000.

Applications

Initial enquiries regarding assistance can only be made through the individual's branch of attendance.

The Royal Masonic Trust for Girls and Boys

£5 million (2,062 grants)

Correspondent: Leslie Hutchinson, Administrator, Freemasons' Hall, 60 Great Queen Street, London WC2B 5AZ (020 7405 2644; fax: 020 7831 4094; email: info@rmtgb.org; website: www.rmtgb.org)

CC Number: 285836

Eligibility

Generally the dependents of Freemasons. The objects of the trust are to relieve poverty and to advance education. The trust also has power, provided sufficient funds are available, to help children who are not the connected to the Freemasons. Such assistance is usually given by way of grants to other children's charities and via the subsidiary funds.

'Non-masonic' support used to be available through the Choral Bursary Scheme but the trustees' annual report from 2013 states that, 'although the support will continue to be provided to existing beneficiaries, the Choral Bursary Scheme was closed to new applicants in 2013.'

Types of grants

Any necessary kind of assistance to children in any kind of educational environment, including state and private schools, colleges and universities and vocational training or apprenticeships. Help towards educational travel or extra-curricular activities is also given. Grants can be one-off or recurring and are offered towards fees, maintenance costs, computer equipment, music and sports activities, instruments, tools and any other specific and identifiable need.

Through the TalentAid scheme support can be given to individuals exceptionally gifted in music, sports or performing arts. Awards are made towards coaching, advanced lessons and fees at specialist institutions or in one-off payments towards equipment and instruments or attendance of events.

Annual grant total

In 2013 the trust had assets of £152.2 million and an income of £21.3 million. There were 2062 beneficiaries supported during the year totalling around £5.9 million. Out of that sum some help has been given in welfare support, therefore we estimate that educational grants totalled around £5 million. Grants can be broken down as follows:

Amount awarded for beneficiaries	1964	£5.4 million
TalentAid	69	£393,000
Choral Bursaries	29	£197,000

Exclusions

No grants are available for student exchanges.

Support towards fees for independent schools can be considered but only in exceptional circumstances.

Applications

Applications should be made in the first instance to the nearest Masonic authority or, where that is not known, a preliminary enquiry may be addressed to the correspondent.

Applications for TalentAid support can be made on a form available on the trust's website from November to April.

Note that new applications for choral bursaries are no longer accepted.

Other information

In 2013 the Girls' and Boys' Special Funds were merged into the General Fund together with some other specific funds.

The trust has welfare and case advisers to assist families. Most of the funds are given to individuals with a Masonic connection.

Through its Stepping Stones scheme the trust also provides support to other charities working for the benefit of children and young people. Assistance is also given to Lifelites Charity providing technology for children's hospices. A number of subsidiary funds which offer further support to children and young people towards charitable work or educational travel overseas are also administered by the trust.

Overseas students (by place of origin)

British Council

Correspondent: Alison Coutts, Administrator, 10 Spring Gardens, London SW1A 2BN (email: trustee@britishcouncil.org; website: www.britishcouncil.org)

CC Number: 209131

Types of grants

For information on the type of grants available see the 'Work, Study, Create' section of the British Council website.

Annual grant total

The British Council provides scholarships for people looking to work, study or volunteer abroad.

Applications

Online application via the British Council website.

The British Institute of Archaeology at Ankara
See entry on page 105

Churches' International Student Network – Hardship Fund

£25,000 (39 grants)

Correspondent: David Philpot, Grants Secretary, 2/27 Pentland Drive, Edinburgh EH10 6PX (020 7901 4890; email: hardship@ctbi.org.uk; website: www.ctbi.org.uk/116)

CC Number: 1113299

Eligibility

Full-time international students from developing countries studying at British or Irish institutions who are facing unexpected financial problems during the final stages of their course (6 months). Both undergraduate and postgraduate students on a degree course lasting more than one year are eligible. Applicants should intend to return to their home country immediately after their course.

Types of grants

Grants are of around £500 but do not exceed £800.

Annual grant total

In 2013 the fund had assets of £26,000 and an income of £25,000. Grants to 39 students totalled £25,000.

Exclusions

Funding is not given to:

▶ Students from developed countries
▶ Permanent residents of Britain, Ireland and EU
▶ Students who began the course without assured funding to meet the education costs
▶ Asylum seekers or refugees
▶ Those whose studies relate to arms manufacture or experimentation on live animals
▶ Students whose fees and living expenses have been covered by major awards
▶ People who have already been awarded a grant from the fund
▶ Individuals who study outside Britain and Ireland or require funding towards a field trip abroad

Applications

Application forms should be requested from the correspondent providing basic details, especially concerning eligibility, and specifying full postal address. Grants are normally considered three times a year, in February (for studies finishing April-July), June (for August-November) and October (for December-March). Requests for application forms should be made by mid-December, mid-April and mid-August, respectively.

Other information

The fund is administered by Churches Together in Britain and Ireland.

Peter Alan Dickson Foundation

£3,300

Correspondent: Pauline Broomhead, Trustee, Robins Roost, Thruxton, Andover SP11 8NL (email: info@padfoundation.org; website: www.padfoundation.org)

CC Number: 1129310

Eligibility

The foundation's education fund provides financial support to individuals who cannot pursue education or develop their skills and abilities because of poverty or other circumstances. The focus specifically, but not exclusively, is placed on people in developing countries.

Types of grants

Individual bursaries to help with tuition fees and related educational expenses. Grants can range from £250 to £1,000.

Annual grant total

In 2012/13 the foundation had an income of £12,000 and an expenditure of £9,900. We estimate that the annual total of grants to individuals for educational purposes was around £3,300.

Exclusions

The foundation will not: give support where central/local/national government should be responsible for the provision of assistance; provide for people in the independent education sector; offer retrospective funding.

Applications

Application forms are available on the foundation's website together with guidelines.

Other information

The foundation also assists charitable organisations, families and communities in relation to educational causes, youth support and development and disaster or poverty relief.

Global Educational Trust
See entry on page 6

Ruth Hayman Trust

£20,000 (94 grants)

Correspondent: The Administrator, PO Box 17685, London N6 6WD (email: info@ruthhaymantrust.org.uk; website: www.ruthhaymantrust.org.uk)

CC Number: 287268

Eligibility

Adults (aged over 16) in state-funded education or training who have come to settle in the UK and who speak English as their second or other language. Applicants must be resident in the UK as citizens of the UK/EU, spouses of citizens or as asylum seekers/refugees.

Types of grants

One-off and recurrent grants of up to £500 (on average £150) are available to help with the cost of fees (registration, course, exam), joining the professional bodies (if it is essential for the course), disclosure and barring service fees. Depending on the finances available, the trust could also assist with the cost of equipment and instruments. Grants towards travel costs are also made to people with disabilities who can provide a statement from their doctor. The trust also suggests that for a limited period the £500 maximum could be increased for those on courses at level 3 and above or for membership of professional associations where fees are very high. Cheques are usually paid to the educational institution directly.

There is an additional annual Rose Grant Special Award of £500 available to 'applicants who can show exceptional academic achievement, an outstanding commitment to the community or human rights as well as financial need.'

Annual grant total

In 2012/13 the trust had an income of £28,000 and awarded a total of £20,000 to 94 individuals. Normally the trust receives about 400 applications each year, of which about 170 are successful.

Exclusions

Grants cannot be given towards travel costs (except for people with a disability), childcare, living expenses, postgraduate education (unless it leads directly to employment) or private education courses (unless the course is only available in specialist private training).

People studying as overseas students are not supported and individuals on distance learning courses can only be supported if they are unable to travel to the place of education.

Applications

Application forms can be found on the trust's website or requested from the correspondent. Grants are awarded about five times a year and applications should be submitted in February, late April, late June, early September or late November. Candidates are required to provide an academic reference.

Applications for the Rose Grant Special Award should be made on the same form providing evidence that the candidate satisfies the additional requirements.

The trust reminds that it is crucial to fill in the application form in full (do not forget to demonstrate financial need, state your first language, include a reference and specify what the support is needed for). Further application guidelines can be found on the trust's website; read them carefully to avoid your application being rejected on technical grounds.

Other information

The full name of the trust is 'The Ruth Hayman Trust for the Advancement of the Education of Adults Resident in the United Kingdom Whose First Language is not English'.

The Nora Henry Trust

£25,000

Correspondent: Fiona MacGillivray, Administrator, Family Action, 501–505 Kingsland Road, London E8 4AU (020 7254 6251; email: grants.enquiry@family-action.org.uk; website: www.family-action.org.uk)

CC Number: 313949

Eligibility

Students from any country with a preference for students from developing countries who are studying subjects which will be of use when the student returns to that country.

Students can study sociology, economics, ecology, philosophy or training of a professional, technological, technical, scientific or artistic nature.

Types of grants

One-off grants usually ranging from £100 to £200 can be given towards books, fees, living expenses, travel and childcare.

Annual grant total

In 2012/13 the trust had assets of £1.6 million, an income of £72,000 and a total expenditure of £58,000.

Grants totalled approximately £25,000.

Exclusions

No grants for study or travel overseas for British students, or for student exchanges.

Applications

On a form available from the correspondent. Applications should be submitted directly by the individual and supported by an academic referee. They are considered all year round.

The David Montefiore Trust

£21,000

Correspondent: Jean MacDonald Bogaardt, Trustee, 17 Market Street, Crewkerne, Somerset TA18 7JU (01460 74401)

CC Number: 260452

Eligibility

Students from developing countries, principally those undertaking postgraduate study in the UK before returning to their own countries. Also asylum seekers who need retraining in this country at any level, from language courses to medical exams.

Types of grants

Normally grants are in the form of single payments in time for the start of the academic year and usually reach up to £500, although can range up to £1,000.

Annual grant total

In 2012/13 the trust had an income of £14,200 and an expenditure of £21,000. We estimate the annual total of grants to be around the same figure.

Applications

Applications must be made through the university or college and provide details

of how all other costs, including living expenses, are going to be met. Our research suggests that applications from individuals will not be considered without confirmation from the university including references and CVs. Applications are considered monthly.

Other information

The trust prefers all correspondence to be received in writing.

The Nurses Association of Jamaica (NAJ) (UK)
See entry on page 108

Prisoners of Conscience Appeal Fund

£46,000 (12 grants)

Correspondent: The Grants Officer, PO Box 61044, London SE1 1UP (020 7407 6644; fax: 020 7407 6655; email: info@prisonersofconscience.org; website: www.prisonersofconscience.org)

CC Number: 213766

Eligibility

Prisoners of conscience and/or their families, who have suffered persecution for their beliefs. The fact that the person is seeking asylum or has been a victim of civil war is not sufficient grounds in itself.

Types of grants

Mainly one-off grants of about £350 each for travel, resources, equipment, vocational conversion courses and re-qualification costs. Bursary grants are also available for tuition fees for postgraduate study and professional conversion courses.

Annual grant total

In 2013 relief grants to 130 individuals and families made in the UK totalled £81,500 with bursaries for 12 individuals totalling an additional £46,000.

Exclusions

No support is given to people who have used or advocated violence or supported a violent organisation.

Applications

Application forms are available from the correspondent and should be submitted by a third party such as human rights organisations, refugee groups, solicitors and organisations in the UK and overseas, from large NGOs to small refugee community organisations. Applicants who do not know of a third party organisation through which they can submit an application should contact the fund for advice. Applications

should include evidence of identification of the applicant and of costs.

Other information

The fund was initially established in 1962 as the relief arm of Amnesty International, but is now a charity in its own right. It is the only agency in the UK making grants specifically to prisoners of conscience – individuals who have been persecuted for their conscientiously-held beliefs, provided that they have not used or advocated violence. Grant recipients include political prisoners, human rights defenders, lawyers, environmental activists, teachers and academics who come from many different countries such as Burma, Zimbabwe, Sri Lanka, Tibet, Iran, Cameroon and Eritrea.

The charity's aim is to raise and distribute money to help them and/or their families rehabilitate themselves during and after their ordeal. Financial grants cover general hardship relief, furniture, medicines, travel costs, family reunion costs, education, requalification and resettlement costs and medical treatment and counselling after torture.

Sloane Robinson Foundation

£94,000

Correspondent: Michael Wilcox, Trustee, Old Coach House, Sunnyside, Bergh Apton, Norwich NR15 1DD (01508 480100; email: info@wilcoxlewis. co.uk)

CC Number: 1068286

Eligibility

Overseas students wishing to study at British universities and British students wishing to study overseas.

At an undergraduate level emphasis is placed on liberal arts, orthodox sciences (but not religion), social sciences and languages. At postgraduate level no restrictions apply. With regards to overseas studies emphasis should be placed on the subjects in which the country offers better courses.

The foundation is also interested in funding research into controversial issues (for example prison policy, decriminalisation of cannabis, population issues) and supporting young people to work in developing countries on projects which transfer knowledge and skills to the local people.

Types of grants

Grants and scholarships according to need.

Annual grant total

In 2012/13 the foundation had assets of £15.6 million and an income of £253,000 and a total charitable expenditure of £372,000. Grants made to individuals totalled £94,000 (all to pupils of Latymer School).

Applications

The foundation is 'continuing to develop long-term relationships with a number of academic institutions, with the ultimate goal of establishing scholarships and bursary schemes.' Our research suggests that applications should be made directly through educational establishments. The trustees meet at least twice a year.

Note that 'only successful applicants are notified, in order to avoid increased administrative costs for the foundation.'

Other information

The foundation mainly provides funding to educational institutions (£278,000 in 2012/13).

Mary Trevelyan Fund

£8,600

Correspondent: Peter Anwyl, Secretary, International Students House, 1 Park Crescent, Regent's Park, London W1B 1SH (020 7631 8309; email: advice@ish.org.uk; website: www.ish.org.uk/welfare-amp-scholarships/mary-trevelyan-fund)

CC Number: 294448–1

Eligibility

Students from developing countries studying in London who are experiencing unexpected financial difficulties. Students must be in their final year of study and intend to return home on completion of their course. Preference is given where the institution is a member of International Students House.

See the fund's website for a list of member institutions and the approved 'developing countries'.

Types of grants

Grants or loans of up to £1,000 are available to those who experience difficulties due to unexpected financial hardship.

Annual grant total

In 2012/13 the fund made awards totalling £8,600.

Exclusions

Students should not require total funding over £2,000. Asylum seekers or people granted asylum in the UK are not supported.

Applications

Application forms are available from the fund's website or can be requested from the correspondent.

Applications are considered throughout the year (at least six times). The fund has previously stated that the application will have a greater chance of success if it is supported by the student's own college/university advice or welfare service.

Other information

This fund is a subsidiary charity of The International Students Trust.

Armenia

Armenian General Benevolent Union London Trust

£66,000 (27 grants)

Correspondent: Dr Berge Azadian, Honorary Secretary, 51C Parkside, Wimbledon, London SW19 5NE (email: info@agbu.org; website: www.agbu.org.uk)

CC Number: 282070

Eligibility

University students of Armenian descent studying full-time at accredited UK educational institutions. Both undergraduate and postgraduate programmes are eligible. Preference can be given for courses in Armenian studies or subjects which may benefit the Armenian community.

There is a specific AGBU Religious Education Assistance Program available to Armenian clergy and lay leaders for professional development.

Types of grants

Scholarships generally range from £1,000 to £3,000 and are awarded annually for up to three years. Support is both need and merit based and is normally intended to cover educational fees or to contribute to essentials, books or maintenance. The trust offers both grants and interest free loans.

Students studying performing arts or religious studies should apply for AGBU Performing Arts Fellowship (study in UK) or AGBU Religious Studies Fellowship, as they will not be eligible for the general scholarship.

Our research suggests that student grants are occasionally given to Armenians with significant financial hardship or for refugees in the UK. Grants have also been given towards teaching, arts and research papers connected with Armenian culture.

Annual grant total

At the time of writing (August 2014) the latest financial information available was from 2012. In 2012 the trust had assets of £4.2 million and an income of £309,000. Student grants and loans totalled £66,000 awarded to 27 individuals.

Exclusions

Citizens of Armenia studying in Armenia are not eligible for the scholarship. The trust does not offer travel grants, support for conferences, semesters of study abroad, non-degree courses, research studies and similar short-term educational or professional experience.

Applications

Applications can be made online on the AGBU Scholarship program (www.agbu-scholarship.org). There is a convenient eligibility checking programme. Applications for scholarships must be made by 31 August and for fellowships by 31 July. Note that application deadlines are very strict and submissions past the designated dates will be disregarded.

Applications for the AGBU Religious Education Assistance Program can be made on a form downloadable from the trust's website.

Other information

Support is also given to Armenian schools, nurseries and cultural groups in the UK and overseas, usually towards running costs for Armenian language, history, religion and culture classes. Occasionally welfare grants can be given to people in need. In 2012 support was given to K. Tahta Armenian Sunday School (£4,000), other organisations (£5,000) and in cultural/intellectual grants (£7,500).

The AGBU scholarship website also suggests a number of other sources of help. The trust itself is connected with the Armenian Education Trust (registered charity number 313930).

The Armenian Relief Society of Great Britain Trust

£100

Correspondent: The Secretary, 209 Syon Lane, Isleworth TW7 5PU

CC Number: 327389

Eligibility

Poor, sick or bereaved Armenians, worldwide.

Types of grants

One-off and recurrent grants of £150 are available to promote the study and research into the history and culture of Armenians or to pay fees or educational costs.

Annual grant total

The majority of grants are usually made to organisations, although the trust does have the capacity to make grants to individuals.

Applications

In writing to the correspondent.

The Benlian Trust

£59,000 (30 grants)

Correspondent: Maral Ovanessoff, Administrator, 15 Elm Crescent, Ealing, London W5 3JW (02085671210; email: benliantrust@gmail.com)

CC Number: 277253

Eligibility

Children of Armenian fathers. Applicants must be members of the Armenian Church studying at universities and colleges in the UK.

Types of grants

Scholarships to Armenian people in higher education. Grants are given towards the cost of fees and/or living expenses. Priority is given to undergraduates. Scholarships are awarded in the range of £1,000 to £4,500.

Annual grant total

In 2012/13 the trust had assets of £2.7 million, an income of £105,000 and a total charitable expenditure of £99,000. Scholarships were made to 30 individuals totalling £59,000.

Applications

Application forms can be requested from the correspondent via post or email. Completed applications should be returned before 30 April (they can be emailed as long as have been signed and scanned). Three references are required (two academic and one social).

Other information

The trust specifies that 60% of its income is to be distributed in scholarships, 25% towards activities connected with the cultural life of the London Community of Armenians, including the maintenance and support of Armenian House, 10% in advancement of medical research, 1/10th to the Armenian Hospital in Istanbul and L'Ecole Mixte Armeniennes (France) in equal shares, and 5% in provision of amenities for nurses at the Middlesex Hospital.

In 2012/13 London Armenian Cultural Fund awarded eight grants totalling £27,000, a total of £13,500 was spent from the hospital fund and four charitable organisations were supported totalling £150.

Mihran and Azniv Essefian Charitable Trust (registered charity number 275074) is a connected charity.

Mihran Essefian Charitable Trust (The Mihran and Azniv Essefian Charitable Trust)

£36,000 (448 grants)

Correspondent: Maral Ovanessoff, Administrator, 15 Elm Crescent, Ealing, London W5 3JW (02085671210)

CC Number: 275074

Eligibility

University students of Armenian origin studying in Armenia or Armenian students in the UK.

Types of grants

The trust offers scholarships to university students. Grants range from around £30 to £200 per student.

Annual grant total

In 2012/13 the trust had assets of £1.6 million, an income of £72,000 and a total charitable expenditure of £41,000. Grants to 448 individuals totalled around £36,000 and can be divided as follows:

Students in Gyumri	182	£22,000 (£80 – £220 per student)
Students in Vanadzor	264	£11,500 (£30 – £60 per student)
Students in Yerevan	2	£3,400

Applications

In writing to the correspondent. The deadline for applications is usually the end of April each year.

Other information

Grants are also given to organisations and institutions promoting educational, cultural and charitable activities of the Armenian community (£5,000 in 2012/13).

Asia

The Bestway Foundation

£80,000 (48 grants)

Correspondent: M. Y. Sheikh, Administrator, Abbey Road, Park Royal, London NW10 7BW (020 8453 1234; fax: 020 8453 8219; email: zulfikaur. wajid-hasan@bestway.co.uk; website: www.bestwaygroup.co.uk/page/Bestway-Foundation.html)

CC Number: 297178

Eligibility

Higher education students who are of Indian, Pakistani, Bangladeshi or Sri Lankan origin.

Types of grants

One-off and recurrent scholarships, grants and loans towards tuition fees. Payments are normally made directly to academic institutions.

Annual grant total

In 2012/13 the foundation had assets of £6.7 million, an income of £737,000 and a charitable expenditure of £426,000. During the year 48 individuals were supported. A total of £154,000 was awarded to individuals and foreign charities. The amount given to students was not specified in the accounts, however previously grants to individuals have totalled around £80,000.

Applications

In writing to the correspondent by post enclosing an sae or by email. Applications are normally considered in January.

Other information

Grants are also made to organisations in the UK and overseas (17 grants were made during the year).

The Hammond Trust

£21,000

Correspondent: Alison Coutts, Secretary to the British Council, British Council, 10 Spring Gardens, London SW1A 2BN (email: Hammond.Trust@britishcouncil. org)

CC Number: 1001818

Eligibility

Students from Asia over the age of 18 who are studying at a recognised institution in the UK. Grants are available to people who would be unable to finish the last six months of the course or a piece of research due to unforeseen financial difficulties beyond their control. Support can only be given where applicants have exhausted any help available from their own authorities or such help is reasonably inadequate. It is expected that candidates will make efforts to meet the commitments from their own resources. Grants are only awarded if students intend to return to their home country (or to a similar country if that is debarred) after completion of the course.

Types of grants

Grants are for living expenses and only available during the last six months of the course. The award can reach up to £2,000.

Annual grant total

In 2012/13 the trust had an income of £340 and a total charitable expenditure of £22,000, which is higher than usual. We estimate that the annual total of grants was about £21,000.

Exclusions

The trust does not provide academic scholarships towards the cost of tuition fees and will not give retrospective awards.

Applications

Application forms are available from the correspondent but applications must be made through the candidate's academic institution. Regrettably, the trust cannot enter into direct communication about individual applications. The course tutor or supervisor must give a report on the applicant in part B of the application form which must be sent through the academic authority and endorsed with an official stamp.

Other information

Students from the following countries are eligible: Armenia, Azerbaijan, Bangladesh, Bahrain, Bhutan, Brunei, Burma (Myanmar), Cambodia, China, Cyprus, East Timor, Georgia, Hong Kong, India, Indonesia, Iran, Iraq, Israel, Japan, Jordan, Kazakhstan, Korea DPR (North), Korea Rep. of (South), Kuwait, Kyrgyzstan, Lebanon, Macau, Malaysia, Maldives, Mongolia, Nepal, Oman, Pakistan, Palestinian Territories, Philippines, Qatar, Russia, Saudi Arabia, Singapore, Sri Lanka, Syria, Taiwan, Tajikistan, Thailand, Turkey, Turkmenistan, United Arab Emirates, Uzbekistan, Yemen, Vietnam.

Australia

The Britain-Australia Society Education Trust

£0

Correspondent: Dale Eaton, Administrator, The Britain-Australia Society, Swire House, Australia Centre, Strand, London WC2B 4LG (020 7630 1075; email: adm@britain-australia.org.uk; website: www.britain-australia.org.uk)

CC Number: 803505

Eligibility

Individuals 18 or under (usually of secondary school age) living in the UK who have a connection with Australia.

Types of grants

Grants contributing towards the expenses (but not fares) of educational projects leading to better British-Australian understanding. Grants are also given to schoolchildren for uniforms/clothing, fees, study/travel overseas and books. Grants range from between £250 to £500.

Annual grant total

In 2012/13 the trust had an income of £100 and had a total expenditure of £0. Although the trust has not had any expenditure for the last three financial years it is still a registered charity and would appear to have funds of at least around £5,500 to be distributed in the future.

Applications

In writing to the correspondent, including details of the funding required. The deadline for applications is 31 March for consideration through May.

Belgium

Royal Belgian Benevolent Society in London

£1,000

Correspondent: Michel Vanhoonacker, Trustee, 8 Northumberland Avenue, London WC2N 5BY (020 7127 4292; email: events@blcc.co.uk)

CC Number: 233435

Eligibility

Belgian nationals who are studying in Britain and have fallen on hard times.

Types of grants

Previously a limited number of small one-off awards (up to £1,500) were available to postgraduate students towards general educational expenses, for example tuition fees or accommodation.

Annual grant total

In 2013 the society had an income of £1,300 and a total expenditure of £2,300. We estimate that during the year over £1,000 was given to students in need. Each year the society receives around 30–40 applications.

Exclusions

The scheme is not generally aimed to assist undergraduates of PhD students.

Applications

The correspondent has informed us that the scheme is on hold and applications are not accepted for the foreseeable future. For the time being enquiries to the society are not welcomed.

Other information

Note: the scheme is currently on hold and applications are not invited.

The scheme is operated through the British Council in Brussels. Some support is also available for general welfare needs.

British Commonwealth

Sir Ernest Cassel Educational Trust (The Cassel Trust)

£32,000

Correspondent: Kathryn Hodges, Secretary, 5 Grimston Park Mews, Grimston Park, Grimston, Tadcaster LS24 9DB (01937 834730; email: casseltrust@btinternet.com; website: www.casseltrust.co.uk)

CC Number: 313820

Eligibility

Overseas students from the Commonwealth countries studying in the UK who are in the final year of their studies and are experiencing unforeseen financial difficulties.

Postdoctoral students of humanities and other fields in the UK universities undertaking research overseas.

Types of grants

The trust offers grants to individuals in the following two categories:

▷ Mountbatten Memorial Grants – for overseas students from the Commonwealth countries who are facing financial difficulties in their final year at a UK university, to help them finish the course by contributing towards their living expenses only
▷ Postdoctoral Travel Grants – awards of up to £1,000 to assist with the travel costs to postdoctoral students who are at university in the UK undertaking research overseas in the humanities and other fields

Annual grant total

In 2012/13 the trust had assets of £1.5 million, an income of £61,000 and a total charitable expenditure of £41,000. Grants to individuals were made in following categories:

Mountbatten Memorial Grants	£17,000
Overseas research grants	£8,000
Mountbatten Memorial Grants provision for exceptional grants	£7,000

Exclusions

Grants are not intended to cover or contribute to the course fees. The trust will not provide retrospective grants, repayment of debts or support to overseas students who are UK-registered for fees purposes. Students on a one year course are unlikely to be supported.

Applications

The Mountbatten Memorial Grants are administered by either Churches International Student Network Hardship Fund or through a Block Grant Scheme currently active in the following universities: Birmingham, Cardiff, Glasgow, Leeds, Leicester, Manchester, Nottingham, Reading, Imperial College London and University College London. Candidates from these institutions should apply directly to their student welfare office responsible for overseas students. Students at any other university should apply to: The Grants Secretary, CISN Hardship Fund, 2/27 Pentland Drive, Edinburgh EH10 6PU (tel: 0131 4454015, email: dphilpot@ cofscotland.org.uk).

Applications should include the following details:

▶ CV and details of the intended career
▶ Details of the course or research degree and completion date
▶ Current financial position and the nature of the unforeseen circumstances causing the difficulty
▶ Any other grants and outstanding applications for financial assistance
▶ A letter of support/statement of attendance from an academic supervisor

The trustees meet once a year to consider applications, usually in July.

Applications for the Postdoctoral Travel Grants are administered by the British Academy and should be made on the small research grant form available from the academy at: The Research Grants Department, The British Academy, 10 Carlton House Terrace, London SW1Y 5AH (tel: 020 7969 5200). Applications are considered in spring each year.

Other information

The trust also provides grants to organisations involved in: higher and adult education; the arts; education of women; education/training of people with disabilities and individuals out of employment; providing opportunities to young people to serve overseas. Grants to organisations totalled £9,200 in 2012/13.

Canada

The Canadian Centennial Scholarship Fund UK (CCSF)

£50,000 (16 grants)

Correspondent: Leith McKay, Trustee, 39 Balham Park Road, Ground Flat SW12 8DX (075000008457; email: info@ canadianwomenlondon.org; website: www.canadianscholarshipfund.co.uk)

CC Number: 313966

Eligibility

Canadian citizens who are in need of financial assistance for a postgraduate study or training in the United Kingdom. Applicants:

> Must demonstrate high academic standards and be currently enrolled in a postgraduate or equivalent course and, at the time of applying, must be attending a full-time UK university or similar institution, and have completed at least one term of study, with at least one term remaining.

Types of grants

The fund offers scholarships ranging from £1,000 to £5,000 which can be used towards fees, travel expenses, books, maintenance and living expenses.

Annual grant total

In 2012/13 the fund had assets of £157,000 and an income of £53,000. Grants to individuals totalled £50,000. Each year 16 individuals are selected for the award.

Exclusions

Applicants undertaking a one-year programme are not accepted.

Applications

Application forms can be downloaded from the fund's website. Candidates who are successful in their initial application will be invited for an interview in London. When applying individuals are requested to provide: a proof of Canadian citizenship (i.e. copy of their passport); a short (up to 500 words) statement about the applicant's course and the impact of their work on Canada; a CV; official transcripts from educational establishments attended; and two references, one of which must be from a current UK supervisor.

Applications can be submitted by post at: CCSF c/o Blake, Cassels and Graydon LLP, 5th Floor, 23 College Lane, London EC4R 2RP; or by email at: applications@ canadianscholarshipfund.co.uk.

Further details and the deadlines for applications can be found on the fund's website. Usually the last submission date is in March. Note that applications received after the deadline are not accepted.

Other information

Among the 16 annual grants the fund gives two special awards: The Belle Shenkman Award for the Study of Arts and the Mary Le Messurier Award for the Study of History.

Unsuccessful applicants are not notified.

Costa Rica

The Ronaldo Falconer Charity

£2,300

Correspondent: The Manager, NatWest Trust Services, 5th Floor, Trinity Quay 2, Avon Street, Bristol BS2 0PT (0551 657 7371)

CC Number: 295853

Eligibility

Further and higher education Costa Rican students, including mature students, who are studying in the UK, with a preference for technical courses and students of any nationality studying in Costa Rica.

Types of grants

Scholarships and bursaries are available.

Annual grant total

In 2012/13 the charity had an income of £7,300 and an expenditure of £2,500. We estimate the total of grants to be around £2,300.

Applications

According to our research the trust does not accept unsolicited applications. Instead, students are recommended to the trustees by a particular university.

Czech Republic

The Anglo-Czech Educational Fund

£35,000

Correspondent: Paul Sheils, Trustee, Moon Beever Solicitors, 24–25 Bloomsbury Square, London WC1A 2PL (020 7637 0661; email: info@ moonbeever.com)

CC Number: 1110348

Eligibility

Students from the Czech Republic who wish to study primarily in the UK, USA and European countries.

Types of grants

Grant and loans.

Annual grant total

In 2012/13 the fund had an income of £187,000 and an expenditure of £134,000. During the year, a grant of £35,000 was awarded to Karlova Univerzita to distribute as grants.

Applications

In writing to the correspondent.

Egypt

Egyptian Community Association in the United Kingdom

£250

Correspondent: Magdy El-Alfy, Trustee, 70 Lillie Road, London SW6 1TN (020 7244 8925; email: secretary@ egyptiangalia.co.uk)

CC Number: 289332

Eligibility

People in need who are Egyptian or of Egyptian origin and are living in or visiting the UK.

Types of grants

One-off and recurrent grants towards course fees, clothing, books, and so on.

Annual grant total

Grants usually total around £500 per year.

Applications

In writing to the correspondent.

Other information

The association arranges seminars and national and religious celebrations, as well as offering other services. It also gives grants to individuals for general welfare purposes. Limited information was available due to no accounts being required at the Charity Commission since 2007.

Greece

Schilizzi Foundation in Memory of Eleutherios and Helena Veniselos (The Schilizzi Foundation)

£53,000

Correspondent: Stephen Schilizzi, Trustee, Chacombe Priory, Chacombe, Banbury OX17 2AW (01295 710356; email: theschilizzifoundation@gmail. com; website: www.schilizzifoundation. org.uk)

CC Number: 314128

Eligibility

Greek nationals pursuing an undergraduate degree course (normally for three years) or vocational training in Great Britain who can demonstrate need and financial hardship. Priority is given to students in their final year of study but postgraduates and other students will be considered too.

Children of Greek nationals resident in Great Britain could also be eligible for support to further their education in the language, history, literature and institutions of Greece.

Types of grants

The foundation's website notes that its present policy is to 'provide financial assistance in two main areas: hardship grants for students currently at British universities and further education scholarships awarded in conjunction with Kings College London.'

Hardship grants are awarded for the tuition fees, cost of books or living expenses. Support can also be given for expenditure outside of Great Britain provided it has been incurred in pursuance of education.

Education scholarships for further education in the UK can be one-off or recurrent and are awarded to selected students, therefore direct applications will not be considered.

Annual grant total

In 2012/13 the foundation had assets of £2.1 million, an income of £72,000 and a total charitable expenditure of £53,000. Hardship awards totalled £36,000 and a further £17,500 was given in scholarship grants.

Applications

Application forms for hardship grants can be requested from the secretary at the following address: The Secretary, The Schilizzi Foundation, Rowan, Turweston, Brackley Northants NN13 54JX. Applications should be then submitted through the student counsellor/adviser at the candidate's college.

India

The Charles Wallace India Trust

£174,000 (52 grants)

Correspondent: Richard Alford, Secretary, 36 Lancaster Avenue, London SE27 9DZ (02086702825; email: cwit@ btinternet.com; website: www.wallace-trusts.org.uk/cwt_india.html)

CC Number: 283338

Eligibility

Students, scholars and professionals of Indian nationality and citizenship (generally between the ages of 25 and 38) studying in the UK in the field of arts, heritage, conservation or humanities. Applicants should normally be resident in India and intend to return to there at the end of their study. Certain short-term awards are available for people aged between 25 to 45.

Types of grants

Grants and scholarships towards educational courses, research or professional development in the fields of arts, heritage, conservation and humanities. Most awards are given at a postgraduate level to supplement other sources of funding or constitute completion of study awards for those whose scholarships have run out.

A limited number of postdoctoral or post-professional research grants are awarded. Support includes fully-funded awards, visiting fellowships in agreed subjects at specific institutions, grants for research and professional visits, grants for doctoral study and grants to attend the Scottish Universities Summer School or specialist training.

Annual grant total

In 2012/13 the trust had assets of £6.2 million and an income of £272,000. A total of £211,000 was spent in charitable expenditure, of which £174,000 was in 52 scholarships and grants.

Exclusions

Studies relating to economic development or leading to professional legal, business or administrative qualifications are not normally considered.

Applications

In writing to the correspondent. Detailed information and application forms for particular funding can be found on the British Council's website (www. britishcouncil.in/study-uk/scholarships/ charles-wallace-india-trust-scholarships) together with respective deadlines. Applicants are required to identify what benefit an award will bring not only to them personally but also to the people of India.

Other information

There are separate, smaller Charles Wallace Trusts for Bangladesh, Burma and Pakistan. All of the trusts are registered charities in the UK with separate and independent boards of trustees.

Note: the British Council facilitates and advises on the visas but the cost must be borne by the applicant. Further enquiries can also be addressed to the British Council in New Delhi at: cwit@in.britishcouncil.org.

Iraq

The British Institute for the Study of Iraq (Gertrude Bell Memorial)

£36,000

Correspondent: Lauren Mulvee, Administrator, 10 Carlton House Terrace, London SW1Y 5AH (020 7969 5274; fax: 020 7969 5401; email: bisi@ britac.ac.uk; website: www.bisi.ac.uk)

CC Number: 1135395

Eligibility

People undertaking research, projects, conferences or development events on Iraq, and Iraqi scholars visiting the UK for study. The charity can support scholars in areas relating to Iraq and neighbouring countries in anthropology, archaeology, geography, history, language and related disciplines within the arts, humanities and social sciences.

Types of grants

Grants are available for research projects, to cultural heritage professionals of Iraq for retraining and re-equipment, also for educational events that develop the understanding of Iraq's society, history and culture.

Research and conference grants are awarded to people in the field of humanities and social sciences. Assistance is available for direct educational expenses (such as equipment, travel costs, consultancy fees) and can be of up to £4,000. Applicants must be employed by, or have an official connection with, a UK higher education institution.

Pilot project grants are given to support up to one year of preliminary research on Iraq, the arts, humanities or social sciences that has a potential to turn into a long-term project. The award can reach up to £8,000. Application criteria are the same as for regular research grants.

Outreach grants, usually of up to £500, can be awarded for various public engagement events and projects (such as lectures or study days) relating to Iraq. Applicants should normally be UK residents.

Visiting Iraqi Scholarships are offered each year to two Iraqi scholars and cultural heritage professionals for research, training and collaborative projects in the UK, particularly those who already work in partnership with UK institutions/academies. These awards are available for institutional fees (excluding tuition fees), living and travel expenses and emergency travel insurance.

Annual grant total

In 2012/13 the charity had assets of £2.7 million, an income of £99,000 and a total charitable expenditure of £134,000. During the year 18 individuals were awarded grants totalling £36,000. The grants can be broken down as follows:

Research/travel/conference grants	£17,000
Pilot project grants	£8,000
Visiting scholarships	£7,500
Outreach grants	£3,700

Exclusions

Visiting Iraqi Scholarships would not cover salary expenses, tuition fees or routine medical expenses. Research grants cannot be offered for institutional overheads, salary costs, PhD studentships or living costs.

Applications

Application forms for different schemes can be found on the charity's website or requested from the correspondent. The deadlines are: 1 October for Outreach grants (applications must be emailed providing two references) and 1 February for Research grants (applications must be made both by email and post) and Visiting Iraqi Scholarships (note that the next available scholarship is in 2016).

Other information

The charity also organises public events, lectures, study days, conferences, also publishes books and a journal.

Pakistan

Viquaran Nisa Noon and Firoz Khan Noon Educational Foundation (Noon Educational Foundation)

£48,000

Correspondent: Dr Paul Flather, Chair, c/o Mansfield College, University of Oxford, Mansfield Road, Oxford OX1 3TF (01865 284480; fax: 01865 284481; email: paul.flather@mansfield. ox.ac.uk)

CC Number: 1017002

Eligibility

People who are from Pakistan, have spent at least 12 years studying in Pakistani schools/colleges/universities and wish to undertake a higher education course in the natural sciences, social sciences or arts and humanities at either Oxford or Cambridge University. Applicants must be able to demonstrate academic merit, excellent command of the English language, financial need and evidence that they have not previously had the opportunity to study abroad at a western university. They must also show that they intend to return to Pakistan and potentially contribute to the local community upon completion of their course.

Types of grants

Full and partial scholarships are generally given for postgraduate study but suitable undergraduates will also be supported.

Annual grant total

In 2012/13 the foundation had assets of £1.9 million and an income of £411,000. The income was higher than in the previous years due to the asset and investment sales. A total of around £48,000 was made in grants to Cambridge and Oxford students.

Applications

There is no specific application form. Candidates should make applications directly to the universities. The foundation's website provides links to the relevant sections. Applicants should indicate that they wish to apply for the Noon Foundation grant on the general scholarships application form that accompanies their application to study at either the University of Oxford or Cambridge. Scholarships are decided by July each year, in preparation for the coming academic year.

Other information

The foundation reminds that 'it receives many more applications for funding than it can offer.'

Poland

The Jeremi Kroliczewski Educational Trust

£11,500

Correspondent: Simeon Arnold, Trustee, Montage Lambert and Co., 41–41A Haven Green, London W5 2NX (020 8997 2288; email: sarnold@ montaguelambert.com)

CC Number: 1051524

Eligibility

Polish students under the age of 25 who are in further/higher education in England or Wales.

Types of grants

Grants are given according to need for general educational purposes, including fees, maintenance and living expenses, books, equipment and other necessities.

Annual grant total

In 2012/13 the trust had an income of £10,000 and an expenditure of £11,900. We estimate the annual total of grants to be around £11,500.

Applications

The trustees have confirmed that the trust's funds are fully committed at least five years in advance therefore new applications are not currently invited.

Prisoners/ ex-offenders

The Aldo Trust

£7,000

Correspondent: c/o NACRO, Coast Cottage, 90 Coast Road, West Mersea, Colchester CO5 8LS (01206 383809; fax: 01206 383809; email: owenwheatley@ btinternet.com)

CC Number: 327414

Eligibility

People in need who are being held in detention pending their trial or after their conviction. The applicant must still be serving the sentence. Applicants must have less than £25 in private cash.

Types of grants

Education grants of £10 to help with items such as books, course fees, equipment, audio/visual and other training equipment and tools for employment. Those eligible can only receive one grant a year.

Annual grant total

In 2012 the trust had an income of £33,000 and a total charitable expenditure of £29,000. The charity supports individuals and organisations for both social welfare and educational purposes. We estimate that grants to individuals for educational purposes totalled around £7,000. The accounts for 2012 were the latest available at the time of writing (August 2014).

Applications

On a form available from the correspondent. Applications must be made through prison service personnel (for example, probation, chaplaincy, education), and should include the name and number of the prisoner, age, length of sentence and expected date of release. No applications direct from prisoners will be considered. Applicants may apply once only in each twelve-month period, and applications are considered monthly.

Other information

NACRO also offers a fund for people on probation; see separate entry in this guide.

The Frank Longford Charitable Trust (Longford Trust)

£44,000

Correspondent: Peter Stanford, Director, The Longford Trust, PO Box, London NW6 9JP (020 7625 1097; email: info@longfordtrust.org; website: www. longfordtrust.org)

CC Number: 1092825

Eligibility

Ex-offenders or those awaiting release in the near future whose sentence was or is still being served in a UK prison who cannot afford education. Applicants must have identified a specific course they want to study at degree level offered by an institute of higher education (including Open University) and have obtained a provisional offer of a place (eligibility remains open for up to five years after release). The chosen course should improve the applicant's career chances and advance the rehabilitation process.

Types of grants

Scholarships are given to enable individuals to continue their rehabilitation through education at a UK university or equivalent institute.

A small number of awards are made under the Patrick Pakenham Awards' Scheme to those who want to study law or criminology.

Both awards are worth up to £5,000 per annum. The Longford Scholarship is extendable for up to three years on receipt of suitable reports of academic progress. Grants are intended to cover both the cost of tuition fees on higher education courses and offer a contribution to living expenses, books, other course material and basic sustenance.

Annual grant total

At the time of writing (August 2014) the latest financial information available was from 2012. In 2012 the trust had an income of £104,000 and awarded scholarships totalling £44,000.

Exclusions

Grants are not made for postgraduate study. Applicants should be ineligible for student loans or other financial support.

Applications

Application forms can be made online on the trust's website or can be downloaded, printed off and posted to the correspondent. Applications for courses beginning in September (including Open University courses starting in February) must be made by June.

Other information

The Longford Trust was established in 2002 by friends, family and admirers of Lord Longford (1905–2001) to celebrate his achievements and to further the goals he pursued in the fields of social and prison reform.

The trust also organises an annual lecture on questions of social and penal reform and awards an annual prize to an outstanding individual or organisation working in the field of prison and social reform.

Each recipient of a scholarship is assigned a mentor who can offer practical and emotional advice, often an ex-prisoner themselves.

Prisoners' Education Trust

£412,000 (1,757 grants)

Correspondent: Rod Clark, Company Secretary, Wandle House, Riverside Drive, Mitcham, Surrey CR4 4BU (020 8648 7760; fax: 020 8648 7762; email: info@prisonerseducation.org.uk; website: www.prisonerseducation.org.uk)

CC Number: 1084718

Eligibility

Individuals over the age of 18 who are serving a custodial sentence in the UK and still have at least six months of their sentence to serve. People leaving prison may also be eligible for resettlement support up to six months after their release.

Types of grants

Grants from the Access to Learning programme to pay fees for distance learning and resettlement courses, including Open University courses (funded by a contract from The Department for Innovation, Universities and Skills), A-levels, GCSE and vocational qualifications, including both accredited and non-accredited courses. Grants are also available for arts and crafts, hobby materials, course related necessities.

Annual grant total

In 2013 the trust had assets of £536,000 and an income of £986,000. A total of £412,000 was awarded in grants in the following categories:

General education courses and arts/ hobby material	£272,000
Open University courses	£134,000
Resettlement grants	£5,600

Applications

By sending a completed application form (which can be downloaded by a prison's education and advice officer from the trust's website) and a letter stating what kind of support is needed and why it would be useful. An endorsement by a prison education manager is essential. Applications are considered each month and the outcome is communicated to all applicants. The trust welcomes initial telephone enquiries prior to the final application.

The trustees' annual report from 2013 further specifies that the trust's:

> Detailed grant approval criteria is shared with prison education staff and applicants upon request, and must include a strong letter of application, an endorsement from a member of staff at the prison, selection of a suitable course, and having the ability to complete the course during his/her sentence.

Other information

The organisation also provides advice about distance learning courses and how they relate to employment paths and possibilities. They support learners in prisons, train people to act as peer learning mentors and commissions research, projects, reports and conferences to help in evaluating and advancing prison education.

Note that applications are welcomed from any prison in the UK (including HMP La Moye, in Jersey).

The Royal London Society

£49,000 (263 grants)

Correspondent: Peter Cox, Grant Administrator, Royal London Society, PO Box 1335, Kent ME14 9RR (01622 230737; email: office@ royallondonsociety.org.uk; website: www.royallondonsociety.org.uk)

CC Number: 214695

Eligibility

People who are serving a prison sentence or ex-offenders recently released from prison who are resident in the South East or Greater London. Candidates who demonstrate efforts to obtain funds elsewhere and make personal contribution (if possible) are favoured.

Types of grants

One-off grants, generally around £300. Support is given towards equipment, tools and work clothing, resettlement education, vocational training and associated needs that will lead to employment, generally in the immediate future or within the next six months.

Annual grant total

At the time of writing (August 2014) the latest financial information available was from 2012. In 2012 the society had assets of £851,000 and an income of £75,000. Grants to 263 individuals totalled £49,000.

Exclusions

Grants are not given for:

- Accommodation costs, rent, leases, licences or deposits
- Household items, furniture or appliances
- Debts or loans
- Driving lessons for domestic purposes
- Computer and associated equipment not related to employment
- Open University or distance learning courses not related to employment
- Personal clothing not related to employment

The trust does not normally consider grants for hobbies and recreation, unless the applicant still has at least 12 months to serve.

Applications

Application forms are available from the society's website. They should be posted to the correspondent together with all the supporting documentation – written references from a prison officer, probation officer, trade instructor, education department or other agency, such as, social services or housing trusts. Applications are considered at quarterly meetings but urgent applications may be dealt with quicker.

Other information

Grants are also made to organisations (£1,300 in 2012).

The trustees annual report from 2012 notes that 'amounts awarded to individuals have not been disclosed in this note as the council believes that to do so would prejudice the working of the society.'

Note: applications not supported by written references are not considered.

SACRO Trust

£4,000

Correspondent: Trust Fund Administrator, 29 Albany Street, Edinburgh EH1 3QN (01316 247270; fax: 01316 247269; email: info@national. sacro.org.uk; website: www.sacro.org.uk)

SC Number: SC023031

Eligibility

People living in Scotland who are subject to a license/court order or who have been released from prison in the last two years.

Types of grants

Grants are usually to a maximum of £300, including those for fees, driving lessons, books and equipment.

Annual grant total

In 2012/13 the trust had an income of £5,300 and awarded 50 grants totalling £7,400. We estimate grants to individuals for educational purposes to be around £4,000. The trust also gives grants for social welfare purposes.

Exclusions

No grants are made where financial help from other sources is available.

Applications

On a form available from the correspondent. Applications can only be accepted if they are made through a local authority, voluntary sector worker, health visitor or so on. They are considered every two months. No payment can be made directly to an individual by the trust; payment will be made to the organisation making the application. Other sources of funding should be sought before applying to the trust.

The Paul Stephenson Memorial Trust

£0

Correspondent: Pauline Austin, Administrator, The New Bridge, 27A Medway Street, London SW1P 2BD (020 7976 0779)

CC Number: 295924

Eligibility

People who have served at least two years of imprisonment and are near the end of their sentence or have been released recently.

Types of grants

One-off grants of up to £100 for tools for work or assistance with college fees.

Annual grant total

In 2012 the trust had an income of £2,000 and a total expenditure of £0. This was also the case the previous year.

The 2012 accounts were the latest available at the time of writing.

Exclusions

Grants are not given for recreational activities, setting up small businesses or becoming self-employed, or for existing debts.

Applications

On a form available from the correspondent, which must be submitted via a probation officer, prison education officer or voluntary associate. Applicants should mention other trusts or organisations that have been applied to and other grants promised or received, including any statutory grants. Trustees usually meet twice a year.

Refugees

The Airey Neave Trust

£45,000

Correspondent: Sophie Butler, Administrator, PO Box 111, Leominster HR6 6BP (email: aireyneavetrust@gmail.com; website: www.aireyneavetrust.org.uk)

CC Number: 297269

Eligibility

People engaged in research projects looking into 'issues related to personal freedom under democratic law against the threat of political violence.' Funding has also been provided towards conferences and seminars on anti-terrorism issues.

Types of grants

Grants for research projects or seminars. For example, previously support has been given for a seminar on counter-terrorism policy and for a project on territorial motivations of terrorist organisations. The trust stresses that only modest funds are available.

Annual grant total

In 2013/14 the trust had an income of £26,000 and an expenditure of £61,000. Previously around £45,000 has been awarded for research purposes.

Exclusions

Financial assistance to refugees is no longer provided.

Applications

Sometimes the trust approaches specific universities requesting research proposals for consideration by the trust but unsolicited proposals are equally welcomed. Applicants should make initial contact by emailing the correspondent.

Other information

The trust has stopped funding for refugees in order to focus all its funds on research grants.

Ruth Hayman Trust
See entry on page 31

Prisoners of Conscience Appeal Fund
See entry on page 32

Religion

Christian

The Daily Prayer Union Charitable Trust Ltd

£26,000

Correspondent: C. Palmer, Administrator, 12 Weymouth Street, London W1W 5BY

CC Number: 284857

Eligibility

Christians undertaking religious training or education.

Types of grants

Grants to support Christian training and education.

Annual grant total

In 2012/13 the trust had an income of £50,000 and assets of £40,000. Grants to individuals totalled £26,000.

Applications

In writing to the correspondent.

Other information

Grants to institutions totalled £15,500.

The NFL Trust

£64,000 (16 grants)

Correspondent: Margot Chaundler, Secretary, 9 Muncaster Road, London SW11 6NY (020 7223 7133; email: nfltrust@mail.com; website: www.nfltrust.org.uk)

CC Number: 1112422

Eligibility

Girls between the ages of 11 and 18 who are attending schools and colleges in the UK (primarily fee charging institutions). Support is given in line with 'Christian principles'.

Types of grants

Recurrent bursaries are awarded subject to means testing and annual financial review. The individual needs of the child and parents' commitment are also taken into account when considering grants. The median value of a bursary in 2012/13 was around £4,700.

Annual grant total

In 2012/13 the trust had assets of £4 million and an income of £124,000. Bursaries were given to 16 pupils totalling £64,000. During the year 11 new bursaries were awarded (all to girls with difficult family circumstances or medical conditions) and ten existing bursaries were reviewed and were to be renewed later in the year. No grants were made form Diana Matthews Trust Fund.

The trustees have already estimated the annual cost of bursaries in 2013/14 to be around £86,000.

Applications

Application forms and further details can be requested from the correspondent. Families of applicants should apply in the academic year before the year in which a bursary is required.

Other information

The trustees of The NFL Trust also administer the designated funds of a small Diana Matthews Trust Fund. They are used to provide educational extras for girls in need, whether or not they benefit from the NFL bursary.

The Podde Trust

£4,000 (19 grants)

Correspondent: Peter Godfrey, Trustee, 68 Green Lane, Hucclecote, Gloucester GL3 3QX (01452 613563; email: thepodde@gmail.com)

CC Number: 1016322

Eligibility

Individuals involved in Christian work in the UK and overseas.

Types of grants

One-off and recurrent grants.

Annual grant total

In 2012/13 the trust had assets of £2,000 and an income of £44,000. The trust awards grants for charitable purposes including the advancement of religion, of education and the relief of poverty. There were 38 grants to individuals totalling £8,900 but no breakdown of the purposes. We estimate grants for educational purposes to be around £4,000. A further £36,500 was given to 40 organisations.

Applications

In writing to the correspondent: note, the trust states that it has very limited resources, and those it does have are mostly already committed. Requests from new applicants therefore have very little chance of success.

Other information

Organisations involved in Christian work are also supported.

The Stewardship Trust Ripon

£8,500

Correspondent: Anne Metcalfe, Trustee, Hutton Hill, Hutton Bank, Ripon HG4 5DT (01765602887)

CC Number: 224447

Eligibility

People connected with Christian causes and studies.

Types of grants

One-off and recurrent grants for people training in Christian ministry, engaged in studies of Christianity or working for Christian causes.

Annual grant total

In 2012/13 the trust had an income of £5,300 and a total expenditure of £55,000. Most of the trust's support goes to organisations. In previous years the total of grants to individuals has reached up to £8,000 – £9,000.

Applications

In writing to the correspondent. Our research suggests that the trust's funds are usually fully committed and new applications are only considered if there is 'extreme need'.

Other information

The trust also supports various churches, societies and the Christian Institute.

Church of England

Saint George's Trust (FSJ (UK) TA SSJE)

£5,800

Correspondent: Linden Sheffield, Administrator, The Almoner's Room, St Andrew Holborn, 5 St Andrew Street, London EC4A 3AB (020 3585 5251; email: lindensheffield@fsje.org.uk; website: www.fsje.org.uk/sgeorges.php)

CC Number: 253524

Eligibility

Members of the Church of England – Anglican clergy, seminarians and students.

Types of grants

Small, one-off grants of up to £350 are made towards specific projects in the UK or abroad. Support can be given to:

- Clergy undertaking a recognised study during their sabbaticals towards travel and accommodation costs
- Seminarians in Anglican theological colleges or on ministerial courses for the costs of pastoral placements that are part of formation (3 members of a college/course may apply each year)

- Students between the ages 18 and 25 towards the work on a Christian mission and service (usually as a gap-year activity)

Annual grant total

At the time of writing (July 2014) the latest financial information available was from 2012. In 2012 the trust had an income of £11,400 and an expenditure of £6,000, which is lower than in the previous few years. We estimate the annual total of grants to be around £5,800.

Exclusions

The trust will not provide any long-term financial support and cannot contribute towards restoration projects or education fees.

Applications

In writing to the correspondent. Applicants should give full details of the project, include estimated costs, note any other funds available and provide a brief letter of reference (from an educational or clerical authority). An sae needs to be provided for a reply from the trust. The trustees encourage applications early in the year.

Other information

In 2006 the administration of the trusts was transferred to The Fellowship of Saint John (UK) Trust Association.

Huguenot

Society of St Onge and Angoumois

£1,200

Correspondent: Pauline Lane-Gilbert, Trustee, Brook Hill Top, Great Wolford, Shipston-on-Stour, Warwickshire CV36 5NW (01608 674379)

CC Number: 208718

Eligibility

Young people in need between the ages of 16 and 25 who live in the UK. Preference is given to those who are descended from French Protestants (Huguenot) and in particular those who have at any time lived in the province of St Onge and Angoumois in France.

Types of grants

One-off grants in the range of £100–£400 to enable beneficiaries to train for a trade or occupation in order to help them to advance in life or earn their living. Support is given for books, equipment, daily travel and clothing for people on a training course or for books, equipment and daily travel for students in further/higher education. Grants are only given on proof of purchase.

Annual grant total

In 2012/13 the charity had an income of £3,200 and an expenditure of £1,400. We estimate that grants totalled around £1,200.

Exclusions

Grants are not available to foreign students studying in the UK.

Applications

Our research suggests that application forms are available from Mr A Squire, 26 Blaisdon, Weston-super-Mare, Somerset BS22 8BN. They should be submitted directly by the individual or by a parent/guardian. Awards are usually considered in April and May.

Other information

The full name of the charity is Charities in Connection with the Society of St Onge and Angoumois.

Jewish

The Anglo Jewish Association

£112,000 (84 grants)

Correspondent: Julia Samuel, Trustee, c/o HW Fisher and Company, Acre House, 11/15 William Road, London NW1 3ER (020 7449 0909; email: info@anglojewish.org.uk; website: www.anglojewish.org.uk)

CC Number: 256946

Eligibility

Undergraduate and postgraduate Jewish students in need who are studying a full-time course at a UK university or further education college, regardless of nation of origin. Preference is given to courses on highly rated institutions.

Types of grants

Scholarships range between £500 and £3,000 a year.

Annual grant total

At the time of writing (July 2014) the latest financial information available was from 2012. In 2012 the association had assets of £1.7 million, an income of £128,000 and awarded grants to 84 individuals totalling £112,000.

Applications

Application forms are available from the association's website or can be requested from the correspondent. Applications should be submitted by 30 April. They must also include two academic references, a CV, a covering letter, a copy of a letter of acceptance from the educational institution and details of the applicant's personal history.

Scholarships are for one academic year and individuals may apply for the part or the whole of an additional academic year by submitting another complete application, prior to the closing date for the relevant year. The award of a second, third or fourth scholarship is not automatic.

Application forms for the Finnart Trust and the Stuart Young Foundation are also available from the association's website.

The association welcomes applicants to contact them via email to discuss the application.

Other information

The association also administers a number of other trusts offering help to students studying in fields of medicine, science or more general areas of study. It has historical links with a number of humanitarian and grantmaking organisations, which can also be supported.

Applicants can be given direct financial support, general advice and guidance on education in the UK or be signposted to other bodies that may help.

Generally, four postgraduate awards per year can be made.

Finnart House School Trust

£92,000 (34 grants)

Correspondent: Jamie Wood, Clerk to the Trustees, Radius Works, Back Lane, London NW3 1HL (07804 854905; email: info@finnart.org; website: www.finnart.org)

CC Number: 220917

Eligibility

Jewish children and young people aged between 14 and 21 who are in need. Bursaries and scholarships are for those with ability, who, because of family circumstances, may otherwise be unable to achieve their potential. The course to be studied must be at a UK institution and end in a recognised qualification.

Types of grants

Bursaries are awarded through schools. Awards may be made regularly each term, or may be one-off. Grants range between £100 and £1,500.

Scholarships are awarded for higher education until the completion of the course and range up to £5,000 a year.

Annual grant total

In 2012/13 the trust had assets of £4.9 million and an income of £136,000. Scholarship grants were awarded to individuals totalling £92,000 and to schools for individuals in need totalling £23,000.

Exclusions

Only members of the Jewish faith can be supported.

Applications

Bursaries are awarded via schools. Scholarship applications are made by the individual on an application pack available to download from the trust's website, to be submitted by April.

Other information

This trust also makes grants for relief-in-need purposes and to organisations which work with children and young people of the Jewish faith who are in need, but its main purpose is to award scholarship grants.

Gur Trust

£9,000

Correspondent: The Administrator, 206 High Road, London N15 4NP (020 8801 6038)

CC Number: 283423

Eligibility

People connected to the Jewish Orthodox faith in the UK.

Types of grants

One-off and recurrent grants for education and personal development. The trust aims to support 'education in and the religion of Orthodox Jewish faith.'

Annual grant total

In 2012/13 the trust had an income of £43,000 and a total expenditure of £39,000. The latest accounts were not available to view at the time of writing (August 2014). We estimate that educational grants to individuals totalled around £9,000.

Applications

In writing to the correspondent. 'Funds are raised by the trustees. All calls for help are carefully considered and help is given according to circumstances and funds then available.'

Other information

The trust also makes grants to organisations, Talmudical colleges and provides relief in need for individuals.

The Jewish Widows and Students Aid Trust

£50,000 (30 grants)

Correspondent: Alan Philipp, Trustee, 5 Raeburn Close, London NW11 6UG

CC Number: 210022

Eligibility

Jewish students from the UK, Ireland, Israel, France and the British Commonwealth who are aged 16 to 30 years old.

Types of grants

The trust also offers interest-free loans ranging from £1,000 to £1,500 mainly for course fees, although living expenses, books, travel or similar necessities can also be supported. Awards are made on the basis of academic excellence and need. On occasions grants can also be given to schoolchildren over the age of 10.

Annual grant total

In 2012/13 the trust had an income of £19,000 and an expenditure of £59,000. Normally around 30 awards are made each year. We estimate that grants to individual students totalled about £50,000.

Applications

In writing to the correspondent including a CV and a confirmation of acceptance at an educational establishment. Applications can be submitted directly by the individual for consideration at any time.

Other information

Grants are also given to widows with young children.

The Montpellier Trust

£600

Correspondent: Michael Allweis, Trustee, 7 Montpellier Mews, Salford M7 4ZW (01613 083928; email: michaelallweis@dwyers.net)

CC Number: 1108119

Eligibility

People in education connected to the Orthodox Jewish faith.

Types of grants

Grants given according to need.

Annual grant total

In 2012/13 the trust had an income of £2,900 and a total expenditure of £2,300. We estimate that educational grants to individuals totalled around £600. Funding is also awarded to charitable organisations and to individuals for social welfare needs.

Applications

In writing to the correspondent.

The Rank Trust

£2,900

Correspondent: Nikki Spencer, Trustee, 16 Eyres Gardens, Ilkeston DE7 8JE (01158 499216; email: nikki.spencer@ robinsons-solicitors.co.uk)

CC Number: 1091456

Eligibility

Students who are of the Jewish faith and are either living or studying within a 50-mile radius of Nottingham city centre.

Types of grants

One-off and recurrent grants to students in college or university.

Annual grant total

In 2013/14 the trust had an income of £167 and a total expenditure of £3,000. We estimate that educational grants to individuals totalled £2,900.

Applications

In writing to the correspondent.

Protestant

William and Mary Hart Foundation

£0

Correspondent: David Marshall, Trustee, 2 Keats Drive, Hucknall, Nottingham NG15 6TE (01159 635428; email: administrator@embaptists.com)

CC Number: 510717

Eligibility

Baptist Christians under the age of 25. Preference shall be given to persons who live in the parish of Collingham or who have a parent or parents living there.

Types of grants

One-off and recurrent grants and loans to schoolchildren, undergraduates and vocational students.

Annual grant total

In 2012 the foundation had an income of £1,900 and had no expenditure. The 2012 accounts were the latest available at the time of writing (August 2014).

Applications

In writing to the correspondent.

The Mylne Trust

£7,000

Correspondent: Paul Jenkins, PO Box 530, Farnham GU9 1BP (email: admin@ mylnetrust.org.uk; website: www. mylnetrust.org.uk)

CC Number: 208074

Eligibility

Members of the Protestant faith who have been engaged in evangelistic work, including missionaries and retired missionaries, and Christian workers whose finances are inadequate. Married ordinands with children are also supported when all other sources of funding have failed to cover their needs.

Types of grants

Grants are given towards educational training at theological colleges, for the cost of books and living expenses to undergraduates and overseas students.

Annual grant total

In 2012/13 grants were made totalling £14,000. The charity gives for both educational and social welfare purposes and we estimate the total awarded to individuals for educational purposes was around £7,000.

Applications

The trust's website provides the following information:

> The trust has reviewed and, in 2013, changed its policy and procedure for making grants. Most grants are now being handled with partners already in Christian mission work. (Applications based on earlier procedures, using the old application forms, will no longer be considered by the trust.)

> *Worldwide except Africa*
> In principle, the only grant applications that will be considered by direct application to the trust are those from candidates for mission work who are studying or planning to study within the UK. Such applicants are invited to contact the Clerk to the Mylne Trust atadmin@mylnetrust.org.uk requesting a current application form.

There are special arrangements for applicants who are based in Africa. Visit the charity's website for more information.

Other information

Applicants are advised to visit the charity's helpful website.

Roman Catholic

The Duchess of Leeds Foundation for Boys and Girls

£45,000

Correspondent: John Sinfield, Administrator, 19 Kenton Road, Harrow, Middlesex HA1 2BW (020 8422 1950)

CC Number: 313103

Eligibility

Roman Catholic children attending Catholic schools who are resident in England, Wales or the Channel Islands and who are either orphaned/fatherless or whose fathers do not support them sufficiently. Our research suggests that help is concentrated on secondary education and children in primary school are helped only in exceptional circumstances.

Types of grants

One-off awards and recurrent grants in the range of around £300–£400 per term. According to our research, support is normally given towards the cost of school fees. Grants may continue until the end of an A-level course.

Annual grant total

In 2013 the foundation had an income of £23,000 and an expenditure of £48,000. We estimate that the annual total of grants to individuals was around £45,000. Usually the charitable expenditure fluctuates around £20,000–£30,000 a year.

Applications

In writing to the correspondent directly by individual or their parents/guardians. The deadline for applications is normally by the end of January.

United Reformed Church

Milton Mount Foundation

£110,000 (15 grants)

Correspondent: Revd Erna Stevenson, Secretary, 11 Copse Close, Slough, Berkshire SL1 5DT (01753 748713)

CC Number: 306981

Eligibility

The children of ministers of the United Reformed Church, the Congregational Federation, the Evangelical Fellowship of Congregational Churches and the Unaffiliated Congregational Churches. The children of members of these churches can also be supported.

Types of grants

Bursaries are available to children aged 11–18 towards school fees and other educational needs, including school uniforms and necessities. Up to one third of the income may be spent on boys as the funds arise from the sale of a girls' school, thereby limiting the number of bursaries available to the sons of ministers. Our research suggests that women taking up further/higher education at a later stage can also receive grants towards books and fees.

Annual grant total

In 2012/13 the foundation had assets of £3 million and an income of £146,000. Annual bursaries and grants to individuals totalled £110,000 and can be broken down as follows:

Bursaries to Bournemouth Collegiate School	£65,000
Bursaries in other schools	£43,000
Outfitting and other allowances	£1,000

The trustees' annual report from 2012/13 states that 'the foundation was able to help 9 girls and 3 boys with school bursaries and one book and two sixth form grants have been awarded.'

Applications

In writing to the correspondent providing information about the family income. Applications are normally considered in May and June.

Sport

The Francis Drake Fellowship

£1,700

Correspondent: Joan Jupp, Administrator, 24 Haldane Close, London N10 2PB (020 8883 8725)

CC Number: 248302

Eligibility

Dependents of deceased flat green bowlers who were members of the fellowship.

Types of grants

Allowances of £52 per month per child is given to children in full-time education, up to the end of their A-levels.

Annual grant total

In 2012 this charity had an income of £2,900 and a total expenditure of £3,800. We estimate that the total awarded to individuals for educational purposes was around £1,700. The latest accounts available at the time of writing (July 2014) were for year ending December 2012.

Applications

In writing to the correspondent, requesting an application form. Applications should be submitted through the bowling club's Francis Drake Fellowship delegate. Applications are accepted two years after the date of the member's death.

Other information

Grants are also given to dependents for welfare.

Vegetarian

The Vegetarian Charity

£5,000

Correspondent: Susan Lenihan, Grants Secretary, 56 Parliament Street, Chippenham, Wiltshire SN14 0DE (01249 443521; email: grantssecretary@ vegetariancharity.org.uk)

CC Number: 294767

Eligibility

People under the age of 26 who are vegetarian or vegan and are sick or in need.

Types of grants

One-off and recurrent grants of £250 to £1,000 for general educational purposes.

Annual grant total

In 2012/13 the charity had assets of £1.1 million and an income of £50,000. Grants paid during the year to individuals and organisations totalled £22,500; a further breakdown was not available. We estimate that grants to individuals for educational purposes was around £5,000.

Applications

On a form available from the correspondent, including details of any other grants received, a CV, a letter of recommendation from a tutor, school reports, covering letter and three references. Applications are considered throughout the year.

Other information

Grants are also made to organisations which promote vegetarianism among young people.

Volunteers

The Alec Dickson Trust

£5,500

Correspondent: Emily Evans, Trustee, 237 Pentonville Road, London N1 9NJ (020 7278 6601; email: alecdickson@ gmail.com; website: www. alecdicksontrust.org.uk)

CC Number: 1076900

Eligibility

Young people under 30 years of age who are involved in volunteering or community service in the UK.

Types of grants

The trust's mission is to support young people who are able to demonstrate that through volunteering or community service they can enhance the lives of others, particularly those marginalised by society. The trust particularly welcomes applications from innovative projects in the spirit of Alec Dickson. Grants of up to £500 are available.

Annual grant total

In 2012/13 the trust had no income and an expenditure £6,000. Grants totalled approximately £5,500.

Grants are mostly given through the charity that administers the fund, Community Service Volunteers which is why the trust has very low income and expenditure figures.

Exclusions

No grants for gap years, projects based outside of the UK or personal development i.e. student course fees.

Applications

On a form available from the correspondent or to download on the trust's website. Applications can be submitted at any time.

Other information

In the spirit of the trust, all the trustees are aged under 30 and have a connection to voluntary or community service.

The Duveen Trust

£8,200

Correspondent: Alan Kaye, Trustee, 1 Beauchamp Court, Victors Way, Barnet EN5 5TZ (020 8216 2520; email: administrator@theduveentrust.org.uk; website: www.theduveentrust.org.uk)

CC Number: 326823

Eligibility

Individuals aged up to 25 who wish to get involved with projects which require initiative and which give something back to the community, and who are in need of financial support. Educational assistance to enable individuals to work in community projects specialising in the social education of young people.

Types of grants

One-off grants of £100 to £500.

Annual grant total

In 2012/13 the trust had an income of £16,500 and made grants totalling approximately £8,200. The trust has stated on its website that it has a grant potential of up to £20,000 per year.

Exclusions

Grants are unlikely to be made to support formal education, except for courses leading to qualifications in youth and community work.

Applications

Application forms and guidelines are available from the correspondent or on the trust's website (www.theduveentrust.

org.uk) and should be accompanied by a report from the organising agency, and a copy of the programme of the scheme that the applicant wishes to participate in.

Emmaus Charitable Trust

£2,000

Correspondent: Doreen and Richard Silman, Trustees, 4 Church Avenue, Lancaster LA1 4SP (01524 36824)

CC Number: 288515

Eligibility

People involved in Christian projects or voluntary work, particularly benefiting children and young people. There is a preference for the North West of England and Greater London.

Types of grants

Small, usually one-off grants for specific projects or voluntary work with particular focus on Christian/church causes.

Annual grant total

In 2012/13 the trust had an income of £8,900 and an expenditure of £4,100. The trust also supports organisations, therefore we estimate the annual total of grants to individuals to be around £2,000.

Applications

In writing to the correspondent.

Other information

The trust mainly makes grants to organisations.

The Torch Trophy Trust

See entry on page 117

Women

Altrusa Careers Trust

£4,500

Correspondent: The Administrator, PO Box 6160, Orkney KW16 3WY (email: admin@altrusacareerstrust.org.uk; website: www.altrusacareerstrust.org.uk)

SC Number: SC009390

Eligibility

Women permanently resident in the UK or the Republic of Ireland who wish to further their career prospects or to retrain after bringing up a family but are prevented from doing so by lack of means.

Types of grants

Grants are of up to £500. Loan schemes are also available.

Annual grant total

In 2012/13 the trust had an income of £1,800 and an expenditure of £4,800. We estimate the annual total of grants to individuals to be around £4,500.

Exclusions

Support is not provided to school leavers and PhD students.

Applications

Application forms are available from the correspondent. Applications will require a passport sized photo of the candidate and names and addresses of two referees. Submissions should be made by 31 March and are only considered once a year. Payments are normally made in July directly to the institution and not the applicant. Do not provide any additional information if it is not requested in the application form. If you have not been contacted by the end of May, you should presume your application to have been unsuccessful.

Other information

The charity's income is derived from donations, gifts and legacies.

Diamond Education Grant (DEG)

£7,000 (18 grants)

Correspondent: The Administrator, 2nd Floor, Beckwith House, 1 Wellington Road North, Stockport, Cheshire SK4 1AF (01614 807686; email: hq@soroptimistgbi.prestel.co.uk; website: sigbi.org/our-charities/deg)

CC Number: 1139668

Eligibility

Women permanently resident in one of the countries of the Federation of Soroptimist International Great Britain and Ireland who wish to refurbish their skills after an employment break or acquire new ones to re-enter the employment market and improve their opportunities of employment/promotion.

Types of grants

Grants, on average of around £390, are available towards the course fees, books or equipment. Grants are normally paid for one year but may be extended in exceptional circumstances.

Annual grant total

In 2012/13 the charity had assets of £102,000 and an income of £27,000. A total of £7,000 was awarded in individual grants to 18 women.

Exclusions

Living expenses cannot be supported.

Applications

Application can be made through the nearest local branch of Soroptimist International. The deadline for applications is 15 April each year.

Other information

Grants are only paid over after the successful applicants have started their courses.

Edinburgh Association of University Women – President's Fund

£14,400

Correspondent: Alison MacLachlan, Trustee, 6/5 Craigleith Avenue South, Edinburgh EH4 3LQ

SC Number: SC004501

Eligibility

Women in their final year of study for a degree (postgraduate or undergraduate) at UK universities who face unexpected financial hardship.

Types of grants

One-off modest grants, usually between £150 and £500. Awards are intended to help with costs of books, equipment and maintenance/living expenses. Applicants receive only one award which is intended to help them to complete the current study.

Annual grant total

In 2013 the charity had an income of £23,000 and an expenditure of £14,700. We estimate that grants to individuals totalled around £14,400.

Exclusions

Grants are not given to begin a new course, towards diplomas, certificates, access courses, study or work outside the UK, childcare, one year undergraduate and one year postgraduate degrees.

Applications

Application forms can be requested by writing to the correspondent. Requests must be submitted directly by the applicant (not third parties). Academic references are required. The trustees usually meet in February, April/May, October and November to consider grants.

Other information

The charity has previously stated that 'applications which disregard the exclusions will not be acknowledged'.

The Girls of The Realm Guild (Women's Careers Foundation)

£14,500

Correspondent: Beth Hayward, Secretary, 2 Watch Oak, Blackham, Tunbridge Wells, Kent TN3 9TP (01892 740602)

CC Number: 313159

Eligibility

Women over the age of 21 who are UK citizens and are seeking assistance to begin or continue studies for a career. Younger applicants (over the age of 16) may be supported for music or dance studies.

Types of grants

One-off grants and loans to help with any costs relating to education or training, preferably leading to a career. Awards can reach up to £1,000 but on average total around £250.

Annual grant total

At the time of writing (July 2014) the latest financial information available was from 2012. In 2012 the charity had an income of £11,100 and an expenditure of £14,800. We estimate that the annual total of grants was around £14,500

Exclusions

Grants are not generally given for PhD or postgraduate studies, particularly if the subject indicates a complete change of direction.

Applications

Application forms and further guidelines can be requested from the correspondent. Candidates are requested to provide an sae. Applications should be submitted between 1 September and 31 January for the following academic year. It is strongly advised to submit applications well in advance. The correspondent has previously stated that timing is crucial: 'so many people write for immediate help which we cannot give'.

Other information

Note that this charity is small and has limited resources.

The Hilda Martindale Educational Trust

£23,000 (15–20 grants)

Correspondent: The Administrator, c/o The Registry, Royal Holloway, University of London, Egham TW20 0EX (01788 434455; fax: 01784 437520; email: hildamartindaletrust@rhul.ac.uk; website: www.royalholloway.ac.uk/ aboutus/governancematters/ thehildamartindaletrust.aspx)

Eligibility

Women over the age of 21 pursuing a profession or career requiring vocational training in the areas where women are underrepresented. Applicants must be British nationals.

Courses/training must be a full academic year in length and preferably start in September/October. Priority is given to undergraduates in their final year of study.

Types of grants

A small number of one-off grants in the range of £200- £3,000 are offered for training courses and are normally paid in three instalments, in October, January and April. Awards can be used for fees, books, equipment, living expenses or childcare and so on.

A limited number of awards can also be given towards the costs of any graduate training (MSc/MA and PhD) in an area which is underrepresented by women (for example science, technology, engineering, architecture, some branches of medicine (such as surgery), leadership roles in all fields) at a UK institution approved by the trustees.

Annual grant total

The trust generally awards grants to 15 to 20 women each year totalling £20,000–£25,000.

Exclusions

Assistance is not given for:
- Short courses
- Access courses
- Courses attended abroad
- Elective studies
- Intercalated BSc years during a UK medical, dental, veterinary or nursing course
- Wholly academic courses
- Academic research
- Special projects in the UK or abroad
- First year undergraduates
- People holding grants from research councils, British Academy and other public sources
- Retrospective awards

Funding can only be given to women who cannot access any other funding. Medical, dental, or veterinary students will only be considered if they are pursuing an area within that field where women are underrepresented.

Applications

Application forms are available from the Council of Royal Holloway website. Applications, together with two references and a personal statement, should be submitted by February for the courses taking place in the following academic year. Submissions can be made by email or via post, providing an sae.

The trustees normally meet in April to consider awards.

Other information

The trust only invites applications from the candidates who exactly suit its eligibility criteria. The correspondent has requested us to direct potential applicants to the Council of Royal Holloway website where the application forms and detailed guidelines can be found and are regularly updated.

Yorkshire Ladies' Council of Education (Incorporated)

£17,000

Correspondent: Phillida Richardson, Administrator, Flat 4, Forest Hill, 11 Park Crescent, Leeds LS8 1DH (01132691471; email: admin@ylce.org; website: www.ylce.org.uk)

CC Number: 529714

Eligibility

British women over the age of 21 who are in need of financial assistance towards their education at a British educational institution and who do not qualify for local authority support.

A separate fund has been set up in association with the Sir James Knott Trust, to enable grants to be offered exclusively to applicants from the North East of England (defined as Tyne and Wear, Northumberland, County Durham inclusive of Hartlepool but exclusive of Darlington, Stockton-on-Tees, Middlesbrough, Redcar and Cleveland).

Types of grants

Grants in the range of £100 to £500 (average grant £200–£300) are given for the course fees only. The award is available for one year but can be renewed for up to three years.

Annual grant total

In 2012/13 the charity had assets of £531,000 and an income of £43,000. A total of £27,000 was spent on charitable activities, of which £17,000 was awarded in scholarships and educational grants.

Exclusions

Members, and the dependents of members, of Yorkshire Ladies' Council of Education are not eligible for support.

Applications

Application forms can be found on the charity's website together with detailed guidelines. A completed form and an sae should be submitted directly by the individual by 1 January, March, June or September for consideration later in the month. The awards committee meets four times a year.

Applicants for grants from the Sir James Knott Trust (who may be asked for proof of residency) should label their form 'SPECIAL FUND'.

Other information

The charity also provides grants to local community bodies and institutions.

The Pratt Charity

£500

Correspondent: Anne Hosker, Gaddum Centre, Gaddum House, 6 Great Jackson Street, Manchester M15 4AX (01618 346069; email: info@gaddumcentre.co. uk)

CC Number: 507162–1

Eligibility

Women over 60 who live in or near Manchester and have done so for a period of not less than five years.

Types of grants

Grants are given towards education, health and relief of poverty, distress and sickness.

Annual grant total

The Gaddum Centre administers and considers applications made to the Pratt Charity. The accounts of the Pratt Charity were not available because they are not consolidated into Gaddum Centre's accounts as the trustees consider that the amounts in the accounts are not significant.

We estimate around £500 was made in grants to individuals for education.

Applications

In writing to the correspondent via a social worker.

Other information

The charity is administered by the Gaddum Centre.

Work/study overseas

Lady Allen of Hurtwood Memorial Trust

£1,000

Correspondent: Caroline Richards, Trustee, 89 Thurleigh Road, London SW12 8TY (01424 844017; website: www.ladyallentrust.org)

CC Number: 277942

Eligibility

Individuals wishing to carry out a specific travel project that will help them gain specific additional knowledge and experience and enhance the quality and nature of their work with children/young people (particularly children with disabilities or children from disadvantaged backgrounds) and their families.

Types of grants

Grants are generally in the region of £1,000.

Annual grant total

In 2012/13 the trust had an income of £600 and an expenditure of £1,200. We estimate the annual grants total to be around £1,000.

Exclusions

Grants are not given for:
- Academic course fees
- Academic research
- Attendance at specific conferences
- Building and equipping centres
- Gap year, sixth form projects or similar travel proposals
- Medical electives
- Supporting individual children

Applications

Application forms and further guidelines are available on the trust's website or can be requested from the correspondent. Applicants must provide a single-sided page outline of a specific project offering positive evidence of how the award will help them and how the knowledge gained will be shared with others. The closing date for applications is 31 January each year. Shortlisting is in February and awards are distributed in March.

The Winston Churchill Memorial Trust

£755,000 (125 grants)

Correspondent: Alexandra Sibun, Trust Secretary, 29 Great Smith Street (South Door), London SW1P 3BL (020 7999 1660; fax: 020 7799 1667; email: office@ wcmt.org.uk; website: www.wcmt.org.uk)

CC Number: 313952

Eligibility

British citizens resident in the UK who are over 18. Preference is given to individuals who are unlikely to obtain funding from other sources.

Types of grants

Grants are made to people with a specific project which involves travelling overseas (normally for four to eight weeks) in order to bring back knowledge and best practice for the benefit of others in their professions, communities and the UK as a whole. Support can cover return travel, daily living, insurance, travel within the countries being visited and occasionally assistance with home expenses. Categories are drawn from the following fields: crafts and makers; designers; education; the arts and older people; early years prevention and intervention; environment and sustainable living; medicine, health and patient care; prison and penal reform; science technology and innovation; young people; and other worthwhile projects not falling within the above categories.

Awards normally range from £2,500 to £10,000 with an average grant of £6,100.

Annual grant total

In 2012/13 the trust had assets of £33.7 million and an income of £1.1 million. A total of £755,000 was awarded in 125 travelling fellowships.

The trust has already decided that approximately 135 fellowships will be awarded in 2014.

Exclusions

Awards are not made for attendance of courses, academic studies, student grants, gap-year projects, electives, degree placements, internships and postgraduate studies (unless real and wider benefits to others in the UK can be clearly demonstrated). Projects involving less than four weeks of travel are not eligible. Existing fellows may not reapply.

Applications

Applications can be made online on the trust's website. They open in May of each year and should be submitted by the end of September for travel in the following year. Shortlisted candidates are invited for an interview in January, in London. The trust invites informal enquiries prior to application.

Other information

The trust also awards up to ten bursaries a year of £2,000 to undergraduates at Churchill College, Cambridge to pupils showing excellence and potential in science, mathematics and the arts who are in financial need. In addition to that, one Archive By-Fellowship of £3,000 is awarded each year. Contact the college for further information.

The trustees' annual report from 2012/13 notes that it has been decided to increase the number of travelling fellowships awarded each year from 100 to 150 by 2015.

The Worshipful Company of Cutlers General Charitable Fund – Captain F. G. Boot Scholarships

£5,000 (7 grants)

Correspondent: Rupert Meacher, Clerk, The Worshipful Company of Cutlers, Cutlers' Hall, 4 Warwick Lane, London EC4M 7BR (020 7248 1866; fax: 020 7248 8426; email: clerk@cutlerslondon.co.uk; website: www.cutlerslondon.co.uk)

CC Number: 283096

Eligibility

Students between the ages of 17 and 25 travelling abroad for at least six months to develop a second language and learn about other cultures. Applicants should either be awaiting entry to further education or be studying abroad as a part of their university degree.

Types of grants

At least five scholarships are awarded each year. Grants can range between £500 and £1,000 depending on the individual's circumstances.

Annual grant total

In 2012/13 Captain F G Boot Scholarships were awarded to seven individuals totalling £5,000.

Exclusions

Grants are not available to Project Trust applicants.

Applications

Application forms can be downloaded from the trust's website. Application forms, completed in handwriting, should be accompanied by two references and posted to the trust before 12 June. Shortlisted applicants will be invited for an interview.

Other information

The charity also: provides a number of specific awards to students at nominated universities/schools/colleges; gives recurrent grants to charitable organisations; offers an annual Surgical Prize to a scientist developing the design or application of surgical instruments or surgical techniques.

The trustees' annual report from 2012/13 also states that 'widows of the members of the Worshipful Company of Cutlers, former members of staff, and their dependents are eligible to receive financial support where there is evidence of need or hardship.'

Gilchrist Educational Trust
See entry on page 9

Go Make it Happen: A Project in Memory of Sam Harding
See entry on page 10

The British and Foreign School Society - International Award Scheme

£0

Correspondent: Belinda Lawrance, Administrator, Maybrook House, Godstone Road, Caterham, Surrey CR3 6RE (01883 331177; email: enquiries@bfss.org.uk; website: www.bfss.org.uk)

CC Number: 314286

Eligibility

Individuals from the UK who wish to engage in educational activities in developing countries. Awards can also be made to students coming to the UK from developing countries to acquire skills and knowledge which will be useful to their home country. Applicants must be in financial need and be supported by one of the link organisations with which the society works. The trust states that 'Link organisations have been encouraged to put forward young people from a more diverse social, cultural and educational background than previously'.

Types of grants

Grants of up to £12,000 depending on the length of the overseas placement. Grants are made to enable volunteers going overseas to teach or undertake other educational activities to support the local community.

Annual grant total

Refer to 'Other information'.

Applications

Applications must be submitted through one of the link organisations with which the society works using the form available on the society's website, where details of application deadlines can also be found.

Other information

The British and Foreign School Society (BFSS) is a grant giving organisation and offers funding for educational projects in the UK and around the world. The society also offers a small number of grants for organisations and individuals through its subsidiary trusts and this award scheme. Eligibility criteria for these subsidiary/linked trusts depend on area of residence and/or particular field of educational activity. In March 2014 we were informed by Steven Ross, a trustee of the society, that money was available from these funds.

Note that the society itself no longer makes grants directly to individuals although it does administer the following 'linked' funds which do:

Alfred Bourne Trust: helps those undertaking education up to the age of 30. The trust has an income of about £1,000 per year. The BFSS is reviewing the arrangements for the administration of this fund and is *not* accepting applications at present.

Berridge Trust: supports the training of teachers of cookery or nutrition. It has an income of about £1,000 per year. Use the BFSS application form for individuals.

The BFSS Trust: Provides annual grants to the student welfare fund at London South Bank University. Grants are made by the university and students should apply to the university direct.

The British School Charity: provides grants in support of education in the Saffron Walden area for students up to the age of 25. Annual income is around £7,000. Most grants go to schools and educational institutions but some grants are made to individuals living in the area. If you are an organisation you should apply using the online grant application form and individuals should apply using the application form for individuals.

Old British School, Bratton: Supports the education of persons under the age of 25 who are in need of financial assistance and who live within a radius of 20 miles from Bratton, Wiltshire. Grants may be made to individuals or organisations. If you are an organisation you should apply using the online grant application form and individuals should apply using the application form for individuals.

The Rowlett Educational Foundation: Supports training and education of students under 25 in Corby from an income of around £1,000 per year. Students living in the area wishing to apply should contact Belinda Lawrance at enquiries@bfss.org.uk in the first instance.

South Church Educational Fund: Supports educational initiatives in the area of the District of Wear Valley from an income of around £1,000. Grants may be made to individuals or organisations. If you are an organisation you should apply using the online grant application form and individuals should apply using the application form for individuals.

Sarah Walker and Spafford Fund: Provides an annual grant to Durham University for student travel. Grants are made by the university to students at the university and students should apply to the university direct.

Details of these funds can also be found in separate entries in this guide or on DSC's subscription website www. grantsforindividuals.org.uk

Visit the BFSS website for information on the set criteria.

The Rotary Foundation Scholarships

£1 million

Correspondent: The Administrator, Rotary International in Great Britain and Ireland, Kinwarton Road, Alcester, Warwickshire B49 6PB (01789 765411; fax: 01789 764916; email: info@ribi.org; website: www.ribi.org)

Eligibility

Scholarships to further international understanding for secondary school students, graduates, undergraduates, teachers and professional journalists.

Types of grants

Global Grant Scholarships overseas are available to graduates and are given towards achieving sustainable high-impact outcomes in the areas of peace and conflict prevention/resolution, disease prevention and treatment, water and sanitation, maternal and child health, basic education and literacy, economic and community development.

District Grant Scholarships are available for smaller scale projects locally or abroad. Clubs and districts create their own scholarships funded through district grants.

The purpose of the scholarships is to further international understanding and friendly relations among people of different countries, rather than to enable beneficiaries to achieve any particular qualification.

Annual grant total

Previously about £1 million has been spent in charitable support.

Applications

Applications can only be made through a rotary club in the district where the applicant lives, studies or works. Applications are normally considered throughout the year but the foundation encourages making enquiries well in advance of the planned activity.

The Sloane Robinson Foundation

See entry on page 32

The WR Foundation

£3,200 (2 grants)

Correspondent: John Malthouse, Trustee, Malthouse and Co., 8B Rumford Place, Liverpool L3 9DD (01512 842000)

CC Number: 1003546

Eligibility

People who need support to 'continue with their work and/or studies'. Our research suggests that grants are mainly awarded to higher education students.

Types of grants

One-off grants normally between £500 and £2,500.

Annual grant total

In 2012/13 the foundation had an income of £40,000 and an expenditure of £34,000. It made two individual grants totalling £3,200.

Applications

In writing to the correspondent.

Other information

Most grants are made to organisations and the amount awarded to individuals varies each year. The charity's income is mainly generated through WR Ltd.

Antarctic

The Trans-Antarctic Association

£16,000

Correspondent: Peters Elworthy and Moore, Accountants, Salisbury House, 2–3 Salisbury Villas, Cambridge CB1 2LA (01223 728222)

CC Number: 205773

Eligibility

Citizens of the UK, Australia and New Zealand seeking to further knowledge or exploration of the Antarctic region.

Types of grants

Grants are given to support expeditions to Antarctica, including travel and equipment costs, also research and publication expenses. Awards normally are up to £1,500.

Our research shows that about one third of the £10,000–£15,000 available each year is awarded to New Zealand nationals.

Annual grant total

In 2013 the organisation had an income of £12,400 and an expenditure of £16,400. We estimate that individual grants totalled around £16,000.

Exclusions

People who are not nationals of the countries named above are not normally supported.

Applications

According to our research, applications should be made by 31 January each year on a form available from the correspondent.

Europe

Erasmus Mobility Grants

Correspondent: The Erasmus Team, British Council, Bridgewater House, 58 Whitworth Street, Manchester M1 6BB (01619 577755; email: erasmus. enquiries@britishcouncil.org; website: www.erasmusplus.org.uk)

CC Number: 209131, SC037733

Eligibility

Students from the EU who wish to study (for a period between 3 and 12 months) or work as a trainee (for a period between 2 and 12 months) abroad. Applicants must be following any higher education studies leading to a recognised degree or other recognised tertiary level qualification up to and including the level of doctorate or be enrolled on a vocational education course, including foundation degree courses, or undertaking apprenticeships.

Academics, trainers, adult education staff, school teachers are eligible for staff mobility programmes (both teaching and training) for a period between two days and two months.

Opportunities are also available to youth workers and young people.

Types of grants

Grants for students carrying out study or work placements. Support is given based on the duration of period abroad and can cover travel costs, foreign language preparation, living costs or other extra costs arising from studying abroad. Amounts awarded will depend on the country where the applicant is travelling and roughly range from 150 to 500 euros per month.

Individuals with special needs, students in traineeship and students from disadvantaged backgrounds are entitled to additional support.

Students from outermost programme countries and regions (Cyprus, Iceland, Malta, overseas countries and territories) will receive higher support to reflect the travel costs.

Annual grant total

The Erasmus+ programme has been allocated an overall budget of £14.7

billion for the seven year period from 2014 to 2020. The sum is divided between education and training (78%), youth (10%), sport (2%) and other (10%) categories.

Exclusions

University students cannot apply during their first year.

The Erasmus+ programme is new, therefore previous participants of Erasmus Life Learning Programme can apply again but the organisations may be more likely to select individuals with no previous experience in Erasmus opportunities.

Applications

Applications have to be made through organisations. Students should contact the Erasmus co-ordinator at their home university to enquire about the programme.

Other information

The Erasmus+ programme started operating from January 2014. It integrates the previously run Erasmus programmes.

The British Council website notes that 'most UK universities and many other UK institutions of higher/further education have some involvement with the Erasmus student mobility programmes. The involvement varies from institution to institution but overall every subject area is covered.' New applications are welcomed from institutions, groups, organisations, charities and so on.

The Peter Kirk Memorial Fund

£18,000

Correspondent: Gillian King, Administrator, 11 Luttrell Avenue, Putney, London SW15 6PA (020 8789 7927; email: mail@kirkfund.org.uk; website: www.kirkfund.org.uk)

CC Number: 1049139

Eligibility

Citizens of any European country aged between 18 and 26 years, (under some circumstances an older candidate up to age 29 might be considered). Applicants must have been in full-time education at some time during the 12 months preceding the application.

Annual grant total

In 2012 the charity had an income of £21,000 and an expenditure of over £22,000. The 2012 accounts were the latest available at the time of writing (August 2014). We know from the charity's website however that in December 2013 scholarships worth

£2,000 each were awarded to nine scholars.

Exclusions

Peter Kirk Scholarships are awarded for independent study projects. Scholarships cannot be used to pay for course work which is required as part of an academic qualification but applicants sometimes find it possible to undertake an independent project alongside studies abroad. Contact mail@kirkfund.org.uk if uncertain of your position.

Applications

On a form available from the correspondent, by email or on receipt of an sae. Application forms can also be downloaded from the charity's website. Projects must be submitted by 5 November, with selection/interviews normally being completed by the end of December (check the website for the most up to date deadlines). Interviews take place in London at the applicant's expense. The fund would prefer applications to be submitted by email if possible.

Other information

The charity has a very helpful and informative website.

Trades Union Congress Educational Trust

£13,800 (10 grants)

Correspondent: Jean Scott, Administrator, Congress House, 23–28 Great Russell Street, London WC1B 3LQ (020 7467 1344; email: jscott@tuc.org.uk; website: www.unionlearn.org.uk/resources/funding/bursaries)

CC Number: 313741

Eligibility

Members of Trades Union Congress (TUC) affiliated trade unions to attend courses at selected colleges and universities. Applicants should not be receiving any other grants.

Types of grants

The trust offers scholarships and bursaries to students at selected institutions:

- Keele University bursaries – ten annual bursaries of £250 for Undergraduate Certificate in Industrial Relations (open to anyone with industrial relations experience); also three annual bursaries of £1,000 for part-time postgraduate courses in industrial relations, industrial relations and employment law, industrial relations and HRM or European HRM and industrial relations
- One Year Awards – at Northern College, Coleg Harlech, Hillcroft

College, Fircroft College and Newbattle Abbey College for one-year residential courses leading to a diploma in labour studies, history or social studies. These courses are financed by mandatory state grants and the TUC provides three additional bursaries of £925
- Ruskin College bursaries – three annual bursaries of £1,000 for an MA in International Labour and Trade Union Studies
- Clive Jenkins European Study Bursary – two bursaries of £800 each to cover travel and subsistence costs for a visit to a European Union country to study aspects of trade unionism, industrial relations or training and employment

The trust also provides Harvard bursaries to female trade unionists, assists union learners working online and provides bursaries to Birkbeck and Middlesex universities.

Annual grant total

At the time of writing (July 2014) the latest financial information available was from 2012. In 2012 the trust had assets of £1.5 million, an income of £65,000 and a total charitable expenditure of £77,000.

During the year the trust awarded 2 Clive Jenkins European Study bursaries, 1 Birkbeck and 3 Keele University bursaries, 3 Ruskin College bursaries and 1 Harvard scholarship. Scholarships and bursaries totalled £13,800.

Applications

For some awards applications need to be made through an educational institution, for others application forms are available online. See the Union Learn website for more details on each of the available bursaries.

Other information

More information about the bursaries can also be obtained by contacting Liz Rees at lrees@tuc.org.uk.

New Zealand
The Link Foundation

£48,000

Correspondent: Liza Fletcher, Administrative Secretary, New Zealand House, 80 Haymarket SW1Y 4PD (07941 000 541; email: admin@nzuklinkfoundation.org.uk; website: www.nzuklinkfoundation.org)

CC Number: 802457

Eligibility

People wishing to participate in a vocational exchange between the UK and New Zealand, through specific joint educational schemes in a range of economic, social, cultural and scientific disciplines. The schemes are advertised through the governing bodies and specialist press belonging to these areas. Applicants must be either nationals or permanent residents of New Zealand or the UK.

Types of grants

Scholarships, grants, allowances and prizes towards educational and cultural exchange linked to a vocation, including for research.

Annual grant total

In 2012/13 the foundation had an income of £106,000 and a total expenditure of £88,000. During the year, the foundation granted fellowships totalling £48,000.

Exclusions

Grants are not made to individuals seeking funds for one-off trips such as medical residencies or to applicants wishing to visit countries other than Britain or New Zealand.

Applications

Application forms or relevant links for schemes can be found on the foundation's website.

Other information

A list of scholarships and fellowships offered by the foundation and its 'Fellowship Partners' are available on its informative website.

Scandinavia

CoScan Trust Fund

£1,500 (Around 15 grants)

Correspondent: Dr Brita Green, Administrator, 103 Long Ridge Lane, Nether Poppleton, York YO26 6LW (email: psgbeg@aol.com; website: www. coscan.org.uk/side7.html)

Eligibility

British people between the ages of 15 and 25 who are undertaking a project of a broadly educational nature involving travel between the UK and Scandinavia and within Scandinavia. Only short visits will be considered.

Types of grants

One-off grants between £75 and £150 to visit a Scandinavian country. Previous grant recipients have included young people looking for vocational experience, attending summer camps/courses, university students, young farmers, members of youth orchestras and scouts or guides.

Annual grant total

Our research suggests that previously approximately 15 grants have been

awarded annually through the travel awards scheme.

Exclusions

Due to limited funds, large scale projects cannot be supported.

Applications

Application forms can be requested from the correspondent. They should be accompanied by a personal letter. Applications are considered once a year and should be submitted by March for consideration in April/May.

Other information

Applicants do not necessarily have to be members of an affiliated society, although a recommendation from one may be helpful.

Sweden

Anglo-Swedish Literary Foundation

£18,000

Correspondent: Ann Nilsen, Cultural Affairs Officer, Embassy of Sweden, 11 Montagu Place, London W1H 2AL (02079176465; website: www. swedenabroad.com/en-GB/Embassies/ London/Contact/Anglo-Swedish-Literary-Foundation)

CC Number: 230622

Eligibility

Individuals connected to studies of Swedish language and literature, translation work and research. The foundation aims develop the 'cultural intercourse between Sweden and the British Islands through the promotion and diffusion of knowledge and appreciation of Swedish culture in the British Islands'.

Types of grants

Grants are given for translation and publishing subsidies, travel to Sweden for educational/research purposes and similar causes.

Annual grant total

In 2012/13 the trust had an income of £7,700 and an expenditure of £18,300. We estimate the annual total of grants to be around £18,000.

Applications

In writing to the correspondent. Applicants should outline their project or activity, state funding required and give details of any other funding applied for/secured. Applications must be received by 1 May or 1 November.

Other information

The foundation established the Bernard Shaw Translation Prize which awards £2,000 every three years for the best

translation into English of a Swedish work, published for the first time by a UK publisher. This prize is administered by the Society of Authors.

National charities classified by occupation of parent

Airline Pilots

The British Airline Pilots' Association Benevolent Fund (BALPA)

£22,000

Correspondent: Antoinette Girdler, Administrator, BALPA House, 5 Heathrow Boulevard, 278 Bath Road, West Drayton UB7 0DQ (020 8476 4029; email: balpa@balpa.org)

CC Number: 229957

Eligibility

Dependents of retired or deceased commercial pilots and flight engineers, who are or have been members of BALPA.

Types of grants

Limited grants are made towards the cost of books, uniforms and associated educational expenses.

Annual grant total

In 2012/13 the charity had assets of £1.5 million and an income of £36,000. It made grants of approximately £44,000 and gave around £15,000 in interest-free loans.

Exclusions

Grants are not given for school fees.

Applications

In writing to the correspondent requesting an application form. Applications are considered quarterly.

Artists

Artists' Orphan Fund (AOF)

£46,000 (17 grants)

Correspondent: Brad Feltham, Secretary, Artists General Benevolent Institute, Burlington House, Piccadilly, London W1J 0BB (020 7734 1193)

CC Number: 219356

Eligibility

Children of a professional artist (for example painter, sculptor, architect, illustrator, engraver, designer and so on), where either one or both parents have died. Applicants must be under the age of 25 and/or in full-time education.

Types of grants

One-off grants for educational costs, maintenance expenses and extra-curricular activities, such as music lessons or sports. Individuals can be supported throughout their education or up to the age of 25 but they must reapply each year.

Annual grant total

In 2012/13 the fund had assets of £1.3 million and an income of £49,000. A total of around £46,000 was awarded in grants to 17 individuals.

Exclusions

Funding is rarely provided for private or boarding education, but will be considered when a child has a scholarship, considerable bursary or the family circumstances present a genuine need for the child to be living outside of the family unit.

Applications

In writing to the correspondent. Applicants should include career details of a qualifying parent and the present financial position of the family. Appropriate candidates will receive an application form to complete which will then be considered upon receipt.

Equity Charitable Trust (formerly Equity Trust Fund)

£71,500 (31 grants)

Correspondent: Kaethe Cherney, Company Secretary, Plouviez House, 19–20 Hatton Place, London EC1N 8RU (020 7831 1926; email: kaethe@ equitycharitabletrust.org.uk; website: www.equitycharitabletrust.org.uk)

CC Number: 328103

Eligibility

Professional performers (under Equity or ITC contracts) with a minimum of ten years' experience as an adult (work performed below the age of 16 is not counted).

Types of grants

Grants to enable people to pursue a new career. They can be used towards books, equipment, instruments, fees, living expenses or childcare.

Annual grant total

In 2012/13 the trust had assets of £9.9 million and an income of £462,000. There were 31 grants for educational bursaries given to individuals with a total value of £71,500.

Exclusions

No grants to amateur performers, musicians or drama students.

Applications

On a form available from the correspondent or downloaded from the trust's website. There are normally three meetings each year, with the first one taking place usually around about the middle of May.

Other information

The trust has an informative website.

The Independent Dancers Resettlement Trust (Dancers' Career Development)

£229,000 (104 grants)

Correspondent: Jennifer Curry, Director of Development, Plouviez House, 19–20 Hatton Place, London EC1N 8RU (020 7831 1449; fax: 020 7242 1462; email: admin@thedcd.org.uk; website: www.thedcd.org.uk)

CC Number: 327747

Eligibility

Professional and independent dancers in the UK, regardless of their artistic background. All applicants must have worked as a professional dancer for a minimum of eight years and have worked a minimum of five years in the UK. In addition to that:

- **Independent dancers** must demonstrate that they have earned an income as a dancer for a minimum of 16 weeks in each year (on average)
- **Company dancers** must have spent at least five years with one or more of the following companies affiliated to the organisation: Adzido Pan African Dance Company, Birmingham Royal Ballet, English National Ballet, Northern Ballet, Phoenix Dance Theatre, Rambert Dance Company, Richard Alston Dance Company, Scottish Ballet, Siobhan Davies Dance Company and The Royal Ballet

Dancers who had to retire due to illness or injury may still be eligible for help even if they are unable to meet the above criteria.

Professional dancers are eligible to apply for up to ten years after they cease performing professionally.

Types of grants

One-off payments and financial assistance for retraining are given to dancers at the end of their career. Support is available for course and training fees, business start-up equipment, maintenance, travel costs, child care costs and so on.

There are certain upper limits for grants: £1,000 for computer support equipment; £5,000 for career support equipment; and a maximum of £15,000 to an individual applicant.

Annual grant total

In 2012/13 the trust had assets of £880,000 and an income of £372,000, mostly in contributions from member companies. Grants to 104 individuals amounted to £229,000 and a further £127,000 was spent in depreciation of equipment on loan to dancers.

Applications

Applications may be obtained from the correspondent or downloaded from the Dancers' Career Development (DCD) website. They should be submitted directly by the individual. Applications must also include a dance career CV, covering letter addressed to the trustees, information on the course or equipment and a detailed application budget. The trustees meet four times a year to consider applications. Deadline dates are publicised on the DCD website and in a monthly e-newsletter. Generally applications for funding should be submitted at least three months prior to the beginning of any training.

Detailed guidelines are available on the DCD website. Informal enquiries prior to the application are also encouraged.

Other information

DCD offers free educational, emotional, careers advice and counselling to eligible dancers. Eight special bursaries to independent dancers were also awarded in 2012/13.

The DCD website contains a lot of useful information including application guidelines, sample budgets and links to organisations which may be able to help individuals who have not spent enough time dancing in the UK to qualify for help from DCD.

DCD is a founding member of the International Organisation for the Transition of Professional Dancers (IOTPD).

Peggy Ramsay Foundation

£50,000

Correspondent: G. Laurence Harbottle, Trustee, Hanover House, 14 Hanover Square, London W15 1HP (020 7667 5000; fax: 020 7667 5100; email: laurence.harbottle@harbottle.com; website: www.peggyramsayfoundation. org)

CC Number: 1015427

Eligibility

Writers for the stage who have been produced publicly, are 'of promise' and are in need of time to write which they cannot afford, or are in need of other assistance. Applicants must live in the British Isles (including Republic of Ireland and the Channel Islands).

Types of grants

One-off grants. Individual grants never ordinarily exceed a standard commissioning fee. Grants are sometimes made for equipment, such as laptops, and for expenditure which makes writing possible.

Annual grant total

In 2012 the foundation had assets of £5.2 million and an income of £255,000. Grants to 53 individuals totalled £101,000. Grants are also made for welfare purposes.

These were the latest accounts available at the time of writing (July 2014).

Exclusions

The foundation does not support production costs. No grants are made for writing not intended for the theatre.

Applications

Applications should provide answers to the following questions:

- When and where was the first professional production of a play of yours
- Who produced the play which qualifies you for a grant
- When and where was your qualifying play produced, what was its run and approximate playing time and has it been revived
- For that production were the director and actors all professionals engaged with Equity contracts
- Did the audience pay to attend

Scripts and publicity material must not be included. Trustees meet quarterly although applications are dealt with between meetings. Applicants will usually receive a decision in six to eight weeks.

Other information

Grants were also made to organisations totalling £22,000.

TACT Education Fund

£12,000

Correspondent: Robert Ashby, Administrator, The Actors Charitable Trust, 58 Bloomsbury Street, London WC1B 3QT (020 7636 7868; email: robert@tactactors.org; website: www.tactactors.org)

CC Number: 802885

Eligibility

Students on performing arts degrees (drama, music, dance and so on) whose one or both parents are/were professional actors.

Types of grants

Maintenance grants of £1,200 per year to students in further and higher education, including mature students and postgraduates.

Annual grant total

In 2012/13 the fund had an income of £12,800 and an expenditure of £12,500. We estimate the annual total of grants to individual students to be around £12,000. The charity is very small and can only fund a few students at a time.

Exclusions

Private school fees cannot be funded.

Applications

Applicants should email the correspondent for more information about the application process.

Bankers

The Bank Workers Charity

£244,000

Correspondent: The Clerk, Pinners Hall, 105–108 Old Broad Street, London EC2N 1EX (0800 023 4834; email: info@bwcharity.org.uk; website: www.bwcharity.org.uk)

CC Number: 313080

Eligibility

Current and ex-employees of banks in the UK and their dependents.

Types of grants

One-off and recurrent grants for fees and other educational expenses.

Annual grant total

In 2012/13 the charity had assets of £46.5 million and an income of £1.6 million. Grants totalled £1.1 million broken down as follows:

Families	£470,000
Retirees	£400,000
Child education	£244,000

Applications

Contact the charity in the first instance to discuss making an application.

Other information

The charity also provides support in three main areas: home, money and wellbeing. They have client advisors who offer information, advice and guidance covering a range of issues as well as offering independent and confidential counselling.

The Alfred Foster Settlement

£14,000

Correspondent: Graham Prew, Administrator, Barclays Bank Trust Co. Ltd, Executorship and Trustee Service, Osborne Court, Gadbrook Park, Rudheath, Northwich CW9 7UE (01606 313118)

CC Number: 229576

Eligibility

Employees and former employees of banks and their dependents who are in need. Applicants must be students aged less than 28 years.

Types of grants

One-off grants, for example, to help with university fees, books, travel costs and living expenses while in further education.

Annual grant total

In 2012/13 the charity had an income of £39,000 and a total expenditure of £29,000. Grants were given to individuals totalling £28,000 and we estimate the total given in educational grants was approximately £14,000.

Applications

In writing to the correspondent. Applications can be submitted directly by the individual or through the school/college or educational welfare agency.

Other information

The charity also makes grants to individuals for welfare purposes.

Barristers

The Barristers' Benevolent Association

£95,000

Correspondent: Janet South, Administrator, 14 Gray's Inn Square, London WC1R 5JP (020 7242 4761; email: susan@the-bba.com; website: www.the-bba.com)

CC Number: 1106768

Eligibility

Past or present practising members of the Bar and their dependents, in England and Wales, who are in need.

Types of grants

Educational grants for dependents are only given in the most exceptional circumstances, for example where the death or disability of a barrister leaves his or her children stranded in mid-education. Grants or loans are given to schoolchildren towards books, educational outings, maintenance or school uniforms or clothing; students in further/higher education for help with books, fees and living expenses; mature students for books, travel, fees or childcare; and people starting work for books, equipment, clothing and travel. Loans are also available.

Annual grant total

In 2012 the charity had assets of £9.5 million and an income of £635,000. £189,000 was given in grants.

These were the latest set of accounts available at the time of writing (July 2014).

Exclusions

School fees are only paid in exceptional circumstances such as if the student is facing imminent examinations.

Applications

On a form available from the website (www.the-bba.com). Applications are considered throughout the year and should include the name and address of the chambers where they last practised as a barrister.

Other information

Grants are also made for welfare purposes.

Book retail

The Book Trade Charity

£4,500

Correspondent: David Hicks, Chief Executive, The Foyle Centre, The Retreat, Abbots Road, Kings Langley, Hertfordshire WD4 8LT (01329 848731; email: david@btbs.org; website: www.booktradecharity.org)

CC Number: 1128129

Eligibility

People in need who have worked in the book trade in the UK for at least one year (normally publishing/distribution/book-selling), and their dependents.

Types of grants

One-off grants of up to £1,000 are given to help retrain people from the book trade who have been made redundant. These grants are given to eligible mature students where a welfare need is evident.

The society is predominantly a relief-in-need charity and retraining is only a small part of their work. Therefore, general educational grants are not usually made.

Annual grant total

In 2013 this charity had assets of £5.7 million consisting for the most part of land and buildings and therefore not available for grant giving. Its income was £508,000 and grants were made totalling £123,000 of which £4,500 was awarded in educational grants.

Applications

On a form available from the correspondent. Applications can be submitted by the individual or through a recognised referral agency (social worker, Citizens Advice, doctor and so on). They are considered as they arrive.

Building trade

Scottish Building Federation Edinburgh and District Charitable Trust

See entry on page 94

Civic and public services

For You By You – The Charity for Civil Servants

£0

Correspondent: The Help and Advisory Team, Fund House, 5 Anne Boleyn's Walk, Cheam, Sutton, Surrey SM3 8DY (0800 056 2424; fax: 020 8240 2401; email: help@foryoubyyou.org.uk; website: www.foryoubyyou.org.uk)

CC Number: 1136870, SC041956

Eligibility

Serving, retired and former civil servants or employees of associated organisations and their financial dependents.

Types of grants

Grants, loans, allowances and gifts in kind can be given according to need. Support is available for retraining, getting back into work and to further the education of the dependents at any stage.

Annual grant total

In 2012/13 the charity had assets of £38.9 million and an income of £8.2 million. A total of £2.9 million was spent in grants and allowances to over

4400 individuals but no awards were made for educational purposes. Previously about £4,000 has been distributed in educational grants.

Exclusions

Grants are not available for private education.

Applications

On an online application form which can be found on the charity's website. Applicants are offered advice, information and help with the application process via freephone at 0800 056 2424. Candidates are encouraged to approach the charity with any questions prior to the application.

Other information

The charity mainly supports individuals for social welfare needs and also provides information, advice and guidance.

Coalminers

Miners' Welfare National Educational Fund (MWNEF)

£97,000 (178 grants)

Correspondent: V. O. S. Jones, Secretary, The Old Rectory, Rectory Drive, Whiston, Rotherham, South Yorkshire S60 4JG (01709 728115; fax: 01709 839164; website: ciswo.org/index.php/education/)

CC Number: 313246, SC038771

Eligibility

People who are or have been employed in the coal mining industry of Great Britain (including any activity conducted by British Coal) and have not undertaken full-time permanent employment since. Individuals who are the dependents of such employees or former employees are also eligible. Applicants must be at least 17 years old.

Types of grants

Grants of not more than £500 a year are given towards higher and further education. Any full time courses of education for which LEA or SAAS support is available are eligible, including undergraduate degrees, Open University courses, full and part time education. Some postgraduate courses may be considered where they are related to and taken directly after a first degree or considered essential for an entry into a profession. Other postgraduate courses of not more than two years in duration, where candidates have achieved at least an upper second class honours degree (at first degree level) can be considered.

Annual grant total

In 2012/13 the fund had assets of £879,000 and an income of £53,000. A total of around £97,000 was awarded in 178 grants

North Yorkshire	53	£28,000
South Yorkshire	31	£17,700
Nottinghamshire	26	£14,500
Scotland	19	£10,600
Central	14	£8,600
South Wales	15	£8,200
HQ and others	11	£6,100
North East	3	£1,600
Western	2	£1,200
Telegraph awards	4	£300

The vast majority of applications were from the dependents of the employees/former employees of the coal mining industry.

Applications

Application forms are available from the correspondent between late August and March. Candidates are required to provide a referee's report from an educational institution, give full personal details and academic achievements, include a confirmation of A-level results and of award of student support. Family or financial circumstances relevant to the application can also be outlined. Grants are considered two or three times a year.

Other information

Applicants must reapply in each academic year of an eligible course.

The trustees remind that 'successful applications from Scottish candidates will be forwarded to the Scottish Coal Industry Special Welfare Fund (SCISWF), where a further grant award of 150% could be awarded on top of the award from MWNEF.'

Commerce

The George Drexler Foundation

£140,000

Correspondent: Jonathan Fountain, 35–43 Lincolns Inn Fields, London WC2A 3PE (020 7869 6080; email: georgedrexler@rcseng.ac.uk)

CC Number: 313278

Eligibility

People who have a direct link with commerce, i.e. who have owned and run their own commercial business. Applicants whose parents or grandparents have this link can also be supported. This does not include professional people such as doctors, lawyers, dentists, architects or accountants. No exceptions can be made. Preference is given to schoolchildren with serious family difficulties so that the child has to be educated away from home, and to people with special educational needs.

Types of grants

One-off and recurrent grants of £1,000 to £10,000. To enrich the educational experiences of younger people; assisting particularly gifted or talented students, undergraduates or postgraduates in developing their individual skills or supporting projects that develop new or enhance existing services or knowledge that benefit society, and particularly those students in medical education.

Annual grant total

In 2012/13 the foundation had assets of £6.1 million and an income of £269,000. Grants to individuals for educational purposes totalled £140,000 and educational grants to organisations totalled £84,500. Grants to individuals to relieve poverty totalled £41,000.

Exclusions

No funding for medical electives, volunteering or gap year projects.

Applications

On a form available from the correspondent, submitted directly by the individual, enclosing an sae. Applications should be submitted in May for consideration in June/July.

Other information

The foundation also provides welfare grants to former employees of the Ofrex Group and their dependents.

The Ruby and Will George Trust

£26,000 (20 grants)

Correspondent: Damien Slattery, 125 Cloverfield, West Allotment, Newcastle upon Tyne NE27 0BE (01912 664527; email: admin@rwgt.co.uk; website: www.rwgt.co.uk)

CC Number: 264042

Eligibility

The dependents of people in need who have been or who are employed in commerce. Preference is given to people who live in the north east of England.

Types of grants

One-off and recurrent grants of up to £2,000 towards maintenance and fees, mainly for those in secondary or further education. Grants relating to fees are usually paid directly to the educational establishment. Occasionally, assistance with maintenance, books and basic travel expenses will be awarded.

Annual grant total

In 2012/13 the trust had assets of £3.4 million and an income of £69,000.

Grants are given to individuals both for educational and welfare purposes. In this accounting year £51,500 was given to 40 individuals and we estimate the total for education was around £26,000.

Exclusions

Expeditions, study visits and student exchanges are not funded.

Applications

The trust has an online application process, though those without access to the internet can still submit a paper-based application. Applicants will need to prove their commerce connection and their income and expenditure. Two references are required.

The trust considers applications four times a year, usually in January, May, July and October. Applications should be submitted two weeks in advance. Note: upcoming deadline dates can be found on the trust's website.

Farming

The Dairy Crest and National Farmers' Union Scholarship Fund

£15,000

Correspondent: Catherine Booth, Administrator, Higher Moorlake Cottage, Moorlake, Crediton, Devon EX17 5EL (01363 776623; fax: 01363 774992; email: aba@adelabooth.co.uk)

CC Number: 306598

Eligibility

Children of farmers or farm workers, ex-farmers, smallholders and ex-smallholders in Cornwall, Devon, Dorset and Somerset who are studying a dairy-related topic at tertiary level or equivalent and intend to follow a career in this field.

Types of grants

Scholarships in the range from £200 to £2,000 can be provided to people studying dairy related topics. Support is given for books, fees, equipment, maintenance/living expenses, travel/study costs and research.

Annual grant total

In 2012/13 the fund had an income of £16,900 and an expenditure of £20,000. Around £15,000 is available for distribution in grants to individuals each year.

Applications

Application forms can be found on the website (www.afcp.co.uk) or requested from the correspondent. Applications should be submitted by 12 August each

year. Eligible applicants will be invited for an interview.

Forestry/ timber

Forest Industries Education and Provident Fund

£3,800

Correspondent: Jane Karthaus, Trustee, Woodland Place, West Street, Belford, Northumberland NE70 7QA (01668 213937; email: jane.karthaus@gmail.com; website: www.confor.org.uk/AboutUs/Default.aspx?pid=150)

CC Number: 1061322

Eligibility

Members of the Forestry and Timber Association (or Confor) and their dependents who are in need. Members must have been involved with the association for at least one year.

Types of grants

One-off grants of up to £750 are made towards education, training or professional development in the field of forestry. Support is also given for educational trips and activities (for example, conferences).

Annual grant total

At the time of writing (August 2014) the latest financial information available was from 2012. In 2012 the fund had an income of £7,100 and an expenditure of £7,900. We estimate that educational grants totalled around £3,800.

Exclusions

Retrospective funding is not given.

Applications

Application forms are available from the fund's website or can be requested from the correspondent.

Other information

Anyone can join Confor who has an interest in trees, woodlands or timber industry. Grants are also made for welfare purposes.

The fund's website also directs beneficiaries to other potential sources of help: The Institute of Chartered Foresters' Educational and Scientific Trust and The Royal Forestry Society.

Furnishing trade

The City of London Linen and Furnishing Trades Benevolent Association

£300

Correspondent: Damilola Bamidele, Grants and Education Manager, 4th Floor, Furniture Makers' Hall, 12 Austin Friars, London EC2N 2HE (020 7256 5954; email: welfare@furnituremakers. org.uk; website: www.furnituremkrs.co. uk/default.aspx)

CC Number: 211522

Eligibility

Children whose parent (or guardian) are, or have been, employed in the UK furnishing industry for a minimum of two years, and are permanently or temporarily unable to maintain them.

Types of grants

One-off grants averaging £250 are given for uniforms, books, instruments, equipment and maintenance and living expenses. Preference is given to children with special needs.

Annual grant total

In 2012 the charity had an income of £1,000 and a total expenditure of £815. The 2012 accounts were the latest available at the time of writing (August 2014).

Applications

To request an application pack write, email or telephone the association giving a brief summary of your employment history and the reasons why you are applying for financial or medical assistance. Applications should be submitted through a third party such as a social worker, teacher, Citizens Advice or school.

Other information

The association states that grants are mainly for the relief of need; education grants are of secondary importance.

Gardeners

Gardeners' Royal Benevolent Society (Perennial)

£29,000

Correspondent: Sheila Thompson, Director of Services, 115–117 Kingston Road, Leatherhead, Surrey KT22 7SU (0800 093 8543, 07901556108; email: info@perennial.org.uk; website: www. perennial.org.uk)

CC Number: 1155156, SC040180

Eligibility

Horticulturalists or those training to become one who are experiencing hardship. The dependent children of horticulturalists who are in full time education.

Types of grants

The charity runs a number of training bursaries with various criteria:
- Sons and daughters bursaries – maximum of £1,500 per year to full-time horticultural students under the age of 40 who are themselves children of horticulturalists
- Hardship bursaries – one-off grants of up to £1,000 to horticultural students experiencing exceptional, unforeseen hardship
- Support for long-term career horticulturalists who find themselves in hardship and are looking to regain satisfactory employment within the industry or elsewhere following adverse circumstance such as an accident or ill health
- Grants are also available for general education for the dependent children of horticulturalists. The regional caseworker should be contacted in the first instance

Annual grant total

In 2013 the charity had assets of £45.1 million, an income of £3.8 million and spent £1.6 million in assisting the beneficiaries. Grants for training and retraining totalled over £20,000 and additional 74 awards were given to support children for education and general welfare needs totalling £18,000. We estimate that annual total of grants for educational purposes was around £29,000.

The biggest part of charity's expenditure is spent in providing advice and advocacy services.

Applications

Applicants are advised to check the charity's website for the application advice relating to separate schemes. Individuals are encouraged to get in touch with the charity to discuss their eligibility and support available.

Other information

In 2010 this charity merged with the Royal Fund for Gardeners' Children. In 2013 the charity had a change in its legal status – became a company limited by guarantee and was registered with the Charity Commission. It continues to be registered with the Office of the Scottish Charity Regulator.

The charity also provides free financial advice, information and advocacy. To access help get in touch with the charity: general advice at 0800 210 0547, services@perennial.org.uk; debt advice at 0800 294 4244, debtadvice@perennial.org.uk.

Additionally, extra funding will be made available for those with 'grandfather rights' towards pesticides qualification to retrain and gain the new certificate before these run out in 2015.

Higher education

The Higher Education Academy

Correspondent: Sean Mackney, Senior Deputy Chief Executive, Innovation Way, York Science Park, York YO10 5BR (01904 717500; fax: 01904 717505; email: enquiries@heacademy.ac.uk; website: www.heacademy.ac.uk)

Eligibility

Anyone who is responsible for the student learning experience working in higher education institutions in the UK that subscribe to the Higher Education Academy, and students of those institutions.

Types of grants

Previously support has been provided: towards teaching development projects that aim to encourage innovations in learning and teaching; in travel awards to staff and students to enable them to engage in events and meetings; and to further good practice in learning, teaching and assessment within higher education.

Annual grant total

Currently grants are not provided.

Applications

Guidelines, terms and conditions and FAQs for the support will be available on the academy's website, should the funding resume.

Other information

The academy's website states that:

> The Higher Education Academy's core funding for 2014–15 and beyond has been reduced in line with many parts of the sector and, regrettably, as a result the HEA is no longer in a position to commit funds for grants and awards from the next academic year, including Teaching Development Grants, the Mike Baker Doctoral Programme and the Professor Sir Ron Cooke International Scholarship Scheme. Grants already underway remain funded.

We are maintaining this entry as the organisation has noted that new plans are being developed and should funding become available grantmaking can resume and will be based in the lines of: curriculum design and innovative pedagogies; and transitions for both students and higher education staff.

The organisation is independent and funded by the four UK higher education funding bodies, by subscriptions and grants.

Horse-racing and breeding

National Trainers' Federation Charitable Trust (N. T. F. Charitable Trust)

£9,000

Correspondent: Janet Byrd, Racing Welfare, 20b Park Lane, Newmarket, Suffolk CB8 8QD (01638 560763; fax: 01638 565240; email: info@racingwelfare.co.uk; website: www.racingwelfare.co.uk)

CC Number: 1004308

Eligibility

Individuals who have had an accident/ been injured in the course of their employment in racing and therefore cannot return to work or perform it in the same capacity. The dependents of such people are also eligible.

Types of grants

Grants are provided for retraining. Individuals can either aim for employment within the racing industry but in a different capacity or enter a new industry altogether. Some examples of courses supported include: plastering, nursing, driving instructing, HGV driving, racing secretary, secretarial and accountancy courses.

Annual grant total

In 2012/13 the trust had an income of £14,600 and an expenditure of £18,000. We estimate the annual total of grants to be around £9,000.

Applications

Application forms can be requested from the correspondent. The trust invites applicants to seek advice of a local welfare officer when completing the application. Candidates should provide a doctor's report stating the reasons why the applicant is no longer suited to work in their present capacity as well as details of the course they are intending to take.

Other information

The trust also supports organisations.

Insurance

The Insurance Charities

£481,000

Correspondent: Annali-Joy Thornicroft, Secretary, 20 Aldermanbury, London EC2V 7HY (020 7606 3763; fax: 020 7600 1170; email: info@theinsurancecharities.org.uk; website: www.theinsurancecharities.org.uk)

CC Number: 206860

Eligibility

University students whose parents have been in the insurance industry for at least five years.

Types of grants

Help may be given to first degree students towards day-to-day expenses, particularly where there is family financial hardship.

Annual grant total

In 2012/13 the charities had assets of £30.1 million and an income of £1.8 million. Grants were made to 259 individuals totalling £962,000. This is the net figure after deducting £95,000 – the contribution made by the Paul Golmick Fund towards grants.

Applications

An initial form can be completed online or downloaded from the charities' website.

Management Accountant

The Chartered Institute of Management Accountants Benevolent Fund

£20,000

Correspondent: Caroline Aldred, Secretary, CIMA, 26 Chapter Street, London SW1P 4NP (020 8849 2221; email: benevolent.fund@cimaglobal.com; website: www.cimaglobal.com)

CC Number: 261114

Eligibility

Children of past and present CIMA members within and outside the UK.

Types of grants

Educational grants and loans for dependent children according to need.

Annual grant total

In 2013 the fund had assets of £2.1 million and an income of £106,000. Grants to 46 individuals totalled £102,000 (14 of these grants included funding for families with dependents). The amount awarded in educational grants was not specified in the accounts. We estimate that educational grants totalled around £20,000.

Applications

On a form available from the correspondent or to download from the website (www.cimaglobal.com/Members/ Fees-benefits-and-career-support/ Services-and-support/CIMA-Benevolent-Fund). Applications can be submitted directly by the individual or through a recognised referral agency (Citizens Advice, doctor, social worker and so on), or through another appropriate third party.

Other information

The charity can also signpost people to relevant services and provide support from a welfare officer. Support is given for general welfare needs as well.

Meat Trade

The Worshipful Company of Butchers' Educational Charity

£4,200

Correspondent: The Clerk, Butchers' Hall, 87–88 Bartholomew Close, London EC1A 7EB (020 7600 4106; fax: 020 7606 4108; email: clerk@butchershall.com; website: www.butchershall.com)

CC Number: 297603

Eligibility
People involved in the meat trade who are studying courses related to the trade.

Applicants for the Nuffield Farming Scholarship must be a UK resident between 22 and 45 years who have been in the industry for at least two years and intend to remain involved in the sector.

Types of grants
One-off grants towards further and higher education fees.

The company also provides one Nuffield Farming Scholarship each year to enable someone who is active in the meat and livestock industries to study a topic of their choice carrying out a tour anywhere in the world to further their knowledge and understanding.

Annual grant total
In 2012/13 the charity had assets of £815,000 and an income of £42,000. Grants to individuals totalled £4,200. Grants to organisations totalled £42,000.

Applications
In writing to the correspondent. Applications should be submitted directly by the individual for consideration monthly.

To apply for the Nuffield Farming Scholarship contact Bob Bansback on bob@bansback.co.uk.

Media

The Chartered Institute of Journalists Orphan Fund

£15,000

Correspondent: Dominic Cooper, Administrator, 2 Dock Offices, Surrey Quays Road, London SE16 2XU (020 7252 1187; fax: 020 7232 2302; email: memberservices@cioj.co.uk; website: www.cioj.co.uk)

CC Number: 208176

Eligibility
Orphaned children of institute members who are in need, aged between 5 and 22 and in full-time education.

Types of grants
Grants are given to schoolchildren towards the cost of school clothing, books, instruments, educational outings and school fees. Grants are also given to students in further or higher education towards the cost of books, help with fees/living expenses and study or travel abroad.

Annual grant total
In 2012 the fund had assets of £1.8 million and an income of £91,000. Grants to individuals totalled £30,000, for welfare and education. We have estimated that grants to individuals for educational purposes totalled £15,000. These were the latest accounts available at the time of writing (July 2014).

Applications
Applications should be submitted by the child's surviving parent or other appropriate third party. Applications are considered quarterly.

Other information
This fund also gives grants for social welfare purposes.

The Grace Wyndham Goldie (BBC) Trust Fund

£22,500

Correspondent: Ms Cheryl Miles, Secretary, BBC, Room M1017, Broadcasting House, Cardiff CF5 2YQ (02920 322000; website: www.bbc.co.uk/charityappeals/grant/gwg.shtml)

CC Number: 212146

Eligibility
Employees and ex-employees engaged in radio or television broadcasting or an associated activity, and their dependents.

Types of grants
One-off grants to help with educational costs such as school or college fees, travelling expenses, school uniforms, books and equipment, living expenses or to supplement existing educational awards.

Annual grant total
In 2012 the trust had assets of £1.2 million and an income of £49,000. Grants totalling £26,700 were made of which £22,500 were for educational purposes and £1,200 were for social welfare. Grants returned totalled £2,800). The 2012 accounts were the most recent available at the time of writing (July 2014).

Exclusions
Recurrent grants are not made.

Applications
On a form available from the correspondent. As the income of the fund is limited, and to ensure help can be given where it is most needed, applicants must be prepared to give full information about their circumstances.

The Newspaper Press Fund (Journalists' Charity)

£10,000

Correspondent: David Ilott, Director and Secretary, Dickens House, 35 Wathen Road, Dorking, Surrey RH4 1JY (01306 887511; fax: 01306 888212; email: enquiries@journalistscharity.org.uk; website: www.journalistscharity.org.uk)

CC Number: 208215

Eligibility
Practising and former journalist and their dependents who are in need because of sickness, accident or other unforeseen circumstances. There are no age restrictions.

Types of grants
One-off and recurrent grants. This fund mainly supports welfare causes, although there is often some crossover with the educational purposes. Help with school, college or university fees is only given in exceptional circumstances.

Annual grant total
In 2013 the charity had assets and an income of £1.5 million and a total expenditure of £2.3 million. At the time of writing (August 2014) full accounts were not available. Normally around 150–200 awards are made each year totalling around £300,000. Most support is given for welfare purposes. We estimate that around £10,000 is spent in supporting individuals' education.

Exclusions
The charity states that their 'aim is to give financial support in times of need however [they] cannot subsidise those who, in the long term, find it difficult to make a living from journalism unless through illness or other misfortune.' Grants are not offered to subsidise an existing lifestyle.

Applications
Application forms can be requested from the correspondent using an online form on the charity's website. They can be submitted directly by the individual or a family member. Applications should include details of the career in journalism and are considered monthly.

The consideration process may take two to six weeks.

Other information
The fund also runs residential and care homes in Dorking.

The Printing Charity (Printers' Charitable Corporation)

£34,000

Correspondent: Henry Smith, Grants Officer, First Floor, Underwood House, 235 Three Bridges Road, Crawley, West Sussex RH10 1LS (01293 649368; fax: 01293 542826; email: henry@ theprintingcharity.org.uk; website: www. theprintingcharity.org.uk)

CC Number: 208882

Eligibility
People who have worked for at least three years in the printing profession, graphic arts or allied trades and their dependents who are in need. A list of eligible trades can be found on the charity's website.

Types of grants
One-off grants of £250 for the costs associated with retraining and seeking future employment, travel to interviews or training.

Annual grant total
In 2013 the charity had assets of £36.4 million and an income of £1.6 million. Educational bursaries totalled £34,000.

Support was also provided through three schemes: Print Futures helped 17 young people; two unemployed individuals were assisted via Chiumento; and 42 persons in the North England were helped in partnership with The Prince's Trust.

Applications
Application forms and guidelines are available from the charity's website. Further information on the application process can also be received by contacting the correspondent. Assistance is means tested so applicants should be prepared to make a full declaration of their finances, including state benefits and funding from other charitable sources. Applications can be made by individuals directly or through a welfare agency.

The trust advises potential applicants to contact them before submitting an application.

Other information
Grants are also given for welfare needs and a great part of the overall charitable expenditure is spent in the provision of

specifically sheltered accommodation for older people.

Medicine

The Dain Fund

£28,000

Correspondent: Marian Flint, Administrator, BMA Charities, BMA House, Tavistock Square, London WC1H 9JP (020 7383 6142; fax: 020 7554 6334; email: info.bmacharities@ bma.org.uk; website: bma.org.uk/about-the-bma/who-we-are/charities)

CC Number: 313108

Eligibility
Children of doctors or deceased doctors (not nurses or physiotherapists and so on) in state, private or higher education and whose families have experienced an unexpected change in financial circumstances following crises such as unemployment, family breakdown or serious illness of a parent or guardian. The fund has also undertaken outreach work to support the children of refugee doctors.

Types of grants
Most grants relate to educational expenses such as school uniforms and study trips for children in state schools where the family is on a low income. Grants are sometimes made for short-term interventions in which school fees are paid for a few terms either until the child finishes GCSEs or A-levels or the child is found a place in the state education system. Occasionally grants are made to students in tertiary education.

Annual grant total
In 2013 the fund had assets of almost £1.6 million and an income of £51,000. Grants were made totalling £28,000.

Applications
On a form available from the correspondent.

Other information
This fund is designed to help families in an emergency and is not a scholarship trust.

The Hume Kendall Educational Trust (Hume Kendall Fund)

£0

Correspondent: Keith Jeremiah, Administrator, 30 Whyteleafe Road, Caterham, Surrey CR3 5EF (email: kjeremiah36@hotmail.co.uk)

CC Number: 313208

Eligibility
Children of any doctors or dentists holding a medical qualification. Generally grants are given in cases of great financial difficulty due to some family tragedy, for example death of the parents or their inability to work.

Types of grants
Supplementary grants towards general educational costs incurred by people at any school, college or university, including those pursuing professional or business career. Grants are normally available up to and including the first degree level.

Annual grant total
In 2012/13 the trust had an income of £4,200. No grants were made in the past two years. Note that the charitable expenditure fluctuates and previously has totalled £12,000 as well as £2,000 a year.

Applications
In writing to the correspondent. Applications can be made at any time.

Other information
Grants are sometimes awarded to private and state schools towards various educational projects.

The RCN Foundation
See entry on page 109

The Royal Medical Benevolent Fund

£413,500

Correspondent: The Senior Case Manager, 24 King's Road, Wimbledon, London SW19 8QN (020 8540 9194; email: info@rmbf.org; website: www. rmbf.org)

CC Number: 207275

Eligibility
Assists GMC-registered, UK resident doctors and their recognised dependents who, through illness or disability are in financial hardship, through the provision of grants, loans and advice services.

Types of grants
This fund assists doctors, medical students and their dependents. Help ranges from financial assistance in the form of grants and interest-free loans to a telephone befriending scheme for those who may be isolated and in need of support. Assistance is tailored to the individual's needs. Support includes:
- One-off grants to help with costs such as home adaptations or specialist vehicles for those with disabilities

- Interest free loans or grants to help where eligible applicants are in financial need
- Specialist money and debt management advice to renegotiate debts and secure all eligible state benefits
- Back-to-work support such as paying childcare or retraining costs
- Support for medical students in exceptional financial hardship
- Support for refugee doctors retraining in the UK

For more detailed information on eligibility for financial help check the financial support section of the fund's website or talk to one of the fund's case workers on 020 8540 9194.

Annual grant total
In 2012/13 the fund had assets of £29 million and an income of £1.9 million. According to the statement of financial activities for year ending 31/03/2013 grants were made to individuals totalling £827,000 for educational and welfare purposes. We estimate that £413,500 was awarded in grants to individuals for educational purposes.

Exclusions
The following are excluded:
- Private healthcare and medical insurance/fees
- Private education
- Legal fees
- Inland revenue payments
- Debts to relatives or friends

Applications
For an application pack and further information, email the correspondent at: help@rmbf.org or telephone the case workers' team on: 020 8540 9194. Two references will be required (at least one of which should be from a medical practitioner). All applicants are visited before a report is submitted to the case committee. Income/capital and expenditure are fully investigated, with similar rules applying as for those receiving state benefits. Applications are considered bi-monthly.

Other information
Every year the RMBF helps hundreds of doctors, medical students and their dependents in a variety of ways.

Voluntary visitors liaise between beneficiaries and the office. The fund has an informative website.

The Royal Medical Foundation

£34,000 (9 grants)

Correspondent: Helen Jones, RMF Office, Epsom College, College Road, Epsom, Surrey KT17 4JQ (01372 821010; email: rmf-caseworker@epsomcollege.org.uk; website: www.royalmedicalfoundation.org)

CC Number: 312046

Eligibility
Dependents, aged up to 18, of medical practitioners who are in need.

Types of grants
Grants of between £500 and £15,000 are given to schoolchildren and college students towards fees. Preference is given to pupils with family difficulties so that they have to be educated away from home, pupils with special educational needs and medical students.

Annual grant total
In 2012/13 the foundation gave grants to individuals totalling £98,000, which were broken down as follows:

Short-term or one-off grants for urgent assistance	29	£45,000
Financial assistance with educational expenses	9	£34,000
Regular payments to medical practitioners and their widows/widowers	4	£15,500
Other grants	2	£650

Applications
On a form available from the correspondent, for consideration throughout the year. Applications can be submitted either by the individual or a family member, through a third party such as a social worker or teacher, or through an organisation such as Citizens Advice or a school. The foundation advises applicants to be honest about their needs. All applicants are means tested.

Other information
The Royal Medical Foundation is a charity founded by Dr John Propert in 1855 and administered by Act of Parliament. Its original objects were to provide an asylum for qualified medical practitioners and their spouses and to found a school for their sons.

Today the foundation's aims and objectives are to assist registered doctors and their families who are in financial hardship. Practical assistance is given in three ways:
- Provision of regular payments to their widows, widowers and their children
- Provision of one-off grants when emergency help is required and
- In exceptional circumstances, assistance with school fees for sons or daughters of registered doctors enabling them to maintain educational stability at times of distress caused by illness, bereavement or financial need in their family

The foundation is managed by a board of directors drawn from various professions and is located at Epsom College.

Metal trades
The Institute of Materials, Minerals and Mining (IOM3)

£50,000

Correspondent: Julija Bugajeva, Head of Finance, The Institute of Materials, Minerals and Mining, 1 Carlton House Terrace, London SW1Y 5DB (020 7451 7300; fax: 020 7839 1702; email: directorate@iom3.org; website: www.iom3.org)

CC Number: 269275

Eligibility
People studying minerals, mining and metallurgy disciplines. Preference is given to current and former members of the institution and their dependents. Membership is a requirement for some grants and some awards are restricted to people under the age of 35 (refer to specific awards for more details).

Types of grants
The institute offers support through one-off and recurrent grants, bursaries, scholarships and various awards. Travel grants are available to members (usually up to the age of 35) to travel long distances to conferences (usually abroad), preferably to present papers. Scholarships and bursaries are awarded in the range of £500 to £14,400.

Annual grant total
At the time of writing (August 2014) the latest financial information available was from 2012. In 2012 the institute had assets of £8.8 million, an income of £6.1 million and spent £2.7 million in direct charitable activities. Grants, scholarships, awards and prizes totalled £50,000.

Applications
Applications can be made online on the institute's website. Separate forms can also be downloaded or requested from the correspondent. Application forms for travel grants are available online and should be emailed to Alison Willis at: alison.willis@iom3.org.

Note: different grants and awards may have different deadlines, eligibility requirements and correspondents. Candidates are advised to see the institute's website for specific details.

Other information
The institute's website has detailed information on all grants available as well as the assistance available from

other bodies. There is a variety of prizes and awards offered.

The institute also runs the School Affiliate Scheme to provide help, advice and teaching materials to schools and to engage children in the science subjects. A new Armourers and Brasiers Tata Sixth Form Materials Prize will be administered by the institute. The first awards will be made from December 2014.

Mining

Mining Institute of Scotland Trust

£12,500

Correspondent: The Secretary, 14/9 Burnbrae Drive, Edinburgh EH12 8AS
SC Number: SC024974

Eligibility
Members or former members of the Mining Institute of Scotland who are taking a university course with a mining element in it. The trust has a preference for supporting people from Fife in the first instance, and, secondly, those who are of Scottish origin, although other people can be considered. Applicants who are not already members of the institute will be invited to join. Members of the Mining Institute of Scotland, and their dependents, can also receive 'hardship grants'.

Types of grants
Educational grants are one-off or recurrent, normally of £1,500 a year. A recent grant was made, for example, towards an engineering course that had a mining element to it. Grants can be for the student's general upkeep, or for course fees, and so on.

Hardship grants are one-off or recurrent of up to £1,000 a year. A recent grant was made, for example, to the son of a member for travel to university.

Annual grant total
The trust has about £25,000 available to give in grants each year for both education and social welfare.

Applications
In writing to the correspondent in the first instance, to request an application form.

Other information
Schools are also supported.

Motor industry

The BMTA Trust Ltd
See entry on page 25

Patent Agents

The Incorporated Benevolent Association of the Chartered Institute of Patent Attorneys

£0

Correspondent: Derek Chandler, Trustee, 95 Chancery Lane, London WC2A 1DT
CC Number: 219666

Eligibility
British members and former members of the institute, and their dependents.

Types of grants
One-off and recurrent grants or loans according to need.

Annual grant total
In 2012/13 the association had assets of £864,000 and an income of £48,500. Grants to individuals totalled £21,000, although no grants were given for educational assistance in this financial year.

Applications
In writing to the correspondent, marked 'Private and Confidential'. Applications can be submitted at any time. Where possible, grants are provided via a third party.

Other information
Grants are also made for welfare purposes.

Police

The Gurney Fund for Police Orphans

£453,000 (126+ grants)

Correspondent: Christine McNicol, Director, 9 Bath Road, Worthing, West Sussex BN11 3NU (01903 237256; website: www.gurneyfund.org)
CC Number: 261319

Eligibility
Children under the age of 18 of deceased or incapacitated police officers from 22 subscribing forces in England and Wales. The list of subscribing forces can be found on the fund's website.

Types of grants
Support is available for long periods of time (up to 20 years). Grants are given for general educational needs, including uniforms, sports kits, school activities, music tuition and instruments, books, equipment, extra-curricular activities and educational travel or school trips. Grants can be both one-off of up to £2,500 or recurrent in the range of £10–£60 per week.

Annual grant total
In 2012/13 the fund had assets of £7.9 million, an income of £488,000 and a total charitable expenditure of £537,000. Weekly allowances and grants to children totalled £453,000.

The fund specifies that 85 grants were awarded for educational trips, books, music lessons, instruments, school uniforms and equipment. Grants totalling £43,000 for fees and £7,900 for books, laptops, stationery and subscriptions, were awarded to 41 students.

During the year there were a total of 187 beneficiaries on the register receiving basic weekly allowances.

Exclusions
Grants are not made to beneficiaries who go on to higher education but the fund may consider assisting with the payment of annual tuition fees and the cost of books and ancillary equipment.

Funding is not normally given for skiing holidays and school fees (here exceptions can be made for children with special educational needs).

Applications
Applications can be made through the force welfare officers, local representatives or the subscribing forces directly. They can be made at any time and are normally considered in February, May, August and November. A copy of the child's birth certificate will have to be provided. Successful candidates will be asked to complete an income and expenditure form and produce receipts if assistance is requested for specific expenditure.

Other information
The fund also awards Christmas gift cheques to all children aged 18 or under and arranges holidays for the beneficiaries. Christmas gifts were awarded totalling £25,000 in 2012/13.

Grants are also made through The Gurney Benevolent Fund.

The National Police Fund

£53,000 (53 grants)

Correspondent: Richard Moule, Administrator, Police Dependants' Trust, 3 Mount Mews, High Street, Hampton, Middlesex TW12 2SH (020 8041 6907; fax: 020 8979 4323; email: office@pdtrust.org; website: www.pdtrust.org)

CC Number: 207608

Eligibility

Children of serving, injured, retired or deceased members of police forces in England, Wales and Scotland who are over the age of 16. The annual household income of the candidate's family should be less than £30,000.

Types of grants

One-off grants generally of up to £1,000. Support is given for general needs (such as, accommodation, learning equipment, books and so on) to students on further/higher education courses (at least one year in duration) or vocational training. Occasionally, albeit rarely, awards may be given to mature students or younger children.

Grants can be renewed only upon further recommendation in favour of renewal by the chief officer.

Annual grant total

At the time of writing (July 2014) the latest financial information available was from 2012. In 2012 the fund had assets of £2.6 million and an income of £119,000. Grants to 53 individuals totalled £53,000.

Exclusions

Grants are not given for A-levels and where support should be obtained from statutory sources.

Applications

Application forms and further information can be requested from the correspondent or obtained from the welfare officer of the police force where the officer is serving or has served. Applications can be made by individuals but must be forwarded by the chief officer. They should be submitted by September. A reference from the student's college or university should be included together with up-to-date weekly expenditure and income of the applicant, details of any benefits received and evidence of academic attainment.

Other information

The fund is administered by the Police Dependants' Trust (registered charity number 251021). Support from this fund can also be given for general welfare needs.

There is also a restricted Mary Holt Fund awarding grants in exceptional cases of distress to widows or orphans of policemen below inspector level at retirement or death. Applications have to be forwarded by the chief constable for approval by the board.

Police Dependants' Trust

£100,000

Correspondent: Chief Executive, 3 Mount Mews, High Street, Hampton, Middlesex TW12 2SH (020 8941 6907; fax: 020 8979 4323; email: office@pdtrust.org; website: www.pdtrust.org)

CC Number: 251021

Eligibility

(i.) Dependents of current police officers or former police officers who have died from injuries received in the execution of duty.

(ii.) Police officers or former police officers incapacitated as a result of injury received in the execution of duty, or their dependents.

Types of grants

One-off grants ranging from £280 to £21,000, averaging about £2,300 each. Grants are available for retraining and to the children of police officers who are at school or university. Under the children's grant scheme funding is given for the purchase of sports and computer equipment, musical instruments and other educational facilities. However, it is important to note that this is primarily a relief-in-need charity, so most of the grants are given for welfare rather than educational purposes.

Annual grant total

In 2012/13 the trust had assets of £24.9 million and an income of over £1 million. Grants to 190 individuals totalled £890,000 and were distributed as follows:

Special purpose grants	£839,000
Children support grants	£51,000

There was no breakdown given of the percentage of educational grants and welfare grants. We have estimated the educational grants to be around £100,000.

Applications

On a form available from the correspondent, to be submitted through one of the force's welfare officers. Applications are generally considered every two months although urgent cases can be addressed between meetings.

Precious metals

Johnson Matthey Public Ltd Company Educational Trust

£70,000

Correspondent: Stephanie Hamilton, Administrator, Johnson Matthey plc, 25 Farringdon Street, London EC4A 4AB (020 7269 8400; email: group.hr@matthey.com)

CC Number: 313576

Eligibility

UK students over the age of 16 who have a parent or grandparent employed by Johnson Matthey or associated with the precious metals industry, and who are studying a scientific or technical subject.

Types of grants

Grants are awarded to college students and undergraduates for fees, books, equipment and maintenance/living expenses. Our research suggests that grants are usually between £400 and £500.

Annual grant total

In 2012/13 the trust had an income of £8,600, which is lower than in previous years, and an expenditure of £74,000. We estimate the annual total of grants to individuals to be around £70,000.

Exclusions

Grants are not normally made to students studying second degrees or mature students.

Applications

In writing to the correspondent. If possible, applications should be submitted by the relevant parent or grandparent on behalf of the individual. Applications are normally invited in October for consideration in December. Advertisements appear in the relevant trade journals.

Other information

The trust was set up in 1967 to commemorate the 150th anniversary of the founding of the company. It is also concerned with promoting research and establishing professorships, lectureships and other teaching posts.

Railway workers

The Railway Benefit Fund

£3,000 (10 grants)

Correspondent: Daniel Jaszczak, Executive Director, Electra Way, Crewe CW1 6HS (email: info@ railwaybenefitfund.org.uk; website: www. railwaybenefitfund.org.uk)

CC Number: 206312

Eligibility
Active and retired members of the British Railways Board, its subsidiaries and related organisations, and their spouses and children.

Types of grants
One-off grants ranging from £100 to £1,500 to schoolchildren, college students, students entering higher education and those with special educational needs towards uniforms, clothing, books and equipment and maintenance/living expenses.

Annual grant total
In 2012 the fund had assets of £3.3 million, an income of £468,000 and made grants totalling £308,000 to individuals for both welfare and education. Ten grants totalling £3,000 were made for education.

These were the latest set of accounts available at the time of writing (July 2014)

Applications
On a form available from the correspondent. Applications can be submitted either directly by the individual or family member, or through a third party such as a social worker, teacher or Citizens Advice. Applicants must be able to provide verification of railway service.

Other information
This is primarily a welfare charity, and educational grants are part of its wider welfare work.

Religious workers

Children of the Clergy Trust

£8,000

Correspondent: The Revd I. Thomson, Trustee, 4 Kierhill Gardens, Westhill, Aberdeenshire AB32 6AX

SC Number: SC001845

Eligibility
Children of deceased ministers of the Church of Scotland.

Types of grants
One-off or recurrent grants according to need. Our research tells us that grants in previous years have ranged from £500 to £1,000 for any educational need.

Annual grant total
In 2013 the trust had an income of £19,300 and a total expenditure of £19,700. Both figures are unusually high compared to those available to view from previous years. We estimate that educational grants to individuals totalled £8,000, with grants also awarded to individuals for social welfare purposes.

Applications
In writing to the correspondent. Applications should be submitted directly by the individual and should include information about the applicant's ministerial parent, general family circumstances and other relevant information.

Other information
The trust is also known as Synod of Grampian Children of the Clergy Trust.

The EAC Educational Trust

£35,000 (28 grants)

Correspondent: Daniel Valentine, Trustee, Sherwood, The Street, Brook, Ashford, Kent TN25 5PG (01580 713055)

CC Number: 292391

Eligibility
Children and young people, normally between the ages of 8 and 16, from single parent families, poor families and, particularly, sons and daughters of Church of England clergymen.

Types of grants
According to our research, grants are almost exclusively given for school fees, including boarding. The trust has a close link with one particular school which specialises in educating the families of clergy but other applications are also accepted, especially for the education of children in choir schools or other establishments with musical or dramatic emphasis. Individual grants almost never exceed one-third of the pupil's annual fees.

Annual grant total
In 2012/13 the trust had assets of £641,000 and an income of £75,000. A total of around £35,000 was awarded in grants to 28 individuals.

Applications
In writing to the correspondent. Applications are normally considered in spring.

Other information
The main objectives of the charity are the relief of poverty and advancement of education for the benefit of the public and particularly amongst the families of clergy of the Church of England, single parent families or other poor families.

The Silcock Trust

£13,000

Correspondent: Alec Hancock, Trustee, 4 Church Street, Old Isleworth, Middlesex TW7 6BH

CC Number: 272587

Eligibility
Mainly children of clergy of the Church of England. Preference may be given to those with learning and/or other difficulties.

Types of grants
Our research indicates that help is available towards the maintenance costs and fees for schoolchildren. Preference will be given to children with serious family difficulties and/or special educational needs. Grants can range from £250 to £2,000.

Annual grant total
The latest financial information available at the time of writing (July 2014) was from 2012. In 2012 the trust had an income of £14,900 and a total expenditure of £13,300. We estimate that the annual total of grants was around £13,000.

Applications
In writing to the correspondent.

Sons and Friends of the Clergy

£757,000

Correspondent: The Rt Revd Graeme Knowles, Administrator, 1 Dean Trench Street, Westminster, London SW1P 3HB (020 7799 3696; fax: 020 7222 3468; email: enquiries@clergycharities.org.uk; website: www.clergycharities.org.uk)

CC Number: 207736

Eligibility

The charity is able to consider grants towards a number of the costs involved with the education of clergy children in both the maintained and the independent sectors. Children for whom grants are sought must be undergoing full-time pre-graduation education and be unmarried and under the age of 25. Visit the charity's website for full details of educational grants, examples, eligibility and exclusions.

Types of grants

Grants may be considered towards school uniforms, travel costs, school trips/language exchanges, music lessons, musical instruments, art/sporting activities, computers (including related software), school fee grants for children attending independent schools, and for children continuing in education after leaving school.

There are specific criteria relating to each category and potential applicants will need to visit the charity's website for a full list of types of grant and their criteria.

Annual grant total

In 2013 the charity had assets of £86 million and an income of £3.7 million. Grants to 1,264 individuals totalled £1.9 million broken down as follows:

General welfare	£532,500
Holidays	£356,500
Resettlement and house expenses	£224,000
University maintenance	£292,500
Education expenses	£194,000
School fees	£146,000
School clothing	£87,000
Christmas	£76,000
Debt	£53,000
Ordinand book grants	£48,000
Bereavement	£19,500

This breakdown includes £40,000 which went to organisations.

Educational grants totalled £757,000 with social welfare grants of £1.2 million being awarded.

Exclusions

For full details of exclusions see the charity's website. Generally, grants are not awarded retrospectively and are based on one year's costs for any particular category. Grants towards school fees are not normally available for those serving outside Great Britain and Ireland. Grants toward the cost of further education courses for the clergy (save for courses on financial management) are not normally considered. No help is given towards school fees for children under the age of 11, unless they are choristers. Grants for clergy children who are continuing in education after leaving school can only be considered for those under the age of 25.

Applications

Before any grants are made, the corporation's educational advisor will usually contact the parents to discuss the application and needs of the child. Visit the charity's website for full details of educational grants under each programme.

Other information

The information in this entry is taken from the charity's website:

> The charity now known as the Corporation of the Sons of the Clergy was founded in 1655 by a group of merchants in the City of London and clergymen who were all sons of the cloth. During the Commonwealth, persecution of clergy who had remained loyal to the Crown was widespread and many who had been deprived of their livings by Cromwell were destitute. The charity's foundation dates from a recognition by a body of sons of clergymen that action was required to meet a pressing need among clergy families for charitable help. The charity's present name is often felt to be a misleading one, but it is in fact an accurate description of its founding fathers.

The trustees' annual report for 2013 states: 'January 2013 saw the beginning of the new charity – the Sons and Friends of the Clergy. This entity came as the culmination of many years of negotiation between the Friends of the Clergy Corporation and the Corporation of the Sons of the Clergy.'

> The landscape of our work is constantly changing as new demands and expectations are placed upon the clergy and their dependents. The bringing together of the two charities, along with the continued generosity of those who support our work, has ensured that we have the capacity to adapt to this changing context. The end of 2013 saw the beginning of our grappling not only with the changing circumstances affecting our beneficiaries but also with a fresh exploration of the most productive and generous ways in which we might help them. This has involved us, staff and trustees alike, in examining once again the definition of poverty as it affects those we wish to help. How this will develop is our work for the coming year, but we note that 2013 saw a steady rise in both the number of cases we considered and also in the total amount of grants awarded. So we continue to explore ways in which we may respond to the challenge for clergy and their dependents in the financial complexities of our age.

The Wells Clerical Charity

£3,500

Correspondent: The Ven. Nicola Sullivan, Trustee, 6 The Liberty, Wells, Somerset BA5 2SU (01749 670777; email: general@bathwells.anglican.org)

CC Number: 248436

Eligibility

People in need under 25 years old who are children of the clergy of the Church of England serving (or who have retired or died and last served) in the former archdeaconry of Wells as constituted in 1738.

Types of grants

Grants are made to support eligible individuals in preparing for entering any profession or employment by paying travel fees, the costs of clothing/uniform or maintenance costs.

Annual grant total

In 2012 the charity had an income of £8,700 and a total expenditure of £7,300. We estimate that grants to individuals for educational purposes totalled around £3,500. These were the latest accounts available at the time of writing (July 2014).

Applications

In writing to the correspondent.

Women's Continuing Ministerial Education Trust

£50,000

Correspondent: Tim Ling, Administrator, Ministry Division, Church House, Great Smith Street, London SW1P 3AZ (020 7898 1408; email: tim.ling@churchofengland.org; website: www.cofe.anglican.org)

Eligibility

Women (ordained or not) who are licensed into a nationally recognised ministry in the Church of England or the Scottish Episcopal Church (with the exception of Readers). Religious sisters and retired clergy who are involved in active ministry can also apply.

Types of grants

Grants are given for continuing ministerial education. Support is given towards general educational needs, conferences, educational fees (where possible, any costs of fees will be awarded). Grants are intended to supplement funds available from the applicant's diocese.

Accommodation, travel costs or childcare is not normally covered, but anticipated costs of those needs should be included in the budget in order to allow better assessment of the application.

Due to limited funds the trust focuses on applications for courses/projects that clearly relate to assisting the minister in their work and professional development.

Annual grant total

Generally about £50,000 is given a year.

Exclusions

The trust does not normally fund courses in IME 4–7 and retreats/sabbaticals.

Applications

Application forms can be accessed from the Church of England website. Applications must be endorsed by the Diocesan CME Officer or Dean of the Women's Ministry. Grants are considered quarterly, in February, May, July and October and the deadline for applications is in the preceding month. Candidates are informed about the outcome of their application in the following month.

Sales representatives

The Royal Pinner School Foundation

£413,000 (163 grants)

Correspondent: David Crawford, Company Secretary, 110 Old Brompton Road, South Kensington, London SW7 3RB (020 7373 6168; email: admin@royalpinner.co.uk; website: www.royalpinner.co.uk)

CC Number: 1128414

Eligibility

Children of commercial travellers, travelling sales and technical representatives and manufacturer's agents, where the family has experienced adversity or hardship. Preference is given to individuals under the age of 25 and orphans.

Types of grants

One-off or recurrent grants are available to individuals at any state, private day or boarding school, college or university.

Support is given towards general educational needs, maintenance costs, clothing, equipment, books, travel expenses in the UK and overseas, undertaking activities in arts and music, also assistance to people starting career/entering a profession, trade or calling.

Awards increase with the level of education, starting at around £450 in primary school up to £900 in the sixth form. Contributions can be made towards independent school fees (grants ranging from £200 to £3,700 per term). Student grants reach up to £6,600 per term (higher amounts may be awarded depending on the circumstances).

Annual grant total

In 2012/13 the foundation had assets of £5.1 million and an income of £188,000. A total of £413,000 was awarded in grants to 163 individuals, broken down as follows:

Children at day and boarding schools	97	£231,000
Students at universities and colleges of higher and further education	60	£118,000
Travel, the arts, outfitting grants and special educational needs	54	£64,000

Exclusions

The foundation does not normally provide loans or support part-time education.

Applications

In writing to the correspondent. The grants committee meets around five times a year.

Other information

Note that no applications can be considered except those applying for the sons and daughters of travelling sales representatives or manufacturer's agents.

Science

Royal Society of Chemistry Benevolent Fund

£193,000

Correspondent: Nicola Cranfield, Administrator, Thomas Graham House, Science Park, Milton Road, Cambridge CB4 0WF (01223432484; website: www.rsc.org)

CC Number: 207890

Eligibility

People who have been members of the society for the last three years, or ex-members who were in the society for at least ten years, and their dependents, who are in need.

Types of grants

This fund is essentially a relief-in-need charity which also makes grants for education. It offers regular allowances, one-off grants and loans towards needs such as school uniforms and educational trips.

Annual grant total

In 2012 the society had assets of £92 million, an income of £49 million and gave grants totalling £385,000 for both educational and welfare purposes.

These were the latest set of accounts available at the time of writing (August 2014).

Exclusions

Anything which should be provided by the government or local authority is ineligible for funding.

Applications

In writing or by telephone in the first instance, to the correspondent. Applicants will be requested to provide a financial statement (forms supplied by the secretary) and include a covering letter describing their application as fully as possible.

Other information

The society also provides advice and guidance services.

Seafarers

Royal Liverpool Seamen's Orphan Institution

£151,000 (101 grants)

Correspondent: Linda Gidman, Administrator, 2nd Floor, Tower Building, 22 Water Street, Liverpool L2 1BA (01512 273417; email: enquiries@rlsoi-uk.org; website: www.rlsoi-uk.org)

CC Number: 526379

Eligibility

Children of deceased British merchant seafarers, who are of pre-school age or in full-time education (including further education). Help can also be given to seafarers who are at home caring for their family alone.

Types of grants

Monthly maintenance and annual clothing grants. Help may also be given for school fees.

Annual grant total

In 2013 the charity had assets of £3 million and an income of £279,000. Grants to individuals totalled £303,000 and is given for both welfare and educational purposes. 101 grants were made to individuals in total.

Applications

On a form available from the correspondent, to be considered at any time.

Other information

It was not possible to obtain a grant total for direct education purposes. However, all grants are given to children and young people who are in attendance at school and further or higher education institutions.

The Royal Liverpool Seamen's Orphan Institution's most recent accounts from 2013 stated the following:

> In 2013 the charity came to an arrangement with the Royal Merchant Navy Education Foundation whereby they would in future take over the support of beneficiaries in further education. This has resulted in transferring 20 beneficiaries over to the Royal Merchant Navy Education Foundation leaving a total of 81 beneficiaries for the Royal Liverpool Seamen's Orphan Institution to support as of 31 December 2013.

The Royal Merchant Navy School Foundation

£137,000 (36 grants)

Correspondent: Commander Charles Heron-Watson, Secretary, Mole Lodge, Mole Road, Sindlesham, Wokingham, Berkshire RG41 5DB (01189 977701; email: office@rmnef.orh.uk; website: www.rmnef.org.uk)

CC Number: 309047

Eligibility

Children in need at any stage of education who have a parent who has served or is serving as a seaman of any grade in the British Merchant Navy. This parent must either have died whilst on duty, or have left the sea because of illness (in which case the child must have been born before the parent left the sea), or be unable to provide fully for the education, maintenance and upbringing of the child.

Types of grants

One–off and recurrent grants are made towards school and university fees, educational extras, school uniforms, some travel to and from the school, equipment and instruments, educational outings, books; some university expenses. Career and personal development endeavours such as Outward Bound-type courses, apprenticeships, career training or pre-school level education are also supported. Grants are tailored to meet

the needs of each individual and are usually paid directly to institutions.

The foundation understands that 'if the need for fee-paying education is established, the families will usually be unable to meet a large percentage of the costs', therefore the foundation 'makes quite large awards in order to meet the needs of individuals.' Families will be expected to make contributions towards the expenses within their means.

Annual grant total

In 2012/13 the foundation had assets of £10 and an income of £299,000 (prior to the transfer the assets and liabilities totalled £11.1 million with £17,500 being in a restricted fund). It had 36 beneficiaries at a secondary education level or beyond and made grants totalling £137,000.

Applications

Initial contact should be made with the correspondent via letter or email. Phone enquiries to discuss individual circumstances are also welcomed. Application forms will then be provided to eligible applicants. Candidates will be paid a home visit and may be required to provide an assessment by a relevant professional. Information about the parent/s' employment and financial situation will also be required.

Other information

In 2013 the assets and liabilities of the foundation were transferred to the Royal Merchant Navy Education Foundation (registered charity number 1153323), a charitable incorporated organisation.

The foundation also assists beneficiaries over the age of 18 who have previously been supported by the Royal Liverpool Seamen's Orphan Institution.

Sailors' Children's Society

£35,000

Correspondent: Deanne Thomas, Chief Officer, Francis Reckitt House, Newland, Cottingham Road, Hull HU6 7RJ (01482 342331; fax: 01482 447868; email: info@sailorschildren.org.uk; website: www.sailorschildren.org.uk)

CC Number: 224505

Eligibility

Seafarers children who are in full-time education and where the families are in severe financial difficulties. Support may be given to two parent families where one of the parents is too ill or disabled to work and the other acts as the carer. Usually, the only source of income for the family is income support or incapacity benefit.

Types of grants

(i) School clothing grants payable per child twice a year, in January and August, to help children to start off the new school year and to buy a new winter coat. (ii) Educational holiday grants.

Annual grant total

In 2012/13 the society had assets of £1.9 million, an income of £570,000 and gave grants totalling £321,000 broken down as follows:

Child welfare grants	£198,000
Clothing grants	£74,000
Special grants	£35,000
Holiday travel grants	£14,000

Applications

On a form available from the correspondent, with details about children, income and expenditure, including copies of relevant certificates, for example, birth certificates and proof of seafaring service. Applications can be submitted directly by the individual or through a social worker, Citizens Advice, other welfare agency, or through seafaring organisations. Applications are considered every other month, beginning in February.

Other information

Previously known as Sailors' Families' Society. The society has an informative website.

Service/ex-service

ABF The Soldiers' Charity (also known as The Army Benevolent Fund)

£1 million

Correspondent: The Director of Grants and Welfare, Mountbarrow House, 6–20 Elizabeth Street, London SW1W 9RB (0845 241 4833; email: info@soldierscharity.org; website: www.soldierscharity.org)

CC Number: 211645

Eligibility

Members and ex-members of the British Regular Army and the Reserve Army (TA) and their dependents who are in need. Serving TA soldiers must have completed at least one year's satisfactory service, and former TA soldiers should have completed at least three years' satisfactory service.

Types of grants

Mature student education/training grants for ex-soldiers who are unemployed and receiving training or education to enhance their prospects of gaining long-term employment. Such assistance is also available to soldiers who became disabled while with the army or after service and need to change their vocation.

Bursaries are also available in exceptional circumstances for the private education of dependents. Preference is given to orphans or children with only one parent, especially if the parent was killed in service. Other priorities include those where a parent is severely disabled or where the child has special needs, which may include where the home environment is such that the child has to be educated away from home.

Annual grant total
In 2012/13 the fund had assets of £45 million, an income of £12.9 million and a total expenditure of £14.7 million. Grants to individuals totalled over £5.2 million the majority of which was made in welfare grants. We have estimated that £1.09 million was given in educational awards comprising £711,000 in Individual Recovery Plan grants for retraining and £379,000 for bespoke employment advice. This leaves £4.4 million awarded for welfare purposes. Grants to organisations totalled £2.8 million.

Applications
The fund does not deal directly with individual cases. Soldiers who are still serving should contact their regimental or corps association, who will then approach the fund on their behalf. Former soldiers should first contact SSAFA or the Royal British Legion. Applications are considered at any time, but all are reviewed annually in July.

Enquiries may be made directly to the fund to determine the appropriate corps or regimental association.

Other information
The charity also gives grants to individuals for relief-in-need purposes and to organisations.

Greenwich Hospital

Correspondent: Charity Administrator, Greenwich Hospital, 1 Farrington Street, London EC4M 7LG (020 7396 0150; email: enquiries@grenhosp.org.uk; website: www.grenhosp.org.uk)

Eligibility
Children and grandchildren of serving or retired officers and ratings of the Royal Navy, Royal Marines and UK Merchant Navy or children and grandchildren of other seafaring professions. A minimum of three years qualifying seafaring service is normally required. Applicants'

academic performance and financial need will be taken into account.

Types of grants
The charity provides bursaries to attend the Royal Hospital School. The awards are only available upon entry and will not be made retrospectively.

Some discounts can also be offered to eligible seafarers who are successful in the January entrance examination and at the interview.

Annual grant total
Our research indicates that generally around £4,000 is awarded in bursaries.

Applications
Initial application forms can be found on the charity's website or can be requested from the admissions officer. Applications should be submitted before the closing date in December and not before 5 April in the year preceding entry to the school. Awards are usually awarded by January.

Further details are available on the charity's website.

Other information
The trust also provides:
- University of Greenwich Undergraduate Awards – three annual bursaries of up to £3,000 for a maximum of four years available to former members of the Royal Navy or Royal Marines or the children of current or former members of the Royal Navy or Royal Marines
- University of Greenwich Postgraduate Awards – one bursary of £3,000 for a retired member of the Royal Navy or the Royal Marines for a Master's degree in MA International Maritime Policy, MA by Research: Maritime Studies, MA International Maritime Policy or MPhil programmes
- Bursaries to study at the Trinity Laban Conservatoire of Music and Dance – to the children of current or former members of the Royal Navy or Royal Marines for a maximum of three years

Help for Heroes

£900,000 (6810 grants)

Correspondent: Grants Team, Administrator, 14 Parker's Close, Downton Business Park, Downton, Salisbury, Wiltshire SP5 3RB (01980 844354; email: grants@helpforheroes.org. uk; website: www.helpforheroes.org.uk)

CC Number: 1120920, SC044984

Eligibility
Current and former members of the armed forces who have been wounded or injured while serving, and their dependants.

Types of grants
Grants towards equipment, facilities or services to assist the individual's rehabilitation. Individuals are supported through Quick Reaction Fund (QRF) and Individual Recovery Plan (IPR). Assistance can be given towards academic and (re)training courses, vocational or employment opportunities and associated needs, such as educational necessities or specialist equipment. QRF support is aimed to be provided within 72 hours in urgent cases.

Support towards specialist sports equipment can be also given from the Battle Back fund.

Annual grant total
In 2012/13 the charity had assets of £107.8 million and an income of £29.4 million. During the year a total of 6,810 individuals were supported in the following categories:

IPR	£900,000
QRF	£500,000
Battle Back	£400,000

We estimate that around £900,000 was awarded for educational or training needs.

Applications
Candidates are encouraged to contact the correspondent to discuss their needs and application procedure.

Other information
The charity works with the armed forces and other military charities. Funding is also given to individuals for general welfare needs and organisations working for the benefit of members of the armed forces.

Individuals and their families or carers are also welcomed to visit one of the 'support hubs' to receive further advice and support on a range of welfare issues. For more details and contact information of the recovery centres see the Help for Heroes website.

Lloyd's Patriotic Fund

£7,500 (7 grants)

Correspondent: Suzanna Nagle, Secretary, Lloyd's Patriotic Fund, Lloyd's, One Lime Street, London EC3M 7HA (020 7327 6144; fax: 020 7327 5229; email: communityaffairs@ lloyds.com; website: www.lloyds.com)

CC Number: 210173

Eligibility
Children of officers and ex-officers of the Royal Navy, the Army, Royal Marines and Royal Air Force. Preference may be given to schoolchildren with serious family difficulties where the child has to

be educated away from home and to people with special educational needs.

Types of grants

Bursaries ranging from around £800 to £1,500 per year are given for school fees.

Annual grant total

In 2012/13 the fund had assets of £1.7 million and an income of £1.3 million. During the year educational grants totalled £7,500 distributed in seven annual bursaries. Educational grants amount to a small proportion of the charitable activities.

Note that in this year the fund received a major donation from the Council of Lloyd's. Normally the income varies and in the past few years has ranged from £83,000 to £477,000.

Applications

Grants are awarded through The Royal Navy and Royal Marines Children's Fund and The Royal Naval Scholarship Fund. All applications should be made through these organisations.

Other information

Grants are also made for welfare purposes and to organisations.

Royal Air Force Benevolent Fund

£120,000

Correspondent: Michael Neville, Administrator, 67 Portland Place, London W1B 1AR (0800 169 2942; email: info@rafbf.org.uk; website: www.rafbf.org)

CC Number: 1081009

Eligibility

The children (aged 8 to 18) of officers and airmen who have died or were severely disabled while serving in the Royal Air Force. Additionally, help may be considered in those circumstances where the parent dies or becomes severely disabled after leaving the Royal Air Force. Students studying for a first degree or equivalent qualification.

Types of grants

Grants to enable the education plans commenced or envisaged by the child's parents to be fulfilled. Children with special needs are given grants to help with schooling fees, equipment and care costs. Children in good health but where parents are in a difficult financial situation can receive grants for such things as the cost of school uniforms.

Annual grant total

In 2012 the charity had assets of £125 million, an income of £21 million and gave grants for education totalling £120,000.

These accounts were the latest available at the time of writing (July 2014).

Exclusions

No grants for private medical costs or for legal fees.

Applications

On a form available directly from the correspondent or on their website via an online application form. Applications can be submitted by the individual or through an ex-service welfare agency such as RAFA or SSAFA. The fund runs a free helpline which potential applicants are welcome to call for advice and support on the application process. Applications are considered on a continual basis.

Other information

The charity provides advice and assistance on a range of issues including benefits, debt advice and relationships. The fund maintains a short-term care home in Sussex and a further three homes in Northumberland, Avon and Lancashire which are operated jointly with the RAFA. They may also be able to help with purchasing a house and they have two holiday homes available at reduced rates for beneficiaries.

Royal Artillery Charitable Fund

£50,000

Correspondent: Lieutenant Colonel I. A. Vere Nicoll, Secretary, Artillery House, Royal Artillery Barracks, Larkhill, Salisbury, Wiltshire SP4 8QT (01980 845233, 01980 845698; fax: 01980 634020; email: rarhq-racf-welfare-sec@mod.uk; website: www.theraa.co.uk)

CC Number: 210202

Eligibility

Current or former members of the Royal Artillery and their dependents who are in need.

Types of grants

This is mainly a relief-in-need charity, which as part of its welfare work supports the children of its members who have started private education before the family's 'breadwinner' became unable to earn – and therefore unable to help them continue their education. It also awards grants for specialist clothing and fees for mature students and people starting work.

Annual grant total

At the time of writing (July 2014) the latest financial information available was from 2012. In 2012 the fund had assets of £14.2 million and an income of £1.1 million. Individual grants totalled £799,000 distributed to 1,772 people.

Educational grants were not specified in the accounts. Most of the support is given for general welfare needs, therefore we estimate the total of educational grants to be around £50,000.

Exclusions

Grants are not normally given towards loans, credit card debts or telephone bills.

Applications

Applications should be made through SSAFA (details of local branches can be found in telephone directories or from Citizens Advice) or other organisations, such as the Royal British Legion or Earl Haig Fund in Scotland (see separate entry), Officers Association, Royal Artillery Association or other regimental charities. Applications can be considered at any time.

Other information

Grants are mostly given for relief-in-need purposes and are also awarded to organisations (£217,000 in 2012).

The fund is the sole corporate trustee of the Royal Artillery Charitable Fund (permanent endowment), the Royal Artillery Benevolent Fund, the Royal Artillery Association and the Kelly Holdsworth Artillery Trust.

Royal British Legion Women's Section President's Award Scheme

£28,000

Correspondent: Welfare Team, The Royal British Legion, 199 Borough High Street, London SE1 1AA (020 3207 2183; email: wswelfare@britishlegion.org.uk; website: www.rblws.org.uk/how-we-help/president-s-award-scheme)

CC Number: 219276

Eligibility

Serving or ex-service personnel, their spouses and dependents who are in need. This includes widows and divorced spouses/partners who have not re-married and are not in another cohabiting relationship.

Dependent children applying for scholarships must be under the age of 21.

Types of grants

The scheme offers:

- Educational scholarships – awards of £1,500 per year (or for a term) for a first degree course towards fees, books, travel costs, living/maintenance expenses and other course related needs

▶ Educational grants – of up to £500 towards educational courses or retraining (people training for a new career can receive small grants towards course costs, books and travel expenses)

Annual grant total

In 2012/13 Royal British Legion Women's Section had assets of £5.3 million, an income of £1 million and expenditure of £1.1 million. During the year over £28,000 has been awarded in scholarships and grants.

Exclusions

Scholarships are not given for postgraduate studies.

Applications

Initial enquiries should be made to the correspondent by telephone or in writing. Applicants will be visited by a welfare team officer who will submit an application form and financial statements. Grants are considered on a regular basis. The correspondent has informed us that all applications are put to a committee for approval and it is they who decide on the amount to be awarded.

Other information

Grants are made through the Women's Section which is an autonomous organisation within the Royal British Legion, concentrating on the needs of widows and ex-servicewomen and dependent children of ex-service personnel. It works in close association with the Legion but has its own funds and its own local welfare visitors.

This scheme also helps with the costs of a welfare break. The Royal British Legion and the Women's section have many grants available for welfare purposes and the charity's website also notes that where they are unable to assist the welfare team will signpost the applicants to other agencies who may help.

The Royal Caledonian Education Trust

See entry on page 135

Royal Naval Benevolent Trust

£16,000

Correspondent: The Grants Administrator, Castaway House, 311 Twyford Avenue, Portsmouth PO2 8RN (02392 690112; fax: 02392 660852; email: rnbt@rnbt.org.uk; website: www.rnbt.org.uk)

CC Number: 206243

Eligibility

Serving and ex-serving men and women of the Royal Navy and Royal Marines (not officers) and their dependents.

Types of grants

Educational grants are available to schoolchildren and people wishing to change their careers. This is a welfare charity which makes these educational grants as part of its wider work.

Annual grant total

In 2012/13 the trust had assets of almost £34 million and an income of £5.3 million. Grants amounted to over £1.5 million, with an additional £1 million given in 'regular charitable payments'. Grants made to individuals for educational purposes have previously totalled around £16,000.

Applications

On a form available from the correspondent, to be submitted through a social worker, welfare agency, SSAFA, Royal British Legion or any Royal Naval Association branch. Applications are considered twice a week.

Other information

The trust has an informative website which states:

> Every year we make grants to individuals to about 3,000 applicants. The grants vary in amount from under £100 up to several thousand pounds with the average being about £550. The total each year is more than £1.6 million.

The Royal Naval Reserve (V) Benevolent Fund

£3,500

Correspondent: Valerie Stamper, Administrator, MP 3.4, NCHQ, Leach Building, Whale Island PO2 8BY (02392 623570)

CC Number: 266380

Eligibility

The children of members or former members of the Royal Naval Volunteer Reserve, Women's Royal Naval Volunteer Reserve, Royal Naval Reserve and the Women's Royal Naval Reserve who are serving or who have served as non-commissioned rates.

Types of grants

One-off grants mainly for schoolchildren who, because of the poverty of their families, need help with clothes, books, equipment or necessary educational visits, and, secondly, for eligible children with aptitudes or disabilities which need special provision. Grants are normally limited to a maximum of £200 for any applicant.

Annual grant total

In 2012/13 the fund had an income of £5,000 and a total expenditure of £8,000. We estimate around £3,500 was made in grants to individuals for education. The 2012 accounts are the latest available at the time of writing.

Applications

In writing to the correspondent.

Other information

The fund also makes grants to individuals for social welfare purposes.

The Royal Navy and Royal Marines Children's Fund

£361,000

Correspondent: Monique Bateman, Director, Castaway House, 311 Twyford Avenue, Stamshaw, Portsmouth PO2 8RN (02392 639534; fax: 02392 677574; email: rnchildren@btconnect.com; website: www.rnrmchildren'sfund.org)

CC Number: 1075015

Eligibility

Young people under 25 who are in need and are the dependent of somebody who has served, or is serving, in the Royal Navy, Royal Marines, the Queen Alexandra's Royal Naval Nursing Service or the former Women's Royal Naval Service.

Types of grants

One-off and recurrent grants are made to schoolchildren, college students, undergraduates and vocational students where there is a special need. Grants given include those towards schools fees, uniforms, clothing, books, equipment, instruments, maintenance, living expenses and childcare.

Annual grant total

In 2012/13 the fund had assets of £9.1 million and an income of £1.27 million. The sum of £732,000 was given in grants to individuals or families for educational and welfare purposes. The average grant per child in this accounting year was £670.

Applications

On a form available from the correspondent or to download from the fund's website. Applications can be submitted directly by the individual or through the individual's school/college, an educational welfare agency, SSAFA or other appropriate third party. They are considered on a monthly basis, though urgent cases can be dealt with between meetings.

The WRNS Benevolent Trust

£3,300

Correspondent: Sarah Ayton, General Secretary, Castaway House, 311 Twyford Avenue, Portsmouth, Hampshire PO2 8RN (02392 655301; fax: 02392 679040; email: grantsadmin@wrnsbt.org.uk; website: www.wrnsbt.org.uk)

CC Number: 206529

Eligibility

Ex-Wrens and female serving members of the Royal Navy (officers and ratings) who joined the service between 3 September 1939 and 1 November 1993 who are in need.

Types of grants

This trust is essentially a relief-in-need charity which offers grants for educational purposes. These are usually given to schoolchildren for uniforms and other clothing and to students in further or higher education, including mature students, towards books, equipment, instruments, computers, fees and maintenance.

Annual grant total

In 2013 the trust had assets of £4 million and an income of £509,000. Educational grants totalled £3,300. Total grants were £305,000.

Exclusions

People who deserted from the service are not eligible.

Applications

Applications can be made direct to the correspondent, or through SSAFA either by the individual, or a friend or relation.

Other information

The following information is taken from the charity's informative and helpful website:

The charity was established in 1942 to help in cases of hardship among the thousands of women who served in the Women's Royal Naval Service. A member is anyone who served in the Women's Royal Naval Service and transferred to the Royal Navy before 1 November 1993, or anyone who has served in the WRNS since 3 September 1939. This amounts to 143,000 women and there are currently 50,000 members.

The trust assists approximately 350 former Wrens and their families each year and in 2013 spent over £300,000 on annual and one-off grants. Over the last seven decades it has helped more than 12,000 women.

All trustees are former Wrens including our current Service and Royal Navy and Royal Marines representatives.

Grants are mostly made in the form of pensions, or for relief in need.

Social work

The Social Workers' Educational Trust

£9,000

Correspondent: The Hon. Secretary, Social Workers' Educational Trust, 16 Kent Street, Birmingham B5 6RD (email: swet@basw.co.uk; website: www.basw.co.uk/financial-support/social-workers-educational-trust)

CC Number: 313789

Eligibility

Qualified social workers, with at least two years of post-qualifying experience, who work or are looking for work in the UK, and are undertaking post-qualifying training to improve their knowledge and skills for social work practice. BASW membership will be taken into account.

Types of grants

One-off and recurrent grants up to £500 for fees, travel costs, childcare and books. Grants for courses of more than one year are made on an annual basis and are dependent on the recipient's successful completion of the year's training and the trust's level of funds. Part-funding of fees or expenses may also be considered should the additional funding be available from another source.

The trust's webpage states that it is usually able to make around 50 grants each year.

Annual grant total

In 2012/13 the trust had an income of £18,700 and a total expenditure of £9,300. We estimate that grants totalled £9,000.

Exclusions

The trust cannot assist those undertaking initial social work training or qualifications. Successful applicants may not reapply within three years of the completion of a supported training course or project.

Applications

On a form available from the correspondent or to download from the trust's website along with guidelines. Applications can be submitted at any time and are normally considered in February, June, September and November.

Other information

The trust also manages funds bequeathed or subscribed in memory of colleagues. 'These funds provide more substantial scholarships which are awarded annually through competition.' Enquiries for these larger annual scholarships should be made to the Hon. Secretary.

Solicitors

The Solicitors' Benevolent Association Ltd

£218,000

Correspondent: John Platt, Administrator, 1 Jaggard Way, London SW12 8SG (020 8675 6440; email: sec@sba.org.uk; website: www.sba.org.uk)

CC Number: 1124512

Eligibility

Solicitors who are or have been on the Roll for England and Wales and have practised, and their dependents, who are in need.

Types of grants

One-off and recurrent grants and interest-free loans where applicable, towards university and other educational costs.

Annual grant total

In 2012 the charity had assets of £16.7 million and an income of £1.9 million. During the year grants and loans were made to 349 individuals. Grants totalled £1 million and loans advanced totalled £612,000, with educational grants totalling £218,000.

These were the latest set of accounts available at the time of writing (August 2014).

Exclusions

Solicitors who have been considered to have brought the profession into disrepute are not eligible.

Applications

On a form available from the charity's website.

Sport

Professional Footballers' Association Educational Fund

£1.2 million

Correspondent: Darren Wilson, Trustee, 20 Oxford Court, Bishopsgate, Manchester M2 3WQ (01612 360575; email: info@thepfa.co.uk; website: www.thepfa.com/education/funding)

CC Number: 306087

Eligibility

Current and former members of the Professional Footballers' Association who wish to retrain in order to continue employment once their football careers have ceased. The fund notes that members who have only ever played at a non-league level are unlikely to receive a grant.

Types of grants

Grants can be given towards a wide variety of educational courses and vocational training, including tuition, exam, registration fees or books. Awards are of up to £1,500 a year, covering up to 50% of the study costs. The funding is capped at £5,000 for each member and a maximum 'lifetime' grant towards book costs is £300.

Annual grant total

In 2012/13 the fund had assets of £20.7 million, an income of £16.8 million and a total charitable expenditure of £15.1 million. Educational and vocational grants totalled £1.2 million.

Exclusions

The fund is unable to provide money for:

- Postgraduate/master's degrees
- Purchase of computers
- Travel and parking expenses
- Accommodation
- Membership fees
- Kits and uniforms
- Tools and equipment
- Postage fees

Applications

Application forms can be obtained from the fund's website or requested from the correspondent. Applications for undergraduate grants should be made at the end of the academic year and for open learning courses at the end of the module. Note that the fund is unable to make 'up-front payments' and grants are only paid upon receiving proof of completion of the course and receipts for the books purchased. Applicants should have paid for the course or training in full themselves before receiving the grant.

Be aware that grants can only be claimed within a year of the delivery and retrospective claims will not be considered.

Other information

The fund also gives grants to organisations to advance the public knowledge of the history and social significance of football, to promote good community and race relations at football events and towards medical initiatives that promote the health of beneficiaries.

Note: members taking out student loans to pay for tuition fees will not receive a grant unless one third (or the maximum of £1,000) is paid back to the Student Loan Company and a confirmation receipt is provided. Individuals receiving a full scholarship covering their tuition fees whilst studying in America, will not be eligible to apply for funding from the fund. A grant will be available in the case of candidates having to make a contribution towards their tuition fees, subject to providing appropriate detailed receipts.

The Rugby Football League Benevolent Fund

£9,100

Correspondent: Steve Ball, Administrator, Red Hall, Red Hall Lane, Leeds, West Yorkshire LS17 8NB (0844 477 7113; email: rfl@rfl.uk.com; website: www.rfl.uk.com)

CC Number: 1109858

Eligibility

People who play or assist, or who have played or assisted, in the game of Rugby League in the UK or for a team affiliated to an association primarily based in the UK and their dependents. Beneficiaries should be in hardship or distress, in particular, as a result of injury through playing or training, or when travelling to or from a game or training session.

Types of grants

Grants are given towards educational courses.

Annual grant total

In 2012 the fund had assets of £453,000 and an income of £221,000. Grants to 89 beneficiaries totalled £87,000. Grants were made to individuals for education totalling £9,100; and to individuals for social welfare purposes totalling £78,000.

The 2012 accounts are the latest available at the time of writing.

Applications

In writing to the correspondent.

Other information

Grants are also made for welfare purposes, including those towards special vehicles and repairs, home improvements, furniture, wheelchairs, gym equipment, computers, hotel accommodation, travel, physiotherapy, home appliances and Christmas presents.

Stationers

The GPM Charitable Trust

£5,000

Correspondent: Keith Keys, Administrator, 43 Spriggs Close, Clapham, Bedford MK41 6GD (07733 262991; email: gpmcharitabletrust@tiscali.co.uk; website: www.gpmtrust.org)

CC Number: 227177

Eligibility

Workers, former workers and their dependents in the printing, graphical, papermaking and media industries.

Types of grants

Grants for retraining, skills enhancement, educational requirement especially following redundancy or other reduction in income.

Annual grant total

In 2012/13 the trust had an income of £8,100 and an expenditure of £23,000. We estimate that the trust gave grants to individuals for educational purposes to the value of £5,000. Further grants were afforded to organisations.

The trust also worked with the Bookbinders Charitable Society on a refurbishment project for sheltered accommodation.

Applications

On a form available to download from the trust's website, or from the correspondent, to be returned by email or post.

Other information

Formed in 2001, the trust brought together the former Lloyd Memorial and NATSOPA (National Society of Operative Printers and Assistants) trusts. The Sheridan Trust, a Manchester-based printing charity, joined in 2010.

The Stationers' Foundation

£90,000 (Around 20 grants)

Correspondent: Pamela Butler, Administrator, Worshipful Company of Stationers and Newspaper Makers, Stationers Hall, Stationers Hall Court, Ave Maria Lane EC4M 7DD (020 7246 0990; email: foundation@stationers.org; website: www.stationers.org)

CC Number: 1120963

Eligibility

UK residents under the age of 25 who are in need and studying stationer's trade, printing, papermaking, publishing and distribution, journalism, librarianship, typography, book and graphic design, photography, conservation of books and manuscripts, packaging, advertising, website creation and all relevant electronic communication and publishing. Preference is given to people who are former pupils of Stationers' Company School, also to sons and daughters of liverymen and freemen of the company.

Types of grants

The foundation offers support through the following schemes:

▶ Scholarships and Awards – a number of various awards to people studying a trade of the guild, or the children of liverymen and freemen towards general educational costs, such as fees, travel in the UK and abroad, projects, living expenses and so on
▶ Postgraduate Bursary – up to 12 annual awards of £6,000 each to postgraduates studying trades of the guild

Annual grant total

In 2013 the foundation had assets of £3.8 million and an income of £340,000. A total of around £90,000 was awarded in educational grants, including £73,000 in postgraduate bursaries and £16,800 in general awards.

Exclusions

People over the age of 25 are only supported in exceptional circumstances.

Applications

Application forms are available from the foundation's website along with detailed guidance notes, specific to each award. Applicants are advised to phone the correspondent in the first instance, to discuss an application. The trustees meet at least quarterly but generally candidates are invited to submit their applications between September and December.

Other information

The foundation also supports a number of specific schools, organises and sponsors Shine School Media Awards, funds three Saturday Supplementary Schools for disadvantaged children in London, holds a welfare fund to support people within the industry and administers a library for the use of people involved in historical studies related to printing, publishing, bookselling, bookbinding, newspaper making and similar trades.

Tailoring

The Merchant Taylors' Company Charities Fund (Livery and Freemen Fund)

£7,900

Correspondent: Nick Harris, Administrator, Merchant Taylors' Hall, 30 Threadneedle Street, London EC2R 8JB (020 7450 4440; email: charities@merchant-taylors.co.uk; website: www.merchant-taylors.co.uk)

CC Number: 1069124

Eligibility

People who attend one of the Merchant Taylors' supported schools or who have some association with the company. Preference may be given to beneficiaries in the inner city London, particularly the boroughs of Lewisham, Southwark, Tower Hamlets, Hackney, and their environs.

Types of grants

Loans and grants to cover direct educational costs of individuals in secondary and further/higher education or training.

Annual grant total

The latest financial information available at the time of writing (July 2014) was from 2012. In 2012 the fund had assets of £698,000 and an income of £293,000. A total of £95,000 was given in grants. Education and training awards totalled £7,900.

Applications

The fund does not normally support individual applications. Awards are made to educational institutions, therefore applications should be made through the individual's school or college.

Other information

Grants are also made to organisations, churches and clergy.

In 2012 the following schools were supported: Foyle College, Merchant Taylors' School Crosby, Merchant Taylors' School Northwood, Royal School of Needlework, St Helen's School, St Paul's Cathedral Choir School and Wolverhampton Grammar School.

Teaching

IAPS Charitable Trust

See entry on page 27

NASUWT (The Teachers' Union) Benevolent Fund

£165,000 (1,027 grants)

Correspondent: Andrew Sladen, Administrator, NASUWT, Hillscourt Education Centre, Rose Hill, Rednal, Birmingham B45 8RS (01214 536150; email: legalandcasework@mail.nasuwt.org.uk; website: www.nasuwt.org.uk)

CC Number: 285793

Eligibility

Members, former members and the dependents of members and former members and dependents of deceased members of NASUWT The Teachers' Union.

Types of grants

Grants of £125 for schoolchildren aged 16 and under and £150 for those 17 and over.

Annual grant total

In 2012 the fund had assets of £2.1 million and an income of £314,000. 1,027 grants were made to individuals totalling £331,000 for education and welfare purposes. The accounts for 2012 were the latest available at the time of writing (August 2014).

Exclusions

No support for private school fees, education courses, repayments of student loans or to assist students with general living expenses.

Applications

All applications must be submitted on behalf of the member by a Benevolence Visitor or another appropriate official of the Union. Arrangements may be made for a benevolence visitor to visit and complete the application form. Applicants must also supply information regarding household income and expenditure.

Other information

Help is also available from this fund for welfare purposes, and they also provide money advice.

Textile workers

The Fashion and Textile Children's Trust

£215,000

Correspondent: Anna Pangbourne, Director, Office 1 and 2, J411/412 The Biscuit Factory, 100 Clements Road, London SE16 4DG (0300 123 9002; fax: 020 7691 9356; email: anna@ftct.org.uk; website: www.ftct.org.uk)

CC Number: 257136

Eligibility

Children and young people under 18 years whose parents work or have worked in the UK fashion and textile retailing and manufacturing industry.

Types of grants

See the trust's website for full details of grants available. The trust concentrates its grant giving on 'the essential costs of education'; in practice this means particularly, but not exclusively, the payment of school fees. There is a preference for those with serious family difficulties so the child has to be educated away from home or at schools which offer vital pastoral care. The trust will also fund places at specialist schools for children with learning difficulties or for those who would benefit from attending a school that focuses on music or sport. Help is given with existing school fees where there has been a 'dramatic' change in family circumstances. Hardship grants are also available for clothing, books, computers, travel costs to attend school and educational trips.

Grants usually range from £200 to £300 for hardship awards and £3,600 spread over the academic year for educational support.

Annual grant total

In 2012/13 the trust had assets of £7.9 million and an income of £456,000. Grants were made to individuals totalling £282,000 broken down as follows:

School fees	£215,000
Welfare/general assistance	£67,000

Exclusions

No grants are given towards child care; study/travel abroad; overseas students studying in Britain; student exchange; or people starting work. No grants are available for those in higher education.

Applications

On a form available from the correspondent or an initial enquiry form from the trust's website(www.ftct.org.uk/grants)

Applications can be submitted at any time either directly by the individual or through a third party such as a social worker, teacher or Citizens Advice. Applicants are encouraged to call the trust in the first instance, to discuss an application.

National charities classified by subject

Actuary

Company of Actuaries Charitable Trust Fund

£18,000 (31 grants)

Correspondent: Patrick O'Keeffe, Administrator, Broomyhurst, Shobley, Ringwood, Hampshire BH24 3HT (01425 472810; email: almoner.cact@btinternet.com)

CC Number: 280702

Eligibility
Further and higher education students progressing towards actuarial qualifications.

Types of grants
One-off grants to help students with course/exam fees so that they can complete their training for the profession.

Annual grant total
In 2012/13 the trust had assets of £389,000, an income of £212,000 and made grants totalling £18,000. The fund made 31 awards to individuals, which were: one bursary of £1,000; 19 bursaries of £750 each; one prize of £300; and ten prizes of £250 each.

Applications
On a form available from the correspondent.

Other information
The trust also gives grants to organisations.

Anderson Barrowcliff Bursary

£4,500

Correspondent: Hugh McGouran, Administrator, Wallace House, Falcon Court, Preston Farm Industries, Estate, Stockton-on-Tees TS18 3TX (01642 260860; email: info@teesvalleyfoundation.org; website: www.teesvalleyfoundation.org)

CC Number: 1111222

Eligibility
Students from Tees Valley on a full-time undergraduate degree in accountancy, maths or business studies at a UK university. Decisions are made based on A-level results, UCAS personal statement and financial circumstances.

Types of grants
Bursary of £4,500 over three years.

Annual grant total
Payments of around £500 per term over three years.

Applications
Application forms are available on the Tees Valley Community Foundation website, when the application round opens.

Other information
This fund is administrated by the Tees Valley Community Foundation.

The successful applicant will have to take part in a six to eight week placement with the Anderson Barrowcliff during the summer vacation.

The Institute of Actuaries Research and Education Fund

£2,800

Correspondent: David Burch, Administrator, Institute of Actuaries, Staple Inn Hall, 1–3 Staple Inn, London WC1V 7QJ (020 7632 2194; email: david.burch@actuaries.org.uk; website: www.actuaries.org.uk)

CC Number: 274717

Eligibility
Actuarial students at any educational establishment approved by the actuarial profession.

Types of grants
Awards, scholarships and grants for professional training and research in actuary.

Annual grant total
In 2013/14 the fund had an income of £5,200 and a total expenditure of £2,900. We estimate that grants totalled £2,800.

Applications
In writing to the correspondent.

Agriculture and related rural issues

The Dick Harrison Trust

£3,800

Correspondent: Robert Addison, Secretary, Hexham Auction Mart Ltd, Mart Offices, Tyne Green, Hexham NE46 3SG (01434 605444, 07702 737560; email: secretary@dickharrisontrust.org.uk; website: www.dickharrisontrust.org.uk)

CC Number: 702365

Eligibility
Further and higher education, mature and postgraduate students training in livestock auctioneering and/or rural estate management who were born in Cumbria, Northumberland or Scotland, or who are (or whose parents or guardians are) at the time of the award living in any of these places.

Types of grants

One-off grants towards fees, books, equipment/instruments, maintenance/living expenses and study or travel abroad.

Annual grant total

In 2012/13 the trust had an income of £739 and an expenditure of £4,000. We estimate that the annual total of grants to individuals was around £3,800.

Applications

Application forms can be found on the trust's website or can be requested from the correspondent. Applicants are requested to provide references and to attend an interview. Applications should be submitted directly by individuals by 31 August.

Other information

Note that the trust is very strict about the application criteria.

The Institute of Chartered Foresters Educational and Scientific Trust

£1,500

Correspondent: The Secretary, Educational and Scientific Trust, Institute of Chartered Foresters, 59 George Street, Edinburgh EH2 2JG (01312 401425; fax: 01312 401424; email: icf@charteredforesters.org; website: www.charteredforesters.org)

Eligibility

Students of forestry and related disciplines.

Types of grants

Grants are available for students and others at an early stage in their career in forestry. The trust offers three types of grant:

- EST Annual Travel Bursary: one award of £500 made to one applicant for travel to benefit professional development
- EST Professional Development Awards: a discretionary award is made to one applicant. Amounts of awards vary, but they are unlikely to exceed £400
- EST Events Bursary: several awards of £100 made for attending the ICF National Conference or Study Tour

The institute says that: 'Funds are limited and may be sufficient to cover only part of the costs.'

Annual grant total

The amount given in grants varies from year to year. We estimate recent grants to have totalled around £1,500.

Exclusions

Grants are not awarded to fund undergraduate or postgraduate studies. For Professional Development and Events Bursary Awards, applications are not considered for projects that have commenced before the quarterly deadline.

Applications

On a form available from the trust's website.

- Applications for the Annual Travel Bursary should be received by 31 March
- Professional Development Awards are considered four times a year and should be received at the latest by 31 March, 30 June, 30 September or 31 December for consideration by trustees
- Events Bursary awards are also considered four times a year and are subject to the same quarterly deadlines

All applications must include a supporting statement from somebody who has a personal knowledge of the applicant and is able to appraise the value of the project to the applicant's professional development.

Nuffield Farming Scholarship Trust

£160,000 (22 grants)

Correspondent: Mike Vacher, Director, Southill Farmhouse, Staple Fitzpaine, Taunton, Somerset TA3 5SH (01460 234012; email: director@nuffieldscholar.org; website: www.nuffieldscholar.org)
CC Number: 1098519

Eligibility

UK residents between the ages of 22 and 45 who have been working for at least two years in farming, horticulture, forestry, rural land-based industries, countryside management, food industries or agricultural associated industries and intend to remain within the sector. Applicants must be three years post-tertiary education. The trust is looking for 'candidates who they believe will contribute and innovate in their respective industries on return from their scholarship, whilst also benefiting as an individual from a unique, often life changing experience.'

Types of grants

Awards are of £6,000 and can be given towards travel and subsistence expenses. Support is intended to encourage the study of practices and techniques employed anywhere in the world within farming, food, horticulture, rural and associated industries.

Annual grant total

In 2012/13 the trust had assets of £814,000 and an income of £361,000. A total of £364,000 was spent on charitable activities, of which £160,000 was awarded in scholarships to 22 individuals. Approximately 20 scholarships are awarded each year.

Exclusions

Funding cannot be given for academic courses, gap years or research projects and to people in full-time education.

Applications

Application forms can be obtained from the trust's website. The closing date for applications is 31 July, scholarships are then awarded in October and must be used within 18 months. Shortlisted applicants are invited for an interview.

Other information

Note that no academic qualifications are required to apply for the scholarship.

A number of other specific awards are offered, such as The Young Nuffield (Bob Matson) Award for young entrepreneurs; Frank Arden Memorial Award to UK residents working in the fields of food, farming or forestry; and various special interest awards. Further details can be found on the trust's website.

The John Oldacre Foundation

£202,000 (11 grants)

Correspondent: Stephen Charnock, Trustee, 35 Broadwater Close, Hersham, Walton-on-Thames KT12 5DD
CC Number: 284960

Eligibility

Undergraduate and postgraduate students who are carrying out research in the agricultural sciences which is meaningful to the UK agricultural industry. The research must be published.

Types of grants

One-off and recurrent grants according to need towards structured research in the UK and overseas. Previously funded research included projects on pig welfare, drought effect on rape, UK food security, potato diseases, soil fertility, wheat vulnerability to environmental stress, sustainable crops and so on.

Annual grant total

In 2012/13 the foundation had assets of £8.7 million and an income of £168,000. During the year 11 awards were made totalling £202,000.

Applications

In writing to the correspondent through the individual's college/university. Applications are usually considered twice a year, in spring and autumn.

Other information

Grants are made through organisations and educational establishments not to individuals directly.

The Royal Bath and West of England Society

£25,000

Correspondent: Dr Jane Guise, Administrator, Showground, Shepton Mallett, Somerset BA4 6QN (01749 822200; email: jane.guise@bathandwest. co.uk; website: www.bathandwest.com)

CC Number: 1039397

Eligibility

People studying any aspect of agriculture, horticulture, forestry, veterinary, conservation or any form of food production or marketing. Other projects that have been supported previously include livestock photography, overseas study tour and rural leadership.

Artists between the ages of 21 and 30 working on artwork on the theme of rural life in the UK.

Types of grants

Scholarships and grants for personal development and projects in furtherance of agriculture and rural economy.

Arts scholarships are worth £3,000 each.

Annual grant total

At the time of writing (July 2014) the latest financial information available was from 2012. In 2012 the society awarded grants and scholarships totalling £25,000.

Applications

Application forms can be requested from the correspondent. They are normally considered twice a year, in spring and autumn.

Application forms for the arts scholarship together with full guidelines can be found on the society's website. Applications should be submitted by post together with an sae and six images of the original work (on a CD) by July.

Other information

The society aims to promote agriculture, rural economy, manufacturing, commerce, arts and crafts through conferences, seminars, study tours, open days, exhibitions and other initiatives to individuals and rural businesses.

Further information on grants and scholarships can also be obtained via email at: mary.holmes@bathandwest.co.uk.

Studley College Trust

£68,000 (57 grants)

Correspondent: Christine Copeman, Secretary, Old Post Office, Hill Road, Lower Boddington, Daventry NN11 6YB (01327 260165; email: studleyct@ btinternet.com; website: www. studleytrust.co.uk)

CC Number: 528787

Eligibility

British or Irish nationals aged 18 to 30 (except in cases of genuine career change) enrolled on a college/university course connected with UK land-based activities (agriculture, horticulture, forestry, fish farming, agri-food technology, agricultural or horticultural marketing, arboriculture and agricultural engineering) whose progress is obstructed by lack of funds. Practical experience and/or strong rural background are required.

The trust is looking to support students in their early qualifications and master's degrees or PhD studies are not likely to be supported.

Types of grants

One-off and recurrent (up to three years) grants towards examination and external test fees, books, study material, transport, travel, clothing, equipment, accommodation and living expenses, food. Grants can be of up to £2,000, according to circumstances.

There are also scholarships sponsored by Tresco Abbey Gardens, Professional Gardeners Guild and Nuffield Farming School.

Annual grant total

In 2012/13 the trust had assets of £2.5 million and an income of £108,000. A total of around £68,000 was paid in grants and bursaries to 57 students.

The trust also specifies that during the year 72 enquiries and 20 applications were received directly from students and 16 direct awards were made. A total of 41 awards were made by the bursary partnership colleges and under the Professional Gardeners Guild training scheme.

Exclusions

No grants are available for hire purchase payments, overdraft and loan repayments, support for dependents or long-term housing costs. Students on industrial experience for over six weeks are not supported.

Applications

The trust has made partnerships with six land-based colleges and students at these should apply through their institution's student support office (a list of partner colleges is available on the trust's website). Applications for sponsored scholarships should be made through the appropriate organisations, details of which can be found on the trust's website.

Applications from other university/ college students and for travelling scholarships or traineeships can be submitted directly to the trust. Application forms can be requested on the trust's website or from the correspondent. The trustees consider applications in July and October, the deadlines are 1 June and 1 October, respectively.

Other information

The trustees' annual report from 2012/13 notes that 'in order to reduce administration costs the trust has increasingly made grants through partnership arrangements with selected land-based colleges and other institutions. Direct applications will still be considered subject to eligibility and availability of funds.'

Archaeology/ antiquarian studies

Society of Antiquaries of London

£49,000 (16 grants)

Correspondent: John Lewis, General Secretary, Burlington House, Piccadilly, London W1J 0BE (020 7479 7080; fax: 020 7287 6967; email: admin@sal.org.uk; website: www.sal.org.uk)

CC Number: 207237

Eligibility

People in higher education (including postgraduates), early career researchers and scholars studying archaeological, antiquarian, architectural subjects, art history, documentary and undertaking research projects focusing on material cultural heritage.

Types of grants

The society offers a number of research and travel grants in the range of £500–£5,000. Awards are given on an annual basis with a potential renewal up to two years.

A number of specific awards named after various benefactors are offered in addition to the general grants. See the society's website for the details of these individual funds.

Annual grant total

In 2012/13 the society had assets of £14.3 and an income of £1.6 million. A total of £49,000 was awarded for research projects to 16 individuals.

Exclusions

Research and travel grants are not made for work contributing to an undergraduate or postgraduate degree.

Some of the awards are not available to students.

Applications

Applications can be made online or downloaded from the society's website. Applications should not exceed four A4 pages and, together with a reference, should be submitted by 15 January for consideration in March. Applicants will be notified of a decision by 31 March.

Other information

The society also awards William and Jane Morris Fund (Church Conservation Grant Awards) grants to churches, chapels and other places of worship in the United Kingdom.

Arts

The Artistic Endeavours Trust

£13,000 (9 grants)

Correspondent: Richard Midgley, Trustee, Macintyre Hudson LLP, 30–34 New Bridge Street, London EC4V 6BJ (020 7429 4100)

CC Number: 1044926

Eligibility

Students undertaking education in the arts or entering artistic professions.

Types of grants

Grants to graduates and undergraduate students for fees, clothing, equipment, books, travel, general subsistence, also living expenses to those who are unable to secure employment for a period not exceeding two years.

Annual grant total

At the time of writing (July 2014) the latest financial information available was from 2012. In 2012 the trust had assets of £19,600 and an income of £26,000. During the year grants totalled £28,000. We estimate that around £13,000 was awarded to individuals. The trustees' annual report from 2012 specifies that nine students and five fringe productions benefited from the grants.

Applications

In writing to the correspondent.

Other information

The trust also gives grants to organisations for various creative projects.

It is possible for donors to indicate a particular individual or individuals who they wish to support and channel the money through the trust.

The William Barry Trust

£29,000 (34 grants)

Correspondent: Keiko Iwaki, Trustee, Flat 56, Avenue Close, Avenue Road, London NW8 6DA (020 7722 3974)

CC Number: 272551

Eligibility

People in vocational studies and training, such as, hospitality, hotel management, technical crafts or artistic occupations (singing, dancing, acting and so on).

Types of grants

One-off cash grants in range of £750 and £1,000. Support is available for general educational expenses, fees and maintenance/living costs.

Annual grant total

In 2012/13 the trust had an income of £418,000 and an expenditure of £384,000, which is higher than in previous years. A total of £29,000 was awarded in grants to 34 individuals.

Exclusions

Grants are not available for career development or postgraduate degrees.

Applications

In writing to the correspondent. Applications can be submitted directly by the individual or a family member.

Other information

The trust also supports organisations and has limitations on individual grants.

Canada House Arts Trust

£4,400

Correspondent: Louise Spence, Trustee, 9 Waters Place, London SW15 1LH (email: mlm.spence@gmail.com; website: www.canadahouseartstrust.org)

CC Number: 1105941

Eligibility

Individuals and groups involved in projects in the visual and performing arts, music, literature, theatre, film, TV and media which have a Canadian focus or theme. Projects must take place in the UK.

Types of grants

Currently funding and grants are suspended. Previously the average grant was between £1,000 and £2,000.

Annual grant total

In 2012/13 the trust had an income of £1,000 and an expenditure of £4,600, which is lower than in previous years. We estimate that the annual total of grants to individuals was around £4,400.

Exclusions

Grants are not given for travel and accommodation expenses or costs for work in development.

Applications

Ordinarily applications are made in writing to the correspondent describing the nature of the project and including estimated costs. The trustees meet quarterly to decide the allocation of funds.

Other information

The trust's website states that 'grant disbursement is on hold until late 2014 and therefore we shall not be in a position to consider any grants for funding.'

The Thomas Devlin Fund

See entry on page 125

See entry on page 125

Henry Dixon's Foundation for Apprenticing – administered by Drapers' Charitable Fund

£43,000 (4 grants)

Correspondent: Andrew Mellows, Charities Administrator, The Drapers' Company, Drapers' Hall, Throgmorton Avenue, London EC2N 2DQ (020 7588 5001; fax: 020 7628 1988; email: charities@thedrapers.co.uk; website: www.thedrapers.co.uk)

CC Number: 251403

Eligibility

Apprentices, students, school leavers and people in vocational training under the age of 25 studying in the fields of technical textiles and art or design, particularly in the inner city London.

Types of grants

One-off grants are made towards vocational training initiatives and apprenticeships, including support towards books, clothing, equipment/ instruments, fees, travel costs and other educational needs.

Annual grant total

In 2012/13 the foundation had assets of £2 million and an income of £45,000. Grants to four individuals were made totalling £43,000.

Applications

Grants are normally made through educational institutions, therefore applications should be made to the university or college rather than the foundation.

Other information

The foundation's funds have been transferred to the Drapers' Charitable Fund and are administrated as a restricted fund. Previously the charity was registered under the Charity Commission number 314292.

The Ann Driver Trust

£17,000

Correspondent: Penny Neary, Administrator, 10 Stratford Place, London W1C 1BA (07939 556574; email: secretary@anndrivertrust.org)

CC Number: 801898

Eligibility

Young people wishing to pursue an education in the arts, particularly music.

Types of grants

Scholarships and bursaries for the advancement of education in the arts, principally music.

Annual grant total

In 2012/13 the trust had an income of £27,000 and assets of £772,000. It made grants totalling £17,000.

Applications

Application forms should be requested by the principal or head of department at the place of study.

Other information

The trust selects different institutes for support in May of each year. A copy of the list of institutes can be obtained from the administrator by sending an sae.

The Exuberant Trust

£3,200

Correspondent: Megan Boyes, Administrator, 11 St Margaret's Road, Oxford, Oxfordshire OX2 6RU (01865 751056; email: admin@exuberant-trust.org.uk; website: www.exuberant-trust.org.uk)

CC Number: 1095911

Eligibility

People in need up to the age of 30 who are from Oxfordshire and are developing their interest in the arts (music drama, dance, arts and crafts, jewellery, multimedia and so on). Preference is given for first time applicants.

Types of grants

One-off grants of up to a maximum of £500 for a specific project or activity. These awards can be made for tools, training, music lessons, general costs, instruments and so on.

Previous grant recipients include: musicians, designers, jewellers, theatre directors, dancers, performing artists, composers, conductors, DJs, film makers, singers, art promoters, concert organisers, instrumentalists, bands and chamber groups.

Annual grant total

In 2013 the trust had an income of £5,000 and an expenditure of £3,400. We estimate that grants to individuals totalled around £3,200. On average around ten individuals are supported annually.

Applications

Full application guidelines are available from the trust's website or can be requested from the correspondent. Applicants are advised to give convincing reasons for applying and are required to provide appropriate references and a budget proposal. Trustees meet four times a year to consider applications. If applying by post, remember to enclose an sae.

Other information

The trust's website states that the charity 'raises funds by organising concerts throughout the year and from donations received from its supporters' and notes that 'successful applicants are encouraged to take part in concerts and other activities in support of the trust.'

The Fenton Arts Trust

£17,500

Correspondent: Shelley Baxter, Trust Manager and Administrator, PO Box 68825, London SE23 9DG (website: www.fentonartstrust.org.uk)

CC Number: 294629

Eligibility

People who are making, or who aspire to make, a worthwhile contribution to the artistic and cultural life of the UK. Grants are made towards the creative arts, principally painting and drama. Students should have British nationality and be aged under 35.

Types of grants

Scholarships and bursaries to charitable bodies and to individuals or organisations which will support work or performance by those early in their careers.

Annual grant total

In 2012/13 the trust had an income of £743,000 and assets totalling almost £4 million. Grants made to individuals totalled £17,500.

Applications

Applications for scholarships and bursaries can come from any institution which provides study opportunities and wishes to offer its students the scholarships and bursaries.

Applications for other grants can be made in writing directly by the individual to the administrator at the address below. Requests should include a fully budgeted proposal with the amount requested and information regarding other sponsors to the project.

Applications should preferably be sent nine months to a year in advance.

The trustees meet to discuss applications four times a year.

Other information

The trust also provides grants to organisations.

The Haworth Charitable Trust

£6,000

Correspondent: Sarah Clark, Trustee, 33 Northampton Street, Bath BA1 2SW

CC Number: 803239

Eligibility

Young musicians and painters in their final year of full-time study or the first year of their professional career. Preference is given to applicants from the north west of England, Herefordshire, Shropshire, The Wrekin and London.

Types of grants

Grants of £1,000 to £2,000 for one year only, paid in instalments over the year. Grants are for any purposes to further the establishment of a career in music, painting and the fine arts. Grants are not made for general welfare purposes.

Annual grant total

In 2012/13 the trust had an income of £2,000 and an expenditure of £6,400. Grants totalled around £6,000.

Exclusions

Loans are not made and mature students cannot be funded.

Applications

Applications should be made by letter, with a CV, to the correspondent, and must be supported by a recommendation of a tutor of a full-time course.

The Philip Bates Trust

£2,000

Correspondent: Karen Moulton, Trustee, 5 Fern Close, Rugby CV23 0UQ (01788 561148; email: info@ philipbatestrust.org.uk; website: www. philipbatestrust.org.uk)

CC Number: 1094937

Eligibility

People under 25 pursuing creative and artistic achievement. Preference is given to musicians and applicants in the West Midlands.

Types of grants

One off, and in exceptional circumstances recurrent, grants of £100 to £300 and musical instrument loans. There are also four prizes for composition awarded each year.

Annual grant total

In 2013 the trust had an income of £2,900 and an expenditure of £4,000. We estimate grants awarded to individuals for educational purposes totalled around £2,000.

Exclusions

Grants to individuals will not be made to more than one sibling per family.

Applications

Applications should be submitted in December or June for consideration in January and July. Where possible, trustees prefer to receive a personal request from the applicant rather than from a parent, guardian or other person on their behalf.

Other information

The trust also supports projects or workshops which aim to develop creative and artistic interests and skills in young people.

Rhona Reid Charitable Trust

See entry on page 109

The Martin Smith Foundation

Correspondent: The Trustees, 29 Beaumont Street, Oxford OX1 2NP (01865 594370)

CC Number: 1150753

Eligibility

People undertaking further, higher or postgraduate training in ecology, environment and natural resources, music or performing arts.

Types of grants

One-off grants, of up to £2,500, towards books, equipment, fees, bursaries or fellowships.

Annual grant total

In April 2014 the foundation was incorporated and its funds were transferred. There was no financial information available at the time of writing (August 2014).

Exclusions

Travel expenses are not funded.

Applications

The trustees state that they do their own research and do not consider unsolicited applications.

The Society for Theatre Research

£4,900

Correspondent: Marion Reed, Hon. Secretary, c/o The Royal Nat Theatre Archive, 83–101 The Cut, London SE1 8LL (email: contact@str.org.uk; website: www.str.org.uk)

CC Number: 266186

Eligibility

People involved with research into the history, historiography, art and practice of the British theatre, including music-hall, opera, dance, and other associated performing arts. Applicants should be aged 18 or over. There are no restrictions on status, nationality, or the location of the research.

Applications are not restricted to those engaged in formal academic work and academic staff, postgraduate students, theatre professionals and private researchers are all equally eligible.

Types of grants

Annual theatre research awards ranging between £200 and £1,000.

Annual grant total

In 2012/13 the charity had an income of £40,000 and assets of £589,000. Research awards totalled £3,100 and grants from the charity's Craig Fund totalled nearly £1,100. The charity also has two prizes awarded annually. The Book Prize totalled £500 and the New Scholars Essay Prize totalled £150.

Exclusions

Exclusively literary topics are not eligible.

Applications

Application forms can be downloaded from the society's website.

The South Square Trust

£18,500 (19 grants)

Correspondent: Nicola Chrimes, Clerk to the Trustees, PO Box 169, Lewes, East Sussex BN7 9FB (01825 872264; email: NoReply@SouthSquareTrust.org.uk; website: www.southsquaretrust.org.uk)

CC Number: 278960

Eligibility

Students over the age of 18 years who are studying full-time practical degree courses in the fine and applied arts, especially those related to gold, silver and metalwork, also music, drama and dance.

Preference is given to students who have been mainly educated in the UK, those in their third year of an undergraduate level or postgraduate students.

Types of grants

The trust assists students directly and also provides scholarships and bursaries to a number of schools/colleges. Individual awards can be given towards fees or for living expenses.

Annual grant total

In 2012/13 the trust had assets of £4.1 million and an income of £193,000. Grants to 19 individuals totalled £18,500.

Exclusions

Grants are not given for:
- People under 18
- Part-time or short courses
- Expeditions or travel outside of the UK
- Courses outside the UK
- Film, architecture and interior design courses
- Foundation courses and research degrees
- Purchase of equipment
- Private lessons

Applications

Application forms can be completed online on the trust's website. Individual applications are invited from 1 January to 30 April each year. Two references (preferably from the applicant's current tutors) and a photograph are required (along with photographs of work if on an arts-related course).

Initial enquiries by telephone are also welcomed.

Other information

Various bursaries have been set up with schools connected with the fine and applied arts. Students at these schools **must** apply through their institution, not directly to the trust. The schools are as follows: London Contemporary Dance School; Bristol Old Vic Theatre School; Guildford School of Acting (GSA); Guildhall School of Music and Drama; London Academy of Music and Dramatic Art (LAMDA); Royal Academy of Dramatic Art (RADA); Birmingham School of Jewellery; Bishopsland Educational Trust; Byam Shaw School of Art; The Royal Academy of Arts Schools; Textile Conservation Centre; West Dean College; Royal Academy of Music; Royal College of Music; and Royal Northern College of Music.

In 2012/13 bursaries and scholarships to seven schools and colleges totalled £113,000.

The Talbot House Trust

£8,600

Correspondent: Jayne Day, Pothecary Witham Weld Solicitors, 70 St George's Square, London SW1V 3RD (020 7821 8211; email: charities@pwwsolicitors.co.uk; website: www.pwwsolicitors.co.uk/funding-applications/11-the-talbot-house-trust)

CC Number: 1010214

Eligibility

UK resident students aged 16 to 25 who come from a household with low income and are undertaking courses in the UK in performing arts, such as drama, dance and music.

Types of grants

One-off grants to students in further/higher education towards the cost of fees. In exceptional circumstances support towards musical instruments, living and maintenance costs or travel expenses may also be given. The grants are intended to be supplementary only and applicants will be expected to raise funds through their own efforts.

Annual grant total

In 2012/13 the trust had an income of £8,100 and a total charitable expenditure of £8,800. We estimate the annual total of grants to be around £8,600.

Exclusions

Postgraduate students are not supported.

Applications

The trust's website state that 'due to the high cost of administering grants to individuals the trustees decided … that in the future the trustees would select one or more colleges or schools to receive a larger grant to be distributed by them.' Individual applicants should enquire at the institution where they plan to study for details of any funding that is available there and *not* directly to the trust.

Other information

In 2012/13 the trust supported the Central School of Ballet and the London Academy of Music and Dramatic Art (LAMDA).

The Wall Trust

£37,000 (18 grants)

Correspondent: Charles Wall, Trustee, Flat 19, Waterside Point, 2 Anhalt Road, London SW11 4PD (020 7978 5838)

CC Number: 291535

Eligibility

Exceptionally talented students of performing arts who are nominated by an organisation with which the trust has a scholarship scheme (see Applications section). Scholarships are given on the basis of outstanding talent and genuine financial need. Individuals aged 16 or over may be undertaking further, higher or postgraduate education or vocational training in music, drama or dance.

Types of grants

The trust provides scholarships (normally ranging between £1,000 and £3,000) towards the cost of tuition and training. Payments are made directly to the educational establishment. Grants are recurrent for the duration of the course (normally three years), provided the candidates continue to progress.

Annual grant total

In 2012/13 the trust had assets of £217,000 and an income of £68,000. A total of £41,000 was spent on charitable activities, of which £37,000 was distributed in scholarships to 18 individuals (five in dance, nine in drama, four in music).

Exclusions

Unsolicited applications are not normally accepted. Funding is supplementary and cannot be given for maintenance/living expenses.

Applications

Applications should only be made via an organisation with which the trust has a scholarship scheme. These are: Central School of Ballet, Drama Royal Academy of Dramatic Art, London Studio Centre, Music Royal Academy of Music, Royal College of Music (London); Royal Northern College of Music (Manchester); The Purcell School (Hertfordshire); and The Royal Ballet School.

Applicants will be auditioned and interviewed by the trustees.

Sydney Dean Whitehead's Charitable Trust

£31,000 (15 grants)

Correspondent: The Administrator, Moore Stephens, Chartered Accountants, 30 Gay Street, Bath BA1 2PA (01225 486100; fax: 01225 448198; email: mark.burnett@moorestephens.com)

CC Number: 207714

Eligibility

Children under the age of 18 who have special artistic talents, especially in music, dance or ballet, and whose 'parents are unable to provide them with an education suitable to their position or abilities.' Preference will be given to applicants who demonstrate efforts of raising funds themselves.

Types of grants

Grants are given mainly towards school fees but support may also be given to help fund one-off purchases (for example musical instruments). The awards range from £500 to £2,500.

Annual grant total

In 2012/13 the trust had assets of £1.1 million, an income of £46,000 and made 15 grants to individuals totalling £31,000.

Applications

Application forms can be obtained from the correspondent providing an sae. They can be submitted directly by the individual. The trustees meet once a year in June.

Other information

Grants are also made to small local charities (£2,300 in 2012/13).

Crafts

Craft Pottery Charitable Trust

£3,200 (6 grants)

Correspondent: Elizabeth Gale, Secretary, Taplands Farm Cottage, Webbs Green, Soberton, Southampton SO32 3PY (02392 632686; email: trust@cpaceramics.co.uk, lizgale@interalpha.co.uk; website: www.cpaceramics.co.uk/about_charitable.php)

CC Number: 1004767

Eligibility

People involved in the field of ceramics (regardless of the membership of the Craft Potters Association).

Types of grants

The trust has two main schemes:

▶ Annual Grant Scheme – awards of up to £1,000

▶ Bursary Scheme – awards of £500 to new graduate makers to undertake an individual postgraduate projects

Both grants and bursaries may be used towards training, travel, conference attendance, preparation of books or films and other projects relevant to the education of the public in craft pottery.

Annual grant total

At the time of writing the latest available financial information was from 2012. In 2012 the trust had assets of £169,000 and an income of £50,000. Grants to six individuals totalled £3,200.

Applications

Application forms and further guidelines can be obtained from the correspondent via email or by post including an sae. The closing date for applications for the annual award is 15 December. These grants are then considered within the following two months.

Other information

Grants are also made to institutions. In 2012 a grant of £2,000 was given to The Craft Potters Association of Great Britain Ltd.

The trust's website also notes that 'each year the CPA organises a Setting Out exhibition, which is designed to launch new graduates on their ceramics careers. Colleges are invited to submit the work of two students for selection for the exhibition.'

The Queen Elizabeth Scholarship Trust

£302,000 (31 grants)

Correspondent: Richard Peck, Secretary, 1 Buckingham Place, London SW1E 6HR (020 7828 2268; email: qest@rwha.co.uk; website: www.qest.org.uk)

CC Number: 802557

Eligibility

People of any age involved in modern or traditional crafts who are British citizens or permanently resident in the UK. Applicants should generally be reasonably well-established in the field, rather than those who are starting off. Preference may be given to activities associated with the Royal Warrant holding firms, although this is not an essential criterion.

Types of grants

One-off grants and staged scholarships over a maximum of four years, each worth between £1,000 and £18,000. Support can be given for further education, such as work experience and training, related travel costs, research visits, special courses and other projects.

Previous grant recipients have included antiques restorers, calligraphers, book conservators, potters, silversmiths, upholsterers, designers and so on.

Annual grant total

At the time of writing (July 2014) the latest financial information available was from 2012. In 2012 the trust had assets of £5 million and an income of £1.4 million. A total of £302,000 was awarded in 31 scholarships.

Exclusions

Grants are not made for tools, equipment, materials, leasing studios/ workshops, staging exhibitions, business start-up or for general further education unrelated to a craft skill.

Applications

Application forms are available on the trust's website (when the application round is open) or can be requested from the correspondent providing an A4 sae. Applications will need to include five to ten high quality images of the candidate's work, a couple of references and estimated costs. Scholarships are awarded twice a year, in spring and summer. See the trust's website for application deadlines.

Dance
The Lionel Bart Foundation

£44,000

Correspondent: John Cohen, Trustee, Clintons, 55 Drury Lane, London WC2B 5SQ (02073796080; email: jc@clintons.co.uk)

CC Number: 1086343

Eligibility

Undergraduate and postgraduate students who are aiming to become actors, composers, lyricists, book writers, playwrights, designers, choreographers, directors and anyone who wishes to make the theatre their career.

Types of grants

Grants towards tuition fees are given in the range of £200–£3,000.

Annual grant total

In 2012/13 the foundation had an income of £47,000 and a total expenditure of £45,000. We estimate that grants to individuals totalled around £44,000. Note that charitable expenditure varies each year and has ranged from £11,500 to £77,000.

Applications

In writing to the correspondent. Applications should be made between January and May each year. Grants are

normally considered at the end of May but applicants are advised to apply in advance of the deadline.

Other information

The foundation also invites applicants through various theatre schools.

The Marie Duffy Foundation

£3,500

Correspondent: Michael Pask, Trustee, 4A Flaghead Road, Poole, Dorset BH13 7JL (01202 701173; email: mduffypask@btinternet.com; website: www.marie-duffy-foundation.com/AboutUs.htm)

CC Number: 1145892

Eligibility

People over 17 with proven excellence in Irish dance, composition or choreography.

Types of grants

Grants and awards for dancers, composers and choreographers to advance or support their education in Irish Dance.

Annual grant total

In 2012/13 the trust had an income of £10,000 and a total expenditure of £8,000. We estimate around £3,500 was made in grants to individuals for education.

Applications

On the application form available to download from the trust's website. Forms should be submitted by 1 September at the latest.

Other information

Grants are also made for Irish Dance projects.

Lisa Ullmann Travelling Scholarship Fund

£11,800 (17 grants)

Correspondent: The Secretary, Breach, Kilmington, Axminster, Devon EX13 7ST (01297 35159; email: jachapman@breachdevon.co.uk; website: www.lutsf.org.uk)

CC Number: 297684

Eligibility

UK residents (for at least five years) over the age of 18 working in the field of movement and dance (choreographers, performers, lecturers/teachers, writers, therapists, administrators and so on) who wish to travel in the UK or abroad to attend a conference, undertake research or a short course of study to develop their skills and knowledge. Travel must originate and end in the UK

Types of grants

Grants are available for travel expenses, generally in the range of £600, but occasionally larger.

Annual grant total

In 2012/13 the fund had an income of £5,100. During the year the trust received 77 applications, of which 62 were eligible. 17 awards were granted to individuals totalling £11,800.

Exclusions

The fund will not support:

◗ Course or conference fees
◗ Applications relating to undergraduate or master's degree courses
◗ Full-time courses or courses extending over one, two or three years, including most diploma, certificate, and postgraduate degree courses (doctoral studies will be considered)
◗ Gap-year travel, degree placements or fieldwork
◗ Joint or group projects (individuals who are part of a larger project team may be considered)
◗ Travel insurance, visas, additional baggage costs, travel to/from the airport
◗ Projects which directly support the work of companies, institutions or organisations
◗ Set up costs of projects or festivals
◗ Previous recipients of a trust's scholarship may be considered for a second award after at least five years have passed and/or in exceptional circumstances

Applications

Application forms and guidelines are available on the foundation's website from 1 September each year or can be requested from the correspondent providing an sae. Four copies of a completed application form should be submitted by post no later than 25 January. Forms sent by email or fax are not acceptable. Individuals will be informed about the outcome of their application by the end of March. Applications should demonstrate passion and commitment. Projects should have clear and achievable outcomes, be carefully thought through and show evidence of preliminary research.

Other information

The fund has selected 17 projects to be supported during 2014/15. A total of £9,600 has been allocated for distribution.

The Jeremy and Kim White Foundation

£900

Correspondent: Kim White, Trustee, 69A Klea Avenue, London SW4 9HZ (email: info@whitefoundation.com; website: www.whitefoundation.com)

CC Number: 1091332

Eligibility

Young people in the performing arts, with a special emphasis on jazz and classical ballet, who are facing serious financial hardship.

Types of grants

One-off scholarships are given according to need.

Annual grant total

In 2013 the foundation had an income of £2,700 and a total expenditure of £1,000. We have estimated that around £900 was distributed in grants to individuals.

Exclusions

The foundation will not provide grants for private arts education.

Applications

Applications should be submitted by email including an explanation of the background of the applicant's financial hardship.

Other information

The foundation also supports an orphanage in India and has established a number of programmes, such as the White Foundation World Sax Competition, the Vevey Youth Ballet and Vevey International Youth Dance Festival.

Music

The Tom Acton Memorial Trust

£2,300

Correspondent: Alan Gage, Trustee, Hamilton House, Cobblers Green, Felsted, Dunmow CM6 3LX (01371 820382)

CC Number: 1088069

Eligibility

People in musical education who are under the age of 30, were born or are resident in Essex and have been largely educated in the county.

Types of grants

Financial assistance is available towards the costs of musical education fees, the purchase or loan of an instrument, travel expenses in respect of musical education

or performance, music related physical and psychological health needs. Grants can reach up to a maximum of £800 and are awarded according to need.

Annual grant total

In 2012/13 the trust had an income of £2,700 and an expenditure of £2,500. We estimate the annual total of grants to be around £2,300.

Applications

Application forms can be requested from the correspondent. Candidates are asked to include a teacher's reference to support the application which should be submitted by the end of May. Applicants successful in their initial application are invited for an audition, usually in July.

The Amber Trust
See entry on page 22

The Australian Music Foundation in London

£20,000

Correspondent: Bronwen Stephens, Arts Administrator, 67 Chestnut Grove, Balham SW12 8JF (077 397 21086; email: bs@australianmusicfoundation.org; website: australianmusicfoundation.org/)

CC Number: 270784

Eligibility

Australian musicians, conductors and composers under 30 years of age for study in Europe, the United Kingdom and the United States of America.

Types of grants

Grants are usually made towards the costs of musical equipment, study and development. This may include: fees for a course of study at an 'outstanding' overseas music institution; contributions towards the maintenance costs of a student attending a full-time course at an overseas institution; or payment for private tuition, language courses, purchase of musical instruments, travel costs or other strategic items necessary for the applicant's musical development. In the case of tuition fees, funds are normally paid directly to the appropriate institution. The foundation's website states: 'Typically awards are in the range of AUD 1,000 to 30,000, or the equivalent amounts in an international currency.'

Annual grant total

In 2012 the foundation had an income of £14,300 and a total expenditure of £27,000. We estimate that grants totalled £20,000.

At the time of writing (July 2014) this was the most recent financial information available for the foundation.

Applications

The application process consists of two stages:

- Stage 1 – An online application form can be found on the foundation's website and should be submitted with accompanying video audition files. There is a £10 administration fee.
- Stage 2 – Applicants who have been successful at Stage 1 will be notified and invited to attend a live audition, usually in September. Awards are then granted to the successful auditionees.

Opening and closing dates for applications are available on the foundation's website, as is a sample application form and a helpful list of FAQs.

Note: Composers should apply using the standard online form, but should instead include scanned copies of scores (or.pdf files), as well as audio files of their music recordings.

Other information

There is a separate award jointly funded by the Australian Music Foundation and Sir Charles Mackerras, which is specifically for young Australian conductors of merit. Potential applicants should request further information from the Australian Musical Foundation.

Awards for Young Musicians

£71,000 (123 grants)

Correspondent: Jane Ordaz Stubbs, Assistant Director, PO Box 2754, Bristol BS4 9DA (01234 750738; fax: 01179 048957; email: jane.ordaz.stubbs@a-y-m. org.uk; website: www.a-y-m.org.uk)

CC Number: 1070994

Eligibility

Musicians aged 5 to 17 who are in financial need and have exceptional musical potential. Applicants must ideally have achieved a distinction in their last music exam or be able to show evidence of this level of ability.

Types of grants

£200 to £2,000 for instruments, music lessons, weekend music schools, music courses, orchestra fees and travel. Awards are not paid directly to students or their families.

Annual grant total

In 2012 the charity had assets of £384,000 and an income of £226,000. Awards to 123 individuals totalled £71,000, of which 89 were made in Strand 1 and 34 in Strand 2.

At the time of writing (July 2014) this was the most recent financial information available for the charity.

Exclusions

No support for singers or students about to enter their first undergraduate year. No retrospective funding.

Applications

On a form available on the charity's website to be submitted by mid-March each year. Dates of deadlines are given on the website. Applications must include three references – one each from the applicant's music teacher, headteacher and recommending organisation – as well as evidence of family income. All applications are means tested.

The applications panel recommends two strands of award beneficiaries: Strand 1, for those awarded funding up to £500, and Strand 2, for those awarded funding of over £500. Applicants in Strand 2 will be invited to audition.

Other information

The charity states that 'funding is limited: even if you are successful in gaining an award, it may not be for the full amount requested'.

Awards for Young Musicians also provides advice, support and mentoring to young musicians.

Josephine Baker Trust

£1,000

Correspondent: David Munro, Trustee, Grange Cottage, Frensham, Farnham, Surrey GU10 3DS (01252 792485; email: munrodj@aol.com)

SC Number: SC020311

Eligibility

People studying vocal music and young singers at the beginning of their career.

Types of grants

Grants ranging from £125 to £250 are awarded to young singers. Support is typically given for the soloist fees at selected concerts.

Annual grant total

In 2012/13 the trust had an income of £25,000 and a total expenditure of £39,000. Normally around £20,000 each year is awarded to individuals.

Applications

In writing to the correspondent. Candidates are required to attend an audition.

Other information

The trust has established links with the Royal Academy of Music and the Royal College of Music.

BBC Performing Arts Fund

£190,000 (19 grants)

Correspondent: Miriam O'Keeffe, Director, 4th Floor Bridge House, MediaCityUK, Salford Quays M50 2BH (01618 360303; email: performingartsfund@bbc.co.uk; website: www.bbc.co.uk/performingartsfund)

CC Number: 1101276

Eligibility

Individuals involved in performing arts, including drama, singing, musical composition, script writing for television, theatre, media presentation, mime and dance. The fund seeks to support people who lack means to achieve their full potential.

Eligibility differs for each scheme so it is recommended that applicants refer to the terms and conditions and other information on open schemes on the fund's website.

Types of grants

The fund is currently inviting applications from organisations to the PAF Fellowship Scheme. The correspondent has advised applicants to consult the fund's website to see when individual applications are welcomed. Each year the fund's work focuses on a different art form: dance, music or theatre.

In 2012/13 the fund ran Community Music and Music Fellowships schemes and in 2013 launched Theatre Fellowships and Community Theatre schemes.

Annual grant total

In 2012/13 the fund had assets of £768,000 and an income of £449,000. A total of £190,000 was awarded to 19 music organisations to provide music fellowships to individuals.

Applications

The fund has recently implemented a three year funding cycle with one art form being funded each year. Eligibility criteria, deadlines and online application forms are available for open schemes on the fund's website. The trustees meet a minimum of four times a year to approve the grants.

The trustees stress that they 'are keenly aware that the bulk of the money we spend comes from all over the UK. It is therefore important to us that all four nations of the UK benefit from our funding as well as the Isle of Man and the Channel Islands.'

Other information

The fund supports individuals, organisations and community groups, for example choirs, community orchestras, samba bands or drumming circles. In 2012/13 the fund awarded 47 community music grants across the UK totalling £252,000.

The charity is mainly funded through the incidental revenue from the voting lines of BBC entertainment programmes such as Strictly Come Dancing, The Voice and Sports Personality of the year. All income is unrestricted.

The Rainer and Doreen Burchett Charitable Foundation (The Burchett Foundation)

£15,000 (10+ grants)

Correspondent: Rainer Burchett, Trustee, Watermillock House, Watermillock, Penrith CA11 0JH (01768 486191; email: burchett.foundation@ gmail.com)

CC Number: 1076739

Eligibility

People in education and those involved in music and athletics.

Types of grants

Grants given according to need.

Annual grant total

In 2012/13 the foundation had an income of £23,700 and an expenditure of £25,600. In previous years the total amount awarded in grants to individuals was around £15,000 and the trust was capable of accommodating over ten students at any given year. Specific information on the grants in 2012/13 was not available on the Charity Commission's record.

Exclusions

Unsolicited applications will not be accepted or acknowledged.

Applications

The foundation has decided to no longer accept unsolicited applications. The trust will be reaching its beneficiaries through a small number of relevant bodies, such as educational organisations.

Other information

The trustees have decided to concentrate the awards on the following three areas: education, music and athletics.

The Busenhart Morgan-Evans Foundation

£7,500

Correspondent: Major Bedford, Trustee, Brambletye, 455 Woodham Lane, Woodham, Addlestone, Surrey KT15 3QQ (01932 344806)

CC Number: 1062453

Eligibility

Young musicians at the start of their professional career.

Types of grants

One-off or recurrent grants towards the cost of equipment, instruments, course fees and also music scholarships.

Annual grant total

In 2012/13 the foundation had an income of £12,500 and an expenditure of £15,500. We estimate the annual total of grants to individuals to be about £7,500.

Applications

Applications should be made through the individual's educational institution at any time.

Other information

Organisations are also supported for music, health and local community causes.

The Choir Schools' Association Bursary Trust Ltd

£208,000 (135 grants)

Correspondent: Susan Rees, CSA Administrator, 39 Grange Close, Winchester, Hampshire SO23 9RS (01962 890530; email: admin@ choirschools.org.uk; website: www. choirschools.org.uk)

CC Number: 1120639

Eligibility

Pupils or proposed pupils between the ages of 7 and 13 at a member school of the Choir Schools' Association.

Ex-choristers over the age of 13 may also be supported from the money donated by the School Fees Insurance Agency.

Types of grants

Grants of up to £1,500 are available to pay the fees of choristers attending member schools of the Choir Schools' Association. Applications are means tested.

Annual grant total

In 2012/13 the trust had assets of £592,000 and an income of £308,000. Grants were awarded totalling around £208,000 to 135 individuals. Support was made possible because of grants to the trust from the Department of Education, the School Fees Insurance Agency (to ex-choristers over the age of 13), the Welsh Assembly Government (to pupils from Wales) and a charitable donation from another charity.

Applications

Applicants should contact the headmaster of the choir school

concerned. Applications should normally be submitted by 15 March, 31 August and 15 December for consideration in May, October and February respectively.

The Else and Leonard Cross Charitable Trust

£20,000

Correspondent: Helen Gillingwater, Trustee, The Wall House, 2 Lichfield Road, Richmond, Surrey TW9 3JR (020 8948 4950; email: helengillingwater@ hotmail.com)

CC Number: 1008038

Eligibility

Young musicians, particularly pianists, between the ages of 11 and 27 who are in need.

Types of grants

Scholarships are normally made through specialist musical institutes to help with fees, living and maintenance expenses, purchase of instruments or performance related costs.

Annual grant total

In 2012/13 the trust had an income of £5,800 and an expenditure of £21,000. We estimate the annual total of grants to individuals to be around £20,000.

Applications

Applications should be made through the individual's educational institution.

Other information

Occasional grants can be given to music related festivals and events.

Miss E. B. Wrightson's Charitable Settlement

£15,500 (34 grants)

Correspondent: N. Hickman, Administrator, Swangles Farm, Cold Christmas Lane, Thundridge, Ware SG12 7SP (email: info@wrightsontrust. co.uk; website: wrightsontrust.co.uk/)

CC Number: 1002147

Eligibility

Young musicians, usually between the ages of 8 and 18, who are in financial hardship.

Types of grants

One-off and recurrent grants ranging from £100 to £800 are given for instruments, lessons, choir/orchestra fees, Saturday conservatoires, travel costs and similar expenses. Recurrent grants would not normally be renewed more than three times per person. The trust prefers to make payments directly to the teachers/instrument dealers/ conservatoires and so on.

Annual grant total

In 2012/13 the trust had assets of £1.1 million, an income of £26,000 and a charitable expenditure of around £18,000. A total of £15,500 was awarded in grants to 34 individuals.

Exclusions

People over the age of 21, undergraduates and postgraduates are not normally supported. Assistance cannot be given for tuition fees.

Applications

Application forms can be found on the trust's website and should be submitted in three copies. Applications should be accompanied with two letters of support from the applicant's tutor/teacher to prove candidate's musical abilities and potential, a CV (for those over 12), reasons for applying, any other sources of funding applied to and any other relevant information about the individual's circumstances and financial situation. The trustees meet regularly to consider applications.

Other information

The trust also supports organisations, makes grants to assist young children in their personal development and runs a boat, Lady Elsa.

Elizabeth Eagle-Bott Memorial Awards

See entry on page 23

EMI Music Sound Foundation

£200,000

Correspondent: Janie Orr, Chief Executive, Beaumont House, Avonmore Road, London W14 8TS (020 7550 7898; email: enquires@ emimusicsoundfoundation.com; website: www.emimusicsoundfoundation.com)

CC Number: 1104027

Eligibility

Young people in the UK who are undertaking music education. Applicants must have been resident in the UK for a minimum of three years and: be a British citizen; a national of a member state of the European Economic Area; have been granted leave to enter or remain in the UK for an indefinite period; or hold a certificate of right of abode in the UK. Due to increased demand the foundation focuses on those in most need.

Note: individuals resident in the UK for the purpose of education or attending a course of study are not eligible.

Types of grants

Grants, usually of up to £2,000, are given towards the purchase of instruments and music equipment in primary, secondary and tertiary education. Funding may also be given to music teachers to further their training and undertake courses.

The foundation also operates a bursary scheme of £5,000 for students at selected musical colleges and institutes. These are: Birmingham Conservatoire, Brighton Institute of Modern Music, Centre for Young Musicians, English National Opera, Irish World Music Centre, National Children's Orchestra, Royal Academy of Music, Royal Welsh College of Music and Drama, Tech Music School, and The Royal Conservatoire of Scotland.

Annual grant total

In 2012/13 the foundation had assets of £8 million and an income of £374,000. During the year 554 individual and school applications were approved totalling £311,000. The amount given to individuals was not specified in the accounts, however we estimate that around £200,000 was awarded, including the bursary awards.

Exclusions

Grants are not provided to:
- Applicants based outside the UK and Ireland
- Non-school based community groups
- Applications for tuition fees and living expenses (other than through the bursary scheme)
- Applications over £2,000
- Independent music teachers
- Cover the teaching of the national curriculum or peripatetic teaching
- Music therapy

Applications

Application forms for instrument/equipment grants can be downloaded from the foundation's website or requested from the correspondent. They should be submitted by individuals or their school via post, together with all the relevant documentation and references a month before the trustees' meeting. The meetings are held twice a year, normally in October and March (for exact dates consult the foundation's website, as they may change). Candidates are invited to approach the foundation with queries prior to application.

Applications for bursaries should be made through the individual's educational establishment.

Other information

The foundation also gives grants to a number of secondary schools to fund music education.

The Gerald Finzi Trust

£15,800 (17 grants)

Correspondent: The Administrator, The Finzi Trust, PO Box 137, Stour Row, Shaftesbury, Dorset SP7 0WX (email: admin@geraldfinzi.org; website: www.geraldfinzi.org)

CC Number: 313047

Eligibility

Musicians and music students between the ages of 18 and 80. Formal training, qualifications or previous professional experience are not prerequisite.

Types of grants

The trust offers grants for the purchase of musical instruments and scholarships for projects in the UK and overseas which 'might show a creative initiative or could involve engaging in some practical experience, education or research, perhaps giving a personal change of direction.' The projects would ideally last between three to eight weeks. If a project involves travel then the trust can meet these expenses along with the cost of accommodation, subsistence and equipment for the period involved. Scholarships awarded in recent years have covered studies in Estonia, Finland, France, Germany, India, Ireland, Italy, South America, Sweden, the UK and the USA.

Grants to individuals in 2012/13 were between £200 and £600 while scholarships ranged between £200 and £2,600.

Annual grant total

In 2012/13 the trust had assets of £182,000 and an income of £66,000. A total of £30,000 was spent on charitable activities. Grants to nine individuals totalled £4,000 and scholarships to eight students totalled £11,800.

Exclusions

Grants are not given for attendance of courses, to support academic degree qualifications and for fees or living expenses. Group applications are not considered and awards are not likely to be made to previous recipients of either a Finzi Scholarship or a Winston Churchill Memorial Trust Fellowship.

Applications

Application forms can be found on the trust's website or requested from the correspondent providing an sae. Applications should include an outline of the proposal and an estimate of the costs involved. The deadline for applications is the beginning of November. Candidates who are successful with their initial application are invited for an interview which is normally held in January, in London.

Other information

Grants are also made to organisations (£5,800 in 2012/13).

In 2013 the first awards of the newly established joint Churchill Finzi Fellowships in Musical Education (in collaboration with the Winston Churchill Memorial Trust) took place presenting a total of £8,000 to two students.

The Jean Ginsburg Memorial Foundation

£9,300

Correspondent: Ian Henry, Trustee, The Garden Flat, Flat 1, 3 Heath Drive, London NW3 7SY (07774435130; email: info@jeanginsburg.com; website: www. jeanginsburg.com)

CC Number: 1104077

Eligibility

Undergraduate and postgraduate students who are training to pursue a career in medicine or people under the age of 30 training as classical musicians, especially pianists.

Types of grants

Scholarships, bursaries and grants towards general educational needs.

Annual grant total

In 2012/13 the foundation had an income of £10 and an expenditure of £18,700. We estimate that about £9,300 was distributed in individual grants.

Applications

In writing to the correspondent, preferably via email.

Other information

The trust also provides scholarships at The Royal Free Medical School, The Royal Academy of Music in London and Somerville College, Oxford University. Previously students in Cardiff, Newcastle and Sheffield universities have been supported.

The Michael James Music Trust

£15,000

Correspondent: Edward Monds, Trustee, Garden House, Cuthburga Road, Wimborne BH21 1LH

CC Number: 283943

Eligibility

Individuals engaged in any musical education, particularly in a Christian context.

Types of grants

One-off and recurrent grants are given towards tuition fees and expenses.

Annual grant total

In 2012/13 the trust had an income of £13,400 and a total expenditure of £16,300. Grants totalled about £15,000.

Exclusions

No grants for the purchase of instruments or equipment.

Applications

On an application form available from the correspondent. Applications should be received by 30 April each year.

Other information

Grants are also made to churches, universities and schools.

The Kathleen Trust

£46,000 (27 grants)

Correspondent: Edward Perks, Administrator, Currey and Co., 21 Buckingham Gate, London SW1E 6LS (020 7828 4091)

CC Number: 1064516

Eligibility

Young musicians of outstanding ability who are in need.

Types of grants

Loans in the form of musical instruments and sometimes bursaries to attend music courses, ranging between £500 and £3,000.

Annual grant total

In 2012/13 the trust had an income of £27,000 and assets of £1.3 million. Grants were made to 27 individuals and totalled £46,000.

Applications

In writing to the correspondent.

Other information

Grants are also made to organisations.

The Macfarlane Walker Trust

£5,700 (4 grants)

Correspondent: Sophie Walker, Administrator, 4 Shooters Hill Road, London SE3 7BD (020 8858 4701; email: sophiewalker@mac.com)

CC Number: 227890

Eligibility

Music students over 18 who are in need, with a preference for those who live in Cheltenham and Gloucestershire.

Types of grants

One-off grants ranging from £500 to £2,500, for the purchase of musical instruments for music students.

Annual grant total

In 2012/13 the trust had an income of £31,000 and an expenditure of £32,000. Four individuals were awarded grants totalling £5,700.

Exclusions

The trust does not provide financial assistance towards tuition fees or gap-year trips. Large charities, animal charities, foreign charities or major building projects are not supported.

Applications

In writing to the correspondent. Applications should be made directly by the individual, giving the reason for applying and an outline of the project with a financial forecast. According to our research, an sae and references from an academic referee must accompany the initial application.

Other information

The charity also supports various projects in the field of music, drama and fine arts. The trust assists in provision of educational facilities particularly for scientific research.

The Music Libraries Trust

£2,900

Correspondent: Edith Speller, Secretary, c/o Jerwood Library of the Performing Arts Trinity Laban, King Charles Court, Old Royal Naval College, Greenwich, London SE10 9JF (020 8305 4422; email: secretary@musiclibrariestrust.org; website: www.musiclibrariestrust.org)

CC Number: 284334

Eligibility

Music librarians in the UK and Ireland involved in education or training and people carrying out research into music librarianship, music bibliography, musicology and related disciplines.

Types of grants

The trust's website states that the charity 'has a regular programme of allocating grants in support of projects, research and course attendance with a preference for supporting those who have been unable to receive financial support from elsewhere.' Previously awards between £100 and £5,000 have been given for initial funding, with second grants being considered in exceptional cases. Support can be provided towards travel expenses, course fees, research, study, wider dissemination of results and other specific projects. Examples of previous awards and suggested potential projects can be found on the trust's website.

Annual grant total

In 2012/13 the trust had an income of £8,500 and an expenditure of £6,000. We estimate that grants to individuals totalled around £2,900.

Exclusions

The trust will not provide funding for general undergraduate and postgraduate studies.

Applications

In writing to the correspondent. Applications can be submitted directly by the individual at any time to be considered in the following trustees' meeting. The meetings take place three times a year. Applications should provide full details of the project, state other sources of funding considered and give a full analysis of anticipated expenses. References may also be required. The trust welcomes informal discussions by email.

Other information

Support is also given to organisations.

In addition to the regular award programme the trust offers: bursaries for students and library staff to attend study weekends and courses organised by International Association of Music Libraries (IAML) UK and Ireland Branch; The Ian Ledsham Bursary to IAML UK and Ireland Branch members who wish to attend IAML's international conferences; and The E.T. Bryant Memorial Prize (in conjunction with IAML UK and Ireland Branch). Further details on the bursaries can be found on the trust's website.

The Ouseley Trust

£58,000 (16 grants)

Correspondent: Martin Williams, Clerk to the Trustees, PO Box 281, Stamford, Lincolnshire PE9 9BU (01780 752266; email: ouseleytrust@btinternet.com; website: www.ouseleytrust.org.uk)

CC Number: 527519

Eligibility

Children, generally between the ages of 9 to 16, who are (or are about to become) choristers in recognised choral foundations in the Church of England, Church of Ireland or Church in Wales.

Types of grants

Grants are given towards the choir school fees for up to two years. They usually range from £1,000 to £5,000. In special circumstances awards may also be given for organ tuition.

Annual grant total

In 2013 the trust had assets of £4.4 million, an income of £259,000 and made grants totalling £88,000. Awards for fees totalled £58,000 given to 16 students.

A further £31,000 was given from specific endowments to be distributed in scholarships and bursaries.

Exclusions

Help is not available for choristers at Brecon, Ely, Norwich, Rochester and St Alban's cathedrals where the trust has donated funds to be used for scholarships. Awards are not made for music lessons or for a period exceeding two years.

Applications via fax or email are not accepted.

Applications

Application forms and guidelines can be requested from the correspondent by the school, church, choir or choral foundation concerned, not by choristers or their parents. A statement of financial resources by the child's parents or guardian will be required as well as references. Applications are considered at the biannual meetings in March and October and should be submitted by 28 February or 30 June, respectively.

The trust stresses that applicants are strongly advised to obtain and study the guidelines for applications.

Other information

The trust's annual report from 2013 states:

> At present, the trustees' policy is to concentrate their resources on making grants for: courses of instruction; endowment grants; choir school fees; and the purchase of music. In addition, careful consideration is given to other applications that involve unique or imaginative ways of fulfilling the trust's object.

The Pratt Green Trust

£0

Correspondent: Revd Brian Hoare, Trustee, 5 Flaxdale Close, Knaresborough, North Yorkshire HG5 0NZ (01423 860750; email: brianhoare@sky.com; website: www. prattgreentrust.org.uk)

CC Number: 290556

Eligibility

Hymn writers, church musicians and others involved in education, research, composition and performance in the area of church music and hymnody.

Types of grants

Scholarships, bursaries, prizes, research expenses, books and other grants.

Annual grant total

In 2012/13 the trust had assets of £12,500 and an income of £39,000. Our research tells us that grants have totalled around £1,000 in previous years, though none were awarded in 2012/13.

Exclusions

No grants towards course fees. Grants for the training of musicians cannot be made unless specifically related to the promotion of hymnody, and such requests will normally be expected to come from a church or related group.

Applications

In writing to correspondent. All applications must be accompanied by a detailed budget covering the project/ purpose for which the grant is requested, together with full details of any other grants or sponsorship applied for. Applications should be supported by a suitable second signatory such as, for example, a college principal or other person with a connection to the purpose and by two references.

Other information

Grants are also made to organisations and projects.

The Royal College of Organists

£13,000

Correspondent: Kim Gilbert, General Manager, PO Box 56357, London SE16 7XL (05600 767 208; email: admin@rco.org.uk; website: www.rco. org.uk)

CC Number: 312847

Eligibility

People studying organ playing or choral directing and similar or those engaged in research in these areas. Most awards are given to members or student members of the Royal College of Organists.

Types of grants

The charity offers various scholarships and awards. One-off and recurrent grants range from £100 to £1,500 and can be awarded for travel costs, purchase of instruments/equipment, music books, additional lessons or courses, tuition fees and other purposes. For specific details of each scholarship, see the 'awards fact sheet', which can be found on the charity's website.

Annual grant total

In 2012/13 the charity had assets of £1.9 million, an income of £468,000 and a total charitable expenditure of £422,000. Scholarships and prizes totalled £13,000.

Applications

Application forms can be downloaded from the charity's website and should be submitted by April (or by February for two specific courses) together with any required documentation, such as a letter of support or an outline of the travel plans.

The Rushworth Trust

£3,100

Correspondent: The Administrator, Liverpool Charity and Voluntary Services, 151 Dale Street, Liverpool L2 2AH (01512 275177)

CC Number: 1076702

Eligibility

Music students living within a 60-mile radius of Liverpool Town Hall. Grants can be awarded to a wide range of musicians, including composers, young conductors, young performers, student singers and instrumentalists, choirs and choir singers and so forth.

Types of grants

One-off grants of up to £300 to help with the cost of the study of music and to develop the taste and appreciation of music. Financial assistance is available for publishing music, promotion, training, equipment/instruments, music tours and concerts. Our research suggests that grants can only be made if the individual is not eligible for grants from any other source and awards are not usually repeated.

Annual grant total

In 2012/13 the trust had an income of £4,700 and an expenditure of £3,300. We estimate the annual total of grants to be around £3,100.

Exclusions

Grants are not available for course fees and maintenance.

Applications

Application forms can be requested from the correspondent and should be submitted in advance of the trustee meetings which are normally held in March, June, September and December.

Other information

The trust has been formed by the merging of The William Rushworth Trust, The Thew Bequest and The A K Holland Memorial Award.

The Stringwise Trust

£1,500

Correspondent: Michael Max, Trustee, Lion House, Red Lion Street, London WC1R 4FP (020 8455 9308)

CC Number: 1048917

Eligibility

People who play stringed instruments, particularly children and aspiring teachers.

Types of grants

Bursaries and scholarships to enable attendance at any training or experiential event.

Annual grant total

In 2012 the trust had an income of £158 and a total expenditure of £1,700. We estimate that grants totalled £1,500.

At the time of writing (July 2014) these were the most recent financial figures available for the trust.

Applications

In writing to the correspondent.

The Society for Wessex Young Musicians Trust

£7,800

Correspondent: Sandrey Date, Trustee, 7 Southbourne Coast Road, Bournemouth BH6 4BE (01202 423429)

CC Number: 1100905

Eligibility

Young musicians who live in Dorset and Hampshire, particularly, but not exclusively, the participants and supporters of the Centre for Wessex Young Musicians.

Types of grants

Grants towards equipment and facilities, also loans, scholarships, bursaries and prizes, not usually provided by the statutory authorities.

Annual grant total

In 2012/13 the trust had an income of £9,700 and an expenditure of £8,000. We estimate that about £7,800 was awarded in grants to individuals.

Applications

In writing to the correspondent.

Performing arts

The Richard Carne Trust

£28,000 (12 grants)

Correspondent: Christopher Gilbert, Administrator, Kleinwort Benson Trustees Ltd, 14 St George Street, London W1S 1FE (0203207 7356; website: richardcarnetrust.org/)

CC Number: 1115903

Eligibility

Young people in the performing arts who are in need. Preference is given to those studying music and theatre.

Types of grants

Grants are given according to need.

Annual grant total

In 2012 the trust had assets of £978,000 and an income of £219,000. Grants to 12 individuals totalled £28,000. A further £118,000 was awarded to musical groups and organisations.

At the time of writing (July 2014) this was the most recent financial information available for the trust.

Applications

The trust's website states: 'Note that the Richard Carne Trust does not respond to individual applications for financial help. Assistance is provided via the various academic and cultural institutions which the trust supports.'

The Elizabeth Evans Trust

£5,000

Correspondent: The Trust Secretary, The Elizabeth Evans Trust, Gwynne House, 6 Quay Street, Carmarthen SA31 3AD (email: hazelthorogood@ theelizabethevanstrust.co.uk; website: www.theelizabethevanstrust.co.uk)

CC Number: 210989–2

Eligibility

Young people aged between 16 and 26 (either at the time of applying or during the academic year in which the award is to be made) accepted onto further/ higher education or training courses who wish to pursue a professional career in the performing arts (acting, singing, instrumental performance or stage management) and can demonstrate a close connection or association with Wales, particularly Carmarthenshire.

Applicants are not means tested but their personal circumstances may determine the amount and extent of an award.

Types of grants

Financial assistance is available for the cost of college/university education, other training at both undergraduate and postgraduate level or for a short-term private project.

Annual grant total

Our research suggests that normally around £5,000 a year is awarded in grants to individuals. The number of recipients fluctuates from around 10 to 15 annually.

Applications

Application and referee forms together with the guidance notes can be found on the trust's website and should be submitted to the correspondent, preferably electronically.

Applications are considered between 1 January and 30 April every year and will be deferred until 1 January if received at other times, unless sufficient reason can be established for expediting the application. Candidates who are successful in their initial application are invited to attend an audit/interview.

Other information

The trust is linked to United Charities.

Theatre

The Actors' Charitable Trust (TACT)

£137,500 (101 grants)

Correspondent: Robert Ashby, General Secretary, The Actors Charitable Trust, 58 Bloomsbury Street, London WC1B 3QT (020 7636 7868; email: robert@tactactors.org; website: www.tactactors.org)

CC Number: 206809

Eligibility

Children (aged under 21) of professional actors who are in financial need with a particular focus on children with special needs, learning disabilities or long-term ill health and families who are living with cancer or other illness, or facing family crisis.

Types of grants

Grants for extracurricular activities, clothing, extra tuition to help with dyslexia or maths and additional therapy for children with disabilities. Grants are also made in the form of gift vouchers and payments to service providers.

Annual grant total

In 2012/13 the trust had assets of £6.3 million and an income of £515,000. Grants for educational and welfare purposes were made to 127 families, with 203 children between them, totalling £275,000. In 2012/13 the average spent per child was around £1,350.

Exclusions

No grants are made towards private school fees or other tuition fees. TACT does not pay independent school fees.

Applications

On a form available from the correspondent or to download from the trust's website. Applicants are strongly advised to contact the trust to discuss their situation before making an application. Applications can be submitted at any time either by the individual or a parent. Awards are decided in July each year.

The Costume Society

£2,900

Correspondent: Jill Salen, Hon Secretary, Rose Cottage, Crofft y Genau, St Fagans, Cardiff CF5 6DU (02920 568622; email: awards@costumesociety.org.uk, costumesociety@tiscali.co.uk; website: www.costumesociety.org.uk)

CC Number: 262401

Eligibility

Students in history and theory of design (fashion and textiles), dress, costume, theatre wardrobe and related fields. Support is given to students engaged in further and higher education, including postgraduate courses.

Types of grants

The society offers five the following awards:

▶ Museum Placement Award – of up to £1,000 to undertake a placement in a public museum in the UK
▶ Symposium Student Bursary – covers costs of full attendance at the Costume Society's annual three-day symposium (excluding transport to and from the event)
▶ The Patterns of Fashion Award – award of £500 open to students in theatre wardrobe and costume design who 'produced a reconstructed garment from a pattern in one of the Janet Arnold *Patterns of Fashion* books that reflect the high standards presented in the books'
▶ The Yarwood Award – of up to £500 plus one-year membership available to master's students 'engaged in high quality research into the history of dress and/or textiles with expenditure relating to the completion of their dissertation.' The award is intended to cover specific expenses, such as 'travel to a library, archive or collection, subsistence while away and archive reproduction fees'

Annual grant total

At the time of writing (July 2014) the latest available financial information was from 2012. In 2012 the society had assets of £307,000 and an income of £224,000. Grants to students totalled £2,900.

Applications

Application procedures and deadlines are different for each of the awards. Detailed eligibility and application guidelines are available on the society's website and are also published in *Costume*, the annual journal of the society. Applicants are encouraged to approach the society with initial enquiries.

Other information

The Student Design Award of £250 is not open to the public and forms a part of the society's symposium. Fashion courses at art schools close to the symposium venue are invited to participate.

The John Thaw Foundation

£60,000

Correspondent: The Administrator, PO Box 477, Amyand Park Road, Twickenham TW1 9LF

CC Number: 1090668

Eligibility

People wishing to pursue a career in the theatre and performing arts. Preference is given to individuals who are underprivileged and disadvantaged.

Types of grants

The foundation provides scholarships and bursaries of around £3,000 towards fees through specifically chosen training programmes at established schools or youth groups.

Annual grant total

In 2012/13 the foundation had assets of £137,000 and an income of £127,000. A total of £138,000 was spent in grants to individuals and organisations. We estimate the annual total of grants to individuals to be around £60,000.

Applications

In writing to the correspondent. Note that awards are mainly made through specific bursary programmes and therefore applications should be made through appropriate institution.

Other information

The foundation works with a number of partner bodies and also supports educational organisations.

The trustees' annual report from 2012/13 notes that the foundation 'continues to avoid ongoing commitments as a general rule in order to maintain as great a degree of financial flexibility as possible.'

Aviation

The Guild of Air Pilots Benevolent Fund

£14,000

Correspondent: Chris Spurrier, Trustee, Derwent, Fox Lane, Eversley Cross, Hook, Hampshire RG27 0NQ (01252

877653; fax: 020 7404 4035; email: gapan@gapan.org; website: www.gapan.org)

CC Number: 212952

Eligibility

Young people who want to become pilots or wish to gain further qualifications in the aviation industry.

Types of grants

Scholarships and bursaries for young people.

Annual grant total

In 2012/13 the guild had assets of £708,000 and an income of £84,000. Educational grants totalling approximately £14,000 were made and a further £1,400 was given in welfare grants.

Applications

On a form available from the guild's website. Details of individual criteria and dates relating to each scholarship are included in the application form. The fund works closely with the other aviation trusts for individuals (both military and civilian). If an applicant has approached another such trust, they should say so in their application to the fund.

Other information

The guild also gives grants for welfare purposes to members of the guild and those who have been engaged professionally as air pilots or air navigators in commercial aviation, and their dependents.

Built environment

Alan Baxter Foundation (ABF)

£3,000

Correspondent: Julia Gavin, Administrator, Alan Baxter and Associates LLP, Cowcross Court, 70–77 Cowcross Street, London EC1M 6EL (020 7250 1555; fax: 020 7250 3022; email: aba@alanbaxter.co.uk)

CC Number: 1107996

Eligibility

People involved in study or research of the built and natural environment.

Types of grants

Grants according to need for general educational costs, research and projects.

Annual grant total

In 2012/13 the foundation had assets of £981,000 and an income of £326,000.

Around £8,300 was spent on charitable activities, of which £3,000 was distributed in grants to students.

Applications

In writing to the correspondent.

Other information

Grants are also made to various organisations supporting education and research relating to the built and natural environment. In 2012/13 a total of £5,300 was awarded in grants to organisations.

Carpentry and construction

The Carpenters Company Charitable Trust

£2,400 (1 grant)

Correspondent: Brigadier Gregson, The Clerk, Carpenters' Hall, 1 Throgmorton Avenue, London EC2N 2JJ (020 7588 7001; email: info@carpentersco.com; website: www.carpentersco.com/pages/charities/carpenters_company_charitable_trust1)

CC Number: 276996

Eligibility

The trust is set up to 'support the craft' i.e. people wishing to set up in or to study carpentry.

Types of grants

Educational grants are awarded up to £2,400 to help with fees, maintenance, equipment and other necessities.

Annual grant total

In 2012/13 the trust had assets of £22 million (comprising mainly of endowment, restricted and designated funds), an income of £1.1 million and a total expenditure of £942,000. One grant of £2,400 was awarded to an individual this financial year.

Applications

On a form available from the correspondent or from the website (www.carpentersco.com/pages/default.aspx). Applications are considered in March, July and November.

Other information

Grants are also made to organisations and 2012/13, grants awarded total £740,000.

Norton Folgate Trust

£205,000 (67 grants)

Correspondent: The Craft and Charities Administrator, Carpenter's Company, Carpenter's Hall, 1 Throgmorton Avenue, London EC2N 2JJ (020 7588 7001; email: info@carpentersco.com; website: www.thecarpenterscompany.co.uk/pages/charities/norton_folgate_charitable_trust/default.aspx)

CC Number: 230990

Eligibility

People in further or higher education at an institution in the UK who are studying the craft of carpentry, fine woodwork, stonemasonry, historic building conservation, any branch of the building industry or related courses.

Types of grants

Grants ranging from £500 to £7,500 can be given to help with school, college or university fees or to supplement existing grants. Support may be available to school pupils towards general educational necessities but most grants are distributed to secondary or tertiary education students, particularly to individuals at the Building Crafts College in Stratford, East London. Some funds may be given towards wood craft tools.

Annual grant total

In 2012/13 the trust had assets of £5.9 million, an income of £267,000 and made grants totalling £241,000. A total of 67 individuals were supported for educational purposes, including 53 grants totalling £159,000 in craft education and 14 grants totalling £46,000 in other education.

Exclusions

Grants are not made retrospectively.

Applications

Application forms are available on the trust's website and have to be submitted by June for the academic year beginning in September. Applicants will be notified of a decision in August.

Students at the Building Crafts College should apply to the following address before May (applicants will be notified of a decision in June): The Bursar, Building Crafts College, Kennard Road, Stratford, London E15 1AH.

People applying for grants for wood craft tools should write to the correspondent.

Other information

Grants are also made for welfare purposes to members of The Worshipful Company of Carpenters and liverymen, freemen, retirees and their dependents. In 2012/13 nine such grants were made totalling £36,000.

Scottish Building Federation Edinburgh and District Charitable Trust

£23,000

Correspondent: Fiona Watson, Administrator, Scott-Moncrieff (Secretaries and Treasurers), Exchange Place 3, Semple Street, Edinburgh EH3 8BL (01314 733500; email: charity@scott-moncrieff.com; website: www.scott-moncrieff.com/charitable_trusts/page7.html)

SC Number: SCO29604

Eligibility

Students studying skills relating to the building industry at the following universities and colleges: Heriot-Watt University; Napier University; West Lothian College; Edinburgh's Telford College; Jewel and Esk Valley College. Dependents of persons who have been involved in the building trade in the Lothians, with a particular emphasis on owners and senior employees of companies.

Types of grants

Scholarships of up to £10,000 for study, research and travel associated with the construction industry and grants for course expenses such as books, equipment and travel.

Annual grant total

In 2013 the trust had an income and expenditure of almost £48,000. Funding is also provided for welfare purposes for those who have been involved in the building trade in the Lothians. We estimate that grants awarded to individuals for educational purposes was around £23,000.

Applications

On forms available from the correspondent or the trust's website.

Applications should be completed and forwarded to the appropriate department of the university or college for scholarships or to the trust for grants. Trustees meet four times a year to consider applications.

Commerce

Gustav Adolph and Ernest Koettgen Memorial Fund

£1,300

Correspondent: Fiona MacGillivray, Family Action, 501–505 Kingsland Road, London E8 4AU (020 7254 6251; email: grants.enquiry@family-action.org.uk; website: www.family-action.org.uk)

CC Number: 313291

Eligibility

Undergraduate students (including mature students) of British nationality whose means are insufficient to obtain higher education or tuition for a higher commercial career. Preference is given to employees of John Batt and Company (London) Ltd or members of their families.

Types of grants

One-off grants from £200 to £500 are available towards the cost of books, fees, living expenses and childcare. According to our research, applicants are only considered if they are in their final year of a course and if they have managed to raise almost the whole amount needed or if they encounter unexpected difficulty, as these grants are only intended to be supplementary.

Annual grant total

In 2012/13 the fund had an income of £1,200 and a total expenditure of £1,400. We have estimated that the annual total of grants was around £1,300. The expenditure in this financial year was lower than usual.

Exclusions

Our research suggests that postgraduate studies are not supported.

Applications

Application forms can be obtained from the correspondent. Applications can be submitted directly by the individual but will need to be supported by an academic reference.

The Worshipful Company of Chartered Secretaries and Administrators Charitable Trust

£5,100 (15 grants)

Correspondent: Erica Lee, Secretary, WCCSA Charitable Trust, 3rd Floor, Saddlers Hall, 40 Gutter Lane, London EC2V 6BR (020 7726 2955; email: assistant.clerk@wccsa.org.uk; website: www.wccsa.org.uk/Education.html)

CC Number: 288487

Eligibility

Chartered secretaries and administrators studying commercial courses in various universities and the apprentices of the Worshipful Company of Chartered Secretaries and Administrators.

Types of grants

The trust awards prizes of up to £500 for success in the examinations of the Institute of Chartered Secretaries and Administrators (ICSA) and in collaborative courses between ICSA and various universities. Support is also available to apprentices of the Worshipful Company of Chartered Secretaries and Administrators.

Annual grant total

In 2012/13 the trust had assets of £1.3 million, an income of £56,000 and a total charitable expenditure of about £31,000. Grants to individuals for educational purposes totalled £5,100, distributed through prizes and awards to 15 individuals.

Applications

In writing to the correspondent. Our research suggests that grants are normally considered every three months, usually January, April, July and October.

Other information

The trustees' report from 2012/13 trust also states that awards are made to 'a range of charities supporting education and social welfare in the City of London and the Inner London Boroughs and to charities working with current or former members of the Armed Services.'

Engineering

The Douglas Bomford Trust

£20,000 (19+ grants)

Correspondent: Paul Miller, Secretary, 46 Howard Close, Haynes, Bedford MK45 3QH (01234 381342; fax: 01234 751319; email: enquiries@dbt.org.uk; website: www.dbt.org.uk)

CC Number: 1121785

Eligibility

People involved in education, research and practice of agricultural engineering and mechanisation who are aiming to become professional engineers or scientists and intend to work applying their expertise to agricultural and land related problems. Priority is given to individuals who work in the areas of particular national or technical importance and those who can receive part of the costs from other sources. Some connection with the UK is required, either through nationality, residency, or place of learning/registration.

Types of grants

The trusts can offer: travel scholarships for educational tours overseas, conferences and for presenting papers at international conferences; recurrent scholarships to undergraduate students; support towards postgraduate study and research; discretionary awards in cases of hardship; and various prizes to students showing high academic achievements or to the authors of papers published in allied journals.

Annual grant total

In 2012/13 the trust had assets of £3.9 million, an income of £124,000 and a total charitable expenditure of £293,000. Grants to individuals totalled £20,000. The amount given can be broken down as follows:

Studentships	7	£8,600
Travel grants	12	£6,400
Discretionary awards	Not specified	£3,000
Other awards	Not specified	£2,000

Applications

There are different grant schemes for travel awards, undergraduate students, postgraduate research and other awards. Application details for each of them can be found on the trust's website.

Other information

Note that 'owing to the high level of applications currently being received relative to the funding available, only those proposals that comply directly with the trust's objectives will be considered or acknowledged.'

The trust also awards grants to organisations (in 2012/13 a total of £273,000) and 'supports student membership of the Institution of Agricultural Engineers as a means of introducing them to the benefits of professional qualifications and of being part of a professional community.'

The Coachmakers and Coach Harness Makers Charitable Trust 1977

£12,700 (9 grants)

Correspondent: Commander Mark Leaning, Administrator, Royal Navy, 1 Rochester Close, Chichester, West Sussex PO19 5DS (07505 089841; email: clerk@coachmakers.co.uk; website: www.coachmakers.co.uk)

CC Number: 286521

Eligibility

People studying/working in the aerospace, automotive and coach making or associated industries.

Types of grants

Grants are available to individuals in technical education and training, including apprenticeships. Awards are usually given towards general educational needs, research, study/travel overseas and maintenance expenses.

Bursaries are given for individuals studying motor vehicle design at The Royal College of Art and aerospace sciences at Cranfield University.

There is also a 'flying scholarship for an individual who, in competition, has shown aptitude and determination to become a pilot' and an annual Award to Industry made 'to promote excellence in design, technical development and commercial significance.'

Annual grant total

In 2012/13 the trust had assets of £1.2 million and an income of £120,000. A total of £12,700 was awarded in grants to nine individuals in the motor and aircraft industries.

Exclusions

The trust's website states that 'awards are as substantial as possible, but bursaries are allocated on an annual basis and, because funds cannot always be guaranteed, the Livery cannot accept commitments to individuals for long-term educational courses.'

Applications

In writing to the correspondent. Applications should normally be submitted in December and October for consideration in January and November respectively.

Other information

In 2012/13 twenty grants were made to institutions totalling £30,000.

Support is also given to freemen and liverymen of the Coachmakers Livery Company and their dependents.

The Worshipful Company of Engineers Charitable Trust Fund

£25,000

Correspondent: Anthony Willenbruch, Clerk, The Worshipful Company of Engineers, Wax Chandlers Hall, 6 Gresham Street, London EC2V 7AD (020 7726 4830; fax: 020 7726 4820; email: clerk@engineerscompany.org.uk; website: www.engineerstrust.org.uk)

CC Number: 298819

Eligibility

Sixth form pupils at schools in Greater London are eligible for scholarships. People studying science and technology of engineering are eligible for various awards and prizes for academic excellence. Engineering students and professionals in education can be assisted in cases of hardship, normally whilst in their final year of study.

Types of grants

The trust supports a number of award schemes to encourage excellence in engineering. It offers two Arkwright Scholarships worth £600 over two years to pupils undertaking sixth form studies at schools in Greater London, potentially leading to higher education in engineering, and can provide general hardship grants to people in engineering education.

Annual grant total

In 2013 the trust had assets of £1.3 million, an income of £85,000 and a total charitable expenditure of around £33,000, distributed in grants to individuals and organisations. Medals, prizes and associated costs amounted to £21,000 while educational grants totalled £4,100.

Applications

Specific application details for different awards can be found on the trust's website. Some schemes require candidates to be nominated by the institution.

Applications for annual awards and prizes should be made in the early part of the year for consideration in the first half of May.

Other information

The trust also supports welfare needs, engineering research and can award grants to organisations in the city of London that further the interest of the history, traditions and customs of the city.

The Benevolent Fund of the Institution of Civil Engineers Ltd

£20,000

Correspondent: Kris Barnett, Chief Executive, 30 Mill Hill Close, Haywards Heath, West Sussex RH16 1NY (01444 417979; fax: 01444 453307; email: benfund@ice.org.uk; website: www.bfice.org.uk)

CC Number: 1126595

Eligibility

Student members of Institution of Civil Engineers (ICE), who are disabled or disadvantaged and are studying on an ICE accredited course at a UK university.

Types of grants

Grants of up to £1,000 per semester for living costs, travel, accommodation, equipment costs and course materials. They are not normally offered to pay course fees.

Annual grant total

In 2013 the fund had assets of £14.5 million, (a significant part of which is designated permanent endowment and cannot be spent on grantmaking), and an income of £1.1 million. Grants were made to 139 individuals in the UK and 18 overseas, totalling £532,000, including support for eight students. There is no breakdown in the accounts for grant purposes but most funding is awarded for social welfare. We have estimated that the amount awarded to individuals for educational purposes was around £20,000.

Exclusions

No grants for students who have not started their university course or have yet to be offered a university place; have mismanaged their finances and simply run out of money; or, are studying for a Civil Engineering degree not accredited by ICE. No support is given to postgraduates.

Funding may not be used to clear old debts, indulge in social activities, or to purchase non-essential equipment and materials.

Applications

On a form available from the correspondent. Applications must be accompanied by a reference or letter of support from the Head of Department, or their nominee. They can be made at any time. All applicants will be visited by one of the fund's volunteer visitors.

Other information

The fund owns properties in West Sussex and has nomination rights to the Hanover Housing Association which it uses to help (ex-)members and their families who are facing difficult circumstances and need somewhere to live.

It also runs a 24-hour helpline (0800 587 3428) which offers support and advice on a wide range of issues including, stress management, debt problems, childcare and substance abuse.

The Institution of Engineering and Technology (IET)

£2.2 million

Correspondent: Andrew Wilson, Administrator, The Institution of Engineering and Technology, 2 Savoy Place, London WC2R 0BL (020 7344 5415; email: governance@theiet.org; website: www.theiet.org)

CC Number: 211014, SC038698

Eligibility

The following list of regulations applies as a general rule to all scholarships and prizes (however candidates should refer to the IET website to ensure they fit the specific criteria of different awards):

- Students must be studying or about to study (in the next academic session) on an IET-accredited degree course at a UK university (for a list of accredited programmes see the IET's website)
- Each candidate should be supported by the head of the educational or training establishment, the course tutor, the university head of department or by a chartered member of the IET (for some awards it is necessary to become a member)
- A candidate who is shortlisted for an award may be required to attend an interview at the IET
- The scholarship will be paid in instalments, as determined by the IET (it will be withdrawn and any unpaid instalments withheld if the holder leaves the course)
- Successful candidates must not hold any other IET scholarship or grant at the same time
- Applicants should demonstrate passion to engineering and/or high academic achievements

Types of grants

The IET offers a range of scholarships, prizes and travel awards ranging up to £10,000. These include undergraduate and postgraduate scholarships, travel grants to members of the IET (for study tour, work in the industry, to attend a conference), apprenticeship and technician awards and various prizes for achievement and innovation. International scholarships for study in India and America and various scholarships at participating universities are also available.

From 2013 a new Diamond Jubilee Scholarship Fund of over £2 million committed over five years has been launched offering £1,000 for each year of the degree to students applying for IET accredited courses in Computing, Electrical, Electronic and Manufacturing Engineering. During the year 540 students received the award.

Annual grant total

In 2013 the charity had assets of £137.2 million and an income of £57.5 million. Grants to individuals totalled around £2.2 million.

Exclusions

There may be certain conditions attached to separate awards, for example, undergraduate grants are not intended to cover placement years and IET postgraduate scholarships are not currently given for MSc degrees (but awards from specific funds offer support). Applicants are advised to read the guidelines for specific awards carefully.

Applications

Further details and application forms are available from the institution's website. Generally applications should be made on an online system. The deadlines vary for different awards.

Other information

The institution also administers a number of restricted funds to assist training and education in engineering and electrical engineering.

The institution's website holds an 'IET Awards Book' with extensive information on all awards available.

The Benevolent Fund of the Institution of Mechanical Engineers (IMechE) – known as Support Network

£54,000

Correspondent: Maureen Hayes, Casework and Support Officer, 1–3 Birdcage Walk, Westminster, London SW1H 9JJ (020 7304 6816; fax: 020 7973 1262; email: info@ supportnetwork.org.uk; website: www. supportnetwork.org.uk)

CC Number: 209465

Eligibility

Financially disadvantaged students or students with disabilities, studying Mechanical Engineering on an IMechE accredited first degree course at a UK University who are IMechE Members. Preference is given to the following: students with disabilities; final year students; students with dependents, particularly lone parents; students aged 25 and over with extra financial commitments; local authority care leavers; students estranged from their parents; students with significant debts before commencing the course; students repeating a year due to causes outside their control and students with no access to other funds.

Types of grants
One-off grants of up to £1,000 for financially disadvantaged students for living costs, travel and accommodation. Grants for equipment costs and course materials such as software and books.

Annual grant total
In 2013 the fund had assets of £20.7 million and an income of £1.4 million. All grants to individuals were listed as relief of poverty and totalled £294,000. Although educational/training grants are not separately listed, this may be because most of the criteria for educational/training grants appear to include a financial qualification as well. We have estimated the educational/training grants to be around £54,000. There were also 287 money advice recipients.

Exclusions
No grants for people who are studying outside the UK, have not been offered a university place or started their studies, or those who have mismanaged their finances and run out of money.

Applications
Applicants should request the appropriate form from the correspondent. Three months are needed to process applications; this should be three months prior to when a decision is required, not necessarily the date of the activity. Closing dates are determined by the approximate dates of the committee meetings, which are held in March, June and September. Applicants requiring an interview will be notified.

Other information
Support Network helps members of IMechE with many of life's challenges. It provides financial help as well as specialist advice and information. Visit the fund's website to find out about the services that it offers.

The Mott MacDonald Charitable Trust

£138,000 (11+ grants)

Correspondent: Steve Wise, Administrator, Mott MacDonald House, 8–10 Sydenham Road, Croydon CR0 2EE (020 8774 2090; email: charitable.trust@mottmac.com; website: mottmac.com/article/5901/mott-macdonald-charitable-trust)

CC Number: 275040

Eligibility
People undertaking higher education in the fields of civil, structural, mechanical, electrical and allied engineering (disciplines directly related to the work of Mott MacDonald company).

Types of grants
Undergraduate bursaries (generally on an annual basis) and recurring scholarships mainly to master's students (or occasionally PhD). The amount of money available to any person is a maximum of £12,000. Awards are given to cover the course fees.

Annual grant total
At the time of writing the latest financial information available was from 2012. In 2012 the trust had assets of £133,000 and an income of £119,000. Eleven scholarships totalling £31,000 and a number of undergraduate bursaries totalling £107,000 were made during the year.

Exclusions
Funding is not given retrospectively.

Applications
In writing to the correspondent. Applications should be submitted by 30 March for the courses starting later in that year. The trustees meet in May. Candidates should have obtained a conditional offer of acceptance and provide details of fees. Each application is acknowledged and if the consideration is taken further the trust will ask for some more clarification.

Applicants employed by Mott MacDonald need to supply two employer references and those that do not work in the company need to supply two academic or one academic and one employer references.

Other information
A further £31,000 was awarded in various special awards. The trust funds four university research projects focusing on providing solutions to the industry and works in partnership with universities to increase the flow of students who at postgraduate level. The trust's website states that they will not be open to new research funding proposals until January 2016.

The Worshipful Company of Scientific Instrument Makers

£31,000

Correspondent: The Clerk, Glaziers Hall, 9 Montague Close, London SE1 9DD (020 7407 4832; email: theclerk@wcsim.co.uk; website: www.wcsim.co.uk)

CC Number: 221332

Eligibility
Schoolchildren, sixth formers, undergraduates and postgraduates with outstanding ability in science and mathematics and a creative and practical interest in branches of engineering connected with instrumentation and measurement.

Students must attend one of the following universities: Brunel, Cambridge, City, Glasgow Caledonian, Imperial, Oxford, Teesside, UCL, UMIST, Warwick.

Types of grants
Mentoring and grants of £500 per year for undergraduates. The Young Engineers Programme supports people to attend national and international events, competitions, prizes and travel support plus apprenticeships. There are also scholarships of £300 for sixth formers.

Postgraduate awards of £2,000 for 'exciting research and design' and a postdoctoral award of £5,000 for up to three years.

Annual grant total
In 2011/12 the trust held assets of £1.6 million and had an income of £58,000. Grants to individuals for educational purposes totalled £31,000 and for social welfare purposes totalled £4,200. This was the latest financial information available at the time of writing (July 2014).

Applications
See the Company's website for details of how to apply to each separate scheme. Students must apply through the university and not directly to the company.

South Wales Institute of Engineers Educational Trust

£6,100

Correspondent: Sandra Chapman, Administrative Officer, Suite 2, Bay Chambers, West Bute Street, Cardiff CF10 5BB (01792 879409/07594 551263; email: sandra.chapman@swieet2007.org.uk; website: www.swieet2007.org.uk)

CC Number: 1013538

Eligibility
People entering and practicing engineering in Wales – school pupils deciding on their career, undergraduate students on engineering courses, graduates starting work in the engineering industry, apprentices and equivalent.

Types of grants
One-off and recurrent grants according to need, generally from £100 to £1,000.

The trust has funded engineering education from pre-GCSE level through to postgraduate/professional qualifications.

Annual grant total

In 2012/13 the trust had assets of £941,000 and an income of £29,000. A total of £27,000 was spent in charitable grants, of which £6,100 was awarded to individuals.

Applications

The trust's office should be contacted directly to find out the details of the current year's awards/prizes and to discuss an application.

Other information

Grants to organisations to support engineering education totalled £21,000 in 2012/13.

The Institution of Works and Highway Management (Bernard Butler) Trust

£18,800

Correspondent: Bernard Butler, Trustee, 10 Vale Close, Lower Bourne, Farnham GU10 3HR (01252 93276; email: info@ bernardbutlertrust.org; website: www. bernardbutlertrust.org)

CC Number: 1063735

Eligibility

People studying or working in the fields of engineering who are in need.

Types of grants

Grants, of at least £1,000, can be one-off or recurrent. Assistance can be given to college/university students (including mature and postgraduate), people in vocational training or individuals who wish to undertake courses to improve their skills and professional qualifications. Support is available towards various course related costs (including fees, necessities, books), travel and accommodation costs to attend seminars/conferences/meetings, also childcare or costs of dependents, and any other project or expenses which will enable individuals to advance their education. The trust is interested in supporting work on 'improving the standards of safety, education and quality of engineering processes and methods of construction.'

Annual grant total

In 2012/13 the trust had assets of £320,000 and an income of £9,600. A total of £18,800 was awarded in grants to individuals.

Applications

Application forms are available from the trust's website or can be requested from the correspondent. They can be submitted at any time. The remit of support available is very wide and the trust welcomes informal enquires to discuss applications.

Other information

Grants can also be made to organisations.

Environmental studies

Alan Baxter Foundation (ABF)
See entry on page 93

The Alice McCosh Trust

£30,000

Correspondent: Grace Carswell, Administrator, 49 Cluny Street, Lewes, Sussex BN7 1LN (email: info@ thealicemccoshtrust.org.uk; website: www.thealicemccoshtrust.org.uk)

SC Number: SC035938

Eligibility

People of any age undertaking work or study related to natural history and/or the environment. Preference will be given to individuals from (or work relating to) Scotland, England and Turkey.

Types of grants

One-off grants in the range of £300 to £1,000, for example, to cover the cost of a school field trip or project, an expedition as part of a research project or the development of new teaching materials for schools or institutes of higher education.

Annual grant total

In 2012/13 the trust had an income of £8,000 and a total expenditure of £31,000. We estimate around £30,000 was made in grants to individuals for education. This is a large increase on the previous year's grants of around £3,000.

Exclusions

Projects involving joining an existing commercial organisation on a pre-paid tour or expedition will not be considered.

Applications

On a form available from the trust's website along with guidelines.

Applications should be emailed to the correspondent between 1 October and 30 November each year. (Applications received at other times, or sent by post, will not be considered). Applications should be concise (no more than four typed pages) and include two referee statements.

The Martin Smith Foundation
See entry on page 82

The Water Conservation Trust

£52,000

Correspondent: The Administrator, HQS Wellington, Temple Stairs, Victoria Embankment, London WC2R 2PN (01189 833689; email: waterloo@aol. com)

CC Number: 1007648

Eligibility

People who are working or studying in the fields of water or environment conservation and industry, and their dependents.

Types of grants

The trust offers one-off grants to individuals and runs a bursary programme for postgraduate studies and research in environment/water at nine UK universities.

Annual grant total

In 2012/13 the trust had assets of £503,000 and an income of £47,000. A total of over £52,000 was spent in grants for educational purposes, broken down as follows:

Bursary and/or dissertation support at various universities	£49,000
School projects and pupil prizes	£2,800
Grants to individuals	£500

Exclusions

Unsolicited applications are not invited.

Applications

When funds are available applicants for scholarships are invited through the water and environmental press. Applications should then be made via specific universities.

Other information

The trust also awards grants to environmental organisations, promotes environmental education in schools and the community and supports activities with environmental focus for people with disability.

Esperanto

The Norwich Jubilee Esperanto Foundation (N. O. J. E. F)

£3,000

Correspondent: Tim Owen, Secretary, c/o Esperanto-Asocio de Britio, Esperanto House, Station Road, Barlaston, Stoke-on-Trent ST12 9DE (email: secretary@nojef.org; website: www.nojef.org)

CC Number: 313190

Eligibility

Young people under the age of 25 who either are British or live in the UK. Our research shows that preference among non-Britons is normally given to those whose native language is not English, since contact with such is more useful to British students of Esperanto.

Research funding available for applicants who are British or at British institution and is only given upon condition that a copy of research will be available (in English or Esperanto) for the Butler Library. Greater grants will be given for research which is in the public domain, for proposals at higher academic level and depending on the extent of attention on Esperanto in the proposal.

Types of grants

The foundation can provide the following financial assistance:

- One-off grants to cover travel, accommodation, entrance fee and related costs for British students attending approved Esperanto events
- Support towards research with a maximum grant of £1,000 for a PhD thesis

Annual grant total

In 2012/13 the foundation had an income of £12,000 and an expenditure of £3,300. We estimate that the annual total of grants was about £3,000.

Exclusions

Financial support cannot be made retrospectively.

Applications

Applications for travel grants should be made by sending a letter in Esperanto to the correspondent giving some details of the travel plans and likely costs. New applicants are also asked to introduce themselves and give details of a referee who could confirm applicants' efforts in learning Esperanto and give an insight on their character.

Applications for research funding should be made by sending a letter to the correspondent with the research proposal including any anticipated costs.

Other information

All grants are given on the condition that a written report in Esperanto will be provided following the event. Further grants for different events will only be considered if the reports are delivered within reasonable time and at respectable length.

Fire-fighting, fire engineering, fire protection or fire research

Institution of Fire Engineers

£10,000

Correspondent: The Administrator, IFE House, 64–66 Cygnet Court, Timothy's Bridge Road, Stratford-upon-Avon CV37 9NW (01789 261463; fax: 01789 296426; email: frstt@ife.org.uk; website: www.ife.org.uk)

SC Number: SC012694

Eligibility

All fire professionals, members of fire research organisations and the fire engineering profession or students of these areas in the UK.

Types of grants

More information on support currently available can be requested from the correspondent via email. Our research suggests that educational grants can be given for assistance with fees, books or research associated with a project/degree/general course work. Scholarships for major pieces of work and research grants are also available.

Annual grant total

The income for the institution is donated by another charity (The Fire Service Research and Training Trust), and varies greatly. The latest financial information at the time of writing (August 2014) was from 2012. In 2012 the institution had an income of £958,000 and spent £788,000 on charitable activities. Grants usually total around £10,000 each year.

Applications

Further guidelines and information on applications are available from the correspondent.

Other information

The institute makes grants on behalf of the Fire Service Research and Training Trust.

Game-keeping

The Gamekeepers Welfare Trust

£0

Correspondent: Philip Holt, Administrator, High Park Farm, High Park, Kirkbymoorside, York YO62 7HS (01751 430100; email: gamekeeperwtrust@binternet.com; website: thegamekeeperswelfaretrust.com)

CC Number: 1008924

Eligibility

Young people in need who wish to make gamekeeping their career. People over 24 will not be considered unless there are extenuating circumstances.

Types of grants

One-off and recurrent grants according to need.

Annual grant total

The latest accounts available were for 2012. During that year, the trust had assets of £144,000 and an income of £27,500. Grants to 23 individuals totalled £4,400. A further £8,400 was given to organisations of which, £7,200 was for educational purposes. In this particular accounting year, there were no grants awarded to individuals for educational purposes.

Applications

On a form available from the correspondent or through the trust's website, along with guidelines. Applications can be made at any time.

Gas engineering

The Institution of Gas Engineers Benevolent Fund

£2,000

Correspondent: Kristina Parkin, Administrator, IGEM House, High Street, Kegworth, Derbyshire DE74 2DA (01509 678167; email: lesley@igem.org. uk; website: www.igem.org.uk)

CC Number: 214010

Eligibility

UK and overseas students wishing to study gas engineering.

Types of grants

Grants are given according to need.

Annual grant total

In 2012 the trust had an income £12,000 and a total expenditure of £4,600. Grants were made totalling approximately £4,000 which was split between educational and welfare grants.

This was the most recent financial information available at the time of writing (August 2014).

Applications

In writing to the correspondent.

Geography

Royal Geographical Society (with the Institute of British Geographers)

£91,000

Correspondent: Grants Office, 1 Kensington Gore, London SW7 2AR (020 7591 3073; fax: 020 7591 3001; email: grants@rgs.org; website: www.rgs. org)

CC Number: 208791

Eligibility

People over the age of 16 who are carrying out geographical research and projects. Teachers, undergraduate and postgraduate students, scientists, also non-academics (for example independent travellers) are all eligible.

The society has previously stated that its grants programme aims to promote geographical research and a wider understanding of the world and therefore applicants are not required to have a geography degree, work in a geography department or define themselves as a geographer, but must share the society's interest in the world, people and environment.

Note: some grants are only open to fellows of the society.

Types of grants

The society administers a large numbers of grants each with separate eligibility criteria and application process. The awards are broken down into the following categories: Established Researchers; Early Career Researchers; Postgraduate; Undergraduate; Expeditions, Fieldwork and Independent Travel; Teaching. For full details of each award see the society's website.

Support can be given for work both in the UK and overseas in the range of £250 -£30,000.

Annual grant total

In 2013 the society had assets of £14.2 million, an income of £4.3 million and made grants totalling £196,000. Out of that sum £91,000 was awarded to individuals and consisted of support for Expeditions and Fieldwork (£89,000) and Education and Teaching (£2,000).

Exclusions

Grants are not made retrospectively or given for fees/living costs associated with degrees.

Applications

All grant details, guidelines, application forms and specific deadlines can be obtained from the society's website. Generally, the application process lasts between three and four months. All candidates are informed about the outcome of their application.

Other information

The society also supports institutions and offers information, advice, resources and training to support anyone planning a fieldwork or scientific expedition.

Greece

The Hellenic Foundation

£7,500

Correspondent: The Trustees, 150 Aldersgate Street, London EC1A 4AB (020 7251 5100)

CC Number: 326301

Eligibility

Students studying the culture, tradition and heritage of Greece, particularly in the subjects involving education, research, music, theatre productions, exhibitions and concerts.

Types of grants

One-off and recurrent grants for projects involving education, research, music and dance, books and library facilities and university symposia.

Annual grant total

In 2012 the foundation had an income of £22,000 and made grants totalling approximately £7,500.

These were the latest accounts available at the time of writing (July 2014).

Applications

In writing to the correspondent.

Historic conservation

The Zibby Garnett Travelling Fellowship

£32,000 (9 grants)

Correspondent: Robert Garnett, Trustee, The Grange, Main Street, Norwell, Newark, Nottinghamshire NG23 6JN (01636 636288; email: info@zibbygarnett. org; website: www.zibbygarnett.org)

CC Number: 1081403

Eligibility

Students, craft apprentices or young professionals working in the fields of historic and decorative crafts, architectural conservation, historic landscape and gardens, traditional building skills, sculpture, artefacts and similar or associated areas, who wish to travel abroad for educational purposes or research.

Types of grants

Grants and bursaries in the range of £300–£3,000 are given to allow individuals to travel overseas for practical study and conservation work. The trustees are looking for 'imaginative and unusual ideas likely to broaden the applicant's understanding of their subject and widen their horizons.' Preference will be given to projects which are not part of the academic curricular but rather applicant's own initiative. The awards are not restricted to British nationals but overseas students should plan projects outside their country of origin.

Annual grant total

In 2012/13 the charity had an income of £22,000 and an expenditure of £33,000. We estimate that the annual total of grants was around £32,000. During the year nine students were awarded.

Exclusions

Grants are not given retrospectively, for placements in the UK, for conferences/formal courses or holidays. Support is intended for practical work in conservation, not new work.

Applications

Application forms can be found on the charity's website. Applications are considered once a year and the submission deadline is 12 noon of the last working day in February annually. Applicants who are successful with their initial application are invited for an interview (usually in March) which is held in London and in Lincoln/Newark.

Anna Plowden Trust

£25,000 (37 grants)

Correspondent: Francis Plowden, Trustee, 4 Highbury Road, London SW19 7PR (020 8879 9841; email: info@annaplowdentrust.org.uk; website: www.annaplowdentrust.org.uk)

CC Number: 1072236

Eligibility

People who want to train for a qualification in conservation of movable heritage and professionals who are looking to develop their skills in conservation.

Types of grants

The trust offers Conservation Bursaries to individuals (usually graduates) seeking to obtain qualifications to enter conservation profession and awards Continuing Professional Development (CPD) grants covering up to 50% of the costs for short, mid-career skills development opportunities.

Annual grant total

In 2012/13 the trust had assets of £539,000 and an income of £74,000. A total of £25,000 was awarded in grants. During the year the trust awarded 12 bursaries and further 25 conservators received the CPD grants.

The trust's website stated that by June 2014 a total of 17 bursaries and 16 CPD grants had already been awarded.

Exclusions

Courses on the conservation of non-moveable heritage are not eligible (for example, building or natural environment conservation).

Applications

Application forms and further guidelines are available from the trust's website. Bursary applications are considered once a year, usually in May. For specific deadlines see the trust's website. Applications for funding are also invited

through advertisements in the national conservation journals.

Other information

The trust also awards an annual Research and Innovation in Conservation Award and provides support through Raising Awareness grant towards the cost of publicising successful conservation projects. For more information on these awards see the trust's website.

As an alternative support the trust's website advises to approach The Clothworkers' Foundation which also offers bursaries for conservators.

Home economics

The British and Foreign School Society - Berridge Trust Fund

£0

Correspondent: Belinda Lawrance, Administrator, Maybrook House, Godstone Road, Caterham, Surrey CR3 6RE (01883 331177; email: enquiries@bfss.org.uk; website: www.bfss.org.uk)

CC Number: 314286

Eligibility

People training to become teachers of cookery or nutrition in England and Wales.

Types of grants

One-off grants according to need.

Annual grant total

In 2013 no grants were made from the fund.

The society's financial statements for the year describe how this reflects the difficulty of attracting suitable applicants who meet the specific requirement to be cookery teachers.

Applications

Applicants should use the application form for individuals, which is available from the BFSS website.

Other information

The British and Foreign School Society (BFSS) is a grant-giving organisation and offers funding for educational projects in the UK and around the world. The society also offers a small number of grants for organisations and individuals through its subsidiary trusts of which this is one. Eligibility criteria for these subsidiary trusts depend on area of residence and/or particular field of educational activity. In March 2014 we

were informed by Steven Ross, a trustee of the society, that money was available from these funds. Visit the BFSS website for information on the set criteria.

Horticulture/ botany

The Merlin Trust

£11,700 (16 grants)

Correspondent: Joanne Everson, Rock Garden Team Leader, Royal Botanic Gardens, Kew Green, Richmond TW9 3AB (020 8332 5585; email: info@merlin-trust.org.uk; website: www.merlin-trust.org.uk)

CC Number: 803441

Eligibility

UK and Irish nationals, aged between 18 and 35, who are horticulturists or botanists or those in their first five years of a career in horticulture who wish to extend their knowledge of plants, gardens and gardening by travelling. Applicants should be able to show that their proposed projects will help them in their careers.

Types of grants

Grants towards visiting gardens in different parts of the country or abroad, or travelling to see wild plants in their native habitats. Any suitable project, large or small, will be carefully considered.

Previous support has been awarded for an expedition to southern Chile to observe the range of beautiful plants, a trip to New York's community gardens and a visit to Peru in search of orchids.

The Valerie Finnis Prize of £500 is also available for the 'Merlin' who demonstrates the most photographic excellence in their final report.

Annual grant total

In 2012/13 the trust had an income of £39,000 and assets of £602,000. Grants totalled £11,700 and were made to 16 individuals.

Exclusions

Grants are not given towards postgraduate study or to fund highly technical laboratory-based research.

Applications

Application forms are available to download from the trust's website. The form should be completed and emailed to the secretary along with a one page description of your project and a CV. A signed copy of the form should also be posted to the secretary. The trust welcomes telephone enquiries. A written report must be presented within three months of the project being completed.

The Royal Horticultural Society (RHS)

£65,000 (100 grants)

Correspondent: Bryan Hislop, Administrator, 80 Vincent Square, London SW1P 2PE (01483 479719, 020 7821 3034; email: bursaries@rhs.org.uk; website: www.rhs.org.uk/Learning/ Education/bursaries.htm)

CC Number: 22879, SC038262

Eligibility

Professional and student gardeners/ horticulturalists, plant and soil scientists, botanists, agroculturalists, landscapers, botanical artists and related professionals. While priority is given to professional horticulturists and students, applications are also considered from serious amateur gardeners. Eligible proposals must be closely identified with horticulture.

Types of grants

Grants can be awarded for horticultural project, expeditions, study tours, voluntary work placements, conferences, educational and training courses, taxonomy, research and so on.

Two separate bursaries are offered: the Susan Pearson Bursary for one year paid traineeship at a UK garden open to public and the Dawn Jolliffe Botanical Art Bursary for painting or drawing plants in their natural habitat or exhibiting work at an RHS show.

Annual grant total

In 2012/13 the society had assets of £84.9 million and an income of £81.3 million. A total of £65,000 was awarded in bursaries. The trust notes that a total of 135 applications were received during the year, of which 74% were awarded a bursary.

Exclusions

Grants are not normally made for salary costs, tuition fees, exam fees or living costs for educational courses.

Applications

Application forms can be obtained from the society's website or the correspondent. Completed forms should be submitted by email by 31 March, 30 June, 30 September or 15 December. Applications for the traineeship and for botanical artwork must be submitted by 31 March.

Other information

Organisations, charities and gardens open to the public may be supported.

The Royal Horticultural Society administers a number of bursary funds, established and maintained through generous bequests and donations, to support professional and student gardeners/horticulturalists.

Hospitality trades

The Geoffrey Harrison Foundation

£7,000

Correspondent: Richard Harrison, Secretary, Oxford House, Oxford Road, Thame, Oxon OX9 2AH (website: www. geoffreyharrisonfoundation.org.uk)

CC Number: 1142242

Eligibility

People in education or training in the hotel, restaurant and hospitality industries. Currently support is mainly aimed at Year 10 and 11 students attending the Junior Chefs Academy courses at selected institutions, and individual students in the 16–18 age groups at Westminster Kingsway College and the University of West London, who show exceptional talent and would benefit from specific support.

Types of grants

Grants to support education and training connected with the catering and hospitality industries.

Annual grant total

In 2012/13 the foundation had assets of £127,000 and an income of £84,000. Student support totalled £7,000.

Applications

In writing to the correspondent.

Other information

The main activity of the foundation is to contribute to the Saturday Morning Junior Chefs Academy courses held at University of West London, Ealing and the Westminster Kingsway College, Victoria. In 2012/13 the amount spent towards the courses totalled £40,000.

The Savoy Educational Trust

£1,600 (5 grants)

Correspondent: Margaret Georgiou, Administrator, Queens House, 55–56 Lincoln's Inn Fields, London WC2A 3BH (020 7269 9692; fax: 020 7269 9694; email: info@ savoyeducationaltrust.org.uk; website: www.savoyeducationaltrust.org.uk)

CC Number: 313763

Eligibility

Individuals undertaking a hospitality related course and those training for management within the hospitality industry.

Types of grants

Grants of up to £500 are available towards college fees, clothing and uniforms, books, equipment, instruments and tools, also educational outings in the UK and study or travel abroad.

There is also a scholarship scheme run in partnership with the Worshipful Company of Innholders which gives around £3,000 per scholarship towards training for management in the hospitality sector. Candidates should normally 'have had a formal education and hold a degree in hotel management (or similar) but those who have attained their positions through a company scheme are not excluded if they can demonstrate aptitude and attitude for promotion.' At least four years of experience in management is required.

Annual grant total

In 2012/13 the trust had both an income and a total expenditure of £1.2 million. Grants to individuals totalled £1,600 and were awarded to five persons. The trust's annual report from 2012/13 notes that:

> The relatively low number of grants awarded ... is primarily due to the fact that individuals do not see their application through to completion ... In seeking to minimise the risk the grant is sent to the individual but made payable to the university, college, supplier, or training provider. The individual is informed of this fact at the early stage of application process and it would appear that in some cases such a condition has served as a deterrent.

Applications

Initially in writing to the correspondent. Eligible applicants will then be provided an application form. Grants are normally considered in March, July, September and December.

Other information

Grants are also made to educational institutions and associations connected with the hospitality industry (£805,000 in 2012/13).

The trust also awards a number of prizes in leading industry competitions. Funding for these awards totalled £80,000 in 2012/13.

International affairs

Gilbert Murray Trust – International Studies Committee

£4,000 (6 grants)

Correspondent: David Faulkner, Trustee, 99 Blacketts Wood Drive, Chorleywood, Rickmansworth, Hertfordshire WD3 5PS (01923 283373; email: david.faulkner57@ntlworld.com; website: www.gilbertmurraytrust.org.uk)

CC Number: 212244

Eligibility

People under the age of 25 who are studying, or have studied, international relations (including international law, security, peace, development studies, global governance) at an institution of higher education in the UK. Applicants above the age of 25 could be considered if there are specific reasons for a delay in their education, such as ill health or financial problems.

Types of grants

Grants of up to £500 are available towards a specific project relevant to the work and purposes of the United Nations (for example, research related visits to a specific country/headquarters of an international organisation, or a short course at an institution abroad) which will directly contribute towards the applicant's studies.

Annual grant total

In 2012/13 the charity had an income of £11,000 and an expenditure of £8,100. We estimate that the annual total of grants was around £4,000. Normally, around six annual awards are offered.

Exclusions

Grants are not intended to support international affairs students with general educational expenses and needs.

Applications

In writing to the correspondent. Applications should include a brief CV, a short statement of career intentions, detailed description of the project with associated costs and sources of additional funding (if required), an assessment by a person 'in a position to judge the applicant in his or her suitability for the award' and, if relevant, reasons for delayed education.

Applications and all the relevant information should be provided in five copies and submitted no later than 2 April.

Other information

The charity's Classical Committee also offers recurring support and awards for various projects and initiatives which seek to promote the studies of ancient Greek civilisation, culture and language.

Iraqi culture and history

The British Institute for the Study of Iraq
See entry on page 38

Italian culture

Il Circolo Italian Cultural Association Ltd

£20,000

Correspondent: Colin Angwin, Secretary, Flat 7, Farley Court, Melbury Road, London W14 8LJ (020 7603 2364; email: grants@ilcircolo.org.uk; website: www.ilcircolo.org.uk)

CC Number: 1108894

Eligibility

Students who have been accepted onto a course at a British higher education institution, either at undergraduate or postgraduate level, pursuing studies, training or research relating to Italian culture (humanities, arts and crafts, sciences and performing arts).

Types of grants

Scholarships for students who wish to further their education in the field of Italian and related studies.

Annual grant total

In 2012 the association had assets of £24,000 and an income of £70,000. Grants to students totalled £20,000.

Charitable organisations received another £20,000, with 'Bazaar donations' totalling £15,000 and music awards a further £1,400.

At the time of writing (July 2014) this was the most recent financial information available for the association.

Applications

In writing to the correspondent. Selected candidates will be interviewed, usually in May.

Languages

John Speak Foundation Foreign Languages Scholarships Trust Fund (John Speak Trust)

£5,700 (4 grants)

Correspondent: Sandy Needham, Bradford Chamber, Devere House, Vicar Lane, Bradford BD1 5AH (01274 230090; email: accounts@bradfordchamber.co.uk; website: www.johnspeaktrust.co.uk)

CC Number: 529115

Eligibility

British born citizens over the age of 18 studying at a recognised college or university, wishing to advance their abilities in foreign language while residing overseas and who, preferably, intend to follow a career in the UK export trade.

A good basic knowledge (at least GCSE or equivalent) of the foreign language is essential. While abroad, candidates will be required to live within the local community rather than with English speakers, volunteer for a business firm in the country or, alternatively, attend a school/university/training course and provide short monthly reports in both English and the foreign language to the trust.

Types of grants

Grant recipients will receive monthly payments for the period of their stay (normally between six and ten months). Usually, the support is given to cover living expenses and sometimes towards travel costs. Awards are aimed at people who are intending to follow a career connected with the export trade of the UK, so applicants should usually be (or should stand a reasonable chance of becoming) a representative who will travel abroad to secure business for the UK. Grants can range from £1,500 to £2,500.

Annual grant total

In 2012/13 the trust had assets of £374,000 and an income of £12,300. A total of £5,700 was distributed in grants to four individuals.

Applications

Applications can be made online on a form available on the trust's website. Potential applicants are invited for an interview with the trustees and will be expected to read, translate and converse in their chosen language. References from a current/prospective employer or the principal/head of languages of the applicant's school may be required.

Leadership

The London Youth Trust (W. H. Smith Memorial)

See entry on page 356

Leather industry

The Leathersellers' Company Charitable Fund

£176,000 (79 grants)

Correspondent: David Santa-Olalla, Clerk, The Leathersellers' Company, 21 Garlick Hill, London EC4V 2AU (020 7330 1444; fax: 020 7330 1454; email: dmsantao@leathersellers.co.uk; website: www.leathersellers.co.uk)

CC Number: 278072

Eligibility

Higher education students on a full-time degree course at any UK university. Applicants must have an unconditional offer for, or be enrolled on, a full time course. Preference is given to people from Greater London and those studying engineering or subjects connected with the leather trade.

Twice a year applications are also welcomed from graduates and undergraduates intending to take Holy Orders.

Types of grants

Grants of up to £4,000 are given to support higher education.

Annual grant total

In 2012/13 the fund had assets of £48.1 million, an income of £1.4 million and a total charitable expenditure of £1.5 million. Grants to students are awarded from a restricted fund. During the year university grants were made to 79 individual students totalling £176,000.

Exclusions

Funding is not given for one year professional conversion courses.

Applications

On an online application form available from the Leathersellers' company's website. Applications should be made by the end of June and references are taken up in August/September. Interviews are held in October. Applicants must also demonstrate efforts of trying to secure funding elsewhere.

Other information

The company also gives grants to organisations for both education and a wide range of welfare causes. In 2012/13 a total of £1.3 million was awarded in 239 grants.

Both successful and unsuccessful applicants are informed in due course and the trust requests not to be contacted with queries regarding the outcome of the application, unless your contact address has changed.

The Doctor Dorothy Jordan Lloyd Memorial Fund

£5,800

Correspondent: Paul Pearson, Company Secretary, Leather Trade House, Kings Park Road, Northampton NN3 6JD (01604 679917; email: paulpearson@uklf.org)

CC Number: 313933

Eligibility

People under the age of 40 working in the leather industry, studying or doing a research on related subjects, and scientist developing the leather production technology. Grants are available to both UK and overseas students (who are required to be fluent in English and intend to return to work their home country).

Types of grants

Grants are available for travel overseas to study the leather science and technology or work on related projects. The support is not intended for students in full/part-time courses rather to encourage short and focused visits.

Annual grant total

In 2012/13 the fund had an income of £5,200 and an expenditure of £6,000. We have estimated the annual total of grants to be around £5,800.

Exclusions

Our research shows that the fellowship may not be offered to an applicant resident in, or a citizen of, a country which restricts free trade in hides, skins or leather.

Applications

In writing to the correspondent. Applications can be submitted directly by the individual for consideration at any time.

Levant

Council for British Research in the Levant

£124,000 (32 grants)

Correspondent: The Administrator, 10 Carlton House Terrace, London SW1Y 5AH (020 7969 5296; fax: 020 7969 5401; email: cbrl@britac.ac.uk; website: www.cbrl.org.uk)

CC Number: 1073015

Eligibility

British citizens or those ordinarily resident in the UK, Isle of Man or the Channel Islands carrying out research in arts, humanities, social and related sciences in connection with the countries of the Levant (Cyprus, Israel, Jordan, Lebanon, Palestine, Syria and adjacent territories).

Types of grants

The charity administers a range of support for scholars, currently:
- Arabic Language Training – grants to cover the cost of full tuition, air travel and accommodation to members of academic staff at a UK university, or academic staff (faculty) with a UK PhD and CBRL membership participating in the CBRL Academic Arabic Programme
- Visiting Research Fellowships and Scholarships – for scholars in university posts, early career postdoctoral candidates and students conducting PhD/DPhil research to spend a period of time at CBRL's overseas institutes to conduct primary research, develop contacts, give lectures and write up project results/ publications derived from a thesis/ research
- Pilot Study Awards – up to £7,500 to enable postdoctoral scholars to undertake initial exploratory work or a feasibility study as a preliminary to making major funding applications to a Research Council, the British Academy or another body
- Travel Grants – up to £800 to cover costs of travel and subsistence of students, academics and researchers undertaking reconnaissance tours or smaller research projects in the countries of the Levant
- Conference and Outreach Funding – lectures, seminars, workshops and conferences in London, Amman, and Jerusalem, as well as occasional meetings elsewhere, mostly initiated by the CBRL (formal applications for support towards conferences, exhibitions, or other forms of outreach are also encouraged)

Awards range from £700 to around £12,000.

Annual grant total

In 2012/13 the charity had assets of £248,000 and an income of £884,000. During the year 32 individuals were awarded grants totalling £124,000 under the following categories: research awards, pump-priming awards, visiting research fellowships, travel grants, scholarships and direct support.

Exclusions

Grants are not normally made towards maintenance, fees, group tours, books or equipment.

Applications

Separate application forms for each of the awards together with extensive guidance notes and conditions are available on the charity's website. Also see the charity's website for application deadlines as these vary.

Other information

This charity has an extremely comprehensive website which should be referred to by any interested applicants.

A report is required to be submitted after the completion of the research which is then made publicly available.

Littoral

The British Institute of Archaeology at Ankara (British Institute at Ankara)

£54,000

Correspondent: Claire McCafferty, Administrator, 10 Carlton House Terrace, London SW1Y 5AH (020 7969 5204; fax: 020 7969 5401; email: biaa@britac.ac.uk; website: www.biaa.ac.uk)

CC Number: 313940

Eligibility

British undergraduates and postgraduates studying the Turkish and Black Sea littoral in academic disciplines within the arts, humanities and social sciences, particularly the archaeology of Turkey. Applicants must be based at a UK university or academic institution.

Scholars from Turkey and the countries surrounding the Black Sea who are studying in the UK can also be supported.

Types of grants

Grants are given for the following purposes:

- Study grants – of up to £2,000 towards travel and subsistence expenses for individuals carrying out doctoral or postdoctoral research
- Fieldwork grants – up to £400 to enable an undergraduate or postgraduate fieldwork project relating to Hellenic studies in its widest sense (participation in a project should take place between May and March)
- Project funding – up to £5,000 a year for a maximum of three years. Applications are invited from project directors who wish to operate within one of the strategic research initiatives currently sponsored by the institute (cultural heritage; society and economy in Turkey; religion and politics in historical perspective; climate and its historical and current impact; migration, minorities and regional identities; and habitat and settlement in prehistoric, historical and environmental perspective)

The institute also offers funding for an annual postdoctoral research fellowship and a research scholarship based at the Institute in Ankara, and also provides scholarships to enable students from Turkey and the Black Sea region to travel to the UK.

Annual grant total

In 2012/13 the institute had assets of £460,000 and an income of £701,000. Grants to individuals were made totalling around £54,000.

Applications

Application forms are available from the institute's website or upon request from the correspondent. The institute notes that 'applications are judged on their academic merit through a stringent process of peer review by appropriate experts.' The deadline for applications is 1 April.

Other information

In 2012/13 the institute also supported institutions (£133,000) and academics from Turkey through a Turkish scholars fund (£2,500).

The institute runs a number of schemes solely for postgraduates, as well as overseeing a number of other funds. See the institute's website for further details.

Marxism, socialism and working class history

The Barry Amiel and Norman Melburn Trust

£30,000

Correspondent: Willow Grylls, Administrative Officer, 8 Wilton Way, London E8 3EE (07921 280378; email: apply@amielandmelburn.org.uk; website: www.amielandmelburn.org.uk)

CC Number: 281239

Eligibility

Groups and individuals working to advance public education in the philosophy of Marxism, the history of socialism, and the working class movement.

Types of grants

Grants to individuals and organisations normally range from £200 to £7,000 and are paid for a range of archiving, research, printing, publishing and conference costs.

Previously funded projects have included the organisation of lectures, discussions, seminars and workshops; the carrying out of research, written work and publications; and the maintenance of libraries and archive material.

Annual grant total

In 2012/13 the trust had an income of £498,000 and a total expenditure of £82,000. At the time of writing (July 2014) the trust's accounts for the year had not yet been submitted to the Charity Commission. Despite the charity's informative website, it has not been possible for us to determine a breakdown of funding between organisations and individuals. We have estimated grants to individuals for educational/research purposes to be around £30,000.

Exclusions

The trust does not award funds to subsidise the continuation or running of university/college courses; to cover transport costs to or from conferences; or to subsidise fees/maintenance for undergraduate/postgraduate students.

Applications

On a form available from the correspondent which must be returned in hard copy. Application guidelines are available to download from the trust's website. Closing dates for applications are noted on the website. The trustees meet twice a year to consider applications, usually in January and June; however, applications for major grants (of more than £6,000) are only considered once a year at the January meeting.

Media

Royal Television Society

£60,000 (20 grants)

Correspondent: Claire Price, Kildare House, 3 Dorset Rise, London EC4Y 8EN (020 7822 2810; fax: 020 7822 2811; email: info@rts.org.uk; website: www.rts.org.uk/royal-television-society-undergraduate-bursary)

CC Number: 313728

Eligibility

UK students studying full time accredited undergraduate degree courses in either television production or broadcast journalism. A full list of eligible universities and courses can be found on the society's website. The trust will **only** consider applicants who:

◗ Are from households with an annual income below £25,000
◗ Are new to higher education
◗ Are home and full time students
◗ Have accepted an offer as their firm choice to study full time on one of the Creative Skillset or Broadcast Journalism Training Council accredited undergraduate programmes
◗ Meet the application deadline

Types of grants

Grants are worth £3,000 and paid in instalments of £1,000 in February of each academic year. Support is provided to assist students with living costs. Successful applicants will also receive a free student membership of the Royal Television Society while studying and one year's free full membership after graduation, a membership of the Hospital Club while studying and the trust will aim to set up a mentoring or placement with one of its industry members in the final year of the applicant's course.

Annual grant total

The society is investing £60,000 a year for the bursary scheme.

Applications

Application forms can be found on the society's website. All applications have to be sent electronically and must be accompanied by a copy of the applicant's UCAS personal statement. Examples of the applicant's work can be attached or given link to. Further guidelines on completing the application form and the shortlisting criteria are on the website. The deadline for applications is 31 May and the outcomes of all applications are communicated to the applicants by the end of the year. Note that the application criteria and deadlines are subject to change and it is best to consult the society's website for any updates before applying.

George Viner Memorial Fund

£15,000 (5 grants)

Correspondent: Gayle Baldwin, Administrator, National Union of Journalists, Headland House, 308–312 Gray's Inn Road, London WC1X 8DP (020 7843 3728; email: georgeviner@nuj.org.uk; website: www.nuj.org.uk/rights/george-viner-memorial-fund)

CC Number: 328142

Eligibility

Students from Black and Asian backgrounds who have received a formal offer of a place on an National Union of Journalists recognised media course in the fields of print, broadcasting, online or photo journalism but have not yet commenced their studies. Applicants must be UK or Irish citizens and intend to continue their education or start a career within UK/Ireland media industry.

Types of grants

Grants are given for tuition fees, travel expenses, accommodation, books, equipment and other necessities. Mentoring and career guidance are also provided. Payments are made directly to institutions.

Annual grant total

In 2012/13 the fund had an income of £31,000 and an expenditure of £15,300. We estimate the annual total of grants to individuals to be around £15,000. Normally about five students are supported annually.

Exclusions

Individuals who have already received a student loan/sponsorship and previous recipients of an award from the fund are not supported.

Applications

Application forms can be obtained from the fund's website once the funding round opens, which happens at the end of May. The deadline for applications is normally in August. It is crucial to include the estimated costs for the course, including fees, travel, accommodation, books and other equipment. Two references will be required. Note that handwritten applications or late submission are not accepted.

Other information

The scholars are also invited to open days, conferences and meetings relating to their chosen field of journalism and have the support of the trustees throughout their course. All grant recipients must attend the annual ceremony, held in February, which is attended by journalists and industry leaders.

Yr Ymddiriedolaeth Ddarlledu Gymreig (The Welsh Broadcasting Trust)

£8,400

Correspondent: Mali Parry-Jones, Secretary, Islwyn, Lôn Terfyn, Morfa Nefyn, Pwllheli, Gwynedd, North Wales LL53 6AP (01758 720132; email: gwybod@ydg.org.uk; website: www.ydg.org.uk)

CC Number: 700780

Eligibility

People who wish to expand and improve their knowledge and skills in television, film, radio and new media. Applicants must either have been fully resident in Wales for at least two years prior to applying, or be born in Wales or be Welsh speakers.

Types of grants

Support can be given towards:

◗ Participation in appropriate training or career full/part-time development courses, such as writing workshops, specialist technical skills, business development
◗ Higher education courses at upper degree level
◗ Travel to accredited festivals/markets
◗ Projects which 'enrich the cultural experience through the medium of television, film, radio and new media'

Annual grant total

At the time of writing (July 2014) the latest financial information available was from 2012. In 2012 the trust had an income of £13,300 and an expenditure of £17,000. We estimate that around £8,400 was awarded in individual grants.

Exclusions

The trust does not fund undergraduate entry to courses.

Applications

Application forms are available from trust's website or can be requested from the correspondent. They should be returned via post by 1 March, 1 July or 1 November.

Other information

Grants are also made to training bodies or companies which offer specific training/educational programmes.

Medicine, including medical research, nursing and veterinary studies

Ted Adams Trust Ltd

£65,000 (59 grants)

Correspondent: Rosie Stables, Administrator, 208 High Street, Guildford, Surrey GU1 3JB (email: tedadamstrust@live.co.uk; website: www. tedadamstrust.org.uk)

CC Number: 1104538

Eligibility

Students of nursing/midwifery, whether pre- or post-registration, working or attending courses in the Guildford area. Individuals or nursing service managers are also eligible to apply for funding towards the course fees or associated costs to further their professional education and development. The trust is 'particularly keen to fund individuals where the outcomes of their course/ study will enhance patient care in the local area.'

Types of grants

Grants can range from £40 to about £4,000 and are awarded towards the course fees, training, travel costs, research and similar expenses and activities undertaken in pursuance of educational and professional development.

The trust also offers special prizes for clinical excellence to final year undergraduate students (including the Diploma in Higher Education, in Nursing Studies and Midwifery Studies at the University of Surrey in Guildford). Potential prize winners are nominated by their mentors. The awards are: £500 to the overall winner in all branches, £250 for each winner in children's nursing, mental health nursing and adult nursing (two awards).

Annual grant total

In 2012/13 the trust had assets of £211,000, an income of £146,000 and made grants totalling £125,000. Grants to 59 individuals totalled £65,000. The directors are aiming for an annual grant distribution level of 340,000.

Exclusions

The trust does not offer support towards living expenses, childcare or debts.

Applications

The trustees state that funds are currently fully committed. No further applications will be considered until further notice. Normally, an online application form can be found on the trust's website or requested from the correspondent, check the trust's website for the latest updates on applications.

Other information

The trust also maintains Ted Adams House for the use of nursing/midwifery students and may fund 'lectures and seminars in association with the University's Department of Health Sciences, which are free to nurses and midwives working in the local area' (these events are advertised on the trust's website). Grants to organisations during the year totalled £60,000.

The trust has stated that the 'funds are currently fully committed. No further applications will be considered until further notice.'

The Worshipful Society of Apothecaries General Charity Ltd

£42,000 (42 grants)

Correspondent: Andrew Smith, Secretary, Apothecaries Hall, Black Friars Lane, London EC4V 6EJ (020 7236 1189; email: clerk@apothecaries.org; website: www.apothecaries.org)

CC Number: 284450

Eligibility

Penultimate and final year medical and pharmaceutical students who are in need. Undergraduates taking courses in history of medicine and the ethics and philosophy of healthcare can also be supported.

The charity also supports a student at the Guildhall School of Music and Drama and provides awards at the London medical schools, Christ's Hospital School and the City of London Academy (Southwark).

Types of grants

One-off and recurrent grants of about £1,000 a year.

Annual grant total

In 2012/13 the charity had assets of £1.4 million and an income of £110,000. During the year 32 undergraduate medical students were given a total of £39,000 in grants and five history of medicine students and five ethics and philosophy healthcare students were supported totalling £3,500.

A further £23,000 was paid in pensions to four individuals.

Applications

Every year the trustees write to the deans of all 28 medical schools, schools of pharmacy and to the Royal Pharmaceutical Society of Great Britain's Benevolent Fund requesting nominations of eligible students, to be submitted by 30 June. Recommendations are considered in July and the grants are disbursed in August. Additional meetings can also be held as required.

Other information

Grants are also made to recognised medical and City of London charities. During the year the Lord Mayor's Charity and 26 other charities were supported totalling £15,500.

The charity also operates a number of restricted funds awarding prizes, scholarships and bursaries.

The trustees' annual report from 2012/13 states that 'in 2013/2014 the trustees are re-organising the grants to medical schools so that more medical students can be supported on the Student Selected Components (SSC) phase of their courses.'

British Society for Antimicrobial Chemotherapy

£7,500 (7 grants)

Correspondent: Tracey Guise, Executive Officer, Griffin House, 53 Regent Place, Birmingham B1 3NJ (01212 361988; fax: 01212 129822; email: tguise@bsac.org.uk; website: www.bsac.org.uk)

CC Number: 1093118

Eligibility

Postgraduate and undergraduate students and members of the society involved in research and training in antimicrobial chemotherapy.

Types of grants

The trust currently offers the following grants:

- Project Grants – up to £10,000 for projects of up to one year duration
- Research Grants – £10,000–£60,000 for projects of up to one year duration

- Overseas Scholarships – up to £1,000 per calendar month, to enable workers from other countries the opportunity to work in UK departments for up to six months
- Vacation Grants – £2,000 for up to ten weeks, designed to give undergraduate experience in research for candidates on a full-time first degree course in the sciences, medicine, veterinary medicine or dentistry
- Travel Grants – up to £1,500, restricted to BSAC members, to enable individuals to attend the annual meetings of ECCMID and ICAAC
- PhD Studentships – up to £25,000 for up to four years to first-class students in the field of antimicrobial chemotherapy (award made biannually)
- Education grants – up to £50,000 for research projects and initiatives of benefit to the field

Annual grant total

In 2012/13 the society had assets of £6 million and an income of £2 million. During the year a total of £7,500 was awarded in travel grants to seven individuals and £154,000 was distributed through institutions in other types of awards, including overseas scholarship (£8,000), vacation grants (£6,500) and one Terry Hennessey Microbiology Fellowship award (£1,500).

Applications

Each programme has specific application forms, guidance notes and deadlines. See the society's website for full details for each programme and note that changes are likely to have been made.

The society also warns that the awards are very competitive, subject to a stringent peer review process and requiring two to three independent referees.

Other information

The society makes large grants to institutions to fund research and liaises with organisations across the globe in promoting medical research.

At the time of writing (August 2014) the society's website was stating that grant categories were under discussion with a decision to be reached no later than 31 August. See the society's website for the latest updates on grants available.

The Jean Ginsburg Memorial Foundation
See entry on page 89

The Nightingale Fund

£11,200 (11 grants)

Correspondent: Rebecca Stanford, Honorary Secretary, Half Thatch, Deers Green, Clavering, Saffron Walden, Essex CB11 4PX (01799550668; email: rlstanford@thenightingalefund.org.uk; website: www.thenightingalefund.org.uk)

CC Number: 205911

Eligibility

Nurses, midwives and community public health nurses who are registered with the Nursing and Midwifery Council and healthcare assistants in the UK.

Types of grants

Grants in the range of £500 to £2,000 are given for the course fees only. Support is given towards further education and training to allow individuals to improve and develop their nursing practice.

Annual grant total

In 2012/13 the fund had assets of £618,000 and an income of £36,000. A total of £11,200 was awarded in educational grants to 11 individuals.

Applications

Application forms can be downloaded from the fund's website and should be emailed to the correspondent together with a current CV. Grants are considered three times a year, in March, July and November. The deadline for applications is six weeks before the meeting. Applicants are required to attend an interview either in person or by telephone.

The Nurses Association of Jamaica (NAJ) (UK)

£2,000

Correspondent: Paulette Lewis, Trustee, PO Box 1270, Croydon, Surrey CR9 3DA (020 8657 1968; email: info@najuk.org; website: www.naj.org.uk/default.aspx)

CC Number: 1063008

Eligibility

Primarily people from black and ethnic minority groups, especially African-Caribbean groups, who are aged 18 or over. The association will consider any studies that promote the practice of nursing, midwifery and health visiting. This may range from students undertaking studies in health education, nursing courses at degree, diploma, certificate and attendance levels, sociology, psychology, nursing and other health and health science related programmes, in particular where the course of study will impact positively on the health and health care of ethnic minority groups. The trust also considers

the following funding priorities: business schools and pre-school education, IT training, special needs education and training for community development. Preference is given to people living in Birmingham, London, Nottingham and internationally.

Types of grants

One-off grants and bursaries ranging between £50 and £300. Support can be given towards necessities, such as books and fees, for educational outings in the UK, study/travel abroad and student exchanges, or towards community projects. Students in health and social care courses may also be given mentoring, coaching and other support from the association.

Priority is given to part-funding for one year or less, although a period of up to two years may be considered.

Annual grant total

At the time of writing the latest financial information available was from 2012. In 2012 the association had assets of £30,000 and an income of £35,000. A total of £4,400 was spent in grants.

Applications

Application forms are available from the association's website. They can be submitted directly by the individual or through a third party, such as a school/college or educational welfare agency, if applicable. All applications need to be supported by a reference. Completed forms can be returned in February or August together with any relevant supporting statements to justify the purpose of the application, costs involved, explaining how the money will be used and providing specific details about the study/project. The awards are usually considered in September and March.

Other information

The biggest part of the overall expenditure was spent on fundraising activities. The association carries out a number of fundraising initiatives, for example health fairs, dinners or conferences.

Grants are made to both individuals and organisations. There is also a small benevolent fund to help members who have health difficulties.

Further information on grants can also be accessed by contacting Lyrell McNish (020 8291 2733) or Charmaine Case (020 8251 7820).

The May Price SRN Award
See entry on page 153

The RCN Foundation

£231,000

Correspondent: Michael Pearce, Administrator, Welfare Service, 20 Cavendish Square, London W1G 0RN (0345 408 4391; email: michael.pearce@rcn.org.uk; website: www.rcnfoundation.org.uk)

CC Number: 1134606

Eligibility

Registered nurses, midwives, health practitioners, health care assistants and people training for these professions. Some bursaries are available for specific areas of medicine, such as orthopaedic and trauma care or palliative care and pain.

Types of grants

Various bursaries of up to £5,000 for learning and development including degrees, training, conference attendance and projects and research.

Annual grant total

In 2012/13 the foundation had assets of £26.9 million and an income of £3.2 million. Grants made for education and training totalled 299,000. Benevolent fund grants (social welfare) totalled £186,000. Grants for individuals totalled £350,000. We consider that all of the benevolent fund grants were awarded to individuals and the total awarded to individuals for educational purposes was £231,000 (the figure given for bursaries).

Applications

The bursaries have different opening and closing dates, potential applicants should check the foundation's website for the most recent information. There are also application forms available to download for the separate bursaries.

Other information

Previously known as The Royal College of Nursing Benevolent Fund, the purpose of the foundation is to enable nurses and nursing to improve the health and wellbeing of the public through:

 ▶ Benevolent funding
 ▶ Education and training bursaries
 ▶ Supporting the development of clinical practice and the improvement of care
 ▶ Developing practice to enable people and communities to make positive choices about their own health and wellbeing
 ▶ Promoting research.

Rhona Reid Charitable Trust

£10,000

Correspondent: K. Clayton, Rathbone Taxation Services, Port of Liverpool Buildings, Pier Head, Liverpool L3 1NW (01512 366666; email: karen.owen-jones@rathbones.com)

CC Number: 1047380

Eligibility

People involved in the study and advancement of medicine (especially ophthalmology), music and the arts.

Types of grants

One-off and recurrent grants according to need for necessities and activities which would be 'supporting excellence in the chosen field.'

Annual grant total

In 2012/13 the trust had an income of £15,800 and an expenditure of £21,500. We estimate the annual total of grants to individuals to be around £10,000.

Applications

In writing to the correspondent. Applications are considered in March and September.

Other information

Grants are also made to organisations and people who are blind, visually impaired or have another disability.

Sandra Charitable Trust

£92,000 (141 grants)

Correspondent: Martin Pollock, Secretary to the Trustees, Moore Stephens LLP, 150 Aldersgate Street, London EC1A 4AB (020 7334 9191)

CC Number: 327492

Eligibility

Nurses and nursing students who are in financial need. Postgraduate, overseas and part-time students can all be supported.

Types of grants

One-off and recurrent grants are given according to need, for courses, equipment and other necessities.

Annual grant total

In 2012/13 the trust had assets of £18.6 million, an income of £550,000 and a total charitable expenditure of around £592,000. Grants to 141 individuals totalled £92,000.

Applications

Application forms can be requested from the correspondent. Previously the trust has stated that its funds are largely committed. The trustees meet on a frequent basis to consider applications.

Other information

Grants are also made to organisations (in 2012/13 a total of £502,000).

The Society for Relief of Widows and Orphans of Medical Men (The Widows and Orphans)

£30,000 (5+ grants)

Correspondent: Charlotte Farrar, Secretary, Lettsom House, 11 Chandos Street, Cavendish Square, London W1G 9EB (01837 83022; email: info@widowsandorphans.org.uk; website: www.widowsandorphans.org.uk)

CC Number: 207473

Eligibility

Support is given in the following order of priority:
 ▶ (i) necessitous dependents of deceased members of the society
 ▶ (ii) necessitous members of the society
 ▶ (iii) necessitous dependents of members of the society
 ▶ (iv) necessitous medical practitioners not being members of the society and their dependents

Types of grants

Our research suggests that one-off and recurrent grants from £500 to £3,000 are available to college students, undergraduates, vocational and mature students for fees, books, maintenance/living expenses, instruments/equipment and clothing (not to mature students). Support is also given to schoolchildren and people starting work for maintenance/living expenses. The society has given help to former doctors for retraining and specific extra costs involved in further education to help them re-enter employment.

Clinical medical students receive higher awards more because of the shorter holidays and the lack of opportunity for supplementing their income through holiday jobs.

Annual grant total

At the time of writing (August 2014) the latest financial information available was from 2012. In 2012 the society had assets of £5.1 million and an income of £169,000. Grants to 78 individuals totalled £60,000. The trustee's annual report specifies that five students received awards. All grant recipients, except for one orphan, were regular practitioners or their dependents. We estimate that around £30,000 was awarded in educational support.

Exclusions

Grants are not normally given for second degrees.

Applications

Application forms (separate for different types of applicants) can be found on the society's website or requested from the correspondent. They can be submitted directly by the individual or a family member and are usually considered in February, May, August and November. Note that applications **must** be submitted via post.

Other information

Support is also given for welfare needs.

Sir John Sumner's Trust

£0

Correspondent: Christine Norgrove, Administrator, 1 Colmore Square, Birmingham B4 6AA (0870 763 1490; email: christine.norgrove@sghmartineau. com)

CC Number: 218620

Eligibility

People studying nursing or medicine, including veterinary studies, who are in need. There is a strong preference for the Midlands.

Types of grants

Grants are normally given towards equipment, instruments, fees or living expenses.

Annual grant total

In 2013/14 the trust had assets of £855,000 and an income of £31,000. During the year, £40,000 was given in 'institutional grants', though it appears no grants were given to individuals.

Exclusions

No grants towards religious or political causes.

Applications

Usually in writing to the correspondent, through the individual's college or social services. Two referees should be provided, one of whom must be from the relevant educational establishment.

Metal work and metal jewellery

The Goldsmiths Arts Trust Fund

£38,000 (28 grants)

Correspondent: The Clerk, The Goldsmiths' Company, Goldsmiths' Hall, Foster Lane, London EC2V 6BN (020 7606 7010; fax: 020 7606 1511; email: charity@thegoldsmiths.co.uk; website: www.thegoldsmiths.co.uk)

CC Number: 313329

Eligibility

University and college students, postgraduates, recent graduates and apprentices studying silversmithing and precious metal jewellery. Specific programmes are also available to support school teachers.

Types of grants

The fund offers bursaries and grants reaching up to over £1,000 to students at universities and colleges of art or apprentices. Support can be given towards exhibitions, specific projects, provision of materials and tools, skills development programmes, masterclasses and courses that advance the arts, design and craftsmanship.

The fund's website also notes that funding is currently focused on four major projects: supporting seven selected primary schools; providing science teachers with free residential courses; allowing primary and secondary school teachers to undertake professional and personal development; and assisting postgraduate medical students who have turned to medicine as their second degree (support administered through BMA only).

Annual grant total

In 2012/13 the fund had assets of £118,000 and an income of £1.1 million. A total of £38,000 was awarded in bursaries and grants to 28 individuals.

Exclusions

According to our research, grants are not normally made for fees or subsistence on standard courses at further or higher education institutions. Awards are not normally available to overseas students studying in the UK.

Applications

Applications should be made in writing to the correspondent, through an organisation such as a college or university. Applications are normally considered quarterly.

Other information

Grants are also given to organisations and individuals who are members of the Goldsmiths' Company for various charitable purposes. In 2012/13 Goldsmith's Craft and Design Council received a grant of £34,000.

The trustees' annual report from 2012/13 states that 'the formation of a new charity, to develop and to operate the Goldsmiths' Centre, means that some of the tasks currently undertaken under the auspices of the Goldsmiths' Arts Trust Fund might, in the medium term, move across to this new charity.'

The South Square Trust
See entry on page 82

Nautical or maritime courses

Reardon Smith Nautical Trust

£117,000

Correspondent: John Cory, Administrator, Cob Cottage, Garth Hill, Pentyrch, Cardiff CF15 9NS (02920890383; email: cory@cobcottage. fsworld.co.uk)

CC Number: 1153623

Eligibility

Residents of Wales up to the age of 25 studying recognised nautical or maritime courses in the UK or abroad. These should relate to shipping, maritime law and commerce, navigation, sailing, oceanography and marine related environmental issues, in particular those which give the individual first hand practical experience of being at sea. Preference is given to residents of city and county of Cardiff.

Types of grants

Grants, scholarships, exhibitions and bursaries towards general educational expenses.

Annual grant total

The trust has been newly re-registered with the Charity Commission and at the time of writing (May 2014) accounts were not yet due. Previously the trust has awarded grants totalling £117,000.

Applications

Applications should be made through a relevant educational establishment or sail training provider.

Other information

The trust has been re-registered with the Charity Commission as a charitable incorporated organisation, therefore the registered charity number has changed.

Sailors' Society

£1,000

Correspondent: Welfare Fund Manager, 350 Shirley Road, Southampton SO15 3HY (02380 515950; fax: 02380 515951; email: welfare@sailors-society. org)

CC Number: 237778

Eligibility

Students or nautical cadets preparing for a career at sea in the merchant navy (of any country) and enrolled at a recognised college or academy of nautical education. Seafarers who have already entered the profession and have been accepted on a course of study by an accredited institution to further their qualifications.

Applicants must be able to demonstrate that they have no other source of funds to pursue their nautical education.

Types of grants

One-off and recurrent grants towards course study fees, related books and necessary course materials.

Annual grant total

In 2012 the society had assets of £13.5 million and an income of £3.3 million. Educational grants to individuals totalled £1,000. Welfare grants awarded to individuals totalled £9,000. The accounts for 2012 were the latest available online.

Applications

On a form available on request to nauticalgrant@sailors-society.org. Any application must be fully supported by the respective course tutor.

Note: beneficiaries who do not complete the full course of study may be required to repay all or any part of the grant.

Other information

The society maintains a network of chaplains at the various key ports around the world, who carry out ship visiting routines and minister to seafarers. It also provides centres and clubs for seafarers and associated maritime workers at strategic seaports.

The society administers the Leith Aged Mariners' Fund and the Dundee Seaman's Friend Society.

Physio-therapy

The Chartered Society of Physiotherapy Charitable Trust

£64,000 (59 grants)

Correspondent: Stuart De Boos, Administrator, 14 Bedford Row, London WC1R 4ED (020 7306 6666; email: debooss@csp.org.uk; website: www.csp. org.uk/charitabletrust)

CC Number: 279882

Eligibility

Qualified, associate and student members of the society.

Types of grants

Grants can be given for fees of academically accredited research courses, UK and overseas presentations, overseas development projects, research visits, master's research dissemination and student elective placements. Educational awards are generally in the range of £150 to £3,000.

Annual grant total

At the time of writing (July 2014) the latest financial information available was from 2012. In 2012 the society had assets of £2.1 million, an income of £902,000 and made grants totalling £832,000. A total of £64,000 was given in 59 educational grants.

Applications

Application for educational awards should be submitted using the CSP ePortfolio which can be accessed on the society's website. The deadlines for applications for different awards vary – for the most up to date information see the society's website.

Other information

Awards can also be made for experienced researchers and those only starting their research career. Research funding comprises Physiotherapy Research Foundation (PRF) awards, paediatric research funding and a special care of older people research award. For specific details and latest available awards in this category, see the society's website. In 2012 scientific awards were given totalling £452,000.

Polish history, literature or art

The Hanna and Zdzislaw Broncel Charitable Trust (The Broncel Trust)

£6,000

Correspondent: The Administrator, 371 Uxbridge Road, London W3 9RH (020 8992 9997; email: info@akpp.co.uk)

CC Number: 1103737

Eligibility

People involved with Polish history, literature, art or social sciences. The trustees are prepared to consider a varied range of requests.

Types of grants

The trust awards scholarships, financial assistance for research and grants for publishing Polish works of literature.

Annual grant total

In 2012/13 the trust had an income of £4,300 and an expenditure of £12,400. We estimate the annual total of grants to individuals to be around £6,000.

Applications

In writing to the correspondent.

Other information

Grants are made to both organisations and individuals. Occasional financial support can be provided for libraries, museums and exhibitions.

Postal history

The Stuart Rossiter Trust Fund

£460

Correspondent: Rex Dixon, Trustee, 39 Braybank, Bray, Maidenhead, Berkshire SL6 2BH (01628 628628; email: rexdixon@btinternet.com; website: www.rossitertrust.com)

CC Number: 292076

Eligibility

Anyone of any nationality undertaking original research into postal history with a view to publication. Applicants can be students seeking a higher degree at university, amateurs or professionals, as long as the research is original, approved, likely to lead to publication for the benefit of a wider public, and adds to the stock of publicly available material. English language is preferred in published or electronic form to promote accessibility.

Types of grants
Grants towards translations, cost of hire of researchers, publication costs and costs of research. Part or the entire grant may be recovered from sales of the publication.

Annual grant total
The latest information available at the time of writing (July 2014) was for 2012. In that financial year, the trust had assets of £425,000 and an income of £28,000. A single grant for research and publications totalled £460.

Exclusions
The trust only gives grants for research into postal history with a view to publication.

Applications
Application forms are available from the correspondent.

Other information
Grants are also made to organisations.

Religion/ ministry

The Andrew Anderson Trust

£24,000

Correspondent: Andrew Anderson, Trustee, 1 Cote House Lane, Bristol BS9 3UW (01179 621588)

CC Number: 212170

Eligibility
People studying theology.

Types of grants
One-off and recurrent grants according to need.

Annual grant total
In 2012/13 the trust had assets of £11.1 million and an income of £284,000. Grants to individuals for welfare and education totalled £49,000.

Applications
The trust states that it rarely gives to people who are not known to the trustees or who have been personally recommended by people known to the

trustees. Unsolicited applications are therefore unlikely to be successful.

The Barnabas Trust

£33,000 (10 grants)

Correspondent: Richard Padfield, Trustee, Lawn Farm, Pillows Green Road, Corse, Gloucester GL19 3NX (01452 840371; email: richard@padfield. me.uk)

CC Number: 900487

Eligibility
The trust defines its objectives as 'being an efficient channel of funds to the individuals and organisations supported by the trust.' People involved in Christian work and missionaries, particularly overseas, are eligible. Support may also be given to individuals on religious education courses.

Types of grants
Grants are given according to need. The trust works 'for individuals and organisations by administering their voluntary income and donations, including banking and recording income, applying for Gift Aid and forwarding funds on to their banks at home or overseas.'

Annual grant total
In 2012/13 the trust had assets of £10,300 and an income of £36,000. A total of £44,000 was spent on charitable activities. Grants were made to ten individuals totalling around £33,000.

Applications
In writing to the correspondent. Our research suggests that normally applications should be submitted by the end of February. The trustees meet quarterly.

Other information
Grants to five organisations totalled £11,000 in 2012/13.

The CPAS Ministers in Training Fund

£8,000

Correspondent: The Trustees, Sovereign Court One (Unit 3), Sir William Lyons Road, University of Warwick, Science Park, Coventry CV4 7EZ (0300 123 0780; email: mail@cpas.org.uk; website: www.cpas.org.uk)

CC Number: 1007820

Eligibility
Evangelical Anglican ordinands who are in financial need during their training. Applicants must be contemplating parochial or ordained pioneer ministry in the UK or Ireland for at least three

years after ordination. Those in Church Army training may also be eligible for a grant.

Types of grants
Recurrent grants, one per academic year, to help with maintenance and personal expenses. They range between £50 and £500.

Annual grant total
In 2012/13 the fund had assets of £6.7 million and an income of £3.7 million. Grants through the Ministers in Training Fund totalled £8,000.

Exclusions
No grants for books or fees.

Applications
Application forms, budget forms and an information sheet are available from the fund's website. Applications should be submitted by the end of September, January or, (for students not in their final year) April. Applicants are asked for two referees and a completed budget form to detail income and expenditure including figures from LEA/CFMT/ diocese. Time should be allowed for references to be taken up.

Other information
The fund gives most of its income to other ecumenical causes such as parish support, publications, training events and children and youth projects.

The Elland Society

£6,000

Correspondent: Revd Colin Judd, Trustee, 57 Grosvenor Road, Shipley BD18 4RB (01274 584775; email: elland@saltsvillage.co.uk; website: www. ellandsocietygrants.co.uk)

CC Number: 243053

Eligibility
Men and women training for the ordained ministry of the Church of England who are evangelical in conviction and outlook (further guidance on the latter requirement is available on the society's website). The society will give priority to the ordinands sponsored by dioceses in the province of York or who will serve their title there.

Types of grants
One-off grants and general cash contributions according to need are given to those who have already started training at residential or non-residential theological college. Previously grants have been awarded for clothing/ footwear, household items, living expenses, travel expenses, study overseas, books and educational equipment. Our

research suggests that grants rarely exceed £500 per person.

Annual grant total

In 2012/13 the society had an income of £7,000 and an expenditure of £6,100. We estimate the annual total of grants to be around £6,000.

Exclusions

Grants are not provided for the items already included in the main church grant.

Applications

Application forms can be downloaded from the society's website or requested from the correspondent.

Other information

The trust prefers communication by email.

Lady Hewley's Charity

£58,000

Correspondent: Neil Blake, Administrator, Military House, 24 Castle Street, Chester CH1 2DS

CC Number: 230043

Eligibility

Young men or women preparing for United Reformed and Baptist Church ministries. Preference will be given to students who were born in the north of England.

Annual grant total

In 2012/13 the trust had assets of £15.5 million and an income of £362,000. Grants to individuals totalled £167,000, of which £58,000 was given in student grants.

Exclusions

No grants will be given when local authority funds are available.

Applications

Applications for grants are invited through contact with respective churches at both local church, regional and province levels. Individual applications are considered twice a year and grants are made according to an individual's personal and financial circumstances.

Lady Peel Legacy Trust

£1,000

Correspondent: Christine Ruge-Cope, Administrator, 21 Chace Avenue, Potters Bar, Hertfordshire EN6 5LX

CC Number: 204815

Eligibility

Men and women, who are in training at a theological college or on a recognised course.

Types of grants

One-off grants generally for the provision of books or, for especially needy candidates, a small cash sum. Grants are occasionally made to clergy undertaking further academic work. Application for book grants should be for books of lasting value to assist in the building up of a priest's working library.

Annual grant total

In 2012/13 although income had increased slightly to £7,500, income was down to £1,700. We estimate grants for individuals for educational purposes was around £1,000.

Applications

On a form available upon written request from the correspondent. The closing dates for applications are 1 April and 1 November each year. Telephone contact is not invited.

Powis Exhibition Fund

£10,600

Correspondent: John Richfield, 39 Cathedral Road, Cardiff CF11 9XF (02920 348200; fax: 02920 387835; email: andrewemery@churchinwales.org.uk)

CC Number: 525770

Eligibility

People who are training as ordinands of the Church in Wales. Applicants must be born or be resident in Wales and speak Welsh.

Types of grants

Grants are available only for the period of study and can range up to £700 per year.

Annual grant total

In 2012/13 the fund had an income of £13,000 and an expenditure of £10,800. We estimate that the annual total of grants was around £10,600.

Applications

Application forms are available from the correspondent or from individual dioceses.

Sola Trust

£287,000 (95 grants)

Correspondent: Simon Pilcher, Trustee, Green End Barn, Wood End Green, Henham, Bishop's Stortford CM22 6AY (01279 850819; email: simon@pilchers. org)

CC Number: 1062739

Eligibility

Individuals training at a theological college or at a church (in a form of an apprenticeship) for full-time Christian

work, as well as to those already involved in full-time ministry.

Types of grants

Grants are usually one-off or up to one year and intended to be supplementary only. Support is available towards books, other necessities, conferences, training courses, retreats and other expenses. Additionally the charity aims to relieve the financial hardship of those involved in Christian ministry.

Annual grant total

In 2012/13 the trust had assets of £378,000 and an income of £546,000, mostly from donations. Grants to 95 individuals totalled £287,000, consisting of:

Theological and ministry training grants	90	£273,000
Other ministry grants	4	£10,500
PhD studies	1	£4,000

The trust further notes that 'the majority of the people and institutions supported were in the UK (with no particular geographical focus within the UK)' with a significant minority being in a variety of European and Australasian countries, South Africa and the USA.

Applications

In writing to the correspondent. Where appropriate, grants may be routed through a church or equivalent body that is providing training to individuals. The trustees meet about ten times a year to consider applications. Applicants are required to provide a budget detailing anticipated income and expenditure and give references, normally from the 'sending' church as well as the college or organisation offering the training concerned.

Other information

A small number of grants are also made to individuals for relief and missionary work. Grants were also made to 45 institutions totalling £218,000 in 2012/13.

The trustees' annual report from 2012/13 states that:

The charity also seeks to facilitate the strategic placement of trained gospel workers – working in new geographical areas (areas of the country where there is little or no biblical ministry at present) and in new types of ministry (for example youth or women's ministry).

The Spalding Trust

£55,000

Correspondent: Tessa Rodgers, Secretary, PO Box 85, Stowmarket IP14 3NY (website: www.spaldingtrust. org.uk)

CC Number: 209066

Eligibility

People undertaking research projects into the great religions of the world, particularly comparative studies, who are in need of financial support. Projects must primarily have a religious concern, rather than sociological or anthropological.

Types of grants

Awards of up to £2,000 for the comparative study of the major religions. Support is available for research projects, publications, occasionally travel costs, conferences and related expenses. Applications may not necessarily be academically orientated, provided they have sufficient practical and beneficial aspect. Recurrent grants extending over one year are only considered in exceptional circumstances.

Annual grant total

In 2013 the trust had assets of £2 million and an income of £94,000. Grants totalled £55,000.

Exclusions

Grants are not given retrospectively and will rarely be provided towards expenses related to the first degree.

Applications

In writing to the correspondent providing:
- An outline of the proposal/course
- A copy of the applicant's CV, specifying their own religious commitment, if any
- Details of the budget and of other possible sources of funding that have been applied for (this should be done using a copy of the financial statement available on the trust's website)
- Preferably two academic references
- Daytime and evening phone numbers and email address

Applications should be submitted by post. Further application guidelines are available on the trust's website. The trustees meet once a year to decide on major proposals but smaller grants are considered on a monthly basis (it may take up to three months to reach a decision).

Other information

The trust also makes grants to institutions, such as libraries, colleges, other educational establishments.

A subsidiary of the trust, the Ellen Rebe Spalding Memorial Fund, makes grants to disadvantaged women and children.

The Foundation of St Matthias

£26,000 (31 grants)

Correspondent: Lynette Cox, Clerk to the Trustees, Hillside House, First Floor, 1500 Parkway North, Newbrick Road, Stoke Gifford, Bristol BS34 8YU (01179 060100; email: stmatthiastrust@ bristoldiocese.org; website: www. stmatthiastrust.org.uk)

CC Number: 311696

Eligibility

Further and higher education students, including mature students and occasionally postgraduates, who are studying in accordance with the doctrine of the Church of England. This includes:
- People who are, or intend to become, engaged in social welfare work as social workers, community workers, youth workers, teachers or supervisors of pre-school groups, etc.
- People who are intending to become ministers of the Church of England or of a church in communion therewith

Preference is given to applicants from the dioceses of Bath and Wells, Bristol and Gloucester, though applicants from elsewhere are considered.

Types of grants

One-off grants usually ranging from £200 to £1,000. Grants can be given for books, fees, maintenance/living expenses, childcare and for some study or travel abroad. Overseas courses may be supported only if the visit is integral to the course or research.

Annual grant total

In 2012 the foundation had assets of £5.6 million and an income of £251,000. Grants to individuals totalled £26,000, of which 27 grants were of less than £1,000 and four were of £1,000 or more. A further £297,000 was awarded to organisations for educational and Christian purposes.

At the time of writing (July 2014) this was the most recent financial information available for the foundation.

Exclusions

No retrospective grants.

Applications

Applicants should telephone in the first instance to discuss the nature of study and so on. Applications must be made on a form available from the foundation's website. They should be submitted by 31 May for consideration in July or 30 September for consideration in November.

Other information

The trust advises applicants to apply to as many sources of funding as possible

as funding is not guaranteed and often, the trust cannot offer the full amount requested. There is a link to other religious education trusts on its website.

The trust is not able to cover the costs of fees, maintenance or travel, etc. of students from overseas, but small contributions may be offered should evidence be supplied that substantial funding is available from other sources.

The Thornton Fund

£7,500

Correspondent: Dr Jane Williams, Trustee, 93 Fitzjohn Avenue, Barnet, Hertfordshire EN5 2HR (020 8440 2211; email: djanewilliams@dsl.pipex.com)

CC Number: 226803

Eligibility

Students at Unitarian colleges or training for Unitarian ministry.

Types of grants

Grants between £250 and £1,500 to help with books, equipment, instruments, living expenses, study exchange and study or travel abroad.

Annual grant total

In 2012 this charity had an income of £19,000 and a total expenditure of £21,000. This was the most up to date information available at the time of writing (July 2014). We estimate grants awarded to individuals for educational purposes to be around £7,500.

Applications

In writing to the correspondent through a third party such as a minister, including the total and annual estimated costs of study. They are considered on an ongoing basis.

Other information

The fund occasionally makes grants to the general assembly of Unitarian and Free Christian Churches for special projects and also to Unitarian ministers for welfare needs.

Torchbearer Trust Fund

£39,500

Correspondent: Phil Burt, Secretary, Capernwray Hall, Carnforth, Lancashire LA6 1AG (01524 733908; fax: 01524 736681; email: info@capernwray.org.uk; website: www.capernwray.org.uk)

CC Number: 253607

Eligibility

People engaged in full-time Christian instruction or training. Preference is given to students and former students of Torchbearer Bible schools.

Types of grants

One-off grants and bursaries according to need.

Annual grant total

In 2012/13 the trust had assets of £157,000 and an income of £72,000. Grants for individuals totalled £79,000. No breakdown was given in the accounts of the amount for educational grants and that for relief in need. We have taken the educational figure as £39,500.

Applications

In writing to the correspondent.

Other information

Grants are also available for missionary work.

Turath Scholarship Fund

£700

Correspondent: Dr Imran Satia, Trustee, 4 West Park Road, Blackburn BB2 6DG (07825 346320; email: scholarship@turath.co.uk; website: www.turath.co.uk/front/turath-scholarship-fund)

CC Number: 1138153

Eligibility

UK citizens between 18 and 24 studying for a skill or doing vocational training that will benefit their community in some way. Preference is given to people studying any aspect of Islamic Science including for example, learning Arabic.

Types of grants

Grants to pay for training or tuition including fees, travel and equipment/tools.

Annual grant total

In 2012/13 the fund had both an income and expenditure of £720. We have retained the entry here as this is a relatively new charity and income and expenditure may well increase in time.

Applications

On a form available on the fund's website to be returned by email.

Seafaring

The Corporation of Trinity House, London

£5,000

Correspondent: Graham Hockley, Secretary, Trinity House, Tower Hill, London EC3N 4DH (020 7481 6914; email: graham.hockley@thls.org; website: www.trinityhouse.co.uk)

CC Number: 211869

Eligibility

Candidates must be between 16 and 18½ years old with five GCSE at grade C or better and must also have passed the Department of Transport medical examination. Applicants must also be British and permanently resident in the British Isles. Applicants must be applying to become an officer in the Merchant Navy.

Types of grants

The Trinity House Merchant Navy Scholarship Scheme provides financial support for young people seeking careers as officers in the Merchant Navy. Cadets undertake a three or four year programme split between nautical college and time at sea in a variety of British-managed vessels. Cadets can train as either Deck or Engineer Officers or pursue a Marine Cadetship encompassing both disciplines. Full scholarships are available for this programme of £7,000, under the Trinity House Cadet Training Scheme.

Annual grant total

The charity's significant assets are no reflection of the money available for grantmaking which is a very small part of its activities.

In 2012/13 the corporation had assets of £166 million and an income of £7.9 million. Grants were made to 33 retired seafarers in financial need at a rate of £676 per year. This totalled £22,300. A further £10,500 was awarded in grants to individuals, some of which was distributed for educational purposes. We estimate this to be around £5,000.

Applications

Details of the scholarship scheme are available upon application in writing to the correspondent.

Other information

The following information is taken from the corporation's website: 'The safety of shipping, and the well being of seafarers, have been our prime concerns ever since Trinity House was granted a Royal Charter by Henry VIII in 1514.'

Today it has three distinct functions:
- The General Lighthouse Authority (GLA) for England, Wales, the Channel Islands and Gibraltar. The remit is to provide Aids to Navigation to assist the safe passage of a huge variety of vessels through some of the busiest sea-lanes in the world
- A charitable organisation dedicated to the safety, welfare and training of mariners
- A Deep Sea Pilotage Authority providing expert navigators for ships trading in Northern European waters

The corporation also makes grants to organisations and to individuals for educational purposes. In this accounting year, the corporation made awards to organisations totalling £3.4 million.

The Honourable Company of Master Mariners and Howard Leopold Davis Charity

£87,500

Correspondent: The Clerk, HQS Wellington, Temple Stairs, Victoria Embankment, London WC2R 2PN (020 7836 8179; email: info@hcmm.org.uk; website: www.hcmm.org.uk)

CC Number: 1127213

Eligibility

People who are serving in the Merchant navy and their dependents, and those intending to serve.

Types of grants

Grants to encourage the education, instruction and training of applicants.

Annual grant total

In 2013 the charity had assets of £3.7 million and an income of £98,000. Grants to individuals totalled £175,000. We estimate that grants for educational purposes totalled around £87,500.

Applications

In writing to the correspondent. Applications can be submitted directly by the individual, through a social worker, Citizens Advice, or other welfare agency, or by a friend or relative. They are considered quarterly.

Other information

This trust is an amalgamation of four separate funds: the Education Fund, the Benevolent Fund, the London Maritime Institution and the Howard Leopold Davis Fund.

The Marine Society and Sea Cadets

£600,000

Correspondent: Claire E. Barnett, 202 Lambeth Road, London SE1 7JW (020 7654 7011; fax: 020 7928 8914; email: info@ms-sc.org; website: www.ms-sc.org)

CC Number: 313013

Eligibility

Professional seafarers, active or retired, members of the Sea Cadet Corps and any other young people considering a maritime career.

Types of grants

It is the society's policy to help where financial hardship is evident. If the applicant is likely to be employed or re-employed then interest-free loans may be given rather than grants. The award of a loan or grant is usually made to an applicant who is attempting to improve his career prospects, or who has to change his career due to unforeseen circumstances. In addition, the society offers a scholarship scheme for seafarers or prospective seafarers.

Annual grant total

In 2012/13 the trust had assets of £21.8 million and an income of £14.4 million. Grants to individuals totalled £1.2 million, although the trust states that 'individual grants given are small and not material within the overall total.'

Exclusions

Recurrent grants are not made.

Applications

On a form obtainable from the correspondent. Applications are considered as they arrive.

Other information

Grants are also made to sea cadet units.

Sport

Athletics for the Young

£20,000

Correspondent: Alan Barlow, Trustee, 12 Redcar Close, Hazel Grove, Stockport SK7 4SQ (01614 839330; email: runalan55@hotmail.com; website: www. englandathletics.org)

CC Number: 1004448

Eligibility

Young people under the age of 23 who are in full time education, active in athletics and eligible to compete for England.

Types of grants

One-off educational grants towards athletic pursuits, including equipment and travel expenses.

Annual grant total

In 2012/13 the trust had an income of £600 and a total charitable expenditure of £33,000. We estimate the annual total of grants to individuals to be around £20,000.

Exclusions

People already receiving funding from other sources are not normally supported.

Applications

Application forms can be downloaded from the England Athletics website or requested from the correspondent. The deadline for applications is mid-February. Note that applications should be completed in handwriting and provide a reference.

Other information

Grants can also be made to organisations and projects benefiting young athletes.

The Dickie Bird Foundation

£4,500

Correspondent: Warren Edward Cowley, Trustee, Flat 3, The Tower, The Tower Drive, Pool in Wharfedale, Otley, West Yorkshire LS21 1NQ (email: info@ thedickiebirdfoundation.co.uk; website: www.thedickiebirdfoundation.org)

CC Number: 1104646

Eligibility

Disadvantaged young people under the age of 17 who are participating in sport.

Types of grants

One-off grants usually ranging from £100 to £1,000, according to need. Grants are usually given for items of sports clothing such as shirts, shorts and footwear, and for equipment and travel within the UK.

Annual grant total

In 2012/13 the foundation had an income of £33,000 and assets of £33,000. Grants made totalled £4,500.

Exclusions

Grants cannot be given for:
- Professional fees of any kind, including club membership, or club fees
- Travel outside the UK
- Scholarships, summer/winter/training camps
- Equipment that is available for use elsewhere
- Overnight accommodation

Applications

Guidelines, which are available on the foundation's website, should be read before submitting an application. Applications also need to be supported by two independent referees.

The R. and D. Burchett Charitable Foundation
See entry on page 87

The Monica Elwes Shipway Sporting Foundation

£3,300

Correspondent: Simon Goldring, Trustee, Trowers and Hamlins LLP, 3 Bunhill Row, London EC1Y 8YZ (020 7423 8000)

CC Number: 1054362

Eligibility

Schoolchildren and university students engaged in sporting activities who live in England and Wales and have limited resources.

Types of grants

One-off grants of up to £300 to schoolchildren and students towards clothing, equipment and fees in relation to sports.

Annual grant total

In 2012/13 the foundation had an income of £2,100 and an expenditure of £3,500. We have estimated that the annual total of grants was around £3,300.

Exclusions

No contribution towards general university fees and no support to individuals with sufficient resources.

Applications

In writing to the correspondent, for consideration throughout the year.

The Brian Johnston Memorial Trust (The Johnners Trust)

£12,000 (22 grants)

Correspondent: Tim Berg, Administrator, c/o The Lord's Taverners, Brian Johnston Memorial Trust, 10 Buckingham Place, London SW1E 6HX (020 7821 2828; email: tim. berg@lordstaverners.org; website: www. lordstaverners.org)

CC Number: 1045946

Eligibility

Young 'promising' cricketers between the ages of 11 and 19 who are in need of financial assistance to further their personal and cricketing development.

Types of grants

Scholarships of around £500 towards travel, equipment and coaching.

Annual grant total

In 2012/13 the trust had assets of £34,000 and an income of £69,000. A total of £39,000 was spent on charitable activities. Brian Johnston Scholarships totalled £12,000 and were given to 22 individuals.

Applications

In writing to the correspondent. Scholarships are awarded on the recommendation of the ECB Performance Department. The awards committee meets at least once a year.

Other information

The trust was set up in April 1995 to 'foster interest in cricket in schools and in the community, and to help encourage cricket for the blind and partially sighted.' Grants are also paid to cricket associations to assist participation of visually impaired and blind cricketers. In 2012/13 three grants were awarded to institutions totalling £12,000.

Young spin bowlers from county academies and emerging cricketer programmes are also supported through the BJMT/ECB Elite Spin Bowling Programme (£16,000 in 2012/13).

Pursuit of Excellence – Sport

£1,000

Correspondent: Hugh McGouran, Administrator, Wallace House, Falcon Court, Preston Farm Industries, Estate, Stockton-on-Tees TS18 3TX (01642 260860; email: info@ teesvalleyfoundation.org; website: www. teesvalleyfoundation.org)

CC Number: 1111222

Eligibility

Young people between the ages of 11 and 24 resident in Darlington, Hartlepool, Redcar and Cleveland, Middlesbrough and Stockton-on-Tees, who are pursuing a chosen sports activity at a high level. Applicants should demonstrate clear potential to progress to full national or international recognition. Support is focused on individuals who are disadvantaged.

Types of grants

Up to £1,000. Applicants can apply once a year for up to five years.

Annual grant total

Grants of £1,000 each.

Applications

Application forms can be downloaded from the Tees Valley Sport website. They should be submitted by the second half of March, June, September or December. For specific deadlines see the charity's website. References will be required.

Other information

This fund is administered by the Tees Valley Community Foundation in partnership with Tees Valley Sport.

44 sports recognised by Sport England and in addition ice and roller hockey are applicable. For a full list see the application guidelines available on the Tees Valley Sport website.

The John Taylor Foundation for Young Athletes

£700

Correspondent: John Taylor Foundation, 6 Sawrey Court, Broughton-in-Furness LA20 6JQ (01484 614367; email: enquiries@johntaylorfoundation. org.uk; website: www. johntaylorfoundation.org.uk)

CC Number: 1101008

Eligibility

Young amateur athletes who are based within the UK. The foundation can only support amateur athletes who compete in the following sports: fell, hill or mountain running; road running; athletics (track and field); cross country running; triathlon; or orienteering.

Types of grants

Grants are given to allow young athletes to pursue opportunities in amateur athletics. They are awarded for activities and equipment.

Annual grant total

In 2012/13 the foundation had an income of £1,700 and a total expenditure of £1,500. We estimate that grants to individuals totalled £700.

Exclusions

Applications from those who do not compete in the sports listed cannot be considered.

Applications

By completing the online form, which can be found on the foundation's website. Applications are considered twice a year.

Other information

The other aim of this foundation is to promote awareness of cardiomyopathy to the public.

The Torch Trophy Trust

£13,000

Correspondent: Hayley Morris, Liaison Officer, 4th Floor, Burwood House, 14–16 Caxton Street, London SW1H 0QT (020 7976 3900; fax: 020 7976 3901; email: hayley.morris@ torchtrophytrust.org; website: www. torchtrophytrust.org)

CC Number: 306115

Eligibility

Volunteers working for any organisation involved in sports or outdoor activities within local communities who want to improve their skills and whose governing body is keen to help out but is unable to provide the necessary funding.

Types of grants

Bursaries from £100 to £1,000 to take courses to qualify as club coaches or officials/administrators. The award will not cover more than 50% of the total costs involved, although exceptional circumstances may be considered.

Annual grant total

At the time of writing (July 2014) the latest financial information available was from 2012. In 2012 the trust had an income of £15,800 and an expenditure of £13,800. We estimate that awards to individuals totalled around £13,000.

Applications

Application forms can be requested from the correspondent or found on the trust's website (when the application cycle begins). A supporting letter from the relevant governing body must be included. For submission deadlines and further details see the trust's website.

Other information

Grants can also be made to organisations, although main support is given to individuals.

The trust also presents annual Trophy Torch Awards to the most outstanding nominated volunteers in the UK.

Surveying

The Company of Chartered Surveyors Charitable Trust Fund (1992)

£0

Correspondent: Amanda Jackson, Administrator, 75 Meadway Drive, Horsell, Woking, Surrey GU21 4TF (01483 727113; fax: 01483 720098; email: wccsurveyors@btinternet.com; website: www.surveyorslivery.org.uk)

CC Number: 1012227

Eligibility

Professional surveyors and further/higher education students of surveying.

Types of grants

The fund offers support to students of the surveying profession and bursaries to pupils in four adopted schools who are going into further education. Awards of around £100 to £500 can be given towards general educational expenses, including books, fees, equipment/instruments, tools or maintenance/living expenses.

There is also an annual award of £4,500 to a surveyor or a university graduate for a 'research project on a subject of current interest which will help foster a better understanding of the built environment.'

Annual grant total

In 2012/13 the fund had assets of £1.5 million, an income of £181,000 and a total charitable expenditure of £107,000. No grants were made directly to individuals during the year. Normally around £5,000 is awarded in educational grants to individuals.

Applications

In writing to the correspondent. The trustees meet four times a year, usually in January, March, June and September. Applications can be submitted throughout the year directly by individuals or through their educational establishment. According to our research, letters of support from the individual's tutor or head of the department must also be provided.

Other information

The fund mainly supports organisations and assists students by giving grants to various universities/colleges to be distributed as bursaries and prizes.

Teaching

The Hockerill Educational Foundation
See entry on page 14

Textiles

British Cotton Growing Association: Work People's Collection Fund

£0

Correspondent: James Evans, Administrator, Directorate of Research and Business Engagement, Support Services, The University of Manchester, Oxford Road, Manchester M13 9PL (01612 758204; email: james.evans@manchester.ac.uk; website: www.staffnet.manchester.ac.uk/services/rbess/governance/research-support-services/finding/cotton)
CC Number: 509075

Eligibility

People undertaking study and/or research in medical, nursing or social disciplines beneficial to the workers in the British textile industry. Previously assistance has been given for: 'occupational health studies of the causative agents of byssinosis and asthma; assistance in organising archives of the cotton industry; the impact of redundancy on textile workers.' Applications for research on the wider impacts of textiles, including dyeing, are welcomed.

Types of grants

One-off or recurrent grants are awarded for research and are available for higher education students, including mature students and postgraduates. The association may also consider fees, maintenance costs or supporting foreign students living and studying in the UK.

Annual grant total

In 2012/13 the charity had assets of £2.1 million, an income of £55,000, and a total expenditure of £300. During the year the recipients of the grants were selected but no grants paid. Normally, about £30,000 is spent in grants each year.

Applications

In writing to the correspondent. Applications should include full details of the research proposal, applicants' background, relevant publications, estimated costs and the names of two referees. Applications are normally invited to be submitted before mid-April for consideration in May.

Coats Foundation Trust

£19,000

Correspondent: Sheila MacNicol, Secretary, Coats Pensions Office, Cornerstone, 107 West Regent Street, Glasgow G2 2BA (01412 076820; email: andrea.mccutcheon@coats.com)
CC Number: 268735

Eligibility

University students living in the UK who are studying textile and thread-related subjects. Those with long-term futures in the UK and without a previous degree are prioritised by the trust.

Types of grants

One-off grants according to need. Grants are made to college students, undergraduates and mature students for fees, books and equipment/instruments. Schoolchildren may also receive grants for books and equipment/instruments.

Annual grant total

In 2012/13 the trust had an income of just £980 and a total expenditure of almost £75,000. We have estimated the figure for the total educational grants to individuals to be around £19,000.

Applications

In writing to the correspondent enclosing a CV, an sae, details of circumstances (e.g. student status, name of college), the nature and amount of funding required and referee names and addresses. There is no formal application form. Only applicants enclosing an sae will receive a reply. Applications are considered four times a year.

Other information

Grants are also made to individuals for welfare purposes and to organisations.

Henry Dixon's Foundation for Apprenticing
See entry on page 80

Wine making

The Wine Guild Charitable Trust

£3,400

Correspondent: Jane Grey-Edwards, Council Secretary, Christmas Cottage, North Street, Petworth GU28 0DF (01798 345262; email: jgrey-edwards@tiscali.co.uk; website: wineguilduk.org/the-charity.php)
CC Number: 1105374

Eligibility

Young people wishing to further their studies in the wine making industry.

Types of grants

Grants, loans or bursaries.

Annual grant total

In 2013 the trust had an income of £5,200 and a total expenditure of £7,000. We estimate that educational grants to individuals totalled £3,400.

Applications

In writing to the correspondent.

Other information

The trust also helps to arrange meetings, lectures and conferences with the aim of sharing knowledge and appreciation of wine with the general public.

Work/study overseas

English Speaking Union of the Commonwealth (English Speaking Union)

£1.1 million

Correspondent: The Administrator, Dartmouth House, 37 Charles Street, London W1J 5ED (020 7529 1550; email: esu@esu.org; website: www.esu.org)

CC Number: 273136

Eligibility

People involved in teaching the English language overseas and other education-related or cross-cultural projects. There are scholarships relating to the clergy, library professionals, literary translators, scientists, young musicians, teachers and students of various subjects.

Types of grants

The charity administers a number of grants and scholarship awards for students and professionals, often in the form of travel scholarships. For details of individual funds, applicants are advised to refer to the charity's website.

It notes that 'the Secondary Schools Exchange programme is the longest-running scholarship and remains a flagship activity.'

Annual grant total

In 2012/13 the charity had assets of £29.7 million and an income of £3.7 million. A total of £1.1 million was spent in scholarships and other educational programmes.

Applications

Applications vary for the different scholarships, therefore applicants should refer to the charity's website.

Some schemes require applicants to attend an interview/audition.

Other information

The charity offers training, initiates youth and academic exchanges, organises educational programmes, conferences and meetings, cultural activities.

Go Make it Happen: A Project in Memory of Sam Harding

See entry on page 10

Local charities

This section lists local charities that give grants to individuals for educational purposes within a specific area. The information in each entry applies only to educational grants and not to other work that the charity may do for relief in need or with organisations; however, it will state in the entry if grants are given for other purposes. The information is concentrated on what a charity actually does rather than what its trust deed allows it to do, as this is a more realistic picture of how charities fund.

All of the entries give or have the potential to give at least £500 a year to individuals for educational purposes, most considerably more than this.

Regional classification

We have divided the UK into nine geographical areas, as numbered on the map on page 122. Scotland, Wales and England have been separated into areas and counties in a similar way to previous editions of this guide. On page 123 we have included a list under each such area or county of the unitary and local authorities they include.

The Northern Ireland section has not been subdivided into smaller areas as there are a limited number of grantmaking charities in that section. Within the other sections, the charities are ordered as follows.

Scotland
▶ Firstly, the charities which apply to the whole of Scotland, or to at least two areas in Scotland.
▶ Secondly, Scotland is sub-divided into five areas. The entries which apply to the whole area, or to at least two unitary authorities within, appear first.
▶ The rest of the charities in the area are listed in alphabetical order of unitary authority.

Wales
▶ Firstly, the charities which apply to the whole of Wales, or to at least two areas in Wales.
▶ Secondly, Wales is sub-divided into three areas. The entries which apply to the whole area, or to at least two unitary authorities within, appear first.
▶ The rest of the charities in the area are listed in alphabetical order of unitary authority.

England
▶ Firstly, the charities which apply to the whole area, or to at least two counties in the area.
▶ Secondly, each area is sub-divided into counties. The entries which apply to the whole county, or to at least two towns within it, appear first.
▶ The rest of the charities in the county are listed in alphabetical order of parish, town or city.

Please note, in the North East section, we have included a section called Teesside incorporating Hartlepool, Stockton-on-Tees, Middlesbrough and Redcar & Cleveland.

London
▶ Firstly, the charities which apply to the whole of Greater London, or to at least two boroughs.

▶ Secondly, London is sub-divided into the boroughs. The entries are listed in alphabetical order within each borough.

In summary, within each county or area section, the grantmaking charities in Scotland and Wales are arranged alphabetically by the unitary or local authority which they benefit, while in England they are listed by the city, town or parish, and in London, by borough.

To ensure you identify every relevant local charity, look first at the entries under the heading for your:
▶ Unitary authority, for people in Scotland and Wales
▶ City, town or parish under the relevant regional chapter heading, for people living in England
▶ Borough, for people living in London

People in London should then go straight to the start of the London chapter, where charities which give to individuals in more than one borough in London are listed.

Other individuals should look at the sections for charities which give to more than one unitary authority or town before finally considering those charities at the start of the chapter that make grants across different areas or counties in your country or region.

Having found the grantmakers in your area, ensure that you read any other eligibility requirements – most charities have other criteria that applicants must meet.

Geographical areas

Northern Ireland

General

Aisling Bursaries

£31,000 (33 grants)

Correspondent: The Administrator, West Belfast Partnership Board, 218–226 Falls Road, Belfast BT12 6AH (02890 809202; email: info@wbpb.org; website: www.westbelfast-partnership. com/what-we-do/education-and-training)

Eligibility

Students in further or higher education who live in the West Belfast. Applicants must be preparing to study or be currently studying on a full-time or part-time course. People returning to education may also be supported. Our research shows that special consideration is usually given to candidates who have significant barriers preventing them from realising their full potential, for example economic or family circumstances.

Types of grants

Grants of £1,000 and £500 are available, normally for a full time and part time bursary respectively, and can be one-off or recurrent.

Annual grant total

In 2012/13 there were 33 bursaries awarded to individuals totalling £31,000.

Exclusions

Grants are not available to students repeating part or all of an academic year unless this has been formally agreed on the basis of medical or personal circumstances. Previous recipients of a full time bursary cannot reapply but previous applicants are welcome to.

Applications

Application forms are available from the correspondent. Our research suggests that the deadlines for applications are usually in June/July and are advertised in the Andersonstown News and on the West Belfast Partnership website.

Other information

Local businesses, companies and individuals in West Belfast are contributing to the funds to make the bursaries available.

The Belfast Association for the Blind

£8,000

Correspondent: R. Gillespie, Hon. Secretary, 30 Glenwell Crescent, Newtownabbey, County Antrim BT36 7TF (02890 836407)

IR Number: XN45086

Eligibility

People who are registered blind in Northern Ireland. Consideration may also be given to those registered as partially sighted.

Types of grants

One-off grants for educational needs such as computers, course fees and so on. Grants are also given for welfare purposes.

Annual grant total

We have no current information for this charity. We know that previously around £16,000 was given in grants to individuals for both educational and social welfare purposes.

Applications

In writing to the correspondent through a social worker. Applications are considered throughout the year.

Other information

Grants are also made to organisations.

The Thomas Devlin Fund

£5,500 (6 grants)

Correspondent: Barbara Woods, Community Foundation for Northern Ireland, Community House, Citylink Business Park, Albert Street, Belfast BT12 4HQ (02890 245927; email: bwoods@communityfoundationni.org; website: www.communityfoundationni. org/Grants/Thomas-Devlin-Fund)

Eligibility

Young people in Northern Ireland between the ages of 15 and 19 who are aiming to pursue a career in the arts and require a small amount of financial assistance to undertake an opportunity or training.

Types of grants

Bursaries of up to £1,750 for specific opportunities and activities which will help to develop young people's skills in music and arts.

Annual grant total

In 2013 the fund received a total of 14 applications, of which six were successful. We have estimated that the annual total of grants to individuals was around £5,500. Normally the trust can support up to ten individuals awarding a total of around £4,000 – £6,000 each year.

Exclusions

Due to high demand, lessons or exam fees are not normally supported and assistance could only be given in exceptional circumstances.

Applications

Application forms can be downloaded from the fund's website and will need to be completed by individuals together with their tutor/teacher. Applicants have to outline how the award would improve their performance and what positive impact it would have on others.

The fund is normally open up in early spring, however the application deadlines are likely to change – see the fund's website for the latest updates.

Other information

This fund was set up in memory of Belfast teenager Thomas Devlin and has its own website www.thomasdevlin.com. The fund is administered by the Community Foundation for Northern Ireland which also administers a number of funds for organisations. The fund is intended to be awarding grants until 2066.

EMMS International

£1,000 (Around 10 grants)

Correspondent: The Administrator, 7 Washington Lane, Edinburgh EH11 2HA (01313 133828; fax: 01313 134662; email: info@emms.org; website: www.emms.org)

SC Number: SC032327

Eligibility

Medical, nursing, dental and therapy (i.e. physiotherapy or occupational therapy) students at universities in Scotland, Northern Ireland or developing countries who wish to undertake a placement abroad for their elective period in a mission hospital in a developing country as an integral part of their course. Preference is given to those with an 'active Christian testimony' and who are involved in a college, university or hospital Christian fellowship.

Types of grants

Bursaries usually range from £200 to £300 but can reach up to £1,000. Our research indicates that higher amounts are more likely to be awarded to applicants working in one of the charity's partnership hospitals in India, Israel, Malawi or Nepal.

Annual grant total

In 2013 the charity had an income of £858,000 and an expenditure of £1.4 million. The charity's website notes that around ten bursaries are awarded annually totalling £10,000.

Exclusions

Students studying at universities in England and Wales are not eligible.

Applications

Application forms and detailed guidelines can be obtained on the charity's website or requested from the correspondent. Applications should include a personal statement, names of two referees (one, preferably, from the local church) and be endorsed with a stamp of the university/college. Awards are made twice a year and applications should be submitted by 31 January for elective periods from April to September and by 31 July for October – March period. Consideration normally takes six to eight weeks. Successful applicants will receive their bursaries four weeks prior to an elective starting.

Other information

The charity states that 'grants are not awarded solely on the basis of academic merit, but also on the student's desire to serve healthcare professionals and patients in a low resource setting at a mission hospital.'

Note that the electives are not organised by the charity on behalf of students but they can be directed to organisations that can help.

Funding is mainly provided to mission hospitals and schools, community health projects, primary health care and staff and volunteer training/education in developing countries. Support may also be given to enable individuals suffering or recovering from a serious illness for a recuperative holiday.

The Fermanagh Recreational Trust

Correspondent: The Administrator, Fermanagh Recreational Trust, Fermanagh House, Broadmeadow Place, Enniskillen BT74 7HR (02866 320210; email: info@fermanaghtrust.org; website: www.fermanaghtrust.org)

CC Number: XR 22580

Eligibility

Individuals based in County Fermanagh.

Types of grants

Grants can be given towards equipment and in educational bursaries for training or other activities which will help individuals to develop their potential, particularly through recreation and sport.

Annual grant total

The total amount of grants awarded was not specified.

Exclusions

Grants are not considered retrospectively.

Applications

Application forms are available to download from the trust's website. They should be submitted by the end of February or August. Two independent references must also be included (this requirement is only waived in exceptional circumstances).

Other information

This fund is administered by the Fermanagh Trust which also administers funds for organisations for a variety of purposes in Fermanagh, particularly involving young people and youth development.

Some of the funds administered by the Fermanagh Trust offer support to individuals, including for voluntary work overseas and bursaries for sport, arts or community service activities.

NIACRO

Correspondent: Gareth Eannetta, Service Manager, Amelia House, 4 Amelia Street, Belfast BT2 7GS (02890 320157; email: gareth@niacro.co.uk; website: www.niacro.co.uk)

IR Number: XN48280

Eligibility

Prisoners, people who have offended and their immediate relatives in Northern Ireland in need of support. People in detention seeking access to education, training and/or employment who cannot obtain help from other sources may be supported financially.

A number of projects are available to children and young people at risk of (re)offending.

Types of grants

Support is given to help individuals access academic qualifications and vocational training which will advance their integration back to the society and the job market. One-off and recurrent grants according to need can be given towards degrees, vocational qualifications, NVQs, HGV driving licenses or other training and associated needs.

Annual grant total

In 2012/13 the association had assets of £1.6 million and an income of £3.8 million. The vast majority of support is available through specific advice services, although some grants can be provided to individuals referred to the organisation. We have been unable to determine the amount given in grants to individuals for educational purposes for this financial year.

Exclusions

Grants are not normally given for computer hardware, capital equipment or set-up costs of small business initiatives.

Applications

Individuals in need of support should contact the correspondent to find out more about the support available and the application procedure.

Other information

The organisation's main activities are providing support, advice and guidance to prisoners, people who have offended and their relatives. A number of projects are undertaken in partnership with other bodies.

The Presbyterian Orphan and Children's Society

£266,000

Correspondent: Paul Gray, Administrator, Glengall Exchange, 3 Glengall Street, Belfast BT12 5AB (02890 323737; email: paulgray1866@gmail.com; website: www.presbyterianorphanandchildrenssociety.org)

IR Number: XN45522

Eligibility

Children aged 23 or under who are in full or part-time education, living in Northern Ireland and Republic of Ireland, usually in single parent families. One parent must be a Presbyterian.

Types of grants

Regular grants paid each quarter. Depending on financial resources, a summer grant and Christmas grant is paid to each family. Exceptional grants of up to £300 (very occasionally up to £500) are also available.

Annual grant total

In 2012 the charity had assets of £9 million and an income of £691,000. Grants were made to individuals totalled £533,000. Grants are also made for welfare purposes.

The charity gives around 3000 regular grants, 1500 special grants and 120 exceptional grants each year.

This was the latest information available at the time of writing (August 2014).

Applications

Applications are made by Presbyterian clergy; forms are available from the correspondent or to download from the charity's website.

The Royal Ulster Constabulary GC – Police Service of Northern Ireland Benevolent Fund

£800,000

Correspondent: The Administrator, Police Federation for Northern Ireland, 77–79 Garnerville Road, Belfast BT4 2NX (02890 764200; email: benevolentfund@policefedni.com; website: www.rucgc-psnibenevolentfund. com)

IR Number: XN 48380

Eligibility

Members and ex-members of the Royal Ulster Constabulary and their dependents. The main objectives of the fund are look after widows and their dependents, injured and disabled officers, pensioners, parents of deceased officers and serving PSNI officers experiencing financial hardship or difficulties.

Types of grants

Support can be given in grants and loans to people in education, including schoolchildren, college students, undergraduates, mature students, individuals with special educational needs. Help can be given towards general educational needs.

Annual grant total

Previously about £800,000 has been spent supporting the beneficiaries.

Exclusions

Our research suggests that loans for debt cases cannot be supported.

Applications

Initial contact should be made to the fund in writing. Eligible applicants will then be advised on further application process. Candidates are visited by the representatives of the fund who then present the case to the management committee, which meets on the first Wednesday of each month. Applicants will be required to provide full financial breakdown and quotes where possible.

Other information

The fund also supports beneficiaries for welfare causes.

Additional help is offered by a number of other organisations, details of which can be found on the Northern Ireland Police Family Assistance (www. northernirelandpolicefamilyassistance. org.uk).

The Society for the Orphans and Children of Ministers and Missionaries of the Presbyterian Church in Ireland

£15,000

Correspondent: Paul Gray, Church House, Fisherwick Place, Belfast BT1 6TW (02890 323737)

Eligibility

Children and young people aged under 26 who are orphaned and whose parents were ministers, missionaries or deaconesses of the Presbyterian Church in Ireland.

Types of grants

One-off grants of £300 to £2,000 for general educational purposes.

Annual grant total

Grants to individuals for educational and welfare purposes total about £30,000.

Applications

On a form available from the correspondent. Applications should be submitted directly by the individual in March for consideration in April.

Other information

The trust also gives welfare grants to the children of deceased ministers, missionaries and deaconesses.

Scotland

General

The Arrol Trust

See entry on page 16

The Avenel Trust

£5,500

Correspondent: Mrs A. Cameron, Trustee, Duich, Dolphinton Road, West Linton, Peeblesshire EH46 7HG

SC Number: SC014280

Eligibility

Children in need under 18 and students of nursery nursing living in Scotland.

Annual grant total

In 2012/13 the trust had an income of £24,000 and an expenditure of £23,000. Grants are awarded to individuals and organisations for both social welfare and educational purposes. We estimate grants to individuals for educational purposes to be around £5,500.

Exclusions

Grants are not given for holidays or household furnishings.

Applications

Applications are considered every two months and should be submitted through a tutor or third party such as a social worker, health visitor or teacher. Applicants are encouraged to provide as much information about their family or individual circumstances and needs as possible in their applications. Applications can only be accepted from people currently residing in Scotland.

The June Baker Trust

£20,000

Correspondent: The Chair, c/o The Scottish Conservation Studio, Hopetoun House, South Queensferry, West Lothian EH30 9SL

CC Number: 1086222

Eligibility

Individuals working in the conservation of historic and artistic artefacts in Scotland, or those training to do so.

Types of grants

Awards are usually in the region of £100 to £300, and are made available for travel, training, fees, purchase of equipment, short courses and other suitable projects to students, mature and vocational students and people starting work.

Annual grant total

In 2013, the trust had an income of £2,000 and a total expenditure of £1,000.

Exclusions

Fees for long, full-time courses are not given.

Applications

On a form available from the correspondent, or online at the Institute of Conservation's website. Applicants may have to attend an interview. A CV and two referees should also be provided. Applications are considered in June, and should be submitted directly by the individual.

The Black Watch Association

£75,000

Correspondent: The Trustees, 6 Atholl Crescent, Perth PH2 6ST (01738 623214; email: bwassociation@btconnect.com; website: www.theblackwatch.co.uk)

SC Number: SC016423

Eligibility

Serving and retired Black Watch soldiers, their wives, widows and children.

Types of grants

One-off grants ranging from £250 to £500. Grants can be made to schoolchildren, people starting work and students in further/higher education for equipment/instruments, fees, books and maintenance/living expenses.

Annual grant total

In 2013 the trust had an income of £153,000 and an expenditure of £165,000. Grants totalled approximately £75,000 for educational purposes.

Exclusions

No grants towards council tax arrears, loans or large debts.

Applications

On an application form to be completed by a caseworker from SSAFA (19 Queen Elizabeth Street, London SE1 2LP. Tel: 020 7403 8783; Fax: 020 7403 8815; Website: www.ssafa.org.uk).

The Buchanan Society

£25,000

Correspondent: The Trustees, 1F Pollokshields Square, Glencairn Drive, Pollokshields, Glasgow G41 4QT

SC Number: SC013679

Eligibility

People with any of the following surnames: Buchanan, McAuslan (any spelling), McWattie or Risk.

Types of grants

Bursaries for students in severe financial difficulties of about £1,000. One-off grants can also be given for general educational purposes.

Annual grant total

In 2012 the society had an income of £57,000. Around 70 people are supported each year. Grants are also made for welfare purposes.

More recent accounts were not available at the time of writing (August 2014).

Applications

On a form available from the correspondent, to be submitted either directly by the individual or a family member, or through a third party such as a social worker or teacher. Applications are considered throughout the year.

Other information

The Buchanan Society is the oldest Clan Society in Scotland having been founded in 1725. Grantmaking is its sole function.

The Carnegie Trust for the Universities of Scotland

£1.8 million

Correspondent: Professor Andy Walker, Secretary and Treasurer, Andrew Carnegie House, Pittencrieff Street, Dunfermline, Fife KY12 8AW (01383 724990; fax: 01383 749799; email: jgray@ carnegie-trust.org; website: www. carnegie-trust.org)

SC Number: SC015600

Eligibility

The trust supports undergraduate or postgraduate students and academic staff at the fifteen Scottish universities (Aberdeen, Abertay, Dundee, Edinburgh, Edinburgh Napier, Glasgow, Glasgow Caledonian, Heriot-Watt, Queen Margaret, Robert Gordon, St Andrews, Stirling, Strathclyde, UHI and West of Scotland).

More specific eligibility requirements apply to different categories (very detailed guidelines are available on the trust's website).

Types of grants

The trust offers support through the following awards:

- Fee assistance - help with the tuition fees for a first degree course at a Scottish university to individuals who lack financial means to attend the course
- Vacation Scholarships- £175 per week to undergraduate degree students at a Scottish university demonstrating exceptional merit to undertake a specific programme of independent research over the summer vacation (2–6 weeks in length). Project should be of direct benefit to the applicant's academic work
- Carnegie-Caledonian PhD Scholarships – the value for the 2013/14 academic year was £15,400 (this figure is expected to rise in future academic years in line with awards funded by the Research Councils). First Class Honours undergraduate degree is a pre-requisite
- St Andrew's Society of New York Scholarships – awarded by the St Andrew's Society for the State of New York. Awards are given to Scottish students towards a year of study in the United States, mainly covering accommodation and travel expenses. Preference is given to individuals who 'have no previous experience of the United States and for whom a period of study there can be expected to be a life-changing experience'
- Research Incentive Grants – from £500 to £7,500 to academics employed by a Scottish university to undertake a short research project. Early career researchers are encouraged and special consideration is given to applicants who are within five years (excluding breaks) of starting their independent academic career
- Carnegie Centenary Professorship – a maximum of two awards each year of up to £40,000 for a period of three to six months to visiting world class scholars who have been nominated. Professorships are tenable at any of the fifteen Scottish universities
- Collaborative Research Grants – of up to £50,000 for a joint research project (researchers from more than one Scottish university) lasting one to two years

Annual grant total

In 2012/13 the trust had assets of £70.6 million and an income of £2.7 million. Grants and awards totalled £1.8 million distributed as follows:

Scholarships	43	£872,000
Research grants	256	£405,000
Fee assistance	154	£261,000
Collaborative research	8	£244,000
Vacation scholarships	92	£72,000
Centenary professorships	1	£40,000

Note: during the year 12 awards were also made for undergraduate expeditions totalling £24,000. The expedition awards have now been discontinued.

Exclusions

Undergraduates who receive government funding towards the costs of their tuition fees (SAAS support) are not eligible. Courses at the Scottish Higher Education Institute delivered and validated by a university outside Scotland, Open University courses, HNC and HND diploma courses, access courses, accelerated degree courses with a graduate entry, Continuing Professional Development (CPD) courses, university courses below degree level (diploma or certificate courses) and second degrees are not supported towards the tuition fees.

Applications

Some applications may be made online on the trust's website, some may need an academic referral or nomination and Vacation Scholarships **must** be applied for via the university. For specific details of each of the awards see the trust's website. A preliminary telephone call may be helpful.

Applications are considered as follows:

- Fee assistance: applications are considered from 1 May to 1 December for assistance with fees for the following academic year
- Carnegie-Caledonian PhD Scholarships: early February
- Vacation Scholarships: applications must be received by 1 April
- St Andrew's Society of New York Scholarships: universities should send applications for the nominated candidates by 15 March
- Research Incentive Grants: 15 September and 15 March
- Carnegie Centenary Professorships: 15 July
- Collaborative Research Grants: 31 January

Other information

In 2016 the Henry Dryerre Scholarship will be offered 'to support students wishing to undertake a PhD in medical or veterinary physiology.'

Carnegie-Cameron Bursaries are available to support fees for one-year taught postgraduate degree courses. Awards are made through universities and any applications should be made to the institution directly (eligibility and submission deadlines will depend on the university).

Churchill University Scholarships Trust for Scotland
See entry on page 17

See entry on page 17

Creative Scotland

£1.8 million (220 grants)

Correspondent: The Administrator, Waverley Gate, 2–4 Waterloo Place, Edinburgh EH1 3EG (0845 603 6000; email: enquiries@creativescotland.com; website: www.creativescotland.com)

Eligibility

People working at a professional level in the arts, screen and creative industries based in Scotland.

Types of grants

A number of funding programmes are available:

- Touring, Festivals and Arts Programming – support for touring of work (including performances and exhibitions), organisation of festivals and presentation of a programme of work
- Professional Development – support of around £1,000 – £5,000 (in exceptional circumstances up to £10,000) to artists and other creative professionals to develop their skills and/or professional practice nationally

and internationally through research and development activities. This includes: conferences, seminars, festivals, professional networking/ information sharing events, technical skills development, workshops, master-classes, seminars and trade fairs, residency to develop professional practice, mentoring and shadowing opportunities, participation in international and European networks, exploratory visits and so on

- Quality Production – grants 'to support the development and creation of high quality work that has a clearly described public outcome.' Awards are of around £1,000 – £20,000 for project development, and £1,000 – £70,000 for production and presentation
- Public Art Sited – for 'development and production of high quality public art projects that bring artists, people and places together'
- Public Art Research and Development – for 'initial research and scoping of a public art project across a range of media and disciplines with priority for activities developing the relationship between the public and the artist and exploring new approaches to the commissioning process'
- International – grants towards the costs involved in performing, touring, translating and exhibiting work (including at recognised showcases and festivals) overseas in order to promote and present high quality work from Scotland. Awards are of £1,000–£20,000 (up to maximum of £40,000 for big scale/impact projects)
- Film and Television – awards to 'emerging and established film and television talent capable of creating distinctive and engaging work that promotes Scotland's creativity'
- Artists' Bursaries – awards of £5,000, £15,000 and £30,000 to artists and other creative professionals at any stage in their career demonstrating 'high level of quality, imagination and ambition in their work'

Annual grant total

From January to April 2014 a total of around £1.8 million was awarded to over 220 individuals, mainly through Professional Development fund, Artists' Bursaries and International fund, also Quality Production and Public Art funds.

Exclusions

Awards are not generally made to students. Most funding is not available to architects/designers, academics, amateur companies, individuals in permanent employment within foundation organisations, flexibly funded organisations or national companies and collections.

For specific exceptions for each of the funds see the guidelines on the Creative Scotland website.

Applications

Application forms, guidelines and deadlines for different funding programmes are available from the Creative Scotland website.

Other information

Creative Scotland is a 'public body that supports the arts, screen and creative industries across all parts of Scotland on behalf of everyone who lives, works or visits here.' Funding is distributed from the Scottish Government and The National Lottery.

The Cross Trust

£75,000 (46 grants)

Correspondent: Kathleen Carnegie, Secretary, McCash and Hunter LLP, Solicitors, 25 South Methven Street, Perth PH1 5ES (01738 620451; fax: 01738 631155; email: kathleencarnegie@ mccash.co.uk; website: www. thecrosstrust.org.uk)

SC Number: SC008620

Eligibility

People aged 16 to 30 who are of Scottish birth or parentage proposing 'a study or project that will extend the boundaries of their knowledge of human life.' Applicants must be in genuine financial need.

Types of grants

The trust offers support from £200 to £2,000 through the following:

- Awards for university or college (including music and art schools) students who can demonstrate outstanding academic achievements and who have taken full advantage of support available from local authorities, student loan opportunities and so on. Second degree and postgraduate studies are only considered in exceptional circumstances. Grants are made towards university or college costs, study/travel overseas, study visits and projects. Attendance at conferences, symposia, extra-curricular courses, voluntary work and gap-year opportunities can also be considered
- Assistance towards projects and expeditions which do not form part of a degree. Candidates are required to provide evidence of efforts to secure funding elsewhere
- Awards for vacation studies in the arts (in its broad sense). The awards are designed 'to enable students of the highest academic merit and limited financial circumstances to attend conferences, symposia, workshops or master classes or to visit libraries, museums, galleries, concerts or centres of excellence in direct and demonstrable connection with their studies.' Around 15–20 awards can be made each year to people studying at Scottish universities
- Awards for medical electives studies abroad (20 awards each year)
- The John Fife Travel Award to people (normally under the age of 30, but in exceptional cases up to 40 years old) studying or working in horticulture. The award is generally up to £500 but a maximum of £1,000 can be awarded in exceptional circumstances

Annual grant total

In 2012/13 the trust had assets of £5.2 million, an income of £215,000 and a total charitable expenditure of £111,000. The trust notes that, although both individuals and organisations can be supported, most of its funding is given to individuals. During the year 138 individual applications were received and out of these 46 were successful. Awards totalled £75,000.

Further 16 applications were made for the medical election grants with 14 awards being made and 13 applications for arts vacation grants with seven awards provided. No John Fife Travel Awards were made.

Exclusions

The trust comments that 'students who have already received support from the trust for a period of elective study abroad are not eligible for further support.'

Applications

Application forms for each of the awards can be found on the trust's website. Applicants are required to provide full information on their financial circumstances, attach a passport photo, provide an academic reference and details of applications for other funding. Further guidance and closing deadlines for applications for each of the awards can be found on the trust's website.

The trustees normally meet four times a year, in March, February, June and November.

Other information

It can take up to three months for a final decision to be made and the trustees request the applicants to refrain from contacting the trust unnecessarily during that period. Each applicant will be notified of the outcome of their application once the final decision has been made. Do contact the trustees if: 'your address, telephone number or email address changed; you decide not to proceed with the course or project to which your application related; or you have received funds or there have been other changes which affect the details of your application.'

Note if you are applying for an award for vacation studies in the arts:

> The trust is familiar with the Carnegie Vacation Scholarship Scheme which is in operation for the benefit of science undergraduates. The Cross Trust scheme is intended to extend vacation support within the fields of the arts and the performing arts on a somewhat different basis. In consequence, in no circumstances will a candidate be considered for both awards and dual applications will be considered void.

EMMS International
See entry on page 126

Esdaile Trust Scheme 1968

£28,000 (60 grants)

Correspondent: Fiona Watson, Administrator, Exchange Place 3, Semple Street, Edinburgh EH3 8BL (01314 733500; fax: 01314 733535; email: fiona. watson@scott-moncrieff.com; website: www.scott-moncrieff.com/services/ charities/charitable-trusts/esdaile-trust)

SC Number: SC006938

Eligibility

Daughters of ministers of the Church of Scotland, daughters of missionaries appointed or nominated by the Overseas Council of the Church of Scotland, and daughters of widowed deaconesses. Applicants must be between the ages of 12 and 25. Preference is given to families with a low income.

Types of grants

Annual grants towards general educational costs, ranging between £150 and £800.

Annual grant total

In 2012/13 the trust had an income of £27,000 and an expenditure of £34,000. Around £28,000 is available for distribution each year. Previously about 60 grants have been made annually.

Applications

Application forms can be obtained from the trust's website and should be completed by a parent/guardian. Applications should be submitted to the correspondent no later than 31 May each year. Grants are distributed by early September.

Other information

The trust also co-operates with the Society for the Benefit of Sons and Daughters of Ministers of the Church of Scotland and the Glasgow Society of the Sons and Daughters of Ministers of the Church of Scotland in the distribution of student grants. The societies can support both boys and girls.

The Caroline Fitzmaurice Trust

£17,500

Correspondent: The Secretaries, 106 South Street, St Andrews KY16 9QD (01334 468604; email: elcalderwood@ pagan.co.uk; website: www. carolinefitzmaurice.org.uk)

SC Number: SC00518

Eligibility

Girls and young women under the age of 23 who live in the geographical area of the diocese of St Andrews, Dunkeld and Dunblane. The trustees will require successful applicants to make an effort in raising funds elsewhere through their own personal attempts and to subsequently contribute to the community wherever they may settle. Applicants must demonstrate a specific financial need and evidence of high promise in educational, social or cultural background.

Types of grants

Grants of between £200 and £5,000 are given if there is a specific need.

Annual grant total

In 2012/13 the trust had an income of £17,700 and an expenditure of £17,800. We estimate that the annual total of grants was around £17,500.

Exclusions

The application guidelines on the trust's website note that 'the trustees will not approve applications which are based on solely financial need, and will require evidence of high promise. They will fund only a proportion of the total costs.'

Applications

Application forms can be obtained from the correspondent and are considered only once a year, usually in early June. The closing date for applications is 30 April annually. Written report from the applicant's referee is required and applicants who are under the age of 18 at the time of the application are additionally asked to provide full information on both parents' financial circumstances.

Other information

Successful applicants are required to provide a written report to the trustees as soon as practicable after the end of each period of funding.

James Gillan's Trust

£2,000

Correspondent: The Trustees, R. & R. Urquhart, 121 High Street, Forres, Morayshire IV36 1AB (01309 672216)

SC Number: SC016739

Eligibility

People training for the ordained ministry in the Church of Scotland who have lived in, or whose parents have lived in, Moray or Nairn for at least three years. There is a preference for those native to the parishes of Dallas, Dyke, Edinkillie, Forres, Kinloss or Rafford.

Types of grants

The trust provides grants, donations, loans, gifts or pensions to individuals. Awards are of up to £1,000.

Annual grant total

In 2012/13 the trust had an income of £7,000 and an expenditure of £3,500. Our research suggests that the trust normally gives approximately £2,000 in grants to individuals each year.

Applications

In writing to the correspondent.

The Glasgow Highland Society

£6,500

Correspondent: The Secretaries, Alexander Sloan C. A, 38 Cadogan Street, Glasgow G2 7HF (01413 540354; email: kt@alexandersloan.co.uk; website: www.alexandersloan.co.uk/ghs)

SC Number: SC015479

Eligibility

Students who have a connection with the Highlands (for example, lived or went to school there) and who are now studying in Glasgow. Grants are normally given for first degrees only, unless postgraduate studies are a natural progression of the degree.

Types of grants

Grants of around £75 help with fees for people at college or university or who are in vocational training (including mature students). Grants may also be given for Gaelic research projects and apprenticeships.

Annual grant total

In 2012 the trust had an income of £4,500 and an expenditure of £7,500. We estimate grants made to individuals for education totalled around £6,500.

The 2012 accounts were the latest available at the time of writing.

Applications

On a form available from the correspondent. Applications should be submitted directly by the individual by 2 November and are considered in December.

Other information

The correspondent has informed us that the trust may be winding down; however a decision has not been made yet. Applications are still being accepted.

The Glasgow Society of the Sons and Daughters of Ministers of the Church of Scotland

£27,000

Correspondent: The Trustees, Exchange Place, 3 Semple Street, Edinburgh EH3 9BL

SC Number: SC010281

Eligibility

Children of ministers of the Church of Scotland who are in need, particularly students and the children of deceased ministers.

Types of grants

One-off and recurrent grants according to need.

Annual grant total

In 2012/13 the charity had an income of £55,000. About £55,000 per year is given in educational and welfare grants to individuals.

Applications

On a form available from the correspondent or downloaded from the charity's website. Applications should be sent in no later than 31 May each year and grants are distributed by early September.

The Grand Lodge of Ancient, Free and Accepted Masons of Scotland

£25,000

Correspondent: The Trustees, c/o Freemasons Hall, 96 George Street, Edinburgh EH2 3DH (01312 255577; email: curator@grandlodgescotland.org; website: www.grandlodgescotland.com)

SC Number: SC001996

Eligibility

Children of members and deceased members.

Types of grants

Grants for people entering further education.

Annual grant total

In 2012/13 the trust had an income of £1.3 million. About £155,000 is given in welfare grants each year and £25,000 in educational grants.

Applications

On a form available from the correspondent, or by direct approach to the local lodge.

Other information

The trust also runs care homes for older people.

Highlands and Islands Educational Trust Scheme

£11,000

Correspondent: The Administrator, Tods Murray LLP, 133 Fountainbridge Road, Edinburgh EH3 9AG

SC Number: SC014655

Eligibility

Students who live in the counties of Argyll, Bute, Caithness, Inverness, Orkney, Ross and Cromarty, Sutherland or Shetland and are of the Protestant faith. Candidates have to be in the fifth/sixth form at school and preparing to go on to higher/further education. Preference is given to Gaelic speakers.

Types of grants

One-off grants in the range of £120 to £160 are available towards the cost of books and maintenance/living expenses to people who are about to start their first degree course at university or college. Applicants' academic results and financial means are taken into account.

Annual grant total

In 2012/13 the trust had an income of £12,900 and a total expenditure of £11,200. We estimate the annual total of grants to be around £11,000.

Applications

In writing to the correspondent. Applications should be submitted through the individual's school and include confirmation of the applicant's faith, details of the occupation and income of parents/guardians, ability at Gaelic (if applicable), information on the course to be undertaken and intended career plans. Applications should be made between March and June for consideration within the following three months.

Jewish Care Scotland

£0

Correspondent: The Trustees, The Walton Community Care Centre, May Terrace, Giffnock, Glasgow G46 6LD (01416 201800; fax: 01416 202409; email: admin@jcarescot.org.uk; website: www.jcarescot.org.uk)

SC Number: SC005267

Eligibility

Schoolchildren, people starting work and students in further or higher education, including mature students, who are Jewish and live in Scotland.

Types of grants

One-off grants are given towards uniforms, other school clothing, equipment, instruments, fees, maintenance and living expenses. There is a preference for schoolchildren with serious family difficulties so that the child has to be educated away from home.

Annual grant total

In 2012 the charity had an income of £720,000 and a total expenditure of £817,000. Educational grants to individuals usually total around £18,000 and social welfare grants around £1,000. In this financial year however, the trustees have declared that there were no grants or donations made. We have retained the entry as grants may well be made again in the near future. The 2012 accounts were the latest available at the time of writing (July 2014).

Exclusions

No grants are given to postgraduates.

Applications

In writing to the correspondent.

Other information

The board also helps with friendship clubs, housing requirements, clothing, meals-on-wheels, counselling and so on.

The Lethendy Trust

£4,000

Correspondent: George Hay, Administrator, Royal Exchange, Panmure Street, Dundee DD1 1DZ

SC Number: SC003428

Eligibility

Young people with a strong connection to the Tayside or North Fife areas.

Types of grants

Grants of £150 to £400 for young people travelling abroad with charitable organisations to carry out charitable activities.

Annual grant total

In 2012/13 the trust had an income of £67,000 and a total expenditure of £80,000. We estimate that the total award given to individuals was approximately £4,000 as the trust also awards grants to organisations.

Exclusions

No support to individuals for school fees or for purely academic based funding requests.

Applications

In writing to the correspondent. The trusts states that there are regular meetings throughout the year to consider applications.

The Dr Thomas Lyon Bequest

£2,500 (3 grants)

Correspondent: The Administrator, The Merchant Company, The Merchants' Hall, 22 Hanover Street, Edinburgh EH2 2EP (01312 209284; fax: 01312 204842; email: info@mcoe.org.uk; website: www.mcoe.org.uk)

SC Number: SC010284

Eligibility

Scottish orphans of members of Her Majesty's Forces and of the Mercantile Marine. Applicants should be between the ages of 5 and 18 and require financial assistance.

Types of grants

Grants ranging from £500 to £1,500 are offered to children in primary and secondary education towards the costs of clothing and school uniforms, books, educational outings and school fees.

Annual grant total

In 2012/13 the charity had assets of £241,000 and an income of £6,100. During the year three individual awards were made totalling £2,500.

Applications

In writing to the correspondent. An application should state the individuals' total income and the regiment/service of their parent as well as the cause and date of their death.

The Catherine Mackichan Trust

£3,500 (8 grants)

Correspondent: David Mackichan, Treasurer, 2 Hutton Avenue, Houston PA6 7JS (email: david.mackichan@sky.com; website: www.mackichantrust.co.uk)

SC Number: SC020459

Eligibility

Grants are available to the students of history, particularly (but not exclusively) Celtic and/or west highland history or medieval history. People who are researching various aspects of Scottish history, including archaeology, genealogy and language studies are equally eligible.

The trust's website also states that 'applicants will receive particular consideration if they demonstrate that they are unable to obtain funding via normal channels, or if their work is an extension of a topic previously funded through one of these channels.'

Types of grants

Grants range from £200 to £500 but in exceptional circumstances greater amounts can be awarded.

Assistance is available to schoolchildren for books or educational outings and to students in further or higher education (including mature and overseas students) towards books and study/travel abroad. Grants are also given to postgraduate students, individuals without formal attachment to any institute of education and amateur historians.

Annual grant total

In 2012/13 the trust had an income of £2,000 and an expenditure of £4,000. We have estimated that around £3,500 was distributed in grants to individuals.

Exclusions

No grants are given to people whose education or research should be funded by the statutory sources. No grants for undergraduate or postgraduate fees or living expenses.

Applications

Application forms can be obtained by contacting the correspondent. Applications should be submitted between 1 January and 16 April. They are usually considered before the end of June. The trust's website mentions that 'it is desirable, but not essential, that the names and addresses of two referees accompany each application.'

Other information

Our research shows that grants are also given to schools and local history societies for local history and archaeological purposes.

Mathew Trust

£10,000

Correspondent: Fiona Bullions, Administrator, Henderson Loggie, Chartered Accountants, Royal Exchange, Panmure Street, Dundee DD1 1DZ (01382 201234; fax: 01382 221240; email: fiona.bullions@hendersonloggie.co.uk)

SC Number: SC016284

Eligibility

People in need who live in the local government areas of the City of Dundee, Angus, Perth and Kinross and Fife.

Types of grants

One-off grants for fees and study/travel abroad are available to college/university students (including mature students), people in vocational or professional training/retraining, people starting work, people struggling to secure employment, also overseas students and people with special educational needs. Awards are usually up to £400 but greater sums may be awarded.

Annual grant total

In 2012/13 the trust had an income of £226,000 and a total expenditure of £216,000. According to our research about £10,000 is given to individuals each year.

Applications

In writing to the correspondent. Applications can be submitted directly by the individual for consideration every two months.

Other information

Grants are also made to organisations.

Maxton Bequest

£0

Correspondent: Donna Cessford, Support Assistant, Education Service 5th Floor, Fife Council, Rothesay House, Rothesay Place, Glenrothes KY7 5PQ (03451 55 55 55 + Ext 44 19 98; email: donna.cessford@fife.gov.uk)

Eligibility

People who are ordinarily resident (or who have parents resident) in Crieff or Kirkcaldy and are in need

Types of grants

Our research suggests that grants of around £100 are available for clothing, books, equipment, educational outings in the UK, fees or living expenses to people pursuing primary, secondary, tertiary education or vocational training.

Annual grant total

Not known.

Applications

Application forms and further guidelines can be requested from the correspondent. The application deadlines vary each year but usually are around October/November.

Other information

The charity's funds form part of the Fife Educational Trust. The fund does not have a registered charity number.

The McGlashan Charitable Trust

£0

Correspondent: Iain McGlashan, Senior Trustee, 11 Melrose Gardens, Glasgow G20 6RB

SC Number: SC020930

Eligibility

Students undertaking postgraduate courses in any subject who are under the age of 30 and either are Scottish-born and studying in/outside Scotland or born elsewhere but enrolled on a degree in Scotland.

Types of grants

Grants of about £1,000 for postgraduate courses. In exceptional circumstances support could be given towards books or other necessities.

Annual grant total

Grants to postgraduate students will only be awarded from April 2014 therefore we cannot estimate the annual total. The correspondent has stated that at least several grants will be available each year.

Applications

Applicants are invited to write to the correspondent demonstrating a clear financial need. Further guidelines will then be given by the trust. Applications must be made during the three month period in March, April and May. Early or late applications will not be considered.

Other information

The trust has changed its grantmaking practice and from April 2014 only postgraduate students are being supported.

Most of the trust's funding goes to support organisations (examples include Royal Conservatoire of Scotland, The Scottish Ensemble, The National Theatre of Scotland and so forth).

The Muirhead Trust

£5,700

Correspondent: The Administrator, c/o Franchi Law LLP, Queens House, 19 St Vincent Place, Glasgow G1 2DT (email: ann@franchilaw.co.uk; website: www.themuirheadtrust.org.uk)

SC Number: SC016524

Eligibility

Female students of Scottish origin and almost exclusively those who are studying in Scotland. Support is available to students of medicine, veterinary science, pharmacy, nursing, dentistry, science and engineering.

Types of grants

Grants of around £2,000 to £3,000 are available for two years, after which the student is eligible for a statutory grant for the further three years.

Annual grant total

In 2012/13 the trust had an income of £7,100 and a total charitable expenditure of £5,900. We estimate the annual total of grants to be around £5,700.

Exclusions

Biomedical or forensic science students are outside the remit of the trust.

Applications

Application forms can be downloaded from the trust's website and should be submitted together with a CV or a resume and an academic transcript. The deadline for applications is 31 August annually.

North of Scotland Quaker Trust

£5,000

Correspondent: The Trustees, Quaker Meeting House, 98 Crown Street, Aberdeen AB11 6HJ

SC Number: SC000784

Eligibility

People who are associated with the Religious Society of Friends in the North of Scotland Monthly Meeting area and their dependents.

Types of grants

Grants are given to schoolchildren and to people studying in further or higher education for books, equipment, instruments and educational outings. Grants for travel and conferences are also available.

Annual grant total

In 2013 the trust had an income of £23,500 and an expenditure of £21,500. We estimate grants to individuals for educational purposes to be around £5,000.

Exclusions

No grants are given to people studying above first degree level.

Applications

In writing to the correspondent.

Other information

Grants are also given for welfare purposes.

Poppyscotland (The Earl Haig Fund Scotland)

£30,000

Correspondent: The Trustees, New Haig House, Logie Green Road, Edinburgh EH7 4HR (01315 501557; fax: 01315 575819; email: enquiries@poppyscotland.org.uk; website: www.poppyscotland.org.uk)

SC Number: SC014096

Eligibility

People in Scotland of working-age who have served in the UK Armed Forces (regular or reserve) and are now unemployed, low-skilled or in low-paid employment.

Types of grants

One-off grants of up to £2,000 for training to improve employment prospects.

Annual grant total

In 2012/13 the fund had an income of £4.4 million and assets of almost £9.9 million. Grants made totalled around £771,000 and were given to 1,500 individuals. Previously grants for educational purposes to individuals have totalled approximately £30,000.

Applications

In writing to the correspondent.

Other information

Poppyscotland is in many respects the Scottish equivalent of the benevolence department of the Royal British Legion in the rest of Britain. Like the legion, it runs the Poppy Appeal, which is a major source of income to help those in need. There is, however, a Royal British Legion Scotland, which has a separate entry in this guide. The two organisations share the same premises and work together.

In 2006 the Earl Haig Fund Scotland launched a new identity – 'Poppyscotland' – and is now generally known by this name.

The Royal Caledonian Education Trust

£88,000 (Around 300 grants)

Correspondent: James MacBain, Chief Executive, Queen Elizabeth House, 4 St Dunstan's Hill, London EC3R 8AD (020 7463 9232; fax: 020 7463 9241; email: admin@rcst.org.uk; website: www.rcst.org.uk)

CC Number: 310952

Eligibility

Children of Scottish people who have served or are serving in the armed forces.

Priority is given to 'families who are facing particular and challenging financial circumstances, health problems and other difficulties at home.' Support may also be given to the children of Scottish people in financial need living in London who are not entitled to parochial relief.

Types of grants

Grants are available to schoolchildren towards school clothing and uniforms, sports equipment, extra-curricular activities, tuition fees for music, drama and arts courses, extra tuition support, books and stationery, after school clubs, school trips and, in cases of very exceptional difficulty, school educational costs. Further and higher education students can be supported towards living expenses, books, special equipment and essential course materials.

The trust has previously stated that they view education in its widest sense and welcome enquires from applicants who are unsure as to whether they can be helped.

Annual grant total

In 2012/13 the trust had assets of £4.4 million, an income of £248,000 and a charitable expenditure of £242,000. Grants to individuals totalled £88,000.

The trust normally makes around 300 awards a year. Currently most of the support is given to the dependents of the army personnel but the trust 'is actively seeking to create a greater balance in its giving between the three armed forces.'

Exclusions

The trust will not provide funding where the need should be met by the statutory provisions.

Applications

Application forms are available from the trust's website or can be requested from the correspondent. The grants committee meets in January, March, June and October to consider the applications.

Other information

In addition to making grants to individuals, the trust also works through its Education Programme with schools, local authorities, armed forces charities and military communities to support the armed forces children, teachers and families in the school environment, especially in relation to children's emotional well-being. During the year around £142,000 was spent in Education Programme.

Scotscare

£398,000 (1000+ grants)

Correspondent: Willie Docherty, Administrator, 22 City Road, London EC1Y 2AJ (020 7240 3718; email: info@scotscare.com; website: www.scotscare.com)

CC Number: 207326

Eligibility

Scottish people, their children and widows, who are in need and have lived within a 35-mile radius of Charing Cross for at least two years.

Types of grants

Training grants for fees, books and computers to enable people to secure qualifications with a view to gaining employment. Student grants for fees, books/equipment and maintenance. Grants are also given for school uniforms and trips.

Annual grant total

In 2012/13 the charity had assets of £49 million and an income of almost £2.2 million. Grants to over 1,000 individuals totalled £398,000 most of which was given for welfare purposes. £22,500 was given in grants to students.

Exclusions

No grants are made for debts or for items that have already been purchased.

Applications

On a form available for download on the charity's website or by contacting the organisation directly.

Other information

The charity runs a dedicated helpline: 0800 652 2989.

The Scottish Chartered Accountants' Benevolent Association

Correspondent: Robert Linton, Administrator, Robert Linton and Co., c/o ICAS 2nd Floor, 7 West Nile Street, Glasgow G1 2PR (01413 011788; email: scaba@robertlinton.co.uk)

SC Number: SC008365

Eligibility

The dependents of members of the Institute of Chartered Accountants of Scotland who are in financial need.

Types of grants

One-off grants for a variety of needs. Recent grants have been given for school fees, maintenance expenses and retraining.

Annual grant total

Grants usually total about £120,000 each year.

Accounts were not available at the time of writing (August 2014).

Applications

An initial letter or telephone call should be made to the correspondent. A member of the fund will then make contact and arrange a visit if appropriate. Following this, an application, report and recommendation will be made to the fund's council for approval.

Other information

Grants are also made for welfare purposes.

Scottish International Education Trust

£20,000 (12 grants)

Correspondent: Gavin McEwan, Administrator, Turcan Connell, Princes Exchange, 1 Earl Grey Street, Edinburgh EH3 9EE (email: siet@turcanconnell.com; website: www.scotinted.org.uk)

SC Number: SC009207

Eligibility

Scottish people who wish to take their studies or training further in order to start a career. Preference is given to postgraduates.

Types of grants

One-off and recurrent grants of up to £2,000 for educational expenses such as fees, books/equipment or travel.

The trust has informed us that awards for travel are currently suspended due to pressure on trust funds.

Annual grant total

IIn 2012/13 the trust had an income of £33,000 and an expenditure of £70,000. No further information was available. Previously grants have been given in the following areas: international affairs; history; drama, dance and ballet; music; law; film-making, cinematography; and science, engineering and technology.

Exclusions

The trust does not normally make grants for:
- Courses leading to qualifications required for entry into a profession (such as teaching or legal practice)
- Purchase of musical instruments
- Undergraduate courses or courses below degree level

Applications

In writing via post or email to the correspondent including CV; details of the course; a statement of aims and two references (further details of information required are available on the trust's website. Applications may be submitted at any time and will be assessed when received. Grants may be awarded at this stage or may be submitted to the board of trustees for a second assessment, therefore if timings are crucial, applications should be submitted by mid-February or mid-July in time for the twice yearly trustee meetings.

Other information

The trust also supports youth organisations and schools, making two grants totalling £4,500 during the year.

Society for the Benefit of Sons and Daughters of the Clergy of the Church of Scotland

£19,000 (59 grants)

Correspondent: Fiona Watson, Administrator, Scott-Moncrieff, Exchange Place 3, Semple Street, Edinburgh EH3 8BL (website: www. scott-moncrieff.com/services/charities/charitable-trusts/society-for-the-benefit-of-sons-and-daughters)

SC Number: SC008760

Eligibility

Children of ministers of the Church of Scotland aged between 12 and 25. Preference is given to low income families.

Types of grants

Grants range from £100 to £1,000 towards general educational purposes. Grants are made for one year only but renewals may be granted following a fresh application.

Annual grant total

In 2013 the society had an income of £31,000 and an expenditure of £46,000. The charity administrator's website states that normally around £19,000 is available for educational grants and most recently 59 individuals were awarded.

Applications

Application forms can be downloaded from the Scott-Moncrieff website and should be posted to the correspondent. Applications should provide full details of the family income and need to be submitted by a parent/guardian before 31 May each year. Grants are distributed by early September.

Other information

The society cooperates with the Glasgow Society of Sons and Daughters of Ministers of the Church of Scotland and the Esdaile Trust in the distribution of grants for the benefit of students.

Other limited funds offering support to dependents are: the John Lang Macfarlane Fund for unmarried and widowed daughters of ministers (with £6,000 available for distribution each year) and the Robertson Chaplin Fund for unmarried sisters over 40 of ordained ministers, with preference given to the aged and infirm (£1,000 available annually).

John Suttie Memorial Fund

£1,600

Correspondent: The Administrator, R. & R. Urquhart Solicitors LLP, 117–121 High Street, Forres IV36 1AB (01309 672216)

SC Number: SC007345

Eligibility

People who live in Moray and Nairn (with preference for people under the age of 30) who are starting on an agricultural or veterinary career.

Types of grants

Grants towards further or higher education in fields of agriculture or veterinary.

Annual grant total

At the time of writing (August 2014) the latest financial information available was from 2012. In 2012 the fund had an income of £12,300 and a total expenditure of £1,700. We estimate that grants totalled around £1,600.

Applications

In writing to the correspondent. Our research suggests that information regarding awards is circulated annually to schools and through agricultural and veterinary organisations.

John Watson's Trust

£150,000

Correspondent: Laura Campbell, Trust Administrator, The Signet Library, Parliament Square, Edinburgh EH1 1RF (01312 250658; email: lcampbell@ wssociety.co.uk; website: www. thewssociety.co.uk/index.asp?pg=145)

SC Number: SC014004

Eligibility

Children and young people under the age of 21 who have a physical/learning disability or are socially disadvantaged and live in Scotland. Preference is given to people living in or connected with Edinburgh or the Lothian region.

Orphans, children from a single parent family or individuals who are burdened with some other special family difficulty,

which is not purely financial, can also be supported towards boarding school costs.

Types of grants

Grants in the range of £30–£2,000 are given towards special tuition, educational trips, computers (especially for people with special educational needs), laptops, books, uniforms, tools, equipment, expenses for further training and education, travel and other activities contributing to education and advancement in life.

School boarding fees may be partially covered but usually in exceptional circumstances, where personal situations makes boarding a necessary option.

Annual grant total

In 2012/13 the trust had an income of £191,000 and a total expenditure of £205,000. Approximately £150,000 is allocated for distribution in grants each year.

Exclusions

Grants are not available for day school or university fees.

Applications

Application forms and full guidelines can be found on the WS Society's website or requested from the correspondent. They can be submitted directly by the individual, or through a third party, for example, a social worker, Citizens Advice, other welfare agency, if applicable. Applications must include details of the candidate's household income, specify the support required and provide references.

The grants committee meets approximately six times a year and the application deadlines are available on the trust's website.

Applications for school trips to outdoor residential centres must be made by the school, not the individual.

Other information

Grants are also made to organisations and groups working with disadvantaged children or young individuals with physical/learning disabilities.

Aberdeen and Perthshire

Aberdeen Endowments Trust

£35,000

Correspondent: David Murdoch, Clerk to the Trust, 19 Albert Street, Aberdeen AB25 1QF (01224 640194; fax: 01224 643918; email: l.clark@abdn.ac.uk)

SC Number: SC010507

Eligibility

People of any age who were born and brought up in Aberdeen, as constituted in 1967. Secondary school pupils in the former Grampian region can be supported according to need and academic performance.

Types of grants

Most of the trust's funding is spent in providing free places at Robert Gordon's Secondary College to pupils who otherwise would not be able to attend it. The trust supports around 60 pupils at Robert Gordon's College.

Educational travel

More than 100 pupils at city primary and secondary schools are given help to participate in school trips each year. Applications can be made at any time of year using forms available from the trust. The trips should have a clear education content and the means-tested awards are paid directly to the school, typically comprising 50% of the trip costs. The trustees are happy to consider applications for group travel.

Secondary School bursaries

Bursaries are awarded in September each year to help disadvantaged families. The awards run for up to four years, to the end of fourth year. In September 2014, 30 new bursaries were awarded for pupils at secondary schools in North East Scotland. Annual payments for these awards range from £160 to £500 per child. Application forms are available from the trust each year and are sent to the headteachers of all North East primary schools.

Further education grants

The trust provides grants to people progressing to further education at college, university or other institutions. Each year around 20 grants are made to students from the city ranging for up to £1,000.

Foreign language education grants

Grants are available to help pupils develop their skills in modern languages through travel or a course of study. Application forms are available from the trust and are sent each year to principal teachers of modern languages in city schools. Applications can be considered at any time. Grants since 2012 have typically been around £300 per pupil.

Annual grant total

In 2013 the trust had an income of £952,000 and made grants totalling £678,000. Out of this amount £643,000 was awarded to support pupils at Robert Gordon's College. The remaining £35,000 was awarded in general grants and bursaries.

Applications

Application forms can be requested from the correspondent. They are normally considered monthly, except in January, July and August.

Other information

Occasionally grants can be made to organisations.

Dr John Calder Trust

£3,000

Correspondent: Clive Phillips, Administrator, St Machar's Cathedral, 18 The Chanonry, Aberdeen AB24 1RQ

SC Number: SC004299

Eligibility

People in need who live in the parish of Machar or within the city of Aberdeen. Individuals who are only resident in the area for their education and people from the area studying elsewhere are both eligible.

Types of grants

Grants are usually of up to £500 and can be given for general educational needs.

Annual grant total

In 2012/13 the trust had an income of £15,000 and a total expenditure of £7,400. We estimate that around £3,000 was awarded in educational grants to individuals.

Applications

Previously the trust has stated that funds were fully committed and that this situation was likely to remain so for the medium to long-term.

Other information

A smaller proportion of charitable expenditure is given to individuals for welfare needs. Organisations may also be supported.

The Anne Herd Memorial Trust

£12,500

Correspondent: The Trustees, 27 Bank Street, Dundee DD1 1RP

SC Number: SC014198

Eligibility

People who are blind or partially sighted who live in Broughty Ferry (applicants from the city of Dundee, region of Tayside or those who have connections with these areas and reside in Scotland will also be considered).

Types of grants

Grants are given for educational equipment such as computers and books. Grants are usually at least £50.

Annual grant total

In 2012/13 the trust had an income of £40,000. The trust gives approximately £25,000 a year in grants for education and welfare.

Applications

In writing to the correspondent, to be submitted directly by the individual in March/April for consideration in June.

The Morgan Trust Scheme 1982

£11,200

Correspondent: The Clerk, Miller Hendry Solicitors, 13 Ward Road, Dundee DD1 1LU (01382 200000; fax: 01382 200098; email: info@millerhendry.co.uk)

SC Number: SC010527

Eligibility

Children whose parents were either born/educated in the former royal burghs of Dundee, Forfar, Arbroath and Montrose, or have been resident in these areas for five years immediately prior to the application (or immediately before their death).

Types of grants

The trust offers maintenance grants to pupils according to need and school scholarships to promising children in day or boarding fee paying schools. Emergency grants may also be awarded to schoolchildren whose parent/guardian has died or suffers a serious loss of income and can no longer support the child's education (such support is continued until the beneficiary finishes school or assistance is deemed no longer necessary). Grants are generally in the range of £200.

Annual grant total

The latest financial information available at the time of writing was from 2012. In 2012 the trust had an income of £13,600 and an expenditure of £11,400. We have estimated that the annual total of grants was around £11,200.

Exclusions

According to our research, grants are not given to people with an income of more than £10,000, unless there are exceptional circumstances.

Applications

Application forms are available from the correspondent. They should be completed by an appropriate third party on behalf of the applicant providing full details of their financial situation. Awards are usually considered in May and November.

Other information

In addition to the above, the trust gives Tom's Prizes awarded by competition or merit and progress in school.

The Gertrude Muriel Pattullo Advancement Award Scheme

£1,800

Correspondent: Private Client Team, Blackadders Solicitors, 30–34 Reform Street, Dundee DD1 1RJ (01382 229222; fax: 01382 342220; email: dundee@blackadders.co.uk)

SC Number: SC000811

Eligibility

Young people aged 16 to 25 who are physically disabled and live in the city of Dundee or the county of Angus.

Types of grants

One-off and recurrent grants, usually of £100 to £500, to schoolchildren and students in further or higher education towards books, equipment, instruments, fees, living expenses and educational outings in the UK.

Annual grant total

In 2012/13 the trust had an income of £5,100 and a total expenditure of £3,800. We estimate that educational grants to individuals totalled £1,800, with funding also awarded to local organisations.

Exclusions

No grants are given towards the repayment of debts.

Applications

On a form available from the correspondent at any time. Applications can be submitted directly by the individual or through any third party.

Aberdeen and Aberdeenshire

Aberdeenshire Educational Trust

£10,000

Correspondent: Maureen Adamson, Administrator, St Leonards-Aberdeenshire Council, Sandyhill Road, Banff AB45 1BH (01261 813336; email: maureen.adamson@aberdeenshire.gov.uk)

SC Number: SC028382

Eligibility

Schoolchildren and students who, or whose immediate family, are resident in the former county of Aberdeenshire. Applicants' household income should not exceed £20,525.

Types of grants

Grants between £10 and £200 are available to individuals in further/higher education, people starting work or individuals undertaking apprenticeships. Postgraduate research or special projects may be supported. Grants are given for travel, fees, books, equipment and so on. Support is also available towards school trips and annual school prizes. There is a preference for education in the visual arts, music and drama.

Annual grant total

In 2012/13 the trust had an income of £135,000. A total of £75,000 was spent on charitable activities supporting both individuals and organisations. Previously around £10,000 a year has been awarded in grants to individuals.

Applications

On a form available from the correspondent. Grants are considered throughout the year. All applications are means tested, therefore applicants are required to provide documentary evidence of their income from the last tax year.

Other information

Grants are mostly made to schools, clubs and educational groups.

Huntly Educational Trust 1997

£13,000

Correspondent: A. Mitchell, Secretary, Peterkins solicitors, 3 The Square, Huntly, Aberdeenshire AB54 8AE (01466 792101)

SC Number: SC026920

Eligibility

Primarily people living in the district of Huntly. Applicants from elsewhere in Scotland may also be supported if there are remaining funds and at the trustees' discretion.

Types of grants

Grants are given towards education and training, including vocational courses. General educational needs can be addressed, including books, equipment, tools, clothing and so on. Awards are of around £200 on average.

Annual grant total

In 2012/13 the trust had an income of £31,000 and an expenditure of £27,000. We estimate that grants to individuals totalled around £13,000. Note that both the income and the charitable expenditure vary every year.

Applications

Application forms can be requested from the correspondent or downloaded from The Gordon Schools' website. Grants are normally considered at monthly meetings.

Other information

The trust also makes grants to local schools, colleges and other educational establishments.

Kincardineshire Educational Trust

£1,800

Correspondent: Grant Administrator, Trust Section, Aberdeenshire Council, St Leonard's, Sandyhill Road, Banff AB45 1BH (01261 813336; email: maureen.adamson@aberdeenshire.gov.uk)

SC Number: SC028381

Eligibility

People who permanently reside or are educated in the former county of Kincardine and schoolchildren whose parents live there.

Types of grants

Grants of up to £100 are given to: schoolchildren towards books, equipment, instruments and educational outings; and people in further or higher education, including mature students and postgraduates, towards books, equipment, instruments, fees, living expenses, student exchanges and educational outings and trips in the UK and overseas. Support is also given to people staring work or apprenticeships and adult education.

Annual grant total

In 2012/13 the trust had an income of £3,600 and a total expenditure of £3,400.

We estimate that grants to individuals for educational purposes totalled around £1,700.

Applications

On a form available from the correspondent, to be received by 30 November for consideration in March. Applications are means tested so documentary evidence of income should be included.

Other information

Grants are also made to clubs, schools and other educational establishments.

Angus

Angus Educational Trust

£8,500

Correspondent: The Administrator, People Directorate, Angus House, Orchardbank Business Park, Forfar DD8 1AE (01307 476339; fax: 01307 461848; website: www.angus.gov.uk/services/view_service_detail.cfm?serviceid=1362)

SC Number: SC015826

Eligibility

People in need residing in the Angus council area who are attending or entering full/part time undergraduate courses in universities. Note: any student entitled to apply for a loan under the Student Loans Scheme must have taken up this option before an application to the trust will be considered.

Types of grants

The trust provides financial assistance towards undergraduate university courses and offers travel grants for those studying on higher education courses outside of Scotland. Young people travelling abroad for other educational purposes can also be supported. Awards are means tested and are intended to supplement existing grants.

Annual grant total

In 2012/13 the trust had an income of £22,000 and a total expenditure of £17,200. The trust also supports organisations, therefore we estimate that grants to individuals totalled around £8,500.

Exclusions

Postgraduate studies and students at colleges are not supported.

Applications

Application forms can be downloaded from the trust's website or requested from the correspondent. Applicants must state full details of their financial situation, provide copies of P60 forms

(for those employed) and enclose a copy of the letter from the awarding authority allocating or rejecting their grant/bursary application. The trustees meet twice a year in March and September to consider applications and can take three to four months to come to a decision.

Other information

Grants are also available to various local clubs, groups working to improve educational opportunities and learning in Angus and rural primary schools for educational excursions.

Assistance for pre-university gap years can also be given, provided the activities are for educational purposes and specific outcomes, length of the stay and associated costs are known at the time of application.

The David Barnet Christie Trust

£6,000

Correspondent: Graham McNicol, Administrator, Thorntons LLP, Brothockbank House, Arbroath DD11 1NJ (01241 872683; fax: 01241 871541)

SC Number: SC004618

Eligibility

Men or women aged up to 40, preferably living in or originating from the Arbroath area (or failing this, Angus), who are about to enter into an engineering apprenticeship, have already taken up such or similar training, or wish to progress by taking further engineering qualifications.

Types of grants

One-off grants of up to £500 to people starting work or students in further or higher education, including mature students and postgraduates, towards books, study or travel abroad, equipment, instruments, maintenance and living expenses.

Annual grant total

In 2012/13 the trust had an income of £8,000 and a total expenditure of £6,500. We estimate that £6,000 in grants was awarded to individuals.

Exclusions

Students from any other area in the UK, EU or overseas are not eligible for funding.

Applications

On a form available from the correspondent. Applications should be submitted directly by the individual by the end of September each year.

The Duncan Trust

£124,000

Correspondent: The Administrator, c/o Thorntons Law LLP, Brothockbank House, Arbroath, Angus DD11 1NE (01241 872683; fax: 01241 871541)

SC Number: SC015311

Eligibility

Students who are training or intend to train for the Ministry of the Church of Scotland on either a regular or modified course. Preference is given to individuals within the Presbytery of Angus and Mearns.

Types of grants

Bursaries and scholarships.

Annual grant total

In 2012/13 the trust had an income of £100,000 and a total charitable expenditure of £124,000. We estimate that the annual total of grants was about the same figure.

Applications

In writing to the correspondent.

Dundee

City of Dundee Educational Trust Scheme

£18,400

Correspondent: Jeffrey Hope, Administrator, Miller Hendry Solicitors, 13 Ward Road, Dundee DD1 1LU (01382 200000; email: JeffreyHope@millerhendry.co.uk)

SC Number: SC015820

Eligibility

Further/higher education students in, or with a strong connection to, Dundee. Priority is given to those who do not receive any statutory awards.

Types of grants

One-off grants ranging from £200 to £300 towards general educational costs.

Annual grant total

In 2013 the trust had an income of £17,100 and an expenditure of £18,800. We estimate that around £18,400 was awarded in grants to individuals.

Applications

Application forms can be requested from the correspondent. Applications, together with a CV, should be submitted at least two weeks before the trustees' quarterly meetings. The meetings are held in March, June, September and December.

Moray

Banffshire Educational Trust

£10,000 (50 grants)

Correspondent: Jean-Anne Goodbrand, Admin Officer, Education and Social Care, The Moray Council, High Street, Elgin, Moray IV30 1BX (01343 551374; fax: 01343 563478; email: jeananne.goodbrand@moray.gov.uk; website: www.moray.gov.uk)

Eligibility

People who live/whose parents live in the former county of Banffshire or who attend schools or further education centres there. Applicants' household earning should be below £34,000 a year.

Types of grants

The trust offers postgraduate scholarships for research work or an advanced/special study; bursaries for further/higher education students, including open university and second/subsequent degrees; grants to mature students to enable them to achieve necessary qualifications to enter university or other institution of further/higher education; financial support towards books, instruments, tools, kits, personal equipment and so on to people undertaking apprenticeships or training; assistance towards study/travel abroad, including fees, books or equipment/instruments; funds for educational outings and visits to schoolchildren and young people attending further education centres; grants for any courses of adult education; and support for research and educational experiments which would be beneficial to the Banffshire county people.

Annual grant total

According to our research, grants totalling around £10,000 are made to about 50 individuals each year.

Applications

Separate application forms for each category and detailed guidelines are available on the trust's website or can be requested from the correspondent. Applications should be submitted by 30 September for consideration in December.

The equal opportunities form should be sent in a separate envelope marked 'private and confidential' to: Alan Taylor, Admin Assistant, Education and Social Care, The Moray Council, High Street, ELGIN, Moray IV30 1BX.

Other information

Support is also given to schools, further education centres, clubs and organisations which operate for the benefit of the people of Banffshire.

Moray and Nairn Educational Trust

£3,000

Correspondent: Administrative Officer, Education and Social Care, The Moray Council, Council Offices, High Street, Elgin IV30 1BX (01343 551374; fax: 01343 563478; email: educationalservices@moray.gov.uk; website: www.moray.gov.uk)

Eligibility

People who or whose parents have lived in the former combined county of Moray and Nairn for at least five years and schoolchildren/young people attending Moray and Nairn schools. Applicants' household earnings must be below £34,000 a year plus an allowance for dependent children.

Types of grants

Bursaries are available to students (including mature and postgraduate) in Scottish universities and people pursuing education at a Scottish Central Institution or Training College. Financial support can also be given for study/travel overseas and to school pupils for educational outings and visits. Grants are normally one-off and can reach up to £200.

Annual grant total

Normally around £6,000 is distributed in grants. We estimate that around £3,000 is given to individuals for educational purposes.

Applications

Application forms can be found on the trust's website and should be submitted before 30 September annually. Note that current guidelines and application forms are subject to change – for the latest updates see the trust's website.

Other information

Grants can also be made to local schools, further education centres or clubs and organisations operating in the area of benefit for facilities, special equipment or promotion of adult education.

Ian Wilson Ski Fund

£0
SC Number: SC026750

Eligibility

Young people under the age of 21 who attend a school run by Moray council (or their statutory successors) or a further education establishment. Preference is given to families with a restricted income.

Types of grants

One-off grants are given for educational purposes promoting outdoor activities. Sport and related studies are eligible.

Annual grant total

In 2012/13 the fund had an income of £11,000. There has been no charitable expenditure for the past few years.

Applications

In writing to the correspondent. According to our research, the number of grants available is limited, therefore applicants are encouraged to apply in plenty of time. It is suggested that applicants apply before the end of the school holidays in October for consideration by the trustees later that month. Applications can be submitted directly by individuals or through their school/college, educational welfare agency, if applicable.

Other information

Group applications can also be supported.

Perth and Kinross

The Guildry Incorporation of Perth

£20,000

Correspondent: Lorna Peacock, Secretary, 42 George Street, Perth PH1 5JL (01738 623195)

SC Number: SC008072

Eligibility

Young people aged 17 to 25 who are in need, living in Perth or Guildtown and following a course of further or higher education in the UK. The guild also supports young people taking part in Raleigh International, Link Overseas Exchange Projects and similar activities.

Types of grants

Grants of up to £800.

Annual grant total

In 2012/13 the guild had an income of £227,000. Our research shows that grants to individuals have previously totalled around £80,000, with approximately £20,000 given for educational purposes.

141

Applications

Application forms can be requested from the correspondent. They are considered at the trustees' meetings on the last Tuesday of every month. Applicants are required to write a short covering letter of around 250 words explaining why they require funding and how the grant they receive could help their local community.

Perth and Kinross Educational Trust

£8,000

Correspondent: The Administrator, Perth and Kinross Council, Chief Executive's Service, 2 High Street, Perth PH1 5PH (01738 476200; email: ECSFST@pkc.gov.uk)

SC Number: SC012378

Eligibility

Students in further or higher education who were born or attended school in Perth and Kinross. Mature students, postgraduates and people undertaking apprenticeships are all eligible.

Types of grants

Grants of up to £150 can be awarded towards books, fees, living expenses and study/travel abroad.

Annual grant total

In 2012/13 the trust had an income of £41,000 and an expenditure of around £44,000. According to our research, previously about £8,000 a year has been given to individuals.

Applications

Application forms can be obtained from the Perth and Kinross Council. Applications should normally be submitted by mid-May for consideration in June. The exact closing date can be found on the application form. Late applications are not considered.

Other information

Organisations may also be supported.

Central Scotland

Clackmannanshire

Clackmannanshire Educational Trust Scheme 1957

£100

Correspondent: Clackmannanshire Council, Administrator, Facilities, Schools and Welfare Team, Services to People, Kilncraigs, Greenside Street, Alloa FK10 1EB (01259 452499; fax: 01259 452440; email: fswsupport@clacks. gov.uk; website: www.clacksweb.org.uk/ learning/clackmannanshireeducational trust)

SC Number: SC008282

Eligibility

People who are resident in the county of Clackmannanshire.

Types of grants

Grants of £50 to £100 towards educational travel (in the UK or overseas) to school pupils or further/higher education students; and for adult education.

Annual grant total

In 2012/13 the trust had an income of £560 and an expenditure of £150. We estimate that grants totalled around £100.

Applications

Application forms are available from the Clackmannanshire Council website or upon request from the correspondent. Applications can be submitted directly by the individual together with two references. Applications are normally considered on the first Thursday of January, April, July and October.

Fife

Fife Educational Trust

£21,000

Correspondent: Education Services, Finance and Procurement, Fife Council, Rothesay House, Glenrothes KY7 5PQ

SC Number: SC004325

Eligibility

People who have a permanent address within the Fife council area and who attended a secondary or primary school there.

Types of grants

Support for individuals below postgraduate level is usually restricted to travel grants where this is an integral part of the course of study, but can also be given for music, drama and visual arts. Grants range from £50 to about £75.

Annual grant total

In 2012/13 the trust had an income of £58,000 and a total expenditure of £42,000. We estimate that the total grant awarded to individuals was approximately £21,000 as the trust also awards grants to organisations.

Applications

In writing to the correspondent. Applicants must give their permanent address, details of schools they attended within Fife with dates of attendance, and details of other money available. Applications are considered in March.

New St Andrews Japan Golf Trust

£5,000

Correspondent: J. Philp, Trustee, 7 Pilmour Links, St Andrews, Fife KY16 9JG

SC Number: SC005668

Eligibility

Children and young people in need who live in the county of Fife and are undertaking sports and recreational activities with a preference for golf.

Types of grants

One-off and recurrent grants ranging from £200 to £1,500 are offered for sports equipment, travel costs, student exchange, accommodation expenses, coaching assistance, university fees or sports scholarships.

Annual grant total

In 2012/13 the trust had an income of £7,800 and a total charitable expenditure of £10,100. We estimate that grants to individuals totalled about £5,000.

Applications

In writing to the correspondent. Contact details of two referees are required.

Other information

The trust supports both individuals and organisations.

Stirling

Stirlingshire Educational Trust

£85,000

Correspondent: Iain Flett, Administrator, 68 Port Street, Stirling FK8 2LJ (01786 474956; fax: 01786 474956; website: www. stirlingeducationaltrust.org.uk)

SC Number: SC007528

Eligibility

People in need who live, or have lived in the past for a period of at least five consecutive years, in Stirlingshire (including Denny/Bonnybridge, Falkirk, Grangemouth, Kilsyth, Polmont, Stirling and environs).

Types of grants

The trust offers:

- Travel post-graduation scholarships – for research work or advanced/special study to postgraduates
- Travel scholarships – for travel within the UK or abroad for educational purposes
- Special grants – to mature students (over the age of 21) for obtaining the necessary educational qualifications to enter university or an institute of further education
- Apprenticeship and professional training grants – to people undertaking apprenticeships or practical experience of a trade/ profession towards 'expenses incurred in occupational/vocational courses at post-school educational establishments, and/or obtaining training/experience at the place of an employer, or such work placement'

Support can be given towards fees, books, travel expenses, equipment/ instruments or other educational necessities and is normally in the range from £150 to £500.

Annual grant total

In 2012/13 the trust had an income of £107,000 and a total expenditure of £105,000. Usually around £85,000 a year is distributed in educational grants.

Applications

Applications can be made online on the trust's website. Applications should be received by February, May, August and November for consideration on the first Wednesday of the following month. An acknowledgement letter will be sent by email following the application providing further information.

Other information

Organisations can also be supported.

Edinburgh, the Lothians and Scottish Borders

City of Edinburgh

The James Scott Law Charitable Fund

£1,500 (5 grants)

Correspondent: The Administrator, The Merchant Company, Merchants' Hall, 22 Hanover Street, Edinburgh EH2 2EP (01312 209284; fax: 01312 204842; email: alistair.beattie@mcoe.org.uk)

SC Number: SC008878

Eligibility

Children between the ages of 5 and 18 who attend primary or secondary Edinburgh Merchant Company Schools.

Types of grants

Grants of up to £2,000 are given for school fees, clothing, books and allowances.

Annual grant total

In 2012/13 the trust had assets of £126,000 and an income of £3,600. During the year, five individuals were awarded grants totalling £1,500.

Applications

Application forms can be requested from the correspondent and should be submitted prior to the trustees' meeting in August. A bursar will usually interview the applicants at their school.

East Lothian

East Lothian Educational Trust

£25,000

Correspondent: J. Morrison, Administrator, Department of Corporate Resources, John Muir House, Haddington, East Lothian EH41 3HA (01620 827273; email: eleducationaltrust@eastlothian.gov.uk; website: www.eastlothian.gov.uk/info/ 828/activities_and_support_for_young_ people/1496/east_lothian_educational_ trust)

SC Number: SC010587

Eligibility

People in education or training who live in the area covered by East Lothian Council (former county of East Lothian).

Types of grants

Support is available to people 'undertaking studies, courses or projects of an educational nature, including scholarships abroad and educational travel.' Grants are normally one-off and means tested. According to our research they range from around £100 to £700 and can be awarded to schoolchildren, further/higher education students (including mature students and postgraduates), people in training, and individuals with special educational needs. Assistance is available for a wide range of educational needs, including uniforms/clothing, fees, study/travel abroad, books, equipment/instruments, maintenance/living expenses, research, accommodation and excursions.

Annual grant total

In 2012/13 the trust had an income of £58,000 and an expenditure of £54,000. We estimate that around £25,000 was given in grants to individuals.

Exclusions

Residents of Musselburgh, Wallyford and Whitecraig are not included. Grants are intended to be supplementary only.

Applications

Application forms can be downloaded from the trust's website or requested from the correspondent. Applicants should provide full costs of the course and associated expenses (such as fees, accommodation, travel, necessities, maintenance, special equipment) and give details of their household income. Applications can be submitted directly by the individual or through a parent/ guardian. Trustees meet four times a year, usually in February, May, August and November.

Other information

Grants are also available to clubs and organisations for various studies or projects of educational nature.

Note that 'if you have used your parents' address for your eligibility as a resident of East Lothian then you will be deemed to be financially dependent on your parents.'

The Red House Home Trust

£10,000 (16 grants)

Correspondent: Fiona Watson, Administrator, Scott-Moncrieff, Exchange Place 3, Semple Street, Edinburgh EH3 8BL (01314 733500; fax: 01314 733500; email: fiona.watson@ scott-moncrieff.com; website: www.scott-moncrieff.com/services/charities/charitable-trusts/red-house-home-trust)

SC Number: SC015748

Eligibility

Young people under the age of 22 who live in East Lothian and are in need of care, live in deprived circumstances or are adjusting to independent living.

Types of grants

Grants in the range of £250 to £1,000 for general needs relating to education and training.

Annual grant total

At the time of writing (July 2014) the latest financial information available was from 2012. In 2012 the trust had an income of £21,000 and an expenditure of £22,000. The trust's website notes that about £10,000 is available for distribution each year. Previously 16 grants have been given during the year.

Applications

Application forms are available from the Scott Moncrieff website or can be requested from the correspondent. They should be returned by post to the correspondent. The trustees normally meet three times a year to review applications and award grants.

Scottish Borders

The Elizabeth Hume Trust

£2,500

Correspondent: J. Brown, Administrator, 26 Whitehall Road, Chirnside, Duns, Berwickshire TD11 3UB

SC Number: SC005995

Eligibility

People in need who live in the parish of Chirnside.

Types of grants

Our research suggests that grants can be made to schoolchildren towards uniforms, other clothing and equipment/ instruments. Undergraduate students can be supported for fees and books.

Annual grant total

At the time of writing (August 2014) the latest financial information available was from 2012. In 2012 the trust had an income of £3 and an expenditure of £10,400. We estimate that educational grants to individuals totalled around £2,500.

Applications

In writing to the correspondent. Applications can be made either directly by an individual or through a third party, such as a family member, social worker or teacher, also through an organisation, for example Citizens Advice, school or church.

Other information

Grants are also awarded for social welfare purposes and to organisations.

Charities Administered by Scottish Borders Council

£10,000

Correspondent: The Administrator, Community Services Council, Newtown St Boswells, Melrose, Roxburghshire TD6 0SA (01835 825020; website: www.scotborders.gov.uk/directory/23/education_trusts)

Eligibility

The Scottish Borders Council administers four educational trusts corresponding to the four former counties of Berwickshire, Peeblesshire, Roxburghshire and Selkirkshire. Applicants should either live in these areas or have family resident there.

Types of grants

Small grants can be given for educational outings and travel, adult education, studies of drama, music and visual arts, research, special equipment/instruments and postgraduate studies. Consult the charity's website for specific details. Grants are usually from £20 to £250.

Annual grant total

Our research suggests that the annual budget for grants is normally about £10,000.

Applications

Application forms for each of the trusts can be found on the Scottish Borders Council website or requested from the correspondent. Applications can be made at any time.

Other information

Awards are made on a first come first served basis. Support can also be given to local clubs.

West Lothian

West Lothian Educational Trust

£6,000 (30 grants)

Correspondent: Fiona Watson, Scott-Moncrieff, Exchange Place 3, Semple Street, Edinburgh EH3 8BL (01314 733500; fax: 01314 733535; website: www.scott-moncrieff.com/services/charities/charitable-trusts/west-lothian-educational-trust)

Eligibility

People who were born in West Lothian or have lived there for the last two years.

Types of grants

Normally, one-off grants from £100 to £300 are given; however recurrent grants may be considered for a training course lasting over a year. Financial support is available for undergraduate and postgraduate studies, apprentices, people entering a trade, travel/study costs within and outside Scotland or for educational outings. Adult education, visual arts, music, drama or educational experiments and research can also be supported.

Annual grant total

The trust's website states that normally, 'after various prize monies and bursaries have been paid, about £6,000 is available for distribution each year.' In 2012/13 the trust had an income of £13,000 and a total expenditure of £14,200. Usually around 30 grants are made annually.

Applications

Application forms are available from the trust's website or can be requested from the correspondent. Applications must be received by 1 February, 1 May and 1 September each year.

It is advised to provide as much information on applicants' financial and personal circumstances as possible, but please **do not** send any additional documentation (such as CVs, references or statements).

Other information

Schools and colleges can be supported towards the cost of special equipment, sports facilities and clubs can be supported for activities of educational nature.

Glasgow and West of Scotland

Ayrshire Educational Trust

£2,400

Correspondent: Catherine Martin, Principal Administration Officer, East Ayrshire Council, Council Headquarters, London Road, Kilmarnock KA3 7BU (01563 576123; fax: 01563 576269; email: CLDEnquires@east-ayrshire.co.uk; website: www.east-ayrshire.gov.uk)

SC Number: SC018195

Eligibility

Individuals who live in the former county of Ayrshire.

Types of grants

Grants are awarded to schoolchildren and further/higher education students. Support is given towards study/travel abroad or in the UK in pursuance of education, equipment for students with special educational needs, educational outings/visits and excursions, also holiday travel for school pupils.

Annual grant total

In 2012/13 the trust had an income of £10,700 and an expenditure of £5,000. We estimate that the annual total of grants to individuals was around £2,400.

Exclusions

The trust will not support people who are studying for a second qualification and will not assist with the cost of uniforms or instruments.

Applications

Application forms can be requested from the correspondent. Applications are normally considered four times a year and can be submitted directly by individuals.

Other information

The trust also supports organisations, groups, clubs or societies, which benefit young people in Ayrshire.

Dunbartonshire Educational Trust

£3,000

Correspondent: The Administrator, West Dunbartonshire Council, Council Offices, Garshake Road, Dumbarton G82 3PU

Eligibility

People who live in the old county area of Dumbarton district and are aged 16 or over. Preference may be given to people who come from deprived areas or those who are otherwise disadvantaged.

Types of grants

Grants are of around £50–£100, larger awards are only made in exceptional circumstances. Previously support has been given in different categories, such as: supplementary bursaries for higher education students; to people entering a profession/vocational training; educational excursions; travel awards; specialist equipment; sports facilities; adult education; assistance to various clubs and groups; education in music, drama and visual arts.

Annual grant total

The trust generally has an annual income of around £3,000 to be distributed in grants.

Applications

On a form available from the correspondent. Applications are considered throughout the year, but students usually apply before the start of their course.

Other information

The trust is small and has little presence in the press.

The Logan and Johnstone School Scheme

£5,000

Correspondent: Deputy Director of Education, Education Services, Wheatley House, 25 Cochrane Street, Merchant City, Glasgow G1 1HL

Eligibility

Students in further and higher education (including mature students, people starting work, undertaking apprenticeships and postgraduates) who live in the former Strathclyde region.

Types of grants

One-off grants are available for books, equipment, instruments and fees. Awards usually range from £200 to £700.

Annual grant total

Our research suggests that about £5,000 is normally given a year.

Exclusions

Grants are not made towards living costs or travel expenses.

Applications

Application forms are available from the correspondent. They should be submitted directly by the individual between April and June for consideration in August.

Colonel MacLean Trust Scheme

£1,000

Correspondent: Deputy Director of Education, Customer and Business Services, Trust Applications, Glasgow City Council, Nye Bevan House, 20 India Street, Glasgow G2 4PF (01412 769918)

Eligibility

Students in further/higher education, including mature students and postgraduates and those undergoing training and apprenticeships who live in the former Strathclyde region.

Types of grants

One-off grants for books, equipment, instruments and fees.

Annual grant total

This charity usually awards around £1,000 in educational grants to individuals.

Applications

On a form available from Glasgow City Council. Applications should be submitted directly by the individual between April and June for consideration in August.

Other information

Visit Glasgow City Council's report (www.glasgow.gov.uk/councillorsand committee), which gives details of endowments funds administered by Glasgow City Council: the Colonel MacLean Trust Scheme 1980 and Logan and Johnston School Scheme 1988.

Renfrewshire Educational Trust

£30,000

Correspondent: The Administrator, Renfrewshire Educational Trust, Finance and Corporate Services, Renfrewshire House, Cotton Street, Paisley PA1 1TR (01416 187104; email: ret.cs@ renfrewshire.gov.uk; website: www. renfrewshire.gov.uk)

SC Number: SC008876

Eligibility

People who live, or have lived for a consecutive period of at least three years in the last ten years, in the Inverclyde, Renfrewshire or East Renfrewshire local authority areas. Applicants' household income must not exceed £34,000 per annum.

In order to qualify for a taught master's award applicants must intend to study on a course which does not attract

145

Student Awards Agency for Scotland (SAAS) funding. Candidates must be in their final year of an undergraduate degree or have graduated in the previous year from either Glasgow Caledonian University, Glasgow School of Art, the University of Strathclyde, the Royal Conservatoire of Scotland, the University of Glasgow or the University of the West of Scotland.

Types of grants

Support is given in three categories:
- School excursions – grants for educational outings to pupils who receive free school meals
- Further and higher education/performing arts/travel grants – awards ranging from £200 to £400 are given towards the fees of higher education courses to 'exceptional students' in music, drama or visual arts and for travel abroad for educational purposes
- Taught master's awards – one grant worth £3,400 is awarded each year to a student on a one year taught master's degree in the UK (the award is paid to the university directly)

Annual grant total

In 2012/13 the trust had both an income and a total charitable expenditure of £34,000. We estimate the annual total of grants to individuals to be around £30,000.

Exclusions

Applicants from households with annual income above £34,000 are not eligible. Support is not available to people who are already in receipt of some kind of award or bursary, including SAAS loans (note that an award from the trust would allow the successful student not to have to take a student loan to cover the cost of fees).

Applications

Application forms for each category are available on the trust's website or can be requested from the correspondent. Application deadline for the taught master's degree award is normally 30 June each year, for school excursions in January and for educational/performing arts/travel grants by the end of January, April, July or October.

The Society for the Education of the Deaf

£38,000

Correspondent: Nancy Ward, Administrator, c/o Alexander Sloan, Chartered Accountants, 38 Cadogan Street, Glasgow G2 7HF (01412 048989; fax: 01412 489931; email: nancy.ward@alexandersloan.co.uk; website: www.gsedd.org.uk)

SC Number: SC003804

Eligibility

Individuals who are deaf and/or speech impaired.

Types of grants

Grants are mainly awarded towards British sign language courses or similar activities and educational courses that will improve applicants' ability to communicate with others. Previously the society has also offered assistance towards specialist equipment such as radio aids, computers and so on.

Annual grant total

In 2012/13 the society had an income of £971,000 and an expenditure of around £40,000. We estimate that grants to individuals totalled about £38,000.

Exclusions

Grants are not given for taster or introductory courses. Grant applications will only be considered from individuals and not course organisers or businesses.

Applications

Application forms can be completed online on the society's website or printed off and sent to the correspondent. Applications can be submitted directly by the individual or through an appropriate third party and are normally assessed within three to eight weeks.

Other information

In 2012 the Glasgow Society for the Education of Deaf and Dumb became a company limited by guarantee and changed its name to the Society for the Education of the Deaf.

The Spiers Trust

£2,000

Correspondent: Carol Kirk, Education and Skills, North Ayrshire Council, Cunninghame House, Irvine KA12 8EE (01294 324483)

Eligibility

Children and young people who live in the parishes of Beith, Dalry, Dunlop, Kilbirnie, Lochwinnoch or Neilston and who attend secondary education there. Preference will be given to students from families with financial difficulties.

Types of grants

Grants ranging between £50 and £200 are available to secondary school and further/higher education students towards the cost of course fees and special tuition in academic, artistic, scientific or technological subject, also travel costs or educational necessities.

Annual grant total

According to our research, the trust gives around £2,000 a year in grants.

Applications

Application forms can be requested from the correspondent and normally should be returned by October. Applicants may be requested to provide some evidence of need.

Other information

The trust generates its income from investments and the rent derived from letting the land adjacent to former school grounds for grazing.

Argyll and Bute

Charles and Barbara Tyre Trust

£25,000

Correspondent: Christine Heads, Clerk to the Governors, William Duncan and Co., Loch Awe House, Barmore Road, Tarbet, Argyll PA29 6TW (01880 820227; email: christine@williamduncantarbert.co.uk; website: www.charlesandbarbaratyretrust.org.uk)

SC Number: SC031378

Eligibility

Children and young people between the ages of 18 and 25 who live within the former county of Argyll (which includes Kinlochleven but excludes Helensburgh and the Island of Bute), have completed their school education and are of the protestant faith.

Types of grants

Grants are given to improve individual's qualifications or for retraining. Support can be offered towards further/higher education, Open University courses, training and development courses which are additional to the applicant's existing degree or qualification. Funding can be given for gaining new skills, leadership and initiative development and similar educational activities.

People with physical or mental disability (whether temporary or permanent) are also entitled to apply for re-creative holiday.

Annual grant total

In 2012/13 the trust had an income of £33,000 and an expenditure of £29,000. We estimate the annual total of grants to individuals for educational purposes to be around £25,000.

Applications

Application forms can be downloaded from the trust's website and should be emailed to the correspondent by 31 May annually. Successful applicants will be notified by the end of August.

Applications received after the closing date are not considered unless in exceptional circumstances.

City of Glasgow

Glasgow Educational and Marshall Trust

£50,000 (60 grants)

Correspondent: The Administrator, 21 Beaton Road, Glasgow G41 4NW (01414 334449; fax: 01414 241731; email: enquiries@gemt.org.uk; website: www.gemt.org.uk)

SC Number: SC012582

Eligibility

People, normally over 18 years old, who are in need and who have lived in the city of Glasgow (as at the re-organisation in 1975) for a minimum of five years (excluding time spent studying in the city with a home address elsewhere). The trust holds a list of the postcodes which qualify for support and can provide it upon request.

The trust states that awards to undergraduate students are made only in exceptional circumstances.

Types of grants

One-off and recurrent grants ranging from £100 to £1,000, although in exceptional cases higher awards have been made. Support can be given to mature students, postgraduates, people in further/higher education and vocational training. Travel expenses, school excursions, books, course fees, living expenses, study/travel abroad, equipment/instruments, childcare for mature students can all be funded.

Grants are normally given for courses where a Students Awards Agency for Scotland grant is not available or where such grants do not cover the total costs.

Annual grant total

In 2012/13 the trust had an income of £98,000 and a total expenditure of £77,000. Previously about 60 awards have been made annually totalling around £50,000.

Exclusions

Retrospective awards are not made and courses run by privately owned institutions are not supported.

Applications

Application forms and full guidelines are available on the trust's website and can be submitted directly by the individual together with two written references. The trustees meet on the first Wednesday of March, June, September and December. Applications for grants for university courses which start in September/ October must be received by 31 July. Candidates are expected to apply for any loans available through the Student Loans Company and should show evidence of savings and other fundraising activity.

Other information

The trust also makes grants to organisations.

James T. Howat Charitable Trust

£11,000

SC Number: SC000201

Eligibility

People who live in Glasgow and are undertaking education which is aimed at addressing unmet local cultural and social needs, other than in municipal, governmental or religious areas.

Types of grants

One-off grants ranging from £100 to £1,000 can be awarded to schoolchildren and further/higher education students. Mature and overseas students can also be assisted. Support can be given towards books, equipment/instruments, course fees, maintenance expenses or study/ travel overseas. Mature students can also get help for the childcare costs and people with special educational needs can receive assistance for educational outings/excursions.

Annual grant total

In 2012/13 the trust had an income of £224,000 and an expenditure of £158,000. Most of the trust's funding is directed to organisations. Previously grants to individuals have totalled around £11,000.

Exclusions

Support is not normally given for medical electives, second or further qualifications, payments of school fees or costs incurred at tertiary educational establishments.

People studying at Glasgow University, Strathclyde University or Royal Scottish Academy of Music and Dance are not likely to be supported, because the trust already makes block payments to the hardship funds of these institutions.

Applications

Applications should be made in writing to the correspondent outlining why the assistance is required and what kind of support is needed. The trustees meet four times a year, normally in March, June, September and December. Applications should be submitted at least a month prior to the meeting.

Other information

The trust mainly supports organisations.

The Trades House of Glasgow

£45,000

Correspondent: The Clerk, Administration Centre, North Gallery – Trades Hall, 85 Glassford Street, Glasgow G1 1UH (01415 531605; website: www.tradeshouse.org.uk)

SC Number: SCO40548

Eligibility

People in need who live in Glasgow.

Types of grants

Grants to encourage promising young people in university or colleges.

Annual grant total

In 2012/13 this charity had an income of £12.8 million and a total expenditure of £793,000. Grants and donations totalled £182,500 and were awarded to both organisations and individuals for social welfare, education and other charitable purposes. We estimate grants to individuals for educational purposes totalled around £45,000.

Applications

In writing to the correspondent.

Other information

The assistance of the needy, the encouragement of youth and support for education, particularly schools and further education colleges in developing craft standards, are now this charity's chief objects.

The Trades House also operates the Drapers Fund which distributes £50,000 annually to children-in-need who are under the age of seventeen. To apply to this fund, supply as much detail as possible highlighting the circumstances of the individual/organisation concerned to: The Manager, The Drapers Fund, The Trades House of Glasgow, Trades Hall, 85 Glassford Street, Glasgow G1 1UH.

Dumfries and Galloway

The Dumfriesshire Educational Trust

£18,000

Correspondent: Janice Thom, Area Committee Administrator, Municipal Chambers, Buccleuch Street, Dumfries DG1 2AD

SC Number: SC003411

Eligibility

People normally living in Dumfriesshire who have had at least five years of education in Dumfriesshire.

Types of grants

Grants of up to £60, usually recurrent, are given to:

▶ Schoolchildren towards educational outings
▶ Students in further/higher education for books, fees/living expenses, study/travel abroad and student exchanges
▶ Mature students towards books and travel

Annual grant total

In 2012 the trust had an income of £52,000 and a total expenditure of £51,000. Our research tells us that grants to individuals usually total around £18,000 a year.

At the time of writing (July 2014) this was the most recent information available for the trust.

Exclusions

Grants are not available for childcare for mature students or foreign students studying in the UK.

Applications

On a form available from the Education Offices at Woodbank or from schools. They are considered quarterly, usually in March, June, September or December, and closing dates are stated on the form. Applications can be submitted directly by the individual, through the relevant school/college/educational welfare agency or through another appropriate third party. The form should be signed by the applicant. For recurrent grants, applicants must reapply each academic year.

The Holywood Trust

£99,000

Correspondent: Richard Lye, Trust Administrator, Hestan House, Crichton Business Park, Bankend Road, Dumfries DG1 4TA (01387 269176; fax: 01387 269175; email: funds@holywood-trust. org.uk; website: www.holywood-trust. org.uk)

SC Number: SC009942

Eligibility

Young people aged 15 to 25 living in the Dumfries and Galloway region, with a preference for people who are mentally, physically or socially disadvantaged.

Types of grants

One-off and recurrent grants of £50 to £500 to schoolchildren, people in further or higher education, vocational students, people with special educational needs and people starting work for books,

equipment, instruments, fees, living expenses, childcare, educational outings and study or travel overseas. Applications which contribute to their personal development are more likely to receive support.

The average award is around £200.

Annual grant total

In 2012/13 the trust had assets of £10.5 million and an income of £2 million. Grants to individuals totalled £99,000. Educational grants to individuals totalled just over £26,000.

Exclusions

No grants are given towards carpets or accommodation deposits.

Applications

On a form available from the correspondent, or which can be downloaded from the trust's website. All applications are considered individually. A supporting statement from an appropriate third party is beneficial. Applicants may apply for more than one grant in exceptional circumstances only.

Other information

The trust also supports individuals with welfare needs and groups and project applications which benefit young people.

John Primrose Trust

£2,000

Correspondent: The Trustees, 1 Newall Terrace, Dumfries DG1 1LN

SC Number: SC009173

Eligibility

Young people in need with a connection to Dumfries and Maxwelltown by parentage or by living there.

Types of grants

Grants to students to help with educational needs or help for people starting work.

Annual grant total

In 2012/13 the trust had an income of £14,700 and a total expenditure of £5,700. The trust awards grants to both individuals and organisations for educational and social welfare purposes. We estimate grants to individuals for educational purposes to be around £2,000.

Applications

On an application form available from the correspondent, to be considered in June and December.

The Stewartry Educational Trust Scheme

£2,000

Correspondent: R. Bellamy, Administrator, Corselet Cottage, Buittle, Castle Douglas, Kirkcudbrightshire DG7 1NR

SC Number: SC017079

Eligibility

People belonging to the Stewartry of Kirkcudbright (i.e. the area of the Stewartry of Kirkcudbright prior to local government re-organisation in 1975).

Types of grants

One-off grants are given to schoolchildren for educational outings in Scotland and for general study costs, also to people starting work and students in further/higher education, including mature students and postgraduates.

Annual grant total

In 2012/13 the trust had an income of £4,900 and an expenditure of £4,400. According to our research, grants usually total around £2,000 a year.

Applications

On a form available from the correspondent. Our research suggests that details of any grants available from other sources should be disclosed. Applications can be made directly by the individual or, if applicable, through a parent/guardian, social worker, Citizens Advice, other welfare agency or appropriate other third party. They should be submitted in February, May or August for consideration in the following month.

Other information

The trust also provides grants to organisations.

John Wallace Trust Scheme

£200

Correspondent: Joanne Dalgleish, Senior Administrator, The Director of Education Services, Woodbank, 30 Edinburgh Road, Dumfries DG1 1NW (01387 260493; fax: 01387 260453; email: Joanne.dalgleish@dumgal. gov.uk; website: www.dumgal.gov.uk/ index.aspx?articleid=10758)

SC Number: SC011640

Eligibility

Young people living in the following areas: the electoral wards of Crichton, Douglas, that part of Dalswinton lying outside the parish of Dumfries, Kirkland,

Kello and Morton – all in the local government area of Nithsdale District.

Types of grants

The trust provides the following:

▶ Supplementary Bursaries – to further/ higher education students, including Open University students, for general educational costs
▶ Travel Grants – for educational visits either within Great Britain or abroad
▶ Agricultural Bursaries – to students at Barony College Parkgate or other institution specialising in agriculture and allied sciences

Financial assistance can be renewed for up to five years.

Annual grant total

In 2012/13 the trust had an income of £7,100 and made grants totalling £200.

Applications

Application forms for bursaries can be downloaded from Dumfries and Galloway Council website or requested from the correspondent. The closing date for applications is 31 December.

People applying for travel grants are requested to do so in writing providing a statement of purpose for the journey, places to be visited, anticipated length and costs of the trip.

Other information

The trust also provides money to the Rector of Wallace Hall Academy for distribution of annual Ferguson Prizes to students following courses in agriculture or allied sciences.

Wigtownshire Educational Trust

£1,500

Correspondent: Council Secretariat, Dumfries and Galloway Council, Department Of Corporate Finance, Carruthers House, English Street, Dumfries DG1 2HP

SC Number: SC019526

Eligibility

People who live in the former county of Wigtownshire who can demonstrate personal hardship and that no other source of funding is available.

Types of grants

Grants ranging from £50 to £300 to schoolchildren, college students, undergraduates, vocational students, mature students, people with special educational needs and people starting work. Grants given include those towards, clothing/uniforms, fees, study/travel abroad, books, equipment/instruments and excursions. Assistance is also given towards gaining practical experience of trades and promoting

education in the visual arts, music and drama.

Annual grant total

This charity awards around £1,500 each year to individuals for educational purposes.

Applications

On a form available from the above address. Applications are considered throughout the year. If the applicant is a child/young person, details of parental income are required.

East, North and South Ayrshire

The John Longwill Education Trust

£270

Correspondent: The Trustees, Clydesdale Bank Chambers, Dalry, Ayrshire KA24 5AB

SC Number: SC005483

Eligibility

Scholars or students who are attending Higher grade school or university in Scotland and who are native to Dalry and of Scottish descent.

Types of grants

Payments of about £100 each.

Annual grant total

In 2013 the trust had an income of £810 and an expenditure of £270. The trustees previously stated that it is an active charity, they are open to applications and the lack of expenditure is due to the very narrow eligibility criteria, which they are looking to widen in the future.

Applications

In writing to the correspondent at any time.

The C. K. Marr Educational Trust Scheme

£409,000

Correspondent: Alan Stewart, Clerk, 1 Howard Street, Kilmarnock KA1 2BW (01563 572727; fax: 01563 527901)

SC Number: SC016730

Eligibility

Students in tertiary education who live in Troon or the Troon electoral wards.

Types of grants

Bursaries, scholarships and educational travel grants to people at college or university, support towards postgraduate

research and assistance to individuals with disability.

Annual grant total

In 2012/13 the trust had an income of £480,000 and a total expenditure of £476,000. Grants totalled £409,000.

Applications

In writing to the correspondent. Applications can be made either directly by the individual or through a third party, such as a university/college or an educational welfare agency, if applicable.

North and South Lanarkshire

Loaningdale School Company

£2,000

Correspondent: Fiona Watson, Administrator, Exchange Place 3, Semple Street, Edinburgh EH3 8BL (01314 733500)

SC Number: SC001065

Eligibility

Children and young people aged 12 to 20 who are in need and live within the Clydesdale local area of South Lanarkshire, especially former pupils of Loaningdale School.

Types of grants

One-off grants ranging from £100 to £1,000 towards furthering the individual's education or employment prospects. Priority is given to creative or outdoor pursuits for young people, young unemployed people and post-school education and training of young people.

Annual grant total

In 2012/13 the charity had an income of just £157, a considerable decrease on previous years. We estimate that grants to individuals totalled around £2,000.

Applications

On a form available from the correspondent or the charity's website, with guidelines for applicants. Applications are considered in March, June, September and December, and should be submitted in the previous month.

Other information

The charity was formed on the closure of Loaningdale School and the income generated is used to provide grants to organisations and individuals. Grants are primarily made to organisations.

Highlands and Islands

The Fresson Trust

£0

Correspondent: T. Whittome, Secretary, The Pilk, 18 Academy Street, Fortrose, Ross-shire IV10 8TW (email: info@ fressontrust.org.uk; website: www. fressontrust.org.uk)

SC Number: SC020054

Eligibility

People who live in or are visiting the Highlands and Islands and wish to further their career in aviation within the area as pilots, engineers or air traffic controllers.

Types of grants

Grants to further education and training. Previously support has been given towards the payment of flying lessons and in the form of a scholarship bursary. One-off grants can be given to help people starting work to buy books, equipment and clothing and help with their travel expenses. Students in further or higher education may be provided with money for books, fees or living expenses. Mature students can receive grants for books, travel, fees and childcare.

Annual grant total

In 2012/13 the trust had an income of £2,700 but no grants were made.

Applications

In writing to the correspondent at any time. Applicants should state how they can assist in the development of aviation in the Highlands and Islands.

Other information

The trust may also support museums and archives relating to aircraft in connection to Highlands and Islands, and organise or promote various events commemorating aviation activities and achievements.

Highland

The Highland Children's Trust

£10,000

Correspondent: The Administrator, 105 Castle Street, Inverness IV2 3EA (01463 243872; email: info@hctrust.co. uk; website: www.hctrust.co.uk)

SC Number: SC006008

Eligibility

Children and young people in need who are under 25 and live in the Highlands.

Types of grants

One-off grants of £50 to £500 are available for the following purposes:
▶ Student hardship funding
▶ School or educational trips
▶ Family holidays
▶ Educational items for children with special educational needs

Annual grant total

This trust awards around £20,000 a year for both education and welfare purposes. We estimate that £10,000 is given for educational purposes.

Exclusions

Grants are not given for postgraduate study, to pay off debts, nor to purchase clothing, footwear, food, furniture or cars and so on.

Applications

On a form available from the correspondent or downloaded from the trust's website, where criteria and guidelines are also posted. They can be submitted at any time either directly by the individual or through a social worker, Citizens Advice or other welfare agency. Applications must include details of income and savings and are considered at board meetings held on a regular basis.

Isle of Lewis

Ross and Cromarty Educational Trust

£5,000

Correspondent: Catriona Maciver, Department of Education and Children's Services, Comhairle Nan Eilean Siar, Sandwick Road, Stornoway HS1 2BW (01851 709546; email: catriona-maciver@ cne-siar.gov.uk; website: www.cne-siar. gov.uk/education)

Eligibility

People who live on the Isle of Lewis. The area is quantified by postal codes HS1 and HS2 (sector 0 and sector 9).

Types of grants

Grants in the range of £30 to £200 are available for general educational expenses and various social, cultural and recreational purposes. Schoolchildren can be assisted towards educational outings and excursions; people entering a trade or a vocational occupation towards equipment/instruments and clothing; higher education students (including postgraduates) may be awarded scholarships. Visual arts, drama, music, dance studies and adult education can also be supported. Application guidelines provide a list of specific sections, where assistance can be requested.

Annual grant total

Our research suggests that the trust normally has an income of about £10,000 each year, all of which is distributed for charitable purposes. We estimate the annual total of grants to individuals to be about £5,000.

Applications

Application forms can be found on the Comhairle Nan Eilean Siar website or requested from the correspondent. Applicants should only apply for one specific cause at a time and provide the details of estimated costs of their activities.

Other information

Local schools, educational establishments and other organisations or clubs can be supported towards the cost of special equipment, facilities, sports equipment and so forth.

Since 1975, Comhairle Nan Eilean Siar local government council operates the sections of the Ross and Cromarty Educational Trust Scheme which relate specifically to the Isle of Lewis. These sections are operated in agreement with Highland Council, which is responsible for the capital of the trust fund.

Orkney Islands

Orkney Educational Trust Scheme 1961

£180

Correspondent: The Director of Education, Orkney Islands Council, Education Department, Council Offices, School Place, Kirkwall, Orkney KW15 1NY (01856 873535; fax: 01856 874615)

Eligibility

People on postgraduate courses, in further education or on apprenticeships who live in the former county of Orkney.

Types of grants

Subsidiary grants of £8 to £50 to help
with travel, material costs and fees/living
expenses for further education students.
Grants are also made to people starting
work to help with books, equipment/
instruments, clothing and travel costs,
and to schoolchildren to help with books
and educational outings. Grants may
also be given for the promotion of
education in the community.

Annual grant total

In 2012/13 the trust had an income of
£2,200 and an unusually low total
expenditure of £186.

Applications

Note: at the time of writing (July 2014)
the Orkney Council website stated: 'this
grant is currently under review. Any
updates will be posted on the council's
website and also in The Orcadian
newspaper.'

Wales

General

The Cambrian Educational Foundation for Deaf Children

£12,000

Correspondent: Pamela Brown, Clerk to the Trustees, Montreux, 30 Lon Cedwyn, Sketty, Swansea SA2 0TH (01792 207628)

CC Number: 515848

Eligibility

People who are deaf or have partial hearing aged under 25, who live or whose parents live in Wales. Beneficiaries can be in special classes (units) in ordinary and special schools in Wales, students in further education and people entering employment.

Types of grants

One-off and occasionally annual grants up to a maximum of £500. Grants have been provided for computers, software, school uniforms, tools/equipment, instruments, books, occasionally for educational outings in the UK and for study or travel abroad, to people starting work and to further and higher education students for books.

Annual grant total

In 2012 the foundation had an income of £18,000 and a total expenditure of £18,300. We estimate that grants to individuals totalled £12,000.

At the time of writing (July 2014) this was the most recent financial information available for the foundation.

Exclusions

Grants are not given for leisure trips.

Applications

Applications are available to download from the foundation's website. If the applicant is under the age of 18, the form should be completed by a parent/ guardian or another authorised person. Applications should be supported in writing by the applicant's teacher or tutor. They are considered throughout the year.

The James Pantyfedwen Foundation (Ymddiriedolaeth James Pantyfedwen)

£158,000 (41+ grants)

Correspondent: Richard Morgan, Executive Secretary, Pantyfedwen, 9 Market Street, Aberystwyth, Ceredigion SY23 1DL (01970 612806; email: pantyfedwen@btinternet.com; website: www.jamespantyfedwenfoundation.org. uk)

CC Number: 1069598

Eligibility

Applicants who have been resident in Wales sometime during the three years immediately preceding the date of application (excluding the term-time address as a college/university student) and who/whose parents, were born in Wales, or who have studied at any educational institution in Wales for at least seven years. Currently some priority is given to students undertaking postgraduate research and candidates training for Christian ministry.

Types of grants

One-off and recurrent grants for postgraduate studies. Most grants are for fees and, in very exceptional circumstances, living costs. The average grant is of around £3,900 but where the fees are higher grants may be awarded of up to £7,000. People training for Christian ministry can also be supported.

Annual grant total

In 2012/13 the foundation had assets of £14.6 million, an income of £538,000 and a charitable expenditure of £401,000. A total of around £156,000 was awarded in grants to 40 postgraduate students plus one Undeb Cymru Fydd scholarships of £1,000.

Candidates for the Christian ministry received grants totalling £1,800.

Exclusions

The foundation does not support the following:

- Undergraduate courses
- Courses at institutions which have not been approved by the department of education
- Higher degrees where students already have a higher degree (this does not exclude progress from a master's degree to a PhD)
- Accounting training courses
- Private tuition
- PGCE courses
- Postgraduate training courses in social work
- CPE Course in law (but legal practice courses are permitted)
- Master's courses of more than one year's duration (where a student is pursuing a two year's master's course on a full-time basis the foundation is prepared to consider assistance for the second and final year of study)

Support is not given to supplement awards provided by the local authorities and research councils.

Applications

Application forms are available on the foundation's website from 1 April. The deadline for applications is 30 June preceding the start date of the course.

Other information

The foundation also supports organisations and churches (grants totalling £11,000 were given to registered religious charities and £59,000 to churches in 2012/13).

The May Price SRN Award

£500

Correspondent: Roger Jones, Administrator, Carmarthenshire County Council, County Hall, Carmarthen SA31 1JP (01267 234567)

CC Number: 514578

Eligibility

People who have lived in Cardiganshire, Carmarthenshire or Pembrokeshire for at least two years and who are pursuing a course in medical or medically related studies.

Types of grants

Grants to help with the cost of books or equipment or to supplement existing grants.

Annual grant total

In 2012/13 the fund had both an income and expenditure of £400. We estimate around £400 was made in grants to individuals for education.

Applications

On a form available from the correspondent, to be returned by 31 October each year.

Reardon Smith Nautical Trust

See entry on page 110

The Michael Sobell Welsh People's Charitable Trust

£700

Correspondent: S. E. Davies, Trustee, Dolenog, Old Hall, Llanidloes, Powys SY18 6PP

CC Number: 255437

Eligibility

People in need who live in Wales.

Types of grants

One-off and recurrent grants which typically range from £40 to £500.

Annual grant total

In 2012/13 the trust had an income of £122 and a total expenditure of £3,200. We estimate that educational grants to individuals totalled £700. Funding is also awarded to organisations and to individuals for social welfare purposes.

Applications

In writing to the correspondent.

Yr Ymddiriedolaeth Ddarlledu Gymreig (The Welsh Broadcasting Trust)

See entry on page 106

Mid-Wales

Ceredigion

The Cardiganshire Intermediate and Technical Educational Fund

£0

Correspondent: Alun Morgan, Administrator, Ceredigion County Council, Canolfan Rheidol, Rhodfa Padarn, Aberystwyth SY23 3UE (01970 633691; email: decsdata@ceredigion.gov.uk)

CC Number: 514597

Eligibility

Individuals who have, at any time, been in attendance for at least two years at a maintained secondary school in the Ceredigion area (the former county of Cardiganshire).

Types of grants

Grants of £100 to £150 a year, to help with secondary school, college or university expenses and fees or to supplement existing grants.

Annual grant total

In 2012/13 the fund had an income of £0 and an expenditure of £0.

This entry has been updated as information still appears on the Charity Commission website.

Applications

Application forms are available from the correspondent from August, to be submitted by 30 November.

Visual Impairment Breconshire

£3,500

Correspondent: Carol Wothers, Administrator, 23 Pen y Fan Close, Libanus, Brecon, Powys LD3 8EJ (01874 625590; website: www.visualimpairment.breconshire.powys.org.uk)

CC Number: 217377

Eligibility

Blind and partially-sighted people living within the district of Breconshire, also their families or carers.

Types of grants

One-off grants for special equipment, services, training and other needs. The charity also offers an annual bursary (up to £500) to enable an individual to pursue an educational or sporting activity.

Annual grant total

In 2012/13 the charity had an income of £2,700 and an expenditure of £3,900. We estimate that about £3,500 was awarded in grants.

Exclusions

Generally the charity will not assist with the expenses which should be provided by the health service or the local authorities.

Applications

In writing to the correspondent. The executive committee meets about six times a year and the annual general meeting is normally held in July.

Other information

The charity also organises audio newsletters and social activities for both individuals and groups.

Powys

The Thomas John Jones Memorial Fund for Scholarships and Exhibitions

£58,000 (33 grants)

Correspondent: David Meredith, Clerk to the Trustees, Cilmery, The Avenue, Brecon, Powys LD3 9BG (01874 623373)

CC Number: 525281

Eligibility

People under the age of 26 pursuing education and training for a higher post in industry who have both been resident and attended secondary school in the former county of Breconshire. Preference is given to applicants undertaking courses of advanced technical education.

Postgraduate applicants must have gained an upper second class degree or above except in exceptional circumstances.

Types of grants

Exhibitions of £1,500 per year for the duration of the course are given to supplement existing awards. Scholarships up to £2,300 (plus £500 for full-time courses) to postgraduate students to cover the tuition fees are available for up to three years. Postgraduate non-technical studies are only supported for one year. Renewals of the award are subject to annual review.

Bursaries are currently suspended.

Annual grant total

In 2012/13 the fund had assets of £1.5 million, an income of £58,000 and awarded educational grants totalling £58,000 to 33 individuals.

Applications

In writing to the correspondent. The trustees meet at least once a year and as required. Applications should include full details of the nature, location, type (full/part-time) and duration of the study and the qualification aimed at. They must be returned to the correspondent by 31 August annually.

Other information

Note that:

Although certain areas of Breconshire were transferred to the counties of Gwent and Mid-Glamorgan when Local Government was re-organised in 1974 students residing in those areas are still eligible to apply for financial assistance from the fund. The areas concerned include Penderyn, part of Hirwaun, Cefn Coed, Pontsticill, most of Brynmawr, Llanelly Hill, Clydach and Gilwern.

Edmund Jones' Charity

£6,000

Correspondent: Ruth Jefferies, Administrator, Steeple House, Brecon, Powys LD3 7DJ (01874 638024; email: edmundjonescharity@gmail.com)

CC Number: 525315

Eligibility

People under the age of 25 who live or work within the town of Brecon.

Types of grants

Grants are available to people undertaking apprenticeships and starting work, mainly towards tools; to college students towards equipment; and to university students towards books. Awards usually range from £50 to £300.

Annual grant total

In 2013 the charity had assets of £423,000 and an income of £39,000. Grants totalled £12,100. The proportion of grants to individuals and organisations was not specified in the accounts. We estimate that grants to individual students totalled around £6,000.

Applications

In writing to the correspondent, giving details of the college/course/ apprenticeship and the anticipated costs, together with the information on any other grants received or applied for. Applications may be submitted by individuals, through their parents or college. According to our research, applications are mainly considered in October.

Other information

Schools and colleges located in the area of benefit may also be assisted.

The Llanidloes Relief-in-Need Charity

£1,300

Correspondent: Elaine Lloyd, Administrator, Woodcroft, Woodlands Road, Llanidloes, Powys SY18 6HX (01686 412636; email: elainelllloyd@ gmail.com)

CC Number: 259955

Eligibility

Students who live in the communities of Llanidloes and Llanidloes Without. No support to students not living within three miles of the town, or to foreign students studying in the area.

Types of grants

Grants to help with the cost of books, living expenses and other essential items for those at college or university.

Annual grant total

In 2013/14 the charity had an income of £240 and an expenditure of £2,700. Grants totalled approximately £2,500 and were split between educational and welfare purposes.

Applications

In writing to the correspondent.

North Wales

Doctor William Lewis' Charity

£540

Correspondent: Dr Michelle Freeman, Administrator, The Diocesan Centre, Cathedral Close, Bangor, Gwynedd LL57 1RL (01248 354999)

CC Number: 216361

Eligibility

Students under the age of 25 who live in the former counties of Anglesey, Caernarvon, Merioneth, Montgomery, Flint and Denbigh.

Types of grants

A portion of the charity's income is used to make awards for students at Oxford, Cambridge or the University of Wales and St David's University College, Lampeter. Grants are also given to applicants who are in training for a profession or trade.

Annual grant total

In 2011/12 the charity had an income of £2,100 and an expenditure of £540. The 2011/12 accounts were the latest available at the time of writing (August 2014).

Applications

On a form available from the correspondent, to be submitted directly by the individual by the beginning of October.

The Wrexham (Parochial) Educational Foundation

£27,000 (59 grants)

Correspondent: Frieda Leech, Clerk to the Trustees, Holly Chase, Pen y Palmant Road, Minera, Wrexham LL11 3YW (01978 754152; email: clerk.wpef@gmail. com)

CC Number: 525414

Eligibility

People between the ages of 16 and 25 who live in the county borough of Wrexham and who are former pupils of one of the following schools: Brymbo and Minera Voluntary Aided Schools, St Giles Voluntary Controlled School and St Joseph's Catholic and Anglican High School.

Types of grants

The foundation provides scholarships, money towards clothing/uniforms, books and equipment/tools, also for travel expenses in the UK and abroad. Help is offered to students in secondary and further/higher education and people starting an apprenticeship or training. Previously grants have included supporting a student with disabilities who was living at home and unable to receive a statutory grant.

Annual grant total

In 2013 the foundation had assets of £12.2 million, an income of £388,000 and a total charitable expenditure of £285,000. A total of £27,000 was awarded in 59 educational grants.

Applications

Application forms can be requested from the correspondent, preferably by email. Applications can be made by individuals directly and should be submitted by 1 October.

Other information

The foundation provides grants to schools within the area of benefit towards equipment/services and also promotes religious education.

The trustees' annual report form 2012/13 states that the 'focus for 2012 was the development of the Centre for Religious Education and Faith Development at St Giles' Church and this has continued during 2013.'

Anglesey

Owen Lloyd Educational Foundation

£4,000

Correspondent: Emlyn Evans, Administrator, Nant Bychan Farm, Moelfre, Gwynedd LL72 8HF (01248 410269)

CC Number: 525253

Eligibility

People between the ages of 16 and 25 in further/higher education who live in Penrhoslligwy and neighbouring parishes.

Larger grants may be given to residents of Penrhoslligwy, as this was the original area covered by the trust deed.

Types of grants

Grants are given to help with the cost of books, fees, living expenses, travel costs (but not for study/travel abroad) and tools/equipment. People starting work and apprenticeships can be supported towards the cost of books, equipment, clothing, travel and so on.

Annual grant total

In 2012/13 the foundation had an income of £9,400 and an expenditure of £8,200. We estimate the annual total of grants to individuals to be around £4,000.

Applications

Application forms can be requested from the correspondent. They should include details of the applicant's financial situation. Applications are normally considered in October with grants being awarded in June.

Other information

Grants are also given to organisations and educational establishments.

Conwy

The Sir John Henry Morris-Jones Trust Fund

£3,000

Correspondent: C. Earley, Clerk to the Trustees, The Bay of Colwyn Town Council, Town Hall, 7 Rhiw Road, Colwyn Bay, Conwy LL29 7TE (01492 532248; email: info@colwyn-tc.gov.uk; website: www.colwyn-tc.gov.uk/town-council/grants-available-and-local-trusts)

CC Number: 504313

Eligibility

People under the age of 19 who are resident in the area of the former borough of Colwyn Bay, as existing on 31 March 1974 (Colwyn Bay, Llysfaen, Mochdre, Old Colwyn and Rhos on Sea). People undertaking full time education outside of the borough but normally resident there are eligible.

Types of grants

One-off scholarships to individuals who demonstrate excellence in one of the following fields: arts, crafts and music, sport, academic and research, commerce and business, science and technology or any other field which would satisfy the trustees.

Annual grant total

In 2012/13 the fund had an income of £3,200 and an expenditure of £3,300. We estimate the annual total of grants to individuals to be around £3,000.

Exclusions

Applications for courses at higher or further education levels are not considered.

Applications

Application forms are available on the fund's website or from the correspondent. They should be submitted by 31 March. Applicants are invited for an interview in May.

Richard Owen Scholarships

£500

Correspondent: Tessa Wildermoth, Administrator, Llandudno Town Council, Town Hall, Lloyd Street, Llandudno, Gwynedd LL30 2UD (01492879130)

CC Number: 525286

Eligibility

People aged under 25 who live in Llandudno. Preference is given to undergraduates at University of Bangor, but not exclusively so.

Types of grants

Grants, ranging from £70 to £100 are given towards clothing, tools, instruments or books for people leaving education and preparing for work. Student bursaries are also available as are grants towards educational travel abroad.

Annual grant total

In 2012/13 the foundation had an income of £500 and a total expenditure of £1,000. We estimate around £1,000 was made in grants to individuals for education.

Applications

On a form available from the correspondent, to be submitted in September for consideration in August.

Denbighshire

The Educational Charity of John Matthews

£12,200

Correspondent: P. B. Smith, Administrator, Lyndhurst, 6 Vernon Avenue, Hooton, Ellesmere Port, Cheshire CH66 6AL (01513 276103; email: pbsberlian@aol.com; website: www.johnmathewscharity.co.uk)

CC Number: 525553

Eligibility

People under the age of 25 who are descendants of the founder of the trust (John Matthew) or are resident in the North Wales areas comprising Chirk, district of Glyndwr, Llanarmon-yn-Ial, Llandegla, Llangollen Rural, Llantysilio, the borough of Wrexham Maelor and the borough of Oswestry, in Shropshire.

Types of grants

Grants of £250 to £2,000 are awarded to young people 'seeking to build upon their talents and improve their educational and career prospects.' Grants have been given to a wide range of applicants, for example musicians, actors, journalists, tree surgeons, medical students and so on. Support can be provided towards specialist equipment, course fees, books, tools and other necessities.

The charity can support undergraduate, postgraduate, second degree students (particularly on courses with a vocational element), people starting work and individuals undertaking apprenticeships. Those who are not able to get other financial support and can demonstrate exceptional talent and passion are favoured.

Annual grant total

In 2013 the charity had an income of £18,700 and an expenditure of £12,500. We estimate that grants to individuals totalled around £12,200.

Exclusions

Financial assistance towards ongoing education within the state or private education system can only be considered in exceptional circumstances.

Applications

Application forms and further guidelines can be found on the charity's website. They should be submitted along with a covering letter giving as much information as possible about the course and the applicant's career aspirations as well as financial and personal circumstances (including proof of identity and residence). The trustees usually meet twice a year, in May and November, but considerations can be made more frequently if needed.

People applying as the descendants of the founder will be required to provide extensive supporting documentation.

Other information

The charity welcomes informal contact prior to the application.

The Freeman Evans St David's Day Denbigh Charity

£500

Correspondent: Medwyn Jones, Town Clerk, Denbigh Town Council, Town Hall, Crown Square, Denbigh LL16 3TB (01745 815984; email: townclerk@ denbightowncouncil.gov.uk)

CC Number: 518033

Eligibility

People in need who live in Denbigh and Henllan.

Types of grants

One-off grants towards the cost of volunteer programmes overseas, educational equipment and so on. In 2012/13 a grant was given towards the fees of a dyslexia assessment.

Annual grant total

In 2012/13 the charity had an income of £33,000 and a total expenditure of £41,000. We believe that one educational grant to an individual totalled £500. Funding was also awarded to a local school, an organisation working to support adults with learning difficulties, and to organisations and individuals for welfare purposes.

Applications

In writing to the correspondent. Applications can be made either directly by the individual or through a third party such as a social worker, Citizens Advice or other welfare agency. The trustees meet regularly throughout the year to consider applications.

The Robert David Hughes Scholarship Foundation

£15,000

Correspondent: Peter Bowler, Trustee, McLintocks, 46 Hamilton Square, Birkenhead, Wirral CH41 5AR (01516 479581)

CC Number: 525404

Eligibility

University students who have connections with the community of former borough of Denbigh. Applicants should either be born in the community of Denbigh or have a parent or parents who have been resident in the area for at least ten years. Full documentary evidence is requested.

Types of grants

One-off and recurrent grants are offered to university students according to need.

Annual grant total

In 2012/13 the foundation had an income of £17,500 and an expenditure of £15,600. We estimate the annual total of grants to individuals to be around £15,000.

Exclusions

Students in colleges of further education are not normally supported.

Applications

In writing to the correspondent. Our research suggests that applications should be submitted by 30 September for consideration in November. Grants are awarded each term upon receipt of completed certificates of attendance, signed by the principal or registrar of the university. Normally, the grant recipients are automatically sent application forms for subsequent years.

The Llanynys Educational Foundation

£450

Correspondent: Robert Kinnier, Administrator, The Post Office, Rhewl, Ruthin LL15 1TH (01824 702730; email: robkinnier@yahoo.co.uk)

CC Number: 507513

Eligibility

People under 25 who live in the community of Llanynys Rural, and that part of the community of Ruthin which was formerly the parish of Llanynys Urban.

Types of grants

One-off and recurrent grants up to £100 for students in further and higher

education to assist with books, fees/ living expenses, and study/travel abroad.

Annual grant total

In 2013/14 the foundation had an income of £500 and an expenditure of £520. Grants totalled approximately £450.

Applications

The charity places advertisements in the local press shortly after A-level results are published. Applications are considered in September. If a large number of requests are received in relation to the funds available, preference is given to first time applicants.

Applicants should include in their application their age; place of residence; course to be followed; qualification pursued; institution attended; and the purpose to which the grant will be put.

Flintshire

The Owen Jones Charity

£600

Correspondent: Dr Jack Wolstenholme, Secretary, 18 St Peter's Park, Northop, Mold, Clwyd CH7 6DP (01352 840739)

CC Number: 525453

Eligibility

College and university students and apprentices from Northop who are in need.

Types of grants

One-off and recurrent grants according to need. Grants have been given to students with inadequate funds to allow them to buy basic food and to apprentices entering a trade for tools and equipment.

Annual grant total

In 2012/13 the charity had an income of £10,000 and a total expenditure of £2,400. We estimate that educational grants to individuals totalled £600. Funding was also awarded to local primary schools and to individuals for social welfare needs.

Applications

On a form available from the correspondent. The charity states on its Charity Commission record that 'financial backgrounds of applicants are checked by questionnaire.'

Gwynedd

The Morgan Scholarship Fund

£700

Correspondent: Strategic Director, Cyngor Gwynedd Council, Shirehall Street, Caernarfon, Gwynedd LL55 ISH (01286 679273; email: davidroberts@gwynedd.gov.uk)

CC Number: 525297

Eligibility

People born or living in the civil parish of Llanengan who are under the age of 25. When funds permit, the area of benefit may be extended to include other parishes in the rural district of Lleyn.

Types of grants

Preference is given to undergraduates of the University College of North Wales. Grants are also distributed for the following purposes; however, for those at college or university; for those going abroad to pursue their education; financial assistance, clothing, tools, instruments or books to help those leaving school, college or university to prepare for, or enter, a profession, trade or calling.

Annual grant total

In 2012/13 the fund had an income of £1,300 and a total expenditure of £800. We estimate that grants to individuals totalled £700.

Applications

On a form available from the correspondent. Applications are considered in September.

The R. H. Owen Memorial Fund (Cronfa Goffa R. H. Owen)

£500

Correspondent: Huw Williams, Trustee, Pant Hyfryd, Ceunant, Llanrug, Caernarfon, Gwynedd LL55 4RY (01286650272; email: huwemyr@btinternet.com)

CC Number: 532326

Eligibility

People in secondary, further or higher education who were born in, or whose parents have lived for at least five years in, the parish of Llanberis and Brynrefail Comprehensive School catchment area.

Types of grants

Recurrent grants are given to schoolchildren, undergraduates, vocational students and people starting work for any academic or vocational need.

Annual grant total

In 2013/14 the fund had both an income and total expenditure of £1,000. We estimate around £500 was made in grants to individuals.

Applications

On a form available from the correspondent which should be submitted directly by the individual. The closing date for applications is 31 August.

The Peter Saunders Trust

£2,500

Correspondent: Peter Saunders, Trustee, Peter Saunders Trust, c/o The Sure Chill Company, Pendre, Tywyn, Gwynedd LL36 6AH (01654713939; email: enquiries@petersaunderstrust.co.uk; website: www.petersaunderstrust.co.uk)

CC Number: 1108153

Eligibility

People throughout Wales (and particularly living in rural Wales between the Dyfi and the Mawddach rivers) who are in need of financial assistance towards their projects. The trust's website states that 'the trust aims to promote excellence and favours projects which show endeavour, a measure of self-reliance and spirit of enterprise' and will prefer projects 'that others might find hard to support, perhaps because they break new ground, involve risk or lack popular appeal.' The trust may initiate projects when 'new thinking is required or when it believes that an opportunity is being missed.'

Types of grants

Grants towards entrepreneurial projects which provide opportunities and learning experiences.

Annual grant total

In 2012/13 the trust had an income of £2,900 and an expenditure of £75,000. Exact amount of grants awarded to individuals was not available; however our research shows that previously grants to individuals have totalled £2,500.

Exclusions

Grants are not available for university education, either at undergraduate or postgraduate level.

Applications

There is no standard application form, instead the applicants are invited to write directly to the correspondent providing the following:

- Their name
- An address for correspondence, telephone number and email address, if available
- Their objective
- The scale of the total funding for their project
- The amount of the award they seek from the trust
- Other sources of funding they have tried
- Other offers of funding they have received
- Other sources of funding about which they know but have not yet tried
- Whether or not they will seek match funding for awards made to them by the trust
- Would any award from the trust replace other source of funds
- What activities are being undertaken to raise funds
- What difference it will make to them if they receive an award from the trust
- The locality which will benefit from any award made by the trust

Other information

The trust's website defines their beneficial area as Wales, with particular focus on 'rural Wales between the Dyfi and the Mawddach rivers.'

The trust helps both individuals and organisations supporting a number of projects and assist Atlantic College and Tring School for the Performing Arts with bursaries.

Dr Daniel William's Educational Fund

£39,000 (174 grants)

Correspondent: Dwyryd Williams, Clerk to the Trust, Bryn Golau, Pencefn, Dolgellau, Gwynedd LL40 2YP (01341 423 459; email: dwyryd@pencefn.freeserve.co.uk)

CC Number: 525756

Eligibility

People under the age of 25 in further/higher education or training. Priority will be given to former pupils of Dr Williams' School, or their descendants, and people who are resident, or whose parents are resident, in the former administrative district of Meirionnydd.

Types of grants

One-off or recurrent grants can be awarded towards the costs of clothing, uniforms, equipment/instruments, books and other necessities to people entering a trade/starting work; for study/travel overseas; towards the study of music and other arts; for general educational costs to further/higher education students and people in training. Grants usually reach up to a maximum of £500.

Annual grant total

In 2012/13 the trust had assets of £306,000, an income of 56,000 and awarded grants to 174 individuals totalling £39,000. The grants were distributed in following categories:

Course fees	53
Music tuition	48
Educational trips	40
Sports tuition	14
Books, clothing and equipment	7
IT equipment	6
Musical instruments	3
Dance and drama tuition	2
Travelling expenses	1

Applications

Application forms can be requested from the correspondent.

Wrexham

Dame Dorothy Jeffreys Educational Foundation

£4,500

Correspondent: Frieda Leech, Administrator, Holly Chase, Penypalmant Road, Minera, Wrexham LL11 3YW (01978 754152; email: clerk.wpef@gmail.com)

CC Number: 525430

Eligibility

People in need aged between 16 and 25 who live or have attended school in the former borough of Wrexham or the communities of Abenbury, Bersham, Broughton, Bieston, Brymbo, Esclusham Above, Esclusham Below, Gresford, Gwersyllt and Minera.

Types of grants

Grants of £50 minimum. Grants for general education purposes are given to schoolchildren, further/higher education students, people starting work and vocational students. Mature students up to the age of 25 can also receive grants.

Annual grant total

In 2013 the trust had an income of £3,900 and an expenditure of £4,700.

Applications

On a form available from the correspondent to be submitted directly by the individual. Applications are considered in November/December and should be submitted by 1 October.

The Ruabon and District Relief-in-Need Charity

£1,600

Correspondent: James Fenner, Administrator, 65 Albert Grove, Ruabon, Wrexham LL14 6AF (01978 820102; email: jamesrfenner@tiscali.co.uk)

CC Number: 212817

Eligibility

People in need who live in the county borough of Wrexham, which covers the community council districts of Cefn Mawr, Penycae, Rhosllanerchrugog (including Johnstown) and Ruabon.

Types of grants

One-off and occasionally recurrent grants of up to £200. Grants are given to schoolchildren towards uniforms/clothing, equipment/instruments and educational visits/excursions.

Annual grant total

In 2013 the charity had an income of £3,300 and an expenditure of £3,400. Grants for education totalled approximately £1,600.

Exclusions

Loans are not given, nor are grants given to investigate bankruptcy proceedings.

Applications

In writing to the correspondent either directly by the individual or a family member, through a third party such as a social worker or teacher, or through an organisation such as Citizens Advice or a school. Applications are considered on an ongoing basis.

South Wales

The Roger Edwards Educational Trust (formerly the Monmouthshire Further Education Trust Fund)

£11,500

Correspondent: Jonathan Stephens, Trustee, Ty Cornel, 11 Castle Parade, USK NP15 1AA (01291 673344; email: rogeredwardstrust@yahoo.co.uk)

CC Number: 525638

Eligibility

Further or higher education students who have attended a local comprehensive/secondary school and have lived in the Greater Gwent area, except Newport, that is, the council areas of Caerphilly (part), Torfaen, Blaenau Gwent and Monmouthshire.

Types of grants

One-off grants, although students can reapply in subsequent years, towards books, fees, living costs, travel and equipment. Grants range between £60 and £360, depending on student's circumstances. Full-time students receiving funding from another source are not funded.

Annual grant total

In 2012/13 the fund had assets of £2.89 million, most of which represented permanent endowment and is therefore not available for grant giving. It had an income of £132,000. Grants were made to individuals for education totalling £11,500.

Applications

Application forms are available from the correspondent, for consideration throughout the year.

Other information

Two thirds of the income of the trust is dedicated to the Monmouthshire Farm School Trust and the remainder is distributed between individuals and local schools.

The Gane Charitable Trust

£6,500

Correspondent: Ken Stradling, Administrator, c/o Bristol Guild of Applied Art, 68–70 Park Street, Bristol BS1 5JY (01179 265548)

CC Number: 211515

Eligibility

Students of arts and crafts, or design and social welfare. There is a preference for applicants from Bristol and south Wales and those in further education.

Types of grants

Grants are available to help meet the educational costs of college students, vocational students and mature students and their children. Grants are given towards fees, books and equipment/instruments. They range from £200 to £500 and are normally one-off.

Annual grant total

In 2012 the trust had assets of £765,000 most of which represented investments and is therefore not available for grant giving. It had an income of £26,000. We estimate grants made to individuals for education totalled around £6,500.

The 2012 accounts are the latest available at the time of writing.

Applications

On a form available from the correspondent. Applications are considered in January, May and September.

Other information

The trust also makes grants to individuals for social welfare purposes and to organisations.

The Glamorgan Further Education Trust Fund

£41,000

Correspondent: Naomi Davies, Administrator, 1st Floor Aberafan House, Education Finance, Port Talbot Civic Centre, Port Talbot, West Glamorgan SA13 1PJ (01639 763553)

CC Number: 525509

Eligibility

Pupils who attend a county secondary school in Glamorgan and female pupils who attend a maintained primary school in the parishes of Llantrisant, Pontypridd, Pentyrch, Llanfabon, Llantwit Fardre, Eglwysilan and that part of the parish of Llanwonno comprising the former Ynysybwl ward of the former Mountain Ash urban district.

Types of grants

Cash grants tenable at any teacher training college, university or other institution of further education (including professional and technical) approved by the council and governed by rules made by the council. Financial assistance, outfits, clothing, tools, instruments or books to assist those leaving school, university or other educational establishments to prepare for or enter a profession, trade or calling.

Annual grant total

In 2012/13 the trust had an income of £36,000 and a total expenditure of £60,000. They awarded £41,000 in grants.

Exclusions

Applicants are not eligible for assistance if they are in receipt of a central government bursary or a mandatory or discretionary award, or are exempt from the payment of the tuition fee.

Applications

On a form available from the correspondent. Applications should be submitted before 31 May each year for consideration in July/August.

The Geoffrey Jones (Penreithin) Scholarship Fund

£7,400

Correspondent: Keith Butler, Trustee, Marchant Harries, 17–19 Cardiff Street, Aberdare CF44 7DP (01685 885500)

CC Number: 501964

Eligibility

Students who have been resident in the parishes or districts of Penderyn, Ystradfellte Vaynor or Taff Fechan Valley, Merthyr Tydfil for at least 12 months.

Types of grants

Assistance with the cost of books, fees, maintenance/living expenses and study/travel abroad is available to students in further or higher education.

Annual grant total

In 2012/13 the fund had both an income and an expenditure of £7,600. We estimate that the annual total of grants was around £7,400. Our research shows that about 25 grants are made each year.

Applications

In writing to the correspondent.

The Monmouthshire Further Education Trust Fund

£10,000

Correspondent: The Trustees, The Community Foundation in Wales, St Andrews House, 24 St Andrews Crescent, Cardiff CF10 3DD (02920 379580; email: info@cfiw.org.uk; website: www.cfiw.org.uk/eng/grants)

Eligibility

Grants of up to £500 are available to provide financial support to individuals under the age of 25 who are pursuing further/higher education or training and who reside in the Gwent area (specifically the County of Monmouthshire as it existed in 1956), excluding Newport.

Types of grants

Applicants can apply for grants ranging between £50 and £500. Successful applicants will be paid upon proof of enrolment on the stated course and/or quotes/invoices for items.

Annual grant total

About £10,000 each year is available for grants to individuals.

Applications

On a form available from the trust's website: www.cfiw.org.uk/eng/grants/25-monmouthshire-further-education-trust-fund

The trust welcomes informal contact prior to applications being formally made.

Caerphilly

The Rhymney Trust

£1,100

Correspondent: David Brannan, Trustee, 11 Forge Crescent, Rhymney, Tredegar NP22 5PR (01685 843094)

CC Number: 517118

Eligibility

People in need who live in Rhymney.

Types of grants

One-off grants, usually under £100, can be given to schoolchildren and college/university students towards general educational needs.

Annual grant total

In 2012/13 the trust had an income of £100 and an expenditure of £2,400. We estimate the annual total of grants to individuals to be around £1,100.

Applications

In writing to the correspondent. Applications can be submitted directly by the individual, usually in June for consideration in August.

Other information

Support is also given to organisations operating within the area of Rhymney for the purposes of education, health and relief or poverty.

Carmarthenshire

The Dorothy May Edwards Charity

£1,100 (7 grants)

Correspondent: Roger Jones, Director of Resources, Carmarthenshire County Council, County Hall, Carmarthen, Dyfed SA31 1JP (01267 234567)

CC Number: 1070293

Eligibility

Persons under the age of 25 years who have attended Ysgol Pantycelyn or Ysgol Bro Dinefwr for at least three years and who live within the catchment area of the old Ysgol Pantycelyn.

Types of grants

Grants, typically ranging between £15 and £125 to:
▶ Provide outfits, clothing, tools, instruments or books on leaving school, university or another educational

establishment to prepare for and to enter a profession, trade or calling

▶ Travel in this country or abroad to pursue education

▶ Study music or other art

▶ Continue education at college or university or at any approved place of learning

Annual grant total

In 2013/14 the charity awarded 7 grants totalling £1,100.

Applications

Application forms should be completed and returned to the Director for Education and Children by the closing date, which is 31 October each year.

The Elizabeth Evans Trust

See entry on page 91

Minnie Morgan's Scholarship

£16,000 (5 grants)

Correspondent: Roger Jones, Trustee, Carmarthenshire County Council, County Hall, Carmarthen, Dyfed SA31 1JP (01267 234567)

CC Number: 504980

Eligibility

People under the age of 25 who have attended any of the secondary schools in Llanelli and who are studying drama or dramatic art at the University of Wales or any school of dramatic art approved by the trustees.

Types of grants

One-off grants, usually around £1,000.

Annual grant total

In 2012/13 the charity had an income of £13,000 and awarded grants to five students totalling £16,000.

Applications

In writing to the correspondent. Applications should be submitted by 31 October each year.

The Mary Elizabeth Morris Charity

£650

Correspondent: Roger Jones, Director of Resources., Carmarthenshire County Council, County Hall, Carmarthen, Dyfed SA31 1JP (01267 234567)

CC Number: 514297

Eligibility

Past and present pupils who are under the age of 25 and have attended Ysgol

Rhys Prichard, and Ysgol Pantycelyn plus those pupils attending Ysgol Bro Dinefwr who live within the catchment area of the old Ysgol Pantycelyn.

Types of grants

Grants to: pupils transferring from Ysgol Rhys Prichard; supplement existing grants of beneficiaries in further or higher education; help towards the cost of education, training, apprenticeships or education for those starting work; and to help with the cost of educational travel at home or abroad.

Annual grant total

In 2013/14, 11 awards totalled £650.

Applications

Application forms should be completed and returned to the Director for Education and Children in either June (for primary school pupils), or 31 October (for secondary school pupils) each year.

The Robert Peel Foundation/Taliaris School Charity

£300

Correspondent: Roger Jones, Director of Resources, Carmarthenshire County Council, County Hall, Carmarthen SA31 1JP (01267 234567)

CC Number: 525382

Eligibility

People under the age of 25 years who, at the time of application, live in the ancient parish of Llandeilo Fawr and have done so for a minimum of two years. Preference is given to applicants who are members of or connected with the Church in Wales.

Types of grants

Awards 'to promote the educational interests' of individuals transferring to a recognised course of further or higher education and also to assist school pupils in need.

Annual grant total

In 2012/13 the foundation had an income of £360 and an expenditure of £300. About three awards are made annually.

Applications

Application forms are available from the correspondent. They should be returned by 31 October.

Other information

The ancient parish of Llandeilo Fawr was a very large parish extending from Capel Isaac and Taliaris in the north west down to the outskirts of Brynamman in the south east and including the township of Llandeilo.

City of Cardiff

The Cardiff Caledonian Society

£9,500

Correspondent: Cathy Rogers, Administrator, 9 Llandinam Crescent, Cardiff CF14 2RB (02921 405800)

CC Number: 257665

Eligibility

People of Scottish nationality and their families, who live in Cardiff or the surrounding district and are in need.

Types of grants

Grants are made to college students, undergraduates, vocational students and mature students, including those towards fees, books and instruments and equipment. Grants are also made to people starting work.

Annual grant total

In 2012/13 the fund had an income of £15,500 and a total expenditure of £19,800. The trustees award grants to individuals for both educational and welfare purposes.

Applications

In writing to the correspondent. Applications can be submitted directly by the individual or through a social worker, Citizens Advice or other welfare agency at any time. Applications are considered on a regular basis.

Cardiff Further Education Trust Fund

£343,000 (1,006 grants)

Correspondent: N. Griffiths, Administrator, Cardiff City Council, City Hall, King Edward VII Avenue, Cardiff CF10 3ND

CC Number: 525512

Eligibility

Young people in need who are over the age of 16, resident in city and borough of Cardiff and have attended a secondary school there for at least two years.

Types of grants

Grants to enable individuals to undertake further education or vocational training. Support towards travel and attendance of special educational courses may also be provided.

Annual grant total

In 2012/13 the fund had assets of £26 million, an income of £144,000 and an expenditure of £411,000. A total of £343,000 was awarded in grants to

161

individuals and 1006 people were supported.

Applications

In writing to the correspondent.

Other information

The trustees' annual report from 2012/13 also notes that 'in order that applications could be kept within the amount of income available annually', the grant was only given to students receiving certain allowances who, without the support, 'would have needed to spend study time securing funds to meet the cost of their courses.'

The fund may also provide special educational premises to Cardiff council and makes grants of £800 a year to University of Wales to enable the institution to award Craddock Wells Exhibitions to its students.

The Howardian Educational Trust

£350

Correspondent: N. Griffiths, Administrator, Cardiff City Council, City Hall, King Edward VII Avenue, Cardiff CF10 3ND (02920 872324)

CC Number: 1019801

Eligibility

Young people who are resident in Cardiff and who attended a primary or secondary school in the city and are in need.

Types of grants

Grants in connection with the costs of further education.

Annual grant total

In 2012/13 the trust had an income of £2,100 and a total expenditure of £700.

Applications

In writing to the correspondent.

Other information

This trust awards grants to both individuals and organisations.

Monmouthshire

Llandenny Charities

£1,300

Correspondent: Dr Graham Russell, Trustee, Forge Cottage, Llandenny, Usk, Monmouthshire NP15 1DL (01633 432536; email: gsrussell@btinternet.com)

CC Number: 223311

Eligibility

Students in full-time higher education who live in the parish of Llandenny and have lived there for more than one year.

Types of grants

Recurrent.

Annual grant total

In 2013 this charity had an income of £2,700 and a total expenditure of £2,300.

Applications

In writing to the correspondent, to be submitted directly by the individual. Applications should be submitted by 15 January for consideration in February.

Other information

Grants are also given to pensioners in need.

Monmouth Charity

£2,500

Correspondent: Andrew Pirie, Trustee, Pen-y-Bryn, Oakfield Road, Monmouth NP25 3JJ (01600 716202)

CC Number: 700759

Eligibility

Further education students who live within a ten-mile radius of Monmouth.

Types of grants

One-off grants usually up to a maximum of £500.

Annual grant total

In 2012/13 the charity had an income of £9,400 and an expenditure of £9,100. Grants are made for both educational and welfare purposes and to individuals and organisations. We estimate the grant total for individuals for educational purposes to be around £2,500.

Applications

The trust advertises in the local press each September/October and applications should be made in response to this advertisement for consideration in November. Emergency grants can be considered at any time. There is no application form. Applications can be submitted directly by the individual or through a social worker, Citizens Advice or other welfare agency.

The Monmouthshire Farm School Endowment

£39,000

Correspondent: The Trustees, Education Finance Dept, County Hall, Croesyceiliog, Cwmbran, Gwent NP44 2XH (01633 644495)

CC Number: 525649

Eligibility

Awards to students in need of assistance who attend Usk Agricultural College, or

any other educational institution that pursues courses of study in agricultural subjects. Preference is given to people aged under 25.

Types of grants

Grants of between £500 and £1,000 to help with the costs of study at the Usk College of Agriculture or any other farm institute, school, university or department of agricultural education approved by the governors. Grants can be for books, equipment/instruments, fees, living expenses and educational outings in the UK.

Annual grant total

In 2012/13 the trust had assets of £662,000 and an income of £39,000. Grants totalled £39,000.

Applications

On a form available from the correspondent which can be submitted at any time directly by the individual including an estimate of costs. Applications are considered in October and January.

The Monmouthshire County Council Welsh Church Act Fund

£3,000

Correspondent: Joy Robson, Head of Finance, Monmouthshire County Council, Innovation House, PO Box 106, Magor, Caldicot (01633 644657; website: www.monmouthshire.gov.uk)

CC Number: 507094

Eligibility

People of any age studying at school, university or any other place of study, who live in the boundaries of Monmouthshire County Council and their dependents. Grants are also made to people starting work.

Types of grants

Applications will be considered from individuals for aid towards a specific activity. The normal level of support to individuals is between £50–£150.

Annual grant total

In 2012/13 the fund had assets of £4.65 million and an income of £77,000. Grants to individuals totalled £3,000.

Applications

On a form available from the correspondent or downloaded from the fund's website, which can be submitted at any time, and must be signed by a county councillor. Applications can be made either directly by the individual or through his or her school, and are usually considered quarterly.

Other information

The fund also makes grants to organisations.

James Powell's Educational Foundation

£4,100

Correspondent: D. Hayhurst, Administrator, Rose Cottage Chapel, Llanvetherine, Abergavenny, Gwent NP7 8PY (01873 821449)

CC Number: 525640

Eligibility

People over the age of 16 who live in the ancient parish of Llantilio Crossenny.

Types of grants

Grants are given for books, equipment/instruments and other essentials, and also towards living and maintenance expenses. Students at school, college or university can be supported, as well as people starting work/entering a trade.

Annual grant total

In 2013 the foundation had an income of £4,400 and an expenditure of £4,300. We estimate the annual total of grants to individuals to be around £4,100.

Applications

Eligible candidates can apply in writing to the correspondent. Applications should be submitted by a parent or guardian, normally by August for consideration in September.

Other information

Note: the foundation awards grants strictly within the area of benefit.

Neath Port Talbot

Elizabeth Jones' Scholarships for Boys and Girls of Aberavon and Margam (Elizabeth Jones' Trust)

£8,000

Correspondent: David Scott, Trustee, 28 Wildbrook, Part Talbot SA13 2UN (01639 887953; email: scott-david11@sky.com)

CC Number: 525517

Eligibility

Young people aged between 16 and 25 who or whose parents live in the borough of Port Talbot and who have attended a county or voluntary school in/around the area of benefit for at least two years. Also students at the Margam College of Further Education.

Types of grants

According to our research, one-off grants ranging from £50 to £400 are available towards general educational costs, including books, equipment/instruments, travel costs and other necessities.

Annual grant total

In 2012/13 the trust had an income of £2,500 and an expenditure of £8,100. We estimate the annual grants total to be under £8,000.

Applications

In writing to the correspondent.

Pembrokeshire

The Charity of Doctor Jones

£12,500

Correspondent: Malcolm Crossman, Trustee, Guinea Hill House, Norgans Hill, Pembroke, Dyfed SA71 5EP (01646 622257)

CC Number: 241351

Eligibility

Young people between the ages of 16 and 25 who/whose parents live in Pembroke or the previous Pembroke borough.

Types of grants

Grants are given to further/higher education students, people in training and those undertaking apprenticeships. Support is available towards general costs associated with the course or training, including outfits, tools, equipment, books, travel expenses, maintenance costs and fees.

Annual grant total

In 2013 the charity had an income of £41,000 and an expenditure of £38,000. Throughout the past four years grants to individuals in education were on average £12,500 a year.

Applications

Application forms can be requested from the correspondent.

Other information

Our research indicates that the charity advertises locally when grants are available, usually twice a year.

Support can also be given to local people for welfare needs. Organisations may be supported but the trustees prioritise helping individuals. The charity also maintains a number of properties in the area and assists the tenants with maintenance and repairs.

Milford Haven Port Authority Scholarships

£6,000 (4 grants)

Correspondent: The Administrator, Gorsewood Drive, Milford Haven, Pembrokeshire SA73 3EP (01646 696100; fax: 01646 696125; email: communications@mhpa.co.uk; website: www.mhpa.co.uk)

Eligibility

Undergraduate students at British universities who have completed most of their secondary education in Pembrokeshire or nearby county.

Types of grants

The charity offers one-off undergraduate scholarships of £1,500 and a placement at the Port of Milford Haven during the summer.

Annual grant total

Four scholarships of £1,500 are awarded every year.

Applications

Application forms can be accessed from the charity's website or requested from the correspondent when the scheme is open. For the scheme opening dates and application deadlines, consult the charity's website. Our research indicates that all communication should be marked 'Scholarship Scheme'.

Narberth Educational Charity

£400

Correspondent: Ann Handley, Administrator, Pembrokeshire County Council, County Hall, Haverfordwest, Dyfed SA61 1TP (01437 775039; email: ann.handley@pembrokeshire.gov.uk; website: pembrokeshire.gov.uk)

CC Number: 1013669

Eligibility

People who live in the community council areas of Narberth, Llawhaden, Llanddewi Velfrey, Lampeter Velfrey (including Tavernspite and Ludchurch), Templeton, Martletwy (including Lawrenny), Begelly, part of Jeffreyston, Minwere and Reynalton. Applicants should have lived there for at least two years and be aged under 25.

Types of grants

Grants, normally ranging from £100 to £150, to help those at school and those transferring to a recognised course or further or higher education.

Annual grant total

In 2013/14 the charity had an income of £3,100 and a total expenditure of £750. We estimate that educational grants to individuals totalled £400, with funding also awarded to local organisations.

Applications

Application forms are available from Student Support, North Wing Reception, Haverfordwest from August onwards and should be returned to the office by 8 October.

Other information

The charity also provides financial assistance for local organisations engaged in youth activities and the promotion of education for young people/children living in the catchment area.

The Tasker Milward and Picton Charity

£2,300 (3 grants)

Correspondent: Anne Evans, Administrator, 11 Albert Street, Haverfordwest SA61 1TA (01437 764073)

CC Number: 525678

Eligibility

Present and former pupils of Tasker Milward VC Sir Thomas Picton Schools in Haverfordwest who are under the age of 25 and in need of financial assistance in pursuance of their education, including physical and social training.

Types of grants

One-off and recurrent grants between £100 and £1,000. Students in higher or further education can receive support towards the cost of the fees, books, living expenses and study or travel abroad.

Annual grant total

In 2012/13 the charity had assets of £1 million. The income and charitable expenditure figures were not provided in the statement of assets and liabilities and the annual report. We have relied on the numbers provided by the Charity Commission's record which states that the charity had both an income and an expenditure of around £45,000. Three individuals were awarded grants. Previously the total of individual grants has averaged at around £2,300 annually.

Applications

Application forms can be requested from the correspondent. Individuals can apply either directly or through their school/college/educational welfare agency, if applicable. Applications are considered twice in the autumn term and once in the spring and summer terms and should be submitted accordingly.

Other information

The charity also provides grants and other financial support to Tasker Milward VC and Sir Thomas Picton Schools.

Swansea

The Swansea Foundation

£25,000

Correspondent: Nigel Havard, Administrator, Council of City County of Swansea, Legal Department, Civic Centre, Oystermouth Road, Swansea SA1 3SN (01792 636291; email: nigel.havard@swansea.gov.uk)

CC Number: 1086884

Eligibility

People in education who are under the age of 25 and live in the city or county of Swansea. Preference is given to people who have attended one of the following schools or colleges: Bishop Gore Comprehensive School, Dynevor Comprehensive School, Swansea College and Swansea Institute of Higher Education.

Types of grants

One-off and recurrent grants according to need.

Annual grant total

In 2012/13 the foundation had an income of £1,800 and an expenditure of £26,000. We estimate the annual total of grants to individuals to be around £25,000.

Applications

In writing to the correspondent.

Torfaen

The Cwmbran Trust

£7,000

Correspondent: Kenneth Maddox, Administrator, Meritor HVBS (UK) Ltd, Grange Road, Cwmbran, Gwent NP44 3XU (01633 834040; email: cwmbrantrust@meritor.com)

CC Number: 505855

Eligibility

People in need who live in the former urban area of Cwmbran, Gwent.

Types of grants

The trust gives one-off and recurrent grants and loans for a wide variety of purposes. Previous grants of an educational nature have included funding for home-study courses and IT

equipment. Grants usually range between £125 and £2,500.

Annual grant total

In 2013 the trust had assets of £2.3 million and an income of £89,000. Grants were made to 43 individuals totalling £32,000 for educational and welfare purposes. There are three interest free loans outstanding. The majority of funding for individuals appears to be for social welfare purposes and we estimate educational grants to be around £7,000.

Applications

In writing to the correspondent. Applications can be submitted directly by the individual or through a social worker, Citizens Advice, welfare agency or other appropriate third party. Applications are usually considered in March, May, July, October and December.

Other information

The trust also awards grants to organisations.

Vale of Glamorgan

The Cowbridge with Llanblethian United Charities

£1,300

Correspondent: Clerk to the Trustees, 66 Broadway, Llanblethian, Cowbridge, Vale of Glamorgan CF71 7EW (01446 773287)

CC Number: 1014580

Eligibility

People in need who live in the town of Cowbridge with Llanblethian.

Types of grants

Grants are made towards clothing, fees, travel and maintenance for people preparing, entering or engaging in any profession, trade, occupation or service.

Annual grant total

In 2012/13 the charities had both an income and total expenditure of £24,000. Based on previous grant giving, we estimate that the total grant awarded to individuals for educational purposes was approximately £1,300.

Applications

In writing to the correspondent. Applications can be submitted directly by the individual or through a school/college or educational welfare agency.

Other information

The charities also award grants to organisations.

North East

General

The Christina Aitchison Trust

£1,000

Correspondent: Revd Roger Massingberd-Mundy, Trustee, The Old Post Office, The Street, West Raynham, Fakenham NR21 7AD

CC Number: 1041578

Eligibility

Young people under the age of 25 who are blind or suffering from any ophthalmic disease or disability.

Types of grants

One-off or recurrent grants for up to £300 to support young people in educational music, riding or sailing activities and other educational purposes. Donations are made in the form of books, equipment, fees, bursaries and fellowships.

Annual grant total

In 2012/13 the trust had an income of £1,900 and an expenditure of £2,200. Grants totalled approximately £2,000 and were split between educational and welfare purposes.

Applications

On a form available from the correspondent, to be submitted in March or September for consideration in April or November.

Other information

Grants are also given to assist people who have an ophthalmic disease or who are terminally ill and to organisations.

M. R. Cannon 1998 Charitable Trust

See entry on page 269

Lord Crewe's Charity

£150,000 (Around 100 grants)

Correspondent: Clive Smithers, Administrator, Rivergreen Centre, Aykley Heads, Durham DH1 5TS (01913 837398; email: enquiries@ lordcrewescharity.co.uk; website: www. lordcrewescharity.org.uk)

CC Number: 1155101

Eligibility

Clergy and their dependents who live in the dioceses of Durham and Newcastle and are in need. Grants may be given more generally to people in need who live in the area of benefit, with preference to people resident in parishes where the charity owns land or has the right of presentation to the benefice.

Types of grants

Grants are given for a whole range of educational needs up to and including first degrees.

Annual grant total

At the time of writing (August 2014) financial information was not yet available following the change in the charity's legal status. Previously around 100 educational grants have been given totalling about £150,000.

Exclusions

Applicants who are not members of clergy are not supported and the trustees ask not to be contacted by people who do not fit the criteria.

Applications for church buildings and church projects are not supported (except in the very small number of parishes in which the charity holds property or has rights of presentation.).

Applications

The charity's website states that there is no 'application form or an open application procedure for grants.' 'The charity works directly with its beneficiaries and with a number of partner organisations.' The application round opens in March and continues until July. Grants are considered in the first two weeks of August and the outcome is communicated to the applicant by the end of the month. For the latest updates on awards see the charity's website.

Other information

From 2014 the charity has become a charitable incorporated organisation and changed its registered charity number (previously 230347).

Small annual grants are made to organisations and support is also given for welfare purposes. Payments are made to Lincoln College of Oxford to be applied in scholarships, fellowships and hardship grants. No other institution can be supported in the same way.

Hylton House Fund

£2,000

Correspondent: Barbara Gubbins, Administrator, County Durham Community Foundation, Victoria House, St John's Road, Meadowfield Industrial Estate, Durham DH7 8XL (01917 806344; fax: 01917806344; email: info@cdcf.org.uk; website: www.cdcf.org. uk)

CC Number: 1047625–2

Eligibility

People in the North East (County Durham, Darlington, Gateshead, South Shields, Sunderland and Cleveland) with cerebral palsy and related disabilities, and their families and carers. Applicants (or their family members, if aged under 18) must be on income support or a low income or have a degree of disability in the family, which creates a heavy financial demand.

Types of grants

Grants of up to £500 towards: education, training and therapy, such as sound and light therapy for people with cerebral palsy to improve quality of life or funding towards further education courses; training and support for carers and self-help groups (where no statutory support or provision is available); provision of aids and equipment, particularly specialist clothing, communication and mobility aids; travel costs, such as taxi and rail fares to attend a specific activity if no alternative transport is available; and respite support for an individual when the needs of the person requires them to either be accompanied by an employed carer or by visiting a specialist centre where full-time extensive care is provided.

Annual grant total

Grants usually total around £4,000. We estimate grants to individuals for educational purposes to be around £2,000.

Exclusions

No grants for: legal costs; ongoing education; medical treatment; decorating and/or refurbishment costs (unless the work is due to the nature of the applicant's disability); motor vehicle adaptations; motor insurance, deposits or running costs; televisions or DVD players; assessments, such as the costs involved in the Scope Living Options Schemes; or retrospective funding. Only one grant can be held in each financial year starting in April.

Applications

On a form available from the correspondent or to download from the foundation's website. All applications must include a reference from a social worker or professional adviser in a related field, with a telephone number and the individual's permission for them to be contacted about an application. A full breakdown of costs should also be included. For specialist equipment and therapy, confirmation from an occupational therapist/doctor/ physiotherapist or other professional advisor that the equipment is suitable, is also required.

Appeals are considered in January, April, July and October and should be received before the start of the month. They can be considered between these dates within a month of application if the need is urgent, but the applicant will need to request this and provide a reason why an exception to the usual policy needs to be made.

S. Y. Killingley Memorial Trust

£5,000

Correspondent: Dermot Killingley, Chair, 9 Rectory Drive, Newcastle upon Tyne NE3 1XT (07720 118603; email: trust@grevatt.f9.co.uk; website: syktrust.org.uk/)

CC Number: 1111891

Eligibility

People aged 18 or over taking part time courses in language, literature, music or any other arts or humanities subject who live and study in the North East of England or are taking a long-distance course based in the North East of England. The aim of the trust is to help people who are likely to benefit the community and could not afford to study without a grant.

Types of grants

Grants for course fees, books, equipment, materials, travel or childcare and similar expenses. Grants have been for as little as £7 up to £1,300 for postgraduate students.

Annual grant total

In 2012/13 there was an income of £5,400 and an expenditure of £5,800. The trust states that around £5,000 is available each year for grantmaking.

Exclusions

No grants for living costs.

Applications

Application forms are available from the correspondent or can be downloaded from the trust's website. This should be submitted by post along with a letter of support from a referee such as a teacher. The selection panel meets about three times a year, usually in January, April and September. Applicants may be asked to attend an informal interview.

Other information

Successful applicants are assigned a mentor to provide them with informal support and advice during the course.

The Northern Counties Children's Benevolent Society

£8,200 (21 grants)

Correspondent: Glynis Mackie, Secretary, 29A Princes Road, Gosforth, Newcastle upon Tyne NE3 5TT (01912 365308; email: info@gmmlegal.co.uk)

CC Number: 219696

Eligibility

Children in need through sickness, disability or other causes who live in the counties of Cheshire, Cleveland, Cumbria, Durham, Greater Manchester, Humberside, Lancashire, Merseyside, Northumberland, North Yorkshire, South Yorkshire, Tyne and Wear and West Yorkshire. Preference is given to individuals who have lost one or both of their parents.

Types of grants

One-off and recurrent grants are available mainly towards school fees and clothing. The society has previously stated that support is also given for necessities, equipment, computers, or, in a limited number of cases, the provision of special equipment of an educational or physical nature for children with disabilities. In almost every case, the need for assistance arises through the premature death of the major wage earner or the break up of the family unit. Applications are treated in strict confidence and the financial circumstances of each applicant are fully and carefully considered by the trustees before an award is made.

Annual grant total

In 2013 the society had assets of £1.5 million and an income of £71,000. Grants totalling £8,200 were awarded to 21 individuals.

Applications

Application forms are available from the correspondent. Grants are normally considered in January, April, July or October. The trustees will usually undertake home visits and may ask a report from a third party, such as a medical professional or a teacher.

The Provincial Grand Charity

£18,500

Correspondent: Michael de-Villamar Roberts, Administrator, Ingham and Co., George Stanley House, 2 West Parade Road, Scarborough, North Yorkshire YO12 5ED (01723 500209)

CC Number: 517923

Eligibility

Children (including adopted and step-children) of present and deceased masons who live or lived in North Yorkshire and Humberside.

Types of grants

Grants for those at school, college or university towards school clothing, books, school fees and living expenses depending on the parental circumstances. Grants range from £100 to £3,000.

Annual grant total

In 2012 the charity had assets of £910,000 and an income of £97,000. Grants to individuals totalled £18,500. The 2012 accounts were the latest available at the time of writing (August 2014).

Applications

In writing to the correspondent, to be considered at quarterly meetings. Applications must be supported by the relative who is a member of the masons.

Prowde's Educational Foundation (Prowde's Charity)

£20,000

Correspondent: Richard Lytle, Administrator, 39 Stanley Street, Southsea PO5 2DS (02392 799142)

CC Number: 310255

Eligibility

Boys and young men aged between 9 and 25 who live in Somerset or the North or East Ridings of Yorkshire. Preference is given to those who are descendants of the named persons in the will of the founder, for those whose parents reside in the foundation's beneficial area and for those whose names were entered in the candidates' book before the date of the scheme. Boys with serious family difficulties causing them to be educated away from home and individuals with special educational needs are also favoured.

Types of grants

One-off grants of around £450 are given to schoolchildren and further/higher education students, including mature students and postgraduates. Support is given towards fees, uniforms and other clothing, books, equipment/instruments and study/travel abroad or in the UK.

Annual grant total

In 2012/13 the foundation had an income of £22,000 and an expenditure of £21,000. We estimate the annual total of grants to individuals to be around £20,000.

Applications

Application forms can be requested from the correspondent and can be submitted by individuals directly or through a third party, such as a parent/guardian or a social worker, if applicable. Applications should include a birth certificate and evidence of enrolment on the course. Grants are normally considered in July and applications should be made by May/June.

The Sherburn House Educational Foundation

£1,000

Correspondent: Stephen Hallett, Administrator, Ramsey House, Sherburn Hospital, Durham DH1 2SE (01913 722551; fax: 01913 720035; email: peter.pybus@sherburnhouse.org; website: www.sherburnhouse.org)

CC Number: 527325

Eligibility

People between the ages of 16 and 21 who live in the civil parish of Sherburn House or other parishes within the county of Durham and are in need.

Types of grants

Grants are given to assist schoolchildren, university or college students and people in other educational institutions or training. The awards are normally between £50 and £450 and are made towards the cost of books, equipment, instruments and fees.

Annual grant total

In 2012/13 the foundation had both an income and an expenditure of around £1,100. We estimate that educational grants totalled around £1,000.

Exclusions

Individuals who have been awarded a grant or refused a grant within the last 24 months cannot be funded. Elementary education is not supported.

Applications

Applications should be made through the individual's school/college, educational welfare agency or other third party, such as social services or Citizens Advice. They are considered throughout the year.

Other information

Grants are also made for welfare purposes. See the foundation's website for more details or refer to the Sherburn House Charity (registered charity number 217652).

Yorkshire Training Fund for Women

£1,800

Correspondent: Ann Taylor, Trustee, 1 High Ash Close, Notton, Wakefield, West Yorkshire WF4 2PF (01226722155; website: ytfund.wordpress.com/)

CC Number: 529586

Eligibility

British women over the age of 16 and over who live in, or have connections to, Yorkshire.

Types of grants

One-off grants in the range of £100–£400 are available to women undertaking training courses that will enable them to become self-sufficient financially. Grants are given towards general necessities, such as books, equipment and instruments.

Annual grant total

In 2013 the fund had an income of £2,600 and an expenditure of £2,000. We estimate that the annual total of grants to individuals was around £1,800.

Exclusions

Grants are not given to cover fees or to people on access courses.

Applications

Application forms can be accessed from the fund's website or requested from the correspondent. They can be submitted by the individual or through a social worker, Citizens Advice or other welfare agency, if applicable. Applicants should provide details of two referees and detailed information of their financial position. Completed forms should be returned by 1 May or by 1 December, providing an sae.

Other information

Support is also given to the Yorkshire Ladies' Council of Education and organisations, especially those working for the benefit of old people.

The fund has previously stated that 'there is a great deal of competition for the grants'.

County Durham

County Durham Community Foundation

£84,000

Correspondent: Mrs Barbara Gubbins, Chief Executive, Victoria House, Whitfield Court, St John's Road, Meadowfield Industrial Estate, Durham DH7 8XL (01913 786340; email: info@cdf.org.uk; website: www.cdcf.org.uk)

CC Number: 1047625

Eligibility

Young people who live in the County Durham area.

Types of grants

Grants are made towards the cost of course fees, tuition fees, books, educational, sporting and musical equipment and travel costs. Bursaries are also awarded.

Annual grant total

In 2012/13 the foundation held assets of £9.6 million and had an income of £3.9 million. Grants for individuals totalled over £167,500 and we estimate the total grants for educational purposes to be £84,000.

Applications

Visit the foundation's website for full details of grant schemes. Application forms are also available to download from the foundation's website.

Other information

Grants are also made to organisations.

The Sedgefield Charities

£5,000

Correspondent: John Hannon, Clerk, East House, Mordon, Sedgefield, County Durham TS21 2EY (01740 622512; email: east.house@btinternet.com)

CC Number: 230395

Eligibility

College, university, vocational and mature students who live in the parishes of Bishop Middleham, Bradbury, Cornforth, Fishburn, Mordon, Sedgefield and Trimdon in County Durham.

Types of grants

One-off grants are made to undergraduates and mature students for books and maintenance/living expenses. Support may also be given towards training fees.

Annual grant total

In 2013 the charity had an income of £15,500 and a total expenditure of £20,200. The charity gives to individuals and organisations and awards grants for both educational and social welfare purposes. We estimate the amount awarded to individuals for educational purposes was around £5,000.

Applications

On a form available from the correspondent, to be submitted by 30 September each year.

The Sedgefield Educational Foundation

£4,200

Correspondent: John Hannon, Clerk, East House, Mordon, Stockton-on-Tees TS21 2EY (01740 622512; email: east.house@btinternet.com)

CC Number: 527317

Eligibility

People between the ages of 18 and 25 who/whose parents, are resident in the parishes of Fishburn, Sedgefield, Bradbury and Morden.

Types of grants

Small grants to people in full-time further/higher education and training. Our research suggests that recurrent grants are available for the duration of the study. Support is given to help with the cost of books, equipment, fees and living expenses. The trustees normally only help with education higher than A-level and support those courses that are not available at schools. Grants can range from £140 to £300 (depending on the applicant's circumstances).

Annual grant total

In 2013 the foundation had an income of £4,500 and an expenditure of £4,400. We estimate the annual total of grants to individuals to be around £4,200.

Applications

Application forms are available from the correspondent. They should be submitted by 30 September for consideration in October.

Other information

Students seeking funds for study or travel abroad and students over 25 may be referred to the Sedgefield District Relief-in-Need Charities, to which welfare applications are also referred (see separate entry).

Durham

Johnston Educational Foundation

£4,000

Correspondent: Aynsley Merritt, CAS Finance Team Room G123–125, Durham County Council, County Hall, Durham DH1 5UE (03000 261862)

CC Number: 527394

Eligibility

People under the age of 25 who live, or whose parents live, in the city of Durham.

Types of grants

Grants of up to £300 to further and higher education students. Support is given towards the cost of books, equipment/instruments, necessities, fees, coaching, accommodation and other educational expenses. Financial assistance is also available for travel and volunteering work. People involved in arts have been also supported.

Annual grant total

In 2012/13 the foundation had an income of £3,000 and an expenditure of £1,100. We estimate the annual total of grants to be around £1,000.

Applications

Application forms can be requested from the correspondent. Our research shows that applications are considered in February, June, October and can be submitted directly by the individual.

Frosterley

The Frosterley Exhibition Foundation

£1,300

Correspondent: Judith Bainbridge, Trustee, 6 Osborne Terrace, Frosterley, Bishop Auckland DL13 2RD (01388527668)

CC Number: 527338

Eligibility

People in full-time education (from secondary school age upwards) whose parents live in the parish of Frosterley. Preference is given to college and university students.

Types of grants

Grants are given towards books, uniforms and any other educational necessities.

Annual grant total

In 2012/13 the foundation had an income of £3,000 and an expenditure of £1,500. We have estimated that the annual total of grants was about £1,300.

Exclusions

Children under the age of 11 are not eligible.

Applications

In writing to the correspondent. Applications should be submitted by the applicant's parent, to whom the cheque will be made. Grants are distributed in September and applications should be made by August.

Stanhope

The Hartwell Educational Foundation

£900

Correspondent: Dorothy Foster, Administrator, Sowen Burn Farm, Stanhope, County Durham DL13 2PP (01388 528577)

CC Number: 527368

Eligibility

People aged between 11 and 21 who live in the civil parish of Stanhope. Eligibility is dependent on parental income.

Types of grants

Grants are primarily awarded on a recurrent basis to students going to college or university for help with fees/living expenses and books. Students from low-income families receive larger grants and one-off grants can also be given to younger pupils attending secondary school towards the cost of uniforms, other clothing, books, and so on.

Annual grant total

In 2012/13 the charity had an income of £1,300 and a total expenditure of just under £1,000.

Applications

Applications should be made by the last Saturday in August, on a form available from the correspondent, for consideration in September/October. Applications can be made either directly by the individual or by a parent/guardian.

East Yorkshire

The Joseph and Annie Cattle Trust

£10,500 (19 grants)

Correspondent: Roger Waudby, Administrator, PO Box 23, Hull HU12 0WF (01964 671742; fax: 01482 211198)

CC Number: 262011

Eligibility

Schoolchildren who have dyslexia and live in Hull or the East Riding of Yorkshire area.

Types of grants

One-off grants of £200 to £500.

Annual grant total

In 2012/13 the trust had assets of £8.3 million and an income of £459,000. Grants for educational and welfare purposes were made to 39 individuals totalling £21,500.

Applications

In writing to the correspondent, only via a welfare organisation, for consideration on the third Monday of every month. Note, if applicants approach the trust directly they will be referred to an organisation, such as Disability Rights Advisory Service or social services.

Other information

Grants are also made to organisations (£305,000 – 2012/13).

The Leonard Chamberlain Trust

£9,500

Correspondent: Alison Nicholson, Secretary, 4 Bishops Croft, Beverley, North Humberside HU17 8JY (01482 865726)

CC Number: 1091018

Eligibility

People who live in Selby or the East Riding of Yorkshire and are in further or higher education.

Types of grants

Grants of £50–£1,000 are given for items such as books.

Annual grant total

In 2013 the charity had assets of £6 million which figure includes mainly permanent endowment and is not available for grant giving. It had an income of almost £182,000 and total expenses of £35,000. Grants awarded to individuals for educational purposes totalled £9,500 and for social welfare purposes totalled £2,500.

Applications

On a form available from the correspondent. They should be returned in August for consideration in September.

Other information

The trust's main purpose is the provision of housing for residents in the area of benefit who are in financial need and it also makes a small number of grants for religious and social welfare purposes.

The Hesslewood Children's Trust (Hull Seamen's and General Orphanage)

£11,000

Correspondent: Rex Booth, Secretary to the Trustees, 1 Canada Drive, Cherry Burton, East Yorkshire HU17 7RQ (01946 550474)

CC Number: 529804

Eligibility

Young people under 25 who live or have firm family connections with the former county of Humberside and North Lincolnshire. The trust also gives to former Hesslewood Scholars.

'Applicants must be in need, but must show their resolve to part fund themselves.'

Types of grants

One-off grants, typically up to £1,000, are given towards: books, school uniforms, educational outings and maintenance for schoolchildren; books for students in higher and further education; and equipment, instruments and clothing for people starting work.

Annual grant total

In 2012/13 the trust had assets of £2.6 million and an income of £85,000.

Grants made to or on behalf of individuals totalled £31,500 of which £11,000 was awarded in educational grants.

Exclusions

Loans are not made.

Applications

On a form available from the correspondent, accompanied by a letter from the tutor or an educational welfare organisation (or from medical and social services for a disability grant). Applications can be submitted by the individual, through their school, college or educational welfare agency, or by another third party such as a Citizens Advice or health centre. Details of the applicant's and parental income must be included, along with an indication of the amount the applicant will contribute and a contact telephone number. Applications are considered in February, June and September.

Other information

Grants are also made to organisations.

The Hook and Goole Charity

£15,000

Correspondent: Diane Taylor, Administrator, The Courtyard, Boothferry Road, Goole DN14 6AW (07539269813; email: hookandgoole@gmail.com)

CC Number: 513948

Eligibility

Students and apprentices aged between 16 to 25 who have lived or attended school in the former borough of Goole or the parish of Hook for at least two years.

Types of grants

Grants of between £150 and £400 are given for educational bursaries. Grants are given for books, tools/equipment, living expenses, educational outings and study or travel overseas.

Annual grant total

In 2012 the charity had an income of £13,000 and an expenditure of £15,500. It made donations of approximately £15,000.

This was the latest financial information available at the time of writing (July 2014).

Applications

On a form available from the correspondent. Applications should be submitted directly by the individual in July/August for consideration in September.

Nancie Reckitt Charity

£5,400

Correspondent: M. Stansfield, Heath House, 19 Northside, Patrington, Hull HU12 0PA (01964 630960)

CC Number: 509380

Eligibility

People under the age of 25 who or whose parents have been resident in the parishes of Patrington, Rimswell and Winestead for at least five years.

Types of grants

Recurrent grants of up to £600 are available to students in further/higher education for general education expenses, including equipment/ instruments, books and fees. Support is also given to people starting work for clothing and equipment/instruments, tools.

Annual grant total

In 2012/13 the charity had an income of £6,300 and an expenditure of £5,600. We have estimated the annual total of grants to be around £5,400.

Applications

Application forms can be requested from the correspondent and submitted directly by the individual. Our research suggests that receipts for items such as books, materials, tools and so forth should be included.

The Sir Philip Reckitt Educational Trust Fund

See entry on page 19

Henry Samman's Hull Chamber of Commerce Endowment Fund

£4,700

Correspondent: Ian Kelly, Administrator, Hull and Humber, Chamber of Commerce, Industry and Shipping, 34–38 Beverley Road, Hull HU3 1YE (01482 324976; fax: 01482 213962; email: info@hull-humber-chamber.co.uk; website: www.hull-humber-chamber.co.uk/the-chamber/henry-samman-fund.aspx)

CC Number: 228837

Eligibility

British citizens who are over the age of 18 and can demonstrate some academic skills in either business methods or a foreign language. Preference is given to young people from Hull and East Riding. Candidates should be studying or planning to study at degree level, although consideration will be given to those slightly under this age limit.

Types of grants

Bursaries to enable individuals to spend a period of 3 to 12 months abroad in connection to their studies of business methods and/or foreign languages. The award is generally of around £100 a month. Longer periods of travel may be funded at the trustees' discretion.

Annual grant total

At the time of writing (July 2014) the latest financial information available was from 2012. In 2012 the fund had an income of £5,200 and an expenditure of £4,900. We estimate that the annual total of grants was around £4,700.

Applications

In writing to the correspondent. Applications should include a covering letter, a CV and outline how the award would benefit the applicant's education and training. Candidates may be required to attend an interview. The trustees meet once a year to consider applications, normally in summer.

Other information

The fund was set up in 1917 originally to encourage the study of Russian, in a commercial context, but has since been extended.

The Sydney Smith Trust

£0

Correspondent: HSBC Trust Company (UK) Ltd, HSBC Trust Company (UK) Ltd, 10th Floor Norwich House, Commercial Road, Southampton SO15 1GX (02380 722214)

CC Number: 252112

Eligibility

Long-term residents of Kingston upon Hull and its immediate vicinity who are undertaking further, higher or vocational training or re-training, and are in need. Applicants must be under 35 and have attended secondary school in Hull.

Types of grants

One-off grants to people starting work and students in further/higher education, including mature students under 35, towards equipment and instruments.

Annual grant total

In 2012/13 the trust had an income of £8,600 and a total expenditure of £10,900. Due to its low income, the trust was not required to submit its accounts to the Charity Commission and so a breakdown of grants was not available. In previous years, however, the trust has distributed all of its grants to institutions, mainly schools. It is likely, based on previous years, that no grants were awarded to individuals.

Applications

In writing to the correspondent at any time. Details of schools attended, qualifications obtained and future plans are required.

Robert Towries Charity

£1,200

Correspondent: Mrs Debbie Ulliot, The Cottage, Carlton Lane, Aldbrough, Hull HU11 4RA (01964 527255; email: roberttowerytrust@googlemail.com)

CC Number: 222568

Eligibility

People under 25 years old who live in Aldbrough and Burton Constable or who have parents living in the area.

Types of grants

One-off grants for educational needs.

Annual grant total

In 2012/13 the charity had an income of £10,500 and a total expenditure of £4,800. The charity makes grants to individuals and organisations for both educational and social welfare purposes. We estimate the total figure for grants awarded to individuals for educational purposes was around £1,200.

Applications

In writing to the correspondent directly by the individual.

Ann Watson's Trust

£51,000

Correspondent: Karen Palmer, Administrator, Flat 4 The College, 14 College Street, Sutton-on-Hull, Hull HU7 4UP (01482 709626; email: awatson@awatson.karoo.co.uk)

CC Number: 226675

Eligibility

People under the age of 25 who live in East Riding, Yorkshire or who attend school in that area.

Types of grants

One-off and recurrent grants according to educational need.

Annual grant total

In 2013 the trust had assets of £18.8 million and an income of £409,000. Educational grants to individuals totalled £51,000. The trust further specifies that 'during the year 47 education grants were made to individuals, schools and organisations.'

Applications

In writing to the correspondent at any time during the year. The trustees meet quarterly.

Other information

Grants are also given to local organisations, churches and to individuals for welfare purposes, and for the provision of accommodation and relief in need of poor women who are members of the Church of England, with preference given to widows or unmarried daughters of clergymen of the Church of England.

In 2013 the trust awarded around £115,000 to institutions.

Christopher Wharton Educational Foundation

£1,500

Correspondent: Jean Reynolds, Trustee, 12 Hudson Close, Stamford Bridge, York YO41 1QR (01759 373842)

CC Number: 506958

Eligibility

People between the ages of 18 and 25 who or whose parents live in the area of Stamford Bridge, Gate Helmsley and Kexby and who are in need.

Types of grants

Grants are of about £100 and can be given to help with further education and training, towards tools, equipment/ instruments or apprenticeships, where help is not normally provided by the local authorities.

Annual grant total

In 2012/13 the foundation had an income of £2,600 and an expenditure of £1,600. We estimate that the annual total of grants to individuals was around £1,500.

Applications

In writing to the correspondent. Applications should normally be submitted by 31 October.

Barmby on the Marsh

Blanchard's Educational Foundation

£1,300

Correspondent: John Burman, Clerk, Heptonstalls Solicitors LLP, 7–15 Gladstone Terrace, Goole, East Yorkshire DN14 5AH (01405 765661; fax: 01405 764201)

CC Number: 529857

Eligibility

People under the age of 25 who/whose parents live in Barmby on the Marsh or who attend/have attended school there.

Types of grants

Our research suggests that grants are available to schoolchildren towards clothing, books and educational outings; to further/higher education students to help with the cost of books and study or travel abroad; to people starting work for books and equipment (but not clothing or travel); and to mature students for books and travel.

Annual grant total

In 2012/13 the foundation had an income of £1,900 and an expenditure of £1,400. We estimate that grants to individuals totalled around £1,300.

Exclusions

Fees, maintenance expenses and childcare costs.

Applications

In writing to the correspondent. The trustees usually meet in July and December.

Beverley

Christopher Eden Educational Foundation

£11,000

Correspondent: Judy Dickinson, Trustee, 85 East Street, Leven, Beverley HU17 5NG (01964 542593; email: judydickinson@mac.com)

CC Number: 529794

Eligibility

Young people under the age of 25 who live in the town of Beverley and the surrounding area or have attended school there. People with special educational needs are given preference.

Types of grants

One-off and recurrent grants in the range of £50–£400 are available to further/higher education students and people undertaking apprenticeships. Financial support is given towards any kind of educational needs, including fees, necessities, books, equipment/ instruments, clothing, travel expenses, sports or art studies and so forth.

Annual grant total

In 2012/13 the foundation had income of £11,700 and an expenditure of £11,500. We estimate the annual total of grants to individuals to be around £11,000.

Applications

In writing to the correspondent. Our research suggests that applications for assistance with university or college costs are considered in October and applications for any other purposes are considered in January, April, July and October. A parent/guardian should complete the application for those under the age of 16. Applications should include full details of the course, information on the applicant's education, income of the parents/ applicant and reasons why the help is needed. Incomplete or incorrect applications will not be considered and are not returned.

Other information

According to our research, the foundation has endowed a berth on a sail training schooner and selects a deserving young person for the berth each year.

The James Graves Educational Foundation

£1,500

Correspondent: Ian Merryweather, Administrator, 10 West Close, Beverley, North Humberside HU17 7JJ (01482 867958; email: ian_merryweather@ hotmail.co.uk)

CC Number: 529796

Eligibility

Students preferably under the age of 18 who live in the parish of St Martin, Beverley.

Types of grants

Grants to help towards the costs of books and other essentials for schoolchildren, particularly those with a church connection and with a specific emphasis on religious education. The maximum grant is £500.

Annual grant total

The trust has both an income and a total expenditure of around £2,000 consistently. About £1,500 is usually given in grants per annum.

This was the most recent financial information available at the time of writing (August 2014).

Applications

In writing to the correspondent. According to the trust not many suitable applications are received each year. Applications are considered twice yearly.

The Wray Educational Trust (Wray Trust)

£6,200

Correspondent: Judy Dickinson, Trustee, 85 East Street, Leven, Beverley, North Humberside HU17 5NG (01964 542593; email: judydickinson@mac.com)

CC Number: 508468

Eligibility

People under the age of 25 who (or whose parents) have lived in the parish of Leven for at least three years.

Types of grants

One-off grants are given to schoolchildren, students in further or higher education and people starting work. Support is available towards general educational costs, including books, equipment/instruments, fees, educational outings, study or travel abroad and musical or sports activities.

Annual grant total

In 2012/13 the trust had an income of £6,600 and an expenditure of £6,400. We estimate that the annual total of grants to individuals was around £6,200.

Applications

Application forms are available from the correspondent, who knows many of the people in the village and is always willing to discuss needs. Applications should be submitted by the beginning of January, April, July and October for consideration during that month.

Other information

Grants are also given to local organisations working for the benefit of young people.

East Riding

The Nafferton Feoffee Charity Trust

£1,100

Correspondent: Margaret Buckton, Trustee, South Cattleholmes, Wansford, Driffield, East Yorkshire YO25 8NW (01377 254293)

CC Number: 232796

Eligibility

People in need who live in the parish of All Saints Nafferton with St Mary's Wansford.

Types of grants

Bursaries are available to local students for things such as educational overseas trips.

Annual grant total

In 2013 the trust had assets of £1.7 million and an income of £56,000. During this accounting year, the trust awarded grants to eight individuals totalling £2,130 with organisations receiving the remaining £18,120 grant expenditure. We estimate that £1,100 was awarded to individuals for educational purposes.

Exclusions

The trust stated that the parish only consists of 3,000 people and every household receives a copy of a leaflet outlining the trust's work. People from outside this area are not eligible to apply.

Applications

In writing to the correspondent at any time, directly by the individual.

Other information

Grants are also made to organisations and to individuals for welfare purposes.

Hedon

The Hedon Haven Trust

£3,000

Correspondent: Ian North, Trustee, 44 Souttergate, Hedon, Hull HU12 8JS (01482 897105; email: iannorth@iannorth.karoo.co.uk)

CC Number: 500259

Eligibility

People at any stage or level of their education, undertaking study of any subject, who live in Hedon near Hull.

Types of grants

One-off grants ranging from £50 to £500 are given to: schoolchildren for educational outings in the UK and abroad; students in further or higher education towards study or travel abroad and maintenance/living expenses.

Annual grant total

In 2013 the trust had an income of £3,400 and an expenditure of £3,000. Grants totalled £3,000.

Applications

In writing to the correspondent at any time, enclosing an sae. Applications can be submitted directly by the individual or through the school/college or educational welfare agency.

Other information

Grants are also made to organisations.

Horbury

The Daniel Gaskell and John Wray Foundation

£5,000

Correspondent: Martin Milner, Clerk, Meadow View, Haigh Moor Road, Tingley, Wakefield WF3 1EJ (07947 611100)

CC Number: 529262

Eligibility

People under 25 in full-time education who are living or who have a parent living in the former urban district council of Horbury.

Types of grants

Grants, typically ranging between £50 and £200, towards books, equipment, field trips, travel, course expenses for those at school, college or university.

Annual grant total

In 2012 the foundation had an income of £19,900 and a total expenditure of £11,500. We estimate that grants to individuals totalled £5,000, with funding also awarded to local schools.

At the time of writing (July 2014) this was the most recent financial information available for the foundation.

Applications

Applications should be made after advertisements are placed in the local press. The trustees meet annually in September, so applications should be received by the end of August.

Humbleton

Heron Educational Foundation (Heron Trust)

£14,700

Correspondent: Brenda Frear, Trustee, 2 The Bungalows, Humbleton Road, Lelley HU12 8SP (01964 670788; email: fay@cold-harbour-farm.freeserve.co.uk)

CC Number: 529841

Eligibility

People under the age of 25 living in the parish of Humbleton and Flinton and Fitling villages.

Types of grants

Grants are available to pupils entering primary/secondary school and further/higher education students. People entering a trade/profession may also be assisted. Support can be given towards general educational needs, mainly for clothing, books and other necessities.

Annual grant total

In 2012/13 the foundation had an income of £12,100 and a total expenditure of £15,000. We estimate that grants to individuals totalled around £14,700.

Applications

In writing to the correspondent.

Kingston upon Hull

Alderman Ferries Charity (Hull United Charities)

£7,200

Correspondent: The Chair, Hull United Charities, The Office, Northumberland Court, Northumberland Avenue, Hull HU2 0LR (01482 323965; email: office@ hulluc.karoo.co.uk; website: www. hullunitedcharities.org.uk/alderman-ferries.html)

CC Number: 529821

Eligibility

People under the age of 25 who are entering secondary, further/higher education or apprenticeships and who have attended school or lived within Kingston upon Hull city boundary for at least two years prior to applying.

Types of grants

Grants ranging from around £300 to £500 are given for fees, books, equipment/instruments, clothing, travel costs and maintenance expenses.

Annual grant total

In 2012/13 the charity had an income of £16,700 and an expenditure of £14,500. We estimate the annual total of grants to individuals to be around £7,200.

Applications

Application forms and detailed guidelines are available on the trust's website or can be requested from the correspondent. The trustees consider grants every December and applications should be submitted by the middle of November.

The Dr A. E. Hart Trust

£20,000

Correspondent: Secretary to the Trustees, Williamsons Solicitors, 45 Lowgate, Hull HU1 1EN (01482 323697; fax: 01482 328132; email: admin@williamsons-solicitors.co.uk; website: www.williamsons-solicitors.co. uk/dr-a-e-hart-trust)

CC Number: 529780

Eligibility

Young people aged 18 and above for educational training within the boundary of the city and county of Kingston upon Hull.

Types of grants

The trust was established for 'the promotion and encouragement of education by way of bursaries and studentships or scholarships for needy students of either sex residing within the boundary of the city and county of Kingston Upon Hull.'

Assistance is offered to those people who are studying for their 1st degree (or equivalent qualification), PGCE, LPC or BPTC.

Annual grant total

In 2012/13 the trust had an income of £21,000 and an expenditure of £25,000. Previously grants to individuals have totalled around £20,000.

Exclusions

Applications cannot be considered for residents living outside the city boundary or students who are resident in Hull only because they are attending an education institution there. Applicants residing in the surrounding areas of Willerby, Hessle, Anlaby, Hedon, etc. will not be funded.

Applications

Application forms can be obtained by contacting the trust. The grants available from this trust are relatively modest, and are most unlikely to have any significant bearing on an applicant's decision to embark on any given course.

Kingston upon Hull Education Foundation

£2,300

Correspondent: Brice McDermid, Administrator, Corporate Finance, City Treasury, Hull City Council, Guildhall Road, Hull HU1 2AB (01482 615010)

CC Number: 514427

Eligibility

People over 13 who live, or whose parents live, in the city of Kingston upon Hull and either attend, or have attended, a school in the city.

Types of grants

Awards of £80 to £250 are available as scholarships, bursaries or grants tenable at any school, university or other educational establishment approved by the trustees; and towards the cost of outfits, clothing, tools, instruments or books to assist the beneficiaries in pursuance of their education or to prepare them for entering a profession, trade, occupation or service on leaving

school, university or other educational establishment.

Annual grant total

In 2012/13 the foundation had an income of £5,000 and an expenditure of £2,500. We have estimated that the total of grants for the year was about £2,300.

Applications

In writing to the correspondent. Applications are considered in November (closing date mid-October) and February (closing date mid-January). A letter of support from the applicant's class or course tutor, plus evidence of their progress and attendance on the course is needed before a grant is made.

Newton on Derwent

Newton on Derwent Charity

£3,000

Correspondent: The Administrator, FAO, Grays Solicitors, Duncombe Place, York YO1 7DY (01904 634771)

CC Number: 529830

Eligibility

People who live in the parish of Newton upon Derwent. Our research suggests that grants are mainly available to higher education students.

Types of grants

One-off grants towards fees. Payments are usually paid directly to the relevant institution.

Annual grant total

In 2013 the charity had an income of £13,200 and an expenditure of £12,300. We estimate that educational grants to individuals totalled around £3,000.

Applications

In writing to the correspondent. Applications are considered throughout the year.

Other information

Grants can also be made to organisations.

Ottringham

The Ottringham Church Lands Charity

£1,500

Correspondent: Mary Fairweather, Trustee, South Field, Chapel Lane, Ottringham, Hull, East Yorkshire HU12 0AA (01964 626908; email: maryfairweather@hotmail.com)

CC Number: 237183

Eligibility

People in need who live in the parish of Ottringham.

Types of grants

Grants are made according to need.

Annual grant total

Income was £10,400 but expenditure only £3,000 in the year 2012/13. The charity also gives grants for social welfare purposes.

Exclusions

No grants are given which would affect the applicant's state benefits.

Applications

In writing to the correspondent at any time. Applications can be submitted either directly by the individual, through a third party such as a social worker or teacher, or through an organisation such as Citizens Advice or a school.

Rawcliffe

The Rawcliffe Educational Charity

£11,500

Correspondent: Julie Parrott, Administrator, 26 Station Road, Rawcliffe, Goole, North Humberside DN14 8QR (01405 839637)
CC Number: 509656

Eligibility

People under the age of 25 who/whose parents live in the parish of Rawcliffe and who have attended one of the local schools.

Types of grants

One-off and recurrent grants of up to £600. Individuals finishing school can be given grants to help upon entering further/higher full-time education. Assistance is given towards the cost of books, equipment/instruments, outfits and clothing, fees, maintenance/living costs and travel expenses. Apprentices and people starting work are also eligible to apply for help with books, equipment, clothing and travel. The study of music and other arts is also supported.

Annual grant total

In 2012/13 the charity had an income of £20,000 and a total expenditure of £11,800. We have estimated the annual total of grants to individuals to be around £11,500.

Exclusions

School fees or study/travel overseas is not normally covered.

Applications

In writing to the correspondent. Applications should include the type and duration of the course to be studied. Candidates must confirm that they are not in receipt of any salary. The awards are normally considered in September.

Other information

Children leaving primary schools and going into secondary education are gifted books.

Riston

The Peter Nevill Charity

£1,400

Correspondent: Julie Rhodes, Trustee, Marleigh, Arnold Lane West, Arnold, Hull HU11 5HP (01964 562872)
CC Number: 506325

Eligibility

Young people under 25 who live, or who have a parent/parents who live, in the parish of Long Riston and Arnold.

Types of grants

Grants of £50 to £200 are given towards books, clothing and other essentials for school-leavers taking up employment and for students in further or higher education.

Annual grant total

In 2012/13 the charity had an income of £3,000 and a total expenditure of £2,900. We estimate that educational grants to individuals totalled £1,400, with funding also awarded to local organisations.

Applications

In writing to the correspondent.

Other information

Grants are made to Riston Church of England Primary School and village organisations serving young people.

North Yorkshire

The Beckwith Bequest

£4,200

Correspondent: Nigel Knapton, 4 Central Buildings, Market Place, Easingwold, York YO61 3AB (07779994712; email: nigel.knapton@townandparish.co.uk)
CC Number: 532360

Eligibility

People resident or educated in the parishes of Easingwold and Husthwaite who are in need of financial assistance.

Types of grants

The charity provides scholarships, bursaries and maintenance allowances. Grants are available to help with general educational costs, including books, equipment/instruments, clothing, travel and so on. Our research indicates that small grants, usually around £100 – £150, are available.

Annual grant total

In 2012/13 the charity had an income of £8,700 and an expenditure of £8,500. We estimate the annual total of grants to individuals to be around £4,200.

Applications

In writing to the correspondent.

Other information

The charity can also provide facilities or other benefits for educational establishments, where these are not already covered by the local authority.

Bedale Educational Foundation (The Rector and Four and Twenty of Bedale)

£1,200

Correspondent: John Winkle, Administrator, 25 Burrill Road, Bedale DL8 1ET (01677 424306; email: johnwinkle@awinkle.freeserve.co.uk)
CC Number: 529517

Eligibility

People aged between 5 and 25 who/whose parents live in the parishes of Aiskew, Bedale, Burrill, Cowling, Crakehall, Firby, Leeming Bar, Langthorne and Rand Grange in North Yorkshire. Preference is given to people with special educational needs or disabilities.

Types of grants

One-off grants in the range of £200–£600 are given to schoolchildren, college students and people in training. Support can be provided towards books, fees, maintenance/living expenses and excursions.

Annual grant total

In 2012/13 the foundation had an income of £1,400 and an expenditure of £2,500. Both figures are the highest in the past five years. We estimate that educational grants to individuals totalled around £1,200.

Applications

Application forms are available from the correspondent. They can be submitted at any time either directly by the individual or his/her parent.

Other information

Grants may also be made to organisations.

Bedale Welfare Charity (The Rector and Four and Twenty of Bedale)

£4,000

Correspondent: John Winkle, Administrator, 25 Burrill Road, Bedale, North Yorkshire DL8 1ET (01677 424306; email: johnwinkle@awinkle. freeserve.co.uk)

CC Number: 224035

Eligibility

People who live in the parishes of Aiskew, Bedale, Burrill with Cowling, Crakehall, Firby, Langthorne and Rand Grange and are in need.

Types of grants

One-off grants, usually ranging from £50 to £5,000, can be given for general educational needs.

Annual grant total

In 2012/13 the charity had an income of £15,300 and a total expenditure of £27,000, which is the highest in the past five years. Note that the expenditure varies every year. Most of the grants are distributed in relief-in-need grants and to organisations, although this does not exclude applications for educational purposes. We estimate that educational grants to individuals totalled around £4,000.

Applications

Application forms are available from the correspondent. They can be submitted at any time either directly by the individual or through a third party, such as a social worker or teacher.

Other information

Grants are also made to organisations and for welfare purposes.

The Gargrave Poor's Lands Charity

£3,800

Correspondent: The Trustees, Kirk Syke, High Street, Gargrave, Skipton, North Yorkshire BD23 3RA

CC Number: 225067

Eligibility

People in need who live in Gargrave, Bank Newton, Coniston Cold, Flasby, Eshton or Winterburn.

Types of grants

One-off and recurrent grants and loans are given to: schoolchildren for uniforms, clothing and outings; and students in further or higher education towards maintenance, fees and textbooks. Help is also available to students taking vocational further education courses and other vocational training.

Annual grant total

In 2012/13 the trust had assets of £411,000 and an income of £44,500. Educational grants totalled £3,800.

Applications

On a form available from the correspondent. Applications can be submitted at any time.

Other information

The charity also gives grants for welfare purposes.

Reverend Matthew Hutchinson Trust (Gilling and Richmond)

£2,500

Correspondent: Christine Wiper Gentry, Administrator, 3 Smithson Close, Moulton, Richmond, North Yorkshire DL10 6QP (01325 377328)

CC Number: 220870/220779

Eligibility

People who live in the parishes of Gilling and Richmond in North Yorkshire.

Types of grants

Grants are given to schoolchildren for fees, equipment and excursions. Undergraduates, including mature students, can receive help towards books whilst vocational students can be supported for study/travel overseas.

Annual grant total

This charity has branches in both Gilling and Richmond, which are administered jointly, but have separate funding. In 2013 the combined income of the charities was £25,500 and their combined expenditure was £11,700.

Applications

In writing to the correspondent. Applications can be submitted directly by the individual or through a trustee, social worker, Citizens Advice or other welfare agency.

Other information

Grants are also made to organisations including local schools and hospitals.

The Kirkby Malhamdale Educational Foundation

£50

Correspondent: Robin Bolland, Trustee, 2 Cove Road, Malham, Skipton BD23 4DH (01729 830501)

CC Number: 1003640

Eligibility

People under 25 who have a parent or guardian living in one of the following parishes in the county of North Yorkshire: Airton, Calton, Hanlith, Kirkby Malham, Malham, Malham Moor, Otterburn and Scosthrop.

Types of grants

One-off grants of £100 to £200 to: schoolchildren for uniforms/clothing, study/travel overseas, books, equipment/ instruments and excursions; college students, undergraduates and children with special educational needs for uniforms/clothing, fees, study/travel overseas, books, equipment/living expenses and excursions; and to people starting work for work clothes, fees, books and equipment/instruments.

Annual grant total

Financial information for the year 2012 was the latest available at the time of writing (August 2014).

In 2012, the foundation had an income of £61 and a total expenditure of £100. We estimate that the total grant awarded to individuals for educational purposes was approximately £50.

Applications

In writing to the correspondent. Applications can be submitted either directly by the individual or through the individual's school/college or an educational welfare agency. Applications are considered three times per year.

The Rowlandson and Eggleston Relief-in-Need Charity

£1,000

Correspondent: Peter Vaux, Administrator, Clowbeck Farm, Barton, Richmond DL10 6HP (01325 377236; email: petervaux@brettanbymanor.co.uk)

CC Number: 515647

Eligibility

People with a disability who are in education in the parishes of Barton and Newton Morrell.

Types of grants

One-off grants of £100 to £500 for educational expenses in cases of need. Expenses can include those towards uniforms/clothing, fees, study/travel abroad, books, equipment/instruments and maintenance/living expenses.

Annual grant total

In 2013/14 the charity had an income of £4,500 and a total expenditure of £3,000. We estimate around £1,000 was given to individuals for educational purposes.

Applications

In writing to the correspondent including details of circumstances and specific need(s), for consideration throughout the year. Applications may be submitted directly by the individual, through a social worker, Citizens Advice or other welfare agency or any third party.

Other information

The charity also provides other facilities and makes grants to individuals for social welfare purposes.

York Children's Trust

£6,700

Correspondent: Margaret Brien, Administrator, 29 Whinney Lane, Harrogate HG2 9LS (01423 504765)

CC Number: 222279

Eligibility

Children and young people under 25 who live within 20 miles of York.

Types of grants

One-off grants of between £100 to £300 are awarded to:
▶ Schoolchildren for uniforms/clothing, equipment/instruments and excursions
▶ College students for study/travel overseas, equipment/instruments, maintenance/living expenses and childcare
▶ Undergraduates for study/travel overseas, excursions and childcare
▶ Vocational students for uniforms/clothing, fees, study/travel overseas, excursions and childcare
▶ Mature students for childcare
▶ People starting work
▶ Those with special educational needs for uniforms/clothing

Preference is given to schoolchildren with serious family difficulties so that the child has to be educated away from home and to people with special educational needs who have been referred by a paediatrician or educational psychiatrist.

Annual grant total

In 2012 the trust had assets of £2.2 million and an income of £93,000. Grants were awarded totalling £49,000, of which educational grants to individuals accounted for £100 and 'Travel and Fostering Talents' grants

another £6,600. The majority of funding was awarded to educational, social welfare, medical, youth and playgroup organisations, though individuals also received £10,400 in grants for social welfare and medical needs.

At the time of writing (July 2014) this was the latest financial information available for the trust.

Exclusions

Grants are not available for private education or postgraduate studies.

Applications

Application forms are available from the correspondent and can be submitted directly by the individual or by the individual's school, college or educational welfare agency, or a third party such as a health visitor or social worker. Applications are considered quarterly, normally in January, April, July and October, and should be received one month beforehand.

Acaster

Knowles Educational Foundation (Acaster Malbis Knowles Education Foundation)

£1,500

Correspondent: J. Jenkinson-Smith, Administrator, The Granary, Mill Lane, Acaster Malbis, York YO23 2UL (01904 706153; email: joycejsmith21@gmail.com)

CC Number: 529183

Eligibility

Children and young people in need living in the ancient parish of Acaster Malbis which includes part of the village of Naburn.

Types of grants

Grants to schoolchildren (other than elementary school pupils), people in further/higher education, individuals undertaking apprenticeships. Awards can be given towards fees, maintenance expenses, travel, other educational essentials. Previously grants have been provided for swimming lessons, field trips and visits abroad.

Annual grant total

In 2013 the foundation had an income of £3,000 and an expenditure of £1,700. We estimate the annual total of grants to individuals to be around £1,500.

Applications

In writing to the correspondent, including invoices for expenses. As each case is considered on its own merit, applicants are asked to supply as much

information as possible. Applications are considered in March, June and October.

Other information

Grants may also be awarded to organisations.

Harrogate

The Haywra Crescent Educational Trust Fund

£1,900

Correspondent: The Student Support Manager, North Yorkshire County Council, Corporate Accountancy Strategic Services, County Hall, Northallerton DL7 8AL (01609 780780)

CC Number: 1042141

Eligibility

People who live in the Harrogate Borough Council area and are in any form of post-16 education.

Types of grants

One-off grants towards books, equipment or travel.

Annual grant total

In 2012/13 the trust had an income of £11,300 and a total expenditure of £10,000. Our research in previous years found that: 'the trust gives about 17% of its annual income to individuals and about 68% to organisations with the balance being used for further investment.' We therefore estimate that educational grants to individuals totalled around £1,900.

Applications

On a form available from the correspondent. Students in post-16 educational courses at secondary schools in Harrogate or at Harrogate College are expected to make their application through their institution. The deadline for applications usually falls at the end of November, for consideration in December.

Kirkbymoorside

The John Stockton Educational Foundation

£800

Correspondent: Elizabeth Kendall, Clerk, Park Garth, School Lane, Nawton, York YO62 7SF (01439 771575; email: marykendall@hotmail.co.uk)

CC Number: 529642

Eligibility

Students and apprentices aged 16 to 25 who live in certain parishes in the

Kirkbymoorside area and have done so for at least two years.

Types of grants

Grants range from £30 to £60. Apprentices can receive help towards the cost of tools. Vocational students and students at university can receive grants towards books, fees, living expenses and study or travel abroad. Students may apply for three years.

Annual grant total

This charity generally has an income of around £900 and a total expenditure of £800. These figures are unlikely to change in any significant way.

Exclusions

Sixth form students do not qualify for grants.

Applications

On a form available from the correspondent, to be submitted by the first week of June or December. Applications can be made directly by the applicant or parent.

Lothersdale

Raygill Trust

£2,500

Correspondent: Roger Armstrong, Armstrong Wood and Bridgman, 12–16 North Street, Keighley, West Yorkshire BD21 3SE (01535 613660; email: mail@awbclaw.co.uk)

CC Number: 249199

Eligibility

Full-time students on a first degree or equivalent course at a university or college who live in the ecclesiastical parish of Lothersdale.

Types of grants

Grants to students in the first three years of their further education.

Annual grant total

In 2012/13 the trust had an income of £11,700 and a total expenditure of £10,400. We estimate that £2,500 was granted to individuals for educational purposes. The trust also made grants to organisations in the Lothersdale area, and to individuals for social welfare purposes.

Applications

In writing to the correspondent. Applicants who do not send thank you letters will not be considered for future grants.

Newton upon Rawcliffe

Poad's Educational Foundation

£3,000

Correspondent: P. Lawrence, Administrator, 23 Larchfield, Stockton Lane, York YO31 1JS (01904 415526)

Eligibility

People from a low income background who are under 25 and live in the ancient town of Newton upon Rawcliffe.

Types of grants

Grants towards course fees, travel, books, incidental expenses and maintenance costs. Grants are towards a broad range of educational needs including support for courses that are not formal and after-school swimming classes.

Annual grant total

In 2012/13 the foundation had an income and expenditure of £3,300. Grants totalled around £3,000.

Applications

In writing to the correspondent.

Scarborough

The Scarborough Municipal Charity

£6,500

Correspondent: Elaine Greening, Administrator, Flat 2, 126 Falsgrave road, Scarborough YO12 5BE (01723 375256; email: scar.municipalcharity@yahoo.co.uk)

CC Number: 217793

Eligibility

People who have live in the borough of Scarborough for at least five years.

Types of grants

Small grants can be given towards general education or training needs and purchase of necessities, including books, fees, uniforms, travel, equipment, maintenance/living expenses and excursions. According to our research, college, undergraduate and mature students and people in vocational training can be supported.

Annual grant total

The latest financial accounts were not available to view at the time of writing (July 2014). In 2013 the charity had an income of £181,000 and a total expenditure of 119,000. In the past five years grants to individuals have totalled

on average around £13,100. We estimate that about £6,500 is awarded in individual grants for educational purposes each year.

Exclusions

In exceptional circumstances support may be given to someone resident outside of the area of benefit or living in the borough temporarily.

Applications

Application forms are available from the correspondent. Our research suggests that they are considered quarterly and the subcommittee of three trustees interview each applicant.

Other information

The trustees are responsible for both the almshouse and the relief-in-need branches of the charity. The majority of trusts expenditure is spent in direct charitable activities maintaining the almshouses and providing services to the tenants.

Scarborough United Scholarships Foundation

£7,400

Correspondent: Anne Morley, Secretary, 169 Scalby Road, Scarborough YO12 6TB (01723 375908)

CC Number: 529678

Eligibility

People under the age of 25 who live in the former borough of Scarborough and have attended school in the area for at least three years.

Types of grants

Grants are available to schoolchildren, college/university students (including mature students), vocational students and people starting work/entering a trade. Support is given towards the cost of uniforms/clothing, books, equipment/instruments, study/travel overseas and educational outings/visits.

Our research suggests that grants are usually given to those at Scarborough Sixth Form College, Yorkshire Coast College or a college of further education 'where a student is following a course which is a non-advanced course.' Occasionally, loans can be made or second degree and postgraduate students supported.

Annual grant total

In 2012/13 the foundation had an income of £8,000 and an expenditure of £7,600. We estimate the annual total of grants to be around £7,400.

Exclusions

According to our research educational fees are not supported.

Applications

Our research shows that the foundation mostly deals with local colleges to ensure potential applicants are made aware of when and how to apply.

Swaledale

Muker Educational Trust

£5,800

Correspondent: Michael McGarry, Administrator, 21 Galgate, Barnard Castle DL12 8EQ (01388 603073; email: office@mbmcgarry.co.uk)

CC Number: 1002488

Eligibility

People who live in the ecclesiastical parish of Swaledale with Arkengarthdale.

Types of grants

The trust offers one-off and recurrent grants to schoolchildren, further/higher education students and people in training. Our research suggests that support ranges from around £15 to £400 and can be given towards books, equipment/instruments, fees, study/ travel overseas and other educational needs.

Annual grant total

In 2012/13 the trust had an income of £6,700 and an expenditure of £6,000. We estimate the annual total of grants to individuals to be around £5,800.

Exclusions

Grants are not usually given for maintenance, clothing or living expenses.

Applications

Application forms can be requested from the correspondent. All communications should be accompanied with an sae. Applications should be submitted by 1 November either directly by the individual or through an organisation such as school or educational welfare agency, if applicable.

Wensleydale

Yorebridge Educational Foundation

£7,000

Correspondent: Robert Tunstall, Treasurer, Kiln Hill, Hawes, North Yorkshire DL8 3RA (01969 667428)

CC Number: 518826

Eligibility

Students under 25 years of age undertaking full-time courses of further education. Students or parents must live in Wensleydale, North Yorkshire. Preference is given to those with parents resident in the parishes of Askrigg, Bainbridge, Hawes, High Abbotside or Low Abbotside.

Types of grants

One-off grants, typically of £200 a year, towards books, fees and living expenses.

Annual grant total

In 2011/12 the foundation had an income of £21,000 and a total expenditure of £15,700. We estimate that educational grants to individuals totalled £7,000, with funding also awarded to organisations.

At the time of writing (July 2014) this was the most recent financial information available for the foundation.

Applications

Applications are considered in September/October each year and should be submitted in writing directly by the individual.

York

The Company of Merchant Taylors of the City of York (Merchant Taylors – York)

£13,700

Correspondent: Nevil Pearce, Clerk, U. H. Y. Calvert Smith, 31 St Saviourgate, York YO1 8NQ (01904 557570; fax: 01904 557571; email: clerk@merchant-taylors-york.org; website: www.merchant-taylors-york.org)

CC Number: 229067

Eligibility

Young people in education or training in the fields of arts, music and craftsmanship who live in York and the surrounding area.

Types of grants

Bursaries, prizes and other grants of up to £1,000 are available for a wide range of activities under the headings of arts, music and craftsmanship to develop applicants' skills and enhance their career prospects.

Annual grant total

In 2012/13 the trust had assets of £476,000 and an income of £89,000. A total of £12,700 was awarded in individual grants and £1,000 in student prizes. The York College bursaries (each £200) were awarded to 12 especially

nominated students across the College's Art and Design Division.

Applications

Application forms can be downloaded from the trust's website or requested from the correspondent. Applications should be submitted at any time to the following address: The Clerk, Charitable Request, Merchant Taylors Hall, Aldwark, York YO1 7BX.

Other information

The trust also maintains the company's hall and premises, almshouses, documents, runs the guild, pays pensions to tailors in the area of benefit and supports individuals and organisations for welfare causes.

The Micklegate Strays Charity

£25

Correspondent: Roger Lee, Trustee, 29 Albemarle Road, York YO23 1EW (01904 653698)

CC Number: 237179

Eligibility

Freemen or dependents of freemen, under 25, of the city of York and who are now living in the Micklegate Strays ward. (This is now defined as the whole of the part of the city of York to the west of the River Ouse.) The applicant's parents must be living in the above area.

Types of grants

Grants of £30 a year are given to schoolchildren and people starting work for uniforms, clothing, books, equipment, instruments, fees, maintenance and living expenses. Grants are also given to students in further or higher education towards study or travel abroad.

Annual grant total

In 2012/13 the charity had an income of £900 and a total expenditure of £50. Grants are given for educational and welfare purposes.

Applications

Applications can be submitted directly by the individual or by a parent. They must include the date at which the parent became a freeman of the city and the address of the parent. Applications are considered twice a year.

Other information

The trust was created by the 1907 Micklegate Strays Act. The City of York agreed to pay the freemen £1,000 a year in perpetuity for extinguishing their rights over Micklegate Stray. This sum has been reduced due to the forced divestment of the trust government stock, following the Charities Act of 1992.

York City Charities

£280

Correspondent: Richard Watson, Clerk, Crombie Wilkinson, 17–19 Clifford Street, York YO1 9RJ (01904 624185; email: r.watson@crombiewilkinson.co.uk)

CC Number: 224227

Eligibility

People in need who live within the pre-1996 York city boundaries (the area within the city walls).

Types of grants

Our research suggests that educational grants can be made to mature students for general purposes from Lady Hewley's Fund and to young people under the age of 21 for general educational purposes (except school trips) from Advancement Branch funds.

Annual grant total

In 2013 the charity had assets of £1.2 million and an income of £237,000. Grants made to individuals totalled £580. The charity has both restricted and endowments funds. We estimate that educational grants totalled around £280.

Applications

In writing to the correspondent. The trustees meet quarterly.

Other information

Most of the charitable expenditure is allocated for the maintenance of almshouses (£189,000 in 2013).

Northumber-land

Coates Educational Foundation

£7,800

Correspondent: Andrew Morgan, Trustee, 14 Bell Villas, Ponteland, Newcastle upon Tyne NE20 9BE (01661 871012; email: amorgan@nicholsonmorgan.co.uk)

CC Number: 505906

Eligibility

People under the age of 25 who live in the parishes of Ponteland, Stannington, Heddon-on-the-Wall, and the former district of Newburn or are current/former pupils of the Richard Coates Church of England Voluntary Aided Middle School.

Types of grants

One-off grants and bursaries to help with the cost of books, equipment/materials, clothing, educational outings, maintenance and fees. Support can be given to schoolchildren and students at college/university. People starting work/entering a trade can also be helped with the cost of books, equipment/instruments, clothing or travel.

Annual grant total

The latest financial information at the time of writing (July 2014) was from 2012. In 2012 the foundation had an income of £18,800 and an expenditure of £15,700. We have estimated the annual total of grants to individuals to be around £7,800.

Applications

Application forms are available from the correspondent. They can be submitted directly by the individual and are normally considered in February and June.

Other information

The foundation also supports local organisations and schools.

The Eleemosynary Charity of Giles Heron

£6,000

Correspondent: George Benson, Trustee, Brunton House, Wall, Hexham, Northumberland NE46 4EJ (01434 681203)

CC Number: 224157

Eligibility

People in need who live in the ancient parish of Simonburn.

Types of grants

One-off grants according to need towards the cost of education, training, apprenticeship and equipment for those starting work and for educational visits abroad.

Annual grant total

In 2012/13 the charity had an income of £13,600 and a total expenditure of £24,000. Grants are made for both educational and welfare purposes to both individuals and organisations. We estimate grants to individuals for educational purposes to be around £6,000.

Applications

In writing to the correspondent directly by the individual.

Other information

Individual grants are also made for welfare purposes.

Rothbury Educational Trust

£5,000

Correspondent: Susan Rogerson, 1 Gallow Law, Alwinton, Morpeth NE65 7BQ (01669 650390)

CC Number: 505713

Eligibility

Higher education students between the age of 18 and 25 who live or have attended school in the parishes of Cartington, Hepple, Hesleyhurst, Rothbury, Snitter, Thropton and Tosson and the parts of the parishes of Brinkburn, Hollinghill and Netherton that lie within the ancient parish of Rothbury.

Types of grants

Small grants towards general educational expenses, including the cost of books, fees, equipment/instruments, clothing and so on.

Annual grant total

In 2012/13 the trust had an income of £7,200 and an expenditure of £5,100. We estimate the annual total of grants to be around £5,000.

Applications

In writing to the correspondent. Our research shows that applications are normally considered in late August/early September and grants are usually advertised in the local newspapers.

Allendale

Allendale Exhibition Endowment

£6,700

Correspondent: Joseph Robinson, Trustee, Amberlea, Catton, Hexham, Northumberland NE47 9QS (01434683586)

CC Number: 505515

Eligibility

People under the age of 25 who live, or whose parents live, in the parishes of Allendale and West Allen.

Types of grants

Grants ranging between £50 and £150 are given to students in further/higher education and training and people starting work. Schoolchildren and individuals studying the arts or music studies can also be supported. Funding is given towards the cost of books, equipment/instruments, maintenance, educational outings or study/travel abroad and student exchange.

Annual grant total

In 2012/13 the trust had an income of £8,800 and a total expenditure of £6,900. We estimate the annual total of grants to be around £6,700.

Applications

In writing to the correspondent. Applications can be submitted directly by the individual and the deadline is normally at the end of October. Usually, application forms are also placed in the library, post office and local shops.

Blyth

Blyth Valley Trust for Youth

£4,600

Correspondent: Nathan Rogerson, Blyth Valley Arts and Leisure, Concordia Leisure Centre, Forum Way, Cramlington NE23 6YB (01670 542222; email: nrogerson@bval.co.uk)

CC Number: 514145

Eligibility

Children and young people under the age of 21 who live or attend school in the borough of Blyth Valley. The trust will provide financial assistance to attend a centre of excellence or similar establishment and further their activities in a chosen field of arts, sciences or sport. Applicants should be of amateur status.

Types of grants

Grants are provided to support activities in the fields of arts, music, sciences or sport/physical recreation. Our research shows that the trust awards one-off grants, usually between £50 and £250. Support may only be given to those who are able to identify specific centres of excellence which they will be attending.

Annual grant total

In 2012/13 the trust had an income of £260 and an expenditure of £4,800. We have estimated the annual total of grants to be around £4,600.

Applications

Application forms can be requested from the correspondent and can be submitted either directly by the individual or by a school/college. Applicants are requested to include full details of the activity and provide references. Our research indicates that applicants should apply early (preferably before February each year) in time for the trustees' meeting, usually held in April.

Haydon Bridge

Shaftoe Educational Foundation

£17,000 (40 grants)

Correspondent: Peter Fletcher, The Clerk, Chesterwood Grange, Chesterwood, Hexham, Northumberland NE47 6HW (01434688872; email: info@shaftoecharities.org.uk; website: www.shaftoecharities.org.uk)

CC Number: 528101

Eligibility

People in further/higher education or vocational training who live, or whose parents live, in the parish of Haydon.

Types of grants

One-off and recurrent grants in the range of about £400 are available to further/higher education students (including mature students) and to people in vocational training or undertaking apprenticeships. Support is available towards the cost of fees, equipment/instruments, tools, books, clothing or other necessities, also study/travel overseas for educational purposes.

Annual grant total

In 2012/13 the foundation had assets of £5.8 million, an income of £146,000 and a total charitable expenditure of £49,000. Grants were made to 40 individuals in education totalling £17,000.

Applications

Application forms can be downloaded from the foundation's website or requested from the correspondent. The trustees meet three times a year, normally in March, July and November.

Other information

The foundation also makes yearly payments to the Almshouse Charity of John Shaftoe (at least £1,700 a year) and supports schools and organisations in the parish of Haydon or local groups seeking support for educational initiatives.

Kirkwhelpington

The Kirkwhelpington Educational Charity

£5,000

Correspondent: Helen Cowan, Administrator, 11 Meadowlands, Kirkwhelpington, Newcastle upon Tyne NE19 2RX (01830 540374)

CC Number: 506869

Eligibility

Young people under the age of 25 who live, or whose parents live, in the civil parish of Kirkwhelpington.

Types of grants

Usually one-off grants in the range of £50–£300 towards education and social or physical training. Our research suggests that assistance to help with the cost of equipment, books, transport and extra courses has been given to individuals going on to some form of training or further education after school. Schoolchildren have also received help with the cost of educational outings and special tuition.

Annual grant total

In 2013 the charity had an income of £6,300 and an expenditure of £10,500, which is considerably higher than in the previous years. We estimate that about £5,000 was awarded in grants to individuals.

Exclusions

Grants are not provided where support is available from the local authority.

Applications

In writing to the correspondent. Candidates should include details of how the money is to be spent, other possible sources of funding secured or applied to, and provide receipts of items/services purchased (where possible). Applications are usually considered in February, May and October.

Other information

Grants are also given to schools and voluntary organisations in the parish providing educational and training facilities for people under the age of 25, where support is not given by the local authorities.

South Yorkshire

The Aston-With-Aughton Educational Foundation

£1,800

Correspondent: James Nuttall, Trustee, 3 Rosegarth Avenue, Aston, Sheffield S26 2DB (01142 876047)

CC Number: 529424

Eligibility

Disadvantaged children in education (other than primary) who/whose parents live in the area of Aston-With-Aughton and who have attended a public elementary school for at least three years.

Types of grants

One-off and recurrent grants are given towards general educational needs, where these are not supported by the local authorities.

Annual grant total

In 2013 the foundation had an income of £8,500 and an expenditure of £3,700, which is the lowest in the past five years. We estimate that individual grants totalled around £1,800.

Applications

In writing to the correspondent. Applications can be made by individuals directly or by their headmaster. Awards are normally considered in March and September, but in urgent cases meetings can be held throughout the year. Applicants are requested to include some details of the purpose of the grant and specify the estimated costs involved.

Other information

Grants may also be made to organisations.

Bolsterstone Educational Charity

£2,500

Correspondent: Cliff North, 5 Pennine View, Stocksbridge, Sheffield S36 1ER (01142 882757; email: cliff.north@virgin. net)

CC Number: 529371

Eligibility

Children and young people under the age of 25 who live in the parishes of St Mary's, Bolsterstone and St Matthias', Stocksbridge.

Types of grants

Grants are given towards books, equipment/instruments and other educational needs, not normally provided by the local authorities.

Annual grant total

In 2012/13 the charity had an income of £10,200 and an expenditure of £5,100. It also supports local schools. We estimate the annual total of grants to individuals total to be around £2,500.

Exclusions

No grants are given to mature students or people starting work.

Applications

In writing to the correspondent. Our research suggests that the applications can be submitted directly by the individual for consideration at the beginning of March, July or November.

Other information

The charity also supports a number of local schools.

The Elmhirst Trust

£800

Correspondent: John Butt, Administrator, 2 Paddock Close, Staincross, Barnsley S75 6LH

CC Number: 701369

Eligibility

People (normally over the age of 30) resident in the boroughs of Barnsley, Doncaster and Rotherham who seek personal and professional development after a change in their lives but are facing financial barriers. Proposals which would benefit the community as a whole are given preference. Our research suggests that the trust strongly prefers to support people who have had little or no post-16 education and are involved in the voluntary sector. Applicants may be undertaking vocational training or retraining in any subject.

Types of grants

Small, one-off grants are awarded towards college or training fees, books and equipment, materials, clothing, travel costs, childcare and any other necessities which can help individuals to pursue their education or training and subsequently move into employment.

Annual grant total

In 2012/13 the trust had an income of £5,000 and an expenditure of £900, which is lower than in previous years. We estimate the annual total of grants to be around £800.

Applications

In writing to the correspondent. Applications should outline what impact the support from the trust would make.

The Robert Woods Exhibition Foundation

£1,000

Correspondent: Dave Telford, Administrator, 15 Woodford Road, Barnby Dun, Doncaster DN3 1BN (01302 883496)

CC Number: 529415

Eligibility

Students in higher education who live in the ecclesiastical parish of Kirk Sandall or Edenthorpe. Applicants must be resident in either parish at the date of application.

Types of grants

Grants of £20 to £50 a year to help with the cost of books for first degree students.

Annual grant total

The foundation has an annual income and expenditure of about £1,000.

Applications

On a form available from local secondary schools or the correspondent. Applications must be submitted by 30 August, for consideration in September.

The Sheffield Bluecoat and Mount Pleasant Educational Foundation

£17,300 (33 grants)

Correspondent: Godfrey Smallman, Administrator, Wrigleys Solicitors, Fountain Precinct, Balm Green, Sheffield S1 1JA (01142 675588; fax: 01142 763176)

CC Number: 529351

Eligibility

People under the age of 25 who have lived within a 20-mile radius of Sheffield Town Hall for at least three years and are in need.

Types of grants

One-off or recurrent grants of can be made for general educational purposes, including necessities, clothing and outfits, equipment/instruments, maintenance expenses, fees, gap-year opportunities, study/travel overseas and study of music, arts, sports or physical education. Support is given to schoolchildren, further/higher education students or people in training and people starting work/entering a trade. In special cases private schooling costs could be assisted.

Annual grant total

In 2012/13 the foundation had assets of £1.4 million, an income of £60,000 and awarded £36,000 in grants. 33 individuals were supported totalling £17,300.

Applications

In writing to the correspondent. Applications should also include all the supporting documents and evidence of financial need. The trustees meet twice a year, usually in April and September.

Other information

The trust also supports local organisations (£19,000 in in 2012/13).

The Sheffield West Riding Charitable Society Trust

£2,000

Correspondent: Malcolm Fair, Diocesan Secretary, Diocesan Church House, 95–99 Effingham Street, Rotherham S65 1BL (01709 309100; email: malcolm. fair@sheffield.anglican.org; website: www.sheffield.anglican.org)

CC Number: 1002026

Eligibility

Clergy children at school and in further education in the diocese of Sheffield.

Types of grants

Only a small proportion of the grants are educational and are given to help with the cost of books, clothing and other essentials.

Annual grant total

In 2013 the trust had an income of £12,700 and a total expenditure of £4,700. We estimate grants to individuals for educational purposes was around £2,000.

Applications

On a form available from the correspondent.

Other information

Welfare grants are also made to the clergy, house-keepers and disadvantaged families in the diocese.

The Swann-Morton Foundation

£6,500

Correspondent: Michael Hirst, Swann-Morton Ltd, Owlerton Green, Sheffield S6 2BJ (01142 344231)

CC Number: 271925

Eligibility

People studying or working in the fields of surgery and medicine, particularly concerned with physical and mental disabilities.

Types of grants

One-off and recurrent grants according to need are available to students of medicine and surgery for general educational expenses and research projects.

Annual grant total

In 2012/13 the foundation had assets of £101,000 and an income of £50,000. A total of £51,000 was spent in charitable expenditure, of which £6,500 was awarded in student grants and electives.

Applications

In writing to the correspondent.

Other information

The foundation welcomes applications from individual students, charities and hospitals.

Armthorpe

Armthorpe Poors Estate Charity

£2,500

Correspondent: Tracey Ellis, 6 The Lings, Armthorpe, Doncaster, South Yorkshire DN3 3RH (01302 355180)

CC Number: 226123

Eligibility

People who are in need and live in Armthorpe.

Types of grants

One-off and recurrent grants of £50 minimum to schoolchildren who are in need for educational outings and to undergraduates for books.

Annual grant total

In 2012/13 the charity had both an income and total expenditure of £10,000. The charity gives to both individuals and organisations for educational and social welfare purposes. We estimate the total grants given to individuals for educational purposes was around £2,500.

Applications

Contact the clerk by telephone who will advise if a letter of application is needed. Applicants outside of Armthorpe will be declined. Undergraduates are required to complete an application form, available from the correspondent, and return it by 31 August.

Barnsley

The Shaw Lands Trust

£9,400 (30 grants)

Correspondent: Jill Leece, Clerk, 35 Church Street, Barnsley, South Yorkshire S70 2AP (01226 213434)

CC Number: 224590

Eligibility

Children and young people under the age of 25 who live within the Barnsley Metropolitan Borough or have attended school there for at least two years. Preference is given to individuals from households with low income.

Types of grants

Grants in the range of £300 – £750. Support can be given to schoolchildren, further/higher education students or people starting work/entering a trade for various educational needs, including books, necessities, equipment/ instruments, tools, outfits/clothing, uniforms, travel in the UK or abroad in pursuance of education and study of music or other arts.

Annual grant total

In 2012/13 the trust had assets of £1.3 million, an income of £46,000 and a total charitable expenditure of £32,000. Educational grants were awarded to 30 students totalling £9,400.

Applications

In writing to the correspondent. The trustees meet twice a year, in April and October.

Other information

At least two thirds of the charity's income is spent supporting local charitable organisations working for young people (£22,600 in in 2012/13) with the remainder being allocated to assist individual students.

Beighton

Beighton Relief-in-Need Charity

£1,500

Correspondent: Diane Rodgers, Trustee, 41 Collingbourne Avenue, Sothall, Sheffield S20 2QR (01142 692875; email: beigtonrelief@hotmail.co.uk)

CC Number: 225416

Eligibility

Students who live in the former parish of Beighton and are in need.

Types of grants

One-off grants according to need.

Annual grant total

In 2013 this charity had an income of £6,700 and a total expenditure of £6,500. It gives to both individuals and organisations for social welfare and educational purposes. We estimate that grants for educational purposes awarded to individuals totalled around £1,500.

Applications

In writing to the correspondent. Applications can be submitted directly by the individual or through a social worker, Citizens Advice, other welfare agency or a third party such as a relative, neighbour or trustee.

Bramley

The Bramley Poor's Allotment Trust

£1,400

Correspondent: Marian Houseman, Administrator, 9 Horton Rise, Rodley, Leeds LS13 1PH (01132 360115)

CC Number: 224522

Eligibility

People in need who live in the ancient township of Bramley, especially people who are elderly, poor and sick.

Types of grants

One-off grants between £40 and £120.

Annual grant total

In 2013 the trust had an income of £3,900 and a total expenditure of £3,000. Grants given to individuals for educational purposes totalled £1,400.

Applications

In writing to the correspondent. The trust likes applications to be submitted through a recognised referral agency (social worker, Citizens Advice, doctor, headmaster or minister). They are considered monthly.

Epworth

Epworth Charities

£500

Correspondent: Katie-Jo Hardacre, Administrator, 34 Low Street, Haxey, Doncaster, South Yorkshire DN9 2LE (01427 330267; email: katesowerby@hotmail.com)

CC Number: 219744

Eligibility

People in need who live in Epworth.

Types of grants

One-off and recurrent grants in the range of £50 and £250 for a specific need. Grants are made to schoolchildren for equipment/instruments and college students, undergraduates, vocational students and mature students for books.

Annual grant total

In 2012/13 the charity had an income of £2,200 and an expenditure of £390, which is the lowest in the past five years. We estimate the annual total of educational grants to be around £150.

Applications

In writing to the correspondent. Applications can be made directly by the individual and are considered on an ongoing basis.

Other information

Grants are also made for welfare purposes.

Sheffield

Church Burgesses Educational Foundation

£117,000

Correspondent: G. J. Smallman, The Law Clerk, 3rd Floor Fountain Precinct, Balm Green, Sheffield S1 2JA (01142 675594; fax: 01142 673176; email: sheffieldchurchburgesses@wrigleys.co.uk; website: www.sheffieldchurchburgesses.org.uk)

CC Number: 529357

Eligibility

People under the age of 25 who/whose parents have lived in Sheffield for at least three years. Generally individuals below tertiary education level.

Types of grants

Grants can be given for a wide variety of general educational needs, such as books, clothing, equipment and other essentials for schoolchildren. Support for attending independent schools can only be made where the need is clearly demonstrated (for example, unexpected familial or financial difficulties, or special needs of the child).

Special grants are given for one-off special projects, church-based youth and education work, gap-year opportunities, summer schools and festivals and extra-curricular activities in arts, music, sports and so on.

Assistance may occasionally be available for those at tertiary education, although no grants are made where a local authority grant is available. Postgraduates could only receive funding if there is a special need for retraining or education in a different subject.

Annual grant total

At the time of writing (July 2014) the latest financial information available was from 2012. In 2012 the foundation had assets of £282,000 and an income of £283,000. Grants to individuals totalled £117,000, consisting of £98,000 in educational grants and £18,900 in special grants.

Exclusions

Individuals based in Sheffield on a temporary basis to attend an educational establishment are not eligible.

As a general rule higher education courses are not supported.

Applications

Application forms are available from the foundation's website or can be requested from the correspondent. The trustees usually meet four times a year, in January, April, August (emergency cases) and October, but grants could be made outside these times as well. Applications will need to include confirmation of attendance at an educational institution, a reference from a music teacher (if applicable), information of the educational trip to be undertaken and other relevant supporting documentation.

Other information

Grants are also made to organisations working with young people, to church schools, bands, orchestras, choirs and for church organised youth activities. Grants to organisations and groups totalled £226,000 in 2012.

The foundation's website notes that the trustees are 'developing schemes with training organisations with a view to helping young men and women through apprenticeships or internships in trades and crafts.'

Sir Samuel Osborn's Deed of Gift Relief Fund

£3,800

Correspondent: Sue Wragg, Fund Manager, South Yorkshire Community Foundation, Unit 3 – G1 Building, 6 Leeds Road, Attercliffe, Sheffield S9 3TY (01142 424294; fax: 01142 424605; email: grants@sycf.org.uk; website: www.sycf.org.uk/apply_for_a_grant/sir_samuel_osborn__s_deed_of_gift_relief_fund)

CC Number: 1140947

Eligibility

Residents of Sheffield, with some preference for former employees of the Samuel Osborn Company (or one if its subsidiaries) and their descendants.

Types of grants

Grants in the range of £250–£1,000 are available towards the costs associated with any training or education, for example, books, equipment and living costs.

Annual grant total

In 2012/13 the fund had assets of £1,300 and an income of £5,000. Grants from the fund totalled £4,800. We have estimated that out of this sum around £3,800 was awarded to individuals for educational purposes.

Exclusions

Individuals with large personal reserves of money will not be funded.

Applications

Application forms can be downloaded from the fund's website or requested from the correspondent. Candidates with a connection to the Samuel Osborn Company should include written evidence. Decisions are normally made within 12 weeks following the application.

Note: due to a high demand for the fund, applications are limited to one grant per year.

Applicants are encouraged to contact the grants team with further enquiries.

Other information

The fund is now administered by the South Yorkshire Community Foundation.

Grants are also made for social welfare purposes.

Sheffield Grammar School Exhibition Foundation

£72,000 (78 grants)

Correspondent: G. J. Smallman, Clerk, 3rd Floor, Fountain Precinct, Balm Green, Sheffield S1 2JA (01142 675594; fax: 01142 675630)

CC Number: 529372

Eligibility

People who have lived within the city of Sheffield boundary for at least three years (excluding residency for educational purposes). There is a preference for people who are attending/ have attended King Edward VII School for at least two years.

Types of grants

Grants are awarded for general educational purposes, including the course costs, study/travel overseas, training and retraining courses, medical electives, childcare costs, field trips, gap-year and character building opportunities, sports or musical training. Support can be given to schoolchildren, further/higher education students and people entering a trade/occupation towards outfits, clothing, tools, books, equipment and instruments.

Annual grant total

In 2012/13 the foundation had assets of £2.7 million, an income of £148,000 and a charitable expenditure of £94,000. Grants to individuals totalled £72,000.

Applications

The trustees' annual report notes that:

Applications are accepted from a wide range of individuals and organisations. Some of the grant programmes have application forms and financial eligibility documentation which requires completion, other applications are taken by letter with supporting documentation.

To obtain further guidance on the application procedure contact the correspondent. The trustees meet in March, June, September and December to consider applications.

Other information

The foundation also assists King Edward VII School of Sheffield where support is not provided by the local authority. Grants are made to organisations but the charity 'does not favour making long-term funding grants.' In 2012/13 a total of £22,000 was awarded in grants to organisations.

Teesside

The Hill Bursary

£4,500

Correspondent: Hugh McGouran, Administrator, Tees Valley Community Foundation, Wallace House, Falcon Court, Preston Farm Industrial Estate, Stockton-on-Tees TS18 3TX (01642 260860; email: info@ teesvalleyfoundation.org; website: www. teesvalleyfoundation.org)

CC Number: 1111222

Eligibility

People residing in Teesside Wide, including Hartlepool, Middlesbrough, Redcar and Cleveland and Stockton on Tees, who are intending to study business economics or accounts on a full-time course at a UK university. Decisions are made based on the A-level results and personal circumstances.

Types of grants

Bursary of £4,500 over three years.

Annual grant total

This fund is administered by the Tees Valley Community Foundation. Successful applicants receive £500 a term for the three years of their degree.

Applications

Application forms are available from the Tees Valley Community Foundation website, once the application round is open. They should normally be submitted by 29 June.

John Bloom Law Bursary

£6,000

Correspondent: Hugh McGouran, Administrator, Wallace House, Falcon Court, Preston Farm Industries, Estate, Stockton-on-Tees TS18 3TX (01642 260860; email: info@

teesvalleyfoundation.org; website: www. teesvalleyfoundation.org)

CC Number: 1111222

Eligibility

Students from Tees Valley studying law on a full-time undergraduate course at a UK university.

Types of grants

A bursary of up to £6,000 over three years.

Annual grant total

Payments are given each term totalling up to £6,000 over three years.

Applications

Application forms are available from the Tees Valley Community Foundation website, once the application round is open.

Other information

This fund is administrated by the Tees Valley Community Foundation.

Pursuit of Excellence – Sport

See entry on page 117

Tees Valley Community Foundation Bursary

£4,500

Correspondent: Hugh McGouran, Administrator, Wallace House, Falcon Court, Preston Farm Industries, Estate, Stockton-on-Tees TS18 3TX (01642 260860; email: info@ teesvalleyfoundation.org; website: www. teesvalleyfoundation.org)

CC Number: 1111222

Eligibility

Students from Tees Valley studying a full-time undergraduate degree at Teesside University. Decisions are made based on A-level (or equivalent) results, UCAS personal statement and financial situation.

Types of grants

Bursary of up to £4,500.

Annual grant total

Awards of up to £4,500 in total are available.

Applications

Application forms can be found on the Tees Valley Community Foundation website, once the application round begins.

Other information

This fund is administrated by the Tees Valley Community Foundation.

Teesside Power Fund Educational Bursary

£4,500

Correspondent: Hugh McGouran, Administrator, Tees Valley Community Foundation, Wallace House, Falcon Court, Preston Farm, Stockton-on-Tees TS18 3TX (01642 260860; email: info@ teesvalleyfoundation.org; website: www. teesvalleyfoundation.org)

CC Number: 1111222

Eligibility

Students who live in Coatham, Dormanstown, Eston, Grangetown, Kirkleatham, Newcomen, Normanby, South Bank or Teesville and wish to follow a full-time course at university in disciplines relevant to energy generation. Qualifying courses should incorporate some elements of the following disciplines: engineering, chemistry, physics or mathematics. Applicants are expected to show high academic achievements and have modest resources.

Types of grants

Bursary of £4,500 over three years.

Annual grant total

This fund is managed by Tees Valley Community Foundation. Grants are paid as £500 a term for three years.

Applications

Application forms are available from the Tees Valley Community Foundation website when the application round is open. They should normally be submitted by the end of June.

Other information

Recipients of this bursary are also encouraged to undertake temporary employment at the power station in Teesside in the summer holidays to get some more experience of the energy generation industry.

The Captain John Vivian Nancarrow Fund

£400

Correspondent: Richard Cross, Strategic Resources, PO Box 506, Middlesbrough, Cleveland TS1 9GA (01642 729558)

CC Number: 506937

Eligibility

Children and young people under the age of 25 living or working in Middlesbrough who are attending or have attended any of the following: Acklam Grange, Brackenhoe/Kings Academy, Hall Garth, Kings Manor, Langbaurgh/Keldholme/Unity City

Academy, Middlesbrough College or Teesside Tertiary College.

Types of grants

The fund provides scholarships, bursaries, maintenance allowances and grants to schoolchildren, students in higher/further education and people entering a trade/profession. Financial assistance is available towards fees, books, clothing, equipment/instruments, travel and educational outings/visits, study of music and other arts, educational research, recreational, social and physical training or in the event of sickness or disability.

Annual grant total

In 2012/13 the fund had an income of £400 and an expenditure of £500. We have estimated that the annual grants total was about £400.

Exclusions

According to our research, grants are not provided where statutory funding is available or to people who have already received a grant from Middlesbrough Council in the current financial year.

Applications

Application forms are available from the correspondent and can be submitted either directly by the individual or by a recommendation from the headteacher.

Other information

Our research suggests that, for the purposes of educational research, assistance may also be provided to people over the age of 25.

Hartlepool

The Preston Simpson and Sterndale Young Musicians Trust

£5,800

Correspondent: Christine Lowson, Hartlepool Borough Council, Civic Centre, Victoria Road, Hartlepool TS24 8AY (01429 523754; email: christine.lowson@hartlepool.gov.uk; website: www.hartlepool.gov.uk/ youngmusicianstrust)

CC Number: 512606

Eligibility

Young musicians between the ages of 15 and 25 who were born in the borough of Hartlepool or have a parent who has lived in the area for at least five years. The grant is designed to support those who have already achieved a good standard in their studies and wish to pursue a career in music. Applicants' achievements should be demonstrated by participation in concerts, membership in bands or orchestras, a minimum

standard of Grade V in the Associated Board Examination or equivalent qualification from Trinity College London and genuine intentions to use musical abilities in their future career (such as commitment to GCSE Music).

Types of grants

Scholarships to musicians studying music at any school, college or university.

Annual grant total

In 2012/13 the trust had an income of £8,200 and an expenditure of £6,000. We estimate the annual total of grants to be around £5,800.

Applications

Application forms and guidelines can be found on the trust's website or requested from the correspondent. Applicants should also provide two written references, one of which must be from music teacher or head of music. Potential candidates are invited for an audition. The deadlines for applications are usually in late autumn but for a current deadline consult the trust's website.

Middlesbrough

Middlesbrough Educational Trust Fund

£100

Correspondent: Richard Cross, Administrator, Strategic Resources, PO Box 500, Middlesbrough, Cleveland TS19GA (01642 729558)

CC Number: 532293

Eligibility

People under the age of 25 who live in Middlesbrough.

Types of grants

A maximum of £250 a year per individual in scholarships, bursaries, maintenance allowances and other financial assistance.

Annual grant total

In 2012/13 the fund had an income of £300 and an expenditure of £200. The fund also supports specified local schools, therefore we estimate the annual total of grants to individuals to be around £100.

Exclusions

Grants are not given where statutory funding is available or to people who have received a grant from Middlesbrough Council in the current financial year.

Applications

Application forms are available from the correspondent. Applicants should have an endorsement from their educational establishment or tutor. Applications are normally considered on a bi-monthly basis.

Other information

The fund aims to provide special benefits for the following educational establishments: Lawson County Infants School, Lawson County Junior School, Southlands County Secondary School. Only where the income cannot be usefully applied for the above mentioned schools, the money is used to support individuals.

Thornaby-on-Tees

Alderman Worsley Bursary

£4,500

Correspondent: Hugh McGouran, Administrator, Wallace House, Falcon Court, Preston Farm Industries, Estate, Stockton-on-Tees TS18 3TX (01642 260860; email: info@ teesvalleyfoundation.org; website: www. teesvalleyfoundation.org)

CC Number: 1111222

Eligibility

Students from Thornaby-on-Tees intending to study on a full-time undergraduate degree at any UK university.

Types of grants

Bursary of up to £4,500.

Annual grant total

Annual award of up to £4,500.

Applications

Application forms can be found on the Tees Valley Community Foundation website, once the application round begins.

Other information

This fund is administered by the Tees Valley Community Foundation.

Yarm

The Yarm Grammar School Trust

£400

Correspondent: Pupil Support, Stockton Borough Council, PO Box 228, Municipal Buildings, Church Road, Stockton-on-Tees TS18 1XE (01642 526604; email: schooladmissions@ stockton.gov.uk; website: www.stockton. gov.uk/childrenandyoungpeople/schools/ financialsupport)

CC Number: 514301

Eligibility

People under 25 years of age who live, or have a parent who lives, in the parish of Yarm and are studying or about to study at a university or a college of further education, etc.

Types of grants

Grants of around £100 are given to provide financial help, outfits, clothing, tools, musical instruments or books so people who leave school, university or any other educational establishment can prepare for, or enter, a profession or trade. Bursaries or maintenance allowances are also awarded to those travelling, whether abroad or in this country, in order to continue their education.

Annual grant total

In 2013/14 the trust had an income of £5,600 and a total expenditure of £700. We estimate that educational grants to individuals totalled £400, with funding also awarded to local schools.

Applications

On a form available to download from the Stockton-on-Tees Borough Council website. A letter of reference from a suitable referee should be submitted along with the form. Applications should be submitted directly by the individual by 31 May for consideration in July, or by 30 November for consideration in January. The Pupil Support Team welcomes telephone enquiries.

Tyne and Wear

The Cullercoats Educational Trust

£2,400

Correspondent: Helen Lawlan, Administrator, 66 Northfield Road, Gosforth, Newcastle upon Tyne NE3 3UN (email: helenlawlan@sky.com)

CC Number: 506817

Eligibility

People who live in the ecclesiastical parishes of St Paul, Whitley Bay and St George, Cullercoats.

Types of grants

Grants are made towards religious instruction in accordance with the doctrines of the Church of England and to promote the education, including social and physical training, of beneficiaries.

Annual grant total

In 2013/14 the trust had an income of £5,300 and a total expenditure of £5,000. We estimate that educational grants to individuals totalled £2,400, with funding also awarded to organisations.

Applications

By letter to the correspondent in February or August for consideration in March or September.

Charity of John McKie Elliott Deceased (The John McKie Elliot Trust for the Blind)

£220

Correspondent: Robert Walker, Trustee, 6 Manor House Road, Newcastle upon Tyne NE2 2LU (01912814657; email: bobwalker9@aol.com)

CC Number: 235075

Eligibility

People who are blind or have a visual impairment and live in Gateshead or Newcastle upon Tyne.

Types of grants

One-off and recurrent grants are given according to need for items, equipment or activities.

Annual grant total

At the time of writing (August 2014) the latest financial information available was from 2012. In 2012 the charity had an income of £1,300 and an expenditure of £470. Both the income and the charitable expenditure vary. We estimate that educational grants totalled around £220.

Applications

In writing to the correspondent.

Other information

The trust also gives grants to individuals in need.

The Sunderland Orphanage and Educational Foundation

£12,000

Correspondent: Peter Taylor, McKenzie Bell, 19 John Street, Sunderland SR1 1JG (01915 674857)

CC Number: 527202

Eligibility

Young people under 25 who are resident in or around Sunderland who have a parent who has disabilities or has died, or whose parents are divorced or legally separated.

Types of grants

(i) Maintenance payments and clothing for schoolchildren.

(ii) Help towards the cost of education, training, apprenticeship or equipment for those starting work.

(iii) Help with travel to pursue education, for the provision of athletic coaching and for the study of music and other arts.

Annual grant total

In 2012/13 the trust had an income of £24,000 and a total expenditure of over £24,000. The foundation makes grants to individuals for both education and welfare purposes. We estimate the total educational grants to be around £12,000.

Applications

Applications should be made in writing to the correspondent. They are considered every other month.

Newcastle upon Tyne

Newcastle upon Tyne Education Fund

£700

Correspondent: Aidan Jackson, Administrator, Room 505, Civic Centre, Barras Bridge, Newcastle upon Tyne NE99 1RD (01912 777510; email: aidan. jackson@newcastle.gov.uk)

CC Number: 518115

Eligibility

People under the age of 25 who/whose parents live in Newcastle upon Tyne and who received a secondary school education in the city. Applicants should be eligible for mandatory or discretionary awards from the local authority.

Types of grants

Grants of around £100–£200 can be awarded to schoolchildren, further/higher education students and people in vocational training. Support is given for equipment/instruments, books, extra-curricular activities, educational outings and study or travel abroad.

Annual grant total

In 2013/14 the fund had both an income and an expenditure of £1,400. We estimate that grants to individuals totalled around £700.

Exclusions

Grants are not given for fees, living expenses, childcare costs or any other non-educational needs.

Applications

In writing to the correspondent. Applications can be considered at any time and should include the candidate's date of birth, details of the secondary school attended and his/her home address in the city. Payments are normally made in a form of cheque to the school or a specific project organiser, not directly to the applicant.

Other information

Organisations may also be supported.

South Tyneside

Westoe Educational Charity

£500 (2 grants)

Correspondent: Debra Collins, BT South Tyneside, Hawthorn, Viking Business Park, Jarrow NE32 3DP (01914 246803)

CC Number: 1074869

Eligibility

People under the age of 25 who/whose parents live in the borough of South Teesside and who are in need of financial assistance.

Types of grants

One-off and recurrent grants, usually around £250, are available to schoolchildren, further/higher education students or people starting work/ entering a trade. Financial support is given towards the costs of uniforms/ clothing, books, equipment/instruments, maintenance/living expenses, travel, study/travel abroad or educational outings. Music and arts studies are also supported.

Annual grant total

In 2012/13 the charity had an income of £4,700 and an expenditure of £3,300. Lately the trustees' financial plan has been to allocate £500 each year to distribute in individual grants. Previously two grants a year have been made to individuals.

Exclusions

According to our research, grants are not normally made for musical instrument tuition.

Applications

In writing to the correspondent.

Other information

The charity also provides support to local schools, where the need is not already addressed by the local authority.

Sunderland

The Mayor's Fund for Necessitous Children

£200

Correspondent: Children's Services Finance Manager, Financial Resources, Room 2.86, Civic Centre, Sunderland SR2 7DN (01915 531826)

CC Number: 229349

Eligibility

Children in need (under 16, occasionally under 19) who are in full-time education, live in the city of Sunderland and whose families are on a low income.

Types of grants

Grants of about £25 for the provision of school footwear, paid every six months.

Annual grant total

In 2012/13 the fund had an income of £100 and a total expenditure of £400. We estimate around £200 was given in grants to individuals for education.

Exclusions

No grants are made to asylum seekers.

Applications

Applicants must visit the Civic Centre and fill in a form with a member of staff. The decision is then posted at a later date. Proof of low income is necessary.

Other information

The fund also makes grants to individuals for social welfare purposes.

West Yorkshire

The Boston Spa Educational Charitable Trust

£2,500

Correspondent: Christopher Walsh, Trustee, 12 Church Lane, Nether Poppleton, York YO26 6LB

CC Number: 702676

Eligibility

People in need who live in Boston Spa, Collingham, Harewood, Alwoodley, Shadwell, Crossgates, Scholes, Barwick-in-Elmet, Bardsey, East Keswick, Whinmoor, Aberford, Thorner, Bramham, Clifford, Walton and Thorp Arch in the north east area of West Yorkshire.

Types of grants

One-off grants are usually given for expeditions and explorations or to students on higher education courses where no grants are available, such as postgraduate courses.

Annual grant total

In 2012/13 the trust had an income of £0 but a total expenditure of approximately £2,700. We estimate that £2,500 was awarded to individuals for educational purposes.

Applications

In writing to the correspondent, to be considered in March, June and November.

Lady Elizabeth Hastings' Educational Foundation

£122,000 (227 grants)

Correspondent: Andrew Fallows, Clerk, Carter Jonas, 82 Micklegate, York YO1 6LF (01904 558212; email: leh. clerk@carterjonas.co.uk; website: www. ladyelizabethhastingscharities.co.uk/ grants/education)

CC Number: 224098–1

Eligibility

Individuals in education who are in need and live in the parishes of Bardsey with East Keswick, Burton Salmon, Collingham with Harewood, Ledsham with Fairburn, Shadwell and Thorp Arch.

Grants can also be made to people who have at any time attended one of the Lady Elizabeth Hastings schools in Collingham, Ledston or Thorp Arch, irrespective of whether they are still resident in the area of benefit.

Types of grants

One-off and recurrent grants according to need can be given to college and university students, schoolchildren or people in vocational training, apprenticeships. Support can be given towards school uniforms, educational outings, sports equipment and musical instruments, university/college fees and associated necessities, tools, books and so on.

Annual grant total

In 2012/13 the foundation awarded 227 grants to individuals totalling £122,000.

Exclusions

Grants to purchase computers are only given in exceptional circumstances; however, college and university grants are generally made without conditions

and may be used towards buying computer equipment.

Applications

Application forms can be found on the foundation's website or requested from the correspondent. Applications can be completed by the individual directly or by a parent/guardian and must be submitted by post at any time a month in advance of the trustees' meeting. The meetings are held four times a year, in early March, June, October and December.

Other information

The foundation is managed by and derives its income from Lady Elizabeth Hasting's Estate Charity. The trust also gives yearly payments to designated local schools, organisations and clergy to be applied for the benefit of people in the area of benefit.

The North Yorkshire Fund Educational Travel Award

£2,000 (2 grants)

Correspondent: Philip Ingham, Trustee, Two Ridings Community Foundation, Primrose Hill, Buttercrambe Road, Stamford Bridge, York YO41 1AW (01759 377400; email: office@trcf.org.uk; website: www.tworidingscommunity foundation.org.uk/grants/travel_award)

CC Number: 1084043

Eligibility

Students on a full-time first degree course at a British university. Applicants must be ordinarily living in the North Yorkshire or within the former West Riding boundary. Preference is given to those who can demonstrate need and/or lasting community benefit.

Types of grants

Two grants ranging from £250 to £1,000 are given each year. Financial assistance is available towards travelling abroad for further education in a directly related field of study, for a language placement, year in industry, international exchange or field trip expenses.

Annual grant total

Up to £2,000 is available for grants each year.

Exclusions

No grants to students who have already taken their final first degree examination at the date any awards are payable.

Applications

On a form available from the foundation's website. Applications open in February and are considered at the end of April. They should be submitted

prior to 12 April. Note that the application requires providing information both online and via post, only when both parts of the application are received can it be considered.

Other information

This award was previously called The Charity of Lady Mabel Florence Harriet Smith.

Two Ridings Community Foundation supports a number of community groups, projects and organisations. This particular award is only a small part of the foundation's activity.

At the time of writing (March 2014) the foundation's website stated that 'this fund was currently closed.' To find out when the award re-opens see the foundation's website.

Frank Wallis Scholarships

£800

Correspondent: Deborah Beaumont, Bradford M. D. C, Department 24, Britannia House Hall Ings, Bradford, West Yorkshire BD1 1HX (01274 434956)

CC Number: 529080

Eligibility

Higher education students whose parents live in the Clayton area and who are leaving Thornton Grammar School or any other school approved by the trustees.

Types of grants

Our research suggests that grants in the range of £50–£100 are available for any course of higher education to assist with the purchase of books, equipment/ instruments and other necessities.

Annual grant total

In 2012/13 the trust had an income of £600 and an expenditure of £1,000. We estimate the annual total of grants to be around £800.

Applications

In writing to the correspondent.

Calderdale

The Bearder Charity

£28,000

Correspondent: Richard Smithies, Administrator, 5 King Street, Brighouse, West Yorkshire HD6 1NX (01484 710571; email: bearders@btinternet.com; website: www.bearder-charity.org.uk)

CC Number: 1010529

Eligibility

People in need who are resident in Calderdale, particularly those who are suffering from poverty, hardship or distress.

Types of grants

Grants for general educational needs, such as equipment/instruments, tools, travel costs, books, fees, clothing and uniforms, educational outings and so forth.

Annual grant total

In 2012/13 the charity had assets of £3.6 million, an income of £195,000 and a total charitable expenditure of £145,000. Grants to individuals for educational purposes totalled £28,000.

Applications

In writing to the correspondent. Applications should outline details of required assistance and anticipated expenses (for example, a project timetable, cost of items required, travel costs and so on). The trustees meet six times a year. Applications can also be made through organisations, such as Citizens Advice or social services, if applicable.

Other information

Grants are also made to individuals for welfare purposes and to local charities.

The Community Foundation for Calderdale

£18,000

Correspondent: Grants Department, The 1855 Building (first floor), Discovery Road, Halifax, West Yorkshire HX1 2NG (01422 438738; fax: 01422 350017; email: grants@cffc.co.uk; website: www.cffc.co.uk)

CC Number: 1002722

Eligibility

Children and young people up to 18 who are living, studying or working in Halifax.

Types of grants

Grants from the 'Noel John Greenwood Halifax Children's Trust' of up to £130 for the costs of school trips, clothing, books or equipment and so on.

Annual grant total

In 2012/13 grants were awarded to 343 individuals totalling £37,000. We estimate grants to individuals for educational purposes totalled around £18,000.

Applications

Individuals should apply through a referring agency, such as Citizens Advice,

on an application form available from the foundation's website. Grants will only be awarded to individuals in the form of a cheque; cash is not given.

Other information

The foundation also gives to organisations and to individuals for relief-in-need purposes.

Elland

Brooksbank Educational Charity

£1,000

Correspondent: A. Blackburn, Trustee, 4 Bryan Road, Elland, West Yorkshire HX5 0QZ (01422 372014)

CC Number: 529146

Eligibility

Children and young people under the age of 25 who live in the area of former urban district of Elland (as constituted on 31 March 1974).

Types of grants

Small grants are mainly given to pupils transferring from primary to secondary school but some assistance may be available to students entering university.

Annual grant total

In 2012/13 the trust had an income of £1,300 and an expenditure of £1,200. We estimate the annual total of grants to be around £1,000.

Applications

In writing to the correspondent. Our research suggests that application forms are also distributed through local junior schools and should be submitted in May for school grants and in September for student grants.

Haworth

Haworth Exhibition Endowment

£250

Correspondent: Dr Andrew Collinson, Trustee, 38 Gledhow Drive, Oxenhope, Keighley BD22 9SA (01535 644447)

CC Number: 507050

Eligibility

People who live, or whose parents lived, in the ancient township of Haworth. Candidates must have attended one of the schools (including Oakbank) in the district of Haworth (including Oxenhope and Stanbury, but excluding Lees and Crossroads) for at least three years.

Types of grants

One-off grants ranging from £25 to £75 to people following A-levels and taking up further education, for books and equipment.

Annual grant total

In 2012/13 the charity had an income of £800 and an expenditure of £300. Grants totalled approximately £250.

Applications

On an application form available from the town hall information desk following an advertisement in the local newspaper. The closing date for applications is 31 August. The trustees meet once a year in October.

Keighley

Bowcocks Trust Fund for Keighley

£3,000

Correspondent: Alistair Docherty, 17 Farndale Road, Wilsden, Bradford BD15 0LW (01535 272657)

CC Number: 223290

Eligibility

People in need who live in the municipal borough of Keighley as constituted on 31 March 1974.

Types of grants

One-off grants according to need.

Annual grant total

In 2012/13 the trust had an income of £9,200 and a total expenditure of £13,000. Grants are given for educational and social welfare purposes and to both individuals and organisations. We estimate grants to individuals for educational purposes totalled around £3,000.

Applications

Initial telephone calls are welcomed. Applications should be made in writing to the correspondent by an appropriate third party.

Leeds

Community Foundation for Leeds – Looked after Children's Fund

£0

Correspondent: Sally-Anne Greenfield, Chief Executive, 1st Floor, 51a St Paul's Street, Leeds LS1 2TE (01132 422426; email: sally-anne@leedscf.org.uk; website: www.leedscf.org.uk)

CC Number: 1096892

Eligibility

Looked after children in Leeds.

Types of grants

Grants of up to £500 are awarded to individuals 'who show promise in academic studies, sports and music.' Support is given for extra educational costs not covered by the statutory allowance, for example school trips, residential trips.

Annual grant total

No grants were awarded in 2012/13.

The correspondent has informed us that at the time of writing (April 2014) the fund was being 're-packaged'.

Applications

Application forms can be requested from the correspondent and should be submitted by a social worker or carer, if applicable. The trustees meet quarterly.

Other information

Looked After Children's Fund is administered by the Community Foundation for Leeds, which also manages other funds.

The Community Shop Trust

£1,500

Correspondent: Lynn Higo, Administrator, Unit 4, Clayton Wood Bank, West Park Ring Road, Leeds LS16 6QZ (01132 745551; fax: 01132 783184; email: info@ leedscommunitytrust.org; website: www. leedscommunitytrust.org)

CC Number: 701375

Eligibility

Children and young people in need who live in Leeds.

Types of grants

Small one-off grants towards the costs associated with education, music and sports are available under the 'Keen Kids' programme. Recent grants have been made towards a computer, learning aids, playgroup fees, a drum kit, DJ mixing decks and sports clothes.

Annual grant total

In 2012 the trust made grants to 435 families totalling £56,000, broken down as follows:

Type of grant	Cases	Items	Amount
Emergency grants	232	347	£40,000
Christmas grants	181	181	£10,500
Holidays	20	20	£4,000
Kosy Kids	2	10	£1,000
Totals	435	558	£56,000

Included in these items are the cost of two computers and five school uniforms which we have taken to be educational grants and estimated the total at £1,500.

The 2012 accounts were the latest available at the time of writing (August 2014).

Applications

In writing to the correspondent through a social worker, Citizens Advice or other welfare agency. Potential applicants are then sent an application form to complete. For this reason the initial letter must give full details of the personal circumstances.

Other information

The trust is also known as the Leeds Community Trust. It runs two shops and distributes the profits to local charities, groups and individuals in need, particularly people in vulnerable situations.

Kirke Charity

£2,500

Correspondent: Bruce Buchan, Trustee, 8 St Helens Croft, Leeds LS16 8JY (01924 465860)

CC Number: 246102

Eligibility

People in need who live in the ancient parishes of Adel, Arthington or Cookridge.

Types of grants

One-off grants of around £100.

Annual grant total

In 2012/13 the charity had an income of £9,200 and an expenditure of £5,200. Grants usually total around £5,000 for education and welfare purposes.

Applications

Applications can be submitted directly by the individual or through a social worker, Citizens Advice or other welfare agency.

Mirfield

Mirfield Educational Charity

£4,100 (7 grants)

Correspondent: Malcolm Parkinson, 7 Kings Street, Mirfield, West Yorkshire WF14 8AW (01924 499251; email: Malcolm.Parkinson@ramsdens.co.uk)

CC Number: 529334

Eligibility

People under the age of 25 who/whose parents live in the former urban district of Mirfield.

Types of grants

One-off grants ranging from £300 to £1,000 are awarded towards educational

costs and opportunities, including tuition fees, travel/study overseas, expeditions, projects, living expenses or necessities.

Annual grant total

In 2012/13 the charity had assets of £1.5 million, an income of £51,000 and a total charitable expenditure of £10,400. Grants to seven individuals totalled £4,100.

Applications

In writing to the correspondent. The trustees meet three times a year, in February, May and October.

Other information

The charity also supports organisations, schools and groups.

Rawdon

The Rawdon and Laneshaw Bridge School Trust (Rawdon Endowment)

£600

Correspondent: Anthea Hargreaves, Trustee, Park Dale, Layton Drive, Rawdon, Leeds LS19 6QY (01132 504061)

CC Number: 529197

Eligibility

People under the age of 21 and living in the former urban district of Rawdon.

Types of grants

Grants for people at college or university (typically for books or equipment) and to needy students pursuing education at lower levels, and changing to higher levels of education.

Annual grant total

In 2012/13 the trust had an income of £1,500 and a total expenditure of £600. We estimate that educational grants to individuals totalled £600.

Applications

In writing to the correspondent. Grants are usually awarded annually in October after applications have been invited in the local press during September.

Other information

The correspondent also administers the Charity of Francis Layton. This is for the advancement in life of deserving and necessitous Rawdon residents under the age of 21. It was formerly to assist with apprentice fees, but now tends to support other educational purposes. In recent years, this charity has had a small annual income and expenditure.

Wakefield

Lady Bolles Foundation

£10,400

Correspondent: Stephen Skellern, Trustee, 6 Lynwood Drive, Wakefield WF2 7EF (01924 250473)

CC Number: 529344

Eligibility

People under the age of 21 who live in the county borough of Wakefield and are in full-time education. At the trustees' discretion support may be continued up to the age of 24.

Types of grants

Grants are given towards uniforms, clothing, fees, educational outings, books, travel or maintenance expenses. Apprentices and people starting work are also supported.

Annual grant total

In 2013 the foundation had an income of £7,900 and an expenditure of £10,600. We estimate the annual total of grants to individuals to be around £10,400

Applications

In writing to the correspondent. Grants are normally considered in February and October.

Feiweles Trust

£6,500

Correspondent: Paul Rogers, Trustee, c/o Yorkshire Sculpture Park, Bretton Hall, Bretton, Wakefield, West Yorkshire WF4 4LG (01924 832519; email: patricia.jorgensen-ghous@ysp.co.uk; website: www.ysp.co.uk)

CC Number: 1094383

Eligibility

Young artists at the beginning of their career.

Types of grants

The trust provides an annual bursary to an artist or artists at the beginning of their career to allow them to work within local schools, normally for three months. Successful applicants work with children of all ages, are supported by the teacher and can use the surroundings and educational resources of Yorkshire Sculpture Park for the residency. Each year a different area of art is undertaken and to date the artists have explored film, sculpture, poetry, drama, dance, music, creative writing, painting, textile art, physical theatre, art as environment and creative writing with illustration. The award is of up to £10,000.

Annual grant total

In 2012/13 the trust had an income of £515 and a total expenditure of £6,600. We estimate that about £6,500 was spent in grants.

Applications

In writing to the correspondent. Our research suggests that applications can be submitted directly by the individual before January for consideration in February/March.

North West

General

The Bowland Charitable Trust

£1,900 (3 grants)

Correspondent: Carol Fahy, Trustee, Activhouse, Philips Road, Blackburn, Lancashire BB1 5TH (01254 290433)

CC Number: 292027

Eligibility

Young people in the north west of England who are in need of assistance towards educational character development opportunities.

Types of grants

Grants towards educational outdoor and character-forming activities for young people. Funding is mainly one-off but recurrent support may also be considered.

Annual grant total

At the time of writing (August 2014) the latest financial information available was from 2012. In 2012 the trust had assets of £12 million and an income of £374,000. During the year three grants were made to individuals totalling £1,900. Note that a major part of the trust's assets is restricted.

Applications

In writing to the correspondent. Applications are considered on a regular basis.

Other information

In 2012 the trust made grants to organisations totalling around £1 million. Support was mainly given for educational, cultural and religious purposes for the benefit of young people and research into the operation of the criminal justice system particularly in relation to young offenders. Occasionally other charitable causes may be assisted.

Crabtree North West Charitable Trust

£300

Correspondent: Ian Currie, Trustee, 3 Ralli Courts, New Bailey Street, Salford M3 5FT (01618 311512)

CC Number: 1086405

Eligibility

Children and young people up to the age of 18 who are in education in the North West.

Types of grants

One-off grants are given according to need towards general educational purposes and sports causes.

Annual grant total

In 2012/13 the trust had an income of £4,000 and an expenditure of £300, which is exceptionally low. In the past five years the total charitable expenditure fluctuated from £300 to £104,000. Our research suggests that individual awards usually total between £5,000 and £10,000 each year.

Applications

In writing to the correspondent.

Other information

Organisations are also supported.

Manchester Publicity Association Educational Trust

£500

Correspondent: Gillian Cosser, Trustee, 7 Heigham Gardens, St Helens, Merseyside WA9 5WB

CC Number: 1001134

Eligibility

People over the age of 16 living in Greater Manchester and the surrounding area who either are studying marketing communications, or already work in or aim to enter marketing, advertising and related occupations.

Types of grants

Our research suggests that grants range between £200 and £500 and are given towards the cost of books or fees for education/training, usually to cover the second half of the year.

Annual grant total

In 2012/13 the trust had an income of £80 and an expenditure of £520. We estimate that grants totalled about £500. Both the income and the total expenditure vary each year.

Applications

Application forms are available from the correspondent. They must be supported by a tutor and are considered on demand.

Norcross Scholarship Fund

£1,900

Correspondent: The Administrator, Rochdale Metropolitan Borough Council, Tax and Treasury Team, Floor 2, Number One Riverside, Smith Street, Rochdale OL16 1XU (01706 924713; email: committee.services@ rochdale.gov.uk; website: www.rochdale. gov.uk/the_council/more_about_the_ council/charitable_trusts.aspx)

CC Number: 526666

Eligibility

People under the age of 30 who are permanently resident within the Rochdale Metropolitan Borough or the former administrative county of Lancaster. Applicants must have already completed a course of study at any university, college or other institution approved by the council and be undertaking a second or further qualification. People who are normally resident in the former borough of Middleton are given preference.

Types of grants

Financial assistance is available towards the cost of the course fees, travel in the UK and abroad, books, equipment/

instruments and other educational expenses.

Annual grant total

In 2012/13 the fund had an income of £8,100 and an expenditure of £2,100 which is lower than in the previous years. We have estimated that the annual total of grants was about £1,900.

Applications

Application forms can be downloaded from the Rochdale Borough Council website or requested from the correspondent.

The Northern Counties Children's Benevolent Society

See entry on page 166

Roundhouse (formerly Cockshot) Foundation

£2,500

Correspondent: Michelle Rothwell, Belle Isle, Windermere, Cumbria LA23 1BG (01539 447087; email: cockshotfoundation@belleisle.net)

CC Number: 1104085

Eligibility

Children attending any institution in the counties of Cumbria, Lancashire and Greater Manchester.

Types of grants

Grants towards the furtherance of education (including social and physical training).

Annual grant total

In 2012/13 the foundation had an income of £4,300 and a total expenditure of £10,300. The foundation gives to organisations and individuals for both educational and social welfare purposes. We estimate the total awarded to individuals for educational purposes was around £2,500.

Applications

In writing to the correspondent.

The Shepherd Street Trust

£31,000 (102 grants)

Correspondent: Judith Turner, Secretary, PO Box 658, Longridge, Preston PR3 2WJ (01200 427625; email: enquiries@shepherdstreettrust.co.uk; website: www.shepherdstreettrust.co.uk)

CC Number: 222922

Eligibility

People under the age of 21 residing within a radius of 50 miles around Preston Town Hall.

Types of grants

Grants are given to cover educational, social and physical training needs. Support can be provided towards travel, course fees, specialist medical attention and equipment, outfits, clothing, tools, instruments/equipment and towards facilities for recreation or other leisure occupations in the interests of social welfare.

Annual grant total

In 2012/13 the trust had assets of £1.3 million, an income of £55,000 and a total charitable expenditure of £41,000. Grants to 102 individuals totalled £31,000.

Applications

Application forms can be downloaded from the trust's website or requested from the correspondent. Candidates are required to provide supporting references from their school, college, a social worker, religious authority or other professional. Applications for grants of less than £500 will be decided by the trustees within four weeks of receipt. Applications for grants exceeding £500 will be discussed at the trustee meetings unless there is a pressing need for funds, in which case, earlier consideration can be made. The trustees meet every two months, in January, March, May, July, September and November.

Other information

The trust also supports other charitable organisations, institutions, groups and assists the children's ward at Preston Royal Infirmary. During the year £10,100 was awarded in 9 grants to organisations.

The Bishop David Sheppard Anniversary Trust

£6,400

Correspondent: Margaret Sadler, Administrator, 5 Hazel Grove, Great Crosby, Liverpool, Merseyside L23 9SH (01513 453972; email: margaret.sadler@hotmail.co.uk)

CC Number: 517368

Eligibility

People between the ages of 21 and 49 who live in the Anglican diocese of Liverpool (which includes Southport, Kirkby, Ormskirk, Skelmersdale, Wigan, St Helens, Warrington and Widnes) and

who are doing second-chance learning at a college or training centre.

Types of grants

Grants are provided for books and equipment needed to complete courses or training programmes.

Annual grant total

In 2013 the charity had an income of £7,600 and an expenditure of £6,600. Grants made totalled approximately £6,400.

Exclusions

No grants to students who have had no break from their education (or schoolchildren), to people with good vocational qualifications or on degree courses, or to organisations.

Applications

On a form available from the administrator to be submitted directly by the individual at any time.

The Winwick Educational Foundation

£2,300

Correspondent: Alastair Brown, Administrator, Forshaws Davies Ridgway LLP, 17–21 Palmyra Square South, Warrington, Cheshire WA1 1BW (01925 230000; email: alastair.brown@fdrlaw.co.uk)

CC Number: 526499

Eligibility

Further education students who live in the parishes of Emmanuel Wargrave, Lowton St Luke's, Lowton St Mary's, Newton All Saints, Newton St Peter's, St John's Earlestown and Winwick.

Types of grants

Small, one-off and recurrent grants are available to further education students towards general educational needs, including books, equipment/instruments and fees. Grants normally range from £75 to £100.

Annual grant total

In 2012/13 the foundation had an income of £4,200 and an expenditure of £4,800. We estimate the annual total of grants to individuals to be around £2,300.

Applications

In writing to the correspondent. Applications should normally be submitted in February and March for consideration in April. They can be made directly by the individual or through a third party, such as the individual's school, college or educational welfare agency, if applicable.

Other information

The foundation supports four specific Church of England primary schools in north Warrington.

World Friendship

£13,000

Correspondent: The Applications Secretary, 15 Dudlow Lane, Liverpool L18 0HH (01517 229700; email: su05@ liv.ac.uk; website: www.worldfriendship. merseyside.org)

CC Number: 513643

Eligibility

International students studying at universities in the diocese of Liverpool. Preference is given to people in the final year of their course and individuals from Anglican dioceses and Christian communities overseas. Applicants must intend to return to their home country.

Types of grants

One-off grants of about £500 towards relieving unexpected hardships which have arisen since the beginning of the course and which would prevent individuals from completing their studies.

Annual grant total

In 2013 the charity had an income of £14,000 and an expenditure of £13,500. We estimate that grants to individuals totalled around £13,000.

Exclusions

Grants are not given to those whose place of study is outside the diocese of Liverpool. Students from an EU country, those who are intending to stay in the UK at the end of their course, or applicants from overseas who are not yet studying in Liverpool are not usually supported.

Applications

Application forms should be sought from student support offices at relevant institutions or can be requested from the correspondent. For details of the relevant contact see the charity's website.

Cheshire

The Sir Thomas Moulson Trust

£3,500

Correspondent: Julie Turner, Administrator, Meadow Barn, Cow Lane, Hargrave, Chester CH3 7RU

CC Number: 214342

Eligibility

Students under 25 who live in the villages of Huxley, Hargrave, Tarvin, Kelsall and Ashton in Cheshire. Preference is given to those resident in the parish of Foulk Stapleford.

Types of grants

One-off grants ranging from £100 to £500 to students in further/higher education towards books, fees/living expenses and study or travel abroad.

Annual grant total

In 2013 the trust had an income of £23,000 and a total expenditure of £15,000. We estimate that around £3,500 was made in grants to individuals for education.

Applications

In writing to the correspondent. Applications should be submitted directly by the individual and are usually considered in September.

The Thornton-le-Moors Education Foundation

£2,300

Correspondent: Roy Edwards, Trustee, Jesmin, 4 School Lane, Elton, Chester CH2 4LN (01928 725188)

CC Number: 525829

Eligibility

People under 25 in full-time education who live in the ancient parish of Thornton-le-Moors which includes the following villages: Dunham Hill, Elton, Hapsford, Ince and Thornton-le-Moors.

Types of grants

The trust gives grants mostly to students going to university for books and also to the local youth groups, mainly the guides, brownies, scouts and cubs.

Annual grant total

In 2013 this charity had an income of £4,500 and a total expenditure of £4,700.

Applications

In writing to the correspondent. Trustees meet twice a year, usually in April and November.

Other information

Grants are also awarded to organisations.

The Verdin Trust Fund

£1,000

Correspondent: John Richards, Administrator, Rose Cottage, 2 Vale Royal Drive, Whitegate, Northwich CW8 2BA (01606 889281; email: johnrichards78@live.co.uk)

CC Number: 221295

Eligibility

People who live within the Vale Royal area of Cheshire West and Chester County.

Types of grants

Most of the funds are given in the form of prizes to local schools, Young Farmers' Associations and courses or gap-years.

Annual grant total

In 2012/13 the fund had both an income and an expenditure of £2,500. Our research shows that generally this fund has about £2,000 a year to distribute in grants to individuals and organisations. We estimate the total of grants to individuals to be around £1,000.

Applications

In writing to the correspondent.

Other information

Grants are also made to organisations.

The Wrenbury Consolidated Charities

£1,000

Correspondent: Helen Smith, Trustee, Eagle Hall Cottage, Smeatonwood, Wrenbury, North Nantwich CW5 8HD (01270 780262; email: helen@ peckfortonhouse.co.uk)

CC Number: 241778

Eligibility

People in need who live in the parishes of Chorley, Sound, Broomhall, Newhall, Wrenbury-cum-Frith and Dodcott-cum-Wilkesley.

Types of grants

Payments on St Mark's Day (25 April) and St Thomas' Day (21 December) to students. Grants are also given for one-off necessities.

Annual grant total

In 2013 the charity had an income of £12,600 and a total expenditure of £12,200. We estimate that grants to students totalled around £1,000. The charity also distributes funds to churches, the village hall, village schools and to older individuals for welfare purposes.

Applications

In writing to the correspondent either directly by the individual or through another appropriate third party on behalf of the individual. The vicar of Wrenbury and the parish council can give details of the six nominated trustees who can help with applications. Applications are considered in December and March.

Alsager

Alsager Educational Foundation

£7,500

Correspondent: Catherine Lovatt, 6 Pikemere Road, Alsager, Stoke-on-Trent ST7 2SB (01270 873680; email: colovatt@hotmail.com)

CC Number: 525834

Eligibility

Children and young people who live in the parish of Alsager.

Types of grants

One-off and recurrent grants ranging from around £200 to £1,000 are available to schoolchildren and further/higher education students. Support is given towards general educational necessities, including books, equipment/instruments, maintenance, clothing, also travel/study abroad and extra-curricular activities.

Annual grant total

In 2012/13 the trust had an income of £16,300 and an expenditure of £15,900. We have estimated the annual total of grants to individuals to be around £7,500.

Exclusions

Our research indicates that postgraduate students and people who do not have a permanent home address in Alsager cannot be supported. Assistance would not be given for extra tuition expenses.

Applications

In writing to the correspondent.

Other information

Both individuals and organisations can be supported. Special benefits are provided to the Alsager Church of England Junior School.

Audlem

Audlem Educational Foundation

£8,000

Correspondent: Louisa Ingham, East Cheshire Council, People Service, Delamere House, Delamere Street, Crewe CW1 2JZ (01270 686223; website: www. audlem.org/services/audlem-education-fund.html)

CC Number: 525810

Eligibility

Children and young people under the age of 25 resident in the Ancient Parish of Audlem, including Buerton and Hankelow and part of Dodcott-cum-Wilkesley and Newhall. Preference is given to individuals who are attending or have attended any maintained school for at least two years.

Types of grants

The foundation awards grants, exhibitions, bursaries, maintenance allowances and other financial support to schoolchildren, further and higher education students or people in training. Grants are made for general educational expenses, educational outings and visits, field courses, equipment/instruments, tools and student exchange.

Annual grant total

In 2012/13 the trust had an income of £10,700 and an expenditure of £12,000. The foundation also supports local schools, therefore we have estimated that the annual total of grants to individuals was around £8,000. Note that the grants total varies each year.

Applications

Application forms can be found on the trust's website or requested from the correspondent. The trustees meet three times a year, usually in November, February and July. Applications should be made in advance of these dates. Candidates are also required to provide a confirmation of attendance and receipts for the items purchased or other financial details of the course/trip taken.

Other information

The trust allocates one third of its income and interest from the investments to support schools in the area of benefit. The remainder is used to award grants to individuals.

Chester

Chester Municipal Charities

£25,000

Correspondent: John Catherall, Administrator, PO Box 360, Tarporley CW6 6AZ (01829 759416; email: info@chestermunicipalcharities.org)

CC Number: 1077806

Eligibility

Young people under the age of 25 who are attending or have attended a school in Chester and who are residents of Chester.

Types of grants

Grants may come in the form of bursaries/grants paid directly to schools/colleges/universities. Grants are made to cover equipment, educational trips and other costs related to education. The charity also provides a limited number of bursaries and a programme of funding support in Early Years education.

Annual grant total

In 2012 the charity had assets of £10 million and an income of £426,000. Grants to both organisations and individuals totalled £159,000. Grants for educational purposes usually total around £25,000.

These were the latest accounts available at the time of writing (July 2014).

Applications

On a form available from the correspondent.

Other information

The charity also manages almshouses.

Congleton

The Congleton Town Trust

£5,000

Correspondent: Joanne Money, Clerk, c/o Congleton Town Hall, High Street, Congleton CW12 1BN (01260 291156; email: info@congletontowntrust.co.uk; website: www.congletontowntrust.co.uk)

CC Number: 1051122

Eligibility

People in need who live in the town of Congleton (this does not include the other two towns which have constituted the borough of Congleton since 1975).

Types of grants

The principal aim of the trust is to give grants to individuals in need or to organisations which provide relief, services or facilities to those in need. The trustees will, however, consider a grant towards education or training if the applicant is in need. Support can be given in the form of books, tools or in cash towards tuition fees or maintenance.

Annual grant total

In 2012 the trust had an income of £24,000 and a total expenditure of £20,000. These were the latest financial details available at the time of writing (July 2014). We estimate grants to individuals for educational purposes totalled around £5,000.

Applications

On a form available from the correspondent or downloaded from the trust's website, to be submitted directly by the individual or a family member. Applications are considered quarterly, on the second Monday in March, June, September and December.

Other information

The trust also administers several smaller trusts and makes grants to organisations.

Warrington

The Police-Aided Children's Relief-in-Need Fund

£0

Correspondent: The Trustees, Warrington Council For Voluntary Services, The Gateway, 89 Sankey St, Warrington WA1 1SR (01925 444263)

CC Number: 223937

Eligibility

Children of pre-school or primary school age living in the borough of Warrington and whose families are in financial or physical need. Applications from students of secondary school age and over will be considered in exceptional circumstances.

Types of grants

Vouchers to help with the cost of clothing and footwear. Vouchers are only redeemable at selected retailers in the borough.

Annual grant total

No accounts have been submitted to the Charity Commission since 2008/09 when the fund had an income of £5,000 and an expenditure of £0.

Applications

The trust stated previously that grantmaking is currently suspended whilst various structural issues are sorted out.

Widnes

Widnes Educational Foundation

£0

Correspondent: Jennifer Turton, Administrator, Halton Borough Council, Municipal Buildings, Kingsway, Widnes, Cheshire WA8 7QF (03033334300)

CC Number: 526510

Eligibility

People under the age of 25 who have lived for at least four years or attended school/college for at least three years in Widnes. Grants are targeted at individuals between the ages of 16 and 25.

Types of grants

The foundation mainly focuses on giving grants to help with educational trips and visits. Cash grants could also be given for books and educational outings for those at school. Very occasionally small grants are given to help with school/college fees or to supplement existing grants. There is no set grant amount as applications are considered on a case by case basis.

Annual grant total

In 2012/13 the foundation had an income of £300 but made no grants.

Applications

Applications should be made through the school or college and must be supported by a third party, such as a teacher.

Other information

Grants can also be made to organisations.

Wilmslow

The Lindow Workhouse Trust

£2,300

Correspondent: Jacquie Bilsborough, Administrator, 15 Westward Road, Wilmslow SK9 5JY

CC Number: 226023

Eligibility

Children with special educational needs who live in the ancient parish of Wilmslow.

Types of grants

One-off grants of up to £500.

Annual grant total

In 2013 the charity had an income of £6,000 and a total expenditure of £4,600. We estimate the total grants awarded to individuals for educational purposes was around £2,300.

Applications

In writing to the correspondent at any time. Applications can be submitted either directly by the individual or a family member, through a third party such as a social worker or teacher, or through an organisation such as Citizens Advice or a school.

Cumbria

The Barton Educational Foundation

£1,000

Correspondent: Alan Wright, Trustee, 15 Church Croft, Pooley Bridge, Penrith, Cumbria CA10 2NL (01768486312)

CC Number: 526927

Eligibility

Tertiary education students who live in parishes of Barton, Martindale, Patterdale, Pooley Bridge or Yanwath, in Cumbria.

Types of grants

One-off and recurrent grants ranging between £25 and £100 are available to students at colleges and universities to help with the cost of books, fees and living expenses. People starting work and apprenticeships can also be supported. Occasionally assistance towards the purchase of books for schoolchildren may be provided.

Annual grant total

At the time of writing (August 2014) the latest financial information available was from 2012. In 2012 the foundation had an income of £1,200 and an expenditure of £1,100. We estimate that grants totalled about £1,000.

Applications

Application forms are available from the correspondent. They can be submitted directly by the individual for consideration, usually, in October.

The Brow Edge Foundation

£2,100

Correspondent: Robert Hutton, Administrator, 20 Ainslie Street, Ulverston, Cumbria LA12 7JE (01229 585888; email: gordon@421.co.uk)

CC Number: 526716

Eligibility

People in need who live in the area of Haverthwaite and Backbarrow, aged between 16 and 25. Preference is given to young people from disadvantaged backgrounds.

Types of grants

Small grants to assist pupils attending schools, institutions or classes for post-16 education.

Annual grant total

In 2012 the foundation had an income of £2,500 and a total expenditure of £2,200. We estimate that grants to individuals totalled £2,100.

At the time of writing (July 2014) this was the most recent financial information available for the foundation.

Applications

In writing to the correspondent, directly by the individual. Applicants must state the type of course of study or apprenticeship they are about to undertake. Applications are usually considered in September.

The Burton-in-Kendal Educational Foundation

£3,000

Correspondent: Allison Cummings, Administrator, 5 Holmefield, Holme, Carnforth, Lancashire LA6 1RY (01524 782331)

CC Number: 526953

Eligibility

People under the age of 25 living in the parishes of Arnside, Beetham and Burton-in-Kendal, in Cumbria. Applicants must have attended a county or voluntary primary school for no less than two years.

Types of grants

Scholarships, bursaries and maintenance allowances are available as well as financial assistance towards study/travel abroad, books, equipment/instruments, maintenance/living expenses or facilities for social and physical training. Our research suggests that average grants range between £10 and £60 and that support can also be made to people with special educational needs.

Annual grant total

In 2012/13 the foundation had an income of £3,000 and an expenditure of £3,200. We estimate the annual total of grants to be around £3,000.

Applications

In writing to the correspondent. Applications are considered twice a year.

Cartmel Old Grammar School Foundation

£5,300

Correspondent: Colin Milner, Administrator, Cartmel Old Grammar School Foundation, Quintaine, Cardrona Road, Grange-over-Sands, Cumbria LA11 7EW (01539535043; email: mrcolinmilner@gmail.com)

CC Number: 526467

Eligibility

Children and young people between the ages of 18 and 25 who live in the parishes of Cartmel Fell, Broughton East, Grange-over-Sands, Lower Holker, Staveley, Lower Allithwaite, Upper Allithwaite and that part of the parish of Haverthwaite east of the River Leven.

Types of grants

Small one-off and recurrent (up to three years) grants of about £90 are awarded to further/higher education students to help with the costs of books, fees/living expenses or study/travel abroad and in the UK. Support is also given for music and arts studies.

Annual grant total

In 2012/13 the foundation had an income of £9,200 and an expenditure of £10,900. We estimate the annual total of grants to individuals to be around £5,300.

Applications

In writing to the correspondent. Applications should be submitted, preferably, by email, otherwise – providing an sae. Application forms are also distributed in local churches and educational establishments. The trustees meet in November and applications should be submitted by the end of September at the latest.

Other information

The foundation also makes payments to the Brow Edge Foundation and Cartmel General Charities for the benefit of the poor (approximately £1,000 annually) and helps local schools.

Edmond Castle Educational Trust

£3,000

Correspondent: Andrew Beeforth, Chief Executive, Cumbria Community Foundation, Dovenby Hall, Dovenby, Cockermouth CA13 0PN (01900 825760; fax: 01900 826527; email: enquiries@ cumbriafoundation.org; website: www. cumbriafoundation.org)

CC Number: 1027991

Eligibility

Disadvantaged children and young people under the age of 21 with a preference to those who are or have been looked after/provided accommodation by/under supervision of Cumbria County Council.

Types of grants

Grants reach up to £500 and are awarded to help with the course fees, computers, equipment, special tuition, childcare and any other activity 'which extend opportunities and which make a difference to the lives of young people.'

Annual grant total

In 2012/13 the trust had an income of £1,500 and an expenditure of £3,100. We estimate the annual total of grants to be around £1,500.

Exclusions

Activities which are the statutory duty of the government are not funded.

Applications

Application forms can be found on the trust's website and are separate for people under 18 or in full time further/ higher education and for people over 18 or in vocational training. Where possible, applications should be supported by a third party, such as a social or youth worker, health visitor and so on. Further application guidelines are available on the trust's website.

Other information

The trust supports both individuals and organisations.

Cumbria Community Foundation

£27,000

Correspondent: The Grants Team, Cumbria Community Foundation, Dovenby Hall, Cockermouth, Cumbria CA13 0PN (01900 825760; fax: 01900 826527; email: enquiries@ cumbriafoundation.org; website: www. cumbriafoundation.org)

CC Number: 1075120

Eligibility

People resident in Cumbria. Other restrictions including geographical and age related pertain depending upon the fund being applied to.

Types of grants

One-off and recurrent grants for various amounts for a wide range of needs including travel abroad and in the UK, educational or training activities or preparations to enter a trade or profession, writing and publishing, the arts

Annual grant total

In 2012/13 the foundation made 97 grants to individuals totalling £55,000. We have estimated grants to individuals for educational purposes to be around £27,000.

Applications

The foundation administers numerous funds that give grants to individuals, they have differing eligibility criteria and application forms. Applicants should check the foundation's website for full details of each scheme, and how to apply.

Other information

The trust administers funds for both individuals and organisations, some of which may open and close regularly. In this accounting year, the total of grants to organisations was in the region of £2 million.

The Mary Grave Trust

£34,000 (52 grants)

Correspondent: The Grants Team, Cumbria Community Foundation, Dovenby Hall, Dovenby, Cockermouth CA13 0PN (01900 825760; email: enquiries@cumbriafoundation.org;

website: www.cumbriafoundation.org/archives/301)

CC Number: 526869

Eligibility

Young people in need aged between 11 and 21 who were born in the former county of Cumberland (excluding those whose parents were resident in Carlisle). Applicants must live, study or have studied (for at least two years, in secondary/further education) within the area of benefit priority being given to Workington, Maryport and Whitehaven areas. Applicants' household income must be less than £539 per week (excluding all benefits).

Students in sixth forms, further education colleges, universities and higher education colleges or in the gaps between these stages can all be considered as well as those at work, in training or involved in youth organisation activities.

Types of grants

Grants of around £1,000 to fund travel overseas in furtherance of education. The full cost of trips up to a set maximum can be provided and additional assistance for clothing and pocket money may also be given. Support is aimed at activities organised by a school/college or other trips, such as field-work expeditions, work-experience visits, specialist study bursaries for art and music schools, gap-year activities and Outward Bound-type courses such as Raleigh International.

Annual grant total

In 2012/13 the trust had assets of £1.5 million and an income of £61,000. Grants to 52 individuals totalled £34,000. The trust has stated that its reserves 'will be depleted over a period of years to minimise the impact of a reduction in grant making.' The grantmaking allocation for 2013/14 has been provisionally set at £48,000.

Exclusions

The trust will not fund:
- Individuals born outside the old county of Cumberland
- Individuals born in Carlisle (unless mother resident outside Carlisle at the time of birth)
- Trips in Cumbria
- Trips in the UK of less than three nights' duration
- Family holidays
- Employees of British Steel or the National Coal Board

Applications

Application forms are available from the trust's website or the correspondent. Applications can be submitted by the individual directly or through a school/college. Applicants are required to submit a full copy of their birth certificate and provide information about their financial circumstances. The trustees meet three times a year and applications should normally be received by 2 April, 1 October and 31 December.

Other information

The fund is administered by the Cumbria Community Foundation but is treated as a separate entity.

Greysouthen Educational Charity

£1,500

Correspondent: John Chipps, Trustee, Brunlea, Overend Road, Greysouthen, Cockermouth, Cumbria CA13 0UA (01900 825235)

CC Number: 512662

Eligibility

People under the age of 25 who live in the parish of Greysouthen.

Types of grants

Support is available to schoolchildren for books, clothing, educational outings, fees and other essentials; to people at college or university towards books, fees/living expenses, childcare costs and study or travel abroad; also to people starting work towards books, equipment/instruments, clothing and travel.

Annual grant total

In 2012/13 the charity had both an income and an expenditure of £3,300. We estimate the annual total of grants to individuals to be around £1,500.

Applications

In writing to the correspondent. Applications can be made either directly by individuals or through their school/university/college, educational welfare agency, if applicable. Applications are normally considered in July/August.

Other information

The trust also pays yearly payments to the Eaglesfield Paddle School and supports organisations in the Greysouthen area.

Hodgson's School Foundation (Wiggonby School Trust)

£24,000

Correspondent: M. Fleming, Administrator, Flemsyam, Aikton, Wigton, Cumbria CA7 0JA (01697 342829)

CC Number: 526850

Eligibility

People under the age of 25 in further education and training who live in the parishes of Aikton, Beaumont and Burgh-by-Sands or are former pupils of Wiggonby School.

Types of grants

Grants are normally around £200 and are given to people engaged in further education/training or people starting work/entering a trade. Support can be given to help with fees, living expenses, books, equipment/instruments and so on.

Annual grant total

In 2012/13 the trust had assets of £148,000 and an income of £27,000. Grants totalled £24,000 and were distributed under the following categories:

Wiggonby School fund	£16,500
Grants and bible to children	£7,100
School prizes	£400

Applications

Applications are normally advertised in the Cumberland News in August. Candidates can request an application from the correspondent. Applications should include the place of further study and details of the qualification aimed for.

Other information

Support is also given to Wiggonby School, where funding is not already provided by the local authority.

Kelsick's Educational Foundation

£106,000

Correspondent: Peter Frost, Clerk, The Kelsick Centre, St Mary's Lane, Ambleside LA22 9DG (01539 431289; fax: 01539 431292; email: john@kelsick.plus.com; website: www.kelsick.org.uk)

CC Number: 526956

Eligibility

Apprentices, further and higher education students under the age of 25 who have been resident in the Lake parishes (Ambleside, Grasmere, Langdale or part of Troutbeck) for at least four years.

Types of grants

The foundation offers grants for additional teaching support, extra assistance for pupils with special needs, music, drama lessons, hire of instruments, travel costs for certain educational trips, for undertaking performing arts or sport activities, books for A-levels, books for college and university courses and any other activity which the trustees consider to be of educational benefit. Apprentices can be supported towards the cost of tools, equipment and extra training. First-year higher education students are eligible for the purchase of a computer and all eligible students attending universities or colleges of further education can apply for subsistence grants. Awards will be given to address essential needs and can be one-off or recurrent, ranging from £25 to £3,000.

Annual grant total

In 2012/13 the foundation had assets of £6.9 million, an income of £352,000 and a charitable expenditure of £254,000. Grants to individuals totalled around £106,000 and the main support was allocated as follows:

Higher education	£64,000
Secondary and further education	£25,000
Primary education	£5,600

Exclusions

Tuition fees and residency expenses cannot be paid by the trust.

Applications

Application forms can be found on the foundation's website. Grants are considered at quarterly meetings in February, May, August and November. The deadlines for applications are 31 January, 30 April, 31 July and 31 October respectively. Candidates must list detailed costs (with receipts) of the items required. Forms should be submitted directly by the individual or by a parent/guardian, if the applicant is under the age of 18.

Other information

Grants totalling £148,000 were awarded to schools and organisations in the area of benefit. Support can also be given to groups where residency and age criteria are satisfied. The foundation's governing document allows using any surplus income for the benefit of people in Patterdale Ward and former county of Westmoreland.

The foundation stresses that considerable attention is given to young people with special needs and the trustees are 'particularly pleased to assist with costs involved with apprenticeships.'

Silecroft School Educational Charity

£1,000

Correspondent: Catherine Jopson, Administrator, Hestham Hall Farm, Millom LA18 5LJ (01229 772525)

CC Number: 509580

Eligibility

People under 25 who were born in the parishes of Whicham, Millom, Millom Without and Ulpha.

Types of grants

Recurrent grants are given for a wide range of educational needs for people at university or college, from books, clothing, equipment and other supplementary awards to foreign travel and other educational visits. However, the trust does not give grants for travel to and from the applicant's place of residence.

Annual grant total

In 2013 the charity had an income of £2,400 and a total expenditure of £1,100. We estimate that educational grants to individuals totalled £1,000.

Exclusions

Grants are not given for schoolchildren, people starting work or to students who have not moved away from home to continue their education.

Applications

On a form available from the correspondent, to be submitted in September for consideration in November. Applications can be made either directly by the individual, or through their school, college or educational welfare agency.

Barrow-in-Furness

The Billincoat Charity

£1,200

Correspondent: Helen Thomson, Administrator, Gummers How, Newton Cross Road, Newton in Furness, Barrow-in-Furness, Cumbria LA13 0NB (email: enquiries@daltontc.wanadoo.co.uk)

CC Number: 233409

Eligibility

People under 21 who live in the borough of Barrow-in-Furness.

Types of grants

One-off grants towards the cost of education, training, apprenticeship or equipment for those starting work. Grants are also made towards the costs of books, equipment/instruments, fees, educational outings in the UK, and study or travel abroad for schoolchildren and people in further and higher education. Schoolchildren can also be supported for uniforms or other school clothing.

Annual grant total

In 2013/14 the charity had an income of £4,600 and a total expenditure of £4,900. We estimate that educational grants to individuals totalled £1,200. Funding is also awarded to individuals for social

welfare purposes as well as to local welfare and educational organisations.

Applications

On an application form available from the correspondent to be submitted in December and June for consideration in January and July. Applications can be submitted by the individual or through their school, college, social services or probation service and so on.

Carlisle

Carlisle Educational Charity

£9,900 (52 grants)

Correspondent: Peter Mason, Assistant Director of Resources, Carlisle City Council, Civic Centre, Rickergate, Carlisle CA3 8QG (01228 817268; email: peterm@carlisle.gov.uk; website: www.carlisle.gov.uk/education_and_learning/carlisle_educational_charity.aspx)

CC Number: 509357

Eligibility

Students in further/higher education under the age of 25 who or whose parents live within the Carlisle district. Financial circumstances of the individual's parents and the extent to which they can support the applicant can be taken into account. Generally, preference is given to students with joint family income below £21,000.

Types of grants

Grants ranging from £50 to £500 are available to students in higher/further education and young graduates undertaking higher studies or professional qualification. Support is given for general educational costs or for students travelling in the UK or abroad for educational purposes associated with their course of study.

Annual grant total

In 2012/13 the charity had an income of £9,900 and an expenditure of £10,500. During the year 52 grants were awarded totalling £9,900.

Applications

Application forms are available on the charity's website or can be requested from the correspondent. Applications should be submitted by February and September for consideration in the following month.

Crosby Ravensworth

The Crosby Ravensworth Relief-in-Need Charities

£2,000

Correspondent: George Bowness, Administrator, Ravenseat, Crosby Ravensworth, Penrith, Cumbria CA10 3JB (01931 715382; email: gordonbowness@aol.com)

CC Number: 232598

Eligibility

People in need who have lived in the ancient parish of Crosby Ravensworth for at least 12 months.

Types of grants

One-off and recurrent grants. As well as relief-in-need grants, funds can also be given to local students entering university if they have been educated in the parish.

Annual grant total

Accounts for the year 2012 were the latest available at the time of writing (August 2014).

In 2012, the charities had an income of £14,000 and a total expenditure of £9,000. We estimate that the total grant awarded to individuals for educational purposes was approximately £2,000 – as the charities also award grants for social welfare purposes and to local organisations.

Applications

In writing to the correspondent submitted directly by the individual including details of the applicant's financial situation. Applications are considered in February, May and October.

Egton-cum-Newland

Egton Parish Lands Trust

£1,000

Correspondent: Joyce Ireland, Administrator, Threeways, Pennybridge, Ulverston, Cumbria LA12 7RX (01229 861405)

CC Number: 221424

Eligibility

Children and young people in need living in the parish of Egton-cum-Newland. Particular favour is given to parents on low incomes whose children wish to go on educational trips.

Types of grants

One-off and recurrent grants of £100 to £1,000 to schoolchildren for equipment/instruments and excursions and to college and university students for books.

Annual grant total

In 2012/13 the charity had an income of £10,600 and a total expenditure of £6,000. Our research tells us that most of the charity's expenditure usually goes in grants to local organisations, schools and groups. We estimate that educational grants to individuals totalled £1,000.

Applications

In writing to the correspondent. Applications should be submitted in April and October for consideration in May and November. They can be made either by the individual or through his/her school, college or welfare agency, or other appropriate third party.

Sedbergh

Robinson's Educational Foundation

£5,300

Correspondent: Ian Jenkinson, Administrator, Milne Moser Solicitors, 100 Highgate, Kendal, Cumbria LA9 4HE (01539 729786; email: solicitors@milnemoser.co.uk)

CC Number: 529897

Eligibility

Children and young people under the age of 25 who live in the parish of Sedbergh, with a preference for people who live in Howgill.

Types of grants

Scholarships, bursaries and maintenance allowances are available to schoolchildren and further/higher education students. One-off grants, in the range of £15 to £1,000 are given towards general educational necessities, including books, fees, equipment, travel costs, study/travel abroad, also music lessons for pupils.

Annual grant total

In 2012/13 the foundation had an income of £12,200 and an expenditure of £10,800. It supports both individuals and organisations, therefore we estimate the annual total of grants to individuals to be about £5,300.

Applications

In writing to the correspondent. Applications can be submitted either directly by individuals or through a social worker/Citizens Advice/welfare agency, if applicable. Grants are normally considered in September.

Other information

The foundation also supports local schools, where assistance is not already provided by the local authority.

Greater Manchester

The Barrack Hill Educational Charity (Barrack Hill Trust)

£4,500

Correspondent: John Asquith, Trustee, 24 Links Road, Romiley, Stockport, Cheshire SK6 4HU (01614 303583; email: cllr.mikewilson@stockport.gov.uk)

CC Number: 525836

Eligibility

Children and young people under the age of 21 who live or whose parents live in Bredbury and Romiley.

Types of grants

One-off grants to assist with general educational expenses. Schoolchildren can be supported towards the cost of uniforms, other school clothing, books and equipment/instruments. Students in full/part-time education can be assisted towards books, study or travel abroad and equipment. People in vocational training may also be helped with the costs of tools, uniforms, equipment and similar needs.

Annual grant total

At the time of writing (July 2014) the latest available financial information was from 2012. In 2012 the charity had an income of £9,300 and an expenditure of £9,100. We estimate the annual total of grants to individuals to be around £4,500.

Applications

Application forms can be requested from the correspondent. They are usually made available from the local libraries towards the end of the school year as well. Awards are normally considered in September and October.

Other information

The charity also makes grants to organisations and schools in the local area.

The Ann Butterworth and Daniel Bayley Charity

£1,700

Correspondent: Anne Hosker, Administrator, Gaddum Centre, Gaddum House, 6 Great Jackson Street, Manchester M15 4AX (01618 346069; fax: 01618 398573; email: gaddumcentre@hotmail.com; website: www.gaddumcentre.co.uk)

CC Number: 526055

Eligibility

Children and young people aged 25 and under who are of the Protestant religion and live in Manchester.

Types of grants

Grants towards the cost of education, training apprenticeships and so on, including for books, equipment, clothing, uniforms and travel. School and university/college fees are not met.

Annual grant total

In 2012/13 the charity had an income of £1,600 and a total expenditure of £1,750. Grants to individuals for educational purposes are estimated to be around £1,700.

Applications

On a form available from the correspondent which must be submitted with support from a sponsor such as a social worker, health visitor or teacher. The charity stated that it receives more applications than it can possibly support.

The Darbishire House Trust

£0

Correspondent: Anne Hosker, Administrator, Gaddum Centre, Gaddum House, 6 Great Jackson Street, Manchester M15 4AX (01618 346069; email: amh@gaddumcentre.co.uk)

CC Number: 234651

Eligibility

Women teachers and ex-teachers who were born in, reside in or work(ed) in Greater Manchester and are now retraining.

Types of grants

Grants towards the costs of education and retraining, including for books, equipment, clothing, uniforms and travel. A one-off contribution to fees may be considered.

Annual grant total

In 2013/14 the fund had an income of £1,100 and an expenditure of £0.

Applications

On a form available from the correspondent which must be completed by a sponsor from an educational establishment.

Forever Manchester (Community Foundation for Greater Manchester)

£3,700

Correspondent: The Awards Team, 2nd Floor, 8 Hewitt Street, Manchester M15 4GB (01612 140940; email: enquiries@communityfoundation.co.uk; website: forevermanchester.com/)

CC Number: 1017504

Eligibility

People in need who live in Greater Manchester.

Types of grants

Grants are usually one-off. Funds for individuals include the Stockport Fund, which supports individuals that contribute positively to the quality of life of people in Stockport and the Seed Fund, which supports individuals who have community ideas.

Annual grant total

Grants totalling £7,400 were made to individuals in 2012/13 for welfare and education. Educational grants totalled approximately £3,700.

Applications

Visit the foundation's website or contact the foundation for details of grant funds that are appropriate for individuals to apply for.

Other information

The Community Foundation for Greater Manchester manages a portfolio of grants for a variety of purposes which are mostly for organisations, but there are a select few which are for individuals. Funds tend to open and close throughout the year as well as new ones being added, and others being spent out. Check the foundation's website for information on current schemes.

Mynshull's Educational Foundation

£7,600

Correspondent: Ann Hosker, Administrator, Gaddum Centre, Gaddum House, 6 Great Jackson Street, Manchester M15 4AX (01618 346069; email: amh@gaddumcentre.co.uk)

CC Number: 532334

Eligibility

Children and young people aged 25 and under who are at school, university or college, on an apprenticeship or attending another educational/training course (except postgraduates). Applicants must be resident or have been born in the city of Manchester and the following adjoining districts: Reddish, Audenshaw, Failsworth, Chadderton, Middleton, Prestwich, Old City of Salford, Stretford, Sale, Cheadle, Heaton Moor, Heaton Mersey and Heaton Chapel.

Types of grants

Grants towards the costs of education, training and apprenticeships, for items such as books, equipment, clothing, uniforms and travel costs.

Annual grant total

In 2012/13 the foundation had an income of £12,900 and a total expenditure of £7,700. We estimate that grants totalled £7,600.

Exclusions

No grants for course fees, rent or any other ongoing expenditure.

Applications

On a form available from the correspondent which must be completed by a sponsor from the educational establishment.

Rochdale Ancient Parish Educational Trust

£20,000

Correspondent: The Administrator, Wyatt Morris Golland and Co., 200 Drake Street, Rochdale, Lancashire OL16 1PJ (01706 864707; website: www.rochdale.gov.uk/pdf/2009–03–19_Form%20Rochdale_Ancient_Parish_Educational_Trust_v4.pdf)

CC Number: 526318

Eligibility

People who live or attend/have attended school in the ancient parish of Rochdale, which includes Bacup, Littleborough, Milnrow, Newhey, Rochdale, Saddleworth, Todmorden, Wardle, Whitworth. There is no age limit but preference is given to people who are under the age of 25.

Types of grants

Grants are one-off and range between £50 and £330. Financial assistance is available towards the cost of clothing, uniforms, books, equipment/instruments and tools to enter a trade/profession or undertake educational/vocational courses. In exceptional circumstances the trust may provide scholarships, bursaries, grants and maintenance allowances to attend a further/higher education course or to travel within the UK/abroad in pursuance of education.

Annual grant total

In 2012/13 the trust had an income of £24,000 and a total expenditure of about £22,000. We estimate the annual total of grants to be around £20,000 but the charitable expenditure varies every year.

Exclusions

People who have already received a grant from Rochdale Ancient Parish Educational Trust or Hopwood Hall College Access Fund in the current academic year.

Applications

Application forms can be requested from the correspondent or found on the trust's website together with detailed guidelines. Applicants are required to submit evidence of enrolment on a particular course and specify the required support with approximate costs.

Seamon's Moss Educational Foundation

£1,200

Correspondent: Roger Drake, Secretary, 32 Riddings Court, Timperley, Altrincham, Cheshire WA15 6BG (01619 697772; email: rogerdrake@talktalk.net)

CC Number: 525823

Eligibility

People under the age of 25 who live in the ancient townships of Altrincham, Bowden and Dunham Massey, in Cheshire. Preference may be given to schoolchildren with serious family difficulties where the child has to be educated away from home.

Types of grants

One-off and recurrent grants up to a maximum of £250 each can be given to support education and training above elementary level. Assistance can be given for general educational needs, including fees, living expenses, books, equipment/instruments, study or travel abroad, and childcare.

Annual grant total

In 2013/14 the foundation had an income of £1,300 and an expenditure of £2,500. We estimate that educational grants to individuals totalled around £1,200.

Applications

In writing to the correspondent. Applications can be submitted directly by the individual. They are normally considered in August. Ineligible applications are not responded to.

Other information

Grants are also given to public elementary schools in the area of benefit.

Billinge

John Eddleston's Charity

£500

Correspondent: Graham Bartlett, Administrator, Parkinson Commercial Property Consultants, 10 Bridgeman Terrace, Wigan, Lancashire WN1 1SX (01942 741800)

CC Number: 503695

Eligibility

Persons under the age of 25 years in need of financial assistance who live in, or whose parents live in, the parish of Billinge.

Types of grants

One-off grants for educational purposes including social and physical training.

Annual grant total

In 2012/13 the charity had assets of £1.7 million and an income of £39,000. Our research tells us that grants to individuals usually total around £1,000 for both education and welfare purposes. Grants are also given to organisations.

Applications

In writing to the correspondent by the end of March. The annual meeting of the trustees takes place after the end of March.

Other information

The charity's trustees' report for 2012 tells us that: 'The charity has very close relationships with The John Eddleston Field Society and John Eddleston Vicarage Moneys, which are charities, all of which nominate trustees and provide funding to enable the charity to carry out its charitable objectives.'

Bolton

The Chadwick Educational Foundation

£1,500

Correspondent: Diane Abbott, Administrator, 71 Chorley Old Road, Bolton, Lancashire BL1 3JA (01204 534421)

CC Number: 526373

Eligibility

People under 25 years of age, living in Bolton and, who are in need.

Types of grants

One-off grants of £100 to £250 for text books, uniforms, equipment/instruments, educational outings in the UK and study or travel abroad. Grants are available for schoolchildren, students, apprentices and people starting work and for music or arts education. The foundation prefers to support the promotion of education in the principles of the Church of England.

Annual grant total

In 2012 the foundation had an income of £75,000 and assets of £50,000. Grants totalled nearly £70,000, of which £1,500 was given to individuals.

These were the latest accounts available at the time of writing (July 2014).

Applications

Application forms are available from the correspondent.

Other information

The foundation made seven grants to educational institutions totalling £69,000.

James Eden's Foundation

£21,000

Correspondent: The Trustees, R. P. Smith and Co., 71 Chorley Old Road, Bolton, Lancashire BL1 3AJ (01204 534421; email: info@ rpsmithbolton.co.uk; website: www. rpsmithbolton.co.uk)

CC Number: 526265

Eligibility

Young people resident in the metropolitan borough of Bolton who are in need of financial assistance, particularly for individuals in further education. Preference is given to people who have lost either or both parents, or whose parents are separated or divorced.

Types of grants

Cash grants of between £400 and £1,500 are given to assist college students and undergraduates with fees, books, equipment/instruments, maintenance/living expenses, educational outings in the UK and study or travel overseas. Parental income is taken into account in awarding grants.

Annual grant total

In 2012/13 the foundation had an income of £16,800 and an expenditure of £22,000. Grants to individuals totalled around £10,000.

Applications

On a form available from the correspondent, to be returned by the individual before September for consideration in October. If an individual has applied previously the trustees are particularly interested to know about his or her progress.

Other information

Grants are also given to organisations.

Golborne

The Golborne Charities – Charity of William Leadbetter

£2,000

Correspondent: Paul Gleave, Administrator, 56 Nook Lane, Golborne, Warrington WA3 3JQ (01942 727627; email: p.gleave56@hotmail.com)

CC Number: 221088

Eligibility

People in need who live in the parish of Golborne as it was in 1892.

Types of grants

One-off grants for equipment such as books, school uniforms and instruments, or for excursions. Grants are usually of between £50 and £80, but occasionally of up to £250. They are usually cash payments, but are occasionally in kind.

Annual grant total

In 2013/14 the charity had an income of £6,500 and a total expenditure of £8,000. We estimate that grants to individuals for educational purposes totalled around £2,000 and for social welfare purposes around £6,000.

Exclusions

Loans or grants for the payments of rates are not made. Grants are not repeated in less than two years.

Applications

In writing to the correspondent through a third party such as a social worker or a teacher, or via a trustee. Applications are considered at three-monthly intervals. Grant recipients tend to be known by at least one trustee.

Leigh

The Leigh Educational Endowment

£14,500

Correspondent: Corporate Director, Progress House, Westwood Park Drive, Wigan, Lancashire WN3 4HH (01942 244991; email: education@wigan.gov.uk)

CC Number: 526469

Eligibility

Children and young people under the age of 25 who live in the former borough of Leigh and are attending any institution of education, approved by the trustees. In practice, further/higher education students who have achieved high A-level results are normally supported.

Types of grants

Grants of between £250 and £500 are available to assist with the course fees, living expenses, books, equipment and other necessities.

Annual grant total

In 2012/13 the trust had an income of £16,100 and an expenditure of £15,000. We estimate the annual total of grants to be around £14,500. Our research suggests that usually around 20 individuals are supported annually.

Applications

Normally, applications should be submitted through the individual's college as a part of a list of suitable applicants for the trustees to choose from. Applications should be made in September after A-level results are released. Grants are considered in October.

Rochdale

The Heywood Educational Trust

£1,700

Correspondent: Michael Garraway, Administrator, Heywood Phoenix Trusts, Heywood Township Office, The Phoenix Centre, Church Street, Heywood, Lancashire OL10 1LR (01706 864707; email: phoenixtrusts@hotmail.co.uk; website: www.rochdaleonline.co.uk/sites/heywood-educational-trust/intro)

CC Number: 526690

Eligibility

People of any age who live in the Heywood area or the village of Birch or those attending or who have previously attended a school in the area. There is no age limit for applicants.

Types of grants

The trust's website says that: Grants from the trust may be given for any purpose which promotes the education, training and development of the applicant. This particularly includes:

- Assistance with the applicant's attendance at any school, university, college of education or other institution of further or higher (including professional and technical) education
- Assistance with travel, whether in the United Kingdom or abroad, to pursue their education
- Assistance with the purchase of necessary items to enable an applicant to enter employment following a course of study

Annual grant total

In 2012/13 the trust had an income of £1,400 and a total expenditure of £1,800. We estimate that educational grants totalled £1,700.

Exclusions

The trust is unable to cover full payment of fees or living expenses and can only provide limited assistance.

Applications

The trust should be telephoned for more information.

Middleton Educational Trust (The Emerson Educational Trust for Middleton)

£12,400

Correspondent: The Administrator, c/o Township Management Service, Middleton Public Library, Long Street, Middleton, Manchester M24 6DU (01706 924707; email: middletonemersontrust@hotmail.com; website: www.rochdale.gov.uk/the_council/more_about_the_council/charitable_trusts.aspx)

CC Number: 510495

Eligibility

People who live or attend/have attended school in the area of the former borough of Middleton.

Types of grants

Support is given to schoolchildren, further/higher education students and people starting work. Grants are given towards the cost of books, equipment/instruments, uniforms/clothing, educational outings in the UK, study/travel abroad and student exchanges, also apprenticeships, fees and maintenance expenses. Our research indicates that grants are one-off and range between £250 and £500.

Annual grant total

In 2012/13 the trust had an income of £7,200 and a total expenditure of £12,600. We have estimated that the annual total of grants was around £12,400.

Applications

Application forms can be downloaded from the Rochdale Borough Council website or requested from the correspondent. Applications can be submitted by individuals directly or through their educational institution or welfare agency, if applicable. Contact details of a course tutor or other academic professional are requested to support the application. Our research suggests that the trustees meet twice a year, usually in April and September.

Salford

The Salford Foundation Trust

£11,000

Correspondent: Peter Collins, Administrator, Foundation House, 3 Jo Street, Salford M5 4BD (01617878170; email: mail@salfordfoundationtrust.org. uk; website: www.salfordfoundationtrust. org.uk)

CC Number: 1105303

Eligibility

Young people between the ages of 5 to 25 who are resident in Salford. Preference is given to applicants who have lived in Salford for a minimum of three years.

Types of grants

Grants of up to £500 to fund opportunities that will enable a young person to learn, develop or gain new skills, take part in a character building experience and so on.

The trust also offers special Tony Wilson Awards which 'are made to children and young people who can demonstrate a special talent or ambition in the fields of art or creative skills.'

Annual grant total

In 2012/13 the trust had an income of £10,400 and a total expenditure of £12,000. We estimate the annual total of grants to be around £11,000. Previously the grants have been made in four categories of performing arts, sports/recreation, skills/talent development and academic/vocational opportunities.

Exclusions

Funding will not be considered for the following:

- Driving lessons
- Childcare costs
- Higher education course fees and living expenses
- Membership fees
- Remedial intervention (speech/language/occupational therapies)
- Retrospective funding
- Standard school/college and sports trips or residential excursions
- Activities with political or religious focus
- Needs that should be financed by statutory services

Group applications, organised group activities and so forth are not supported.

Applications

Application forms are available from the trust's website or can be requested from the correspondent and can be submitted directly by the individual or a third party (but not someone who will directly benefit from the grant). Applications are decided in four rounds per year: 3 February – 7 March, 5 May – 6 June, 4 August – 5 September, 3 November – 5 December. Note that applications can only be submitted by post and have to include two references.

Other information

Among the trust's patrons have been musician Peter Hook, actress Maxine Peake and Sarah Storey MBE.

Stockport

The Ephraim Hallam Charity

£2,900

Correspondent: Stephen Tattersall, Administrator, 3 Highfield Road, Poynton, Stockport, Cheshire SK12 1DU (01625 874445; email: smt@lacywatson. co.uk)

CC Number: 525975

Eligibility

People under 25 resident in Stockport.

Types of grants

Grants to support people at any institution of further or higher education, including the study of music and arts, travel costs, vocational training and people starting work

Annual grant total

In 2012 the charity had an income of £12,500 and a total expenditure of £5,900. We estimate that grants to individuals totalled £2,900, with funding also awarded to local youth organisations.

At the time of writing (July 2014) this was the most recent financial information available for the charity.

Applications

In writing to the correspondent.

Sir Ralph Pendlebury's Charity for Orphans

£2,100

Correspondent: Stephen Tattersall, Administrator, Lacy Watson and Co., Carlyle House, 107–109 Wellington Road South, Stockport SK1 3TL

CC Number: 213927

Eligibility

Orphans who have lived, or whose parents have lived, in the borough of Stockport for at least two years and who are in need.

Types of grants

Our research suggests that grants can be given to schoolchildren towards the cost of clothing, holidays, maintenance and books. Awards are usually of £5 or £6 a week plus clothing allowance twice a year. The main priority for the charity is relief-in-need.

Annual grant total

At the time of writing (August 2014) the latest financial information available was from 2012. In 2012 the charity had an income of £7,800 and a total expenditure of £4,400. We estimate that around £2,100 was awarded in grants for educational purposes.

Applications

In writing to the correspondent. Applications should be made by a parent/guardian.

Other information

Grants are also made for social welfare purposes.

Tameside

Ashton-under-Lyne United Scholarship Fund (The Heginbottom and Tetlow and William Kelsall Grants)

£0

Correspondent: Scott Littlewood, Finance Officer, Education and Cultural Services, Council Offices, Wellington Road, Ashton-under-Lyne OL6 6DL (01613 422878)

CC Number: 526478

Eligibility

People under the age of 25 who are attending or have attended a secondary school in the borough of Ashton-under-Lyne or who live, or whose parents live, in the former borough.

Types of grants

Financial assistance to students in any institution of further education. Only small grants can be awarded towards general educational expenses.

Annual grant total

In 2012/13 the trust had an income of £5,000. In the past two years there was no charitable spending.

Exclusions

Our research suggests that grants are not available to individuals receiving any grant or award other than a local authority or state grant.

Applications

In writing to the correspondent. Applications can be submitted by the individual directly.

Other information

Various grants are administered under this fund. The above refers to the Heginbottom and Tetlow Grants and William Kelsall Grants. There are also two smaller awards: the Thomas Taylor Grant to those studying full-time for a degree or diploma in electrical engineering; and J. B. Reyner Grants to those attending approved colleges of music.

The fund awards prizes at county or voluntary secondary schools in the area of benefit and uses the remainder to support individuals.

The Dowson Trust and Peter Green Endowment Trust Fund

£0

Correspondent: Scott Littlewood, Finance Officer, Educational and Cultural Services, Council Offices, Wellington Road, Ashton Under Lyne OL6 6DL (01613 422878)

CC Number: 525974

Eligibility

People aged under 25 who live in the former borough of Hyde.

Types of grants

Grants to those undertaking approved courses at universities or teacher training colleges.

Annual grant total

In 2012/13 the trust had an income of around £300 and an expenditure of £0. We have retained the entry as grants may well be made again in the near future.

Accounts were not available at the time of writing (July 2014).

Applications

In writing to the correspondent. Applications should be submitted by the individual by 30 September for consideration in October.

Timperley

The Timperley Educational Foundation

£800

Correspondent: Philip Turner, Trustee, 103 Sylvan Avenue, Timperley, Altrincham, Cheshire WA15 6AD (01619 693919)

CC Number: 1018845

Eligibility

Pupils, students or apprentices under the age of 21 and in need, who have a parent resident in the parish of Timperley. Assistance is also given to educational establishments and youth organisations within the parish.

Types of grants

One-off and recurrent grants to meet general expenses for students in further/higher education, including those being instructed in the doctrines of the Church of England. Schoolchildren may receive assistance on the recommendation of the headteacher only.

Annual grant total

In 2013 the foundation had an income of £1,000 and an expenditure of £1,600. Grants are made to individuals and organisations.

Applications

On a form available from the correspondent, either directly by the individual or, more usually, through the individual's parent/guardian, school, college or educational welfare agency. Applications are usually considered in August prior to the academic year for which support is needed, although this is not always essential. Application forms for new university entrants, however, must be received by 31 August.

Tottington

The Margaret Ann Smith Charity

£1,500

Correspondent: The Clerk, Woodcock and Sons, West View, Princess Street, Haslingden, Rossendale, Lancashire BB4 6NW (01706 213356)

CC Number: 526138

Eligibility

People who live in the urban district of Tottington, Bury as defined on 23 June 1964.

Types of grants

Grants of about £200 to help towards the cost of overseas exchange visits. There is

an emphasis on Commonwealth countries.

Annual grant total

This trust awards around £1,500 to individuals for educational purposes.

Applications

In writing to the correspondent. Applications should be submitted directly by the individual or through the individual's school/college or an educational welfare agency.

Isle of Man

The Manx Marine Society

£5,000

Correspondent: Capt. R. K. Cringle, 10 Carrick Bay View, Ballagawne Road, Colby, Isle of Man IM9 4DD (01624 838233)

Eligibility

Young Manx people under 18 who wish to attend sea school or become a cadet.

Types of grants

One-off grants for people about to start a career at sea towards uniforms, books, equipment/instruments and fees.

Annual grant total

About £5,000 a year is awarded to individuals for educational purposes.

Applications

In writing to the correspondent. Applications are considered at any time and can be submitted by the individual or through the school/college or educational welfare agency.

Other information

The trustees also award grants for social welfare purposes.

Lancashire

Baines's Charity

£4,000

Correspondent: Duncan Waddilove, 2 The Chase, Normoss Road, Blackpool, Lancashire FY3 0BF (01253 893459)

CC Number: 224135

Eligibility

People in need who live in the ancient townships of Carleton, Hardhorn-cum-Newton, Marton, Poulton-le-Fylde and Thornton.

Types of grants

One-off grants ranging from £100 to £250. 'Each case is considered on its merits.'

Annual grant total

In 2013 the charity had an income of £17,000 and a total expenditure of £18,000. Grants are made to individuals and organisations for both welfare and educational purposes. We estimate the amount paid in grants to individuals for educational purposes was £4,000.

Applications

On a form available from the correspondent, either directly by the individual, or through a social worker, Citizens Advice or other welfare agency. Applications are considered upon receipt.

Educational Foundation of John Farrington

£1,000

Correspondent: Dennis Johnson, Trustee, 35 Ribblesdale Drive, Grimsargh, Preston PR2 5RJ (01772 703050; email: dvicj@talktalk.net)

CC Number: 526488

Eligibility

People under the age of 25 who live, or have a parent who lives, in any of the following areas: former urban district of Fulwood, parishes of Goosnargh, Grimsargh, Haighton, Longridge, the city of Preston, Ribbleton and Whittingham. According to our research, preference is given to people with special educational needs and Ribbleton area residents.

Types of grants

Small grants of up to £250 to assist with the cost of general educational expenses, including books, equipment/instruments, fees, educational outings and visits. Our research indicates that help may also be available towards childcare expenses and to develop personal qualities and social awareness, for example through leadership courses, community development activities, camping expeditions and so forth.

Annual grant total

In 2012/13 the foundation had an income of £2,700 and an expenditure of £1,100. We have estimated that the annual total of grants was about £1,000.

Exclusions

Grants are not available to postgraduate students or to people who already receive a local authority grant. It is essential that the activity or course supported will contribute towards the applicant's educational development.

Applications

In writing to the correspondent. Our research shows that the foundation provides a leaflet outlining the format and contents of an application letter which can be submitted by the individual directly or through a third party such as a school/college, educational welfare agency/social worker, if applicable. Applications are considered twice a year.

Fort Foundation

£350

Correspondent: Edward Fort, Trustee, Fort Vale Engineering Ltd, Calder Vale Park, Simonstone Lane, Simonstone, Burnley BB12 7ND (01282 440000)

CC Number: 1028639

Eligibility

Young people in Pendle Borough and district, especially those undertaking courses in engineering.

Types of grants

One-off grants of £50 to £1,000 to schoolchildren, college students, undergraduates and vocational students for uniforms/clothing, study/travel overseas, books and equipment/instruments and excursions.

Annual grant total

In 2012/13 the trust had an income of £305,000 and a total expenditure of £94,000. It had assets of £517,000. Grants were made to individuals for education totalling £350.

Exclusions

Grants are not made for fees.

Applications

In writing to the correspondent, directly by the individual. Applications are considered at any time.

Other information

Grants are also made to organisations and small groups.

The Harris Charity

£1,400

Correspondent: David Ingram, The Secretary, c/o Moore and Smalley, Richard House, 9 Winckley Square, Preston PR1 3HP (01772 821021; fax: 01772 259441; email: harrischarity@mooreandsmalley.co.uk; website: theharrischarity.co.uk/)

CC Number: 526206

Eligibility

People in need under 25 who live in Lancashire, with a preference for the Preston district, who are in further or higher education.

Types of grants

One-off grants of £250 to £1,000 for equipment/instruments, tools, materials and so on.

Annual grant total

In 2012/13 the charity had assets of £3.5 million, an income of £181,000 and made grants totalling 53,000 of which £2,800 was awarded to individuals. We estimate that £1,400 of this was for educational purposes.

Exclusions

No grants are available to cover the cost of course fees or living expenses.

Applications

On an application form downloaded from the charity's website, where guidance and criteria can also be found. Applications are considered during the three months after 31 March and 30 September and can be submitted directly by the individual or through a school/college or educational welfare agency.

Other information

The original charity known as the Harris Orphanage Charity dates back to 1883. A new charitable scheme was established in 1985 following the sale of the Harris Orphanage premises in Garstang Road, Preston. The charity also supports charitable organisations that benefit individuals, recreation and leisure and the training and education of individuals.

The Khaleque and Sarifun Memorial Trust

£1,000

Correspondent: Ahmed Zaman, Trustee, 8 Cobden Villas, Oldfield Avenue, Darwen BB3 1QY (01254 777403)

CC Number: 518794

Eligibility

People who live in the borough of Blackburn (including overseas students studying there).

Types of grants

Grants are made to schoolchildren, further and higher education students and postgraduates towards the cost of uniforms or other school clothing, books, equipment/instruments and maintenance/living expenses. Foreign students in further and higher education in the UK can also be supported. Grants range from £50 to £1,100.

Annual grant total

In 2012/13 the trust had an income of £13,300 and a total expenditure of £8,300. Both figures were unusually high compared to those available to view from previous financial years. Our research tells us that grants are mainly given to support educational projects in Bangladesh and India. We estimate educational grants to individuals to have totalled £1,000.

Applications

In writing to the correspondent directly by the individual with a supporting letter from the individual's school or college. Applications should be submitted in October for consideration in November.

Peter Lathom's Charity

£5,500

Correspondent: Christine Aitken, Administrator, 13 Mallard Close, Aughton, Ormskirk, Lancashire L39 5QJ (01515 202717)

CC Number: 228828

Eligibility

People under 25 resident in West Lancashire.

Types of grants

Cash grants according to need for education and training.

Annual grant total

In 2013 this charity had assets of £1.4 million, an income of £53,000 and a total expenditure of £47,000. Educational grants awarded to individuals totalled £5,500. There were no welfare grants made in the year due to a lack of applications.

Applications

On a form available from the correspondent, to be submitted by 30 September. Awards in all cases are based on financial need as applications always exceed distributable income. Grants are awarded in November/December of each year.

John Parkinson (Goosnargh and Whittingham United Charity)

£2,000

Correspondent: John Bretherton, Clerk to the Trustees, Lower Stanalea Farm, Stanalea Lane, Goosnargh, Preston PR3 2EQ (01995 640224)

CC Number: 526060

Eligibility

People under the age of 25 who live in the parishes of Goosnargh, Whittingham and part of Barton.

Types of grants

One-off grants of up to £150 are available to people starting work,

entering a trade or preparing for a profession/occupation. Support can be given for tools, books, outfits, payment of fees towards training and courses, also travel expenses or maintenance costs to those who have to travel outside Lancashire to attend an interview or training. Our research suggests that students in further or higher education may be given help towards the cost of books.

Annual grant total

In 2013 the charity had an income of £5,400 and expenditure of £2,100, which is lower than in the past few years. We estimate that grants to individuals totalled around £2,000.

Applications

In writing to the correspondent. Applications are normally considered in May and November.

The Peel Foundation Scholarship Fund

£1,700

Correspondent: Catharine Oldroyd, Barnfield, Billinge End Road, Blackburn BB2 6QB (01254 56573)

CC Number: 526101

Eligibility

Students under the age of 25 resident in or in the neighbourhood of Blackburn who are entering higher education course to obtain a degree. The trustees choose successful applicants based on academic excellence, career ambitions and financial need.

Types of grants

Grants are for general student expenses. The fund can also support people entering a professional trade.

Annual grant total

In 2012/13 the fund had an income of £2,500 and an expenditure of £1,900. We have estimated that the annual total of grants was around £1,700.

Applications

Application forms can be requested from the correspondent. Candidates must be nominated by the headteacher or principal of their school or college. Our research shows that applicants may be called for an interview. Candidates must begin their course in the term following the award of scholarships (usually in September), unless excused by the trustees for sufficient cause. Applications are normally considered in July and August and should be submitted in advance.

Other information

The beneficial area more specifically is defined as: the whole borough of

Blackburn, except the civil parish of North Turton; the borough of Hyndburn, those parts of the former urban districts of Rishton and Oswaldtwistle which are close to the boundary with Blackburn; the Ribble Valley borough, the civil parishes of Balderstone, Billington, Clayton-le-Dale, Dinckley, Mellor, Osbaldeston, Ramsgreave, Salesbury and Wilpshire.

Superintendent Gerald Richardson Memorial Youth Trust

£7,500

Correspondent: David Williamson, Trustee, Northdene, Stoney Lane, Hambleton, Poulton-le-Fylde FY6 9AF (01253 590510)

CC Number: 504413

Eligibility

Children and young people under the age of 25 who live or work within 15 miles of Blackpool Town Hall. There is a preference for people with physical or mental disabilities.

Types of grants

Our research suggests that the trust can provide one-off and recurrent grants, typically in the range of £50 to £250. Awards are aimed to encourage children and young people to attend courses and activities of an educational, cultural, sporting, adventuresome or character-building nature. Assistance towards the cost of equipment, instruments, special educational needs, projects, study or travel overseas can also be provided.

Annual grant total

In 2012/13 the trust had an income of £11,100 and an expenditure of £15,300. The trust also supports organisations, therefore we estimate the annual total of grants to be around £7,500.

Applications

In writing to the correspondent. Individuals can apply directly or through a school/college, welfare agency/carer, if applicable. Applications are considered monthly but should be submitted at least two months before the requested amount is required.

Other information

The trust provides funds to youth organisations and schools. Generally, requests for help with major capital projects or where aid from the trust would be insignificant are rejected.

The Shaw Charities

£1,000

Correspondent: Mrs E. Woodrow, Administrator, 99 Rawlinson Lane, Heath Charnock, Chorley, Lancashire PR7 4DE (01257 480515; email: woodrows@tinyworld.co.uk)

CC Number: 214318

Eligibility

People in need who live in Rivington, Anglezarke, Heath Charnock and Anderton.

Types of grants

Grants to students on first degree courses for books.

Annual grant total

In 2012/13 the charity had an income of £7,000 and a total expenditure of £2,500. We estimate around £1,000 was made in grants to individuals for education.

Applications

On a form available from the correspondent to be submitted for consideration in March and November.

Other information

Educational funding from The Shaw Charities is given through the subsidiary charity The Shaw Educational Endowments. The charities also make grants for social welfare purposes.

Tunstall Educational Trust

£2,600

Correspondent: Joyce Crackles, Trustee, Mill Farm, Burrow, Carnforth, Lancashire LA6 2RJ (01524 274239)

CC Number: 526250

Eligibility

Pupils above elementary level living in Burrow, Cansfield and Tunstall.

Types of grants

One-off and recurrent grants are given according to need and are available to schoolchildren (above the elementary education level) 'to encourage them to continue at school.' Our research suggests that the trust mainly makes travel grants.

Annual grant total

In 2013 the charity had an income of £5,600 and an expenditure of £5,400. We estimate the annual total of grants to individuals to be around £2,600.

Applications

In writing to the correspondent. Trustees normally meet in June and November to consider applications.

Other information

Public elementary schools and organisations in Tunstall may also be supported.

Bickerstaffe

Bickerstaffe Education Trust

£1,100

Correspondent: Merrick Rimmer, Trustee, Primrose Cottage, Hall Lane, Bickerstaffe, Ormskirk, Lancashire L39 0EH (01695 727848; email: hilaryrosbotham@hotmail.co.uk)

CC Number: 1108104

Eligibility

Mainly children and young people resident in the parish of Bickerstaffe or attending Bickerstaffe Voluntary Controlled School.

Types of grants

Grants given according to need.

Annual grant total

In 2012 the trust had an income of £9,100 and a total expenditure of £2,200. We estimate that educational grants to individuals totalled £1,100, with funding also awarded to organisations.

At the time of writing (July 2014) this was the most recent financial information available for the trust.

Applications

In writing to the correspondent.

Blackburn with Darwen

It's Your Wish – The John Bury Trust

£20,000

Correspondent: Pamela Rodgers, Trustee, 2 Eckersley Close, Blackburn, Lancashire BB2 4FA (07985 894499; email: info@thejohnburytrust.co.uk; website: www.johnburytrust.co.uk)

CC Number: 1108181

Eligibility

Young people between the ages of 10 and 25 who reside within the boundaries of Blackburn with Darwen borough council.

Types of grants

Grants are given to 'promote the mental, spiritual, moral and physical development and improvement' of the individuals. Support can be for a wide range of causes, including purchase of equipment, other necessities, short-term projects, study/travel overseas, expeditions, personal development opportunities, gaining new skills, travel costs, extra-curricular activities and so on.

Annual grant total

In 2012/13 the trust had an income of £16,400 and an expenditure of £20,000. We estimate the annual total of grants to individuals to be about the same amount.

Applications

Application forms can be downloaded from the trust's website together with full terms and conditions. Applicants who are successful in the initial consideration are invited for an interview.

Other information

All grants are expected to be spent within a 12-month period of receiving the award.

Blackpool

Blackpool Children's Clothing Fund

£4,500

Correspondent: Alan Rydeheard, Trustee, 96 West Park Drive, Blackpool FY3 9HU (01253 736812)

CC Number: 215133

Eligibility

Schoolchildren aged 4 to 16 who live and attend an educational establishment in the borough of Blackpool.

Types of grants

Clothing, footwear and equipment for disadvantaged children in Blackpool. The trust gives vouchers which can be redeemed in participating local retailers and school shop suppliers.

Annual grant total

In 2012/13 the fund had an income of £2,600 and an expenditure of £4,700. We have estimated that the annual total of grants was about £4,500.

Applications

In writing to the correspondent. If applicable, applications should be made by a third party, such as education or social work service, on behalf of the applicant. Individuals in need identified by the local education authority are also considered. Applications are administered by the members of student support team.

The Swallowdale Children's Trust

£0

Correspondent: Alexa Alderson, Administrator, 13 Newlands Avenue, Blackpool FY3 9PG

CC Number: 526205

Eligibility

People who live in the Blackpool area who are under the age of 25. Orphans are given preference.

Types of grants

One-off grants are given to: schoolchildren, college students, undergraduates, vocational students and people starting work, including those for clothes/uniforms, fees, study/travel abroad and equipment/instruments.

Annual grant total

In 2012/13 the trust held assets of £999,000 and had an income of £40,000. During the year, the trust awarded 210 hardship grants to individuals, totalling £22,000. Grants amounting to £10,400 were made to Lancashire Outward Bound and to Life Education Centres, with the aim of assisting young people 'to achieve a more positive approach to life.' No grants were awarded to individuals to assist in education.

Applications

On a form available from the correspondent, with the financial details of the individual or family. Applications must be made through a social worker or teacher. They are considered six times per year.

Burnley

Edward Stocks Massey Bequest Fund

£7,000

Correspondent: Saima Afzaal, Burnley Borough Council, Town Hall, Manchester Road, Burnley, Lancashire BB11 1JA (01282 425011; email: safzaal@ burnley.gov.uk)

CC Number: 526516

Eligibility

People who live in the borough of Burnley and higher education students who have been previously educated in the borough.

Types of grants

The primary purpose of the fund is to assist local individuals and voluntary organisations in the fields of education, science, music and arts. Two Higher Education Student Support Scholarships are considered each year to support students in higher education who have been previously educated in the borough of Burnley.

Annual grant total

In 2012/13 the fund had assets of £979,000 and an income of £34,000. Total charitable expenditure was around £52,000, of which grants to individuals and student scholarships totalled £7,000.

Exclusions

Our research suggests that support is not given to people already in receipt of funding from the local authority. It is required that other sources of funding are explored before applying to the trust.

Applications

Application forms can be requested from the correspondent. Applications should be submitted by the end of May for consideration within the following two months. Students seeking scholarships should be nominated by their previous educational establishment and demonstrate great academic achievements, contribution to school/ college and/or financial need.

Other information

Support is mostly given to organisations and groups.

The fund also gives grants to the Burnley Mechanics Institute trust.

Darwen

The W. M. and B. W. Lloyd Trust

£15,000

Correspondent: John Jacklin, Trustee, Gorse Barn, Rock Lane, Tockholes, Darwen, Lancashire BB3 0LX (01254 771367)

CC Number: 503384

Eligibility

People in need who live in the old borough of Darwen in Lancashire. Preference is given to single parents.

Types of grants

One-off and recurrent grants according to need. Grants are made to schoolchildren, college students, undergraduates, vocational students and mature students, including those for uniforms/clothing, books, study/travel abroad, equipment/instruments, excursions and awards for excellence.

Annual grant total

In 2012/13 the trust had an income of £95,000 and a total expenditure of £63,000. We estimate grants to individuals for educational purposes to be around £15,000.

Applications

In writing to the correspondent to be submitted either directly by the individual or through a relevant third party. Applications are considered quarterly in March, June, September and December. Applicants are advised to enquire about the other funds (detailed in this entry) administered by the trustees and available to people living in Daren.

Other information

Grants are made to both individuals and organisations for educational and social welfare purposes.

The trustees also administer the following funds:

- The Peter Pan Fund for the benefit of people with mental disabilities
- The Darwen War Memorial and Sick Poor Fund originally to help war widows and dependents after the 1st World War and the sick poor of Darwen
- The Darwen Disabled Fund which was originally designed to assist with the social welfare of people with physical disabilities in Darwen
- The Ernest Aspin Donation to support sporting activities and in particular training and educating young people in sport
- The T. P. Davies Fund which is for the benefit of the residents of Darwen
- Darwen Probation Volunteers Fund supports people in Darwen who have come under the probation and aftercare service, and their families

Leyland

The Balshaw's Educational Foundation

£1,500

Correspondent: Phil Hamman, Administrator, 25 Lonsdale Close, Leyland, Lancashire PR25 3BU (01772 424029)

CC Number: 526595

Eligibility

People living in the parish of Leyland.

Types of grants

Help with educational needs including the cost of books, clothing and other essentials for schoolchildren. Grants may also be available for those at college or university.

Annual grant total

In 2013 the foundation had an income of £2,000 and an expenditure of £1,700. Grants made totalled approximately £1,500.

Applications

In writing to the correspondent.

Lowton

The Lowton United Charity

£2,000

Correspondent: John Naughton, Secretary, 51 Kenilworth Road, Lowton, Warrington WA3 2AZ (01942 741583)

CC Number: 226469

Eligibility

People in need who live in the parishes of St Luke's and St Mary's in Lowton.

Types of grants

Help with the cost of books, clothing and other essentials for schoolchildren. Grants are also available for those at college or university.

Annual grant total

Grants for individuals total about £4,000 each year. About half of grants are given at Christmas for relief-in-need purposes and the rest are given throughout the year.

Exclusions

Grants are not given to postgraduates.

Applications

Usually through the rectors of the parishes or other trustees.

Over Kellet

Thomas Wither's Charity

£3,500

Correspondent: David Mills, Clerk to the Trustees, 51 Greenways, Over Kellet, Carnforth, Lancashire LA6 1DE (01524 732194)

CC Number: 526079

Eligibility

People under the age of 25 who live in the parish of Over Kellet.

Types of grants

Originally grants were given to people starting work/entering a trade and people undertaking apprenticeships. Currently the funds are also available to support general educational needs. Support can be given for various educational necessities, including clothing, outfits, equipment, tools, and towards courses, workshops and other training helping to get into employment.

Annual grant total

In 2013 the charity had an income of £5,700 and an expenditure of £3,700. We estimate the annual total of grants to individuals to be around £3,500.

Applications

Application forms can be requested from the correspondent. They should be submitted by 1 May or 1 November each year.

Preston

Roper Educational Foundation

£0

Correspondent: Mark Burrow, Administrator, Blackhurst Swainson Goodier LLP, 3–4 Aalborg Square, Lancaster LA1 1GG (01524 386500; email: mwb@bsglaw.co.uk)

CC Number: 526428

Eligibility

Children and young people under the age of 26 who live in St Wilfrid's Parish, Preston or who have attended school in the parish for at least two years. Preference may be given to current or former pupils of St Wilfrid's Roman Catholic Primary School.

Types of grants

The foundation can support schoolchildren, further/higher education students and people in vocational training/apprenticeships or entering a trade/starting work. Support is given for general educational needs.

Annual grant total

At the time of writing (July 2014) the latest financial information available was from 2012. In 2012 the foundation had assets of £793,000 and an income of £65,000. A total of £43,000 was awarded in grants but no individual awards were made this year. In the past few years grants to individuals have on average totalled £4,500.

Applications

Application forms can be requested from the correspondent. Applications can be submitted directly by the individual for consideration in February, July and October. The foundation advertises grants through notices in the local and diocesan newspapers and by writing to eligible schools.

Other information

Grants are also made to voluntary-aided Roman Catholic schools in the county borough of Preston.

Rishton

The George Lawes Memorial Fund

£600

Correspondent: Director of Financial Services, Scaitcliffe House, Ormerod Street, Accrington, Lancashire BB5 0PF (01254 388111)

CC Number: 224118

Eligibility

People under the age of 21 who live in the township of Rishton and are in financial need.

Types of grants

One-off grants to help schoolchildren and further and higher education students, including mature students, with books, equipment, clothing/uniforms, fees, maintenance/living expenses, educational outings in the UK and study or travel abroad.

Annual grant total

In 2012/13 the fund had an income of £600 and a total expenditure of approximately £700. We estimate that £600 was awarded in grants for educational purposes.

Applications

In writing to the correspondent directly by the individual. Applications should be submitted around November/December for consideration in December.

Merseyside

The Girls' Welfare Fund

£2,500

Correspondent: Mrs S. M. O'Leary, Trustee, West Hey, Dawstone Road, Heswall, Wirral CH60 4RP (email: gwf_charity@hotmail.com)

CC Number: 220347

Eligibility

Girls and young women, usually those aged between 15 and 25 years, who were born in Merseyside. Applications from outside this area will not be acknowledged. Preference will be given to those who are pursuing vocational or further education courses rather than other academic courses.

Types of grants

Both one-off and recurrent grants of £100 to £1,000 for leisure and creative activities, sports, welfare and the relief of poverty. Grants may be given to schoolchildren and students for uniforms/clothing, college students and undergraduates for uniforms/clothing, study/travel overseas and books, vocational students for uniforms/clothing, books and equipment/instruments and to people starting work for clothing and equipment/instruments. The fund is particularly interested in helping individual girls and young women of poor or deferred education to establish themselves and gain independence.

Annual grant total

In 2013 the fund had an income of £9,800 and a total expenditure of £10,700. We estimate grants to individuals for educational purposes totalled around £2,500.

Exclusions

Grants are not made to charities that request funds to pass on and give to individuals.

Applications

In writing to the correspondent or by email. Applications can be submitted directly by the individual or through a social worker, Citizens Advice, other welfare agency or college/educational establishment. Applications are considered quarterly in March, June, September and December, and should include full information about the college, course and particular circumstances.

Other information

The trust also gives grants to individuals in need and organisations helping girls and young women in Merseyside.

The Holt Education Trust

£18,300 (71 grants)

Correspondent: Anne Edwards, Administrator, P. H. Holt Foundation, 151 Dale Street, Liverpool L2 2AH (01512 372663; email: info@holteducationtrust.org.uk; website: www.phholtfoundation.org.uk/education-trust.aspx)

CC Number: 1113708

Eligibility

Higher education students in need who have lived most of their life in Merseyside and still have a home there. Normally first degree, academic, full-time basis courses are supported but applicants who can only study part-time because of family circumstances will be considered. In some subjects, including medicine, second degree students can also be assisted.

Types of grants

One-off grants ranging from £50 to £300 to help with the college or university

fees, books, equipment, study trips and, more frequently, childcare, accommodation and travel.

Annual grant total

In 2012/13 a total of £18,300 was awarded in grants to 71 students.

Exclusions

The trust's website reminds that the trustees will 'not normally give grants for courses which can be considered as in-service training; which employers could fund.'

Applications

Application forms can be requested from the correspondent and have to be accompanied by written evidence of enrolment on the relevant course. The trustees consider the applications twice a year.

Other information

This trust is part of the P H Holt Foundation.

The trust's website states that 'candidates can apply to the trust once every academic year, [however] once the trust has started to help it normally renews the grant in each year the course lasts, provided the applicant's circumstances have not changed.'

The Sheila Kay Fund

£30,000

Correspondent: Victoria Symes, Administrator, c/o PSS, 18 Seel Street, Liverpool L1 4BE (01517 025545; email: gill.gargen@skffund.org.uk; website: www.sheilakayfund.org/site)

CC Number: 1021378

Eligibility

People in need living in Merseyside (Liverpool, Knowsley, Sefton, St Helens, Wirral) who have a background of work (paid or voluntary) in social/community/voluntary sector and are pursuing education but lack means.

Priority is given to those who have left school with few, if any, qualifications, also people from minority communities who have experienced difficulties in entering education, unemployed people or individuals on low incomes.

Types of grants

One-off and recurrent grants are made ranging between £50 to £300 for people engaged in social, youth and community work (paid or voluntary) who cannot afford the relevant education or training. Support has been previously awarded for the course fees, childcare, travel expenses and books or materials.

The trust helps people at a wide variety of educational stages, including higher education in social, community and

youth work, access courses, GNVQ's, GSE's, counselling qualifications, introductory courses to Maths, English and IT, and Community courses such as Credit Union, Playwork and Capacity Building. Priority will be given to funding short/part-time courses or conferences.

Annual grant total

In 2012/13 the fund had assets of £14,500 and an income of £40,000. Educational awards totalled over £7,000, consisting of £5,600 in grants towards higher education costs, £900 in books and £700 in travel grants. A further £23,000 was spent to enable adults to access learning opportunities.

Exclusions

Grants are not given to anyone qualified to a degree standard and beyond.

Applications

Application forms are available on the fund's website and can be submitted by email or post at any time. References are required.

Other information

The trust also offers guidance, information or support materials to individuals and community/voluntary groups and can refer applicants to other funds to obtain further grant support.

The trust notes that 'grants from the fund to students are only considered in exceptional circumstances when the applicant is faced with extreme difficulties.'

Community Foundation for Merseyside

£7,000

Correspondent: Sue Langfeld, Administrator, Community Foundation for Merseyside, Third Floor, Stanley Building, 43 Hanover Street, Liverpool, Merseyside L1 3DN (01512 322444; email: info@cfmerseyside.org.uk; website: www.cfmerseysde.org.uk)

CC Number: 1068887

Eligibility

People in need who live in Merseyside.

Types of grants

The foundation currently administers three funds which provide grants to individuals for education:

- John Goore Fund – grants of up to £350 to people in higher education and training, particularly adults who need to retrain and improve their skills after a period of unemployment or redundancy
- Joseph Harley Bequest Fund – support is given to young people under the age of 25 who live in

Formby for educational projects and activities which are not normally assisted by the public bodies and local authorities

▸ Sefton Education and Learning Fund – grants of up to £250 are offered to young people under the age of 25 who are resident in Sefton towards the cost of educational materials and courses

Annual grant total

In 2012/13 the foundation had assets of £7.4 million, an income of £3.2 million and a charitable expenditure of £2.3 million. A total of £41,000 was awarded in grants for both educational and welfare purposes to 61 individuals. We estimate that around £7,000 was available to individuals in education.

Applications

Application forms can be found on the foundation's website. For further information on the application procedure and required supporting documents for each of the funds, consult the website or contact the correspondent.

Other information

The foundation administers a number of funds for various purposes. Most of the funding is given to organisations (in 2012/13 £1.9 million to 369 voluntary and community groups); however, individuals in need can also be supported. The funds tend to open and close regularly, therefore potential applicants should contact the foundation directly for the most recent updates.

John James Rowe's Foundation for Girls

£15,500

Correspondent: Gill Gargan, Administrator, 18–28 Seel Street, Liverpool L1 4BE (01517 025555)

CC Number: 526166

Eligibility

Girls between the ages of 10 and 22 who live in Merseyside and whose parents are separated/divorced, whose home conditions are especially difficult, or who have lost one or both of their parents.

Types of grants

Assistance is given for girls at secondary school, further/higher education students and those entering a profession/trade or undertaking apprenticeships. One-off grants are made for equipment/instruments, clothing, tools, books, also boarding expenses and the cost of holidays. The maximum award is of about £200.

Annual grant total

In 2012/13 the foundation had an income of £13,200 and an expenditure of £15,700. We estimate that grants to individuals totalled around £15,500.

Applications

Application forms can be requested from the correspondent or downloaded from The Sheila Kay Foundation's website (www.sheilakayfund.org). Applications can be made at any time directly by the individual.

The Rushworth Trust
See entry on page 91

Great Crosby
The Halsall Educational Foundation

£1,400

Correspondent: Hugh Hollinghurst, Trustee, 37 St Michaels Road, Crosby, Merseyside L23 7UJ (01519 247889)

CC Number: 526236

Eligibility

Girls who are leaving sixth form education and entering higher education and live, or whose parents live, in the ancient township of Great Crosby.

Types of grants

One-off towards books, stethoscopes and so on.

Annual grant total

In 2012 the foundation had an income of £1,400 and a total expenditure of £1,500. This was the latest information available at the time of writing (August 2014). We estimate that educational grants to individuals totalled £1,400.

Exclusions

Grants are made only to girls living in the ancient township of Great Crosby.

Applications

In writing to the correspondent. Applications should be submitted between March and 30 June, for possible interview in September.

Liverpool
The Liverpool Council of Education (Incorporated)

£10,000

Correspondent: Roger Morris, Trustee, P. H. Holt Foundation, 151 Dale Street, Liverpool L2 2AH (01512 372663)

CC Number: 526714

Eligibility

Pupils, students and teachers in Liverpool.

Types of grants

Grants, usually of around £50 to £350, are given according to need.

Annual grant total

In 2012/13 the charity had an income of £19,600 and an expenditure of £22,000. We estimate that individual grants totalled around £10,000.

Applications

In writing to the correspondent. Our research suggests that the charity shares its details with the schools in Liverpool at the beginning of each school year and the closing date for applications is normally the last week of January.

Other information

The charity acts as a trustee to various charitable funds providing educational support to schools, pupils and teachers in Liverpool.

Lydiate
The Charity of John Goore

£1,500

Correspondent: Edward Bostock, 124 Liverpool Road, Lydiate, Liverpool L31 2NB (01515 264919; email: info@cfmerseyside.org.uk; website: www.cfmerseyside.org.uk/John-Goore-Fund---Individuals)

CC Number: 238355

Eligibility

Higher education students and people in training/retraining who live in Lydiate.

Types of grants

Grants, ranging up to £350, are awarded towards the costs of books, equipment/instruments, travel expenses, clothing required for courses or interviews, for short courses, relevant accreditations and other items or activities which advance education or training.

Annual grant total

In 2012/13 the charity had an income of £6,600 and an expenditure of £6,500. We estimate the annual total of grants for educational purposes to be about £1,500.

Applications

Application forms can be downloaded from the charity's website or requested from the correspondent and are considered throughout the year. Our research indicates that, together with the application, it is required to submit a written proof of residence in Lydiate and a letter of acceptance from the higher education establishment.

Other information

The charity also makes grants to organisations and to individuals for welfare purposes.

St Helens

The Rainford Trust

£500 (1 grant)

Correspondent: William H. Simm, Executive Officer, c/o Pilkington Group Ltd, Prescot Road, St Helens, Merseyside WA10 3TT (01744 20574; email: rainfordtrust@btconnect.com)

CC Number: 266157

Eligibility

People in need who are normally resident in the borough of St Helens.

Types of grants

One-off and recurrent grants ranging from £100 to £750 are paid directly to the college or other third party organisation. Grants can be for schoolchildren for equipment/instruments, fees, maintenance/living expenses and educational outings in the UK. Further and higher education students and mature students can receive grants for books, equipment/instruments, fees, childcare and educational outings in the UK.

Annual grant total

In 2012/13 the trust had assets of £8.6 million and an income of £212,000. During the year only one grant was made to an individual for educational purposes and this was in the amount of £500.

Applications

In writing to the correspondent, for consideration throughout the year. Applications can be made directly by the individual, or through his or her school, college or educational welfare agency. The trust sends out a questionnaire, if appropriate, after the application has been made.

Other information

Grants are mostly made to organisations.

Wirral

Lower Bebington School Lands Foundation

£2,200

Correspondent: S. R. Green, Trustee, Poulton Hall, Bebington, Wirral, Cheshire CH63 9LN (01513 343000)

CC Number: 525849

Eligibility

Higher/further education students residing in the area of the parish of St Andrew, Lower Bebington, as it was in 1924.

Types of grants

Small grants of up to £300 are available towards general educational costs, including books, equipment/instruments, necessities, fees and living expenses.

Some assistance may also be available towards facilities not normally provided by the local authorities for public school pupils.

Annual grant total

In 2012/13 the trust had an income of £3,200 and an expenditure of £2,400. We have estimated the annual total of grants to be around £2,200.

Applications

Application forms can be obtained from the correspondent. Our research suggests that applications should be submitted by August each year but may be considered at other times if funds are available.

Other information

The trustees inform that 'owing to poor drafting when state education was introduced [the beneficial area] cannot be adjusted to suit current boundary' and further suggest that applicants should 'see the Poulton Lancelyn Lands Foundation (1998) which covers omitted areas'.

The Thomas Robinson Charity

£1,000

Correspondent: Charles F. Van Ingen, Administrator, 1 Blakeley Brow, Wirral, Merseyside CH63 0PS

CC Number: 233412

Eligibility

People in need who live in Higher Bebington.

Types of grants

One-off grants in the range of £50 to £500.

Annual grant total

In 2012 the charity had both an income and a total expenditure of £3,000. We estimate around £1,000 was made in grants to individuals for education.

The 2012 accounts are the latest available at the time of writing.

Applications

In writing to: The Vicar, Christ Church Vicarage, King's Road, Higher Bebington, Wirral CH43 8LX. Applications can be submitted directly by the individual or a family member, through a social worker, or a relevant third party such as Citizens Advice or a school. They are considered at any time.

Other information

The charity also makes grants to individuals for social welfare purposes.

Midlands

General

The Beacon Centre for the Blind

£900

Correspondent: Phil Thomas, Company Secretary, Wolverhampton Road East, Wolverhampton WV4 6AZ (01902 886781; email: enquiries@beacon4blind. co.uk; website: www.beacon4blind.co.uk)

CC Number: 216092

Eligibility

People who are registered blind or partially sighted and live in the metropolitan boroughs of Dudley (except Halesowen and Stourbridge), Sandwell and Wolverhampton, and part of the South Staffordshire District Council area.

Types of grants

One-off grants up to a maximum of £250 for specific items or improvements to the home.

Annual grant total

In 2012/13 the charity had assets of £8.6 million, an income of £2.1 million and a total expenditure of £2.4 million. 7 grants were made to individuals totalling £1,900 of which we estimate, £900 was awarded for educational grants. Grants are also made to individuals in need.

Applications

In writing to the correspondent stating the degree of vision and age of the applicant, and their monthly income and expenditure. Applications can be submitted through a social worker or a school, and are considered throughout the year.

Other information

The charity provides domiciliary care for up to 71 elderly blind and partially sighted people who attend the day centre each week to participate in therapeutic activities. The charity also provides a gym, outreach and a talking newspaper.

The Birmingham and Three Counties Trust for Nurses

£4,000

Correspondent: David Airston, Administrator, 16 Haddon Croft, Halesowen B63 1JQ (01216 020389; email: ruthmadams_45@msn.com)

CC Number: 217991

Eligibility

Nurses on any statutory register, who have practised or practise in the city of Birmingham and the counties of Staffordshire, Warwickshire and Worcestershire.

Types of grants

One-off grants up to £300 per annum to nurses taking post-registration courses (post-basic nurse training or back-to-nursing course). Grants are made towards books, travel and/or fees.

Annual grant total

In 2012/13 the trust had an income of £5,300 and a total expenditure of £14,000. Previous grants have mostly been made for welfare purposes.

Applications

On a form available from the correspondent to be submitted directly by the individual. Applications are considered at any time.

The Francis Bernard Caunt Education Trust

£40,000

Correspondent: James Kitchen, Trustee, Larken and Co., 10 Lombard Street, Newark NG24 1XE (01636 703333; email: info@larken.co.uk; website: www. larken.co.uk)

CC Number: 1108858

Eligibility

People aged between 16 and 25 who are, or whose parents or guardians are, resident within a 12 mile radius of Newark on Trent Parish Church.

Applicants should have attended or attend Newark schools or colleges or Southwell or Tuxford schools in the previous eight years for at least two years and be intending to study part-time or full-time for at least one year on a recognised academic or vocational course.

Types of grants

Grants and loans of £500–£2,000.

Annual grant total

In 2012/13 the trust had assets of £1.4 million, an income of £48,000 and made grants totalling £40,000.

Applications

On the application form available from the website (www.larken.co.uk/about/in-the-community.html) with a letter of reference from a headteacher, employer or other appropriate person such at a career adviser.

The Charities of Susanna Cole and Others

£4,000

Correspondent: Peter Gallimore, Trustee, 19 Oak Tree House, 153 Oak Tree Lane, Bournville, Birmingham B30 1TU (01214 714064)

CC Number: 204531

Eligibility

Quakers in need who live in parts of Worcestershire and most of Warwickshire and are 'a member or attendee of one of the constituent meetings of the Warwickshire Monthly Meeting of the Society of Friends'. Preference is given to younger children (for education).

Types of grants

One-off and recurrent grants for education or re-training.

Annual grant total

In 2012 the charity had an income of £12,000 and a total expenditure of £8,500. Grants are made for welfare and educational purposes. We estimate grants to individuals for educational purposes to be around £4,000. The 2012 accounts were the only ones available at the time of writing (July 2014).

Applications

In writing to the correspondent via the overseer of the applicant's Quaker meeting. Applications should be received by early March and October for consideration later in the same months.

Thomas Monke

£2,000

Correspondent: Christopher Kitto, Administrator, 29 Blacksmiths Lane, Newton Solney, Burton on Trent, Staffordshire DE15 0SD (01543 267995)

CC Number: 214783

Eligibility

Young people under the age of 25 who live in Austrey, Measham, Shenton and Whitwick.

Types of grants

One-off and recurrent grants towards the cost of goods, tools, books, fees and travelling expenses for educational purposes.

Annual grant total

In 2013 the charity had an income of £4,200 and an expenditure of £4,100. Grants for educational purposes totalled around £2,000.

Exclusions

Expeditions, scholarships and university course fees are not funded.

Applications

Application forms are available from the correspondent and should be submitted directly by the individual before 31 March, in time for the trustees' yearly meeting held in April.

The Newfield Charitable Trust

£3,800 (10 grants)

Correspondent: David Dumbleton, Clerk, Rotherham and Co. Solicitors, 8–9 The Quadrant, Coventry CV1 2EG (02476 227331; fax: 02476 221293; email: d. dumbleton@rotherham-solicitors.co.uk)

CC Number: 221440

Eligibility

Girls and women (under 30) who are in need of care and assistance and live in Coventry or Leamington Spa.

Types of grants

Grants towards school uniforms and other school clothing, educational trips, books and childcare costs. Most grants are under £500.

Annual grant total

In 2012/13 the trust had assets of almost £1.5 million and an income of £53,000. During the year, the trustees received a total of 146 applications, from which 139 applicants were awarded. Grants totalled nearly £35,000 and were distributed as follows:

Educational	10	£3,800
Clothing	56	£13,800
General	73	£17,200

Exclusions

No grants for postgraduate education.

Applications

Write to the correspondent for an application form. Applications are accepted from individuals or third parties e.g. schools, social services, Citizens Advice, etc. A letter of support/reference from someone not a friend or relative of the applicant (i.e. school, social services, etc.) may be required. Details of income/expenditure and personal circumstances should also be given.

Applications are considered eight times a year.

The Norton Foundation

£1,270 (13 grants)

Correspondent: Richard Perkins and Company, 50 Brookfield Close, Hunt End, Redditch B97 5LL (01527 544446; email: correspondent@ nortonfoundation.org; website: www. nortonfoundation.org)

CC Number: 702638

Eligibility

Young people under 25 who live in Birmingham, Coventry or Warwickshire and are in need of care, rehabilitation or aid of any kind, 'particularly as a result of delinquency, maltreatment or neglect or who are in danger of lapsing or relapsing into delinquency'.

Types of grants

One-off grants of up to £500 are available to schoolchildren and further and higher education students for school clothing, books, equipment, instruments, fees, maintenance and living expenses and educational outings in the UK.

Annual grant total

In 2012/13 the trust had assets of £4.4 million and an income of £119,000. Grants were made totalling £96,000, of which £13,000 was given in individual grants, £24,000 was awarded in discretionary grants and the remaining £60,000 was given to organisations. Grants to individuals were distributed as follows:

Household	104	£9,900
Clothing	22	£1,700
Education and training	13	£1,270

Applications

By letter which should contain all the information required as detailed in the guidance notes for applicants. Guidance notes are available from the correspondent or the foundation's website. Applications must be submitted through a social worker, Citizens Advice, probation service, school or other welfare agency. They are considered quarterly.

Sir John Sumner's Trust

See entry on page 110

The Anthony and Gwendoline Wylde Memorial Charity

£2,000

Correspondent: Kirsty McEwen, The Clerk, 3 Waterfront Business Park, Dudley Road, Brierley Hill, West Midlands DY5 1LX (0845 111 5050; email: kirsty.mcewen@higgsandsons.co. uk; website: www.wyldecharity.weebly. com)

CC Number: 700239

Eligibility

People in need with a preference for residents of Stourbridge (West Midlands) and Kinver (Staffordshire).

Types of grants

One-off grants in the range of £50 and £500 are given to college students and undergraduates for clothing, fees, books, equipment/instruments, maintenance/ living expenses, voluntary work overseas and excursions.

Annual grant total

In 2012/13 the charity had an income of £47,000 and a total expenditure of £42,000. Based on previous giving, we estimate that the total grant awarded to individuals, for educational and social welfare purposes, was approximately £4,000.

Exclusions

No grants towards bills or debts.

Applications

In writing to the correspondent. Applications can be submitted directly by the individual or a family member and are considered on an ongoing basis.

Other information

The charity also awards grants to organisations.

Derbyshire

Coke's Educational Charity

£2,000

Correspondent: Andrew Cree, Administrator, Damson Lodge, Longford, Ashbourne, Derbyshire DE6 3DT (01335 330074)

CC Number: 527028

Eligibility

People under the age of 25 who live in the parishes of Alkmonton, Hollington, Hungry Bentley, Longford and Rodsley.

Types of grants

One-off and recurrent grants for general educational purposes. Support is available to people who have completed their secondary education and are entering a university/college or starting a career.

Annual grant total

In 2013 the charity had an income of £4,600 and an expenditure of £3,200. We estimate the annual total of grants to individuals to be around £2,000.

Applications

In writing to the correspondent.

Other information

Local schools can also be supported towards the purchase of educational materials, items or activities.

The Dronfield Relief-in-Need Charity

£1,000

Correspondent: Dr Anthony Bethell, Trustee, Ramshaw Lodge, Crow Lane, Unstone, Dronfield, Derbyshire S18 4AL (01246 413276)

CC Number: 219888

Eligibility

People under 25 who live in the ecclesiastical parishes of Dronfield, Holmesfield, Unstone and West Handley.

Types of grants

One-off grants up to a value of £100 are given, including those for social and physical training.

Annual grant total

This charity gives around £1,000 each year in grants to individuals for educational purposes.

Applications

In writing to the correspondent though a social worker, doctor, member of the clergy of any denomination, a local councillor, Citizens Advice or other welfare agency. The applicants should ensure they are receiving all practical/financial assistance they are entitled to from statutory sources.

Other information

Grants are also given to local organisations.

Hilton Educational Foundation

£6,300

Correspondent: Sue Cornish, Administrator, 6 Willow Brook Close, Hilton, Derby DE65 5JE (01283 734110)

CC Number: 527091

Eligibility

Young people under the age of 25 in further or higher education who live, or whose parents live, in the parish of Hilton.

Types of grants

One-off grants, usually of around £100–£150, are given towards travel, clothing, books and equipment needed for studies, also towards the studies of music and other arts.

Annual grant total

In 2012/13 the foundation had an income of £11,600 and an expenditure of £9,100. Previously about three quarters of the overall expenditure has been awarded in grants to individuals, therefore we estimate the annual total of grants to be about £6,300.

Applications

In writing to the correspondent. Applications can be submitted directly by the individual. They should normally be made in March and October and are considered in the same month.

Other information

Grants are also available to schools in the local area.

Risley Educational Foundation

£12,200 (50 grants)

Correspondent: Margaret Giller, The Clerk to the Trustees, 27 The Chase, Little Eaton, Derby DE21 5AS (01332 883361)

CC Number: 702720

Eligibility

People under the age of 25 who are in further education and live in the parishes of Breaston, Church Wilne, Dale Abbey, Draycott, Hopewell, Risley, Sandiacre or Stanton-by-Dale.

Types of grants

Grants of about £250 are available to further education students towards the cost of books, equipment/instruments, travel for educational purposes, study of music and arts.

Annual grant total

In 2012/13 the foundation had assets of £750,000 and an income of £51,000. The total charitable expenditure reached £27,000, of which £12,200 was awarded in grants to 50 individuals.

Applications

In writing to the correspondent. The trustees' annual report from 2012/13 also states that 'the charity advertises widely within the area of benefit to ensure that individuals are aware of the grants available.' According to our research, applications are normally considered on a quarterly basis.

Other information

The trust also supports local schools allowing up to 5% of the annual income to be awarded to the Church of England Sunday schools and up to 25% to other local schools. The remainder is then allocated for individual grants.

In 2012/13 grants totalling £11,100 were made to seven schools for the instruction of their pupils in music and a total of £2,400 to 5 Sunday schools.

Scargill's Educational Foundation

£9,000

Correspondent: Stephen Marshall, Administrator, Robinsons Solicitors, 10–11 James Court, Friar Gate, Derby DE1 1BT (01332 254105; email: stephen.marshall@robinsons-solicitors.co.uk)

CC Number: 527012

Eligibility

People under the age of 25 who live in the parishes of West Hallam, Dale Abbey, Mapperley and Stanley (including Stanley Common).

Types of grants

The main beneficiary of the charity is Scargill Church of England Primary School. Priority is also given to three other schools in the area. After that, help is available for groups and also for individuals for the following purposes:

(i) Grants, usually up to about £45, for sixth form pupils to help with books, equipment, clothing or travel.

(ii) Grants, usually up to about £175, to help with school, college or university fees or to supplement existing grants.

(iii) Grants to help with the cost of books and educational outings for schoolchildren.

(iv) For the study of music and other arts and for educational travel.

Annual grant total

Around £8,000 to £10,000 is given in educational grants to individuals each year.

Applications

On a form available from the correspondent.

Ault Hucknall

Hardwick Educational Charity

£2,700

Correspondent: C. E. Hitch, Administrator, Stainsby Mill Farm, Heath, Chesterfield, Derbyshire S44 5RW (01246 850288)

CC Number: 526995

Eligibility

People between the ages of 16 and 26 (inclusive), whose parent(s) live in the civil parish of Ault Hucknall.

Types of grants

Our research suggests that help with the cost of books is given to students in further/higher education and training. People starting work/entering a trade can be assisted towards the cost of books, equipment and instruments.

Annual grant total

At the time of writing (August 2014) the latest financial information available was from 2012. In 2012 the charity had an income of £1,600 and an expenditure of £2,900. We estimate that grants totalled around £2,700.

Exclusions

According to our research, grants are not normally available for student exchanges, maintenance, fees or to support mature students.

Applications

In writing to the correspondent. Applications are considered in April and October.

Buxton

The Bingham Trust

£16,000

Correspondent: Roger Horne, Trustee, Blinder House, Flagg, Buxton, Derbyshire SK17 9QG (01298 83328; email: binghamtrust@aol.com; website: www.binghamtrust.org.uk)

CC Number: 287636

Eligibility

People in need, primarily those who live in Buxton. Most applicants from outside Buxton are rejected unless there is a Buxton connection.

Types of grants

One-off grants ranging from £200 to £1,500. Grants are made to individuals for a wide variety of needs, including further education.

Annual grant total

In 2012/13 the trust had assets of £4.3 million and an income of £180,000. Grants to individuals for welfare and education totalled £32,000. There was no breakdown of how much was awarded in educational/social welfare grants and we estimate the total in educational grants to be around £16,000.

Exclusions

No grants are made for debts or higher education study. In exceptional circumstances the trust may support people in higher education if they are suffering from disabilities and require specialised equipment for them.

Applications

On a form available from the correspondent or to download from the trust's website. Applications should include a supporting letter from a third party such as a social worker, Citizens Advice, doctor or minister. They are considered during the first two weeks of January, April, July and October and should be received before the end of the previous month.

Queries can be sent to the email address given or made to the trust's secretary Emma Marshall on 07966 378 546.

Other information

The trust gives primarily to organisations.

Derby

The Derby City Charity

£500

Correspondent: Lindsay Kirk, Administrator, Derby City Council, Constitutional Services, 5th Floor, Saxon House, Friary Street, Derby DE1 1AN (01332 643656; email: lindsay.kirk@ derby.gov.uk)

CC Number: 214902

Eligibility

People under 25 who live in the city of Derby and are in need.

Types of grants

Grants for education, training, apprenticeships, and for equipment for those starting work.

Annual grant total

In 2012/13 the charity had an income of £3,500 and an expenditure of £2,000. We estimate around £500 in grants was given to individuals for education.

Exclusions

Assistance is not given where other funds are available or towards books or fees for pupils and students if the LEA already has a scheme covering such items.

Applications

On a form available from the correspondent on written request.

Other information

The charity also gives grants to individuals for social welfare purposes.

Holmesfield

The Holmesfield Educational Foundation

£4,200

Correspondent: Geraldine Austen, Administrator, Greenways, Holmesfield, Dronfield S18 7WB (01142 890686)

CC Number: 515723

Eligibility

People living in the parish of Holmesfield, under the age of 25.

Types of grants

Books, clothing, equipment and other essentials.

Annual grant total

In 2012 the foundation had an income of £4,500 and made grants totalling approximately £4,200.

These were the latest financial details available at the time of writing (July 2014).

Applications

In writing to the correspondent.

Matlock

The Ernest Bailey Charity

£1,100

Correspondent: The Chief Executive, Derbyshire Dales District Council, Town Hall, Bank Road, Matlock DE4 3NN (01629 761100; email: legal@ derbyshiredales.gov.uk)

CC Number: 518884

Eligibility

People in need who live in Matlock (this includes Bonsall, Darley Dale, South Darley, Tansley, Matlock Bath and Cromford).

Types of grants

Most applications have been from local groups, but individuals in need and those with educational needs are also supported. Educational grants are one-off and generally of around £100 to £200. Grants are given to students in further/higher education towards books, fees, living expenses and study or travel abroad. Mature students can apply towards books, travel, fees or childcare. People with special educational needs are considered. Each application is considered on its merits.

Annual grant total

In 2012/13 the trust had an income of £2,600 and an expenditure of £2,500. Grants totalled approximately £1,100 for educational purposes.

Applications

On a form available from the correspondent. Applications can be submitted directly by the individual and/or can be supported by a relevant professional. They should be returned by the end of September for consideration and award in October. Applications should include costings (total amount required, funds raised and funds promised). Previous beneficiaries may apply again, with account being taken of assistance given in the past.

Spondon

The Spondon Relief-in-Need Charity

£3,600

Correspondent: Lynn Booth, Secretary and Treasurer, PO Box 5073, Spondon, Derby DE21 7JZ (01332 678533; email: info@spondonreliefinneedcharity.org; website: www. spondonreliefinneedcharity.org)

CC Number: 211317

Eligibility

People in education who live in the ancient parish of Spondon within the city of Derby.

Types of grants

Small grants are made to schoolchildren, college students, undergraduates and mature students, including those towards uniforms/clothing, study/travel abroad, books, equipment/instruments, excursions, awards for excellence and childcare.

Annual grant total

In 2013 the trust had assets of £683,000, an income of £30,000 and a total expenditure of £26,000. Grants are made for educational and welfare purposes. In this accounting year, educational grants totalled £3,600 consisting of 16 school

uniform grants totalling £1,780 and student grants totalling £1,850.

Exclusions

This grant is not intended to supplement an LEA grant.

Applications

On a form available from the correspondent to be submitted either directly by the individual or a family member, through a third party such as a social worker or through an organisations such as Citizens Advice or a school. Each form must be accompanied by a letter of support from a sponsor such as a doctor, health authority official, social worker, city councillor, clergyman, headteacher, school liaison officer, youth leader or probation officer. The sponsor must justify the applicant's need. This is particularly important. The applicant should provide as much information on the form as possible. It is better to ask for a visit by a trustee if possible. The trustees meet quarterly. A guide is available from the secretary.

Hereford-shire

The Hereford Society for Aiding the Industrious

£5,000

Correspondent: Sally Robertson, Secretary, 18 Venns Close, Bath Street, Hereford HR1 2HH (01432 274014 – Thursdays only; email: hsaialms@ talktalkbusiness.net)

CC Number: 212220

Eligibility

People in need who live in Herefordshire, with preference for Hereford City and its immediate environs. Applicants may be undertaking primary, secondary, further or higher education, non-vocational training or vocational training or re-training, in most subjects.

Types of grants

Normally one-off grants ranging between £50 and £1,000 and occasionally interest-free loans. Grants can be made towards: schoolchildren for educational outings; people starting work towards books and equipment/instruments; students in further/higher education towards books, fees and living expenses; and mature students towards books, travel, fees and childcare.

Annual grant total

In 2012/13 the trust had assets of £1 million and an income of £107,000. It was not clear from the accounts the total amount given in grants/loans to individuals and we have estimated this to be around £5,000 for educational purposes.

Exclusions

Grants are rarely given towards gap year travel.

Applications

In writing to the correspondent. If eligible, an application form will be sent and the applicant will probably be asked to attend an interview (between 2.00pm and 4.00pm on Thursday). Grants are rarely given directly to the applicant; instead they are given to the bookseller, college and so on. The trust has stated that applications should be 'precise' and 'honest'. Applications are considered every month.

Other information

The trust's main areas of activity are grants and loans to individuals and maintaining almshouses. Donations are also given to Herefordshire charities for specific projects rather than for running costs.

The Herefordshire Community Foundation (known as Hereford-shire Foundation)

£2,500

Correspondent: Dave Barclay, Director, The Fred Bulmer Centre, Wall Street, Hereford, Herefordshire HR4 9HP (01432 272550; email: dave.barclay@ herefordshire-cf.co.uk; website: www. herefordshirefoundation.org)

CC Number: 1094935

Eligibility

People in need who live in Herefordshire.

Types of grants

One-off and recurrent grants according to need.

Annual grant total

In 2012/13 the foundation had assets of £1.7 million and an income of £171,000. Previous research suggest that approximately £5,000 is given each year to individuals.

Applications

HCF administers a number of different funds. These all have their specific application processes and criteria.

Applications should be addressed to 'The Herefordshire Foundation' and if a grant is awarded the applicant will be advised of which fund (or funds) it came from. It is rare for any of these funds to make an award of more than £1,000.

Applications for under £1,000 are welcomed as a 'free-format' letter but this of course should include some standard information such as contact details, what is the grant to be used for and when, a budget/costs and why the grant is needed. Contact us if you wish to discuss details before you apply.

Other information

Grants are also made to organisations.

Jarvis Educational Foundation

£2,700

Correspondent: Betty Maura-Cooper, Administrator, 4 Church Street, Hay-on-Wye, Hereford HR3 5DQ (01497 821023; email: bettymchay@googlemail.com)

CC Number: 526881

Eligibility

People who are under the age of 25 and live the parishes of Staunton-on-Wye, Bredwardine and Letton in Herefordshire.

Types of grants

One-off grants ranging from £100 to £1,000 can be given:

- To individuals at secondary school, university or college where education authority support is not available
- To provide outfits, clothing, tools, instruments or books to help people enter a trade, profession or calling on leaving education
- To enable such people to travel to pursue their education

Annual grant total

In 2012 the foundation had an income of £23,000 and a total expenditure of £64,000. Due to its low income, the foundation was not required to submit its accounts to the Charity Commission. Therefore, a breakdown of grants distributed during the year was not available; however, in previous years educational grants to individuals have totalled £2,700.

At the time of writing (July 2014) this was the most recent financial information available for the foundation.

Applications

In writing to the correspondent for consideration at any time.

Other information

The foundation also owns land and property, which are used for the purpose of a voluntary school.

The Emma Russell Educational Foundation

£450

Correspondent: Charles Masefield, Trustee, The Cloisters, Worcester Road, Ledbury, Herefordshire HR8 1PL (01531 632638; email: cwm@masefield.co.uk)

CC Number: 527246

Eligibility

People under 25 who live in the Ledbury area for help towards further education or training.

Types of grants

Grants to help people with expenses at university and those undertaking apprenticeships and training generally.

Annual grant total

In 2012/13 the foundation had an income of £800 and an expenditure of £500. Grants made totalled approximately £450.

Applications

On a form available from the correspondent. Awards are made in October.

Bosbury

Bosbury Educational Foundation

£21,000

Correspondent: Jane Bulson, Willow End, Southfield Lane, Bosbury, Ledbury HR8 1PZ

CC Number: 527140

Eligibility

Young people leaving school who live in the parish of Bosbury and have done so for at least three years.

Types of grants

Grants of up to £250 towards books are given to young people 'on leaving school' going on to further education. Students undertaking university courses of three years or longer are invited to apply for a further grant in their final year. Grants may also be given towards school uniform for children in need.

Annual grant total

At the time of writing (August 2014) the latest financial information available was from 2012. In 2012 the foundation had an income of £21,000 and an expenditure of £23,000. We estimate that grants totalled about £21,000.

Applications

In writing to the correspondent. Full details of the course should be included. Applications can be submitted directly by the individual and are considered at any time.

Other information

Note: the parish of Bosbury consists of around 500 people. In previous years the trust has stated that it is being inundated by applications from outside the parish which cannot be considered due to the deeds of the trust. These applications will not be acknowledged.

Hereford

The Hereford Municipal Charities

£1,800

Correspondent: The Trustees, 147 St Owen Street, Hereford HR1 2JR (01432 354002; email: herefordmunicipal@btconnect.com)

CC Number: 218738

Eligibility

People in need who live in the city of Hereford.

Types of grants

One-off grants of up to £200. Grants are given to help with the cost of education and starting work.

Annual grant total

In 2013 the charity had an income of £307,000 and a total expenditure of £285,000. Most of the charity's expenditure is allocated to the running of its almshouses and we estimate that grants to individuals for educational purposes totalled around £1,800.

Exclusions

No grants towards debts or nursery fees.

Applications

On a form available from the correspondent to be submitted directly by the individual or through a relevant third party. Applications are considered five times a year but can be authorised within meetings if they are very urgent.

Middleton-on-the-Hill

The Middleton-on-the-Hill Parish Charity

£900

Correspondent: Clare Halls, Secretary, Highlands, Leysters, Leominster, Herefordshire HR6 0HP (01568 750257; email: leystershalls@aol.com)

CC Number: 527146

Eligibility

People living in the parish of Middleton-on-the-Hill.

Types of grants

One-off and recurrent grants for both welfare and educational purposes.

Annual grant total

In 2013 the charity had an income of £4,300 and a total expenditure of £3,500. We estimate that educational grants to individuals totalled £900. Grants are also distributed to individuals for social welfare purposes and to local organisations.

Applications

In writing to the correspondent.

North Canon

The Norton Canon Parochial Charities

£2,500

Correspondent: Mary Gittins, Administrator, Ivy Cottage, Norton Canon, Hereford HR4 7BQ (01544 318984)

CC Number: 218560

Eligibility

Young people who live in the parish of Norton Canon.

Types of grants

Grants have been given towards books and educational outings for schoolchildren, books, fees/living expenses and study or travel abroad for students in further or higher education and equipment/instruments, books, clothing and travel for people starting work.

Annual grant total

Grants total around £10,000 per year and are given to both individuals and organisations for educational and welfare purposes.

Applications

In writing to the correspondent at any time.

Ross

Ross Educational Foundation

£2,600

Correspondent: Margaret Bickerton, Administrator, 3 Silver Birches, Ross-on-Wye, Herefordshire HR9 7UX (01989 563260)

CC Number: 527229

Eligibility

People under the age of 25 who live (or whose parents live) in the town of Ross Wye and the civil parish of Ross Rural.

Types of grants

Small one-off and recurrent grants are available to higher education students and people in further education or vocational training. Support is given towards books, equipment and instruments, tools and other necessities, educational travel. People studying music and other arts may also apply. Grants usually range from £25 to £120.

Annual grant total

In 2013 the foundation had an income of £3,200 and an expenditure of £2,800. We estimate that grants to individuals totalled around £2,600

Exclusions

Our research suggests that accommodation costs and day-to-day travel expenses are not normally considered.

Applications

In writing to the correspondent. Applications can be submitted directly by the individual, normally in February and August for consideration in April and October respectively.

Leicester-shire and Rutland

The Dixie Educational Foundation

£11,600

Correspondent: Peter Dungworth, Clerk to the Trustees, 31 Oakmeadow Way, Groby, Leicester LE6 0YN (01162 913683; email: pdungworth@hotmail.co.uk)

CC Number: 527837

Eligibility

People under the age of 25 who or whose parents/guardians live, or have lived for at least two years, in the civil parishes of Barlestone, Cadeby, Carlton, Market Bosworth, Osbaston, Shenton, Sutton Cheney or in such civil parishes situated in the former rural district of Market Bosworth, as the trustees decide.

Types of grants

One-off grants in the range of £75 and £150 are available to further education students for general educational costs, including clothing, books, equipment/instruments, educational outings in the UK or study/travel abroad.

The trust also awards Sir Wolstan Dixie Exhibition scholarship for pupils 'who demonstrate academic excellence in the examination for entry into Year 7 of The Dixie Grammar School.'

Annual grant total

In 2012/13 the foundation had assets of £686,000 and an income of £106,000. A total of £74,000 was spent on charitable activities, of which £11,600 was awarded in individual grants.

Applications

In writing to the correspondent. Applications can be submitted directly by individuals, their parents/guardians, through a school/college or educational welfare agency, if applicable. Applicants should provide their date of birth, residential qualification, brief details of educational background and present course of study or apprenticeship together with details and estimates of the required assistance. Our research suggest that applications should be received at least two weeks before each of the termly meetings which are held on the first Friday of March, June and November.

For Sir Wolstan Dixie Exhibition Scholarship the parents of candidates should contact the bursar (01455292244 or bursar@dixie.org.uk) for a declaration of income form to access the eligibility and then apply as usual.

Other information

The foundation also provides up to one third of its income to Primary School of Market Bosworth, The High School of Market Bosworth and associated schools in the local area. Local societies and organisations helping young people are also supported (£63,000 in 2012/13).

The Thomas Rawlins Educational Foundation

£2,400

Correspondent: Gill Bertinat, 21 Haddon Close, Syston, Leicester LE7 1HZ (01509622800)

CC Number: 527858

Eligibility

People under the age of 25 living in Barrow upon Soar, Quorn, Woodhouse and Woodhouse Eaves only.

Types of grants

Our research shows that grants normally range from £50 up to £250. Support is given to school pupils to help with books, equipment, school uniform, maintenance or fees, but not other school clothing or educational outings; to students in further and higher education to help with books, equipment, instruments, study or travel abroad or fees, but not for student exchange or for foreign students studying in the UK; also to people starting work to help with the cost of books, equipment and instruments, travel and clothing.

Annual grant total

In 2012/13 the foundation had both an income and an expenditure of £2,700. Our research indicates that about £2,400 is spent in grants to individuals.

Applications

Application forms can be requested from the correspondent and should be submitted directly by the individuals or their parents/guardians at any time.

The Harry James Riddleston Charity of Leicester (Riddleston Charity)

£0

Correspondent: Elizabeth Bass, Clerk to the Trustees, 44 High Street, Market Harborough, Leicestershire LE16 7AH (01858 463322; website: www. harryriddleston.org.uk)

CC Number: 262787

Eligibility

People in need between the ages of 21 and 34 (in exceptional circumstances those over 18) who live in Leicestershire or Rutland. Applicants must run their business within the beneficial area and demonstrate its potential to succeed.

Types of grants

The charity provides interest free loans of up to £10,000 for between five and ten years to enable young people to start/ expand a business or to further their vocational or educational training. The loan becomes repayable in full within the term granted.

Annual grant total

In 2012/13 the charity had assets of £1.1 million, an income of £27,000 and a charitable expenditure of £19,800. During the year loans advanced totalled £90,000.

Applications

Application forms can be requested from the correspondent. Candidates will need two guarantors for a loan of up to £6,000 and three for a loan between £6,000 and £10,000. All eligible applicants are interviewed by the trustees, normally in February, May, August and November.

The Rutland Trust

£3,500

Correspondent: Richard Adams, Clerk, 35 Trent Road, Oakham, Rutland LE15 6HE (01572 756706; email: adams@apair.wanadoo.co.uk)

CC Number: 517175

Eligibility

People, usually under 35, in need who live in Rutland and are at any level or stage of their education.

Types of grants

One-off grants ranging between £50 and £400. There are no restrictions on how the grants may be spent. In the past, grants have been made towards music and school trips for needy young people, for European exchange trips, and for young people to take part in educational, missionary and life-experience programmes overseas. Grants may also be spent on books, equipment, fees, bursaries, fellowships and study visits.

Annual grant total

In 2013 the trust had an income of £20,000 and a total expenditure of £14,000. Grants are also made for welfare purposes and to organisations. We estimate grants awarded to individuals for educational purposes totalled around £3,500.

Applications

An initial telephone call is recommended.

The Sir John Sedley Educational Foundation

£10,000

Correspondent: Elaine Everington, Administrator, 29 Mill Grove, Whissendine, Oakham, Leicestershire LE15 7EY (01664474593; email: ellemai@ btinternet.com)

CC Number: 527884

Eligibility

People under the age of 25 in further and higher education living in the parish of Wymondham and peripheral areas.

Types of grants

The foundation provides scholarships, bursaries, financial assistance towards the cost of books, clothing, equipment/ instruments and travel costs. Financial help is also available for people starting work/entering a trade.

Annual grant total

In 2012/13 the foundation had an income of £15,200 and an expenditure of £20,000. It supports both individuals and organisations, therefore we estimate the annual grants to individuals total to be around £10,000.

Applications

In writing to the correspondent. Our research suggests that it is preferable if a supplier's quotation for the requested item is included.

Other information

The trustees have a discretionary power to allocate up to one quarter of the income towards the benefit of the local schools. The foundation also supports charitable organisations and maintains a hall for the benefit of the local area.

The Marc Smith Educational Charity

£2,500

Correspondent: Diana Jones, Secretary, 21 Highcroft, Husbands Bosworth, Lutterworth, Leicestershire LE17 6LF (01858 880741; email: dianajones929@ gmail.com)

CC Number: 1045965

Eligibility

People under the age of 25 who live or have attended school in the ancient parishes of Claybrooke Magna, Claybrooke Parva, Ullesthorpe or Wibtoft, or whose parents live there.

Types of grants

Support is given to people in further education or training and individuals undertaking apprenticeships or starting work. Schoolchildren moving from primary to upper schools can also be supported, usually for clothing.

Annual grant total

In 2013 the charity had an income of £6,200 and an expenditure of £4,500. We estimate the annual total of grants to individuals to be around £2,500.

Applications

According to our research, applications from pupils should be made in writing to the correspondent and are normally considered in May. Applications from further education students are normally considered in September and should be submitted at a meeting, which applicants are invited to through local advertisements near to the time of the meeting.

Other information

Grants may also be made to local schools for educational projects and to organisations, depending on the income of the charity.

The Wyvernian Foundation

£3,200

Correspondent: Andrew York, Administrator, 6 Magnolia Close, Leicester LE2 8PS (01162 835345; email: andrew_york@sky.com)

CC Number: 509225

Eligibility

People who live or have lived in the city or county of Leicester for three years (excluding those who are temporary resident while undertaking studies), generally higher and further education students (including mature students).

Types of grants

One-off and recurrent grants of up to £250 towards the cost of fees, living expenses, study or travel abroad, books, equipment and childcare.

Annual grant total

In 2012/13 the foundation had an income of £2,600 and an expenditure of £3,400. We have estimated the annual total of grants to be around £3,200.

Applications

Application forms can be obtained by sending a covering letter with an sae to the correspondent. Applications should be submitted by early February, May, August and December each year for consideration in the following months.

Ashby-de-la-Zouch

The Mary Smith Scholarship Fund

£0

Correspondent: R. Wright, Administrator, Leicestershire County Council, Education Finance, Room 139, County Hall, Glenfield, Leicester LE3 8RF (01163 057643; email: edfinance@leics.gov.uk; website: www. ashbyschool.org.uk)

CC Number: 527890

Eligibility

People in need of financial assistance who are under the age of 25 and live in Ashby-de-la-Zouch, or are former students of either Ashby School or Ivanhoe High School.

Types of grants

The fund awards scholarships, bursaries, maintenance allowances and assists people entering a profession with the cost of clothing/outfits, equipment/ instruments, books and tools. Funding to travel abroad in pursuance of education and help to study music or other arts can also be provided. Grants normally range from £25 to £150.

Annual grant total

In 2012/13 the fund had an income of £3,200. There was no charitable spending in that year; however our research indicates that usually around £2,500 is awarded in grants.

Exclusions

Funding is not available towards university tuition fees, living expenses, accommodation, regular travel costs or school trips.

Applications

Application forms can be obtained from the correspondent or downloaded from the fund's website.

Other information

The fund's website notes that 'it is a condition of any award that a report is sent to the governors by 31 December detailing how the money was spent. Governors will not consider applications from anyone who has previously received an award but not submitted a report.'

Cossington

Babington's Charity

£8,000

Correspondent: Helen McCague, Trustee, 14 Main Street, Cossington, Leicester, Leicestershire LE7 4UU (01509 812271)

CC Number: 220069

Eligibility

People in need in the parish of Cossington.

Types of grants

One-off and recurrent grants according to need.

Annual grant total

In 2012 the trust had an income of £28,000 and a total expenditure of £22,000. We have estimated the grant total to be around £21,000 with £16,000 going to individuals of which £8,000 was awarded for educational purposes. The accounts for 2012 were the latest available at the time of writing (July 2014).

Applications

In writing to the correspondent.

Other information

Gives to individuals and organisations for both education and social welfare purposes.

Great Glen

Great Glen Town Charity

£130

Correspondent: Major Gerald Hincks, Trustee, 19 Naseby Way, Great Glen, Leicester LE8 9GS (01162 593155)

CC Number: 701901

Eligibility

People who live in the parish of Great Glen and are in need.

Types of grants

One-off and recurrent grants are available towards education and training. People going to university, those starting work and individuals undertaking voluntary work in their gap-year can all be supported.

Annual grant total

In 2013 the charity had an income of £2,000 and an expenditure of £280. We estimate that educational grants to individuals totalled around £130.

Applications

In writing to the correspondent. Applications from outside the beneficial area will not be acknowledged.

Other information

Organisations may also be supported. The charity has a welfare branch which distributes grants at Christmas to older residents at a rate of £15 per individual and £30 per couple.

Groby

Thomas Herbert Smith's Trust Fund

£7,000

Correspondent: Andrew York, Administrator, 6 Magnolia Close, Leicester LE2 8PS (01162 835345; email: andrew_york@sky.com)

CC Number: 701694

Eligibility

People who live in the parish of Groby in Leicestershire.

Types of grants

One-off and recurrent grants ranging from £100 to £500.

Annual grant total

In 2012/13 the fund had an income of £16,000 and a total expenditure of £20,000. We estimate that grants made to individuals for education totalled around £7,000.

223

Applications

On a form available from the correspondent, for consideration throughout the year. Applications can be submitted either directly by the individual, or through a social worker, Citizens Advice or other appropriate third party.

Other information

Grants are also made to individuals and organisations for social welfare purposes.

Harborough

The Market Harborough and The Bowdens Charity

£54,000 (23 grants)

Correspondent: James Jacobs, Steward, Godfrey Payton and Co., 149 St Mary's Road, Market Harborough, Leicester LE16 7DZ (01858 462467; email: admin@mhbcharity.co.uk; website: www. mhbcharity.co.uk)

CC Number: 1041958

Eligibility

Disadvantaged young adults entering further/higher education (including postgraduate courses) or undertaking vocational training or apprenticeships. Applicants should normally be aged between 19 and 30 and live within Market Harborough or immediately outside the area.

Types of grants

Grants of up to £5,000 for fees and maintenance/living expenses. Associated equipment costs may also be covered.

Annual grant total

At the time of writing (August 2014) the latest financial information available was from 2012. In 2012 the trust had assets of £15.8 million and an income of £629,000. Grants totalling £54,000 were awarded to 23 individuals for educational purposes.

Applications

Application forms for different types of applicants are available on the charity's website. Applications should be supported by two suitable referees, such as employers, teachers or tutors. Applications for vocational and undergraduate support should normally be submitted by mid-April with interviews taking place in June.

Other information

Grants are also given to individuals for welfare purposes, to organisations, institutions and towards preservation of historic churches in the area.

Keyham

Keyham Educational Foundation

£1,300

Correspondent: David Witcomb, Trustee, Tanglewood, Snows Lane, Keyham, Leicester LE7 9JS (01162 595663)

CC Number: 527965

Eligibility

People under the age of 25 who live, or whose parents live, in the parish of Keyham and who are in need.

Types of grants

Small, one-off grants can be given to people in secondary and tertiary education for general educational needs, including books, equipment/instruments, travel, educational outings, study of arts and other educational expenses. Awards usually are of around £100.

Annual grant total

In 2013 the foundation had an income of £1,400 and an expenditure of £1,500. We estimate the annual total of grants to individuals to be around £1,300.

Applications

In writing to the correspondent. Applications are normally considered in March and October. They can be submitted by the individual or through a third party, such as parent/guardian. Urgent applications can be considered at other times. If the applicant does not live in Keyham, information about their connection with residents should be provided with the application.

Other information

Village groups participating in educational classes may also be supported.

Leicester

Alderman Newton's Educational Foundation

£78,000

Correspondent: Jim Munton, Clerk, Leicester Charity Link, 20A Millstone Lane, Leicester LE1 5JN (01162 222200; fax: 01162 222201; email: info@charity-link.org; website: www.charity-link.org/trust-administration/trusts-we-support/alderman-newtons-educational-foundation)

CC Number: 527881

Eligibility

People in need who are under the age of 25 and live (or whose parents live) in the city of Leicester.

Types of grants

Grants are given to schoolchildren, further/higher education students and people starting work/entering a trade. Support can be offered towards general educational needs, including school uniforms, clothing, books, equipment, instruments, tools, fees, maintenance, study of music and arts, educational outings and study or travel overseas.

Annual grant total

In 2012/13 the foundation had assets of £3.9 million and an income of £169,000. A total of £78,000 was awarded in grants and bursaries to individuals.

Applications

Application forms are available from the foundation's website or from the correspondent. They must be accompanied by three references and provide information on applicants' and/or their parents' income. Applications can be submitted directly by individuals and are considered regularly throughout the year.

Other information

The foundation also makes grants to schools in Leicester and Leicestershire.

Loughborough

The Dawson and Fowler Foundation

£29,000

Correspondent: Lesley Cutler, Clerk to the Trustees, PO Box 73, Loughborough, Leicestershire LE11 0GA (07765 934117; email: dawsonfowler@fsmail.net)

CC Number: 527867

Eligibility

Young people between the ages of 11 and 25 who have lived in the borough of Loughborough (including Hathern), normally for at least three years.

Types of grants

The foundation offers:

▷ School uniform grants – of up to £100 once a year for pupils in years 7, 8, 9, 10 and 11

▷ School grants – lump sums given to local schools and academies to be distributed in grants of up to £200 to pupils in need towards books, equipment, instruments and similar necessities, also residential trips, educational outings, conferences and interview expenses (individual awards for endowed schools are of up to £500)

▷ Other educational grants – to people in further/higher education, apprenticeships, people involved in scouting, guiding, sports, volunteering (for the cost of uniforms), individuals undertaking personal development/ character building schemes and so on

The foundation also provides scholarships to the endowed schools.

Annual grant total

In 2013 the foundation had assets of £752,000 and an income of £42,000. Grants to schools, academies and individuals totalled over £29,000 and can be broken down as follows:

Uniform grants	£20,000
Grants to state schools	£5,900
Scholarships and grants (endowed schools)	£2,500
Other grants for course	£800

Exclusions

Grants are not normally given for accommodation, subsistence, day to day travelling costs, tuition, examination fees or childcare costs. Applications from groups of students or classes of pupils cannot be considered.

Applications

Application forms are available from the correspondent or can be asked for at the applicant's school office. The trustees meet quarterly and applications should be made in advance to avoid disappointment. The school uniform subcommittee normally considers uniform applications in July or August prior to the start of the academic year.

Other information

The trustees have previously stated that they would like to encourage independent applications.

Mountsorrel
Mountsorrel Educational Fund

£84,000 (154 grants)

Correspondent: Paul Blakemore, Clerk to the Trustees, KDB Accountants and Consultants Ltd, 21 Hollytree Close, Hoton, Loughborough LE12 5SE (01509 889369/07984 363069; website: mountsorrelunitedcharities.co.uk/)

CC Number: 527912

Eligibility

People under the age of 25 who have been (or whose parent/guardian has been) resident in the parish of Mountsorrel for at least a year or who are current or former pupils of Christ Church and St Peter's Church of England School.

Types of grants

One-off and recurrent grants in the range of £100–£1,000 towards general education and training needs, including books, equipment, specialist clothing, music tuition, educational visits and training schemes or apprenticeships.

Annual grant total

At the time of writing (July 2014) the latest financial information available was from 2012. In 2012 the fund had assets of £87,000 and an income of £114,000 (the fund's income is provided by Mountsorrel United Charities). Grants to individuals totalled around £84,000, broken down as follows:

Higher education and training	85	£74,000
A-level college students	34	£5,100
Other	12	£3,000
Music	23	£2,300

Applications

In writing to the correspondent (providing an sae), or via the fund's website. The trustees meet twice a year in November and April. Further guidelines can be obtained from the correspondent.

Other information

Grants to Christ Church and St Peters Church of England School totalled £5,400 in 2012.

Oadby
The Oadby Educational Foundation

£21,000

Correspondent: Rodney Waterfield, Hon. Secretary and Treasurer, 2 Silverton Road, Oadby, Leicester LE2 4NN (01162 714507)

CC Number: 528000

Eligibility

People with a home address within the former urban district of Oadby who were educated in Oadby.

Types of grants

One-off grants in the range of £50 and £200 are made to schoolchildren, college students and undergraduates, including those towards uniforms/clothing, study/ travel abroad and equipment/ instruments. People of any age can receive one-off grants towards expeditions and voluntary work, such as Operation Raleigh or Voluntary Service Overseas.

Annual grant total

In 2012 the foundation had assets of £1 million and an income of £46,000. £21,000 was given in educational grants and no grants for welfare were made during the year. These were the latest accounts available at the time of writing (July 2014).

Applications

On a form available from the correspondent. They should be submitted either through the individual's school, college or educational welfare agency, or directly by the individual. Applicants must have a home address in the parish of Oadby.

Other information

Grants are also made to organisations.

Peatling Parva
Richard Bradgate's Charity

£700

Correspondent: Brian Higginson, Trustee, The Old Rectory, Main Street, Peatling Parva, Lutterworth LE17 5QA (01162 478240)

CC Number: 217379

Eligibility

People living in the parish of Peatling Parva who are in need.

Types of grants

Our research indicates that grants can be given to students in further and higher education towards books or fees and living expenses. People starting work or undertaking apprenticeships can be supported for books and equipment/ instruments.

Annual grant total

In 2012/13 the charity had an income of £1,700 and an expenditure of £1,600. We estimate that educational support totalled around £700.

Applications

In writing to the correspondent. Applications are usually considered in October/November.

Other information

Support may also be given to organisations or to support other parishioners facing special difficulties, particularly the elderly.

Smisby
The Smisby Parochial Charity

£400

Correspondent: Mrs S. Heap, Clerk, Cedar Lawns, Forties Lane, Smisby, Ashby-de-la-Zouch, Leicestershire LE65 2SN (01530 414179)

CC Number: 515251

Eligibility

People in need who live in Smisby.

Types of grants

Grants are given to schoolchildren, people starting work, further and higher education students, mature students and postgraduates towards books and equipment. Grants are in the range of £10 and £500.

Annual grant total

In 2012/13 the charity had an income of £30,000 and a total expenditure of £9,000. Grants totalled approximately £4,000 with £400 awarded for educational purposes.

Applications

In writing to the correspondent.

Other information

Grants are also awarded in support of local village projects and events. In 2012/13 this amount totalled approximately £3,700.

Wigston

The Norton, Salisbury and Brailsford Educational Foundation

£400

Correspondent: Michael Charlesworth, Trustee, 2 Midland Cottages, Wigston, Leicestershire LE18 2BU (01162 811245)

CC Number: 527930

Eligibility

People under the age of 25 who live in Wigston.

Types of grants

One-off grants towards the cost of books, tools, equipment and travel, including travel abroad.

Annual grant total

Accounts for 2012 were the latest available at the time of writing (August 2014).

In 2012, the foundation had an income of £2,000 and a total expenditure of £400.

Applications

On a form available from the correspondent. Applications are considered three times a year, usually in March, September and November.

Other information

The foundation also awards grants to organisations.

Wymeswold

The Wymeswold Parochial Charities

£2,000

Correspondent: Mrs J. Collington, Administrator, 94 Brook Street, Wymeswold, Loughborough LE12 6TU (01509 880538)

CC Number: 213241

Eligibility

People in need who have lived in Wymeswold for the last two years.

Types of grants

One-off grants are given for educational and relief-in-need purposes.

Annual grant total

The income of this charity is around £5,000 each year. Grants total about £4,000 per year for educational and social welfare purposes.

Applications

In writing to the correspondent at any time.

Lincolnshire

The Alenson and Erskine Educational Foundation

£4,100

Correspondent: Edwina Arnold, Administrator, Crooks Cottage, Wrangle Bank, Wrangle, Boston PE22 9DL (01205 270352; email: wranglepc@aol.com)

CC Number: 527671

Eligibility

People under the age of 25 who live in the parishes of Old Leake, New Leake and Wrangle. Preference is given to people who have attended county or voluntary school for at least two years. Candidates should normally have been resident in the area of benefit for at least five years.

Types of grants

Grants can be given to further/higher education students towards educational necessities and fees or to school leavers entering a trade/profession to help with the cost of books, equipment, clothing or travel.

Annual grant total

In 2013 the foundation had an income of £3,900 and an expenditure of £4,300. We estimate the annual total of grants to be around £4,100.

Exclusions

Grants are not given for A-levels.

According to our research, schoolchildren (other than those with special educational needs) are only considered if family difficulties are serious.

Applications

Application forms can be requested from the correspondent. They can be submitted by individuals directly via post or email and are usually considered in October/November. Applicants can only claim for what they have bought and not what they would like to buy and must submit receipts with their application.

Allen's Charity (Apprenticing Branch)

£4,500

Correspondent: Keith Savage, Administrator, Lenton Lodge, 94 Wignals Gate, Holbeach, Spalding PE12 7HR (01406 490157)

CC Number: 213842–1

Eligibility

Children and young people in need who live in the parish of Long Sutton. Higher education students between the ages of 18 and 25 are also supported.

Types of grants

Grants towards apprenticeships and related costs. Students can be assisted towards general educational necessities.

Annual grant total

In the past the charity has made grants totalling around £4,500.

Applications

Application forms can be requested from the correspondent. The scheme is normally advertised in the local press and promoted by local employers.

Other information

This charity is linked to Allen's Charity (registered charity number 213842).

Cowell and Porrill

£7,000

Correspondent: Roger Hooton, Clerk, 33 Glen Drive, Boston, Lincolnshire PE21 7QB (01205 310088)

CC Number: 240438

Eligibility

People under the age of 25 who live, or whose parents live, in the parishes of Benington and Leverton.

Types of grants

Awards are usually in the range of £250 and £600. Support is given for general educational needs to people at any level or stage of their education and undertaking the study of any subject.

Annual grant total

In 2013 the charity had an income of £15,300 and an expenditure of £14,100. We estimate that the annual total of grants to individuals was around £7,000.

Applications

In writing to the correspondent. Our research shows that applications can be submitted directly by the individual by the end of July for consideration in September.

Other information

The charity also provides almshouses for the poor residents of Benington and Leverton and can support local schools, where assistance is not already provided by the local authorities.

Gainsborough Educational Charity

£4,000

Correspondent: Maria Bradley, Clerk to the Trustees, Burton and Dyson Solicitors, 22 Market Place, Gainsborough DN21 2BZ (01427 610761; email: maria.bradley@ BurtonDyson.co.uk; website: www. burtondyson.com/gainsborough-educational-charity.htm)

CC Number: 527299

Eligibility

Children and young people between the ages of 11 and 25 who live, or whose parents live, in Gainsborough, Lea, Morton or Thonock.

Types of grants

The trust provides grants, bursaries and allowances to help with the cost of uniforms and specialist clothing, fees, books, equipment/instruments and other necessities to schoolchildren, further/higher education students and people starting work. Travel costs in the UK and abroad for educational purposes and music/arts studies are also supported.

Annual grant total

In 2012/13 the charity had an income of £5,900 and a total expenditure of £5,500. It also supports a local school, therefore we estimate the annual total of grants to individuals to be around £4,000.

Exclusions

Grants are not given towards the purchase of computers.

Applications

Application forms can be downloaded from Burton and Dyson Solicitor's website or requested from the correspondent. A completed application form, together with a reference from an academic tutor, can be submitted directly by the individual in advance of the trustees' meetings, which are held twice a year, normally in March and November.

Other information

One quarter of the charity's annual income is given to the Queen Elizabeth Grammar School at Gainsborough, where support is not already provided by the local authority.

The Hesslewood Children's Trust (Hull Seamen's and General Orphanage)

See entry on page 169

The Kirton-in-Lindsey Exhibition Foundation

£3,000

Correspondent: Penelope Hoey, Administrator, Woodbine Cottage, 6 Queen Street, Kirton Lindsey, Gainsborough DN21 4NS (01652 640075)

CC Number: 529749

Eligibility

People who live in the parishes of Blyborough, Grayingham, Hibaldstow, Kirton-in-Lindsey, Manton, Northorpe, Redbourne, Scotter, Scotton or Waddingham and who have attended one of the following primary schools for at least two years: Hibaldstow, Kirton-in-Lindsey, Messingham, Scotter or Waddingham.

Types of grants

Grants are given towards the cost of books and other essentials. The foundation offers the awards of Junior and Senior Exhibitions. The Junior ones are available to secondary school pupils and the Senior ones – to higher education students. Awards are also available to students in technical, industrial or professional training. Additional support is given to children resident in the beneficial area to continue their education at evening schools, day or evening classes.

Annual grant total

In 2012/13 the foundation had an income of £3,400 and an expenditure of £3,200. We have estimated that the

annual total of grants to individuals was around £3,000.

Applications

Application forms are available from the correspondent.

Other information

Foundation also provides books or fittings for a school library in the parish of Kirton-in-Lindsey for the use of scholars.

Kitchings Educational Charity

£6,000

Correspondent: M. Sankey, Trustee, 50 Station Road, Bardney, Lincoln LN3 5UD (01526 398555)

CC Number: 527707

Eligibility

Children and young people under the age of 25 who live in Bardney, Bucknall, Southrey or Tupholme and are in need of financial assistance.

Types of grants

Small grants to schoolchildren and further/higher education students to assist with the costs of books, equipment/instruments or other general educational necessities.

Annual grant total

In 2012/13 the charity had an income of £11,000 and an expenditure of £12,000. It also supports local schools, therefore we estimate the annual total of grants to individuals to be about £6,000.

Exclusions

Our research suggest that support would not be given to students who choose to take A-levels (or equivalent) at college when they could take the same course at their school.

Applications

In writing to the correspondent enclosing an sae. Applications can be submitted directly by the individual or through the applicant's school, university/college or educational welfare agency, if applicable. Applications are normally considered in October and should be received by the end of September.

Other information

The charity also provides financial support to The Bardney Joint Church of England and Methodist Primary School or The Bucknall Primary School, where support is not already provided by the local authority.

The Kitchings General Charity

£2,800

Correspondent: J. Smith, Secretary, 42 Abbey Road, Bardney, Lincoln LN3 5XA (01526 398505)

CC Number: 219957

Eligibility

Students, especially mature (over 25 years of age), part-time, and vocational students, living in the parish of Bardney (covers Stainfield, Apley, Southrey, Tupholme and Bucknall).

Types of grants

Grants are given for playgroup fees, books, excursions, uniforms and sports equipment. Grants are usually in the range of £200 and £500 but can be up to £1,000.

Annual grant total

In 2013 the trust had an income of £38,000 and made educational grants totalling £2,800.

Applications

In writing to the correspondent giving details of age, course name, college and brief description of education to date. Applications are considered in May, October and January.

Other information

Grants are also given to local schools and organisations, and to individuals for welfare purposes.

The Kochan Trust

£25,500 (26 grants)

Correspondent: Revd Roger Massingberd-Mundy, Honorary Secretary, The Old Post Office, The Street, West Raynham, Fakenham, Norfolk NR21 7AD (01328 838611; fax: 01328 838698)

CC Number: 1052976

Eligibility

People studying veterinary science or creative arts, music and performance who live in Lincolnshire and are in need of financial assistance.

Types of grants

One-off grants are given according to need. Support can be given for tuition fees, purchase of an instrument, research of veterinary science or other educational expenses.

Annual grant total

In 2012/13 the trust had an income of £28,000 and an expenditure of £33,000. Grants to 11 veterinary students in training were awarded totalling £14,500 and 15 music and arts students were given grants for instruments or tuition fees totalling £11,000.

Applications

In writing to the correspondent. The trustees meet four times a year, usually in January, April, July and November. Applications should give some details about the candidate and state what the grant is needed for. They can be made by individuals directly or through a third party, such as a school/college or educational welfare agency, if applicable.

Other information

Grants can also be made to local churches. In 2012/13 no such applications were made.

Lincolnshire Community Foundation

£6,000

Correspondent: Sue Fortune, Grants Manager, 4 Mill House, Moneys Yard, Carre Street, Sleaford, Lincolnshire NG34 7TW (01529 305825; email: lincolnshirecf@btconnect.com; website: www.lincolnshirecf.co.uk)

CC Number: 1092328

Eligibility

People in need in Lincolnshire although eligibility differs depending on the scheme applied for, as outlined in the following section.

Types of grants

Funds currently administered by the foundation include:
- Make A Start (MAST) – grants of up to £250 for people aged 16 and over in receipt of benefits or working no more than 16 hours a week to assist with re-entry into employment, education or training
- Colin Batts' Family Trust – available to individuals and not for profit community groups to provide opportunities for young people

Annual grant total

In 2012/13 the foundation had assets of £3.4 million and total expenditure of £895,000. Educational grants to individuals from the MAST (Make-a-Start) Fund totalled over £6,000.

Exclusions

Grants cannot be awarded retrospectively.

Applications

For the MAST scheme applications are usually made by registering interest with the correspondent who will then organise an assessment.

Be aware that community foundations schemes can open and close at very short notice so it is worth checking the foundation's website before applying.

The Mapletoft Scholarship Foundation

£3,500

Correspondent: Patrick Purves, Administrator, The Old Vicarage, Church Street, Louth, Lincolnshire LN11 9DE (01507 605883; email: pmp@bmcf.co.uk)

CC Number: 527649

Eligibility

People who have attended primary school in the parishes of North Thoresby, Grainsby and Waithe, for no less than five years and who are engaged or about to engage in higher education.

Types of grants

Grants up to about £150 to help with further/higher education books and fees/living expenses or to supplement existing grants. Travel grants are also available. Grants are recurrent.

Annual grant total

In 2012/13 the foundation had an income of £4,200 and an expenditure of £3,800. We estimate that grants given totalled £3,500.

Applications

Applications should be received no later than 30 September for consideration in November.

Sir Thomas Middlecott's Exhibition Foundation

£15,000

Correspondent: Frank Wilson, Administrator, 57A Bourne Road, Spalding PE11 1JR (01775 766117; email: info@middlecotttrust.org.uk; website: www.middlecotttrust.org.uk)

CC Number: 527283

Eligibility

Students who live in the parishes of Algarkirk, Fosdyke, Frampton, Kirton, Sutterton and Wyberton in Lincolnshire, who are in further/higher education and are aged under 25. Applicants must have attended a maintained primary school in the area for at least two years.

Types of grants

Grants are given to students in further/higher education towards books, clothing and equipment/instruments.

Annual grant total

In 2012/13 the trust had assets of £734,000 and an income of £30,000. Grants were made totalling £15,000.

Applications

On a form available from the correspondent, or from the foundation's website (www.middlecotttrust.org.uk/information) to be submitted directly by the individual via post. Applications are considered in October and should be submitted by the end of September.

Phillips Charity

£1,900

Correspondent: Keith Savage, Clerk, Lenton Lodge, 94 Wignals Gate, Holbeach, Spalding PE12 7HR (01406 490157)

CC Number: 213843

Eligibility

People living in the parishes of Long Sutton and Sutton Bridge, aged between 11 and 20.

Types of grants

Grants of up to £200 are given:

- To schoolchildren for books, equipment, clothing or travel
- To students in further/higher education towards the cost of books and travel or study overseas
- For help with the study of music and other arts, as well as for overseas study

Annual grant total

In 2012 the charity had an income of £5,000 and a total expenditure of £3,800. We estimate that educational grants to individuals totalled £1,900, with funding also awarded to individuals with social welfare needs.

At the time of writing (July 2014) this was the most recent financial information available for the charity.

Exclusions

Grants are not given for school fees or maintenance, student fees/living expenses or for people starting work. The charity stresses that it can only support people living at Long Sutton and Sutton Bridge.

Applications

On a form available from the correspondent. They are considered at trustees' meetings, which are usually held in July and September.

The Pike and Eure Educational Foundation

£1,700

Correspondent: Susan Smith, Clerk to the Trustees, 18 Oxford Close, Washingborough, Lincoln LN4 1DT (01522 792406)

CC Number: 527725

Eligibility

Young people between the ages of 16 and 25 who are in need and live in the parishes of Washingborough and Heighington in Lincolnshire.

Types of grants

One-off grants for students in further or higher education or apprenticeships towards books, equipment/instruments or scholarships. The foundation also makes grants to young people who need assistance to participate in sport and other outdoor related activities.

Annual grant total

In 2012 the foundation had an income of £4,600 and a total expenditure of £1,800. We estimate that grants totalled £1,700.

At the time of writing (July 2014) this was the most recent financial information available for the foundation.

Exclusions

People starting work are not eligible.

Applications

On a form available from the correspondent, submitted directly by the individual, with information about the nature of the course, location, and the occupation of the parent(s). Applications should be submitted in early August for consideration in October.

The Educational Foundation of Philip and Sarah Stanford

£2,000

Correspondent: Eleanor Hine, Clerk, 86 Brigsley Road, Waltham, Grimsby, South Humberside DN37 0LA (01472 827883)

CC Number: 529755

Eligibility

People under 25 who live in the ancient parishes of Aylesby, Barnoldby-le-Beck, Bradley, Irby-upon-Humber and Laceby.

Types of grants

Grants of £60 to £100 towards books, clothing or equipment/instruments for college students and undergraduates.

Annual grant total

Accounts for the year 2012 were the latest available at the time of writing (August 2014). In 2012, the foundation had an income of £21,000 and a total expenditure of £8,000. We estimate that the total grants awarded to individuals is approximately £2,000.

Exclusions

Grants are not given for subjects and courses available in schools, or for help with student fees, travel nor living expenses.

Applications

On a form available from the correspondent, submitted directly by the individual, including reasons for the application and plans for the future. The closing date is 1 October each year. Applications must be in the applicant's own handwriting.

Other information

Grants are also made to organisations and the foundation provides bibles and food vouchers.

The Sutton St James United Charities

£4,000

Correspondent: Keith Savage, Clerk to the Trustees, Lenton Lodge, 94 Wignals Gate, Holbeach, Spalding, Lincolnshire PE12 7HR (01406 490157; email: keithsavage@btinternet.com)

CC Number: 527757

Eligibility

People under 25 who are in need and live in the parish of Sutton St James and the surrounding area.

Types of grants

(i) Grants, of up to £100, to all pupils living in the village at age 11 when transferring to secondary schools, to help with books, equipment, clothing, etc.

(ii) Grants, of up to £100, to help students aged 16 who are taking A-levels and further education courses.

(iii) Grants, of up to £600 a year, to students entering university to help with general expenses and to supplement existing grants.

Help is also given to people entering a trade or profession.

Annual grant total

In 2012/13 the charity had an income of £15,000 and a total expenditure of over £17,000. Grants are made to individuals and organisations for educational and welfare purposes. We estimate that the amount awarded to individuals for educational purposes was around £4,000.

Applications

On a form available from the correspondent. Applications are considered in April/May for primary schoolchildren and December/January for A-level and university students.

Dame Margaret Thorold's Apprenticing Charity

£3,000

Correspondent: The Trustees, Tallents Solicitors, 2 Westgate, Southwell NG25 0JJ (01636 813411)

CC Number: 527628

Eligibility

People aged 18 to 25 living in the ancient parishes of Sedgebrook, Marston and Cranwell who are undertaking an apprenticeship.

Types of grants

Small cash grants to assist students in further or higher education, especially vocational training. Grants may be recurrent or one-off and are towards books, fees/living expenses or study/travel abroad.

Annual grant total

In 2013 the charity had an income of £2,000 and an expenditure of £3,300. Grants made totalled approximately £3,000.

Applications

Applications should be submitted in writing by the individual or parent/guardian or through the school/college/educational welfare agency, by mid-January for consideration in February. If appropriate, a letter of support from the employer or place of training should be included with the application.

Barkston

Barkston Educational Foundation

£2,500

Correspondent: Tallents Solicitors, 2 Westgate, Southwell, Nottinghamshire NG25 0JJ (01636 813411)

CC Number: 527724

Eligibility

People under 25 who live, or whose parents live, in the parish of Barkston.

Types of grants

Grants for educational purposes, including social and physical training.

Annual grant total

In 2012/13 the foundation had an income of £6,300 and an expenditure of £5,300. The trust also supports Barkston School, therefore we estimate the annual total of grants to individuals to be around £2,500.

Applications

In writing to the correspondent.

Other information

The foundation provides special benefits for Barkston School, where the needs are not met by the local authorities.

Boston

The Sutterton Educational Foundation (Sutterton Education Trust)

£1,200

Correspondent: Deirdre McCumiskey, Administrator, 6 Hillside Gardens, Wittering, Peterborough PE8 6DX (01780 782668)

CC Number: 527771

Eligibility

Elementary schoolchildren in the parish of Sutterton.

Types of grants

Small grants are given towards general educational costs, including books, clothing, educational outings and other necessities.

Annual grant total

In 2012/13 the foundation had both an income and an expenditure of £2,600. We estimate the annual total of grants to be around £1,200.

Applications

In writing to the correspondent.

Other information

The foundation also provides maintenance and improvements of the premises of any public elementary school in the area of benefit where these are not provided by the local authority.

Corby Glenn

The Willoughby Memorial Trust

£0

Correspondent: Timothy Clarke, Administrator, Estate Office, Grimsthorpe, Bourne, Lincolnshire PE10 0LY (01778 591205)

CC Number: 527647

Eligibility

People who live in the Corby Glen area of Lincolnshire.

Types of grants

Grants to promote the study, education and knowledge of people in the Corby Glen area.

Annual grant total

In 2012 the fund had assets of £842,000, an income of £37,000 and made no grants to individuals from its educational fund. The 2012 accounts were the latest available at the time of writing (August 2014).

Applications

On a form available from the correspondent, to be submitted by the individual's headteacher.

Other information

This trust mainly gives grants to schools and organisations, although it budgets a small amount each year for grants to individuals.

Deeping

Deeping St James United Charities

£4,400

Correspondent: Julie Banks, Clerk, The Institute, 38 Church Street, Deeping St James, Peterborough PE6 8HD (01778 344707 (Tues/Thurs 9am-12pm); email: dsjunitedcharities@btconnect.com; website: www.dsjunitedcharities.org.uk)

CC Number: 248848

Eligibility

School pupils, college/university students and people in training under the age of 25 in the parish of Deeping St James (including Frognall).

Types of grants

Schoolchildren in the three local schools are assisted to enable them to take part in additional educational activities and opportunities, such as school trips or educational outings in the UK. Expenses for school uniforms can also be covered.

University/college (or equivalent) students, generally aged 18 to 25, undertaking their first degree/qualification can be supported each year for three years of their studies towards books or equipment/instruments from the Tyghe Educational Foundation's funds.

Annual grant total

In 2013 the charity had assets of £2.6 million and an income of £99,000. Educational grants totalled £4,400.

Exclusions

The charity's annual report from 2013 states that 'the trustees decided in 2012 that, in future, it may not be possible to continue giving grants for educational trips abroad.' In 2013 no such grants were made.

Applications

Applications for schoolchildren grants should generally be directed to the school, although families may approach the charity directly as well.

Application forms for tertiary education students are available online or can be requested from the correspondent. They should be submitted as soon as a place on the course has been granted.

Other information

The trust is an amalgamation of a number of small charities from the local area. This trust also gives grants to individuals for welfare purposes and local organisations, groups, clubs or societies. Regular support is given to all three schools in Deeping St James for the benefit of their pupils.

Applicants are encouraged to get in touch with the charity via phone, email or by calling in to the office if they have any questions or need further assistance.

The charity is also funding counselling sessions with Citizens Advice for local residents. The sessions are held on a fortnightly basis at the Institute (to book an appointment call: 01780 763051).

Dorrington

Dorrington Welfare Charity

£500

Correspondent: Susan Tong, Trustee, Penneshaw Farm, Sleaford Road, Dorrington, Lincoln LN4 3PU (01526 833395; email: susantong@btinternet.com)

CC Number: 216927

Eligibility

People under the age of 25 who have lived in the village of Dorrington for at least a year.

Types of grants

Traditionally one-off grants have been made in amounts of up to £200.

Annual grant total

In 2013, the charity had an income of £2,500 and a total expenditure of £2,500. We estimate that £500 was awarded in grants for educational purposes.

Applications

In writing to the correspondent or any trustee directly by the individual. Applications are considered at any time.

Other information

Grants are also awarded for social welfare purposes.

Fleet

The Deacon and Fairfax Educational Foundation

£2,500

Correspondent: Jill Harrington, Administrator, 11 West End, Holbeach, Spalding PE12 7LW (01406 426739)

CC Number: 527639

Eligibility

People who live in the parish of Fleet (Lincolnshire), aged between 16 and 25 and attending further education.

Types of grants

Grants are given to further and higher education students.

Annual grant total

In 2012/13 the foundation had an income of £2,700 and an expenditure of £2,700. Grants totalled approximately £2,500.

Applications

In writing to the correspondent directly by the individual.

Other information

Grants are also made to schools in the area.

Frampton

Frampton Educational Foundation

£4,000

Correspondent: Mark Hildred, Administrator, Moore Thompson, Bank House, Broad Street, Spalding PE11 1TB (01775 711333)

CC Number: 527784

Eligibility

People who have lived in the ancient parish of Frampton for at least five years.

Types of grants

One-off and recurrent grants according to need.

Annual grant total

In 2012/13 the foundation had an income of £5,400 and an expenditure of £4,300. Grants totalled around £4,000.

Applications

In writing to the correspondent. Applications are considered in early October and students must reapply each year.

Other information

Grants are also given to local schools.

Gainsborough

Tyler Educational Foundation

£4,100

Correspondent: E. Bradley, Administrator, 22 Market Place, Gainsborough, Lincolnshire DN21 2BZ (01427 010761)

CC Number: 527691

Eligibility

People under the age of 21 who live in the parishes of Morton and Thornock and are in financial need. Preference may be given for Church of England related causes and activities.

Types of grants

Grants are available for general educational purposes.

Annual grant total

In 2012/13 the foundation had an income of £8,400 and an expenditure of £8,400. We estimate that grants to individuals totalled around £4,100.

Applications

In writing to the correspondent.

Other information

Organisations may also be supported.

Holbeach

Farmer Educational Foundation

£10,000

Correspondent: Michael Griffin, Administrator, 39 Church Street, Warmington, Peterborough PE8 6TE (email: griffin325@btinternet.com)

CC Number: 527636

Eligibility

Children and young people who live in the parish of Holbeach, South Lincolnshire.

Types of grants

Grants are given up to £150 to help students in higher/further education and sometimes to assist schools serving Holbeach with projects.

Annual grant total

In 2012/13 the foundation had an income of £27,000 and assets of almost £628,000. Grants made to individuals totalled approximately £20,000.

Applications

On a form available from Holbeach Library, to be submitted by the individual at the end of August.

Applications are considered in September.

Horncastle

George Jobson's Trust

£3,700

Correspondent: Sarah Steel, Administrator, Chattertons Solicitors, 5 South Street, Horncastle LN9 6DS (01507 522456)

CC Number: 213875

Eligibility

Children and young people in need who live or attend/have attended school in the parish of Horncastle.

Types of grants

Recurrent grants between £50 and £500 to people in education and training for general educational needs, including books, courses, equipment/instruments and various projects.

Annual grant total

In 2012/13 the trust had assets of £1.1 million, an income of £120,000 and a total charitable expenditure of £7,500. The trust also supports organisations, therefore we estimate that grants to individuals did not exceed £3,700.

Exclusions

Our research suggests that grants are not normally awarded to postgraduate students.

Applications

Application forms can be requested from the correspondent and submitted directly by the individual or through a social worker/welfare agency, if applicable.

Other information

Most of the trust's funding goes to schools, youth organisations and students at college.

Kesteven

The Kesteven Children in Need

£500

Correspondent: Alexandra Howard, Trustee, Nocton Rise, Lincoln LN4 2AF (01522 791217; email: enquiries@kcin. org; website: www.kcin.org)

CC Number: 700008

Eligibility

Children/young people up to the age of 16 who live in Kesteven.

Types of grants

Grants of up to £500 towards books, clothing and educational outings.

Annual grant total

In 2013, the charity had an income of £12,500 and a total expenditure of £15,000. The majority of grants are usually awarded for welfare purposes, so we estimate that approximately £500 was awarded for educational purposes.

Applications

Generally through local social workers, health visitors, teachers and education officers. Information should include the family situation, the age of the child and his/her special needs. Applications are considered throughout the year.

Lincoln

Leeke Church Schools and Educational Foundation

£41,000 (86 grants)

Correspondent: Anne Young, Administrator, 23 Upper Long Leys Road, Lincoln LN1 3NJ (01522 526466; email: leekeclerk@gmail.com)

CC Number: 527654

Eligibility

People under the age of 25 who live, or whose parents live, in the city of Lincoln. People studying in Lincoln with a home address elsewhere are ineligible.

Preference can be given to students from families on low income, minimum wage, state benefits, with a single parent or living independently.

Types of grants

One-off and recurrent grants, normally in the range of £150 to £500 each term. Grants are given to schoolchildren, further/higher education students and people entering a trade/profession. Support is aimed to help with the cost of uniforms, outfits, books, equipment/instruments, fees, educational outings in the UK, educational leisure time activities, study or travel abroad and student exchanges.

Annual grant total

In 2012/13 the foundation had assets of £797,000 and an income of £55,000. Grants to 86 individuals totalled £41,000.

Exclusions

Grants are not given for private education – there must be a financial need.

Applications

In writing to the correspondent. Applications can be submitted by the individual for consideration at any time. Educational costs should be listed either giving the real amount or a fair estimate.

Other information

The foundation also made one grant to a school totalling £2,000 in 2012/13.

The trustees' annual report from 2012/13 also notes that 'the trustees' current policy is to prioritise grants to individual students in need. As a result of this, they award the grants to schools towards the end of the financial year.'

Lindsey

The Joseph Nickerson Charitable Foundation

£15,300

Correspondent: Eric White, Administrator, Villa Office, Rothwell, Market Rasen, Lincolnshire LN7 6BJ (01472 371216; email: j.n.farms@ farmingline.com)

CC Number: 276429

Eligibility

Young people, normally aged 18 or over, in further or higher education. Preference may be given to people from Lincolnshire.

Types of grants

Grants to assist with general educational expenses.

Annual grant total

In 2012/13 the foundation had an income of £42,000 and a total charitable expenditure of £32,000. A total of £15,300 was awarded in grants to individuals.

Applications

In writing to the correspondent. Our research suggests that applications for courses starting in September should be made by the end of June for consideration in July.

Other information

The foundation also supports various charitable purposes and organisations (£6,400 in 2012/13), finances outings and activities for senior citizens and young people in Rothwell village (£5,700 in 2012/13) and provides building overheads and repairs (£3,800 in 2012/13).

Moulton

The Moulton Poors' Lands Charity

£200

Correspondent: Richard Lewis, Clerk, Maples and Son Solicitors, 23 New Road, Spalding, Lincolnshire PE11 1DH (01775 722261)

CC Number: 216630

Eligibility

People in need who live in the civil parish of Moulton.

Types of grants

Our research tells us that the charity mainly makes relief-in-need grants and that very occasionally education grants are available.

Annual grant total

In 2012 the charity had assets of £919,000 and an income of £31,000. During the year, £11,200 was awarded in grants, the majority of which we believe was to individuals for welfare purposes. We estimate that educational grants to individuals amounted to no more than £200. A total of £3,000 was awarded to two local primary schools.

At the time of writing (August 2014) this was the most recent financial information available

Applications

In writing to the correspondent, usually through a trustee. Applications are usually considered in April and December.

Other information

The charity also manages almshouses, the rent from which makes up a small part of its income.

Navenby

The Navenby Town's Farm Trust

£3,000

Correspondent: Leonard Coffey, Secretary, 17 North Lane, Navenby, Lincoln LN5 0EH (01522 810273)

CC Number: 245223

Eligibility

University students and young people doing their A-levels who are in need and live in the village of Navenby.

Types of grants

Recurrent grants while at university, but only following reapplication every year.

Annual grant total

About £12,000 a year is awarded to individuals and organisations. We estimate that around £3,000 is given to individuals for educational purposes.

Exclusions

No grants can be given outside the village.

Applications

On a form available from the correspondent, the post office, or the local newsagents. Applications are considered in September. Unsolicited applications are not responded to.

Other information

Grants are also made for welfare purposes.

North Lincolnshire

Withington Education Trust

£2,100

Correspondent: Benjamin Lawrence, Trustee, Frederick Gough School, Grange Lane South, Bottesford, Scunthorpe DN16 3NG (01724 860151)

CC Number: 507975

Eligibility

People under the age of 21 who live in the area of the North Lincolnshire Council area (comprising Scunthorpe, Glanford and Boothferry).

Types of grants

Grants can be given for a wide range of educational needs, including academic or training courses, fees, maintenance expenses, and non-formal educational pursuits, for example, music, artistic activities, dance, sports and international opportunities. Grants usually range from £50 to £300.

Annual grant total

In 2012/13 the trust had an income of £4,800 and an expenditure of £2,300. We have estimated the annual total of grants to be around £2,100.

Exclusions

Grants towards fees for private schooling are not normally given. Our research suggests that general educational necessities, such as books or equipment, are not usually covered.

Parishes of East Halton, North Killingholme, South Killingholme and that part of the district of Boothferry which lies north of the river Ouse are excluded from the area of benefit.

Applications

In writing to the correspondent. Applications can be made at any time

and preferably should be supported by the applicant's school or college. Awards are considered each term.

Other information

The trust was set up in 1979 in memory of Peter Withington, headteacher of Frederick Gough Comprehensive School.

Potterhanworth

Christ's Hospital Endowment at Potterhanworth

£14,200

Correspondent: Yvonne Woodcock, Clerk to the Governors, The Conifers, Barff Road, Potterhanworth, Lincoln LN4 2DU (01522 790942)

CC Number: 527669

Eligibility

People under the age of 25 who live, or whose parents live, in the parish of Potterhanworth, Lincolnshire.

Types of grants

Grants are available to schoolchildren towards the cost of educational visits and extra-curricular activities, such as music, arts, sports and other social and physical training. Further education students and people in vocational training, including apprenticeships, can be supported for general educational needs. Further education awards were of about £100 each.

Annual grant total

At the time of writing (July 2014) the latest financial information available was from 2012. In 2012 the trust had assets of £347,000 and an income of £32,000. Grants totalled around £14,200, broken down as follows:

Educational visits and tuition fees, etc.	£11,800
Further education students (11 awards)	£1,100
School, pre-school, brownies and Little Potters	£1,100
Books to primary school leavers	£300

Exclusions

Grants are not normally given to cover the cost of school fees or school books.

Applications

In writing to the correspondent. Applications can be made either directly by individuals or through a third party, for example a parent/guardian or the individual's educational institution. Applications are normally considered once a year in November and should be received before 31 October. Where applicable, valid receipts for the items/services purchased must be included.

Other information

The trust also supports local schools and nurseries.

Quadring

Cowley and Brown Charity

£1,000

Correspondent: K. J. Watts, Clerk, 99 Hawthorn Bank, Spalding, Lincolnshire PE11 1JQ (01775 760911)

CC Number: 217099

Eligibility

People in education who live in the ancient parish of Quadring. Support is generally given to individuals under the age of 25.

Types of grants

Small grants can be given towards the cost of books, clothing and other educational essentials.

Annual grant total

In 2013 the charity had an income of £4,400 and an expenditure of £3,800. Both figures are the highest in the past few years. We estimate that educational grants to individuals totalled around £1,000.

Applications

In writing to the correspondent. Applications are usually considered in July and November.

Other information

Support is also given to schools, organisations and for general relief-in-need purposes or in Christmas gifts to pensioners.

Scunthorpe

The James Reginald Heslam Settlement

£3,700

Correspondent: Donald Johnson, Executive, 2 Park Square, Laneham Street, Scunthorpe DN15 6JH (01724 281616; email: don.johnson@sbblaw.com)

CC Number: 256464

Eligibility

People in need who are resident in, or originally from, Scunthorpe and immediate district.

Types of grants

One-off grants of up to £1,000 towards books, computers, laptops, other electronic equipment and fees for further education.

Annual grant total

In 2012/13 the trust had an income of £1,400 and an expenditure of £3,900. We estimate that the annual total of grants to individuals was around £3,700.

Applications

In writing to the correspondent by post or email. Our research suggests that applications should include a CV and details of the applicant's financial situation.

South Holland

The Moulton Harrox Educational Foundation

£6,700

Correspondent: Richard Lewis, Administrator, Maples and Son Solicitors, 23 New Road, Spalding, Lincolnshire PE11 1DH (01775 722261)

CC Number: 527635

Eligibility

People up to 25 who live in the South Holland district council area.

Types of grants

Grants for school pupils and college students, including mature students, to help with books, equipment, fees, clothing, educational outings and study or travel abroad. Preference is given to schoolchildren with serious family difficulties so the child has to educated away from home, and to people with special educational needs. One-off and recurrent grants according to need. Individuals must reapply in order to receive the grant in the following year.

Annual grant total

In 2012/13 the foundation had an income of £38,000 and a total expenditure of £34,000. Grants were made to individuals for education totalling £6,700; and to organisations £24,000.

Applications

On a form available from the correspondent. Applications should be submitted before 31 August for consideration in September.

Spalding Relief-in-Need Charity

£14,000

Correspondent: Richard Knipe, Clerk and Solicitor, Dembleby House, 12 Broad Street, Spalding, Lincolnshire PE11 1ES (01775 768774; email: patrick.skells@chattertons.com)

CC Number: 229268

Eligibility

People in need who live in the area covered by the district of South Holland. Preference is given to residents of the urban district of Spalding and the parishes of Cowbit, Deeping St Nicholas, Pinchbeck and Weston.

Types of grants

One-off grants in the range of £100 to £400. Normally payments are made directly to suppliers.

Annual grant total

In 2013 the charity had assets of £1.3 million, an income of £49,000 and gave grants totalling over £32,000. The support can be broken down as follows:

Individuals	£29,000
Individuals, TV licences	£2,200
Individuals, annual grants	£1,400

Exclusions

Grants are not intended to be made were support can be obtained from statutory sources.

Applications

Application forms can be requested from the charity. They can be submitted directly by the individual or assisted by a social worker/Citizens Advice/other welfare agency, if applicable. Grants are considered fortnightly.

Other information

Support is also given to organisations and to individuals for welfare purposes.

This charity is connected with the Spalding Almshouse Charity (registered charity number 220077) and share the same body of administration, the Spalding Town Husbands.

Stickford

The Stickford Relief-in-Need Charity

£7,500

Correspondent: Katherine Bunting, Clerk, The Old Vicarage, Church Road, Stickford, Boston, Lincolnshire PE22 8EP (01205 480455)

CC Number: 247423

Eligibility

Schoolchildren in need who live in the parish of Stickford.

Types of grants

School clothing grants. Grants are also made for welfare purposes.

Annual grant total

In 2013 the charity's income was almost £20,000 and expenditure £16,300. We estimate that grants to individuals totalled around £15,000 with awards being made for both educational and social welfare purposes.

Applications

In writing to the correspondent. Applications should be submitted directly by the individual and are considered all year.

Sutton St Edmund

The Sutton St Edmund Charities United Educational Foundation

£1,700

Correspondent: Jane Ripley, Clerk, 231 Broadgate, Sutton St Edmund, Spalding, Lincolnshire PE12 0LT (01945 700268; email: the.clerk@btinternet.com)

CC Number: 527706

Eligibility

Children or young people who live in the ancient parish of Sutton St Edmund.

Types of grants

Recurrent grants are given to further and higher education students for books, equipment/instruments, fees and maintenance/living expenses. The amount given in individual grants is dependent on the number of applicants and the amount of available income.

Annual grant total

In 2013/14 the foundation had an income of £6,300 and a total expenditure of £1,900. We estimate that educational grants totalled £1,700.

Applications

In writing to the correspondent either directly by the individual, or through a parent or guardian, including details of the course attended i.e. A-level, NVQ, degree, and so on. Applications should be submitted by mid-February each year and grants are paid in April.

Waddingham

James Thompson's Educational Charity (Waddingham Endowment Trust)

£1,700

Correspondent: Brian Milton, Trustee, South View, Moor Road, Snitterby, Gainsborough DN21 4TT (01673 818314)

CC Number: 1039838

Eligibility

People in need who are under the age of 25 and live in the parish of Waddingham.

Types of grants

Small grants of up to £250 are available to schoolchildren and higher/further education students. Financial help is given towards general educational costs, including clothing, books, equipment/instruments, educational outings, travel and living expenses.

Annual grant total

In 2012/13 the trust had both an income and an expenditure of around £3,500. We have estimated the annual grants total to be about £1,700.

Exclusions

Our research indicates that grants are not made to children below primary school age.

Applications

In writing to the correspondent. Applications can be made either directly by individuals or by their parent/guardian. Our research suggests that applications are usually considered in September and should be submitted in advance.

Other information

The charity also supports schools which serve the Waddingham parish.

Northamp-tonshire

Arnold's Education Foundation

£6,500

Correspondent: Jane Forsyth, Administrator, 4 Grange Park Court, Roman Way, Grange Park, Northampton NN4 5EA (01604 876697)

CC Number: 310590

Eligibility

People in need who are under 25 and live in the parishes of Stony Stratford, Buckinghamshire; Nether Heyford, Upper Heyford, Stowe-Nine-Churches, Weedon Bec, Northamptonshire; and the ancient parish of St Giles, Northampton. Preference for members of the Church of England.

Types of grants

One-off and recurrent grants for the study of music and the arts, as well as social and physical training. Grants are made: for schoolchildren towards the cost of clothing, books, educational outings, maintenance and school fees; towards the cost of books, fees/living expenses, travel exchange and study or travel abroad for students in further or higher education; and towards books, equipment/instruments, clothing and travel for people starting work. Grants range from £200 to £500.

Annual grant total

In 2012 the trust had an income of £4,200 and made grants totalling approximately £6,500.

These were the latest accounts available at the time of writing (July 2014).

Applications

On a form available by writing to the correspondent.

Church and Town Allotment Charities (The Kettering Charities (Apprenticing)

£6,000

Correspondent: Anne Ireson, Administrator, Kettering Borough Council, Council Offices, Bowling Green Road, Kettering NN15 7QX (01536 534398; email: anneireson@kettering.gov.uk)

CC Number: 207698

Eligibility

People in further/higher education who are over the age of 16 and live in Kettering or Barton Seagrave.

Types of grants

Financial support is available towards general educational needs, including books, equipment/instruments and other necessities. People in vocational training, people starting work, mature students and individuals with special educational needs can all be assisted.

Annual grant total

In 2012/13 the charity had an income of £14,800 and an expenditure of £12,200. We estimate the annual total of grants to individuals for educational purposes to be around £6,000.

Applications

In writing to the correspondent. Applications can be made by individuals directly or through their parents/guardians, educational establishment or welfare agency, if applicable. Details of the applicant's financial situation should also be included. The trustees usually meet twice a year, in February and November.

Other information

'The trustees are keen to encourage applications from mature students, as well as school leavers and students in higher education, to reflect the national trend for more mature students entering higher education.'

Support is also given to the Kettering parish church and to local retired people who live alone to help with the cost of fuel in winter.

The Charity of Hervey and Elizabeth Ekins

£12,000

Correspondent: Richard Pestell, Administrator, 41 Thorburn Road, Northampton NN3 3DA (01604 408712; email: pestells@btinternet.com)

CC Number: 309858

Eligibility

People who (i) have lived in the borough of Northampton or the parish of Great Doddington for no less than three years; (ii) attended a state school for no less than one year and (iii) attended a Church of England church on a regular basis.

Preference will be given to boys and girls residing in the ecclesiastical parishes of St Peter, Weston Favell, St Peter and St Paul, Abington and Emmanuel, Northampton.

Types of grants

Grants are given to schoolchildren, students in further or higher education and to people starting work towards books, equipment and educational outings in the UK and overseas.

Grants are also given for music tuition fees. Preference is given to those entering the ministry of the Church of England.

Grants average around £200, but in exceptional circumstances can be for as much as £500. Other grants are given to a school for larger projects.

Annual grant total

In 2012/13 the charity had assets of £992,000 and an income of £35,000. Grants to individuals totalled £12,000 and were broken down as follows:

Higher education	£7,400
Music and residential activities	£4,500

Exclusions

Grants are not given for school fees.

Applications

In writing to the correspondent directly by the individual, including details of school and church attended.

Other information

One grant to Weston Favell CE Primary School totalled £7,000 and grants to churches totalled £1,800.

The Horne Foundation

£177,000 (88 grants)

Correspondent: Ros Harwood, Trustee, PO Box 6165, Newbury RG14 9FY (email: hornefoundation@googlemail. com)

CC Number: 283751

Eligibility

Higher education students in need who live in Northamptonshire.

Types of grants

The foundation awards bursaries to higher education students towards course fees, living expenses and other educational costs. Grants are of up to of £5,000.

Annual grant total

In 2012/13 the foundation had assets of £7.2 million, an income of £173,000 and a total charitable expenditure of £197,000. Grants were made to 88 individuals totalling £177,000.

Applications

In writing to the correspondent. The trustees meet every three months.

Other information

The foundation also supports organisations towards educational projects that involve new buildings and through regular smaller donations to local projects in the Northampton and Oxfordshire area. In 2012/13 a total of £20,000 was awarded in two grants.

The trustees' policy is to distribute an amount approximately equal to the investment income received.

The Isham Educational Foundation

£600

Correspondent: Frances Allbury, Administrator, 1 Hedgerow Lane, Mawsley, Kettering, Northamptonshire NN14 1TN (01536 790870; email: lhhpcouncil@btinternet.com)

CC Number: 309839

Eligibility

People under the age of 25 who live in the ancient parishes of Faxton, Hanging Houghton and Lamport and are in need.

Types of grants

One-off and recurrent grants between £50 and £1,000 can be given towards education costs, uniforms, clothing, equipment/instruments, tools or books. Further/higher education students and people entering a trade/starting work can be supported. Our research suggests that school pupils can be given assistance for books, equipment, clothing, travel or

school fees but not for maintenance, preference being given to those with serious family difficulties so the child has to be educated away from home.

Annual grant total

In 2013 the foundation had an income of £1,400 and an expenditure of £1,200. We estimate that grants to individuals totalled around £600.

Applications

In writing to the correspondent. Applications can be submitted directly by the individual or by a parent/ guardian and are usually considered in July and November.

Other information

Local schools may also be supported.

The Dorothy Johnson Charitable Trust

£19,500

Correspondent: Ms Zinaida Silins, Clerk to the Trust, Hybank, 12 Old Road, Walgrave, Northampton NN6 9QW (01604 780662; email: zinaida@ zinaidasilins.com)

CC Number: 298499

Eligibility

People under 25 who were born and are living, have lived or were educated at some time in Northamptonshire.

Types of grants

One-off and recurrent grants in the range of £100 and £500. Grants are made to schoolchildren, college students, undergraduates, vocational students, postgraduates and people with special educational needs, towards clothing/ uniforms, fees, study/travel abroad, books, equipment/instruments, maintenance/living expenses and excursions.

Annual grant total

In 2012/13 the trust had an income of £21,000 and an expenditure of £20,000. Grants totalled approximately £19,500.

Applications

In writing to the correspondent. Applications are considered three times a year.

Parson Latham's Educational Foundation

£1,700

Correspondent: Graham Sands, Clerk, Magnolia Cottage, 1 Main Street, Cotterstock, Peterborough PE8 5HD (01832 226025; email: grahamsands@ btconnect.com; website: www. parsonlathamscharity.org.uk)

CC Number: 309843

Eligibility

Young people living in the parish of Oundle and seeking to enter further/higher education or apprenticeships/vocational courses. Applicants must have attended one of the following schools: Oundle Primary School, Oundle Middle School or Prince William School, for at least two years.

Types of grants

According to our research, small grants of up to £250 are available towards general educational costs, including books, clothing, uniforms, equipment/instruments, tools, maintenance/living expenses, educational outings and fees.

Annual grant total

In 2012/13 the foundation had an income of £3,500 and an expenditure of £3,600. We have estimated the annual total of grants to individuals to be around £1,700.

Exclusions

Our research indicates that grants are not given to overseas students studying in the UK or for student exchange.

Applications

Application forms can be found on the foundation's website or can be requested from the correspondent. Applications should be submitted directly by the individual by the end of August.

Other information

The foundation also makes grants to organisations.

Northamptonshire Community Foundation

£8,500 (17+ grants)

Correspondent: Victoria Miles, Chief Executive, Within Royal and Derngate, 19 Guildhall Road, Northampton NN1 1DP (01604 230033; email: enquiries@ncf.uk.com; website: www.ncf.uk.com)

CC Number: 1094646

Eligibility

- Northamptonshire Champions Fund – people under the age of 25 (under the age of 35 for people with disability) who are competing/have a potential to compete within 18 months for England or Great Britain at regional or, ideally, national level. Applicants must live, train, coach or officiate in Northamptonshire. Performers from all sports recognised by Sport England (an extensive list is available online) are assisted. Athletes with disabilities over the age of 35 can still apply if they can demonstrate that they have taken up the sport for

which they are applying for, within the last three years
- Arts and Music Fund – young people wishing to take part in Royal and Derngate's Youth Theatre

Types of grants

Two funds offer help to individuals:
- Northamptonshire Champions Fund – bursaries are available to 'Northamptonshire's emerging sports stars' to help with the costs of sports-based activities, including travel expenses, clothing, equipment and training/coaching. Grants range between £200 and £1,000 in the first year and up to a maximum of £400 in subsequent years. Funding can be used to help applicants to remain in education if they are experiencing financial difficulties and to athletes on a low income generally or to athletes with disabilities who require an assistor or carer in order to compete
- Arts and Music Fund – bursaries of up to £165 to contribute towards the cost of fees

Annual grant total

In 2012/13 the foundation had assets of £3.1 million, an income of £1.3 million and a total expenditure of £624,000. Out of all the funds which the foundation administers two give grants to individuals. The Champions Fund made 17 awards totalling £4,900 and the Arts and Music Fund gave bursaries totalling £3,600.

Exclusions

Overseas travel or expeditions are not supported and help is not available where statutory or public funding should be provided.

Applications

Application forms together with detailed guidelines can be found on the foundation's website and should be submitted in **two copies**, one electronically and one by post. Applications can be made at any time and should be accompanied by an independent reference for Northamptonshire Champions Fund and an academic reference for Arts and Music Fund.

The foundation invites potential applicants to approach its staff members for an informal advice or feedback on applications prior to final submission. Applicants are reminded that the funds may open and close at short notice and are asked to check the foundation's website for any changes before applying.

Other information

The foundation manages a number of funds the majority of which are supporting organisations.

Foundation of Thomas Roe

£1,000

Correspondent: Ursula Morris, Administrator, Highfield Grange, Highfield Park, Creaton, Northampton NN6 8NT (01604 505554; email: ursula@ursulamorris.co.uk)

CC Number: 309801

Eligibility

Young people in need under the age of 25 who live in the parishes of Brixworth and Scaldwell, Northamptonshire.

Types of grants

One-off grants of about £50–£150 are available to schoolchildren, students in further/higher education and people starting work/entering a trade. Support is given for school uniforms and other school clothing, books, educational outings in the UK, study or travel abroad, maintenance, fees, living expenses and equipment/instruments.

Annual grant total

At the time of writing (August 2014) the latest financial information available was from 2012. In 2012 the foundation had an income of £2,200 and an expenditure of £1,900. We estimate that educational grants to individuals totalled around £1,000.

Applications

Application forms are available from the correspondent. They are normally considered in March and September each year.

Other information

Assistance is also provided to schools in the local area.

Sir Thomas White's Northampton Charity

£76,000

Correspondent: Angela Moon, Administrator, Hewitsons LLP, Elgin House, Billing Road, Northampton NN1 5AU (01604 233233; fax: 01604 627941; email: angelamoon@hewitsons.com)

CC Number: 201486

Eligibility

People who live within the extended borough of Northampton.

Types of grants

(i) Nine-year interest-free loans to people aged between 21 and 34 for education and new businesses (and home improvements). (ii) Grants to young people aged between 16 and 25 attending school, college or university.

The fund was originally set up for the provision of tools for people entering a trade or profession.

Annual grant total

In 2013 the trust had assets of £3.4 million and an income of £262,000. Interest free loans and educational grants are available. 30 loans totalling £75,000 and £76,000 in student grants were made.

Applications

Apply in writing for a form in November, following a public notice advertising the grants.

Other information

Previously called Sir Thomas White's Loan Fund.

The Wilson Foundation

£8,000 (31 grants)

Correspondent: The Administrator, The Maltings, Tithe Farm, Moulton Road, Holcot, Northamptonshire NN6 9SH (01604 782240; fax: 01604 782241; email: polly@tithefarm.com; website: www. thewilsonfoundation.co.uk)

CC Number: 1074414

Eligibility

Young people (normally 10 to 21 years of age) who were born or have lived in Northamptonshire for at least a year, particularly those who are disadvantaged or underprivileged.

Types of grants

Scholarships can be given for trips and expeditions or Outward Bound courses which help build the individual's character and can make a lasting impact on his/her life. Support could also be given towards educational necessities, such as school uniforms and clothing, equipment or books.

Grants can range from £100 to about £3,000 with an average grant of around £200.

Annual grant total

In 2012/13 the foundation had assets of £5.2 million, an income of £76,000 and a total charitable expenditure of £68,000. During the year 31 individuals were awarded grants totalling £8,000.

Applications

Application forms can be downloaded from the foundation's website and once completed should be sent to the correspondent. At least one reference must be supplied. The trustees meet at least twice a year.

Other information

Grants are also made to organisations for various projects benefiting young people (a total of £60,000 to 18 institutions in 2012/13).

Blakesley

The Blakesley Parochial Charities

£2,000

Correspondent: Derek Lucas, Administrator, Bradworthy, Main Street, Woodend, Towcester NN12 8RX (01327 860517)

CC Number: 202949

Eligibility

People who are in need and live in Blakesley.

Types of grants

One-off and recurrent grants according to need for post-16 education and apprenticeships.

Annual grant total

In 2013 the charity had an income of £6,700 and a total expenditure of nearly £5,000. We estimate that educational grants to individuals totalled around £2,000.

Applications

In writing to the correspondent. Applications are considered in September.

Other information

The charities also make grants for welfare purposes.

Brackley

The Brackley United Feoffee Charity

£6,000

Correspondent: Rosemary Hedges, Administrator, 7 Easthill Close, Brackley, Northamptonshire NN13 7BS (01280 702420; email: caryl.billingham@tesco. net)

CC Number: 238067

Eligibility

People under the age of 25 who live in the parish of Brackley.

Types of grants

One-off grants in the range of £100 and £1,000 to: schoolchildren for uniforms/ clothing, study/travel abroad, books, equipment/instruments, excursions and childcare; college students and undergraduates for study/travel abroad, books and excursions; and to people with special educational needs for excursions and childcare.

Previous educational grants (2006/07) have included funding for educational trips to developing countries, music lessons, purchasing of musical instrument and contributions towards fees to attend a musical college.

Annual grant total

In 2012/13 the trust had an income of £34,000 and a total expenditure of over £26,000. We estimate grants to individuals for educational purposes to be around £6,000.

Applications

In writing to the correspondent either directly by the individual or through the individual's school, college or educational welfare agency. Trustees meet every three to four months.

Other information

The charity awards grants to individuals and organisations for both educational and social welfare purposes.

Brington

The Chauntry Estate

£5,000

Correspondent: Rita Tank, Administrator, Walnut Tree Cottage, Main Street, Great Brington, Northampton NN7 4JA (01604 770809)

CC Number: 200795

Eligibility

People who live in the parish of Brington. Applicants must have lived in the parish for at least five years.

Types of grants

One-off grants for purchase of uniforms for children transferring to secondary schools, books and equipment for students in further/higher education or apprenticeships, and assistance towards items of school equipment not provided by LEA. Grants are also available for mature students.

Annual grant total

In 2012/13 the trust had both an income and a total expenditure of just over £10,000. We estimate grants to individuals for educational purposes to be around £5,000.

Applications

In writing to the correspondent. Ineligible applications are not acknowledged.

Other information

Grants are also awarded for social welfare purposes.

Burton Latimer

The Burton Latimer United Educational Foundation

£1,500

Correspondent: Rebecca Hall, Administrator, 23 Spring Gardens, Burton Latimer, Kettering NN15 5NS (01536 722113)

CC Number: 309818

Eligibility

People who live in Burton Latimer.

Types of grants

A general grant is made to students in further or higher education, usually to be used for books; grants to people undertaking training with low earnings to be used at their discretion; and a few grants to schoolchildren towards the cost of field study courses for GCSE work.

Grants are also made to mature students undertaking full or part-time training. In the case of part-time training, this depends on the applicant's income.

Annual grant total

In 2012 the foundation had an income of £2,800 and a total expenditure of £3,200. We estimate that educational grants to individuals totalled £1,500, with funding also awarded to the three primary schools in the town.

At the time of writing (July 2014) this was the most recent financial information available for the foundation.

Exclusions

People who live in other parts of (or outside of) the borough of Kettering are not eligible.

Applications

Application forms are available from the correspondent and must be submitted directly by the individual. Applications are usually considered in October. Applications unrelated to educational needs will not be considered.

Byfield

The Poors Allotment

£350

Correspondent: Pam Hicks, Administrator, 1 Edwards Close, Byfield, Daventry, Northamptonshire NN11 6XP

CC Number: 220321

Eligibility

People in need who live in the parish of Byfield.

Types of grants

Our research suggests that grants are mainly given to undergraduates for books and study/travel overseas.

Annual grant total

At the time of writing (August 2014) the latest financial information available was from 2012. In 2012 the charity had both an income and a total expenditure of around £800. We estimate that educational grants totalled around £350.

Applications

Application forms are available from the correspondent. They can be made directly by the individual or through a relevant third party at any time for consideration in March, June, September and December.

Other information

The charity also makes grants for welfare purposes.

Chipping Warden

Relief in Need Charity of Reverend William Smart (Chipping Warden Smarts Charity)

£500

Correspondent: Nigel Galletly, Trustee, 3 Allens Orchard, Chipping Warden, Banbury, Oxfordshire OX17 1LX (01295 660365)

CC Number: 239658

Eligibility

People in need who live in the parish of Chipping Warden, Northamptonshire. Preference is given to elderly people and young people in education.

Types of grants

One-off grants can be given according to need.

Annual grant total

At the time of writing (August 2014) the latest financial information available was from 2012. In 2012 the charity had an income of £4,100 and a total expenditure of £2,900. We estimate that educational grants to individuals totalled around £500.

Exclusions

People outside the area of benefit cannot be supported.

Applications

In writing to the correspondent. Applications can be made either directly by the individual or through a third party, such as a social worker. They are considered at any time.

Other information

Grants are mainly made for welfare purposes and can also be given to organisations.

East Farndon

The United Charities of East Farndon

£2,800

Correspondent: C. L. Fraser, Administrator, Linden Lea, Main Street, Market Harborough, Northamptonshire LE16 9SJ (01858 464218; email: fraser_cameron@hotmail.com)

CC Number: 200778

Eligibility

Students in need who live in East Farndon.

Types of grants

One-off grants of up to £50 for people starting work, schoolchildren and college students. Grants given include those for books, equipment and instruments, as well as to schoolchildren for excursions.

Annual grant total

In 2013 the charity had an income of £7,800 and an expenditure of £5,600. We estimate that grants awarded to individuals for educational purposes totalled around £2,800.

Applications

In writing to the correspondent directly by the individual or a family member for consideration as they are received.

Other information

Grants are also made for welfare purposes.

Harringworth

The Harringworth Educational Foundation

£1,500

Correspondent: Paul Manning, Trustee, Vale House, Gretton Road, Harringworth, Corby NN17 3AD

CC Number: 309835

Eligibility

Individuals under the age of 25 who live in Harringworth. Applicants must be pupils of a public elementary school in the area.

Types of grants

Grants are awarded to 'encourage children to continue their attendance at school.' Students entering a trade/profession can be supported as well. Our research shows that one-off grants between £50 and £300 are given for books and equipment/instruments.

Annual grant total

In 2012/13 the foundation had an income of £2,100 and an expenditure of around £1,600. We estimate that the annual total of grants was about £1,500.

Exclusions

Grants are not normally given for school clothing or fees.

Applications

In writing to the correspondent, either directly by the individual or through the individual's school/college or educational welfare agency, if applicable. Applications should normally be submitted in February for consideration in March.

Other information

The Harringworth Parochial Charities (registered charity number 241784) offers support towards general charitable causes in the area.

Isham

Isham Apprenticing and Educational Charity

£50

Correspondent: A. S. Turner, Trustee, 36B South Street, Isham, Kettering, Northamptonshire NN14 1HP (01536 722500)

CC Number: 309885

Eligibility

Young people under the age of 25 who/ whose parents live in the parish of Isham, Northamptonshire.

Types of grants

Small grants are given to advance education and/or training. Our research suggests that help can be provided towards the cost of books, clothing, educational outings, maintenance and school fees for schoolchildren; and for books, equipment/instruments, clothing and travel for people starting work or undertaking apprenticeships.

Annual grant total

In 2013 the charity had an income of £1,800 and an expenditure of £100. We estimate that about £50 was awarded in grants to individuals.

Applications

In writing to the correspondent. Applications can be made directly by individuals or their parents/guardians. Awards are considered on a regular basis.

Other information

Organisations may also be supported.

Litchborough

Litchborough Parochial Charities

£3,000

Correspondent: Maureen Pickford, Trustee, 18 Banbury Road, Litchborough, Towcester NN12 8JF (01327 830110)

CC Number: 201062

Eligibility

Young people resident in or connected to the ancient parish of Litchborough following a formal programme of study.

Types of grants

One-off and recurring grants to help with the course fees.

Annual grant total

In 2012/13 the charity an income of £6,200 and an expenditure of £6,100. The trust also provides support to individuals in need, therefore we estimate the annual total of educational grants to be around £3,000.

Applications

In writing to the correspondent.

Other information

Grants are also given for widows' pensions and to assist the pensioners with the costs of heating bills.

Middleton Cheney

Middleton Cheney United Charities

£2,000

Correspondent: Linda Harvey, Administrator, 1 The Avenue, Middleton Cheney, Banbury, Oxfordshire OX17 2PE (01295712650)

CC Number: 202511

Eligibility

People who live in Middleton Cheney and are in need.

Types of grants

Our research suggests that one-off grants are available to schoolchildren for equipment/instruments and to students in higher/further education (including mature students) for books and study or travel abroad. Awards are in the range of £100 to £200.

Annual grant total

In 2013 the charity had an income of £3,800 and an expenditure of £4,000. We estimate that educational support to individuals totalled around £2,000.

Applications

In writing to the correspondent. Applications can be submitted directly by the individual and are considered four times a year.

Other information

Support may also be given to organisations.

Northampton

Beckett's and Sergeant's Educational Foundation

£88,000 (134 grants)

Correspondent: Angela Moon, Administrator, Hewitsons LLP, Elgin House, Billing Road, Northampton NN1 5AU (01604 233233; fax: 01604 627941; email: angelamoon@hewitsons. com)

CC Number: 309766

Eligibility

People under the age of 25 who either live in the borough of Northampton, or are attending/have attended for at least two years All Saints CEVA Primary School, or who are attending schools or further/higher education institutions within the borough.

The trustees have discretion to award grants to further/higher education students ordinarily resident in but undertaking courses beyond the borough of Northampton.

Types of grants

Grants are of up to £1,000 and can be given for a wide range of educational and training purposes, including educational trips, books, equipment, study of music or other arts and supplementing existing grants.

Annual grant total

At the time of writing (July 2014) the latest financial information available was from 2012. In 2012 the foundation had assets of £2.9 million, an income of £219,000 and gave grants to 134 individuals totalling £88,000.

Applications

Application forms can be requested from the correspondent in writing. Awards are normally considered four times a year.

Other information

Grants may also be given to other Church of England schools and organisations that are connected with the Church of England, in the local area. In 2012 grants to seven organisations totalled £39,000.

Blue Coat Educational Charity

£7,500

Correspondent: Richard Pestell, Trustee, 41 Thorburn Road, Northampton NN3 3DA (01604 401237; email: pestells@btinternet.com)

CC Number: 309764

Eligibility

Schoolchildren, students and people entering work who are under the age of 25 and live in the borough of Northampton.

Types of grants

One-off and recurrent grants for general educational purposes, including the costs of clothing, educational outings, books, fees, study/travel abroad or student exchange, and equipment/instruments or tools. Grants can reach up to £500 per individual.

Annual grant total

In 2012/13 the charity had an income of £9,000 and an expenditure of £15,100. It also supports local schools, therefore we estimate that the total of grants awarded to individuals was around £7,500.

Exclusions

Grants are not available to mature students or overseas students studying in Britain.

Applications

In writing to the correspondent. Our research suggests that applications are usually considered in February, July and November.

Other information

Grants are also made to the Church of England schools in Northampton.

Old

The Old Parish Charities

£0

Correspondent: Judith Willis, Clerk to the Trustees, 5 Townson Close, Old, Northampton NN6 9RR (01604 781252)

CC Number: 252168

Eligibility

People who live in the parish of Old.

Types of grants

Help with the cost of books, clothing and other essentials for schoolchildren. Help is also available for students at college or university.

Annual grant total

In 2012 the charities had assets of £1.1 million and had an income of £67,000. During the year, £670 was given in grants for the 'general benefit' of residents of the parish. No grants were given for the advancement of education.

At the time of writing (August 2014) this was the most recent financial information available for the charities.

Applications

In writing to the correspondent.

Other information

The charities also manage a community centre, bungalows and a playing field in the village, and state their objectives as follows: 'The first obligation of the trustees is to meet the outgoings and repair and maintain the homes. Up to one third of any remaining income may be distributed as grants for the advancement of education. The balance may be applied for relief of those in need among the residents. Any residue may be used for the general benefit of parish inhabitants'.

Ringstead

The Ringstead Gift

£500

Correspondent: Louise Smith, 1 Chapel Street, Ringstead, Kettering, Northamptonshire NN14 4DL (01933 626011; email: harlousophsmith@aol.co.uk)

CC Number: 239517

Eligibility

People up to the age of 25 whose parents live in the parish of Ringstead.

Types of grants

One-off grants in kind to schoolchildren, college students, undergraduates and vocational students, including those for uniforms/clothing, study/travel abroad, books and equipment/instruments.

Annual grant total

In 2012/13 the charity had an income of £2,000 and a total expenditure of £2,000. We estimate that £500 was awarded in grants for educational purposes.

Applications

In writing to the correspondent, to be submitted either directly by the individual or a family member, through a third party, such as a social worker or teacher, or through an organisation, such as Citizens Advice or a school. Applications are considered in June and November and should be submitted at least two weeks prior to this.

Scaldwell

The Scaldwell Charity

£1,200

Correspondent: James Kearns, Clerk to the Trustees, Wilson Browne Solicitors, The Manor House, 12 Market Square, Higham Ferrers, Rushden NN10 8BT (01933 410000; fax: 01933 410401; email: jkearns@wilsonbrowne.co.uk)

CC Number: 277208

Eligibility

People in need who live in the parish of Scaldwell.

Types of grants

Help with the cost of books, clothing and other essentials for schoolchildren; books, fees and travel expenses for students in further or higher education; books, equipment and clothing for people starting work; and books, travel and fees for mature students.

Annual grant total

In 2013 the charity had an income of £3,400 and a total expenditure of £2,400. We estimate that educational grants to individuals totalled £1,200, with funding also awarded to organisations.

Applications

In writing to the correspondent, including details of financial circumstances. Applications are normally considered in March, July and November.

Welton

Welton Village Hall (formerly The Welton Town Lands Trust)

£1,000

Correspondent: Carol Bertozzi, Trustee, 5 Well Lane, Welton, Daventry, Northamptonshire NN11 2JU (01327 702213; email: caroline@paddockend.com)

CC Number: 304449

Eligibility

Students in higher education who are in need and have lived in the village of Welton for at least two years.

Types of grants

One-off grants of up to £75 to assist students in higher education for the cost of books, equipment and so on.

Annual grant total

In 2013/14 the charity had an income of £6,900 and a total expenditure of £4,700.

Grants given to individuals totalled approximately £1,000.

Exclusions

Grants are not made to school aged children unless they have a mental or physical disability or to individuals pursuing a hobby.

Applications

In writing to the correspondent.

Other information

The trust also makes grants to local schools and churches.

Nottingham-shire

The John and Nellie Brown Farnsfield Trust

£6,000

Correspondent: Alan Dodd, Trustee, Roan House, Crabnook Lane, Farnsfield, Newark NG22 8JY (01623 882574)

CC Number: 1078367

Eligibility

People in need who live in the Farnsfield, Edingley Halam and Southwell area of Nottinghamshire.

Types of grants

Grants are given according to need.

Annual grant total

In 2012/13 the trust had an income of £5,100 and a total expenditure of £25,000. Grants are made to individuals and organisations for both educational and social welfare purposes. We estimate the grant total for the year made to individuals for educational purposes to be around £6,000.

Applications

In writing to the correspondent.

Nottingham Gordon Memorial Trust for Boys and Girls

£13,300

Correspondent: Anna Chandler, Charity Administrator, Cumberland Court, 80 Mount Street, Nottingham NG1 6HH (01159 015562; fax: 01158 599652; email: anna.chandler@freeths.co.uk)

CC Number: 212536

Eligibility

Children and young people under the age of 25 who are in need and live in Nottingham and the area immediately around the city. Preference can be given to individuals who are of the former Nottingham Gordon Memorial Home for Destitute Working Boys.

Types of grants

Grants are given to schoolchildren and further/higher education students. Assistance is awarded towards general education and training needs, books, equipment/instruments, tools, maintenance/living expenses, educational outings in the UK and study/travel abroad and school uniforms or other clothing.

Annual grant total

At the time of writing (August 2014) the latest financial information available was from 2012. In 2012 the trust had assets of £1.1 million and an income of £46,000. A total of £36,000 was awarded to individuals, of which £8,200 was given in educational grants and £5,100 in grants for trips in the UK and overseas.

Applications

Application forms are available from the correspondent. They can be submitted through the individual's school, college, educational welfare agency, health visitor, social worker, probation officer or similar professional. Our research suggests that individuals, supported by a reference from their school/college, can also apply directly. The trustees meet twice a year, although applications can be considered all year round.

Other information

The trust also supports organisations in the Nottingham area and provides relief in need for individuals.

The Nottingham Roosevelt Memorial Travelling Scholarship Fund

£17,400

Correspondent: Ellen Burns, Trustee, 8 Mornington Crescent, Nuthall, Nottingham NG16 1QE (01159 755669; website: www.rooseveltscholarship.org)

CC Number: 512941

Eligibility

People between the ages of 21 and 30 (cut-off date is 1 August of the current year) who work and/or live in the city or county of Nottingham and are primarily engaged in trade, commerce or 'the professions'.

Types of grants

A scholarship to enable an individual to visit the USA for a period between one and three months. 'Scholars are expected to travel widely throughout the USA and learn about the American way of life – an ambassadorial role. 'It is expected that some aspects linked to the work of the applicant will be investigate during the trip. The value of each scholarship can be up to about £3,200, plus a return flight to New York.

Annual grant total

At the time of writing (July 2014) the latest financial information available was from 2012. In 2012 the fund had an income of £9,300 and an expenditure of £17,600. We estimate the annual total of grants to be around £17,400.

Applications

Detailed guidelines, application forms and submission deadlines can be found on the fund's website. Applications are usually invited in spring. The fund prefers to receive them via email. Shortlisted candidates are required to attend interviews.

Other information

Applicants do not need to be in full-time education/employment or have any formal qualifications.

Further queries can be submitted online on the fund's website.

The Puri Foundation

£0

Correspondent: Nathu Ram Puri, Trustee, Environment House, 6 Union Road, Nottingham NG3 1FH (01159 013000)

CC Number: 327854

Eligibility

Individuals in need living in Nottinghamshire who are from India (particularly the towns of Mullan Pur near Chandigarh and Ambala). Employees/past employees of Melton Medes Group Ltd, Blugilt Holdings or Melham Inc. and their dependents, who are in need, are also eligible. The foundation wants to support people who have exhausted state support and other avenues, in other words to be a 'last resort'. Eligible people can receive help at any stage of their education, including postgraduates and mature students.

Types of grants

One-off and recurrent grants according to need. The maximum donation is usually between £150 and £200.

Annual grant total

In 2012/13 the foundation had assets of £2.8 million and an income of £325,000. There were no grants to individuals made. Grants to organisations totalled £277,000, of which £234,000 was given to an organisation operating in India.

Applications

In writing to the correspondent, either directly by the individual or through a social worker.

Arnold

Arnold Educational Foundation

£18,000

Correspondent: Brian West, Administrator, 73 Arnot Hill Road, Arnold, Nottingham NG5 6LN (01159 206656; email: b.west909@btinternet. com; website: stmarysarnold.org.uk/arnold_parochial_charities.html)

CC Number: 528191

Eligibility

People under the age of 25 who/whose parents live in the ancient parish of Arnold (which includes Daybrook and Woodthorpe) and who require financial assistance.

Types of grants

Mainly further/higher education students can be assisted with the cost of books, equipment/instruments, course fees or educational expeditions. According to our research, schoolchildren may only be assisted in special circumstances towards the cost of books, clothing or other essentials.

Annual grant total

In 2012/13 the trust had an income of £16,400 and an expenditure of £18,900. We estimate the annual total of grants to be around £18,000.

Applications

Application forms can be found on the St Mary's Arnold website or requested from the correspondent. The receipts for purchased items must be included.

Bingham

The Bingham Trust Scheme

£1,000

Correspondent: Gillian Bailey, Trustee, 20 Tithby Road, Bingham, Nottingham NG13 8GN (01949 838673)

CC Number: 513436

Eligibility

People under the age of 21 living in Bingham.

Types of grants

Grants in the range of £50 and £150 to help with expenses incurred in the course of education, religious and physical welfare and so on. They are

made in January and early July each year.

Annual grant total

In 2012/13 the scheme had both an income and a total expenditure of £1,300. Grants would seem to be made mainly for educational purposes.

Applications

Application forms are available from the correspondent. They can be submitted directly by the individual or a family member by 30 April and 31 October each year.

Bingham United Charities 2006

£3,300

Correspondent: Susan Lockwood, Administrator, 23 Douglas Road, Bingham, Nottingham NG13 8EL (01949 875453; email: lockwoodsue79@gmail. com)

CC Number: 213913

Eligibility

People in need who live in the parish of Bingham.

Types of grants

For a range of educational purposes.

Annual grant total

In 2013/14 the charity had an income of £10,800 and an expenditure of £6,800. Grants totalled £6,500 and were divided between welfare and education.

Exclusions

Applicants must live in Bingham.

Applications

Application forms are available from the secretary (details as above). However applications supported by a professional, medical, or social care agency can often be dealt with more quickly.

Other information

Grants are also given to organisations and individuals for welfare purposes.

Carlton-in-Lindrick

The Christopher Johnson and the Green Charity

£1,000

Correspondent: Robin Towle, Hon. Secretary and Treasurer, 135 Windsor Road, Carlton-in-Lindrick, Worksop, Nottinghamshire S81 9DH (01909 731069; email: 1cert@tiscali.co.uk)

CC Number: 219610

Eligibility

Schoolchildren in need who live in the village of Carlton-in-Lindrick.

Types of grants

One-off grants ranging from £10 to £250 for school trips, books and so on.

Annual grant total

Grants usually total about £2,000 each year and are given for educational and welfare purposes.

Applications

In writing to the correspondent either directly by the individual, via a third party, such as a social worker, doctor or district nurse, or through Citizens Advice or other welfare agency. Applications are considered throughout the year.

Collingham

William and Mary Hart Foundation
See entry on page 44

Mansfield

Faith Clerkson's Exhibition Foundation

£2,500

Correspondent: C. P. McKay, Administrator, 68 Hillside Road, Beeston, Nottingham NG9 3AY (07771 978622)

CC Number: 528240

Eligibility

People going to university or entering further education who have lived in the borough Mansfield or the urban district of Mansfield Woodhouse for at least two years.

Types of grants

Small grants are available to help higher/further education students and others leaving school with general educational costs, including books, equipment, clothing or travel.

Annual grant total

In 2012/13 the foundation had an income of £3,000 and a total expenditure of £2,700. We estimate the annual total of grants to be around £2,500.

Exclusions

According to our research, grants are not available towards the course fees.

Applications

In writing to the correspondent. The trustees normally meet in June and October.

North Muskham

Mary Woolhouse

£2,900

Correspondent: Robert Patterson, Administrator, Coniston, Main Street, North Muskham, Newark NG23 6HQ (01636705517)

CC Number: 528185

Eligibility

People under the age of 25 who or whose parents live in the parishes of North Muskham and Bathley.

Types of grants

Our research suggests that one-off grants are given to schoolchildren and college students towards the cost of books and equipment/instruments. The support includes education in the doctrines of the Church of England and social or physical training.

Annual grant total

The latest financial information available was from 2012. In 2012 the charity had both an income and an expenditure of £6,000. We estimate that grants to individuals totalled around £2,900.

Applications

In writing to the correspondent. Applications can be submitted directly by the individual at any time.

Other information

Local schools are also supported, where the need is not addressed by the local authorities.

Nottingham

Audrey Harrison Heron Memorial Fund

£5,000

Correspondent: NatWest Trust Services, 5th Floor, Trinity Quay 2, Avon Street, Bristol BS2 0PT (0551 657 7371)

CC Number: 504494

Eligibility

Girls and women under the age of 25 living in the city of Nottingham.

Types of grants

One-off and recurrent grants between £50 and £2,000 to help with the cost of books, equipment/instruments, clothing, travel in the UK and overseas, also school, college or university fees.

Annual grant total

In 2012/13 the fund had an income of £4,800 and an expenditure of £5,200. We estimate the annual total of grants to be around £5,000.

Applications

Application forms can be requested from the correspondent. Applications can be submitted either directly by the individual or through a third party, such as school/college/educational welfare agency, if applicable. Our research shows that applications are considered all year round.

Other information

Grants could also be awarded to societies or charitable organisations which share the fund's objectives.

Peveril Exhibition Endowment

£2,000

Correspondent: Graham Scott, Clerk to the Trustees, Stone Cottage, 5 New Road, Burton Lazars, Melton Mowbray, Leicestershire LE14 2UU (email: peverilfund@gmail.com; website: www. peveril.org.uk)

CC Number: 528242

Eligibility

Children and young people aged between 11 and 25 who/whose parents have lived in Nottingham for at least one year and who are attending, or about to attend, secondary or further education. Preference is given to people who permanently reside in Nottingham rather than on temporary or transitional basis.

Types of grants

One-off and recurrent grants are available to secondary school pupils and further/higher education students. Awards are given for general educational expenses and can reach up to £1,000.

Annual grant total

In 2012/13 the charity had an income of £5,900 and an expenditure of £2,200. We estimate the annual total of grants to be around £2,000.

Applications

Application forms can be requested from the correspondent and can be submitted at any time for consideration within the following six weeks. Academic references or financial details of the family may be requested and taken into account.

Tuxford

Read's Exhibition Foundation

£4,800

Correspondent: A. Hill, Administrator, Sandy Acre, Eagle Road, Spalford, Newark NG23 7HA (01522 778250)

CC Number: 528238

Eligibility

Children and young people, including university students, who have attended school and lived in the parish of Tuxford.

Types of grants

Mainly help for students in further or higher education. Assistance is also given towards the cost of education, training, apprenticeships or equipment for those starting work and towards essentials for schoolchildren.

Annual grant total

In 2012/13 the foundation had an income of £4,300 and an expenditure of £5,000. We have estimated that the total of grants given was around £4,800.

Exclusions

Elementary school pupils.

Applications

In writing to the correspondent. The trustees have stated that invoices for school equipment must be submitted on application before any grant is issued. Applications are considered throughout the year.

Other information

All applications will be considered upon the receipt of invoices.

Warsop

The Warsop United Charities

£1,100

Correspondent: Mrs J. R. Simmons, Newquay, Clumber Street, Warsop, Mansfield, Nottinghamshire NG20 0LX

CC Number: 224821

Eligibility

People in need who live in the urban district of Warsop (Warsop, Church Warsop, Warsop Vale, Meden Vale, Spion Kop and Sookholme).

Types of grants

Grants for those at school, college or university.

Annual grant total

In 2012 this charity had an income of £8,000 and total expenses of £2,200. We estimate grants for educational purposes to be around £1,100. This was the latest financial information available at the time of writing (July 2014).

Applications

In writing to the correspondent. Trustees meet three or four times a year.

Other information

Grants are also made for relief-in-need purposes.

Shropshire

The Atherton Trust

£900

Correspondent: Paul Adams, Administrator, Whittingham Riddell LLP, Belmont House, Shrewsbury Business Park, Shrewsbury SY2 6LG (01743 273273; email: pa@whittinghamriddell.co.uk)

CC Number: 515220

Eligibility

People in need who live in the parishes of Pontesbury and Hanwood and the villages of Annscroft and Hook-a-Gate in the county of Shropshire.

Types of grants

One-off grants are given towards fees, living expenses or study or travel abroad for students in further and higher education and towards equipment or instruments for people starting work.

Annual grant total

In 2012/13 the trust had an income of £4,400 and an unusually high total expenditure of £11,400. Our research tells us that the trust generally gives around £900 annually to individuals for educational purposes.

Applications

On a form available from the correspondent, to be submitted directly by the individual. Applications are considered quarterly in February, May, August and November.

Other information

The trust also supports organisations that give, or agree to give when required, support and services to people who need aid due to loss of sight, limb or health by accident or inevitable causes.

Bowdler's Educational Foundation

£2,500

Correspondent: Tim Collard, Clerk to the Trustees, c/o Legal Division, Shropshire County Council, Shirehall, Abbey Foregate, Shrewsbury SY2 6ND (01743 252756; email: tim.collard@shropshire.gov.uk)

CC Number: 528366

Eligibility

People under the age of 25 who live in the county of Shropshire, with a priority for those living in the Shrewsbury area.

Types of grants

Grants, to a maximum of £100 to £200, for:

- School pupils, to help with books, equipment, clothing or travel
- Help with school, college or university fees or to supplement existing grants
- Help towards the cost of education, training, apprenticeship or equipment for those starting work

Annual grant total

In 2012 the foundation had an both an income and a total expenditure of £2,700. We estimate that grants totalled £2,500.

At the time of writing (July 2014) this was the most recent financial information available for the foundation.

Applications

On a form available from the correspondent.

The Careswell Foundation

£8,000

Correspondent: Bridget Marshall, Administrator, 24 The Crescent, Town Walls, Shrewsbury SY1 1TJ (01743 351332; email: terri.gill@lindermyers.co.uk)

CC Number: 528393

Eligibility

People under the age of 25 who live in Shropshire, the parish of Bobbington or Staffordshire and have attended any of the following schools: Adam's Grammar School (Newport), Bridgnorth Endowed School, Idsall School (Shifnal), Shrewsbury School, Thomas Adam's School (Wem) and secondary education schools for the Donnington area.

Types of grants

Grants, usually of up to about £150, are available to further/higher education students to assist with general educational expenses, including books, equipment and other necessities.

Annual grant total

In 2012/13 the foundation had an income of £11,600 and an expenditure of £8,300. We estimate the annual total of grants to be around £8,000.

Applications

In writing to the correspondent. Our research suggests that applications should be submitted by September for consideration in October.

Charity of Charles Clement Walker (The Walker Trust)

£93,000

Correspondent: Edward Hewitt, Administrator, 2 Breidden Way, Bayston Hill, Shrewsbury SY3 0LN (01743 873866)

CC Number: 215479

Eligibility

People who live in Shropshire. Applicants should have been resident in the area for at least 12 months prior to application. Preference is given to individuals who are on a low income or state benefits, people estranged from their families, single parents and young people leaving care.

Types of grants

Grants can be given towards further/higher education and training courses undertaken within or outside the area of benefit, also for gap-year projects, music, drama and arts costs and expeditions or travel. Individual grants range from £150 up to about £2,000.

Annual grant total

In 2012/13 the trust had assets of £6.1 million and an income of £233,000. Grants to individuals totalled over £93,000, broken down as follows:

Music and drama	£45,000
College course	£31,000
University course	£12,000
Foreign travel	£2,600
Health and disability	£1,800

During the year over 70 grants were made to individuals and organisations, out of those 22 were for music, drama or art studies.

Applications

In writing to the correspondent. Applications are considered four times a year, normally in January, April, July and October. They must reach the correspondent at least one month before help is required. Decisions on urgent cases can be made between meetings.

Other information

Grants are also made to organisations (£60,000 in 2012/13).

The Clungunford Educational Foundation

£1,800

Correspondent: Wendy Shearman, Administrator, Rose Cottage, Hopton Heath, Craven Arms SY7 0QD (01547 530447)

CC Number: 505104

Eligibility

People under the age of 25 who live in the parish of Clungunford.

Types of grants

Educational activities such as school trips, driving lesson costs, equipment and books for school or university.

Annual grant total

In 2013 the foundation had an income of £1,900 and an expenditure of £2,000. Grants totalled around £1,800.

Applications

In writing to the correspondent or any trustee. An information sheet is distributed to each household in the parish at two or three-year intervals and to all newcomers.

Millington's Charity (Millington's Hospital)

£5,000 (11 grants)

Correspondent: Keith Fearnside, Administrator, Copthorne Road, Shrewsbury, Shropshire SY3 8JW (01743 360904)

CC Number: 213371

Eligibility

Further/higher education students under the age of 25 who live or have been educated in Shropshire and who, or whose parents/guardians, are members of the Church of England.

Types of grants

One-off grants ranging from £100 to £400 are given to help people in further/higher education (including religious instruction). Support is given towards general educational expenses associated with college or university attendance, including equipment, books, maintenance/living costs and study/travel abroad. Help can also be given for a specific educational project, musical instruments or extra activities within the chosen course.

Annual grant total

In 2013 the charity had assets of £1 million and an income of £157,000. Grants to 11 individuals in further education totalled £5,000.

Exclusions

Grants are not normally given towards fees.

Applications

Application forms can be obtained from the correspondent upon written request. Candidates are required to give details of their parents' income, other funding secured/applied to and provide references. Awards are made at quarterly meetings, usually in early March, June, September and December.

Other information

Most of the charity's expenditure is spent in providing almshouses with an on-site warden assistance to the members of the Church of England who are in need (£180,000 in 2012/13).

The Shropshire Youth Foundation

£5,000

Correspondent: Karen Nixon, Administrator, The Shirehall, Abbey Foregate, Shrewsbury, Shropshire SY2 6ND (01743 252724; email: karen.nixon@shropshire.gov.uk)

CC Number: 522595

Eligibility

People under the age of 25 years who live in the county of Shropshire.

Types of grants

One-off grants up to £200 can be provided towards educational leisure time activities and opportunities developing physical, mental and spiritual capacities of individuals, for example voluntary service.

Annual grant total

In 2012/13 the foundation had an income of £9,400 and an expenditure of £10,400. We have estimated the annual total of the grants to individuals to be around £5,000.

Exclusions

Financial help is not available towards the course fees.

Applications

Application forms can be requested from the correspondent. The trustees meet twice a year, usually in January and June.

Other information

The main objective of the foundation is to assist youth clubs and similar organisations with specific projects benefiting local young people.

Bridgnorth

The Bridgnorth Parish Charity

£2,000

Correspondent: Elizabeth Smallman, Clerk, 37 Stourbridge Road, Bridgnorth WV15 5AZ (01746 764149; email: eeesmallman@aol.com)

CC Number: 243890

Eligibility

People living in Bridgnorth parish, including Oldbury and Eardington, who are in need.

Types of grants

One-off grants according to need, including those towards playgroup fees, school visits, funeral expenses and heating costs.

Annual grant total

Accounts for the year 2012 were the latest available at the time of writing (August 2014).

In 2012, the charity had an income of £8,000 and a total expenditure of £9,500. We estimate that the total grants awarded to individuals was approximately £2,000 as the charity also awards grants for social welfare purposes and to organisations.

Applications

In writing to the correspondent either directly by the individual or through a doctor, nurse, member of the local clergy, social worker, Citizens Advice or other welfare agency.

Ercall Magna

Ercall Magna Education Endowment

£400

Correspondent: Pauline Lloyd, Administrator, 35 Talbot Fields, High Ercall, Telford, Shropshire TF6 6LY (01952 770353; email: geoff@gloyderdrome.com)

CC Number: 505544

Eligibility

People between the ages of 16 and 25 who are in full-time education and have been living in the civil parish of Ercall Magna for at least one year.

Types of grants

Recurrent grants of about £20–£40 for individuals at college or university towards the costs of books, equipment/instruments, outfits, fees, living expenses, and study/travel abroad. Applicants must be staying in full-time education for at least one academic year after applying. People entering a trade/profession may also be supported.

Annual grant total

In 2012/13 the charity had an income of £900 and an expenditure of £430. We have estimated the annual total of grants to be £400.

Applications

Application forms are available from the correspondent. They should be submitted in advance for consideration in September. Candidates are asked to provide an explanation of what the grant would help to achieve.

Hodnet

The Hodnet Consolidated Eleemosynary Charities

£2,000

Correspondent: Mrs S. W. France, Administrator, 26 The Meadow, Hodnet, Market Drayton, Shropshire TF9 3QF (01630 685907)

CC Number: 218213

Eligibility

Students in need who live in Hodnet parish.

Types of grants

Grants for books to students in further/higher education.

Annual grant total

In 2012 the charities had an income of £4,000 and a total expenditure of £5,000. We estimate that grants awarded to individuals for educational purposes totalled around £2,000. The 2012 accounts were the latest available at the time of writing (August 2014).

Applications

In writing to the correspondent for consideration throughout the year. Applications can be submitted directly by the individual or through a social worker, Citizens Advice or other welfare agency.

Other information

This is essentially a relief-in-need charity that also gives money to students for books.

Hopesay

Hopesay Parish Trust

£3,000

Correspondent: David Evans, Trustee, Park Farm, The Fish, Hopesay, Craven Arms, Shropshire SY7 8HG (01588 660545; email: annedalgliesh@aol.com; website: www.2shrop.net/live/welcome.asp?id=3167)

CC Number: 1066894

Eligibility

People under the age of 25 in any level of education who live, or whose parents live, in the parish of Hopesay, Shropshire.

Types of grants

Grants are typically between £25 and £500 for any educational need, including extra-curricular, gap-year activities, vocational opportunities, tuition fees, travel costs, books, materials, equipment, instruments and so on. Except in cases of financial hardship, grants will not normally exceed half the cost of any activity. The trustees prefer not to enter into extended commitments but will look favourably on repeat applications on an annual basis for extended periods of study.

Annual grant total

In 2013 the trust had an income of £2,800 and an expenditure of £3,500. Grants usually total around £3,000 per year. In the past about 20 individuals a year have been supported. We estimate that educational grants to individuals totalled around £3,000.

Exclusions

Grants are not made where the funding is the responsibility of central or local government, whether or not the individual has taken up such provision. Retrospective applications are not considered.

Applications

Application forms are available from the correspondent or can be downloaded from the Hopesay Parish council website. The application form covers the essential information required, and the trustees will ask for further details if necessary. Applications can be made at any time directly by the individual or by a third party, such as a parent/guardian, teacher/tutor, or through an organisation, such as Citizens Advice or a school.

Other information

The trust gives priority to educational grants. At the trustees' discretion, any surplus income may be applied for other charitable purposes but only within the parish.

Newport

Charity of Annabelle Lady Boughey

£400

Correspondent: Stuart Barber, Administrator, Merewood, Springfields, Newport TF10 7EZ (01952 814628; email: bougheyroddamha@btinternet.com)

CC Number: 213899

Eligibility

Individuals connected with the civil parish of Newport, including the town of Newport and areas of Chetwynd Aston, Church Aston, Edgmond, Forton, Lilleshall, Moreton, Sambrook, Tibberton and Woodcote (TF10 postcode area).

Types of grants

Our research suggests that one-off grants can be given to schoolchildren and students in further/higher education, also mature students. Support is mainly given towards educational trips connected with non-vocational courses in any subject, study or travel abroad and also for instruments/equipment.

Annual grant total

In 2012/13 the charity had an income of £1,200 and an expenditure of £700. We estimate that around £400 was awarded in grants to individuals. The charitable expenditure usually totals around £1,000.

Applications

Our research indicates that initial telephone calls are welcomed and application forms are available on request. They can be submitted directly by the individual and are usually considered in March, June, September and November. Submissions should be made in the preceding month.

Other information

Grants can also be made to organisations.

Oswestry

The Educational Charity of John Matthews
See entry on page 156

Shrewsbury

John Allatt's Educational Foundation

£1,200

Correspondent: Peter Power, Clerk to the Trustees, Sheinton House, Sheinton Street, Much Wenlock TF13 6HY (01952727662; email: power535@btinternet.com)

CC Number: 528294

Eligibility

Children and young people between the ages of 11 and 25 who live in the parishes of Betton Strange, Bicton and Berrington, Leaton and Albrighton, Meole Brace, Shelton and Oxon, or Shrewsbury plus Bayston Hill.

Types of grants

Small grants, usually around £100–£150, are available for specific educational projects, gap year activities or in cases of financial hardship to help with general educational costs and necessities. Grants for undergraduate and postgraduate courses can also be considered.

Annual grant total

In 2012/13 the foundation had an income of £1,600 and an expenditure of £1,400. We estimate the annual grants total to be around £1,200.

Applications

In writing to the correspondent. The trustees meet twice a year, in January and July. Applications should be submitted in advance of these dates. Our research suggests that a letter of support from the individual's educational establishment is also required.

Telford

Maxell Educational Trust

£2,500

Correspondent: Ian Jamieson, Administrator, Maxell Europe Ltd, Apley, Telford, Shropshire TF1 6DA (01952 522222; email: hr@maxell.eu)

CC Number: 702640

Eligibility

Young people aged 9 to 25 years who live, or whose family home is, in Telford, or who attend school or college there. Projects should ideally have an industrial or technological element.

Types of grants

One-off grants for schoolchildren, college students and people with special educational needs, towards books and equipment/instruments.

Annual grant total

In 2012/13 the trust had an income of £6,000 and an expenditure of £6,500. We estimate that around £2,500 was made in grants to individuals for education.

Applications

In writing to the correspondent. Applications are considered throughout the year and should be submitted either by the individual or a parent/guardian, through a third party, such as a teacher, or through an organisation, such as a school or an educational welfare agency.

Staffordshire

Consolidated Charity of Burton upon Trent

£39,000 (39 grants)

Correspondent: J. P. Southwell, Clerk, Dains LLP, 1st Floor, Gibraltar House, Crown Square, First Avenue, Burton upon Trent DE14 2WE (01283 527067; fax: 01283 507969; email: clerk@ consolidatedcharityburton.org.uk; website: www.consolidatedcharityburton. org.uk)

CC Number: 239072

Eligibility

People who live in Burton upon Trent and the neighbouring parishes of Branston, Outwoods and Stretton.

Schools and colleges participating in the bursary scheme are Abbot Beyne School, Burton College, The de Ferrers Academy, John Taylor High School, Paget High School and Stapenhill Sixth Form Centre.

Types of grants

The charity provides around 30 annual undergraduate bursaries of £400 per year for up to three years (provided satisfactory academic development is demonstrated). One-off grants of up to £300 are also available for further education and vocational training, overseas trips, personal development, sports activities and arts scholarships.

Annual grant total

In 2013 the charity had assets of £12.3 million and an income of £497,000. A total of £89,000 was awarded to individuals during the year. Bursaries were given to 31 individuals over three years totalling £37,000 and further 8 grants were given for general educational purposes totalling £1,700.

Exclusions

Grants are not awarded for postgraduate study.

Applications

Application forms are available from the charity's website or can be requested from the correspondent. Candidates should include evidence of acceptance on the course or activity and an accompanying letter of support from a school or college.

Applications for bursaries must include a personal statement and be submitted through the applicant's educational institution. Academic abilities, need and activities undertaken in the community are all taken into consideration.

The trustees meet regularly to consider grants.

Other information

The charity also runs 32 almshouses in the local area, makes grants to local organisations and to individuals for relief-in-need purposes. Grants to organisations totalled £55,000 in 2013.

Lady Dorothy Grey's Foundation

£24,000

Correspondent: Richard Jones, Trustee, Batfield House, Batfield Lane, Enville, Stourbridge, West Midlands DY7 5LF (01746 78350)

CC Number: 508900

Eligibility

Children and young people under the age of 25 who/whose parents live in the parishes of Bobbington, Enville or Kinver, with a preference for Enville.

Types of grants

Grants are given towards general educational expenses, including the cost of books, equipment/instruments, fees, maintenance expenses, clothing and uniforms, educational outings or study/travel abroad. Our research suggests that one-off and recurrent grants normally range from £150 to £500 and can be given to schoolchildren or further/higher education students.

Annual grant total

In 2012/13 the foundation had assets of £89,000 and an income of £27,000. A total of £24,000 was awarded in grants to individuals.

Applications

In writing to the correspondent. Applications can be made either directly by individuals or through their parents/guardians. According to our research, applications should be submitted by 31 August for consideration in October.

Maddock, Leicester and Burslem Educational Charity

£9,000

Correspondent: Graham Hill, Administrator, Grindeys LLP, Glebe Court, Stoke-on-Trent, Staffordshire ST4 1ET (01782 846441)

CC Number: 528586

Eligibility

Schoolchildren and further/higher education students who live in Stoke-on-Trent or Newcastle-under-Lyme.

Types of grants

Small grants, usually of up to £200, are available towards the cost of clothing/outfits, books, equipment/instruments, tools, educational outings, travel/study abroad for educational purposes and study of music and other arts. Schoolchildren, higher/further education students and people starting work are supported. Our research suggests that help may also be available towards the course fees for those at college or university.

Annual grant total
In 2012/13 the charity had an income of £7,600 and an expenditure of £9,100. We have estimated the annual total of grants to be around £9,000.

Exclusions
According to our research, postgraduates or mature students are not normally supported.

Applications
Application forms can be requested from the correspondent and submitted by individuals directly or through their educational establishment. Our research indicates that applications should include details on what the grant is required for, what the aims of the applicant are, if any other funding is applied for/secured, and also have a comment from the school/college/university. The funding is publicised in over 20 local schools.

Realise Foundation

£780 (2 grants)

Correspondent: Kerry Shea, Administrator, Dudson Centre, Hope Street, Hanley, Stoke-on-Trent ST1 5DD (01782 683030; email: kerry@ staffsfoundation.org.uk; website: www. staffsfoundation.org.uk)

CC Number: 1091628

Eligibility
Students over the age of 16 studying at any institute of further or higher education in Leek town, the borough of Newcastle-under-Lyme, Stafford town or the city of Stoke-on-Trent, or following a course related to a future employment aim. Applicants have to be British citizens and have been resident in North Staffordshire or Strafford town for at least five years.

Types of grants
One-off grants of up to £500 are given for goods and services to assist students who are at risk of having to leave their course due to financial difficulties. Support can be given for IT packages, equipment for learning, books, instruments, course fees, travel costs, educational outings, childcare and other necessities.

In 2012 the fund established the Jane Price Award and the first two grants were awarded for special sports equipment and for travel abroad and accommodation cost.

Annual grant total
In 2012/13 the fund had assets of £396,000 and an income of £13,500. Two

grants were made totalling £780. It is both endowed and restricted fund, therefore grantmaking activities are limited.

Exclusions
Students must be undertaking an independent study – no funding is available for those financed by an employer.

The website also states that the charity:

> Will not fund laptops alone, unless there is a specific reason as to why [the individual] must have a different specification laptop, which could include being on a course that dictates [they] would need a different specification. This could be an IT course or any form of arts course, including art, design or music.

Touchscreen laptops or tablets are not funded either.

Applications
Application forms can be downloaded from the foundation's website. Together with the application it is required to provide a proof of ID (excluding student ID), proof of address and any document proving financial hardship. Applications should be signed by a representative from the student funding office (eligible officers and their contact details can be found on the website). The fund has two rounds of applications – one at the beginning of the academic year and another at the beginning of the summer term, post-Easter.

Other information
This fund is managed by the Staffordshire Community Foundation.

The Strasser Foundation

£5,000

Correspondent: The Trustees, c/o Knights Solicitors, The Brampton, Newcastle-under-Lyme, Staffordshire ST5 0QW (01782 619225)

CC Number: 511703

Eligibility
Schoolchildren and students in the local area, with a preference for North Staffordshire.

Types of grants
Usually one-off grants for books, equipment and other specific causes or needs for educational purposes.

Annual grant total
In 2012/13 the trust had both an income and a total expenditure of £21,000. We estimate that grants to individuals for education totalled around £5,000.

Exclusions
Grants are rarely made to people at doctoral level.

Applications
In writing to the correspondent. The trustees meet quarterly. Applications are only acknowledged if an sae is sent.

Other information
The trust also makes grants to individuals for social welfare purposes.

Bradley
The Bradley Trust

£2,500

Correspondent: Jayne Oakley, Administrator, c/o Oakley Accounting Solutions, 128 Old Croft Road, Stafford ST17 0NL (07861 393501; email: oakleyas@gmail.com)

CC Number: 528448

Eligibility
People from the parish of Bradley in Stafford who are in further and higher education.

Types of grants
Grants ranging up to £2,000.

Annual grant total
In 2012 the trust had assets of £1.4 million and an income of £37,000. Grants totalled £6,500, of which £2,500 was distributed in 'university grants'. Grants were also awarded to village organisations and schools attended by children in Bradley.

At the time of writing (July 2014) this was the most recent financial information available for the trust.

Applications
On a form available from the correspondent. Applications are considered once a year in September and should be submitted along with proof of acceptance/attendance at university in August.

Other information
The trust also maintains the village hall for use by the people of Bradley, who benefit from attending meetings and activities subsidised by the trust.

Leigh
Spencer's Educational Foundation Trust

£2,000

Correspondent: Emma Beaman, Administrator, 4 Bents Lane, Leigh, Stoke-on-Trent ST10 4PX (01889 502353)

CC Number: 528442

Eligibility

People under the age of 25 who live in the village of Leigh.

Types of grants

Grants of around £150 are given to people in secondary, further or higher education towards educational necessities, maintenance costs, fees or travel in pursuance of education. Individuals starting work/entering a trade can be assisted with the cost of books, clothing and equipment/instruments.

Annual grant total

At the time of writing (August 2014) the latest financial information available was from 2012. In 2012 the trust had an income of £6,100 and a total expenditure of £2,100. We estimate that grants to individuals totalled around £2,000.

Exclusions

Applications from people outside the area of benefit will not be considered.

Applications

Application forms can be requested from the correspondent. They are normally considered in September and should be received by August. Our research suggests that grants are paid in arrears after a reference from the educational body is received.

Other information

Some support may be given to local schools where help is not already provided by the local authorities.

Rugeley

The Chetwynd Educational Foundation (part of the Chetwynd Charities)

£700

Correspondent: Carl Bennett, Trustee, Sherwood, East Butts Road, Rugeley, Staffordshire WS15 2LU (01889 800727)

CC Number: 234806

Eligibility

People going into higher education who live in the ancient parish of Rugeley.

Types of grants

To students who are proceeding to higher education, university, college or technical college. The correspondent states: 'There is no means test. All applications are considered on their merits. The grant is used mainly to buy books and other equipment. Any applicant who needs to purchase musical instruments or such equipment will also be considered for a further grant from

our general fund. This would also apply to provision of special clothing.' Grants are also given towards study or travel abroad for students in further/higher education and towards fees for mature students. Grants are one-off and usually for amounts of £40 or £50 each.

Grants are usually made up to degree level; however, if the applicant intends to take a Master's degree further help may be given.

Annual grant total

In 2013 the foundation had an income of £3,700 and an expenditure of £2,900. We estimate grants awarded to individuals for educational purposes to be around £700.

Applications

In writing to the correspondent. Applications are usually made directly by the individual and are considered in April and October. 'We normally expect to be informed of the applicant's results and the schools attended. Most applicants inform us of the course and subjects. We enjoy learning of their progress and the correspondence is friendly.'

Other information

Grants are also given for welfare needs and to organisations.

The Rugeley Educational Endowment

£30,000

Correspondent: Financial Directorate, Staffordshire County Council, Finance Directorate, Wedgwood Buildings, Tipping Street, Stafford ST16 2DH (01785 276332; email: john.wood@ staffordshire.gov.uk)

CC Number: 528603

Eligibility

People in need who are under the age of 25 and live in the former urban district of Rugeley as constituted on 31 March 1974. Beneficiaries must have attended any comprehensive school in the area of benefit for at least two years.

Types of grants

According to our research, one-off grants up to a maximum of £100 can be given towards the cost of school and work related clothing, books, educational outings and projects, travel costs in the UK or abroad in pursuance of education, study of music or other arts, sports activities and for equipment/instruments or tools. Support is given to schoolchildren, students in higher or further education and to people preparing to enter a trade/start work.

Annual grant total

In 2012/13 the charity had an income of £80,000 and a total expenditure of £61,000. At the time of writing (August 2014) full accounts from 2012/13 were not available to view. We estimate that the annual total of grants to individuals was around £30,000.

Applications

Our research suggests that applications should be made through the headteacher of the school attended.

Other information

The charity has specific funds awarding prizes to pupils attending The Fair Oak Comprehensive School in Rugeley. The remainder of the endowment is used to provide educational grants.

Stafford

The Stafford Educational Endowment Charity

£10,000

Correspondent: Financial Directorate, Staffordshire County Council, Wedgwood Buildings, Tipping Street, Stafford ST16 2DH (01785 276333; email: john.wood@staffordshire.gov.uk)

CC Number: 517345

Eligibility

Pupils and former pupils of secondary schools in Stafford, who are under 25 years of age and are in need.

Types of grants

Small one-off grants for books, travel, educational outings, educational equipment and similar expenses incurred by schoolchildren, students and people starting work. There is a preference to award grants for benefits not normally provided for by the LEA.

Annual grant total

In 2012/13 the charity had an unusually high income of £75,000 and a similarly high total expenditure of £79,000. At the time of writing (July 2014) the charity's yearly accounts had not yet been received by the Charity Commission. Our research tells us that, in previous years, grants to individuals have totalled around £10,000. Funding is also awarded to secondary schools in Stafford.

Exclusions

Grants are unlikely to be given for course fees or the ordinary living costs of students.

Applications

Through the headteacher of the secondary school attended.

Tamworth

The Rawlet Trust

£5,000

Correspondent: Christine Gilbert, Administrator, 47 Hedging Lane, Wilnecote, Tamworth B77 5EX (01827 288614; email: christine.gilbert@mail. com)

CC Number: 221732

Eligibility

Young people under the age of 25 who are in need and live, or have parents living, in Tamworth.

Types of grants

One-off grants ranging between £30 and £200 towards the cost of books, fees, living expenses, student exchange and study or travel abroad. Grants have also been made for equipment, instruments, clothing or travel for people starting work.

Annual grant total

In 2012/13 the trust had an income of £24,000 and an expenditure of £21,000. The trust was not required to submit accounts to the Charity Commission, but we estimate grants to individuals for educational purposes to have totalled £5,000. The trust also awarded funding for social welfare purposes and to organisations.

Applications

On a form available from the correspondent, to be submitted either directly by the individual or through a third party such as a social worker or Citizens Advice. The clerk or one of the trustees will follow up applications if any further information is needed. The trustees meet in January, April, July and October to consider applications.

Other information

Grants are also made to organisations.

Trentham

The Lady Katherine and Sir Richard Leveson Charity

£400

Correspondent: Adam Bainbridge, Trustee, 67 Jonathan Road, Stoke-on-Trent ST4 8LP (01782 643567)

CC Number: 1077372

Eligibility

People in need under 25 years who live in the ancient parish of Trentham.

Types of grants

One-off grants are given to: schoolchildren for equipment/ instruments, educational outings in the UK and study or travel abroad; people starting work for equipment/ instruments; and further and higher education students and postgraduates for books, equipment/instruments, educational outings in the UK and study or travel abroad.

Annual grant total

In 2013, the charity had an income of £2,500 and a total expenditure of £800. We estimate that £400 was awarded in grants for educational purposes.

Applications

In writing to the correspondent, either directly by the individual or through a third party, such as an educational welfare office or school/college. Applications can be submitted at any time, though August is most popular.

Other information

The charity also makes grants to organisations and to individuals for social welfare purposes.

Tutbury

The Tutbury General Charities

£1,500

Correspondent: Jeanne Minchin, Administrator, 66 Redhill Lane, Tutbury, Burton-on-Trent, Staffordshire DE13 9JW (01283 813310)

CC Number: 215140

Eligibility

Students and people starting apprenticeships or other training who live in the parish of Tutbury.

Types of grants

One-off grants in the range of £40 and £80.

Annual grant total

In 2012/13 the charities had an income of £9,200 and an expenditure of £6,500 Grants are made for welfare and educational purposes both to individuals and organisations.

Applications

The charities have application forms, available from the correspondent, which should be returned by 1 October for consideration in November. A letter of acceptance from the place of education is required.

Other information

The clerk of the trust states that details of the trust are well publicised within the village.

Warwick-shire

Arlidge's Charity

£2,300

Correspondent: A. Pointon, Administrator, 17 Ferndale Drive, Kenilworth CV8 2PF (01926 855399)

CC Number: 528758

Eligibility

People under the age of 25 who live in the county of Warwick (preference is given to residents of Kenilworth) and who are, or one of whose parents are, members of Congregational Church or the United Reformed Church.

Types of grants

Help to students in further/higher education towards the cost of books, fees and travel or study abroad. Grants may be recurrent.

Annual grant total

In 2012/13 the charity had an income of £2,400 and an expenditure of £2,700. We estimate the annual total of grants to be around £2,300.

Exclusions

According to our research, schoolchildren and people entering work are not normally supported.

Applications

In writing to the correspondent. Applications should include details of the course to be taken and information of any other funding secured or applied to. Grants are normally considered in October.

Other information

The Charity Commission's record specifies that:

> 1/7th of the yearly income of the charity is dedicated to the current Minister of the Abbey Hill United Reformed Church either for application by him in furthering the religious and other charitable work of the congregation meeting for religious worship at the said church or in augmentation of his stipend.

Dunchurch and Thurlaston Educational Foundation

£1,200

Correspondent: Paul Smith, Clerk, 11 Bilton Lane, Dunchurch, Rugby, Warwickshire CV22 6PY (01788 810635; email: pppsmith80@hotmail.com)

CC Number: 528738

Eligibility

People under the age of 25 who/whose parents live in the parishes of Dunchurch and Thurlaston.

Types of grants

One-off grants, rarely of more than £200, are available to further/higher education students, people entering a trade/occupation and schoolchildren. Awards are available for general educational needs, including books, equipment/instruments, educational outings, travel in pursuit of education in the UK and abroad and the study of music or other arts. Our research suggests that people starting work and individuals in tertiary education can be funded for fees and maintenance or living expenses.

Annual grant total

In 2012/13 the foundation had an income of £2,800 and an expenditure of £2,500. We estimate that educational grants to individuals totalled around £1,200.

Applications

In writing to the correspondent. Applications can be made directly by the individual or a parent/guardian. They can be submitted at any time.

Other information

This trust also gives grants to local schools for repairs and supports voluntary organisations providing assistance to people under the age of 25 in the area of benefit.

The Hatton Consolidated Charities

£4,500

Correspondent: M. H. Sparks, Clerk, Weare Giffard, 32 Shrewley Common, Shrewley, Warwick CV35 7AP (01926 842533)

CC Number: 250572

Eligibility

People who live in the parishes of Hatton, Beausale and Shrewley. Applications from outside these areas will not be considered.

Types of grants

One-off grants usually in the range of £50 to £500. Recent grants have been given to college students, undergraduates, vocational and mature students towards books, equipment and instruments. People with special educational needs have also been supported.

Annual grant total

In 2012/13 the charity had an income of £10,300 and an expenditure of £9,200. Grants are given for both educational and social welfare purposes and we estimate that grants awarded to individuals for education totalled around £4,500.

Exclusions

Grants are not given to schoolchildren.

Applications

In writing to the trustees or the correspondent, directly by the individual or a family member. Applications should include details of the course and envisaged expenditure.

The Leigh Educational Foundation

£20,000

Correspondent: James Johnson, Clerk to the Trustees, 3 Barford Woods, Barford Road, Warwick CV34 6SZ (01926 419300; email: johnson.jf@virgin.net)

CC Number: 701462

Eligibility

People in need who are under the age of 25 and who (or whose parents) are resident in the parishes of Stoneleigh, Ashow, Leek Wootton and Burton Green.

Types of grants

One-off or recurrent grants according to need, normally ranging from £100 to £1,000. Grants are given to schoolchildren, college students, undergraduates, vocational students and people starting work. Support is offered towards general educational needs, including uniforms/clothing, fees, study/travel abroad, books, equipment/instruments and maintenance/living expenses.

Annual grant total

In 2013 the foundation had assets of £947,000 and an income of £36,000. A total of £25,000 was spent in charitable expenditure. Previously most of the funding was allocated to individuals, therefore we estimate that individual grants totalled around £20,000.

Applications

Application forms and full guidelines are available from the correspondent (in hard copy or electronic format). Applications can be submitted directly by the individual. They are considered four times a year, in February, May, August and November.

Other information

Institutions are also eligible to apply.

The Middleton United Foundation Trust

£2,300 (15 grants)

Correspondent: Elaine Foulkes, Administrator, Horse Shoes, Crowberry Lane, Middleton, Tamworth B78 2AJ (01213 083107)

CC Number: 528699

Eligibility

Young people under the age of 25 who are in need and live, or whose parents live, in the parish of Middleton or the immediate vicinity.

Types of grants

One-off and recurrent grants usually of up to £300 each. Schoolchildren, further and higher education students and postgraduates can be supported for books, equipment/instruments, educational outings in the UK and study or travel abroad. In addition, schoolchildren can be helped with uniforms/other school clothing and students in further and higher education can be supported with maintenance and living expenses. People starting work can be helped with books and equipment/instruments. Grants can also be made towards the costs of developing a hobby.

Annual grant total

In 2012/13 the trust had an income of £2,600 and an expenditure of £2,700. The trust gave out grants of approximately £2,300.

Applications

In writing to the correspondent, giving as many details as possible, for example, the purpose and size of grant requested, the cost of books/equipment, the age of the applicant and a description of the course.

Other information

Grants are occasionally made to organisations.

Perkin's Educational Foundation

£11,000 (70 grants)

Correspondent: The Clerk to the Governors, c/o Lodders Solicitors LLP, 10 Elm Court, Arden Street, Stratford-upon-Avon, Warks CV37 6PA (01789 293259; website: www. williamperkinscharity.org)

CC Number: 528678

Eligibility

People aged 16 to 24 who have been living in Bidford-on-Avon, Broom, Cleeve Prior, Harvington or Salford Priors for at least two years immediately prior to their application.

Types of grants

Grants are mainly given to people entering further/higher education and to individuals undertaking vocational training or apprenticeships. Help is available towards the cost of books, equipment/instruments, clothing, other necessities, also fees, living expenses, study or travel abroad. Awards are usually of around £150–£200.

Annual grant total

In 2013 the foundation had an income of £13,900 and an expenditure of £19,600. Grants to individuals totalled around £11,000. Previously about 70 individuals have been awarded each year.

Exclusions

Awards are not usually made to students under the age of 18 doing GCSE or A-level courses, or to candidates who have reached the age of 25.

Applications

Application forms can be requested in writing from the correspondent or downloaded from the foundation's website. Applications must be signed by the applicant personally and first time applicants should provide a statement of recommendation from their headteacher, college principal or employer. Completed forms should be returned to the clerk by 15 October. Late submissions are not accepted.

The Watson Scholarship for Chemistry

£2,000

Correspondent: Ruth Waterman, School Partnerships Support Officer, Learning and Achievement, Saltisford Office Park, Ansell Way, Warwick CV34 4UL (01926 742075; email: ruthwaterman@ warwickshire.gov.uk)

Eligibility

People who have a home address in Warwickshire, an A grade A-level in chemistry and a confirmed place on a first degree course in chemistry or one in which chemistry is the main subject.

Types of grants

Grants of up to £200, to be paid in the second semester of the first year of the course, after the university had confirmed the satisfactory progress of the student.

Annual grant total

In 2013/14 the trust gave £2,000 in grants to individuals. Not all those that applied were supported.

Exclusions

Students doing pharmacy or medicine will not be supported unless their main subject is chemistry.

Applications

Application forms are sent to schools/colleges in the area in September/October, or they are available from the correspondent. Forms must be signed by the headteacher of their school/college. The closing date for applications is changeable so contact the correspondent for details.

Baginton

The Lucy Price Relief-in-Need Charity

£15,000

Correspondent: Delia Thomas, Clerk, 19 Holly Walk, Baginton, Coventry CV8 3AE (07884 182904)

CC Number: 516967

Eligibility

Only people in need who are between the ages of 5 and 25 and live in the parish of Baginton, Warwickshire.

Types of grants

Grants are made for: (i) attendance at university, living away from home; (ii) attendance at university or colleges of further education, living at home; (iii) attendance at local schools or sixth form college or A-level courses; (iv) school uniforms; (v) travel or visits of an educational nature at home or abroad organised by school or university; (vi) occasionally for equipment, instruments or books specially required for people starting work; and (vii) special educational needs requiring special courses or equipment. Grants made under (i), (ii) and (iii) are for the academic year and are paid in three equal instalments. Grants made under (iv), (v), (vi) and (vii) may be applied for at any time.

Annual grant total

In 2012 the charity had an income of £3,900 and a total expenditure of £33,000. We estimate that educational grants to individuals totalled £15,000. Grants are also given for welfare purposes.

At the time of writing (July 2014) this was the most recent financial information available for the charity.

Applications

Application forms can be obtained from the correspondent either directly by the individual or by the applicant's parents if they are under 16 years old.

Barford

The Barford Relief-in-Need Charity

£3,000

Correspondent: Terry Offiler, Administrator, 14 Dugard, Barford, Warwick CV35 8DX (01926 624153)

CC Number: 256836

Eligibility

Young people who live in the parish of Barford.

Types of grants

Grants for those at school, college or university. Occasional financial assistance is provided for specific purposes such as Raleigh International and Outward Bound-type courses.

Annual grant total

In 2013, the charity had an income of £12,400 and a total expenditure of £10,800. The charity makes grants to both individuals and organisations for educational and social welfare purposes. We estimate that grants to individuals for education totalled around £3,000.

Exclusions

No loans are given.

Applications

In writing to the correspondent, directly by the individual or a family member. Applications are considered upon receipt. One of the trustees will visit to elicit all necessary information. Applications are usually considered in May and October.

Bilton

The Bilton Poor's Land and Other Charities

£2,000

Correspondent: Robin Walls, Trustee, 6 Scots Close, Rugby CV22 7QY (01788 810930)

CC Number: 215833

Eligibility

People in need who live in the ancient parish of Bilton (now part of Rugby).

Types of grants

This charity is not primarily an educational charity, concentrating rather on the relief of need. However, some grants are made for books, fees and other costs.

Annual grant total

In 2012/13 the charity had an income of £21,500 and a total expenditure of £17,500. The charity makes grants to both individuals and organisations for social welfare and educational purposes. We estimate that grants to individuals for educational purposes totalled around £2,000.

Applications

In writing to the correspondent, by the individual or through a relevant third party such as a minister, although often applications are forwarded by social services. They are considered in February, May and October.

Coleshill

The Simon Lord Digby Educational Endowment

£0

Correspondent: Juliet Bakker, Administrator, The Vicarage, High Street, Coleshill, Birmingham B46 3BP (01675 462188)

CC Number: 528710

Eligibility

Students of secondary school or higher education age who live in the parish of Coleshill.

Types of grants

One-off grants are given to schoolchildren for school uniforms and other school clothing, books and educational outings, and to students in further/higher education for help with books. Preference is given to schoolchildren with serious family difficulties.

Annual grant total

In 2013 grants were made to local organisations totalling £16,600 but no grants were made to individuals.

Exclusions

No grants to mature students.

Applications

On a form available from the correspondent. Applications should be submitted directly by the individual or parent/guardian for consideration in March or November, and include a breakdown of expenses, the amount requested and details of applications to any other grants.

Exhall

The Exhall Educational Foundation

£2,300

Correspondent: Alice Farnhill, Secretary, St Giles' Parish Office, Church Hall, St Giles' Road, Ash Green, Coventry CV7 9GZ (02476 365258; email: alice.farnhill@gmail.com; website: exhalleducationalfoundation.blogspot.co.uk/)

CC Number: 528663

Eligibility

People under the age of 25 who live, or whose parents live, in the parish of Exhall or Keresley End.

Types of grants

One-off and recurrent grants for specific educational purposes (for example, course, activity, materials or travel). Average award is of £200. The foundation can cover full costs or, in more expensive cases, offer supplementary assistance. Previously grants have been awarded for books, dance classes, music tuition, field trips, educational outings, expeditions, travel costs and so on.

Annual grant total

In 2013 the foundation had an income of £3,100 and an expenditure of £2,500. We estimate the annual total of grants to individuals to be around £2,300.

Applications

Application forms are available from the foundation's website or can be requested from the correspondent. Applications are considered twice a year, in mid-March and mid-October. They can be submitted by post or by email in advance of the trustees' meeting.

Other information

Schools in the area of benefit are eligible to apply for support.

The area of benefit comprises: Ash Green, Black Bank, Exhall, Goodyers End, Keresley End, Little Bedworth Heath, Neal's Green and Wagon Overthrow. The trustees encourage potential applicants to get in touch if in doubt about their geographical eligibility.

Kenilworth

William Edwards Educational Charity

£49,000 (103 grants)

Correspondent: John Hathaway, Clerk to the Trustees, Heath and Blenkinsop Solicitors, 42 Brook Street, Warwick CV34 4BL (01926 492407; email: heath.blenkinsop@btopenworld.com)

CC Number: 528714

Eligibility

People under the age of 25 who/whose parents have lived in the town of Kenilworth, or those who have attended a school in the town.

Types of grants

Grants are given for school uniforms, school trips, other educational needs and in bursaries for postgraduate students and people on vocational courses.

Annual grant total

In 2012/13 the charity had assets of £6.2 million, an income of £236,000 and an expenditure of £258,000. Grants to individuals totalled £27,000 and bursaries totalled £22,000. The charity further specifies that during the year 124 applications were received from individuals, of which 100 were successful. Further three awards were given under the bursary scheme.

Applications

In writing to the correspondent.

Other information

In 2012/13 the trust also made grants to schools totalling £98,000.

Shipston-on-Stour

Shipston-on-Stour Educational Charity

£2,000

Correspondent: Mr D. Squires, Administrator, Pinnegar House, 49 Telegraph Street, Shipston-on-Stour CV36 4DA (email: ds@pinnegards.com)

CC Number: 507400

Eligibility

People under 25 who live, or whose parents live, in the parish of Shipston-on-Stour.

Types of grants

One-off grants, ranging from £30 to £120, are given to students undertaking further and higher education, postgraduate courses and apprenticeships. Support can be for uniforms/clothing, books, tools, instruments/equipment, educational outings in the UK or study or travel abroad.

Annual grant total

In 2012 the charity had an income of £3,000 and a total expenditure of £2,100. We estimate that grants totalled £2,000. At the time of writing (July 2014) this was the most recent financial information available for the charity.

Applications

On a form available from the correspondent. Applications should be submitted directly by the individual by the first week of September for consideration at the end of that month.

Stoke Golding

Stoke Golding Boy's Charity

£6,800

Correspondent: Ruth Fisher, Trustee, 21 Hinckley Road, Stoke Golding, Nuneaton, Leicestershire CV13 6DU (01455 212489)

CC Number: 519728

Eligibility

Young men and boys under the age of 25 who live in Stoke Golding. Our research suggests that some preference may be given to people with special educational needs.

Types of grants

One-off grants, generally around £200, depending on availability and circumstances. Support is given for a wide range of educational needs.

Annual grant total

In 2013 the charity had an income of £7,000 and an expenditure of £6,900. We estimate that around £6,800 was available for distribution in grants to individuals, as the charity normally spends the whole of the annual interest in grants.

Applications

In writing to the correspondent. Applications can be made directly by the individual and normally should be submitted by mid-March for consideration in April.

Stratford-upon-Avon

The Stratford-upon-Avon Municipal Charities – Relief in Need

£0

Correspondent: Ros Dobson, Clerk to the Trustees, 155 Evesham Road, Stratford-upon-Avon CV37 9BP (01789 293749; email: municharities@yahoo.co.uk; website: www.municipal-charities-stratforduponavon.org.uk)

CC Number: 214958

Eligibility

People in need living in the town of Stratford-upon-Avon.

Types of grants

Occasionally, one-off grants up to £500 are given towards the cost of: (i) school uniforms, other school clothing, books, maintenance and school fees for schoolchildren; (ii) books for students in further and higher education; and (iii) books, equipment and instruments for people starting work.

Annual grant total

In 2012 this charity had an income of over £55,000 (including an amount of £54,000 transferred from the Charity of William Tyler), and awarded no educational grants to individuals. Grants to organisations totalled £31,000. The 2012 accounts were the latest available at the time of writing (August 2014).

Applications

On a form available from the correspondent, including details of the course costs and the financial circumstances of the applicant and parent(s) if appropriate. Applications for schoolchildren must be made through the school.

Thurlaston

Thurlaston Poor's Plot Charity

£1,200

Correspondent: Kathleen Owens, Clerk, Congreaves, Main Street, Thurlaston, Rugby CV23 9JS (01788 817466; email: kathleenowens@outlook.com)

CC Number: 232356

Eligibility

Students who are in need and live in Thurlaston.

Types of grants

Grants are given for help with the cost of books.

Annual grant total

In 2013 the charity had an income of £2,600 and a total expenditure of £2,500. We estimate that educational grants to individuals totalled £1,200. Grants are also distributed to older residents of the village for lifelines and extra fuel charges.

Applications

In writing to the correspondent directly by the individual. Applications are usually considered in January, September and November.

Warwick

Austin Edwards Charity

£5,000

Correspondent: Jackie Newton, Administrator, 26 Mountford Close, Wellesbourne, Warwick CV35 9QQ (01789 840135; website: www.austinedwards.org.uk)

CC Number: 225859

Eligibility

People living in the old borough of Warwick (generally postcode CV34).

Types of grants

Grants of up to £300. Our research indicates that support is normally provided to students at college or university (including mature students) or people starting work. Grants are given towards the expenses for clothing, equipment, books, travel, course fees and study/travel overseas.

Annual grant total

In 2012/13 the charity had an income of £10,700 and an expenditure of £10,200. We have estimated the annual total of grants to be around £5,000.

Exclusions

Grants cannot be provided for follow-on courses, postgraduate courses or additional degrees. The charity's website also reminds that 'where grants are applied for in respect of study courses, the trustees will only consider providing funding for one course per applicant.'

Applications

In writing to the correspondent. Applications should state the purpose and amount of the grant required and provide details of any applications made to other charities. The trustees normally meet once a year in July but can consider applications throughout the year.

Other information
Grants are also given for welfare causes.

The King Henry VIII Endowed Trust – Warwick

£1,300 (1 grant)

Correspondent: Jonathan Wassall, Clerk and Receiver, 12 High Street, Warwick CV34 4AP (01926 495533; email: jwassall@kinghenryviii.org.uk; website: www.kinghenryviii.org.uk)

CC Number: 232862

Eligibility
People who live in the former borough of Warwick. The area of benefit is roughly the CV34 postcode but exceptions apply so see the full list of eligible areas within the guidelines or contact the correspondent for clarification.

Types of grants
Grants can be given to schoolchildren for excursions and educational outings. College and university students may be supported for study/travel overseas and vocational students for fees.

Grants are intended to be supplementary and applicants are expected to raise additional funds themselves. Payments are normally made upon submission of receipts.

Annual grant total
At the time of writing (July 2014) the latest financial information available was from 2012. In 2012 the trust had assets of £24 million and an income of £1.4 million. Two grants to individuals totalled £2,600, one of which we estimate to be educational. In previous years individual awards were made to 20–30 persons totalling under £20,000. The money for charitable activities is generated from the permanent endowment.

Exclusions
Grants are not made where support should be provided by the local or central government. Funding is not given retrospectively.

Applications
Application forms are available from the correspondent or from the trust's website. Applications should provide full details of the costs involved and the time schedule of the activity, where relevant. Awards are considered on a quarterly basis, usually in March, June, September and December. The closing dates for applications are the beginning of March/June and the second half of August/November. You will normally receive the outcome of your application within a week of the relevant meeting. In urgent cases applications can be 'fast-tracked' (emergency should be specified in the application).

Other information
The income is distributed to Anglican churches in Warwick (50%) Warwick Independent Schools Foundation for allocation in scholarships and bursaries (30%) and to organisations and individuals in the town (20%). Town grants to various institutions and groups totalled £160,000, the foundation received £342,000 and the churches were awarded £565,000 in 2012.

Note:

> Where the trust believes that there are more suitable charities within the town to assess applications it will either forward the application directly to another charity or recommend that the applicant approaches them directly. Young people under 24 years old applying for support at university or college will be referred directly to the Warwick Apprenticing Charities

(see separate entry).

Warwick Apprenticing Charities

£66,000 (60 grants)

Correspondent: C. E. R. Houghton, Clerk, Moore and Tibbits Solicitors, 34 High Street, Warwick CV34 4BE (01926 491181; email: commercial@moore-tibbits.co.uk; website: www.warwickapprenticingcharities.org.uk)

CC Number: 528745

Eligibility
People under the age of 25 who have finished school and live within the town of Warwick. Residents of Warwick aged 16 to 18 who are still at school can apply for assistance in attending Outward Bound courses.

Types of grants
One-off 'advancement in life' grants are available to people undertaking apprenticeships, further/higher education students or those undertaking any other form of training which will help to advance their career. Support is given towards general educational needs, including fees, maintenance expenses, books, equipment/instruments, materials, special clothing, travel costs and so on.

Annual grant total
In 2013 the charity had assets of £1 million and an income of £66,000. Grants also totalled around £66,000 and consisted of 60 'advancement in life' awards (£57,000) and support for Outward Bound courses (£8,700).

Applications
Application forms are available on the charity's website or can be requested from the correspondent. Candidates are invited to attend an interview. The trustees meet at least twice a year to approve and allocate grants.

Charity of Sir Thomas White, Warwick

£24,000

Correspondent: Belinda Shuttleworth, Clerk and Receiver, 12 High Street, Warwick CV34 4AP (01926 350555; email: connect@sirthomaswhite.org.uk; website: www.sirthomaswhite.org.uk)

CC Number: 1073331

Eligibility
People between the ages of 18 and 35 who are ordinarily resident in the town of Warwick who are establishing a business or undertaking tertiary education.

Types of grants
Interest-free loans of up to £1,500 per year for three years for university students. Interest-free loans up to £10,000 for five years for young business people who are setting-up a business in Warwick for the duration of the loan.

Annual grant total
In 2012 the charity had assets of £360,000 and an income of £208,000. Interest-free loans advanced during the year totalled £24,000.

The overall balance for interest-free loans repayable to the charity amounted to £126,000.

At the time of writing (July 2014) this was the most recent financial information available for the charity.

Applications
On a form available from the correspondent or from the charity's website.

▶ Applications for educational loans should include details of the course to be undertaken and the applicant's financial requirements for the duration of the course. An interview with a small panel of trustees will be arranged and applications must be received by the charity at least three weeks prior to the interview date. Successful applicants are required to sign a loan agreement and two adults are required to guarantee repayment of the loan

▶ Applications for business loans should be submitted along with a business plan. An interview will be arranged with a small panel of trustees to discuss the business idea and applications must be received by the charity at least three weeks prior to the interview date. Successful applicants must sign a joint and several bond, as must their sureties. The number of sureties required ranges from two to four, depending on the amount requested

West Midlands

The Chance Trust

£900

Correspondent: Revd Iain Shelton, Trustee, 192 Hanover Road, Rowley Regis B65 9EQ (01215 591251; email: robertshelton954@hotmail.com; website: www.warleydeanery.co.uk)

CC Number: 702647

Eligibility

People in need in the rural deaneries of Warley and West Bromwich (the area covered by the southern parts of Sandwell borough).

Types of grants

One-off grants ranging from £50 to £400 can be given to help access the education. Our research suggests that occasionally support can be made to university students for up to three years.

Annual grant total

In 2012/13 the trust had an income of £2,900 and an expenditure of £1,900. We estimate that around £900 was given in educational grants. Normally the trust spends around £2,500–£3,000 per year in grants to individuals for both educational and relief-in-need purposes.

Exclusions

Grants are not normally provided where statutory funding is available.

Applications

In writing to the correspondent. Applications should specify the need and the amount required. They are usually considered in January and July.

Other information

Grants are also made for welfare purposes.

The W. E. Dunn Trust

£1,900 (4 grants)

Correspondent: David Corney, Trustee, The Trust Office, 30 Bentley Heath Cottages, Tilehouse Green Lane, Knowle, Solihull B93 9EL (01564 773407)

CC Number: 219418

Eligibility

People who live in the West Midlands who wish to further their education, but have special difficulties which prevent them from doing so. These can include, for example, prisoners who are using education as part of their rehabilitation, or students who have physical disabilities or who have lived through particularly difficult circumstances.

Types of grants

One-off grants usually ranging from £50 to £200.

Annual grant total

In 2012/13 the trust had assets of £4.5 million and an income of £330,000. Grants totalling £53,000 were distributed to 337 individuals in the following areas:

Clothing and furniture	145	£21,000
Domestic equipment	125	£21,000
Radio, TV and licences	39	£5,900
Social and welfare	20	£2,700
Education	4	£1,900

Exclusions

Grants are not made to settle or reduce debts already incurred.

Applications

In writing to the correspondent. Applications for educational grants from mature students should be submitted directly by the individual and other applications should be submitted through the individual's parent/guardian or school/college/educational welfare agency. They are considered two or three times a month depending on the number of applications.

Other information

Grants were also made to 176 organisations totalling £153,500 in 2012/13.

Grantham Yorke Trust

£10,500 (21 grants)

Correspondent: Christine Norgrove, Administrator, Martineau, 1 Colmore Square, Birmingham B4 6AA (0870 763 2000; email: christine.norgrove@ sghmartineau.com)

CC Number: 228466

Eligibility

People under 25 who were born in what was the old West Midlands Metropolitan County area (basically: Birmingham, Coventry, Dudley, Redditch, Sandwell, Solihull, Tamworth, Walsall or Wolverhampton).

Types of grants

One-off grants are given to:
- Schoolchildren and students for uniforms and other school clothing, books, equipment, instruments, fees, maintenance and living expenses,

childcare, educational outings in the UK, study or travel overseas and student exchange
- Students leaving school or further education for equipment and clothing, which will help them enter, or prepare for, their chosen profession or trade
- People starting work for maintenance and living expenses and childcare
- Education focused on preventing unplanned pregnancy, drug, alcohol and gambling abuse, child abuse or youth offending

Annual grant total

In 2012/13 the trust held assets of £6.5 million and had an income of £221,000. A total of £21,000 was awarded in 43 grants to individuals. We estimate the educational grants total to be around £10,500.

Applications

On a form available from the correspondent. Applications can be submitted either directly by the individual or a relevant third party, or through the individual's school, college or educational welfare agency.

Other information

The trust also makes grants to organisations and to individuals for welfare purposes.

The James Frederick and Ethel Anne Measures Charity

£7,500

Correspondent: Laura Reid, Clerk to the Trustees, Harris Allday, 2nd Floor, 33 Great Charles Street, Birmingham B3 3JN

CC Number: 266054

Eligibility

The following criteria apply:
1. Applicants must usually originate in the West Midlands
2. Applicants must show evidence of self-help in their application
3. Trustees have a preference for disadvantaged people
4. Trustees have a dislike for applications from students who have a full local authority grant and want finance for a different course or study
5. Trustees favour grants towards the cost of equipment
6. Applications by individuals in cases of hardship will not usually be considered unless sponsored by a local authority, health professional or other welfare agency

Types of grants

One-off or recurrent grants, usually between £50 and £500.

Annual grant total

In 2012/13 the charity had assets of £963,000 and an income of £36,000. Grants were made totalling £31,000. The charity gives to both individuals and organisations and we estimate grants to individuals for educational purposes to be around £7,500.

Applications

In writing to the correspondent. No reply is given to unsuccessful applicants unless an sae is enclosed.

The Mitchells and Butlers Charitable Trusts

£18,100 (49 grants)

Correspondent: Ms H. Woodall, Administrator, Mitchells and Butlers, 27 Fleet Street, Birmingham B3 1JP (01214 984129; website: www.mbtrusts. org.uk)

CC Number: 528922

Eligibility

Students resident in the UK who are over the age of 11 and who live in the city of Birmingham and Smethwick. Preference may be given to the employees and children of the employees of Mitchells and Butlers and 'successors in business' of the company. External applicants are invited to apply, provided they can demonstrate financial hardship. Applicants from low income households are favoured.

Types of grants

The trust's Welfare Fund offers support to schoolchildren and further/higher education students, including mature students and individuals with special educational needs. Financial assistance is available towards the course fees, living expenses, course related necessities and expenses, such as books, equipment, clothing and uniforms, travel costs and so forth.

The trust's Scholarship Fund can assist students in courses relating to brewing industry, licenced retailing, catering and hotel management. Support can be given towards general educational expenses, including books or the cost of equipment. Previously students in Leeds Metropolitan University and University College Birmingham have been supported.

Annual grant total

In 2012/13 the trust had assets of £3.1 million and an income of £100,000. A total of £77,000 was spent on charitable activities with £18,100 being awarded from the Welfare Fund in educational grants to 49 individuals. No grants were made from the Scholarship Fund this year.

Applications

Application forms for the Welfare Fund can be found on the trust's website and should be submitted a month in advance of the trustees' meeting which is normally held in July. Inclusion of a letter of support from a teacher, educational welfare officer or other professional would benefit the application

Applications for the Scholarship Fund should be made through a relevant university.

Other information

Educational grants to institutions totalled £26,000 in 2012/13.

The trust also has the Mitchell Fund, which is used to assist employees and former employees (or the dependents of both) in the brewing and catering industries or the licensed retail industry who are in need.

The Perry Family Charitable Trust

£7,000

Correspondent: Sir Michael Perry, Trustee, Bridges Stone Mill, Alfrick Pound, Worcester WR6 5HR (01886 833290; email: perrytrust@aol.com)

CC Number: 1094675

Eligibility

People in need under the age of 25 whose parents or guardians have been resident in the West Midlands for not less than three years.

Types of grants

Small grants may be awarded towards travel for educational purposes in the UK or overseas, clothing, instruments, tools, books and other essentials. People starting work/entering a trade can be supported.

Annual grant total

In 2012/13 the trust had an income of £49,000 and a total expenditure of £30,000. We estimate that grants to individuals for educational purposes totalled around £37,000.

Applications

In writing to the correspondent.

Other information

The trust also supports organisations and aims to address welfare needs of people with disabilities, the elderly, those in poor health, or suffering from poverty.

Birmingham

Birmingham Bodenham Trust

£12,000

Correspondent: Justin Pinkney, Administrator, Finance (WS), PO Box 16306, Birmingham B2 2XR (01213 038744)

CC Number: 528902

Eligibility

Young people under the age of 19 who have special educational needs. Preference may be given to people in Birmingham area.

Types of grants

Grants are given for special equipment and facilities which would advance the individual's education and training, including recreation and leisure. Support can be given towards holidays and trips, course fees, books, toys, IT equipment, summer schools and so on.

Annual grant total

In 2012/13 the trust had an income of £22,000 and an expenditure of £24,000. We estimate the annual total of grants to individuals to be around £12,000.

Applications

In writing to the correspondent. Applications are considered at quarterly meetings.

Other information

Support can also be given to individuals and organisations engaged in innovative projects on education, training, recreation or medical care of young people with special needs.

The Letisha and Charlene Education Award (LCEA)

£570 (7 grants)

Correspondent: The Administrator, Birmingham and Black Country Community Foundation, Nechells Baths, Nechells Park Road, Nechells, Birmingham B7 5PD (01213 225560; email: info@letishaandcharlene.com; website: www.letishaandcharlene.com)

CC Number: 1048162

Eligibility

Students over the age of 16 who live in north-west Birmingham. Applicants must be settled in the UK and enrolled on a course at an educational establishment either on a full-time or part-time basis.

Types of grants

Grants, usually around £200, are awarded to reimburse the expenses of course and accommodation fees, computer equipment, books and course materials, travel expenses, childcare costs and so forth and will usually be given upon the submission of receipts.

Annual grant total

In 2012/13 the fund awarded £570 in grants to seven students.

Applications

Application forms can be downloaded from the trust's website or requested from the correspondent. The award is launched annually at the beginning of the academic year and the deadline for applications is usually six weeks later. Applications, together with a personal statement, evidence of the applicant's current financial situation and an academic reference, can be submitted by the individual directly. Individuals successful in their initial application will be invited for a short interview.

Other information

This fund is administered by The Birmingham and Black Country Community Foundation.

Sir Josiah Mason's Relief in Need and Educational Charity

£2,000

Correspondent: Edward Kuczerawy, Financial Controller, Mason Court, Hillborough Road, Birmingham B27 6PF (01212 451002; fax: 01217 071090; email: enquiries@sjmt.org.uk; website: www.sjmt-rin.org.uk)

CC Number: 1073756

Eligibility

People under 25 who live or study in the West Midlands area and are in genuine financial hardship.

Types of grants

One-off grants of up to £500 for exam or tuition fees, study materials, books and equipment or tools for training or apprenticeships.

Annual grant total

In 2012/13 the charity had assets of £4 million and an income of £97,000. Grants to individuals totalled £2,000 and to organisations £44,000.

Exclusions

No grants for living costs.

Applications

On a form available from the charity's website or from the correspondent to be returned by email or post. Applications

are reviewed every three months, usually in March, June, September and December. The date of the next meeting is published on the website.

William Piddock's Foundation

£2,800

Correspondent: Andrew Peet, Trustee, Birmingham and Midland Institute, 9 Margaret Street, Birmingham B3 3BS (01212 363591; fax: 01212 124577; email: accounts@bmi.org.uk)

CC Number: 528920

Eligibility

People under the age of 25 who are in further or higher education and who/whose parents are or were resident in Birmingham during the secondary education of the applicant.

Types of grants

Financial assistance is available towards the cost of clothing/outfits, equipment/instruments, tools, books and travel expenses in the UK and overseas for educational purposes. Further/higher education (including music and arts) students and people entering a trade/starting work are supported. Our research suggests that both one-off and recurrent grants, usually ranging from £50 to £500, can be provided.

Annual grant total

In 2012/13 the foundation had an income of £5,500 and an expenditure of £5,800. It also helps local schools, therefore we estimate the annual total of grants to individuals to be around £2,800.

Applications

Application forms can be requested from the correspondent and can be submitted directly by the individual. Our research suggests that an academic reference is also required and candidates are asked to attend an interview. Applications are normally considered in August/September and should be submitted at least a month in advance.

Other information

The foundation also supports any school within the area of benefit where assistance is not provided by the local authority.

Reuben Foundation
See entry on page 357

Joseph Scott's Educational Foundation

£2,200

Correspondent: Derek Duffield, Trustee, 29 Jasmin Croft, Birmingham B14 5AX (01214 445479; email: joseph_scott_ef@hotmail.co.uk)

CC Number: 528919

Eligibility

Young people who live and 'have been educated for at least 2 years at a school provided by the Birmingham education authority or at a legally designated academy or free school within the boundaries, for the time being, of the city of Birmingham.'

Types of grants

One-off grants are given to students in further/higher education and mature students towards books and fees/living expenses.

Annual grant total

In 2013/14 the foundation had an income of £1,900 and a total expenditure of £2,300. We estimate that educational grants to individuals totalled £2,200.

Exclusions

No grants are given to postgraduates.

Applications

On a form available from the correspondent for consideration quarterly, usually in March, June, September and November.

Castle Bromwich
The Mary Dame Bridgeman Charity Trust

£750

Correspondent: Jeremy Dutton, Administrator, 60 Whateley Crescent, Birmingham, West Midlands B36 0DP

CC Number: 701557

Eligibility

People under 25 who are in need and living in the ecclesiastical parishes of St Mary, St Margaret and St Clement, Castle Bromwich.

Types of grants

One-off grants ranging from £100 to £400 towards clothing, books and educational outings for schoolchildren; and books, fees, living expenses and study or travel abroad for students in further/higher education. There is a preference for schoolchildren with serious family difficulties so that the child has to be educated away from home and people with special educational needs.

Annual grant total

In 2013/14 the charity had an income of £3,300 and a total expenditure of £3,400. Grants are awarded to individuals and organisations for both educational and social welfare purposes. We estimate that educational grants to individuals totalled around £750.

Exclusions

Grants are not given if they will affect any statutory benefits.

Applications

In writing to the correspondent either directly by the individual, through the individual's school, college, educational welfare agency or through a parent. The trustees meet twice a year in May and November.

Coventry

The Children's Boot Fund

£8,000

Correspondent: Janet McConkey, Trustee, 123A Birmingham Road, Coventry CV5 9GR (02476 402837; email: martin_harban@btconnect.com)

CC Number: 214524

Eligibility

Schoolchildren in the city of Coventry, aged 4 to 16.

Types of grants

Grants for school footwear for children in need. No other type of help is given. Grants are made directly to footwear suppliers in the form of vouchers.

Annual grant total

In 2012/13 the fund had an income of £7,500 and an expenditure of £16,000. Grants are also made for social welfare purposes. We estimate that grants to individuals for educational purposes in this accounting year totalled around £8,000.

Applications

Application forms are available from schools in the area and should be completed, verified and signed by the headteacher of the child's school. Applications are considered four times a year.

General Charity (Coventry)

£40,000 (105 grants)

Correspondent: Victoria Tosh, Clerk to the Trustees, General Charities Office, Old Bablake, Hill Street, Coventry CV1 4AN (02476 222769; email: cov.genchar@btconnect.com)

CC Number: 216235

Eligibility

Children and young people under the age of 25 who are in need and live in the city of Coventry. Preference may be given to children of the freemen of the city.

Types of grants

Grants are given towards fees, books or specialised equipment, also to support music education.

Annual grant total

At the time of writing (August 2014) the latest financial information available was from 2012. In 2012 the charity had assets of £8.7 million, an income of £1.3 million and gave educational grants to individuals totalling around £40,000, broken down as follows:

School fees	9	£24,000
Books and equipment	95	£10,900
Music award	1	£5,000

A medical award for four years was also given to one PhD student at University of Warwick totalling £75,000.

Exclusions

Our research suggests that maintenance costs are not supported. Cash grants are not given.

Applications

Application forms can be requested from the correspondent, normally in late August/early September. They should be submitted for consideration in November. The outcome of the application is communicated in December.

Other information

The charity consists of the charities formerly known as The Relief in Need Charity, Sir Thomas White's Pension Fund and Sir Thomas White's Educational Fund. The trustees are also responsible for the administration of Lady Herbert's Homes and Eventide Homes Ltd providing accommodation for the elderly in the city of Coventry.

Grants are also made for welfare purposes and in pensions to people over the age of 60 in the city of Coventry. Most of the charity's assistance is given to organisations. Annual payment is made to the Coventry School Foundation (£491,000 in 2012).

The Andrew Robinson Young People's Trust

£9,800

Correspondent: Clive Robinson, Trustee, 31 Daventry Road, Coventry CV3 5DJ (02476 501579)

CC Number: 1094029

Eligibility

Young people who live in Coventry, particularly those who are facing social or economic disadvantages, or suffer from ill health.

Types of grants

One-off and recurrent grants to advance the religious education of young people and their faith within the Catholic Church. The support is also given to assist individuals in their personal development through various leisure activities and trips related to the Catholic faith.

Annual grant total

In 2012/13 the trust had an income of £17,700 and an expenditure of £19,800. We estimate the annual total of grants to individuals to be around £9,800.

Applications

In writing to the correspondent.

Other information

The trust also makes grants to organisations and provides support to relieve poverty.

Soothern and Craner Educational Foundation

£12,000

Correspondent: Gillian Waddilove, Trustee, The Hollies, Priory Road, Wolston, Coventry CV8 3FX (02476 544255; email: admin@ soothernandcraner.org.uk; website: www. soothernandcraner.org.uk)

CC Number: 528838

Eligibility

Girls and young women who live in Coventry or who are Quakers connected to Coventry Quaker Meeting. Studies may be undertaken away from Coventry but the connection with the city is crucial.

Types of grants

Grants are mainly given to further education students and people in vocational training for general educational costs, including equipment/ instruments, outfits, books and so on. Our research indicates that support is intended to supplement existing grants or where no mandatory award is available.

Annual grant total

In 2012/13 the foundation had an income of £11,900 and an expenditure of £12,100. We estimate the annual total of grants to individuals to be around £12,000. Normally, the foundation can distribute around £7,000 to £8,000 in grants each year.

Exclusions

Support will rarely be given to people studying at or above the first degree level.

Applications

The foundation's website provides two application forms – for those still in school and for school leavers. Applicants should have two references available. Applications can also be made on behalf of groups (by a teacher or group leader) for educational activities. The trustees request the applicants to use ordinary post rather than recorded delivery in order to avoid delays. The trustees meet in July each year with additional meetings held as required.

Dudley

Baylies' Educational Foundation

£28,000 (Up to 100 grants)

Correspondent: David Hughes, Clerk to the Trustees, 53 The Broadway, Dudley, West Midlands DY1 4AP (01384 259277; email: bayliesfoundation@hotmail.co.uk; website: www.dudleyrotary.org.uk/baylies.html)

CC Number: 527118

Eligibility

People under the age of 25 living in the area of Dudley Metropolitan Borough Council who are in need. It is necessary to demonstrate genuine financial need for a specific purpose and be unable to secure support from other sources.

Types of grants

One-off grants, usually around £200–£300, can be given to help with the university/college fees and course related necessities (books, equipment/instruments, tools, clothing), travel expenses, educational trips abroad or in the UK, school uniforms, towards music and drama lessons or sports activities, also to unemployed people for retraining or individuals facing family difficulties to help them continue their education.

Annual grant total

In 2012/13 the foundation had assets of £1.1 million and an income of £40,000. A total of around £28,000 was awarded in grants to individuals. The foundation states that during a typical year up to 100 grants are made.

Applications

Application forms are available on the foundation's website or can be requested from the correspondent.

Other information

Local schools can also be supported.

Daniel Parsons Educational Charity

£13,600

Correspondent: David Hughes, Trustee, 53 The Broadway, Dudley, West Midlands DY1 4AP (01384 259277; email: parsonscharity@hotmail.com)

CC Number: 1068492

Eligibility

People under the age of 25 who/whose parents live in Dudley and its neighbourhood or who have attended school in that area.

Types of grants

One-off grants in the range of £200 to £500 towards education and training.

Annual grant total

At the time of writing (July 2014) the latest financial information available was from 2012. In 2012 the charity had an income of £18,500 and an expenditure of £13,900. We estimate that the total of annual grants was around £13,600.

Applications

Application forms can be requested from the correspondent or downloaded from Rotary Club of Dudley website. They can be submitted to the correspondent at any time.

The Sedgley Educational Trust

£2,200

Correspondent: Chris Williams, Administrator, 12 Larkswood Drive, Dudley DY3 3UQ (01902 672880)

CC Number: 1091563

Eligibility

People in need who live in the ecclesiastical parishes of All Saints Sedgley, St Chad's Coseley and St Mary the Virgin Sedgley.

Types of grants

One-off and recurrent grants according to need are available to people in education, including religious education in accordance with the doctrines of the Church of England.

Annual grant total

In 2012/13 the trust had an income of £2,700 and an expenditure of £2,400. We have estimated that the annual total of grants was around £2,200.

Applications

In writing to the correspondent.

King's Norton

The King's Norton United Charities

£2,500

Correspondent: Canon Rob Morris, Administrator, The Rectory, 273 Pershore Road, Kings Norton, Birmingham B30 8EX (01214 590560; email: parishoffice@kingsnorton.org.uk; website: www.knuc.org.uk)

CC Number: 202225

Eligibility

The charity is able to assist only those who live within the boundary of the ancient parish of Kings Norton, formerly in Warwickshire and Worcestershire, now in Warwickshire and the West Midlands. This area includes the current Church of England parishes of Kings Norton, Cotteridge, Stirchley, parts of Bournville, Balsall Heath, Kings Heath, Moseley (St Anne's and St Mary's), Brandwood, Hazelwell, Highters Heath, Wythall, West Heath, Longbridge, Rubery and Rednal.

Types of grants

One-off and recurrent grants according to need. The charity's website states that grants are usually between £50 and £350 and are typically for one-off purchases of essential household items, for short-term bridging support or for educational needs such as help with fees or to cover unforeseen expenses. The trustees may consider making larger grants in specific cases.

Annual grant total

Grants usually total around £5,000 for educational and welfare purposes.

Applications

The trustees prefer to receive requests for grants through organisations or agencies working on behalf of families or individuals in need. An organisation or individual applying on another's behalf will then be expected to take responsibility and to account for the correct use of the grant.

The trustees meet twice each year to consider grant requests and to distribute regular amounts to the discretionary funds of the incumbents of member parishes. Other selected organisations or agencies, based within the ancient parish of King's Norton and who assist in relieving genuine poverty or hardship, may also be awarded discretionary grants. Grant applications for smaller amounts (currently up to £250) may also be agreed and paid by the chair, vice-chair and treasurer on behalf of the main meeting.

Meriden

Meriden United Charities

£80

Correspondent: Mavis Edwards, Administrator, Meriden United Charities, 3 Thebes Close, Millisons Wood, Coventry CV5 9QW (01676 522107; email: Mavis@PMEdwards.com)

CC Number: 234452

Eligibility

Young people who have lived in the parish of Meriden for at least two years.

Types of grants

Grants are given to schoolchildren, college students, undergraduates, vocational students and people with special educational needs. They include those for uniforms/clothing, fees, books and equipment/instruments.

Annual grant total

In 2013, the charities had an income of £2,000 and a total expenditure of approximately £300. We estimate that approximately £80 was awarded in grants for educational purposes.

Applications

Applications can be submitted either directly by the individual or a family member or through a third party, such as a social worker or teacher. The existence of the charities is made known by a notice in the Meriden magazine and by a notice in the library.

Other information

Grants are also awarded for social welfare purposes and for local organisations.

Oldbury

The Oldbury Educational Foundation (The Oldbury Charity)

£5,300

Correspondent: Elaine Burke, Administrator, Shakespeare's Legal LLP, Somerset House, 37 Temple Street, Birmingham B2 5DJ (01212 373000)

CC Number: 527468

Eligibility

Schoolchildren in the borough of Oldbury.

Types of grants

Small grants are available to help with general educational costs, including books, clothing, equipment/instruments and travel expenses. Our research suggests that most grants are awarded to pupils at Warley High School, but pupils at other schools in Oldbury can also apply.

Annual grant total

In 2012/13 the foundation had an income of £6,900 and an expenditure of £5,500. We estimate the annual total of grants to be around £5,300.

Applications

In writing to the correspondent.

Rowley Regis

The Mackmillan Educational Foundation

£1,000

Correspondent: V. J. Westwood, Administrator, 18 Westdean Close, Halesowen, West Midlands B62 8UA (01216 022484; email: vicwestw@ blueyonder.co.uk)

CC Number: 529043

Eligibility

People under 25 who live in the ancient parish of Rowley Regis.

Types of grants

Grants to people at school and college.

Annual grant total

In 2012/13 the trust had both an income and a total expenditure of £1,500. We estimate that grants made to individuals for education totalled around £1,000.

Applications

In writing to the correspondent.

Sandwell

The George and Thomas Henry Salter Trust

£23,000

Correspondent: J. Styler, Administrator, Lombard House, Cronehills Linkway, West Bromwich, West Midlands B70 7PL (01215 533286)

CC Number: 216503

Eligibility

Students in further or higher education who are in need and resident in the borough of Sandwell.

Types of grants

Grants usually range between £100 and £1,000 and are given to help students pursue their education, including general, professional, vocational or technical training, in the UK and abroad.

Annual grant total

In 2012 the trust had assets of £1.4 million and an income of £31,000. Educational grants totalled £23,000.

These were the latest accounts available at the time of writing (July 2014).

Applications

Initially by letter to the correspondent. Applicants must provide full written details of their circumstances and study courses. The trustees meet regularly and will occasionally interview applicants.

Stourbridge

The Palmer and Seabright Charity

£7,500

Correspondent: Susannah Griffiths, c/o Wall, James and Chappell, 15–23 Hagley Road, Stourbridge, West Midlands DY8 1QW (01384 371622)

CC Number: 200692

Eligibility

People living in the borough of Stourbridge.

Types of grants

One-off and recurrent grants are made to college students, undergraduates and mature students for fees, books, equipment/instruments and maintenance/living expenses. Grants are also given to schoolchildren for fees.

Annual grant total

In 2013, this charity had assets of £268,000, an income of £48,000 and made grants totalling £18,800 (which included £3,200 in Christmas gifts). We estimate grants to individuals for educational purposes to be around £7,500.

Applications

On a form available from the correspondent. Applications can be submitted either directly by the individual or a family member, through a third party such as a social worker or teacher, or through an organisation such as Citizens Advice or a school.

The Scott Educational Foundation

£0

Correspondent: Alan Cutler, Trustee, 21 Primrose Hill, Stourbridge DY8 5AG (01384 443644)

CC Number: 511001

Eligibility

People under 25 who live in the old borough of Stourbridge (excluding Amblecote). Preference is given to those who have attended a maintained school in the area for more than two years.

Types of grants

Grants of £100 to £600 are given to schoolchildren towards school uniform, other school clothing, books, educational outings in the UK, maintenance and fees. Grants to students in further or higher education are given towards books, equipment/instruments, fees, living expenses and study or travel abroad. Grants to people starting work are for equipment or instruments. Grants are mainly one-off; for recurrent grants a repeat application must be made.

Annual grant total

In 2013 the foundation had no expenditure.

Exclusions

Grants are rarely made to postgraduate students.

Applications

On a form available from the correspondent. Applications can be submitted either directly by the individual or a parent, guardian, local authority or through the individual's school/college/educational welfare agency. Preferably they should be received by June or November for consideration in July and January, otherwise there are no other requirements.

Other information

The foundation may also make grants to schools within the borough of Stourbridge.

Sutton Coldfield

Sutton Coldfield Municipal Charities

£11,000 (309 grants)

Correspondent: Helen Kimmet, Administrator, Lingard House, Fox Hollies Road, Sutton Coldfield, West Midlands B76 2RJ (01213 512262; fax: 01213 130651; email: helen.kimmet@ suttoncharitabletrust.org; website: www. suttoncoldfieldmunicipalcharities.com)

CC Number: 218627

Eligibility

People in need under the age of 25 living in the Four Oaks, New Hall and Vesey wards of Sutton Coldfield.

Types of grants

Grants are given to: schoolchildren for uniforms/other school clothing, books, equipment/instruments, fees and educational outings in the UK; and further and higher education students for books, equipment/instruments, fees, maintenance/living expenses, childcare, educational outings in the UK and study or travel abroad. Grants are also given to people with a wide range of special educational needs.

Annual grant total

In 2012/13 the charity had assets of almost £48 million and an income of £1.7 million. There were 28 grants to individuals in need, hardship or distress totalling £21,000, 3 grants for individual educational and personal needs totalling £1,500 and 278 school clothing grants totalling £9,500.

Applications

In writing or on a form available from the correspondent. Applications for educational grants should be made directly by the individual or through a parent or carer. They are considered every month, except April, August and December. Telephone enquiries are welcomed. Applications for school clothing are distributed to parents or carers through local schools before Easter each year.

Other information

The principal objective of the charities is the provision of almshouses, the distribution of funds and other measures for the alleviation of poverty and other needs for inhabitants and other organisations within the boundaries of the former borough of Sutton Coldfield.

Walsall

W. J. Croft for the Relief of the Poor

£900

Correspondent: Matthew Underhill, Administrator, Constitutional Services, Walsall MBC, Civic Centre, Darwall Street, Walsall WS1 1EU (01922 652087; email: underhillm@walsall.gov.uk; website: cms.walsall.gov.uk/charities)

CC Number: 702795

Eligibility

Residents of the borough of Walsall who are in hardship, need or distress.

Types of grants

Grants for school uniforms, including shoes.

Annual grant total

In 2012/13 the trust had an income of £2,700 and a total expenditure of £2,000. We estimate that grants for school uniforms and shoes totalled around £900. Grants are also distributed to individuals for welfare purposes.

Applications

Contact the correspondent for an application form or download one from the Walsall Council website. Applications for school uniform grants are considered in July/early August.

The Fishley Educational and Apprenticing Foundation

£32,000 (42 grants)

Correspondent: Neil Picken, Clerk to the Trustees, Constitutional Services, Walsall Council, The Civic Centre, Darwall Street, Walsall WS1 1TP (01922 654369, 01922 652018; email: charities@ walsall.gov.uk; website: cms.walsall.gov.uk/charities)

CC Number: 529010

Eligibility

Young people in need who are under the age of 25 and live, work or study in Walsall.

Types of grants

Grants are available towards general educational needs, including tuition fees, specialist equipment, books, clothing, field trips, study of music and arts, study/travel overseas and so on. Pupils and further/higher education students are supported.

Annual grant total

In 2012/13 the foundation had assets of £487,000 and an income of £32,000. Grants totalled £32,000. During the year 46 applications were considered and 42 were successful.

Applications

Application forms can be accessed from the foundation's website or requested from the correspondent via phone. Grants are considered at least twice a year. Applications must be supported by a member of teaching staff.

Note that applications for grants towards educational trips should be made through the educational establishment.

C. C. Walker Charity

£300

Correspondent: Neil Picken, Clerk to the Trustees, Constitutional Services, Walsall Council, The Civic Centre, Darwall Street, Walsall WS1 1TP (01922 654369; email: charities@walsall.gov.uk; website: cms.walsall.gov.uk/charities)

CC Number: 528898

Eligibility

People who are under the age of 25 and live or study in the borough of Walsall. Preference is given to those people whose one or both parents have died and who were born in Walsall and/or whose parents or surviving parent have lived there at any time since the birth of the applicant.

Types of grants

Grants according to need for any educational purpose. Grants have been given towards clothing for schoolchildren and books, fees, living expenses and equipment for students in further/higher education.

Annual grant total

In 2012/13 the charity had an income of £18,800 and an expenditure of £300, which is lower than usual. We estimate that the annual total of grants was about £300.

Applications

Application forms are available from the charity's website or can be requested from the correspondent. The trustees meet at least twice a year. Grants are normally considered in January, June and October.

Walsall Wood (Former Allotment) Charity

£9,500

Correspondent: Craig Goodall, Administrator, Democratic Services, Walsall Council, Council House, Lichfield Street, Walsall WS1 1TW (01922 654765; email: goodallc@walsall. gov.uk; website: www.walsall.gov.uk/ charities)

CC Number: 510627

Eligibility

Residents of the borough of Walsall who are in need.

Types of grants

Grants for school uniforms and clothing, including footwear.

Annual grant total

In 2012/13 the charity had an income of £23,000 and an expenditure of £19,100.

We estimate the annual total of grants to be around £9,500.

Applications

Application forms can be downloaded from the charity's website or requested from the correspondent via phone. Applications should state what assistance is needed and how it would help. Any additional evidence of applicants' personal circumstances, such as proof of income or letters of support from professional people who are familiar with the case, will benefit the application. The trustees meet approximately six times a year.

Other information

The charity is administered by the Walsall Council Democratic Services team, which also administers a number of other funds.

Individuals for welfare purposes are also supported.

The Blanch Woolaston Walsall Charity

£850

Correspondent: Matthew Underhill, Administrator, Constitutional Services, Walsall Council, The Civic Centre, Darwall Street, Walsall WS1 1TP (01922 652087; email: underhillm@walsall.gov. uk)

CC Number: 216312

Eligibility

People in need living in the borough of Walsall. Educational grants will only be given to those under 21 years of age. There is no age limit for relief-in-need grants.

Types of grants

Around 20 one-off grants are made each year ranging from £50 to £300 for school uniforms and small household items. The trustees cannot undertake to repeat/renew any grants.

Annual grant total

In 2012/13 the charity had both an income and an expenditure of £1,800. Grants made totalled approximately £1,700 and was split between educational and welfare purposes.

Exclusions

No grants are made for the payment of rates, taxes or other public funds (including gas, electricity and so on).

Applications

On a form available from the correspondent. Applications are considered four times a year.

Warley

Palmer Educational Charity (The Palmer Trust)

£6,500

Correspondent: David Flint, Administrator, Birmingham Diocesan Offices, 175 Harborne Park Road, Birmingham B17 0BH (01214 260400)

CC Number: 508226

Eligibility

Children and young people under the age of 25 who live in the Warley Deanery.

Types of grants

Grants are available to schoolchildren and further/higher education students. Our research suggests that support can mainly be given towards the cost of books directly related to Christianity and religious education.

Annual grant total

In 2013 the charity had an income of £8,400 and an expenditure of £6,800. We estimate the annual total of grants to be around £6,500.

Applications

In writing to the correspondent. According to our research, applications should be submitted through the PCC or clergy of Warley Deanery and are normally considered in March and October.

Other information

Primarily grants are made to the Church of England schools in the Warley Deanery. Local churches and organisations may also be supported.

West Bromwich

The Akrill, Wilson and Kenrick Trust Fund and West Bromwich Educational Foundation

£0

Correspondent: Sandwell MBC, Children and Young People's Services, Shaftsbury House, 402 High Street, West Bromwich, West Midlands B70 9LT (01215 698283; email: matthew_driver@ sandwell.gov.uk)

CC Number: 528996

Eligibility

Students under 25 years of age, who are in need and live in West Bromwich.

Types of grants

(i) Scholarships and maintenance allowances for schoolchildren and students. (ii) Grants, clothing, tools, instruments and books for people leaving school or another educational establishment and starting work. (iii) Grants towards educational travel abroad. (iv) Grants for the study of music and other arts.

Annual grant total

Despite an income of £1,700 for two years running, in 2012/13 and 2013/14 there was no expenditure made by the trustees of this charity.

Applications

On an application form, available by writing to the correspondent.

Yardley

Yardley Educational Foundation

£116,000

Correspondent: Derek Hackett, Clerk, Edzell House, 121 Chester Road, Castle Bromwich, Birmingham B36 0AE (01212463625; email: dhhackett@ blueyonder.co.uk; website: www. yardleyeducationfoundation.org)
CC Number: 528918

Eligibility

Children and young people in need between the ages of 11 and 19 who have lived in the ancient parish of Yardley for at least two years. For specific geographical area covered by the foundation, see the map supplied on the foundation's website.

Types of grants

Secondary school pupils aged 11–16 can be supported towards school uniforms, school clothing, sports equipment, educational outings in the UK and study or travel overseas. Grants are normally of around £80. Young adults aged 16–19 can be assisted towards further vocational training and apprenticeships. The foundation also provides book vouchers of £25 redeemable at Waterstones.

Applications for different types of grants can also be considered, these include adventure trips, Duke of Edinburgh Award, Operation Raleigh, purchase of musical instruments, student exchange programmes or cost of attending interviews at universities.

Annual grant total

In 2012/13 the foundation had assets of £4.1 million and an income of £182,000. A total of around £116,000 was spent on charitable activities, of which educational support amounted to £99,000 and book vouchers totalled £16,000. The foundation received over 1,500 applications for grants.

Applications

Application forms are available from the correspondent and should be submitted through the individual's school or college, usually in May or June for consideration in July and August.

Other information

The foundation also states that 'the clerk to the trustees has close liaison with the secondary schools throughout the parish and is in constant touch with them to ascertain their needs.'

Worcester-shire

The Alfrick Educational Charity

£4,200

Correspondent: Andrew Duncan, Clerk, Bewell, Alfrick, Worcestershire WR6 5EY (01905 731731; email: a.duncan@wwf.co. uk)
CC Number: 517760

Eligibility

People who live in the parish of Alfrick, Lulsley and Suckley and are under 25. Preference is given to those who live in Alfrick.

Types of grants

Grants are given to further and higher education students for books, maintenance/living expenses and educational outings in the UK.

Annual grant total

In 2012/13 the charity had an income of £9,500 and a total expenditure of £8,600. We estimate that educational grants to individuals totalled £4,200, with funding also awarded to schools in the area of benefit, including Suckley Primary School.

Applications

In writing to the correspondent directly by the individual. Applications can be submitted at any time.

The Bewdley Old Grammar School Foundation

£9,500

Correspondent: Shana Kent, Administrator, Bewdley Old Grammar School Foundation, Bewdley High School, Stourport Road, Bewdley DY12 1BL (01299 403277)
CC Number: 527429

Eligibility

People under the age of 25 living in Bewdley, the parish of Rock and Ribbesford and Stourport-on-Severn.

Types of grants

Grants are available to schoolchildren and further/higher education students to help with general educational costs, including books, uniforms/clothing, necessities and maintenance. Music and arts studies are also supported.

Annual grant total

In 2012/13 the foundation had an income of £8,700 and an expenditure of £9,700. We have estimated the annual total of grants to be around £9,500.

Applications

In writing to the correspondent. Applications should be made by the individual directly or through a referral agency, if applicable.

The Ancient Parish of Ripple Trust

£1,700

Correspondent: John Willis, Secretary, 7 Court Lea, Holly Green, Upton-upon-Severn, Worcestershire WR8 0PE (01684 594570; email: willis.courtlea@ btopenworld.com)
CC Number: 1055986

Eligibility

Students in higher education who live in the parishes of Ripple, Holdfast, Queenhill and Bushley.

Types of grants

Small cash grants are made.

Annual grant total

In 2012/13 the trust had both an income and an expenditure of around £13,000. Accounts were not required to be submitted to the Charity Commission due to the low income. The trust gives to both individuals and organisations and for educational and welfare purposes. We estimate the grants for individuals totalled approximately £3,500 with £1,700 being awarded in educational grants.

Applications

In writing to the correspondent. The trustees meet twice a year to consider applications, and the funds are advertised locally before these meetings.

Walwyn's Educational Foundation

£4,400

Correspondent: Charles Walker, Administrator, 29 Brookmill Close, Colwall, Malvern WR13 6HY (01684 541995; email: cdw1810@btinternet.com)

CC Number: 527152

Eligibility

Young people aged 16 and over living in the parishes of Colwall and Little Malvern and 'pursuing approved courses in tertiary education' up to first degree level (including vocational training). Grants may be available for secondary school, training college and higher education students, also people starting work/entering a trade. Professions insisting on qualifications beyond first degree (for example, teaching profession) will be considered on their merits.

Types of grants

Small grants, usually around £150, are available towards general educational expenses including the cost of books, fees, equipment/instruments, living expenses and study or travel abroad.

Annual grant total

In 2012/13 the foundation had both an income and an expenditure of £4,600. We have estimated that the annual total of grants was about £4,400. Normally awards total around £4,000 each year.

Exclusions

Mature students are not supported.

Applications

Application forms can be requested from the correspondent. They are considered in September and can be submitted directly by the individual.

Worcester Municipal Exhibitions Foundation (Worcester Municipal Charities)

£6,600 (15 grants)

Correspondent: Mary Barker, Administrator, Kateryn Heywood House, Berkeley Court, The Foregate, Worcester WR1 3QG (01905 317117; email: admin@wmcharities.org.uk; website: www.wmcharities.org.uk/index.html)

CC Number: 527570

Eligibility

People in financial hardship who are resident or have been educated in the city of Worcester and parishes of Bransford, Leigh, Powick and Rushwick for at least two years.

Types of grants

One-off grants are given to schoolchildren, people starting work, further and higher education students (including mature students), apprentices and people entering a trade/profession. Support can be given for fees, books, equipment/instruments, educational outings in the UK, study or travel overseas and student exchanges, also for clothing to people starting work and for schoolchildren (excluding uniforms).

Grants can range from £20 to £1,000.

Annual grant total

In 2013 the foundation had assets of £1.1 million and an income of £143,000. Educational grants to 15 individuals totalled £6,600.

Exclusions

Grants are not given:
- To people outside the area of benefit
- To those attending private or fee paying institutions unless there is no reasonable public alternative
- For travel abroad where the main purpose of the visit is to benefit the local inhabitants and the educational benefits for the student are a by-product
- At second degree level except where these it is essential for certain fields of employment

The foundation no longer assists with the cost of school uniforms and related enquiries should be made directly to the individual's school.

Applications

Application forms and guidelines can be found on the foundation's website. They can be submitted by the individual or through a school, college or educational welfare agency, if applicable. Grants are considered monthly. For exact dates of the meetings and corresponding application deadlines see the foundation's website.

Other information

Grants are also given to schools and educational organisations. In 2013 a total of £91,000 was awarded in 7 grants to organisations which provide educational facilities within the area of benefit.

Worcester Consolidated Municipal Charity (registered charity number 205299) provides support to individuals and organisations for welfare purposes.

Alvechurch

The Alvechurch Grammar School Endowment

£10,000 (27 grants)

Correspondent: David Gardiner, Administrator, 18 Tanglewood Close, Blackwell, Bromsgrove, Worcestershire B60 1BU (01214 453522; email: enquiries@alvechurchgst.org.uk; website: www.alvechurchgst.org.uk/index.htm)

CC Number: 527440

Eligibility

Children and young people under the age of 25 who/whose parents are resident in the old parish of Alvechurch (Hopwood, Rowney Green, Bordesley and parts of Barnt Green) and who require financial assistance.

Types of grants

Scholarships, exhibitions, bursaries and maintenance allowances ranging from £50 to about £750. Support may be given for specific expenses or purchases, such as outfits/clothing, school uniforms, tools, equipment/instruments, books or travel in pursuance of education, and educational outings both in the UK and abroad. Applications are invited form people in further/higher education and training but schoolchildren and people starting work can also be supported. The trust is willing to sponsor a wide range of educational activities including various projects, personal development, training, language courses, sports, volunteering experience and so on.

Annual grant total

In 2012/13 the charity had an income of £21,000 and an expenditure of £13,400. We estimate the annual total of grants to individuals to be around £10,000. Previously about 27 individual awards have been given annually.

Exclusions

Assistance is only available where support cannot be received from the local authority.

Applications

Application forms can be found on the charity's website or requested from the correspondent. Applications are considered three times a year in January, May or September and should be submitted by the first day of each month.

Other information

Grants are also made to local organisations working for the benefit of young people.

Cropthorne

Randolph Meakins Patty's Farm and the Widows Lyes Charity

£1,500

Correspondent: Mrs J. Ayliffe, Orchard House, Main Street, Cropthorne, Pershore, Worcestershire WR10 3LT (01386 860011)

CC Number: 500624

Eligibility

People in need who live in the village of Cropthorne (Worcestershire).

Types of grants

One-off grants according to need.

Annual grant total

In 2012/13 the charity had an income of £4,200 and an expenditure of £3,300. Grants totalled approximately £3,000, which is divided between education and welfare purposes.

Applications

In writing to the correspondent.

Evesham

John Martin's Charity

£266,000

Correspondent: John Daniels, Clerk to the Trustees, 16 Queen's Road, Evesham, Worcester WR11 4JN (01386 765440; fax: 01386 765340; email: enquires@ johnmartins.org.uk; website: www. johnmartins.org.uk)

CC Number: 527473

Eligibility

People resident in Evesham in Worcestershire. Applicants or a parent/ guardian must have lived in the town for at least 12 months at the date of application. Applications from those over 25 are income assessed.

Types of grants

Individual students, between the ages of 16 and state retirement age, may apply for educational grants to support study in a wide variety of courses at local colleges in addition to universities and colleges throughout the country and the Open University. Qualifying courses include HND, degree, postgraduate and part-time vocational courses. Grants are also made towards:

▸ School uniform costs – grants may be available to assist with the cost of school uniforms for children aged 4–18
▸ Educational visits and music, arts and sports activities – grants may be available to students aged 4–18 for activities including school trips, music lessons/instrument hire and sporting activities
▸ 'Standards of Excellence' awards – grants for students aged 4–18 for achieving a 'standard of excellence' in a sporting or arts/music area

Annual grant total

In 2012/13 the charity had assets of £20.5 million and an income of £749,000. Grants were made to individuals totalling £266,000 for the promotion of education. Grants to organisations and schools for the promotion of education totalled an additional £54,000.

Exclusions

The charity does not currently provide grants for full-time courses below degree level.

Applications

On a form available from the correspondent or downloaded from the charity's website, where criteria is also posted. Applications are considered from July to September for further and higher education grants. Grants for part-time vocational courses are available throughout the year.

Note the following statement from the charity: 'Since 1 July 2009 we have rejected 70% of all Student Grant Applications because the required evidence to prove residency in the town of Evesham was not supplied. Read the Application Form.'

Other information

Grants are also made to organisations and to individuals for welfare purposes. The charity has an informative website.

Feckenham

The Feckenham Educational Foundation

£2,000

Correspondent: J. Bate, Administrator, Wychway, Droitwich Road, Hanbury, Bromsgrove B60 4DB (01527 821285)

CC Number: 527565

Eligibility

People under the age of 25 who live in the ancient parish of Feckenham.

Types of grants

Schoolchildren and students can be supported towards general educational needs and people preparing to enter a trade or profession can be assisted towards the cost of outfits, clothing, tools or books.

Annual grant total

In 2012/13 the foundation had an income of £3,300 and an expenditure of £2,400. We estimate that the annual total of grants was about £2,000.

Applications

In writing to the correspondent.

Worcester

The United Charities of Saint Martin

£2,600

Correspondent: Michael Bunclark, Administrator, 4 St Catherine's Hill, London Road, Worcester WR5 2EA (01905 355585)

CC Number: 200733

Eligibility

People in need who live in the parish of St Martin, Worcester.

Types of grants

One-off grants are given for general educational purposes.

Annual grant total

In 2013 the charities had an income of £6,600 and a total expenditure of £5,300. We estimate grants awarded to individuals for educational purposes to be around £2,600. The charity also makes grants to individuals for social welfare purposes.

Applications

In writing to the correspondent.

South West

General

The Adams Youth Trust

£72,000

Correspondent: Margaret Pyle, Administrator, Greendale Court, Clyst St Mary, Exeter, Devon EX5 1AW (01395 233433)

CC Number: 1067277

Eligibility

Young people principally in the West Country (Cornwall, Devon, Somerset and Wiltshire).

Types of grants

Grants to provide opportunities for education, advancement of personal skills and training.

Annual grant total

In 2012/13 the trust had an income of £7,300 and an expenditure of £113,000. We have estimated that grants and scholarships totalled around £72,000.

Applications

In writing to the correspondent at any time.

Other information

The trust also makes grants to organisations.

The charity holds only unrestricted funds from an original donation of £1 million.

The Christina Aitchison Trust

See entry on page 165

Viscount Amory's Charitable Trust

£5,200 (7 grants)

Correspondent: The Trust Secretary, The Island, Lowman Green, Tiverton, Devon EX16 4LA (01884 254899)

CC Number: 204958

Eligibility

People in need in the south west of England, with a preference for small charities in Devon (due to limited funds).

Types of grants

One-off and recurrent grants according to need.

Annual grant total

In 2012/13 the trust had assets of almost £12.5 million and an income of £390,000. The trust made 14 grants to individuals totalling £11,200, of which £5,200 was awarded for educational purposes. A further £369,000 was given to organisations.

Applications

In writing to the correspondent, for consideration every month.

M. R. Cannon 1998 Charitable Trust

£36,000

Correspondent: Chris Mitchell, Trustee, 53 Stoke Lane, Westbury-on-Trym, Bristol BS9 3DW (01173 776540)

CC Number: 1072769

Eligibility

Young people who wish to undertake vocational training or studies. Preference is given to individuals from Bristol, County Durham, Dorset, North Devon and North Yorkshire.

Types of grants

One-off and recurrent grants are given according to need.

Annual grant total

In 2012/13 the trust had assets of £3.5 million, an income of £38,000 and a total charitable expenditure of £40,000. Grants to individuals totalled £36,000.

Applications

In writing to the correspondent.

Other information

Support can also be given to medical/health charities, conservation and countryside related initiatives or small local projects. Grants made to 17 institutions totalled £4,200 in 2012/13.

Devon and Cornwall Aid for Girls Trust

£12,500

Correspondent: Frederick Webb, Administrator, 33 Downham Gardens, Tamerton Foliot, Plymouth, Devon PL5 4QF (01752 776612; email: fjwebb@talktalk.net)

CC Number: 202493

Eligibility

Young women between the ages of 16 and 23 who live in the counties of Devon and Cornwall. Preference is given to girls who have lost one or both of their parents.

Types of grants

One-off and recurrent grants ranging from £100 to £350 are offered to further and higher education students or people in vocational training to help with the cost of books, clothing, fees, instruments/tools, IT equipment, travel or living expenses.

Annual grant total

In 2012/13 the trust had an income of £12,500 and a total expenditure of £12,700. We estimate the annual total of grants to individuals to be around £12,500.

Exclusions

Grants are not normally awarded for postgraduate and mature students, second qualifications or part-time studies.

Applications

In writing to the correspondent. Applications can be submitted directly by the individual at any time.

Dyke Exhibition Foundation

£3,000

Correspondent: Christopher Stanley-Smith, Administrator, Grove View, Hodshill, Southstoke, Bath BA2 7ED (email: christopher.stanley-smith@brewin.co.uk)

CC Number: 306610

Eligibility

Further and higher education students (between the ages of 16 and 25) who are resident in Somerset, Devon or Cornwall. Applicants must either have been born in the area, have been resident there for at least three years, or have been attending school in the area of benefit for at least two years prior to application.

Preference is given to individuals who are in most need and those who are, or are about to become, undergraduates of Oxford University or other university.

Types of grants

Grants are given towards fees, accommodation, books and equipment, travel costs or similar necessities. Awards usually range between £100 and £300 a year for up to three years.

Annual grant total

In 2012/13 the foundation had an income of £3,500 and an expenditure of £3,200. We have estimated that the annual total of grants to individuals was around £3,000.

Applications

Application forms can be obtained by sending an sae to the correspondent. Completed application forms must be submitted by the end of February for consideration in April.

The Elmgrant Trust

£3,600 (21 grants)

Correspondent: Amanda Critchlow Horning, Secretary, Elmhirst Centre, Dartington Hall, Totnes, Devon TQ9 6EL (01803 863160; email: info@elmgrant.org.uk; website: www.elmgrant.org.uk)

CC Number: 313398

Eligibility

People living in the South West (counties of Cornwall, Devon, Dorset, Gloucestershire, Somerset and Wiltshire).

Types of grants

The trust offers one-off grants in the region of £150 to help schoolchildren with the cost of books, equipment/instruments, fees and educational outings/visits. Further/higher education students are also assisted with the cost of books, equipment/instruments, fees, maintenance/living expenses, educational outings in the UK and childcare.

Annual grant total

In 2012/13 the trust had assets of £2.1 million, an income of £59,000 and a total charitable expenditure of £25,000. Grants to 21 individuals totalled £3,600.

Exclusions

The trustees will not provide support towards the following:

- Postgraduate study or related expenses
- Second and subsequent degrees
- Overseas student grants
- Expeditions, travel and study projects overseas
- Training in counselling courses

Grants will not be given to organisations or individuals who have already received a grant from the trust within the previous two years.

Applications

In writing to the correspondent. Applications should provide full details of the project/course/event, including anticipated costs, relevant dates and documents, such as a letter of acceptance on a course and a letter of support from a tutor/educational establishment/social worker. An outline of the applicants' current financial circumstances would also be helpful.

The trustees meet three times a year on the last Saturday of February, June and October. It is crucial to submit the application at least one month prior to the meeting.

Other information

The trust also supports organisations, groups and educational establishments throughout the UK with strong preference for those in the South West. Various projects, particularly related to education, arts and social sciences are eligible. Large-scale national organisations would not be assisted.

A. B. Lucas Memorial Awards

£1,000

Correspondent: Martin Dare, Trustee, Green Meadows, Lower Odcombe, Yeovil BA22 8TZ (01935 863522; email: martindare@btinternet.com)

CC Number: 282306

Eligibility

People who are undertaking the study of dairy agriculture and live in the administrative counties of Cornwall, Devon, Somerset, Dorset and those parts of Avon that were previously part of Somerset.

Types of grants

Provision of scholarships, grants, loans and otherwise to young people for studies of agriculture and particularly dairy farming.

Annual grant total

Grants usually total around £1,000 each year. In 2012/13 the trust had an income of £2,100 and an expenditure of around £1,000.

Applications

In writing to the correspondent.

Avon

R. W. Barnes Educational Fund

£8,000 (4 grants)

Correspondent: Julie Newman, Administrator, Quartet Community Foundation, Royal Oak House, Royal Oak Avenue, Bristol BS1 4GB (01179 897700; fax: 01179 897701; email: applications@quartetcf.org.uk; website: www.quartetcf.org.uk)

CC Number: 1080418

Eligibility

Undergraduate students on mathematics, physics, engineering (aeronautical, electrical, electronic or mechanical), astronomy or oceanography related courses at Bath or Cambridge universities, Imperial College, other Russell group universities or other universities in the top 40 university rankings, as compiled by 'The Complete University Guide'. Applicants must be UK nationals by birth, demonstrate that their family income is below £40,000 a year and live within either of the following post code areas: all of BS, BA, and TA, DT9, DT10, SP3/7/8, SN10/12/13/14/15, GL9.

Priority is given to students with no family history of higher education, those attending Imperial College, Bath or Cambridge Universities, individuals studying mathematics or physics and people living within BA8, BA9 BA11 post code areas.

Types of grants

Recurrent grants of up to £2,500 a year (for a maximum of four years) are available towards university fees and living costs. Awards are subject to satisfactory academic result.

Annual grant total

The amount of grants awarded from this particular fund was not specified in the Quartet Community Foundation's annual accounts; however, previously awards have totalled around £8,000.

Exclusions
Grants are not awarded to applicants studying civil or chemical engineering.

Applications
Application forms can be downloaded from the Quartet Community Foundation's website and should be returned by August, either by post or email. Applicants will be informed about the outcome in September.

Other information
This fund is managed by Quartet Community Foundation.

Bristol Trust for the Deaf

£500

Correspondent: A. M. Burrows, Administrator, 13 Wellington Walk, Bristol BS10 5ET (01179 505631)

CC Number: 311507

Eligibility
People with hearing impairments who live in and around the city of Bristol.

Types of grants
The trustees normally make grants to assist in the training of people working with individuals who are deaf to ensure that the greatest number of people benefit from the limited resources available. In certain circumstances applications from individuals are considered. Grants range from £50 to £250 and are given for books, equipment/instruments and fees for students, mature students and postgraduates. Schoolchildren can receive grants for equipment/instruments.

Annual grant total
In 2013 the trust had an income of £5,000 and a total expenditure of £1,500. We estimate that around £1,000 was made in grants to organisations and individuals for education. Grants are usually made to organisations, although there is some scope for grants to be made to individuals.

Applications
In writing to the correspondent, directly by the individual. Applications are considered in May and November and should be submitted in April and October, but special consideration can be given at other times to urgent needs.

Other information
This trust mainly supports Elmfield School for Deaf Children, Hearing Impaired Service and Bristol Centre for Deaf People.

Nailsea Community Trust Ltd

£1,500

Correspondent: Ann Tonkin, Administrator, 8 Blakeney Grove, Nailsea, Bristol BS48 4RG (website: www.nailseacommunitytrust.co.uk)

CC Number: 900031

Eligibility
Grants are made to schoolchildren, college students and undergraduates for study/travel abroad.

Types of grants
One-off grants, usually up to £500.

Annual grant total
This organisation makes grants to individuals and organisations for both social welfare and educational purposes. We estimate grants to individuals for educational purposes to be around £1,500.

Applications
On a form available from the correspondent. Applications can be submitted either directly by the individual or via a relevant third party, such as a school, social worker or Citizens Advice. Applications are considered at meetings held every three months.

Bath and North East Somerset

Richard Jones Charity (Richard Jones Foundation)

£3,000

Correspondent: Peter Godfrey, Administrator, 'Two Shillings', 24D Tyning Road, Saltford, Bristol BS31 3HL (01225 341085; email: peter@godfreyfamily.org.uk)

CC Number: 310057

Eligibility
People under the age of 30 who live in the parishes of Chew Magna, Newton St Loe, Stanton Drew, Stanton Prior and Stowey-Sutton (all in the area of Bath and North East Somerset).

Types of grants
Small educational grants are available to schoolchildren, college/university students, people starting work, also mature and postgraduate students. One-off and recurrent grants, usually from £30 to £400, are available for course books and equipment/instruments, tools. Occasionally pupils may be helped with the cost of school clothing and further/higher education students supported towards educational travel.

Annual grant total
In 2012/13 the charity had an income of £11,200 and an expenditure of £3,300. We estimate the annual total of grants to individuals to be around £3,000.

Exclusions
Individuals attending private schools are not supported.

Applications
Application forms are available from the correspondent and can be submitted directly by the individual. Grants are normally considered in April and October and applications should be submitted in March and September respectively. Specific dates of the trustees' meetings and the application deadlines are normally advertised in parish magazines and on parish noticeboards. Candidates may be invited for an interview.

Other information
Small awards are also made to elderly people in need at Christmas time. Schools, clubs and other organisations supporting the youth in the area of benefit may also receive grants towards equipment.

Previously the correspondent has stated:

> The majority of our beneficiaries are students at universities and colleges of further education. We would like to attract more applications from school leavers starting to learn a trade for grants towards tools and equipment … We do on occasions assist school pupils with the cost of extra music lessons and, if they can exhibit exceptional talent, towards the cost of musical instruments. We have also given grants to children for educational visits, camps, etc. organised by their schools but it seems that most of the state schools in the area are able to fund needy pupils from their own resources for such activities. We do not, generally speaking, assist pupils at private schools. Very occasionally grants may be made towards the cost of school uniform. Grants have also been given in the past few years to participants in Operation Raleigh expeditions, Outward Bound courses and other ventures of a similar nature.

Ralph and Irma Sperring Charity

£23,000

Correspondent: Ms M. Jorden, Clerk to the Trustees, Thatcher and Hallam Solicitors, Island House, Midsomer Norton, Bath BA3 2HJ (01761 414646; email: sperringcharity@gmail.com)

CC Number: 1048101

Eligibility

People in need who live within a five-mile radius of the Church of St John the Baptist in Midsomer Norton, Bath.

Types of grants

One-off and recurrent grants according to need.

Annual grant total

In 2012/13 the charity had assets of £6.1 million and an income of £331,000. Awards to local causes amounted to £94,000. The charity makes grants to both individuals and organisations although there is no stipulation as to how the income is divided. We have estimated the amount awarded to individuals for educational purposes to be approximately £23,000.

Applications

In writing to the correspondent, to be considered quarterly.

Bristol

The Christ Church Exhibition Fund

£20,000

Correspondent: Ian Millsted, Administrator, 1 All Saints Court, Bristol BS1 1JN (01179 292709; email: ccl.charity@btconnect.com)

CC Number: 325124

Eligibility

Grants are given to:

▷ Boys and girls over the age of 11 who live in the city of Bristol and are attending fee-paying schools. Assistance is not, however, given on first entry to fee-paying education. Grants for schoolchildren are calculated in relation to family income and actual fees

▷ Students in higher education up to the age of 25 who have received at least two years' secondary education in Bristol or who have long residential connections with the city

Types of grants

Grants, generally between £200 and £1,000 a year, are given for fee-paying secondary education, where parents are unable to maintain payments because of changed family or financial circumstances. Grants are awarded to help with the cost of school uniforms, other school clothing, books and educational outings. Occasional help is given to talented pupils at state schools who need help to pay for music lessons. Grants of between £100 and £300 a year are awarded to students unable to obtain discretionary awards or for higher education courses not qualifying for grants. Grants are awarded only for

courses in the UK and can be given to help with the cost of books or towards fees and living expenses.

Annual grant total

In 2012 the fund had an income of £10,700 and a total expenditure of £28,000. Based on financial information that is available from previous years, we estimate grants to individuals to have totalled around £20,000.

At the time of writing (July 2014) this was the most recent financial information available for the fund.

Exclusions

Grants are not given for trips abroad, for courses outside the UK or for postgraduate study.

Applications

On a form available from the correspondent from Easter onwards. Applications should be submitted directly by the individual (student) or by a parent (schoolchildren). Meetings are held in June/July for junior grants, and in September for seniors. Applications should include length of residence in Bristol, how long in present school (schoolchildren) and whether a definite place offer has been received (student).

Other information

Choristers of Christ Church with St Ewen, Bristol, are also eligible for support.

Edmonds and Coles Scholarships (Edmonds and Coles Charity)

£8,000

Correspondent: Helen Parker, Administrator, The Society of Merchant Venturers, Merchants' Hall, The Promenade, Clifton Down, Bristol BS8 3NH (01179 738058; email: hparker@merchantventurers.com; website: merchantventurers.com/charitable-activities/edmonds-and-coles-scholarships/)

CC Number: 311751

Eligibility

People in need who are under the age of 25 and live in the area of benefit, which includes: Aust, Avonmouth, Bishopston, Brentry, Charlton Mead, Coombe Dingle, Cotham, Durdham Down, Hallen, Henbury, Henleaze, Horfield, Kingsweston, Kingsdown, Lawrence Weston, New Passage, Northwick, Pilning, Redland, Redwick, Sea Mills, Severn Beach, Shirehampton, Southmead, Stoke Bishop, Tyndalls Park, Westbury-on-Trym, Westbury Park and Woolcott Park.

Types of grants

Small grants, usually in the range of £100–£1,000, are available towards general educational expenses, including the cost of books, equipment/instruments or travel. Support can be given to people at school, college/university, or those undertaking vocational training. According to our research, grants can be made for university fees but not school fees.

Annual grant total

In 2012/13 the charity had an income of £11,000 and an expenditure of £8,100. We estimate the annual total of grants to individuals to be around £8,000.

Exclusions

At primary and secondary school level, grants are not normally given to enable children to enter private education when parents cannot afford the cost. Help may be given in respect of children already in private education when there is a change in financial circumstances (for example, death of a parent, marriage break-up, unemployment and so on) and there are good reasons for avoiding disruption of the child's education.

Applications

Application forms are available from the charity's website or the correspondent. They can be submitted by the individual or an appropriate third party, if the applicant is under 16. Grants are usually considered in February, July and September.

Other information

Our research shows that this charity consults and co-operates with Bristol Municipal Charities in some cases.

Anthony Edmonds Charity

£9,500

Correspondent: F. Greenfield, Administrator, 43 Meadowland Road, Bristol BS10 7PW (01179 098308; email: fran.greenfield@blueyonder.co.uk; website: www.edmondscharity.org.uk)

CC Number: 286709

Eligibility

Young people up to the age of 25 who live in any of the ancient parishes of Henbury, Westbury and Horfield.

Types of grants

Grants are to help with activities of a broadly educational nature, including apprenticeships, courses and less formal projects that can be academic, artistic, technical, social or sporting.

Annual grant total

In 2011/12 the charity had an income of £22,500 and made grants of approximately £9,500.

Accounts were not available at the time of writing (July 2014).

Applications

On a form available from the correspondent, submitted directly by the individual. The trustees meet to consider applications in March and September.

The Gane Charitable Trust

See entry on page 159

The Redcliffe Parish Charity

£4,000

Correspondent: Paul Tracey, Administrator, 18 Kingston Road, Nailsea, Bristol, North Somerset BS48 4RD (01275 854057; email: redcliffeparishclerk@mail.com)

CC Number: 203916

Eligibility

Schoolchildren in need who live in the city of Bristol.

Types of grants

One-off grants usually of £25 to £50. 'The trustees generally limit grants to families or individuals who can usually manage, but who are overwhelmed by circumstances and are in particular financial stress rather than continuing need.' Grants can be for children's school trips and school uniforms.

Annual grant total

In 2012/13 the charity had an income of £9,600 and a total expenditure of £8,200. We have estimated that educational grants totalled around £4,000.

Exclusions

No support for adult education, school fees or repetitive payments.

Applications

In writing to the correspondent. Applications should be submitted on the individual's behalf by a social worker, doctor, health visitor, Citizens Advice or appropriate third party, and will be considered early in each month. Ages of family members should be supplied in addition to financial circumstances and the reason for the request.

Other information

Grants to schoolchildren occur as part of the charity's wider welfare work.

The Stokes Croft Educational Foundation

£20,000

Correspondent: Frances Webster, Administrator, 7 Remenham Park, Bristol BS9 4HE

CC Number: 311672

Eligibility

People aged 11 to 50 with family connections with the Unitarian Church in Bristol, the Stokes Croft (Endowed) School or the Western Union of Unitarian and Free Christian Churches.

Types of grants

Grants are given for maintenance allowances, overseas travel, books, clothing, and equipment/instruments for beneficiaries looking to enter a particular profession, trade or calling. Grants range from £50 to £500.

Annual grant total

In 2013 the foundation had an income of £23,000 and an expenditure of almost £22,000. Educational grants totalled around £20,000.

Applications

In writing to the correspondent.

Wraxall Parochial Charities

£4,000

Correspondent: Mrs A. Sissons, Clerk to the Trustees, 2 Short Way, Failand, Bristol BS8 3UF (01275 392691)

CC Number: 230410

Eligibility

Residents of the parish of Wraxall and Failand, Bristol who are at any level of their education, in any subject, and are in need.

Types of grants

One-off grants in the range of £50 and £100.

Annual grant total

In 2013 the charity had an income of £26,000 and a total expenditure of £18,000. We estimate that grants to individuals for educational purposes totalled around £4,000.

Applications

In writing to the correspondent, directly by the individual. Applications are considered in February, June, September and November.

Other information

Grants are also made for welfare purposes and to organisations.

North Somerset

Charles Graham Stone's Relief-in-Need Charity

£1,500

Correspondent: John Gravell, Administrator, Administrator, Easton Grey, Webbington Road, Cross, Axbridge BS26 2EL (01934 732266)

CC Number: 260044

Eligibility

Vocational students who live in the parishes of Churchill and Langford, North Somerset.

Types of grants

One-off grants, typically of £50 to £150, towards fees, books, equipment and instruments.

Annual grant total

In 2013 the charity had an income of £4,300 and a total expenditure of £9,400. The charity's main activity is the distribution of grants to individuals for social welfare purposes. We estimate that educational grants totalled £1,500.

Exclusions

No grants for payment of national or local taxes or rates.

Applications

In writing to the correspondent with a full explanation of the personal circumstances. Applications should be submitted by the end of February or August for consideration in the following month. Initial telephone calls are not welcomed.

South Gloucestershire

Almondsbury Charity

£1,400 (5 grants)

Correspondent: Peter Orford, Administrator, Shepperdine Road, Oldbury Naite, Oldbury-on-Severn, Bristol BS35 1RJ (01454 415346; email: peter.orford@gmail.com; website: www. almondsburycharity.org.uk)

CC Number: 202263

Eligibility

People in further or higher education who have a permanent residence or attend an educational establishment in the old parish of Almondsbury.

Types of grants

One-off grants are made, usually for buying books.

Annual grant total

In 2012/13 the charity had assets of £2.2 million and an income of £66,000. There were 10 grants made to individuals totalling £2,800. There was no breakdown of whether the grants were for social welfare or educational purposes.

Exclusions

No grants for school or course fees.

Applications

On a form available from the correspondent or the charity's website. Cash grants are never made directly to the individual; the grant is either paid via a third party, such as social services, or the trust pays for the item directly and donates the item to the individual. Trustees meet six times a year usually in January, March, May, July, September and November (exact dates available on the website) and applications should be submitted at least two weeks beforehand.

Other information

Grants were also made to schools and organisations totalling £17,700.

The Chipping Sodbury Town Lands

£8,000

Correspondent: Nicola Gideon, Administrator, Town Hall, 57–59 Broad Street, Chipping Sodbury, Bristol BS37 6AD (01454 852223; email: nicola. gideon@chippingsodburytownhall.co.uk; website: www.chippingsodburytownhall. co.uk)

CC Number: 236364

Eligibility

People in need who are aged up to 25 years and live in Chipping Sodbury or Old Sodbury.

Types of grants

One-off and recurrent grants to aid the promotion of education, including further education courses.

Annual grant total

In 2013 the charity had assets of £8.9 million, an income of £360,000 and gave grants totalling £127,000, of which £31,000 was given to individuals. The charity gave approximately £8,000 in educational grants.

Applications

In writing to the correspondent. Grant aid is advertised locally in schools, clubs, associations, churches and other religious orders, in the local press, and the Town Hall.

Cornwall

Blanchminster Trust

£268,000 (329 grants)

Correspondent: Jane Bunning, Clerk to the Trustees, Blanchminster Building, 38 Lansdown Road, Bude, Cornwall EX23 8EE (01288 352851; fax: 01288 352851; email: office@blanchminster. plus.com; website: www.blanchminster. org.uk)

CC Number: 202118

Eligibility

People who live (or have at least one parent who lives) in the parishes of Bude, Stratton and Poughill (the former urban district of Bude-Stratton). Current or immediate past pupils of Budehaven Community School living outside the area are also considered.

Types of grants

One-off grants are made to schoolchildren, people starting work, further and higher education students, mature students and postgraduates towards uniforms or other school clothing, books, equipment/instruments, fees, maintenance/living expenses, childcare, educational outings in the UK, study or travel overseas and student exchanges.

Annual grant total

In 2013 the trust had assets of £10 million. It should be noted that this is in the form of investment property, only the surplus income from which is available for grant giving. In this accounting year, the charity had an income of £510,000 and made 329 educational grants totalling £268,000.

Exclusions

Grants are not given to foreign students studying in Britain.

Applications

On a form available from the correspondent. Applications are considered monthly and should be submitted directly by the individual. Where possible the application should include a request for a specific amount and be supported with quotes for the costs of items and so on needed and/or written support from a social worker or other welfare agency. Applications must include evidence of financial need.

Other information

Grants are also made to individuals for welfare and community projects.

The Elliot Exhibition Foundation

£1,000

Correspondent: Samantha Hocking, Student Services, Services for Children, Young People and Families, County Hall, Truro, Cornwall TR1 3AY (01872 324144; email: ask.elliott@cornwall.gov. uk)

Eligibility

Students going into higher education at any British university or higher education establishment, whose parents/guardians live in the city of Truro, the town council areas of Liskeard and Lostwithiel or the parish of Ladlock.

Applicants must be under the age of 19 on 1 July preceding the award of the exhibition. Preference is given to applicants who have attended a maintained school for at least two years.

Applicants with parents/guardians who live in the county of Cornwall may also be considered if insufficient candidates meeting the above criteria apply.

Types of grants

Awards of up to £150.

Annual grant total

Grants usually total around £1,000.

Exclusions

No funding for postgraduate degrees, international students or travel abroad.

Applications

On a form available from the correspondent, to be submitted directly by the individual by 30 September for consideration in November.

The Ken Thomas Charitable Trust

£0

Correspondent: Christopher Riddle, Trustee, Molesworth House, Whitecross, Wadebridge, Cornwall PL27 7JE (01208 815562; email: christopherriddle@ royalcornwall.co.uk)

CC Number: 287260

Eligibility

Young people connected with the agricultural industry who live in Cornwall and the Isles of Scilly, aged from 20 to 30 years.

Types of grants

One-off cash grants, advice and assistance to enable beneficiaries to travel out of the county of Cornwall to further their experience in matters allied to agriculture and horticulture, either in this country or abroad.

Annual grant total

In 2012/13 the trust had an income of £1,200 and had no expenditure. The trust has previously stated that it is operational, although small-scale in its operation.

Applications

On a form available from the correspondent, to be submitted by the individual. Applications are considered throughout the year.

Linkinhorne

The Roberts and Jeffery Foundation

£500

Correspondent: Beryl Martin, Trustee, The Old Dry, Minions, Liskeard, Cornwall PL14 5LJ (01579 362773; email: berylmartin@rocketmail.com)

CC Number: 271577

Eligibility

Schoolchildren living in the parish of Linkinhorne who are in secondary education and/or training.

Types of grants

Our research suggests that grants are made to every eligible child and there is an option to return the money if it is not needed. Awards are for uniforms, other school clothing and educational outings in the UK. Some support may be given to improve the health of children in primary schools or otherwise help where there is a financial need.

Annual grant total

In 2012/13 the foundation had an income of £1,500 and an expenditure of £1,000. We estimate that educational grants to individuals totalled around £500.

Applications

In writing to the correspondent. Applications can be made directly by the individual or a parent/guardian. The foundation also receives a list of children moving to secondary school. Awards are normally considered in April and October.

Other information

Support could also be made to organisations.

St Newlyn East

Trevilson Educational Foundation

£3,500

Correspondent: Marjorie Vale, Trustee, Fiddlers Reach, 34 Station Road, St Newlyn East, Newquay, Cornwall TR8 5NE (01872 510318; email: maggie.vale@gmail.com)

CC Number: 306555

Eligibility

People under the age of 25 who live in the parish of St Newlyn East and are in need.

Types of grants

Grants are available to schoolchildren, further/higher education students and people starting or undertaking apprenticeships. Help is given towards books, equipment/necessities, educational outings and other essentials. Awards usually range from £50 to £500.

Annual grant total

In 2013 the foundation had an income of £15,700 and an expenditure of £3,600. We estimate that grants to individuals totalled around £3,500. Note that both the income and expenditure vary annually. Over the past five years the charitable expenditure fluctuated between £470 and £27,000.

Applications

In writing to the correspondent.

Devon

Adventure Trust for Girls

£6,300

Correspondent: Beryl Cuff, Administrator, 28 Lovelace Crescent, Exmouth, Devon EX8 3PR (01395 223606; email: ecuff@btinternet.com)

CC Number: 800999

Eligibility

Girls and young women between the ages of 10 and 20 who live or attend school within eight miles of Exmouth Town Hall, south of the M5 and east of the Exe.

Types of grants

One-off grants, usually ranging from £50 to £400, can be provided to girls who wish to travel either on their own or with friends/group/organisation. A wide range of trips can be supported, including summer schools, camps, school exchange programmes and any other adventure that would develop the individual's personality, self-confidence, physical abilities, leadership and team working skills.

Assistance can also be given to girls from low income households to participate in school trips and educational outings.

Annual grant total

In 2012/13 the trust had an income of £7,300 and an expenditure of £6,500. We estimate the annual total of grants to be around £6,300.

Exclusions

Areas to the west of the river Exe are excluded. Our research suggests that grants would not be given towards organised school ski trips.

Applications

Application forms can be requested from the correspondent. Our research indicates that applications should be submitted two months in advance of the trustees' meetings, which are normally held every second month.

Individuals who require assistance with the cost of school trips should apply through their school.

Albert Casanova Ballard Deceased (A. C. Ballard Deceased Trust)

£17,200 (91 grants)

Correspondent: Margaret Mary, Trustee, Pengelly, 6 Victory Street, Keyham, Plymouth PL2 2BY (01752 569258)

CC Number: 201759

Eligibility

Boys aged between 11 and 16 who are entering or attending secondary education and live in the city of Plymouth, within seven miles from the Ballard Institute.

Types of grants

One-off grants are offered towards general educational expenses, including school uniforms, other clothing, books and equipment/instruments.

Annual grant total

In 2012/13 the trust had assets of over £1 million, an income of £51,000 and a total charitable expenditure of £43,000. Grants to 91 individuals totalled £17,200.

Applications

Application forms can be requested from the correspondent providing an sae up until April. Applications should be made by the individual's parent/guardian and need to be submitted in advance for consideration in May/June.

Application forms should be sent to the following address: c/o Bishop Fleming Accountants, Salt Quay House, 4, North East Quay, Sutton Harbour, Plymouth PL4 0BN.

Other information

Grants can also be given to organisations, clubs and schools operating in the area of benefit. In 2012/13 a total of £25,400 was awarded to 31 bodies.

Bideford Bridge Trust

£194,000

Correspondent: P. R. Sims, Steward, 24 Bridgeland Street, Bideford, Devon EX39 2QB (01237 473122)

CC Number: 204536

Eligibility

People in need who live in Bideford and the immediate neighbourhood.

Types of grants

One-off grants ranging from £150 to £500 to: schoolchildren for books and equipment/instruments; people starting work for books; further and higher education students for books, equipment/instruments and fees; and mature students for books and equipment/instruments.

Annual grant total

In 2012 the charity had assets of £15 million and an income of £1 million. The accounts for 2012 were the latest available at the time of writing (July 2014). Book grants, student bursaries and grants for vocational training courses and apprenticeships totalled £98,000. A further £96,000 was given in business start-up grants to people from disadvantaged backgrounds.

The majority of the assets are held as property and are not available for distribution, though they do produce income for the charity.

Exclusions

Grants are not given to postgraduates or for computers for personal use.

Applications

On a form available from the correspondent, to be submitted at any time during the year by the individual, although a sponsor is usually required. Applications are considered monthly.

Cranbrook Charity

£1,200

Correspondent: Stephen Purser, Trustee, Venn Farm, Bridford, Exeter EX6 7LF (01647 252328; email: purseratvenn@ hotmail.com)

CC Number: 249074

Eligibility

People in need who live in the parishes of Dunsford, Doddiscombsleigh and 'that part of the parish of Holcombe Burnell as in 1982 constituted part of the parish of Dunsford'. Promotion of education for people under 25 living in the area of benefit.

Types of grants

One-off and recurrent grants to those in need. Recently, grants of £80 have been given every six months for relief-in-need and educational purposes.

Annual grant total

In 2012/13 the charity had an income of £10,000 and an expenditure of £5,400. We estimate that grants for educational purposes to individuals totalled around £1,200.

Applications

In writing to the correspondent.

Other information

Grants are made for both individuals and organisations for educational and social welfare purposes.

The Devon Educational Trust

£27,000

Correspondent: The Clerk to the Trustees, PO Box 86, Teignmouth TQ14 8ZT (email: devonedtrust@ talktalk.net; website: www.devon.gov.uk/ index/learning/leaving_school/ studentfinance/alternative_funding/ trusts_and_charities.htm)

CC Number: 220921

Eligibility

Pupils and students under the age of 25 who live, or whose parents' normal place of residence is, in Devon. Preference is given to applicants from low income families. Applicants or their parents must have been living in Devon on a permanent basis for at least 12 months.

Types of grants

One-off grants of between £100 and £500 to:

- Schoolchildren for uniforms/clothing and equipment/instruments
- College students and undergraduates for special clothing, study/travel costs, books, equipment/instruments and maintenance/living expenses
- Vocational students and people starting work for uniforms/clothing, books, equipment/instruments and maintenance/living expenses

During 2012 grants were also awarded to:

- Young people with specific learning difficulties to assist with the costs of one-to-one specialist tuition
- Young people who are visually impaired for the provision of computer equipment and software

Annual grant total

In 2012 the trust had assets of £1 million and an income of £39,000. The trust's financial report for the year stated that charitable grants totalled £32,000 and that £5,200 was given to eight institutions. A total for grants to individuals was not included in the report, but from the figures available, we estimate that they totalled around £27,000.

At the time of writing (July 2014) this was the most recent financial information available for the trust.

Exclusions

Assistance is not normally given to those embarking on a second or higher degree course. However, in some cases the trustees may make a small grant to assist with living costs or the purchase of books, equipment and so on. No assistance is available for the payment of university fees and only in exceptional cases will the trustees consider paying school or boarding fees.

Applications

On a form available from the correspondent or to download from the Devon County Council website, including details of two references. The trustees meet three times a year, usually in March, July and November, and applications should be submitted four weeks before the date of the next meeting.

Other information

In cases where an application does not fit the trust's criteria, the applicant may be referred to another educational trust for consideration.

The Exeter Advancement in Life Charity

£7,600

Correspondent: M. R. King, Clerk, Chichester Mews, Exeter Municipal Charities, 22A Southernhay East, Exeter, Devon EX1 1QU (01392 201550; fax: 01392 201551; email: admin@ exetermunicipalcharities.org.uk)

CC Number: 1002151

Eligibility

Children and young people under the age of 25 who are in need and live in the city of Exeter or within 15 miles of the city centre. Preference may be given to schoolchildren with serious family difficulties so that the child has to be educated away from home.

Types of grants

One-off and recurrent grants up to £500 a year. Support can be given to schoolchildren towards clothing and uniforms, books, equipment/ instruments, fees or educational outings in the UK. Further/higher education students (including mature and postgraduate) can be assisted with the cost of books, equipment/instruments, course fees and related necessities, also study or travel overseas. People in vocational training/starting work can receive help with equipment/ instruments, travel costs, outfits and materials. Grants towards study/travel overseas are subject to a minimum study period of six months (unless it is an obligatory part of an approved course).

Annual grant total

The latest financial information available at the time of writing (July 2014) was from 2012. In 2012 the charity had an income of £7,600 and an expenditure of £7,800. We estimate the annual total of grants to be around £7,600.

Applications

Application forms are available from the correspondent. They can be submitted directly by the individual or through a third party, such as a parent/guardian or educational welfare agency, if applicable. Candidates should provide an academic reference and outline their financial circumstances. Prospective grant recipients are interviewed in February, May, August and November.

Note: this charity is comprised of two educational trusts: John Dinam School Endowment and Lady Ann Clifford Trust. These two trusts have the same criteria, described above, with the exception that the Endowment can make grants outside Exeter – up to 15 miles from the city centre. Applicants can only receive a grant from one of these trusts. Those living outside the city should apply to John Dinam School Endowment.

Other information

This charity is part of Exeter Municipal Charities. Support for welfare needs is available through The Exeter Relief-in-Need Charity.

The Gibbons Family Trust

£15,700 (20 grants)

Correspondent: Cathy Houghton, Trust Manager, 14 Fore Street, Budleigh Salterton, Devon EX9 6NG (01395 445259; email: enquiries@gibbonstrusts. org; website: www.gibbonstrusts.org)

CC Number: 290884

Eligibility

People up to 25 in Devon and the Isle of Thanet area of Kent with a preference for those from East Devon.

Types of grants

Grants towards the maintenance and educational advancement, training and recreation of children and young people.

Annual grant total

In 2013/14 the trust had assets of £2 million and an income of £83,000. Grants to 20 individuals totalled £15,700 and to organisations £160,000.

Exclusions

No grants for private school fees, gap-year projects or other types of overseas trips.

Applications

On a form available to download from the trust's website with a short covering letter and a supporting statement from a third party, such as a school, club, doctor or social worker. Applications must be posted and are not accepted by email.

The Heathcoat Trust

£154,000

Correspondent: Mrs C. J. Twose, Secretary, The Factory, Tiverton, Devon EX16 5LL

CC Number: 203367

Eligibility

Mainly students in secondary and further education who live and study in Tiverton and the mid-Devon area. Occasionally students can be supported for study outside the area if the courses are not available locally. Applicants need to have a personal connection with either the John Heathcoat or the Lowman Companies.

Types of grants

One-off and recurrent grants towards fees.

Annual grant total

In 2012/13 the trust had assets of £19.3 million and an income of £534,000. Grants made to individuals totalled £567,000 and were distributed as follows:

Consolidated grant	£284,000
Educational	£154,000
Death grants	£34,000
Hospital visiting	£29,500
Chiropody	£24,000
Opticians' charges	£20,000
Dentists' charges	£12,000
Communication grant	£5,000
Cases of hardship	£3,000
Employees sickness	£3,000

Applications

In writing to the correspondent. For A-level applicants who attend East Devon College, application forms are available and should be submitted between April and June each year.

Other information

Grants were also made to charitable organisations (£186,000 in 2012/13).

Hele's Exhibition Foundation

£1,500

Correspondent: Sally Luscombe, Trustee, Brook Cottage, 65 Fore Street, Plympton, Plymouth PL7 1NA (01752 344857)

CC Number: 306657

Eligibility

People under 25 who live, firstly, in the former parishes of Plympton St Maurice, Plympton St Mary and Brixton, and, secondly, in other parts of Devon (excluding Plymouth) if there are insufficient applications from the initial areas.

Types of grants

Cash grants to help with books, equipment, clothing or travel; grants to help with school, college or university fees or to supplement existing grants; and help towards the cost of education, training, apprenticeships or equipment for those starting work.

Annual grant total

In 2012/13 the foundation had an income of £1,800 and an expenditure of £2,200. £1,500 is usually given in grants each year.

Applications

In writing to the correspondent.

Dulce Haigh Marshall Trust

£3,400

Correspondent: Colin Power, Trustee, Elmfield, Lustleigh, Newton Abbot TQ13 9TW (01647277276)

CC Number: 286273

Eligibility

Cellists and other string players who are in need of financial assistance, live in Devon, and are under the age of 25.

Types of grants

Grants ranging between £200 and £500 towards tuition fees or the purchase of instruments.

Annual grant total

In 2012/13 the trust had an income of £600 and a total expenditure of £3,600. We have estimated that the annual total of grants was around £3,400.

Exclusions

Grants are not given to people who or whose parents have sufficient income to meet their needs. People who do not demonstrate sufficient commitment to learning their instrument will not be supported.

Applications

Application forms are available from the correspondent and should be returned before 1 May. Grants are usually distributed in August each year. Applications can be made directly by the individual and should include a teacher's report. Students may be asked to attend an audition.

The Vivian Moon Foundation

£8,800 (43 grants)

Correspondent: The Administrator, The Vivian Moon Foundation, Simpkins Edwards, 21 Boutport Street, Barnstaple, Devon EX31 1RP (email: info@ vivianmoonfoundation.co.uk; website: www.vivianmoonfoundation.co.uk)

CC Number: 298942

Eligibility

People over the age of 18 who have links with North Devon and have an offer of a place on a course of further educational, professional or vocational training which will lead to employment or improve individuals' skills and their career opportunities. Preference is given to people who intend to return to North Devon to work and, ideally, have an employment secured there at the end of their training.

Types of grants

One-off and recurrent grants ranging between £150 and £300 are available to people in further education and training, including college students, vocational students, mature students, people starting work, unemployed people seeking to get into employment or working people who wish to develop their skills. Both full-time and part-time, also sandwich and correspondence courses can be supported. Most applicants are funded partially and on a course or annual basis.

Annual grant total

In 2012/13 the foundation had assets of £597,000 and an income of £18,500. A total of £8,800 was awarded in grants to 43 individuals.

Exclusions

First degree applicants are unlikely to be supported, unless in extraordinary circumstances.

Applications

The foundation prefers to receive applications online through its website in order to speed up the process. Applicants who are unable to apply in such way can book computer time at a Pathfinder centre in Barnstaple (01271 345851) or Bideford (01237 405250), or request an application from the correspondent. Applications should provide an email address of one referee. Grants are considered in January, May and September.

Other information

North Devon comprises the area administered by either Torridge or North Devon District Council.

The Pain Trust (The Pain Adventure Trust)

£44,000 (40 grants)

Correspondent: The Secretary, 15 Rolle Street, Exmouth, Devon EX8 1HA (01395 275443; email: admin@pain-trust. org.uk; website: www.pain-trust.org.uk)

CC Number: 276670

Eligibility

Boys and young men aged between 11 and 21 (on the day of the expedition or activity, not on the date of application) who live in the East Devon area or within eight miles of Exmouth Town Hall, excluding the area to the west of the estuary of the river Exe. In considering awards the trust takes into account whether the applicants: are away from home for the first time; are having their first trip abroad; show self-sufficiency and integration within a group; are pursuing a new activity never attempted before. Preference may be given to activities undertaken as a part of the group rather than individually.

Types of grants

One-off grants towards travel and adventure to further physical development, character building, leadership training or fostering a team spirit. Examples of projects include: bungee jumping in New Zealand, skiing in Europe and the USA, train rides to China via Russia, camping on Dartmoor, canoeing in Norway, surfing in Australia, assisting charity projects in Brazil, community work in Zambia and so on.

Annual grant total

In 2012/13 the trust had assets of £74,000 and an income of £60,000. A total of £44,000 was awarded in grants to 24 individuals and 12 groups. During the year 40 grants were made for the benefit of 288 boys.

Exclusions

The following are not supported:
- Competitive sport or the pursuit of excellence in sport
- Purchase of equipment
- Activities considered to be within the responsibilities of the government/ local authorities
- Activities which could be considered to be a part of the national curriculum
- Retrospective applications
- Activities during term time for those in full-time education

Applications

Application forms are available on the trust's website. The trust invites potential applicants to contact the correspondent to discuss their application or for further guidance. Applications must be submitted at least 16 days before a meeting, the dates of which can be found on the website. Last year there were eight meetings held. Applications must be accompanied by a detailed itinerary with costs and demonstrate adequate evidence of background research into the proposed expedition. Repeat applications can be considered as long as they fulfil the objectives for funding.

The Christine Woodmancy Charitable Foundation

£500

Correspondent: Jill Hill, Administrator, Thompson and Jackson, 4–5 Lawrence Road, Plymouth PL4 6HR (01752 665037; email: jill@thompsonandjackson. co.uk)

CC Number: 1012761

Eligibility

Children and young people under the age of 21 who live in the Plymouth area and are in need.

Types of grants

One-off grants to help maintain and educate young people in need.

Annual grant total

In 2012/13 the foundation had an income of £15,000 and a total expenditure of £13,000 However, in previous years grants have tended to be given mostly to organisations rather than individuals.

Applications

In writing to the correspondent, to be submitted either directly by the individual or via a school or educational welfare worker. Applications should include background information and provide evidence of financial need.

Bovey Tracey
Bovey Tracey Exhibition Foundation

£1,500

Correspondent: Mrs E. A. Crosby, Administrator, 32 Churchfields Drive, Bovey Tracey, South Devon TQ13 9QU (01626 835524; email: ecrosby143@ btinternet.com)

CC Number: 306653

Eligibility

Full-time students in further or higher education, over 16, who live in Bovey Tracey and have done so for at least three years.

Types of grants

Grants ranging between £65 and £75 for students attending approved places of further and higher education to help with the cost of, amongst other things, books, fees and living expenses, equipment and uniforms. Grants can generally be spent on whatever is required by the recipient. Grants are generally recurrent.

Annual grant total

This charity awards around £1,500 to individuals for educational purposes each year.

Exclusions

Grants are not given to students on government sponsored schemes.

Applications

On a form available from the correspondent from 1 April, to be returned by 31 July for consideration in August. Applications should be made directly by the individual.

Braunton
Chaloner's Educational Foundation

£1,300

Correspondent: Louise Langabeer, Administrator, Slee Blackwell Solicitors, 10 Cross Street, Barnstaple, North Devon EX31 1BA (01271 349943; email: louise. langabeer@sleeblackwell.co.uk)

CC Number: 286580

Eligibility

People under the age of 25 who live in the parish of Braunton and are in need.

Types of grants

Grants of £140 are made towards equipment, instruments, tools, books, fees, maintenance/living expenses, and study or travel overseas. Support is available to people starting work and individuals in further or higher education. Tertiary students can also be supported for educational outings in the UK.

Annual grant total

In 2012/13 the foundation had an income of £2,600 and an expenditure of £1,400. We estimate the annual total of grants to be around £1,300.

Applications

Application forms can be requested from the correspondent. They can be submitted directly by the individual and are normally considered in February, June or October.

Broadhempston
The Broadhempston Relief-in-Need Charity

£500

Correspondent: Rosalind Brown, Administrator, Meadows, Broadhempston, Totnes, Devon TQ9 6BW (01803 813130)

CC Number: 272930

Eligibility

For educational purposes for children in need who live in the parish of Broadhempston.

Types of grants

One-off or recurrent grants ranging from £40 to £100. Grants are made towards children's educational trips and aids for educational purposes.

Annual grant total

In 2012/13 the charity had both an income and a total expenditure of approximately £1,500. We estimate that

the total grant awarded for educational purposes was £500.

Applications

In writing to the correspondent directly by the individual to be considered in June and December.

Other information

The charity also awards grants for social welfare purposes, especially to assist local families in buying fuel and groceries. Finally, they also provide meals to the elderly parishioners.

Colyton
The Colyton Parish Lands Charity

£100

Correspondent: Sarah Charman, Administrator, Fermain House, Dolphin Street, Colyton, Devon EX24 6LU (01297 553148; website: www.colytonfeoffees-townhall.org.uk)

CC Number: 243224

Eligibility

Young people in need in the ancient parish of Colyton.

Types of grants

One-off and recurrent grants in support of education and training.

Annual grant total

In 2012/13 the charity had an income of £60,000 and a total expenditure of £33,000. Grants awarded totalled £500 with approximately £100 being awarded for educational purposes.

Applications

In writing to the correspondent to be submitted either directly by the individual or a family member, through a third party, such as a social worker or teacher, or through a welfare agency such as Citizens Advice. Applications are considered monthly.

Other information

The charity also awards grants for social welfare purposes and for the maintenance of the town hall and other properties owned by the charity.

Combe Martin
The George Ley Educational Trust

£3,000

Correspondent: James Williams, Trustee, Brendon, Western Gardens, Combe Martin, Ilfracombe, Devon EX34 0EY

CC Number: 306788

Eligibility
People who live in Combe Martin who are in higher education.

Types of grants
Grants for books and equipment.

Annual grant total
In 2013, the trust had an income of £5,000 and a total expenditure of £3,300. We estimate that the total of grants awarded to individuals was approximately £3,000.

Exclusions
Grants are not given for main expenses such as fees or living costs.

Applications
In writing to the correspondent. A committee meets to consider applications in May and September. Reapplications for future grants can be made by people who have already been supported by this trust.

Cornwood

Reverend Duke Yonge Charity

£3,000

Correspondent: Janet Milligan, Administrator, 8 Chipple Park, Lutton, Nr Cornwood, Ivybridge, Devon PL21 9TA

CC Number: 202835

Eligibility
People in need who live in the parish of Cornwood.

Types of grants
One-off grants according to need.

Annual grant total
In 2013 the charity had an income of £15,500 and a total expenditure of £12,000. We estimate that grants awarded to individuals for educational purposes totalled around £3,000.

Applications
In writing to the correspondent via the trustees, who are expected to make themselves aware of any need. Applications are considered at trustees' meetings.

Other information
Grants are also made to individuals in need and organisations.

Culmstock

Fuel Allotment Charity

£1,500

Correspondent: Jennifer Sheppard, Administrator, Rexmead, Culmstock, Cullompton, Devon EX15 3JX (01823 680516; email: jenny@rexmead.eclipse.co.uk)

CC Number: 205327

Eligibility
Students in need who live in the ancient parish of Culmstock.

Types of grants
Recurrent grants according to need. Books and equipment for college courses.

Annual grant total
In 2013/14 the trust had an income of £4,900 and an expenditure of £4,700. Grants usually total around £1,500.

Applications
In writing to the correspondent directly by the individual.

Other information
Grants are also given for welfare purposes.

Great Torrington

The Great Torrington Town Lands Poors Charities

£2,000

Correspondent: Ian Newman, Administrator, Town Hall Office, High Street, Great Torrington, Devon EX38 8HN (01805 625738; email: greattorringtoncharities@btconnect.com)

CC Number: 202801

Eligibility
People in need who live in Great Torrington.

Types of grants
Grants are usually made to students towards a year out (voluntary work). Requests are also considered for school uniform costs for schoolchildren and for other costs for mature students.

Annual grant total
In 2012/13 the charity had assets of £6.4 million, an income of £267,000. The amount spent on charitable activities for this charity totalled £156,000 and we estimate grants to individuals for educational purposes to be around £2,000.

Applications
In writing to the correspondent, with all relevant personal information.

Other information
The main purpose of this charity is the provision of accommodation. Grants are provided for pensioners, those in need and organisations with various purposes.

Plymouth

Joan Bennett's Exhibition Endowment

£0

Correspondent: Vanessa Steer, Clerk and Treasurer, 184 Mannamead Road, Plymouth PL3 5RE (01752 703280; email: v_steer@yahoo.co.uk; website: www.plymouth.gov.uk)

CC Number: 306609

Eligibility
Young people resident in Plymouth.

Types of grants
Grants for further or higher education students, for tools, equipment, books, clothing and instruments to assist people starting apprenticeships or work. Assistance can also be given with travel costs.

Annual grant total
The fund usually has an annual income of £250 to £500. No grants have been made in recent years but the trust states that they are open to applications.

Applications
In writing to the correspondent.

John Lanyon Educational Foundation

£300

Correspondent: Frederick Webb, Administrator, 33 Downham Gardens, Tamerton Foliot, Plymouth, Devon PL5 4QF (01752 776612; email: fjwebb@talktalk.net)

CC Number: 306773

Eligibility
People in need who live within Plymouth city boundaries and are aged 16 to 23 years, with a preference for people from low-income families who are in higher education or leaving school or university and starting work.

Types of grants

One-off and recurrent grants ranging from £100 to £300, for instance, towards books, equipment/instruments, fees and maintenance/living expenses.

Annual grant total

In 2013/14 the foundation had an income of £1,000 and a total expenditure of approximately £300. We estimate that all £300 of the expenditure was awarded in grants.

Exclusions

No grants for postgraduates, part-time or home study courses, mature students or study outside the UK.

Applications

On a form available from the correspondent, directly by the individual, for consideration in any month.

The Olford Bequest

£3,000

Correspondent: John Coates, Administrator, 24 Dolphin House, Sutton Wharf, Plymouth PL4 OBL (01752 225724; email: johnbcoates@btinternet.com)

CC Number: 306936

Eligibility

Young people from Plymouth schools.

Types of grants

Allowances for five students from Plymouth schools, who have gained exhibitions or scholarships to universities. Two of these grants must be awarded to students at Devonport High School for Boys.

Annual grant total

In 2012/13 the charity had an income of £3,800 and an expenditure of £3,400. Grants totalled about £3,000.

Applications

In writing to the correspondent.

Orphan's Aid Educational Foundation (Plymouth)

£1,400

Correspondent: Vanessa Steer, Clerk and Treasurer, 184 Mannamead Road, Plymouth PL3 5RE (01752 703280; email: v_steer@yahoo.co.uk; website: www.plymouth.gov.uk)

CC Number: 306770

Eligibility

Children who live in the city and county borough of Plymouth who are of school age and from a one-parent family.

Types of grants

One-off grants of up to £250 for the purchase of school uniforms and shoes.

Annual grant total

In 2012 this charity had an income of £2,400 and a total expenditure of £1,400. The 2012 accounts were the latest available at the time of writing (August 2014).

Exclusions

No grants for school fees or maintenance, for people starting work or for mature students.

Applications

On a form available from the correspondent by email or post, including information about income, expenditure and dependents. Applicants are usually interviewed.

Plymouth Charity Trust

£700

Correspondent: Samantha Easton, Trust Manager, Charity Trust Office, 41 Heles Terrace, Prince Rock, Plymouth PL4 9LH (01752 663107; email: info@plymouthcharitytrust.org.uk)

CC Number: 1076364

Eligibility

People living in the city of Plymouth who are under the age of 25 and require financial assistance. In exceptional cases individuals who are otherwise qualified but reside outside the city of Plymouth, or are only temporarily resident there, may be supported at the trustees' discretion.

Types of grants

One-off grants ranging between £50 and £100 are made to people at all levels of education. Support is mainly given for books and equipment/instruments but other needs may also be considered. The trust usually makes the award in the form of vouchers or credit at a relevant shop – payments are not made directly to the applicant.

Annual grant total

In 2012/13 the charity had assets of £2 million and an income of £361,000. Grants to individuals totalled around £4,700, consisting of donations (£1,500), Christmas vouchers (£1,800) and residents' outings subsidy (£1,300). We estimate that about £700 was awarded for educational purposes.

Exclusions

Our research suggests that no grants are given to other charities, to clear debts or for any need that can be met by Social Services.

Applications

Application forms are available from the correspondent. They can be submitted directly by the individual or through a third party, for example, school or educational welfare agency. Applications are normally considered on the first Monday of every month.

Other information

The trust also gives grants to individuals for welfare purposes and provides housing accommodation.

Plympton

The Maudlyn Lands Charity

£2,000

Correspondent: Anthony Peter Golding, Clerk to the Trustees, Blue Haze, Down Road, Tavistock, Devon PL19 9AG (01822 612983)

CC Number: 202577

Eligibility

People in financial need who live in Plympton St Mary and Sparkwell.

Types of grants

One-off grants to help with educational costs.

Annual grant total

In 2012 this charity had both an income and an expenditure of around £8,000. This was the most up to date information available at the time of writing (July 2014). We estimate that the total awarded to individuals for educational purposes was around £2,000.

Applications

In writing to the correspondent. Applications are considered in November.

Other information

This trust also gives grants to individuals for welfare purposes, and to organisations.

Sheepwash

The Bridgeland Charity

£1,000

Correspondent: Mrs D. Tubby, Administrator, Bramble Cottage, East Street, Sheepwash, Beaworthy, North Devon EX21 5NW (01409 231694)

CC Number: 206377

Eligibility

Young people in need who live in the parish of Sheepwash.

Types of grants

One-off grants ranging from £50 to £500. Loans are also made.

Annual grant total

In 2012/13 the charity had an income of £3,500 and a total expenditure of £2,500. We estimate that the total of grants awarded to individuals for educational purposes was approximately £1,000, as the charity also awards grants for social welfare purposes.

Applications

In writing to the correspondent through a third party, such as a social worker or teacher, for consideration throughout the year.

Other information

The charity also supports local schools and community projects.

Sidmouth

Sidmouth Consolidated Charities

£5,000

Correspondent: Ruth Rose, Administrator, 22 Alexandria Road, Sidmouth, Devon EX10 9HB (01395 513079; email: ruth.rose@eclipse.co.uk)

CC Number: 207081

Eligibility

People in need who live in Sidmouth, Sidford, Sidbury or Salcombe Regis.

Types of grants

One-off grants for educational needs, such as computers and books for university students.

Annual grant total

In 2013 the charity had assets of £1.2 million, almost all of which was permanent endowment and unavailable for grant giving. The charity's income was £36,000 and £21,000 was spent in awarding grants to both individuals and organisations for educational and social welfare purposes. We estimate that grants to individuals for educational purposes totalled around £5,000.

Applications

In writing to the correspondent, either directly by the individual, or through a social worker, Citizens Advice or welfare agency. Applications are considered at monthly meetings.

Silverton

The Richards Educational Charity

£39,000 (139 grants)

Correspondent: Geoffrey Knowles, Secretary, Silvertrees, 26 Hederman Close, Silverton, Exeter EX5 4HW (01392 860109; email: jmthomas1951@ yahoo.co.uk)

CC Number: 306787

Eligibility

Young people under 25 who live in the parish of Silverton.

Types of grants

Recurrent grants in the range of £5 to £750 are given to schoolchildren and college students for study/travel abroad, books, equipment/instruments, maintenance/living expenses and excursions. They are also given to undergraduates, vocational students, mature students, and people starting work for fees, study/travel abroad, books, equipment/instruments, maintenance/living expenses and excursions

Annual grant total

In 2012 the charity had assets of £1.2 million and an income of £257,000 (including proceeds from sales of investments). Educational grants to individuals totalled £39,000 and were distributed as follows:

University students	20	£19,000
Schoolchildren	86	£11,800
Career training	14	£5,500
Pre-school	17	£2,200
Further education	2	£600

A further £1,100 was awarded in 3 grants to groups.

At the time of writing (July 2014) this was the most recent financial information available for the charity.

Applications

Application forms are available at the village post office. They should be submitted directly by the individual or a parent. They are considered regularly.

Other information

Information about the charity is made known throughout the parish, particularly through the places of education for children in Silverton.

Silverton Parochial Charity

£9,000

Correspondent: Michelle Valance, Secretary to the Trustees, 9 Davis Close, Silverton, Devon EX5 4DL (01392 860408; email: secretary@ silvertonparochialtrust.co.uk)

CC Number: 201255

Eligibility

People in need in the parish of Silverton only.

Types of grants

One-off grants, with no minimum or maximum limit.

Annual grant total

In 2012/13 the charity had an income of £29,000 and a total expenditure of £37,000. We estimate that grants to individuals for educational purposes totalled around £9,000.

Exclusions

No grants are made towards state or local authority taxes.

Applications

Application forms are available to download from the charity's website. They can also be obtained from the Silverton Post Office or the Community Hall, or prospective beneficiaries can write to the correspondent. Completed forms can be submitted to the correspondent by the individual or by a carer or welfare department, and so on. The trustees will need details of the applicant's financial situation. Applications are considered monthly.

Other information

Grants are also made to people in need who live in the parish and to organisations providing assistance for them. The charity has an informative website.

South Brent

Parish Lands (South Brent Feoffees)

£9,000

Correspondent: J. I. G. Blackler, Administrator, Luscombe Maye, 6 Fore Street, South Brent TQ10 9BQ (01364 646180)

CC Number: 255283

Eligibility

Individuals who live or have lived in the parish of South Brent.

Types of grants

One-off and recurrent grants. Awards are generally in the range of £50 to £300 and can be given for general educational needs. Our research suggests that mainly further education students can be supported.

Annual grant total

In 2013 the charity had assets of around £58,000 and an income of £52,000. A total of £37,000 was given in grants. We estimate that educational grants to individuals totalled around £9,000.

Applications

Application forms can be requested from the correspondent. They can be submitted at any time either directly by the individual or through a third party, such as a family member, social worker, teacher, or an organisation, such as Citizens Advice or a school.

Other information

Grants are also given to organisations and for welfare purposes. The trustee's annual report from 2013 further specifies that one third of the income of the charity is to be applied for upkeep of the parish church, one third for the benefit of deserving people in need living in the parish and one third to form the endowment of the Parish Lands Educational Foundation (to support the education and advancement in life of the parish children).

Sowton

Sowton In Need Charity

£500

Correspondent: Noel Waine, Trustee, Meadowsweet, Sowton, Exeter EX5 2AE (01392 368289; email: wn894@ btinternet.com)

CC Number: 204248

Eligibility

Educational purposes for people in need who live in the parish of Sowton.

Types of grants

One-off grants for any specific educational or personal need. Grants have been given towards tuition fees.

Annual grant total

In 2012 the trust had an income of £1,000 and an expenditure of £2,000. We estimate around £500 was made in grants to individuals for education. The 2012 accounts were the latest on record at the time of writing.

Applications

In writing to the correspondent, to be submitted either directly by the individual or through a social worker,

Citizens Advice, other welfare agency or any third party.

Other information

Grants are also given to organisations and for individuals for welfare purposes.

Taunton Dean

Ayshford Educational Foundation

£500

Correspondent: Peter Walter, Administrator, Eastbrook, Burlescombe, Tiverton EX16 7JT (01823 672545; email: pwalter@talk21.com; website: sites.google.com/site/burlescombeparish/ local-services/ayshford-trust)

CC Number: 306659

Eligibility

Students over 18 resident in the parishes of Burlescombe, Holcombe Rogus and Uffculme.

Types of grants

Grants of up to £300 for books and equipment for further and higher education and apprenticeships.

Annual grant total

In 2013/14 the foundation had both an income and a total expenditure of £1,000. We estimate that around £500 was made in grants to individuals for education.

Applications

In writing to the correspondent before 31 December for consideration by the trustees in January. Awards will be made when receipts are submitted.

Dorset

Cole Anderson Charitable Foundation

£5,000

Correspondent: Martin Davies, Administrator, Rawlins Davy, Rowlands House, Hinton Road, Bournemouth BH1 2EG (01202 558844; email: martin. davies@rawlinsdavy.com)

CC Number: 1107619

Eligibility

Students studying medicine, architecture or music who live in Bournemouth and Poole.

Types of grants

Grants are given according to need.

Annual grant total

This foundation generally gives around £10,000 to individuals for educational and welfare purposes.

Applications

In writing to the correspondent.

Ashley Churchill and Thorner Educational Trust

£5,200

Correspondent: Kay Dawson, Administrator, Clerk's Office, Whetstone's, West Walks, Dorchester, Dorset DT1 1AW (01305 262662; email: info@actet.org.uk; website: www.actet. org.uk)

CC Number: 306229

Eligibility

Children and young people under the age of 25 who live within five miles of the County Hall in Dorchester or in the civil parish of Crossways. Applicants' household income should be below £30,800 a year.

Types of grants

One-off grants, normally of up to £500, are available to schoolchildren and further/higher education students to help with the cost of fees, books, equipment/ instruments, materials, travel expenses, study/travel abroad and other necessities.

Annual grant total

In 2012/13 the trust had an income of £6,300 and a total expenditure of £5,400. We estimate the annual total of grants to individuals to be around £5,200.

Applications

In writing to the correspondent. Applications should outline how the grant will benefit the applicant, include details of parental income and confirmation of course attendance. They can be submitted by the individual directly, through a school/college/ university or through a welfare agency, if applicable. Our research shows that information about applications is also publicised in local schools. The trustees normally meet in September, January and April.

The Beaminster Charities

£2,300

Correspondent: John Groves, Administrator, 24 Church Street, Beaminster, Dorset DT8 3BA (01308 862192; email: jan@hand-n-head. freeserve.co.uk)

CC Number: 200685

Eligibility

Schoolchildren in need who live in Beaminster, Netherbury and Stoke Abbott.

Types of grants

Grants in the range of £50 and £1,000 are made to schoolchildren and college students for study/travel abroad, books and equipment/instruments. About 50 grants are made each year.

Annual grant total

In 2012 this charity had an income of £11,300 and a total expenditure of £9,600. We estimate that the total awarded to individuals for educational purposes was around £2,300. The latest accounts available at the time of writing (July 2014) were for year ending December 2012.

Applications

Applications can be submitted in writing to the correspondent by the individual or through a recognised referral agency, such as a social worker, Citizens Advice or doctor. The trustees meet throughout the year.

Other information

Grants are also made to organisations.

The Bridge Educational Trust (1996)

£57,000 (52 grants)

Correspondent: The Administrator, c/o Piddle Valley School, Piddletrenthide, Dorchester, Dorset DT2 7QL (email: admin@bridgeeducationaltrust.org.uk; website: www.bridgeeducationaltrust.org.uk)

CC Number: 1068720

Eligibility

People in need who were born or are resident in the county of Dorset, primarily from the parishes of Alton Pancras, Piddlehinton, Piddletrenthide and Plush. Normally the candidates should be approaching the end of their school education or be recent school leavers.

Special consideration is given to:

- People who are suffering from hardship or are in difficult family circumstances
- Cases where the education, course or activity would not be possible without assistance
- Younger children with special educational needs
- Older people who are making a late start after interrupted education

Types of grants

One-off and recurrent grants (for a maximum of three years) are offered to people in education at school, college or other educational establishment. Grants are not normally paid to individuals directly. Average grants range from £50 to over £1,000 and are awarded towards fees, study/travel abroad, books, equipment/instruments, excursions and visits, childcare and other expenses.

The trust's website also reminds that 'expeditions or travel groups for young people which are organised for scientific or cultural purposes may be eligible, provided they meet the educational element.'

Annual grant total

In 2012/13 the trust had assets of £1.8 million, an income of £682,000 and made grants totalling £57,000 to 52 individuals for educational purposes. Grants were awarded in the following categories:

Mature students	11	£18,100
University/college students	15	£14,900
Pupils with special educational needs	1	£12,200
Individuals introduced by other support agencies	7	£5,800
Single parents	2	£2,800
Educational visits/expeditions/ courses	5	£2,400
Individuals recommended by the probation service	9	£800
Grants for various short-term problems	2	£400

Exclusions

The trust does not:
- Make loans
- Provide grants for fees which can be covered by student loans
- Give retrospective grants
- Support postgraduate degrees
- Assist people living in temporary student accommodation while studying at an educational establishment in Dorset, unless their permanent home is also in Dorset

Applications

Application forms can be requested from the correspondent or online and should be submitted at least three to four weeks before a trustees' meeting. The meetings are normally held in March, July and November. Applications should include details of the applicant's financial circumstances, estimated costs of the item/activity, outline why a particular course or activity is pursued and explain why the help is required. Applicants who are no longer resident in Dorset are requested to provide documentary evidence of place of birth. New application is required for the second and subsequent years of the course.

Submissions can be made by email to the correspondent or by post at: Piddle Valley First School, Piddletrenthide, Dorset DT2 7QL.

Other information

The trustees' annual report from 2012/13 states that:

> In view of the high number of applications received, the trustees focus their support on residents of the Piddle Valley, and those in the rural shire county of Dorset, rather than the South East Dorset conurbation (Bournemouth, Christchurch, etc.), which they believe is in accord with the benefactor's wishes.

The Cecil Charity

£15,000

Correspondent: Lord Rockley, Trustee, Lytchett Heath House, Lytchett Heath, Poole BH16 6AE (email: charity@lytchettheath.co.uk)

CC Number: 306248

Eligibility

Young people under the age of 25 who live within a ten-mile radius of the parish church at Lytchett Matravers.

Types of grants

Grants, scholarships and bursaries at any secondary school, university, college or other place of education. The provision of clothing, books and equipment, and studying abroad.

Annual grant total

In 2012/13 the charity had an income of £20,000 and an expenditure of £16,000. Grants totalled approximately £15,000.

Applications

An application form is available from the correspondent and can be submitted directly by the individual. Applications are considered in August, November and March.

Clingan's Trust

£30,000

Correspondent: David Richardson, Clerk, Avon House, 4 Bridge Street, Christchurch, Dorset BH23 1DX (01202 484242; email: enquiries@williamsthompson.co.uk; website: www.clinganstrust.co.uk)

CC Number: 307085

Eligibility

People under the age of 25 who are in need, and live and have been educated in the old borough of Christchurch, which includes parts of Bournemouth and the surrounding areas. See the map supplied on the trust's website for the exact areas.

Types of grants

One-off grants between £100 and £1,000 for any educational need for people under 25. Preference is given to schoolchildren with serious family difficulties where the child has to be educated away from home and people with special educational needs.

Annual grant total
In 2012 the trust had an income of £61,000 and a total expenditure of £49,000. At the time of writing, the trust's accounts for the year were not available to view on its Charity Commission record and so a breakdown of grants was not available. We estimate that educational grants to individuals totalled £30,000.

At the time of writing (July 2014) this was the most recent financial information available for the trust.

Exclusions
The trust is normally unable to consider applicants who have applied for a grant within six weeks of the next meeting.

Applications
On a form available from the correspondent or to download from the trust's website. Applications can be made directly by the individual, unless they are under the age of 14. They are subject to deadlines, which are listed on the website, and are considered at meetings, usually held quarterly.

Other information
Funding is also occasionally awarded to organisations.

The Dixon Galpin Scholarships

£400

Correspondent: Andrea Houghton, Administrator, Dorset County Council, County Hall, Colliton Park, Dorchester, Dorset DT1 1XJ (01305 224381; email: m.granlund@dorsetcc.gov.uk)

CC Number: 306325

Eligibility
People who were born in Dorset or who have lived in the county for at least 12 months prior to the application.

Types of grants
Average grants range from £100 to £150. The charity provides scholarships, bursaries, grants or maintenance allowances to assist students attending full or part-time courses at universities or other establishments of further education. The awards are made to undertake a vacation study, to travel overseas for educational purposes approved by the college authorities or to buy books, instruments or equipment. Support is also given to people attending summer schools organised by a university and people attending short courses or weekend schools organised by the Southern and Western Districts of

the Workers' Education Association (or other similar body).

Annual grant total
In 2012/13 the charity had an income of £3,000 and an expenditure of £500. We have estimated the annual total of grants to be around £400. Our research shows that annual total of grants normally fluctuates between £2,000 and £3,000.

Exclusions
People from the boroughs of Bournemouth and Poole are excluded form eligibility criteria.

Applications
Application forms are available upon request from the correspondent. They are considered in February, May and October and must include details of the student's financial circumstances, information about the course/ expedition/vacation study, including costs involved and anticipated benefits the course will provide.

Other information
Dorset County Council also administers The Marras Prize – each year grants totalling up to £1,000 are given to people aged 16 to 19 who are assessed to be the most deserving from the point of behaviour, honesty and truthfulness. Two smaller trusts are also administered, each making grants totalling less than £500 a year.

Gordon Charitable Trust

£5,000

Correspondent: Gerry Aiken, Trustee, 45 Dunkeld Road, Bournemouth BH3 7EW (01202 768337; email: gerry_aitken@hotmail.com)

CC Number: 200668

Eligibility
Young people between the ages of 15 and 25 living in the county of Dorset who are in further/higher education or undertaking apprenticeships. Preference is given to individuals who have lived, or whose parents have lived, in the borough council areas of Bournemouth, Poole and Christchurch.

Types of grants
The trust provides scholarships, bursaries and other financial help 'to a very limited extent.' Grants are one-off or recurrent for three or four years (depending on the course) of up to £1,000 per year per individual. Support is towards the cost of books, clothing, equipment/instruments, and maintenance/living expenses. People starting work and music/arts students are also supported.

Annual grant total
In 2012/13 the trust had an income of £1,400 and an expenditure of £5,100. We estimate the annual total of grants to be around the same figure.

Applications
In writing to the correspondent.

Other information
Our research indicates that the trust is reliant upon donations from other sources, therefore its income is limited and variable.

Lockyer's Charity Trust

£1,500

Correspondent: Richard Tattershall, Administrator, 89 Redwood Road, Upton, Poole BH16 5QG (01202 632505)

CC Number: 306246

Eligibility
People who live in Lytchett Minster, Upton and Organford, aged up to 25. Applicants must have lived in the parish for two years before applying and it must be their main residence.

Types of grants
Help towards books, equipment and educational outings in the UK for students in further or higher education, apprentices or people starting work.

Annual grant total
This trust awards around £1,500 a year to individuals for educational purposes.

Applications
On a form available from the correspondent, submitted directly by the individual or by a parent or guardian. Applications are considered in February, June and November and should be submitted in the preceding month.

Francis Ramage Prize Trust

£0

Correspondent: Andrea Houghton, Administrator, Dorset County Council, County Hall, Colliton Park, Dorchester, Dorset DT1 1XJ (01305 224381; email: m.granlund@dorsetcc.gov.uk)

CC Number: 1085755

Eligibility
Young people up to the age of 19 who live in the administrative area of Dorset and attend a school maintained by Dorset Local Authority. Priority is given to children from low income families, then children with special educational needs.

Types of grants

One-off and recurrent grants according to need for study or travel abroad, study or experience in the UK, travel, training, coaching, rehearsals, books, equipment/tools, clothing and uniforms.

Annual grant total

In 2013/14 the trust had an income of £180 and had no expenditure.

Applications

On a form available from the correspondent.

The William Williams Charity

£98,000

Correspondent: Ian Winsor, Administrator, Stafford House, 10 Prince of Wales Road, Dorchester, Dorset DT1 1PW (01305 264573; email: enquires@williamwilliams.org.uk; website: www.williamwilliams.org.uk)

CC Number: 202188

Eligibility

People in need who live in the ancient parishes of Blandford, Shaftesbury or Sturminster Newton.

Types of grants

One-off grants of £500 to £1,000 for those embarking on higher education or recognised training schemes or apprenticeships.

Annual grant total

In 2013 the charity had £7.9 million and an income of £307,000. Grants to 219 individuals totalled £140,000 with £42,000 given for welfare and £98,000 for education.

Exclusions

Applicants' parental/household income cannot exceed £35,000 net per annum.

Applications

On a form available from the correspondent or the charity's website along with guidelines. Applications are considered at least four times a year.

Other information

Grants totalling £56,000 were made to 13 organisations.

Blandford

Blandford Forum Charities

£250

Correspondent: Irene Prior, Administrator, Barnes Homes, Salisbury Road, Blandford Forum, Dorset DT11 7HU (01258 451810)

CC Number: 230853

Eligibility

People under the age of 25 who are living, or who have been educated for at least two years, in the borough of Blandford Forum.

Types of grants

(i) Cash grants, to a usual maximum of about £400, for school pupils to help with books, equipment, clothing or travel.

(ii) Grants, to a usual maximum of about £400, to help with school, college or university fees or to supplement existing grants.

(iii) Help towards the cost of education, training, apprenticeships, clothing or equipment for those starting work.

Annual grant total

In 2012/13 the Apprenticing and Education Foundation Charity had assets of £18,600, an income of £10,000 and made grants totalling £250. The total grants amount has been declining in recent years.

Applications

In writing to the correspondent.

Other information

The Blandford Forum Charities include the Relief-in-Need fund, the Blandford Forum Almshouse Charity, Blandford Forum Apprenticing and Educational Foundation Charity and George Ryves Apprenticing Charity.

T.E.D. George Fund – The Blandford Children Fund

£0

Correspondent: The Administrator, Blandford Forum Almshouse Charity, Barnes Homes, Salisbury Road, Blandford Forum, Dorset DT11 7HU (01258 451810; email: clerkbfc@ googlemail.com)

CC Number: 230853–6

Eligibility

Children who were under the age of 12 on 1 January in the year of application and are resident in the borough of Blandford Forum.

Types of grants

Small, one-off or recurrent grants towards the cost of books, educational trips, also clothing, school uniforms and other necessities.

Annual grant total

In 2012/13 the fund had assets of £43,000 and an income of £700. No grants were made during the year. Over the past few years expenditure has fluctuated between £75 and £5,000.

Note: the grants are only made from the investment income, not the total assets.

Applications

Application forms can be requested in writing to the correspondent. Applications are usually considered in January and should include details of parents' occupation, the net family income, purposes for which the grant will be used and a birth certificate. During the consideration process the trustees may consult the Mayor of Blandford.

The fund also reminds that the trustees may need to visit the applicant's home as a part of the application process.

Other information

This fund is linked to Blandford Forum Charities (registered charity number 230853).

The trustees emphasize the age criterion.

Charmouth

The Almshouse Charity

£900

Correspondent: Anthea Gillings, Administrator, Swansmead, Riverway, Charmouth, Bridport, Dorset DT6 6LS (01297 560465)

CC Number: 201885

Eligibility

People in further and higher education who, or whose immediate family, live in the parish of Charmouth.

Types of grants

One-off and recurrent grants, generally of £25 to £250 towards school uniforms, overseas voluntary/education work and university books.

Annual grant total

In 2013 the trust had an income of £3,800 and a total expenditure of £3,600.

Applications

In writing to the correspondent or other trustees. Applications can be submitted directly by the individual or through a third party, such as a rector, doctor or trustee. They are usually considered at quarterly periods; emergencies can be considered at other times. Applications should include details of the purpose of the grant, the total costs involved, and an official letter or programme/itinerary.

Other information

Grants are also given to individuals for relief-in-need purposes and to youth clubs for specific purposes.

Corfe Castle

Corfe Castle Charities

£31,000 (20 grants)

Correspondent: Jenny Wilson, Clerk to the Trustees, The Spinney, Springbrook Close, Corfe Castle, Wareham, Dorset BH20 5HS (01929 480873)

CC Number: 1055846

Eligibility
People in need who live in the parish of Corfe Castle.

Types of grants
One-off grants or interest free loans to students in further or higher education. In recent years grants have been given for books, fees, maintenance/living expenses, educational outings in the UK and study or travel overseas. Schoolchildren have also received one-off grants for uniforms or other school clothing.

Annual grant total
In 2012/13 the charity had assets of £3.2 million and an income of £241,000. There were 20 educational grants made to individuals totalling almost £31,000.

Applications
On a form available from the correspondent, to be submitted directly by the individual. The trustees meet monthly, but emergency requests are dealt with as they arise.

Other information
Grants are also made to organisations.

Dorchester

Dorchester Relief-in-Need Charity

£700

Correspondent: Robert Potter, Trustee, 8 Mithras Close, Dorchester, Dorset DT1 2RF (01305 262041; email: robjoy1@talktalk.net)

CC Number: 286570

Eligibility
People in need who live in the ecclesiastical parish of Dorchester.

Types of grants
One-off grants to those in need. Recent grants have been given for school uniforms and excursions, and to people starting work for books and equipment.

Annual grant total
In 2013/14 this charity had an income of £3,000 and a total expenditure of £1,700. We estimate that grants to individuals for educational purposes totalled around

£700 and for social welfare purposes £1,000.

Applications
Application forms are available from the correspondent and can be submitted through a school/teacher, social worker, health visitor, Citizens Advice or social services.

Other information
This charity also gives grants for relief-in-need purposes.

Litton Cheney

The Litton Cheney Relief-in-Need Trust

£2,200

Correspondent: B. Prentice, Administrator, Steddings, Chalk Pit Lane, Litton Cheney, Dorchester DT2 9AN (01308 482535; email: bpprentice@gmail.com)

CC Number: 231388

Eligibility
University students and people starting work who live in the parish of Litton Cheney.

Types of grants
Grants of £100 are made each year for 16-year-olds who are about to start a career and to 18-year-olds who are about to start at university. Grants are towards books and equipment.

Annual grant total
In 2013 the trust had an income of £5,800 and an expenditure of £4,600. Grants totalled £4,400 which was split between educational and welfare purposes.

Exclusions
No grants for people taking A-levels, or for schoolchildren.

Applications
In writing to the correspondent.

Poole

The Poole Children's Fund

£400

Correspondent: Julia Palmer, Administrator, 52 Hennings Park Road, Poole BH15 3QX (01202 261921)

CC Number: 277300

Eligibility
Children up to 18 who are disadvantaged, disabled or otherwise in need and live in the borough of Poole.

Types of grants
Help towards the cost of holidays and other recreational and educational facilities, including grants for educational outings for schoolchildren and for study or travel abroad for students in further and higher education. Grants can be in the range of £10 to £80 and are usually one-off.

Preference for children with behavioural and social difficulties who have limited opportunities for leisure and recreational activities of a positive nature, for schoolchildren with serious family difficulties so the child has to be educated away from home, and for people with special educational needs.

Annual grant total
Over the past five years, this charity's income has been decreasing and in 2012 (the latest information available at the time of writing – August 2014) had dropped to just £15. Total expenditure was £860 and grants were awarded to individuals for both educational and social welfare purposes.

Applications
On a form available from the correspondent completed by a third party such as a social worker, health visitor, minister or teacher. Applications are considered throughout the year. They should include details of family structure including: ages; reason for application; family income and any other sources of funding which have been tried; what agencies (if any) are involved in helping the family; and any statutory orders (for example, care orders) relating to the child or their family members.

Other information
The charity currently has only one trustee.

Weymouth and Portland

The Sir Samuel Mico Trust

£35,000

Correspondent: Howard Jones, Administrator, Edwards and Keeping Unity Chambers, 34 High East Street, Dorchester, Dorset DT1 1HA (01305 251333; email: howardjones@ edwardsandkeeping.co.uk; website: www. weymouthtowncharities.org.uk)

CC Number: 202629

Eligibility
Young people between the ages of 16 and 24 who reside in the borough of Weymouth and Portland and have been born in the borough, or have resided

there for at least ten years. The trust particularly welcomes applications for those on apprenticeships and those wishing to take up professional careers.

Types of grants

One-off and recurrent grants are made to students in further or higher education or those undertaking apprenticeships. Grants are given towards educational course fees, living costs for those on educational courses, equipment, books and assisted places on the Tall Ships Youth Trust ships.

Annual grant total

In 2012 the trust had assets of £838,000 and an income of £39,000. It made grants to individuals totalling almost £35,000. The 2012 accounts were the latest available at the time of writing (August 2014).

Applications

On a form available to download from the trust's website or from the correspondent. Applicants must be able to show that they are in difficult financial circumstances and have a desire to extend their education.

Gloucester-shire

Barnwood House Trust

£125,000 (about 350 grants)

Correspondent: Gail Rodway, Grants Manager, Ullenwood Manor Farm, Ullenwood, Cheltenham, Gloucestershire GL53 9QT (01452 611292; fax: 01452 634011; email: gail.rodway@ barnwoodtrust.org; website: www. barnwoodtrustorg)

CC Number: 218401

Eligibility

People in need over the age of 18 who live in Gloucestershire, have a long-term mental or physical disability that affects their quality of life, are on a low income and have little or no savings. Applicants are expected to seek statutory support first.

Types of grants

Opportunities Fund offers one-off grants ranging from £200 to £2,000 (average award of £700) to provide individuals with the opportunity to attempt something new that will enable them to move on to employment, volunteering or give them the ability to help others. It may also be used to fund training or equipment that will enhance their ability to pursue a current hobby. Grants can be given for training courses, purchase of equipment for sports or other hobbies,

towards books, exam fees, educational necessities, specialist work clothing and so on.

Annual grant total

In 2013 the trust had an income of £3.5 million and a total expenditure of £2.6 million. Each year around 700 individuals are supported totalling over £250,000. We estimate that opportunities grants total about £125,000.

Applications

Application forms can be downloaded from the trust's website or requested from the correspondent. All applications should be made through, or endorsed by, a social or healthcare professional (an occupational therapist, social worker, health visitor, district nurse or community psychiatric nurse). Applications are considered at quarterly meetings, normally in March, June, September and December.

Other information

Small grants are made to local organisations with similar aims. The trust is also engaged in providing housing accommodation.

The Wellbeing Fund of the trust offers support to enable individuals to live independently.

Lumb's Educational Foundation

£15,900

Correspondent: Neville Capper, Trustee, 54 Collum End Rise, Leckhampton, Cheltenham GL53 0PB (01242 515673; email: lumbsfoundation@virginmedia. com)

CC Number: 311683

Eligibility

People between the ages of 16 and 25 who live in the borough of Cheltenham and the surrounding parishes. Students from Gloucestershire, especially studying arts and music, can also be considered.

Types of grants

One-off grants in the range of £50–£1,000 towards general education and training. Support can be given for the course fees, books, clothing, equipment/instruments and educational visits in the UK or study/travel abroad. People starting work can be helped with the cost of uniforms/outfits, books and equipment/instruments. Gap-year and similar official travel projects are supported.

Annual grant total

At the time of writing (July 2014) the latest financial information available was from 2012. In 2012 the foundation had an income of £14,700 and an

expenditure of £16,100. We estimate the annual total of grants to individuals to be around £15,900.

Exclusions

People who are permanently resident outside the area of benefit are ineligible. Grants are not made towards trips that are not of educational nature. Living expenses or school fees are not supported.

Applications

Application forms can be requested from the correspondent. Once completed they should be returned with a supporting letter, including details of income, expenditure, parents' financial situation and the purpose of the grant. The trustees usually meet in February, April, July, September and November. Candidates are interviewed. Each application is assessed according to need and funds available at the time.

Charlton Kings

Higgs and Cooper's Educational Charity

£18,000

Correspondent: Martin Fry, Administrator, 7 Branch Hill Rise, Charlton Kings, Cheltenham GL53 9HN (01242 239903; email: martyn.fry@dsl. pipex.com)

CC Number: 311570

Eligibility

People under the age of 25 who were born or live in the former Charlton Kings civil parish. Preference is given to people from single parent families.

Types of grants

Grants are awarded to people in secondary education, further/higher education students and people starting work/entering a trade. Support is mainly given towards educational outings, study/travel overseas, but also for general educational expenditure, including books, equipment/instruments, fees and so on. Grants can also be given for postgraduate degrees and training.

Annual grant total

In 2012/13 the charity had an income of £17,500 and an expenditure of £19,100. We estimate that the annual total of grants to individuals was around £18,000. Normally around 30 individuals are awarded each year.

Exclusions

Trips beyond Europe are not likely to be supported.

Applications

Application forms can be requested from the correspondent. They can be submitted directly by the individual and are considered six times a year. Our research suggests that the charity publicises its grants locally in order to increase awareness, as at times there has been a lack of applications.

Other information

The charity also supports local schools, youth clubs and other voluntary organisations broadly connected with the education or recreational pursuits of young people in the area of benefit.

Cirencester

John Edmonds' Charity

£7,700 (Around 10 grants)

Correspondent: Richard Mullings, Administrator, 7 Dollar Street, Cirencester, Gloucestershire GL7 2AS (01285 650000)

CC Number: 311495

Eligibility

People under the age of 25 who were born in Cirencester. Our research indicates that people who currently live or were educated in Cirencester are also eligible for support.

Types of grants

Help is given to people entering a trade/starting work. Assistance is towards the cost of education, training or apprenticeships, including fees, equipment/tools, clothing/outfits, travel costs or maintenance expenses. Grants could be made to schoolchildren and students as well. Awards can range from £100 to £500 and are one-off.

Annual grant total

The latest financial information available at the time of writing (July 2014) was from 2012. In 2012 the charity had an income of £7,800 and an expenditure of £7,900. We estimate that around £7,700 was awarded in grants to individuals. Our research suggests that about ten awards are made each year.

Applications

Application forms can be requested from the correspondent.

Highnam

William Andrews Foundation

£1,300

Correspondent: Jean Rosam, Administrator, 66 Maidenhall, Highnam, Gloucester GL2 8DL (01452 416946; email: jrosam@highnambband.co.uk)

CC Number: 311522

Eligibility

People in need aged under 25 years who live in the parish of Highnam.

Types of grants

One-off and recurrent grants ranging from £50 to £200 for schoolchildren, students and young people starting work. Help is specifically given towards school uniforms, textbooks, equipment, educational visits in the UK, travel overseas and fees.

Annual grant total

In 2013 the income of this charity was £1,000 and its total expenditure was over £1,300. Grants awarded to individuals for educational purposes totalled around £1,300.

Applications

In writing to the correspondent, directly by the individual or their parent, in time to be considered at the annual general meeting in July. Applications should include the reason for the request, place of residence, details of education, the age of the applicant and general financial information (for example, low income).

Stroud

The Stroud and Rodborough Educational Charity

£20,000

Correspondent: Shani Baker, Clerk to the Trustees, 14 Green Close, Uley, Dursley, Gloucestershire GL11 5TH (01453 860379; email: info@stroudrodboroughed.org; website: www.stroudrodboroughec.org)

CC Number: 309614

Eligibility

Children and young people in need who are under the age of 25 and resident in the parishes comprising the Stroud rural district (Bisley-with-Lypiatt, Chalford, Cranham, Horsley, Kings Stanley, Leonard Stanley, Minchinhampton, Miserden, Oakridge, Painswick, Pitchcombe, Randwick, Rodborough, Stonehouse, Thrupp, Whiteshill, Woodchester and Nailsworth urban district).

Types of grants

Grants can be given towards general educational needs, including study/travel overseas, educational activities, equipment/instruments, clothing, books, music and drama lessons, course related necessities and so on. Primary schoolchildren have also been assisted to undertake educational and residential school trips. Grants range from £10 to £500.

Annual grant total

In 2012/13 the charity had assets of around £494,000 and an income of £104,000. A total of £51,000 was spent on charitable activities. We estimate that around £20,000 was given to individuals in educational grants. Around £1,000 was awarded in educational prizes.

Exclusions

Support is not given in the cases where funding should be provided by the local authority.

Applications

Application forms are available on the charity's website or from the correspondent. The trustees meet four times a year, normally at the end of January, April, July and October. Applications should provide a reference from a teacher and be submitted in advance of the meetings.

Other information

The priority of the charity is to assists Marling School, Stroud High School and Archway School, where support is not already provided by the local authority. The charity also gives grants to local charitable organisations working for the benefit of young people and administers a number of prize funds tenable at the local schools.

Weston-sub-Edge

Weston-sub-Edge Educational Charity

£13,000

Correspondent: Rachel Hurley, Administrator, Longclose Cottage, Weston-sub-Edge, Chipping Campden, Gloucestershire GL55 6QX (01386 841808; email: cjhurley@wseg.wanadoo.co.uk; website: www.westonsubedge.com/?page_id=143)

CC Number: 297226

Eligibility

People under the age of 25 who or whose parents live in Weston-sub-Edge, or who have at any time attended (or whose parents have attended) Weston-sub-Edge Church of England Primary School.

Types of grants

Grants range from £10 to £500 and can be awarded to eligible candidates at any stage of education (including people starting work) for books, equipment/ instruments, fees, educational outings or study/travel abroad. Further/higher education students can be helped with maintenance/living expenses and, in cases of special financial need, schoolchildren can be assisted with the costs of uniforms and other school clothing.

Previously grants have been given for nursery fees, music, dance, drama and sports lessons, after school clubs and trips, residential trips, Brownies/Clubs, extra tuition and grants to university students.

Annual grant total

In 2012/13 the charity had an income of £10,000 and an expenditure of £13,300. We estimate the annual total of grants to individuals to be around £13,000.

Applications

Application forms can be requested from the correspondent and should include the details, duration and purpose of the course. Applications should be submitted by individuals directly if they are over 16, or by their parent/guardian otherwise. Individuals are invited to apply either during or just before the term in which the course/activity takes place and at least ten days prior to the meetings, which are held in January, March, May, July, September and November.

Somerset

Huish's Exhibition Foundation

£1,900

Correspondent: Kate James, Administrator, Porter Dodson Solicitors, Quad 2000, Blackbrook Park Avenue, Taunton TA1 2PX (01823 625800; email: kate.james@porterdodson.co.uk)

CC Number: 310245

Eligibility

Pupils leaving one of the following schools in the county of Somerset: King's College, Taunton; Queen's College, Taunton; Richard Huish College, Taunton; Taunton School, Taunton; Wellington School, Wellington. Applicants should normally have a GCSE or A-level in Religious Studies.

Types of grants

Grants of about £300 a year are available to students entering university education. The grants are made for the duration of the university course.

Annual grant total

In 2013 the foundation had an income of £3,800 and an expenditure of £2,100. We estimate that individual grants totalled around £1,900, which is a bit lower than the expenditure in previous years.

Applications

Applications should be made through the applicant's school.

The Ilminster Educational Foundation

£15,100 (44 grants)

Correspondent: Edward Wells, Administrator, 20 Station Road, Ilminster, Somerset TA19 9BD (01460 53029)

CC Number: 310265

Eligibility

People under the age of 25 who live or have attended an educational institution for at least two years in the parish of Ilminster.

Types of grants

Grants of around £200–400 are available to schoolchildren for educational outings in the UK/overseas and to students at Ilminster based universities or colleges for general educational expenses.

Annual grant total

In 2012/13 the foundation had assets of £161,000 and an income of £48,000. A total of £15,100 was awarded in grants to 44 students.

Exclusions

According to our research, grants are not made for A-level courses.

Applications

In writing to the correspondent. Our research suggests that applications are normally considered in October and November. They should be submitted in advance of those dates.

Other information

The foundation also makes grants to five local schools, special grants to individuals and an annual grant for the general benefit of the parish of Ilminster.

Keyford Educational Foundation

£700

Correspondent: J. Pegg, Administrator, The Blue House, The Bridge, Frome, Somerset BA11 1AP (01373 455338; email: bhouse1ap@btinternet.com)

CC Number: 309989

Eligibility

Young people aged up to 25 who live in the parishes of Frome or Selwood.

Types of grants

One-off grants from £50 to £100. Schoolchildren and students in further and higher education can be helped with uniforms/other school clothing, books, equipment/instruments, fees, educational outings in the UK and study or travel abroad.

Annual grant total

In 2012 the foundation had an income of £2,700 and an expenditure of £1,900. Grants of around £700 are made to individuals annually. Half of the yearly income is designated to Frome College.

Accounts were not available at the time of writing (August 2014).

Applications

On a form available from the correspondent, to be submitted either directly by the individual, through the individual's school, college or educational welfare agency or through another appropriate third party, such as their parent/guardian, social worker or Citizens Advice. The foundation requires a recommendation from the teacher or tutor and a telephone or personal interview. Applications are considered every other month, from January onwards.

Other information

This trust incorporates the Ancient Blue Coat Foundation.

John Nowes Exhibition Foundation

£2,000

Correspondent: Philip Crowther, Administrator, Battens Solicitors, Mansion House, 54–58 Princes Street, Yeovil, Somerset BA20 1EP (email: p. crowther@battens.co.uk)

CC Number: 309984

Eligibility

Children and young people between the ages of 16 and 25 living in the Yeovil parishes (including Yeovil Without) who have a household income of less than £30,000 per annum.

Types of grants

Grants ranging from £150 to £500. The foundation provides scholarships, bursaries, maintenance allowances and grants to support schoolchildren, further and higher education students and people starting work or entering a trade/profession. Financial assistance is also available to travel/study abroad in pursuance of education, to study music or other arts. The foundation can support people in primary, secondary and further education in provision of facilities for recreation, social and physical training, including coaching in athletics, sports and games, where help is not provided by the local authorities.

Annual grant total

In 2012/13 the foundation had an income of £5,600 and an expenditure of £2,200. We estimate that the annual total of grants was about £2,000.

Applications

Application forms can be requested from the correspondent and should be submitted by 31 August each year.

Prowde's Educational Foundation

See entry on page 167

Blackford

Blackford Educational Charity

£2,500

Correspondent: Simon Kraeter, Trustee, Hugh Sexey Middle School, Blackford, Wedmore, Somerset BS28 4ND (01934 710041)

CC Number: 277339

Eligibility

Children and young people who live in the parish of Blackford. Our research suggests that primary and secondary schoolchildren and higher/further education students can be supported.

Types of grants

Small grants are available for general educational expenses, including books, equipment/instruments and educational outings/visits.

Annual grant total

In 2012/13 the charity had both an income and an expenditure of about £5,000. We estimate the annual total of grants to individuals to be around £2,500.

Applications

Application forms can be requested from the correspondent. Our research shows that applications can be submitted directly by the individual in January, May or September for consideration in the following month and must be accompanied by receipts for the expenses incurred.

Other information

The charity also assists primary and secondary schools in the parish of Blackford where these are not already supported by the local authority.

Draycott

Card Educational Foundation

£700

Correspondent: Helen Dance, Clerk and Treasurer, Leighurst, The Street, Draycott, Cheddar, Somerset BS27 3TH (01934 742811)

CC Number: 309976

Eligibility

People in need in the hamlet of Draycott, aged between 4 and 30 years.

Types of grants

Grants range from £50 to £200 and can be for books, equipment/instruments, fees and study or travel abroad. Other grants can be made to: schoolchildren for uniforms or other school clothing, educational outings in the UK and student exchanges; people starting work for uniforms, maintenance/living expenses and educational outings in the UK; further and higher education students for maintenance/living expenses; and mature students and postgraduates for maintenance/living expenses, educational outings in the UK and student exchanges.

Annual grant total

In 2012/13 the charity had an income of £1,500 and a total expenditure of £1,400. We estimate that grants awarded to individuals totalled around £700.

Exclusions

No grants towards ski trips or school transport.

Applications

In writing to the correspondent including a clear statement of residence in the hamlet. Applications can be submitted either directly by the individual or through a third party such as a parent or teacher. They are considered at the end of November and should be submitted at least two weeks before.

Other information

Grants are also made to organisations.

Evercreech

Arthur Allen Educational Trust

£5,600

Correspondent: Allison Dowding, Trustee, Meadow's Edge, High Street, Stoney Stratton, Shepton Mallet, Somerset BA4 6DY (01749 831077; email: adowding.epc@virgin.net)

CC Number: 310256

Eligibility

Further and higher education students between the ages of 16 and 25 who were born or live in the parish of Evercreech.

Types of grants

One-off and recurrent grants in the range of £50–£2,000 are available to students attending college, university or sixth form college, also vocational students or people starting work. Support is given towards travel expenses, books, equipment/instruments, study/travel abroad, clothing, maintenance/living expenses and fees.

Annual grant total

In 2013 the trust had an income of £5,900 and an expenditure of £5,800. We estimate that the annual total of grants to individuals was around £5,600.

Applications

Application forms can be either downloaded from the Evercreech village and district website (www.evercreech.org.uk/arthur-allen-education-trust), requested from the correspondent, or collected from the Evercreech Pharmacy. The closing date for applications is 1 October each year and the awards are made in late October/early November. Two references are required.

Ilchester

Ilchester Relief-in-Need and Educational Charity (IRINEC)

£15,700

Correspondent: Kaye Elston, Clerk, 15 Chilton Grove, Yeovil, Somerset BA21 4AN (01935 421208; website: www.ilchesterparishcouncil.gov.uk/Core/IlchesterPC/Pages/IRINEC_3.aspx)

CC Number: 235578

Eligibility

Students in financial need who live in the parish of Ilchester only.

Types of grants

One-off grants to university students for fees and maintenance/living expenses, also travel, books and field trips. College students can be supported towards the cost of travel.

Annual grant total

At the time of writing (August 2014) the latest financial information available was from 2012. In 2012 the charity had assets of £382,000 (mainly as a permanent endowment) and an income of £35,000. Educational grants totalled £15,700.

Exclusions

Grants are not available where support should be received from the statutory sources.

Applications

Application forms can be requested from the correspondent. They should be submitted directly by the individual. Additional information can be obtained from the correspondent. The trustees consider grants at their monthly meetings. Evidence of financial need will be required.

Other information

Grants are also given for relief-in-need purposes. Organisations may be supported.

Rimpton

The Rimpton Relief-in-Need Charities

£700

Correspondent: John Spencer, Trustee, Field End House, Home Farm Lane, Rimpton, Yeovil, Somerset BA22 8AS (01935 850530)

CC Number: 239816

Eligibility

People who live in the parish of Rimpton only.

Types of grants

One-off or recurrent grants according to need. Recent grants have been made to cover student expenses, for exchange visits and to students representing their country at sport.

Annual grant total

Grants to individuals for educational purposes usually total about £700 each year. Grants for welfare are also made.

Applications

On a form available from the correspondent, to be submitted either by the individual, a family member, or through an appropriate third party.

Taunton Deane

Taunton Heritage Trust

£14,400 (88 grants)

Correspondent: Karen White, Clerk to the Trustees, Huish Homes, Magdalene Street, Taunton, Somerset TA1 1SG (01823 335348 (Mon-Fri, 9am-12pm); email: tauntonheritagetrust@btconnect. com; website: www.tauntonheritagetrust. org.uk)

CC Number: 202120

Eligibility

People living in the borough of Taunton Deane that are of school age (generally up to the age of 16). Our research suggests that requests from colleges of further education on behalf of individuals may also be considered depending on circumstances and need.

Types of grants

Grants to schoolchildren are made according to need, towards school uniforms, educational visits and, in exceptional circumstances, computers.

Annual grant total

In 2013 the trust had assets of £5.5 million and an income of £546,000. A total of £14,400 was awarded in 88 educational grants.

Exclusions

Retrospective funding or replacement of statutory support (supplementary grants may be available)is not given. The trust cannot provide support towards school trips, school bags, stationery, course fees, course books or further/higher education.

Applications

Application forms are available on the trust's website or can be requested from the correspondent but must be completed by a recognised referral agency (such as schools, educational welfare agency, social services or Citizens Advice) on behalf of the candidate. They should be typed (not handwritten) and posted in four copies. Grants are considered on the first Wednesday of each month and all applications should be received by Friday preceding that date. Specific items must be itemised and costed (see further guidelines on the website).

Other information

The prime role of the charity is to provide sheltered accommodation for people over the age of 60. Grants are also made for welfare purposes and to organisations.

Wiltshire

William (Doc) Couch Trust Fund

£0

Correspondent: Rosemary MacDonald, Administrator, The Community Foundation for Wiltshire and Swindon, Ground Floor, Sandcliffe House, 21 Northgate Street, Devizes, Wiltshire SN10 1JX (01380 729284; email: info@ wscf.org.uk; website: www.wscf.org.uk/ grants-communityfoundationgrant-williamdoccouchfund.asp)

CC Number: 1123126–1

Eligibility

Children and young people under the age of 25 who live in Wiltshire and have a disability or are otherwise disadvantaged.

Types of grants

Grants to assist children and young people pursuing further/higher education towards general educational costs, including equipment, training and educational activities.

Annual grant total

In 2012/13 the fund had assets of £4.3 million. No individual grants were made.

Applications

The fund's website notes that 'in line with the original trust deed, some funds will also be used to make grants to individual disadvantaged children and young people through the Community Foundation for Wiltshire & Swindon other grant programmes.' Individuals should contact the correspondent to check their eligibility. Alternatively, the website offers details of other funds administered by the Community Foundation.

Other information

The funds of the charity have been transferred and are now administered by the Community Foundation for Wiltshire and Swindon. The fund's website notes that the transfer 'allowed to align the fund with the Community Foundation's objectives which concentrate on addressing disadvantage through the funding of voluntary organisations.' Constituted voluntary organisations, registered charities and other social enterprises, working with children and young people up to the age of 24 who live in Wiltshire and have disabilities or other needs, can be given grants of up to £5,000 (a total of £29,000 in 2012/13).

SOUTH WEST – WILTSHIRE

Colonel William Llewellyn Palmer Educational Charity

£500 (1 grant)

Correspondent: The Administrator, Wiltshire Council, Department of Resources, County Hall, Trowbridge, Wiltshire BA14 8JN (01225 718584)

CC Number: 1015681

Eligibility

Children and young people under the age of 25 who live or attend/have attended schools maintained by the local authority in Bradford-on-Avon.

Types of grants

One-off grants are available towards general educational expenses, such as purchase of equipment/instruments, books, uniforms/clothing, also for recreational projects, holiday schemes and music lessons.

Annual grant total

In 2012/13 the charity had assets of £1.6 million and an income of £56,000. A total of £15,000 was awarded in educational grants to individuals and organisations, of which £500 grant was made to one individual and £10,000 to ten group applications.

Applications

Our research suggests that applications should not be made directly to the correspondent. Individual applications have to be made on behalf of the candidate by their school as a part of a block application of all pupils who wish to apply. Such block applications should be submitted to the correspondent normally by October for consideration at a meeting in November. Grants are then distributed via the school.

Other information

Grants are also made to local schools. A total of £4,500 was awarded to three schools in 2012/13.

The Rose Charity

£4,800

Correspondent: Charles Goodbody, Trustee, 94 East Street, Warminster, Wiltshire BA12 9BG (01985 214444; email: cgoodbody@mulaw.co.uk)

CC Number: 900590

Eligibility

Schoolchildren in need who live in Warminster and the surrounding villages.

Types of grants

One-off grants, ranging from £50 to £500, towards general educational costs, such as books, necessities, uniforms and other clothing, educational outings and so forth. According to our research, music lessons can also be supported.

Annual grant total

In 2012/13 the charity had an income of £4,100 and an expenditure of £5,000. We estimate the annual total of grants to be around £4,800 but the amount awarded varies each year.

Applications

In writing to the correspondent. Our research suggests that applications are considered throughout the year and should be supported by the social services/welfare agency or school/college.

Salisbury City Educational and Apprenticing Charity

£3,600

Correspondent: The Clerk to the Trustees, Trinity Hospital, Trinity Street, Salisbury, Wiltshire SP1 2BD (01722 325640; email: clerk@almshouses.demon.co.uk; website: www.salisburyalmshouses.co.uk)

CC Number: 309523

Eligibility

Young people under the age of 25 who live in the district of Salisbury (with a preference to those resident in the city of Salisbury, and/or in secondary education).

Types of grants

One-off grants ranging from £100 to £200 are made to schoolchildren for educational outings in the UK and study or travel abroad, and to further and higher education students (but not mature students or postgraduates) for books, equipment/instruments, educational outings in the UK and study or travel abroad.

Interest-free loans are also made towards the cost of tools and equipment needed to start a trade.

The charity interprets the term education in the widest sense, and offers help towards the cost of expeditions and other educational projects designed to develop character, such as Project Trust, scout jamborees and adventure training.

Annual grant total

In 2013, the charity had an income of £4,000 and a total expenditure of £4,000. Fourteen grants to individuals for educational purposes were awarded totalling £3,600.

Exclusions

Grants are not made for school uniforms, maintenance/living expenses or student exchanges. There is no support for second degree courses.

Applications

On a form available, along with guidance notes, from the charity's website (www.salisburyalmshouses.co.uk/grants). Applicants are advised to contact the clerk as early as possible to discuss an application. Applications are considered monthly and can be submitted through the individual's school, college or educational welfare agency.

Sarum St Michael Educational Charity

£52,000 (37 grants)

Correspondent: The Clerk to the Governors, First Floor, 27A Castle Street, Salisbury SP1 1TT (01722 422296 (Monday to Thursday mornings); email: clerk@sarumstmichael.org; website: www.sarumstmichael.org)

CC Number: 309456

Eligibility

People over the age of 16 who live or study in the diocese of Salisbury or adjoining dioceses, including Bath and Wells, Exeter, Oxford and Winchester (for exact geographical areas see the map supplied on the charity's website). The trust can support:

▶ Individuals in need of financial assistance towards their higher/further education or training
▶ People who are/are about to become teachers or otherwise work with religious education
▶ Research and development of religious education

Types of grants

Grants are available for first degrees (including mature students), diplomas, access courses, Open University courses, vocational courses, postgraduate degrees, gap-year activities and projects. Support can be given towards general educational expenses, including fees, necessities, books, equipment, travel, dissertation expenses and so on. Clergy can also apply for grants to attend conferences and travel.

Bursaries for potential teachers of religious education are £1,000 for each year of the first degree and £2,000 for the PGCE (or equivalent) year. A further £3,000 'golden handshake' is available to candidates who:

Have been awarded a PGCE (or equivalent), completed their Newly Qualified Teacher induction and either, in the case of primary teachers, have secured a post of responsibility with the coordination of religious education across the school as its most significant element, or, in the case of secondary teachers, have taught religious education for at least 60% of their contracted teaching time for three years (both evidenced through a letter from the headteacher).

Annual grant total

In 2013 the charity had assets of £5.5 million, an income of £203,000 and a total charitable expenditure of £162,000. Grants to 37 individuals totalled £52,000 and were awarded in the following categories:

Financial assistance for education	£36,000
People who work/intend to work in religious education	£14,300
Assistance with provision of a chapel and chaplaincy for students	£1,000
Provision of teaching resources	£500

Exclusions

The charity will not:
- Make retrospective grants
- Contribute towards maintenance (unless an integral part of a residential course)
- Pay money for buildings, fixtures or fittings

Grants for persons attending educational establishments are continued only if the applicant remains at that establishment.

Applications

Application forms can be obtained from the charity's website. Grants are considered four to five times a year, normally in January, April, July, September and November. Exact dates of the meetings are available online. Applications can be submitted directly by individuals, preferably by email.

Other information

The charity aims to distribute the money in the following proportions: 45% in individual grants and bursaries; 45% in grants to institutions; 7% in support to schools/universities; and 3% to assist parishes and other religious establishments.

Alfred Ernest Withy's Trust Fund

£0

Correspondent: Maggie Russell, Grants Administrator, The Community Foundation for Wiltshire and Swindon, Ground Floor, Sandcliffe House, 21 Northgate Street, Devizes, Wiltshire SN10 1JX (01380 729284; email: maggie.russell@wscf.org.uk; website: www.odm.wiltshirecf.org.uk)

CC Number: 1123126–2

Eligibility

People in need between the ages of 16 and 25 who have lived within the boundaries of Swindon or Wiltshire councils for five years and who (or whose parents/guardians) are in receipt of means tested benefits.

Types of grants

Grants of up to £1,000 are given for vocational education. Awards are particularly aimed towards equipment/tools, training costs, books but can also be given for childcare, transport costs or other needs.

Annual grant total

In 2012/13 the fund had assets of £235,000 and an income of £173,000. During the year no grants were made, due to the fund being transferred. The correspondent has informed us that in 2014 the fund has already made 3 grants totalling £5,900.

Exclusions

Retrospective payments are not made and grants are not given where support should be provided by the statutory sources.

Applications

To receive an application form and detailed guidelines candidates should make an initial enquiry on the fund's website or contact the correspondent. References will be required for the application. Grants are considered four times a year, in January, April, July and October.

Other information

The fund is administered by The Community Foundation for Wiltshire and Swindon (registered charity number 1123126) and is part of the vocational grants in the One Degree More programme.

Chippenham

Chippenham Borough Lands Charity

£15,000

Correspondent: Philip Tansley, Administrator, Jubilee Building, 32 Market Place, Chippenham, Wiltshire SN15 3HP (01249 658180; fax: 01249 446048; email: admin@cblc.org.uk; website: www.cblc.org.uk)

CC Number: 270062

Eligibility

People in need who are living within the parish of Chippenham at the date of application, and have been for a minimum of two years immediately prior to applying.

Types of grants

Usually one-off grants according to need, for things such as help towards travel costs, the provision of equipment to undertake a course or help towards actual course fees, depending on the nature of the course and the individual's personal circumstances.

Annual grant total

In 2012/13 this charity had assets of £13.2 million and an income of £436,000. Grants were given to 58 individuals totalling over £37,000. Grants are awarded to both individuals and organisations for educational, social welfare and other charitable purposes. We estimate total grants paid to individuals for educational purposes was around £15,000.

Exclusions

The charity is unable to help towards the cost of undergraduate degree courses. Equally, grants are not given in any circumstances where the trustees consider the award to be a substitute for statutory provision.

Applications

On a form available from the correspondent. Once received the application will be looked at in detail by an education officer. It is possible that the charity will visit, or ask applicants to call in at this stage. Applications are considered every month and can be submitted directly by the individual or through a third party such as a teacher.

Other information

The charity was first established in 1554 when Queen Mary granted a Royal Charter to Chippenham. She gave Crown Land to the borough and the income was to be used to pay for two members of parliament and for the upkeep of the bridge over the River Avon. A full history of the charity can be found on its informative and helpful website.

Conock

The Ewelme Exhibition Foundation (Ewelme Exhibition Endowment)

£106,000 (66 grants)

Correspondent: James Oliver, Clerk and Trust Manager, 126 High Street, Oxford OX1 4DG (01865 244661; fax: 01865 721263; email: clerk@ewelme-education-awards.info; website: www.ewelme-education-awards.info)

CC Number: 309240

Eligibility

Young people (both in state and independent education) aged between 11 and 21 who live in Berkshire, Buckinghamshire, Conock in Wiltshire, Oxfordshire and Ramridge in Hampshire, and demonstrate exceptional talent or need.

Types of grants

The foundation provides the following means-tested support:

- Bursaries – a limited number of awards towards independent school fees available to gifted young people
- Grants – awards are available to people in secondary and tertiary education towards vocational training, development of skills, funding for equipment, tools, master-classes and other general necessities
- Academic scholarships – of around £1,800 per year to young people with exceptional talent or specific educational needs, or individuals facing sudden and unforeseen financial circumstances or bereavement. Awards are normally made on entry to secondary education at 11 or 13 but later applications are also considered and may be continued up to the completion of A-levels

In the state sector the foundation provides funds for additional tuition, educational visits, sports, music and arts, also books and equipment for skills training. The trustees note that a large proportion of the endowment income is currently used to support young people in independent education and mostly at secondary education level.

Annual grant total
In 2013 the foundation had assets of £229,000 and an income of £129,000. Grants to 66 individuals totalled £106,000.

Applications
Application forms can be requested from the correspondent via email. Applications are advertised in the regional press in late September/October and the closing date for submissions is the end of November. Candidates are invited to an interview in February. The foundation requires to provide details of the parental income and a testimonial from the school's headteacher.

Other information
The foundation is one of the three charities, which together make up the Ewelme Trusts.

Grants are also made to local schools (£10,200 in 2013).

East Knoyle
The East Knoyle Welfare Trust

£800

Correspondent: Sabrina Sully, Trustee, Old Byre House, Millbrook Lane, East Knoyle, Salisbury SP3 6AW

CC Number: 202028

Eligibility
People in need who are under the age of 25 and live in the parish of East Knoyle.

Types of grants
Any need is considered, including grants to school leavers for tools, working clothes and books.

Annual grant total
Grants awarded to individuals for educational purposes usually total around £800.

Applications
At any time to the correspondent or any other trustee.

Other information
Grants are also made for welfare purposes.

Swindon
The W. G. Little Scholarship and Band Concert Fund

£19,000

Correspondent: Darren Stevens, Administrator, Swindon Borough Council, Civic Offices, Euclid Street, Swindon SN1 2JH (01793 445500; email: customerservices@swindon.gov.uk)

CC Number: 309497

Eligibility
Secondary school pupils who have lived within the boundary of Swindon Borough Council for at least 12 months. Priority is given to pupils who are transferring form primary to secondary school. Only applicants who have previously received a grant from the trust are currently eligible.

Types of grants
Grants are given towards school clothing and are usually of about £50.

Annual grant total
In 2012/13 the fund had an income of £22,000 and an expenditure of £19,500. We estimate that around £19,000 was awarded in grants. Normally several hundreds of grants are distributed each year.

Applications
The Swindon Borough Council's website (www.swindon.gov.uk/el/el-studentfinance/Pages/Financial-Assistance—School-Uniforms.aspx) notes that new applicants are currently not accepted. Individuals who have received a grant in 2012/13 and who are under the age of 16 will be sent notification letters and forms.

Other information
The fund is administered by the Swindon Borough Council. The council's website states that:

The use of the fund is being greater aligned to the original aims of the trust, and only those who have previously received an award in 2012/13 will be eligible to re-apply for 2014/15. It is anticipated that 2015/16 will be the final year of this award process. Awards are not available for new applicants.

The information provided on the Charity Commission record states that the primary aims of the trust are 'under review with the aim of adding in other funds and updating activities.'

Organisations could also be supported, provided their service users are aged 11 to 25 and live within the borough boundary.

Ethel May Character Award

£0

Correspondent: Darren Stevens, Finance Manager, Swindon Borough Council, Civic Offices, Euclid Street, Swindon SN1 2JH (01793 445500; email: customerservices@swindon.gov.uk)

CC Number: 1002739

Eligibility
Schoolchildren and students under the age of 25 of good character and studious application, who attend school or college full or part-time in the boundary of Swindon Borough Council.

Types of grants
One-off grants according to need. Grants are often £150 towards equipment or dancewear.

Annual grant total
In 2013/14 the charity had an income of £300 and a total expenditure of £0.

Applications
In writing to the correspondent.

Tisbury
Educational Foundation of Alice Coombe and Others (Alice Coombe's Education Charity)

£2,400

Correspondent: Kathleen Wright, Administrator, Court Street Farm Cottage, Court Street, Tisbury, Salisbury, Wiltshire SP3 6LN (01747 871774; email: kmmwright@hotmail.com)

CC Number: 309359

Eligibility
Children and young people under the age of 25 who live in the ancient parish of Tisbury and West Tisbury.

Types of grants

One-off grants, usually in the range of £20–£250, are available to secondary schoolchildren, higher/further education students, people in teacher training college or undertaking vocational training. Awards are given towards school uniforms, clothing, books, educational visits, and study or travel abroad for those in further/higher education. People starting work can be given help towards books, equipment/instruments, clothing and travel to interviews.

Annual grant total

In 2013 the foundation had an income of £2,400 and an expenditure of £2,600. We estimate the annual total of grants to be around £2,400.

Exclusions

Applications from outside the area of benefit are not considered.

Applications

In writing to the correspondent. Applications can be made directly by the individual or through their school/college, vicar, health visitor, educational welfare agency, if applicable, or other third parties. Applications are considered throughout the year.

Other information

Local schools may also be supported.

South East

General

Anglia Care Trust

£500

Correspondent: Jane Simpson, Secretary, 65 St Matthew's Street, Ipswich, Suffolk IP1 3EW (01473 213140; email: admin@ angliacaretrust.org.uk; website: www. angliacaretrust.org.uk)

CC Number: 299049

Eligibility

Offenders, ex-offenders, people at risk of offending, and their families, who live in East Anglia and are in need.

Types of grants

One-off grants may be provided towards rehabilitation. Grants usually range from £10 to £70 and can be given to help people entering education or (re)training. They are given towards fees, books, equipment, tools, clothing or other learning aids. Sums of money are not usually paid direct but itemised bills will be met directly. Applicants are usually already being supported by, or are known to, ACT and should have exhausted all possible sources of statutory funds.

Annual grant total

In 2012/13 the trust had assets of £1.1 million and an income of £1.4 million. The trustees' annual report from 2012/13 notes that 'grant giving is a very small part of the activities of the charity, supported from its current unrestricted reserves.' Generally grants to individuals total under £1,000.

Exclusions

Awards are not available for schoolchildren.

Applications

In writing to the correspondent. All applications must be supported by a probation officer or other professional person. The committees meet at least four times a year.

Other information

For this entry, the information relates to the money available from ACT. For more information on what is available throughout East Anglia, including advice and advocacy, housing services and other support, contact the correspondent and see the trust's website.

The Blatchington Court Trust (BCT)

£69,000 (203 grants)

Correspondent: Dr Geoffrey Lockwood, Clerk to the Trustees, 6A Hove Park Villas, Hove, East Sussex BN3 6HW (01273 727222; fax: 01273 722244; email: info@blatchington-court.co.uk; website: www.blatchington-court.co.uk)

CC Number: 306350

Eligibility

People under the age of 30 who live in the Sussex area and are visually impaired.

Types of grants

One-off and recurrent support to people at any school, university, college or other institution of further education and training, approved by the trustees. The trust provides equipment, mobility aids, books and other study necessities (including those for the study of music and other arts) which will assist in the pursuit of education, training and employment or business development. Assistance will also be given in connection with preparation to enter a school, profession, trade, occupation or service. Occasionally the trust will fund one-to-one swimming or riding lessons if it is felt that this would be beneficial to the child. Loans may also be provided.

Note that 'any equipment which is provided by the trust can only be for home use and the individual is not permitted to take it in to school.'

Annual grant total

In 2012/13 the trust had assets of £12.2 million, an income of £521,000 and a total charitable expenditure of £345,000. A total of £69,000 was awarded in grants to individuals, consisting of 74 computer grants totalling £38,000 and 129 personal grants totalling £31,000.

Exclusions

The trust does not give cash grants or bursaries and will not normally provide funding for wheelchairs, school fees, holidays or travel costs.

Applications

Application forms should be requested from the correspondent. Applications should normally be made by 1 February, 1 June, 1 August and 1 October each year.

Other information

In addition to the financial support, the trust offers advocacy, counselling, family advice, education, training and assistance in finding an employment. The trust also runs 'an annual awards scheme to assist charities, groups, companies and statutory bodies throughout the UK in their work with young visually impaired people.'

The Chownes Foundation

£16,000

Correspondent: Sylvia Spencer, Secretary, The Courtyard, Shoreham Road, Upper Beeding, Steyning, West Sussex BN44 3TN (01903 816699)

CC Number: 327451

Eligibility

Individuals and small charities primarily in Sussex, particularly Mid-Sussex, being the former home of the founder.

Types of grants

One-off and recurrent.

Annual grant total

In 2012/13 the foundation had assets of £1.5 million and an income of £26,000. Grants were made to individuals totalling £33,000, broken down as £17,000 relief of poverty; and £16,000 other charitable activities.

Applications

The trustees prefer a one page document and will request further information if they require it.

Other information

The majority of the charity's funds are committed to long-term support for poor and vulnerable beneficiaries, so only very few applications are successful.

The Eric Evans Memorial Trust

£4,000

Correspondent: John Kinder, Trustee, 55 Thornhill Square, London N1 1BE (email: info@ericevanstrust.com; website: www.ericevanstrust.com)

CC Number: 1047709

Eligibility

Young people who live in East Anglia or London. Preference is given to underprivileged individuals and people with disabilities.

Types of grants

Educational grants linked to sport activities.

Annual grant total

In 2012/13 the trust had an income of £50 and an expenditure of £9,000. We estimate the annual total of grants to individuals to be around £4,000.

Applications

In writing to the correspondent. Applications can be made directly by individuals or through their school/ college, welfare agency, if applicable. Our research suggests that applications are considered quarterly.

Other information

The trust supports both individuals and organisations.

The Ewelme Exhibition Endowment

See entry on page 294

The Hale Trust

£0

Correspondent: Lady Broughton, Administrator, Rosemary House, Woodhurst Park, Oxted, Surrey RH8 9HA

CC Number: 313214

Eligibility

Young people under the age of 25 who live in Greater London, Kent, Surrey or Sussex. According to our research, the trust assists children whose lives are affected by mental, physical or sensory disabilities, behavioural or psychological problems, living in poverty or situations of deprivation, or illness, distress, abuse or neglect.

Bursaries are given to children under the age of 18 where there are medical requirements, family problems, special educational needs or limited means.

Types of grants

Assistance is given to schoolchildren, further/higher students, people starting work/entering a trade, apprentices or individuals in any educational institution approved by the trustees. Financial support is given towards clothing/outfits, school uniforms, tools, equipment/ instruments, books and other necessities, also for travel/study abroad and educational outings in the UK.

Our research suggests that bursaries of £400 per term are also available for people under the age of 18 but they cannot exceed £1,200 a year per individual or last for more than three years. They are paid to the school and not the individual.

Annual grant total

In 2012/13 the trust had an income of £1 and made no grants. There has been no charitable giving for the past two years.

Exclusions

Grants are not normally given for unspecified expenditure, deficit funding, the repayment of loans or second degrees/postgraduate studies.

Applications

In writing to the correspondent. Our research indicates that applications should be submitted through the individual's school, college or educational welfare agency, if applicable. Applications for one-off grants should be submitted in time for the trustees' meetings, which are held in February, June and October.

Candidates for bursaries should apply to: Sheila Henderson, Foyle Farm, Merle Common, Oxted, Surrey RH8 9PN. The trust aims to interview all applicants for bursaries. Grants are paid to the school.

Other information

This trust also supports charitable organisations which help individuals, particularly disadvantaged children or children with disabilities, to improve their life conditions and develop their physical and mental skills through leisure time activities.

The Walter Hazell Charitable and Educational Trust Fund

£9,000

Correspondent: Rodney Dunkley, Trustee, 20 Aviemore Gardens, Northampton NN4 9XJ (01604 765925)

CC Number: 1059707

Eligibility

Employees and past employees of the printing trade in Buckinghamshire and Berkshire. Spouses, widows, widowers and children and any other financial dependents can also be supported.

Types of grants

One-off and recurrent grants are given to further/higher education students towards the cost of books, necessities, equipment/instruments or other course-related expenses.

Annual grant total

In 2012/13 the fund had an income of £17,300 and an expenditure of £19,000. We estimate the annual total of grants to individuals to be around £9,000.

Exclusions

According to our research, grants are not made towards the course fees.

Applications

In writing to the correspondent.

Other information

This fund also awards Christmas payments to ex-employee pensioners of BPC Hazells.

Kentish's Educational Foundation

£28,000

Correspondent: Margery Roberts, Clerk to the Trustees, 7 Nunnery Stables, St Albans, Hertfordshire AL1 2AS (01727 856626)

CC Number: 313098

Eligibility

Young people in need between the ages of 11 and 35, particularly (but not exclusively) those who are permanently resident in Hertfordshire or Bedfordshire. Preference can be given to people with the family name Kentish or people related to the founder Thomas Kentish (died 1712).

Types of grants

One-off and recurrent grants ranging from £200 to £1,000 are available to individuals in any school, university/ college or other institution of education approved by the trustees, also to people starting work/entering a trade, apprentices and individuals with special needs. Support is given towards general course related expenses, such as books, equipment/instruments, outfits/clothing, uniforms, study of music or arts, travel/ study in pursuance of education, educational outings and so on. Postgraduate studies can be assisted but only in special cases.

Annual grant total

In 2012/13 the foundation had an income of £25,000 and an expenditure of £29,000. We estimate that the annual total of grants to individuals was around £28,000.

Exclusions

Support is normally available up to first degree level.

Applications

Application forms can be requested from the correspondent and can be submitted by individuals directly or through their parents/guardians. Applicants should also provide a copy of their school/tutor report and copies of birth or marriage certificates (for applicants claiming kinship). Grants are normally considered in October/November, therefore applications should be received by the end of August.

The Mijoda Charitable Trust

£12,000

Correspondent: Jacquie Hardman, Trustee, Oak House, 38 Botley Road, Chesham HP5 1XG (01494 783402; email: jacquie_hardman@hotmail.com)

CC Number: 1002565

Eligibility

People who live in Buckinghamshire or Hertfordshire who are undertaking further, higher or postgraduate education in music, the arts or medicine. Beneficiaries are usually under 40 years of age.

Types of grants

One-off and recurrent grants of up to £250 towards fees and study or travel overseas.

Annual grant total

In 2013/14 the trust had an income of £18,800 and an expenditure of £12,300. Grants totalled around £12,000.

Applications

In writing to the correspondent. A reply will only be sent if an sae is enclosed.

Nichol-Young Foundation

£10,000

Correspondent: The Administrator, Bates Wells and Braithwaite, 27 Friars Street, Sudbury, Suffolk CO10 2AD (01787 880440)

CC Number: 259994

Eligibility

Individuals in need who are in full-time education, with a preference for those who live in East Anglia.

Types of grants

One-off and recurrent grants, generally of around £500, to those 'who perhaps feel marginalised by society or who wish to improve their life skills so that they in turn can then be of benefit to others.' Awards are given for general educational needs, educational trips, medical electives and other such projects undertaken by individuals. Grants may also be given for computers, equipment and tools.

Annual grant total

In 2012/13 the foundation had an income of £37,000 and a total expenditure of £22,000. We estimate that grants to individuals totalled around £10,000.

Applications

In writing to the correspondent. Applications are normally considered on a quarterly basis. Unsuccessful applicants will only be contacted if an sae is provided. Where possible, payments are paid through an educational institution.

Other information

The foundation also gives grants to small charitable organisations.

Note: the foundation has previously noted that telephone enquiries are not welcomed.

Bedfordshire

Ashton Schools Foundation

£7,300

Correspondent: Yvonne Beaumont, Administrator, Grove House, 76 High Street North, Dunstable, Bedfordshire LU6 1NF (01582 660008; email: dunstablecharity@yahoo.com)

CC Number: 307526

Eligibility

Children and young people under the age of 25 living within the Dunstable area (defined as a radius of six miles

from the parish church of the ecclesiastical parish of St Peter).

Types of grants

One-off and recurrent grants, scholarships and bursaries towards general educational needs, including books, equipment/instruments, clothing, maintenance, other necessities, also study/travel overseas, educational outings, study of music or other arts. Schoolchildren, further/higher education students or people starting work/ entering a trade can be supported.

Annual grant total

In 2012/13 the trust had an income of £21,000 and a total expenditure of £14,700. We estimate the annual total of grants to individuals to be around £7,300.

Applications

In writing to the correspondent.

Other information

The trust also provides annual grants to Manshead, Ashton Middle and Ashton Lower schools in Dunstable.

Chew's Foundation at Dunstable

£5,300 (20–25 grants)

Correspondent: Yvonne Beaumont, Administrator, Grove House, 76 High Street North, Dunstable, Bedfordshire LU6 1NF (01582 660008; email: dunstablecharity@yahoo.com)

CC Number: 307500

Eligibility

Children and young people, normally under the age of 25, living within the boroughs of Dunstable and Luton and parish of Edlesborough who/whose parents are 'in sympathy' with the Church of England and other Christian churches. Our research suggests that a certificate of baptism is required.

Types of grants

The trust provides scholarships to individuals in education and can assist people undertaking apprenticeships. Support is given towards general educational costs, including books, school uniforms, educational outings, equipment/instruments and so forth.

Annual grant total

In 2012/13 the foundation had an income of £16,500 and an expenditure of £11,000. Previously around 20–25 grants a year have been awarded to individuals. We estimate the annual total of grants to individuals to be around £5,300.

Applications

In writing to the correspondent. According to our research, applications should normally be submitted by the end of May to receive a grant around July. Late applications may be considered in December. Details of parental income and the number of dependent children of school age in the family will be taken into account.

Other information

The foundation also maintains the Chew's House and the old library (now the little theatre).

The Harpur Trust

£91,000 (19 grants)

Correspondent: Lucy Bardner, Grants Manager, Princeton Court, The Pilgrim Centre, Brickhill Drive, Bedford MK41 7PZ (01234 369503; fax: 01234 369505; email: grants@harpurtrust.org. uk; website: www.harpurtrust.org.uk)

CC Number: 1066861

Eligibility

Adults who are returning to study after a minimum of five years away from formal education and are resident in the borough of Bedford. Schoolchildren who are in receipt of free school meals are eligible for school uniform when transitioning from state upper school to middle school.

Undergraduate bursary applicants should meet the criteria set by their university or college.

Preference is given to people in need, hardship or distress.

Types of grants

Grants are made to help with the cost of further education and training leading to career development. Support can be given for fees, travel costs and necessities. The trust also gives grants towards school uniforms and provides bursaries at the schools it runs as well as undergraduate bursaries for school leavers at the partner schools. Contact the school directly to discuss these awards.

Annual grant total

In 2012/13 the trust had assets of £120.1 million and an income of £49.5 million. Grants to individuals totalled £91,000. During the year 38 organisations and 19 individuals were awarded grants.

The awards can be broken down as follows:

University bursary programme	£58,000
College bursary programme	£20,000
School uniform grants	£13,000
Grant to an individual	£300

Exclusions

The trust will not give grants for PGCE courses and certificates of education or

for recreational courses, including academic courses taken for recreational purposes only.

Applications

Adults returning to education may use the form available on the trust's website. It should be submitted by the end of May for courses beginning in September/October. Successful candidates are invited for an interview. Applicants must determine their entitlement to statutory funding before making an application.

Applicants for the university/college bursaries should apply via their schools.

The school uniform grants scheme is advertised to all eligible families in the borough by Bedford schools.

The trustees consider grants five times a year. Applicants are 'encouraged to contact the trust informally for initial guidance on their applications and much advice is given verbally.'

Other information

In July 2012 the trust has been incorporated as a company limited by guarantee. Its previous registered charity number was 204817.

Most grants are given to registered charities, voluntary organisations and other groups but a small number of grants can be offered to individuals pursuing or continuing vocational education and training, particularly adults returning to education.

The trust has made plans to establish a new small grants application process by June 2014.

The David Parry Memorial Trust

£840

Correspondent: Ann Swaby, Trustee, The Mary Bassett Lower School, Bassett Road, Leighton Buzzard, Bedfordshire LU7 1AR (07710 272520)

CC Number: 1020762

Eligibility

Schoolchildren aged 5 to 18, in the areas centred around Leighton Buzzard and Linslade whose families are experiencing severe financial hardship.

Types of grants

Grants to enable pupils to take part in extra-curricular activities and visits. Help towards books may also be given.

Annual grant total

In 2012 this charity had an income of just £60 and a total expenditure of £840. The 2012 accounts were the latest available at the time of writing (August 2014).

Applications

Applications can only be made on behalf of the families by the head of the school that the pupil attends and not directly by the parents. They are considered all year round.

The Sandy Charities

£3,500

Correspondent: P. J. Mount, Clerk, Woodfines Solicitors, 6 Bedford Road, Sandy, Bedfordshire SG19 1EN (01767 680251; email: pmount@woodfines.co. uk)

CC Number: 237145

Eligibility

People in need who live in Sandy and Beeston.

Types of grants

One-off grants only, ranging from £100 to £1,000. Schoolchildren can receive grants towards school uniforms and other school clothing and educational outings; and college students, undergraduates and vocational students towards books and equipment/instruments.

Annual grant total

In 2012/13 the charities had an income of £9,600 and a total expenditure of £14,800. We estimate the total amount awarded to individuals for educational purposes was around £3,500.

Applications

In writing to the correspondent who will supply a personal details form for completion. Applications can be considered in any month, depending on the urgency for the grant. They should be submitted either directly by the individual or via the individual's school, college or educational welfare agency.

Other information

Grants are also made to organisations and to individuals for welfare purposes.

Bedford

Alderman Newton's Educational Foundation (Bedford branch)

£4,000

Correspondent: Lynn McKenna, Bedford Borough Council, Committee Services, Borough Hall, Cauldwell Street, Bedford MK42 9AP (01234 228193; email: lynn. mckeena@bedford.gov.uk; website: www. bedford.gov.uk/aldermannewton)

CC Number: 307471

Eligibility

People aged 13 to 25 who have lived in the borough of Bedford (including rural areas) for at least three years. Support is available to schoolchildren, higher/further education students and people entering a trade/profession.

Types of grants

The foundation reimburses the expenses for educational necessities such as books, equipment/instruments, stationery, outfits, special clothing and so forth. The upper limit of money available is £500 but in exceptional circumstances can be increased up to £750. Grants are only given when receipts for the items specified in the application are produced.

Annual grant total

In 2012/13 the foundation had an income of £5,400 and an expenditure of £4,300. We have estimated the annual total of grants to be around £4,000.

Exclusions

Grants exceeding £750 or travel expenses to and from school would not normally be supported.

Applications

Application forms are available from the foundation's website and can be submitted at any time. A letter from applicants' educational establishment is required to confirm their attendance and need for the items requested. Details of the applicants' or their parents' income should also be included.

Clapham

Ursula Taylor Charity

£1,000

Correspondent: Mavis Nicholson, Secretary to the Trustees, 39 George Street, Clapham, Bedford MK41 6AZ (01234 405141; email: mavis. nicholson1@ntlworld.com)

CC Number: 307520

Eligibility

Children and young people between the ages 11 and 25 who live in the parish of Clapham and are in full-time education or training.

Types of grants

Grants are made to schoolchildren, people starting work, individuals undertaking apprenticeships and students in further/higher education. Support can be given for books, course fees, equipment/instruments, tools, clothing and other educational needs.

Annual grant total

In 2013 the charity had an income of £2,600 and an expenditure of £1,200. We

estimate the annual grants total to be around £1,000.

Exclusions

Our research suggests that grants are not given for bus passes and school uniforms.

Applications

Application forms together with further guidance are available from the correspondent. According to our research submissions can be made either directly by the individual or through the charity's trustees. Applications are considered four times a year in February, April, June and November. Candidates should provide receipts for the items purchased.

Clophill

Clophill United Charities

£3,900

Correspondent: Gillian Hill, Clerk, 10 The Causeway, Clophill, Bedford MK45 4BA (01525 860539)

CC Number: 200034

Eligibility

People who live in the parish of Clophill and are in need.

Types of grants

One-off and recurrent grants can be given 'in times of need'. Support can be provided towards various school activities and trips in the UK or abroad. Assistance can be given to people aiming for employment.

Annual grant total

In 2013 the charity had an income of £17,100 and a total expenditure of £15,900. We estimate that educational grants to individuals totalled around £3,900.

Exclusions

Grants are not given where statutory funds are available.

Applications

Application forms can be obtained from the correspondent. The trustees normally meet every two months.

Other information

Grants are also made to organisations and to individuals for welfare causes.

Flitwick

The Flitwick Town Lands Charity

£4,000

Correspondent: David Empson, Trustee, 28 Orchard Way, Flitwick, Bedford MK45 1LF (01525 718145; email: Deflitwick8145@aol.com)

CC Number: 233258

Eligibility

Students between 18 and 25 who live in the parish of Flitwick.

Types of grants

Grants are awarded to students of around £100 to £250. As a general rule, educational grants are awarded to students at the start of their second year of study in higher education. In exceptional circumstances, one-off grants may be given to an organisation, for reasons such as providing sports equipment to a youth group.

Annual grant total

In 2012/13 the charity had an income of £11,000 and total expenditure of £9,000. Grants are given for both education and welfare purposes.

Applications

On a form available from the correspondent.

Kempston

The Kempston Charities

£1,000

Correspondent: Christine Stewart, Administrator, 15 Loveridge Avenue, Kempston, Bedford MK42 8SF (01234 302323)

CC Number: 200064

Eligibility

People in need who live in Kempston (including Kempston rural).

Types of grants

One-off grants according to need.

Annual grant total

In 2012 this charity had an income of £3,900 and a total expenditure of £3,700. Grants are awarded to individuals for both educational and social welfare purposes. Grants are also given to local schools and other local organisations. We estimate grants given to individuals for educational purposes was around £1,000. The 2012 accounts were the latest available at the time of writing (August 2014).

Exclusions

No recurrent grants are made.

Applications

In writing to the correspondent. Applications should be made either directly by the individual or through a social worker, Citizens Advice or other welfare agency. They are considered in March, July and November.

Oakley

Oakley Educational Foundation

£2,100

Correspondent: Louise Tunley, Administrator, c/o Steve Monico Ltd, 19 Goldington Road, Bedford MK40 3JY (01234 402040)

CC Number: 307464

Eligibility

Young people between the ages of 16 and 25 who live in the parish of Oakley.

Types of grants

Small grants are available to people leaving school, individuals starting work, further and higher education students (including mature students and postgraduates.) Support can be given for general educational costs, including books, equipment/instruments, tools, educational outings in the UK and study/travel abroad.

Annual grant total

In 2012/13 the foundation had an income of £3,800 and an expenditure of £2,300. We estimate that grants to individuals totalled around £2,100.

Exclusions

According to our research, grants for travel fares are not normally provided.

Applications

Application forms are available upon request from the correspondent. Our research suggests that they should be submitted by 1 May and 1 November together with the receipts of the items purchased.

Potton

The Potton Consolidated Charities

£29,000

Correspondent: Dean Howard, Administrator, 69 Stotfold Road, Arlesey, Bedfordshire SG15 6XR (0146273520; email: pcc.clerk@hotmail. co.uk; website: www.potton-consolidated-charity.co.uk)

CC Number: 201073

Eligibility

People between 16 and 25 who live in the parish of Potton.

Types of grants

Book grants of about £200 for students in further or higher education. People between the ages of 16 and 18 may apply for travel educational grants. People between the ages of 18–25 may apply for higher educational grants.

Annual grant total

In 2013/14 the charity had assets of £4 million and an income of £146,000. Educational grants to individuals totalled £29,000.

Applications

Directly by the individual on a form available from the correspondent. Applications are considered in November and should be received by 31 October.

Other information

In 2013/14 grants were also made to organisations for education totalling £51,000. Welfare grants were also made to organisations totalling £20,000.

Berkshire

Wellington Crowthorne Charitable Trust
See entry on page 20

The Polehampton Charity

£1,600

Correspondent: Caroline White, Administrator, 65 The Hawthorns, Charvil, Reading RG10 9TS (01189 340852; email: thepolehamptoncharity@ gmail.com; website: www. thepolehamptoncharity.co.uk)

CC Number: 1072631

Eligibility

People who live in the ecclesiastical parishes of Twyford and Ruscombe.

Types of grants

(i) Educational grants – these cover the purchase of books, tools, instruments and so on which are essential for the completion of apprenticeships, or courses or training at universities, colleges of further education and other recognised educational establishments. They also cover assistance to allow young people to study music or other arts, and to make provision for recreational and sports training, not normally provided by local authorities.

Grants are also given for school uniforms and school educational outings.

(ii) Educational bursaries – these are to assist those who are under 25 and are undertaking courses of further education for which no local authority or similar grants are available.

Grants are in the range of £100 to £250.

Annual grant total

In 2013 the charity had an income of £97,000. The trustees annual report states: 'During the year, grants by the charity totalled £80,000. Of this, £46,500 went to local schools. The trustees made grants for books and equipment totalling £1,600, with £1,700 to individuals and £31,000 to local groups and organisations.'

Applications

Applications should be submitted either directly by the individual or a family member, through a third party such as a social worker or teacher, or through an organisation such as Citizens Advice or a school. They should include a list of the books and/or equipment needed. Applications can be made at any time and are considered at trustee meetings.

Reading Dispensary Trust

£1,500 (8 grants)

Correspondent: Walter Gilbert, Clerk, 16 Wokingham Road, Reading RG6 1JQ (01189 265698; email: admin@rdt. btconnect.com)

CC Number: 203943

Eligibility

People in need who are in poor health, convalescent or who have a physical or mental disability and live in Reading and the surrounding area (roughly within a seven-mile radius of the centre of Reading).

Types of grants

One-off grants towards course fees, books, computer equipment and software.

Annual grant total

In 2012 the trust had assets of £1.2 million and an income of £48,000. A total of £25,000 was awarded in 145 grants to individuals, most of which were given for social welfare purposes. During the year there were 5 grants awarded for course fees and books, and a further 3 grants for computer equipment and software. We estimate these grants totalled around £1,500.

At the time of writing (August 2014) this was the most recent financial information available for the trust.

Applications

On a form available from the correspondent. Applications should generally be submitted through a doctor, nurse, social worker, Citizens Advice or other appropriate third party. They are considered on a monthly basis.

Other information

Grants are also given to organisations.

The Spoore Merry and Rixman Foundation

£178,000 (129 grants)

Correspondent: Helen MacDiarmid, Clerk to the Trustees, PO Box 4229, Slough SL1 0QZ (020 3286 8300; email: clerk@smrfmaidenhead.org; website: www.smrfmaidenhead.org.uk)

CC Number: 309040

Eligibility

People under the age of 25 who are in need and live in the former (pre-1974) borough of Maidenhead or the ancient parish of Bray, including Holyport and Woodlands Park.

Types of grants

Grants can be given for school uniforms, equipment/instruments, tools, books, musical instruments and sporting equipment, school visits, facilities for recreational or social training not normally provided by the local authorities, tuition in music or other arts, travel expenses in the UK and overseas, apprenticeships, residential courses and special needs courses and aids, such as laptops for dyslexic children.

Our research suggests that grants are for amounts of up to £5,000 each, although in special cases, such as the death of parents, this figure can be exceeded. Families receiving income support can be given up to £3,000 for a student in higher education. Grants of £1,000 (if living at home) or £1,500 (if living independently) per year are offered to people undertaking an apprenticeship.

The foundation encourages young people to return to or remain in education when they may have dropped out and not achieved GCSE passes.

Annual grant total

At the time of writing (July 2014) the latest financial information available was from 2012. In 2012 the foundation had assets of £9.2 million and an income of £339,000. A total of £178,000 was awarded in grants to 129 individuals. The trustees' annual report from 2012 notes that 'it has been determined that

all funds held are to be classified as permanent endowment funds.'

Applications

Application forms can be accessed on the foundation's website. They can be submitted by post (together with an sae) or online, either directly by the individual or through a school, college or educational welfare agency, if applicable. Applications for school uniforms should be submitted by a parent/guardian with a supporting statement from a social worker/teacher/ Citizens Advice/health professional. Parents are also required to provide a statement of their annual income. The trustees' meetings are held in the middle of January, April, July and October. Applications should be submitted at least two weeks before the scheduled meeting.

Note: applicants are requested not to send applications via recorded or registered post as the charity operates with a PO Box address and there is no one to sign a receipt.

Other information

Grants are also made to schools, youth clubs and initiatives involving children. Awards to 43 institutions totalled £106,000 in 2012.

The foundation's website states that 'the trustees are considering setting up bursaries for students from low income families which could cover the entire cost of a university course.'

Every child leaving a local authority maintained primary school in Maidenhead and Bray receives a dictionary from the trust.

The Wokingham United Charities

£2,500

Correspondent: P. Robinson, Clerk, 66 Upper Broadmoor Road, Crowthorne, Berkshire RG45 7DF (01344 351207; email: peter.westende@btinternet.com)

CC Number: 1107171

Eligibility

Schoolchildren in need who live in the civil parishes of Wokingham, Wokingham Without, St Nicholas, Hurst, Ruscombe and that part of Finchampstead known as Finchampstead North.

Types of grants

One-off grants between £25 and £150. Grants have been given towards school uniforms and educational visits.

Annual grant total

Grants for individuals totalled around £5,000. We estimate grants for

educational purposes to be around £2,500.

Applications

On a form available from the correspondent. Applications are considered each month (except August) and can be submitted directly by the individual, or through a social worker, school liaison officer or similar third party.

Pangbourne

The Breedon Educational and Vocational Foundation

£1,500

Correspondent: Richard Stone, Trustee, Westfields, Woodview Road, Pangbourne, Reading RG8 7JN (01189 844452; email: stonerc@aol.com)

CC Number: 309069

Eligibility

Children and young people who live in the civil parish of Pangbourne, Berkshire who are in full-time or further education.

Types of grants

One-off and recurrent grants: (i) to help with books, equipment, clothing or travel for schoolchildren, students or people starting work; or (ii) to help with school, college or university fees or to supplement existing grants.

Annual grant total

In 2011/12 the trust had an income of £1,200 and an expenditure of £1,500. The 2011/12 accounts were the latest available at the time of writing (August 2014).

Applications

On a form available from the correspondent. Applications are considered in March, July and December each year.

Windsor and Maidenhead

The Prince Philip Trust Fund

£780 (4 grants)

Correspondent: Kevin McGarry, Secretary, 10 Cadogan Close, Holyport, Maidenhead, Berkshire SL6 2JS (01628 639577; email: kmmcgarry@talktalk.net; website: www.rbwm.gov.uk/web/ members_grants_prince_philip_trust. htm)

CC Number: 272927

Eligibility

Young people from the royal borough of Windsor and Maidenhead undertaking voluntary work or training schemes. Support is also given to individual pupils selected to represent their district, county or country in an activity considered worthy of the fund's support.

Types of grants

One-off grants of around £200 towards educational opportunities and travel, particularly to undertake voluntary service. Loans may also be provided.

Annual grant total

In 2012/13 the fund had assets of £1.5 million and an income of £77,000. Four individuals were supported totalling £780.

Exclusions

Grants are not made for tuition fees.

Applications

In writing to the correspondent. Application letter should include full details of the project, the amount of grant sought, sources of other funding secured or applied to, the amount of funds in hand, budget projection, the names of two referees and a letter of acceptance on a course (if applicable). The trustees meet twice a year, usually in April and November.

Other information

Grants are mainly made to organisations and various projects. In 2012/13 a total of around £74,000 was awarded to 41 organisations.

The trustees state that 'their policy has always been to provide grants at a modest level' and 'they believe that grants at a higher level would not necessarily provide the same motivation.'

Buckingham-shire

The Amersham United Charities

£250

Correspondent: C. Atkinson, Clerk to the Trustees, 25 Milton Lawns, Amersham, Buckinghamshire HP6 6BJ (01494 723416)

CC Number: 205033

Eligibility

People under the age of 21 who live in the parishes of Amersham and Coleshill.

Types of grants

One-off grants for those at school, college or university, or about to start work, to help with the cost of fees (students only), books, equipment, clothing and travel.

Annual grant total

In 2012/13 £500 was distributed from the 'Young Persons and Poor Fund' in donations for educational and social welfare purposes.

Applications

In writing to the correspondent.

Other information

The main work of the charities is the administration and management of 13 almshouses.

Norman Hawes Memorial Trust

£4,700

Correspondent: Sue Bruce, Schools Support Officer, Milton Keynes Council, Education Department, 502 Avebury Boulevard, Milton Keynes MK9 3HS (01908 253614; email: sue.bruce@milton-keynes.gov.uk)

CC Number: 310620

Eligibility

Young people between the ages of 15 and 18 who are in full-time education in Milton Keynes and North Buckinghamshire.

Types of grants

Financial assistance to students travelling abroad for educational purposes. Grants range between £50 and £200.

Annual grant total

In 2012/13 the trust had an income of £3,600 and an expenditure of £4,800. We have estimated that the annual total of grants was around £4,700.

Applications

Application forms are available from the correspondent. They can be submitted either by individuals or through their school/college/educational welfare agency, if applicable. Considerations take place in November and February/March, therefore applications should be made in September/October and January/February respectively.

The Saye and Sele Foundation

£7,200

Correspondent: Richard Friedlander, Clerk, Parrot and Coales LLP, 14 Bourbon Street, Aylesbury, Buckinghamshire HP20 2RS (01296 318500; fax: 01296 318531; email: law@parrottandcoaleslp.co.uk)

CC Number: 310554

Eligibility

People under the age of 25 who live in the parishes of Grendon Underwood and Quainton.

Types of grants

One-off and recurrent grants to help schoolchildren, college or university students and people entering a trade/profession. Awards are made to help with the cost of books, equipment/instruments, tools, clothing, training expenses, sport activities. Previously grants have been made towards computers for people from low-income families and equipment for people with disabilities. Grants are generally around £200.

Annual grant total

In 2013 the foundation had an income of £17,200 and an expenditure of £14,700. We estimate that grants to individuals totalled around £7,200.

Applications

In writing to the correspondent. Applications are normally considered in January, April, July and October.

Other information

The foundation also provides building space in the community and can support local schools.

The Stoke Mandeville and Other Parishes Charity

£18,400

Correspondent: Caroline Dobson, Administrator, 17 Elham Way, Aylesbury HP21 9XN (01296 431859; email: smandopc@gmail.com)

CC Number: 296174

Eligibility

People in need who live in the parishes of Great and Little Hampden, Great Missenden and Stoke Mandeville. The vast majority of funding is given to the residents of Stoke Mandeville.

Types of grants

Grants can be given for general educational essentials, including the cost of books, clothing and other necessities. Support is available to schoolchildren (of up to £300 a year) and further/higher education students (of up to £600 a year). People starting work may also be assisted.

Annual grant total

In 2013 the charity had assets of £1.8 million and an income of £96,000. Educational grants totalled £18,400.

Applications

On a form available from the correspondent. Grants are normally considered in January, April, July and October. Individuals must reapply each year for additional grants.

Other information

The charity gives grants to individuals for welfare causes and can also support organisations.

Town Lands

£2,300

Correspondent: Julian Barrett, Trustee, South Cottage, 18 Broughton Road, Salford, Milton Keynes MK17 8BH (01908 583494)

CC Number: 256465

Eligibility

People in need who live in the parish of Hulcote and Salford.

Types of grants

Grants are one-off and range from £100 to £200. They can be awarded for the cost of school uniforms and other school clothing, books, educational outings and maintenance for schoolchildren; books and help with fees/living expenses for students in further/higher education; books, travel expenses and fees for mature students; and books, equipment/instruments, clothing and travel for people starting work.

Annual grant total

At the time of writing (August 2014) the latest financial information available was from 2012. In 2012 the charity had an income of £7,700 and an expenditure of £9,600. We estimate that educational grants to individuals totalled around £2,300.

Applications

In writing to the correspondent. Applications can be submitted directly by the individual or through any other parishioner.

Other information

Grants are also made to organisations supporting the community.

Aylesbury
William Harding's Charity

£143,000 (185 grants)

Correspondent: John Leggett, Clerk to the Trustees, 14 Bourbon Street, Aylesbury, Buckinghamshire HP20 2RS (01296 318501; fax: 01296 318531; email: John.leggett@parrottandcoalesllp.co.uk)

CC Number: 310619

Eligibility

People under the age of 25 who live in the town of Aylesbury.

Types of grants

One-off grants are made to schoolchildren towards uniforms, clothing, fees, study/travel overseas, books, educational outings, equipment/instruments, maintenance/living expenses or for special educational needs. Further/higher education students and people in vocational training can also be supported. Facilities for recreation, social or physical training may be provided to people in primary, secondary or further education.

Annual grant total

At the time of writing (July 2014) the latest financial information available was from 2012. In 2012 the charity had assets of £23.6 million and an income of £834,000. During the year 185 pupils were supported totalling £143,000.

Applications

Application forms can be requested from the correspondent. They can be submitted directly by the individual or through a third party, such as a family member/social worker/teacher, or through an organisation, for example, Citizens Advice or other welfare agency. The trustees normally meet on a monthly basis to consider applications. Details of family income should also be provided.

Other information

The charity also owns almshouses, provides relief in need and supports local educational institutions, youth groups and organisations.

Thomas Hickman's Charity

£24,000

Correspondent: John Leggett, Clerk, Parrott and Coales, 14–16 Bourbon Street, Aylesbury, Buckinghamshire HP20 2RS (01296 318500; email: doudjag@pandcllp.co.uk)

CC Number: 202973

Eligibility

People who live in Aylesbury town and are in need, hardship or distress.

Types of grants

According to our research grants can be given for school uniforms.

Annual grant total

In 2013 the charity had assets of £18.6 million and an income of £635,000. Grants were made to 95 individuals totalling £48,000. We estimate that grants for educational purposes totalled up to £24,000.

Applications

Application forms can be requested from the correspondent. They should be submitted either directly by the individual or through a third party, such as a family member, social worker, school or Citizens Advice. The trustees meet on a regular basis and applications are considered as they arise.

Other information

The charity provides almshouses to the elderly, supports individuals for welfare purposes and makes grants to organisations. Awards to institutions totalled £49,000 and almshouse expenditure reached £270,000.

Aylesbury Vale
Charles Pope Memorial Trust

£1,400

Correspondent: Roger Kirk, Trustee, 77 Aylesbury Road, Bierton, Aylesbury, Buckinghamshire HP22 5BT (01296 415312; email: info@cpmtrust.co.uk; website: www.cpmtrust.co.uk)

CC Number: 287591

Eligibility

Applicants may be of any age but must have lived or been educated in the Aylesbury Vale District Council administrative area for two years or more. A reference from a relevant music teacher is required.

Types of grants

Small grants are available to students to assist with the cost of musical education, including tuition fees, instruments, musical scores and books.

Annual grant total

In 2012/13 the trust had both an income and a total expenditure of around £1,400.

Applications

On a form available from the correspondent, submitted directly by the individual or by a parent or guardian.

Applications are usually considered in March, June and November and should be received in the middle of February, May and 1 October. A reference is required from a relevant music tutor. If it is close to the time when applications are to be considered, it is helpful if the reference can be sent with the application. In other cases the secretary will contact the referee direct. Applicants need to show some musical competence and commitment.

Calverton

Unknown Donor (Calverton Apprenticing Charity)

£700

Correspondent: Karen Phillips, Administrator, 78 London Road, Stony Stratford, Milton Keynes MK11 1JH (01908 563350; email: karen.phillips30@yahoo.co.uk)

CC Number: 239246

Eligibility

People under the age of 21 who live in the parish of All Saints, Calverton. Preference is given to apprentices.

Types of grants

Grants, generally in the range of £100 to £150, are available to college students, undergraduates, apprentices and people starting work. Support can be given for uniforms/clothing, fees, books and equipment/instruments.

Annual grant total

In 2013/14 the charity had an income of £2,200 and a total expenditure of £2,800. We estimate that educational grants to individuals totalled around £700. Our research suggests that grants for educational purposes usually total around £1,000 annually.

Applications

Application forms can be requested from the correspondent. They can be submitted directly by the individual or a family member.

Other information

The charity also makes grants to organisations and for welfare purposes to older people in need.

Cheddington

Cheddington Town Lands Charity

£2,000

Correspondent: Stuart Minall, 10 Hillside, Cheddington, Leighton Buzzard LU7 0SP (01296 661987)

CC Number: 235076

Eligibility

People in need who live in Cheddington.

Types of grants

One-off and recurrent grants according to need.

Annual grant total

In 2012/13 the charity's income was £13,000 and total expenditure £17,000. One third of the charity's income is paid to the parish church and the remaining income divided between local organisations and individuals for welfare and educational purposes. We estimate educational grants to be around £2,000.

Applications

In writing to the correspondent, directly by the individual or a family member.

Emberton

Emberton United Charity

£1,500

Correspondent: Warwick Clarke, Trustee, Old Pits, West Lane, Emberton, Olney, Bucks MK46 5DA (01234 713174)

CC Number: 204221

Eligibility

People under 25 in higher education who live in the parish of Emberton.

Types of grants

One-off and recurrent grants, usually of up to £350, towards books and equipment/instruments, but not fees.

Annual grant total

In 2013 the charity had an income of £38,000 and an expenditure of £38,500. Educational grants awarded to individuals totalled £700.

Applications

In writing to the correspondent, directly by the individual.

Other information

Grants are also given for welfare purposes.

Great Linford

The Great Linford Advancement in Life Charity

£200

Correspondent: Michael Williamson, Treasurer, 2 Lodge Gate, Great Linford, Milton Keynes MK14 5EW (01908 605664)

CC Number: 310570

Eligibility

People under 25 who live in the civil parish of Great Linford.

Types of grants

Grants of up to £200 are given for many educational purposes, such as scholarships and bursaries, clothing, equipment, musical instruments, books and travel. Grants are also awarded for young people preparing to enter a trade or profession after leaving school or university.

Annual grant total

In 2013 the charity had an income of £2,300 and an unusually low total expenditure of £450. We estimate that grants to individuals totalled £200, with funding also awarded to organisations.

Applications

In writing to the correspondent, either directly by the individual or through their school, college or educational welfare agency. Applications must include details of the purpose for which the request is being made and official estimates. They are usually considered in January, May and September.

Olney

The Olney British School Charity

£0

Correspondent: Donald Saunders, Trustee, 17 Long Lane, Olney, Buckinghamshire MK46 5HL (01234 711879; email: donaldsaunders@talktalk.net)

CC Number: 310538

Eligibility

People in need under the age of 25 who live, or whose parents live, in Olney, who are engaging in education beyond A-level or training after leaving school.

Types of grants

Grants to those 'who are preparing for, entering upon or engaged in any profession, trade, occupation, or service, by providing them with outfits, or by paying fees, travelling or maintenance expenses, or by such means for their advancement in life or to enable them to earn their living'. Students in further/ higher education can receive grants for books or study or travel abroad.

Annual grant total
In 2013/14 the charity had an income of £2,100, which is considerably higher than in recent years. The charity has had no expenditure since the 2009/10 financial year.

Applications
In writing to the correspondent. Applications must be received by 31 August for consideration in September.

Radnage

Radnage Poor's Land Educational Foundation

£1,000

Correspondent: Ian Blaylock, Clerk to the Trustees, Hill Top, Green End Road, Radnage, High Wycombe, Buckinghamshire HP14 4BY (01494 483346)

CC Number: 310582

Eligibility
People in need below 25 years, who live in the parish of Radnage.

Types of grants
One-off grants ranging from £100 to £500. Grants are given to schoolchildren and further and higher education students and include those for uniforms, books, equipment/instruments, fees, maintenance/living expenses, educational outings in the UK, study or travel abroad and student exchanges. Grants are also given to people starting work for books.

Annual grant total
In 2013, the foundation had an income of £3,000 and a total expenditure of £1,500. We estimate that the total grant awarded to individuals was approximately £1,000.

Applications
In writing to the correspondent, either directly by the individual or through a school, college or education welfare agency, for consideration in February, June, September and December.

Other information
Local schools are also supported.

Stoke Poges

Stoke Poges United Charities

£1,500

Correspondent: Anthony Levings, Clerk, The Cedars, Stratford Drive, Wooburn Green, High Wycombe HP10 0QH (email: anthony@levings123.wanadoo.co.uk)

CC Number: 205289

Eligibility
Children in primary and secondary school and apprentices/people starting work who live in the parish of Stoke Poges.

Types of grants
Grants, typically ranging between £30 and £1,500, are given for tools, clothing, books and other school equipment.

Annual grant total
In 2013 the charities had an income of £46,000 and a total expenditure of £6,300. We estimate that educational grants to individuals totalled £1,500. Funding is also awarded to local organisations and to individuals for social welfare needs.

Applications
In writing to the correspondent, to be submitted either directly by the individual or through a social worker, Citizens Advice, other welfare agency or any appropriate third party.

Stokenchurch

The Stokenchurch Education Charity

£39,000

Correspondent: Martin Sheehy, Administrator, Fish Partnership LLP, The Mill House, Boundary Road, Loudwater, High Wycombe HP10 9QN (01628 527956; email: martins@fishpartnership.co.uk)

CC Number: 297846

Eligibility
People under the age of 25 who live in the parish of Stokenchurch.

Types of grants
Grants normally range from £5 to £500 and are available for educational expenses and training, including awards for clothing, tools, books, equipment/instruments and study of music and other arts. Schoolchildren, further/higher education students and people entering a trade/starting work or undertaking apprenticeships can be supported.

Annual grant total
In 2012/13 the charity had assets of £2 million and an income of £59,000. Grants to individuals for educational purposes totalled £39,000.

Exclusions
Grants are not normally made for private tuition and where statutory grants are available. Applications from outside the parish cannot be considered.

Applications
Application forms can be requested from the correspondent. Ordinarily the trustees place an advertisement in the local press and two public places in Stokenchurch in August to invite applications. They should be returned by 30 November each year. Grants are paid in or around April.

Other information
Organisations may also be supported. Any excess income is given to village groups which benefit local inhabitants. In 2012/13 five community grants totalled £8,900.

Stony Stratford

The Ancell Trust

£2,000

Correspondent: Karen Phillips, Secretary, 78 London Road, Stony Stratford, Milton Keynes MK11 1JH (01908 563350; email: karen.phillips30@hotmail.co.uk)

CC Number: 233824

Eligibility
People in need in the town of Stony Stratford.

Types of grants
Grants are given to students for books and are occasionally made to individuals for welfare purposes and to organisations.

Annual grant total
In 2012/13 the trust had an income of £10,000 and a total expenditure of £7,500. We estimate the grant total to be around £7,000 with approximately £3,500 paid to organisations and around £2,000 paid to individuals for educational purposes.

Applications
In writing to the correspondent at any time.

Other information
The charity owns the sports ground in Stony Stratford which provides cricket, football, bowls, croquet and tennis facilities.

Arnold's Education Foundation

See entry on page 235

Winslow

Rogers Free School Foundation

£1,000

Correspondent: Paul Mostyn, Trustee, 2 Byford Way, Winslow, Buckingham MK18 3RJ (01296 670419; email: p. mostyn@live.co.uk)

CC Number: 310557

Eligibility

People at any stage of education who live in the parish of Winslow.

Types of grants

Grants are given towards help with school uniforms, other school clothing, educational outings in the UK, books, fees, study or travel abroad, or for maintenance allowances.

Annual grant total

In 2012 the foundation had an income of £3,000 and a total expenditure of £2,000. This was the latest financial information available at the time of writing (July 2014). We estimate that educational grants to individuals totalled £1,000, with funding also awarded to educational organisations.

Applications

On an application form, available from the correspondent. Applications can be submitted either directly by the individual or through a parent.

Wolverton

Wolverton Science and Art Institution Fund

£2,100

Correspondent: Karen Phillips, Administrator, 78 London Road, Stony Stratford, Milton Keynes MK11 1JH (01908 563350; email: karen.phillips30@hotmail.co.uk)

CC Number: 310652

Eligibility

People who live, study or work in the parishes of Wolverton or Stantonbury.

Types of grants

The fund awards scholarships, bursaries and grants to schoolchildren, people starting work, further and higher education students, mature students and postgraduates. Particular preference is given to the arts, science and related subjects. Our research suggests that grants can range between £100 and £500 and are given towards the cost of school uniforms, other clothing, books, equipment/instruments, fees and educational outings in the UK.

Annual grant total

In 2012/13 the fund had an income of £6,200 and an expenditure of £4,300. We have estimated that the annual total of grants to individuals was about £2,100.

Exclusions

Our research indicates that grants are not available to cover the salary expenses of a project.

Applications

Application forms are available from the correspondent and can be submitted either directly by the individual or through a school/college/educational welfare agency, if applicable. According to our research, applications are considered in February, April, August and October and should be received in the preceding month.

Other information

The fund allocates up to one third of the income to provide benefits to educational organisations not normally provided by the local authorities.

Cambridgeshire

Bishop Laney's Charity

£24,000 (101 grants)

Correspondent: Richard Tyler, Secretary, 8 Barton Close, Witchford, Ely, Cambridgeshire CB6 2HS (01353 662813; email: richard_i_tyler@hotmail.com; website: www.whitingandpartners.co.uk/Bishop-Laney-Charity-Vocation)

CC Number: 311306

Eligibility

People in need under the age 25 who live in the parishes of Soham and Ely. Consideration might be given to people under 25 who live in other parts of Cambridgeshire where funds permit.

Types of grants

Grants are given towards education and training, especially apprentices and people starting work. Where possible awards are recurrent and can be given towards uniforms/clothing, books and equipment/instruments, also study or travel abroad, excursions in the UK and maintenance/living expenses. Grants to individuals are of around £150–£250.

Annual grant total

In 2013/14 the charity had assets of £3.1 million and an income of £109,000. A total of £24,000 was awarded in 101 grants to individuals.

Applications

Application forms are available from the Whiting and Partners website or can be requested from the correspondent. They can be submitted directly by the individual and are normally considered in July, September, October and December. Applications should include a copy of the applicant's birth certificate, proof of attendance at college/university/training and details of the items needed.

Other information

The charity can also give grants to educational establishments.

The trustees are looking to increase the number of applications.

The Leverington Town Lands Educational Charity

£10,000

Correspondent: Rosemary Gagen, Clerk to the Trustees, 78 High Road, Gorefield, Wisbech, Cambridgeshire PE13 4NB (01945 870454; email: leveoffees@aol.com)

CC Number: 311325

Eligibility

Schoolchildren and people in further/higher education who live in Leverington, Parson Drove and Gorefield.

Types of grants

One-off grants according to need.

Annual grant total

In 2012/13 the charity had both an income and expenditure of £22,000. We estimate around £10,000 was made in grants to individuals for education.

Applications

On a form available from the correspondent for consideration in September.

Other information

Grants are also made to local schools.

The Henry Morris Memorial Trust

£3,300

Correspondent: Peter Hains, Trustee, 24 Barton Road, Haslingfield, Cambridge CB23 1LL (email: mail@henrymorris.plus.com; website: www.henrymorris.plus.com)

CC Number: 311419

Eligibility

Young people between the ages of 13 and 19 who live or attend/have attended school or college in Cambridge/Cambridgeshire.

Types of grants

The trust is offering grants for short travel expeditions with a specific purpose and to help with the cost of materials and running expenses for a home-based project. Some examples of previously supported activities include: making a video diary of the village shop, investigating local wartime airfields, comparing two local windmills (home-based projects); a visit to a famous harpist in Dresden to listen and learn, a comparison between Coventry's and Dresden's old cathedrals, an enquiry into the story surrounding the fate of the 44 Jewish children of Izieu (travel awards).

Grants are from £20 to £200. Candidates are encouraged to fundraise towards their goal themselves.

Annual grant total

In 2013 the trust had an income of £4,700 and an expenditure of £3,500. We estimate that the annual total of grants was around £3,300.

Exclusions

Grants will not normally be made towards the full cost of a gap-year project, foreign exchange, school coursework, a holiday or a project planned and managed by a school/other organisation (for example, Raleigh International). The cost of permanent equipment is not usually covered.

Applications

Application forms are available from the local schools or from the trust's website. They can be submitted directly by the individual by 31 January for consideration in February/March. Candidates under the age of 18 will need full approval from a parent/guardian. Potential grant recipients are invited for an interview in Cambridge.

Other information

The trustees are looking for independently planned and managed projects and particularly seek to encourage 'individual candidates wishing to pursue topics of particular fascination to them'. All travel and accommodation arrangements have to be made by the applicants themselves.

Couples and groups are also encouraged to apply together.

The Charities of Nicholas Swallow and Others

£0

Correspondent: Nicholas Tufton, Clerk, 11 High Street, Barkway, Royston, Hertfordshire SG8 8EA (01763 848888)

CC Number: 203222

Eligibility

People in need who live in the parish of Whittlesford (near Cambridge) and adjacent area.

Types of grants

One-off grants according to need.

Annual grant total

In 2012/13 the charity had assets of £651,000 and an income of £59,000. No educational grants were awarded in this financial year.

Applications

In writing to the correspondent directly by the individual.

Other information

The principal activity of this charity is as a housing association which manages bungalows and garages.

Elsworth

The Samuel Franklin Fund Elsworth

£1,000

Correspondent: Serena Wyer, Administrator, 5 Cowdell End, Elsworth, Cambridge CB23 4GB (01954 267156; email: serena.wyersff@gmail.com)

CC Number: 228775

Eligibility

People who live in the parish of Elsworth, are entering further education, vocational training or are starting in a trade/occupation and require financial assistance.

Types of grants

One-off and recurrent grants in the range of £10 to £1,000 are given to individuals undertaking further education or vocational training.

Annual grant total

In 2013 the fund had assets of £137,000 and an income of £34,000. During the year support was provided to 32 beneficiaries totalling £17,900. Most of this sum was awarded for welfare purposes. We estimate that around £1,000 was given to individuals in education.

Applications

In writing to the correspondent. Applications should provide brief details of assistance required.

Other information

Grants are also made to local organisations and for general welfare purposes.

Hilton

Hilton Town Charity

£1,200

Correspondent: Phil Wood, Administrator, 1 Sparrow Way, Hilton, Huntingdon, Cambridgeshire PE28 9NZ (01480 830866; email: phil.n.wood@btinternet.com)

CC Number: 209423

Eligibility

People who live in the village of Hilton, Cambridgeshire.

Types of grants

Only a limited number of grants are given for educational purposes. Individuals at any stage or level of their education, undertaking study of any subject can be supported.

Annual grant total

In 2013 the charity had an income of £4,500 and a total expenditure of £5,300. We estimate that educational grants to individuals totalled around £1,200.

Applications

In writing to the correspondent.

Other information

Grants are also available for organisations which serve the direct needs of the village and for welfare purposes.

Little Wilbraham

The Johnson, Bede and Lane Charitable Trust

£1,000

Correspondent: Linda Stead, Trustee, 76 High Street, Little Wilbraham, Cambridge CB21 5JY (01223 813794; email: lindastead9@googlemail.com)

CC Number: 284444

Eligibility

People in need who live in the civil parish of Little Wilbraham.

Types of grants

Our research suggests that one-off grants, usually between £50 and £150, can be given to schoolchildren and university/college students. Support can be awarded towards fees, equipment/instruments, excursions, music lessons, school outings and so on.

Annual grant total

In 2012/13 the trust had an income of £4,400 and a total expenditure of £4,100. We estimate that around £1,000 was awarded in educational grants to individuals.

Applications

In writing to the correspondent. Applications can be made directly by the individual or through a third party, such as a social worker, Citizens Advice or a neighbour. Applications are considered on an ongoing basis.

Other information

Grants are also made to organisations and for welfare purposes.

Sawston

John Huntingdon's Charity

£11,500

Correspondent: Jill Hayden, Charity Manager, John Huntingdon House, Tannery Road, Sawston, Cambridge CB2 3UW (01223 492492; email: office@ johnhuntingdon.org.uk)

CC Number: 1118574

Eligibility

Schoolchildren, college students and people with special educational needs who live in the parish of Sawston in Cambridgeshire.

Types of grants

One-off grants, usually ranging from £25 to £250 and occasionally up to £500 or more. Grants are given to: schoolchildren for uniforms/clothing, school trips and books; college students for books and equipment/instruments; and people with special educational needs for uniforms/clothing, books, equipment/instruments and excursions.

Annual grant total

In 2013 the charity had assets of £8.4 million which mainly represents permanent endowment and is not available for grant giving. It had an income of £363,000 and a total expenditure of £335,000. Grants to individuals totalled £23,500 and we estimate that those awarded for educational purposes totalled £11,500.

Applications

On an application form available from Sawston Support Services at the address above or by telephone. Office opening hours are 9am to 2pm Monday to

Friday. Grants are considered on an ongoing basis.

Other information

The charity provides almshouses for those in financial need in the area of benefit. It also gives grants for social welfare purposes.

Werrington

The Werrington Educational Foundation

£500

Correspondent: John Burrell, Clerk, 15 Gildale, Werrington, Peterborough PE4 6QY (01733 577652)

CC Number: 311838

Eligibility

People under 25 who live in the parish of Paston (Werrington).

Types of grants

Grants towards the cost of essentials for schoolchildren, books, fees/living expenses and study or travel abroad for students, and towards books, equipment and clothing for people starting work. The trustees are required to have regard to the promotion of education in accordance with the principles of the Church of England. In the past, the foundation has had few individual applications and has given grants to the schools in the beneficial area. When individual applications are received they are given priority.

Annual grant total

In 2012 the foundation had an income of £1,000 and a total expenditure of £1,200. We estimate that educational grants to individuals totalled £500. Funding was also awarded to local schools.

At the time of writing (August 2014) this was the most recent financial information available for the foundation.

Applications

On a form available from the correspondent. Applications are considered in May and October.

Whittlesey

The Whittlesey Charity

£1,000

Correspondent: Phil Gray, Administrator, 33 Bellamy Road, Oundle, Peterborough PE8 4NE (01832 273085)

CC Number: 1005069

Eligibility

People under the age of 25 who live in the ancient parishes of Whittlesey Urban and Whittlesey Rural.

Types of grants

Any grant is considered, but the trustees say they would have to be satisfied that all alternative sources had been investigated. Previously grants have been made to allow people to travel abroad for trips such as a scouts jamboree and travel to the World Martials Arts Championships.

Annual grant total

Grants to individuals for educational purposes usually total around £1,000.

Applications

Applications can be submitted directly by the individual, school or college, or other appropriate third party. Applications are usually considered in February, May and September, but urgent applications could be dealt with at short notice. Note that the charity will not respond to ineligible applicants.

Other information

The charity makes grants to organisations and individuals, for relief in need, educational purposes, public purposes and it also makes grants to churches.

Wisbech

Elizabeth Wright's Charity

£4,000

Correspondent: Dr Iain Mason, Trustee, 13 Tavistock Road, Wisbech, Cambs PE13 2DY (01945 588646; email: Eliz. wrightcharity1725@gmail.com)

CC Number: 203896

Eligibility

People who live in the parishes of St Peter and Paul and St Augustine, Cambridgeshire.

Types of grants

Grants for students of music and other arts and towards vocational education or training in other areas. Primary, secondary and further education students can receive grants for projects in the areas of religious education, citizenship, arts, music and drama or Christian and youth work.

Annual grant total

The latest financial information available at the time of writing (August 2014) was from 2012. In 2012 the charity had an income of £38,000 and an expenditure of £33,000. Previously grants to individuals for educational purposes have totalled around £4,000.

Exclusions

Grants are not given for people starting work.

Applications

In writing to the correspondent. Applications can be submitted directly by the individual at any time.

Other information

The charity also makes grants to schools and organisations and supports individuals for welfare purposes.

East Sussex

Catherine Martin Trust

£13,500

Correspondent: The Administrator, Catherine Martin Trust, The Parish Office, Hove Vicarage, Wilbury Road, Hove, East Sussex BN3 3PB (email: audrey.good14@hotmail.co.uk)

CC Number: 258346

Eligibility

Children and young people under the age of 21 who are in full-time education, British born and have lived in the old borough of Hove and Portslade for at least one year. Support is intended to help individuals whose parents cannot work due to ill health or are deceased. It is necessary to demonstrate that applicants' next of kin or another person/persons acting as guardians do not have sufficient means to support the child.

Types of grants

Recurrent grants are available to schoolchildren and further/higher education students for educational expenses, including books, equipment/instruments, clothing, fees, travel and maintenance costs.

Annual grant total

In 2012/13 the trust had an income of £14,800 and an expenditure of £13,900. We estimate that the annual total of grants to individuals was around £13,500.

Applications

In writing to the correspondent. Applications can be made by the individual directly or through a third party, such as a relative, solicitor, school/college or educational welfare agency, social/health worker, if applicable. Applications are usually considered in March, June, August, September and December.

The Mrs A. Lacy Tate Trust

£10,500

Correspondent: The Trustees, Heringtons Solicitors, 39 Gildredge Road, Eastbourne, East Sussex BN21 4RY (01323 411020)

CC Number: 803596

Eligibility

Schoolchildren in need who live in East Sussex.

Types of grants

One-off and recurrent grants according to need.

Annual grant total

In 2012/13 the trust had assets of £686,000 and an income of £56,000. Grants were made to 75 individuals totalling £21,000. We estimate that grants to individuals for educational purposes were around £10,500.

Applications

In writing to the correspondent.

Other information

Grants are also made to individuals in need for relief-in-need purposes and to organisations.

Brighton and Hove

The Brighton Educational Trust

£2,500

Correspondent: Mary Grealish, Administrator, Brighton and Hove City Council, Central Accounting, Room 201, Kings House, Grand Avenue, Hove, East Sussex BN3 2SR (01273 291259)

CC Number: 306963

Eligibility

People under the age of 25 who have lived in Brighton and Hove for at least two years.

Types of grants

Small, one-off grants, usually between £10 and £250. The trust provides scholarships, maintenance allowances, assists with living expenses and gives support towards the cost of books, clothing, equipment/instruments, tools, educational outings and visits or travel costs in the UK and abroad in pursuance of education. Facilities for recreation, social and physical training for primary, secondary and further education students are provided, where these are not normally paid for by the local authorities. Financial assistance is also available to people starting work/

entering a trade and students of music and arts.

Annual grant total

In 2012/13 the trust had an income of £4,600 and an expenditure of £2,700. We estimate the annual total of grants to be about £2,500.

Exclusions

No grants are available for postgraduate students.

Applications

Application forms can be requested from the correspondent. The trustees meet twice a year, in April and October. Applications should be received by the end of March and September respectively. Our research indicates that applicants should also provide a letter of support from the place of study.

The Brighton Fund

£15,000

Correspondent: Mary Grealish, Administrator, Brighton and Hove City Council, Central Accounting, Room 201, Kings House, Grand Avenue, Hove (01273 291259; website: www.brighton-hove.gov.uk)

CC Number: 1011724

Eligibility

People in need who live in the Brighton and Hove administrative boundary.

Types of grants

One-off cash grants are given for nursery childcare costs, excursions and school uniforms.

Annual grant total

In 2012/13 the fund had an income of £46,000 and a total expenditure of £32,000. Grants are awarded to individuals for both educational and social welfare purposes. We estimate grants made for educational purposes to be around £15,000.

Applications

On a form, available from the correspondent or the fund's website, to be submitted either through an organisation such as Citizens Advice or a school or through a third party such as a social worker or teacher. Applications are considered upon receipt.

The Oliver and Johannah Brown Apprenticeship Fund

£6,500

Correspondent: Mary Grealish, Administrator, Brighton and Hove City Council, Central Accounting, Room 201

311

Kings House, Grand Avenue, Hove, East Sussex BN3 2LS (01273 291259)

CC Number: 306335

Eligibility

People under the age of 25 who have lived in Brighton and Hove for at least five years and are in training for a profession, trade, occupation, service or are undertaking an apprenticeship.

Types of grants

One-off grants of about £10 to £600 are given to help with the cost of fees, outfits/uniforms, travel costs, maintenance expenses, equipment/ instruments, books or other educational needs.

Annual grant total

In 2012/13 the fund had an income of £12,500 and an expenditure of £6,700. We estimate the annual total of grants to individuals to be around £6,500.

Exclusions

According to our research, overseas students studying in Britain cannot be supported.

Applications

In writing to the correspondent. Applications can be submitted by the individual directly and are normally considered in September and April. A letter of support from the place of study/ workplace should also be provided.

The Hallett Science Scholarship

£0

Correspondent: Mary Grealish, Administrator, Brighton and Hove City Council, Central Accounting, Room 201, Kings House, Grand Avenue, Hove, East Sussex BN3 2LS (01273 291259)

CC Number: 306361

Eligibility

People under the age of 25 who have lived in Brighton and Hove for at least two years and are undertaking courses or research projects in pure or applied science. Awards are available to students on a full-time course outside Brighton or full/part-time course at the Brighton Polytechnic (Technology) or Brighton Technical College.

Types of grants

One-off grants of £250 to £500 are given for materials and equipment and, occasionally, travel.

Annual grant total

In 2012/13 the fund had an income of £3,300. The correspondent has stated that there is around £2,000 available for distribution each year; however, during the 2012/13 there was no charitable

spending, due to difficulties in finding eligible beneficiaries.

Applications

Application forms are available from the correspondent. They can be submitted directly by the individual and are considered in April and September.

Other information

Recent low expenditure is due to the difficulty finding eligible applicants, the fund is definitely active and open for applications.

Miss Laura Soames Charity for Education of Girls (Soames Girls Educational Trust)

£3,600

Correspondent: Mary Grealish, Administrator, Brighton and Hove City Council, Central Accounting, Room 201, Kings House, Grand Avenue, Hove, East Sussex BN3 2LS (01273 291259; email: mary.grealish@brighton-hove.gov.uk)

CC Number: 306962

Eligibility

Girls and young women under the age of 25 who live in Brighton and Hove.

Types of grants

One-off grants in the range of £250–£500 are available towards general educational costs, including maintenance expenses, course fees, travel, books, equipment/ instruments, materials and clothing. School pupils and university/college students can be assisted.

Annual grant total

In 2012/13 the charity had an income of £6,900 and an expenditure of £3,800. We estimate that the annual total of grants was about £3,600.

Applications

In writing to the correspondent. Our research suggests that applications are considered twice a year, usually in April and September.

Hastings

The Isabel Blackman Foundation

£36,000 (45 grants)

Correspondent: The Administrator, Stonehenge, 13 Laton Road, Hastings, East Sussex TN34 2ES (01424 431756)

CC Number: 313577

Eligibility

People in education who live in Hastings and St Leonards district and require financial assistance.

Types of grants

Scholarships are available to schoolchildren for educational outings and further/higher education students (including mature students and postgraduates) for books, equipment/ instruments, fees, maintenance/living expenses or childcare costs.

Annual grant total

In 2012/13 the foundation had assets of £5.2 million, an income of £300,000 and a total charitable expenditure of £158,000. A total of £36,000 was awarded in educational grants to 45 individuals.

Applications

In writing to the correspondent. Applications can be made directly by individuals. The trustees' annual report from 2012/13 also states that 'applications for grants are more likely to succeed where it can be shown that the applicants are helping themselves as well as seeking assistance.'

Other information

The foundation also gives grants for education, health, culture, religion, environment, youth or welfare causes. It mainly supports organisations.

The Magdalen and Lasher Educational Foundation

£58,000

Correspondent: Gill Adamson, Administrator, 132 High Street, Hastings, East Sussex TN34 3ET (01424 452646; email: mlc@oldhastingshouse.co. uk; website: www.magdalenandlasher.co. uk)

CC Number: 306969

Eligibility

People under 25 who live in the borough of Hastings or who have attended schools in the borough for more than two years.

Types of grants

Scholarships, bursaries or maintenance allowances at higher education institutions for any profession, trade or calling; scholarships and maintenance allowances for education abroad; financial assistance to study music or other arts.

Annual grant total

In 2012/13 the foundation had assets of £4 million and an income of £160,000. 41 bursaries totalling £40,000 and individual grants totalling £18,000 were made.

Applications

On a form available from the correspondent. The trustees meet every three months.

Other information

The foundation also supports state schools in Hastings.

Mayfield

The Mayfield Charity

£1,000

Correspondent: Brenda Hopkin, Administrator, Appletrees, Alexandra Road, Mayfield, East Sussex TN20 6UD (01435 873279)

CC Number: 212996

Eligibility

People in need who live in the ancient parish of Mayfield.

Types of grants

One-off grants of £50 to £1,000 to: schoolchildren for uniforms, clothing, equipment, instruments and excursions; college students for study/travel abroad and equipment/instruments; and undergraduates for study/travel abroad.

Annual grant total

In 2012 the charity had an income of £4,000 and a total expenditure of £4,500. We estimate around £1,000 was given in grants to individuals for education.

The 2012 accounts were the latest available at the time of writing.

Applications

In writing to the correspondent at any time either directly by the individual or a family member, through a third party such as a social worker or teacher, or through an organisation such as Citizens Advice or a school. Proof of need should be included where possible.

Other information

The charity also makes grants to individuals for social welfare purposes.

Newick

The Lady Vernon (Newick) Educational Foundation

£2,500

Correspondent: Colin Andrews, Trustee, 91 Katherine Way, Seaford, East Sussex BN25 2XF (01323 351561)

CC Number: 306410

Eligibility

People under 25 living in and/or attending school in Newick only.

Types of grants

Scholarships, bursaries, maintenance grants and educational equipment.

Annual grant total

In 2012/13 the foundation had an income of £3,500 and an expenditure of £3,000. Grants totalled around £2,500.

Applications

In writing to the correspondent, either directly by the individual if aged 18 or over, or by the parent/guardian or through an organisation such as a school or educational welfare agency. Details of the purpose of the grant and the amount anticipated to be spent should be included in the application. They are considered in April and October and should be received in the preceding month.

Warbleton

Warbleton Charity

£500

Correspondent: John Leeves, Administrator, 4 Berners Court Yard, Berners Hill, Flimwell, Wadhurst, East Sussex TN5 7NE (01580 879248)

CC Number: 208130

Eligibility

People living in the parish of Warbleton who are either taking part in vocational training courses in further education or starting apprenticeships.

Types of grants

One-off grants according to need. Recent awards have been made for books and equipment.

Annual grant total

In 2013 the charity had an income of £2,500 and a total expenditure of £2,000. We estimate around £500 was made in grants to individuals for education.

Exclusions

Students on academic courses are not eligible.

Applications

In writing to the correspondent either directly by the individual or through an appropriate third party. Applications are considered on a regular basis.

Other information

Grants are also made for welfare purposes.

Essex

The Hervey Benham Charitable Trust

£900 (3 grants)

Correspondent: John Woodman, Clerk to the Trustees, 18 Wren Close, Stanway, Colchester CO3 8ZB (email: admin@ herveybenhamtrust.org.uk)

CC Number: 277578

Eligibility

People who live in Colchester or North East Essex and wish to further their artistic, and particularly musical, talent but are prevented by physical, environmental or financial difficulties.

Types of grants

One-off and recurrent musical scholarships ranging from £150 to £2,000. Support is given towards equipment/instruments, fees, study or travel abroad, album launch and other expenses.

Annual grant total

In 2012/13 the trust had assets of £1.2 million and an income of £27,000. A total of £4,000 was awarded in grants, of which £900 was given to three individuals. Around £5,000 was spent in administration costs.

Exclusions

Applications are only accepted within the trust's beneficial area and grants are not given for mainstream education.

Applications

In writing to the correspondent. The trustees meet twice a year and had a third meeting replaced by a postal consensus. Applications should outline what kind of assistance is requested, any other sources of funding available and any other details of individual's personal and financial circumstances.

Other information

The trust also supports organisations and various projects (a total of £3,000 in 2012/13).

The Butler Educational Foundation

£6,000

Correspondent: Nicholas Welch, Administrator, Duffield Stunt, 71 Duke Street, Chelmsford, Essex CM1 1JU (01245 262351)

CC Number: 310731

Eligibility

Children and young people living in the parishes of Boreham and Little Baddow who have attended a public elementary school in the area for at least two years.

Types of grants

Grants are available for general educational expenses, including clothing/uniforms, books, tools, equipment/instruments, maintenance costs, educational visits, fees, equipment for special projects and so on. Financial assistance is available to secondary school pupils, further/higher education students, people entering a trade/starting work or individuals undertaking apprenticeships.

Annual grant total

In 2012/13 the foundation had an income of £8,400 and an expenditure of £8,300. We estimate the annual total of grants to individuals be around £6,000.

Exclusions

Primary schoolchildren are not supported.

Applications

In writing to the correspondent. The trustees meet three times a year, usually in January, April and October. Our research suggests that normally one of the trustees will visit the applicant.

Other information

The foundation may also assist school libraries in the provision of books and fittings.

George Courtauld Educational Trust

£2,300

Correspondent: Bryony Wilmshurst, Administrator, c/o Cunningtons, Great Square, Braintree, Essex CM7 1UD (01376 326868)

CC Number: 310835

Eligibility

People under the age of 21 who live in, or have parents who live in, the parishes of Braintree, Bocking, Black Notley, Great Notley, Rayne and Cressing. Also eligible are those under the age of 21 who have at any time attended a school in the parishes.

Types of grants

One-off grants up to £250 are given to schoolchildren and further and higher education students for uniforms/other school clothing, books and equipment/instruments. Grants given include those in the areas of music and other arts and individuals preparing to enter a profession or trade after leaving school or higher education.

Annual grant total

In 2012 the trust had an income of £1,700 and a total expenditure of £2,500. We estimate that grants totalled £2,300.

At the time of writing (July 2014) this was the most recent financial information available for the trust.

Applications

On a form available from the correspondent. Applications can be submitted at any time, directly by the individual, including an independent letter of support and a written quotation.

Earls Colne and Halstead Educational Charity

£9,200 (40 grants)

Correspondent: Martyn Woodward, Clerk to the Trustees, St Andrew's House, 2 Mallows Field, Halstead, Essex CO9 2LN (01787 479960; email: earlscolnehalstead.edcharity@yahoo.co.uk; website: www.echec.org.uk)

CC Number: 310859

Eligibility

Children and young people between the ages of 5 and 25 who have lived for at least one year or attended school in the charity's catchment area in North Essex.

The following parishes are eligible: Alphamstone, Ashen, Belchamp Otten, Belchamp St Paul, Belchamp Walter, Birdbrook, Borley, Bulmer, Bures Hamlet, Castle Hedingham, Coggeshall, Colne Engaine, Earls Colne, Foxearth, Gestingthorpe, Gosfield, Great Henny, Great Maplestead, Great Yeldham, Greenstead Green and Halstead Rural, Helions Bumpstead, Lamarsh, Liston, Little Henny, Little Maplestead, Little Yeldham, Middleton, Ovington, Pebmarsh, Pentlow, Ridgewell, Sible Hedingham, Stambourne, Steeple Bumpstead, Stisted, Sturmer, Tilbury Juxta Clare, Toppesfield, Twinstead, White Colne and Wickham St Paul, the town of Halstead (all in the District of Braintree) and Chappel, Mount Bures and Wakes Colne (all in the District of Colchester).

Types of grants

The charity offers Book Grants for books, equipment/instruments, tools, outfits usually to further/higher education students; and Projects Grants for various educational projects and educational outings for schoolchildren. Priority is given to people studying for a recognised higher education qualification or who are already performing to a high level in the arts or sports.

Annual grant total

In 2012/13 the charity had assets of £1.2 million and an income of £61,000. A total of £9,200 was distributed in grants to 40 individuals.

Exclusions

Tuition fees are not normally supported.

Applications

Application forms can be found online or requested from the correspondent. Applications for Book Grants can be made at any time and for the Project Grants should be submitted in advance of the trustees' meetings which are held in February, July and November.

Other information

The charity also gives grants to local schools for educational travel or other purposes and supports voluntary bodies working for the benefit of young people in the charity's beneficial area. A total of £27,000 was awarded to organisations in 2012/13.

The Fawbert and Barnard's Educational Foundation

£500

Correspondent: Christine Baxter, Trustee, Fawbert and Barnard's (Undl) Primary School, London Road, Harlow CM17 0DA (01279 429427; email: admin@fawbert-barnards.essex.sch.uk)

CC Number: 310757

Eligibility

Young people, usually under the age of 25, who live in Harlow and surrounding areas.

Types of grants

The foundation may give small grants (usually of about £25) to school pupils towards books, equipment, clothing or travel and to college/university students towards fees, books, equipment or to supplement existing grants. Support is also available to people starting work towards the cost of education, training, apprenticeships or equipment.

Annual grant total

In 2013 the foundation had an income of £1,800 and an expenditure of £900. Normally the total charitable expenditure is above £1,000.

Exclusions

Grants are not given for school fees.

Applications

In writing to the correspondent. The trustees usually meet in February, June and October.

Other information

Our research shows that most of the funding is allocated to Fawbert and Barnard School. Grants are rarely made directly to individuals.

Great Bursthead Exhibition Foundation (Billericay Educational Trust)

£14,000

Correspondent: Jennifer Moore, Clerk to the Trustees, The Billericay School, School Road, Billericay, Essex CM12 9LH (01277 655191; email: info@ billericayeducationaltrust.co.uk; website: www.billericayeducationaltrust.co.uk)

CC Number: 310836

Eligibility

Young people under the age of 25 who live within a six-mile radius of Billericay (including Noak Bridge, Ramsden Bellhouse, Ramsden Heath and Stock) and are in need.

Types of grants

One-off or recurring grants may be given for up to three years to further/higher education students and people in vocational training or those starting work. Help is given towards general educational necessities, including clothing, tools, instruments and equipment, books, also tuition fees, travel for educational purposes in the UK or abroad, the study of music or other arts, recreational activities or physical training.

Annual grant total

In 2012/13 the foundation had an income of £15,300 and an expenditure of £14,400. We estimate that around £14,000 was given in grants to individuals.

Applications

Application forms can be downloaded from the foundation's website and should be submitted by June for consideration in July. Applicants are invited to an informal meeting.

Other information

Previously grants have also been given to schools to help with specific educational projects.

The Canon Holmes Memorial Trust

£10,300

Correspondent: John Brown, Trustee, 556 Galleywood Road, Chelmsford

CM2 8BX (01245 358185; email: canonjbrown@mac.com)

CC Number: 801964

Eligibility

Children between the ages of 7 and 13 who live or have recently lived in the Roman Catholic diocese of Brentwood and cannot continue their education because their parents/guardians are experiencing financial difficulties as a result of employment problems, marital breakdown, illness or death.

Types of grants

Short-term scholarships and bursaries to continue school education in the moment of crisis. Grants can be given for private school fees.

Annual grant total

In 2012/13 the trust had an income of £11,700 and an expenditure of £10,500. We estimate the annual total of grants to individuals to be around £10,300.

Applications

In writing to the correspondent. Applications should be made by a parent or guardian and grants will be made directly to the school.

Ann Johnson's Educational Foundation

£17,000

Correspondent: J. P. Douglas-Hughes, Clerk, 58 New London Road, Chelmsford, Essex CM2 0PA (01245 493939; fax: 01245 493940; email: douglas-hughesj@gepp.co.uk)

CC Number: 310799

Eligibility

People living or educated in Chelmsford and the surrounding parishes, who are under 25.

Types of grants

Help with the cost of books, clothing and other essentials for schoolchildren, including school fees. Grants are also available for those at college or university and towards the cost of books, equipment and instruments, clothing and travel for people starting work.

Annual grant total

In 2012/13 the foundation had an income of £32,000 and a total expenditure of over £22,000. We estimate grants to individuals to total around £17,000.

Applications

On a form available from: Ravenscroft, Stock Road, Galleywood, Chelmsford, Essex CM2 8PW (01245 260757). The governors meet quarterly to consider applications.

Other information

The foundation also gives funding to local schools. The accounting year of the foundation appears to have changed from end December to end September.

The Pilgrim Educational Trust

£1,000

Correspondent: Bryony Wilmshurst, Administrator, Cunningtons, Great Square, Braintree CM7 1UD (01376 326868)

CC Number: 1083109

Eligibility

People aged between 16 and 20 years (inclusive) who attend a Braintree or Bocking senior school, namely Alec Hunter High School, Braintree College of Further Education, Notley High School or Tabor High School.

Types of grants

One-off grants are given for costs incurred in connection with A-level courses.

Annual grant total

In 2012/13 the trust had an income of £1,300 and an expenditure of £1,100. We estimate the annual total of grants to be around £1,000.

Applications

In writing to the correspondent. Applications must include an independent letter of support.

Canewdon

The Canewdon Educational Foundation

£3,200 (40 grants)

Correspondent: Alan Lane, Administrator, Trust House, Anchor Lane, Canewdon, Rochford, Essex SS4 3PA (07706 877 437)

CC Number: 310718

Eligibility

People under the age of 25 who live in the parish of Canewdon and are in full-time education.

Types of grants

Grants to assist with primary and secondary education or to support people starting work/entering a trade/undertaking apprenticeships. Help is given towards the purchase of books, tuition in music, dance, drama and swimming, extra tuition, boarding costs, travel expenses, dyslexia assessment, school uniforms, school trips and other needs.

Annual grant total

The latest financial information available at the time of writing (July 2014) was from 2012. In 2012 the foundation had assets of £637,000 and an income of £31,000. Grants to 40 individuals totalled around £3,200, broken down as follows:

School trips	6	£900
Dance, drama and singing lessons	9	£800
Swimming tuition	15	£650
Textbooks for courses	3	£300
Travel expenses to college	4	£300
College boarding	2	£100
Football club fees	1	£40

Exclusions

Individuals from outside the parish of Canewdon will not be supported.

Applications

In writing to the correspondent. Information sheets are normally delivered to each household in the parish giving details of how, and to whom, applications should be made. The trustees meet monthly. Note that unsolicited applications will not be responded to.

Other information

Primarily, 20% of the unrestricted fund income after the deduction of the trustees' expenses is paid to the Canewdon Poor's Charity (registered charity number 210406). In 2012 the amount given totalled £1,200.

Grants are also made to organisations (including youth clubs) and local primary schools (£5,800 in 2012).

Chelmsford

Chelmsford Educational Foundation (CEF)

£9,500

Correspondent: Richard Emsden, Administrator, 19 Rushleydale, Chelmsford CM1 6JX (07941 958652; email: remsden@gmail.com)

CC Number: 310815

Eligibility

People who live or have been educated in the borough and former rural district of Chelmsford.

Types of grants

Grants are given to people in education and training towards general needs, such as books, fees, tools, equipment, instruments, also travel/study abroad, study of music, and for any other activities that will help the applicant to achieve employment or qualifications. Awards usually are of up to £500.

Annual grant total

In 2013 the foundation had an income of £21,000 and an expenditure of £20,000. We estimate that grants to individuals totalled around £9,500.

Exclusions

Grants are not normally given for school fees.

Applications

In writing to the correspondent. Our research suggests that candidates are interviewed.

Other information

Grants are also available to organisations and schools.

Coggeshall

Sir Robert Hitcham's Exhibition Foundation

£7,000

Correspondent: Nicholas Johnson, Trustee, 75 Queen Street, Coggeshall, Colchester CO6 1UE (01376 562915)

CC Number: 1095014

Eligibility

People under the age of 25 who live in Coggeshall and have left school and are moving on to higher education or training.

Types of grants

Small grants are given towards books, equipment/instruments, clothing/uniforms/outfits, tools and living costs to students and people starting work/entering a trade.

Annual grant total

In 2012/13 the foundation had an income of £6,700 and a total expenditure of £7,100. We have estimated the annual total of grants to individuals to be around £7,000.

Applications

Application forms can be requested from the correspondent. Our research suggests that applications are normally considered in early September and should be submitted by the end of August.

Finchingfield

Sir Robert Kemp's Education Foundation

£1,500

Correspondent: Jo Davies, Trustee, Bramble Cottage, Mill End, Spains Hall Road, Finchingfield, Essex CM7 4NH (01371 810642)

CC Number: 310804

Eligibility

People in need who are under 25 and live, or whose parents live, in the parish of Finchingfield.

Types of grants

Grants are given towards, for example, books, clothing, equipment, educational trips, music for individual students or people starting work.

Annual grant total

In 2012 the foundation had an income of £2,200 and a total expenditure of £3,200. We estimate that educational grants to individuals totalled £1,500, with funding also awarded to organisations.

At the time of writing (July 2014) this was the most recent financial information available for the foundation.

Applications

On a form available from the correspondent. Applications should be submitted in April and October for consideration in May and November.

Gestingthorpe

The Gestingthorpe Educational Foundation

£1,500

Correspondent: Peter Collett, Administrator, Orchard House, Audley End, Gestingthorpe, Halstead, Essex CO9 3AU (01787 469187; email: peterccollett@btinternet.com)

CC Number: 310725

Eligibility

People who live in the ancient parish of Gestingthorpe, preference being given to those under 25.

Types of grants

One-off grants are given to: schoolchildren and further education students for books equipment/instruments, fees, educational outings in the UK and study or travel abroad; to mature and vocational students for books and fees; and to higher education students for books. Grants are in the range of £10 to £225.

Annual grant total

Grants awarded to individuals for educational purposes usually total around £1,500.

Applications

In writing to the correspondent directly by the individual, including receipts for any payments made. Applications are usually considered in April and October.

Ongar

Joseph King's Charity

£41,000 (60 grants)

Correspondent: Catherine Kenny, Secretary, 36 Coopers Hill, Ongar, Essex CM5 9EF (01277 366167)

CC Number: 810177

Eligibility

People under 25 years of age who live in the civil parish of Chipping Ongar.

Types of grants

Help with the cost of books, clothing and other essentials for schoolchildren. Help may also be available for students at college or university. Preference is given to the advancement of the Christian religion.

Annual grant total

In 2012 the charity had assets of £1.8 million and an income of £69,000. Educational grants to 60 individuals totalled £41,000. A further £2,200 was given in grants to three schools and a Sunday school, and towards 'Sunday Special' activities at St Martin's Church, Chipping Ongar.

At the time of writing (July 2014) this was the most recent information available for the charity.

Applications

In writing to the correspondent.

Other information

One twentieth of the charity's remaining income after management expenses have been deducted is given to St Martin's and St Peter's Parochial Church Council for King's Ecclesiastical Charity.

Hampshire

Aldworth's Educational Trust (Aldworth Trust Foundation)

£2,300 (23 grants)

Correspondent: D. Reavell, 25 Cromwell Road, Basingstoke RG21 5NR (01256 473390; email: reavell@btinternet.com)

CC Number: 307259

Eligibility

Children and young people who are either resident or were educated/are attending school in the borough of Basingstoke and Deane.

Types of grants

Grants can be awarded for travel, books, equipment and clothing. The charity has informed us that most of their grants go to 'school children whose parents cannot afford the costs of residential visits which primary schools make.'

Annual grant total

In 2012/13 the trust had an income of £4,100 and an expenditure of £4,500. Grants to individuals totalled £2,300 with an average grant being £97.

Applications

In writing to the correspondent.

The Ashford Hill Educational Trust

£7,500

Correspondent: Graham Swait, Administrator, Oakview, Yeomans Lane, Newtown, Newbury RG20 9BL (01635 276098)

CC Number: 1040559

Eligibility

People who live in the parish of Ashford Hill with Headley or the surrounding area.

Types of grants

Grants are generally given to promote social and physical education. They are given towards the cost of formal education, enhancement of employment prospects, group activities, music, adult education and sporting and recreational activities.

Annual grant total

In 2012 the trust had an income of £6,900 and made grants totalling approximately £7,500.

These were the latest accounts available at the time of writing (July 2014).

Applications

On a form available from the correspondent. Applications are considered in January, March, July and October.

Bramshott Educational Trust

£3,100

Correspondent: Richard Weighell, Trustee, 107 Haslemere Road, Liphook GU30 7BU (01428 724289; email: info@bramshotteducationaltrust.org.uk; website: www.bramshotteducationaltrust.org.uk)

CC Number: 277421

Eligibility

Children and young people under the age of 25 who live, or have a parent/guardian who lives, in the ancient parish of Bramshott, which includes Liphook, Bramshott, Passfield, Conford and the parts of Hammer Vale located in Hampshire.

Types of grants

Grants of up to £250 are awarded for general educational needs which in the past have included equipment/instruments, tools, school uniforms/clothing, books, educational trips/visits, specialist courses and tuition, also extra-curricular activities such as music or ballet lessons.

Annual grant total

In 2012/13 the trust had an income of £6,600 and an expenditure of £5,300. The trustees have discretion to allocate funds to support local schools, therefore we estimate the annual total of grants to individuals to be around £3,100.

Exclusions

The trust's eligibility guidelines remind that 'in order to support as many applicants as possible, the trustees do not fund the whole amount required and do not award grants for expenditure which would reasonably be provided by the local authority.'

Applications

Application forms can be found on the trust's website or requested from the correspondent. The deadlines for submission are 15 March for consideration in April and 15 September for consideration in October.

Other information

Up to one third of the yearly income can be allocated to help local schools.

The Cliddesden and Farleigh Wallop Educational Trust

£8,500

Correspondent: Alison Mosson, Administrator, 11 Southlea, Cliddesden, Basingstoke RG25 2JN

CC Number: 307150

Eligibility

People under 25 who are in need of financial assistance and live within the original boundaries of the parishes of Cliddesden and Farleigh Wallop only.

Types of grants

One-off and recurrent grants. Education is considered in its broadest sense, from help with school projects and trips, to college/university courses and music lessons.

Annual grant total

In 2013 the trust had an income of £12,600 and a total expenditure of £17,600. We estimate that educational grants to individuals totalled £8,500, with funding also awarded to organisations.

Applications

In writing to the correspondent. Applications should be submitted through a school or directly by the individual or their guardian to reach the secretary by the end of April, August or December, accompanied by fully documented receipts.

Dibden Allotments Fund

£2,400 (7 grants)

Correspondent: Valerie Stewart, Administrator, 7 Drummond Court, Prospect Place, Hythe, Southampton SO45 6HD (02380 841305; email: dibdenallotments@btconnect.com; website: daf-hythe.org.uk)

CC Number: 255778

Eligibility

People in need who live in the parishes of Hythe, Dibden, Marshwood and Fawley.

Types of grants

One-off and recurrent grants according to need. Recent grants have been awarded for school uniforms, other school clothing, books, equipment, fees and living expenses for students in further and higher education, educational outings for schoolchildren and childcare for mature students.

Annual grant total

In 2012/13 the fund had assets of £9.1 million and an income of £349,000. There were 7 grants made for educational purposes to individuals totalling £2,400.

Applications

On a form available on the fund's website, where its criteria, guidelines and application process are also posted. It is helpful to supply a supporting statement from a 'professional' such as a health or social worker, midwife or teacher.

Other information

Grants are also made to charitable and voluntary organisations.

Gordon Charitable Trust

See entry on page 285

The Robert Higham Apprenticing Charity

£8,200

Correspondent: Roy Forth, Administrator, PO Box 7721, Kingsclere RG20 5WQ (07796 423108; email: kclerecharities@aol.co.uk)

CC Number: 307083

Eligibility

People aged between 16 and 25 attending sixth forms, colleges and universities who live in the parishes of Kingsclere, Ashford Hill and Headley.

Types of grants

Grants towards books, specialist equipment and clothing or travelling expenses for those preparing for, or engaged in, any profession, trade, occupation or service or towards books, study or travel abroad for those studying for A-levels. Grants can be one-off or recurrent and are given according to need.

Annual grant total

In 2013 the charity had an annual income of nearly £8,000 and made grants totalling approximately £8,200.

Applications

On a form available from the correspondent. Applications must include a letter outlining the applicant's further education plans. Applications are not accepted from parents.

The Foundation of Sarah Rolle

£4,000

Correspondent: Gregory McCann, Secretary, Mount View, East Dean Road, Lockerley, Romsey SO51 0JQ (01794 340698)

CC Number: 307157

Eligibility

Schoolchildren, people starting work and further and higher education students under 25 who live, or whose parents live, in the parishes of East Tytherley and Lockerley.

Types of grants

Grants, ranging from £50 to £250, for uniforms/other school clothing, books, equipment/instruments, educational outings in the UK and study or travel abroad.

Annual grant total

In 2012 the foundation had assets of £302,000 and an income of £26,000. Educational grants to individuals totalled £4,000. A further £13,200 was awarded

to groups and organisations, including two local primary schools.

At the time of writing (July 2014) this was the most recent information available for the foundation.

Exclusions

Grants are not given for school or college fees or living expenses.

Applications

On a form available from the correspondent, to be submitted either directly by the individual or through a parent. Applications should be submitted by January or July for consideration in February or August respectively.

The Earl of Southampton Trust

£500

Correspondent: Sue Boden, Clerk to the Trustees, 24 The Square, Titchfield, Hampshire PO14 4RU (01329 513294; email: earlstrust@yahoo.co.uk; website: eost.org.uk/)

CC Number: 238549

Eligibility

People in need who live in the ancient parish of Titchfield (now subdivided into the parishes of Titchfield, Sarisbury, Locks Heath, Warsash, Stubbington and Lee-on-the-Solent).

Types of grants

One-off grants ranging from between £25 and £1,000 to schoolchildren, college students, mature students and to people with special educational need towards tuition fees, uniforms and books.

Annual grant total

In 2012/13 the trust had assets of £1.6 million and an income of £99,000. A total of £27,000 was awarded in 55 grants, the majority of which was awarded for social welfare purposes. We estimate that grants for school uniforms totalled around £500. During the year, no grants were made towards tuition fees.

Exclusions

Grants are not given for study or travel abroad, student exchange, tertiary and postgraduate education.

Applications

On a form available to download from the trust's website. They should be submitted through a school or other educational establishment, welfare agency or another appropriate third party. Applications must include financial details of the applicant and the trustees may request further information. Applications are considered monthly.

Other information

The trust runs almshouses and a day centre for old people.

The trust's main office is open 9.30am – 1.00pm every Tuesday, Wednesday and Thursday.

Sir Mark and Lady Turner Charitable Settlement

£3,300

Correspondent: Elizabeth Fettes-Neame, Administrator, Kleinwort Benson Trustees Ltd, 14 St Georges Street, London W1S 1FE (020 3207 7337; email: elizabeth.fettes-neame@kleinwortbenson.com)

CC Number: 264994

Eligibility

University students in need, with a preference to those living in Highgate, North London.

Types of grants

One-off and recurrent grants between £100 and £500 are given for university tuition fees and necessities, including books or equipment/instruments.

Annual grant total

In 2012/13 the charity had an income of £9,600 and an expenditure of £13,200. We estimate that the annual total of grants to individuals for educational purposes was about £3,300.

Applications

In writing to the correspondent. Our research suggests that applicants should include either their telephone number or email address and submit the application by the end of April or October for consideration in early June or December, respectively.

Other information

Grants are also made for welfare purposes. Both individuals and organisations can be supported.

Alverstoke

The Alverstoke Trust

£500

Correspondent: Jane Hodgman, Administrator, 5 Constable Close, Gosport, Hampshire PO12 2UF (02392589822)

CC Number: 239303

Eligibility

People in need who live in the parish of Alverstoke. In exceptional circumstances people resident in the borough of Gosport can be supported.

Types of grants

One-off grants, usually of up to £200, are available to college students, undergraduates, vocational students and people with special educational needs. Grants given include those for fees, study/travel abroad and books.

Annual grant total

In 2013 the trust had an income of £1,800 and a total expenditure of £1,200. We estimate that educational support totalled around £500.

Exclusions

Our research indicates that the trust does not make loans, grants to other charities or recurring awards.

Applications

In writing to the correspondent. Applications can be made by individuals directly or through a third party, such as Citizens Advice, a social worker or welfare agency, if applicable. Awards can be considered at any time.

Andover

Miss Gale's Educational Foundation (The Gale Trust)

£15,000

Correspondent: John Butcher, Trustee, Barker Son and Isherwood, 32 High Street, Andover SP10 1NT (email: gales.trust@yahoo.co.uk)

CC Number: 307145

Eligibility

Children and young people in need who are under the age of 25, live in or near Andover and are attending/have attended any school in the area. Preference is given to girls and applicants from families with serious difficulties.

Types of grants

The foundation provides small, one-off grants to schoolchildren, higher/further education students and people starting work/entering a profession. Financial assistance is available towards general educational expenses, including the cost of uniforms/clothing, books, equipment/ instruments, tools, educational outings and study/travel abroad.

Annual grant total

In 2013 the foundation had both an income and an expenditure of £15,100. We have estimated that the annual total of grants was just under £15,000.

Exclusions

Our research suggests that grants are not normally given towards the cost of school or college fees or living expenses.

Applications

In writing to the correspondent. Applications can be made by individuals directly or through their educational establishment or welfare agency, if applicable. According to our research, applicants are required to specify the individual's date of birth, give reasons why the family are not able to provide themselves and explain what the grant is required for.

Fareham

The William Price Charitable Trust

£15,400 (94 grants)

Correspondent: Christopher Thomas, Administrator, 24 Cuckoo Lane, Fareham, Hamps PO14 3PF (01329 663685; email: mazchris@tiscali.co.uk; website: www.pricestrust.org.uk)

CC Number: 307319

Eligibility

Children and young people under the age of 25 who live in the parishes of St Peter and St Paul, Holy Trinity with St Columba and St John the Evangelist (the same area as the original Fareham town parish but not the whole area of the Fareham borough).

Types of grants

Grants are intended to support such areas which 'do not command adequate priority in education.' The trustees will favour projects which 'enrich the quality of life and widen horizons, encourage participation and appreciation of the arts, develop good citizenship and encourage help in the community and local environment.' Support can equally be given towards fees, travel costs, outfits/clothing, books or other necessities. In accordance with the provisions of the trust the trustees also seek to promote education in the doctrines of the Church of England. Major grants for educational benefits are normally in the range of £1,000 while the minor 'hardship' grants for urgent needs are of about £100.

Annual grant total

In 2012/13 the trust had assets of £6.5 million, an income of £188,000 and a total charitable expenditure of £114,000. Grants to individuals totalled £15,400. A total of £12,100 was awarded in 'hardship grants' to 91 people and three students were supported through larger bursaries, grants for college/ university fees and overseas projects totalling £3,300.

Applications

Where possible applications should be made through a school/college; however, individual applications will be considered, particularly from people in further/higher education. Application forms can be downloaded from the trust's website or requested from the correspondent. Bursaries and college/ university grants are considered twice a year, normally in March and September, and applications should be received by the first day of these months. Applications for smaller 'hardship grants' can be made at any time and will be paid through a school/college.

Other information

Grants are also made to churches and schools/colleges (£88,000 in 2012/13) and there is an annual grant to the Fareham Welfare Trust (£10,000).

The trustees have established a bursary for the two private schools in the area offering one-off emergency help with fees. These grants are designed to help children whose parents have run into financial difficulties. Applications should be made by the schools. In 2012/13 one such bursary of £1,500 was awarded.

Gosport

Thorngate Relief-in-Need and General Charity

£3,000

Correspondent: Kay Brent, Administrator, 16 Peakfield, Waterlooville PO7 6YP (02392 264400; email: kay.brent@btinternet.com)

CC Number: 210946

Eligibility

People in need who live in Gosport.

Types of grants

One-off grants mostly between £100 and £500.

Annual grant total

In 2012/13 the charity had an income of £8,800 and a total expenditure of £12,300. Grants are made for both welfare and educational purposes. We estimate grants for educational purposes for individuals to be around £3,000.

Exclusions

No grants are made towards legal expenses.

Applications

On a form available from the correspondent. Applications can be made either directly by the individual or through a social worker, Citizens Advice,

the probation service or other welfare agency.

Other information

Grants are also made to organisations.

Isle of Wight

The Broadlands Home Trust

£2,000

Correspondent: Mrs M. Groves, Administrator, 2 Winchester Close, Newport, Isle of Wight PO30 1DR (01983 525630; email: broadlandstrust@ btinternet.com)

CC Number: 201433

Eligibility

Girls and young single women (under the age of 22) in need who are at school, starting work or are in further or higher education.

Types of grants

One-off grants of £100 to schoolchildren, vocational students, people with special needs and people starting work, including those for uniforms/clothing, books, equipment/ instruments and educational trips.

Annual grant total

In 2012/13 the trust had an income of £11,800 and a total expenditure of £9,600. The charity gives grants for both educational and social welfare purposes and we estimate the total educational grants to be around £2,000.

Exclusions

No grants for married women or graduates.

Applications

On a form available from the correspondent, to be submitted either directly by the individual or a family member. Applications are considered quarterly in January, April, July and October.

Portsmouth

The Bentley Young Person's Trust

£1,000

Correspondent: John Turner, Trustee, Hazel Bank, Morland, Penrith, Cumbria CA10 3BB (01931 714304; email: john@ fundaid.net)

CC Number: 1069727

Eligibility

People under the age of 26 who live in Portsmouth and surrounding areas or who have a connection with the area.

Types of grants

Grants to help develop the 'physical, mental and spiritual capacities' of young people.

Annual grant total

In 2012/13 the trust had an income of £3,400 and a total expenditure of around £2,300. We estimate that the annual total of grants to individuals was about £1,000.

Exclusions

Direct educational fees are not provided.

Applications

In writing to the correspondent.

Other information

Grants are also made to organisations.

Reuben Foundation

See entry on page 357

Wield

Wield Educational Charity

£2,800

Correspondent: Teresa Burnhams, Trustee, The Dairy, Upper Wield, Alresford SO24 9RT

CC Number: 288944

Eligibility

Schoolchildren under the age of 18 living in the parish of Wield.

Types of grants

Grants are provided towards educational activities which are not available within the school curriculum. Our research suggests that people with special educational needs are given preference.

Annual grant total

In 2012/13 the charity had an income of £7,700 and an expenditure of £5,900. It also supports schools, therefore we have estimated the annual total of grants to individuals to be around £2,800.

Exclusions

School fees or maintenance costs are not normally supported.

Applications

In writing to the correspondent.

Other information

The charity also provides support to the local schools where assistance is not already given by the local authority.

Hertfordshire

The 948 Sports Foundation

£4,600 (9 grants)

Correspondent: Julia Dekker, Administrator, Old Albanian Sports Club, Woollam Playing Fields, 160 Harpenden Road, St Albans AL3 6BB (01727 864476; email: Julia. dekker@ntlworld.com; website: www. the948sportsfoundation.org)

CC Number: 1088273

Eligibility

Young people who attend schools, colleges and universities in St Albans and the surrounding areas.

Types of grants

Grants of up to £1,000 are given according to need to allow individuals to participate in sports and recreational activities.

Annual grant total

In 2012/13 the foundation had assets of £538,000 and an income of £21,000. A total of £10,300 was spent on charitable activities, of which £4,600 was awarded to nine individuals.

Exclusions

Retrospective grants are not made and funding is not normally given for holidays or general grants.

Applications

Application forms can be downloaded from the foundation's website or requested from the correspondent. They should be submitted by post at least ten days before the trustees' meeting. Candidates are required to provide copies of accreditation from sport associations and demonstrate evidence of efforts to secure funding from other sources. Awards are only made upon production of an invoice/purchase order/a copy of a receipt.

Other information

Grants are also made to St Albans schools and organisations towards projects, equipment and facilities. In 2012/13 four organisations were supported totalling £5,900.

The Digswell Arts Trust

£1,600

Correspondent: Steve Rogers, Trustee, 10 Old Garden Court, St Albans, Hertfordshire AL3 4RQ (01727 811412; email: sje_rogers@hotmail.com; website: www.digswellartstrust.com)

CC Number: 305993

Eligibility

Young people living in Welwyn, Hertfordshire and the surrounding areas 'who intend to or have become artists or craftsmen who are in need of financial assistance by the provision of materials or the payment of fees, travelling expenses or maintenance allowances or by other means for their advancement in life and to enable them to earn their living.'

Types of grants

One-off and recurrent according to need. The payment of fees, travel expenses or maintenance allowances.

Annual grant total

In 2012/13 the trust had assets of £36,000 and an income of £35,000. Grants made to individuals totalled £1,600.

Applications

In writing to the correspondent.

Fawbert and Barnard School's Foundation

£5,000

Correspondent: Pamela Rider, Trustee, 22 South Brook, Sawbridgeworth, Hertfordshire CM21 9NS (01279 724670)

CC Number: 310965

Eligibility

People between the ages of 16 and 25 who live within a three-mile radius of Great St Mary's church in Sawbridgeworth or who attend/have attended school in that area for at least three years.

Types of grants

One-off grants and bursaries to assist further/higher education students. Awards are made to help with the cost of books or materials associated with a course. Grants are usually in the range of £100 to £200.

Annual grant total

In 2013 the foundation had an income of £9,900 and an expenditure of £10,200. We estimate the annual total of grants to individuals to be around £5,000.

Applications

Application forms can be requested from the correspondent. Applications should normally be submitted by 30 September; they are considered in October.

Other information

As the grant is awarded once only, students who do not apply during their first year can apply at any time during their period of study.

Support can also be given to organisations.

Hertfordshire County Nursing Trust (Hertfordshire Nursing Trust)

£27,000

Correspondent: Nicholas Tufton, Trustee, 11 Highway Street, Barkway, Royston, Hertfordshire SG8 8EA (01763 848888; email: nicholas@ntufton.co.uk; website: www.hertsnursing.co.uk)

CC Number: 207213

Eligibility

Nurses who have worked within the community of Hertfordshire for at least 18 months. As defined by the Queen's Nursing Institute, the 'community' means 'working outside a hospital setting'

Types of grants

Financial assistance is available to both individual nurses and groups for various activities, projects and full-time or part-time courses which contribute to applicant's professional development. It is reminded that any available funding from NHS sources must be exhausted prior to application. Recently grants have been awarded for the following activities/projects/courses: counselling, palliative care, cancer care, mental health, childcare, learning disabilities, asthma tissue viability, systemic psychotherapy, pain management, gerontology nurse prescribing and general nursing degrees.

Annual grant total

In 2012/13 the trust had assets of £805,000 and both an income and a total charitable expenditure of £55,000. Educational grants to individuals totalled £27,000.

Exclusions

Grants are not made retrospectively and cannot be provided for subsistence expenses for conferences or academic courses, such as travel, hotel, food costs and so on.

Applications

Application forms can be found on the trust's website. A completed application form should be accompanied with full details and costs of the course or conference attended. The trustees require the application to be signed by the applicant's manager to confirm his/her support and agreement with the project.

Applications should demonstrate the benefit of the funding to the applicant and their care abilities. In the case of applications for equipment, the application should demonstrate how it benefits the patients/families/carers.

The trust's website also notes that:

Applications should be for one activity or project ... consideration will not be given to several different courses or conferences in one year. In the case of academic courses, funding must be sought for each academic year and in certain instances for each academic module.

Other information

The trust owns Rosemary House, which comprises ten flats. The flats are let at a rent well below the market levels to nurses who are working or have worked in the community of Hertfordshire. Other welfare support is available to working and retired nurses.

Grants are also made to the Queen's Nursing Institute.

The Hertfordshire Educational Foundation

£10,000

Correspondent: Justin Donovan, Administrator, c/o Finance Accountancy Group, 3rd Floor, North West Block, County Hall, Hertford, Herts SG13 8DN

CC Number: 311025

Eligibility

Pupils and students up to 21 years who have a home address in Hertfordshire.

Types of grants

The foundation administers three types of grant scheme:
1   Travel scholarships to individuals aged 17 to 21 to undertake approved courses of study, expeditions, voluntary work and other projects in overseas countries. The usual duration is for a minimum of one month and individuals should be able to demonstrate how their project will benefit the local community they are visiting. Scholarships range between £100 and £500
2   Grants for school visits, usually ranging between £25 and £50. Help for pupils in exceptional circumstances, whose parents have difficulty in paying the board and lodging cost of visits arranged by their schools
3   The Sir George Burns Fund. Grants to enable young people who are disabled or underprivileged aged 16 to 21 to participate in expeditions, educational visits and so on, or to purchase special items of equipment needed for them to become involved in recreational and educational activities. Grants are usually in the range of £50 to £700 and previous awards have covered the costs of laptops and computer software, travel expenses, courses and conferences

Annual grant total

In 2012 the foundation had an income of £21,000 and an expenditure of £22,000. Educational grants to individuals total around £10,000 each year.

The 2012 accounts were the latest available at the time of writing.

Applications

On forms available from the correspondent. Applications should be submitted at least a month before the individual travels. The deadlines for travel scholarships and Sir George Burns Fund applications are the end of February, May and October. Guidelines and application forms are available from the foundation's website.

Other information

The foundation has also provided grants to organisations.

Hitchin Education Foundation

£22,000

Correspondent: Brian Frederick, Administrator, 33 Birch Close, Broom, Biggleswade SG18 9NR (01767 313892)

CC Number: 311024

Eligibility

People who live in the former urban district of Hitchin and surrounding villages, aged under 25.

Types of grants

One-off grants are given towards the costs of uniforms, books, scholarships and other educational facilities.

Grants are means tested, so income and size of family are taken into account.

Annual grant total

In 2012/13 the foundation had assets of £1.3 million and an income of £99,000. £22,000 was made in grants to individuals consisting of £2,900 in grants of less than £400 and £19,500 in grants of over £400.

Exclusions

Grants are not available for fees, travel, living expenses or mature students.

Applications

On a form available from the correspondent, either directly by the individual, or through the individual's school, college, educational welfare agency or any third party. They are considered monthly.

Other information

Grants were also made available to four educational establishments.

The James Marshall Foundation

£104,000 (181 grants)

Correspondent: Teresa Whittle, Clerk to the Trustees, Trustees' Office, Unit 6, 17 Leyton Road, Harpenden, Hertfordshire AL5 2HY (01582 760735; email: jmfoundation@btconnect.com; website: www.wheathampstead.net/jmf)

CC Number: 312127

Eligibility

People under the age of 25 who live in Harpenden and Wheathampstead and are in financial need. Priority is given to individuals over the age of 16.

Types of grants

Grants to help with the cost of education, training, apprenticeships, work-related expenses or character building opportunities. Support can be given to schoolchildren, people starting work and further/higher education students, including mature students and postgraduates. The awards are very wide ranging in scope and can include help towards uniforms/other school clothing, books, accommodation, equipment/ instruments, fees, educational outings in the UK, study or travel abroad, vocational courses, GNVQ, BTEC, extra-curricular activities, school trips or music, arts and sports tuition.

All applications are based on family income, unless the applicant is fully self-supporting. Grants generally range from £50 to £2,000, but can be of up to £4,000.

Annual grant total

In 2012/13 the foundation had assets of £3.1 million and an income of £188,000. Grants were made totalling around £104,000 to 181 individuals (£65,000 in Harpenden and £38,000 in Wheathampstead).

The grants were made in the following categories:

Primary/secondary/further education	116
Degree courses	39
Computer	15
Other	6
Personal development	4
Medical student	1

Applications

Application forms and further guidance can be requested from the correspondent. Applications can be submitted directly by the individual at any time and are considered every six to eight weeks. Applicants should provide details of their parental or other income and state the purpose for the requested grant.

The Platt Subsidiary Foundation

£3,100

Correspondent: Alan Taylor, Secretary, 57A Loom Lane, Radlett, Hertfordshire WD7 8NX (01923 855197)

CC Number: 272591

Eligibility
People under the age of 25 who live in the parishes of Aldenham, Christ Church, Radlett, St John the Baptist or St Martin's (Shenley) and are in need.

Types of grants
Grants in the range of £200–£800 can be given to people planning expeditions away from home, for example gap-year schemes, volunteering opportunities adventure trips and so on. Community projects are particularly favoured.

Annual grant total
In 2013 the foundation had an income of £7,700 and an expenditure of £6,400. We have estimated that the annual total of grants to individuals was around £3,100.

Applications
Application forms can be requested from the correspondent. The deadline for applications is normally by the end of March. Applicants are required to attend an interview in April.

Other information
Grants may also be made to organisations.

The Ware Charities

£4,500 (10 grants)

Correspondent: Susan Newman, Administrator, 3 Scotts Road, Ware, Hertfordshire SG12 9JG (01920 461629; email: suedogs@hotmail.com)

CC Number: 225443

Eligibility
Schoolchildren, college students and people starting work who live in the area of Ware Town Council, the parish of Wareside and the parish of Thundridge.

Types of grants
Grants are given to schoolchildren, college students, people with special educational needs, people starting work and overseas students, including those for uniforms/clothing, fees, study/travel abroad, books, equipment/instruments and excursions. Grants are also made to undergraduates and vocational students for uniforms/clothing.

Annual grant total
In 2012/13 the charities had assets of £1.2 million and an income of £62,000.

Grants made totalled £30,000 of which £21,000 went to organisations which provide or undertake services or facilities to people residing in Ware who are in need, hardship or distress and £9,000 went to individuals for social welfare or educational purposes.

Applications
In writing to the correspondent at any time, to be submitted directly by the individual or a family member. Applications must include brief details of the applicant's income and savings and be supported and signed by a headteacher, GP, nurse or social worker.

Berkhamsted

Bourne's Educational Foundation

£800

Correspondent: Priscilla Watt, Clerk, Flat 11, Cavalier Court, Chesham Road, Berkhamsted HP4 3AL (01442 863804; email: priscilla.watt@googlemail.com)

CC Number: 310966

Eligibility
People under the age of 25 who live in the ecclesiastical parish of Great Berkhamsted or are attending/have attended Berkhamsted Victoria Church of England Primary School.

Types of grants
Grants to students in primary, secondary, further and higher education for books, equipment/instruments, uniforms and other clothing, educational outings in the UK, study or travel abroad and for the study of music or other arts. People entering a trade/starting work may also be supported.

Annual grant total
In 2013/14 the foundation had both an income and a total expenditure of £900. We estimate that about £800 was given in educational grants.

Exclusions
Our research suggests that mature students are not normally supported and funding for school fees for schoolchildren is not provided.

Applications
Application forms are available from the correspondent. They can be submitted directly by the individual or through a social worker, Citizens Advice or other welfare agency, if applicable. Candidates should include all relevant information on parental income. Applications are usually considered in March and October.

Salter's Educational Foundation

£1,500

Correspondent: Priscilla Murray Watt, Administrator, Flat 11, Cavalier Court, Chesham Road, Berkhamsted HP4 3AL (01442863804; email: priscilla.watt@googlemail.com)

CC Number: 311081

Eligibility
People under the age of 25 living in the ancient parish of Berkhamsted St Peter who are in need of financial assistance.

Types of grants
Small grants of up to £200 are available for general educational expenses, including clothing, books, equipment/instruments, educational outings, study/travel abroad and in the UK.

Annual grant total
In 2012/13 the foundation had an income of £1,700 and an expenditure of £1,600. We estimate the annual total of grants to be around £1,500.

Exclusions
Our research indicates that grants are not available for people starting work, mature students, towards maintenance fees or school fees for schoolchildren.

Applications
In writing to the correspondent. According to our research, applications can be submitted either directly by the individual or through a social worker, Citizens Advice or other welfare agency, if applicable.

Cheshunt

Robert Dewhurst's School Foundation

£10,000

Correspondent: Jill Hempleman, Administrator, 215 Northbrooks, Harlow, Essex CM19 4DH (01279 425251; email: jillhempleman@yahoo.co.uk)

CC Number: 310972

Eligibility
Children and young people under the age of 25 who live within the ancient parish of Chestnut. Preference is given to people who have attended Dewhurst St Mary's Church of England Primary School for at least two years.

Types of grants

One-off grants to secondary schoolchildren, further/higher education students and people starting work to help with general educational costs, including books, equipment/instruments, tools, materials, clothing, travel, fees and educational outings in the UK.

Annual grant total

In 2012/13 the foundation had an income of £10,500 and an expenditure of £23,800, which is much higher than usual. We estimate that the total of grants to individuals was about £10,000.

Applications

In writing to the correspondent. Applications can be submitted directly by the individual or through a school/welfare agency, if applicable.

Other information

The foundation also provides support to Dewhurst St Mary's Church of England Primary School.

Dacorum

The Dacorum Community Trust

£15,000

Correspondent: The Grants and Finance Officer, The Hub Dacorum, Paradise, Hemel Hempstead HP2 4TF (01442 231396; email: admin@dctrust.org.uk; website: www.dctrust.org.uk)

CC Number: 272759

Eligibility

People in need who live in the borough of Dacorum.

Types of grants

Generally one-off grants up to £500 to schoolchildren for uniforms/clothing, equipment/instruments and excursions, to college students, undergraduates and people starting work, for clothing and equipment/instruments and to vocational students, mature students and those with special educational needs, for uniforms/clothing, equipment/instruments and childcare.

Annual grant total

In 2012/13 the trust had assets of £136,000 and received an income of £107,500. There were 673 grants made totalling £65,000. Direct grants totalled £41,000 and gifts in kind were costed at £23,000. We have estimated the educational grants total to be around £15,000.

Exclusions

Grants are not normally given for the costs of further or mainstream education

and only in exceptional circumstances for gap-year travel.

Applications

On a form available from the correspondent or to download from the trust's website. Applications can be submitted by the individual, through a recognised referral agency (such as social services or Citizens Advice) or through an MP, GP or school. Applications are considered in March, June, September and December. The trust asks for details of family finances. A preliminary telephone call is always welcome.

Other information

The trust also gives to organisations.

Harpenden

The Harpenden Trust

£13,300 (121 grants)

Correspondent: Dennis Andrews, Trustee, The Trust Centre, 90 Southdown Road, Harpenden AL5 1PS (01582 460457; email: admin@theharpendentrust.org.uk; website: www.theharpendentrust.org.uk)

CC Number: 1118870

Eligibility

Children in need who live in the 'AL5' postal district of Harpenden.

Types of grants

One-off grants are available for school field trips, special equipment and to help towards involvement in charitable work.

Annual grant total

In 2012/13 the trust had assets of £4 million and an income of £217,500. Grants were made to 794 individuals totalling £58,500 and were distributed as follows:

General grants	543	£30,000
Utilities grants	71	£13,300
Youth grants	121	£13,300
Christmas parcels	180	£1,700

Grants for educational purposes benefited 121 children and totalled £13,300. The remaining £45,000 was given to individuals for welfare purposes. A further £45,500 was given to organisations.

Applications

In writing to the correspondent, either directly by the individual or through a third party such as a social worker or Citizens Advice.

Other information

The trust's helpful and informative website states:

> The trust's objective – to help Harpenden people in need, individually and collectively remains the same as when it

was founded in 1948. More than 60 years on there are still Harpenden people suffering hardship, financial or otherwise; people in need of the help of a good neighbour. The Harpenden Trust is here to be that good neighbour, with the active support of the town's residents. Recently the trust has been able to extend its help to community organisations and groups whose aims are to enhance the lives of Harpenden people, especially the young and the elderly.

Hatfield

Wellfield Trust

£3,000

Correspondent: Jeanette Bayford, Administrator, Birchwood Leisure Centre, Longmead, Hatfield, Hertfordshire AL10 0AN (01707 251018; email: wellfieldtrust@aol.com; website: www.wellfieldtrust.co.uk)

CC Number: 296205

Eligibility

People in need who live in the parish of Hatfield and are undertaking vocational courses, such as computer or hairdressing training. Schoolchildren in the parish may also be supported.

Types of grants

One-off grants of £100 to £500 to schoolchildren, college students, mature students, people with special educational needs and people starting work, including those towards, the cost of uniforms/clothing, fees, books, equipment/instruments, excursions and childcare.

Annual grant total

In 2012/13 grants to individuals totalled £15,500 with a further £1,700 given towards projects.

The majority of grants are given for welfare purposes and we have estimated the total given for educational purposes to be around £3,000.

Exclusions

Grants are not made for council tax arrears, rent or funeral costs.

Applications

On a form available from the correspondent or to download from the trust's website, only via a third party such as social services or Citizens Advice. Most of the local appropriate third parties also have the application form available. Applications are considered monthly and should be received by the first Monday of every month.

Other information

The trust also gives to organisations, has a room at a local leisure centre which can be hired free of charge to charitable organisations and a scooter loan scheme. It has a helpful and informative website.

Hertford

Newton Exhibition Foundation

£13,500

Correspondent: Anne Haworth, Administrator, 117 Ladywood Road, Hertford SG14 2TA (01992 550121; email: clerk@newtonexhibition foundation.co.uk)

CC Number: 311021

Eligibility

Young people under the age of 25 who are attending/have attended school in the town of Hertford. Preference is given to members of the Church of England. Our research also suggests that grants may be awarded to otherwise eligible applicants who, because of special learning difficulties or disabilities, are attending/have attended schools outside the town.

Types of grants

According to our research, grants between £20 and £400 can be awarded to schoolchildren and further/higher education students (including postgraduates). Financial support is available for general educational purposes, such as uniforms/clothing, books, equipment/instruments, fees, educational outings in the UK and study or travel overseas.

Annual grant total

In 2012/13 the foundation had an income of around £11,700 and a total expenditure of £14,000. We have estimated the annual total of grants to be about £13,500.

Applications

In writing to the correspondent. Our research indicates that the application should include the name(s) of schools attended, full details and costs of the support required, and information about any other grants obtained or applied for. Applications can be submitted either directly by individuals or through their school, welfare agency/social worker, if applicable.

Hertingfordbury

Walter Wallinger Charity

£1,900

Correspondent: Alastair Liddard, Administrator, Longmores, 24 Castle Street, Hertford SG14 1HP

CC Number: 312137

Eligibility

People aged 6 to 24 who have lived, or were educated, for at least two years in the ancient parish of Hertingfordbury, Hertford and are in financial need.

Types of grants

Grants, usually to a maximum of £300, are awarded to help with the costs of books or educational outings for schoolchildren, and towards books and study or travel abroad for students. Help is also given towards the cost of education, training, apprenticeship or equipment for those starting work.

Annual grant total

In 2012 the charity had an income of £2,300 and a total expenditure of £2,000. We estimate that grants totalled £1,900.

At the time of writing (July 2014) this was the most recent financial information available for the charity,

Applications

On a form available from the correspondent to be submitted by the individual or a parent/guardian. They are usually considered in May and November.

Hexton

Hexton Village Trust

£250

Correspondent: Patrick Cooper, Trustee, Hexton Manor, Hexton, Hitchin, Hertfordshire SG5 3JH (01582 882991)

CC Number: 285832

Eligibility

People who live in the parish of Hexton and are in need.

Types of grants

The trust 'supports individuals and community activities within its charitable objects'. Educational support is likely to be given to help with the cost of books, clothing and other essentials for schoolchildren. Grants may also be available for those at college or university.

Annual grant total

In 2012/13 the trust had an income of £1,700 and an expenditure of £1,100. We estimate that educational grants to individuals totalled about £250.

Applications

In writing to the correspondent.

Other information

Support is also given to organisations for general charitable purposes and to individuals for welfare needs.

Letchworth Garden City

The Letchworth Civic Trust

£39,000 (212 grants)

Correspondent: Sally Jenkins, Administrator, 66 Highfield, Letchworth Garden City, Hertfordshire SG6 3PZ (01462 686919; email: letchworthct@ gmail.com; website: letchworthct.org.uk/)

CC Number: 273336

Eligibility

Schoolchildren and students attending college or university who are in need and have lived in Letchworth Garden City for two years or more.

Types of grants

University students who have lived in Letchworth for at least two years will usually receive a grant of £300. Third year students may re-apply for a 'top up' grant of £100. Schoolchildren can receive help of up to £60 with the cost of educational trips and study or travel where their parents cannot afford the whole amount.

Average grants were as follows:

University students	£219
School students	£52
Other individuals	£380

Annual grant total

In 2012/13 the trust had assets of £644,000 and an income of £72,000. Grants were distributed as follows:

University students	166	£36,000
School students	43	£2,300
Other individuals	3	£1,100

Applications

Forms are available to download from the trust's website. Applications are considered in January, March, June, September, October and December. Applications can be submitted as an individual or through an appropriate third party.

Other information

Grants are also made to people who are in need, sick or requiring accommodation, and to groups and societies, but not religious or political groups.

Royston

The Leete Charity

£5,000

Correspondent: Susan Thornton-Bjork, Administrator, Royston Town Council, Town Hall, Melbourn Street, Royston, Hertfordshire SG8 7DA (01763 245484; email: enquires@roystontowncouncil. gov.uk; website: www. roystontowncouncil.gov.uk)

CC Number: 311084

Eligibility

People under the age of 25 going into further education who are either resident in Royston or attending school there.

Types of grants

Small grants to help with the costs of books, travel expenses, equipment/instruments and other educational necessities.

Annual grant total

In 2012/13 the charity had an income of £2,400 and an expenditure of £5,300. We estimate the annual total of grants to be around £5,000.

Exclusions

According to our research, grants are not normally available to people starting work or mature students.

Applications

Application forms are available from the Royston Town Council offices at the town hall or can be downloaded from the council's website. It is requested to submit all the relevant information about the applicant's financial situation and their general background to speed up the consideration. Estimated costs of the items the funding is requested for would also be helpful.

Wormley

The Wormley Parochial Charity

£3,500

Correspondent: Carol Proctor, Trustee, 5 Lammasmead, Broxbourne, Hertfordshire EN10 6PF

CC Number: 218463

Eligibility

Students of any age in the parish of Wormley as it was defined before 31 March 1935.

Types of grants

Grants to schoolchildren or college students, people undertaking training or apprenticeships, towards essential clothing, equipment, instruments or books.

Annual grant total

In 2012 this charity had an income of £15,000 and a total expenditure of nearly £7,000. We estimate that grants for individuals for educational purposes totalled around £3,500. The accounts for 2012 were the latest available at the time of writing (July 2014).

Exclusions

The charity does not give loans.

Applications

In writing to the charity either directly by the individual or through a social worker, Citizens Advice, welfare agency or a third party such as a friend who is aware of the situation. Applications are considered in April and October.

Kent

The Reverend Tatton Brockman's Charity

£2,000

Correspondent: Janet Salt, Administrator, Greatfield House, Ivychurch Road, Brenzett, Romney Marsh, Kent TN29 0EE (01797 344364)

CC Number: 307681

Eligibility

People under the age of 25 who are in full-time education and live in the ancient parishes of Brenzett, Cheriton, and Newington-next-Hythe in the county of Kent.

Types of grants

One-off grants in the range of £100 to £500 to help with the cost of fees, study or travel abroad, books, equipment and instruments for schoolchildren, students in further/higher education, vocational students and people with special educational needs.

Annual grant total

In 2012/13 the charity had an income of £21,000 and a total expenditure of £22,000. We estimate that educational grants to individuals totalled £2,000.

Applications

In writing to the correspondent, directly by the individual. Applications are normally considered in May and November.

Other information

The charity's main financial concern is its support of four Church of England primary schools in the area of benefit; however, the correspondent has previously stated: 'We would very much like to make a greater number of grants to individuals but efforts to encourage more applications have, so far, met with very limited success.' Furthermore, 'it should be stated that in allocating grants the trustees shall have regard to the principles and doctrines of the Church of England'.

John Collings Educational Trust

£17,000

Correspondent: Anthony Herman, Trustee, 11 Church Road, Tunbridge Wells, Kent TN1 1JA (01892 526344)

CC Number: 287474

Eligibility

Children, normally up to the age of 14, who are in need.

Types of grants

Support towards general educational needs, including books, fees, equipment/instruments and other essentials for schoolchildren.

Annual grant total

In 2012/13 the trust had an income of £27,000 and an expenditure of £43,000. According to our research grants to individuals usually total around £17,000.

Exclusions

Grants are not available to people at college or university.

Applications

In writing to the correspondent. Previously the trust has noted that its income is accounted for and new applicants are unlikely to benefit.

Other information

Grants can also be made to organisations.

The Mike Collingwood Memorial Fund

£2,400

Correspondent: Peter Green, Trustee, Acorn House, 12 The Platt, Sutton Valence, Maidstone, Kent ME17 3BQ (01622 843230; website: www. wealdofkentrotary.org.uk/MCMF.html)

CC Number: 288806

Eligibility

Young people who live within a 20-mile radius of 'The Who'd a Thought It' pub in Grafty Green, Kent, where the Rotary Club of the Weald of Kent holds its weekly meetings.

Types of grants

Support can be given to undertake projects, trips and challenges in the UK and abroad, practise towards excellence in a chosen sport or vocation, and similar activities. The fund aims to give learning opportunities which may not be essential for a course, but are a good learning experience and will contribute to the applicant's future career.

Grants and loans are available. Due to the limited amount available, support is only supplementary and the applicants are expected to raise the balance by other means, ideally, with an entrepreneurial spirit and personal effort.

Annual grant total

In 2012/13 the fund had an income of £3,600 and an expenditure of £2,600. We estimate the annual total of grants to individuals to be around £2,400.

Exclusions

The fund is not able to help with recurring costs such as university fees.

Applications

Application forms can be found on the Rotary Club of The Weald of Kent website or requested from the correspondent. Awards are normally made in February and October and applications should reach the trustees a month in advance.

Applications can be submitted by email at: mcmf@wealdofkentrotary.org.uk, or by post to: Derek Lamb, 68 Oak Lane, Headcorn TN27 9TB.

Headley-Pitt Charitable Trust

£5,500

Correspondent: Thelma Pitt, Administrator, Old Mill Cottage, Ulley Road, Kennington, Ashford, Kent TN24 9HX (01233 626189; email: thelma.pitt@headley.co.uk)

CC Number: 252023

Eligibility

Individuals in need who live in Kent, with a preference for those residing in Ashford.

Types of grants

One-off grants usually in the range of £100 and £300. Recent grants have been given to schoolchildren, college students, undergraduates, vocational students, mature students, people with special educational needs, people starting work and overseas students, for various educational purposes.

Annual grant total

In 2012/13 the trust had assets of £2.4 million and an income of £79,000. Grants made to individuals totalled £11,000. We estimate that grants made to individuals for educational purposes totalled around £5,500.

Applications

In writing to the correspondent, either directly by the individual or through an appropriate third party.

Other information

Grants are also made to organisations and to individuals for welfare purposes.

Hothfield Educational Foundation

£5,000

Correspondent: Pater Patten, Trustee, The Paddocks, Hothfield, Ashford TN26 1EN (01233 620880; email: marianne.highwood@btinternet.com)

CC Number: 307670

Eligibility

People under the age of 25 who live in, or have attended school at, the parish of Hothfield. People resident immediately outside the area of benefit or those over 25 may be supported at the trustees' discretion if there are surplus funds.

Types of grants

One-off and recurrent grants are given according to need, in the range of £10–£3,000. Funding is given to help with the cost of books, school clothing, uniforms, educational trips and other essentials for schoolchildren. Further and higher education students can be supported towards books, fees, living expenses and study or travel abroad. People starting work may receive grants towards books, equipment, instruments and clothing.

Annual grant total

In 2013 the foundation had an income of £8,600 and an expenditure of £10,300. We estimate the annual total of grants to individuals to be around £5,000.

Applications

In writing to the correspondent. Applications are considered on an ongoing basis.

Other information

Grants are also made to local organisations.

The Hugh and Montague Leney Travelling Awards Trust

£6,200

Correspondent: Lyn Edwards, Awards Group, Education and Libraries, Bishops Terrace, Bishops Way, Maidstone, Kent ME14 1AF (01622 605111; email: leneytrust@hotmail.co.uk)

CC Number: 307950

Eligibility

Children and young people over the age of 16 who are attending/have attended within the previous 12 months any county, voluntary or independent school in the county of Kent. The trustees will give preference to individuals in their final year of school showing qualities of leadership. The project should be of a humanitarian nature, in less developed regions of the world, lasting at least four weeks and benefiting the local community.

Types of grants

The trust provides awards of up to £2,500 to travel to all parts of the world in pursuance of education and to gain skills and knowledge for a future career.

Annual grant total

In 2012/13 the trust had an income of £8,000 and an expenditure of £6,400. We estimate the annual total of grants to be around £6,200.

Applications

In writing to the correspondent. The closing date for applications is 31 January each year. Our research indicates that applications should be submitted by the headteacher or come through an educational welfare agency, if applicable.

Other information

Grants are not intended to cover all costs and other efforts of fundraising, such as sponsorships, parents' contributions and individual initiative will be taken into account.

The William Strong Foundation

£700

Correspondent: Brian Barkley, Trustee, 5 Blatchington Road, Tunbridge Wells TN2 5EG (01892 525047; email: hildascats@sky.com)

CC Number: 307944

Eligibility

Young people between the ages of 11 and 21 who live in the of the former urban or rural district of Tonbridge, the borough of Tunbridge Wells area and the former urban district of Southborough.

Preference may be given to beneficiaries who intend to take up a nautical career or occupation.

Types of grants

Grants are mainly one-off and range from £60 to £250. Support can be given to secondary schoolchildren for uniforms and other school clothing, books and equipment/instruments; to people starting work for books, clothing and equipment/instruments; and to further and higher education students for fees, books, equipment/instruments and maintenance/living expenses.

Annual grant total

In 2013/14 the foundation had an income of £1,700 and a total expenditure of £800. We estimate that around £700 was distributed in grants to individuals.

Exclusions

Grants are not normally given for gap-year opportunities.

Applications

In writing to the correspondent directly by the individual or a parent/guardian. Applications should include details of the applicant's household income and annual outgoings. Applications are normally considered in June and July and should be submitted between January and March.

Yalding Educational Foundation

£2,400

Correspondent: Kim Keeler, Administrator, Hamilton, Vicarage Road, Yalding, Maidstone ME18 6DR (01622 817919)

CC Number: 307646

Eligibility

Individuals who have attended primary school in the parishes of Courier Street, Laddingford and Yalding for at least two years.

Types of grants

The foundation provides grants, awards and prizes of around £200 to people in higher or further education to assist with general educational costs, including fees, books, clothing, equipment/instruments and other necessities.

Annual grant total

In 2012/13 the foundation had an income of £7,400 and an expenditure of £5,000. It also supports local schools, therefore we estimate the annual total of grants made to individuals to be about £2,400.

Applications

In writing to the correspondent. Our research suggests that applications should provide details of the school attended in the parish, the college or university to be attended, the course to be taken and the length of the course. The trustees meet several times a year.

Other information

The foundation also sponsors a spoken English competition in local primary schools and provides them with general financial assistance.

Benenden

The Gibbon and Buckland Charity

£11,000

Correspondent: David Harmsworth, Trustee, Hemsted Oaks, Cranbrook Road, Benenden, Cranbrook TN17 4ES (01580 240683; website: benendenparishcouncil.org/grants-for-young-persons/)

CC Number: 307682

Eligibility

People between the ages of 16 and 25 who have lived in Benenden for at least three years.

Types of grants

Grants are given to students entering further/higher education, also people starting work and apprenticeships. Awards are of around £150–£300 and can be given for general educational needs or gap-year and similar projects.

Annual grant total

In 2013 the charity had both an income and an expenditure of around £24,000. Previously around £11,000 has been awarded in educational grants to individuals.

Applications

Application forms can be requested from the correspondent, downloaded from the Benenden parish council's website and are also placed in the village shop. The trustees meet twice a year with additional meetings being called as the need arises. Applications should be made by 30 September.

Other information

The charity also supports a Benenden Primary School and provides Bibles to year six pupils in the school.

Borden

The William Barrow's Charity

£25,000 (28+ grants)

Correspondent: Stuart Mair, Administrator, George Webb Finn, 43 Park Road, Sittingbourne, Kent ME10 1DY (01795 470556; email: stuart@georgewebbfinn.com)

CC Number: 307574

Eligibility

Further and higher education students in need who are under the age of 25 and who/whose parents live in the parish of Borden.

Types of grants

Grants are available for general educational necessities, such as books, equipment/instruments, tools and also travel/study overseas or maintenance expenses for students studying away from home. According to our research, schoolchildren can be supported towards the cost of school uniforms/other clothing, educational outings and other necessities. Grants are usually in the range of £350 to £500 and can be given as one-off awards or as two-yearly allowances.

Annual grant total

In 2013 the charity had assets of over £6 million, an income of £215,000 and a charitable expenditure of £84,000. A total of around £25,000 was awarded to individuals for educational purposes (£16,600 from Eleemosynary Fund and £8,700 from Educational Fund).

Applications

In writing to the correspondent. The trustees meet at least four times a year, normally in January, April, July and October.

Other information

The charity also provides funds for alterations/repairs or general school expenses to Borden C.E. Primary School and Borden Grammar School premises.

The Eleemosynary Fund gives funding to the elderly, people with disabilities and students away in college/university to help with living costs and the Education Fund supports institutions/schools and individuals in education.

Canterbury

The Canterbury United Municipal Charities

£1,500

Correspondent: Aaron Spencer, Furley Page Solicitors, 39–40 St Margaret's Street, Canterbury, Kent CT1 2TX (01227 863140; email: aas@furleypage.co.uk)

CC Number: 210992

Eligibility

People in need who have lived within the boundaries of what was the old city of Canterbury for at least two years.

Types of grants

Small one-off and recurrent grants are made to further and higher education students for books and equipment/instruments.

Annual grant total

In 2012 this charity had an income of £9,100 and a total expenditure of £6,400. We estimate that the total awarded to individuals for educational purposes was around £1,500. The latest accounts available at the time of writing (July 2014) were for year ending December 2012.

Applications

In writing to the correspondent through the individual's school/college/ educational welfare agency or directly by the individual. Applications are considered on an ongoing basis and should include a brief statement of circumstances and proof of residence in the area.

Other information

Grants are also given to individuals for welfare purposes and to organisations with similar objects.

Streynsham's Charity

£3,500

Correspondent: The Clerk to the Trustees, PO Box 970, Canterbury, Kent CT1 9DJ (0845 094 4769)

CC Number: 214436

Eligibility

Young people who live or attend school in the ancient parish of St Dunstan's, Canterbury, and are under the age of 21.

Types of grants

One-off grants up to a maximum of about £300. Help with the cost of books, clothing, educational outings, maintenance and other essentials can be given to schoolchildren. Grants are also available for those at college or university, (including mature students), for books, fees, travel and living expenses. People starting work can receive help towards books, equipment/ instruments, clothing and travel.

Annual grant total

In 2012 grants awarded to individuals for educational purposes totalled £3,500. Grants to individuals for social welfare purposes totalled £20,500 and organisations were awarded £5,600. The latest accounts available at the time of writing (July 2014) were for year ending December 2012.

Applications

In writing to the correspondent. Applications can be made directly by the individual, through the individual's school/college/educational welfare agency or through another appropriate third party on behalf of the individual. They are usually considered in March and October but can be made at any time and should include an sae and telephone number if applicable.

Dover

The Casselden Trust

£400

Correspondent: Leslie Alton, Administrator, 26 The Shrubbery, Walmer, Deal, Kent CT14 7PZ (01304 375499)

CC Number: 281970

Eligibility

People in need who live in the Dover Town Council area.

Types of grants

One-off and recurrent grants, up to a maximum of £250.

Annual grant total

In 2012/13 the trust had an income of £1,800 and a total expenditure of £2,000. The trust makes grants to both individuals and organisations for general charitable purposes. We estimate that educational grants to individuals totalled £400.

Applications

In writing to the correspondent.

Fordwich

The Fordwich United Charities

£2,000

Correspondent: Dr Roger Green, Trustee, 15 Water Meadows, Fordwich, Canterbury, Kent CT2 0BF (01227 713661; email: rogergreen@fordwich.net)

CC Number: 208258

Eligibility

People who live in the parish of Fordwich, aged 16 to 25.

Types of grants

One-off grants of £150 are given towards books for college students.

Annual grant total

In 2013 the charity had an income of £15,700 and an expenditure of £8,400. It gives to individuals and organisations for both educational and social welfare purposes. We estimate grants awarded to individuals for educational purposes to be around £2,000.

Applications

The deadline for applications is 1 September and a decision will be made within a month.

Godmersham

Godmersham Relief in Need Charity

£2,500

Correspondent: David T. Swan, Administrator, Feleberge, Canterbury Road, Bilting, Ashford, Kent TN25 4HE (01233 812125)

CC Number: 206278

Eligibility

Students who live in the ancient parish of Godmersham in Kent.

Types of grants

One-off and recurrent grants to help with the costs of equipment, instruments, books, study or travel overseas and extracurricular activities, such as music lessons and sports coaching.

Annual grant total

In 2013 the charity had an income of £6,500 and a total expenditure of £5,400. Grants are given for both educational and relief-in-need purposes.

Applications

In writing to the correspondent, either directly by the individual or through an appropriate third party.

Hawkhurst

Dunk's and Springett's Educational Foundation

£3,400

Correspondent: Andrew Davis, Clerk to the Trustees, Fothersby, Rye Road, Hawkhurst, Kent TN18 5DB (01580 388973; email: dunksclerk@outlook.com; website: dunksclerk.simplesite.com/ 295401684)

CC Number: 307664

Eligibility

Children and young people under the age of 25 who live in the ancient parish of Hawkhurst and are in need.

Types of grants

One-off and recurrent grants to individuals in full-time education towards general needs.

Annual grant total

At the time of writing (July 2014) the latest financial information available was from 2012. In 2012 the foundation had an income of £9,200 and a total expenditure of £6,900. We estimate the annual total of grants to individuals to be around £3,400.

Applications

In writing to the correspondent. Applications are welcomed once the grants are advertised in a local newspaper.

Other information

The clerk to the trustees is responsible for both Dunk's charities. Should you need to contact the correspondent, it is helpful to specify that the query is for the educational foundation not the almshouses charity.

Hayes

Hayes (Kent) Trust

£3,700

Correspondent: Andrew Naish, Administrator, 2 Warren Wood Close, Bromley BR2 7DU (020 8462 1915; email: hayes.kent.trust@gmail.com)

CC Number: 221098

Eligibility

Students who live in the parish of Hayes and can demonstrate that they are in need.

Types of grants

One-off grants, generally in the region of £75 to £1,500, are given according to need.

Annual grant total

In 2012/13 the trust had assets of £966,000 and an income of £45,000. Grants were awarded to individuals as follows:

Relief in need	9	£3,400
Advancement of education	5	£3,700
Relief in sickness	1	£700

The trust also granted £14,700 to organisations for educational purposes; £10,000 to organisations for relief in sickness; and £500 to organisations for welfare purposes.

Applications

In writing to the correspondent. Applications should include the full name of the applicant, postal address in Hayes (Kent), telephone number and date of birth. Applications can be made either directly by the individual, or through a third party such as the individual's college, school or educational welfare agency.

Hythe

Anne Peirson Charitable Trust

£4,500

Correspondent: Ina Tomkinson, Trustee/Secretary, Tyrol House, Cannongate Road, Hythe, Kent CT21 5PX (01303 260779)

CC Number: 800093

Eligibility

People who live in the parish of Hythe who are at any level of their education, in any subject, who are in need.

Types of grants

One-off grants ranging between £50 and £600 given mainly to early years children and schoolchildren for books, educational outings, fees and equipment.

Annual grant total

In 2013 the trust had an income of £13,200 and a total expenditure of £18,000. Grants are awarded to individuals and organisations for both educational and social welfare purposes. We estimate the amount given to individuals for educational purposes was around £4,500.

Exclusions

No grants are made where statutory support is available.

Applications

In writing to the correspondent via either Citizens Advice, a social worker, health visitor, school headteacher or other appropriate third party. Grants are considered at quarterly meetings of the trustees, but emergency applications can be considered in the interim.

Isle of Thanet

The Gibbons Family Trust

See entry on page 277

Medway

Arthur Ingram Trust

£108,000 (74 grants)

Correspondent: Margaret Taylor, Administrator, Medway Council, Gun Wharf, Dock Road, Chatham, Kent ME4 4TR (01634 732876; email: margaret.taylor@medway.gov.uk)

CC Number: 212868

Eligibility

Young people in need between the ages of 14 and 21 who are in full-time education and live in the Medway council area.

Types of grants

According to our research, grants can be made to:

- Students aged between 14 and 16 whose parents are on a low income and who need assistance with school uniform, books and towards school trips which are identified as being linked to exam-related studies (the maximum grant is £300)
- Students continuing at school or in further education establishments/ training and have attendance of at least 90% unless there are exceptional reasons for absence, such as long-term illness (the maximum grant is £400)
- Students whose courses have been recognised as requiring specialist equipment can be granted advanced payments in kind to the school/ college (maximum grant is £150)
- Independent students where parental assistance is not possible or appropriate and the student is independent through no fault of their own
- Sixth form students who have been nominated by the school (applications for these bursaries cannot be requested directly from the trust)

Annual grant total

In 2012/13 the trust had assets of £2.1 million, an income of £85,000 and a total charitable expenditure of £117,000. Grants to individuals totalled £108,000 and were made in the following categories:

Bursary grants	31	£95,000
Continuing education	28	£10,800
Uniforms	14	£2,000
Independent students	1	£150

Applications

Application forms can be requested from the correspondent. Applications can be made by the individual or through a third party, such as a teacher, school/ college or educational welfare agency, if applicable. General grants can be submitted at any time and are considered on an ongoing basis. Continuing education applications should normally be submitted between July and March and bursaries can be applied for from April to June. Each application is means tested and evidence of income is required.

Other information

Grants are also given to local schools towards equipment, books and field trips (in 2012/13 a total of £8,700). Our research suggests that emergency grants to school voluntary funds are also provided.

New Romney

Southland's Educational Charity

£4,000

Correspondent: U. Whiting, Administrator, c/o Town Hall, High Street, New Romney, Kent TN28 8BT (01797 362348)

CC Number: 307783

Eligibility

People who live in the parish of New Romney under the age of 25.

Types of grants

Grants are given towards the cost of books, equipment, instruments, fees, maintenance/living expenses, educational outings in the UK and study or travel overseas for students in further and higher education. Grants are in the range of £100 to £500.

Annual grant total

In 2012/13 the charity had an income of £3,800 and an expenditure of £4,400. Grants made totalled approximately £4,000.

Applications

On a form available from the correspondent.

Rochester

Cliffe-at-Hoo Parochial Charity

£2,600

Correspondent: Paul Kingman, Clerk, 52 Reed Street, Cliffe, Rochester, Kent ME3 7UL (01634 220422; email: paul. kingman@btopenworld.com)

CC Number: 220855

Eligibility

People in need who live in the ancient parish of Cliffe-at-Hoo.

Types of grants

One-off grants according to need for any educational purpose.

Annual grant total

In 2012/13 the charity had an income of £7,900 and a total expenditure of £5,600. We estimate that around £2,600 worth of grants were given for educational purposes.

Applications

In writing to the correspondent, to be submitted either directly by the individual or a family member, or through a third party such as a social worker or teacher.

Richard Watts and The City of Rochester Almshouse Charities

£18,000 (16 grants)

Correspondent: Jane Rose, Clerk, The Office, Watts Almshouses, Maidstone Road, Rochester, Kent ME1 1SE (01634 842194; fax: 01634 409348; email: jane. rose@richardwatts.org.uk; website: www. richardwatts.org.uk)

CC Number: 212828

Eligibility

People in need who live in the city of Rochester and urban Strood.

Types of grants

One-off grants towards specific items required for the course or training, such as books, equipment, special educational needs, musical instruments, educational outings, tours, outfits, school uniforms or similar support. Schoolchildren, university students and people in further education or training can be assisted.

Annual grant total

In 2013 the charity had assets of £20.4 million and an income of £1.1 million. A total of £18,000 was awarded in 16 educational grants. Note that most of the charity's expenditure is spent in maintaining the almshouses.

Applications

Application forms can be requested from the correspondent and can be submitted at any time directly by individuals. Grants are considered on a regular basis. Candidates will be interviewed before the final decision is reached.

Other information

The charity also runs almshouses and gives grants to schools and organisations which benefit the local community. In 2013 educational grants to institutions totalled £3,000.

Sandgate

Educational Foundation of James Morris

£2,500

Correspondent: Maria Wells, Trustee, 4 Bybrook Field, Sandgate, Folkestone CT20 3BQ (01303 248092; email: robjhudson@ntlworld.com)

CC Number: 307559

Eligibility

Young people who live within the boundaries of Sandgate on a permanent basis.

Types of grants

Our research suggests that one-off and recurrent grants can range from £75 to £275 and are awarded to help further and higher education students with fees, books, equipment/instruments and maintenance/living expenses. Support is also offered towards the cost of school uniforms, books and equipment/ instruments for schoolchildren and towards books and fees for people starting work. Mature students can receive help towards books, fees and maintenance/living expenses and vocational students can receive help towards fees.

Annual grant total

In 2012/13 the foundation had an income of £2,900 and an expenditure of £2,700. We estimate that the annual total of grants was around £2,500.

Applications

In writing to the correspondent. Applications can be made either directly by the individual or through their school/college, educational welfare agency, if applicable. Our research shows that applications should include particulars of the university or college that the applicant is attending or planning to attend, together with details of the course of study and ultimate ambitions. Applications should be submitted by 15 September for consideration in October.

Sevenoaks

The Kate Drummond Trust

£1,500

Correspondent: David Batchelor, Trustee, The Beeches, Packhorse Road, Sevenoaks, Kent TN13 2QP (01732 451584)

CC Number: 246830

Eligibility

Young people, especially girls, living in Sevenoaks.

Types of grants

One-off grants are given towards education, recreation or training.

Annual grant total

In 2012/13 the charity had an income of £7,500 and a total expenditure of £7,000. We estimate grants to individuals for educational purposes totalled around £1,500 and for social welfare purposes around £2,000.

Applications

In writing to the correspondent, with an sae if a reply is required.

Other information

This charity also gives grants to organisations.

Wilmington

The Wilmington Parochial Charity

£1,500

Correspondent: Regina Skinner, Administrator, 101 Birchwood Road, Dartford DA2 7HQ (01322 662342)

CC Number: 1011708

Eligibility

People in need, living in the parish of Wilmington, who are receiving a statutory means-tested benefit, such as income support, housing benefit or help towards their council tax.

Types of grants

One-off grants according to need. Grants are awarded to: (i) schoolchildren for books and educational outings but not clothing, uniforms or fees; (ii) students in further/higher education for books, fees, living expenses and study and travel abroad, but not to foreign students or for student exchange; and (iii) mature students for books and travel but not fees or childcare.

Annual grant total

Educational grants total about £1,500 each year.

Applications

Applications should be submitted by the individual, or through a social worker, Citizens Advice or other welfare agency. The trustees meet in February and November. Urgent applications can be considered between meetings in exceptional circumstances.

Other information

Grants are also given to local schools at Christmas and to individuals for welfare.

Norfolk

Anguish's Educational Foundation

£430,000 (2,793 grants)

Correspondent: David Walker, Clerk to the Trustees, 1 Woolgate Court, St Benedicts Street, Norwich NR2 4AP (01603 621023; email: david.walker@ norwichcharitabletrusts.org.uk; website: www.norwichcharitabletrusts.org.uk)

CC Number: 311288

Eligibility

Individuals under the age of 25 who are permanent residents of Norwich and the parishes of Costessey, Hellesdon, Catton, Sprowston, Thorpe-next-Norwich and Corpusty in the County of Norfolk. Preference is given to individuals who live in the city of Norwich and have lost either one or both parents.

Types of grants

Grants can be made towards school clothing, school trips; maintenance costs for university students; fees for school and further education; music, dance and sport training (if applicants are likely to reach professional standard); books and equipment/instruments; support for childcare, dyslexia and scotopic therapy.

Most assistance is still given to school pupils, but further education fees and university students are increasingly supported. A few grants are made each year for educational travel including school trips and occasional overseas visits. However, the trustees believe that the most urgent need of parents is help with the cost of school clothing and the majority of grants are made for this purpose.

Annual grant total

In 2012/13 the foundation had assets of £18.7 million and an income of £850,000. Educational grants to 2,793 individuals totalled £430,000, broken down as follows:

School clothing	36%	£153,000
Further education and school fees	31%	£131,000
School trips	18%	£79,000
University student maintenance support	14%	£61,000
Musical and dance training	1%	£3,400
Dyslexia and scotopic therapy and child minding		£1,500
Books and equipment		£1,100

Exclusions

Postgraduates are not supported.

Applications

In writing to the correspondent directly by the individual. Parents or candidates will generally be required to attend the office for a short interview. Informal enquiries are welcomed prior to application.

Other information

In 2012/13 a total of £52,000 was also given in grants to organisations.

The Brancaster Educational and Almshouse Charity

£1,300

Correspondent: Dorothy Wooster, Administrator, Strebla, Mill Road, Brancaster, King's Lynn PE31 8AW (01485 210645; email: rodolf@btinternet. com)

CC Number: 311128

Eligibility

People living in the ancient parishes of Brancaster, Titchwell, Thornham, and Burnham Deepdale only.

Types of grants

Grants to schoolchildren for excursions and to undergraduates for books.

Annual grant total

In 2012 the charity had an income of £10,500 and a total expenditure of £5,100. We estimate that educational grants to individuals totalled £1,300. Funding is also awarded to Brancaster School, towards the costs of equipment, and towards the maintenance of the charity's almshouses and their residents.

At the time of writing (July 2014) this was the most recent financial information available for the charity.

Applications

In writing to the correspondent.

The Norfolk (le Strange) Fund and Provincial Charities

£3,800

Correspondent: Michael Spalding, Administrator, 23 Woodfield Close, Shadingfield, Beccles, Suffolk NR34 8PD (01502 575722; email: mike6623@ btinternet.com)

CC Number: 209020

Eligibility

Dependents of Freemasons of the Province of Norfolk.

Types of grants

Help with the cost of books, clothing and other essentials for schoolchildren. Grants may also be available for those at college or university.

Annual grant total

In 2012 the charity had an income of £9,400 and a total expenditure of £18,200. We estimate that educational grants to individuals totalled £3,800. Funding is also awarded to organisations as well as to individuals for relief-in-need purposes.

At the time of writing (July 2014) this was the most recent financial information available for the charity.

Applications

In writing to the correspondent. Applications are considered every two months. The charity does not respond to unsuccessful applications made outside its area of interest and prefers applicants to enquire and apply by post or email, rather than by phone.

The Norwich French Church Charity

£8,000

Correspondent: Samantha Loombe, Hansells Solicitors, 13–14 The Close, Norwich NR1 4DS (01603 275814; email: samanthaloombe@hansells.co.uk)

CC Number: 212897

Eligibility

Children and young people primarily of French Protestant descent who are under the age of 25 and live in Norwich. Applicants from Norfolk can also be considered.

Types of grants

Grants, ranging from £250 to £500, for schoolchildren and college students for uniforms/other school clothing, books, equipment/instruments, maintenance/ living expenses, childcare, educational outings in the UK, study or travel abroad, etc. A preference is given to applicants with a Huguenot descent.

Annual grant total

In 2012 the charity had an income of £13,000 and an expenditure of £9,000. We estimate around £8,000 was made in grants to individuals for education.

The 2012 accounts were the latest available at the time of writing.

Applications

On a form available from the correspondent which can be submitted directly by the individual or through the individual's college or educational welfare agency, or another appropriate third party, at any time.

The Sir Philip Reckitt Educational Trust Fund

See entry on page 19

Red House Youth Projects Trust

See entry on page 13

The Charity of Joanna Scott and Others

£41,000

Correspondent: Sam Loombe, Administrator, Hansells, 13–14 The Close, Norwich NR1 4DS (01603 224800)

CC Number: 311253

Eligibility

People under the age of 25 who are being educated or live within five miles of Norwich City Hall. Preference is given to families in financial need.

Types of grants

Grants are given towards the costs of uniforms/other school clothing, books, equipment/instruments, fees, maintenance/living expenses, childcare, educational outings in the UK, study or travel abroad and student exchanges. Grants range between £15 and £2,000. The charity also offers interest-free loans.

Annual grant total

In 2012/13 the charity had assets of £2.3 million, an income of £8,000 and made grants to individuals totalling £47,000.

Applications

On a form available from the correspondent. Applications are usually considered in March, July, September and November, but smaller applications are considered daily. Supply a copy of the appropriate circular from the school or college to assist the trustees.

Other information

Grants are also given to organisations and schools.

The Shelroy Trust

£3,000 (11 grants)

Correspondent: Norfolk Community Foundation, St James Mill, Whitefriars, Norwich NR3 1TN (01603 623958)

CC Number: 327776

Eligibility

Youth of East Norfolk and Norwich for voluntary services overseas. Projects must have a Christian and/or humanitarian objective.

Types of grants

One-off grants, ranging from £200 to £300.

Annual grant total

In 2012/13 the trust had an income of £28,500 and total expenditure of £27,000. Youth sponsorship grants totalled around £3,000.

Applications

In writing to the correspondent at any time. Individuals applying for grants must provide full information and two referees are required. Applications can be made directly by the individual or through a social worker, Citizens Advice or other appropriate third party. They are considered at the trustees' quarterly meetings in March, June, September and December. The trust is not able to reply to unsuccessful applicants unless an sae is provided.

Other information

Grants are also made to organisations.

West Norfolk and King's Lynn Girls' School Trust

£20,000 (24 grants)

Correspondent: Miriam Aldous, Administrator, The Goodshed, Station Road, Little Dunham, King's Lynn PE32 2DJ (01760 720617; website: wnklgirlsschoolstrust.org.uk/)

CC Number: 311264

Eligibility

Girls and young women over the age of 11 who are at a secondary school or in their first years after leaving school or further education, who live in the borough of King's Lynn and West Norfolk. Awards to older candidates will be made in exceptional circumstances.

Types of grants

One-off and recurrent grants. Grants are provided for school uniforms, books, equipment/instruments, and educational outings in the UK and overseas.

Annual grant total

In 2012/13 the trust had assets of £286,000, an income of £26,000 and made grants to individuals totalling almost £20,000. Grants were broken down into the following categories:

Music fees	6
Educational trips	4
Swimming costs	3
Travel expenses	2
Book grants	2
College fees	2
Help whilst studying at college	2
New instruments	1
Childcare	1
Purchase of a computer	1

Applications

On a form available on the trust's website. Application forms should be completed together with a supporting letter outlining the proposed venture or study course, and include two independent references, one of which must be a teacher or tutor who can vouch for the suitability of the course.

Other information

This trust also gives grants to secondary schools within the area.

Burnham Market

The Harold Moorhouse Charity

£7,500

Correspondent: Christine Harrison, Trustee, 30 Winmer Avenue, Winterton-on-Sea, Great Yarmouth, Norfolk NR29 4BA (01493 393975; email: haroldmoorhousecharity@yahoo.co.uk)

CC Number: 287278

Eligibility

Individuals in need who live in Burnham Market in Norfolk only.

Types of grants

One-off grants are made ranging from £50 to £200 for educational equipment and school educational trips.

Annual grant total

This charity gives around £15,000 each year for both educational and welfare purposes.

Applications

In writing to the correspondent. Applications should be submitted directly by the individual in any month.

Burnham Thorpe

Richard Bunting's Educational Foundation (The Bunting's Fund)

£2,300

Correspondent: Anthony Taylor, Trustee, 3 Stratton Place, Shop Lane, Wells-Next-The-Sea, Norfolk NR23 1JR (01328 712155)

CC Number: 311175

Eligibility

Children and young people in need who are under the age of 25 and live in the parish of Burnham Thorpe.

Types of grants

The foundation provides grants, scholarships, bursaries and maintenance allowances to individuals at school, university or any other educational establishment. Financial assistance is available towards the cost of clothing, school uniforms, books, equipment/instruments, tools, educational outings, travel/study abroad, student exchange and other educational necessities or expenses. People entering a trade/starting work and students of music or

other arts are also supported. Our research shows that grants reach up to £400.

Annual grant total

In 2012/13 the foundation had an income of £4,500 and an expenditure of £2,500. We estimate the annual total of grants to be around £2,300.

Applications

In writing to the correspondent. Our research suggests that applications can be made either directly by the individual (if over 18) or by a parent/guardian. Applications are considered in February and September, but emergencies can be dealt with on an ongoing basis.

Other information

The foundation can give financial assistance towards the provision of facilities for recreation, social or physical training for students in primary, secondary or further education, where these are not normally provided by the local authorities.

Buxton with Lammas

Picto Buxton Charity

£2,000

Correspondent: Stephen Pipe, Administrator, Beam End, Mill Street, Buxton, Norwich NR10 5JE (01603279823)

CC Number: 208896

Eligibility

People in need who live in the parish of Buxton with Lamas.

Types of grants

One-off grants of £100 to £200 to schoolchildren for uniforms/clothing, books and excursions and to college students, undergraduates, vocational students, mature students and people starting work towards books.

Annual grant total

In 2012/13 the charity had an income of £28,500 and a total expenditure of £10,500. We estimate around £2,000 was given in grants to individuals for education.

Applications

In writing to the correspondent directly by the individual or a family member, or through a third party such as a social worker or teacher. Applications are considered at any time.

Other information

Grants are also available for social welfare purposes and to organisations or groups within the parish boundary.

Diss

Diss Parochial Charity

£500

Correspondent: Sylvia Grace, Honorary Clerk, 2 The Causeway, Victoria Road, Diss IP22 4AW (01379 650630)

CC Number: 210154

Eligibility

People in need who live in the town and parish of Diss.

Types of grants

One-off grants can be given to schoolchildren towards fees, books and excursions, and to college students and undergraduates towards fees and books. Grants normally range from £30 to £200.

Annual grant total

In 2013 the charity had assets of £633,000 and an income of £30,000. Grants to individuals totalled £2,800 with further £3,300 being paid in bereavement support grants and £600 in bereavement Christmas gifts. Previously the majority of grants have been welfare-related, with a couple of awards made for educational purposes.

Applications

In writing to the correspondent. Applications can be made directly by the individual, through the individual's school/college/educational welfare agency, if applicable, or through another appropriate third party on behalf of the individual. They are considered upon receipt.

Other information

The charity also supports local organisations and maintains almshouses.

East Tuddenham

The East Tuddenham Charities

£800

Correspondent: Janet Guy, Administrator, 7 Mattishall Road, East Tuddenham, Dereham, Norfolk NR20 3LP (01603 880523)

CC Number: 210333

Eligibility

People in further and higher education who live in East Tuddenham.

Types of grants

Help with the cost of books, clothing and other essentials.

Annual grant total

Grants are made to individuals usually totalling around £2,000 a year, mostly for welfare purposes.

Applications

In writing to the correspondent.

Other information

The main activity of this charity is the maintenance of almshouse accommodation.

Feltwell

Sir Edmund Moundeford Charity

£2,400

Correspondent: Barry Hawkins, Administrator, The Estate Office, 15 Lynn Road, Downham Market, Norfolk PE38 9NL (01366 387180)

CC Number: 1075097

Eligibility

Individuals in need who live in Feltwell.

Types of grants

One-off cash grants and grants in kind are made to schoolchildren, college students and vocational students, including those for clothing/uniforms, books and equipment/instruments.

Annual grant total

In 2012 the charity had assets of £3.5 million and an income of £120,000. Educational grants awarded to individuals totalled £2,400 and grants for fuel totalled £9,800. Accounts for 2012 were the latest available at the time of writing (August 2014).

Applications

In writing to the correspondent either directly by the individual or through an organisation such as Citizens Advice or a school. Applications are considered at meetings held quarterly.

Other information

The main purpose of this charity is the provision of almshouse accommodation.

Garboldisham

The Garboldisham Parish Charities

£1,500

Correspondent: P. Girling, Treasurer, Sandale, Smallworth Common, Garboldisham, Diss, Norfolk IP22 2QW (01953 681646; email: pandw6@btinternet.com)

CC Number: 210250

Eligibility

People under 25 who have lived in Garboldisham for at least two years.

Types of grants

One-off and recurrent grants including gifts in kind are made to schoolchildren, college students, undergraduates, vocational students, people with special needs and people starting work. Grants given include those for uniforms/clothing, study/travel abroad, books, equipment/instruments and maintenance/living expenses. Grants are in the range of £30 to £600.

Annual grant total

In 2013/14 the charity had both an income and expenditure of £6,000. We estimate that grants awarded to individuals for educational purposes totalled around £1,500.

Applications

Applications can be submitted directly by the individual including specific details of what the grant is required for. They are usually considered in July and December.

Other information

This charity also makes grants to organisations and to individuals for social welfare purposes.

Harling

Harling Town Lands Educational Foundation

£1,000

Correspondent: David Gee, Clerk, Hanworth House, Market Street, East Harling, Norwich NR16 2AD (01953 717652; email: gee@harlingpc.org.uk)

CC Number: 311209

Eligibility

Young people resident in Harling who are in need.

Types of grants

One-off grants for those attending higher or further education (including professional and technical education) for books, clothing, equipment and so on.

Annual grant total

In 2012/13 the foundation had an income of £3,200 and a total expenditure of £2,100. We estimate that educational grants to individuals totalled £1,000. Funding was also awarded to educational institutions, including East Harling County Primary School.

Applications

In writing to the correspondent at any time from any appropriate source. A brief financial statement will also be required.

Hempnall

The Hempnall Town Estate Educational Foundation

£8,200

Correspondent: Marjorie Emery, Trustee, 17 Roland Drive, Hempnall, Norfolk NR15 2RB (01508 499460)

CC Number: 311218

Eligibility

People under the age of 25 who live in Hempnall and have done so for a year.

Types of grants

Grants are made to help with:
- Costs of educational outings for schoolchildren
- Expenses incurred while at college or university such as books, help with fees and study or travel abroad
- Help with the cost of vocational courses
- Other activities, including athletic expenses and the study of the arts

Grants to individuals are usually made on a percentage basis on production of receipts for courses, books and so on, with a maximum ceiling which is reviewed annually. Each application is considered entirely on merit, but if a grant is made to one person on a particular course, then everyone making an application for the same course receives exactly the same amount or percentage.

Annual grant total

In 2012 the foundation had an income of £15,200 and a total expenditure of £16,800. We estimate that educational grants to individuals totalled £8,200, with funding also awarded to the village primary school and other organisations.

At the time of writing (July 2014) this was the most recent financial information available for the foundation.

Applications

In writing to the correspondent, including evidence of the course being taken and relevant receipts. Applications should be made by 1 March, 1 July and 1 November to be considered during these months.

Hilgay

The Hilgay United Charities (Non-Ecclesiastical Branch)

£1,500

Correspondent: A. Hall, Administrator, Windrush, Church Road, Ten Mile Bank, Downham Market, Norfolk PE38 0EJ (01366 377127; email: hilgay.feoffees@aol.com)

CC Number: 208898

Eligibility

People starting an apprenticeship or work who live in the parish of Hilgay.

Types of grants

One-off and recurrent grants towards apprenticeships or training to help beneficiaries enter employment.

Annual grant total

In 2013 the charity had an income of £24,000 and an expenditure of almost £24,000. Grants to individuals generally total around £2,000 with 75% for education, training and apprenticeships and the remainder for general grants.

Applications

In writing to the correspondent, directly by the individual. Applications are considered in June each year.

Other information

The charity also gives to local schools.

Horstead with Stanninghall

The Horstead Poor's Land

£2,200

Correspondent: W. B. Lloyd, Administrator, Watermeadows, 7 Church Close, Horstead, Norwich NR12 7ET (01603 737632; email: chadlloyd@btopenworld.com)

CC Number: 364730

Eligibility

People in need who live in Horstead with Stanninghall.

Types of grants

One-off grants, usually up to a maximum of £2,000, can be made for any purpose.

Annual grant total

In 2012/13 the charity had an income of £7,700 and a total expenditure of £8,900. We estimate that educational grants to individuals totalled £2,200. Funding was also awarded to local organisations and to individuals for social welfare needs.

Applications

Applications can be submitted directly by the individual, through a school or college, or other appropriate third party giving details of the applicant's financial resources. Applications are considered at any time.

King's Lynn

The King's Lynn General Educational Foundation

£2,000

Correspondent: Andrew Cave, Administrator, Wheelers, 27–29 Old Market, Wisbech, Cambridgeshire PE13 1NE (01945 582547; email: andrew.cave@wheelers-accountants.co.uk)

CC Number: 311104

Eligibility

People aged under 25 who have lived in the borough of King's Lynn for not less than two years, or those who have attended school in the borough for not less than two years, who are going on to further education.

Types of grants

One-off grants of £75 to £200 for people at school, college or university or any other further education institution towards the cost of books, equipment, fees and living expenses.

Annual grant total

In 2012 the foundation had both an income and a total expenditure of £2,100. We estimate that educational grants to individuals totalled £2,000.

At the time of writing (August 2014) this was the most recent financial information available for the foundation.

Applications

On a form available from R G Pannell, 21 Baldwin Road, King's Lynn, Norfolk PE30 4AL, to be submitted by 30 August each year. The application should be supported by the applicant's previous educational establishment.

Norwich

Norwich Town Close Estate Charity

£166,000

Correspondent: David Walker, Clerk to the Trustees, 1 Woolgate Court, St Benedicts Street, Norwich NR2 4AP (01603 621023; email: david.walker@norwichcharitabletrusts.org.uk; website: www.norwichcharitabletrusts.org.uk)

CC Number: 235678

Eligibility

People under the age of 25 living in Norwich.

Types of grants

Grants are given to schoolchildren, further and higher education students, mature students and postgraduates for fees and maintenance/living expenses.

Annual grant total

In 2012/13 the charity had assets of £21 million and an income of £844,000. Grants given for educational purposes totalled £61,000. Grants were broken down as follows:

Pensions	£100,000
Education	£61,000
Relief in need	£3,100
TV licence fees	£2,800

Applications

In writing to the correspondent by June/early July each year. Applications are considered in August.

Sir Peter Seaman's Charity

£2,500

Correspondent: Air Commodore Kevin Pellatt, Administrator, Great Hospital, Bishopgate, Norwich NR1 4EL (01603 622022)

CC Number: 311101

Eligibility

Young men up to the age of 21 who live in Norwich.

Types of grants

One-off and recurrent grants generally between £100 and £300. Grants can be towards all kinds of educational purposes, including starting a new job/career or to help with educational trips such as Duke of Edinburgh Award Scheme, Raleigh International, etc.

Annual grant total

In 2012/13 the charity had an income of £5,500 and an expenditure of £3,000. Grants made totalled approximately £2,500.

Applications

In writing to the correspondent. Applications can be submitted directly by the individual and are considered quarterly in March, June, September and December.

Outwell

The Outwell Town Lands Educational Foundation

£3,000

Correspondent: Debbie Newton, Administrator, 90 Wisbech Road, Outwell, Wisbech PE14 8PF (01945 774327; email: outwellpc@btinternet.com)

CC Number: 311211

Eligibility

People who live in the ancient parish of Outwell.

Types of grants

Recurrent grants are usually made to: (i) those staying at school beyond normal school-leaving age; (ii) those attending courses of further education at technical colleges, other colleges (e.g. agricultural and teacher training) and universities; and (iii) those taking an apprenticeship course or other work leading to a trade qualification. Grants range from £50 to £200 and are for general educational purposes.

Annual grant total

About £3,000 is available for grants each year.

Applications

On a form available from the correspondent. Applications should be submitted directly by the individual in September for consideration in October. Proof of satisfactory attendance may be requested. Grants are paid at the end of January.

Oxborough

Thomas Hewers Educational Foundation

£150

Correspondent: Elizabeth Mason, Trustee, 31 Oxborough Village, Oxborough, King's Lynn, Norfolk PE33 9PS (01366 328874)

CC Number: 311184

Eligibility

People under the age of 25 who live in the ancient parish of Oxborough, Norfolk.

Types of grants

Educational grants for those at school, college or university. The maximum grant is usually around £200.

Annual grant total

In 2013 the foundation had an income of £560 and an expenditure of £310. We estimate that individual grants totalled around £150.

Applications

In writing to the correspondent. Applications are usually considered in November.

Other information

Grants can also be made to local organisations.

Saxlingham

The Saxlingham United Charities

£4,000

Correspondent: Jane Turner, Administrator, 4 Pitts Hill Close, Saxlingham, Nethergate NR15 1AZ (01508 499623)

CC Number: 244713

Eligibility

People under 21 who have lived in Saxlingham Nethergate for at least five years.

Types of grants

Grants of £50 to £100 towards the cost of books, clothing or tools to young people starting work or in further or higher education.

Annual grant total

In 2012/13 the charity had an income of £5,000 and a total expenditure of £8,300. Grants are made for welfare and educational purposes. We estimate grants for educational purposes were in the region of around £4,000.

Applications

In writing to the correspondent. Applications can be submitted directly by the individual and are usually considered in October.

Snettisham

Hall's Exhibition Foundation

£61,000 (83+ grants)

Correspondent: Christopher Holt, Administrator, 4 Bewick Close, Snettisham, King's Lynn, Norfolk PE31 7PJ (01485 541534; email: administrator@hallsfoundation.co.uk; website: www.hallsfoundation.co.uk)

CC Number: 325128

Eligibility

People between the ages of 11 and 25 (as of 1 September in the year of the course) who have been resident in the village of Snettisham for at least one year and are in need of financial assistance.

Types of grants

Grants are available in the following categories:

- Students over the age of 11 moving on to secondary education – up to £200
- Young people over the age of 16 going on to further education/ undertaking A-levels or training courses – up to £200 per each year of the course
- Students over the age of 18 undertaking higher education at universities/colleges – up to £2,000 per each year of the course. The foundation states that in the future 'all students attending higher education courses will be deemed independent of parental support and will be eligible for the full grant.' The grant is awarded in half – at the start and at the end of the academic year

Grants can be awarded for general educational purposes, including books, materials, clothing, travel, accommodation or any other expenses, as decided by the individuals and their parents/guardians.

Additional grants covering up to half the costs may be available for travel abroad as part of the studies. Grants for musical instruments:

Can be awarded to students over the age of 18 following a recognised course of study or other form of musical scholarship acceptable to the trustees. A grant may be made up to half the cost of an instrument (to a maximum of £500) plus an interest free loan for the other half (up to £500).

Annual grant total

In 2012/13 the foundation had assets of £1.4 million, an income of £67,000 and a total charitable expenditure of £63,000. Grants to individuals totalled about £61,000 and awards to organisations amounted to £2,400. The grants were distributed in the following categories:

Students over the age of 18 undertaking higher education at universities/colleges	29	£49,000
Young people over the age of 16 going on to further education/ undertaking A-levels or training courses	37	£7,400
Students over the age of 11 moving on to secondary education	17	£3,400
Other grants	Not specified	£3,200

Exclusions

No additional grants are made for word processors, computers, normal travelling expenses or work experience costs. Grants must be returned if any year of the course is not completed.

Applications

Application forms are available on the foundation's website or can be requested from the correspondent. More application forms are also distributed in the local area. They can be submitted either directly by the individual or through an appropriate third party.

Other information

The trustees note in their annual report from 2012/13 that:

The foundation gives priority to individual applicants, but should money be available, having satisfied the demands of all individual applicants, then grants requests can be considered from those local organisations and bodies which exist for the benefit/education of such young people.

South Creake

The South Creake Charities

£1,500

Correspondent: Sarah Harvey, Administrator, Byanoak, Leicester Road, South Creake, Fakenham, Norfolk NR21 9PW (01328 823391)

CC Number: 210090

Eligibility

People in further or higher education who are in need and live in South Creake.

Types of grants

One-off grants range from £100 to £200 and are given to help schoolchildren and further and higher education students with the cost of books, equipment/ instruments, fees and educational outings in the UK.

Annual grant total

In 2012/13 the charity had an income of £5,000 and a total expenditure of £3,500. Grants are given for both educational and social welfare purposes. We estimate that grants awarded to individuals for educational purposes was around £1,500.

Applications

In writing to the correspondent. Applications should be submitted directly by the individual and are considered in November; they should be received before the end of October.

Other information

Grants can also be given to schools and playgroups.

South Walsham

Richard Harrold (Harrold's Charity)

£1,700

Correspondent: Pauline James, Trustee, Ivy Cottage, Burlingham Road, South Walsham, Norwich NR13 6DJ (01603270425; email: paulinejames@aol.com)

CC Number: 311107

Eligibility

People under the age of 25 who live in South Walsham and are at college, university, undertaking an apprenticeship or entering a profession/ trade.

Types of grants

Grants are available towards the cost of clothing, uniforms, equipment/ instruments, tools, books, travel expenses or fees. Our research suggests that grants can be one-off or recurrent and range from £25 to £250.

Annual grant total

In 2012/13 the charity had an income of £2,700 and an expenditure of £1,900. We estimate the annual total of grants to be about £1,700.

Applications

In writing to the correspondent. Our research shows that applications are normally considered in January, April and September.

Swaffham

Swaffham Relief In Need Charity

£2,000

Correspondent: Richard Bishop, The Town Hall, Swaffham, Norfolk PE37 7DQ (01760 722922; email: reliefinneed@swaffhamtowncouncil.gov.uk)

CC Number: 1072912

Eligibility

People in need who live in Swaffham.

Types of grants

Grants are given for welfare purposes, including for school uniforms.

Annual grant total

In 2012/13 the charity had an income of £11,300 and a total expenditure of £8,800. We estimate that of this, £4,000 was made in grants to individuals for both educational and social welfare purposes. The charity also grants money to organisations.

Applications

In writing to the correspondent.

Walpole

The Walpole St Peter Poor's Estate

£1,800

Correspondent: Edward Otter, Administrator, 1 Sutton Meadows, Leverington, Wisbech, Cambridgeshire PE13 5ED (01945 665018)

CC Number: 233207

Eligibility

People in need aged 16 and over who are at college or university and live in the old parishes of Walpole St Peter, Walpole Highway and Walpole Marsh.

Types of grants

One-off and recurrent grants for educational purposes.

Annual grant total

In 2012 the charity had both an income and expenditure of £3,800. Grants for education totalled around £1,800.

More recent accounts were not available at the time of writing (August 2014).

Applications

In writing to the correspondent. Applications should be submitted directly by the individual and are considered in November.

Other information

Grants are also made to older people.

Wiveton

The Charities of Ralph Greenaway

£500

Correspondent: Robert Harris, Administrator, East Barn, Hall Lane, Wiveton, Holt, Norfolk NR25 7TG (01263 740090; email: robertpharris@btinternet.com)

CC Number: 207605

Eligibility

Young people living in the parish of Wiveton or associated closely with it, up to university age, including young people who are starting work.

Types of grants

One-off grants are given towards books, equipment, clothing, study/travel abroad, excursions and so on.

Annual grant total

In 2013/14 the charity had an income of £3,000 and a total expenditure of £3,000. We estimate that £500 was awarded in grants for educational purposes.

Applications

Applications, on a form available from the correspondent, should be submitted directly by the individual and are considered twice a year. However, if a need arises, a special meeting can be convened.

Other information

Grants are also awarded to organisations, and for social welfare purposes for those over 60 who live in the village.

Woodton

Woodton United Charities

£2,000

Correspondent: Peter Moore, Trustee, 6 Triple Plea Road, Woodton, Bungay, Suffolk NR35 2NS (01508 482375; email: peter.bmoore@btinternet.com)

CC Number: 207531

Eligibility

People in need who live in the parish of Woodton. The charity is particularly interested in supporting young people undertaking apprenticeships or going on to further/higher education.

Types of grants

One-off and recurrent grants can be given according to need, mainly for books and equipment. Previous grants have included tools for an apprentice and books for an A-level student.

Annual grant total

In 2013 the charity had an income of £5,100 and a total expenditure of £4,300. We estimate that educational support totalled around £2,000.

Applications

In writing to the correspondent. Applications can be made directly by the individual, including full details and the nature of the need. They can be submitted at any time.

Other information

Grants are also given for welfare causes.

Oxfordshire

The Bampton Exhibition Foundation

£2,000

Correspondent: Gerald Mills, Trustee, 21 Southlands, Aston, Bampton OX18 2DA (01993 850670; email: geraldmills1937@gmail.com)

CC Number: 309238

Eligibility

People under 25 who live in Bampton, Aston, Cote, Weald or Lew and are in need.

Types of grants

Grants are given to schoolchildren, people with special educational needs, students in further/higher education, vocational students and postgraduates for projects/courses which would be otherwise beyond the means of applicants. Support that can be given includes books, equipment/instruments, fees, maintenance/living expenses, educational outings in the UK, study or travel abroad and so on.

Annual grant total

In 2013/14 the foundation had an income of £10,000 and a total expenditure of £8,000. We estimate that the total grant awarded to individuals was approximately £2,000.

Applications

In writing to the correspondent at any time, including details regarding the proposed project/course, any expenses involved and relevant references. Applications can be submitted either directly by the individual, through the individual's school, college or educational agency, or through another appropriate third party such as a teacher or parent.

Other information

The foundation also awards grants to organisations and spends some of its income on the maintenance of a partly listed building.

Charney Bassett and Lyford Educational Trust

£1,000

Correspondent: Frances Rothwell, Administrator, Old Walls, Buckland Road, Charney Bassett, Wantage OX12 0ES

CC Number: 1076943

Eligibility

People who live in Charney Bassett and Lyford who are in need.

Types of grants

Grants towards educational need.

Annual grant total

About £1,000 is given each year in grants to individuals for educational purposes.

Applications

In writing to the correspondent.

Other information

Grants are also made to organisations.

Culham St Gabriel's Trust (The Culham Institute)

£177,000 (49 grants)

Correspondent: Mark Chater, Director, Culham St Gabriel's, 60–62 Banbury Road, Oxford OX2 6PN (01865 612035; email: enquiries@cstg.org.uk; website: www.cstg.org.uk)

CC Number: 309671

Eligibility

People who are or intend to become teachers in religious education or are otherwise involved in work, development, research and studies of the Church of England.

Types of grants

Grants are aimed to help further/higher education students and to promote life-long learning of teachers. Financial support is available towards books, equipment, necessities and the costs of classes, lectures, various development opportunities.

Annual grant total

In 2012/13 the trust had assets of £14.3 million and an income of £813,000. A total of £432,000 was spent in grant giving activities, of which £177,000 was awarded to 49 individuals.

Exclusions

Grants are not given for work outside the UK, for general running costs, deficit reduction or religious instruction (as distinct from education).

Applications

Application forms can be obtained from the trust's website and should be submitted by February, May and October (specific dates may be subject to change; see the trust's website for further information).

Other information

Grants are also made to organisations (16 awards totalling £254,000 in 2012/13) and for various programmes (7 awards totalling £231,000 in 2012/13).

Ducklington and Hardwick with Yelford Charity

£1,200

Correspondent: Joyce Parry, Administrator, 16 Feilden Close, Ducklington, Witney, Oxfordshire OX29 7XB (07993 705121)

CC Number: 237343

Eligibility

People in need or hardship who live in the villages of Ducklington, Hardwick and Yelford.

Types of grants

Grants of up to £200 can be awarded to people 'embarking on courses'. University/college students can be assisted towards the cost of books, also travel/study overseas; and individuals undertaking apprenticeships/starting work are given help for equipment, clothing and similar necessities.

Annual grant total

In 2013 the charity had an income of £2,700 and an expenditure of £5,000. We estimate that educational support to individuals totalled around £1,200.

Applications

In writing to the correspondent. The trustees meet in March and November but applications can be made at any time.

Other information

Grants are also made to organisations, clubs, schools and so on.

The Faringdon United Charities

£2,500

Correspondent: Vivienne Checkley, Administrator, Bunting and Co., 7 Market Place, Faringdon, Oxfordshire SN7 7HL (01367 243789; fax: 01367 243789)

CC Number: 237040

Eligibility

People in need who live in the parishes of Faringdon, Littleworth, Great and Little Coxwell, all in Oxfordshire.

Types of grants

One-off grants to: schoolchildren for study/travel abroad, equipment/instruments and excursions; mature students for books; people with special educational needs for equipment/instruments; and people starting work for equipment/instruments.

Annual grant total

In 2012/13 the charity had an income of £13,500 and total expenditure of £9,000. Grants are awarded to individuals and organisations for both educational and social welfare purposes. We estimate the total awarded to individuals for educational purposes was around £2,500.

Applications

In writing to the correspondent throughout the year. Applications can be submitted either through Citizens Advice, a social worker or another appropriate third party, directly by the individual or by a third party on their behalf, for example a neighbour or parent.

Henley Educational Trust

£18,600 (124 grants)

Correspondent: Claire Brown, Clerk, Syringa Cottage, Horsepond Road, Gallowstree Common, Reading, Oxon RG4 9BP (01189 724575; email: henleyeducationalcharity@hotmail.co.uk; website: www.henleyeducationalcharity. com)

CC Number: 309237

Eligibility

People under the age of 25 who live in the parishes of Bix, Henley, Remenham or Rotherfield Greys, or who attend/have attended Badgemore Primary School, Gillotts Secondary School, Henley College, Nettlebed Primary School, Sacred Heart RC Primary School, Trinity Primary School or Valley Road Primary School for at least two years.

Types of grants

Grants can be given to schoolchildren for uniforms, educational outings, music lessons and instruments, educational extra-curricular activities; to people entering a trade/starting work for fees, clothing, equipment/instruments, maintenance expenses or travel costs; young people under 25 can be assisted with the study/travel overseas costs, voluntary work, gap year activities. Pre-school fees for up to three extra sessions may also be provided. Payments are made directly to organisations not the individuals and usually are around £100–£200.

Annual grant total

In 2012/13 the trust had assets of £3.2 million, an income of £147,000 and a total charitable expenditure of £120,000. There were 124 grants made to individuals totalling £18,600.

Exclusions

Funding for pre-school fees is only provided where the extra sessions can be supported by an educational or

healthcare professional and are essential to the child's development. The trust will not help merely to allow the parent/guardian to engage in employment.

Applications

Application forms can be obtained from the trust's website. The trustees meet six times a year, in January, March, May, June, September and November. For specific dates see the trust's website. Note that email applications are not accepted. Candidates are required to provide evidence of their financial circumstances and a letter of support from an educational or healthcare professional.

Other information

Up to one third of the trust's income may be given to local schools, where support is not already provided by the local authority (£30,000 in 2012/13). Funding can also be given to organisations towards wider educational purposes (£71,000 in 2012/13).

The Hope Ffennell Trust

£6,000

Correspondent: Louis Letourneau, Trustee, Church End, Wytham Abbey, Wytham, Oxon OX2 8QE (01865 203475)

CC Number: 309212

Eligibility

People under the age of 25 years who live in the parishes of Wytham and North Hinksey.

Types of grants

Help towards outings and educational visits, books and the study of music.

Annual grant total

In 2012 the trust had an income of £7,300 and made grants totalling approximately £6,000.

These were the latest set of accounts available at the time of writing (July 2014).

Applications

In writing to the correspondent.

The Stevens Hart and Municipal Educational Charity (Henley Municipal Charities)

£2,200

Correspondent: Jean Pickett, Administrator, Henley Municipal Charities, Rear, 24 Hart Street, Henley-on-Thames, Oxon RG9 2AU (01491 412360; email: henleymcharities@aol. com)

CC Number: 292857

Eligibility

Children and young people in need of financial assistance who live in the parishes of Bix and Rotherfield Greys or the town of Henley-on-Thames.

Types of grants

Our research shows that grants are awarded up to a maximum of £300 and can be given towards the cost of books, clothing and other educational necessities. Support is mainly for schoolchildren but students at college or university may also be assisted.

Annual grant total

In 2012/13 the charity had an income of £5,300 and an expenditure of £4,400. It provides assistance to local schools, therefore we estimate the annual total of grants to individuals total to be around £2,200.

Applications

In writing to the correspondent.

Other information

The charity also supports local schools in maintenance and special benefits not normally provided by the local authorities.

The Thame Welfare Trust

£6,000

Correspondent: John Gadd, Administrator, 2 Cromwell Avenue, Thame, Oxfordshire OX9 3TD (01844 212564; email: johngadd4@gmail.com)

CC Number: 241914

Eligibility

People in need who live in Thame and immediately adjoining villages.

Types of grants

One-off grants of amounts up to £1,000 are given to help towards a wide variety of needs to schoolchildren, college students, undergraduates, vocational students, mature students, people with special educational needs and people starting work.

Annual grant total

In 2012/13 the trust had an income of £18,500 and a total expenditure of £24,000. Grants are made to organisations and individuals for relief-in-need and education. We have estimated the educational grants total to be around £6,000.

Applications

In writing to the correspondent mainly through social workers, probation officers, teachers, or a similar third party, but also directly by the applicant.

Banbury

The Banbury Charities

£46,000 (329 grants)

Correspondent: Nigel Yeadon, Administrator, 36 West Bar, Banbury OX16 9RU (01295 251234)

CC Number: 201418

Eligibility

People under 25 who live in the former borough of Banbury.

Types of grants

Grants are given to people preparing for or entering a profession or trade and students in higher and further education, particularly for books and equipment. Also grants are given to assist young people under the age of 25 who are studying the arts, literature or science.

Annual grant total

In 2013 the charities had assets of £5.6 million and an income of £1.6 million. Grants were made to 329 individuals for both education and welfare purposes at an average of £279 per grant, totalling £92,000.

Applications

In writing to the correspondent. Applicants are encouraged to obtain a letter of support from their social worker, carer, teacher or other person in authority to give credence to their application.

Other information

Banbury Charities is a group of eight registered charities. These are as follows: Bridge Estate Charity; Countess of Arran's Charity; Banbury Arts and Educational Charity; Banbury Almshouses Charity; Banbury Sick Poor Fund; Banbury Welfare Trust; Banbury Poor Trust; and Banbury Recreation Charity.

Barford

Bakehouse or Shepherd's Charity

£4,000

Correspondent: Helen Honour, Administrator, The Cottage, 5 Mead Road, Barford St John, Banbury, Oxfordshire OX15 0PW

CC Number: 309173

Eligibility

Young people under the age of 25 who/ whose parents have lived in the parish of Barford St John or Barford St Michael for at least three years.

Types of grants

Grants of £150 to £300 towards the cost of education, training and apprenticeships. The charity offers support towards general educational expenses, including maintenance allowances, outfits, fees, equipment and so on for those starting work.

Annual grant total

In 2012/13 the charity had an income of £10,400 and an expenditure of £4,100. We have estimated that the annual total of grants was around £4,000.

Exclusions

Our research indicates that grants are not made for schoolchildren.

Applications

In writing to the correspondent.

Bletchington

The Bletchington Charity

£2,500

Correspondent: Sue Green, Administrator, Causeway Cottage, Weston Road, Bletchington, Kidlington, Oxon OX5 3DH (01869 350895)

CC Number: 201584

Eligibility

People in need who live in the parish of Bletchington.

Types of grants

Grants to students and apprentices to help with the purchase of books, instruments or tools necessary for their course.

Annual grant total

In 2012 the charity had an income of £11,000 and a total expenditure of just under £10,000. This was the most up to date information available at the time of writing (July 2014). We estimate grants to individuals for educational purposes totalled around £2,500.

Applications

Applications can be made in writing to the correspondent by the individual.

Other information

The charity also seeks to support any medical and social needs that will benefit the village community as a whole.

Charlbury

Charlbury Exhibition Foundation

£9,000

Correspondent: Kathryn Jones, Trustee, Took House, Sheep Street, Charlbury, Chipping Norton, Oxfordshire OX7 3RR (01608810793)

CC Number: 309236

Eligibility

People under the age of 25 who live in the ancient township of Charlbury and are going into further or higher education, including vocational courses and apprenticeships.

Types of grants

Recurrent grants for up to three years. Our research shows that grants are of about £100 a year per individual but depend on the foundation's income. Support is given towards general educational costs, necessities and maintenance expenses.

Annual grant total

In 2012/13 the foundation had an income of £13,900 and an expenditure of £9,200. We have estimated that the annual total of grants was around £9,000. The amount given in grants varies each year.

Applications

In writing to the correspondent. Applications should be submitted by October and include the individual's age, school, details of course, university/college and so on. People attending short training courses sponsored by Charlbury youth organisations can also apply.

Other information

The foundation owns a property and a field in Charlbury, Oxfordshire and uses the rental income from these assets to award grants.

Eynsham

Bartholomew Educational Foundation

£2,000

Correspondent: Robin Mitchell, Clerk to the Trustees, 20 High Street, Eynsham, Witney, Oxfordshire OX29 4HB (01865 880665; website: www.eynsham.org/edcharity.html)

CC Number: 309278

Eligibility

People under the age of 25 who live in the parish of Eynsham.

Types of grants

Grants are available towards educational travel abroad; study of music and other arts; the cost of tools, equipment/instruments, books and clothing to apprentices and trainees; to schoolchildren and university/college students for general educational needs. Awards are usually in the range of £50 to £200.

Annual grant total

In 2013 the foundation had an income of £3,800 and an expenditure of £2,300. The foundation states that about £2,000 is available for distribution in grants annually.

Applications

In writing to the correspondent stating the candidate's name, address, age, what the grant is for, costs involved and so on. Applications for people under the age of 18 should be made by a parent/guardian. Apprentices and trainees should also send a list of the items required with their prices and the date when the training will commence.

The trustees meet four times a year, usually in February, May, August or September and November. Applications should be submitted a month before the next meeting.

Other information

Local educational bodies can also be supported, after individuals' needs have been met.

Oxford

The Thomas Dawson Educational Foundation

£1,800

Correspondent: Mrs K. K. Lacey, Clerk and Receiver, 56 Poplar Close, Garsington, Oxford OX44 9BP (01865 368259)

CC Number: 203258

Eligibility

Children and young people in need who have lived in the city of Oxford (postcodes OX1 to OX4) for three years, with a preference for those resident in the parish of St Clements.

Types of grants

Help with the cost of books, clothing, fees and other essentials for schoolchildren and for people at college or university. Grants are also available for people preparing for entering or engaging in a profession, trade, occupation or service. Grants generally range from £40 to £1,500.

Annual grant total

In 2012/13 the foundation had assets of £10.2 million, the majority of which is permanent endowment and unavailable for grant giving. It had an income of £551,000 and made grants to individuals totalling £1,800. Grants to organisations totalled £32,000.

Exclusions

No grants are given for medical sponsorships or electives, or towards accommodation, travel or living expenses.

Applications

In writing to the correspondent, with evidence regarding course fees. Note: applicants can only apply for one degree course.

Other information

Grants are also made to schools and youth, family and volunteer organisations.

The City of Oxford Charity

£15,000 (38 grants)

Correspondent: David Wright, Administrator, 11 Davenant Road, Oxford OX2 8BT (01865 247161; email: enquiries@oxfordcitycharities.fsnet.co.uk; website: www.oxfordcitycharities.org)

CC Number: 239151

Eligibility

Children and young people under the age of 25 who have lived in the city of Oxford for at least three years.

Types of grants

One-off grants are given to schoolchildren and college or university students. Assistance can be given for school uniforms, books, fees, equipment/instruments, materials, school trips and also special educational needs.

Annual grant total

In 2013 the charity had assets of £5.3 million, an income of £342,000 and made grants totalling £87,000. Educational grants totalled £15,000 awarded to 38 individuals/schools.

A major part of the charity's expenditure is spent in maintaining its almshouses.

Applications

Application forms can be downloaded from the charity's website or requested from the correspondent. Grants are considered quarterly in March, June, September and December. Applications from pupils must be accompanied by a letter of support from an educational social worker/health visitor/welfare worker/similar professional.

Other information

The charity is an amalgamation of a number of charities working for the benefit of the people of Oxford city. It also accepts applications from schools to help with the costs of educational trips for children from low income families, gives support for welfare causes and maintains almshouses in the local area.

Rotherfield Greys

The Rotherfield Greys Educational Charity

£0

Correspondent: Sam Samuels, Trustee, Cowfields Farm, Rotherfield Greys, Henley-On-Thames RG9 4PX (01491 628819; email: samsamuels@btconnect. com)

CC Number: 284643

Eligibility

People aged between 5 and 25 who live in the ecclesiastical parish of St Nicholas, Rotherfield Greys.

Types of grants

One-off grants are available to schoolchildren and further and higher education students to cover the cost of books, equipment/instruments, fees, educational outings in the UK, and study and travel abroad. There is a preference for Church of England-oriented education.

Grants are given in the range of £100 to £250.

Annual grant total

In 2012/13 the charity had an income of £1,900 but had no expenditure.

Applications

On a form available from the correspondent for consideration in March and September. Applications must include proof of residential qualification.

Wallingford

Wallingford Relief in Need Charity

£2,000

Correspondent: Andrew Rogers, Town Clerk, 9 St Martin's Street, Wallingford, Oxfordshire OX10 0AL (01491 835373; email: wallingfordtc@btconnect.com)

CC Number: 292000

Eligibility

People in need who live in the former borough of Wallingford.

Types of grants

Help with the cost of bills, clothing and other essentials. The charity gives one-off grants only.

Annual grant total

Grants average in total around £6,500 per year. We estimate that grants for educational purposes is generally about £2,000.

Applications

On a form available from the correspondent, submitted either directly by the individual or through a local organisation. Trustees meet about every three months, although emergency cases can be considered at other times. Urgent cases may require a visit by a trustee.

Other information

The majority of grants are given for welfare needs.

Wheatley

The Wheatley Charities

£3,000

Correspondent: R. F. Minty, Trustee, 24 Old London Road, Wheatley, Oxford OX33 1YW (01865 874676)

CC Number: 203535

Eligibility

People who are under 25 and live in the parish of Wheatley.

Types of grants

Grants are given to help young people prepare for any trade or occupation or to promote their education.

Annual grant total

In 2012 the charities had an income of £4,500 and a total expenditure of £6,400. We estimate that grants to individuals for educational purposes totalled around £3,000. The accounts for 2012 were the latest available at the time of writing (July 2014).

Applications

In writing to the correspondent.

Other information

Grants are also awarded to individuals for social welfare purposes.

Wootton

The Parrott and Lee Educational Foundation

£1,500 (5 grants)

Correspondent: Charles Ponsonby, Treasurer, Woodleys House, Woodstock, Oxford OX20 1HJ (01993 811717)

CC Number: 309586

Eligibility

People under the age of 25 who attended Wootton-by-Woodstock Primary School and/or live in Wootton-by-Woodstock.

Types of grants

Annual grants (which in 2012 averaged £300) particularly towards course fees, maintenance, travel, outfits, books and equipment to people in tertiary education. In 2012, grants were awarded to young people in the areas of interpreting, social work, media, environmental science and product design.

Annual grant total

In 2012 the foundation had assets of £910,000 and an income of £32,000. A total of £1,500 was awarded in five educational grants to individuals. A further £17,500 was given to Wootton-by-Woodstock Primary School.

At the time of writing (August 2014) this was the most recent financial information available for the foundation.

Applications

On a form available from the correspondent, which should be submitted directly by the individual. They are considered half-yearly, normally in March and September.

Suffolk

The Annie Tranmer Charitable Trust

£13,000 (17 grants)

Correspondent: M. R. Kirby, Administrator, 51 Bennett Road, Ipswich IP1 5HX (01473 743694; email: mary. kirby@timicomail.co.uk)

CC Number: 1044231

Eligibility

Young people who live in Suffolk who are keen to develop their physical, mental and spiritual capacities through their leisure time activities.

Types of grants

One-off and recurrent grants according to need, towards for example, educational outings, fees, equipment/ instruments and travel overseas. Grants range from £40 to £1,000.

Annual grant total

In 2012/13 the trust had assets of £3.5 million and an income of £119,000. Grants to 17 individuals totalled £13,000.

Applications

In writing to the correspondent, including details of the specific need, finances and alternative funding sources.

343

Other information

Grants are also made to other local agencies for the benefit of individuals.

Calthorpe and Edwards Educational Foundation

£8,800

Correspondent: R. Boswell, Administrator, Chegwidden, Beauford Road, Ingham, Bury St Edmunds IP31 1NW (01284 728288)

CC Number: 310464

Eligibility

People between the ages of 18 and 25 who live in the parishes of Ampton, Great Livermere, Little Livermere, Ingham and Timworth, Troston, Ixworth, Culford, Great Barton, West Stow, Wordwell, Fornham St Genevieve and Fornham St Martin.

Types of grants

Small scholarships and bursaries are available to further/higher education students for the purchase of books, equipment, necessities or expenses for study/travel overseas. Grants are paid termly with a total of around £300 per year and can be awarded for up to three years. People starting work/entering a trade can be assisted with the cost of books, instruments, tools, equipment and clothing/outfits.

Annual grant total

In 2012/13 the foundation had an income of £9,200 and an expenditure of £9,000. We estimate the annual total of grants to be around £8,800.

Applications

Application forms can be requested from the correspondent and submitted directly by the individual. Grants are normally considered in October.

The Fauconberge Educational Foundation

£1,000

Correspondent: Dr Barry Darch, Trustee, The Moorings, 9 Waveney Road, Beccles NR34 9NW (01502 711318)

CC Number: 310459

Eligibility

Children and young people between the ages of 11 and 18 who live within a five-mile radius of Beccles Town Hall, are in need of financial assistance and are 'engaged in a course of study intended to prepare them for higher or further education or for an advanced qualification.'

Types of grants

Grants for schoolchildren and further education or vocational students. Support is given to help with the school fees, books, equipment, educational outings in the UK and study or travel abroad. Schoolchildren can also receive help for uniforms and clothing. The grants are given as one-off payments and range from £50 to £500.

Annual grant total

In 2012/13 the foundation had an income of £1,700 and an expenditure of £1,300. We estimate that the annual total of grants was around £1,000.

Exclusions

University students are not eligible.

Applications

Our research shows that vacancies are normally advertised in the local papers and noticeboards. Application forms are available from the correspondent and can be submitted at any time by a parent/guardian or through a teacher. Applications should include the family's financial position and the number of children.

Other information

The foundation also makes occasional grants to local secondary schools.

Hope House and Gippeswyk Educational Trust

£7,500

Correspondent: John Clements, Trustee, 4 Church Meadows, Henley, Ipswich IP6 0RP

CC Number: 1068441

Eligibility

Children and young people in need who are under the age of 21 and live in Ipswich or the surrounding area.

Types of grants

One-off grants towards the costs of school uniforms/clothing, books, educational outings, travel, fees, maintenance/living expenses and other necessities, Support is given to schoolchildren and higher/further education students.

Annual grant total

In 2012/13 the trust had an income of £10,300 and an expenditure of £15,100. The trust also supports organisations, therefore we estimate the annual total of grants to individuals to be around £7,500.

Applications

In writing to the correspondent. Our research indicates that applications

should be submitted through the individual's school/college or welfare agency, if applicable, for consideration throughout the year.

Other information

Financial assistance can be given to both individuals and organisations.

The Mills Educational Foundation

£12,000

Correspondent: Deborah Stace, Administrator, 45 Saxmundham Road, Framlingham, Woodbridge, Suffolk IP13 9BZ (01728 724370; email: info@themillscharity.co.uk; website: www.themillscharity.co.uk)

CC Number: 310475

Eligibility

Children and young people up to the age of 24 who live in Framlingham and the surrounding district, or attend a school there.

Types of grants

One-off grants ranging from £50 to £550. Schoolchildren and further/higher education students can be supported for uniforms, other school clothing, books, equipment, instruments, educational outings in the UK and study or travel abroad. People starting work can receive grants for uniforms, other clothing, equipment and instruments.

Annual grant total

In 2012/13 the foundation had an income of £6,700 and an expenditure of £12,500. Grants given totalled approximately £12,000.

Applications

In writing to the correspondent.

Other information

Local primary schools are also supported.

Brockley

The (Brockley) Town and Poor Estate

£1,050

Correspondent: Jane Forster, Trustee, Brooklands, Chapel Lane, Brockley, Bury St Edmunds, Suffolk IP29 4AS (01284 830558; email: binnybops@btinternet.com)

CC Number: 236989

Eligibility

Schoolchildren who live in Brockley village.

Types of grants

Grants are given for the purchase of uniforms. In previous years an educational book has also been given to all students in the village on reaching the age of 15.

Annual grant total

In 2013 the charity had an income of £2,600 and a total expenditure of £2,100. Grants are made for educational and welfare purposes and totalled £2,100.

Applications

In writing to the correspondent to be submitted directly by the individual or a family member.

Bury St Edmunds
Old School Fund

£1,900

Correspondent: Michael Dunn, Administrator, 121 Southgate Street, Bury St Edmunds IP33 2AZ (01284 769483)

CC Number: 310348

Eligibility

People under 25 who live in, or whose parents live in, Bury St Edmunds and are undertaking further or higher education in any subject and are in need.

Types of grants

One-off and recurrent grants of between £100 and £250 towards the cost of books, fees and living expenses.

Annual grant total

In 2012 the fund had an income of £3,400 and a total expenditure of £3,800. We estimate that educational grants to individuals totalled £1,900, with funding also awarded to local schools.

At the time of writing (July 2014) this was the most recent financial information available for the fund.

Exclusions

Grants are not made for benefits which are normally provided by the local education authority.

Applications

An introductory letter and reference to the correspondent requesting an application form is preferred. Deadlines for applications are subject to the dates of trustee meetings.

Dennington
The Dennington Consolidated Charities

£500

Correspondent: William Blakeley, Clerk, Thorn House, Saxtead Road, Dennington, Woodbridge, Suffolk IP13 8AP (01728 638031)

CC Number: 207451

Eligibility

Grants are awarded to those embarking on tertiary education and vocational training living in the village of Dennington.

Types of grants

One-off and recurrent grants.

Annual grant total

Accounts for the year 2012 were the latest available at the time of writing (August 2014).

In 2012, the charity had an income of £15,000 and a total expenditure of £6,000. Approximately £500 is awarded in grants for educational purposes each year and £3,000 for social welfare.

Exclusions

The charity does not make loans, nor does it make grants where public funds are available unless they are considered inadequate.

Applications

In writing to the correspondent. Applications are considered throughout the year and a simple means test questionnaire must be completed by the applicant. Grants are only made to people resident in Dennington (a small village with 500 inhabitants). The charity does not respond to applications made outside this specific geographical area.

Other information

Grants are also awarded to organisations and for the maintenance of services in the parish church.

Dunwich
The Dunwich Town Trust

£0

Correspondent: Angela Bell, Administrator, The Old Forge, St James Street, Dunwich, Saxmundham, Suffolk IP17 3DU (01728 648107)

CC Number: 206294

Eligibility

People in need who live in the parish of Dunwich.

Types of grants

Grants for education range from £600 to £3,500 depending on the needs and type of course.

Annual grant total

In 2013 the trust had assets of £2.5 million and an income of £97,000. Grants to individuals totalled £14,100 and were awarded as follows:

Contact care alarms	£2,000
Winter grants	£9,500
Education grants	£0 (2012: £3,400)
General relief	£2,700
Unrestricted fund	£0 (2012: £60,000)

There were no grants for educational purposes in this financial year (2013) but we anticipate grants will be made in future years.

Applications

Write to the correspondent and request an application form.

Other information

Formerly known as 'Dunwich Pension Charity'. The trust makes grants to both individuals and organisations.

Earl Stonham
Earl Stonham Trust

£1,500

Correspondent: Sam Wilson, Administrator, College Farm, Forward Green, Stowmarket, Suffolk IP14 5EH (01449 711497; email: sam_wilson@ talk21.com)

CC Number: 213006

Eligibility

People with educational needs who live, or whose parents live, in the parish of Earl Stonham.

Types of grants

One-off grants up to a maximum of £200.

Annual grant total

In 2012/13 the trust had an income of £8,000 and an expenditure of £6,800. Grants can be made for educational and welfare needs and for both individuals and organisations. We estimate that grants to individuals for educational purposes totalled around £1,500.

Applications

In writing to the correspondent, to be submitted directly by the individual.

Gislingham

The Gislingham United Charity

£2,000

Correspondent: Robert Moyes, Administrator, 37 Broadfields Road, Gislingham, Eye, Suffolk IP23 8HX (01379 788105; email: r.moyes1926@ btinternet.com)

CC Number: 208340

Eligibility

Children who attend Gislingham Church of England School.

Types of grants

Grants are given to schoolchildren for excursions and to college and mature students for books.

Annual grant total

In 2013 the charity had an income of £16,500 and an expenditure of £9,000. We estimate that grants to individuals for educational purposes totalled around £2,000.

Applications

Applications can be submitted directly by the individual or verbally via a trustee. Applications must include reasons for the application, the amount requested and the applicant's address.

Other information

The charity also gives grants to individuals in need and supports village organisations and ecclesiastical causes.

Hadleigh

Ann Beaumont's Educational Foundation

£7,500 (59 grants)

Correspondent: Rose Welham, Administrator, 55 Castle Road, Hadleigh, Ipswich IP7 6JP (email: rosewelham55@ aol.com)

CC Number: 310397

Eligibility

Students under the age of 25 years who are in need of financial assistance and live in the parish of Hadleigh.

Types of grants

Grants to help with course books, equipment or educational trips for people at school, college, university or those starting work.

Annual grant total

In 2012/13 the foundation had assets of £1.3 million, an income of £43,500 and made 59 grants to individuals totalling £7,500.

Applications

In writing to the correspondent, together with evidence of the cost of the books or equipment required. Applications are considered four times a year.

Other information

9 grants were made to organisations during the year.

Halesworth

The Halesworth United Charities

£1,000

Correspondent: Janet Staveley-Dick, Clerk, Hill Farm, Primes Lane, Blyford, Halesworth, Suffolk IP19 9JT (01986 872340)

CC Number: 214509

Eligibility

People in need who live in the ancient parish of Halesworth.

Types of grants

One-off grants according to need. Recent examples include travel abroad for educational purposes, medical equipment or tools needed for a trade.

Annual grant total

Grants usually total between £2,000 and £3,000.

Applications

In writing to the correspondent, directly by the individual or through a social worker, Citizens Advice or other welfare agency. Applications can be submitted at any time for consideration in January, July and December, or any other time if urgent.

Other information

Grants are also made to individuals for welfare purposes and to organisations.

Hundon

Hundon Educational Foundation

£8,000

Correspondent: Bernard Beer, Administrator, Beauford Lodge, Mill Road, Hundon, Sudbury CO10 8EG (01440 786942)

CC Number: 310379

Eligibility

Children and young people under the age of 25 living in the parish of Hundon.

Types of grants

Financial support is available to pre-schoolchildren, school pupils, further/ higher education students, people in training and those starting work/entering a trade. Grants are given towards the costs of the course fees, educational outings/visits and for general educational purposes, including books, clothing, equipment/instruments. Our research indicates that grants range from £50 to about £500.

Annual grant total

In 2013 the foundation had an income of £9,000 and an expenditure of £8,200. We estimate the annual total of grants to be around £8,000.

Exclusions

The foundation is strictly limited to beneficiaries within the specified area.

Applications

In writing to the correspondent. Applications can be submitted by individuals directly or by their parent/ guardian. The trustees meet two or three times a year. Our research suggests that the foundation is well advertised in the village.

Kirkley

Kirkley Poor's Land Estate

£5,700

Correspondent: Lucy Walker, Administrator, 4 Station Road, Lowestoft, Suffolk NR32 4QF (01502 514964; email: kirkleypoors@gmail.com; website: kirkleypoorslandestate.co.uk/)

CC Number: 210177

Eligibility

Individuals in need who live in the parish of Kirkley.

Types of grants

One-off grants ranging from £200 to £300 to help towards university expenses.

Annual grant total

In 2012/13 the charity had assets of £2 million and an income of £87,000. Grants were made totalling £62,000 and were distributed as follows:

Grants to individuals (education)	£5,700
Grocery voucher scheme	£15,700
Grants to organisations	£41,000

Applications

In writing to the correspondent.

Lakenheath

George Goward and John Evans

£3,500

Correspondent: Laura Williams, Administrator, 8 Woodcutters Way, Lakenheath, Brandon, Suffolk IP27 9JQ (01842 860445)

CC Number: 253727

Eligibility

People under the age of 25 who live in the parish of Lakenheath, Suffolk.

Types of grants

Our research suggests that grants are in the range of £25 and £300. Support can be given for people leaving school/ starting work for equipment and other necessities and to further/higher education students to help with the maintenance/living expenses and books. Schoolchildren can also receive grants towards uniforms, clothing and educational outings.

Annual grant total

At the time of writing (August 2014) the latest financial information available was from 2012. In 2012 the charity had an income of £37,000 and a total expenditure of £16,000. We estimate that grants to individuals for educational purposes totalled around £3,500.

Applications

In writing to the correspondent. Applications can be submitted either directly by the individual or through a third party, such as a family member, social worker, teacher, or an organisation, for example, Citizens Advice. Applications should generally be submitted by February and August for consideration in March and September, respectively. Candidates should provide brief details of their financial situation and include receipts for the items purchased.

Other information

One eighth of the charity's income is allocated to Soham United Charities. Grants are also made to other organisations, local primary, secondary, nursery and Sunday schools, and to individuals for welfare purposes.

Lowestoft

Lowestoft Church and Town Educational Foundation

£12,000

Correspondent: Matthew Breeze, Norton Peskett Solicitors, 148 London Road North, Lowestoft, Suffolk NR32 1HF

CC Number: 310460

Eligibility

Children and young people between the ages of 5 and 25 who or whose parents are resident in the parish of Lowestoft and who have attended school in the area for at least three years.

Types of grants

Small, one-off grants are available to schoolchildren, higher/further education students or people entering a trade/ starting work. Support is given towards the cost of uniforms/clothing, books, equipment/instruments, tools, travel expenses, educational outings, study/ travel abroad in pursuance of education, and other general educational needs.

Annual grant total

In 2012/13 the foundation had an income of £18,200 and an expenditure of £18,400. We have estimated the annual total of grants to individuals to be around £12,000.

Applications

Application forms can be requested from the correspondent and submitted directly by the individual. Our research indicates that the application will need to be verified by the applicant's place of education.

Other information

Up to one third of the foundation's funding is directed to support local schools, where assistance is not already provided by the local authority.

Mendlesham

The Mendlesham Educational Foundation

£40,000

Correspondent: S. C. Furze, Administrator, Beggars Roost, Church Road, Mendlesham, Stowmarket IP14 5SF

CC Number: 271762

Eligibility

People under 25 who live in the parish of Mendlesham.

Types of grants

One-off and recurrent grants are given towards pre-school fees for children with serious family difficulties, and books and equipment for students in further/higher education or apprenticeships.

Annual grant total

In 2012 the foundation had an income of £63,000 and an expenditure of £86,000. Grants totalling around £40,000 were made to individuals for education; and to organisations £40,000.

The 2012 accounts are the latest available at the time of writing.

Exclusions

Grants are not given for school fees or maintenance. They are not normally available towards the cost of school educational outings or for special educational needs.

Applications

On a form available from the correspondent, including details of education to date, details of course to be taken, other grants applied for, estimated expenditure, parents' financial position and other dependent children in the family. Applications should be made by the individual or through a parent/ guardian by mid-September.

Other information

Grants are also made to organisations and Mendlesham CP School.

Pakenham

Town Estate Educational Foundation (Pakenham Educational Trust)

£2,500

Correspondent: Margaret Cohen, Clerk, 5 St Marys View, Pakenham, Bury St Edmunds, Suffolk IP31 2ND (01359 232965; email: maggiecohen59381@aol. com)

CC Number: 310364

Eligibility

Residents of the parish of Pakenham who are undertaking post-school education or training and require financial assistance.

Types of grants

Small grants (normally in the range of £50–£300) are given to people attending university and college courses or vocational training, including apprenticeships. Support can be given for general educational needs, including books, equipment, tools, accommodation and fees. Grants may also be given towards activities such as

Duke of Edinburgh Award Scheme, cathedral camps, sports scholarships and so on.

Annual grant total

In 2012/13 the charity had an income of £5,200 and a total expenditure of £5,300. We estimate that grants to individuals totalled around £2,500.

Applications

Application forms can be obtained from the correspondent or the Pakenham post office. They can be submitted directly by individuals by mid-November. The trustees meet in early December to consider applications but if necessary, urgent meetings can also be held in mid-summer.

Other information

Grants are also given to local schools and organisations working for educational causes.

Risby

The Risby Fuel Allotment

£500

Correspondent: Penelope Wallis, Trustee, 3 Woodland Close, Risby, Bury St Edmunds IP28 6QN (01284 81064)

CC Number: 212260

Eligibility

People in need who live in the parish of Risby.

Types of grants

Grants are given to higher education students.

Annual grant total

In 2012/13 the charity had an income of £3,700 and a total expenditure of £3,500. The charity predominantly makes grants for welfare purposes and for fuel contributions. We estimate educational grants to individuals to have totalled around £500.

Applications

In writing to the correspondent. Applications can be submitted by the individual and are considered in March and October. Applications made outside the specific area of interest (the parish of Risby) are not acknowledged.

Stutton

The Charity of Joseph Catt

£3,500

Correspondent: Keith R. Bales, Trustee, 34 Cattsfield, Stutton, Ipswich, Suffolk IP9 2SP (01473 328179)

CC Number: 213013

Eligibility

People in need who live in the parish of Sutton.

Types of grants

One-off grants and loans according to need.

Annual grant total

In 2012 this charity had an income of £9,900 and a total expenditure of £14,600. We estimate that grants for individuals for educational purposes totalled around £3,500. The accounts for 2012 were the latest available at the time of writing (July 2014).

Applications

Applications can be submitted by the individual, or through a recognised referral agency (e.g. social worker, Citizens Advice or doctor) and are considered monthly. They can be submitted to the correspondent, or any of the trustees at any time, for consideration in May and November.

Other information

The charity also supports local almshouses.

Walberswick

The Walberswick Common Lands

£1,500

Correspondent: Jayne Tibbles, Administrator, Lima Cottage, Walberswick, Southwold, Suffolk IP18 6TN (01502 724448; website: walberswick.onesuffolk.net/walberswick-common-lands-charity/)

CC Number: 206095

Eligibility

People in need who live in Walberswick village.

Types of grants

Grants are given in the range of £35 and £1,200 to schoolchildren for maintenance/living expenses and to college students for study/travel abroad, maintenance/living expenses and equipment.

Annual grant total

In 2013 the charity had assets of £125,000, an income of £72,000 and total expenditure of £78,000. Educational grants to individuals totalled almost £1,500. Grants for social welfare purposes awarded to individuals totalled £3,900 and grants to organisations £26,000.

Applications

In writing to the correspondent, either through the individual's school/college/educational welfare agency, or directly by the individual or through a parent or relative. Applications are considered in February, April, June, August, October and December.

Surrey

The Archbishop Abbot's Exhibition Foundation

£5,000

Correspondent: Richard Middlehurst, Administrator, 17 Ashdale, Bookham, Leatherhead, Surrey KT23 4QP (01483 302345; email: rhm@awb.co.uk)

CC Number: 311890

Eligibility

People aged between 11 and 28 who live or attend school in the boroughs of Guildford or Waverley in Surrey. Preference is given to male applicants.

Types of grants

Scholarships, bursaries or maintenance allowances at schools or universities; provision of clothing and equipment to assist entry into a trade or profession; scholarships for travelling abroad.

Grants range from £250 to £800 and are one-off.

Annual grant total

In 2012 the foundation had an income of £6,000 and made grants totalling around £5,000.

These were the latest accounts available at the time of writing (July 2014).

Applications

On a form available from the correspondent.

The Egham Education Trust

£2,800

Correspondent: Max Walker, Administrator, 33 Runnemede Road, Egham TW20 9BE (01784 472742; email: eghamunicharity@aol.com)

CC Number: 311941

Eligibility

People under the age of 25 who have lived in the electoral wards of Egham, which is now Egham, Englefield Green, Virginia Water and Hythe, for at least five years.

Types of grants

One-off and recurrent grants in the range of £100 and £500 are made to schoolchildren, undergraduates, vocational students, mature students and people with special educational needs. Grants may also be given for activities such as the Duke of Edinburgh Award Scheme.

Annual grant total

In 2013, the trust had an income of £8,000 and a total expenditure of £3,000. We estimate that £2,800 was awarded in grants to individuals.

Applications

On a form available from the correspondent. Applications must include details of other grants and loans. The deadline for applications is the 15th of each month.

The Mary Stephens Foundation

£5,000

Correspondent: John Stephenson, Trustee, Doghurst Cottage, Doghurst Lane, Chipstead, Surrey CR5 3PL (01737 556548)

CC Number: 311999

Eligibility

People under the age of 25 who live, or whose parents live, in the ancient parish of Chipstead and Hooley, or who have attended Chipstead County First School.

Types of grants

One-off and recurrent grants up to a maximum of £1,200 a year. Help to people in further education is in the form of books, uniforms and travel expenses. Limited help is given towards fees on a scholarship basis. Grants are given to those qualifying to obtain further education in the broadest possible way, such as for music lessons and field courses.

Annual grant total

In 2012/13 the foundation had an income of £7,200 and an expenditure of £5,900. Grants totalled about £5,000.

Exclusions

The foundation does not issue grants to pre-schoolchildren or provide loans.

Applications

Applications are considered at quarterly meetings and should be made directly by the individual, or by the individual's head of school or church leader.

The Witley Charitable Trust

£1,700

Correspondent: Daphne O'Hanlon, Trustee, Triados, Waggoners Way, Grayshott, Hindhead, Surrey GU26 6DX (01428 604679)

CC Number: 200338

Eligibility

Children and young people (normally under the age of 20) who are in need and live in the parishes of Witley, Milford and a small part of Brook.

Types of grants

One-off, modest grants ranging from £25 to £300. Most recently the trust has supported a pupil to attend a local pre-school.

Annual grant total

At the time of writing (August 2014) the latest financial information available was from 2012. In 2012 the trust had an income of £5,500 and an expenditure of £3,500. We estimate that grants for educational purposes totalled around £1,700.

Exclusions

The trust does not give loans or support for items which should be provided by statutory services.

Applications

In writing to the correspondent. Applications should be submitted through social workers, schools, Citizens Advice and so on but not directly by the individual. Awards are usually considered in early February and September, although emergency applications can be considered throughout the year.

Other information

Grants are also given for welfare purposes.

Charlwood

John Bristow and Thomas Mason Trust

£500

Correspondent: Marie Singleton, Trust Secretary, 3 Grayrigg Road, Maidenbower, Crawley RH10 7AB (01293 883950; email: trust.secretary@ jbtmt.org.uk; website: www.jbtmt.org.uk)

CC Number: 1075971

Eligibility

Only people who live in the ancient parish of Charlwood (as constituted on 17 February 1926).

Types of grants

Grants are given to schoolchildren, college students, undergraduates, vocational students, mature students, people with special educational needs and to people starting work. Help is given for the cost of uniforms/other school clothing, books, equipment/ instruments, fees, maintenance/living expenses, childcare, education outings in the UK, study or travel abroad and student exchanges.

Annual grant total

In 2013 the trust had assets of £2.7 million representing mainly endowment funds with only £85,000 being unrestricted. The trust had an income of £95,000 and made grants totalling almost £93,000, of which £500 went to individuals for educational purposes and almost £700 to individuals for social welfare purposes. The remainder was awarded to organisations.

Applications

On a form available from the correspondent or to download from the trust's website. Applications can be submitted directly by the individual or through an appropriate third party. They will normally be considered within two weeks but can be dealt with more quickly in urgent cases.

Chertsey

The Chertsey Combined Charity

£5,500

Correspondent: M. R. O'Sullivan, Secretary, PO Box 89, Weybridge, Surrey KT13 8HY (email: info@charity.me.uk)

CC Number: 200186

Eligibility

People in need who live in the electoral divisions of the former urban district of Chertsey.

Types of grants

Grants are often given to help towards the cost of books, clothing and other essentials for those at school. Grants may also be given to people at college or university.

Annual grant total

In 2013/14 the charity had assets of £1.9 million – most of which is in the form of permanent endowment. The charity had an income of £61,000 and a total expenditure of £66,000. Grants to individuals total £11,000, we estimate that half (£5,500) was awarded for educational purposes.

Applications

On a form available from the correspondent.

Other information

The charity also makes grants to organisations (£28,000 in 2013/14).

Chessington

Chessington Charities

£2,000

Correspondent: Mrs L. Roberts, Administrator, St Mary's Centre, Church Lane, Chessington, Surrey KT9 2DR

CC Number: 209241

Eligibility

People in need who live in the parish of St Mary the Virgin, Chessington. Applicants must have lived in the parish for at least one year.

Types of grants

Recent grants included those for school uniforms, shoes and school trips. Grants are given in the range of £30 to £250 and are usually one-off.

Annual grant total

In 2013 the charity had both an income and a total expenditure of almost £8,000. We estimate grants for individuals for educational purposes totalled around £2,000.

Exclusions

Grants are not given to pay debts. Applicants must live in the parish of St Mary the Virgin; this excludes those that live in the rest of the Chessington postal area.

Applications

On a form available from the correspondent to be submitted either directly by the individual or through a social worker, Citizens Advice or other agency. Christmas gifts are distributed in November. Other applications are considered throughout the year. A home visit will be made by a trustee to ascertain details of income and expenditure and to look at the need.

Other information

Grants are also given to local organisations which help people who are elderly or who have disabilities. Individual welfare grants are also available.

Chobham

Chobham Poor Allotment Charity

£590 (3 grants)

Correspondent: Elizabeth Thody, Administrator, 46 Chertsey Road, Windlesham GU20 6EP (01276 475396)

CC Number: 200154

Eligibility

People living in the parish of Chobham and West End.

Types of grants

Grants ranging between £100 and £500 are normally made towards the cost of school uniforms and educational outings, trips, visits.

Annual grant total

In 2012/13 the charity had assets of £422,000, an income of £45,300 and a total expenditure of £41,000. Three individual grants were awarded totalling £590.

Applications

In writing to the correspondent.

Other information

The main activities of the charity are the provision and maintenance of allotments, almshouses and relief in need. The charity is also involved in provision/maintenance of recreational and educational facilities. The trustees can support both individuals and organisations, nevertheless only a small amount each year is awarded in educational grants.

East Horsley

Henry Smith Charity (East Horsley)

£800

Correspondent: Nicholas Clemens, Administrator, East Horsley Parish Council Office, Kingston Avenue, East Horsley, Surrey KT24 6QT (01483 281148; email: henrysmithcharity@ easthorsley.net)

CC Number: 200796

Eligibility

Children from poor or disadvantaged backgrounds who have lived in East Horsley for at least two years.

Types of grants

Grants can be given to children to support them through their schooling and to orphaned children for small scholarships.

Annual grant total

Each year the charity receives an amount allocated by Henry Smith's (General Estate) Charity which is divided according to need between welfare and educational grants.

Applications

In writing to the correspondent through a third party such as a social worker, teacher or vicar. Applications are considered in December.

Elmbridge

The R. C. Sherriff Rosebriars Trust

£3,600

Correspondent: Sam Thompson, Administrator, Charity House, 5 Quintet, Churchfield Road, Walton-on-Thames, Surrey KT12 2TZ (01932 229996; email: arts@rcsherrifftrust.org. uk; website: www.rcsherrifftrust.org.uk)

CC Number: 272527

Eligibility

Amateur and professional artists (composers, craftspeople, curators, designers, directors, film-makers, musicians, performers, producers, promoters, theatre technicians, visual artists, writers and so on) in the borough of Elmbridge.

The trust's grantmaking guidelines specify that 'managers, education officers, fundraisers, marketing staff, press officers and workshop leaders may apply for individual grants towards training and personal development only.'

Types of grants

Grants and bursaries, usually of up to £500 a year for up to three years, to assist with:

- Professional development and training (including travel grants), such as short courses in specific skills, work placements with other artists or specified periods of travel and/or study
- Research and development for arts projects
- Publication or production of a specific piece of work
- Capital items (for example, equipment)

Annual grant total

The latest financial information available at the time of writing (July 2014) was from 2012. In 2012 the trust had assets of £3.6 million, an income of £209,000 and made 38 grants totalling £45,000. Grants under £1,000 to individuals and organisations totalled £7,200.

The trust's website states that approximately £60,000–£70,000 is available each year for distribution in awards to individuals and organisations.

Exclusions

Grants are not given retrospectively. The project should take place at least one month after the application submission deadline. Support is not given for non-art related activities, fundraising events, higher education courses, long-term vocational training (for example, drama school) or ongoing training programmes (such as piano lessons or regular dance classes).

Applications

Initial contact should be made with the correspondent prior to formal application to ensure that the project meets the eligibility criteria. Application forms are available to download from the trust's website. The trustees meet quarterly to consider applications. For specific deadlines see the trust's website, although generally they are in the middle of January, April, July and October.

Other information

Grants are also made to arts organisations and for various arts projects. Part of the trust's expenditure is allocated for the publication of a magazine *Art Focus* (£8,000 in 2012) and for organising and managing arts initiatives (£56,000 in 2012).

Further guidance, information and advice can also be obtained from the correspondent by phone.

Epsom

Epsom Parochial Charities

£1,500

Correspondent: Patricia Vanstone-Walker, Administrator, 42 Canons Lane, Tadworth, Surrey KT20 6DP (01737 361243; email: vanstonewalker@ntlworld.com)

CC Number: 200571

Eligibility

Educational support for the people of Epsom.

Types of grants

One-off and recurrent grants according to need are given to: schoolchildren, college students, undergraduates, vocational students, mature students, people starting work and people with special educational needs, including those towards clothing/uniforms, fees, books, equipment/instruments maintenance/living expenses and excursions.

Annual grant total

IIn 2012 the charity had an income of £83,000 and assets of £1.6 million. Grants were made to individuals for education and welfare purposes totalling £2,400.

These were the latest accounts available at the time of writing (August 2014)

Applications

On a form available from the correspondent, to be submitted directly by the individual. Applications are considered in March, June, September and December and should be submitted in the preceding month.

Other information

Grants are also given from Epsom Parochial Charities for relief in need.

Leatherhead

Leatherhead United Charities

£10,000 (50–60 grants)

Correspondent: David Matanle, Clerk to the Trustees, Homefield, Forty Foot Road, Leatherhead, Surrey KT22 8RP (01372 370073; email: luchar@btinternet.com)

CC Number: 200183

Eligibility

People in need who live in the area of the former Leatherhead urban district council (Ashtead, Bookhams, Fetcham and Leatherhead). Preference is given to residents of the parish of Leatherhead as constituted on 27 September 1912.

Types of grants

Our research indicates that grants are normally one-off and can range from £100 to £750. Support is available for general educational expenses. This charity does not deal with educational needs only, 'grants are made for the relief of need generally'.

Annual grant total

At the time of writing (July 2014) the latest accounts were not available to view. In 2013 the charity had an income of £298,000 and a total expenditure of £233,000. In the past grants to individuals totalled around £20,000 a year, distributed in 50–60 awards. We estimate that grants for educational purposes totalled around £10,000.

Applications

Application forms can be requested from the correspondent. They can be submitted by the individual directly or by a family member. Awards are considered throughout the year.

Other information

Grants are also made to organisations.

Reigate

The Pilgrim Band Trust

£7,000

Correspondent: Gregory Andrews, Trustee, Clevelands, 13 Furzefield Road, Reigate RH2 7HG (01737 244134; email: pilgrim.band@virgin.net)

CC Number: 1140954

Eligibility

Children and young people between the ages of 8 and 18 living in Reigate and surrounding areas who want to learn to play an instrument. Young musicians are also supported. Preference may be given to individuals or families with limited means or children with disabilities.

Types of grants

The trust gives an opportunity to children and young people to learn music by loaning instruments and providing one-to-one or group tuition sessions for acoustic and electric guitars, piano, singing, drums and steel pans. Grants can also be provided for tuition fees to young musicians.

Annual grant total

In 2012/13 the trust had assets of over £4 million, an income of £122,000 and a total charitable expenditure of £95,000. Around £7,000 was given in scholarships and tuition.

Applications

In writing to the correspondent.

Other information

The trust also supports local schools, with priority to state schools and local music festivals. Most of the charitable expenditure is spent for the activities of the Pilgram Band.

Thorpe

The Thorpe Parochial Charities

£1,000

Correspondent: Dorothy Jones, Administrator, 9 Rosefield Gardens, Ottershaw, Chertsey, Surrey KT16 0JH (01932 872245)

CC Number: 205888

Eligibility
People in need under 21 years who live in the ancient parish of Thorpe.

Types of grants
Grants are occasionally given towards books for students in further or higher education. Relief-in-need grants are also available.

Annual grant total
About £3,000 is given in grants each year to individuals with most of the awards being made for social welfare purposes.

Applications
In writing to the correspondent by the end of October. Applications are usually considered in November. The grants are usually given out at Michaelmas.

Woking

The Deakin Charitable Trust

£0

Correspondent: William Hodgetts, Trustee, Station House, Connaught Road, Brookwoood, Woking GU24 0ER (01483 485444)

CC Number: 258001

Eligibility
People studying music who are living in the immediate Woking area.

Types of grants
Bursaries are given to students of music.

Annual grant total
In 2012/13 the trust had assets of £864,000 and an income of £67,500. There were no grants awarded to individuals. This entry has been retained as it is likely that music bursaries will be awarded again in the future.

Applications
In writing to the correspondent.

Other information
Most of the trust's income goes in grants to organisations.

West Sussex

The Bassil Shippam and Alsford Trust
See entry on page 19

Angmering

William Older's School Charity

£3,000

Correspondent: The Hon. Secretary, Parish Office, Church House, Arundel Road, Angmering, Littlehampton BN16 4JS

CC Number: 306424

Eligibility
People aged 23 or under who live in the ecclesiastical parish of Angmering. The applicant's parents must reside in Angmering.

Types of grants
One-off and recurrent grants up to £500. Grants are given to schoolchildren towards the cost of equipment/ instruments and fees, and to students in further or higher education towards books, equipment/instruments, childcare and educational outings in the UK.

Annual grant total
In 2012 the charity had an unusually high income of £17,300 and an unusually high total expenditure of £22,000. In previous years, grants to individuals have totalled around £3,000, with further grants also given to organisations.

At the time of writing (July 2014) this was the most recent financial information available for the charity.

Applications
In writing to the correspondent giving details of income and expenditure, the course being studied and residence in Angmering. Applications are usually considered in January, May and October.

Crawley

Crawley and Ifield Educational Foundation

£4,900

Correspondent: Hilary Ward, Administrator, St Marys Rectory, Forester Road, Crawley, West Sussex RH10 6EH (01293 547261)

CC Number: 1042834

Eligibility
People under 25 who are in financial need and live in Ifield, Southgate, Crawley or Rusper.

Types of grants
One-off and recurrent grants, with a preference for those which will promote the individual's religious education, such as Sunday School.

Annual grant total
In 2012 the foundation had an income of £108 and a total expenditure of £10,000. This was the most recent information available at the time of writing (August 2014). We estimate that grants to individuals totalled £4,900, with funding also awarded to local schools.

Applications
In writing to the correspondent.

London

General

The Aldgate and Allhallows Foundation

£44,000 (46 grants)

Correspondent: Richard Foley, Clerk, 31 Jewry Street, London EC3N 2EY (020 7488 2518; email: aldgateandallhallows@ sirjohncass.org; website: www. aldgateallhallows.org.uk)

CC Number: 312500

Eligibility

Young people under the age of 25 who have lived in the city of London or the London borough of Tower Hamlets for at least three years and are studying full-time in further or higher education (including postgraduates) on a course of at least one year that will result in a recognised qualification. Priority is given to people from disadvantaged backgrounds.

The foundation also notes that 'individuals from a refugee background are welcome to apply, providing they have been granted indefinite leave to remain in the UK or full refugee status.'

Types of grants

Most of the foundation's support is distributed by way of undergraduate bursaries to students at Queen Mary University, London. Some grants are available to individuals studying at other courses or institutions. Support can be given towards books, equipment, travel expenses, maintenance and tuition fees. Awards are normally of up to £1,000 and are made for one year only but can be renewed following a receipt of a progress report from the university or college.

Annual grant total

In 2013 the foundation had assets of £7.6 million, an income of £73,000 and a total charitable expenditure of £289,000. Grants to 46 individual students totalled £44,000.

Exclusions

Grants are not normally given for:
- Courses at private colleges
- Fees at independent schools
- Repeated years of study
- Study for a qualification at the same or lower level than those an individual already possesses
- Fees for higher education courses, unless they are for second degrees and a student loan is not available
- Medical electives
- Individuals with time limited leave to remain in the UK

Applications

Initially in writing to the correspondent specifying the applicants' 'name, address, phone number, email address, age, course, how long they have lived in the city of London or Tower Hamlets, how they heard about the trust, and what they need a grant for.' Eligible candidates will then be sent an application form which should include full details of their financial circumstances. Applications are considered throughout the year and can be made at any time by individuals directly or through an appropriate third party. Applicants may be invited for an interview. The foundation welcomes informal contact via phone or email prior to application.

Other information

Grants were also made to 14 schools and institutions working for the benefit of young people in the local area (£245,000 in 2013).

It is noted in the trustees' annual report from 2013 that they 'wish to maintain this blend of group and individual support.'

Sir William Boreman's Foundation

£11,000 (17 grants)

Correspondent: Andrew Mellows, Head of Charities, The Drapers' Company, Drapers' Hall, Throgmorton Avenue, London EC2N 2DQ (020 7588 5001; fax: 020 7628 1988; email: charities@ thedrapers.co.uk; website: www. thedrapers.co.uk/Charities/Grantmaking-trusts/Sir-William-Boremans-Foundation.aspx)

CC Number: 312796

Eligibility

Children and young people under the age of 25 with a household income of £25,000 or less who live in the London boroughs of Greenwich and Lewisham or in that part of the London borough of Newham which was formerly in the Metropolitan Borough of Woolwich. Preference is given to the borough of Greenwich, to practising members of the Church of England and to sons and daughters of seamen, watermen and fishermen, particularly those who have served in the armed forces. Boys and young men pursuing a career in seafaring are also favoured. Applicants must be UK nationals or have full refugee status.

Types of grants

One-off grants usually of up to £1,000 are given to higher/further education students and people starting work towards living expenses, travel costs, educational necessities, books, equipment/instruments, childcare costs. Schoolchildren are eligible for assistance with the cost of school uniforms, sports kits, travel costs and educational outings/visits.

Annual grant total

In 2012/13 the foundation had assets of £3.3 million and an income of £94,000. The total charitable expenditure was around £87,000, of which around £11,000 was awarded to 17 individuals.

Exclusions

Grants are not made for:
- Students aged over 25 or pre-school children
- Non-UK citizens and asylum seekers (only those with full refugee status may apply)
- Postgraduate students who have attained a 2.2 or lower
- Overseas study/travel or exchange visits
- Retrospective grants
- Tuition fees

- Non-education related loans or debts
- Setting up business ventures
- Performing arts courses (acting, dance, drama)
- Private school fees

Applications

Application forms can be found on the foundation's website or can be requested from the correspondent. The trustees welcome unsolicited applications which should be submitted at least four weeks before the meetings held in November, February and June each year. Further guidelines are available on the foundation's website. Our research suggests that applicants are expected to have applied for a grant from their local authority and to have received a decision on this before applying to the foundation. Some applicants may be asked to attend a brief interview with the governors.

Other information

The foundation also supports organisations. In 2012/13 about £76,000 was distributed to 17 institutions and organisations.

The Castle Baynard Educational Foundation

£5,000

Correspondent: Mauricia Cebulec-Gardner, Trustee, 17 Fleetwood, 2 Northwold Road, London N16 7HG (020 7249 2490)

CC Number: 312502

Eligibility

People in need under the age of 25 who/ whose parents are resident or employed in the Castle of Baynard ward of the City of London or in the former county of Middlesex, or who are/have been in full-time education at any educational establishment closely connected with the corporation of London. Preference may be given to the City of London School and The City of London School for Girls or to people with special educational needs.

Types of grants

Grants range from £100 to £500 and are available to schoolchildren, further/ higher education students and people starting work. Financial assistance is given towards the cost of books, equipment/instruments, tools, materials, events and educational outings, clothing/ outfits, also travel expenses and research.

Annual grant total

In 2012/13 the foundation had an income of £8,300 and an expenditure of £9,100. We estimate the annual total of grants to individuals to be around £5,000.

Exclusions

Support is not normally available for the course fees or general maintenance.

Applications

In writing to the correspondent. Applicants should provide an sae and include the following details: the purpose of the grant; a CV; evidence of financial need; and a reference of support to confirm their current educational status and financial circumstances. Applications are normally considered in March, June, September and December.

Other information

The foundation also supports a Sunday school at St Andrew by the Wardrobe.

The City and Diocese of London Voluntary Schools Fund

£16,500 (233 grants)

Correspondent: Inigo Woolf, Administrator, 36 Causton Street, London SW1P 4AU (02079321165; email: inigo.woolf@london.anglican.org; website: www.london.anglican.org/ schools)

CC Number: 312259

Eligibility

Children and young people under the age of 25 who have attended Church of England voluntary aided schools in the diocese of London (i.e. north of the river) for at least two years.

Types of grants

Due to limited funds, support is mainly given towards the costs of school journeys/field trips, music tuition and maintenance costs. Occasionally grants can be given for general educational expenses. Schoolchildren, further/higher education students, people in vocational training or individuals entering a trade/ starting work can be supported. Grants can range up to £500 and are usually one-off.

Annual grant total

In 2012/13 the fund had assets of £693,000 and an income of £124,000. A total of £16,500 was spent in grants to 233 individuals.

Exclusions

Retrospective applications are not considered.

Applications

Application forms can be found on the fund's website or requested from the correspondent. Applications should include two references and specify what kind of assistance is required. Applications for individuals under 16

should be completed by a parent/ guardian. The deadlines are: 28 February for summer term journeys, 30 June for autumn term journeys and 30 October for spring term journeys.

Other information

The fund also accepts group applications for school journeys.

The City of London Corporation Combined Education Charity

£27,000

Correspondent: Barbara Hamilton, Head of Adult Education, Community and Children's Services, City of London, PO Box 270 EC2P 2EJ (020 7332 1755; email: adulteducation@cityoflondon.gov. uk; website: www.cityoflondon.gov.uk/ corporation/lgnl_services/advice_and_ benefits/grants/student_awards.htm# hersef)

CC Number: 312836

Eligibility

To further the education of people attending secondary schools or higher educational institutions in the City of London or other London boroughs. Priority will be given to courses related to civil engineering and construction, but other branches of engineering, building studies, manufacturing, IT and design will also be considered. A list of approved courses is available from the correspondent.

Types of grants

Support may take the form of: a bursary over an academic year, with possible renewal for further years during the period of eligibility (living, travel and/or tuition expenses); specific grants to assist in the completion of short course or educational project work; and help with the costs of attendance at courses or conferences in the UK or overseas.

Grants for staff at maintained schools and academies in London to undertake studies either at educational institutions or other establishments that will further their development as teachers will also be provided.

Annual grant total

In 2012/13 the charity held assets of £970,000 and had an income of £32,000. Grants of £27,000 were made to individuals. Note that the investment income consists of distributions from the Charities Pool, which is an investment mechanism that operates similarly to a Unit Trust. The City of London Corporation pools small charitable investments together to receive better returns.

Applications

On a form (www.cityoflondon.gov.uk/corporation/lgnl_services/advice_and_benefits/grants/student_awards) available from the correspondent, submitted either directly by the individual, or via their school, college or educational welfare agency. Applications must show evidence of financial hardship and be accompanied by a covering letter of support from the head of the institution. Applications should be submitted before March.

Other information

This charity was previously called the Higher Education Research and Special Expenses Fund (HERSEF), which received no applications in the year 2010/11. In 2011 a new scheme was approved whereby this fund merged with Archibald Dawnay Scholarships, Robert Blair Fellowships for Applied Science and Technology and Alan Partridge Smith Trust to form the City of London Corporation Combined Education Charity (retaining the charity registration number for HERSEF).

John Edmonds (Battersea United Charities – The John Edmond Charity)

£1,200

Correspondent: Stephen Willmett, Trustee, Battersea United Charities, Battersea District Library, Lavender Hill, London SW11 1JB (07960 483842)

CC Number: 312153

Eligibility

Children and young people under the age of 25 who live in the former metropolitan borough of Battersea. Preference may be given for individuals whose families have lived in Battersea for a long time.

Some additional help may be available to older women.

Types of grants

Small, one-off and recurrent grants, generally of £50–£500. Support is given to schoolchildren towards uniforms, school clothing, books, equipment/instruments, educational outings in the UK and study or travel abroad. Students in further and higher education (including postgraduates and vocational students) can receive grants towards books, equipment/instruments, excursions, fees, maintenance and childcare. Assistance is also given to people entering a trade/starting work.

Annual grant total

In 2012/13 the charity had an income of £4,100 and an expenditure of £2,500. We estimate that educational grants to individuals totalled around £1,200.

Applications

Application forms are available from the correspondent. They can be submitted at any time directly by the individual or through a school/college/university. Applications are considered bi-monthly.

Other information

Grants are also given to organisations. Some support in food parcels may be available to pensioners at Christmas.

The Eric Evans Memorial Trust

See entry on page 298

Francon Trust

£18,300 (7 grants)

Correspondent: Colonel Derek Ivy, Administrator, Smithtown, Kirkmahoe, Dumfries DG1 1TE (01387 740455)

CC Number: 10033592

Eligibility

Students in tertiary education and vocational training who were born or brought up and live in London. Support is aimed at 'school examination high achievers' entering vocational training or proceeding to the first degree courses, particularly in medicine, architecture, accountancy, insurance, banking, law or other professional business or trade fields, including science and engineering.

Types of grants

Our research suggests that grants range from £1,000 to £3,000 and are normally given in the form of interest-free loans which become gifts on completion of the course after six months of employment in a related occupation. Grants may be in the form of a single payment or a series of successive payments, depending upon circumstances.

Annual grant total

In 2012/13 the trust had assets of £1.2 million, an income of £28,000 and awarded grants totalling £18,300. The trust states that 'approximately seven students per annum are supported.'

Applications

Applicants should contact the correspondent by sending a brief letter. Application forms will then be provided. The trust's annual report from 2012/13 states that:

> Potential students for first degree courses are selected in accordance with the guidelines, based upon applications and

recommendations from headteachers in support of bright students who have little or no financial means. Potential students are identified by contact with headteachers and then, after due application, are interviewed by the trustees to decide those who should receive support.

Other information

The trustees' annual report from 2012/13 notes that 'starting in 2014 some four new students per year may be supported.'

Grants are also given for social welfare needs.

The Hale Trust

See entry on page 298

The Hornsey Parochial Charities

£18,000

Correspondent: Lorraine Fincham, Administrator, PO Box 22985, London N10 3XB (020 8352 1601; fax: 020 8352 1601; email: hornseypc@blueyonder.co.uk)

CC Number: 229410

Eligibility

People under 25 who have lived for at least one year in the ancient parish of Hornsey in Haringey and Hackney.

Types of grants

Grants of between £350 and £1,200 for bursaries, maintenance allowances, clothing, instruments and books.

Annual grant total

In 2013 the charity had assets of £1.6 million and an income of £51,000. Educational grants averaged around £650 and totalled approximately £18,000.

Applications

Individuals can write requesting an application form that, on being returned, can usually be dealt with within a month.

Other information

Grants are also made for welfare purposes.

The Island Health Charitable Trust

£0

Correspondent: Sonia Lapwood, Administrator, Island Health Trust, Carter Lemon Camerons LLP, 10 Aldersgate Street, London EC1A 4HJ (020 7406 1000; email: info@islandhealthtrust.org; website: www.islandhealthtrust.org)

CC Number: 1127466

Eligibility

The trust's website states: 'We also welcome applications from individuals working locally who want to attend courses to improve their qualifications or to run courses to promote in Tower Hamlets and Newham.'

Types of grants

One-off grants and recurrent grants according to need for up to three years. The maximum grant available is £5,000.

Annual grant total

In 2012/13 the trust had assets of £3.6 million and an income of £301,000. Although grants were made to two organisations totalling £13,500 it appears no grants to individuals were made during the year.

Exclusions

Grants are not given to university students for living expenses or tuition fees, to cover the travel costs of training abroad, or are made in any case where statutory funding is available.

Applications

On the application form available with guidance notes on the trust's website.

The London Youth Trust (W. H. Smith Memorial)

£2,000

Correspondent: Philip Sadd, Administrator, The Worshipful Company of Carpenters, Carpenters' Hall, 1 Throgmorton Avenue, London EC2N 2JJ (020 7588 7001; fax: 020 7382 1683; email: info@carpentersco.com; website: www.londonyouthtrust.org.uk)

CC Number: 230990–1

Eligibility

People under the age of 25 who are resident in London and are studying at the Building Crafts College.

Types of grants

The trust offers support through three grant schemes:

- LYT scholarships – £6,500 for students enrolled on the high fee, flagship courses (fine woodwork, stonemasonry and historic building conservation) at the Building Crafts College
- LYT bursaries – £15–£20 per week to support students in training and those entering employment for travel costs, basic welfare needs, purchase of tools/ equipment
- LYT prizes – two prizes of £250 each

Annual grant total

In 2012/13 the trust had assets of £635,000 and an income of £5,600. A total of £2,000 was awarded in grants.

Applications

Applications should be made via the Worshipful Company of Carpenters. The company's website notes that applicants should write to the following address: The Bursar, Building Crafts College, Kennard Road, Stratford, London E15 1AH. Grants are considered in May.

Other information

In September 2012 the funds of the trust were passed over to the Worshipful Company of Carpenters. It remains as a restricted fund administered by the company via the Norton Folgate Trust.

Need and Taylor's Educational Charity

£6,300

Correspondent: Julie Cadman, St Paul's Church Office, St Paul's Road, Brentford TW8 0PN (020 8568 7442; email: clerk@ brentfordchiswickmc.org.uk; website: www.brentfordchiswickmc.org.uk)

CC Number: 312269

Eligibility

Children in need who are under the age of 21 and live in the former borough of Brentford and Chiswick (as constituted immediately before 1 April 1965). The charity uses the child's eligibility for free school meals as an indicator of 'need'.

Types of grants

One-off grants between £80 and £100 are provided to schoolchildren towards the cost of uniforms, other clothing including PE kits, coats and shoes, school bags and educational equipment (calculators, art tools and so on).

Annual grant total

In 2012/13 the charity had an income of £14,000 and an expenditure of £12,800. It supports a number of local schools and we estimate the annual total of grants to individuals to be around £6,300.

Applications

Application forms can be found on the charity's website and have to be accompanied by the 'applicant's letter'. The application needs to be signed by the headteacher and include specific amounts requested for each individual item and prices inclusive of VAT. The trustees meet quarterly.

Other information

Grants are also made to schools, where support is not already provided by the local authorities.

The Philological Foundation

£18,000 (20 grants)

Correspondent: Carolyn Keen, Trustee, 20 Upper Montagu Street, London W1H 2PF (email: thephilological@gmail. com)

CC Number: 312692

Eligibility

Children and young people under the age of 26 who are, or have been, pupils at a state-funded secondary school in the City of Westminster or the London borough of Camden. Particular regard is paid to former pupils of the St Marylebone Grammar School.

Types of grants

Grants are offered towards tuition fees, study/travel costs, educational necessities, such as books, equipment/ instruments, materials, clothing and so forth. Schoolchildren, further/higher education students and individuals in vocational training or people starting work/entering trade can be assisted. Awards are normally in the range from £150 to £2,000.

Grants for education are considered at the following levels: GNVQ, GCSE, A-level, access and foundation courses, diploma, first and postgraduate taught degrees.

Annual grant total

In 2012/13 the foundation had assets of £959,000 and an income of £130,000. Around £47,000 was spent on charitable activities, of which £18,000 was distributed in grants to 20 individuals.

Exclusions

Support will not be given to individuals who could be assisted by a statutory loan.

Applications

Applicants are invited to email the correspondent to request further information and application forms. The trustees meet at least five times a year, normally during the third week of September, December, February, April and June. Applications should be submitted by the 22nd of the month two months prior to a meeting. Applicants will need to provide proof of their attendance at any school or educational establishment in either Westminster or Camden, evidence of their financial circumstances, academic results and some details of what help is required together with estimated costs.

The foundation has previously stated that 'if non-eligible students apply (for example, those aged over 25 or those who did not attend a secondary school in Westminster or Camden) the application will not be acknowledged.' The foundation discourages late applications which will be postponed or refused altogether.

Other information

Grants are also made to state-funded primary and secondary schools within the area of benefit for the provision of various recreational and leisure activities, educational outings and visits, facilities or equipment (about £25,000 in in 2012/13).

The Pocklington Apprenticeship Trust (Acton, Ealing and Hammersmith and Fulham branch)

£750

Correspondent: Mary Church, Trustee, 48 St Dunstans Avenue, London W3 6QB (020 8992 8311)

CC Number: 312186

Eligibility

Young people aged 25 or under who have lived in Acton, Ealing or Hammersmith and Fulham for at least five years. Special consideration is given to people who have a disability or special educational needs.

Types of grants

Grants in the range of £100 and £300 are given towards tools, equipment, training course fees, textbooks, stationery, computer accessories, special clothing, etc.

Annual grant total

About £500 to £1,000 is available each year.

Applications

On a form available from the correspondent, for consideration in May/June. Applicants should provide evidence of financial hardship; this could be being in receipt of state benefits or because of personal circumstances. Applicants can apply on their own behalf or through a sponsor who might be a teacher, tutor, youth leader or social worker.

Other information

Although it is primarily for the benefit of young people, the trustees have stated that it will also be worth older people applying who, because of a disabling condition later in life, have had to consider an alternative job to that which they have been used to.

Richard Reeve's Foundation

£72,000 (232 grants)

Correspondent: Shirley Scott, Clerk and Company Secretary, 2 Cloth Court, London EC1A 7LS (020 7726 4230; email: enquiries@ richardreevesfoundation.org.uk; website: www.richardreevesfoundation.org.uk)

CC Number: 1136337

Eligibility

People under the age of 25 (in exceptional cases this may be extended to 40) who (or whose parents) have lived, studied or worked in the London boroughs of Camden, City of London and Islington for the last 12 months or for at least two of the last ten years.

Types of grants

Grants ranging from £100 to £1,000 are given to students identified by the partner institutions (see 'Applications').

Previously individuals in further education could be supported towards maintenance costs, special tuition or treatment, UK based field trips that are required as an essential part of the course, the cost of training, apprenticeships or tools/equipment for those starting work, and sometimes course fees.

Annual grant total

In 2012/13 the foundation had assets of £23.1 million, an income of £626,000 and a total charitable expenditure of £267,000. Grants to 232 individuals totalled £72,000. All awards were made to individuals studying at the specified universities and colleges through their support schemes.

Note: lately the foundation was not making any grants to individuals directly but the governors 'anticipate making funds available for grants to students in further education again.'

Exclusions

The foundation does not normally provide grants for:

- Computers
- Holidays
- Clothing
- Childcare costs
- Fees at private schools or colleges (except in some exceptional cases and where it is agreed that education within the state system would be inappropriate)
- Overseas trips or placements
- Second degrees
- Postgraduate courses (except those that are essential for certain careers)
- International students who are resident in the UK on a student visa

Applications

Students studying at the partner institutions (City and Islington College, City University London or Westminster Kingsway College) should apply through their student services.

Otherwise, application forms and guidelines can normally be downloaded from the foundation's website (when the grants are available) or requested from the correspondent. Applications are considered at the trustees' meetings in March, June, October and December with the deadlines for each meeting being published online. Consult the foundation's website to see when individual applications (other than from partner educational establishments) are invited again.

Other information

The foundation also supports local organisations, charities and schools. In 2012/13 grants to organisations totalled £196,000. It has been decided to allocate larger amounts of money to a smaller number of projects delivering a quality programme, in some cases over a three year period.

Reuben Foundation

£36,000

Correspondent: Patrick O'Driscoll, Trustee, 4th Floor, Millbank Tower, 21–24 Millbank, London SW1P 4QP (020 7802 5014; fax: 020 7802 5002; email: contact@reubenfoundation.com; website: www.reubenfoundation.com)

CC Number: 1094130

Eligibility

Children and young people from disadvantaged backgrounds who attend the University of Oxford, University College London or any of the Ark Schools (partnership schools) and show academic potential.

Types of grants

Scholarships for undergraduates at partnership schools. Awards are available at each institution over three years from October 2012 (30 at Oxford, 15 at UCL and 6 at ARK Schools). Scholarships at the University of Oxford are of around £7,500 a year.

In connection with UK Friends of the Association for the Wellbeing of Israel's Soldiers 'Impact scholarships' are available to discharged combat unit soldiers to pursue higher education.

Annual grant total

At the time of writing (August 2014) the latest financial information available was from 2012. In 2012 the foundation had assets totalling £66.5 million and an income of £3.9 million. Grants to 20 individuals totalled £73,000 given for both educational and healthcare purposes. We estimate that about £36,000 was awarded in educational support.

Applications

The foundation has partnerships with Oxford, UCL and ARK schools to identify the applicants. Interested pupils enrolled at any of these schools should make enquiries at the school and not to the foundation.

Other information

The foundation was established in 2002 as an outlet for the philanthropic giving of billionaire property investors David and Simon Reuben. The foundation was endowed by the brothers with a donation of $100 million (£54.1 million), with the income generated to be given to a range of charitable causes, particularly in the fields of healthcare and education.

The majority of grants are given to organisations (over £2 million to 415 bodies in 2012). Support is also given to individuals for welfare (mainly medical) causes.

Scotscare

See entry on page 136

The Sheriffs' and Recorders' Fund

£17,000 (105 grants)

Correspondent: The Secretary, c/o Central Criminal Court, Old Bailey, Warwick Square, London EC4M 7BS (020 7248 3277; email: secretary@srfund. net; website: www.srfund.org.uk)

CC Number: 221927

Eligibility

People on discharge from prison, and families of people imprisoned. Applicants must live in the Greater Metropolitan area of London.

Types of grants

One-off grants for education and training at any level.

Annual grant total

In 2012/13 the fund had assets of £1.3 million and an income of £245,000. Grants were made to 1,193 individuals totalling £166,500. There were 105 grants totalling £17,000 made for education and training purposes.

Applications

On a form available from the correspondent, submitted through probation officers or social workers. They are considered throughout the year.

Other information

Grants are also made for welfare purposes and for special projects.

St Clement Danes Educational Foundation

£8,400 (8 grants)

Correspondent: Deb Starkey, Administrator, St Clement Danes School, Drury Lane, London WC2B 5SU (020 7641 6593; email: dstarkey@stcd.co.uk)

CC Number: 312319

Eligibility

After meeting the needs of St Clement Danes Primary School, grants are awarded to (in order of priority):
- Ex-pupils of St Clement Danes Church of England Primary School
- People who are under 25 years of age and have lived within the diocese of London, with preference for the City of Westminster, for the majority of their education

Types of grants

Grants to assist with the costs of books, materials, travel, uniform and associated costs for study at college or university. Normally grants sit alongside other grants obtained.

Annual grant total

In 2013 the foundation had assets of £3.4 million and an income of £155,000. 8 grants were awarded to students totalling £8,400.

A further £113,000 was given to St Clement Danes Church of England Primary School.

Exclusions

Grants towards fees are not usually given to pupils in primary and secondary education. No grants to overseas students.

Applications

On a form available from the correspondent. Applications can be submitted directly by the individual, or by a parent/guardian if the individual is under 18, for consideration in February, May, October or November. They need to be submitted six weeks before the trustees' meeting.

Sir Walter St John's Educational Charity

£7,000 (8 grants)

Correspondent: Susan Perry, Manager, Sir Walter St John's Educational Charity, Office 1A, Culvert House, Culvert Road, London SW11 5DH (020 7498 8878; email: manager@swsjcharity.org.uk; website: www.swsjcharity.org.uk)

CC Number: 312690

Eligibility

People under the age of 25 (in practice, aged 16 to 24) who have been resident in the boroughs of Lambeth and Wandsworth for at least six months. Preference is given to the Battersea area. Grants can only be given to students who are following a validated, approved or recognised course and can demonstrate good prospects of successfully completing it. Individual grants will only be given in exceptional circumstances and where the award would have a critical effect on the applicant's opportunity to study.

Types of grants

Support is available for core expenditure for attendance on the course – registration fees, travel expenses, books, equipment/instruments. The upper limit for grants is £500 to students aged 16–18 and £750 to students aged 19–25. Lone parents who are in receipt of benefit can receive grants of up to £1,500 towards childcare. Grants above £1,500 may be awarded in exceptional circumstances to students on foundation or access courses in arts, dance and drama who have good prospects of progressing to higher education afterwards. Students with a disability are eligible for grants to meet additional education/training expenditure.

Annual grant total

In 2012/13 the charity had assets of £3.9 million, an income of £138,000 and a total charitable expenditure of £35,000. One grant of £2,000 was made to an individual pursuing further education.

A block grant totalling £5,000 was given to the South Thames College to be distributed to seven students and an additional grant of £2,000 for the purchase of computers to be loaned by single parents.

Exclusions

Grants are not normally given to schoolchildren under the age of 16 or full-time university students. Maintenance expenses are not supported and the charity will not usually contribute towards the cost of a computer or laptop.

Applications

Applicants are invited to contact the correspondent for an initial discussion. Eligible applicants will be sent an application form which has to be returned together with the supporting information and evidence.

Students at South Thames College should contact the college's student services directly to find out specific criteria for applications.

Other information

Currently the charity is focusing its funding to support local organisations providing education and training opportunities for children and young people in the area of benefit. Only a small amount of money is allocated annually to support individual students. Block grants are also made to local colleges for distribution to their students.

Truro Fund

£8,500

Correspondent: Richard Martin, Clerk to the Trustees, St Botolph's Church, Aldgate High Street, London EC3N 1AB (020 7929 0520; email: lm800aat@ hotmail.com)

CC Number: 312288

Eligibility

Children and young people under the age of 21 living or attending an educational establishment in Greater London.

Types of grants

One-off bursaries, scholarships and maintenance allowances are available to schoolchildren, further/higher education students, people entering a trade/ profession, and people starting work/ business or apprenticeships. Support is given towards the cost of outfits/ clothing, books, equipment/instruments, materials, tools, travel/study abroad, also for music and arts studies.

Annual grant total

In 2012/13 the fund had an income of £8,600 and an expenditure of £10,500. Normally around £8,500 is available to distribute in grants and around 12–15 small awards are given every six months.

Exclusions

Our research suggests that grants are not intended to cover fees.

Applications

In writing to the correspondent. Applications should include three references (at least one of which should be from the applicant's educational establishment), evidence of the date of birth (either a photo page from a British passport or a birth certificate), full financial details and any information concerning immigration status (if applicable).

The trustees meet twice a year in April and September to consider applications.

Other information

The fund is an amalgam of three small charities – The Rt Hon the Dowager Baroness Truro's Fund (The Truro Fund), The East London Industrial School Fund and the Regent's Park Boy's Home Fund.

The British and Foreign School Society Trust Fund

£3,500

Correspondent: Belinda Lawrance, Administrator, Maybrook House, Godstone Road, Caterham, Surrey CR3 6RE (01883 331177; email: enquiries@bfss.org.uk; website: www. bfss.org.uk)

CC Number: 314286

Eligibility

Students in Bermondsey, Bethnal Green, Poplar, Southwark and Stepney. In practice students need to be studying at London South Bank University, who currently administer grants from this fund.

Types of grants

Grants of £150 to £1,300.

Annual grant total

In 2013 the fund awarded a total of £3,500 to the student welfare fund at London South Bank University.

Exclusions

Grants are not given for private education.

Applications

Applications should be made directly to the University Welfare Fund at London South Bank University.

Other information

The British and Foreign School Society (BFSS) is a grant giving organisation and offers funding for educational projects in the UK and around the world. The society also offers a small number of grants for organisations and individuals through its subsidiary trusts. Eligibility criteria for these subsidiary trusts depend on area of residence and/or particular field of educational activity. In March 2014 we were informed by Steven Ross, a trustee of the society, that money was available from these funds. Visit the fund's website for information on the set criteria.

Sir Mark and Lady Turner Charitable Settlement

See entry on page 319

The Turner Exhibition Fund

£180

Correspondent: The Administrator, Veale Wasbrough Vizards, Barnards Inn, 86 Fetter Lane, London EC4A 1AD (020 7405 1234; email: jcuxson@vwv.co.uk)

CC Number: 312891

Eligibility

Girls and women (over the age of 10) who are members of the Church of England, have attended a school wholly or partly maintained out of public funds for at least two years and are now living in the diocese of London or the Lambeth, Lewisham, Southwark, Southwark within Greenwich and Wandsworth boroughs.

Types of grants

Small cash grants are available to assist candidates in meeting the expenses incurred while pursuing their education or training at any stage after leaving primary school. Support can be given towards fees, purchase of books and equipment, travel costs to and from college or other needs.

Our research suggests that the fund prefers to award individuals undertaking a first course of education or training, rather than postgraduate students.

Annual grant total

In 2013/14 the fund had an income of £2,600 and an expenditure of £180. Note that charitable spending varies drastically over the years. During the past five years charitable expenditure has been about £1,400 on average.

Applications

In writing to the correspondent. Applications should specify the details of the course of education and training which the applicant intends to pursue and the availability of other funding. According to our research, applications are usually considered in June and October and application forms are issued on request approximately two months before each meeting.

The Wiseman and Withers Exhibition Foundation

£1,500

Correspondent: David Fisher, Clerk, 5 Upton Road, Bexleyheath, Kent DA6 8LQ (020 8306 0278; email: dcfisher08@hotmail.co.uk)

CC Number: 312820

Eligibility

People who live in the London borough of Greenwich and that part of the London borough of Newham which was formerly in the metropolitan borough of Woolwich. Applicants must be under the age of 26.

Types of grants

Grants of between £50 and £200, to provide equipment needed for courses of further education.

Annual grant total

This charity awards around £1,500 each year to individuals for educational purposes.

Exclusions

No grants towards travel or major awards to finance full-time education.

Applications

In writing to the correspondent. The trustees meet twice a year.

Barking and Dagenham

The Catherine Godfrey Association for those with Learning and other Disabilities

£0

Correspondent: Kathryn Pettitt, Trustee, 25 Wraglings, Beldams Lane, Bishop's Stortford CM23 5TB

CC Number: 207370

Eligibility

People who have learning difficulties and/or other disabilities, including physical disabilities, and people with mental health issues. Applicants must be in financial need and live in Barking and Dagenham or the surrounding areas. Support is also given to carers.

Types of grants

Grants for outdoor activities and holidays in Britain to those who cannot afford them.

Annual grant total

In 2012/13 and in the previous financial year, this charity's income was in single figures. There has been no expenditure for the past five years. It remains on the Central Register of Charities and possibly still has money available for grant-giving.

Applications

In writing to the correspondent. Applications need to be co-signed by a social worker or similar and have to be submitted between September and December for consideration in January.

Barnet

Elizabeth Allen Trust

£8,600 (14 grants)

Correspondent: Helen Rook, Clerk to the Trustees, PO Box 270, Radlett, Herts WD7 0DJ (01727 823206; email: elizabethallentrust@fsmail.net)

CC Number: 310968

Eligibility

People in need under the age of 25 who live, attend a college of further education or are employed in the borough of Barnet. Priority is given to applicants from the pre-1965 urban district of (High) Barnet.

Types of grants

One-off grants, normally of up to £300, are offered to schoolchildren, further/higher education students and people starting work/entering a trade. Financial assistance is given for general educational expenses, including books, fees, maintenance expenses, equipment/instruments, tools, clothing/outfits, uniforms, travel in pursuance of education, also for the study of music and arts.

Annual grant total

In 2012/13 the trust had assets of £741, 000 and an income of £25,000. A total of £8,600 was awarded in grants. During the year 21 applications were received, of which 14 were successful.

Exclusions

Grants are not given for private school fees, postgraduate studies, gap-year activities or where funding can be received from the local authority.

Applications

Application forms can be requested from the correspondent, with an sae provided. Applications should include details of the parents' finances and the use of the applicant's student loan. The trustees meet four times a year to consider applications. It is advised that applications for the current year should be made by April.

Other information

The trust also supports local schools.

The Mayor of Barnet's Benevolent Fund

£3,000

Correspondent: Ken Argent, Grants Manager, London Borough of Barnet, Building 4, North London Business Park, Oakleigh Road South, London N11 1NP (020 8359 2020; email: ken.argent@ barnet.gov.uk; website: www.barnet.gov. uk/info/930094/grants_for_individuals/ 262/grants_for_individuals)

CC Number: 1014273

Eligibility

Schoolchildren who have lived in the London borough of Barnet for at least a year and whose parents are in receipt of an income-related statutory benefit.

Types of grants

Small, one-off grants of up to £60 can be given towards school uniforms to pupils transferring from primary to secondary school or starting a new secondary school. Up to two awards can be given to each applicant.

Annual grant total

In 2012/13 the fund had an income of £11,800 and a total expenditure of £11,600. Both figures are the highest in the past five years. Nevertheless, the income and the expenditure vary annually. Most support is given in relief-in-need grants, therefore we estimate that educational grants totalled around £3,000.

Exclusions

Pupils at schools operating their own schemes of financial assistance are not eligible for a grant from the fund.

Applications

In writing to the correspondent via post or email. Applications can be submitted directly by the individual or through a third party, such as a social worker, health visitor or an advice agency. Candidates should provide full details of their name, address, contact number, confirmation of residence in the borough, number and ages of the family members, family income, proof of entitlement to a benefit, summary of the applicant's circumstances, details of support requested, a quotation for any items required and information on other sources of funding approached. Consideration takes about a month. Payments are not made to the applicant directly, but to the school or supplier.

Other information

Grants are mainly made for welfare purposes.

The Hyde Foundation

£10,600 (19 grants)

Correspondent: Robin Marson, Administrator, 1 Hillside, Codicote, Hitchin SG4 8XZ (020 8449 3032; email: marson36@homecall.co.uk)

CC Number: 302918

Eligibility

People in education up to first degree level in the ancient parishes of Chipping Barnet and Monken Hadley.

Types of grants

One-off grants in the range of £100 to £6,000. Grants are given to college students, undergraduates, vocational students, mature students, people with special educational needs and people starting work. Grants given include those for music lessons, fees, travel abroad, books, equipment and maintenance/living expenses.

Annual grant total

In 2013 the foundation had assets of £689,000 and an income of £40,000. Grants were made to individuals totalling £10,600, to assist them in further education and cultural activities.

Applications

In writing to the correspondent, who will forward an application form. Trustees meet quarterly in January, April, July and October to consider applications which should be received at the end of December, March, June and September respectively.

Other information

Grants are also given to local schools and organisations.

The Valentine Poole Charity

£2,000

Correspondent: Victor Russell, Clerk, The Forum Room, Ewen Hall, Wood Street, Barnet, Hertfordshire EN5 4BW (020 8441 6893; email: vpoole@ btconnect.com)

CC Number: 220856

Eligibility

Young people in need under the age of 26 who live in the former urban districts of Barnet and East Barnet (approximately the postal districts of EN4 and EN5).

Types of grants

One-off grants to schoolchildren for uniforms and people starting work for books, equipment and instruments.

Annual grant total

In 2013 the charity had assets of £629,000 and an income of £68,000. The trustees annual report states that 32 families received a Christmas grant which totalled £1,870; payment of pensions totalled £19,500; and £20,600 was spent on relief in need and advancement in life purposes. We consider the majority of these latter payments would have been for social welfare purposes and have estimated advancement in life grants to have been around £2,000. In this year there were no grants awarded to organisations.

Applications

On a form available from the correspondent for consideration in March, July and November. Applications should be submitted by a school, welfare agency or other relevant third party, not directly by the individual.

Bexley

Bexley United Charities – Charity of the Reverend Thomas Smoult

£230

Correspondent: Kenneth Newman, Clerk to the Trustees, 13 High Street, Bexley, Kent, Da5 1AB (07831 838 054)

CC Number: 205964–1

Eligibility

People under the age of 25 who live in the borough of Bexley and are in need.

Types of grants

Grants can be given to individuals who are preparing for or entering a trade/ profession. Small awards are offered towards fees, travelling and maintenance expenses, educational necessities or other needs.

Annual grant total

In 2012/13 the charity had assets of £34,000 and an income of £20. A total of £230 was awarded in grants.

Applications

In writing to the correspondent.

Other information

The charity is administered by Bexley United Charities.

Accommodation and relief-in-need support to individuals can be provided from Bexley Almshouse and Relief in Need Charity and North Cray Parish Charities.

Brent

The Wembley Samaritan Fund

£800

Correspondent: Jack Taylor, Administrator, c/o Sudbury Neighbourhood Centre, 809 Harrow Road, Wembley, Middlesex HA0 2LP (020 8908 1220)

CC Number: 211887

Eligibility

People in need who live in the electoral wards of Wembley (Tokyngton, Alperton, Sudbury, Sudbury Court and Wembley Central). The charity is particularly aimed at children.

Types of grants

One-off grants mostly for school uniforms, warm clothing, nursery equipment and the costs of school outings.

Annual grant total

In 2013 this charity had an income of £3,500 and a total expenditure of £1,600. We estimate grants to individuals for educational purposes in this financial year was around £800.

Applications

By telephone or in writing to the correspondent.

Other information

Grants are also made to local organisations.

Bromley

The Downham Feoffee Charity

£8,000

Correspondent: Jo Howard, Administrator, 35 Fieldside, Ely, Cambridgeshire CB6 3AT (01353 665774; email: downhamfeoffees@ hotmail.co.uk)

CC Number: 237233

Eligibility

Residents of the ancient parish of Downham.

Types of grants

Grants for students attending higher education or other education or training.

Annual grant total

In 2012/13 the charity had assets of £4.15 million and an income of £79,000. The charity gave £8,000 in educational grants, £500 to individuals in need and £3,500 to public organisations, although its main focus is the provision of housing and allotments.

Applications

In writing to the correspondent.

Camden

Bromfield's Educational Foundation

£18,000 (74 grants)

Correspondent: Alison Shaw, Administrator, 5 St Andrew Street, London EC4A 3AB (020 7583 7394; email: info@standrewholborn.org.uk; website: www.standrewholborn.org.uk)

CC Number: 312795

Eligibility

People in need under 25 who have lived (or whose parents or guardians have lived) in the Holborn area of the London borough of Camden for at least two years.

Types of grants

One-off and termly grants for clothing, books, equipment/instruments, music lessons, computers and maintenance/ living expenses.

Annual grant total

In 2012 the foundation had assets of £1.6 million and an income of £47,000. The 2012 accounts were the latest available at the time of writing (August 2014). Grants to individuals totalled almost £18,000. 16 families received termly grants from the foundation, almost all of which included a child with a disability. 58 children were also provided with a school uniform grant.

Exclusions

No grants for school, college or university fees. Applications for postgraduate studies will not be considered.

Applications

On a form available from the foundation's website. Details of income and expenditure and personal information are required, supported by documentary evidence which will be treated in the strictest confidence. Applications can be submitted at any time, and will be considered within 21 days.

Other information

Priority is given to families of children with disabilities. Almost all of the families who receive termly grants are caring for a disabled child. Grants are also given to organisations.

Hampstead Wells and Campden Trust

£2,000

Correspondent: Sheila Taylor, Director and Clerk, 62 Rosslyn Hill, London NW3 1ND (020 7435 1570; email: grant@hwct.co.uk; website: www.hwct. org.uk)

CC Number: 1094611

Eligibility

Grants to individuals, whether one-off payments or pensions, can only be made to residents of the former metropolitan borough of Hampstead (the area of benefit). A temporary stay in Hampstead, or in hospital in the area is not in itself a sufficient qualification.

Types of grants

Grants are given to people at any stage of their education, or who are entering a trade or profession, for uniforms and other clothing, books, equipment, instruments, maintenance, living expenses, childcare and educational outings in the UK.

Annual grant total

In 2012/13 the trust had assets of £1.3 million, an income of over £552,000 and gave grants to 3,176 individuals totalling £197,000, including eight education grants totalling £2,000. 93 pensions totalling over £72,000 were also awarded.

Exclusions

The trustees are unable to offer assistance with course or school fees.

Applications

Applications may be made by letter or on the trust's application form which can be downloaded from its website. Applications by letter will only be accepted if they include the following details: the client's name, date of birth, occupation, address and telephone number, details of other household members, other agencies and charities applied to, result of any applications to the Social Fund, household income, and details of any savings and why these savings cannot be used. Applications should be supported by a statutory or welfare agency. Decisions are made within two weeks.

Other information

We advise referring to the trust's website which at the time of writing (July 2014) was in the process of being updated.

St Andrew Holborn Charities

£60,000

Correspondent: Alison Shaw, Administrator, 5 St Andrew Street, London EC4A 3AB (020 7583 7394; email: info@standrewholborn.org.uk; website: www.standrewholborn.org.uk)

CC Number: 1095045

Eligibility

People who are under the age of 25 and who have lived in the area of benefit for at least two years.

Types of grants

One-off grants up to £500 for educational needs including books, computers, instruments, uniforms, travel and living costs. Recurrent grants can be made for children with disabilities.

Annual grant total

In 2012 the charity had assets of £8.8 million and an income of £225,000. Grants totalled around £60,000. Altogether funding for individuals totalled £121,000.

These were the latest accounts available at the time of writing (July 2014).

Exclusions

No grants for private school fees or postgraduate studies.

Applications

On a form available from the correspondent or to download from the charity's website. There are separate forms for under 18s and over 18s.

Other information

This charity is the result of an amalgamation of three organisations: The City Foundation, The Isaac Duckett Charity and The William Williams Charity. Grants are also made to local organisations.

City of London

The Thomas Carpenter Educational and Apprenticing Foundation (Thomas Carpenter's Trust)

£26,000 (12 grants)

Correspondent: Richard Martin, Administrator, St Botolph's Church, Aldgate High Street, London EC3N 1AB (020 7929 0520; email: lm800aat@ hotmail.com)

CC Number: 312155

Eligibility

People under the age of 25 who/whose parents have lived or worked for three years in Bread Street and adjoining wards in the City of London, or who attend educational establishment in that area.

Types of grants

Grants of around £500–£3,000 towards general course related costs, including outfits, fees, books, equipment/tools, study of music or other arts, travel/study abroad and so on. People in schools, universities/colleges or those starting work/entering trade can be supported.

Annual grant total

In 2012/13 the foundation had an income of £34,000 and a total expenditure of £30,000. We estimate that grants to individuals totalled around

£26,000. Around 12 students are awarded grants each year.

Exclusions

Grants are not normally given towards electives or field trips which are not part of a full-time study course.

Applications

Application forms can be requested from the correspondent. They should normally be submitted before 31 July by the individual's parent or guardian, details of whose financial circumstances should be included.

Other information

Applications from local groups for recreational, social and physical training or equipment will also be considered.

The Mitchell City of London Educational Foundation

£70,000 (44 grants)

Correspondent: Lucy Jordan, Administrator, Ash View, High Street, Orston, Nottingham NG13 9NU (08456001558; email: mitchellcityoflondon@gmail.com)

CC Number: 312499

Eligibility

People aged 11 to 19 who are either attending school in the City of London or whose parents have lived or worked there for at least five years.

The City is classified as the area of almost all postcodes EC3 EC4 and a small area of EC1, EC2.

Types of grants

Awards are given as sixth form bursaries for A-level or IB students within independent education, or in grants to children from single parent families who are within independent education and have been at the school of choice for one year. Support is available towards general educational needs. Choral bursaries may also be provided.

Awards of £2,000 are made to students in need.

Annual grant total

In 2012/13 the foundation had an income of £88,000 and made grants to individuals totalling £70,000. The awards consisted of:

Sixth form bursaries	27 (12 first year and 15 second year)
Pupils from single parent families	12
Choral bursaries	3
Students in need	2

The foundation also notes that 113 applications and enquiries for awards did not meet the terms of reference of the charity and seven applications were unsuccessful.

Exclusions

The foundation does not support further or higher education at any other establishment. Second and master degrees or gap-year and other projects are not assisted.

Applications

Application forms can be requested from the correspondent. They can be submitted either directly by the individual or through a third party, such as a parent/guardian, school or an educational welfare agency, if applicable. Grants are normally considered in March and September.

Other information

The Mitchell City of London Charity provides welfare support to individuals in need.

Croydon

The Church Tenements Charities– Educational and Church Branches

£6,100 (Around 20 grants)

Correspondent: June Haynes, Administrator, Croydon London Borough Council, Taberner House, Park Lane, Croydon CR9 3JS (020 8726 6000 EXT 62317; email: june.haynes@croydon.gov.uk)

CC Number: 312554

Eligibility

People under the age of 25 who are living or studying in the London borough of Croydon (including people from overseas studying in Croydon) who are experiencing financial hardship.

Preference is given to people requesting funding below £500 who have not received support from the local authorities or where the applicants have made some effort to raise funds themselves.

Types of grants

Small, one-off grants in the range of £50–£500 mainly to people in primary, secondary and post-school education and training. Support is given towards books, stationery, uniforms, travelling to and from the place of education, music tuition and instruments, also educational outings, study/travel abroad or school fees. People entering a trade may also be supported.

Annual grant total

In 2012/13 the charity had an income of £53,000 and a total expenditure of £51,000. Over the previous four years grants to individuals totalled on average around £6,100 distributed between approximately 20 people each year.

Applications

Application forms can be requested from the correspondent. They are normally considered quarterly, in January, April, July and October. It is helpful to provide as much supporting information as possible.

Other information

The charity also gives grants to youth services, ecclesiastical organisations and supports Archbishop Tenison's School.

The Frank Denning Memorial Charity

£4,700

Correspondent: Maxine Cooper, Democratic Services Officer, Croydon Council, Chief Executive's Department, Zone 4G, Bernard Weatherill House, 8 Mint Walk, Croydon CR0 1EA (020 8726 6000 Ext 60125; email: Maxine. Cooper@croydon.gov.uk; website: www. croydon.gov.uk/advice/grants/frankdenning)

CC Number: 312813

Eligibility

Students between the ages of 19 and 25 (by 30 April in the year of their application) who/whose parents are resident in the London borough of Croydon and who want to undertake an educational project overseas. The applicant's travel plans must commence between 1 May and 30 April of the year of application.

Types of grants

One-off travelling scholarships of up to £1,000 are available to full-time university or college students for undertaking a specific project abroad as a part of their course of study.

Annual grant total

In 2012/13 the charity had an income of £4,700 and an expenditure of £4,900. We estimate the annual total of grants to be around £4,700.

Exclusions

Support is not available for holidays and journeys that have been completed or have already started at the time of application.

Applications

Application forms are available on the charity's website. Applicants who are successful in their initial application are invited for an interview to discuss their proposal with the trustees.

Ealing

Acton (Middlesex) Charities

£2,000

Correspondent: Revd David Brammer, The Rectory, 14 Cumberland Park, London W3 6SX (020 8992 8876; email: acton.charities@virgin.net; website: www.actoncharities.co.uk)

CC Number: 312312

Eligibility

Students whose home residence is in the former ancient parish of Acton. They must be between 18–25 years of age and have entered a full-time course in the UK, usually of at least three years, which will lead to a recognised qualification.

Types of grants

Grants of £300 per year to assist with books or equipment.

Annual grant total

In 2013 the charity had an income of £9,000 and an expenditure of £8,000. We estimate that grants to individuals for educational purposes totalled around £2,000.

Applications

On a form available from the correspondent. Proof that the student is entered on an educational course is required.

Other information

The charity also provides welfare and arts grants and supports local schools and carnivals.

The Educational Foundation Of Francis Courtney

£1,000

Correspondent: Janis Gaylor, Clerk, 5 Holly Farm Road, Southall UB2 5SY (020 8574 5980)

CC Number: 312547

Eligibility

People under the age of 25 who live in Southall.

Types of grants

One-off grants are given to assist in further education only. Help may be given towards books, fees/living expenses and study or travel abroad. Mature students may also receive help in special circumstances.

Annual grant total

Accounts for the year 2012 were the latest available at the time of writing (August 2014).

In 2012, the foundation had an income of £3,000 and a total expenditure of £2,000. We estimate that the total grant awarded to individuals for educational purposes was approximately £1,000.

Exclusions

No grants for clothing, equipment or childcare.

Applications

On a form available from the correspondent, indicating the size of contribution the individual can make and an indication of what the grant is for. The applicant's place of study must approve the completed form, which should be submitted directly by the individual. Applications are considered before the individual begins further education.

Other information

Grants are also awarded to organisations.

Educational Foundation of William Hobbayne

£0

Correspondent: Anita Sheehan, Administrator, Community Centre, St Dunstan's Road, London W7 2HB (020 8810 0277; email: hobbaynecharity@btinternet.com)

CC Number: 312544

Eligibility

Children and young people who live in Hanwell (W7 area) in the London borough of Ealing. Preference may be given to children in junior school.

Types of grants

Grants are generally of up to £100 for the costs of school trips, educational outings, books/equipment and travel expenses. University students, including those taking Open University/long distance courses, can also be supported.

Annual grant total

In 2012/13 the foundation had an income of £5,200 and an expenditure of £5,300. No grants were awarded to individuals during the year.

Applications

Application forms and further guidelines can be requested from the correspondent. Applications must be made by a sponsor (usually the school, scout or guide group and so on), and are considered monthly.

Other information

The foundation receives its funding from the Eleemosynary Charity of William

Hobbayne (registered charity number 211547), which supports individuals in need, living in Hanwell. The funds available to the educational foundation are limited.

Grants are mainly made to organisations and groups in the area of benefit (in 2012/13 one grant of £5,200) Applications from individuals are rare.

Enfield

Enfield Church Trust for Girls

£2,700

Correspondent: Maureen Anderson, Trustee, 12 Amberley Gardens, Enfield, Middlesex EN1 2NE (02083640377)

CC Number: 312210

Eligibility

Girls and young women in need who are under the age of 25 and live, work or attend school/college/university in the ancient parish of Enfield (as constituted immediately before 1 April 1965).

Types of grants

Grants towards general educational needs and recreational, leisure pursuits. For example, in the past the trust has bought a radio-linked hearing aid to enable a deaf 12-year-old girl to continue normal schooling and would consider providing support towards course fees when local education authority grants are not available, assisting students for books and study or travel abroad, giving grants for childcare and other child costs to single parents who are studying, training or early on in their careers, supporting schoolchildren for school uniform, books, educational outings and maintenance. The trustees are particularly concerned to help disadvantaged young women and girls. Grants usually range from £70 to £300 and are one-off, although beneficiaries are free to reapply each year.

Annual grant total

At the time of writing (July 2014) the latest financial information available was from 2012. In 2012 the trust had an income of £3,900 and an expenditure of £2,900. We estimate the annual total of grants to be around £2,700.

Exclusions

Grants are not generally given for mature students or towards school fees.

Applications

Application forms are available from the correspondent and are considered throughout the year.

The Old Enfield Charitable Trust

£75,000 (Around 50 grants)

Correspondent: Karen Wellings, Administrator, The Old Vestry Office, 22 The Town, Enfield, Middlesex EN2 6LT (020 8367 8941; email: enquiries@toect.org.uk; website: www.toect.org.uk)

CC Number: 207840

Eligibility

People in need who live in the ancient parish of Enfield.

Types of grants

Grants to students and other residents who are undertaking education or training. Help is towards living costs, equipment, stationery, childcare costs, travel expenses and so on. People starting work/entering a trade are also supported.

Annual grant total

In 2012/13 the trust had an income of £632,000 and a total expenditure of £645,000. At the time of writing (August 2014) full accounts were not available to view. Normally educational grants are given to about 50 individuals each year totalling between £50,000 and £100,000.

Exclusions

The trust will not provide support where the local authority or central government should be assisting. Grants are not normally given for second degrees or master's degree courses.

Applications

Application forms are available upon request from the correspondent. Applicants are normally interviewed by the trustees. Candidates are expected to take up the student loan offers and approach their educational institution for funding before applying to the trust.

Other information

Community grants are also made to organisations. The trust also administers Ann Crowe's and Wright's Almshouse Charity which owns 10 Almshouses that are let to needy people already resident in the ancient parish of Enfield.

Greenwich

Greenwich Blue Coat Foundation

£16,100 (26 grants)

Correspondent: M. Bake, Clerk to the Trustees, 136 Charlton Lane, London SE7 8AB (020 8858 7575; email: bluecoat@baker5.co.uk; website: www.bluecoathistory.co.uk/page829.html)

CC Number: 312407

Eligibility

Young people up to 25 years of age who have lived or have been educated in the London borough of Greenwich for at least two years previous to their application. Preference is given to individuals with limited means.

Types of grants

One-off and recurrent grants, normally of around £500, are given to help individuals to further their education, develop life skills or enter a chosen career path. Financial assistance can be given for the course fees, equipment/instruments or other course related expenses.

Annual grant total

In 2012/13 the foundation had assets of £1.7 million and an income of £31,000. A total of £16,100 was awarded in grants to 26 individuals. Two beneficiaries were awarded grants exceeding £1,000 with a total of £2,607.

Exclusions

Maintenance or travel costs are not normally supported.

Applications

Application forms can be downloaded from the foundation's website or requested from the correspondent. Candidates are required to provide the name of a referee. The trustees usually meet four times a year in January, April, July and November.

Other information

The trustees remind that the foundation 'only has a relatively small sum of money available annually and does not therefore usually make large individual awards.'

Hackney

The Hackney Parochial Charities

£25,000

Correspondent: Benjamin Janes, Clerk to the Trustees, The Trust Partnership, 6 Trull Farm Buildings, Trull, Tetbury GL8 8SQ (01285 841900; email: office@thetrustpartnership.com)

CC Number: 219876

Eligibility

People in need who live in the former metropolitan borough of Hackney.

Types of grants

Help towards the cost of books, equipment, tools and examination fees for apprentices and young people at college or university who are not in receipt of a full grant. Grants are one-off, although applicants can re-apply annually.

Annual grant total

In 2012/13 the charities had assets of £5.4 million and an income of £187,000, of which at least £58,000 was distributed in grants to organisations. We have estimated the grants for individuals for educational purposes to be approximately £25,000.

Applications

In writing to the correspondent. Grants for individuals will be considered by the trustees by email on a monthly or bi-monthly basis.

Other information

In 2008 the charities took over the administration of Hackney District Nursing Association. In 2012/13 the trustees made no grants out of the Hackney District Nursing Association's funds.

Hammersmith and Fulham

Dr Edwards' and Bishop King's Fulham Charity

£2,300

Correspondent: The Clerk to the Trustees, Percy Barton House, 33–35 Dawes Road, London SW6 7DT (020 7385 9387; fax: 020 7610 2856; email: clerk@debk.org.uk; website: www.debk.org.uk)

CC Number: 1113490

Eligibility

People undertaking training courses who live in the old metropolitan borough of Fulham. This constitutes all of the SW6 postal area and parts of W14 and W6.

Types of grants

One-off grants are made to individuals for accredited training courses which are likely to lead to employment, support with childcare and other needs.

Annual grant total

In 2012/13 grants to individuals totalled £136,000 with most grants being awarded for relief-in-need purposes. We could not find a figure for how much was awarded to individuals for educational purposes but we do know from the charity's accounts that 1% of the total grant spend was given for education. We have used this figure as that given to individuals because the breakdown of organisations given in the accounts does not appear to include any educational grants. We have therefore concluded that grants for educational purposes were made to individuals only.

Exclusions

The charity does not fund postgraduate courses or give cash grants (unless they are to be administered by an agency).

Applications

Application forms are available from the correspondent or on the charity's website. Applications must be submitted in hard copy either directly by the individual or through an appropriate third party. It is important to note that individuals applying directly for a grant will be visited at home by the grants administrator.

The committee which considers relief-in-need applications, including educational grant applications, meets ten times a year, roughly every four to five weeks. The charity suggests that applications be submitted around two to three weeks before the next meeting.

Other information

The charity gives money to both individuals and organisations, with its main responsibility being towards the relief of poverty rather than assisting students.

Haringey

The Tottenham Grammar School Foundation

£289,000 (1,343 grants)

Correspondent: Graham Chappell, Clerk to the Foundation, PO Box 34098, London N13 5XU (020 8882 2999; fax: Available on request; email: trustees@ tgsf.org.uk; website: www.tgsf.org.uk)

CC Number: 312634

Eligibility

Young people under the age of 25 who/ whose parents normally live in the borough of Haringey and who have attended a school in the borough.

Types of grants

The foundation has three types of award and there are different eligibility criteria for each:

- The Somerset Award – generally one-off grants of £200 to students on full-time courses at colleges of further education (or equivalent)
- The Somerset Undergraduate Award – recurrent payments of £200 a year (up to three years) to university students following a full-time degree or an equivalent higher education course of at least two years' duration
- The Somerset Special Award – a wide range of grants, to postgraduate students, young sports people at a county standard or higher, musicians at a conservatoire standard and individuals with special needs

Annual grant total

In 2012/13 the foundation had assets of £21.2 million and an income of £372,000. Grants to individuals totalled £289,000.

Exclusions

Awards are not normally offered to support apprenticeships or courses being followed at schools (including school sixth forms).

Applications

Separate application forms for general and undergraduate awards can be downloaded from the foundation's website. Applications can also be made through a fast-track online system on the foundation's website.

Applications for special grants must be made in writing to the correspondent providing the date of birth, relevant documentation, letters of support and other information specific for different categories (see the foundation's website for details). There is an application form for awards to children with special needs, which should be completed by a parent/guardian.

Candidates are invited to apply from 1 May each year (for the academic year commencing the following September) until 31 January.

Other information

Grants are also made to charities, voluntary groups and other organisations who work with young people in the borough of Haringey. Local schools are also supported for the costs of school trips, special educational needs (for example music and dance therapy, out of school activities), musical instruments and other expenses. Awards to institutions totalled £373,000 in 2012/13.

The foundation operates a scholarship and sponsorship scheme awarding a limited number of grants each year, normally in partnership with Mountview Academy of Theatre Arts (to students permanently resident in Haringey for the cost of fees for some Mountview part-time courses) and The Harington

Scheme (preparing young people with learning difficulties for careers in horticulture). In 2012/13 scholarships totalling £56,000 were awarded to the Harington Scheme and £30,000 in bursaries to 337 Mountview Academy students. Applications for these awards should be made through the relevant institutions.

The trustees' annual report from 2012/13 notes that they have:

> Decided to increase the annual value by £50 for each of the standard awards. Therefore, for the period covered by next year's report, the individual Somerset Undergraduate Award's total value will be up to a maximum of £750 payable in annual instalments of £250. The Somerset (Further Education) Award will be £250.

The foundation's website offers a helpful FAQ section.

Hillingdon

Uxbridge United Welfare Trusts

£17,600 (45 grants)

Correspondent: J. Duffy, Grants Officer, Trustee Room, Woodbridge House, New Windsor Street, Uxbridge UB8 2TY (07912 270937; email: grants.officer@ uuwt.org; website: www.uuwt.org)

CC Number: 217066

Eligibility

People under the age of 25 who are in need and live in (or has a parent who lives in) or have a very strong connection with the Uxbridge area. The area of benefit covers Cowley, Harefield, Hillingdon, Ickenham and Uxbridge.

Types of grants

One-off grants for people in school, further/higher education and individuals undertaking vocational training or apprenticeships. Grants can be given towards specific needs, items or services, including course costs, books, school uniforms, school trips, travel and transport expenses, computer equipment, instruments, living expenses and so on.

Annual grant total

At the time of writing (August 2014) the latest financial information available was from 2012. In 2012 the charity had assets of £6.4 million and an income of £583,000. Grants and awards totalled £78,000. Educational grants from a restricted Lord Ossulton Fund amounted to £17,600 distributed to 45 individuals.

Exclusions

Our research suggests that grants are not normally given for school fees. Funding is not intended to be provided where statutory support is available.

Applications

Application forms can be requested from the correspondent. They can be submitted directly by the individual or through a social worker, Citizens Advice or educational welfare agency, if applicable. Awards are considered each month. A trained staff member will visit applicants for an interview to better assess their application.

Other information

Grants are also awarded for welfare purposes and may be given to support organisations. The charity also runs almshouses. In 2012 a total of £136,000 was spent in almshouse expenses.

Islington

Worrall and Fuller Exhibition Fund

£6,500

Correspondent: Martyn Craddock, Administrator, 90 Central Street, London EC1V 8AJ (07799 282 413; email: mcraddock@slpt.org.uk)

CC Number: 312507

Eligibility

Children and young people between the ages of 5 and 25 who are resident in the old borough of Finsbury (now part of Islington). Preference is given to those who live in the parish of St Luke, Old Street, or whose parents have had their business or employment there in previous years.

Types of grants

The fund awards scholarships, bursaries, maintenance allowances, grants to schoolchildren, further/higher education students and people entering a trade/starting work. Financial assistance is given towards the cost of books, clothing/outfits, uniforms, equipment/instruments, other necessities, also travel/study abroad in pursuance of education. Arts and music studies can be supported.

Annual grant total

In 2012/13 the fund had an income of £17,000 and an expenditure of £13,300. It can also support organisations, therefore we estimate the annual total of grants to individuals to be around £6,500.

Applications

In writing to the correspondent.

Other information

The fund can also offer grants for the maintenance of local schools.

Kensington and Chelsea

The Campden Charities

£354,000

Correspondent: Christopher Stannard, Clerk, Studios 3&4, 27a Pembridge Villas, London W11 3EP (020 7243 0551 Grants officer: 020 7313 3797; website: www.campdencharities.org.uk)

CC Number: 1104616

Eligibility

Individuals applying for funding must:
- Be living in the former parish of Kensington
- Have been living continuously in Kensington for two years or more
- Be a British or European citizen or have indefinite leave to remain in Britain
- Be renting their home

Working age members of the family must also be in receipt of an out-of-work benefit or on a very low income.

Types of grants

The charity considers funding to all ages of applicant; however, it divides its funding into three basic categories:
- Young people (16–24)
- People of working age
- People of retirement age

The charity will give grants for many direct and indirect educational causes, including course and training fees, childcare costs, travel expenses and equipment.

Annual grant total

In 2012/13 grants made directly to individuals for educational purposes totalled £354,000, of which over £223,200 was awarded for vocational education with a further £131,100 being awarded to encourage academically able young people from disadvantaged backgrounds to attend university.

Exclusions

The charity will not give funding for:
- Direct payment of council tax or rent
- Debt repayments
- Fines or court orders
- Foreign travel or holidays
- Career changes
- Personal development courses
- Postgraduate studies
- Computers
- Individuals whose immediate goal is self-employment
- Goods and services catered for by central government

Applications

Preliminary enquiries should be made by telephone or in writing to the education assistant, who will then informally interview applicants. The trustees of the education committee, who meet monthly, then make final decisions, based on the formal interviews of the applicants.

Applicants should also be willing for a grants officer to visit them at home.

Other information

Grants are also awarded to organisations and individuals for welfare purposes.

The Pocklington Apprenticeship Trust (Kensington)

£13,000

Correspondent: Ali Omar, Administrator, Floor 1 Room 127, Town Hall, Hornton Street, London W8 7NX (email: ali.omar@rbkc.gov.uk; website: www.rbkc.gov.uk/educationandlearning/familyinformationservice/charitabletrusts.aspx)

CC Number: 312943

Eligibility

Young people aged 21 years or younger who were either born in Kensington and Chelsea or whose parent/parents have lived there for at least ten years. Applicants must have a financial need, which is described on the trust's webpage as when 'either the parents/carers/young person receive entitlements such as Housing Benefit, Jobseekers' Allowance, income support or other similar equivalents.'

Types of grants

One-off grants, usually of between £200 and £300, are awarded to schoolchildren, students in further/higher education, vocational students, people starting work and for special educational needs. Grants are typically awarded for books, equipment, instruments and commuting expenses. People starting work may also receive support for uniforms and clothing.

Annual grant total

In 2013/14 the trust had an income of £6,000 and a total expenditure of £13,500. We estimate that grants to individuals totalled £13,000.

Exclusions

Help is only given to attend classes outside the borough if the classes are unavailable within it.

Applications

On a form available from the correspondent. Applications are considered at Administration Committee meetings, deadlines for which are updated on the Royal Borough of Kensington and Chelsea website.

Other information

There is also support for those who meet the age criteria who are in the care or under the supervision of the borough.

Westway Trust

£20,400

Correspondent: Mark Lockhart, Administrator, 1 Thorpe Close, London W10 5XL (020 8962 5720; email: info@westway.org; website: www.westway.org)

CC Number: 1123127

Eligibility

Support is available to people who live in the borough of Kensington and Chelsea. Adults out of work undertaking courses leading to employment are eligible for educational grants, individuals over the age of 16 wishing to undertake training courses can apply for sports training grants and people who wish to participate in Westway organised sports activities but lack means can receive a sports bursary.

Types of grants

The trust offers the following support:
- Education grants – up to £1,000 towards fees, books, travel costs and childcare
- Sports training grants – up to £500 towards 'training courses which could lead to employment in the sport and fitness industry by gaining qualifications such as NVQs and coaching certificates'
- Sports bursaries – training bursary (fitness membership, access to gyms and sports programmes), coaching bursary (equipment, travel competition entry costs) or education bursary (NGB training courses to enter employment as a coach/instructor in the sport and fitness industry). The bursaries are of up to £500, the average award being around £80–£120, and are awarded where candidates can show evidence of registered disability or receipt of universal credits

Annual grant total

In 2012/13 the trust had assets of £28 million, income of £7.2 million and made grants totalling £394,000. Out of this amount £19,700 was distributed in educational grants to individuals and £700 in grants for childcare. No sports grants to individuals were awarded this year.

Applications

Application forms are available on the trust's website or can be requested from the correspondent. The sports bursary scheme is open for applications on 1 May and 1 October each year and applications are considered within six weeks of the closing date.

Note that application criteria are subject to change and for the latest updates see the trust's website.

Other information

The majority of grants are made to local community groups and organisations (a total of £374,000 in 2012/13).

Applicants successful in their application for a sports training grant will be expected to do ten hours of voluntary work on the trust's sport projects. Recipients of the sports bursary are required to 'assist in promoting activities and events through showcase events whenever possible (minimum 1 event per year)'.

Lambeth

Walcot Educational Foundation (Lambeth Endowed Charities)

£95,000 (123 grants)

Correspondent: Daniel Chapman, Grants Manager, 127 Kennington Road, London SE11 6SF (020 7735 1925; fax: 020 7735 7048; email: office@walcotfoundation.org.uk; website: www.walcotfoundation.org.uk)

CC Number: 312800

Eligibility

People, normally under 30 years of age, who are on low income and live in the borough of Lambeth. Individuals currently living outside the area but who are still considered to be Lambeth residents will also qualify for assistance.

Types of grants

The foundation offers:
- Student grants -one-off or recurrent awards of up to £2,000 per academic year to help young people over the age of 18 with the costs of first degree or vocational training, that has a strong likelihood of leading to work. Grants can be given for: course fees (not for private institutions), associated travel costs, books, special clothing, equipment, study/field trips and childcare
- Moving into employment grants – one-off grants for vocational training and related activities are available to people who have been out of work for most of the previous five years and have not gained a degree or qualification in the past ten years. The support is intended to help to move people back into work and can be given for costs associated with further education or vocational courses, work

experience, necessities, such as clothing and equipment/instruments
- Talented young people awards – to children between the ages of 10 and 18 who have exceptional talents in sports, music, drama, dance or other areas can apply for a grant of £500 to help with tuition fees, equipment or summer schools

Annual grant total

In 2012/13 the foundation had assets of £70.4 million, an income of £2.2 million and a charitable expenditure of £1.7 million. A total of £1.2 million was awarded in 197 grants for educational purposes, of which 123 individuals were supported totalling £95,000.

Exclusions

Grants are not given for:
- Postgraduate studies
- Second degrees
- Personal development courses
- Study at private institutions
- Repayment of debts
- Career changes
- Course fees in cases where it is not clear that the applicant will be able to raise the balance of funds to complete the entire course
- The cost of goods/services already purchased or those provided by central/local government
- Council tax, rent or other taxes
- Household goods, furnishing, clothing, unless directly related to work or education progress
- Travel abroad and holidays
- Gifts or toys
- Funeral costs
- Court orders or fines

If the applicant already has significant work experience with a reasonable level of responsibility, or a vocational qualification (at NVQ-4 or equivalent), the foundation will not fund further study.

Applications

Application forms are available on the foundation's website or from the correspondent. Applications can be made at any time and a referral may be required by a member of staff in educational institutions, social care officer or other professional. The trustees meet six times a year and it is aimed to respond to applications from individuals within six weeks.

Other information

The foundation is made up of four charities – The Cynthia Mosley Memorial Fund, Hayle's Charity, Walcot Educational Foundation and The Walcot Non-Educational Charity. The general financial information given above represents the funds of the four charities and the information on grants for educational purposes concerns the Walcot Educational Foundation only.

The foundation also provides additional services to beneficiaries including careers advice, debt and budgeting advice, capacity building and low cost psychotherapy. Various projects, schools and organisations working for individuals can also be supported.

Lewisham

Lee (Educational) Charity of William Hatcliffe

£10,000

Correspondent: Gordon Hillier, Oakroyd, Bowers Place, Crawley Down, Crawley, West Sussex RH10 4HY (01342 713153; email: gandbhillier@tiscali.co.uk)

CC Number: 312801

Eligibility

Young people under the age of 25 living in Lewisham, with some preference for those living in the ancient parish of Lee.

Types of grants

One-off support for education and training purposes.

Annual grant total

In 2012/13 the charity had an income of £21,000 and a total expenditure of £11,700.

Applications

In writing to the correspondent.

Lewisham Educational Charity

£100

Correspondent: Joy Segun, Administrator, Clerk's Office, Lloyd Court, Slagrove Place, London SE13 7LP (020 8690 8145)

CC Number: 1025785

Eligibility

People under the age of 25 who/whose parents live in the ancient parish of Lewisham (which does not include Deptford or Lee).

Types of grants

One-off grants can be given for any educational need. Applications are preferred for specific items rather than contributions to large fee costs.

Annual grant total

In 2012/13 the charity had an income of £770 and an expenditure of £180. We have estimated that individual grants totalled about £100.

Exclusions

Support is not normally given where statutory assistance is available.

Applications

Application forms are available from the correspondent. They can be submitted directly by the individual or through their school, college or educational welfare agency, if applicable. Awards are considered on a regular basis.

Other information

Some support is also occasionally given to local schools.

Merton

Alf and Hilda Leivers Charity Trust

£13,000

Correspondent: The Administrator, Rosewood End, Windsor Road, Chobham, Surrey GU24 8NA

CC Number: 299267

Eligibility

Young people in need up to the age of 18 who live or attend school/college in the London borough of Merton. The trust particularly aims to assist in the fields of education, arts, drama, music or athletics.

Types of grants

One-off and recurrent grants to help with the cost of books, clothing, equipment/instruments, educational outings and other essentials for those at school.

Annual grant total

In 2012/13 the trust had an income of £15,000 and an expenditure of £13,700. We estimate that around £13,000 was awarded in educational grants to individuals.

Applications

In writing to the correspondent. Our research shows that applications can be submitted by individuals, their headteacher or a social care worker, if applicable. Applications should specify what funding is requested and give full details of the applicant's circumstances. Grants are usually considered between April and June, although urgent cases can be considered at any time.

Other information

Grants are also made to organisations.

Richmond upon Thames

The Barnes Workhouse Fund

£9,400 (23 grants)

Correspondent: Miranda Ibbetson, Administrator, PO Box 665, Richmond, Surrey TW10 6YL (020 8241 3994; email: mibbetson@barnesworkhousefund.org.uk; website: www.barnesworkhousefund.org.uk)

CC Number: 200103

Eligibility

Students and schoolchildren who have been resident in the ancient parish of Barnes (in practice SW13) for at least six months. Applications are actively encouraged from individuals looking to return to education.

Types of grants

One-off grants of up to £1,000 are available for students in further education where local or national authority assistance is unavailable for costs such as fees, maintenance, educational equipment and books, travel costs and childcare.

Annual grant total

In 2013 the fund had assets of £9.4 million most of which represented permanent endowment and is therefore not available for grant giving. It had an income of £615,000. Grants were made to 23 individuals for education totalling £9,400; to individuals for social welfare purposes £17,900; and to organisations £191,000.

Applications

On a form available from the fund's website, to be submitted directly by the individual. Applications are considered upon receipt. If students apply for more than £750 this will be considered at bi-monthly trustee meetings held in January, March, May, July, September and November. Students under the age of 25 must provide details of their parents'/carers' income.

Other information

Grants are also made to organisations and for other purposes, such as welfare.

The Hampton Wick United Charity

£5,000

Correspondent: Roger Avins, Clerk to the Trustees, Hunters Lodge, Home Farm, Redhill Road, Cobham, Surrey KT11 1EF (01932 596748)

CC Number: 1010147

Eligibility

People under 25 who are in need and live in Hampton Wick and most of South Teddington, within the parishes of St John the Baptist, Hampton Wick and St Mark, South Teddington.

Types of grants

One-off cash grants (with the possibility of future reapplication) to help with the cost of, for example, books, equipment, clothing and course fees.

Annual grant total

We have no current information on the grant giving of this charity. We know that previously over £20,000 a year was awarded to individuals in educational and welfare grants. Grants are also awarded to organisations. We estimate the amount given to individuals for educational purposes is around £5,000.

Applications

In writing to the correspondent. The trustees normally meet three times a year to consider applications.

The Petersham United Charities

£1,000

Correspondent: Canon Tim Marwood, The Clerk, The Vicarage, Bute Avenue, Richmond, Surrey TW10 7AX (020 8940 8435)

CC Number: 200433

Eligibility

People under 25 who live in the ecclesiastical parish of Petersham, Surrey as constituted in 1900.

Types of grants

One-off grants of £75 to £500 are given for any educational need.

Annual grant total

Accounts for the year 2012 were the latest available at the time of writing (August 2014). In 2012, the charity had an income of £5,000 and a total expenditure of £3,000. We estimate that the total award given to individuals for educational purposes was approximately £1,000.

Applications

In writing to the correspondent. Applications are considered in January, April, July and October and can be submitted either directly by the individual or through a social worker, Citizens Advice or other welfare agency.

Other information

Grants are also given for relief-in-need purposes and to organisations.

The Richmond Parish Lands Charity

£121,000

Correspondent: The Clerk to the Grants Committee, The Vestry House, 21 Paradise Road, Richmond, Surrey TW9 1SA (020 8948 5701; fax: 020 8332 6792; website: www.rplc.org.uk)

CC Number: 200069

Eligibility

People above school age who are in need and have lived in the TW9, TW10 or SW14 areas of Richmond for at least six months prior to application and have no other possible sources of help.

Types of grants

One-off and recurrent grants to help people obtain vocational, professional or academic qualifications or to retrain after employment. Grants can range from £50 towards course books to larger recurrent grants over several years for course fees.

Annual grant total

The charity is a grant maker and housing provider. In 2012/13 the charity had assets of £69.3 million and an income of £3.5 million. It made grants to over 1,000 individuals totalling £269,000. Grants for educational purposes totalled £121,000.

Exclusions

No grants to schoolchildren.

Applications

On a form available from the Clerk to the Education Committee, to be submitted directly by the individual. This includes details of current employment, income and expenditure, details of the course/expenses applied for and a statement in support of the application. Two references are required and applicants are usually asked to attend an interview. Applications should be based on financial need and parental income is taken into account up to the age of 25 years. There are two charities which are also administered by the Richmond Parish Lands Charity:

The Barnes Relief in Need Charity (BRINC) – cc.no 200318
BRINC small grant forms are available for existing RPLC small grants referral agencies. In addition some Mortlake based organisations will be invited to become referral agencies for individuals in need. Application forms for organisational and individual grants are available from the correspondent.

The Bailey and Bates Trust – cc.no 312249
Grants are made for relief-in-need purposes for individuals living in the postcode area SW14. Contact the correspondent for further details of how to apply. However, note that charitable expenditure for this trust has been particularly low since 2005.

Other information

Grants are also made to organisations. The charity has an informative website.

The Thomas Wilson Educational Trust

£29,000 (23 grants)

Correspondent: Karen Hopkins, Administrator, 23 Tranmere Road, Twickenham TW2 7JD (020 8893 3928)

CC Number: 1003771

Eligibility

People under 25 who live in Teddington and neighbourhood.

Types of grants

Grants of £100 to £4,500 are given to schoolchildren towards clothing, books, educational outings and fees (only in exceptional circumstances) and to students in further or higher education, including overseas students (depending on how long they have been a resident in Teddington), towards books, fees, living expenses and study or travel abroad. Help may also be given to mature students under 25.

Annual grant total

In 2012 the trust had an income of £60,000 and a total expenditure of £47,000. A total of £29,000 was distributed in educational payments to 23 individuals. Of these, 19 were university or higher education students and four were pupils from a local primary school who received assistance to attend educational school trips.

At the time of writing (July 2014) this was the most recent financial information available for the trust.

Applications

On a form available from the correspondent. Applications can be submitted directly by the individual or by a parent or guardian. They are considered throughout the year.

Southwark

The Christchurch Church of England Educational Fund

£300

Correspondent: The Administrator, c/o Marshall House, 66 Newcomen Street, London SE1 1 YT (020 7407 2967; fax: 020 7403 3969; email: catherine@marshalls.org.uk)

CC Number: 312363

Eligibility

People under the age of 25 who live in the parish of Christchurch and in the former borough of Southwark.

Preference may be given to schoolchildren with serious family difficulties where the child has to be educated away from home and to people with special educational needs.

Types of grants

Grants are for promoting education 'in accordance with the principles of the Church of England.' The awards are made towards general educational needs, such as school uniforms, other clothing, books and educational outings, study and travel overseas, student exchanges, equipment and instruments or travel costs. Schoolchildren, further/higher education students and people starting work can be supported. Grants normally range from £50 to £150 and are one-off.

Annual grant total

In 2013 the fund had an income of £6,300 and an expenditure of £630, which is much lower than in previous years (over the past five years the average charitable expenditure was around £5,400). We estimate that around £300 was awarded in individual grants.

Exclusions

Grants are not normally made for fees or maintenance/living expenses.

Applications

In writing to the correspondent. Candidates should include details of any other applications made. Grants are normally considered in May and November.

Other information

The administration of the fund has been transferred to the Newcomen Collett Foundation (registered charity number 12804).

Grants may also be given to organisations.

Charity of Thomas Dickinson

£1,400

Correspondent: David Freeman, Trustee, Flat 99 Andrewes House, Barbican, London EC2Y 8AY (020 7628 6155)

CC Number: 802473

Eligibility

Young people aged 25 or under and in financial need who are living in, studying in or have at least one parent working in the ancient parishes of: St Giles without Cripplegate; St Sepulchre, St George the Martyr or St Olave, Southwark; or St Mary Magdalene, Bermondsey.

Types of grants

One-off grants ranging from £100 to £500 are given to:

- Schoolchildren for uniforms and educational outings in the UK and overseas
- Students in further or higher education for books
- Vocational students for equipment and instruments
- Individuals with special educational needs for uniforms/clothing

Annual grant total

In 2012 the charity had an income of £2,700 and a total expenditure of £2,900. We estimate that educational grants to individuals totalled £1,400, with funding also awarded to organisations.

At the time of writing (July 2014) this was the most recent financial information available for the charity.

Applications

On a form available from the correspondent, submitted either directly by the individual or via their school/college/educational welfare agency. Applications are considered in February/March, June/July and October/November.

Newcomen Collett Foundation

£30,000 (86 grants)

Correspondent: Catherine Dawkins, Administrator, 66 Newcomen Street, London SE1 1YT (020 7407 2967; fax: 020 7403 3969; email: grantoffice@newcomencollett.org.uk; website: www.newcomencollett.org.uk/index.html)

CC Number: 312804

Eligibility

People under the age of 25 who have lived in the London borough of Southwark for at least two years. Priority is given to individuals who have grown up in the borough of Southwark and are continuing their education/training beyond school-leaving age.

Types of grants

Grants are available to students in tertiary education or undertaking apprenticeships and to people pursuing courses in arts, music, dancing and so on. Support can be given towards equipment/instruments, college fees, course related necessities (such as travel, books or supplies) and vocational training expenses. Awards are one-off or recurrent and usually about £500.

Support towards school uniforms is given through the Southwark Education Welfare and Attendance Office.

Annual grant total

In 2012/13 the foundation had assets of £2.6 million, an income of £170,000. A total of £91,000 was paid in grants to individuals and organisations. Normally around £30,000 can be awarded in grants to individuals annually. During the year 42 students were supported and further 44 grants totalling £5,200 were given by referral through the Southwark Education Welfare and Attendance Office.

Exclusions

Grants are not given for independent school fees, overseas travel, postgraduate degrees or for retrospective expenditure.

Applications

Application forms are available from the foundation's website or can be requested from the correspondent. Applicants can apply directly providing a supporting statement from a tutor or other qualified person. Applications are considered four times a year, in March, June, September and December. They should be submitted a month in advance of the meeting (for specific dates consult the foundation's website).

Other information

Grants are also given to schools and organisations.

St Olave's United Charity, incorporating the St Thomas and St John Charities

£27,000

Correspondent: Angela O'Shaughnessy, Administrator, 6–8 Druid Street, off Tooley Street, London SE1 2EU (020 7407 2530; email: st.olavescharity@btconnect.com)

CC Number: 211763

Eligibility

People under the age of 25 who live in the ancient parishes of Southwark

St Olave and St Thomas, and Bermondsey Horsleydown St John. In practice this means residents of Bermondsey (part SE1 and all SE16).

Types of grants

Grants to college students and mature students for books. Grants for schoolchildren for items such as clothing, travel and fees are only given in very exceptional circumstances.

Annual grant total

In 2012/13 the charity had assets of almost £13.8 million and an income of £381,000. Educational grants to individuals totalled almost £27,000.

Applications

In writing outlining the need. Applications should be made through a school or similar organisation.

Other information

Grants are also made to organisations and to individuals for relief-in-need purposes and in this financial year, over £297,000 was awarded in social welfare grants.

Tower Hamlets

Stepney Relief-in-Need Charity

£11,000

Correspondent: Mrs J. Partleton, Clerk to the Trustees, Rectory Cottage, 5 White Horse Lane, Stepney, London E1 3NE (020 7790 3598)

CC Number: 250130

Eligibility

People in need who live within the old metropolitan borough of Stepney.

Types of grants

One-off grants of £200 to £500, including those for uniforms/clothing, books and fees for attendance at college or university.

Annual grant total

In 2012/13 the charity had both an income and a total expenditure of £22,800. Grants are given to individuals for both social welfare and educational purposes. We estimate the total awarded for educational purposes was around £11,000.

Applications

An application form is available from the correspondent and may be submitted either directly by the individual or through a relative, social worker or other welfare agency. The trustees usually meet

four times a year, but some applications can be considered between meetings at the chair's discretion.

Waltham Forest

Henry Green Scholarships in Connection with Council Schools

£3,100

Correspondent: Duncan Pike, Head of Resources for Children, Waltham Forest Town Hall, Forest Road, Walthamstow, London E17 4JF (email: jenny.hall@ walthamforest.gov.uk; website: www. walthamforest.gov.uk/Pages/Services/wf-ect.aspx)

CC Number: 310918

Eligibility

People under the age of 25 who live in Waltham Forest and are attending a full-time course at the universities of Oxford, Cambridge or London and have attended one or more of the following schools for at least two years: Connaught School for Girls, George Mitchell Secondary Phase All-through School, Leyton Sixth Form College, Leytonstone School, Norlington School for Boys or The Lammas School.

In making their decision the trustees may give consideration to the results of any examinations passed by the applicants, their school record, the headteacher's report, financial needs and their ability to profit by further education.

Types of grants

Small grants for educational necessities, books, equipment/instruments or living expenses. Our research suggests that on average grants are from £50 to £200.

Annual grant total

In 2012/13 the charity had an income of £3,600 and an expenditure of £3,300. We estimate the annual total of grants to be around £3,100.

Applications

Application forms can be requested from the correspondent or found on the charity's website. Applications can be submitted directly by the individual by the end of May and will need a supporting statement from the headteacher. Applicants successful in their initial application are invited for an interview which is normally held in September.

Sir William Mallinson Scholarship Trust

£0

Correspondent: Alice Everett, Administrator, Waltham Forest College, 707 Forest Road, London E17 4JB (020 8501 8134)

CC Number: 312489

Eligibility

People under 25 who live in the former metropolitan borough of Walthamstow.

Types of grants

Grants of £150 to £500 to people starting work for equipment, instruments and travel expenses and students in further or higher education for study or travel overseas and student exchange.

Annual grant total

In 2012/13 the trust had an income of £1,700. There was no expenditure during the year.

The accounts were not available to view at the time of writing (July 2014).

Applications

On a form available from the correspondent.

Sir George Monoux Exhibition Foundation

£4,600

Correspondent: Duncan Pike, Administrator, Walthamstow Town Hall, Forest Road, Walthamstow, London E17 4JF (020 8496 3592; email: jenny. hall@walthamforest.gov.uk)

CC Number: 310903

Eligibility

Further and higher education students in need of financial assistance who are under the age of 25, live in the London borough of Waltham Forest and are pupils or former pupils of the following schools: Belmont Park School, Brookfield House School, Buxton All-through School Secondary Phase, Chingford Foundation School, Connaught School For Girls, Frederick Bremer School, George Mitchell Secondary Phase All-through School, Heathcote School and Science College, Holy Family Catholic School and 6th Form, Joseph Clarke School, Kelmscott School, Leyton Sixth Form College, Leytonstone School, Rush Croft School, Sir George Monoux Sixth Form College, The Lammas School, Waltham Forest College, Walthamstow Academy, Whitefield School and Centre, William Morris School and Willowfield School.

In making their decision the trustees may take into consideration the results of any examinations taken by the applicants, their school record, the headteacher's report, their financial needs and their ability to profit by further education.

Types of grants

One-off awards ranging from £50 to £100 are available for activities not normally covered by the local authority. Such activities include student exchanges and other educational visits overseas, as well as educational visits in the UK. The foundation also aims to 'encourage students to develop their project work.'

Annual grant total

In 2012/13 the foundation had an income of £1,400 and an expenditure of £4,800. We estimate that the annual total of grants was around £4,600.

Applications

Application forms are available from the foundation's website or can be requested from the correspondent. The application must be accompanied with a supporting statement and signature of a referee from the applicant's school/college/university and should be submitted before the end of May. Candidates successful in their initial application are invited for an interview which is normally held in September.

Wandsworth

Supporting Children of Wandsworth Trust

£600

Correspondent: Adrian Butler, Trustee, 82 Reigate Road, Epsom KT17 3DZ (020 8393 5344; email: adrian.butler2@ntlworld.com)

CC Number: 1063861

Eligibility

Children and young people between the ages of 3 and 18 inclusive who have lived in the borough of Wandsworth for at least two years.

Types of grants

Our research suggests that small grants (up to a maximum of £200) can be given towards various items, such as musical instruments, sporting equipment, special clothing, educational trips and personal development opportunities. Grants are made for educational and welfare purposes to help children 'achieve their full potential'.

Annual grant total

In 2012/13 the trust had an income of £1 and an expenditure of £700, which is lower than in the previous years. We estimate that individual grants totalled

about £600. Generally about £1,500 is available for distribution in grants.

Applications

Application forms are available from the correspondent. They should include recommendation letters from clubs, social workers or other professionals/professional bodies, if possible. The trustees meet every two to three months, although urgent applications can be considered between meetings.

Westminster

The Hyde Park Place Estate Charity (Civil Trustees)

£11,000

Correspondent: Shirley Vaughan, Clerk, St George's Hanover Square Church, The Vestry, 2a Mill Street, London W1S 1FX (020 7629 0874; website: www.stgeorgeshanoversquare.org)

CC Number: 212439

Eligibility

People under 25 who are residents of the borough of Westminster and are studying at schools or colleges in Westminster.

Types of grants

Grants of £50 to £500 for schoolchildren, college students and vocational students towards clothing, books, living expenses and excursions.

Annual grant total

In 2012/13 the charity had assets totalling £11.9 million, an income of £439,000 and made grants totalling £154,000 for the relief of hardship, the relief of sickness and the advancement of education, of which £132,000 went to organisations and £22,000 to 160 individuals. We estimate that grants to individuals for educational purposes was around £11,000.

Exclusions

Refugees, asylum seekers and overseas students are not eligible.

Applications

All applications should be made through a recognised third party/organisation and include a case history and the name, address and date of birth of the applicant. Applications are considered on an ongoing basis.

The Paddington Charitable Estates Educational Fund

Correspondent: Sarah Craddock, Administrator, 15th Floor, City of Westminster, Westminster City Hall, 64 Victoria Street, London SW1E 6QP (020 7641 2770)

CC Number: 312347

Eligibility

People aged under 25 who are living in Paddington and who are in need of financial assistance to enable them to pursue their education.

Types of grants

The fund has a number of schemes that support both individuals and organisations.

The pocket money scheme allocates a block grant to the admissions and benefits office of the education department of Westminster City Council, which then distributes about 25 to 30 grants to individuals nominated by schools and educational welfare officers, of £2 per week for children aged 11 to 14 and £2.50 for children aged over 14.

Long-term recurrent grants are made for school and course fees for children who are particularly gifted, or in need of special tuition, to enable them to attend special schools.

One-off grants are also made towards one-off course fees and maintenance, travel, clothing and other expenses.

Scholarships and bursaries are available towards educational trips and to allow young people to enter into a trade or profession or to study music and other arts.

Annual grant total

In 2012 the fund had an income of £75,000 and an expenditure of £70,000. No further information was available at the time of writing (August 2014).

Applications

Applications should be made in writing by a social services or welfare organisation on behalf of an individual. If in doubt a telephone call to the correspondent would be useful to establish whether a case is eligible.

Other information

Grants are also made to schools in Paddington for repairs or physical alterations.

Saint Marylebone Educational Foundation

£35,000 (6 grants)

Correspondent: Caroline Grant, Clerk to the Trustees, c/o St Peter's Church, 119 Eaton Square, London SW1W 9AL

CC Number: 312378

Eligibility

People aged between 8 and 18 who have lived or been educated in the former borough of St Marylebone and the City of Westminster for at least two years. Preference may be given to individuals experiencing unforeseen circumstances affecting their financial situation or for whom boarding school is a preferred option due to a parental illness or specific educational need.

Support is also given to postgraduate students at the Royal Academy of Music and the Royal College of Music.

Types of grants

Generally recurrent grants for school pupils to help with fees or other educational needs. Awards usually range from £500 to £5,500.

Annual grant total

In 2012/13 the foundation had assets of £716,000 and an income of £151,000. A total of £75,000 was spent on charitable activities. Grants to six pupils totalled £35,000.

A further £15,000 was awarded to ten postgraduates at the two music schools, grants being made through the institutions.

Exclusions

Grants for further/higher education are not provided.

Applications

In writing to the correspondent. Applications should be made by the applicant's parent/guardian or by the individual, if aged over 18. Applications can also be submitted through a third party such as a teacher, school or welfare agency, if applicable. Applications are considered in January and July.

Postgraduate students should apply through one of the specified schools.

Other information

Grants are also made to the St Marylebone Bridge School and St Marylebone Church of England Secondary School, also other non-fee paying schools within the City of Westminster.

The trustees inform that 'applications from tertiary students, other than the limited number interviewed annually at the two music colleges sited in Westminster, were declined due to the limited funds.'

Statutory grants and student support

A comprehensive guide to benefits is beyond the scope of this book. There are a number of organisations which provide comprehensive guides, information and advice to students wishing to study in the UK and overseas. Contact details for these organisations can be found in the 'Contacts and sources of further information' section on page 391.

The following is a basic guide to the statutory entitlements for people in education. The situation is extremely complex and changes continually, but the state is still the largest provider of educational support and will continue to be so. Potential applicants should check the situation before applying. Note that this information is correct as of September 2014. You are advised to check the relevant sources (signposted in this section) for the latest information.

This chapter covers:

▷ schoolchildren (aged 16 and under) – free school meals, school clothing grants, and school transport;
▷ further education – Discretionary Learner Support, Residential Support Scheme, Care to Learn and 24+ Advanced Learner Loans;
▷ welfare reforms;
▷ student support – from the government, LEAs, supplementary grants, NHS bursaries, social work bursaries and teacher training funding.

Schoolchildren (aged 16 and under)

The following benefits are all separately administered by individual local education authorities (LEAs) which set their own rules of eligibility and set the level of grants. The following information covers the basic general criteria for benefits, but you should contact your LEA directly for further information and advice (see 'Education authority contacts' on page 395 to find your local LEA).

Free school meals

In England and Wales, LEA-maintained schools must provide a free midday meal to pupils if they or their parents receive:

▷ Income Support;
▷ Jobseeker's Allowance;
▷ Employment and Support Allowance;
▷ support as asylum seekers;
▷ Universal Credit.

The school must also provide a free meal if a pupil's parents receive Child Tax Credit and their income is below a certain level or if they get the Guarantee Credit part of the Pension Credit. Children who receive a qualifying benefit in their own right are also entitled to free school meals.

School clothing grants

All schools are expected to consider cost a high priority when deciding on a uniform policy, as no school uniform should be so expensive that families feel excluded.

In England, LEAs have the discretion to give grants to help towards the cost of buying school uniforms for pupils in maintained schools, colleges for further education and sixth form colleges. They will set their own criteria for eligibility; this can include uniform and non-uniform clothes, shoes and sports kits. In some schools and colleges, help may be available from the governing body or parents' association.

Some LEAs, however, do not give financial help to buy school uniforms on the grounds that there is no legal basis for a pupil to wear a school uniform. In this instance, you may have to challenge your LEA if the school requires a pupil to wear a uniform and you cannot afford the cost. Information on challenging an LEA can be found on the Citizens Advice Adviceguide website (www.adviceguide.org.uk).

It is worth remembering that many schools address the issue of the cost of school uniforms by selling good quality second-hand items directly to parents. Some schools also have hardship funds to enable parents to purchase uniforms, while others run schemes for purchasing uniforms through the school, where uniforms can be paid for in weekly instalments. Contacting the school before buying new items may significantly help to reduce the cost.

You can check if your local authority provides school clothing grants on the www.gov.uk website.

School transport

Generally, children who are between 5 and 16 years old qualify for free school transport if they go to their nearest suitable school and live at least two miles from the school if they are under 8 years old or three miles from the school if they are over 8 years old, or if there is no safe walking route to school. There are lower requirements for families on low incomes and some LEAs may provide free transport for other reasons. Check with your local LEA for more information (for a list of LEAs, see 'Education authority contacts' on page 395).

People who are over 16 years old and in further education may qualify for help with transport costs; this varies by LEA.

Local authorities also have to consider any disability or special educational needs when deciding whether transport is necessary for a child. If a child has a statement of special educational needs (SEN) and has transport requirements written into their statement, the local authorities must meet them. Discretionary grants may also be available from LEAs to cover travel expenses for parents visiting children at special schools.

Pupils living in London can also qualify for free transport on London buses and trams if they are in full-time education or work-based learning. For more information, a helpline is available on 0845 330 9876, or information can be found online at www.tfl.gov.uk.

Further education

Discretionary Learner Support

You may be eligible for Discretionary Learner Support if you are over 19 years old, on a further education course and facing financial hardship. This can help to pay for childcare, accommodation and travel, course materials and equipment and other hardship needs. Contact your learning provider, as each institution administers this scheme individually.

Residential Support Scheme

If you have to live away from home to attend a level 2 or 3 qualification course you can be eligible for up to £4,079, depending on household income and where the course is located.

Care to Learn

You can get grants of up to £175 per week if you are a parent under the age of 20 at the start of your course (which must be publicly funded). Contact the Learner Support helpline on 0800 121 8989 to get an application form and guidance notes.

24+ Advanced Learning Loans

If you are 24 years old or older you can apply for a loan to help with the costs of a college or training course at level 3 or above. Similar to higher education loans, you don't pay anything back until you are earning more than £21,000 a year. Contact your training organisation or college for more details on this loan, which is available from August 2013.

Further information

Department for Education: Piccadilly Gate, Store Street Manchester, M1 2WD

Department of Business, Innovation and Skills (further and higher education): 1 Victoria Street, London SW1H 0ET (tel: 020 7215 5000; email: enquires@bis.gsi.gov.uk; website: www.bis.gov.uk).

Welsh Assembly Education and Skills: Cathays Park, Cardiff CF10 3NQ (tel: 03000 603300/03000 604400; email: learningwales@wales.gsi.gov.uk; website: www.learning.wales.gov.uk).

Education Scotland: Denholm House, Almondvale Business Park, Almondvale Way, Livingston EH54 6GA (tel: 01412 825000; email: enquires@educationscotland.gov.uk; website: www.educationscotland.gov.uk).

Department of Education for Northern Ireland: Rathgael House, Balloo Road, Rathgill, Bangor, County Down BT19 7PR (tel: 02891 279279; email: mail@deni.gov.uk; website: www.deni.gov.uk).

Welfare reforms

The coalition government has implemented extensive welfare reforms. As well as reassessing everyone on Employment and Support Allowance, most means-tested benefits are being rolled into one single means-tested benefit called Universal Credit, which is currently being introduced in stages throughout the UK. Disability Living Allowance is gradually being replaced with Personal Independence Payments (PIPs). A PIP checker tool is available on the www.gov.uk website and can be used to see how PIPs will affect you.

- Council Tax Benefits are now the responsibility of local authorities, rather than being worked out according to a national formula.
- A benefits cap is being introduced which puts a limit on the total amount of money from benefits you can receive if you are of working age.

Other changes include amendments to the rules about appealing against a benefits decision, new conditions about looking for work and means-testing for Child Benefit. Also, large parts of the Social Fund have been abolished.

If you think you might be affected by any of these changes, we advise you to contact your local Citizens Advice for information and advice. There is a list of local advice centres and some self-help guides at www.adviceguide.org.uk.

Student support

Following drastic changes in the way universities are funded in England, different rules apply depending on whether you started university pre-2012 when the old funding system was in place, or 2012 or after when the new system came in.

Advice is available from your LEA (see 'Education authority contacts' on page 395). However, note that the busiest time for LEAs is the period between mid-August (when A-level results come out) and about mid-November (by which time most awards have been given). It is probably best not to contact your LEA for detailed advice at this time unless absolutely necessary. Students should also check with their university or college for other available funds.

Students who began university before September 2012

Full-time students are entitled to a Tuition Fee Loan of up to £3,500 per year, a Maintenance Loan of up to £4,950 (£6,928 in London), and a Maintenance Grant of up to £2,984. Most of this is dependent upon your household income and whether or not you are living at home. Funding is slightly different for part-time students.

Repayments are automatically deducted from your pay when your income is over £15,795 a year and payments are at a rate of 9% of any given income over this amount. Check www.gov.uk for more information.

Students who began university after September 2012

As tuition fees have tripled, you are entitled to a Tuition Fee Loan of up to £9,000 (less for part-time students) and a Maintenance Loan of up to £5,500 (up to £7,765 in London). You are also entitled to a Maintenance Grant of up to £3,354; this is dependent upon household income and will reduce the amount of Maintenance Loan to which you are entitled.

Repayments are linked to your income and begin when you are earning more than £21,000, with 9% of everything above this amount being deducted.

Funding is slightly different for part-time students. See the www.gov.uk website for more information.

Supplementary grants

Some students are entitled to extra help, and this can be applied for through supplementary grants:

- **National Scholarship Programme:** If your household income is less than £25,000 a year, you can apply for this bursary which provides a

minimum of £2,000 of help with tuition fees and accommodation or a free foundation year. Contact your college or university to find out how and when to apply. Please note that from 2015/16 the programme ceases supporting undergraduates and will be repurposed to support postgraduate students.

- **Childcare Grant:** Full-time higher education students with children can apply for a childcare grant of up to 85% of childcare costs (maximum amounts apply), dependent upon income. Apply by completing form CCG1 available on the www.gov.uk website.
- **Parents' Learning Allowance:** Full-time students with children can get up to £1,523 a year to help with costs such as books, study materials and travel. Applications are made as part of the main student finance application.
- **Adult Dependants' Grant:** Students can apply for a grant of up to £2,757 if they have an adult who depends upon them financially. The amount given varies according to the student and the dependent's income and can be applied for as part of the main student finance application.
- **Disabled Students' Allowance:** If you have a disability, long-term health condition, mental health condition or specific learning disability, you can apply for specialist equipment allowance, a non-medical helper allowance and a general allowance using the Disabled Students' Allowance form available from the www.gov.uk website.

Information and applications for student finance in England can be found on the www.gov.uk website. You can also contact your LEA, a list of which can be found on page 395. Further useful contacts include:

- **Student Finance England:** PO Box 210, Darlington, DL1 9 HJ (tel: 0300 100 0607; website: www.gov.uk/student-finance)
- **Student Finance Wales:** PO Box 211, Llandudno Junction, LL30 9FU (tel: 0300 200 4050; website: www.studentfinancewales.co.uk)

- **Student Finance Northern Ireland:** tel: 0300 100 0077; website: www.studentfinanceni.co.uk
- **Student Awards Agency for Scotland:** Gyleview House, 3 Redheughs Rigg, Edinburgh, EH12 9HH(tel: 0300 555 0505; website: www.sass.gov.uk)
- **For students from other EU countries:** PO Box 89, Darlington, DL1 9AZ (tel: 01412 433570; website: www.gov.uk/ studentfinance)

NHS bursaries

Full-time NHS students can apply for a bursary and a grant from the NHS. Part-time students are eligible for reduced bursaries and grants. Grants are for £1,000 and bursaries can be up to £5,460 depending on course intensity, where you study and live and your household income.

Eligible courses that lead to professional registration are:

- medicine or dentistry;
- chiropody, podiatry, dietetics, occupational therapy, orthoptics, physiotherapy, prosthetics and orthotics, radiography, radiotherapy, audiology and speech and language therapy;
- dental hygiene or dental therapy;
- nursing, midwifery or operating department practice.

Social Work Bursaries

Social Work Bursaries do not depend upon your household income and can help with living costs and tuition fees.

For students in England: Rigway House, Northgate Close, Middlebrook, Bolton, BL6 6PQ (tel: 0300 330 1345; website: www.nhsbsa.nhs.uk)

For students in Wales: Care Council for Wales (CCW), South Gate House, Wood Street, Cardiff CF10 1EW (tel: 0300 3033 444; email: info@ccwales.org.uk; website: www.ccwales.org.uk)

For students in Scotland: Scottish Social Services Council (SSSC), Compass House, 11 Riverside Drive, Dundee DD1 4NY (tel: 01382 207 101; email: enquiries@sssc.uk.com; website: www.sssc.uk.com)

For students in Northern Ireland: Social Service Inspectorate (SSI), The

Department of Health, Social Services and Public Safety, Castle Buildings, Stormont, Belfast BT4 3SJ (tel: 02890 520500; email: webmaster@dhsspsni. gov.uk; website: www.dhsspsni.gov.uk)

Teacher Training Funding

Funding is available for full-time or part-time students on initial teacher training (ITT), postgraduate certificate in education (PGCE) and school-centred initial teacher training (SCITT) courses through the main student finance avenue. Training bursaries are available from the Teaching Agency to students who achieved at least a 2:2 at undergraduate level. These bursaries are dependent upon what subject or phase is being studied, as some are priority areas. They can range from £4,000 up to £20,000 for a trainee with a first class degree who is training to teach physics, chemistry maths, computing or languages.

Department for Education: (tel: 0800 389 2500; website: www.education. gov.uk/get-into-teaching)

Further advice and information services are listed in the 'Contacts and sources of further information' on page 391).

Types of schools in the UK and their funding

This section contains information about and details of the types of schools that exist in the UK, how they are funded and how funding can be obtained to attend them.

Local authority maintained schools

These schools are funded by the local education authority and include foundation schools, community schools, voluntary-controlled schools, voluntary-aided schools, nursery schools and some special schools. They all follow the national curriculum and are inspected by Ofsted.

The gov.uk website supplies some information about the different types of schools, how to find one and apply for a place. See: www.gov.uk/types-of-school/overview for more information.

Academies

Academies are independently managed schools which are funded directly by the Education Funding Agency and operate outside the control of the local authority. They are set up by sponsors from business, faith or voluntary groups in partnership with the Department for Education and the local authority. In January 2013 more than half of all secondary schools had converted, or were in the process of converting, to academy status. Many factors have caused academies to be a controversial current issue; therefore there exists a wide range of information available about academies from all perspectives. The Department for Education supplies some here: www.education.gov.uk/schools/leadership/typesofschools/academies.

Free schools

These schools are non-profit, independent, state-funded schools which are not controlled by the local authority. They are similar to academies but are usually new schools, set up as a response to a demand that is not being met by existing schools.

The New Schools Network provides advice about free schools, including how to set one up. See www.newschoolsnetwork.org or call 020 7537 9208 for more information.

Independent schools

Independent schools are independent in their finances and governance, and are funded by charging parents fees (on average £10,500 a year, or £25,000 for boarders). They set their own curriculum and admissions policies and are inspected by Ofsted or other approved inspectorates. According to the Independent Schools Council, around 6.5% of schoolchildren in the UK are educated in independent schools, with the figure rising to 18% of pupils for those over the age of 16.

Most independent schools offer scholarships and bursaries to some applicants, ranging from 10% of fees to full fees paid (very occasionally). They are subject to fierce competition and are usually awarded on the basis of academic merit, as well as individual need.

A number of independent schools also offer music scholarships, varying from 10% of fees to full fees paid (including free musical tuition). Candidates are usually expected to offer two instruments at at least grades 6 to 8. Contact the Director of Music at the school you are interested in for more details.

The Independent Schools Directory

The Independent Schools Directory lists all the UK independent schools.

Tel: 020 8906 0911

Website: www.indschools.co.uk

The Independent Schools Council Information Service

The Independent Schools Council Information Service is the main source of information on independent schools. It has a website containing detailed information to help families to select the right school and find possible sources of funding.

Tel: 020 7766 7070

Website: www.isc.co.uk

The Independent Schools Yearbook

The Independent Schools Yearbook contains details of schools with a membership of one or more of the Constituent Associations of the Independent Schools Council. It is published by A&C Black and can be bought online.

Tel: 020 7631 5988

Email: isyb@acblack.com

Website: www.isyb.co.uk

The Independent Association of Prep Schools

The Independent Association of Prep Schools is the professional association for head teachers of the leading 600 independent prep schools in the UK and worldwide.

Tel: 01926 887833

Email: iaps@iaps.org.uk

Website: www.iaps.org.uk

The Council of British International Schools

The Council of British International Schools is a membership organisation of British schools of quality, Europe and worldwide which provide a British education.

Tel: 020 8240 4142

Email: members@cobis.org.uk

Website: www.cobis.org.uk

Boarding schools

Boarding Schools Association

The Boarding Schools Association serves and represents boarding schools and promotes boarding education in the UK, including both state and private boarding schools.

Very occasionally the local authority may pay for a child's boarding fees, if they have a particularly difficult home situation. Seventy-five children were supported in this way in 2011/12, and the new Assisted Boarding Network, which is backed by the government, is pushing for this number to rise to 1,000 by 2018.

Contact the Director of Education or the Chief Education Officer for the area in which you live, or if you live outside the UK, the area with which you have the closest connection.

Tel: 020 7798 1580

Website: www.boarding.org.uk

Maintained boarding schools

These are state schools that take boarders as well as day pupils; they only charge for the cost of boarding, not for tuition. Boarding costs are generally between £8,000 and £13,000 a year. According to the State Boarding Schools Association, there are 37 state boarding schools in England. They are a mix of all-ability comprehensive schools, academies and grammar schools. They all follow the national curriculum and take the same examinations as pupils in day state schools.

State Boarding Schools Association

Tel: 020 7798 1580

Email: info@sbsa.org.uk

Website: www.sbsa.org.uk

Music, dance and stage schools

Choir schools

Choir Schools Association

The Choir Schools Association is a group of 44 schools which are attached to cathedrals, churches and college chapels around the country. The majority are fee-paying, with 9 out of 10 choristers qualifying for financial help with fees through the schools.

Tel: 01359 221333

Email: info@choirschools.org.uk

Website: www.choirschools.org.uk

Music schools

There are various specialist music schools in the UK, with no overall umbrella body. Contact the school directly for information about fees and funding.

Music and Dance Scheme

This government scheme is designed to help exceptionally talented young musicians and dancers between the ages of 8 and 19. Means-tested fee support and grants are distributed through specialist centres of education and training and conservatoires. More information on the scheme can be obtained by contacting the Department of Education or the place of education.

Access to Excellence

Website: www.education.gov.uk/ schools/teachingandlearning/ curriculum/subjects/b0068711/mds

MMA

MMA is the national association for music teaching professionals. It publishes the *MMA Music Directory* annually, a comprehensive guide to music departments and music scholarships in the UK, which can be purchased on its website.

Tel: 01227 475600

Email: admin@mma-online.org.uk

Website: www.mma-online.org.uk

Foundations for Excellence

The Foundations for Excellence website provides information, guidance and signposting in the areas of health and wellbeing for young musicians and dancers.

Website: www.foundations-for-excellence.org

Dance schools

Council for Dance and Education Training

Information on dance education and training can be obtained from the Council for Dance and Education Training. It is the quality-assurance body of the dance and musical theatre industries and provides information on its recognised schools and teachers.

Tel: 020 7240 5703

Email: info@cdet.org.uk

Website: www.cdet.org.uk

Dance Schools UK

Dance Schools UK provides a directory of dance schools and teachers across the UK and Ireland.

Website: www.danceschools-uk.co.uk

Stage schools

Drama UK

Drama UK was formed out of the National Council for Drama and the Conference of Drama Schools and provides accreditation for vocational drama courses and support for organisations which offer accredited training. It acts as an advocate for the sector and encourages the industry and training providers to work together. Its website provides information about drama training.

Tel: 020 3393 6141

Email: info@dramauk.co.uk

Website: www.dramauk.co.uk

Free Index

Free Index provides a list of stage schools in the UK.

Website: www.freeindex.co.uk/categories/entertainment_and_lifestyle/performing_arts/stage_schools

Other possible sources of help with fees

Allowances for Crown Servants

The Foreign and Commonwealth Office gives grants to enable children of diplomats and other government servants working abroad to attend boarding schools in the UK.

Tel: 020 7008 1500

Allowances for Armed Forces Personnel

The Children's Education Advisory Service (CEAS) provides expert and impartial advice about the education of Service children.

Children whose parents are members of Her Majesty's Forces are eligible for an allowance towards boarding education, whether their parent(s) is (are) serving at home or abroad. This is the Continuity of Education Allowance which is available for children who are 8 years old and older. Families are expected to contribute a minimum of 10% towards the fees. Contact CEAS to obtain advice and the relevant application form.

Address: Trenchard Lines, Upavon, Pewsey, Wiltshire SN9 6BE

Tel: 01980 618244 (civilian)/ GPTN 94 344 8244 (military)

Extra funding is also available for day-school allowances, special educational needs, guardian's allowances and children's visits to parents serving overseas.

Multinational companies

Some multinational companies and organisations help with school fees if parents have to work overseas. A few firms make grants, run scholarship schemes or provide low-interest loans for employees who are resident in the UK. Consult your employer for further information.

Alternative routes to employment: apprenticeships

Following the government announcement to reform apprenticeship standards in October 2013, we thought it would be pertinent to include a section about apprenticeships in this guide for those looking for alternative routes into employment. In this section, there will be information on apprenticeships and how to apply for one.

What is an apprenticeship?

Briefly, an apprenticeship is a job that also provides rigorous skills training in order to equip a school-leaver with enough experience to work in their chosen field, and improve their career prospects. At the end of an apprenticeship, the apprentice is awarded a nationally recognised qualification.

Types of apprenticeship

There are approximately 1,500 job roles available in ten different sectors including: agriculture, horticulture and animal care; business, administration and law; construction, planning and the built environment; education and training; engineering and manufacturing technologies; health, public services and care; information and communications technology; and retail and commercial enterprise.

Qualification framework

There are a number of elements and qualification criteria to each apprenticeship and this is referred to as the Framework. Each apprenticeship framework has three main strands:

- a competence-based element;
- a technical element;
- a skills element.

The skills element includes a module on employment rights and responsibilities, and a module on Personal Learning and Thinking Skills.

Training duration

Generally, an apprenticeship takes between one and four years to complete. The length varies depending on existing skills levels of the apprentice, the qualification being obtained and the industry sector.

Main benefits

The main benefits of becoming an apprentice are:

- you earn a wage during your entire apprenticeship;
- there is a guaranteed, nationally recognised qualification awarded to you as you complete each stage of your training;
- you gain skills and knowledge which can be used across a range of jobs and industries;
- once the apprenticeship has finished there's the opportunity to carry on working, maybe get promoted or go on to higher education in a college or university;
- you can learn at your own pace and get support as and when you need it.

Entry requirements

Different apprenticeships have different entry requirements depending on the type of work you will do. However, the most important requirements are that:

- you must be living in England and not taking part in full-time education;
- you must be aged 16 or over;

▶ if you took your GCSEs more than five years ago and didn't gain a top grade (A or A*), or you don't have good GCSE grades in maths and English you will need to take a literacy and numeracy test.

Are there any costs involved?

The National Apprenticeship Service supports, funds and co-ordinates the delivery of apprenticeships throughout England. It will pay the costs of your training depending on your age, with any remaining costs met by the employer if you are aged 23 or under.

How to apply

To apply for an apprenticeship or traineeship, visit the apprenticeship vacancies website apprenticeshipvacancymatchingservice.lsc.gov.uk/navms/Forms/Candidate/Apprenticeships.aspx.

Application Support

If you would like some help on registering, searching and applying for your chosen apprenticeship, then please read the 'How to write a winning apprenticeship application' guide at www.apprenticeships.org.uk/~/media/Collateral/IAG/Apprenticeships-writing-130614.ashx.

References and further information

All the information presented on this page was taken from the National Apprenticeship Service. For more information, or to view what previous apprentices have to say about their experiences, please visit www.apprenticeships.org.uk.

Company sponsorship and career development loans

This chapter looks at two possible sources of finance for some students.

1   Company sponsorships: these apply particularly to people in their last year at school who are intending to study a business-related, engineering, or science-based subject at university.

2   Career development loans: these can be a useful means of helping to finance vocational courses for periods of up to two years, particularly if the course offers the prospect of obtaining a steady, reasonably well-paid job at the end.

Company sponsorships

Sponsorship of degree courses

A number of companies sponsor students who are taking degree courses at universities, usually in business, engineering, technology or other science subjects. These are generally for students who are resident in the UK and are taking a first degree course (or a comparable course).

Sponsorship generally takes the form of cash support (i.e. a bursary or scholarship) while at university, with a salary being paid during pre-university and vacation employment or during periods of industrial training at the company concerned. (If the sponsorship is for a sandwich course the placements will be for longer than the vacation and will form an integral part of the course.) Sponsorships are highly competitive but can be of great value to students who, for any reason, do not receive the full grant. They may also help students avoid having to take out a loan.

Each company has its own sponsorship policy. Some sponsorships are tied to a particular course or institution; others are only given for specific subjects. The value of the sponsorship also varies. Additional help can be available in the form of discretionary educational gifts or degree prizes.

Sponsorships do not necessarily offer a permanent job at the end of the course (unless the student is classed as an employee). Equally, the student does not usually have to take up a job if offered by the company, although there may be at least a moral obligation to consider one.

Students should not decide on a course simply because there may be sponsorship available, they should choose the course first and seek sponsorship afterwards if appropriate.

In most sponsorships it is the student, not the company, who has to make arrangements to get on the course. Indeed some companies will only sponsor students who have already been accepted on a course. However, most university departments have well-established links with industry and actively encourage students who are seeking sponsorship.

Students should apply for sponsorships as early as possible in the autumn term of the final academic year before moving to university.

The Engineering Development Trust

The Engineering Development Trust (EDT) (Charity Commission no. 1156066 and in Scotland SC039635) is a nationwide education charity providing opportunities for young people in science, technology, engineering and mathematics (STEM).

The charity's website, with links to the appropriate information, states:

If you are over 16 there are 3 EDT schemes on offer:

- *4 day Residential STEM courses at University help you get connected to the right degree – click on Headstart (for 16/17 yr olds)*

- *6 month real life STEM projects in industry help you focus on future careers – click on Engineering Education Scheme (for 16/17 yr olds)*

- *Year-long work placements fast track your career – click on The Year in Industry (for students completing A levels/Scottish Highers or equivalent)*

EDT also offers schemes for under 16s.

If you are aged 11–16 speak to your school about what EDT schemes are on offer.

EDT could help you…

- *think differently about STEM*

- *find out about courses and careers in STEM*

- *build key skills for life.*

Please note for First Edition, Go4SET, Open Industry and Engineering Education Scheme please find out if your school runs the programme.

For comprehensive information, including full contact details you should visit the website: www.etrust.org.uk

Further information

Individuals are best advised to identify major institutions working in the industry they intend to follow and see what schemes are available. For example, for engineering opportunities visit engopps.com.

Professional and career development loans

The following information is taken from the National Careers Service website: www.nationalcareersservice.direct.gov.uk/advice/curses/funding

A Professional and Career Development Loan (PCDL) is a commercial bank loan which can be applied for to pay for courses, training and other learning that will help enhance your job skills or career. It has to be paid back once you have left your course, but interest is not paid for the period when you are learning. This is paid by the government, and for one more month after you complete the course. You can apply to borrow between £300 and £10,000.

Eligibility

To qualify for a PCDL you must:

- be aged 18 or over;
- have been living in the UK for at least three years before your course starts;
- plan to work in the UK, European Union (EU) or European Economic Area (EEA) after the course.

Your course must:

- only last up to two years, or three years if it includes one year of work experience;
- be provided by an organisation on the PCDL Register – check with your course provider;
- help with your career – but your course does not have to lead to a qualification.

Note that it is very important your course is registered because you will need the course name and provider registration number when you fill in the loan pack. If the course is not registered, the action you need to take will depend on who is running the course:

For a public provider

Complete the loan application pack and the bank will verify that the course is suitable, and arrange for the course to be added to the register.

For a private or international provider

Ask the course provider if they will register the course with the Skills Funding Agency.

A Professional and Career Development Loan might not be right for everyone – make sure you have looked at the full range of funding options. For instance, you may be able to get financial support that you won't have to repay, such as Discretionary Learner Support (which may be available from your college).

Ordering a PCDL application pack

A PCDL application pack can be ordered by contacting an adviser by email or telephone.

To order by telephone call 0800 100 900. An adviser will check that you and your intended course are eligible and will then take the details needed to get a pack sent out to you.

If you order by email, make sure you include your full name and address, your age and confirm that you meet the residency requirements outlined above. Include the full name of the course, the qualification type and the course provider, so that eligibility check can be made on the course before an application pack is sent.

For more information about Professional and Career Development Loans see www.gov.uk/career-development-loans/overview.

Funding for gap years and overseas voluntary work

Gap years have traditionally been a popular choice with school-leavers looking to travel, volunteer, work or broaden their horizons in some other way before embarking on university life. With increasingly high costs of education many feel the need to be extra careful in choosing a career path. A short pause between leaving school and continuing education may be a smart rather than just adventurous decision. A 'mini-gap', for example, during the summer holidays can equally add valuable experience and skills to a CV and is looked upon by many universities and potential employers as an advantage in what is a very competitive job market.

There are some opportunities to participate in voluntary work, expeditions and other activities which can be funded or partly funded through charities, bursaries and schemes. For further information on support available in this area see 'Gap year/voluntary work overseas' on page 16. The charities in this section are divided into two categories:

1. Those with full entries – these mainly fund gap year activities;
2. Those that are cross-referenced – these prefer to give more widely in other areas as part of their charitable objectives.

Generally, most grantmaking charities have quite specific criteria which they apply to all eligible applicants; it is important to keep this in mind and not assume that you can apply just because you wish to travel to a particular area or place. Likewise, many may have a particular preference for a certain type of project, for example conservation or one that involves working for the benefit of the local community. They may also give within a specific catchment area, so it can be useful to look at local grantmakers first. Many of the local charities in this guide will give grants under terms such as 'travel overseas' or 'personal development activities'. This allows them to give broadly to a number of different activities which may fall into these categories, such as gap year projects, voluntary work overseas and so on.

It cannot be over-emphasised that it is your responsibility to check that you are eligible for funding from any charity to which you intend to apply. Please do not apply if you are in doubt of your eligibility; or where appropriate, contact the organisation for further clarification.

If you are successful in gaining financial support, remember that it is always good practice to keep charities informed of the progress of your project and what you have achieved by doing it. This might even be a requirement of accepting their funding. You may also be asked to act as an ambassador to the charity when returning to the UK by giving talks or presentations on your experiences. This might be something to think about when making your application, particularly if the organisation is keen to involve past participants in promoting its scheme.

It may help your cause if you raise some of the funds yourself; this might give you an edge over other applicants and prove how dedicated and determined you are to succeed. You may also find it useful to break down the total cost of your application and apply to several different grantmakers for smaller amounts of money, as this could increase your chances of securing the right amount of funding.

There are other alternatives to funding gap year projects and voluntary work overseas. Many large volunteer organisations provide funded or partly funded volunteering and exchange schemes that will allow you to take part in voluntary work at minimum cost. Some can offer bursaries to cover specific costs such as the project fee or flight fare, and others may ask you to fundraise a block amount of money but will pay for all your necessary costs in return.

Below are a few funded or partly funded voluntary schemes available to young people living in the UK.

The European Voluntary Service (EVS)

EVS is a fully funded youth volunteering scheme run by the British Council, the UK's national agency for the Erasmus+ programmes. EVS provides opportunities for young people to volunteer in another European country for two weeks to twelve months.

The scheme is open to all young people aged 17 to 30 who are:
- resident in one of the European member states;
- members of the European Economic Area;
- resident in any country neighbouring the EU and participating in the programme.

EVS placements take place in all member countries of the European Union, the European Economic Area, pre-accession countries and countries neighbouring EU, including Western Balkans, Eastern Partnership countries, Russian Federation or Southern Mediterranean.

Most placements last from six to twelve months and priority is usually given to longer-term placements; however, short-term placements are also available. Placements can be organised in variety of sectors, such as social, cultural, environmental and sports and are selected by the volunteers themselves.

All EVS projects are fully funded by European Commission grants, which are applied for by the applicant's sending organisation. The grant covers the costs of travel, food and accommodation, insurance, training and living expenses and provides volunteers with a modest living allowance.

In order to take part in an EVS project, volunteers have to find a suitable host organisation to volunteer with and a sending organisation from their own country to sponsor them. A list of sending organisations, host organisations, projects and other information regarding EVS can be found on their website: www.britishcouncil.org.

Note that applicants are advised to plan their projects in advance (preferably six months), as the process can take this long to complete.

In addition to applying for a volunteer placement with EVS directly, it is also possible to organise a placement through certain volunteering organisations that are linked to the EVS programme. The Inter-Cultural Youth Exchange (www.icye.org.uk) and International Voluntary Service (www.ivsgb.org) will help volunteers through application processes and will sometimes carry out administration work on their behalf. If you are interested in volunteering with EVS, it may be worthwhile contacting one of these organisations for help.

Lattitude Global Volunteering

Lattitude Global Volunteering is a UK-based volunteering organisation and registered charity (Charity Commission no. 272761) that organises volunteer placements for young people in developing countries and offers bursaries and funded projects for applicants in need of financial help. Volunteers can take part in a number of different projects such as camps and outdoor education, and environmental, medical and community projects. Lattitude Global Volunteering can also offer graduate placements that focus on a specific skill or professional area, which can be designed by the applicant themselves.

General bursary scheme

Bursaries of £100 to £2,000 can be given to British nationals (although those who do not hold a UK passport may be considered under special circumstances) aged 17 to 25. Applicants must be able to prove why they would have difficulty in raising money in comparison to other Lattitude candidates.

Specific funds are also available to people in Scotland and Greater London.

Full details of all the scheme can be found on Lattitude's website.

Lattitude Global Volunteering, 42 Queen's Road, Reading, Berkshire RG1 4BB; tel: 01189 594914; website: www.lattitude.org.uk, email: volunteer@lattitude.org.uk

The Jack Petchey Foundation

The foundation supports young people who have to raise money in order to be involved in a voluntary project or participate in events that will benefit others in society. Grants covering up to 50% of the overall expenses (but no more than £300 per person) are only available to those aged 11 to 25 who live in Essex or London. Full details of eligibility criteria and how to apply can be found on the foundation's website: www.jackpetcheyfoundation.org.uk.

Project Trust

Project Trust is an educational charity which specialises in overseas volunteering placements for school-leavers. People between the ages of 17 and 19 are given training and support to undertake voluntary teaching and social care projects abroad lasting about 8 to 12 months. Living allowances are provided by the trust or the overseas host. More details on the opportunities available can be found on the website: projecttrust.org.uk, by email: info@projecttrust.org.uk, or phone: 0879230444.

Other helpful contacts

www.igapyear.com

iGapyear.com provides advice on how to put together a proposal for a funding application as well as offering other information on gap year and volunteering opportunities.

www.gapyear.com

A social network where travellers can meet, chat and share experiences.

www.idealist.org

Idealist.org is an independent, online network of non-profit and voluntary organisations that provide information on voluntary opportunities worldwide.

www.wwv.org.uk

Worldwide Volunteering has a search-and-match database of voluntary organisations and volunteer placements worldwide.

www.europa.eu/youth/en

General information on volunteering opportunities as well as details of organisations accredited to run EVS projects.

www.eurodesk.eu/edesk

The website holds information on European policies and opportunities for young people.

www.yearoutgroup.org

Year Out Group is an association of organisations running gap year and volunteering projects. The website provides general information for people planning to take a year out and offers the details of member organisations.

Volunteer organisations

www.vso.org.uk

www.frontier.ac.uk

raleighinternational.org

Contacts and sources of further information

Many people in education and training need financial advice and help from time to time. It is usually best to contact the following people or organisations as a starting point:

- the educational institution you are studying at;
- your local education authority (addresses are in the previous section of this guide);
- your local Citizens Advice or other welfare agencies.

These should point you in the right direction for more specialist advice if you need it. However, the following organisations and publications may be useful and should be available from all main libraries. Readers should also look at the specialist sections of this guide where relevant.

General

Citizens Advice

England: 0844 411 1444

Wales: 0844 477 2020

Scotland: 0808 800 9060

Northern Ireland: contact local bureau

Provides free, independent, confidential and impartial advice to everyone on their rights and responsibilities. Find your local bureau at www.citizensadvice.org.uk

or get advice online at www.adviceguide.org.uk.

Department for Education

Piccadilly Gate, Store Street, Manchester M1 2WD (tel: 03700 002288; website: www.gov.uk/dfe)

Department of Business, Innovation and Skills (further and higher education)

1 Victoria Street, London SW1H 0ET (tel: 020 7215 5000; email: enquires@bis.gsi.gov.uk; website: www.gov.uk/bis)

Department of Education for Northern Ireland

Rathgael House, Balloo Road, Rathgill, Bangor, County Down BT19 7PR (tel: 02891 279279; email: mail@deni.gov.uk; website: www.deni.gov.uk)

Education Scotland

Denholm House, Almondvale Business Park, Almondvale Way, Livingston EH54 6GA (tel: 01412 825000; email: enquires@education scotland.gov.uk; website: www.educationscotland.gov.uk)

Gov.uk

Website: www.gov.uk

General advice and information on government services.

The Money Advice Service

Holborn Centre, 120 Holborn, London EC1N 2TD (tel: 0300 500 5000 – English; 0300 500 5555 – Welsh; Text Relay: 18001 0300 500 5000 [Mon–Fri 8am–8pm, Sat 9am–1pm]; email: enquiries@moneyadviceservice.org.uk; website: www.moneyadvice.org.uk; an online chat facility is also available.)

The Money Advice Service helps people manage their money, through a free and impartial advice service. It also works in partnership with other organisations to help people make the most of their money. It is an independent service set up by the government.

The Prince's Trust

Prince's Trust House, 9 Eldon Street, London EC2M 7SL (tel: 0800 842 842; email: info@princes-trust.org.uk; website: www.princes-trust.org.uk

A youth charity that helps change young lives. The trust can help people under 30 who are not expecting to achieve 5 GCSEs grades A–C or who are not in education, training or not working more than 16 hours a week.

Welsh Assembly Education and Skills

Cathays Park, Cardiff CF10 3NQ (tel: 03000 603300 – English; 03000 604400 – Welsh; email: Customer Help@Wales.GSI.Gov.uk; website: www.wales.gov.uk)

Children

Child Poverty Action Group (CPAG)

Child Poverty Action Group, 94 White Lion Street, London N1 9PF (tel: 020 7837 7979; email: info@cpag. org.uk; website: www.cpag.org.uk)

Child Poverty Action Group in Scotland, Unit 9 Ladywell, 94 Duke Street, Glasgow G4 0UW (tel: 0141 552 3303; email: staff@cpagscotland. org.uk)

CPAG publishes a number of guides which include information on state benefit and entitlements for both schoolchildren and students.

National Youth Advocacy Service

Egerton House, Tower Road, Birkenhead, Wirral CH41 1FN (tel: 01516 498700; helpline: 0800 808 1001 [Mon–Fri 9am–8pm, Sat 10am–4pm]; email: main@nyas.net or help@nyas.net; website: www.nyas. net)

Youth Access

1–2 Taylors Yard, 67 Alderbrook Road, London SW12 8AD (tel: 020 8772 9900; email: admin@youth access.org.uk; website: www.youth access.org.uk – an online directory of information, advice and support services for young people).

Further and continuing education

City & Guilds

1 Giltspur Street, London EC1A 9DD (tel: 0844 543 0033; email: learner support@cityandguilds.com; website: www.cityandguilds.com)

City and Guilds provides support to learners and training providers.

Department for Business, Innovation, and Skills

Department of Business, Innovation and Skills (further and higher education): 1 Victoria Street, London

SW1H 0ET (tel: 020 7215 5000; email: enquires@bis.gsi.gov.uk; website: www. gov.uk/bis)

National Institute of Adult Continuing Education (NIACE)

Chetwynd House, 21 De Montford Street, Leicester LE1 7GE (tel: 01162 044200; email: enquiries@niace. org.uk; website: www.niace.org.uk).

National Institute of Adult Continuing Education Wales

3rd Floor, 33–35 Cathedral Road, Cardiff CF11 9HB (tel: 02920 370900; email: enquiries@niacedc.org.uk; website: www.niacedc.org.uk).

NIACE is the national organisation for adult learning.

Higher Education

The National Union of Students (NUS)

NUS UK, Macadam House, 275 Gray's Inn Road, London WC1X 8QB (tel: 0845 521 0262; website: www.nus.org. uk; email: online form).

NUS Scotland

Papermill Wynd, McDonald Road, Edinburgh EH7 4QL (tel: 01315 566598; email: mail@nus-scotland. org.uk)

NUS-USI

42 Dublin Road, Belfast BT2 7HN (tel: 02890 244641 email: info@ni students.org)

NUS Wales

2nd Floor, Cambrian Buildings, Mount Stuart Square, Cardiff CF10 5FL (tel: 02920 435390 email: office@nus-wales.org.uk)

The Open University (OU)

The Open University, PO Box 197, Milton Keynes MK7 6BJ (tel: 0845 300 6090; email: online form; website: www.open.ac.uk).

Scholarship Search

Website: www.scholarship-search. org.uk

Search scholarships in the UK for pre-university, undergraduate and postgraduate learning.

Student Awards Agency for Scotland

Gyleview House, 3 Redheughs Rigg, Edinburgh EH12 9HH (tel: 0300 555 0505; website: www.saas.gov.uk; email: online form).

Student Cashpoint

Website: www.studentcashpoint.co.uk

A website giving information on student grants, loans, bursaries, scholarships and awards.

University and Colleges Admissions Service (UCAS)

Rosehill, New Barn Lane, Gloucestershire GL5 3LZ (tel: 0371 468 0468; website: www.ucas.com).

UCAS uses social media for direct contact.

Applications for full-time university degree courses must be made through UCAS (part-time degree courses and the Open University are not covered by UCAS – apply directly to the university).

Careers

National Careers Service

Website: www.nationalcareersservice. direct.gov.uk; tel: 0800 100 900; an online chat service is also available

Provides information, advice and guidance to help people make decisions on learning, training and work opportunities. The service offers confidential and impartial advice, supported by qualified careers advisers.

Not Going to Uni

Mountcharm House, Ground Floor 102–104 Queens Road, Buckhirst Hill IG9 5BS (tel: 0203 691 2800; email: info@notgoingtouni.co.uk; website: www.notgoingtouni.co.uk)

Opportunities for school and college leavers outside of the traditional university route, including apprenticeships, sponsored degrees, diplomas, gap years, distance learning and jobs.

Prospects

Graduate Prospects, Booth Street East, Manchester M13 9EP (tel: 0161

277 5200; website: www.prospects.ac.uk)

Graduate careers website for jobs, postgraduate courses, work experience and careers advice.

Students with disabilities

Disability Rights UK

Ground Floor CAN Mezzanine, 49–51 East Road, London N1 6AH (tel: 0800 328 5050; email:students@disabilityrights.org; website: www.disabilityrightsuk.org)

National pan-disability organisation led by disabled people that provides advice to disabled students.

Lead Scotland

Princes House, 5 Shandwick Place, Edinburgh EH2 4RG (tel: 01312 289441; email: enquires@lead.org.uk; website: www.lead.org.uk)

Set up to widen access to learning for disabled young people and adults and carers across Scotland.

Study overseas

The British Council

British Council Customer Service UK, Bridgewater House, 58 Whitworth Street, Manchester M1 6BB (tel: 01619 577755; email: general. enquiries@britishcouncil.org; website: www.britishcouncil.org).

Advice and publications on educational trips overseas.

Erasmus

British Council, Erasmus Team, 1 Kingsway Cardiff CF10 3AQ (tel: 02920 924311; email: erasmus@british council.org; website: www.british council.org/erasmus).

Erasmus enables higher education students, teachers and institutions in 31 European countries to study for part of their degree in another country.

Overseas students

Refugee Women's Association

Print House, 18 Ashwin Street, London E8 3DL (tel: 020 7923 2412; email: info@refugeewomen.org.uk; website: www.refugeewomen.org.uk)

Provides advice and guidance on education, training, employment, health and social care for refugee women throughout London.

United Kingdom Council for International Students' Affairs (UKCISA)

9–17 St Albans Place, London N1 0NX (advice line: 0207 788 9214; website: www.ukcisa.org.uk).

UKCISA provides information for overseas students on entering the UK, as well as general advice.

Other funding or sources of help

Community Foundations

12 Angel Gate, 320–326 City Road, London EC1V 2PT (tel: 020 7713 9326; website: www.ukcommunity foundations.org). These local organisations sometimes have a pot of money available for individuals to apply for. Use this website to identify your local community foundation.

Money Saving Expert

Website: www.moneysavingexpert. com

British consumer finance information and discussion website providing information and journalistic articles enabling people to save money.

Prisoners Education Trust

Prisoners Education Trust, Wandle House, Riverside Drive, Mitcham. Surrey CR 4BU (tel: 020 8648 7760; website: www.prisonerseducation. org.uk)

Access to a grants programme to enable prisoners in England and Wales to study through distance learning. Also provides advice and

support, and influences policy and best practice.

Education authority contacts

This section provides a list of council offices and of the main government departments. Check online for specific education departments or for further information relating to children and young people in education.

Government departments

England

Department for Business, Innovation and Skills: 1 Victoria Street, London SW1H 0ET (tel: 020 7215 5000; email:enquiries@bis.gsi.gov.uk; website: www. gov.uk/bis).

Department for Education: Piccadilly Gate, Store Street, Manchester M1 2WD (tel: 03700 002288; email: online form; website: www.education. gov.uk).

Isle of Man

Department of Education and Children: Mount Havelock, Isle of Man IM1 2QF (tel: 01624 685685; email: enquiries@.gov.im; website: www.gov.im/education).

Northern Ireland

Department of Education for Northern Ireland: Rathgael House, 43 Balloo Road, Bangor BT19 7PR (tel: 02891 279279; email: mail@deni.gov. uk; website: www.deni.gov.uk).

Scotland

Education Scotland: Denholm House, Almondvale Business Park, Almondvale Way, Livingston EH54 6GA (tel: 01412 825000; Text Relay: 01506 600 236 [Mon–Thurs 8:30am–5pm, Fri 8:30am–4:30pm]; email: enquires@educationscotland. gov.uk; website: www.education scotland.gov.uk).

Wales

Welsh Assembly Education and Skills Department: Cathays Park, Cardiff CF10 3NQ (tel: 0300 0603300 – English; 0300 0604400 – Welsh; email: CustomerHelp@Wales.GSI. Gov.UK; website: www.wales.gov.uk).

Local education authorities

England

London

Barking and Dagenham: c/o Civic Centre, Rainham Road North, Dagenham RM10 7BN (tel: 020 8215 3004; email: 3000 direct@lbbd.gov.uk; website: www.barking-dagenham.gov. uk).

Barnet: North London Business Park (NLBP), Oakleigh Road South, London N11 1NP (tel: 020 8359 2000; email: first.contact@barnet.gov.uk; website: www.barnet.gov.uk).

Bexley: Civic Offices, 2 Watling Street, Bexleyheath, Kent DA6 7AT (tel: 020 8303 7777; website: www. bexley.gov.uk).

Brent: Town Hall, Forty Lane, Wembley HA9 9HD (tel: 020 8937 1234; email: cutomer.services@brent. gov.uk; website: www.brent.gov.uk).

Bromley: Education Department, Civic Centre, Stockwell Close, Bromley BR1 3UH (tel: 020 8464 3333; website: www.bromley.gov.uk).

Camden: 5 Pancras Square, London N1C 4AG (tel: 020 7278 4444 [Mon–Fri 8am–6pm]; website: www. camden.gov.uk).

City of London: PO Box 270, Guildhall, London EC2P 2EJ (tel: 020 7606 3030; email: online form; website: www.cityoflondon.gov.uk).

Croydon: Bernard Weatherhill House, 8 Mint Walk, Croydon CR0 1EA (tel: 020 8726 6000 [Mon–Fri 9am–5pm]; website: www.croydon.gov.uk).

Ealing: Customer Services, Perceval House, 14–16 Uxbridge Road, Ealing W5 2HL (tel: 020 8825 5000 or 0845 121 2208; website: www.ealing.gov. uk).

Enfield: Civic Centre, Silver Street, Enfield EN1 3XY (tel: 020 8379 1000; website: www.enfield.gov.uk).

Greenwich: Customer Services. The Woolwich Centre, Wellington Street, Woolwich, London SE18 6QH (tel: 020 8854 8888; website: www. greenwich.gov.uk).

Hackney: Hackney Service Centre, 1 Hillman Street, London E8 1DY (tel: 020 8356 3000; email: info@hackney. gov.uk; website: www.hackney.gov. uk).

Hammersmith and Fulham: Town Hall, King Street, Hammersmith, London W6 9JU (tel: 020 8748 3020; Text Relay: 0800 7311888; website: www.lbhf.gov.uk).

Haringey: Education Department, Civic Centre, High Road, Wood Green, London N22 8LE (tel: 020 8489 1000 [Mon–Fri 9am–5pm]; email: online form; website: www. haringey.gov.uk).

Harrow: Civic Centre, Station Road, Harrow, Middlesex HA1 2XF (tel: 020 8863 5611; website: www.harrow.gov. uk).

Havering: Town Hall, Main Road, Romford RM1 3BB (tel: 01708 434343; website: www.havering.gov. uk).

Hillingdon: Civic Centre, High Street, Uxbridge, Middlesex UB8 1UW (tel: 01895 250111; website: www. hillingdon.gov.uk).

Hounslow: Civic Centre, Lampton Road, Hounslow TW3 4DN (tel: 020 8583 2000; email: customerservices@ hounslow.gov.uk; website: www. hounslow.gov.uk).

Islington: 222 Upper Street, Islington, London N1 1XR (tel: 020 7527 2000; website: www.islington.gov.uk).

Kensington and Chelsea: Customer Services, Town Hall, Hornton Street, London W8 7NX (tel: 020 7361 3000; email: RBKC CustomerServices@rbkc.gov.uk; website: www.rbkc.gov.uk).

Kingston upon Thames: Guildhall 2, High Street, Kingston-upon-Thames, Surrey KT1 1EU (tel: 020 8547 5000; email: information@kingston.gov.uk; website: www.kingston.gov.uk).

Lambeth: Brixton Customer Centre, Olive Morris House, 18 Brixton Hill, London SW2 1RD (tel: 020 7926 1000; email: infoservice@lambeth.gov. uk; website: www.lambeth.gov.uk).

Lewisham: Town Hall, Catford, London SE6 4RU (tel: 020 8314 6000; website: www.lewisham.gov.uk).

Merton: Merton Civic Centre, London Road, Morden, Surrey SM4 5DX (tel: 020 8274 4901 [Mon–Fri 9am–5pm]; website: www. merton.gov.uk).

Newham: Dockside, 1000 Dockside Road, London E16 2QU (tel: 020 8430 2000; website: www.newham. gov.uk).

Redbridge: Town Hall, 128–142 High Road, Ilford, Essex IG1 1DD (tel: 020 8554 5000; email: customer.cc@ redbridge.gov.uk; website: www. redbridge.gov.uk).

Richmond-upon-Thames: Civic Centre, 44 York Street, Twickenham TW1 3BZ (tel: 020 8891 1411; website: www.richmond.gov.uk).

Southwark: PO BOX 64529, London SE1P 5LX (tel: 020 7525 5000; website: www.southwark.gov.uk).

Sutton: Civic Offices, St Nicholas Way, Sutton SM1 1EA (tel: 020 8770 5000; email: online form; website: www.sutton.gov.uk).

Tower Hamlets: Education and Community Services, Town Hall, Mulberry Place, 5 Clove Crescent, London E14 2BG (tel: 020 7364 5020; email: online form; website: www. tower hamlets.gov.uk).

Waltham Forest: Customer Services Centre, 137 Hoe Street, Walthamstow E17 4RT (tel: 020 8496 3000; email: wfdirect@walthamforest.gov.uk; website: www.walthamforest.gov.uk).

Wandsworth: Education and Social Services Department, Town Hall, Wandsworth High Street, London SW18 2PU (tel: 020 8871 6000; website: www.wandsworth.gov.uk).

Westminster: City Hall, 64 Victoria Street, London SW1E 6QP (tel: 020 7641 6000; website: www.westminster. gov.uk).

Midlands

Derbyshire

Derby City Council: The Council House, Corporation Street, Derby DE1 2FS (tel: 01332 293111; email: cutomerservices@derby.gov.uk; website: www.derby.gov.uk).

Derbyshire County Council: Education Offices, County Hall, Matlock DE4 3AG (tel: 01629 533190; email: contact.centre@derbyshire.gov. uk; website: www.derbyshire.gov.uk).

Herefordshire

Herefordshire Council: Plough Lane, Hereford, Herefordshire HR4 0LE, (tel: 01432 260500; email: info@ herefordshire.gov.uk; website: www. herefordshire.gov.uk).

Leicestershire and Rutland

Leicester City Council: City Hall, 115 Charles Street, Leicester LE1 1FZ (tel: 0116 454 1000; email: online form; website: www.leicester.gov.uk).

Leicestershire County Council: County Hall, Glenfield, Leicester LE3 8RA (tel: 01162 323232 [Mon–Thurs 8:30am–5pm, Fri 8:30am–4:30pm]; website: www.leics. gov.uk).

Lincolnshire County Council: Education Department, County Offices, Newland, Lincoln LN1 1YL (tel: 01522 552222; email: customer_ services@lincolnshire.gov.uk; website: www.lincolnshire.gov.uk).

North East Lincolnshire Council: Municipal Offices, Town Hall Square, Grimsby DN31 1HU (tel: 01472 326291; website: www.nelincs.gov.uk).

North Lincolnshire Council: Civic Centre, Ashby Road, Scunthorpe, North Lincolnshire DN16 1AB (tel: 01724 296296 or 01724 297000; email: customerservice@northlincs.gov.uk; website: www.northlincs.gov.uk).

Rutland County Council: Catmose, Oakham, Rutland LE15 6HP (tel: 01572 722577; email: enquiries@ rutland.gov.uk; website: www.rutland. gov.uk).

Northamptonshire

Northamptonshire County Council: County Hall, Northampton NN1 1ED (County Hall has one reception at George Row opposite All Saints Church) (tel: 0300 126 1000; email: online form; website: www. northamptonshire.gov.uk).

Nottinghamshire

Nottingham City Council: Loxley House, Station Street, Nottingham NG2 3NG (tel: 01159 155555; website: www.nottinghamcity.gov.uk).

Nottinghamshire County Council: County Hall, Loughborough Road, Nottingham NG2 7QP (tel: 0300 500 8080[Mon–Fri 8am–8pm, Sat 8am–12pm]; email: enquiries@ nottscc.gov.uk; website: www. nottinghamshire.gov.uk).

Shropshire

Shropshire County Council: Shirehall, Abbey Foregate, Shrewsbury SY2 6ND (tel: 0845 678 9000; email: online form; website: www.shropshire.gov. uk).

Telford and Wrekin Council: Addenbrooke House, Ironmasters Way, Telford TF3 4NT (tel: 01952 380000 [Mon–Fri 8am–5:15pm];

email: contact@telford.gov.uk; website: www.telford.gov.uk).

Staffordshire

Staffordshire County Council: Number 1 Staffordshire Place, Stafford ST16 2LP (tel: 0300 111 8000; email: contactus@staffordshire. gov.uk; website: www.staffordshire. gov.uk).

Stoke-on-Trent City Council: Civic Centre, Glebe Street, Stoke-on-Trent ST4 1RN (tel: 01782 234234; email: Enquiries@stoke.gov.uk; website: www.stoke.gov.uk).

Warwickshire

Warwickshire County Council: Shire Hall, Warwick CV34 4SA (tel: 01926 410410[Mon–Fri 8am–8pm, Sat 9am–4pm]; website: www. warwickshire.gov.uk).

West Midlands

Birmingham City Council: Education Office, Council House, Victoria Square, Birmingham B1 1BB (tel: 01213 031111; email: contact@ birmingham.gov.uk; website: www. birmingham.gov.uk).

Coventry City Council: Earl Street, Coventry CV1 5RS (tel: 02476 834333; email: coventrydirect@ coventry.gov.uk; website: www. coventry.gov.uk).

Dudley Metropolitan Borough Council: Council House, Priory Road, Dudley, West Midlands DY1 1HF (tel: 0300 555 2345; email: online form; website: www.dudley.gov.uk).

Sandwell Metropolitan Borough Council: Sandwell Council House, PO Box 2374, Oldbury, West Midlands B69 3DE (tel: 0845 358 2200 [Mon–Fri 8am–8pm, Sat 8:30am–1:30pm]; email: contact@ sandwell.gov.uk; website: www. sandwell.gov.uk).

Solihull Metropolitan Borough Council: Manor Square, Solihull, West Midlands B91 9QU (tel: 01217 046000; email: connectcc@solihull. gov.uk; website: www.solihull.gov.uk).

Walsall Borough Council: Education Department, The Civic Centre, Darwall Street, Walsall WS1 1TP (tel: 01922 650000; email: infor@walsall. gov.uk; website: www.walsall.gov.uk).

Wolverhampton Borough Council: Education Services, Civic Centre, St Peter's Square, Wolverhampton WV1 1SH (tel: 01902 556556; email: city.direct@wolverhampton.gov.uk; website: www.wolverhampton.gov. uk).

Worcestershire

Worcestershire County Council: County Hall, Spetchley Road, Worcester WR5 2NP (tel: 01905 763763; email: hub@worcestershire. gov.uk; website: www.worcestershire. gov.uk).

North East

County Durham

Darlington Borough Council: Town Hall, Feethams, Darlington, County Durham DL1 5QT (tel: 01325 380651; email: customerservices@darlington. gov.uk; website: www.darlington.gov. uk).

Durham County Council: County Hall, Durham, County Durham DH1 5UL (tel: 03000 260000; email; help@durham.gov.uk; website: www. durham.gov.uk).

East Yorkshire

East Riding of Yorkshire Council: County Hall, Cross Street, Beverley* East Riding of Yorkshire HU17 9BA (tel: 01482 393939; email: customer. services@eastriding.gov.uk; website: www2.eastriding.gov.uk).

Hull City Council: Guildhall, Alfred Gelder Street, Hull HU1 2AA (tel: 01482 300300; email: info@hullcc.gov. uk; website: www.hullcc.gov.uk).

North Yorkshire

North Yorkshire County Council: County Hall, Northallerton, North Yorkshire DL7 8AD (tel: 0845 241 1307; website: www.northyorks.gov. uk; an online chat option is also available).

Northumberland

Northumberland County Council: County Hall, Morpeth NE61 2EF (tel: 0845 600 6400 [Mon–Fri 7am–8pm, Sat 9am–3pm, (excluding bank holidays)]; email: ask@ northumberland.gov.uk; website: www.northumberland.gov.uk).

City of York Council: West Offices, Station Rise, York Y01 6GA (tel: 01904 551550 [Mon–Fri 8:30–5:30pm]; email: ycc@york.gov. uk; website: www.york.gov.uk).

South Yorkshire

Barnsley Borough Council: Town Hall, Church Street, Barnsley, South Yorkshire S70 2TA (tel: 01226 770770 [Mon–Fri 8am–6pm]; email: online@ barnsley.gov.uk; website: www. barnsley.gov.uk).

Doncaster Council: Civic Office, Waterdale, Doncaster DN1 3BU, (tel: 01302 736000; email: general. enquiries@doncaster.gov.uk; website: www.doncaster.gov.uk).

Rotherham Borough Council: Riverside House, Main Street, Rotherham S60 1AE (tel: 01709 382121; website: www.rotherham.gov. uk).

Sheffield City Council: Town Hall, Pinstone Street, Sheffield S1 2HH (tel: 01142 734567 [Mon–Fri 8am–6pm]; email: online form; website: www.sheffield.gov.uk).

Teesside

Hartlepool Borough Council: Customer Services, Civic Centre, Victoria Road, Hartlepool TS24 8AY (tel: 01429 266522; email: customer. service@hartlepool.gov.uk; website: www.hartlepool.gov.uk).

Middlesbrough Borough Council: PO Box 500, Middlesbrough TS1 9FT (tel: 01642 245432; email: contactcentre@middlesbrough.gov.uk; website: www.middlesbrough.gov.uk).

Redcar and Cleveland Borough Council: Redcar and Cleveland House, Kirkleatham Street, Redcar TS10 1RT (tel: 01642 774774; email: contactus@redcar-cleveland.gov.uk; website: www.redcar-cleveland.gov. uk).

Stockton-on-Tees Borough Council: Municipal Buildings, Church Road, Stockton-on-Tees TS18 1LD (tel: 01642 393939; website: www. stockton-bc.gov.uk).

Tyne and Wear

Gateshead Borough Council: Civic Centre, Regent Street, Gateshead NE8 1HH (tel: 01914 333000; email: customerservices@gateshead.gov.uk; website: www.gateshead.gov.uk).

Newcastle upon Tyne City Council: Civic Centre, Barras Bridge, Newcastle upon Tyne NE1 8QH (tel: 01912 787878; email: csc@newcastle. gov.uk; website: www.newcastle.gov. uk).

North Tyneside Borough Council: Quadrant, The Silverlink North, Cobalt Business Park, North Tyneside NE27 0BY (tel: 0345 2000 101; website: www.northtyneside.gov.uk).

South Tyneside Borough Council: Town Hall and Civic Offices, Westoe Road, South Shields, Tyne and Wear NE33 2RL (tel: 01914 277000; email: customerhelp@southtyneside.gov.uk; website: www.southtyneside.info).

Sunderland City Council: Civic Centre, Burdon Road, Sunderland SR2 7DN (tel: 01915 205555 [Mon–Fri 8am–6:30pm]; email: enquiries@sunderland.gov.uk; website: www.sunderland.gov.uk).

West Yorkshire
City of Bradford Metropolitan District Council: City Hall, Centenary Square, Bradford BD1 1HY (tel: 01274 432111; website: www.bradford.gov.uk).

Calderdale Borough Council: Town Hall, Crossley Street, Halifax, West Yorkshire HX1 1UJ (tel:01422 288001; email: customer.first@calderdale.gov.uk; website: www.calderdale.gov.uk, an online chat facility is also available).

Kirklees Council: 2nd Floor, Civic Centre 3, Market Street, Huddersfield HD1 1WG (tel: 01484 221000, website: www.kirklees.gov.uk; an online chat facility is also available).

Leeds City Council: Civic Hall, Calverley Street, Leeds, West Yorkshire LS1 1UR (tel: 01132 22 4444; website: www.leeds.gov.uk).

Wakefield District Council: Wakefield One, PO Box 700, Wakefield WF1 2EB (tel: 0345 850 6506; email: customerservices@wakefield.gov.uk; website: www.wakefield.gov.uk).

North West

Cheshire and Chester
Cheshire East Council: Westfields, Middlewich Road, Sandbach CW11 1HZ, (tel: 0300 123 55 00); email: online form; website: www.cheshireeast.gov.uk).

Cheshire West and Chester Council: HQ, 58 Nicholas Street, Chester CH1 2NP (tel: 0300 123 8 123; website: www.cheshirewestandchester.gov.uk.

Halton Borough Council: Municipal Building, Kingsway, Widnes, Cheshire WA8 7QF (tel: 0303 333 4300; email: online form; website: www3.halton.gov.uk).

Warrington Borough Council: Education and Lifelong Learning, New Town House, Buttermarket Street, Warrington WA1 2NH (tel: 01925 443322; email: contact@warrington.gov.uk; website: www.warrington.gov.uk).

Cumbria
Cumbria County Council: The Courts, Carlisle, Cumbria CA3 8NA (tel: 01228 606060; email: info@cumbria.gov.uk; website: www.cumbria.gov.uk).

Greater Manchester
Bolton Borough Council: Town Hall, Victoria Square, Bolton BL1 1RU (tel: 01204 333333; email: online form; website: www.bolton.gov.uk).

Bury Council: Town Hall, Knowsley Street, Bury, Lancashire BL9 0SW (tel: 01612 535000; website: www.bury.gov.uk).

Manchester City Council: Town Hall, Albert Square, Manchester, Lancashire M60 2LA (tel: 01612 345000; website: www.manchester.gov.uk).

Oldham Council: Civic Centre, West Street, Oldham OL1 1UG (tel: 0161 770 3000; website: www.oldham.gov.uk).

Rochdale Metropolitan Borough Council: Number One Riverside, Smith Street, Rochdale OL16 1XU (tel: 01706 647474 [Mon–Fri 8:30am–5pm]; email: council@rochdale.gov.uk; website: www.rochdale.gov.uk).

Salford City Council: Civic Centre, Chorley Road, Swinton, Salford M27 5AW (tel: 01617 944711; website: www.salford.gov.uk).

Stockport Metropolitan Borough Council: Town Hall, Edward Street, Stockport SK1 3XE (tel: 01614 804949; email: stockportdirect@stockport.gov.uk; website: www.stockport.gov.uk).

Tameside Council: The Council Offices, Wellington Road, Ashton-under-Lyne OL6 6DL (tel: 01613 428355; website: www.tameside.gov.uk).

Trafford Council: Trafford Town Hall, Talbot Road, Stretford, Manchester M32 0TH (tel: 01619 122000; email: access.trafford@trafford.gov.uk; website: www.trafford.gov.uk).

Wigan Borough Council: Town Hall, Library Street, Wigan WN1 1YN (tel: 01942 244991; website: www.wigan.gov.uk).

Lancashire
Blackburn with Darwen Borough Council: Town Hall, King William Street, Blackburn, Lancashire BB1 7DY (tel: 01254 585585; email: info@blackburn.gov.uk; website: www.blackburn.gov.uk).

Blackpool Council: PO Box 4, Blackpool FY1 1NA (tel: 01253 477477; email: customer.first@blackpool.goc.uk; website: www.blackpool.gov.uk).

Lancashire County Council: PO Box 78, County Hall, Fishergate, Preston, Lancashire PR1 8XJ (tel: 0300 123 6701; email: enquiries@lancashire.gov.uk; website: www.lancashire.gov.uk).

Merseyside
Knowsley Borough Council: Customer Contact Centre, the Kirkby Centre, Norwich Way, Kirkby L32 8XY (tel: 01514 896000; email: customerservices@knowsley.gov.uk; website: www.knowsley.gov.uk).

Liverpool City Council: Municipal Buildings, Dale Street, Liverpool L69 2DH (tel: 01512 333000; website: www.liverpool.gov.uk).

St Helens Council: Contact Centre, Wesley House, Corporation Street, St Helens, Merseyside WA10 1HF (tel: 01744 676789 [Mon–Fri 8am–8pm, Sat 10am–2pm]; email: contactcentre@sthelens.gov.uk; website: www.sthelens.gov.uk).

Sefton Metropolitan Borough Council: Town Hall, Lord Street, Southport PR8 1DA (tel: 0845 140 0845; email: online form; website: www.sefton.gov.uk).

Wirral Borough Council: Town Hall, Brighton Street, Wallasey, Wirral CH44 8ED (tel: 151 606 2000 [Mon–Fri 8:45am–5pm]; website: www.wirral.gov.uk).

South East

Bedfordshire

Central Bedfordshire Council: Priory House, Monks Walk, Chicksands, Shefford, Bedfordshire SG17 5TQ (tel: 0300 300 8301; email: customers@centralbedfordshire.gov.uk; website: www.centralbedfordshire.gov.uk).

Luton Borough Council: Town Hall, George Street, Luton, Bedfordshire LU1 2BQ (tel: 01582 546000; website: www.luton.gov.uk).

Berkshire

Bracknell Forest Council: East Hampstead House, Time Square, Market Street, Bracknell, Berkshire RG12 1JD (tel: 01344 352000 [Mon–Fri 8:30am–5pm]; email: customer.services@bracknell-forest.gov.uk; website: www.bracknell-forest.gov.uk).

Reading Borough Council: Civic Centre, Reading RG1 7AE (tel: 01189 373737; email: online form; website: www.reading.gov.uk).

Slough Borough Council: Landmark Place, High Street, Slough SL1 1JL (tel: 01753 475111; website: www.slough.gov.uk).

West Berkshire Council: Council Offices, Market Street, Newbury, Berkshire RG14 5LD (tel: 01635 42400; email: customerservices@westberks.gov.uk; website: www.westberks.gov.uk).

Windsor and Maidenhead: Education Department, Town Hall, St Ives Road, Maidenhead SL6 1RF (tel: 01628 683800; email: online form; website: www.rbwm.gov.uk).

Wokingham Borough Council: Education and Cultural Services, Shute End, Wokingham, Berkshire RG40 1BN (tel: 01189 746000; email: online form; website: www.wokingham.gov.uk).

Buckinghamshire

Buckinghamshire County Council: County Hall, Walton Street, Aylesbury, Buckinghamshire HP20 1UA (tel: 0845 370 8090 or 01296 395000 [Mon–Fri 9am–5:30pm]; email: customerservices@buckscc.gov.uk; website: www.buckscc.gov.uk).

Milton Keynes Council: Civic Offices, 1 Saxon Gate East, Central Milton Keynes MK9 3EJ (tel: 01908 691691; email: info@milton-keynes.gov.uk; website: www.milton-keynes.gov.uk).

Cambridgeshire

Cambridgeshire County Council: Shire Hall, Castle Hill, Cambridge CB3 0AP (tel: 0345 045 5200 [Mon–Fri 8am–6pm, Sat 9am–1pm]; email: info@cambridgeshire.gov.uk; website: www.cambridgeshire.gov.uk).

Peterborough City Council: Town Hall, Bridge Street, Peterborough PE1 1HF (tel: 01733 747474; email: ask@peterborough.gov.uk; website: www.peterborough.gov.uk).

East Sussex

Brighton and Hove City Council: King's House, Grand Avenue, Hove BN3 2LS (tel: 01273 290000; email: info@brighton-hove.gov.uk; website: www.brighton-hove.gov.uk).

East Sussex County Council: County Hall, St Anne's Crescent, Lewes, East Sussex BN7 1UE (tel: 0345 60 80 190; email: online form; website: www.eastsussex.gov.uk).

Essex

Essex County Council: County Hall, Market Road, Chelmsford CM1 1QH (tel: 0845 7430430; email: contact@essex.gov.uk; website: www.essex.gov.uk).

Southend-on-Sea Borough Council: Civic Centre, Victoria Avenue, Southend-on-Sea, Essex SS2 6ER (tel: 01702 215000; email: council@southend.gov.uk; website: www.southend.gov.uk).

Thurrock Council: Civic Offices, New Road, Grays, Thurrock, Essex RM17 6SL (tel: 01375 652652; email: general.enquiries@thurrock.gov.uk; website: www.thurrock.gov.uk).

Hampshire

Hampshire County Council: Education County Office, The Castle, Winchester SO23 8UJ (tel: 0845 603 5638; email: info@hants.gov.uk; website: www.hants.gov.uk).

Isle of Wight Council: Education Department, County Hall, High Street, Newport, Isle of Wight PO30 1UD (tel: 01983 821000; website: www.iwight.com).

Portsmouth City Council: Civic Offices, Guildhall Square, Portsmouth PO1 2BG (tel: 02392 822251; email: cityhelpdesk@portsmouthcc.gov.uk; website: www.portsmouth.gov.uk).

Southampton City Council: Civic Centre, Southampton SO14 7LY (tel: 02380 833000; email: enquiries@southampton.gov.uk; website: www.southampton.gov.uk).

Hertfordshire

Hertfordshire County Council: County Hall, Pegs Lane, Hertford SG13 8DQ (tel: 0300 123 4040; email: online contact form; website: www.hertsdirect.org).

Kent

Kent County Council: County Hall, Maidstone, Kent ME14 1XQ (tel: 03000 41 41 41 [Mon–Fri 8am–6pm]; email: county.hall@kent.gov.uk; website: www.kent.gov.uk).

Medway Council: Gun Wharf, Dock Road, Chatham, Kent ME4 4TR (tel: 01634 306000 [Mon–Fri 8:30am–5pm]; website: www.medway.gov.uk).

Norfolk

Norfolk County Council: County Hall, Martineau Lane, Norwich, Norfolk NR1 2DH (tel: 0844 800 8020; email: information@norfolk.gov.uk; website: www.norfolk.gov.uk).

Oxfordshire

Oxfordshire County Council: County Hall, New Road, Oxford OX1 1ND (tel: 01865 792422; email: online form; website: www.oxfordshire.gov.uk).

Suffolk

Suffolk County Council: Endeavour House, 8 Russell Road, Ipswich, Suffolk IP1 2BX (tel: 08456 066 067 [Mon–Fri 8:30am–6pm]; website: www.suffolkcc.gov.uk).

Surrey

Surrey County Council: County Hall, Penrhyn Road, Kingston-upon-Thames KT1 2DJ (tel: 03456 099 099 [Mon–Fri 8am–6pm]; email: contac.centre@surreycc.gov.uk; website: www.surreycc.gov.uk).

West Sussex

West Sussex County Council: Education Department, County Hall, Chichester PO19 1RQ (tel: 01243 777100; email: online form; website: www.westsussex.gov.uk).

South West

Avon

Bath and North East Somerset Council: Lewis House, Manvers Street, Bath BA1 1JG (tel: 01225 477000; email: enquiries@bathnes.gov.uk; website: www.bathnes.gov.uk).

Bristol City Council: City Hall, College Green, Bristol BS1 5TR (tel: 01179 222000 [Mon–Thurs 8:30am–6pm, Fri 8:30am–4:30pm]; website: www.bristol-city.gov.uk).

North Somerset Council: Town Hall, Walliscote Grove Road, Weston-Super-Mare BS23 1UJ (tel: 01934 888888; email: customer.services@n-somerset.gov.uk; website: www.n-somerset.gov.uk).

South Gloucestershire Council: Badminton Road, Council Offices, Badminton Road, Yate BS37 5AF (tel: 01454 868009 [Mon–Thurs 8:45am–5pm, Fri 8:45am–4:30pm]; website: www.southglos.gov.uk).

Cornwall

Cornwall County Council: County Hall, Treyew Road, Truro, Cornwall TR1 3AY (tel: 0300 1234 100; email: enquiries@cornwall.gov.uk; website: www.cornwall.gov.uk).

Council of The Isles of Scilly: Town Hall, St Mary's, Isles of Scilly TR21 0LW (tel: 01720 424000; email: enquiries@scilly.gov.uk; website: www.scilly.gov.uk).

Devon

Devon County Council: County Hall, Topsham Road, Exeter, Devon EX2 4QD (tel: 0345 155 1015; email: customer@devon.gov.uk; website: www.devon.gov.uk).

Plymouth City Council: Armada Way, Plymouth PL1 2AA (tel: 01752 668000; email: enquiries@plymouth.gov.uk; website: www.plymouth.gov.uk).

Torbay Borough Council: Town Hall, Castle Circus, Torquay, Devon TQ1 3DR (tel: 01803 207201; website: www.torbay.gov.uk).

Dorset

Bournemouth Borough Council: Town Hall, Bourne Avenue, Bournemouth BH2 6DY (tel: 01202 451451; email: enquiries@bournemouth.gov.uk; website: www.bournemouth.gov.uk).

Dorset County Council: County Hall, Colliton Park, Dorchester DT1 1XJ (tel: 01305 221000 [Mon–Fri 8:30am–5:30pm]; email: online form; website: www.dorsetforyou.com).

Borough of Poole Council: Education Department, Civic Centre, Poole, Dorset BH15 2RU (tel: 01202 633633; website: www.poole.gov.uk).

Gloucestershire

Gloucestershire County Council: Shire Hall, Westgate Street, Gloucester GL1 2TG (tel: 01452 425000; email: customerservices@gloucestershire.gov.uk; website: www.gloucestershire.gov.uk).

Somerset

Somerset County Council: County Hall, Taunton, Somerset TA1 4DY (tel: 0845 345 9122; email: generalenquiries@somerset.gov.uk; website: www.somerset.gov.uk).

Wiltshire

Swindon Borough Council: Civic Offices, Euclid Street, Swindon SN1 2JH (tel: 01793 445500; email: customerservices@swindon.gov.uk; website: www.swindon.gov.uk).

Wiltshire County Council: Education Department, County Hall, Bythesea Road, Trowbridge, Wiltshire BA14 8JN (tel: 0300 456 0100; email: customerservices@wiltshire.gov.uk; website: www.wiltshire.gov.uk).

Northern Ireland

Belfast: Education and Library Board, 40 Academy Street, Belfast BT1 2NQ (tel: 02890 564000; email: info@belb@belb.co.uk; website: www.belb.org.uk).

CCMS (Council for Catholic Maintained Schools): 160 High Street, Holywood, County Down BT18 9HT (tel: 02890 426972; website: www.onlineccms.com).

North Eastern Education and Library Board: County Hall, 182 Galgorm Road, Ballymena BT42 1HN (tel: 028 2565 3333; website: www.neelb.org.uk).

South Eastern Education and Library Board: Grahamsbridge Road, Dundonald, Belfast BT16 2HS (tel: 02890 566200; email: info@seelb,org.uk; website: www.seelb.org.uk).

Southern Education and Library Board: 3 Charlemont Place, The Mall, Armagh BT61 9AX (tel: 02837 512200; email: selb.hq@selb.org; website: www.selb.org).

Western Education and Library Board: 1 Hospital Road, Omagh, Co. Tyrone BT79 0AW (tel: 02882 411411; email: info@welbni.org; website: www.welbni.org).

Scotland

Aberdeen City Council: Ground Floor, Marischal College, Broad Street, Aberdeen AB10 1AB (tel: 0845 608 0910; website: www.aberdeencity.gov.uk)

Angus Council: Education Department, Angus House, Orchardbank Business Park, Orchardbank, Forfar DD8 1AX (tel: 08452 777 778; website: www.angus.gov.uk).

Argyll and Bute Council: Education Department, Kilmory, Lochgilphead, Argyll PA31 8RT (tel: 01546 605522; email: enquiries@argyll-bute.gov.uk; website: www.argyll-bute.gov.uk).

Clackmannanshire Council: Kilncraigs, Alloa, Clackmannanshire FK10 1EB (tel: 01259 450000; email: customerservice@clacks.gov.uk; website: www.clacksweb.org.uk).

Comhairle nan Eilean Siar: Council Offices, Sandwick Road, Stornoway, Isle of Lewis HS1 2BW (tel: 0845 6007090; email: enquiries@cne-siar.gov.uk; website: www.cne-siar.gov.uk).

Dumfries and Galloway Council: Council Headquarters, Council Offices, English Street, Dumfries DG1 2DD (tel: 030 33 33 3000; email: cis@dumgal.gov.uk; website: www.dumgal.gov.uk).

Dundee City Council: Education Department, Dundee House, 50 North Lindsay Street, Dundee DD1 1QE (tel: 01382 434000; email: customerservices@dundeecity.gov.uk; website: www.dundeecity.gov.uk).

East Ayrshire Council: Council Headquarters, London Road, Kilmarnock, East Ayrshire KA3 7BU (tel: 0845 724 0000; email: online form; website: www.east-ayrshire.gov.uk).

East Dunbartonshire Council: Broomhill Industrial Estate, Kilsyth Road, Kirkintilloch G66 1QF (tel: 0300 123 4510; email:

customerservices@eastdunbarton.gov.uk; website: www.eastdunbarton.gov.uk).

East Lothian Council: Education and Community Services, John Muir House, Haddington, East Lothian EH41 3HA (tel: 01620 827827; email: customerservices@eastlothian.gov.uk; website: www.eastlothian.gov.uk).

East Renfrewshire Council: Education Department, Eastwood Park, Rouken Glen Road, Giffnock G46 6UG (tel: 01415 773001; website: www.east renfrewshire.gov.uk).

Edinburgh City Council: Education Department; Waverley Court, 4 East Market Street, Edinburgh EH8 8BG (tel: 01312 002000; website: www.edinburgh.gov.uk).

Falkirk Council: Municipal Buildings, West Bridge Street, Falkirk FK1 5RS (tel: 01324 506070; email: contact.centre@falkirk.gov.uk; website: www.falkirk.gov.uk).

Fife Council: Education service, Fife House, North Street, Glenrothes, Fife KY7 5LT (tel: 03451 550000 [Mon–Fri 8am–6pm]; email: online form; website: www.fife-education.org.uk).

Glasgow City Council: Customer Care Team, City Chambers, Glasgow G2 1DU (tel: 01412 872000; website: www.glasgow.gov.uk).

Highland Council: Glenurquhart Road, Inverness IV3 5NX (tel: 01349 886606; website: www.highland.gov.uk).

Inverclyde Council: Municipal Buildings, Greenock PA15 1LY (tel: 01475 717171; website: www.inverclyde.gov.uk).

Midlothian Council: Midlothian House, Buccleuch Street, Dalkeith EH22 1DN (tel: 01312 707500 [Mon–Thurs 8:45am–4:45pm; Fri 8:45am–4pm]; email: online form; website: www.midlothian.gov.uk).

Moray Council: Educational Services, Council Offices, High Street, Elgin IV30 1BX (tel: 01343 543451; email: access.point@moray.gov.uk; website: www.moray.gov.uk).

North Ayrshire Council: Cunninghame House, Friars Croft, Irvine KA12 8EE (tel: 01294 310000 [Mon–Fri 8:30am–5:30pm]; email:

contactus@north-ayrshire.gov.uk; website: www.north-ayrshire.gov.uk).

North Lanarkshire Council: Education Department, Municipal Buildings, Kildonan Street, Coatbridge ML5 3BT (tel: 01698 403200; website: www.northlan.gov.uk).

Orkney Islands Council: Council Offices, School Place, Kirkwall, Orkney KW15 1NY (tel: 01856 873535 ext. 2902, 2903 or 2904; email: online form; website: www.orkney.gov.uk).

Perth and Kinross Council: Pullar House, 35 Kinnoull Street, Perth PH1 5GD (tel: 01738 475000; email: enquiries@pkc.gov.uk; website: www.pkc.gov.uk).

Renfrewshire Council: Renfrewshire House, Cotton Street, Paisley PA1 1UJ (tel: 0300 300 0330; email: customerservices.contact@renfrewshire.gov.uk; website: www.renfrewshire.gov.uk).

Scottish Borders Council: Council Headquarters, Newtown St Boswells, Melrose TD6 0SA (tel: 0300 100 1800; email: enquiries@scotborders.gov.uk; website: www.scotborders.gov.uk).

Shetlands Islands Council: Office Headquarters, 8 North Ness Business Park, Lerwick, Shetland ZE1 0LZ (tel: 01595 693535; email: info@shetland.gov.uk; website: www.shetland.gov.uk).

South Ayrshire Council: Council Headquarters, County Buildings, Wellington Square, Ayr KA7 1DR (tel: 0300 123 0900; website: www.south-ayrshire.gov.uk).

South Lanarkshire Council: Education Dept, 5th Floor, Council Offices, Almada Street, Hamilton, South Lanarkshire ML3 0AA (tel: 0303 123 1015; email: customer.services@southlanarkshire.gov.uk; website: www.southlanarkshire.gov.uk).

Stirling Council: Old Viewforth, 14–20 Pitt Terrace; Stirling FK8 2ET (tel: 0845 277 7000; email: info@stirling.gov.uk; website: www.stirling.gov.uk).

West Dunbartonshire Council: Learning and Education, Council Offices, Garshake Road, Dumbarton G82 3PU (tel: 01389 738282; email: online form; website: www.west-dunbarton.gov.uk).

West Lothian Council: West Lothian Civic Centre, Howden South Road, Livingston, West Lothian EH54 6FF (tel: 01506 280000; email: customer.service@westlothian.gov.uk; website: www.westlothian.gov.uk).

Wales

Blaenau Gwent County Borough Council: Education/Lifelong Learning, Municipal Offices, Civic Centre, Ebbw Vale NP23 6XB (tel: 01495 311556; email: info@blaenau-gwent.gov.uk; website: www.blaenau-gwent.gov.uk).

Bridgend County Borough Council: Education, Leisure and Community Services, Civic Offices, Angel Street, Bridgend CF31 4WB (tel: 01656 643643; email: talktous@bridgend.gov.uk; website: www.bridgend.gov.uk).

Caerphilly County Borough Council: Pontllanfraith House, Blackwood Road, Pontllanfraith, Blackwood, Gwent NP12 2YW (tel: 01443 815588 or 01495 226622; email: info@caerphilly.gov.uk; website: www.caerphilly.gov.uk).

The City and County Council of Cardiff: Education Department, County Hall, Atlantic Wharf, Cardiff CF10 4UW (tel: 02920 872087; website: www.cardiff.gov.uk).

Carmarthenshire County Council: County Hall, Carmarthen, Carmarthenshire SA31 IJP (tel: 01267 234567; email: direct@carmarthenshire.gov.uk; website: www.carmarthenshire.gov.uk).

Ceredigion County Council: Neuadd Cyngor Ceredigion Penmorfa, Aberaeron, Ceredigion SA46 0PA (tel: 01545 570881; email: online form; website: www.ceredigion.gov.uk).

Conwy County Borough Council: Bodlondeb, Conwy, North Wales LL32 8DU (tel: 01492 574000; email: information@conwy.gov.uk; website: www.conwy.gov.uk).

Denbighshire County Council: Education Services, County Hall, Wynnstay Road, Ruthin LL15 1YN (tel: 01824 706101 [Mon–Fri 8:30am–5pm]; website: www.denbighshire.gov.uk).

Flintshire County Council: Education and Children's Services, County Hall, Mold, Flintshire CH7 6NB (tel: 01352

752121; email: online form; website: www.flintshire.gov.uk).

Gwynedd Council: Gwynedd-Ni, Council Offices, Shirehall St, Caernarfon LL55 1SH (tel: 01766 771000; website: www.gwynedd.gov. uk).

Isle of Anglesey County Council: Council Offices, Llangefni, Anglesey LL77 7TW (tel: 01248 750057; website: www.anglesey.gov.uk).

Merthyr Tydfil County Borough Council: Civic Centre, Castle Street, Merthyr Tydfil CF47 8AN (tel: 01685 725000 [Mon–Fri 8:45am–5pm]; email: customer.care@merthyr.gov.uk; website: www.merthyr.gov.uk).

Monmouthshire County Council: PO Box 106, Caldicot NP26 9AN (tel: 01633 644644; email: contact@ monmouthshire.gov.uk; website: www.monmouthshire.gov.uk).

Neath Port Talbot County Borough Council: Education Department, Civic Centre, Port Talbot SA13 1PJ (tel: 01639 686868; email: contactus@ npt.gov.uk; website: www.neath-porttalbot.gov.uk).

Newport County Borough Council: Education Department, Civic Centre, Godfrey Road, Newport, South Wales NP20 4UR (tel: 01633 656656 [Mon–Fri 8am–6pm]; email: info@ newport.gov.uk; website: www. newport.gov.uk).

Pembrokeshire County Council: Education Department, County Hall, Haverfordwest, Pembrokeshire SA61 1TP (tel: 01437 764551; email: enquiries@pembrokeshire.gov.uk; website: www.pembrokeshire.gov.uk)

Powys County Council: Education Dept, County Hall, Llandrindod Wells, Powys LD1 5LG (tel: 01597 826000; website: www.powys.gov.uk).

Rhondda Cynon Taff County Borough Council: Headquarters The Pavilions, Cambrian Park, Clydach Vale, Tonypandy CF40 2XX (tel: 01443 744000 [Mon–Fri 8:30am–5pm]; email: customerservices@rctcbc.gov.uk; website: www.rhondda-cynon-taff. gov.uk).

City and County of Swansea: Education Department, Civic Centre Oystermouth Road, Swansea SA1 3SN (tel: 01792 636000; email: education.

department@swansea.gov.uk; website: www.swansea.gov.uk).

Torfaen County Borough Council: Torfaen County Borough Council, Civic Centre, Pontypool NP4 6YB (tel: 01495 762200; email: your.call@ torfaen.gov.uk; website: www.torfaen. gov.uk).

The Vale of Glamorgan County Borough Council: Education Department, Civic Offices, Holton Road, Barry CF63 4RU (tel: 01446 700111; email: online form; website: www.valeofglamorgan.gov.uk).

Wrexham County Borough Council: Learning and Achievement Department, 16 Lord Street, Wrexham LL11 1LG (tel: 01978 292000; email: contact-us@wrexham. gov.uk; website: www.wrexham.gov. uk).

Index

What else can DSC do for you?

Let us help you to be the best you possibly can be. DSC equips individuals and organisations with expert skills and information to help them provide better services and outcomes for their beneficiaries. With the latest techniques, best practice and funding resources all brought to you by our team of experts, you will not only boost your income but also exceed your expectations.

Publications

With over 100 titles, we produce fundraising directories and research reports, as well as accessible 'how to' guides and best practice handbooks, all to help you help others.

Training

The voluntary sector's best-selling training – 80 courses covering every type of voluntary sector training.

In-house Training

All DSC courses are available on your premises, delivered by expert trainers and facilitators. We also offer coaching, consultancy, mentoring and support.

Conferences and Fairs

DSC conferences are a fantastic way to network with voluntary sector professionals whilst taking part in intensive, practical training workshops.

Funding Websites

*DSC's funding websites provide access to thousands of trusts, grants, statutory funds and corporate donations. You won't get more funders, commentary and analysis anywhere else. Demo our sites **free** today.*

Trust**funding**.org.uk

Government**funding**.org.uk

Company**giving**.org.uk

Grantsfor**individuals**.org.uk

Visit our website today and see what we can do for you:

www.**dsc.org.uk**

Or contact us directly: publications@dsc.org.uk

@DSC_Charity
For top tips and special offers